James Durham

Christ crucified, or the marrow of the gospel:

Evidently holden forth in seventy two sermons on the whole fifty third chapter of Isaiah

James Durham

Christ crucified, or the marrow of the gospel:
Evidently holden forth in seventy two sermons on the whole fifty third chapter of Isaiah

ISBN/EAN: 9783337713935

Printed in Europe, USA, Canada, Australia, Japan

Cover: Foto ©ninafisch / pixelio.de

More available books at **www.hansebooks.com**

Christ Crucified:
OR, THE
MARROW of the GOSPEL,

Evidently holden forth in

Seventy two SERMONS
ON THE
Whole Fifty third Chapter of *Isaiah*.

WHEREIN

The Text is clearly and judiciously opened up, and a great many most Apposite, profoundly Spiritual, and very Edifying Points of Doctrine, in a delectable Variety, drawn from it; With choice and excellent Practical Improvements made of them.

Wherein also several Adversaries of the Truth, as *Socinians, Arminians, Antinomians,* &c. are smartly, solidly and succinctly Reasoned with, and Refuted.

Wherein moreover, many Errors in Practice incident to Professors, otherwise Sound and Orthodox in their Opinions, are Discovered; And not a few grave, deep, and very concerning Cases of Conscience, soberly and satisfyingly Discussed.

By that able Minister of the New Testament, Mr. JAMES DURHAM, sometime Minister of the Gospel at *Glasgow*, and solemnly called to a publick Profession of Divinity in the University there, and also his Majesty's Chaplain in Ordinary, when he was in *Scotland*.

1 Cor. ii. 2. *For I determined not to know any thing among you, save Jesus Christ, and him crucified.*
Gal. iii. 1. *O foolish Galatians, who hath bewitched you, that ye should not obey the truth, before whose eyes Jesus Christ hath been evidently set forth, crucified among you?*
1 Cor. i. 23. *But we preach Christ crucified, unto the Jews a stumbling-block, and unto the Greeks foolishness; but unto them which are called, both Jews and Greeks, Christ the power of God, and the wisdom of God.*
2 Cor. v. 21. *For he hath made him to be sin for us, who knew no sin; that we might be made the righteousness of God in him.*
1 Pet. ii. 24. *Who his own self bare our sins in his own body on the tree, that we being dead to sin, should live unto righteousness: by whose stripes ye were healed.*
Augustinus in *Psal.* 120. Sacerdos noster a nobis accepit, quod pro nobis offerret: accepit a nobis carnem; in ipsa carne victima pro nobis factus est, holocaustum factus est, sacrificium factus est.

The SIXTH EDITION, carefully Corrected.

GLASGOW, Printed by ARCHIBALD M'LEAN and JOSEPH GALBRAITH, for JAMES WILKEN, Merchant in *Paisley*. MDCCLXI.

Unto all afflicted and Cross-bearing serious Christians; and more particularly to the Right Honourable and Truly Noble Lord WILLIAM *Earl of* CRAWFORD.

IT is one of the greatest practical debates and contests betwixt God and his own people, privileged with a special interest in him, which they are naturally inclined longest to keep up, and are lothest to let fall, *viz*. Whether he shall guide and govern them, and shape out their lot to them, while they sojourn here in the world, as he himself, in his own infinite wisdom, shall think fit, having a blank submission put by them into his hand, to be filled up with what kind and quality, with what measure and quantity, and with what continuance and duration of troubles, trials and afflictions himself pleaseth? Or, whether he should, as to some things at least, consult their will and pleasure, and, as it were, take their advice, and allow them a liberty to prescribe to him, how he should guide and dispose of them? And, indeed, to be here denied to their own will, and absolutely submitted to the will of God, is one of the highest and most difficultly practicable points of self-denial, (to which, notwithstanding, all the disciples and followers of Christ are expresly called, and wherein he hath great delight and complacency, as favouring strong of intire trust and confidence in him) yet, if we consider these few things, it will be found that there is all the reason in the world, why they should come in his will, and sweetly submit themselves to it in all things, how cross soever to their own inclination, without any the least reluctation or contradiction; which is our privilege, and the restoration of our degenerated nature to its divine and primitive integrity.

First, If it be *considered*, that he hath most sovereign, absolute and incontroulable dominion over you, as the potter hath over the clay; for *ye are the clay, and he is the Potter*: Nay, he hath more absolute dominion over you than the potter hath over the clay, for the potter maketh not the clay, both the clay and the potter being made by him; but *he hath made you, and not you yourselves; ye are all the work of his hands*, Psal. 100. 3. Isa. 64. 8. He hath made you living creatures, rational creatures, and new creatures; *If any man be in Christ, he is a new creature*, 2 Cor. 5. 17. which is the very flower of the creation: And *ye are his workmanship, created in Christ Jesus unto good works*, Eph. 2. 10. If therefore it be unsuitable and incongruous for the clay *to say to him that fashioned it, What makest thou?* or for *a man's work to say to him, that he hath no hands*, Isa. 45. 9. it's sure much more for you to say to your great Potter and Fashioner, What makest thou of us? why dealest thou so and so with us? *Wo to him that striveth with his Maker; let the potsherds strive with the potsherds of the earth: Hath not the potter power over the clay? And are you not in the hand of the Lord; as the clay is in the hands of the potter?* Rom. 9. 21. Jer. 18. 6. He might have made you *vessels to dishonour, vessels of wrath. fitted for destruction*, without being justly chargeable with any injury done to you; and when he hath, in the sovereignty of his most wonderful free grace, made you *vessels to honour*, and *vessels of mercy, which he hath afore prepared unto glory*, will ye dare to quarrel with him for disposing in his own way of your external condition in this world, and of these moveables and accessories that are wholly extrinsick, and not at all essential to your salvation and true happiness? (For, let all the pleasures, riches and honours of the world, even all the delights of the sons of men, in their very extract, spirits and quintessence, and when in a manner distill'd in a lembick, till they be made to evaporate the purest perfumes of their utmost perfections, be heaped on the Christian; as they make him no better Christian, nor make any addition at all to his true happiness; so, when he is deplumed and stripped naked of them all, every bird as it were of these earthly comforts taking back again from him its own feather, he is made never a whit the worse Christian, nor his happiness in the least impaired) It were certainly much more becoming you to say, It is the Lord, who can do us no wrong, and who hath undeservedly done us much good;' let him do to us what seemeth good in his sight.

Secondly, If it be *considered,* that he is of infinite wisdom, and knows much better what is good for you, than ye do yourselves, who often mistake what is good for you, through your corruption, ignorance, partiality or prejudice; but he, by the most absolute perfection of his blessed nature, is infinitely removed from all possibility of mistaking what is good in itself, or good for you: And if you will adventure your estate and livelihood in the world on able and faithful lawyers, when ye yourselves are much unacquainted with, and ignorant of law, and are disposed to think that the suit that is commenced against you will ruin you, while they think otherwise; and if you will commit your health and life to skilful and painful physicians or chirurgeons, and receive from the one many unpleasant and lothsom potions and pills, and suffer from the other such painful incisions and injections, such searchings, lancings and pancings, such scarifications, cauterizings and amputations; from all which ye have so great an aversation, if not abhorrency: Will ye not much rather, and much more confidently commit the conduct and care of yourselves, and of all that concerns you, to him, *of whose understanding there is no search,* as to what is good for his own people, and *whose faithfulness* in his dealing with them, *reacheth to the very clouds, and never faileth?* Psal. 36. 5. Psal. 89. 33. The skilfullest of these may mistake, none of them being infallible; and the most faithful of them may possibly at some times and in some things be found unfaithfully neglective, none of them being perfect: But it is simply impossible for him, either to mistake or to be unfaithful; for otherwise he should deny himself, and so cease to be God, whereof once to admit the thought thereof, is the highest blasphemy. Let therefore your confident trusting of men in their respective professions and callings, make you blush at, and be ashamed of your distrustings and jealousings of God, and of your quarrellings with him, even when ye know not for the time what he is doing with you, and when what is done would have been none of your own choice, but doth very much thwart and cross your natural inclination. Is it not enough that he is infinitely wise in himself, and for you? may you not therefore safely trust in him, and with unsolicitous confidence, commit the conduct of yourselves and of all your concerns to him, as knowing that he cannot himself be misled, nor misgovern you? may you not in faith, without distrustful and perplexing fear, follow him, as faithful *Abraham followed him, not knowing whither he went,* Heb. 11. 18. and cast all your care on him, *who careth for you,* 1 Pet. 5. 7. and hath made it your great care to *be careful for nothing,* Phil. 4. 6. and thus even sing care away?

Thirdly, If it be *considered,* that ye have in your own experience (as the rest of the people of God have in theirs) found, that in all his bypast dealings with you, even these that for the time were most afflicting, his will and your true welfare have been unseparably joined together, and that but very seldom and rarely your own will and welfare have trysted together; so that ye have been constrained, when at yourselves and in cold blood, to bless him that you got not your will in such and such things, however for the time ye were displeased with the want of it, and have been made to think, that if ever ye had any good days or hours along

your

your pilgrimage, your most crossed and afflicted ones, wherein God took most of his will, and gave you least of your own, have been your best days and hours: Dare you say, upon serious and just reflections, that it hath been otherwise? or that ye have not reason, as to all bygone cross providences, even the most apparently crushing of them, since the day that ye were first brought under the bond of his covenant to this day, to set up as it were your stone, and to call it *Ebenezer, The stone of help,* saying, *Hitherto the Lord hath helped us?* 1 Sam. 7. 12. May you not, and should you not then humbly and confidently trust him, that ye shall thro' grace have reason as to present and future ones, how sadly and surprizingly soever they are or may be circumstantiated, to say, *Jehovah-jireh, the Lord will see or provide?* Gen. 22. 14. O but it be a sweet, pleasant, spiritually wholsom and refreshful air that breathes in that walk betwixt Ebenezer and Jehovah-jireh, wherein a few turns taken by the most afflicted Christians in their serious, composed, spiritual and lively contemplation, would, thro' God's blessing, very much contribute quickly to reconcile them to all their respective crosses, how cross soever, and to the keeping of them in better, firmer, and more constant spiritual health!

Fourthly, If it be *considered,* that by your pettish, fretful, male-contented and unsubmissive contendings, strivings and strugglings with him, ye will not help yourselves, ye may well make your own burden the more uneasy, and your chain the heavier; *Should it be according to your mind?* Job 34. 33. *Shall the earth be forsaken for you? or shall the rock be removed out of his place?* Job 18. 4. *Will ye disannul his judgment? will ye condemn him, that ye may be righteous?* Job 40. 8. *Will ye strive against him, who giveth not account of any of his matters?* Job 33. 13. Will ye tax his wisdom, as if he did not understand what is convenient for you? *Will ye teach God knowledge?* Job 21. 22. Is it fit that he should come down to your will, rather than ye should come up to his? shall God change and break all his wisely laid measures and methods of governing his people, and take new ones to gratify your peevish humours? He will not be diverted from his purpose; *When he is in one way, who can turn him? what his soul desireth, that he doth; for he performeth the thing that is appointed for you,* Job 23. 13, 14. He is more just to himself, (to speak so) and more merciful to you, than to degrade as it were his infinite wisdom so far, as to suffer himself to be swayed against the dictates of it, by such short-sighted and forward tutors as you; the great Physician of souls is more compassionate and wise than to permit his distempered, and sometimes even in a manner distracted patients, to prescribe their own course of physick; but he will needs do, what he thought fit and resolved to do, *whether ye choose, or whether ye refuse,* Job 34. 33. only he would (to say so) have your consent unto, and your approbation of what he doth, for the greater peace and tranquillity of your minds: *Surely therefore it is meet,* meekly and submissively, *to be said to God,* whenever and however he chastiseth, *I have borne chastisement, I will not offend any more; that which I know not, teach thou me; if I have done iniquity, I will do no more,* Job 34. 31, 32. It is the surest and shortest way to get our will, in so far as may be for our weal, to allow him to take his own will and way with us; for he hath a special complacency in this, and therein gives wonderful vent to the bowels of his tender compassion toward his chastised and humbly submissive children: *Surely* (saith he) *I have heard Ephraim bemoaning himself thus, Thou hast chastised me, and I was chastised, as a bullock unaccustomed to the yoke: turn thou me, and I shall be turned; for thou art the Lord my God. Surely after that I was turned, I repented; and after that I was instructed, I smote upon my thigh: I was ashamed, yea, even confounded, because I did bear the reproach of my youth. Is Ephraim my dear son? is he a pleasant child? for since I spake against him, I do earnestly remember him still: therefore my bowels are troubled for him; I will surely have mercy on him, saith the Lord,* Jer. 31. 18, 19, 20. Thus, when ye come submissively to his hand, he comes as it were sweetly to yours: And as ye gain nothing by your striving with him, so ye lose nothing, but gain much, by your soft stooping and silent submitting to him; If ye *humble yourselves in the sight of the Lord, he shall lift you up,* James 4. 10. *Humble yourselves therefore under the mighty hand of God, that he may exalt you in due time,* 1 Pet. 5. 6.

Fifthly, If it be *considered,* that ye stand in need of all the troubles and afflictions that ye meet with; whenever *ye are in heaviness through* one or mo, or *manifold temptations,* it is alway, and only, *if need be,* 1 Pet. 1. 6. And if ye be well seen in the state and posture of your soul-affairs, what graces of the Spirit are to be quickned and drawn forth into more lively and vigorous exercise, what of these precious spices in your gardens are to be blown upon, not only by the more gentle and soft south-winds of consolations, but also by the more sharp and nipping north-winds of afflictions, and to be beaten as it were in the mortar thereof, that they may send forth their pleasant and fragrant smell; what religious duties are either much neglected, or but very lifelesly, coldly, formally, lazily, superficially and heartlesly performed, and to what a higher pitch and peg of spirituality in the manner of performing them they are to be skrewed up; what lusts and corruptions are to be further mortified and subdued; how little your hypocrisy, your self-love and self-seeking, your pride, passion, impatience, unpliableness and unsubmittedness to the will of God, your carnalness, earthly-mindedness, your immoderate and inordinate love to the things of the world, your murmuring and fretting at, your dissatisfaction and discontent with your present lot; how little these and many other corruptions are crucified and brought at under: If, I say, ye be well seen and versed in the knowledge of your spiritual condition, ye will upon serious and thorow reflections find, that ye stand in need of every affliction ye meet with, as to all the circumstances thereof; or, if ye do not, in so far ye are unacquainted with, and strangers to yourselves, and to the state and posture of your spiritual affairs; nay, ye will easily find, that all, even your heaviest crosses and afflictions, have enough ado to work you up to what you should be at; and tho' sometimes ye may be disposed to think that ye could hardly bear any more, yet ye will upon due search find that ye could have wanted nothing of what ye have met with, without a greater prejudice than the cross hath brought along with it. We are naturally froward and peevish, bent to fretfulness and discontent, inclining rather to restless endeavouring to have our lot brought up to our spirits, than to be at suitable pains to have our spirits brought down to our lot, and therefore have much need to be tamed and calmed by the cross; this rugged and uneasy temper of spirit being the great hinderer, yea opposite of that stayed and sweet contentation of heart with and in every state, which is the very life of a Christian's life, *consisting* (as the Lord saith) *not in the abundance of the things which we possess,* Luke 12. 15. but in our satisfiedness with them, whether abundant or not: To the attaining unto which blessed temper, the shortest cut, and most compendious way, is, in the *first* place, to be well-pleased and satisfied with God himself, and with a solidly secured interest in him; and to endeavour, in the *next* place, to be well-pleasing in his sight, to be gracious in his eyes, to stand well in his thoughts, even *to do always these things that please him,* John 8. 29. to which desirable frame of soul, if we were once thro' grace brought, (whereto our bearing of the yoke, and putting our shoulders under the cross, is not a little thro' God's blessing contributive) O how good-natured then and easy to please would we be found to be, and how ready to construe well of all that he doth to us! seldom out of humour, so speak so. Now, if we stand in need of all the afflictions we are trysted with, in all their most sad and sorrowful circumstances, (as certainly we do, because God, who cannot lie or mistake, hath said it) why should we not submit ourselves to his will in measuring them out to us? or what just reason can there be to be dissatisfied with, or to complain of God's giving to, or

ordering

ordering that for us, whereof we stand in need, and which we cannot want, without being considerably prejudged and worsted by the want?

Sixthly, If it be *considered*, that in all your chastisements and afflictions God is graciously driving the blessed design of your spiritual *good* and *profit*, making them *all to work together* for that desirable end, causing them *turn to your salvation, thro' the help of the prayers of others of his people, and the supply of the Spirit of Jesus Christ*, Rom. 8. 28. Phil. 2. 19. Giving you assurance by his faithful word of promise, that thereby *your iniquity shall be purged*, and *that this shall be all the fruit* (O strange and admirable condescension of grace! *all the fruit!) to take away sin*, Isa. 27. 9. and that he will not chastise you *as parents according to the flesh do their children*, to wit, *for their own pleasure;* who, however they may have a general design of good to their children in their chastising of them, yet, thro' a remainder of corruption in the best of them, they are often subjected to such hurries and transports of passion, when it comes to the act of chastisement, that they much forget to consult the good and advantage of the chastised child, and too much gratify their own pleasure and humour; but that he will chastise *for your profit, that ye may be made partakers of his holiness*, Heb. 12. 10. Now, if this be his design in chastising, and if this be the promised fruit of your chastisements and afflictions, why should ye not therein submit to his pleasure, which hath your own profit inseparably joined within it, if ye your selves do not sinfully lay obstructions in the way thereof, as otherwise, so particularly by your being displeased with this his pleasure, which yet his grace in his own people suffers not to be invincible nor final? I do not say, that our chastisements and afflictions do of themselves produce this profit, and bring forth this fruit: for alas! we may from doleful experience have ere now arrived at a sad perswasion, that we are proof against all applications, excepting that of sovereign, efficacious and all difficulty-conquering free grace, and that nothing will do at us save that alone; whatever means be made use of, this only must be the efficient producer of our profit: It is a piece of God's royal and incommunicable prerogative, which he hath not given out of his own hand to any dispensation, whether of ordinances, never so lively and powerful in themselves; or of providences, never so cross, loudly alarming and clearly speaking, abstractly from his own blessing, effectually *to teach to profit*, Isa. 48. 17. and therefore he doth (as well he may) claim it to himself alone, as his peculiar privilege, while he saith, *I am the Lord thy God that teacheth thee to profit*. Since then this is his design in all the chastisements inflicted on his own people, and since he only by his grace can make it infrustrably take effect, let him have our hearty allowance and approbation, to carry it on vigorously and successfully; and let us pray more frequently and fervently, that, by his effectually teaching, our profiting may be made more and more to appear under our chastisements; and withal, *in the multitude of our* sad *thoughts* about them, let *his comforts delight our souls*, and this comfort in particular, that in them all he graciously designs and projects *our profit*, even the making of us more and more *to partake of his holiness*.

Seventhly, If it be *considered*, that all our trials and troubles are but of time-continuance, and will period with it; they are but *for a season*, 1 Pet. 1. 6. yea, but *for a moment*, 2 Cor. 4. 17. *He will not contend for ever*, knowing well, if he should do so, *the spirits would fail before him, and the souls which he hath made*, Isa. 57. 16. Tho' they should follow close on you, and accompany you to your very dying day, yet then they will leave you, and take their last good-night and everlasting farewel of you; *sorrow and sighing will* then for ever *fly away*, and *all tears* on whatever account *shall then be wiped from your eyes*, Rev. 7. 17. and 21. 4. It is a great alleviation and mitigation of the most grievous affliction, and of the bitterest and most extreme sorrow, to think, that not only it will have a term-day and date of expiration,

but

but it will quickly, in a very short time, even in a moment, be over and at an end (as a holy martyr said to his fellow-sufferer in the fire with him, *It is but winking, and our pain and sorrow is all over*) and that there shall be an eternal tack of freedom from it; and that everlasting solace, satisfaction, and joy without the least mixture of sorrow and sadness, shall succeed to it, and come in the room thereof: It is but for the little space of *threescore years and ten*, or *fourscore*, Psal. 90. 10. (which length most people never come) that his people are subjected to trouble; and what is that very short moment and little point of time, being compared with a vast and incomprehensibly long eternity? in respect of which, *a thousand years are but as one day, or as a watch in the night, when it is past*, Psal. 90. 4. And no doubt the little while's trouble, sadness and sorrow of sojourning and militant saints, is, in the depth of divine wisdom, ordered so, that it may the more commend and endear that blessed calm and tranquillity, that fulness of purest joys, and these most perfect pleasures at his right hand, that triumphant saints shall for evermore enjoy.

Eighthly, If it be *considered*, that all along the little moment that your trials and afflictions abide with you, they are, even the saddest and most severe of them, moderate, and thro' his grace portable and *light*; *In measure he debateth with you, and stays his rough wind in the day of his east wind*, Isa. 27. 8. And whatever difficulty ye sometimes find under sore pressures, to get it solidly and practically believed, yet *God is faithful who hath promised, and will not suffer you to be tempted above that which ye are able, but will with the temptation make a way to escape, that ye may be able to bear it*, 1 Cor. 10. 13. He is a God of judgment, (Isa. 30. 18.) and discretion, that suits his peoples burdens to their backs, and wisely proportions their straits to their strength: *He puts not new wine into old bottles*, Mat. 9. 17. neither doth he break the bruised reed, Isa. 42. 3. and even *when he hides his face, and is wroth with his children, and smites them for their iniquity*, Isa. 42. 17, 18. it is only fatherly wrath; And however dreadful that may be, and difficult to be born, yet there is nothing vindictive in it; it is a Father's anger, but contempered with a Father's love, where also love predomines in the contemperature. And indeed the most extreme, and the very heaviest of all our afflictions, are moderate, and even *light*, being compared, *1st*, With what your sins deserve, exceedingly far *beneath the desert whereof ye are punished*, Ezra 9. 23. even so far, that ye may without all compliment most truly say, *That it is because his compassions fail not, that ye are not consumed*, Lam. 3. 22. that ye are kept out of hell, and free from everlasting burnings, to which your many, various, and grievously aggravated provocations, have made you most justly liable: So that ye have reason to think any affliction, short of everlasting destruction from the presence of God, to be a highly valued piece of moderation, and to say, *Wherefore doth a living man complain, a man for the punishment of his sin?* Lam. 3. 39. We will bear the indignation of the Lord, because we have sinned against him, Mic. 7. 9. 2dly, With what others of the people of God have readily met with; for *we have not resisted to the blood, striving against sin*, Heb. 12. 4. We have it may be all this while been but *running with the footmen*, when they have been put *to contend with horses*, Jer. 12. 5. 3dly, With what ourselves have sometimes dreaded and been put to deprecate, when horrid guilt hath stared us in the face, and when God apprehended to be very angry, even threatning to *smite us with the wound of an enemy*, and *with the chastisement of a cruel one*, to *run upon us a giant, to break all our bones*: And again to *shew himself marvellous upon us, by taking us by the neck, and shaking us in pieces*, Jer. 30. 14. Job 16. 14. & 12. Job 10. 16. 4thly, With what our blessed Lord Jesus suffered for his people, who, all the while he sojourned here on earth, was a *Man of sorrows, and acquainted with grief*, Isa. 53. 4. and might most justly have said, beyond all men, *I am the man that hath seen affliction by the rod of his wrath: Is there any sorrow*

row like unto mine, in the day when the Lord hath afflicted me? And 5thly, Being compared with that *far more exceeding and eternal weight of glory, which they work for you*, 2 Cor. 4. 14. Seeing then that the sharpest and sorest of your afflictions are, in these and many other respects, very moderate, gentle, easy and light; is there not reason why ye should in them, without grudging, sweetly submit yourselves to his will, heartsomly saying, It might have been much worse, this falls infinitely short of what we have deserved, blessed be God that it is only thus, and no worse.

Ninthly, If it be *considered*, that often, when in any more than ordinary spiritual and lively frame of soul, ye have in prayer desired the Lord, that he would take any way, and make use of any means he pleased (wherein your sin might not be) to make you more serious in the exercise of godliness, more effectually to mortify your corruptions, and to further your conformity to his image in holiness; and that ye should thro' his grace be content, putting as it were a blank in his hand, to be filled up as himself in his own infinite wisdom should think fit, declaring that ye were satisfied, on the terms proposed by Jesus Christ, to be his disciples, and to take up not only *a cross*, or *the cross* in general, but, Mat. 16. 24. *your cross* in particular, the cross that should be shaped out for you, however circumstantiated: And when under some very sad affliction, he on the matter bespeaks thus, I am now about to grant you your own desire, tho' it may be in such a way, and by such a mean, as either would have been none of your own choosing, had it been left to your choice, or possibly such as ye did not think of; will ye be displeased with me, or mistake my hearing of your prayers, fulfilling of your petitions, and granting you according to your own heart's desire, because I do it in my own way, and by means of my own choosing, wherein ye left and allowed me a latitude, and not in your way and by your means, which ye then renounced, as not thinking yourselves competent judges thereof? Alas! here we are often found at best to border upon a practical rewing, retracting, and lifting up again of the blank submission which we professed to lay down before him; and to say, by our fretting, repining, dissatisfaction, immoderate heaviness and despondency of spirit, that we were somewhat rash, and not so well advised, when we subscribed and gave in such a submission, and surrender of ourselves to him; that we did not think he would have taken such advantage of us, or would have put us thus sore to it; and that, if we had thought he would have done so, we would have been better advised, before we had thus submitted to him, and with our own consent put ourselves in his reverence; and that, if it had been any thing *but this*, we could have born it (whereas he saith, Nothing *but this*) Whereby we do not only, not a little reflect upon him, as dealing unkindly, and doing what we would not have expected at his hand; but also make a sad and humbling discovery of much unsoundness in ourselves, as to our offering up of such general desires, and as to our making of such absolute submissions to him: Let us therefore, in order to the justifying of him as both righteous and kind, and to the vindicating of ourselves, at least from allowing of any unsoundness, dissimulation, or unfair and meerly complimental dealing with God, in our submitting ourselves to him in the general, without any *But's* or *If's*, any *restrictions* or *exceptions*, hold at the submission given; sharply expostulating with, and severely chiding ourselves for this discovered practical contradiction and contravention; and we shall find that he hath done nothing unworthy of himself, nor in the least prejudicial to us, but what is according to our own most deliberate desires, and greatly to our advantage.

It were a very wide mistake, if, from what is discoursed in this *Consideration*, any should conclude, that we intend either to commend or allow Christians praying directly and expresly for crosses and afflictions, let be for such and such afflictions in particular: For, beside that we neither find it commanded in the scriptures, nor allowedly (if at all) precedented or practised by the saints recorded there; and that it seems to be a sinful limiting of the sovereign God to a particular mean: We may easily know, from sad experience, with what difficulty, repining and fainting we often bear these crosses and afflictions that we are most clearly called to take on, and that are unavoidably laid upon us; and how lamentably little, for most part, we profit by them: What hope or assurance could we then have, that we should either carry christianly under, or make suitable improvement of such crosses as we should unwarrantably seek, and pray for to ourselves? It is true, we find some of the saints, and these, stars of the first magnitude, as Moses, Job, Elias, David and Jonas, in their distempered, malecontent, or fainting fits, passionately, preposterously and precipitantly praying, or rather wishing for death; (for which they were not for the time in so good case) but that was not for death, under the notion of affliction, but rather to prevent future and further afflictions, or to have a period put to presently incumbent ones. If it should here be said, Why may not saints pray for afflictions, since they seem to be promised in the covenant of grace, as Psal. 89. 30, 31, 32. Hos. 2. 6, 7. and v. 14. and since God hath graciously promised to bless all the afflictions of his people, and to make them turn to their spiritual good, profit and advantage, as Rom. 8. 28. and Heb. 12. 10. and elsewhere? To the *first* part of the *objection*, it may be briefly answered, That these, and other such, are not properly and formally promises of the covenant of grace, but rather covenant-threatnings, (for the covenant of grace hath its own threatnings, suited to the nature thereof, as well as the covenant of works hath its) tho' dipped (to say so) in covenant-grace and mercy: And to the *other* part of it as briefly, That God hath promised to bless and to cause to profit by such afflictions and chastisements as himself thinks fit to inflict and lay on, but not these which we seek and pray for to ourselves: Neither doth that scripture, Psal. 119. v. 75. *I know——that in faithfulness thou hast afflicted me*, say any thing towards strengthning the objection, or invalidating the answers given to it; for, the Psalmist only there humbly and thankfully acknowledgeth God's faithfulness in fulfilling his threatning, in afflicting him when he went astray; and in performing his promise, in blessing his affliction to him for preventing his after-straying, and making him learn better to keep his commandments; in both which he is faithful. All that is either expressed or meant in this *consideration*, is, That the saints often pray God, that he would take his own way, and use his own means to bring about these great ends mentioned; wherein there is indeed at least a tacit insinuation, that if he in his wisdom see it meet to make use of the rod and affliction in order thereto, that they will not allow themselves to decline the same, nor to mistake him in it; but that rather they shall, through grace, be satisfied with, and bless him for fulfilling their petitions, and granting them according to their own hearts desires, tho' it be by such means: Which is not praying for afflictions, but a resolved and declared submission to infinite Wisdom's love-choice of his own midses to effectuate and bring to pass the prayed-for ends.

Tenthly, If it be *considered*, that it now neither grieveth nor troubleth any of all the glorified, triumphing, and palm-bearing company before the throne of God, and of the Lamb, that they were exercised with so many and so great trials and tribulations, while they were here below: It troubleth not John the Baptist, that he was imprisoned, basely murdered and beheaded there in a hole, without having access to give any publick testimony before his death, and at the desire of a wanton dancing damsel, thro' the instigation of her adulterous and incestuous mother: Nor Stephen, (commonly called the Proto-martyr) that he was stoned to death as a blasphemer, for giving testimony to the most precious and comfortable truth of Christ's being the Messiah: Nor Paul, that he was thrice beaten with rods, and

and received five times forty stripes save one; that he was in so many perils by sea and land, in the city, in the country, and in the wilderness, by the Heathen, by his own countrymen, and by false brethren; that he was stoned, and suffered all these other things, whereof he gives us an historical abridgment in his 2d Epist. to the Corinthians, chap. 11. Nor doth it trouble any of all these *worthies, of whom the world was not worthy*, that they were cruelly mocked, imprisoned, scourged, tortured, or tympanized and racked, stoned, tormented, sawn asunder, killed with the sword, tempted, driven to dens and caves of the earth, and put to wander up and down in sheep-skins and goat-skins, whose martyrology the apostle briefly compendeth, Heb. 11. Nor doth it trouble any other of all the martyrs, saints and servants of Jesus, who have in the several ages of the church suffered so many and so great things while they were here in the world; nay, all these their sufferings go to make up a considerable part of their song of praise in heaven: (where the history of these wars, of and for the Lord, will be very pleasant to them to read, however sore and bloody they were on earth) And not only so, but these of them who have suffered most, wonder much that they have suffered so little, and that they are come to so excellent and glorious a kingdom, thorow so little tribulation in the way to it: Believe it, there will be as much matter of thanksgiving and praise to God found treasured up under the plyes and foldings (to say so) of the most cross and afflicting providences that ever the people of God met with here in the world, as under these that for the time were more smiling and satisfying; Let us then, valuing all things we meet with, according to the aspect they have on our spiritual and eternal state, (which is sure the justest and safest valuation of them) heartily allow him to take his own will and way in afflicting us.

Eleventhly, If it be *considered*, that as this submission to the will of God, in cross and afflicting providences, is chronicled in the sacred records, to the perpetual commendation of several of the saints; namely, of Aaron, of whom it is said, when God had slain his two sons in a strange and stupendous manner, even by fire from heaven, for their presumptuous offering of strange fire before him, that *he held his peace*, Lev. 10. 3. Of old Eli, when he received a sad message concerning himself and his house by the hand of young Samuel, who said, *It is the Lord, let him do what seemeth him good*, 1 Sam. 3. 18. Of Job, after, by four several messengers, (each of them coming immediately upon the back of the other, so that he scarcely got leave to breathe betwixt, or the former to finish his lamentable narration) the terribly alarming tidings were brought him, concerning the plundering of his oxen and asses by the Sabeans, and the killing of his servants with the sword; concerning the consuming of his sheep and servants by the fire of God falling from heaven upon them; concerning the carrying away of his camels, and the killing of his servants by the Caldeans; and concerning the smothering to death of all his sons and daughters, while feasting together, by the falling of the house upon them; who said, *The Lord giveth, and the Lord taketh away, blessed be the name of the Lord; In all this not sinning, nor charging God foolishly*, Job 1. 21, 22. Of David, who, in a croud of crosses, saith to God, *I was dumb, I opened not my mouth, because thou didst it*, Psal. 39. 9. 2 Sam. 15. 25, 26. and who, when forced to flee from Jerusalem, by his unnatural and rebellious son Absalom, and sending back the ark thither, with admirable composure and sweet stooping of soul, said, *If I shall find favour in the eyes of the Lord, he will bring me again, and shew me both it and his habitation: But if he say thus, I have no delight in thee, behold, here am I, let him do with me as seemeth good to him*: Of Hezekiah, when that heavy message was brought to him by the prophet Isaiah concerning the Babylonish captivity, wherein his royal posterity were to have their deep share; who said, *Good is the word of the Lord which thou hast spoken;* who said moreover, *Is it not good, if peace and truth*

truth be in my days? 2 Kings 20. 19. if the threatned doom and sentence shall be for a while suspended, and not presently execute: And of these Christians, who, after they had with much weeping earnestly intreated the apostle Paul, deservedly very dear to them, not to go up to Jerusalem, where the prophet Agabus had foretold he should be apprehended and put in bonds, and perceived that he was inflexibly resolved at any rate of hazard to go thither, ceased, and submissively said, *The will of the Lord be done,* Acts 21. 14. As, I say, it is thus chronicled to their commendation, so it is a piece of most beautiful and amiable conformity to the practice of our blessed Lord Jesus, of whom we ought to *be followers as dear children* (Eph. 5. 1.) in all these things, wherein he is proposed as a Pattern for our imitation, who in a great and grievous agony of trouble, and when most terribly assaulted by a strong combination of cross and afflicting providences, and after conditionate deprecating of that bitterest cup and blackest hour, pleasantly, sweetly and submissively subjoined, and saith to his Father, *Nevertheless not my will, but thine be done; Not as I will, but as thou wilt,* Luke 22. 42. Mat. 26. 32.

Twelfthly and finally, If it be *considered,* that when the whole contexture and web of providences, and more especially about the catholick, visible, militant church, and every individual member thereof, shall be wrought out, and in its full length and breadth (as it were) spread forth in the midst of all the redeemed, perfected, glorified and triumphant company of saints, standing round about, and with admiration beholding it; there will not be found (to say so) one misplaced thread, nor one wrong-set colour in it all, but every thing will be found to have fallen in, in the fittest place, and in the most beautiful season and order thereof: O so rare, so remarkable, so renowned and so ravishing a piece, as it will by them all unanimously, and with one voice, be judged and declared to be, even worthy of the most exquisite art and infinite skill of the great Worker thereof! The severest criticks, and most difficultly satisfiable of them all, while here below, about more publick and more particular cross providences, will then fully and to the height be satisfied, and will all, without any the least hesitation or jarring, readily and chearfully bear him this concordant testimony, that *he hath done all things well,* Mark 7. 37. every thing in particular, and all things in general, tho', when he was a doing of them, they often presumptuously took upon them rashly to censure, and to offer their impertinent and crabbed animadversions on, and their amendations and alterations of several of them; and will most cordially bless him, that he wrought on in his own way, about his church, and each of themselves, without consulting them, or following their way, which would have quite marred the beauty, and darkned the lustre and splendor of that most close and curious divine contexture.

Every one of these considerations hath much reason in it, to persuade to this intire and absolute submission to God's will and pleasure, in what is cross to you, afflicted and sorrowful Christians; but O how much weight and strength of sound spiritual reason is there in them all united together, (beside the many other excellent considerations, dispersed up and down these choice Sermons, stuffed full with strong cordials, fitted both to recover and preserve you from fainting under your many several afflictions) powerfully to persuade and prevail with you, even the most averse, untoward, way-ward, and cross-grain'd (to say so) of you all, without further debate, demur, or delay, in these things that are most afflicting to you, and do most thwart your inclination, to come in his will, and pleasantly, without any the least allowed reluctancy or gainsaying, to submit to him! How might you thus possess your souls in patience, and how quiet, calm, sedate and composed might ye be, more especially in troublesom times, amidst these things wherewith others are kept in a continual hurry, almost to the hazard of being distracted by them?

Let

Let them all, *my noble Lord*, prevail with your Lordship in particular, reverently to adore, silently to stoop unto, and sweetly to acquiesce in, the Lord's sovereign, holy, and wise ordering your many and various complicated trials; and more especially his late removing your excellent Lady, the desire of your eyes, the Christian and comfortable companion of your youth, by his stroke: As indeed all the ties of nearest and dearest relations, betwixt husbands and wives, parents and children, brothers and sisters, &c. are capable of dissolution, and will all, ere long, by death be actually dissolved; there being but one tie and knot of marriage-union betwixt precious Jesus Christ and the believer, that by divine ordination is eternally incapable of any dissolution, even by death itself; which tho' it dissolve the strait union that is betwixt the soul and the body, yet doth not at all loose the straiter bond of union that is betwixt him and both of them, but it remains still inviolable; and by vertue thereof, the believer's vile dead body shall be raised again at the last day, conform to his own glorious body, and be re-united to the perfected-soul, which two old intimates will then meet in far better case than when they were parted and pulled asunder: For he is an Husband that cannot grow old, sick or weak, neither can he die; he is a Husband whose bride and spouse is never a widow, neither hath he any relicts: The drawing on of which matchless match and marvellous marriage, is one great design of these sweet sermons, wherein pregnant reasons are adduced by this *friend of the Bridegroom*, to persuade sinners to embrace the offer thereof made to them in the gospel; and to make them, who, by his own gracious and powerful insinuations on their hearts, have entertained his proposal, toward making up, and final closing of the match, to bless themselves in their choice, and to bless him, that ever he was pleased to stoop so very low as to become a Suiter to them, with a peremptory resolution to admit of no refusal, but infrustrably to carry their hearts consent to take him for their *Lord, Head* and *Husband*, to be to them a *Saviour*, a *Physician* and *Treasure*, even their *All in all*, their *All above all;* which day of espousals, as it was *the day of the gladness of his heart*, so it will never be any grief of heart to them. Let all mutinous thoughts about his dealings with you be silenced with, *It's the Lord;* let not too much dwelling on the thoughts of your affliction, to the filling of your heart still with sorrow, incapacitate you for, nor divert you from, humble asking the Lord, what he aims at by all these dispensations, what he would have you to learn out of them, what he reproveth and contends for, what he would have you amending your hands in, and what he would have you more weaned, self-denied, and mortified in, and what he would have you a further length and a greater proficient in : He hath told you *the truth, that these things are expedient for you;* study to find them to be so in your experience. Sure he hath, by them, written in great, legible and capital characters, yea, even as with a sun-beam, vanity, emptiness, uncertainty, mutability, unsatisfactoriness and disappointment upon the forehead of all creature-comforts, and with a loud voice called your Lordship, yet more seriously than ever, to seek after solid soul-satisfaction in his own blessed and all-sufficient Self, where it is most certainly to be found, without all peradventure or possibility of misgiving: Make haste, *my Lord*, yet to come by a more close confining of all your desires and expectations of happiness and satisfaction to your soul, to God only, contracting and gathering them in, from the vast and wearisom circumference of earthly comforts, and concentring them all in himself as their point; study thro' grace, in a sweet soliloquy, to bespeak your soul, thus, *My soul, wait thou only upon God, for my expectation is from him,* Psal. 62. 5. O blessed confinement of desires and expectations of happiness and satisfaction to the soul! where it is as impossible to meet with disappointment, as it is impossible not to meet with it from every airth whence it is looked for. Alas! it is the scattering of our expectations and desires of happiness among other

objects

objects beside him, that breeds us all the disquiet, anxiety and vexation; whereas, if we kept ourselves thro' grace under a more close and constant confinement to him, when this and that, and the other creature-comfort, whether person or thing, were taken from us, there would be no deduction made from, nor any diminution made of our true happiness; none of these, how dear and desirable soever, being essentially constitutive of it, nor so much as trenching thereupon; and he, in whom only all our happiness lies, being *the same yesterday, to day, and for ever, without any variableness or shadow of turning.* There are some whom he loveth so well, that he cannot (to speak so) find in his heart to see them thus to parcel out their affections, and to dote upon any painted imaginary happiness in creature-comforts; and therefore, on design, he doth either very much blast them, as to the expected satisfaction from them; or quite remove them, that, by making such a vacuity, he may make way for himself to fill it, and happily to necessitate the person, humbly, prayerfully, and believingly, to put him to the filling of it: And it is a great vacuity that he, *who fills heaven and earth,* cannot fill; a little of whose gracious presence, and manifested special love, can go very far to fill up the room that is made void, by the removal of the choicest and most desirable of all earthly comforts and enjoyments. Happy they, who, when they lose a near and dear relation or friend, or any idol they are fond of, are helped of God to make Jesus Christ, as it were, succeed to the same as its Heir, by taking that loss as a summons to transfer and settle their whole love on him, the Object incomparably most worthy of it, as being *altogether lovely,* or *all desires!* Cant. 5. 16. There is no earthly comfort, person or thing, but hath somewhat in it that is not desirable, and that it would be the better to want; but there is nothing in him that is not truly desirable, nor any thing out of him that is worthy to be desired

I am, *my noble Lord,* the more easily prevailed with and encouraged to address the dedication of these *Sermons* to your Lordship, more particularly when I remember *the unfeigned faith that first dwelt in your grandmother,* as another *Lois;* and in your mother, as another *Eunice;* and more lately in your own choice Lady, who, as another *beloved* Persis, *laboured much in the Lord:* And tho' she had but a very short Christian race (in which she was much encouraged by coming into your Noble Father's family, and her beholding how hard your blest Mother did run and press toward the mark, even when in the last stage, and turning in a manner the last stoop of her Christian course) yet it was a very swift one, where she did quite out-run many that were in Christ long before her; (all three Ladies of honour, almost (if I need to say almost) without parallels in their times, in the serious and diligent exercise of godliness, and patterns worthy to be imitated by others) and I trust in your Lordship's self also, yea, and in several others of your elder and younger noble relations (for grace hath such a draught of souls amongst you, as it useth not often to have in societies of so noble extract, *for not many noble are called*) which, as it deservedly draweth respect to such of you, as are thus privileged, from the observers of it, so it layeth a mighty strong obligation upon you, to be much for God, and in service to your generation, according to his will. Further, when I observe your Lordship's christian and exemplary carriage, under such a conjunction and combination of so very cross, and almost crushing calamitous providences, choosing rather contentedly and satisfiedly to be (if it so please the Lord, and O! that it may not) the last of that ancient and honourable family, than to be found endeavouring to keep it from sinking by any sinful and unwarrantable course, particularly by defrauding just creditors (tho' the debt was not of your Lordship's own contracting) under whatever specious pretexts and advantages of law; whereof many make no bones, who,

if

if they may keep up their superfluities, care not to ruin their friends ingaging in sure-tyship for their debt, and to live on the substance of others. Moreover, when with great satisfaction I notice how much your Lordship makes it your business to follow your noble ancestors, in so far as they were *followers of Christ*, which many great men, even in the christian world, alas, do not much mind, not considering that it is true nobility, where God is the chief and top of the kin, and where religion is at the bottom; and what renown'd *Raleigh* saith, *Hinc dictus nobilis quasi præ aliis virtute notabilis*; and what another saith, *Qui ab illustrium majorum splendida virtute degenerarunt nobilia portenta sunt.* And finally, when I consider, that in your Lordship's retirement and abstraction from wonted converse and dealing in business, you will have access at leisure to read them, whereby you may thro' God's blessing be sweetly diverted from pensive and not so profitable poring on your affliction, and be much instructed, convinced, reproved, directed, edified, strengthned and comforted. Read them then, my Lord, carefully (as I take it for granted you will) ponder and digest them well, and I am hopeful, that they shall thro' grace prove contributive to the bringing upon you a considerable growth of holiness, and to the making of *your ways and doings* more than ever such, that others of his people observing the same, shall be comforted, and made to think and say, *Verily God hath not done in vain all that he hath done to yonder Nobleman.*

That these substantial and marrowy gospel-sermons may come along to you all, nay to all the readers of them, and to your Lordship more particularly, with showers of gospel-blessings, is the earnest desire of,

Dearly beloved afflicted Christians, and my very noble Lord in particular,

Nov. 15. 1682.

Your Companion in Tribulation, desirous also to be in the Kingdom and Patience of Jesus Christ, and your Servant in the Gospel for his sake.

J. C.

xvi

Unto the Readers, and more particularly unto the Inhabitants of the City of Glasgow, of all Ranks.

THOUGH the whole field of the sacred and infallibly inspired scriptures, be very pleasant and beautiful (a spiritual cool and cleansing, a fructifying, fresh, refreshful and wholesom air, breathing continually there) yet if we may compare some parts thereof with others, those wherein *the Treasure, precious Jesus Christ*, lieth most obvious and open, are certainly most pleasant and beautiful; and amongst these, such as hold forth his sufferings, and himself as crucified, most evidently before mens eyes, have a peculiar and passing pleasantness and beauty in them: If so, then sure this 53d chapter of the prophecies of Isaiah cannot, but be lookt at as a transcendently pleasant, beautiful, sweet-smelling and fragrant piece of divine scripture-field, wherein the evangelick prophet discourseth of the sufferings of Christ, as particularly and fully, as plainly and pathetically, even to the very life, as if he himself had been a spectator and eye-witness of them. However, this sweetest chapter from beginning to end, as also the three last verses of the foregoing, be by the greatly learn'd Grotius most miserably perverted, while he industriously diverts it from the Messiah, and by stretching and curtailing thereof at his pleasure, (as the cruel tyrant Mazentius did the men he laid on his bed, to make them of equal length with it) wholly applies it to the prophet Jeremiah in the first place only, not denying that it hath accommodation to Christ, of whom too he takes but little or no notice in all his annotations thereon: The impertinencies and wreslings of which application, are convincingly holden forth by famous Doctor Owen (who looks on this portion of scripture as the sum of what is spoken in the Old Testament, concerning the satisfactory death of Jesus Christ) that mell of Socinians, in his *Vindiciæ Evangelicæ* against Bidle and the Racovian Catechism, who was a burning and shining light in the reformed churches, tho' now, alas! to their great loss, lately extinguished: And indeed the dealing of that very learn'd man professing himself to be a Christian, with this most clear, and to all true Christians most comfortable scripture, is the more strange and even stupendous, considering, 1. That several passages in it, are in the New Testament expresly applied to Christ, *Matth.* 8. 17. *Mark* 15. 28. *Luke* 22. 27. *Acts* 8. 28, &c. 1 *Pet.* 2. 22. & 24. but not one so much as alluded to, in reference to Jeremiah. 2. That the ancient Jewish Doctors and the Chaldee Paraphrast (as Dr. Owen, in the foresaid learn'd and savoury book, gives an account) do apply it to him. 3. That a late Doctor of great note and honour among the Jews, Abarbinel affirmeth, That in truth he sees not how one verse of the whole (several of which he toucheth on) can be expounded of Jeremiah; and wonders greatly that any wise man can be so foolish as to commend, let be to be the author of such an exposition, (as one Rabbi Gaon had been) which is (saith he) so utterly alien, and not in the least drawn from the scripture. 4. That several Jews do profess, that their Rabbins could easily have extricated themselves from all other places of the prophets (a vain and groundless boast) if Isaiah in this place had but held his peace, as Hulsius (very lately, if not present) Hebrew-Professor at Breda, declares some of them did to himself. 5. That a Rabbi, by his own confession, was converted from a Jew to a Christian, by the reading of this 53d of Isaiah, as the

excellent

excellent Mr. Boyle, in his delicate discourses on the stile of the holy scriptures, informs us; yea, that divers Jews have been convinced, and converted to the Christian faith by the evidence of this prophecy, as learn'd and laborious Mr. Pool affirms in his lately published English Annotations on this scripture. 6. That the Socinians themselves have not dared to attempt the accommodation of the things here spoken of, to any other certain and particular person than the Messiah, tho', being so much tortured thereby, that they shewed good-will enough to it. And 7. That himself had before written a learn'd *Defence of the catholick faith concerning Christ's satisfaction* against Socinus, wherein also he improved to notable purpose several verses of this same chapter: But, in these later annotations, being altogether silent as to any use-making of them that way, he, as much as he can, delivers that Desperado and his disciples from one of the sharpest swords that lies at the very throat of their cause (for if the chapter may be applied to any other, as he applies it wholly to Jeremiah, no solid nor cogent argument can be drawn from it for confirming Christ's satisfaction;) and by his never re-inforcing of that *defence* of his, against the assault made upon it by the Socinian Crellius, (tho' he lived 20 years thereafter) he seems for his part quite to have abandoned and delivered it up into the hands of those declared enemies of Christ's *satisfaction*, yea and of his *Godhead*. It's true indeed, that the learn'd Vossius defends that defence, against the assault of Ravenspergerus, a *Groning* Divine, but it is on a quite different account from that of Crellius: by which *annotations* of his, as by several others on other scriptures, how much (on the matter at least) great Grotius hath, by abusing his prodigious wit, and profound learning, subserved the cursed cause of blasphemous Socinus, and further hardened the already, alas much and long hardened poor Jews; and what bad service he hath done to our glorious Redeemer, and to his church satisfied-for, and purchased by his blood, by his sad sufferings, and sore soul-travel, most clearly and comfortably discoursed in this chapter, let the Lord himself, and all that love him in sincerity, judge: I wish I could, and had reason to say no worse of this admirably learn'd person here, than that, *Quandoque dormitat* Homerus.

Which very many and various, very great and most grievously aggravated sufferings, were endured by him, not only in his body, nor only in his soul, by vertue of the sympathy it had with his body, from the intimate strait union betwixt them; but also, and mainly, in his blessed human soul immediately: Since he redeemed, satisfied for, and saveth his people's souls as well as their bodies; and the soul having principally sinned, and being the spring and source of sin; sinners withal deserving punishment in their souls as well as in their bodies; and being, without the benefit of his mediation, to be punished eternally both in their souls and bodies, and mainly in their souls; there is no doubt, the same cogent reason for the Mediator's suffering in both parts of the human nature assumed by him, that there is for that nature's suffering which sinned: Which, his sad complaints of the exceeding trouble of his soul, putting him to say these strange and stupendous words, *What shall I say?* and of the great *sorrow* and *heaviness* thereof, *even to death*, his *amazement*, *strong cries* and *tears*, with his *agony* and *sweat of blood*, John 12. 27. Mat. 26. 38. Mark 14. 33. Luke 22. 44. Heb. 5. 7. (and that before any pain was caused to his body by men) and his conditional deprecating of that bitter cup, put beyond all reach of rational contradiction: And to think or say, that only the fear of his bodily sufferings quickly approaching him, did make these sad impressions upon him, and draw these strange expressions from him, would make him, who is Lord and Master, to be of far greater abjectness of Spirit than many of his servants the martyrs were, and to fall hugely below that holily heroick and magnanimous courage and resolution, wherewith they adventured on extream sufferings, and most exquisite torments; which would be very unworthy of, and a mighty reflection upon him, who is the vailant *Captain of salvation, made perfect through suffering, who drank of the brook in the way, and therefore lifted up the head*, Heb. 2. 10. Psal. 110. 7. But here is the great and true reason of the difference betwixt his sad and sorrowful deportment under his sufferings, and their solacious, cheerful and joyful deportment under theirs; that they, through his sufferings and satisfaction, were perswaded and made sensible of God's being pacified towards them, and were mightily refreshed by his gracious comforting presence with them amidst their sufferings; while he on the contrary looked upon himself as one legally obnoxious to punishment, sifted before the terrible tribunal of the justice of God, highly provoked by, and very angry at the sins of his people, who was in a most signal manner pouring out upon his soul the vials of his wrath and curse, which made him lamentably and aloud to cry out of desertion, tho' not in respect of the personal union, as if that had been dissolved, nor yet as to secretly supporting, yet as to such a measure at least of sensibly comforting and rejoicing presence, *My God, my God, why hast thou forsaken me?* (here faith was in its meridian, tho' it was dark mid-night as to joy) wherewith, as such, his body could not be immediately affected, spiritual desertion not falling under bodily sense. Whence we may see how justly the doctrine of Papists is to be exploded, who deny all suffering in his soul immediately, to salve their darling dream of his local descent as to his soul, while his body was in the grave, into hell, and to *limbus patrum*, to bring up thence into heaven the souls of the fathers, whom, without giving any reason, or alledging any fault on their part, they foolishly fancy, after their death till then, to have been imprisoned there, tho' quiet and under no punishment of sense, yet deprived of all light and vision of God, and so under the punishment of loss, the greatest of punishments, even by the confession of some of themselves, whereby they put these holy and perfected souls (for there they say there is no more purgation from sin, that being the proper work of their profitable Purgatory) in worse case, all that length of time after their death, than they were when alive on the earth, where doubtless they had often much soul-refreshing fellowship with God, and the light of his countenance lifted up upon them.

Neither were these his sufferings in soul and body only to confirm the doctrine taught by him, (if that was at all designed by him as an end of his sufferings, so much stumbled at in the time, (which yet I will not debate, let be peremptorily deny) his doctrine being rather confirmed by his miracles and resurrection) and to leave us an example and pattern how we should suffer (as non christian and blasphemous Socinians aver) which were mightily to depretiate, and disparage, nay, to enervate and quite to evacuate his sufferings, by attributing no more to them than is attributable to the sufferings of his servants and martyrs: (its true his example was an infallible directory, the example of all examples, but theirs not so; yet this doth not at all influence any alteration of the nature of the end) but also and mainly by them, undergone for his people, and in their room, and as sustaining their persons, vice and place, truly and properly by the sacrifice of himself to satisfy Divine Justice for their sins: And who, I pray, can put any other comment on these scripture-expressions, without manifest perverting and wresting of them, *He hath made him to be sin for us, who knew no sin; Christ hath redeemed us from the curse of the law, being made a curse for us; Who his own self bare our sins in his own body on the tree*, 2 Cor. 5. 21. Gal. 3. 13. 1 Pet. 2. 24. (which is by the apostle subjoined as a superior end of his sufferings to that of leaving us an example, discoursed by him immediately before) *He was wounded for our transgressions; he was bruised for our iniquities, and the chastisement of our peace was upon him; The Lord laid upon him the iniquity of us all; For the transgression of my people was he stricken; When thou shalt make his soul an offering for sin; He shall bear the sins of many; In whom we have redemption through his blood; Who is the propitiation for our sins;* Isa. 53. 5, 6, 8, 10, 12. Eph. 1. 17. Col. 1. 14. 1 John 2. 2. and the like.

Nor did he undergo these sad sufferings for all men in the world, to satisfy justice for them, and to reconcile them to God, but only for the elect, and such as were given unto him.

For, *First, The chastisement of their peace* only, *was laid on him, who are healed by his stripes,* as it is v. 5. of this 53d of Isaiah, *For the iniquities of my people was he stricken,* saith the Lord, v. 8. The same who are called the Mediator's people, Psal. 110. 3. (for saith blessed Jesus to his Father, John 17. 10. *All mine are thine, and thine are mine*) *Who shall,* without all peradventure or possibility of misgiving, *be made willing in the day of his power:* He only *bare the iniquities of those whom he justifieth by his knowledge,* vers. 11. For, otherwise the prophet's reasoning would not be consequent; he only *bare the iniquities of as many transgressors as he makes intercession for,* verf. 12. And that he doth not make intercession for all, but for these only who are given to him, that is, all the elect, is undeniably manifest from John 17. 9. where himself expresly saith, *I pray not for the world, but for these whom thou hast given me.* Now, God's eternal electing love, and his giving the elect to the Mediator in the covenant of redemption, to be satisfied for, and saved by him, and his intercession for them, are commensurable and of equal extent, as is most clear from John 17. 6. where he saith, *Thine they were,* (to wit, by election) *and thou gavest them to me,* to wit, in and by the covenant of redemption, (God's decree of election being in order of nature prior to this donation, or gift of the elect in the covenant of redemption) compared with v. 9. where he saith, *I pray for them, I pray not for the world, but for them whom thou hast given me, for they are thine:* It is observable, that he saith twice over, *I pray for them,* manifestly and emphatically restricting his intercession to them, and excluding all others from it. Why then should not also his sacrifice (the price of the redemption of these elected and given ones, agreed upon in that covenant betwixt these two mighty Parties) be commensurable with the former three? especially since he saith, v. 19. *For their sakes sanctify I myself,* or separate myself to be a sacrifice. 2. Christ's satisfaction and his intercession being the two parts of his priestly office, and his intercession being founded on his satisfaction, as it's clear, v. 12: of this 53d of Isaiah; yea, a very learn'd man affirms, That Christ's appearance in heaven, and his intercession, are not properly sacerdotal acts, but in so far as they lean on the vertue of his perfected sacrifice: What just, relevant, or cogent reason, can there be, to make a disjunction betwixt these parts of his office, and to extend the most difficult, operous and costly part to all men, and to narrow the other, which is the more easy part, as that whereby he only deals for the application of what he hath made a purchase of by his satisfaction, which put him to much sad and sore soul-travel, and to restrict it to the elect and gifted ones? 3. Doth not the scripture hold forth his death, and the shedding of his blood, as the great demonstration of his special love to his own elect people? as is clear else-where, so particularly *John* 15. 13. *Greater love than this hath no man, that a man lay down his life for his friends;* nay, purchased reconciliation through the death of Christ, is by the Holy Ghost made a greater evidence of divine love, in some respect, than the glorification of the reconciled, according to what the apostle saith, Rom. 5. 10. *For if, when we were enemies, we were reconciled to God by the death of*

Son, much more being reconciled, we shall be saved by his life. 4. All the other gifts of of God to sinners, even the greatest spiritual ones, fall hugely below the giving of Jesus Christ himself, *that Gift of God* by way of eminency, as the apostle reasoneth irrefragably, for the comfort of believers, *Rom.* 8. 32. *He that spared not his own Son, but delivered him up for us all, how shall he not with him also freely give us all things?* Will he give the greatest gift, and not give the lesser? as justification, adoption, sanctification and glorification; which, how great soever in themselves, are yet lesser than the giving of Christ himself to the death; and if it be undeniably certain that he giveth not these to all, which are the lesser and lower gifts, why should it be thought that he hath given the higher and greater? 5. Shall that grand expression of the special love of God be made common, by extending it to all the world, the greatest Profligates and Atheists not excepted, no, not Pharaoh, nor Ahab, nor Judas the traitor, nor Julian the apostate, nay, nor any of all the damned reprobates, who were actually in hell when he died and shed his blood? 6. If he died thus for all, it seems that the new song of the redeemed, *Rev.* 5. would have run and sounded better thus, Thou hast redeemed *us all and every man*, of every kindred, and tongue, and people, and nation, to God by thy blood, than as it there stands by inspiration of the Holy Ghost, *Thou wast slain, and hast redeemed us to God, by thy blood, out of every kindred, and tongue, and people, and nation;* but who may presume by such an universality to extend and ampliat what he hath so restricted, and to make that common to all, which God hath peculiarized to a few favourites? But the author having spoken to much better purpose on this head in these Sermons, I need add no more here.

I shall only further say of these astonishing, in a manner non-plussing and surpassing great sufferings of blessed Jesus, that, *as* they were equivalent to what all the elect deserved by their sins, and should have suffered in their own persons throughout all eternity, consistently with the innocency and excellency of his Person, and with the dignity of his mediatory office; therefore it is said, *v.* 9. *And he made his grave with the wicked, and with the rich in is death;* or as it is in the original, *in his deaths*, in the plural number, as if he had died the death of every one of the elect; or as if there had been a conjunction and combination of all their deaths in his one death; and *v.* 6. That *the Lord laid on him the iniquity of us all*, or, as the word is, *made the iniquity of us all to meet on him*, there having been a solemn tryst, convocation and rendezvous (as it were) of all the iniquities of all the elect, more common and more peculiar, in all their various aggravating circumstances; not so much as one committed since Adam's first transgression, or to be committed to the day of judgment, being absent in the punishment of them upon his Person: No wonder that such a load of innumerable thousands and millions of iniquities made him heavily to groan, and that the consideration thereof made great *Luther* say, *That Christ was the greatest sinner in all the world*, to wit, by imputation of the guilt of all the sins of the elect to him, and by his having had the punishment of them all laid upon his Person: So we may from them be instructed in these things.

First, Concerning the height of holy displicence and detestation, that the Majesty of God hath at sin, the only thing in the whole world that his soul hates, and which, in the vile and abominable nature of it, hath an irreconcilable antipathy with, and enmity against his infinitely pure, holy, and blessed nature; and hath a tendency, could it possibly be effected, to seek after the destruction and annihilation of the very Being of God, and is interpretatively *deicide*; the language of it being, *O that there were not a God!*

God! that he cannot behold it in his own sinless, innocent, and dearly beloved Son, tho' but by imputation (for he was not made formally the sinner, as *Antinomians* blasphemously aver) but he will needs in so terrible a manner, testify his great dislike of, and deep displeasure at it, and take such formidable vengeance on it, even in his Person: Ah! the nature of sin, which God, who is of pure eyes, cannot, wherever it be, behold, without perfect abhorrency of it, is but little thorowly understood and pondered; Would we otherwise dare to dally and sport with it, or to take the latitudes in committing of it at the rate we do? I have sometimes thought that it is an error in the first concoction (to say so) of religion in many professors of it, and pretenders to it, that we have never framed suitable apprehensions of the most hateful, vile and abominable nature of sin, (which hath a great influence on the superficiariness and overliness of all duties and practices of religion) and that many of us had need to be dealt with, as skilful school-masters use to deal with their scholars that are foundered in the first principles of learning, left they prove but smatterers all their days; to bring them back again to these, even to be put to learn this first lesson in religion better, and more thorowly to understand the jealousy of God as to this cursed thing *Sin*; for which, tho' he graciously, for the sake of these sufferings of Christ, pardon the guilt of it to his people, and hear their prayers, yet will needs *take vengeance on their inventions,* Psal. 99. 8. be they never so seriously, holily, and eminently serviceable to him, and to their generation according to his will; whereof Moses the man of God is a memorable instance: That *Ancient* conceived rightly of the nature of sin, who said, *That if he behoved necessarily, either to commit the least sin, or go to hell to be tormented there eternally, he would rather wish to desire to go to hell, if he could be there without sin.*

Secondly, Concerning the severity of divine justice in punishing sin, whereof its punishment in the Person of the Son of God, at such a rate, is one of the greatest, clearest and most convincing evidences imaginable, to whom he would not abate one farthing of the elect's debt, but did with holy and spotless severity exact the whole of it; and tho' he was the *Father's Fellow,* yet he would needs have him *smitten with the awakned sword* (Zech. 13. 17.) of sin-revenging justice and wrath: As if all the executions that had been done in the earth on men for sin, as on the old world of the ungodly, drowned by the deluge; on the miscreant inhabitants of Sodom and Gomorrah, and of these other *Cities,* upon whom he showered down liquid flames of fire and brimstone, even somewhat of hell in a manner out-of heaven (*cœlum pluebat Gehennam*) burning them quick, and frying them to death in their own skins; on Corah, Dathan and Abiram, and their associates, upon whom the earth opened and swallowed them up in a most stupendous manner alive, the rest being consumed by fire sent down from heaven; on the one hundred eighty five thousand men of *Senacherib's* army, all slain in one night by an angel; and on the Israelites, who by many and various plagues were wasted and worn out to the number of six hundred thousand fighting men in the space of forty years; reflections on which made Moses, a witness of all, with astonishment to cry out, *Who knows the power of thy anger?* Psal. 90. 11. As if, I say, all these terrible executions of justice, had been done by a sword asleep, or in the scabbard, in comparison of the execution it did on Jesus Christ the elect's Cautioner against whom it *awakened,* was unsheathed, furbished, and made to glitter: So that we may say, Had all the sons and daughters of Adam, without the exception of so much as one, been eternally destroyed, it would not have been a greater demonstration of the severity of the justice of God in punishing sin.

Thirdly, Concerning the greatness, incomprehensible vastness, and unparallelableness of the love of God to the elect world, which he so loved (O wonderful *so*! eternity will but be sufficient to unfold all that is infolded in that mysterious *so*; an *ἵνα* that hath not an *ὡς*, an *ita* that hath not a *sicut*, a *so* that hath not an *as*) *That he gave his only begotten Son,* 1 John 3. 16. to suffer all these things, and to be thus dealt with for them: And of the Mediator, who was content, tho' *thinking it no robbery to be equal with God, to empty himself, and be of no reputation, to take on him the shape of a Servant,* Phil. 2. 6, 7, 8. to be *a Man of sorrows and acquainted with grief;* to be *chastized, smitten, wounded and bruised for their iniquities,* Isa. 53. 3, 5. to step off the throne of his declarative glory, or of his glory manifested to the creatures, and in a manner to creep on the footstool thereof in the capacity of a worm, and to *become obedient even unto the death,* the shameful and cursed death of the cross: This is indeed matchless and marvellous love, *Greater than which no man hath, to lay down his life for his friend,* John 15. 13. But he, being *God-Man,* laid down his life for his *enemies,* that he might make them friends, Rom. 5. 10. *O the height and depth, the breadth and length of the love of Christ!* Eph. 3. 9. 10. whereof, when all that can be said, is said, this must needs be said, *That it's a love that passeth* not only expression, but *knowledge;* it's dimensions being altogether unmeasurable: So that we may say, if it had seemed good to the Lord, and been compatible with his spotless justice, and with his infinite wisdom, as supreme Rector and Governor of the world, giving a law to his creatures, to have pardoned the sins of the elect, in the absoluteness of his dominion, that knows no boundary, but what the other divine attributes set to it, without any intervenient satisfaction to his justice at all, (which needs not to be debated here, especially since God hath determined, and in the scriptures of truth made publication of his determination, that he will not pardon sin without a satisfaction, and particularly without this satisfaction made by Jesus Christ) It would not have been a greater and more glorious demonstration of the freeness and riches of his love than he hath given, in pardoning them, thro' the intervention of so difficult and toilsom, of so chargeable and costly a satisfaction, as is the sad sufferings, and the sore soul-travel of his own dear Son; who yet is pleased to account sinners coming to him, and getting good of him, satisfaction for all that soul-travel: And indeed, which of these is the greatest wonder, and demonstration of his love, whether that he should have undergone such soul-travel for sinners, or that he should account their getting good of it, satisfaction of the same, is not easy to determine; but sure, both in conjunction together make a wonder passing great, even a most wonderful demonstration of love.

Fourthly, Concerning what dreadful measure all they may look for, who have heard of these sufferings of Christ, and make not conscience in his own way to improve them for their being reconciled to God thereby, and whose bond to justice will be found still standing over their heads uncancelled in their own name, as proper debtors, without a cautioner. When the innocent Son of God, *who had never done wrong, and in whose mouth no guile was ever found,* Isa. 53. 9. having but become Surety for the elect's debt, was thus hotly pursued, and hardly handled, and put (through sad soul-trouble) to cry, *What shall I say?* John 12. 27. and falling a-groof on the ground with the tear in his eye, in much sorrow and heaviness even to death, and in a great agony, causing a sweat of blood, tho' in a cold night, and lying on the earth, conditionally

to

to pray for the paſſing of that cup from him, and for his being ſaved from that hour ; ſo formidable was it to his holy human nature, which had a ſinleſs averſation from, and an innocent horror at what threatned ruin and deſtruction to it ſelf ſimply conſidered ; and which, had it not been mightily ſupported by the power of the Godhead united thereto in his Perſon, would have quite ſhrunk and ſuccumbed under ſuch an heavy burden, and been utterly ſwallowed up by ſuch a gulf of wrath : What then will ſinners, even all the dyvour debtors, not having ſeriouſly ſought after, nor being effectually reached by the benefit of his ſuretyſhip, do, when they come to grapple with this wrath of God, when he will fall upon them as a giant, breaking all their bones, and as a roaring lion, *tearing them to pieces, when there will be none to deliver?* Pſal. 50. 22. *Will their hands be ſtrong, or their hearts be able to endure in the day that he ſhall deal with them?* Ezek. 22. 14. Then, O then, they *will be afraid, and fearfulneſs will take hold of them,* and make them ſay, *Who can ſtand before the devouring fire, and who can dwell beſide the everlaſting burnings?* Iſa. 34. 14. and *to cry unto the hills and mountains to fall on them, and to hide them from the face of the Lamb, and of him that ſits on the throne, for the great day of his wrath is come, and who is able to ſtand?* Rev. 6. 16, 17. then it will be found in a ſpecial manner to be *a fearful thing to fall into the hands of the living God,* Heb. 10. 31. All ſuch may ſee, in the great ſufferings of Chriſt, as in the cleareſt glaſs, what they are to look for, and moſt certainly to meet with ; for if it was thus *done in the green tree, what ſhall be done in the dry?* Luke 23. 31. O it is a ſad, even one of the ſaddeſt ſubjects of thought, to think, that a rational creature ſhall be eternally ſupported, preſerved and perpetuated in its being, by the one hand of God's omnipotency, that it may be everlaſtingly capable of terrible vengeance, to be inflicted by the other hand of his juſtice !

Fifthly, Concerning the very great obligation that lieth on believers to love Jeſus Chriſt, who hath thus commended his love to them, by undergoing all theſe ſad ſufferings for their ſakes ; even out of love to them to become a curſe, to bleed out his precious life, and to pour out his ſoul to death for them ; which to do he was under no neceſſity, nor in the leaſt obliged by them, being infinitely removed from all poſſibility of being reached by any obligation from his creatures, whom he loved, and for whom he deſigned this grand expreſſion of his love, the laying down of his life for them, before they or the world had any being ; nay, being by their ſins infinitely diſobliged : Ah, that moſt of theſe whom he loved ſo much, ſhould love him (*who is altogether lovely*) their duty, his friends and intereſts for his ſake ſo little ; even ſo very little, that, if it were poſſible, he could rue and repent of what he hath done and ſuffered, to commend his love to them, they would tempt him to it ! And indeed there is nothing that more ſpeaks forth the freeneſs of his love than this, that he ſhould love them ſo fervently, and continue thus to love them, even *to the end*, who are often ſo very cool in their love to him : Sure ſuch, when in any meaſure at themſelves, cannot but love themſelves the leſs, and lothe themſelves the more, that they love him ſo little ; and earneſtly long for that deſireable day, wherein he ſhall be *admired in* and by *all them that believe*, and when they ſhall get him loved as well as ever they deſired to love him, and as well as he ſhall will them to love him, and when they ſhall be in an eternal extaſy and tranſport of admiration at his love.

Sixthly, Concerning the little reaſon that believers have to think much of their ſmall and petty ſufferings undergone for him : For what are they all, even the greateſt and moſt grievous of them, being compared with his ſufferings for them ? They are but as little chips of the cross, in comparison of the great and heavy end of it, that lighted on him, and not worthy to be named in one day with his: All the sad and sorrowful days and nights that all the saints on earth have had, under their many and various, and sadly circumstantiated crosses and sufferings, do not by thousands of degrees come near unto, let be to equal that one sad and sorrowful night, which he had in *Gethsemane* (beside all the sorrows and griefs he endured before that time) where he was put to conflict with the awakned sword of sin-revenging justice, that did most fiercely lay at him, without sparing him : Which terrible combat lasted all that night, and the next day, till three a-clock in the afternoon, when that sharpest sword, after many sore wounds given him, killed him outright at last, and left him dead upon the place (who yet, even then, when seemingly vanquished and quite ruined, 'was a great and glorious Conqueror, having *by death overcome and destroyed him that had the power of death, that is the devil ; and having spoiled principalities and powers, making a shew of them openly, and triumphing over them in his cross*, Heb 2. 14. Col. 2. 15. the spoils of which glorious victory believers now divide, and shall enjoy to all eternity.) Ah that ever the small and inconsiderable sufferings of the saints, should so much as once be made mention of by them, where his strange and stupendous sufferings offer themselves to be noticed.

Seventhly, Concerning the unspeakably great obligations that lieth on believers, readily, pleasantly and cheerfully, not only to do, but also to suffer for Christ, as he shall call them to it, even to do all that lieth in their power for him, and to suffer all that is in the power of any others to do against them on his account, who did willingly, and with delight, do and suffer so much for them : They have doubtless good reason heartily to pledge him in the cup of his cross, and to drink after him, there being especially such difference betwixt the cup that he drank, and that which they are put to drink ; his cup was steered thick with the wrath of God, having had the dregs thereof, in a manner, wrung out to him therein ; so that it was no wonder, that the very sight of it made him conditionally to supplicate for its departure from him, and that the drink of it put him in a most grievous agony, and cast him in a top-sweat of blood : Yet, saith he on the matter, either they or I must drink it, they are not able to drink it, for the drinking of it will distract them, and put them mad, will poison and kill them eternally ; but I am able to drink it, and to work out the poison and venom of it, and though it shall kill me, I can raise up, and restore myself to life again ; therefore, Father, come away with it, and I will drink it up, and drink it out, This to the everlasting welfare of these dear souls ; *Not my Will, but thine be done ;* for, thus it was agreed betwixt thee and me in the covenant of redemption ; when as theirs is love from bottom even to brim (whatever mixture may sometimes be of paternal and domestick justice, proper and peculiar to God's own family, and which, as the Head and Father thereof, he exerciseth therein) not so much as one gut or scruple of vindictive wrath being left therein : Ah ! it's both a sin and shame, that there should be with such, even with such, so much shyness and shrinking, to drink after him in the cup of his cross ; especially considering, that there is such an high degree of honour put upon the suffering believer for Christ, above and beyond what is put on the simple believer in him, so that in the scripture-account, the suffering believer is not *only*, but *also*, according to what the apostle saith, *Phil.* 1. 29. *To you it is given in the behalf of Christ, not only to believe on him, but also to suffer for his sake.*

Eighthly, Concerning what mighty obligation lieth on believers to mourn and weep, to be sad and sorrowful for sin: How can they look on him, whom they have thus bruised, wounded and pierced by their sins, without the tear in their eye, without mourning for him, and being in bitterness, as a man is for his first born, and for his only begotten son? when they think (as all of them, on serious consideration, will find reason to think) that if their sins keeped the tryst and rendezvous, when all the sins of all the elect did meet, and were laid on him; then sure, there came no greater company, and more numerous troop of sins, to that solemn rendezvous, from any of all the redeemed than came from them; and that he had not a heavier load and burden of the sins of any than he had of theirs, whereby he was even pressed, as a cart is pressed down under the sheaves, and was made most grievously to groan, even with the groanings of a deadly wounded man; and that if he was wounded and pierced by their iniquities, then surely he was more deeply wounded and pierced by the iniquities of none, than by theirs: O! what mourning should this cause to them? even such mourning as was at *Hadadrimmon* in the valley of *Megiddo*, on the occasion of the sad slaughter and death of that good and desirable king Josiah? This is indeed one of the most genuine and kindly, one of the most powerful and prevalent, one of the sweetest and strongest springs of, and motives to, true gospel-repentance sorrow and mourning for sin.

Ninthly, Concerning the notable and none-such obligation that lieth on believers, to study the crucifixion and mortification of sin: Was it not their sins that crucified and killed precious Jesus Christ, the Prince of life? was it not their sins that violently drove the nails thorow his blessed hands and feet, and thrust the spear thorow his side, to the bringing forth of water and blood? Shall they not, in their burning zeal and love to him, and in the height of holy indignation at themselves, be avenged on that which brought such vengeance on him? shall they not seriously seek to be the death of that which brought him to death, and whereof, the death and destruction, was one of his great designs therein, on which he was so intent, that in the prosecution of it, he did amidst his dying pangs and agonies breathe out his soul? O let it never be heard for shame, that ever any of them shall find the least sweetness in that accursed thing, that was so bitter to him; that ever any of them shall be found to dally with, or to hug that serpent and viper in their bosom, that so cruelly stung him to death.

But this being the great subject of these following sermons, wherein *the preacher*, being in a good measure wise, hath *sought to find out acceptable words*, (Eccl. 12. 10, 11.) *and words* I hope *of uprightness and truth;* (O that they may be to the readers *as goads and nails fastned by him who is the great Master of assemblies!*) I shall insist no further; only I may humbly say, that to my knowledge, none hath preached on this whole *chapter* to better purpose every way; many may have done virtuously, but it's probable he will be found to *excel them all:* Nay, if I should say, that, for any thing I know, this book for so much is amongst the best books of this nature the world hath seen, I suppose hardly will any judicious Christian, thorowly exercised to godliness, after he hath read it all over, and pondered it, think that I have greatly, if at all, hyperbolized.

There are in these choice Sermons, depths as it were for elephants to swim in (whereof his surprizing, sublimely spiritual, and very deep divine discourses, concerning the nature of Christ's *intercession*, and the right improvement of it, in the last six Sermons, is a notable instance) and shallows for lambs to wade in; there is in them *milk for babes in Christ, and stronger meat for such as are of full age, who by reason of use have*

D

their

their senses exercised to discern both good and evil, Heb. 5. 13, 14. Nay, I may in a good measure say of these Sermons, as it's said of the learned discourses of a late great man, *That in the doctrinal part of several of them, ye will find the depth of polemical divinity; and in his inferences from thence the sweetness of practical; some things that may exercise the profoundest scholar and others that may edify the weakest Christian; nothing readily is more nervous and strong than his reasonings, and nothing more sweetly and powerfully affecting than his applications:* There is in them much for information of the judgment, for warming of the affections, and for direction toward a gospel becoming conversation; there is much for clearing and expeding the doubts and difficulties of more weak and darkned Christians, and much for edifying, confirming and establishing of more grown ones; there is much for conviction, reproof, warning, humbling, for stirring up and provoking to the serious exercise of godliness, and much for the comforting and refreshing of such as stand in need, and are capable of consolation; there is much for discovering, rouzing, awakning and alarming of carnal, secure, unsound, hollow-hearted and hypocritical professors of religion, and much for beating and hammering down of the pride of conceity self justifying professors; much for training up of young beginners, and much for advancing and carrying on in their Christian course such as are entred into it, and have made any tolerable progress therein: In a word, he doth in a great measure *approve himself to God, as a workman that needs not be ashamed, rightly dividing the word of truth* (2 Tim. 2. 15.) and as a skilful and faithful steward, giving to every one his portion in *due* kind, measure and season.

It may be some readers will think, that there are in these Sermons several coincidencies of purposes, and repetitions: To which I shall but presume to say, That, beside that there is a great affinity amongst many of the purposes delivered by the prophet in this piece of his prophecies, if not a holy coincidency of them, and a profitable repetition now and then of the same thing in different expressions; as there is in some other scriptures, without any the least imputation to them, as that truly noble and renowned Gentleman Mr. Boyle, sheweth, in his elaborate, eloquent and excellent *Considerations, touching the stile of the holy Scriptures;* and that the same midses, and near by the same expressions, may very pertinently be made use of, to clear and confirm different points of doctrine; It will be found, that if there be in so many sermons or discourses on subjects of such affinity, any coincidencies or repetitions, they are at such a convenient distance, and one way or other so diversified, and appositely suited to the subject of his present discourse, that the reader will not readily nauseate, nor think what is spoken in its place, impertinent, superfluous or needless, tho' somewhat like it hath been said by him in some other place: Or, if there be any not only seeming, but real repetitions of purposes and expressions, as *they have not been grievous* (Phil. 3. 1.) to the preacher, so he, with the apostle Paul, judged them *needful* at the time for the hearers.

And now, as for you, *much honoured, right worthy, and very dearly beloved Inhabitants of the City of* Glasgow, let me tell you, that I have sometimes of late much coveted to be put and kept in some capacity to do the churches of Christ, and you in particular, this piece of service, in putting to the press these sweet Sermons on this choice Scripture before I die: And indeed, after I had gone thorow a good number of them, not without considerable toil and difficulty (having, all alongst, had no notes of his own, but the Sermons as they were taken hastily with a current pen from his mouth, by ane of his ordinary hearers, no scholar, who could not therefore so thorowly and distinctly

ſtinctly take up ſeveral of the purpoſes handled by the preacher) the Lord was pleaſed to give me a ſtop, by a long continued ſharp affliction, not altogether without ſome little more remote and gentle threatnings of death; but he, to whom the iſſues from death do belong graciouſly condeſcended to ſpare me a little, that I might gather ſome ſtrength to go thorow the remainder of them. I have much reaſon to think, that if poor I had been preaching the goſpel to you theſe twenty years paſt, wherein we have been in holy providence ſeparated (which hath been the more afflicting to me, that ye were in my heart to have lived and died with you; and if it had ſo ſeemed good in the eyes of the Lord, it would have been to me one of the moſt refreſhing and joyful providences I could have been tryſted with in this world, to have had fair acceſs, thro' his good hand upon me, and his gracious preſence with me, to have preached the goſpel to you a while before my going hence and being no more) I would not by very, very far, have contributed ſo much to your edification, as theſe few Sermons may, and I hope thro' God's bleſſing ſhall. Several of you heard them preached by him, when he was alive amongſt you; and now, when he is dead, he is in a manner preaching them over again to you (O that ſuch of you as then were not taken in the preaching of them, might be ſo now in the ſerious reading of them!) and by them ſpeaking to theſe of you that did not then hear them, who, as I ſuppoſe, are now the far greateſt part of the city inhabitants: You will find yourſelves in them again and again ranked and claſſed, according to your different ſpiritual eſtates, and the various caſes and conditions of your ſouls, and wonderful diſcoveries made of yourſelves to yourſelves, that I ſomething doubt if there be ſo much as one ſoul among the ſeveral thouſands that are in *Glaſgow*, but will find itſelf, by the reading of theſe Sermons, ſpoken to, ſuitably to its ſtate and caſe, as if he had been particularly acquainted with the perſon and his ſpiritual condition (as indeed he made it a conſiderable part of his work, as the obſerving Reader will quickly and eaſily perceive, to be acquainted very thorowly with the ſoul-ſtate and condition of ſuch at leaſt of the Inhabitants as were more immediately under his own inſpection and charge) and, as if he had ſpoken to the perſon by name; O how inexcuſable will ſuch of you be, as had your lot caſt to live under the miniſtry of ſuch an able *Miniſter of the New Teſtament*, of ſuch *a Scribe very much inſtructed into the kingdom of Heaven, who as a good houſholder knew well how to bring out of his treaſure things new and old!* Mat. 13. 52. If you were not bettered and made to profit thereby; God and angels, and your own conſciences, will witneſs, how often and how urgently the Lord Jeſus called to you by him, and ye would not hear. And how inexcuſable will ye alſo be, that ſhall diſdain or neglect to read *theſe Sermons* (as I would fain hope none of you will) that were ſometime preached in that place by that faithful ſervant of Chriſt, who was your own Miniſter, which layeth ſome peculiar obligation on you beyond others to read them? or if ye ſhall read them and not make conſcience to improve them to your ſouls edification and advantage, which contain more genuine, pure, ſincere, ſolid, and ſubſtantial goſpel, than many thouſands have heard, it may be in an age, though hearing preachings much of the while; even ſo much, that if any of you ſhould be providentially deprived of the liberty of hearing the goſpel any more preached, or ſhould have acceſs to read no other ſermons or comments on the ſcriptures, theſe ſermons, through God's bleſſing, will abundantly ſtore and enrich you in the knowledge of the *uncontrovertably great myſtery of godlineſs, God manifeſted in the fleſh,* 1 Tim. 3. 16. and *according to the ſcriptures make you wiſe unto ſalvation, through faith which is in Chriſt Jeſus,* 2 Tim. 3. 15. much inſiſted on in them: I would therefore

fore humbly advise (wherein I hope ye will not mistake me, as if by this advice I were designing some advantage to my self, for indeed I am not at all that way concerned in the sale of them) that every one of you that can read, and is easily able to do it, would buy a copy of these Sermons; at least, that every family that is able, wherein there is any that can read, would purchase one of them; I nothing doubt, but ye will think that little money very well bestowed, and will find your old minister, desirable *Durham*, delightful company to discourse with you by his sermons, now when he is dead, and you can see his face, and hear him speak to you by *viva voce* no more; whose voice, or rather the voice of Christ by him, was, I know, very sweet to many there, now asleep, and to some of you yet alive; who, I dare not doubt, never allow yourselves to expect with confidence and comfort to look the Lord Jesus in the face, but as seriously and sincerely ye make it your business to be found in his righteousness, so much cleared and commended to you; and in the study of holiness in all manner of conversation, so powerfully pressed upon you, here.

That these sweet and savoury gospel-sermons may come to you all, and more particularly to you, my dear friends at *Glasgow*, *with the fulness of the blessing of the gospel*, (Rom. 15. 29.) even of *the word of his grace, which is able to build you up, and to give you an inheritance among them that are sanctified*, (Acts 20. 32.) is the serious desire of

Your servant in the Gospel,

J. C.

SERMON I.

SERMON I.

Isaiah liii. 1. Who hath believed our report? and to whom is the arm of the Lord revealed?

WE hope it shall not be needful to insist in opening the scope of this chapter, or in clearing to you of whom the prophet meaneth, and is speaking: It was once questioned by the eunuch, Acts viii. 32. when he was reading this chapter, *Of whom do the prophet speak this? of himself, or of some other man:* And it is so clearly answered by Philip, who, from these words, began and preached to him of Jesus Christ, that there needs be no doubt of it now. To Christians these two may put it out of question, that Jesus Christ and the substance of the gospel is compended and summed up here. 1. If we compare the letter of this chapter with what is in the four evangelists, we will see it so fully, and often so literally made out of Christ, that if any will but read this chapter and compare it with them, they will find the evangelists to be commentators on it, and setting it out more fully. 2. That there is no scripture in the old testament so often and so convincingly applied to Christ as this is, there being scarce one verse, at least not many, but are by the evangelists or apostles made use of for holding out of Christ.

If we look then to the sum of the words of this chapter, they take in the sum and substance of the gospel; for they take in these two, 1. The right description and manifestation of Jesus Christ, And, 2. The unfolding and opening up of the covenant of redemption. Where these two are, there the sum of the gospel is; but these two are here, therefore the sum of the gospel is here. *First,* Jesus Christ is described, 1. In his person and natures; as God, being eternal; as Man, being under suffering. 2. In all his offices; as a Priest, offering up himself as a sacrifice to satisfy justice; as a prophet, venting his knowledge to the justifying of many thereby; and as a King, dividing the spoil with the strong. 3. In his humiliation, in the cause of it, in the end of it, in the subject of it, in the nature and rise of all, God's good pleasure. And, 4. In his exaltation, and outgate promised him on the back of all his sufferings and humiliation.

2*dly,* The covenant of redemption is here described and set out, 1. In the particular parties of it, God and the Mediator. 2. As to the matter about which it was, the seed that was given to Christ, and whose iniquities met on him. 3. As to the mutual engagements on both sides, the Son undertaking to make his soul an offering for sin, and the Father promising that the efficacy of his satisfaction shall be imputed and applied for the justification of sinners; and the terms on which, or the way how this imputation and application is brought about, to wit, *By his knowledge:* All are clearly held out here.

This is only a touch of the excellency of this scripture, and of the materials (to say so) in it, as comprehending the substance and marrow of the gospel. We shall not be particular in dividing the chapter, considering that these things we have hinted at, are interwoven in it.

The first verse is a short introduction to lead us in to what follows. The prophet hath in the former chapter been speaking of Christ as God's Servant, that should be extolled and made very high; and, before he proceed more particularly to unfold this mystery of the gospel, he cries out by way of regret, *Who hath believed our report?* Alas, (would he say) for as good news as we have to carry, few will take them off our hand! Such is mens unconcernedness, yea, malice and obstinacy, that they reject them. *And to whom is the arm of the Lord revealed?* To point at the necessity of the power of God to accompany preaching, and even the most lively ordinances to make them effectual. How few are they, that the power of God captivates to the obedience of this truth?

For the first part of this verse, *Who hath believed our report?* To open it a little, ye shall take these four or five considerations, ere we come to the doctrines.

Consider, 1. The matter of this report, in reference to its scope; 'tis not every report, but a report of Christ, and of the covenant of redemption and of grace. In the original it is, Who hath believed *our hearing* actively; that is, that which we have proposed to be heard; and the word is turned *tidings,* Dan. xi. 44. and *rumour,* Jer. li. 46. It is the tidings and rumour of a suffering Mediator, interposing himself betwixt God and sinners: and it may be *hearing* is mentioned, to point out the confidence which the prophet had in reporting these news; he first heard them from God, and in that was passive; and then, actively, he proposed them to the people to be heard by them. 2. Consider that the prophet speaketh of this report, not as in his own person only, but as in the person of all that ever preached, or shall preach this gospel; therefore this to give a redug̃ of the Jews unbelief, because Isaiah foretold it long before. 4. Consider, that when he complaineth of the want of faith to the report and tidings of the gospel, it is not of the want of historical faith, as if the people would not give Christ a hearing at all, but is of the want of saving faith; therefore, *Jo*. xii. 37, 38. it is said, *Though he had done many miracles before them, yet they believed not on him;* and this prophetick scripture is subjoined as the reason of it, *That the saying of Esaias might be fulfilled, who said, Lord, who hath believed our report?* applying the *believing*, spoken of here, to that saving faith, whereby folk believe and rest upon Jesus Christ. 5. Consider, that tho' there be no express party named, to whom the prophet complaineth, yet no doubt, it is to God; therefore, *Jo*. xii. 38. and *Rom*. x. 16. when this scripture is cited, it is said, *Lord who hath believed our report* so it is the prophet's complaint of the little fruit himself had, and that the ministers of the gospel should have, in preaching of the gospel, regreting and complaining of it to God, as a sore matter, that it should come to so many, and so few should get good of it, so few should be brought to believe, and to be saved by it.

Tho' these words be few, yet they have four great things in them, to which we shall reduce them, for speaking more clearly to them. 1. That the great subject of preaching, and preachers great errand, is, to report concerning Jesus Christ, to bring tidings concerning him. 2. That the great duty of hearers (implied) is, to believe this report, and, by vertue of it, to be brought to rest and rely on Jesus Christ. 3. That the great, tho' the ordinary sin of the generality of the hearers of the gospel, is unbelief; *Who hath believed?* that is, it is few that have believed; it is a rare thing to see a believer of this report. 4. That the great complaint, weight and grief of an honest minister of the gospel, is this, that his message is not taken off his hand, that Christ is not received, believed in, and rested on; this is the great challenge ministers have against the generality of people, and the ground of their complaint to God, that whatever they report concerning Christ, he is not welcomed, his kingdom thrives not.

That we may speak to the first, considering the way of eminency, a report above, and beyond all other reports; these are news worthy to be carried by angels, *Behold* saith one of them, Luke ii. 20. *I bring you good tidings of great joy, which shall be to all people.* And what are these tidings, so prefaced to with a *Behold! For unto you is born this day, in the city of* David, *a Saviour, which is Christ the Lord,* these are the good tidings, that Jesus Christ is come, and that he is the Saviour by office. We shall not insist on this; only, 1. We will find a little view of this subject in the following words, which hold forth clearly Christ, God and Man in one Person, so compleatly qualified, and excellently furnished for his offices. 2. It is also clear, if we look to the excellent effects that come by his being so furnished; as, his satisfying of justice, his setting free of captives, his triumphing over principalities and powers, his destroying the works of the devil, &c. there cannot be more excellent works or effects spoken of. 3. It is clear, if we look to him, from whom this report cometh, and in whose breast these news bred, (if we may speak so) they are the result of the counsel of the God-head; and therefore, as the report here is made in the Lord's name, so he is complained to, when it is not taken off the prophet's hand. And, 4. It is clear, if we look to the mysteriousness of these news; angels could never have conceived them, had not this report come: these things tell, that they are great, glorious, and good news, glad tidings, as it is in the end of the former chapter, *That which hath not been told them, shall they see; and that which they have not heard, shall they consider.*

The first *Use* is, To draw our hearts to be in love with the gospel, and to raise our estimation of it. Peoples ears are itching after novelties, and ye are much worn out of conceit with these news; but is there in any news such an advantage as in these? when God sendeth news to men, they must be great news, and such indeed are these.

Use 2. Therefore be afraid to entertain lothing of the plain substantial truths of the gospel; if ye had never heard them before, there would be-like, be some *Athenian* itching to hear and speak of them; but they should not be the less thought of, that they are often heard and spoken of.

Use 3.

Use 3. Therefore think more of the gospel, seeing it containeth the substance of these good news and glad tidings; and think more of gospel ordinances, whereby these good tidings are so often published and made plain to you.

2. More particularly *observe*, That Jesus Christ, and what concerneth him, the glad and good news of a Saviour, and the reporting of them is the very proper work of a minister, and the great subject of a minister's preaching, his proper work is to make him known: or take it thus, Christ is the native Subject, on which all preaching should run. This is the report the prophet speaketh of here, and in effect it was so to John and the other apostles, and should be so to all ministers; Christ Jesus, and what concerns him in his person, natures and offices; to know, and make him known to be God and man; to make him known in his offices to be Priest, Prophet, and King; to be a Priest in his suffering and satisfying justice; to be a prophet in revealing the will of God; to be a King, for subduing folks lusts and corruptions; and to know, and make him known, in the way by which sinners, both preachers, and hearers may come to have him to themselves, as follows in this chapter. This, this is the subject of all preaching, and all preaching should be levelled at this mark; Paul is 1 Cor. ii. 2. peremptory in this, *I determined to know nothing among you, but Jesus Christ and him crucified;* as if he had said, I will meddle with no other thing, but betake myself to this: not only will he forbear to meddle with civil employments, but he will lay aside his learning, eloquence, and human wisdom, and make the preaching of Christ crucified his great work and study; the reason of this is, because Christ standeth in a fourfold relation to preaching: 1. He is the *Text*, to say so, of preaching; all preaching is to explain him, Acts x. 43. *To him give all the prophets witness*, and so do the four evangels, and the apostolic epistles, which are as so many preachings of him; and that preaching which standeth not in relation to him, is beside the text and mark. 2. He is holden out as the *Foundation* and groundwork of preaching, so that preaching without him wants a foundation, and is the building as it were, of a castle in the air, 1 Cor. iii. 10. *I have laid the foundation, and another build*——*reon: but let every man take heed how he bu*—— *for other foundation can no man lay than that which is laid, which is Jesus Christ.* Importing, that all preaching should be squared to, and made to agree with this ground stone. 3. He standeth as the great *End* of preaching, not only that hearers may have him known in their judgments, but may have him high in their hearts and affections, 2 Cor. iii. 4. *We preach not ourselves*, that is not only do we not preach ourselves as the subject, but we preach not ourselves as the end of our preaching; our scope is not to be great, or much thought of, but our end in preaching is to make Christ great. 4. He standeth in relation to preaching, as he is the *power and life* of preaching, without whom, no preaching can be effectual, no soul can be captivate and brought in to him; hence, 1 Cor. i. 23, he saith, *We preach Christ crucified, to the Jews a stumbling-block*, they cannot abide to hear him; *and to the Greeks foolishness; but to them that are saved, the Power of God, and the Wisdom of God.*

Use 1. For ministers, which we shall forbear insisting on; only, 1. Were Christ the subject and substance of our report, were we more in holding out him, it is like it might go better with us. 2. There is need of wariness, that the report we make, suit well the foundation: And, 3. The neglect of this may be the cause of much powerless preaching, because Christ is not so preached as the subject-matter, and end of preaching; many truths are (alas) spoken without respect to this end, or but with little respect to it.

Uses particular for you that are hearers, are these, 1. If this be the great subject of ministers preaching, and that which ye should hear most gladly, and if this be most profitable for you, we may be particular in some few directions to you, which will be as so many branches of the use. And, 1. Of all truths that people would welcome and study, they would welcome and study these that concern Christ, and the covenant of grace most, as foundation-truths, and seek to have them backed by the Spirit. We are afraid there is a fault among Christians, that most plain and substantial truths are not so heeded, but some things that may further folk in their light, or tickle their affections, or answer a case, are almost only sought after; which things (it is true) are good; but if the plain and substantial truths of the gospel were more studied, and made use of, they have in them that which would answer all cases. It is a sore matter, when folks are more taken up with notions and speculations, than with these soul-saving truths, as, that Christ was born, that he was a true Man, that he was, and is King, Priest, and Prophet of his Church, &c. and that other things are heard with more greediness; but if these be the great subject of ministers preaching, it should be your great study to know Christ, in his person, natures, offices, and covenant; what he is to you, and what is your duty to him, and how you should walk in him, and with him; this was *Paul*'s aim, *I count* (faith he) *all things loss and dung for the excellency of the knowledge of Christ, that I may know him and the power of his resurrection, and the fellowship of his sufferings*, &c. Phil. iii. 8, 9, 10. It is my design, (as if he had said) not only to make him known, but to know him myself. There is little faith in Christ, and distinctness in use-making of his offices, and folks take but little pains to know these things: Therefore, on the one side, let me exhort you, to make this more the subject of your enquiry; and on the other side, take it for your reproof, that there is such a readiness to snuff when plain truths are insisted on, or when they are not followed to some uncouth or strange way; which says, we are exceeding unthankful to God for giving us the best things to speak, hear, and think of.

2. Think much of the preaching of Christ, and to have ministers to preach of him, he is the best news, and God hath sent ministers on this errand, to make them known to you: had he sent them to tell you all the secret things to come that are in God's purpose, and all the hid works of nature, it had not been comparable to these news; what would you have been! O what would sabbath-days and week-days, your lying down and rising up, your living and dying been, if these news had not been? ye should have had a sinful and sad life, and a most comfortless and terrible death; therefore think this gospel a thing of more worth than ye do, and count their feet beautiful on the mountains, that bring these news and glad tidings, as it is Isa. lii. that good report of making peace betwixt God and sinners should be much thought of, and prized, and counted a greater favour than we use to count it. 3. By this ye may know who thrives and profits best under the gospel, even these that learn most of Christ: which consists not in telling over of words. But *first*, In actual improving of him, as it is, Eph. iii. 20. *Ye have not so learned Christ*, but so as to improve what is in him. 2*dly*, In an experimental finding of these effects in us, that are spoken of to come by Christ, which is that which the apostle meaneth, Phil. iii. 10. *That I may know him, and the power of his resurrection, and the fellowship of his sufferings, that I may be conformable to his death*. I am afraid that of the many that hear this gospel, there are but few that know Christ this way. But if he be the great thing that should be preached by us, and that ye should learn, (1) What is the reason that so many should be ignorant of him, that the most part look rather like *Turks* and *Pagans*, than like *Christians*? God help us, what shall we say of the condition of the most part of people, when the preaching the gospel has not gained this much ground on us, as to make us know Christ, in his person, natures, offices, our need of him, and the use we should make of him? But, 2. If we will try how he is improven, it is to be feared there be far fewer that know him in this respect; do not many men live, as if they had never heard tell of him? Though they hear that pardon of sin is to be gotten through him, and that vertue to subdue sin must flow from him, yet they live as if no such thing were in him: if your consciences were posed, besides the evidences that are in your practice, this would be found to be a sad truth. And, (3.) If we will yet try further, what experience folk have of Christ, what vertue they find flowing from his resurrection, what fellowship there is in his sufferings, what conformity to his death, what benefit redounds to them from his offices of King, Priest, and Prophet, to the slaying of sin, and quickning to holy duties, what benefit of fruit from his death; alas! no more, with most, than if he had never died: what profit or real influence, as to any spiritual change, do any to count upon find? and think ye all these things to be but words? they know him not, that feel not something of the efficacy of his death and resurrection in themselves.

3. *Observe*, That the report concerning Christ, is the main subject and errand that has been, and is, and will be common to all the ministers of the gospel, to the end of the world; it's *our report*, it was the report of all the prophets, Acts x. 43. *To him bear all the prophets witness, that thro' his name, whosoever believeth on him should have remission of sins:* they all agree, and have a joint testimony in these. 1. In one subject, Christ, and the same things concerning him, as, that the pardon of sin is to be gotten in him, and through faith in him and no other way, &c. 2. In one commission, they have all one commission, though they be not all equal; all are not apostles, yet all are ambassadors, there is the same authority for us to report, and you to receive the gospel, as if *Isaiah* or *Paul* were preaching; the authority depending on the commission, and not on the persons of men who carry it. 3. In one common end which they all have, and in one common object they are sent to. 4. In this, that they all hold of one common Master, being gifts of one and the same Mediator, Eph. iv. *When he ascended on high, he led captivity captive, and gave gifts to men, to some Apostles*, &c.

The last use is, To teach you, not to think the less

less of the testimony, or matter testified, because of these that testify to you; if *Isaiah* or *Paul* were testifying to you, ye would get no other tidings, though their life and way would be of another sort and stamp than ours are: Alas! for the most part, we are warranted, as well as they, to make Christ known to you, therefore take heed of rejecting the testimony of this Christ, that we bear witness unto; it is the same Christ that the law and the prophets bear witness to, *there is not another name given under heaven, whereby a sinner can be sav'd;* it is through him, that whosoever believes on him may receive the remission of sins; in this ye have not only us, but the prophets and apostles, to deal with, yea Jesus Christ, and God himself; and the rejecting of us, will be found to be the rejecting of them. It is the same testimony, on the matter, that it was in *Isaiah* his time; and therefore, tremble and fear, all ye that slight the gospel; ye have not us for your party, but all the prophets, and *Isaiah* among the rest, and our Lord Jesus Christ, who hath said, *He that receiveth you, receiveth me, and he that despiseth you despiseth me.* There will be many aggravations of the guilt of an unbeliever and this will be a main one, even the testimony of all the prophets that concur in this truth which they have rejected. Take heed to this, all ye Atheists, that know not what it is to take with sin; and all ye hypocrites, that coin and counterfeit a religion of your own; and all ye legal persons, that lean to your own righteousness; what will ye say, when it shall be found, that ye have rejected all these testimonies? ye must either say, ye counted them false witnesses, which ye will not dare to say; or that ye accounted them true, and yet would not receive their testimony: and the best of these will be found sad enough; for if ye counted them true, why did not ye believe them? this will be a very pungent dilemma.

Use 2. For comfort to poor believers. They have good ground to receive and rest upon Jesus Christ; there is never a prophet, apostle or preacher of the gospel, but he hath sealed this truth concerning Christ. What needs any sinner fear at him, or be fearful to close with him? will ye give credit to the testimony of *Isaiah* and of *Peter*, Acts x. 43. and of the rest of the prophets and apostles? Then receive their report, and set yourselves to be among the number of believers, that their testimony may be rested on. We are persuaded there is one of two that will follow on this doctrine, either a strong encouragement to, and confirmation of believing, and quietly resting on Jesus Christ for pardon of sin; or a great ground of aggravation of, and expostulation with you for your guilt, who care not whether ye receive this report or not. We shall say no more for the time, but God bless this to you.

SERMON II.

Isaiah liii. 1. *Who hath believed our report? and to whom is the arm of the Lord revealed?*

THE prophet *Isaiah* is very solicitous about the fruit of his preaching, when he hath preached concerning Christ; as indeed it is not enough for ministers to preach, and for people to hear, except some fruit follow; and now, when he hath been much in preaching, and looketh to others that have been much in that work, he sadly regrets the little fruit it had, and would have among them, to whom Christ was and should be spoken of; a thing that in the entry should put us to be serious, lest this complaint of *Isaiah* stand on record against us; seeing he complains of the hearers of the gospel, not only in his own time, but in our time also.

We told you, there were four things in this first part of the verse. 1. The great errand that ministers have to a people, it is to report concerning Christ; and beside that we observed from this head before, looking to the scope, we shall observe further,

1. The end that ministers should have before them in preaching Christ and the gospel, is, that the hearers of it may be gained to Jesus Christ by hearing, so as they may be brought to believe on him; it is, in a word, to gain them to saving faith in Christ.

2. It is implied, that Jesus Christ is only to be proposed as the object of faith, to be rested on by the hearers of the gospel; and is the only ground of their peace: there is no name that can be mentioned for the salvation of souls, but this name only; and there is no other gospel can be proposed, but that which holdeth him out to people.

3. Observe, (which is much the same with the former observation and to which we would speak a little more particularly) that by preaching of the gospel, Jesus Christ is laid before the hearers of it, as the object of their faith, and proposed to be believed

lieved upon by them; else there would be no ground of this complaint against them. But wherever this gospel is preached, there Christ is laid, as it were, at the foot or door of every soul that heareth it, to be believed and rested on; this is the great errand of the gospel, to propose to people Jesus Christ, as the the object and ground of faith, to lay him down to be rested on for that very end. When the apostle is speaking, Rom. x. 8. of the doctrine of faith, he saith, *It is not now, Who shall ascend into heaven? nor who shall descend into the deep? but the word is near thee, even in thy mouth, and in thy heart: what word is that? the word of faith which we preach.* Now, saith he, Christ, by the preaching of the gospel, is brought so near folks, that he is brought even to their hearts and to their mouths; so near, that (to speak so) people have no more to do, but to stoop and take him up, or to roll themselves over upon him; yea, it bringeth him in to their very heart, that they have no more to do, but to bring up their heart to consent to close the bargain, and with the mouth to make confession of it: and these words are the more considerable, that they are borrowed from Deut. xxx. where Moses is setting death and life before the people, and bidding them choose; tho' he would seem to speak of the law, yet, if we consider the scope, we will find him to be on the matter speaking of Jesus Christ, holden forth to that people under ceremonial ordinances, and shewing them that there was life to be had in him that way, and according to God's intent, they had life and death put in their choice.

I know there are two things necessary to the acting and exercising of faith. The *1st* is objective, when the object or ground is proposed in the preaching of the gospel. The *2d* is subjective, when there is an inward, spiritual, and powerful quickning, and framing of the heart, to lay hold on, and make use of the object and offer. It is true, that all, to whom the offer cometh, are not quickned; but the doctrine saith, that, to all to whom the gospel cometh, Christ is proposed, to be believed on by them, and brought near unto them, so that we may say, as Christ said to his hearers, *The kingdom of God is come near unto you;* both Christ and John brought, and laid the kingdom of heaven near to the Jews, and it is laid as near to you in the preached gospel: This is it then that the doctrine says, 1. That the gospel holdeth out Christ, as a sufficient ground of faith to rest upon. And, 2. With a sufficient warrant to these who hear it to make use of him, according to the terms on which he is offered. And, 3. It brings him so pressingly home, as he is laid to the doors and hearts of sinners who hear the gospel; that whoever hath the offer, he must necessarily either believe in, and receive Christ, or reject him, and cast at the report made of him in the gospel.

I shall first a little confirm this doctrine, and then secondly make use of it.

First, I shall confirm it from these grounds, (1.) From the plain offers which the Lord maketh in his word, and from the warrant he giveth his ministers to make the same offers; it is their commission to pray them, to whom they are sent, to be reconciled; to tell them, *that God was in Christ reconciling the world to himself,* as it is, 2 Cor. v. 19, 20. and in Christ's stead to request them to embrace the offer of reconciliation; to tell them, that Christ died for the sinners that will embrace him, and that he will impute his righteousness unto them; and Chap. vi. 1. *We beseech you* (saith he) *that ye receive not this grace in vain;* which is not meant of saving grace, but of the gracious offer of grace and reconciliation through him; this is ministers work, to pray people not to be idle hearers of this gospel; For, saith he, *I have heard thee in a time accepted, and in a day of salvation have I succoured thee; behold, now is the accepted time; behold, now is the day of salvation.* The force of the argument is this, If ye will make this gospel welcome, ye may get a hearing; for now is the day of salvation, therefore do not neglect it. So Psal. lxxxi. 10. 11. (where God maketh the offer of himself, and that very largely) *Open thy mouth wide and I will fill it.* The offer is of himself, as the words following clear; *My people would not hearken to my voice, and Israel would none of me;* for they that refuse his word, refuse himself; and hence, Isa. lxv. 1. he saith, *I am found of them that sought me not; I said, Behold me, behold me, unto a nation that was not called by my name;* and to the Jews, *I have stretched out my hands all day long to a rebellious people.* (2.) We may clear and confirm it from these similitudes, by which the offer of this gospel is, as it were, brought to the doors of people: and there are several similitudes made use of to this purpose; I shall name but four. 1. It is set down under the expression of wooing, as, 2 Cor. xi. 2. *I have espoused you as a chaste virgin to Christ;* this is ordinary, and supposeth a marriage, and a bridegroom, that is by his friends wooing and suiting in marriage; so that (as we shew) wherever the call of the gospel comes, it is a bespeaking of souls to him, as, Cant. viii. *What shall we do for our sister in the day that she shall be spoken for?* 2. It is set out under the expression of inviting to a feast; and hearers of the gospel are called to come to Christ, as strangers or guests are called to come to a wedding-feast, Mat. xxii. 2, 3, 4. *All things are ready come to the wedding*, &c. Thus the gospel calleth not to an empty house that wants meat, but to a banqueting house where Christ is made ready as the cheer, and there wants no more but feasting on him: so it is set out under the similitude of eating and drinking, John vi. 27. *He that eats me, even he shall live by me.* 3. It's set out often under the expression or similitude of a market, where all the wares are laid forth on the stand, Isa. lv. 1. *Ho, every one that thirsts, come to the waters*, &c. And, lest it should be said, or thought, that the proclamation is only to the thirsty, and such as are so and so qualified; ye may look to what followeth, *let him that hath no money come; yea, come, buy without money and without price.* And to the offer that is made to those of Laodicea, Rev. iii. who, in appearance, were a hypocritical and formal people, yet to them the counsel and call comes forth, *Come buy of me eye-salve, gold tried in the fire*, &c. It says the wares are even in their offer, or even offered to them. 4. It is set out under the similitude of a standing and knocking at a door, because the gospel brings Christ as knocking and calling hard at sinners doors, Rev. iii. 20. *Behold, I stand at the door and knock; if any man will hear my voice, and open the door, I will come into him, and sup with him, and he with me.* So, Cant. v. 2. By the sleepy bride it is said, *It is the voice of my beloved that knocketh;* and Psal. xxiv. last four verses, 'tis cried, *Lift up your heads, ye gates, and be lift up, ye everlasting doors, that the King of glory may come in;* which is an earnest invitation to make way for Christ Jesus, wanting nothing but an entry into the heart, whereby we may see how near Christ comes in the gospel, and is laid to folks hand. 3. We may confirm it from the nature of faith, and of the obedience that is required to be given to the command of believing: Wherever this gospel comes, it tyeth and obligeth all the hearers to believe on Christ, that is, to receive and welcome him; and there could be no receiving of him, if he were not making an offer of himself. Thus it is said, John i. 11, 12. *He came unto his own, but his own received him not; but as many as received him, to them gave he power to become the sons of God.* He came to both these who received him, and to these who received him not; but he gave to believers only this privilege of sonship. If we look to all the names of faith; as *coming to Christ, eating and drinking of him, receiving of him, resting on him*, &c. they all suppose that Christ is near to be catched hold of, and within speaking and trysting terms to people that hear the gospel. 4. It may be confirmed from the many sad complaints that the Lord hath for not receiving him, and not believing his word, and from the dreadful designations, by which he holds out the sin of unbelief, all which will make out this, that God lays Christ at sinners door in his word; hence, John v. 40. our Lord says, *Ye will not come unto me that ye may get life:* and Mat. xxiii. at the close, *O Jerusalem, Jerusalem, how often would I have gathered thee, and ye would not?* This was it that did aggravate their sin, that he would, and they would not; so Psal. lxxxi. *My people would not hearken to my voice, and Israel would none of me;* and, Luke vii. it is said, the *Scribes and Pharisees rejected the counsel of God against themselves;* and Acts xiii. 54. when the Jews rejected Christ, it is said, *they judged themselves unworthy of everlasting life;* and therefore the Apostles say, that they will *leave them, and turn to the Gentiles.* 5. We may confirm it from this, that in respect of the gospel, and offer made in it, Christ comes alike near to all that hear it; for if he be near to some, then he is near to all, I mean in regard of an objective nearness; there is the same warrant to speak and make the offer to all, before there be some discovery made for qualifying the doctrine to some. It is true, there is a difference in respect of the power that accompanieth the gospel; but as it layeth out the offer of Christ, and life through him, it comes alike near to all the hearers of it: the invitation comes to all, and in the same terms, to them that refuse, as well as to them that receive him; the same gospel is preached to both. A 6th confirmation is from the nature of God's administration of his external covenant, which is sealed in baptism to both; not one covenant to one, and another covenant to another; but the same covenant, on condition of believing, to both: behold, then, in the preaching of this gospel, that Christ comes near you, even to your door, in respect of the mediate ordinances; as near as he did to Abraham and David, altho' God had his extraordinary ways of manifesting himself to them, not common to others: yea, this day, the gospel is more clear objectively to you than it was to Abraham, who rejoiced to see Christ's day afar off, when it was vailed; yea, the gospel is as clearly preached to you, as those, who are now before the throne of God, had it preached to them, as to the matter of it, tho' we will make no equality as to the manner of it.

Use 1. Advert to this, when ye come to hear the gospel preached, and think how you are living in trysting terms with God, and how near Christ come:

unto

unto you; the word of faith lays him so near, that ye have no more to do but receive the offer of him, to believe and close with him, and step in upon him, as it were, to come as living stones to be built upon him as a sure foundation.

But it will be asked, How comes this gospel so near? How does it bring in Christ so near to sinners? *Ans.* In these five steps, 1. As it makes the report of Christ, and brings the tidings of such things, as that he is born, and that he hath suffered, and for such an end, that we may partake of the benefit of them on such terms; it makes the proclamation narratively, and tells what he did, what good may be gotten of him, and how we may come by it. 2. As it brings an offer of these good things on the terms on which they are to be gotten, so it never tells that Christ is come, but it says also, Here is life to be gotten in him by you, if ye will take the way proposed to come by it; therefore, when the proclamation comes forth, *that all things are ready*, the next word is, *Come to the wedding*; And when, in the one word, he says, *I stand at the door and knock*; at the next he says, *If any man will open the door, I will come in to him, and sup with him, and he with me*; and when, Isa. xxviii. it is said, *He is a precious Corner-stone, a tried Foundation-stone laid in Zion*; the next word is, *He that believes on him shall not make haste*, or, as the Apostle hath it, *shall not be ashamed or confounded*; this makes the gospel glad tidings, because it comes always with an offer of Christ, and of life in him. 3. When the offer is made, and the precious wares are exposed to sale in this cried fair of grace, a command comes out, Choose life, come buy the wares, believe, receive the offer, as is clear in all the places we named before; it leaves not folk indifferent to receive or not, but chargeth them, as they would be obedient to a command, to receive him, 1 John iii. 23. *This is his commandment that ye should believe on the name of his Son Jesus Christ*; this is the great gospel command, and ministers have not only the telling of these news, and warrant to make the offer, but a commission to command to receive it; and therefore the fitting and flighting of the offer, is a sin opposite to the command. 4. It not only makes the offer, and backs the offer with a command to embrace it, but it sweetens the command with many gracious promises knit to it, as Isa. lv. *Hear and your soul shall live, and I will make an everlasting covenant with you, even the sure mercies of David*: And whenever the command of believing comes, it is always with a promise; as Paul deals with the jaylor, Acts xvi. *Believe, and thou shalt be saved*; and Mark xvi. at the close, the Lord says, *They that believe shall be saved*, to encourage to faith in him. 5. It presses the offer, and commands embracing of it with the promise, with a certification; for the offer is not conditional, but alternative, Mark xvi. *If ye believe not, ye shall be damned*; so Deut. xxx. death and life are proposed, and they are bidden choose: If the gospel be not effectual in its commands and promises, it will be effectual in its threatnings; the word of God will triumph one way or the other, and not return to him void, as is very clear, Isa. lv. 11. and 2 Cor. ii. 15, 16. it triumphs in some, while they are brought by the promise to give obedience to the command of believing, and to them it becomes the savour of life unto life; and to others it triumphs, as to the execution of the threatning on them for their unbelief, and to them it becomes the savour of death unto death. In a word, Christ Jesus comes so near people in this gospel, that he must either be chosen, and life with him; or refused, to the destruction and death of the refuser; ye have the same Christ, the same word, the same covenant, the same obligation to believe, proposed to you, that believers from the beginning of the world had; and another ye will not get, and what more can the gospel do to bring Christ near to you? when it brings him so near, that ye have him in your offer, and the authority of God and his promises interposed to persuade you to accept of the offer; and threatnings added, to certify you, that if ye accept it not, ye shall perish: in which respect, we may say, as the prophet Isaiah doth, Chap. v. *What could God do more to his vineyard, which he hath not done?* as to the holding out of the Object of faith, Jesus Christ to be rested on by you.

But some will, it may be, object here, 1. But if there come not life and power with the offer, it will not do the turn; we cannot believe, nor receive the offer. *Ans.* Whose fault is this, that ye want ability? It is not God's fault; ye have a sure ground to believe, his word is a warrant good enough, the promises are free enough, the motives sweet enough; the great fault is a heart of unbelief in you, that ye will not believe in Christ, nor open to him when he is brought to your door. I doubt, yea, I put it out of doubt, when all that ever heard the gospel shall stand before the throne, that there shall be one found that shall dare to make this excuse that they were not able to receive Christ; the gospel brings Christ so near them, that they must either say, yea, or nay; It is not so much, I cannot, as, I will not believe: and that will be found a wilful and malicious refusal.

2. It may be objected, But how can this gospel come to all alike, seeing it cannot be, that these that will never get good of the gospel, have it as near to them, as these that get the saving fruit of it? *Ans.* Not to speak of God's purpose, or what he intends to make of it, nor of the power and fruit that accompanies it to some, and not to all; it is certain, the gospel, and Christ in its offer, comes alike near to all that hear it: It objectively reveals the same glad tidings to all, with the conditional offer of life, and with the same command and encouragement, and certification, in threatnings as well as promises: In these respects, Christ is brought alike near to all; and when God cometh to reckon, he will let sinners know in that day, that the gospel came to their door, and was refused: yea, it comes, and where it comes will take hold of some, to pluck them out of the snare, and be ground of faith to them; and to others it will be a ground of challenge, and so the savour of death unto death: for tho' it take not effect as to its promises in all, nor in its threatnings to all; yet as to either death or life, it will take effect in every one, so as, if life be refused, death steps in the room of it.

But it may be asked, Why will God have Christ in the offer of the gospel brought so near the hearers of it? *Ans.* 1. Because it serves to commend the grace and love of God in Christ Jesus: when the invitation is so broad, that it is to all; it speaks out the royalty of the feast, upon which ground, 2. Cor. vi. 1. it is called *grace*, the offer is so large and wide. 2. Because it serves for warranting and confirming the elect in the receiving of this offer; for none of the elect could receive him, if he were not even laid to their door. It is this, which gives us warrant to receive that which God offers: it is not because we are elected or beloved of God before time, or because he purposed to do us good, that we believe; these are not grounds of faith, being God's secret will: but we believe, because God calleth and maketh the offer, inviteth and promiseth, knowing that he is faithful, and we may trust him; hence David says, *I will never forget thy word*, and *In God will I praise his word*; for the word in its offer speaks alike to all, and to none particularly: Indeed, when it comes to the application of promises for consolation, that is to be made according to the qualifications in the persons, but the offer is to all. 3. Because by this means the Lord hath the fairer access to found his quarrel and controversy against unbelievers, and to make their dittay and doom the clearer in the day of the Lord, when it is found that they never received the offer, *My people would not hearken to my voice, and Israel would none of me; therefore I gave them up to their own hearts lusts, and they walked in their own counsels:* and this is an approbation given to justice here, It's well-wair'd, seeing they would not receive thee, that they get worse in thy room.

Use 2. Seeing Christ comes near you in this gospel, and this is one of the market-days, I intreat you, while he is near, receive him, call upon him while he is near; or, take it in the plain words of the apostle, Open to him, take him in, give him welcome, while he bodes himself, to say so, on you. There is not a conscience in any man that hears this gospel, but he will have this testimony from him in it, that he came near them, was in their sight, and within their reach and grips, as it were, if they would have put out their hand to receive him: and seeing it is so, O receive this gospel, give him room; while he is content to sup with you, take him in, make sure your union with him: this is the end why this report is made, and Christ is laid before you, even that you may lay yourselves over on him.

I would follow this *use* a little, by way of exhortation and expostulation jointly, seeing the doctrine will bear both; for when Christ is brought so near, even to the mouth and to the heart, it will be great ground of reproof and expostulation, if he shall be rejected. Be exhorted therefore to be in earnest, seeing, 1. It is a matter of such concernment to you: many nations, kings, and kingdoms have not had Christ so near them as ye have; neglect not such an opportunity. Do ye think that all that is said in the gospel, concerning this, is for nought? Is it for no use, that such a report is made, and preaching continued so long among you? And if it be for any use, is it not for this, that ye may receive the report, and may, by doing so, get your souls for a prey? To what use will preaching be, if this use and end of it be missed? Will your hearing the gospel make your peace with God, if Christ be not received? 2. Consider the advantage ye may have by receiving the gospel, that others have not. Is it a little thing to be called to God's feast, to be married to Christ, to be made friends with God, and to enjoy him for ever? The day comes, when it will be thought an advantage; and are there motives to persuade to any thing, like those that are to induce to that? 3. Consider what it is that we require of you: it is no strange nor hard thing, it is but believing; and this is nothing else, but that the report concerning Christ be received, yea, that he be received for your own good; that is it that the gospel calls you to, even to betake you to a Physician for cure, to

betake

betake you to a Cautioner for your debt. If you could escape a reckoning and wrath another way, it were something; but when there is no other way to obtain pardon of sin and peace, or to escape wrath, and obtain favour and friendship with God, but this, and when this way (to speak so) is made so easy, that it is but to stoop down, and to take up Christ at your foot, as it were, or to roll yourselves on him, how inexcusable will ye unbelievers be, when ye shall be arraigned before his tribunal? But, 4. Look a little farther to what is coming: If ye were to live always here, it were hard enough to live at a feud with God; but have ye faith of a judgment after death? if so, how will ye hold up your faces in that day, that now refuse Christ? will not horrible confusion be the portion of many then? and will any ground of confusion be like this, the slighting of Christ? when he shall be seen coming to judge slighters of him, what horror will then rise in consciences, when he shall appear and be avenged on them that were not obedient to this gospel? as is most clear, 2 Thess. i. *When our Lord Jesus shall be revealed in flaming fire, with his mighty angels from heaven, to take vengeance on all that know God, and obey not the gospel.* 5. Consider, that death and life are now in your option, in your hand as it were, chuse or refuse: I speak not, nor plead here for free-will, but of your willing electing of that which ye have offered to you; for one of two will be, either shall ye willingly chuse life, which is a fruit of grace, or refuse life, and chuse death, which will be found the native fruit of your corruption: ye may have life by receiving Christ, who is laid to your door; and if ye refuse him, death will follow it: as now in hearing this gospel, ye carry in chusing or refusing, so will the sentence pass on you at the great day; and so your sentence, in a manner, is written down with your own hand, as it is said, Acts xiii. 46. *Ye judge yourselves unworthy of eternal life*, not out of humility, but maliciously. Now, when the matter is of such concernment, beware of playing the fool; if ye will continue presumptuous and secure, following your idols, what will the Lord say, but, Let it be so, ye get no wrong when ye get your own choice? and he but, as it were, ratifies the sentence which ye have past on yourselves. 6. I shall add but this one word more, and beseech you that ye would seriously lay this to heart, as a weighty thing, considering the certification that follows on it: It is not only death, but a horrible death, wrath, and wrath with its aggravation from this ground; like that of Capernaum, that was lifted up to heaven in this respect, having Christ brought so near them. To whom this gospel is not the favour of life unto life, it shall be the favour of death unto death: and think not this a common motive, tho' it be commonly used; it will bring wrath upon wrath, and vengeance upon vengeance on the hearers of this gospel, beyond that of Sodom, if ye be rejecters of it. Sure, none of you would think it an easy thing to be punished as Sodom was, nor digest well the curse that came on them: Is there any of you, but ye would think it uncouth and strange, yea stupendous, to enter into their judgment, and to have your lands turned into a stinking loch, and yourselves eternally tormented with them? But there is more wrath and vengeance following on the sin of unbelief, and rejecting of Christ, when he comes to your door in this gospel. To close up all, Consider, that Christ is near you, and hath been long near you, and wooing you: ye know not how many days or years ye shall have; how soon this gospel may be taken from you, or ye from it; how soon ye may be put in the pit, where ye will gnash your teeth, gnaw your tongues, and blaspheme God: therefore be serious while Christ is in your offer, and roll yourselves over upon him, while ye have him so near you; welcome this *hearing* or *report*, while it sounds in your ears, that there may be no just ground of this complaint against you, *Lord, who hath believed our report?*

SERMON III.

Isaiah liii. 1. *Who hath believed our report? and to whom is the arm of the Lord revealed?*

THE most part of men and women think not much of the preached gospel; yet, if it were considered, what is the Lord's end in it, it would be the most refreshful news that ever people heard, to hear the report of a Saviour: that is, and should be, great and glad tidings of great joy to all nations; and we should be so composed to hear such news from God, and concerning his will and our own weal, as to be suitably affected with them. It is a wonder that God hath sent such a report to people, and in it hath laid Christ so near them, that he puts him home to them, and lays him before them, even at their feet as it were; and as great a wonder, that when the Lord hath condescended to give such a Saviour, and

brought

brought him so near, that all he calleth for is faith, to belive the report, or rather faith in him of whom the report is; which is the second thing in the words.

The second thing is, The duty that lies on people to whom the Lord sends the gospel, or this report concerning Christ: and ye may take it in this general, That it lies on all that hear the gospel, to believe the report that it brings concerning Christ, and by faith to receive him, who is holden out to them in it: this is clearly implied; Isaiah and all ministers are sent to report concerning him, and to bear witness of him, and it is the duty of all hearers to believe it; and this is the ground of his and their complaint, when people do not believe it: by comparing this text with Rom. x. 16. and John xii. 38. we shew, that it is saving faith that is here to be understood.

I shall take up this doctrine in three branches, which we will find in the words, and which will make way for the use. 1. *That a people to whom Christ is offered in the gospel, may warrantably accept of Christ;* or, *The offering of Christ in the gospel, is warrant enough to believe in him:* Otherways there had been no just ground of expostulation and complaint for not believing; for tho' the complaint will not infer that they had ability to believe, yet it will infer they had a warrant to believe; for the complaint is for the neglect of the duty they were called to. 2. *That they, to whom Christ is offered in the gospel, are called to believe;* it is their duty to do it: thus, believing, in all that hear this gospel, is necessary, by necessity of command; even as holiness, repentance, &c. are. 3. *That saving faith is the way and mean, by which these, that have Christ offered to them in the gospel, come to get a right to him, and to obtain the benefits that are reported of to be had from him;* thus, believing is necessary, as a mids, to the end of getting Christ, and all that is in him: this is also here implied in the regret made of the want of faith, which prejudgeth men of Christ, and of the benefits of the gospel.

We shall shortly put by the *first* of these, which is, That all that hear the gospel preached, have warrant to believe and receive Christ, for their eternal peace, and for making up of the breach betwixt God and them: this preached gospel gives you all warrant to accept of Jesus Christ, and ye would not seek after, nor call for another. I shall first premise two distinctions to clear this, and then, secondly confirm it. As for the first of the two distinctions that serve to clear it, we may take up the gospel more largely and complexly, in a covenant form, holding out Christ and his benefits, on condition of believing; or, we may take it up as it holds out a promise, without particular mentioning of a condition: now, when we say, that the gospel commands and warrants all that hear it to accept the offer, we do not mean the last, that all that hear the gospel have warrant to accept the promise, without a condition, but the first, that is, that all the hearers of the gospel are commanded to accept of Christ offered; there is, by the preaching of it, a warrant to close with the report, and then to meddle with, and take hold of the promises, and the things promised: so that it is the gospel, conditionally proposed, that gives warrant to believe, as believing rests on Christ for obtaining life in him. The second distinction is, That we would consider faith, as it rests on Christ or obtaining union with him, and right to the promises; or, as it applies and makes use of the benefits to be gotten in and by Christ: the offer of the gospel gives not to all a warrant to apply the benefits to be gotten by Christ instantly; but it warrants them to close with him first, and then to apply his benefits.

Secondly, For confirmation of this truth, That the general preaching of the gospel is a warrant for believing and exercising faith on Jesus Christ, for making our peace with God; it is clear from these grounds, 1. From the nature of the gospel, it is the word of God, as really inviting to do that which it calls for, as if God were speaking from heaven; it is the word of God, and not the word of man, and hath as real authority to call for obedience, as if God spake it immediately from heaven; and the word of promise is as really his word, as the word of command, and therefore to be rested on and improven, as well as we are to endeavour obedience to the command: and if we think that God's testimony is true, and if we lay any just weight on these three witnesses testifying from heaven, and on these other three testifying from earth, 1 John v. 7. then we may rest on Jesus Christ offered in this gospel, and believe, that these who rest on him shall have life; for it is, as we said, as really God's word, as if he were speaking it audibly from heaven, 2. It may be confirmed from these solemn things, the *word* and *oath* of God, whereby he hath mightily confirmed the external offer of the gospel, even the two immutable things, wherein it is impossible for him to lie, that these who are fled for refuge to lay hold on the hope set before them, may have strong consolation, as it is, Heb. vi. 18. And God having thus said and sworn anent this external covenant, for this very end, that the hearers of the gospel may know, that they who receive Christ offered therein, shall have life, it is warrant sufficient to believe on him for life: it is also for this end that he hath put seals to the covenant, circumcision and the passover in the old, and baptism and the Lord's supper in the new testaments; which are extended, not only to the elect, but to professors in the visible church, that every one, who is baptized and admitted to the communion, may have confirmation of this, that the offer, that God maketh of life through Christ, is a true and real offer, and will be made good to the persons that shall receive it, and so perform the condition. 3. It may be confirmed from the end for which God appointed the word and ministry in his church, even to make the offer of Christ and life through him, John xx. 31. *These things are written, that ye might believe that Jesus Christ is the Son of God, and that believing ye might have life through his name;* the word is both written and preached for this very end. 4. And *lastly*, It is confirmed from the experience of all the saints, and from the ground on which they believed, which was the same that we have; they had no other ground but the same gospel and word that we have; it was not the secret operation or instinct of the Spirit, it is that indeed which works faith; but it was the word which was the ground of their faith, for there is no warrant for faith but in the word: and as many believers as have gone before us, are as so many instances and experiences to confirm this truth to us.

Use. It serves for good use to such as may fall to doubt and dispute what warrant they have to believe: we say, ye have as good warrant as Abraham, David, Paul, or any of the godly that lived before you, had: ye have the same gospel, covenant and promises; it was always God's word preached, which was the ground of faith; and there needs not be much disputing, what is God's purpose; for we are not called to look to that in the matter of believing, more than in the matter of our duty: and as it were evil reasoning to dispute what may be God's purpose in the matter of our duty, when we are called to it; it is as bad reasoning to dispute his purpose in the matter of faith: And therefore we leave this use with a word of advertisement, that this gospel, as it lays Christ before you, it gives you warrant to receive him, and rest upon him; and we may say as Paul did, Acts xiii. 38, 39. *Be it known unto you therefore, men and brethren, that thro' this man is preached unto you forgiveness of sins, and by him all that believe are justified from all things, from which ye could not be justified by the law of* *Moses.* There is the way held out for obtaining pardon of sin, and peace; the Lord hath made the offer, and laid a fair bridge over the gulf of distance betwixt God and sinners, tho' ye should never get good of it, and tho' ye should never set a foot on the bridge: none needs to fear to step forward; behold, our Lord Jesus hath holden out the golden scepter, his call may be warrant enough to come; the preaching of this gospel stops all disputing, and banisheth debating of the business: it calls all the hearers of it, and gives them warrant to come forward, and it is such a warrant, as they will be found slighters of the great salvation offered, who had this door opened to them, and did not step forward; for, as the apostle says, 2 Cor. vi. *Behold, now is the day of salvation, behold now is the accepted time:* and Heb. ii. 2. *If the word spoken by angels was stedfast, and every transgression and disobedience received a just recompence of reward, how shall we escape if we neglect so great salvation? which at the first began to be spoken by the Lord,* &c. It is the same gospel that from the beginning hath been preached to sinners, and that is the reason why the gospel is called grace, in that 2 Cor. vi. 1. *We beseech you that ye receive not this grace of God in vain;* and Gal. ii. at the close, *I do not frustrate the grace of God;* For many get the warrant and pass to come and receive Christ, who put it up in their pocket, as it were, and make no use of it, as the man that hid the talent in his napkin; the banns of marriage are proclaimed, and the warrant given forth, and yet they halt, and come not to the wedding.

We shall add the second branch, which is, That this gospel where it comes and offers Jesus Christ to sinners, men and women are not only warranted to come; but required and commanded to come. The great duty that the gospel calls for, is believing; it leaves it not indifferent to believe or not, but peremptorily lays it on as a command: ye hear many preachings, and Christ often spoken of; now this is the great thing called for from you, even believing in Christ; and while it is not performed, there is no obedience given to the gospel.

We shall first confirm, and then make use of this branch of the doctrine.

1. For confirmation, take these grounds, 1. From the manner how the gospel proposeth faith, it is by way of command in the imperative mood, *Believe, Come, ye that are weary,* &c. *Come to the wedding, Open,* &c. wherein somewhat of the nature of faith is held out, all these being the same with believing. 2. It is not only commanded as other

ther things are, but peculiarly commanded; and there is a greater weight laid on the obedience of this command, than on the doing of many other commanded duties: it is the sum of all Christ's preaching, Mark i. *Repent ye and believe the gospel:* it is the only command which Paul proposes to the jaylor, Acts xvi. *Believe in the Lord Jesus,* &c. 3. It is, as it were, the peculiar command that Jesus Christ hath left to his people, 1 John iii. 23. *This is his commandment, that we should believe on the name of his Son Jesus Christ;* and this command of believing on him, is the peculiar command left to, and laid on ministers to press. 4. It will be clear, if we consider, that the great disobedience that he quarrels for, is, when there is not believing, when sinners will not come to him, this is his quarrel, John v. 40. *Ye will not come to me, that ye may have life;* and here, *Who hath believed our report?* so Mat. xxiii. *I would have gathered you, and ye would not;* and John xii. 37. *Tho' he did many mighty works among them, yet they believed not on him.* 5. Look to the nature of the offer made by Christ, and to the end of it, and ye will find that the great thing called for, is the receiving of it, which is nothing but believing: and all our preachings of Christ, and his benefits, are useless without it: without this, he wants the satisfaction he calls for, for the travel of his soul; and without it the hearers of this gospel profit not, 1 Pet. i. 9. *Receiving the end of your faith, the salvation of your souls;* the subordinate end of preaching, to wit, the salvation of our souls, cannot be attained without faith.

The *uses* are three. 1. It serveth to be a ground for us to propose the main gospel-duty to you, and to teach you, what is the great and main thing ye are called to; it is even to believe in Jesus Christ, to exercise faith on him: it is not only that your life should be civil and formal, that ye should read, pray, frequent ordinances, learn the catechism, and such like; but this is it, to believe on Jesus Christ for the obtaining of life and remission of sins through him; and it is not a thing indifferent to you, but commanded, and with this certification, that if ye believe not, ye shall never get life nor pardon of sin: and therefore as we tell you that remission of sins is preached to you thro' Christ, so we command and charge you to believe on him, and receive this gospel, wherein he is offered for the remission of sins.

For clearing of this use, and that we may have the more ready access to application, we shall speak a word to these three, 1. To several kinds of true faith, three whereof are not saving; or to the ordinary distinctions of faith. 2. To the scripture-expressions, that hold out the nature of saving faith. 3. To some difference betwixt this saving faith, and false and counterfeit faith, or these acts of true faith more generally taken, which yet are not saving.

For the *first* of these, When we speak of faith, we shall draw it to these four kinds ordinarily spoken of, and shall not alter nor add to the common distinctions of faith, tho' there may be more given. The *first* is *historical* faith: which may be called true, being it whereby we assent to the truth of a thing, because of his supposed fidelity that telleth it; as when an author writes a history, we give it credit upon report that he was an honest man that wrote it: so historical faith is, when people hearing the word preached or read, they assent to the truth of it all; and do not question, but that Christ came to the world; that he was God and Man in one person; that he died and rose the third day, and ascended into heaven; that they that believe on him shall be saved, &c. and taking the word to be God's word, they may give to it a higher assent than they give to any man's word, because God is worthy, infinitely worthy of more credit than any man, yea than all men, and angels too: There may be, I say, in this historical faith of divine truths, a higher or greater assent than there is in believing of any human history, which may be the reason why many mistake historical faith, and yet it is but of the same kind, and a thing which many reprobates have, as John ii. at the close, it is said, *Many believed on him when they saw the miracles which he did, but Jesus did not commit himself unto them:* they were brought to believe, from the signs which they saw, that he was more than a meer man, and that it was the word of God which he spoke, and yet it was but a historical faith; yea this faith may be and is in devils, who are said, James ii. 9. *To believe and tremble.* There are many, who, if they believe Christ to be God and Man, and the word to be true, think it enough; yet James, having to do with such, tells them, that the devils believe as much as that, and more thorowly than many that have historical faith; he knows God to be true, and one that cannot lie, and he finds it to his cost; he knows that such as believe cannot perish, for he cannot get one of them to hell; he knows that there is a time set, when Christ will come to judge the world and himself among the rest, and therefore he says often to him, *Torment me not before the time:* and as the devil hath this faith, so there are many in hell that have

it

it too; the rich glutton had it, therefore he bids go tell his brethren, that they come not to that place of torment; and it is told him, They have Moses and the prophets, &c. which says, that he then felt the truth of many things he would not believe before. This I speak, that ye may know, that this historical faith is the first step of faith; but it may be in hell, and so in many in whom saving faith is not: it is really a wonder that folks that are called Christians should own this to be saving faith, and think they are well come to, when they are only come the devil's length in believing; yea, there are many that never came this length, else they would tremble more. The *second* sort of faith, is the faith of *miracles*, which is often spoken of in the New Testament; as when the Lord saith, *If ye had faith as a grain of mustard-seed, ye should say to this mountain, Be thou removed and cast into the sea, and it should be done.* There was an active faith to work miracles, and a passive faith, to receive the particular effect the miracle did produce; some had the faith of miracles to heal, and others to be healed; this is an extraordinary thing, and folks may go to heaven without it, and go to hell with it, though they cannot go to heaven without historical faith; hence it is said, *Many shall come to me in that day, and shall say, We have cast out devils in thy name; to whom he will say, Depart from me, ye workers of iniquity.* And the Apostle saith, 1 Cor. xiii. 2. *If I had all faith, and could remove mountains, if I want charity, it avails me nothing.* This faith of miracles availeth not alone to salvation, because it acts not on Christ holden out in the promises, as a Saviour to save from sin; but on Christ, as having power and ability to produce such an effect: which may be, where there is no quitting of a man's own righteousness; and, if there be not grace in the person that hath it, it is an occasion of pride. We call you then to historical faith, as necessary, tho' not sufficient; but not to this faith of miracles, it being neither necessary nor sufficient. A *third* sort of faith is *temporary* faith, spoken of Matt. xiii.

and set out under the parable of the seed sown on stony-ground, which soon springs up, but withers; so some hearers of the gospel receive the word with joy, and are affected with it, but endure not: The difference betwixt this and historical faith, is, that historical faith, as such, consists in the judgment, and reaches not the affections; at best, it reaches not the affection of joy, for tho' the devils tremble, yet they are never glad; temporary faith reaches the affections, and will make a man to tremble at the threatnings, as Felix did; so some way to delight himself in the promises of the gospel, and to smack them, as it were, from the apprehension of the sweet taste and relish he finds in them. It is even here (as it were) told a whole man, that a Physician is come to town, he is neither up nor down with it; but tell it to a sick man, and he is fain, from an apprehended possibility of the cure, yet the apprehended possibility of the cure never sends him to the Physician, nor puts him to apply the cure. The *fourth* sort is *saving* faith, which goeth beyond all the rest, and brings the sick man to the physician, and to make use of the cure: there may be some measure of true saving faith, where there is not much temporary faith, or moving of the affections; and there may be a considerable measure of temporary faith, where there is no saving faith at all; even as a fallen-star may seem to glance more than a fixed one that is overclouded, yet it hath no solid light. Know then, that faith is called for, but take not every sort of faith for saving faith: it would make tender hearts bleed, to see so many mistaken in the matter of their faith; there are some who say, they had faith all their days. O that ye were convinced of the lamentable deceit and delusion that ye are under, and that ye could distinguish betwixt faith and presumption, betwixt historical and temporary faith, and true saving faith: tho' the two former be not delusions; but in so far as ye rest on the same, and take them for saving faith, ye are deluded; for saving faith puts you out of yourselves, to rest on Jesus Christ.

SERMON IV.

Isaiah liii. 1. *Who hath believed our report? and to whom is the arm of the Lord revealed?*

THE gospel is a sweet message, and ought to be glad news, when it comes to a people; and therefore, when this report of our Lord Jesus Christ is made to sinners, O! but it is a sad complaint that follows on the refusal and not welcoming of it: there is no better news a minister can carry, than these brought to the shepherds by the angels, Luke ii. 10, 11. *Fear not, behold we bring you glad tidings of great joy to all people; unto you is born, in the city of David, a Saviour, which is Christ the Lord:* but, were it an Isaiah, it will weight him, when he looks on a fruitless ministry

and

and despised gospel, and will make him complain, *Who hath believed our report?* O that we may experimentally know the chearfulness and gladness that follows the gospel where it is embraced; and that we may not know the sorrow and sadness that will follow the challenge for despising of it. One of these two preached gospel will be, either it will be joyful news to you, or sad ground of complaint to God against you.

We entered to speak of the great duty of a people that hear the gospel, and the great mean whereby these news become delightsom, and that is by faith to receive the report of the gospel, or to believe on Christ reported of in it: This is clearly implied, for the regret which holds out the sin, is, *Who hath believed our report?* and therefore the great duty must be, to believe, and by faith to receive the report. We come now to speak of the *Use*. And because it is the great design of the whole gospel, yea, it is the design of the law also, both of which level at this end and scope, even faith in Christ; it will be expedient, and noways impertinent, that we insist a little on this, especially when so many thousands are utterly ignorant of faith, being strangers to what believing in Christ is, and so great strangers to the native end of the gospel, and out of the way of getting good by the preaching of it; so that, to this day, they have not learned this one lesson, to wit, concerning faith in Christ, and other lessons will be to little or no purpose, till this be learned.

We shall not insist to speak at large of the doctrine of faith, but only, in a plain way, glance at what this great duty is, that is required of the hearers of the gospel; it is believing in Christ savingly, or saving faith, for no other thing will hold off the complaint against you: ye will be complained of, tho' ye would believe with all other faith; therefore it is this faith that is here meaned.

That we may come the sooner to that which we would be at, we shall premise two or three words. *First*, when we speak of believing here, we presuppose these things that are necessary for clearing the object of faith, and capacitating us to believe, tho' they be not saving faith: As namely, 1. That the offer of the gospel must come to people, that the Object of faith be held out to them, that it be told them, that there is a way for a sinner's justification through Christ Jesus, and that sinners may be accepted before God on his account, or through him. There must also, 2. Be an understanding of this, a conceiving in the judgment what it is; folks cannot believe, except they hear, and understand what they hear, in so far as distinctly to fix their faith on the thing known; they must know and understand the Mediator's fulness, the Covenant's freeness, and the efficacy of faith to make Christ theirs. Yea, 3. It is necessary there be some acquaintance with our own condition; as that we are naturally under sin; that we are lost, and under the curse; sick, and utterly unable, and even desperate to get ourselves recovered, by any thing that is in, or by any thing that we can do of ourselves; that we are for ever undone, if we get not a Saviour, that our mouth may be stopped. 4. Not only must we know this, but it is necessary there be a historical faith of it, to believe that there is fulness and sufficiency in Christ, that he is able to cure, and take away the guilt of sin in all that rest on him; these must be believed in general, ere ever sinners can rest on him for their own salvation; which supposes, that there may be an historical, where there is not a saving faith. Now, when all this length is gone, saving faith is that which the gospel calleth for, and it is the heart's acting, according to what sound light and conviction it hath, on Jesus Christ, as holden out in the promise, for obtaining of life and salvation through him; so that, when the soul is lying still under its conviction, and knows it cannot have life but by resting on Christ, and hears that there is a sufficiency in him for up-making of all its wants, then the work of the Spirit prevails with the soul, to cast itself over on him, for obtaining of life, and of every other thing needful; it brings the soul to embrace and lay hold on him, not only as one able to save sinners, but to save itself in particular: and this is the native work of faith, that unites the soul to Christ, and puts it over the bound-road, or march of all delusion; it is like a sinking man's leaping to catch hold of a rock or rope; it is the bringing of a lost sinner, from the serious apprehension of his own naughtiness and undone estate, to cast himself over on Jesus Christ, for the obtaining of life through him.

2*dly*, When we speak of faith, we would premise this, That even this true and saving faith, which is not only in kind true, that is, such as hath a real being, but is saving, may be considered in its different acts or actings, for its different needs or necessities: Tho' the covenant be one, yet the acts of faith are many, we having to do with pardon of sin, with sanctification in its parts, vivification, and mortification, with peace, &c. faith differently acts on Christ and the promise for obtaining of these. Now, the faith that we would insist on, is, that faith that rests on Christ for pardon of sin, on which all the rest of the acts of faith depend; it is that faith, whereby a sinner receives Christ, and casts himself over on him; that faith, whereby union with Christ is made up.

3*dly*, We would premise, That there is a great difference betwixt faith, and the effects of it, as peace, joy, assurance of God's love, and these other spiritual privileges that follow believing. It is one thing actually to believe, another thing to have the peace and joy that follows upon, and flows from believing; the one being as the putting out of the hand to receive the meat, and the other as the feeding on it. It is the first of these we mean, and intend to speak of, even that faith, wherey we grip Jesus Christ himself, and get a right to all these privileges, in and through him.

4*thly*, We premise, That even this saving faith hath its degrees, as all other faith hath; some have more weak faith, some stronger; some have that full assurance, spoken of, Heb. x. or a plerophory, not only as to the Object, that it is sufficient; but as to the apprehending and obtaining of life through that Object; so that they are able to say, *Neither height, nor depth, nor any thing else, shall be able to separate them from the love of God in Christ Jesus*. We say then, that saving faith hath its degrees, tho' the degree be not that which we speak of; but it is the kind of this faith, whether weaker or more strong, whereby a lost sinner rolls itself over on Christ; the faith which puts the sinner off the ground it stood on, over on him; the faith, which brings the soul from the covenant of works, to a new holding of life by Christ and his righteousness. We shall then speak a little, 1. To what we conceive this act of saving faith is not, for precaveating of mistakes. 2. What way the scripture expresses it. When then we say that such a thing is not saving faith, ye would know that thing is not it that ye must lippen to; and when we say such a thing is saving faith, ye would labour to act and exercise faith according to it.

1*st*, For what saving faith is not. 1. It is not the knowing that Christ is God and Man; that he was born, was crucified, dead, and buried, and rose again. Ask some, What true saving faith is? They will say, It is a true knowledge: Ask them again, How long it is since they believed? They will say, Since ever they knew good by ill. Ye would know that apprehensive or literal and speculative knowledge is needful, but it will not be taken for saving faith. 2. It is not a touch of warmness or liberty in the affections in a natural way, which may be in unregenerate men, yea possibly in Pagans, as in a Felix, who, in the mean time, have not so much as temporary faith; because it

rises not from the word, but from dispensations of Providence, or from temporary things; and if it rise from the promises of the word, if there be no more, it is but temporary faith. 3. It is not convictions, which many take for faith, and take it for granted, if they be convinced of sin, they believe, and will say, Whom should they believe on but Christ? and yet they never follow the conviction, to put in practice what they are convinced of. 4. It is not simply a resolution to believe, as others take saving faith to be, who being convinced that their own righteousness will not do their turn, resolve to believe on Christ for righteousness, but they will take a convenient time to do it; and many maintain their peace with this, tho' it be no true peace: but a bare resolution to believe is not faith; ye use to say, There are many good wishers in hell. I remember the words of a dying man in this place, who thought he believed before; and being asked, What difference he conceived to be betwixt the faith he had before, and the faith he now had attained to? He answered, Before, I thought or resolved to believe, but never practised it; now I practise believing. There is such a subtilty and deceit in the heart, that if it resolve to believe, and if it observably thwart not with faith, it will sit down on that, as if all were done; therefore the word is, *To day if ye will hear his voice*, that is, to day if ye will believe, *harden not your heart.* This resolving to believe, is like a man sinking in the water, and having a rope cast out to him, he resolves to grip it, but does it not; so many think they have the promise beside them, and resolve to make use of it, but do not presently make use of it, and the ship sinks down, and they perish, while the promise abides and swims above. 5. It is not prayer. There are many, they think they believe, when they some way repent, pray, and put their hand to other duties; and they know no more for believing but something of that kind. It is true indeed, prayer may help to believe, yet it is not always with faith: it is not every one that saith, *Lord, Lord,* that believeth; many will seek to enter, that shall not be able. Folks very often have these two miserable mistakes about prayer, either they put it in the room of Christ, or in the room and place of faith, not considering that they are different things; for faith exerciseth itself on Christ as Mediator, and prayer taketh him up as God, the true Object of divine worship; tho', if it be founded on Christ as Mediator, it hath no access: the acting of saving faith is properly on Christ held forth in the word, and prayer is a putting up of suits according to the word. There are many,

that

that know no more what use to make of Christ, than if he had never been incarnate, nor had come under that relation of a Mediator, and make their prayers serve to make up all; whereas faith not only respects Christ as God but his merits as Mediator, and his offices. 6. Nor is faith only a believing this word of God to be true, tho' we could wish many were come that length; it would make a man tremble, to hear the blasphemous words that some will have, when they are asked concerning their believing the truth of the bible; but tho' ye were that length, it were not enough, the devils believe and tremble. The faith, that we call you to, is more than historical; it is to resting on Christ, to cordial receiving of the message which he sends to you: as, suppose a king should send an embassage to a person, to woo her to be his wife; it is one thing to know that there is such a king, another thing to believe that he is real in his offer, and that the woman by consenting to marry him, may be, and will be happy, and (which is yet more) actually to receive the message, and to consent to go and marry him. It is here as when Abraham's servant is sent to Rebekah, Gen. xxiv. she and her friends believe all the report that the servant made of his master and of his son, that it was true; and then it is given to her option, if she will go with the man, and she consents to go, and actually goeth; this is it we press you to, to go with us, and close the bargain, and to accept of him, and of life through him. By the same similitude ye may know what saving faith is, and what is the difference betwixt it and temporary faith: when the great, rich, and brave offer comes to be made to Rebekah, by a man with many camels, gold and bracelets; when she believes that it is true, and that it is made to her, she is fain, and it may be over fain, if not somewhat vain also; that is like *temporary faith*: But when it comes to the articles of the contract, be it is said to sinners, Ye must be subject to Christ and follow his will, and not your own; this, this casts the bargain. Thus many, when they hear there is a possibility of life to be had in Christ, and much more when they hear it is to be had on good, easy, and free terms, it will make them smile; but when it comes to that, Psal. xlv 10. *Hearken, O daughter, and consider, forsake thy father's house*, or the fashions of thy father's house; it halts there, and they suspend and demur to close the bargain; but *saving faith* goes further on, and with Rebekah, finally closes the bargain.

Secondly, The next thing is, What is saving faith? Or, What is it to believe in Christ? And would to God ye were ready to believe, and as ready to receive the invitation, as to ask the question, and that in asking the question ye were in earnest; for, by the way, many have asked the question, *What shall we do to be saved?* where, if they had been in earnest, they might have been soon resolved: The answer is at hand, *Believe in the Lord Jesus Christ, and thou shalt be saved*. But, to them that desire further clearness or confirmation in this concerning business, we shall speak a little; yet ye must know, that it is such a thing as is impossible to be made plain to a proud-humoured or unhumbled sinner; it is the poor humbled soul that will take it up; and, to such a soul, half a word will help to take it up.

The plainest way to set it out, as we conceive, is, to name some scripture-expressions, and similitudes, that hold it forth: The first whereof is in that of Mat. xi. 28. *Come to me, all ye that are weary and heavy laden*; And John vi. 35. *He that cometh to me shall never hunger, and he that believeth on me shall never thirst*. Readily these expressions hold out these three; *First*, An evil which men cleave to. *Secondly*, A good that is offered to them. *Thirdly*, A passing from the evil to the good, and so, *Come to me*, implies, 1. A hazard that folks are in, by being at a distance from Christ. 2. That there is access to Jesus Christ for remedying that evil, and removing of that hazard. 3. A passing from the one to the other, a passing from our own righteousness to Christ's righteousness, a passing from our natural condition to Jesus Christ, a real passing from death in ourselves to life in him. Most part think faith to be a conceit, a humour, or a guessing, that they think they may have, and never know how; but it is a real thing, a coming from our own righteousness (as I said) to his, from a covenant of works, to rest on Christ and his righteousness, held forth in the covenant of grace. This is somewhat explained, Rom. vii. where two husbands are spoken of: a woman cannot marry another man till her first husband be dead; so, till a sinner be dead to the law, he cannot marry Christ; there must be a divorcing from the law and covenant of works, ere ye can close with Christ.

The second expression is, John i. 12. where faith is held forth as *a receiving* of Christ, *To as many as received him, he gave them power to become the sons of God, even to as many as believed on his name*: And it is well express'd in the Catechism, to be a receiving of Christ as he is offered in the gospel; this supposes, that Christ is offered to us, and that we are naturally without him. The gospel comes and says, Why will ye die, O house of Israel? Come and receive a Saviour; and the act of faith

faith is a gripping to that offer, a receiving and embracing of it, a being well content to take a free discharge through his blood.

A third expression is, Phil. iii. 12. where faith is set out as an *apprehending* of Christ, and Heb. vi. 18. it is called a *laying hold* on the hope set before us, and Isa. lvi. 4. a *taking hold* of the covenant: All which suppose folk to have a choice, as it were laid to them, and Christ to be holden out as a city of refuge, and a shelter from that which we are in hazard of: Christ is held out in the gospel as the city of refuge; and the exercise of faith is to run from the hazard to him, as a child, that is chased by an unknown and uncouth body, flees unto the mother's arms, or as the man-slayer fled from the avenger of blood to the city of refuge: And faith, having run to him, casts itself, on him, or thrusts itself (as it were) into him.

A fourth expression is, *rolling or casting* of ourselves over upon the Lord, as Psal. lv. 22. *Cast thy burden on the Lord*; and Psal. xxxvii. 5. *Commit thy way to the Lord*; it is on the margin, *Roll thy self on the Lord*, or *rest*, as it is v. 7. and ease thyself on the Lord. The gospel lays Christ, as it were, at folk's feet, and faith rolls them over on him; it is even the soul's finding itself through the work of the Spirit, unable to stand under the burden, rolling itself on Christ, as a crazy and weak body casts itself on a down-bed for ease. This is a very emphatick, significant, and active expression of faith; setting out a man quitting his own legs or feet, as unable to stand on them, and laying himself over on Christ; this is it that we call you to, even to quit your own feet, and to roll yourselves over on Christ.

A fifth expression is, Rom. x. 3. where it is called *a submitting to the righteousness of God*; which is held out in the gospel thus, as if a king were proclaiming a pardon to rebels, and saying to them, For as many hainous crimes as ye have committed, and are guilty of, if ye will take with them, and betake yourselves to my grace and mercy, sincerely resolving to be henceforth faithful and dutiful subjects to me, I will freely pardon you; which gracious offer they most gladly accept of, and submit themselves to it. *Submitting* is an acquiescing in the terms of the gospel, as it is proposed; it is even as if ye should say, We hold the bargain, and are well content and satisfied with it. In a word, faith carves not to God the way to salvation, but sweetly submitteth to the way he hath carved out.

A sixth expression is, *Hiding of ourselves in God, or in Christ*; so the word, *trust* in God, signifies, to hide ourselves in him as in a place of refuge, according to that, Prov. xviii. *The name of the Lord is a strong tower; the righteous run into it, and are preserved*, or hid; or, they flee to it, as doves do to their windows: And this is it the apostle saith, Phil iii. 9. *That I may be found in him, not having my own righteousness*, &c. So that, if ye ask, What is faith? It is a man betaking himself to Christ, that when he shall be called for, it may be answered, Lord, I am in Christ, not having mine own righteousness, &c. it is not to be lippening to the man's good hopes, to his good prayers, or to his good meaning, but to Christ's satisfaction, and God's promise; by faith, when rightly exercised, the sinner holds and hides himself in Christ, till (to speak so) a bit of the man cannot be seen; and this is well set out by the Lord, when he says, Isa. xxvi. 20. *Come, my people, enter into your chambers, shut the doors about you, hide yourselves for a little while,* &c. Come in under the Mediator's wings, lock in yourselves by faith there, and so make all sure.

A seventh expression is, 2 Chron. xxx. 8. where, when Hezekiah is writing to the degenerate tribes to come home again, he bids them, *Yield themselves to the Lord*; in the original it is, *Give the hand to Lord*: even as two men, who have been at odds and variance, or have broken the tyes that were betwixt them, come to renew the friendship, they chop hands; now, God is brought in, stretching out his hands to you, Isa. lxv. 2. therefore come and close with him, yield to him, give him the hand, or chop hands with him, and make the bargain and engagement sicker for the time to come. All these similitudes, borrowed from men, are partly to make the nature of faith obvious and clear, partly to strengthen and confirm believers faith.

An eighth expression is, that of *opening* to Christ, Cant. v. 2. *Open to me my dove*, &c. Rev. iii. 20. *Behold, I stand at the door and knock; if any man open the door to me*, &c. Acts xvi. it is said, *The Lord opened the heart of Lydia*: When the word comes, sinners hearts are locked on God; Christ comes by his word, and knocks hard to be in, bids open and take in the Saviour; and faith discerns his voice, and gives him entry. It is the letting of the word sink, the making of him welcome; it is not only the crediting of the word as true, but the receiving of him whom the word offers, for the end for which he is offered; and this is, when the work of the Spirit, with the word, wakens up a stichilling, or slightering (to say so) within, and makes the heart to open to take in Christ; as one worded it well and significantly, *My heart cleeked as a lintseed boll to Christ*. And wherever Christ hath a design of grace on the soul, and comes with power, he continues

tinues knocking, rapping, and calling hard and loud, till doors and gates be cast open to him.

A ninth expression or similitude, under which faith is held forth, is that which is ordinary *of a marriage*, or of *covenanting* or consenting, whether in marriage or otherwise, but more especially in marriage: When Christ taketh on him the place of an wooer, ministers are his ambassadors, the word is their instructions, wherein he bids them go tell sinners, that *all things are ready*, and to pray them to come to the marriage, or to marry and match with him; and faith is a coming away to this Husband, a receiving of the word of invitation, a consenting to the marriage: It is not so much a local, as a qualitative change or mutation; we change fashions, we subscribe the contract on the terms it is laid out to us: In the bargain of grace, something is offered by God, and that is, Christ and his fulness; and there is something done on our side, and that is, accepting of him by faith: And this is not so much a saying with the tongue, as it is a believing with the heart; as it is Rom. x. 10. *With the heart man believes unto righteousness*: it is the heart's present subscribing the marriage-contract, and going away with Christ, to live and cohabit with him; tho' confession will be readily with the mouth also, as he calls for it.

A tenth expression, or similitude, is that of *buying, Ho, every one* (crieth the prophet Isa. lv. 1.) *that thirsts, come to the waters; and he that hath no money, come, buy*, &c. so Rev. iii. 18. *Buy of me eye-salve*, &c. It says this much, that God in the gospel sets forth, as in a market, to sinners, rich and rare wares, and good cheap, or at very low and easy rates; and that believing is like buying up of the wares: Life eternal is holden out on condition of believing on Christ, and the poor sinner thinks that a good bargain, for it takes no money from him; Rev. xxii. 17. this is called *willing, Whosoever will, let him come and take of the water of life freely*; the soul hath a good will to the thing. It is held forth by several other expressions in the scripture; it is called a *cleaving to the Lord, or sticking to him*, Josh. xxiii. 8. and Acts xi. 23. it is called *hearing, hearkning*, and *inclining of the ear*, Isa. lv. 2, 3. an attentive, concerned, and holily greedy listning to, and taking hold of this offer; it is a cleaving to the Lord, as woodben or ivy cleaves to an oak, because its life depends upon it: And, Deut. xxx. and Josh. xxiv. it is called a *choosing of the Lord*, and that upon deliberation, as knowing that we have need of him, that he is a Saviour suited compleatly to all the necessities of our souls, and that we are warranted to believe on him; it is the native act and exercise of faith to choose Christ among all the wooers that are courting the soul: So likewise it is set out under *trusting and committing*, Psal. xxxvii. *Commit thy way to the Lord, trust in him*; *I know*, saith Paul, 2 Tim. i. 12. *he is able to keep that which I have committed to him*: it is to give Christ the credit of your salvation; it is one thing to give a man the credit that he is true, and another thing to con-credit him with our greatest concerns; we will credit many, whom we will not thus con-credit ourselves to, nor commit our concerns to; the former (when these are applied to God) is historical faith, but this latter is saving faith, when we dare trust and lippen ourselves to him, and to his word; and we think this expression holds forth as much of the nature of saving faith as any of the former, if we could take it up, when we dare con-credit ourselves to him, because he hath said the word. Thus also, to act and exercise faith on him, for temporal, or for spiritual things, it is to expect the event from God, but so, as we expect and look for it on this ground, that Christ hath purchased it, and we have accepted him on his offer, which gives us a right to these things needful for us, and purchased by him: It is said, Matth. xxii. 5. when the invitation comes, that *some made light of it*; but faith, on the contrary, is a laying weight on it, and con-crediting of ourselves to God on that ground: it is called, Rom. vi. *A delivering up of ourselves to the word*, and to him in it; it is even to put a blank in Christ's hand, to be filled up as he pleases.

Ye see then what ye are called to, it is to open to Christ, to come to him, to marry him, to roll yourselves on him, to commit yourselves to him, to give him credit, &c. And is there any of these unreasonable or prejudicial to you? and if they be very reasonable and advantageous, (as indeed they are) we would exhort you to come to him, to receive him, to apprehend him, to flee to him, to take hold of him, to marry him, &c. believe on him, and by believing, be united to him, and get a right to him, and to all his purchase; give him the credit of saving your souls. This we call for from you; and if ye do it not, the complaint in the text will stand against you, *Who hath believed our report?*

Isaiah liii. 1. *Who hath believed our report? and to whom is the arm of the Lord revealed?*

IT is a great matter once to get the gospel brought amongst a people, and such messengers, as may make the savoury report of Jesus Christ unto them; yet this is not all, there is a greater work behind, and that is, to get Christ believed on, and to get the report concerning him received by the people to whom it is made; this being the greatest and gravest work of the prophets, and of the ministers of the gospel, and the most eminent, not so much to get a word to say, as to get the word believed; and this is Isaiah's complaint, that tho' he himself brought the report concerning Christ, and foresaw many more would bring it, yet, that the exercise of faith in these who should hear it would be very rare.

We spoke of the great thing called for from a people, to whom this gospel comes, and the report of Christ is made; and that is, to believe on him, to receive and rest on him, of whom the report is made; except this be, tho' there were never so many preachers, and encouragements to preach, tho' ye should flock to the ordinances every day, the ground of complaint will still remain, if there be not saving faith in Jesus Christ, which is the substance of the gospel.

After confirmation of this point, we shew what faith is, from the several names the scripture giveth it; and wherein the exercise of saving faith is holden out: All which imply these three. 1. A great hazard and danger that the hearers of the gospel are in, whether they be sensible of it in such a measure at least or not, we speak not now, yet they are so really; so much *fleeing, coming, laying hold, apprehending,* &c. insinuate. 2. A fulness and sufficiency in Christ Jesus, holden forth to them, as the object of their faith, as one that can deliver out of that danger, and can right whatever is wrong. 3. An act, wherein mainly the exercise of faith is holden forth, and 'tis the act of the soul under that danger and distress, betaking itself to Christ's fulness for help: it is a fleeing from the curse of the law to him, as to the city of refuge; so every name that faith gets, sets out a man acting and moving some way for Christ's remedying the evil and removing the hazard he is in.

Having spoken a little to this, that faith is the main duty that is called for, we may now follow the exhortation to press you to it; it being to no purpose to speak of Christ, and of faith in him except he be received. This is the end of the word written and taught, John xx. at the close, even to believe in the name of the son of God, and by believing to receive life in and thro' him.

And therefore, 2*dly*, Seeing this is the main duty called for by the gospel, that by faith ye should receive it, and Christ offered in it; we earnestly exhort you to it. It is not so much to this or that particular duty, tho' these be implied; it is not so much to attendance on ordinances, nor to submission to discipline and censures, tho' these also be duties that we exhort you to; but it is to obedience to the great command of faith even to believe on him whom the Father hath sent and sealed: It is to receive this gospel, to submit to the righteousness of faith, to open to him that is knocking at the door, to yield to him, and to give him the hand, that bygone quarrels may be removed, and taken out of the way: except this be, we profess to you in his name, that ye bring not forth the fruit that this gospel calleth for from you, and that no less will be acceptable to God, nor taken off your hand by him.

And to add here the *third* branch of the doctrine, we say, That no less will do your turn, as a necessary mean for attaining the promise, and that which is promised: 1. Look to all the promises, whether of pardon of sin, or of peace with God, of joy in the holy Ghost, of holiness and conformity to God; there is no access to these, or to any of them, but by faith: this is the very proper condition of the covenant of grace, and the door whereby we step in to it; and if ye think pardon of sin, peace with God, and holiness to be necessary, then this great gospel-duty of believing is no less necessary; for the Lord saith, John iii. 36. *He that believeth not is condemned already*. 2. Look to the performance of any duty, or mortification of any lust or idol, and faith is necessary to that, 1 John iii. 5. *It is by faith we obtain victory over the world:* it was by faith (Heb. xi.) that all the worthies, spoken of there, wrought righteousness, &c. 3. When any duty is done, of whatsoever nature it be, there is no acceptation of it without faith; it is not our praying, or coming to the church, that will make duty to be accepted, but it is faith; *The word profited them not,* saith the Apostle, Heb. iv. 2. *because it was not mixed with faith*. And that, for making the duty acceptable, faith is necessarily requisite, we may clearly see, Heb. xi. 6. where it is expresly said, that *without faith it is impossible to please God;* and how is it that Abel offers a more excellent sacrifice than Cain? it was nothing

sure

sure in Cain's sacrifice itself that made it be casten, nor any thing in Abel's that made it be received or acceptable, but faith in the Messiah to come, that was found to be in the one, and was amissing in the other. Is there not reason then to press this duty on you, and to exhort you not to think this a common and easy thing, tho' the most part think it to be so? If we look to the benefits of it, to the difficulty of it, and to the rarity of it in the world, there is no duty had need more to be press'd than this, even that Christ Jesus should get the burden of your immortal souls cast on him by his saving faith. I shall therefore, in the further prosecution of this, 1. Shew, what mainly you would eschew and avoid, as that whereat folk more ordinarily stumble. 2. What it is we would press to, and on what grounds.

For the *first*, I know the deceits and mistakes in men about the exercise of faith are so many, that they are more than can well or easily be reckoned up; yet we shall in some generals, spoken of before, hint at a few of them: For, so long as ye continue in the same snares, they must still be pointed out to you, and endeavours still used to undeceive and extract you out of them; and therefore, 1. Beware of resting on a doctrinal faith, which before I called *historical*. We know it is hard to convince some that they want faith, yet we would have you to consider, that it is not every kind of faith, but saving faith, that will do your turn; it is the want of that, which the prophet complains of: And therefore to open this a little, ye would consider, that there may be really such a faith, as is an assent to the truth of the word, in a natural man, yea in a reprobate; but that faith will never unite to Christ, nor be waited with the pardon of sin. (1.) I do not say, that every one that is in the visible church hath this doctrinal faith, to believe a heaven and a hell, that the scripture is the word of God, and that all that believe in Christ shall get pardon of sin, and life; the carriage, alas! of many testifies that they have not this much: whatever fleeting notions they may have of these things, or whatever esteem they may seem to put on the gospel, and whatever profession they may make, that they believe the truth of it, yet in their deeds they deny it; for if there were a fixedness in the doctrinal faith of the gospel in men, they durst not for their souls live as they do. Neither yet, (2.) Do we say, that all they that have this doctrinal faith of the gospel, or somewhat of it, do believe every passage in it alike, but often as they please them, they believe them: Hence, many believe what the word speaks of mercy, and of pardon of sin, and will not question that, but what it speaks of holiness and of the severity of God's reckoning with men for sin, they do not so credit that part of the word: it is true, where the faith of the one is, the faith of the other will some way be; but because the one agrees better with their corruption than the other, therefore the one is not received as the other: and it is very frequent with such, to be found diminishing from one place, and adding to another, of the word of God. Nor, (3.) Do we say, that all men do, in a like and equal degree, believe the truth of the word; there is in some more knowledge, in some less, in some more convictions, in some fewer; and tho' we preach to you all, yet there are some that believe not this to be God's ordinance, albeit there are many who will not be saved, that take this word to be the word of God, and believe what is the meaning of it, because the word itself says it is so: And the reason of this is, 1. Because there is nothing that is not saving, but a natural man may have it; now, this doctrinal faith is not saving, and so a natural man may have it, yea, the devils believe and tremble: and James does not dispute with these to whom he writes, on this account, that they believe not this, but tells them, that historical faith was not enough; and we think a man in nature may have a great persuasion of the truth of the word of God, and that which it says will come to pass, and yet still continue but a natural man. A 2d reason is, because the scripture speaks so often of many sorts of faith that are not saving, as Exod. xiv. at the close, it is said, *The people believed the Lord*, and Psal. cvi. 12. *Then they believed his word, and sang his praise*: and John ii. 23. *Many believed on Christ, to whom he did not commit himself*; there was faith in them which his signs and miracles extorted from them, which was not saving; and Matt. xiii. two or three such acts of faith are spoken in the parable of the sower, that were not saving, however sound they might be in their own kind; and, 1 Cor. xiii. we have such a faith spoken of, as a man dare not deny the truth of the word, tho' he should bring his body to be burnt by his avouching of the same. A 3d reason is, because as much credit may be given to the word, as is given to any other history that is creditable, believed; and it is on this ground that we believe there were such men as Cæsar, Pompey, Wallace, &c. and it being certain, that there may be impressions on the consciences of hearers, that this is God's word, backed with some common work of the Spirit, and that is generally received to be the word of God in the part of the world we live in; what wonder is it, that folk believe thus, and think it a fixed historical or doctrinal faith of the word, so as they may even dare to suffer death for it? and yet, in the mean time, may want saving faith; the devils being as sure as any natural man is, that God is true, and that his word will be performed; and therefore they say to Christ, *Art thou come to torment us before the time?* The pangs of a natural conscience in men will assure them of a judgment coming, tho' they tremble to think on it.

And therefore, ere we proceed further, take a word of *use* from this, and it may let you see the great and very general mistake of the most part of the hearers of the gospel, in resting on this doctrinal faith. If ye tell them that they have no faith, they will not by any means take with that; they believe there is a Saviour, and that he is God and man, and that such as believe on him shall be saved; and on this they rest: It is such as these, who think they have believed all their days, since ever they had any knowledge; because the word was always, or very long since, received in the place where they lived, for the word of God; and they believe it to be so also, and know no difference betwixt believing the word, and believing on Christ holden out in it: tho' alas! many of you believe not this much; for if ye were among the Jews, ye might be soon brought to question the truth of the gospel: but tho' ye had the real faith of the truth of the word, take not that for saving faith; for as there is a real sorrow, that is not the saving grace of repentance unto life, so there is a sort of real faith, that hath a real object, and a real being in the judgment, which yet is not a real closing with Christ, and so not saving faith: as, suppose a man, pursued by his enemy, should see a strong castle-door standing open, or one in hazard at sea should see dry land, if he should stand still while the enemy were pursuing him, or abide still in the sinking vessel, the sight of the castle-door open, or of the dry land, would not save him; so it is not the believing that there is a Saviour come into the world to save sinners, that will save, except there be a resting on him, as he is holden out in the word of the gospel. Historical faith is only (as it were) a looking on the Saviour, but saving faith grips to him, and rests on him: Historical faith looks on Christ, but acts not on him, closes not with him; and therefore such as have it only, and no more, sink and perish without getting good of him. We would think it a great matter, to get many of you as far on in believing as the devil is, who believes and trembles; the little trembling that is, shews that there is but little of this historical faith: yet, as I have often said, this is not all, ye may have this, and yet, if ye halt there, ye will certainly perish, if ye were never so confident to be saved; the Apostle doth well distinguish these,

Heb. xi. 6. *He that cometh to God, must believe that he is, and that he is a rewarder of them that diligently seek him:* where these two are presupposed, 1. Believing that God is, or hath a being: And, 2. Believing that his promise is sure and sicker; that he is faithful that hath promised, and will make his word good. And then, 3. On both these follows a coming to him, as a rewarder of diligent seekers of him. The first two take in historical faith: for to believe that God is, is natural; and to believe that God is faithful in his promise, may be in natural men: but to come to him, to get the hazard that the soul is in, removed, through Jesus Christ, is a thing few do attain. This then is the *first* thing we would be aware of, not aware to believe the truth of the word, but to be aware of resting on it as saving faith: it is not enough to look on Christ, and to grant that it is he, but the man must never be satisfied till he get himself rolled on Christ, and the weight of his salvation and peace laid on him in his own way.

The *second* thing ye would beware of is some common and quickly transient work on the affections, that may accompany historical faith; whether the affection of grief, or the affection of joy be stirred thereby, both are unsafe to be rested on, when we can't prove our resting on Christ, or where there is no relevant ground to prove it by. Tho' ye should tremble as Felix did, and be under alarming convictions of conscience and fears of your hazard, or though ye should be affected with joy, as the temporary believer may be, and sometimes is, what will that profit you? It is a great mistake to take some small work on the affections, which at the best is but an effect of historical faith, for a saving work of the Spirit. Or, 2. If it be not an effect of historical faith, it is an effect of a challenge of conscience, and smiting of the heart, as in Saul, who could say to David, *Thou art more righteous than I, my son David.* Or, 3. It is some common work of the Spirit, such as was in Simon Magus, of whom it is said, *He believed,* and who could say, *Pray for me;* for folks to conclude on this ground, that they are brought out of nature into a state of grace, is to build upon a sandy foundation: The Apostle speaketh, 2 Cor. vii. 10. of worldly sorrow, as well as of godly sorrow; and as there may be a worldly sorrow, so there may be carnal joy, a piece of fainness, to speak so, in prayer, or at hearing of a preaching, or at a communion, which is not saving faith: some hear the word with joy, Matt. xiii. who yet *endure not;* and John Baptist's hearers rejoiced in his light for a season; even as a sick man, who hearing (as we hinted before) that

a physician

a physician, who is skillful and able to cure him, is come to town, he grows fain in the contemplation of a cure of his disease; but here is the stick, when the physician tells the man that he must be so and so abstemious, and keep himself under such a strict diet, he dow not abide that, and so all his joy evanishes: There is something like this in temporary faith, where some remote expectation of salvation will cause a carnal joy and fainness: but when it comes to this, that a man is called to quit his lusts, or his estate, or in the world to undergo trouble and persecution for the gospel, *by and by he is offended*, he thinks (to say so) *A fowl in his hand is worth two flying;* and therefore, when the storm blows in his teeth, he turns his back, and runs away; especially we will find this to be with men in sickness, they will have mints at seriousness, and sometimes flashes of sorrow under convictions and challenges, and sometimes flashes of joy, that will evanish when they come to health again. When we speak of some common work on the affections, we would take in liberty, and some warmness of spirit in prayer, which, no question, even unrenewed men may find more at one time than another; as when they are in some great hazard or strait, they will be more than ordinary serious in that duty, and yet that may be but an effect of nature: This proves a great stumbling and neck-break to many, that they think they are well enough, if now and then they get utterance in prayer, as sometimes they will get words beyond what they expected; and when, upon reflecting, they find that they have been in earnest, tho' it hath been with moral seriousness, that blows them up; so they put prayer in the place of saving faith, and when they pray with warmness, they trow they believe, when in the mean time they never knew what it was in good earnest to lay themselves over on Christ Jesus: Therefore, when we invite you to believe, this is another thing we would bid you beware of, that ye put not a flash of sense in the room of faith.

3. There is yet a more subtile, tho' no less dangerous mistake, that ye would beware of, and that is, when faith is confounded with obedience, and is looked on in justification as a piece of new obedience, but defective, yet wherein they are defective, they think there is worth in their faith to make up that want, and to supply that defect; and so, by faith they think they will obtain the acceptation of their works, and of their persons on account of their works: they look upon their works as pleasing to God, but because they are not perfect, they will believe, or exercise faith, to make up their defects; to which the way of grace is quite contrary, which makes the tree first good, and then the fruit. This way, that many take, is not to draw the evidences of believing from works of holiness, which is warrantable; but the founding of faith, or their hope of heaven, on works: and the use they make of their faith, is, to ward off challenges for the imperfection of their works, and to make faith procure acceptance (as I just now said) to their works, and acceptance to their person for their works sake.

4. Beware of that which ye ordinarily call a certain assurance, or sure knowledge of your salvation, and that all the promises are yours, whereby ye think yourselves in no hazard; a hope and assurance of heaven that ye can give no ground for, nor proof of; only ye think ye are sure of pardon of sin, and coming to heaven, and that ye are obliged to maintain that groundless hope: but that is not saving faith, for it is a hope of heaven that can give you no right to Christ; there must first be a fleeing to him, and closing with him before ye can have any true and well-grounded hope of heaven: but your hope and confidence is, never to question the matter; ye are like Laodicea, who thought herself rich, and to stand in need of nothing, when she was beggarly poor; or like these men, who, when God was threatning them with judgment, yet would needs presume to think that they leaned on the Lord. I think, among all the persons that God hath indignation against, it is in a special manner against these who have this sort of hope, and to whom God discovereth the groundlesness of it, and yet they will still stoutly maintain, and stand fast by their hope: it is to these he speaks, Deut. xxvi. 16. who despise and tush at God's threatnings, and say, *We shall have peace, though*

call *presumption* and *hope of the hypocrite that will perish*, Job. viii. 13. the confidence of such shall be rejected and swept away as a spider's web, and shall be rooted out of their tabernacles, and bring them to the king of terrors. They think they believe always; when they are not troubled nor disquieted, they never want faith, but have a great deal of it; which yet is but a guessing, which cannot support and uphold them when they come to a strait; when they are more secure, they believe very well, and they think when they are more waken'd and disquieted, they believe less, and their fancied faith ebbeth quite on them: when they hear of any exercise of mind, or trouble of conscience in others, they wonder that they will not believe, and all this work is to maintain their deep security and strong delusion; this is then the *fourth* thing ye would beware of, for it is not the faith that will turn away the complaint, *Who hath believed our report?* and yet how many are there of this sort, who say they shall have peace, and please themselves with this their good hope, say the word what it will. O! be perswaded, that this is nothing else but woful unbelief and presumption; and we preach to you terror and the curse of God, tho' ye cry peace to yourselves: the Lord complains of such persons, Jer v. 12. saying, *They belied the Lord;* he sent his prophets to denounce judgments in the days of Josiah, when there was a fair profession of religion and reformation, yet they would believe and hope that no evil should overtake them.

That which we aim at in this part of the use is, to make way for what follows, even to give you a cleanly ground for exercising of faith on Jesus Christ, when all these stumblings and mistakes are rolled out of the way: We therefore exhort you, to lay your hand to your heart, and narrowly to try, if ye have called, or accounted any of these to be saving faith, for there are hundreds, nay thousands, that perish under these pretexts, deceiving themselves, and deluding others, with a faith they were born and brought up with, and they have no more but their groundless hope to prove their faith by, and that they will stick by it, be said to them what will; but be not deceived, for God will discover you; ye think a strong presumption is faith, and that ye can by such a faith, drink in the promises; but God will make you vomit them up, and ye shall be declared to be void of faith in the great day: therefore be more jealous over your faith, and seek to have your grips of Christ sickered, which is done, when, from the belief of your hazard and self-emptiness, and of Christ's fulness,

ye go to him, and close with him, to make up all ye want in him; and this faith is especially qualified by the account on which we go to him, and rest on him: even as a conscientious duty is that which flows from a command, as obedience to it, so one of the main things that qualifies this faith is, a receiving Christ as Christ, or as he is holden out in the gospel: which is therefore well put in the description given of faith in the Catechism; and it is called *a believing on him whom the Father hath sent*, which is not to believe on Christ simply, but as he is holden out in the word of the gospel. Presumption may look on Christ and his fulness, and few or none will readily dare to give him a direct and down-right refusal, or to reject him professedly and avowedly, when they hear of such happiness that is to be had in him; but that which we say qualifies faith, is, to desire, receive and embrace him, according as he is holden out in the gospel, *for wisdom, righteousness, sanctification, and redemption,* 2. Cor. i. 30. when he is lippened to with an eye to the promise, and when that, which makes us rest on him, is the word of God: for, tho' Christ be the material Object of faith, yet the word is the formal object whereby we get a right to him; and there is no gripping or getting hold of Christ, but in, and according to his word: and therefore the generality of people (who, on the matter, take the Antinomian way) think they have no more to do, but to apply Christ, and to count him their own at the very first; but, thro' their not exercising faith on the word of promise they miss him. This is, as I have said, a main qualification of saving faith, even to rest on Christ as he is holden out in the word, and by the word to take hold of him, and rest upon him: Saving faith doth not simply rest on Christ because he is merciful, and hath all fulness in him, but it rests on him and his fulness, as received in the word, and offered by God in his word; Faith takes God's faithfulness in his word, and lays hold on him by that: Christ is the thing that makes happy, but God's faithful promise is the right by which we get a title to that thing. We would never love nor like that faith, that knows not the use of the word; that betakes itself to Christ, or the thing in the word, but meddles not, nor hath any dealings with the word that holds them out; when as it is only this word that gives us warrant to expect that his fulness shall be made furthcoming for our up-making, and for the supply of all our needs. Many desire, and expect good of God, but get it not, because their expectation is not founded on his word, and God's faithfulness in his word is not closed withal. In a word, I would have you to

Serm. VI.   Isaiah liii. Verse 1.   53

think, that faith is neither an easy, nor an insuperably difficult thing, but that it is easy to go wrong, and difficult to go right; and that, without God's special and powerful guiding, ye cannot believe, nor exercise faith, nor walk in the way of believing in him, and dependence on him; that ye may be helped to make a right use of Christ, and to build upon him, that ye may not slip nor stumble, and fall on the stumbling-stone laid in Zion, on which so many fall every day, and break themselves to pieces.

SERMON VI.

Isaiah liii. 1. *Who hath believed our report? and to whom is the arm of the Lord revealed?*

IF it were not recorded in the infallible scriptures of truth, we would hardly believe that there could be so much powerful and sweet preaching of the most excellent instruments that ever were employed, and yet that there should be so little fruit following on it; who would believe that Isaiah, so excellent, so sweet, and so evangelick a prophet, should have preached so many pleasant, plain, and powerful sermons to a people from the Lord, and yet that he should have so many sad complaints as he hath? chap. vi. xxviii. and lviii. that he should be forced to bring in the Lord, saying, *All the day long have I stretched out my hands to a rebellious people,* chap. lxv. and that here himself should have it to say, *Who hath believed our report?* It is scarce one man here or there that hath savingly believed on Christ. And this is the third thing in the words, that now we would speak to; and it is a very sad, tho' a very clear truth.

The doctrine is this, *That there may be much powerful preaching of the gospel, and yet unbelief generally among the hearers of it.* Or, take it with dependence on the former two, Namely, 1. That the great work of the ministry, is, to propose and make Christ known to a people. 2. That the great duty of a people, that have Christ proposed to them, is to believe on him. Then this 3d follows on the back of these, *That a people may have Christ proposed to them, brought to their heart and mouth; and tho' it be but believing that is called for from them, yet that cannot be obtained from most of them.* This gospel-duty of believing is often slighted by the hearers of the gospel; this is clearly holden forth here, *Who hath believed our report?* we have called for faith, but it is a rare thing, among the multitude of hearers, to get one that believeth savingly.

To make out, and prove this a little further, we would consider this complaint, with these aggravations of it, which will make it the more clear, and so the more to be wondered at; as, 1st, These of whom the complaint is made; it is not heathens, but God's own people, as the Lord complains, Psal. lxxxi. 11. *My people would not hearken to my voice and Israel would have none of me;* our Lord Jesus complains of Jerusalem, Matt. xxiii. at the end, *O Jerusalem, Jerusalem, how often would I have gathered thee, and thou wouldst not!* That the Lord's own professing people should not believe, nor receive the report that is made of him, heightens the complaint, and aggravates their guilt exceedingly. 2dly, It is not a complaint as to one sermon, or as to one time, but it is a complaint frequently repeated, as to many fruitless sermons, and as to many times, yea generations: Isaiah preached long, in many kings reigns; and yet all along in his prophecy he complains of it, as chap. vi. 11. *How long Lord, shall their eyes be blind, and their ears heavy?* &c. and chap. xxviii. 9. *Whom shall I teach doctrine? them that are weaned from the milk, and drawn from the breasts; precept must be on precept, and line upon line, here a little, and there a little;* and chap. lxv. 2. *All day long I have stretched out my hands to a rebellious people;* and here again, *Who hath believed our report?* Much and long, or many years preaching, much plain and powerful preaching, and yet little or no fruit, they are snared and taken, and fall backward, for all that; and this was not in Isaiah's days only, but in Christ's days, John xii. 37, 38. and in Paul's days, Rom. x. 16. where the same very words in the text are repeated: nay it runs down from the first spreading of the gospel, even to these latter days wherein we live; many hear, but few receive the report. 3dly, Consider how many they are that complain: it is not one or two, or a few, but all the preachers of the gospel; it is not, Lord, who hath believed *my* report, but, Who hath believed *our* report? It is complained of by Isaiah here, and in several other places named before; it is complained of by Micah, chap. vii. 1. *Wo is me, for I am as they who have gathered the summer-fruits, as the grape gleanings of the vintage, there is no cluster to eat, the good man is perished out of the earth, and there is none upright among men,* &c. It is complained of by Hosea, chap xi. 7. *Tho' they called them to the most High, none at all would exalt him,* that is, none would give him the glory

H

of his grace, in believing on him; ah sad word! as is that also in Psal. lxxxi. the Lord calls, *Hear, O my people, and I will testify to thee; open thy mouth wide, and I will fill it: but my people would not hearken to my voice, and Israel would none of me*. And what prophet is there almost (if I need say almost) but hath one way or other this complaint, that tho' the Lord stretched out his hands all day long, yet it was to a rebellious and gain-saying people: Look forward, and see what our Lord says of John Baptist, and of himself, *Whereto shall I liken this generation? it is like children sitting in the market-places, saying one to another, We have piped to you, and ye have not danced; we have mourned to you, and ye have not lamented;* that is, there is much preaching of men endowed with several gifts, but none of them does the people much good: John preached with much holy austerity, like one mourning; the *Son of man* most sweetly, like one piping; yet neither the one nor the other prevailed; there are some Boanerges, sons of thunder, alarming and thundering preachers; some Barnabusses, sons of consolation, sweetly comforting preachers; yet all gain but little on the hearers; our Lord saith, Matt. xxiii. *O Jerusalem, Jerusalem, how often would I have gathered you!* this is the ordinary complaint, *Ye would not*. A 4th aggravation is, if we consider who they are that meet with this unbelief and unfruitfulness in them they preach to: if it were poor coldrise preachers, such as we, alas! in a great measure, are, or such as the Scribes and the Pharisees were, or if it were they who had learning only, and not piety, it were not so great matter to see them meet with unbelief and unfruitfulness in their hearers: but it is even these whom the Lord sent and sharpened, as arrows out of his quiver, as this prophet was; it is even his preaching that is fruitless in a great measure: and was there ever a more sweet, plain, powerful, and delectable preacher than Isaiah was? that even the very reading of his preachings may affect the readers; yet is there any that complains more, or so much as he doth, in the chapters before cited? It is like, ye will think, that if Isaiah were preaching now, he would be as a stone, that would not be moved thereby, and yet his preaching got the same return and entertainment that ours gets now; and Hosea called his hearers to the most high, yet none at all would exalt him: it was their work to stretch out their hands all the day long, but they hardened their necks, and refused to return, Jer. viii. and Zech. vii. But *5thly*, Consider all these are servants and preachers under the old testament,

and you may be disposed to think, that under the gospel, when the vail is laid by, and when Christ himself, their Lord and Master, and his apostles come to preach the gospel, it should be otherwise: yet John the Baptist, who was Christ's harbinger, who was a burning and shining light, a stayed and fixed man, not a reed shaken with the wind, (as many of us are) a prophet, yea, more than a prophet; yet, when he preached, many of his hearers *rejected the counsel of God against themselves*, Luke vii. John comes preaching austerely, and they say he hath a devil; and if there was any rejoicing in his light, it was but for a season; and Paul that chosen vessel, how often was he persecuted? and he hath the same complaint, in the same words that Isaiah hath here of his hearers, especially the Jews, Acts xiii. 46. and xxviii. 28. and was constrained to tell them, that he and his fellow-preachers behoved to quit them, and betake themselves to the Gentiles; and how doth he complain of the Corinthians and Galatians, of their being bewitched, and suddenly seduced, and drawn away from the truth and simplicity of the gospel, by some self-seeking lown ministers, coming with a glancing counterfeit among them. We shall close this with the consideration of our Lord Jesus, who was a none-such preacher, of whom it it said, Matt. vii. 29. that *He spake with power, and not as the Scribes*, and Luke iv. when he is opening that sweet text, Isa. lxi. 1, 2, 3. it is said, *They all wondered at the gracious words that proceeded out of his mouth*; and the officers that came to take him, say, that *never man spake as he spoke*; and yet this same is his complaint, Matt. xxiii. 37. *How often would I have gathered you, and ye would not!* and, John i. 11. it is said, *He came to his own, and his own received him not*: Chorazin, Bethsaida, and Capernaum were lifted up to heaven by the Lord's preaching to them in person; and yet wo after wo is denounced against them, because they believed not, for all his preaching and miracles; and it is a wonder, if we look thorow the history of the gospel, how many a sweet preaching he had, and with what weight and power he spoke, and sometimes with tears, and withal backed his word with miracles, that made his hearers acknowledge the finger of God; and yet how few were brought to believe on him? so that he was put to take up this very complaint of Isaiah here, John xii. 38. Is it not a wonder, when he and his apostles have preached so much, and so long, that the Church is so little a flock, and that believers are so few in number, even after his ascension? need we any further proof,

that

that the gospel, where it comes, gets but little welcome? the carriage of many among ourselves is a sad proof of it; for we are afraid that many of you do not believe to this day, tho' there hath been amongst you, much, long or many years, and powerful preaching of the gospel, but are still living without faith, and perishing.

If this be not enough to clear the *doctrine*, 1. See how Christ speaks of it Matt. xiii. in the parable of the sower of the seed, where there are three sorts of ground that never bring forth good fruit; and there he speaks not only of the time of his own personal ministry, but of all times. 2. Look to the ordinary and daily effect, or rather consequent, of this preached gospel, and it will prove it: Do not many perish? do not many croud thick in the broad way that leads to destruction? do not but very few fruits of faith appear? is there not little, lamentably little, real change in the way and walk of most to be seen? To clear it yet further, go thro' the several ranks of persons, that in God's account are unbelievers, and lay them by; O! there will be exceeding few believers in Christ found. *First*, Then, lay by the grosly profane, that are never so much as civilized: *Secondly*, The ignorant, stupid, and senseless, that never have mind they have souls, are never feared for wrath, nor in the least exercised to make their peace with God: *Thirdly*, The earthly minded, that mind no other thing save the world: *Fourthly*, These of a civil outward carriage, that have some good works, and as they think, good days too, and yet come not near to Christ to close with him: *Fifthly*, The hypocrites, and that of all sorts; both the presuming hypocrites, that will thank God they are better than their neighbours, and yet lippen not to Christ, and free grace thro' him, but seek to establish their own righteousness, gross as it is; and the legal hypocrites, that never denied their own righteousness, nor submitted to the righteousness of Christ: Lay aside all these, I say, and we leave it to your own consciences to judge, how few will be found to have saving faith; and therefore I am persuaded, if there be any truth of God delivered to you, that this is a truth, that tho' the gospel be preached to many, yet there are but few hearers of it, that do actually believe in Jesus Christ, to the saving of their souls.

Use 1. The first use of it is, To beseech you to let this sink deep into your minds, as the truth of God, for these reasons, 1. Because it is a most useful truth; and if it were believed, it would make folks very watchful over themselves, and to tremble for fear lest they be found among the multitude that believe not; and put them to secure and sicker their interest in God, and not to rest on a fashion and form of religion, without observing what fruit followeth on the gospel. Among the many evils that undo not a few, we think this is not the least, that this truth is never thorowly fixed in them; they think there are many Heathens and Turks without the Church, and many gross swearers, drunkards, and others such within it, that will perish, but none others, or at least, that they are but very few, who among a professing people perish; neither can they be induced to think it is such a hard matter to get one, or a very few that are believers in a country-side; so that, if Isaiah were now alive to cry, *Who believes our report?* each of them would be ready to answer, I believe. 2. Because, for as certain and useful a truth as this is, yet generally it is not believed; folks cannot think that so few believe, and that believing is so difficult and rare a thing: I would ask you this question, Was it ever a difficulty to any of you to believe? if not, what is it that makes believing so rare? what should move the prophet thus to complain, *Who hath believed our report?* I shall shortly give you some evidences that many of you do not really believe this truth. The *first* is, That so few of you tremble at the word of God; the historical faith that the devils have, makes them tremble, but ye have not that much; this is given as a property of a suitable hearer of the gospel, to whom the Lord will look, Isa. lxvi. 1, 2. that he is one *who trembles at the word*; but the most part of you, that hear this gospel, are like these pillars on which this house stands, who are never so much as once moved at the word: ye either take not faith to be an absolutely necessary thing, and that ye cannot but perish without it, or ye think that the faith ye were born with will do your turn; ye do not believe that ye are naturally under the power of the devil, and led captive by him at his will, and that without holiness, and a spiritual gracious frame, and stamp on your heart and way, ye shall never see God: what wonder then, that ye come not to rest on Christ, when the very letter of the gospel is not credited. A *second* Evidence is, That there is so little preparation made to prevent your eternal hazard: it is said of Noah, Heb. xi. that *Noah, being warned of God, prepared an ark*: and this is attributed to his faith; it is not possible that ye would live so negligently and carelesly, if ye believed that the curse of God were pursuing you, and that ye will be brought to reckon for that which ye have done in the body, and that ye will meet with God as an enemy; if this were believed tho' your hearts were harder than they are, it would make you tremble, and put you to other sort of thoughts and seriousness. A *third* evidence is, That there is no fruit of faith among many of you; for, where it is, it will not be got altogether smothered, but will kythe and shew itself one way or other: And if ye will still assert your faith, I would say to you, as James doth to these to whom he writes, *Shew me your faith by your works*. If ye shall say, God knows: I answer, that ye shall find that to be a truth, that he knows; and he will make you know that he does so: but alas! that poor shift will not avail you, when it comes to the push. O try your faith then by your works; see what mortification of lusts, what repentance from dead works, what growth in knowledge, what shining of holiness in your conversation, is attained to. Many of you, as to your very knowledge, are as if ye lived among Heathens, many of whom have been as free of vice, and more profitable to others, than many of you are, and cared as little for the world as many of you do: How comes it to pass, then, that ye have lived as if ye could have faith, and yet have no fruit? Ye must either say, that faith is not necessary, or that ye may have faith without fruit; for we are sure your fruit is not the fruit of faith. To live honestly as you call it, what is that? There are many Heathens, who have gone beyond you in that. We will not say, that moral honesty is nothing, but sure it is not all; all the fruits of meer moral honesty are but sour fruits, that will set your teeth on edge: neither is it your hearing of the word only, but your believing and doing of it, that will profit you. It is very sad, that most plain obvious duties are not at all followed, as the studying of knowledge, the exercising of repentance, one of the very first duties, which is never separated from faith; the humbling of the soul before God, the lothing of yourselves for all ye have done, the love of God, &c. for there may be challenges for gross evils in Heathens; and fear is not repentance, but godly sorrow, that causeth repentance, not to be repented of. A *fourth* evidence is, The want of that work of God's Spirit that accompanies faith. Faith is a special work of the Spirit, and the gracious gift of God; it is wrought by the exceeding mighty power of God, whereby he raised Christ from the dead; and by that same power he worketh in them that believe. Now, know ye ever what this work meaned? Found ye it ever to be a difficult work to believe? knew ye ever what it was to have the Spirit of God constraining your heart to believe? I speak not of any extraordinary thing; but certainly faith is not natural, nor cometh from pure nature: and wherever it is, it manifests itself by works, and evidenceth the power of the Spirit in the working thereof. There are some sad evidences of, and bitter fruits that spring from this root, to wit, folks being strangers to the experimental knowledge of the work of faith; As, 1. When men know no more difficulty to get Christ, and to rest on Christ, than to believe a story of Wallace or of Julius Cæsar. 2. When folks say that they believed all their days, and believed always since ever they knew good by ill; and tho' their faith be no true saving faith, but a guessing, yet they will not quit it; yea, it is impossible for men to get them convinced that they want faith. 3. When men never knew what it is to be without faith; it is one of the great works of the Spirit, John xvi. 8. to convince of the want of faith: folks will be easily convinced, that breach of the Sabbath, that stealing, that bearing false witness, &c. are sins, where the special work of the Spirit is not; but how many of you have been convinced of the want of faith? We are constrained to say this sad word, when we look on this text, that it is lamentably fulfilled in your eyes, and in this our congregation: Think not that we wrong such of you who have believed our report; Ah! it is few, even very few of you, that receive and believe this gospel.

Use 2. The second use is for conviction. If it be ordinary for the great part of the hearers of the gospel not to believe, let it sink in your hearts, that it is no extraordinary thing that hath befallen you. Are ye not such hearers, as many of these were, who heard Isaiah and Jesus Christ? and if so, will not this follow, that there are many, yea, even the thick and throng of the hearers of the gospel, that believe not; and who, if Christ were gathering sinners by this preached gospel, would not be gathered? If, where the gospel comes, many do not believe; then here in this city, where the gospel is preached to a great multitude of professing members of the visible church, there are readily many that do not believe: or, let me ask of you a reason why ye do except yourselves; either this truth holds not so universally, or many of you must fall under it, or else give a reason why you fall not under it; the truth, which Isaiah preached, hath been preached to you, and yet ye remain unbelieving, and despisers of the invitation to the marriage of the King's Son, as the Jews did. We are not now speaking of Jews, Turks, nor Heathens, nor of the Churches in general, nor of other congregations, but of you in Glasgow, that have this gospel preached amongst you; and we say of you, that there

there are few that believe our report. Think it not our word; the application flows natively from the text, not from necessity of the thing, but from the ordinary course of mens corruption. Are not the same evidences of the want of faith, which we spoke of, among you? how many are there in their life prophane? how many rest on civility and formality? is there not as little repentance now, as was in Isaiah's time? as little denying of our own righteousness, and making use of Christ's; tho' the word be taught by line upon line, here a little, and there a little? It may be, tho' ye think that the doctrine is true in the general, ye will not, ye cannot digest the application, that among so many of you visible professors of faith there are but few real believers; therefore we shall follow the conviction a little further, by giving you some considerations, to make it out, that we have but too just ground to make application of the doctrine to you, especially considering the abounding of corruption that is amongst you, that ye may be put to fear the wrath that attends sin, and to flee to Christ, for refuge, in time. 1. Consider of whom it is that the prophet is speaking, and of what time: Is it not the times and days of the gospel? had not the Spirit (in dictating this text of scripture) an eye on Scotland, and on Glasgow? and do not our Lord Jesus Christ and Paul apply it in their days? and why then may not we also in ours? and when the Spirit speaks expresly of the last times, that they shall be perilous, and of the falling away of many, should it not give us the hotter alarm? 2. Do not all things agree to us, as to them? is not this gospel the same? is our preaching any better than theirs? nay, had they not much more powerful preaching? and if that preaching, which was much more powerful, had not efficacy, as to many, to work faith in them, what may we expect to do by our preaching? are not your hearts as deceitful? are not your corruptions as strong? are ye not as bent to backsliding, as they were? what sort of folk were they, that were unfruitful hearers? were they not members of the visible church as ye are, circumcised under the Old Testament, as ye are baptized under the New? was it not those who had Christ and his apostles preaching to them? yea, they were not among the more ignorant sort, who did not believe, but Scribes and Pharisees, and these not of the prophanest sort only, but such as came to church, and attended on ordinances, as ye do: yea, were such as had gifts, and cast out devils, and preached in Christ's name, as you may see, Luke xiii. 6. Now, when there are so many, and of such ranks, who get no good of the word, and of such, a great many that will seek to enter, and shall not be able, to whom Christ will say, Depart, I know you not, ye workers of iniquity; what can be the reason that many of you do so confidently assert your faith, when there are scarcely any characters of unbelief, but ye have them? Or, what can be your advantage, in keeping yourselves carnally secure, when the strong man in the mean time is in the house? and to shut your eyes, and make your necks stiff, and to resolve, as it were, not only to ly still, but to die in your unbelief? I persuade myself, that many of you, ere long, will be made to wonder, that ever ye thought yourselves believers, and will be galled when ye think upon it, that whatever was said to you, ye would needs maintain your presumptuous faith. When we bid you suffer the conviction to sink, let none put it from themselves to others, but let every one take it home to himself; altho' we would not have any of you casting loose what is indeed made fast and well secured, nor overturning a slender and weak building, tho, it were, to speak so, but of two stone height, if it be founded on a right foundation, on the Rock; but we speak to you, that cannot be brought to suspect yourselves, when ye have just reason to do so: sure, this challenge and charge belongs to some, yea to many, and we would ask what ground have ye to shift it? How can ye prove your faith, more than others, that have none at all? That ye hope ye have faith, will not do your turn, that's no solid proof: Ye cannot come to Christ, except made suitably sensible of your distance; and of that ye have never been convinced as yet. Do ye think to roll yourselves on Christ sleeping, and ye know not how? Certainly, when the pins of your tabernacle come to be a loosing, ye shall find that your fancied faith shall not be able to keep out a challenge: Ye could never endure to think yourselves to be Christ's enemy, or that ye wanted faith; but when death comes, conscience will awaken, and the challenge will needs be in upon you, whether ye will or not. Many of you think that ye get wrong, when your faith is questioned or reproved, as if it were an odd and rare thing to be graceless, or to be living as members of the visible church, and yet want faith; and it irritates you, to be expostulated with in private for your lying in unbelief; but suffer this word now to take hold of you, I beseech you; and if ye could once be brought to suspect yourselves, and to think thus with yourselves, What if I be one of those many that believe not? I fear I be in hazard to be mistaken about my faith; and

from

from that, put to follow on to see how ye will be able to ward off the challenge, and to prove your believing to be sound, we would think ye were far on? O if ye had the faith of this truth, that, among the many hearers of the gospel, there are but few that believe, and were brought thereby to examine and try yourselves! There is no truth, that Christ insists more on, than this, that *Strait is the gate, and narrow is the way to heaven, and* that *but few find it ;* and that there are few that believe, and few that be saved. If ye did once in earnest look on yourselves as in hazard, and were brought to reflect on matters betwixt God and you, it might be, the Lord would follow the conviction. We desire him to do it, and to him be praise.

SERMON VII.

Isaiah liii. 1. *Who hath believed our report? and to whom is the arm of the Lord revealed?*

IT's a sad matter, and much to be lamented, when the carrying of such good news, as is the report of Jesus Christ in the gospel, becomes unprofitable to them that hear it, and thereby burdensom to them that carry it; folk would think, that such glad tidings, as make the heavenly host of angels to sing, would be very joyful and welcome news to sinners, and also most heartsom to them that carry them; and where the former is, there the latter will be also; where the word becomes useless and unprofitable to hearers, it is burdensom, as to the concomitant and effect, to honest ministers that speak it. Tho' Isaiah brought these news, in a very plain, powerful, pleasant, and sweet manner, to the people he preached to, and that frequently; yet, in the midst of his sweet prophecies, he breaks out with this complaint, *Who hath believed our report?* He is crying glad tidings; yet, taking a look of the unbelief of his hearers now and then, he complains of it to God, in his own name, and in the name of all the ministers of the gospel, that should come after him.

We shew, that it was a very ordinary thing, where the gospel comes in greatest plenty and power, for the hearers thereof to meet it with much unbelief; a truth that was verified in Isaiah his time, and that he foresaw would be verified in the days of the gospel: and therefore it is *our* report; not only is it the report of Isaiah, but it is the report of Christ and of Paul, who make the same complaint, and cite the same words of Isaiah; and, need we doubt of the truth of it, when Isaiah in the Old, and Paul in the New Testament, thus complain? Not to speak of their, and our Lord and Master, who *came to his own, and his own received him not;* and of whom, when he came, they said, *This is the heir, come let us kill him;* need we, I say, doubt of the truth of the doctrine, or to think it strange to see it so in our time, and that we have the same complaint, when the means (at least the instruments) are incomparably far below what they were then, tho' it be still the same gospel?

The prophet's scope is, to give advertisement and warning to the hearers of the gospel, for the time to come, of this rife evil, even the abounding of unbelief in them that hear it; 1. That he may prevent the scandal of the unfruitfulness of the word where it comes. 2. That he may add a spur of excitement to the hearers of the gospel, to endeavour to make use of it, and not to rest upon means, how powerful and lively soever they be, but to press forward to the end they aim and shoot at. 3. That he may put his to the trial, and that they may be brought to look in upon themselves, whether they be ... or be, in the black roll of them that receive not the reports: and we think, if any thing put folks to be suspicious of themselves, and to commune with their own hearts about their souls estate, this should do it; especially, when they consider how this evil agrees to all times, and yet more especially to the times of the gospel, and how it is an evil that abounds, not only among the prophane, but among these who are civil, and zealous too for the righteousness of the law: It should make them put themselves to the trial, and not to take every thing to be faith, that they fancy to be faith; for either this doctrine is not true, that wherever the gospel comes, it meets with unbelief in most part of its hearers, and cannot be applied to this generation; or, that there is much faith in this generation that we live in, that will not be counted saving faith: If all of you were believers, there were no ground for this complaint; and if we will take folks on their own word, we can hardly get a person, but will say, he believes; so that the generality of mens hearts run quite contrary to this truth; and therefore we say, it is the scope of this doctrine, and the like, to give folks the alarm, and to put them to suspect and try themselves. I do not mean, that any should cast the work of faith where it is indeed, for that is also a part of our unbelief; and ordinarily, when unbelief falleth on the one side, the devil maketh it up on the other, and makes tender souls question their faith, when they begin to believe, as if they could mend unbelief with unbelief: But it is to such that we speak, who cannot be brought to suspect their faith. Certainly ye will wonder one day, that ye should have heard such a plain truth, and yet would not so much as ask your own hearts, whether there was reason to suspect your want of faith; as it is said, that Christ marvelled at their unbelief who heard him, so may we at yours, and ere long ye shall also marvel at yourselves, on this account.

Before we prosecute this use and the rest any further, we shall speak to another doctrine, and it is the last that flows from these words, tending to the same scope to make us fear at unbelief, which the prophet makes such a heavy ground of complaint. The doctrine then is, *That if there were never so many under unbelief, and never so many who refuse to receive Jesus Christ, yet unbelief is a sin, and a most sinful sin; which tho' folks had no more, will seclude them from heaven.* There were no ground for this complaint, if it were not so; even as the prophet would have had no ground to complain of the people's unbelief, if there were not many unbelievers; so unbelief is a very great sin, in whomsoever it is, and makes them exceeding sinful. Or, take the doctrine thus, *It is a very great sin for a people, to whom Christ is offered in this gospel, not to receive him, and rest upon him for salvation, as he is offered to them therein.* And it ariseth from this ground, That where Christ is not received there the ministers of the gospel have ground of complaint; for it supposes a great defect of their duty, seeing it is their duty to believe, yea, the great gospel-duty, on which all other duties hang, and which is called for by many ties and obligations: *This is his commandment,* saith John, in his first epistle, chap. iii. 23. *that ye believe on the name of his Son Jesus Christ,* therefore it must be a great sin not to believe.

There are shortly three things comprehended in this doctrine (speaking now of unbelief, not only as oppposite to historical faith, which we commonly call *infidelity,* but as it is opposite to *saving faith,* which we shew is that which is called for here) 1. That unbelief, or not receiving of Christ, is a sin, or a thing in its own nature sinful: It is a sin, as well as adultery, murder, stealing, lying, sabbath-breaking, &c. are; yea, and in the aggravations of it, a sin beyond these: it is as contrary to the word and will of God, and is as contrary to the Divine Majesty, as drunkenness, murder, adultery, or any other sin is; the positive command of believing being as peremptory, plain, and particular, as these negative ones are, the breach of it must be as sinful. 2. That there is such a kind of sin as unbelief, beside other sins, and such a distinct duty as believing, that if folks could do all other duties, if this duty of believing be wanting, they will be still sinful, and there will be still ground of complaint: and if faith be a particular duty required, and distinct from other duties and graces, as it is clear Gal. v. 21. then unbelief must be a particular sin, distinct from other sins, tho' it hath influence on other sins, as faith hath on other duties; so, Rev. xxi. 8. it is ranked among the most abominable sins. The reason why we mark this, is, because there may be some, in whom some gross sins, as adultery, bloodshed, and the like, do reign, and they get that name to be called *adulterers, murderers,* &c. Others may possibly be free of these, who yet have unbelief reigning in them; and therefore they get that name to be called *unbelieving,* and are ranked with the grossest evil-doers. 3. That even many in the times wherein the scriptures were written, and in every age since are found guilty of this sin, and condemned for it, who are as to several other things commended: hence it is said, Rom. x. 3. of the Jews, that *they had a zeal of God,* which in itself is good, *though not according to knowledge;* yet it was their main let and obstruction in the way to life, that *being ignorant of God's righteousness, they went about to establish their own:* For as much zeal as they had for the law of Moses, seeing they did not receive Jesus Christ and his righteousness by faith, it made any other good thing they had unacceptable. And the reason why we mark this, is, that folks may see that it is not only for gross sins, and with gross sinners, that the gospel complains and expostulates; but it is also for not submitting unto, and not receiving the righteousness of Christ: and therefore ye are far mistaken, that think yourselves free from just grounds of challenge, because, forsooth, ye are free of murder, adultery, drunkenness, and the like. Do ye not consider, that unbelievers, are in the same rank and roll with abominable whoremongers, sorcerers, idolaters, and dogs? And is not unbelief contrary to the command of God, as well as murder, adultery, and these other gross sins? And therefore folks think little of unbelief, tho' it be very rise, if they be free of other gross sins. 4. We shall add a fourth thing which the doctrine implies, That unbelief, tho' there were no other sin, is exceeding sinful, and is, *First,* the great ground that makes God expostulate with the hearers of the gospel, and that makes them come under the complaint, John v. 40. *Ye will not come*

come to me, that ye may have life; and Matt. xxiii. 37. *How often would I have gathered you, and ye would not!* And, for substance, it is the Lord's great complaint of most of his professing people, Psal. lxxxi. 10, 11. *I am the Lord thy God; open thy mouth wide, and I will fill it; but my people would not hearken to my voice, and Israel would none of me;* And then follows, *O that my people had hearkned to my voice!* There is no sin the Lord complains more of than this, and it is the great complaint of all his servants. *Secondly,* Behold how the Lord threatens this sin, and punishes for it; see Psal. xcv. 7. and Heb. iii. 7. and Heb. iv. 8. where he swears in his wrath against unbelievers, that they shall not enter into his rest; adultery and murder do not more certainly keep men from heaven than this sin of unbelief doth, yea, they are classed together, Rev. xxi. 8. see also Luke xii. 46. where the severest judgment that is executed is upon unbelievers; and in the man that had the offer of Christ, and did not receive it, and put on the wedding-garment, Matt. xxii. 12, 13. see it also in the words that are pronounced against Chorazin, Bethsaida, and Capernaum, Matt. xi. and our blessed Lord Jesus loves not (to speak so) to pronounce woes, but to bless his people; yet when they have the offer of life thro' him, and will not receive it, he pronounces wo after wo upon them; and of what sort were they? even beyond these that came upon Tyre and Sidon, upon Sodom and Gomorrah: we think such threatnings as these should make folks not to think unbelief a light, or little sin; or, that there is any ground of quietness so long as they are in a self-righteous condition, and have not their peace made with God through Christ. *Thirdly,* Look further, to the greatness of this, in the strange names that the Lord puts upon it, 1 John v. 11. *He that believes not, hath made God a liar:* and is there any sin that hath a grosser name or effect than this? for it receives not the report which he hath given of his Son: he tells folks that happiness is to be gotten in him only, and they think to be happy tho' they take another way; they believe not the report, for if they believed it, they would receive Christ as their life. See further what names are given to it, Heb. vi. 6. and Heb. x. 20. which tho' they be there given, with other aggravations of sinning *wilfully, with despite,* &c. with respect to the unpardonable sin, yet who are they that live under the gospel and believe not, but in a great measure they will be found capable of most of them at least? *It is called a crucifying of the Son of God afresh, a putting him to open shame,* &c. and who are they that do this,

and on what ground? It is unbelievers thro' their unbelief; they think not Christ worth the having, and reject all that is spoken of him, and cry, *Away with him,* as the Jews did; and as to their particular guilt, they crucify him, for they cannot refuse him, without affronting him; and can there be such an affronting of him, as when he condescends so very low, to think so little of him? *Fourthly,* Consider the expressions, under which he sets out his being affected (to say so) with this sin; he was so affected with it, Mark iii. 5. that it is said, *He was grieved for their unbelief:* He had had many sorrows and griefs, and suffered many things, but this grieved him someway more than all did, And it's said, Mark vi. 6. That *he marvelled, because of their unbelief;* it's not said that he marvelled at their adulteries, and their gross sins; but that, when he was taking such a convincing way to demonstrate to them his God-head, yet they would not believe on him, he marvelled at that; So, Luke xix. 41. it is said, that when he came near to Jerusalem, *he wept over it;* and why? the following words tell us, *O that thou had known in this thy day, the things that belong to thy peace!* That is, O that thou hadst believed, and received the gospel, at least in this thy day, (tho' thou did it not before) when thou wert, and art so plainly and powerfully called to this duty; and ye may know that it behoved to be some great thing that made him to weep, when all that the devil and Pontius Pilate, and the Jews could do, made him not to weep. It is said, Matt. xi. that he *upbraided* these cities that *he* had preached much in, on this ground; sure, when *he* that gives liberally, and upbraids none, does upbraid for this sin, it shews how much *he* was pressed with it. And, Luke xiv. 21. it is said of this sin, that it *angered* him, and he is not easily angered: Sinners need not fear to anger him, by coming to him; but when they come not, he is angry. It is said, Matt. xxii. 7. He was *wroth* at this sin; and it is on this ground, that, Psal. ii. 12. we are bidden, *Kiss the Son, lest he be angry,* that is, to exercise faith in him; for if we do it not, he will be angry, and we will perish. There are other aggravations of this sin, which we leave till we come to the application.

Use 1. Is there not as much here, tho' folks had no more but their unbelief, as may make them know, it is an evil and bitter thing, and as may make them fear at it, and flee from it, and to fear lest they be found under the guilt of it, when called to a reckoning; especially when unbelief is so rife, that but few suspect themselves or fear it: there is hardly any ill, but ye will sooner take with it, than this of unbelief; and there is no duty nor grace that ye more readily think ye perform and have, than this of faith; and it is come to that height, that folks think they believe always, and know not what it is to misbelieve: Do ye think that this presumptuous and fancied faith will be counted for faith, or that Christ, who sifts faith narrowly, will let it pass for saving faith? no certainly.

Use 2. Is there not here ground of advertisement, wakening, rousing, and alarming to many, that think themselves free of other challenges; if the Spirit were coming powerfully to convince of sin, it would be of this, *Because they believe not*, as it is, John xvi. 9. and we are persuaded many of you had need of this conviction, that never once questions your having of faith, or care not whether ye have it or not. Put these two doctrines together, That unbelief is an abominable sin, and that it is notwithstanding a very rife sin, and let them sink deep into your hearts, and they will put you to other thoughts of heart; if this plain truth of God prevail not with you, we know not what will do it :—But the time cometh, when ye shall be undeniably convinced of both, that unbelief is a great sin, and that it is a very rife sin; and of this also, that it is an abominable and lothsom thing, and very prejudicial and hurtful to you.

Use 3. And therefore, a third use, If it be so, let us ask this question, How comes it to pass, that so many, in trying their state, and in grounding of it, lay so little weight on faith, and think so little of unbelief? I am speaking to the generality of you, and let not others wrong themselves, nor mistake the intent of this scripture; how is it, I say, that the generality of you that hear this gospel come under this common and epidemic temper, or rather distemper, to maintain your peace and confidence, when ye can (in the mean time) give so little proof of it? Think ye that faith cannot be amissing, or mistaken, or that it is ordinary and common, or that it is indifferent, whether ye have it or not? we are persuaded that many of you think, that if ye have a good mind, (as ye call it) and a square civil honest walk, and keep still your good hope, that all will be well; ye never doubt, nor question whether ye have received Christ or not: but if unbelief ly in your bosom, (I mean not, doubting desperation, or questioning of the God-head, but the not receiving of Christ, and his righteousness) tho' ye had more than ordinary hypocrites have, ye will for this sin of unbelief find yourselves under the standing curse of God; for our Lord says, John iii. 18. *He that believes not, is condemned already;* and v. 36. *The wrath of God abideth on him.*

In pressing of this *Use*, I shall shew, by a few aggravations of this sin, why the Lord layeth so much weight upon it, and that, not so much as it opposeth faith, as it is a condition of the covenant of grace, and a mean to unite us to Christ; but mainly as it is a sin thwarting his command : And, 1. It thwarteth with both the law and the gospel ; it thwarteth with the commands of the first table, and so is a greater sin than murder or adultery, nay than sodomy, tho' these be great, vile and abominable sins; which may be thought strange, yet it is true; it makes the person guilty of it more vile before God, than a Pagan-Sodomite; the nature of the sin being more hainous, as being against the first table of the law, in both the first and second commands thereof; it being by faith in God, that we make God our God, and worship God in Christ acceptably. Next, it is not only a sin against the law, but a sin against the gospel, and the prime flower (to speak so) of the gospel; it comes in contradiction to the very design of the gospel, which is to manifest the glory of the grace of God, in bringing sinners to believe on Christ, and to be saved through him; but he can do no great things of this sort amongst unbelieving people, because of their unbelief; it bindeth up his hands as it were, (to speak so with reverence) that he cannot do them a good turn. 2. It strikes more narrowly against the honour of God, and of the Mediator, and doth more prejudice to the ministry of the gospel, and causeth greater destruction of souls, than any other sin. It's impossible, notwithstanding of other sins, that Christ may have satisfaction for the travel of his soul, and there may be a relation bound up betwixt him and sinners notwithstanding of them; but if this sin of unbelief were universal, he should never get a soul to heaven: the salvation of souls is called, *the pleasure of the Lord;* but this obstructs it, and closeth the door betwixt sinners and access to God. It strikes also at the main fruit of the ministry, it makes them complain to God, that the word is not taken off their hand: it frustrates the very end of the ministry, and it comes nearest the destruction of immortal souls; we need not say, it brings on, but it holds and keeps on the wrath of God on sinners for ever, *He that believeth not* (as we shewed before from John iii.) *is condemned already, and the wrath of God abideth on him.* 3. More particularly, There is nothing in God, (even that which is most excellent in him, if we may speak so, not excepted) but it strikes against it: it strikes against his grace, and frustrates that; when Christ is not received, some sort and degree of despite is done to the Spirit of grace; unbelievers

thwart

thwart with him in the way of his grace, and will have no spiritual good from him: it comes in opposition to his goodness; for, where unbelief reigns, he hath no access, in a manner, to communicate it: It strikes against his faithfulness; there is no weight laid on his promises, it counts him a liar: In a word, it strikes against all his attributes. 4. There is no sin that hath such a train of sad consequences following on it: it is that which keeps all other sins lively; for none hath victory over any sin but the believer: the unbeliever lies as a bound slave to every sin, and it is impossible to come to the acceptable performance of any duty without faith, for none can come suitably to any duty without a promise; and can any. but a believer comfort himself in use making of any promise?

We shall close our discourse, with speaking a word to that which we hinted at before, even to let you see, not only the ripeness of unbelief, but the great hazard that flows from it, and the exceeding great evil of it. If we be only convinced of the ripeness of it, it will not much trouble us, except we be also convinced, and believe the hazard of it: but if we were convinced of both, thro' God's blessing it might affect us more, and necessitate us to make more use of Christ. Ye that stand yet at a distance from Christ, can ye endure to ly under this great guilt, and ground of controversy that is betwixt him and you? do ye think little to hazard on his upbraidings and woes, even such woes as are beyond these that came on Sodom, the heavy curse and malediction of God? And yet we say to you who are most civil, discreet, formal, and blameless in your conversation, If there be not a fleeing in earnest to Christ, and an exercising of faith on him, the wrath of God not only waits for you, but it abides on you. O tremble at the thoughts of it; it were better to have your head thrust in the fire, than your souls and bodies to be under the wrath and curse of God for ever. It is not only the ignorant, prophane, drunkard, swearer, adulterer, whoremonger, &c. that we have to complain of, and expostulate with, but it is the unbeliever, who, tho' he be lift up to heaven, shall be cast down to the pit of hell. If ye ask, What is all this that we would be at? It is only this, in a word, We would have you receiving Christ: If ye think that unbelief is an exceeding great evil, and that it is an horribly hazardous thing to ly under it, then haste you out of it to Christ; O! haste, haste you out of it to Christ; *kiss the Son lest he be angry;* embrace him, yield to him; there is no other possible way to be free of the evil, or to prevent the hazard.

SERMON VIII.

Isaiah. liii 1. *Who hath believed our report? and to whom is the arm of the Lord revealed?*

IT is a great encouragement and delight to the ministers of the gospel, and it is comfortable and refreshing to hearers, when the message of the gospel is received, and our Lord Jesus Christ is welcomed; but on the contrary, it is burdensom and heavy, when there are few or none that believe and receive the report, when their labour and strength is spent in vain, and when all the assemblings of them together, that hear the word of the gospel, is but a treading of the Lord's courts in vain: if there were no more to prove it, this complaint of Isaiah, speaking in his own name, and in name of all the ministers of the gospel, is sufficient; for as comfortable messages as he carried (and he carried as comfortable messages as any that we hear of) yet there was a general not-profiting by the word of the gospel in his mouth. When we meet with such words as these, our hearts should tremble, when we consider how general and rife an evil unbelief, and the not receiving of Christ, is; how horrible a sin, how abominable to God, and how hazardous and destructive to ourselves, it is; and how rare a thing it is to see, or find any number believing and receiving this message of the gospel.

We spoke from these words to these *doctrines; First,* That where the gospel comes, it makes offer of Jesus Christ to all that hear it. *Secondly,* That the great thing called for, in the hearers of the gospel, is faith in him. *Thirdly,* That yet notwithstanding unbelief is an exceeding rife evil in the hearers of the gospel. *Fourthly,* That it is a very sinful, heavy, and sad thing, not to receive Christ, and believe in him. All which are implied in this short, but sad complaint, *Who hath believed our report?*

We would now prosecute the *use* and scope of this. The last *use* was an use of conviction of, and expostulation with, the hearers of the gospel, for their being so fruitless under it; serving to discover a great deceit among hearers, who think they believe, and yet do it not; whence it is, that so many are mistaken about their souls state, and most certainly the generality are mistaken, who live as if believing were a thing common to all professors of faith; while, as it is so rare, and there are so very few that believe.

The next *use* is, an use of exhortation to you, That seeing unbelief is so great an evil, ye would by all means eschew it; and seeing faith is the only way to receive Christ, and to come at life thro' him, ye would seek after it, to prevent the evil of unbelief: this is the scope of the words, yea, and of all our preaching, that when Christ, and remission of sins thro' him, is preached to you, ye would by faith receive him, and rest upon him, for obtaining right to him and to the promises, and for preventing of the threatnings and curses that abide unbelievers. We shall not again repeat what faith is,; only, in short, it comes to this, that seeing Christ hath satisfied justice for sinners, and his satisfaction is offered in the gospel to all that will receive it, even to all the hearers of the gospel; that sinners, in the sight and sense of their lost condition, would flee into him, receive and rest upon him, and his satisfaction, for pardon of sin, and making of their peace with God. Is there need of arguments to persuade you to this? If ye be convinced of your sinfulness, and of your lost estate without Christ, and that there is a judgment to come, when sinners must appear before him, and be judged according to that which they have done in the body; and if ye have the faith of this, that sinners, that are not found in Christ, cannot stand (as, by the way, wo to that man that is not found in him, if it were a Paul; for even he, he is only happy by being found in him, not having his own righteousness, but Christ's) and withal, that there is no other way to be found in him but by faith, (which is that which Paul hath for his main scope, Phil. iii. 9, 10.) Then, to be found in him by faith, should be your main work and study; this is that we should design and endeavour, and to this we have access by the gospel; and it is in short, to be denuded of, and denied to our own righteousness, as to any weight we lay upon it for our justification before God, and to have no other thing but Christ's righteousness, offered in the gospel, and received by faith, to rest upon for justification, and making of our peace with God: This is it that we command you to flee to, and by all means to seek an interest in, that when the gospel makes offer of Christ, and righteousness thro' his satisfaction, and commands you to believe in him, when it lays him to your door, to your mouth and heart, that ye would roll and lay yourselves over on him, for the making of your peace, and the bearing you thro' in the day of your reckoning before the tribunal of God.

That we may speak the more clearly to this *use*, we shall shortly shew you, 1. What ground a lost sinner hath to receive Christ, and to lippen to him. 2. What warrants and encouragements a sinner hath to lean and lippen to this ground. 3. We shall remove a doubt or two, that may stand in the way of sinners resting on this ground. 4. We shall give some directions to further you to this. And, 5. We shall give you some characters of one that is tenderly taking this way of believing. And because this is the way of the gospel, and we are sure there is not a word ye have more need of, or that, thro' God's blessing, may be more useful, and there is not a word more uncontrovertible, which all of you will assent to the truth of, to wit, that there is a great good in believing, and a great evil in unbelief, we would exhort you the more seriously to lay it to heart: O! think not that our coming to speak and hear, is for the fashion, but to profit; cast yourselves therefore open to the exhortation, and let the word of faith sink down into your hearts, considering that there is nothing you have more need of than of faith, and that ye will not find it safe for you to hazard your souls on your own righteousness, or to appear before God without Christ's righteousness; and that the only way to come by it is faith: This may let you see the necessity of believing, and that it is of your concernment to try how it is with you as to that; and therefore, again and again, we would exhort you in the fear of God, that ye would not neglect so great a salvation, which through faith is to be obtained, but lay it to heart, as ye would not have all the servants of God, who have preached the gospel to you, complaining of you. It is our bane, that we suspect not ourselves; and indeed it is a wonder, that these who have immortal souls, and profess faith in Christ, should yet live so secure, and under so little care, and holy solicitude to know, whether they have believed or not, and should with so little serious concernedness, put the matter to a trial: But we proceed to the particulars we proposed to speak to.

And first to this, That ye have a good solid ground to believe on; for clearing of which, we would put these together. 1. The fulness and sufficiency of the Mediator Jesus Christ, in whom all the riches of the gospel are treasured up, in whom, and by whom our happiness comes, and who wants nothing that may fit him to be a Saviour, *who is able to save to the uttermost all that come unto God by him.* 2. The well-orderedness, freeness, and fulness of the covenant of grace, wherein it is transacted, that the fulness, that is in the Mediator Christ,

Christ, shall be made forthcoming to believers in him; and by which lost sinners, that by faith flee unto him, have a solid right to his satisfaction, which will bear them out before God; by which transaction, Christ's satisfaction is made as really theirs, when by faith it is closed with, as if they had satisfied and paid the price themselves, 2 Cor. v. 21. *He, who knew no sin, was made sin for us, that we might be made the righteousness of God in him.* And this consideration, of the legality and order of the covenant, serves exceedingly to clear our faith as to the ground of it, because by this covenant it is transacted and agreed upon, that Christ shall undergo the penalty, and that the believer in him shall be reckoned the righteous person: if there be a reality in Christ's death and satisfaction to justice, if he hath undergone the penalty and paid their debt, there is a reality in this transaction, as to the making over of what he hath done and suffered, to believers in him; and the covenant being sure and firm as to his part, he having confirmed it by his death, it is as sure and firm, as to the benefit of it, to the believer in him. 3. The nature of the offer of this grace in the gospel, and the nature of the gospel, that makes the offer of the fulness that is in Christ by virtue of the covenant: It is the word of God, and hath his authority, when we preach it according to his command, as really as when he preached it himself in Capernaum, or any where else: even as the authority of a king is with his ambassador, according to that, 2 Cor. v. penult v. *We are ambassadors for Christ; as tho' God did beseech you by us;* There is the Father's warrant and name interposed; and for the Son's, it follows, *We pray you in Christ's stead be ye reconciled to God.* Add to this, the nature of the offer, and the terms of it; there is no condition required on our part, as the precise condition of the covenant, but believing: Now, when these are conjoined, we put it to your conscience, if ye have not a good ground to lippen to, and a sufficient foundation to build on; and if so, it ought to be a powerfully attractive motive to draw you to believe in him, and to bring you to rest on him by believing.

Secondly, We have also many warrants and encouragements to step forward, and when Christ in his fulness lays himself before you, to roll over yourselves on him, and to yield to him: If we could speak of them suitably, they are such as may remove all fearring that any might have in coming to him, and may serve to leave others inexcusable, and unanswerably to convince them that the main obstruction was in themselves, and that they would not come unto him for life; he called to them, but none would exalt him. 1. Do ye not think that the offer of this gospel is a sufficient warrant, and ground of encouragement to believe on him? and if it be so to others, ought it not to be a sufficient warrant and encouragement to you? when he says, Psal. lxxxi. 10. *Open thy mouth wide, and I will fill it:* what excuse can ye have to shift or refuse the offer? if ye think Christ real in his commands, is he not as real in his offers? 2. He hath so ordered the administration of this gospel, as he hath purposely prevented any ground that folks may have of fearring to close with Christ; he hath so qualified the objects of this grace in the gospel, that these in all the world that men would think should be secluded, are taken in to be sharers of it; for it is *sinners, lost sinners, self-destroyers, ungodly, the sheep that have wandered, the poor, the needy, the naked, the captives, the prisoners, the blind,* &c. according to that of Isa. lxi. 1, 2. *The Spirit of the Lord God is upon me; he hath sent me to preach glad tidings to the meek or poor, to bind up the brokenhearted, to proclaim liberty to the captive, the opening of the prison to them that are bound,* &c. And, Isa. lv. 1. these, who are invited to come to the cried fair of grace, are such as are *thirsty,* and such as *want money*; who among men use to be secluded, but in grace's market they only are welcome; it is to them that grace says, *Ho, come,* and Rev. xxii. 17. *Whosoever will, let him come and take of the water of life freely.* It is not only, to say so with reverence, these whom he willeth, but it is, *whosoever will:* and so, if thou wilt come, grace puts the offer into thy hand, as it were, to carve on; to let us know, that he allows strong consolation to believers, and that either the hearers of this gospel shall believe, or be left without all excuse. He hath it to say, as it is, Isa. v. *What could I have done to my vineyard, that I have not done?* if ye had the offer at your own carving, what could ye put more in it? it cannot be more free than without money, it cannot be more seriously pressed than with a *Ho,* and *Oyes,* to come. Sometimes he complains, as John v. 40. *Ye will not come to me, that ye might have life;* and sometimes weeps and moans, because sinners will not be gathered, as Luke xix. 41, 42. and Matt. xxiii. 37. Can there be any greater evidences of reality in any offer? A third warrant is from the manner and form of Christ's administration: he hath condescended to make a covenant and many promises, to draw folks to believe; to which he hath added his oath, swearing by himself, when he had not a
greater

greater to swear by, for our confirmation and consolation, as it is, Heb. vi. 16, 17. And among men, ye know, that an oath puts an end to all controversy; and what would ye, or could ye seek more of God than his saying, writing, and swearing? he hath done all this, *that the heirs of promise may have strong consolation, who are fled for refuge to the hope set before them.* O! will ye not trow and credit God, when he swears? Among other aggravations of unbelief, this will be one, that by it ye make God not only a liar, but perjured; a heavy, hainous, and horrid guilt on the score of all unbelievers of this gospel. 4. To take away all controversy, he hath interposed his command, yea, it is the great command, and in a manner, the one command of the gospel, 1 John iii. 23. *This is his commandment, that ye believe on the name of his Son Jesus Christ;* and therefore the offer of the gospel, and promulgation of it, cometh by way of command, Ho, come, believe, &c. whereby the Lord would tell the hearers of the gospel, that it is not left to their own option, or as a thing indifferent to them, to believe, or not to believe; but it is laid on them by the necessity of a command to believe; and if ye think ye may and should pray, sanctify the Sabbath, or obey any other command, because he bids you, there is the same authority enjoining and commanding you to believe, and as great necessity lieth on you to give obedience to this command, as to any other; do not therefore think it humility not to do it, for obedience is better than sacrifice.

For your further encouragement to believe, I would say three words, which ye would also look upon as warrants to believe, and by them know that it is a great sin not to believe. 1. Ye have no less ground or warrant than ever any that went before you had; David, Moses, Paul, &c. had no better warrant; my meaning is, ye have the same covenant, the same word and promises, Christ and his fulness, God and his faithfulness offered to you, the same warrant that God hath given to all his people since ever he had a Church; and do ye not think but it will be a sad and grievous ground of challenge against you, when ye shall see others, that believe on the same grounds that ye have, sit down in the kingdom of heaven, and yourselves, as proud rebels, shut out? Whatever difference there be as to the main work of grace, and of God's Spirit on the heart in the working of faith, yet the ground of faith is the word, that all hear who are in the visible Church; and ye having the same ground and object of faith in your offer, there will be no excuse for you, if ye do not believe. A 2d encouragement is, That the ground of faith is so solid and good, that it never disappoints any one that leans to it; and count the gospel a fecklefs and insignificant thing who will, it shall have this testimony, which damned unbelievers shall carry to hell with them, that *it was the power of God to salvation to them that believed;* and that there was nothing in the gospel itself that did prejudge them of the good of it, but that they prejudged themselves, who did not lippen to it: Therefore the word is called, *Gold tried in the fire;* all the promises having a being from Jehovah himself, one jot or one title of them cannot fail, nor fall to the ground. 3. If ye were to carve out a warrant to yourselves, as I hinted before, what more could ye desire? what miss ye in Christ? what clause can ye desire to be insert in the covenant, that is not in it? It contains pardon of sin, healing of your backslidings, and what not? and he hath said, sealed, and sworn it; and what more can ye require? Therefore we would again exhort you, in the name of Jesus Christ, and in his stead, not to to neglect so great a salvation, O! receive the grace of God, and let it not be in vain.

In the *third* place, Let us speak a word or two to some objections or scruples, which may be moved in reference to what hath been said. And, 1*st*, It may be some will say, that the covenant is not broad enough, because all are not elected, all are not redeemed nor appointed to be the heirs of salvation; upon which ground, temptation will sometimes so far prevail, as to waken up a secret enmity at the gospel: But, 1. How absurd is this reasoning? Is there any that can rationally desire a covenant so broad, as to take in all, as necessarily to be saved by it? there is much greater reason to wonder that any should be saved by it, than there is if all should perish: beside, we are not now speaking to the effects, but to the nature of the gospel; so that, whoever perish, it is not because they were not elected, but because they believed not; and the bargain is not of the less worth, nor the less sure, because some will not believe; and to say, that the covenant is not good enough, because so many perish; it is even as if ye should say, it is not a good bridge, because some will not take it, but adventure to go thorow the water, and so drown themselves. 2. I would ask, Would ye overturn the whole course of God's administration, and of the covenant of his grace? Did he ever *a priori*, or at first hand, tell folks that they were elected? who ever got their election at the very first revealed to them? or, who are now before the throne, that ever made the

keeping

up of this secret from them, a bar or impediment to their believing? God's eternal purpose or decree is not the rule of our duty, nor the warrant of our faith, but his revealed will in his word. Let us seek to come to the knowledge of God's decree of election *a posteriori*, or by the effects, which is a sure way of knowledge; our thwarting with his word, to know his decree, will not excuse, but make us more guilty; *He hath shewed thee, O man*, saith Micah, chap. vi. 8. *what is good; and what doth the Lord require of thee*, &c. And if any will scruple and demur on this ground to close the bargain, let them be aware that they provoke him not to bring upon them their own fears, by continuing them under that scrupling and demurring condition. Ye cannot possibly evite hazard, by looking on only, and not making use of Christ; therefore do not bring on your own ruin by your fear, which may be by grace prevented, and by this way of believing shall be certainly prevented.

But, 2*dly*, Some may object and say, I am indeed convinced that believing is my duty; but that being a thing that I cannot do, why therefore should I set about it? *Ans*. 1. This is a most unreasonable and absurd way of reasoning; for, if it be given way to, what duty should we do? we are not of ourselves able to pray, praise, keep the Lord's day, nor to do any other commanded duty? shall we therefore abstain from all duties? Our ability or fitness for duty, is not the rule of our duty, but God's command; and we are called to put our hand to duty, in the sense of our own insufficiency, acknowledging God's sufficiency; which if we did, we should find it go better with us: and may not the same be expected in the matter of believing, as well as in other duties? 2. None, that ever heard this gospel, shall in the day of judgment have this to object; none shall have it to say, that they would fain have believed, but their meer infirmity, weakness, and inability, did impede them; for, tho' it be our own sin and guilt that we are unable; yet, where the gospel comes, that is not the controversy, but that folks would not come to Christ, would not be gathered, that when he would, they would not; for, where there is a will, to will and to do go together: But it is enmity at the way of believing, security, stupidity, senselesness, and carelesness what become of the immortal soul, that ruins folks: for the soul, that would fain be at Christ, shall be helped to believe: the reason is, because the nature of the covenant of grace, and of the Mediator thereof, is such, that all to whom he gives to will, he gives them also to perform; and his faithfulness is engaged so to do. It must therefore return to one of these two, That either ye will not receive him, or else ye are willing, tho' weak; and if ye be willing. *Faithful is he that hath called you, who also will do it*; but if it halt at your perverseness and wilful refusal of the offer, there is good reason that in God's justice ye should never get good of the gospel: Nay, there is never one, to whom the gospel comes, and who doth not believe, but formally, as it were, he passeth sentence on himself as the word is, Acts xiii. 46. to judge yourselves unworthy of eternal life; which the apostle gathers from this ground, that they did not, neither would accept of Jesus Christ offered to them in the gospel: as the event is that follows on the offer, so will the Lord account of your receiving of it.

Fourthly, As for directions, to help and further you to believe; it is not easy, but very difficult to give them, it being impossible to satisfy the curiosity of nature; neither can any directions be prescribed, that without the special work of God's Spirit can effectuate the thing; the renewing of the will, and the working of faith, being effects and fruits of omnipotent grace: Yet, because something lies upon all the hearers of the gospel as a duty, and it being more suitable and congruous, that in the use of means, than when means are neglected, believing should be attained; and because oftentimes these that desire this question to be answered, to wit, How they may win at believing? are such as have some beginnings of the work of grace and of faith; we shall speak a few words to such as would be at believing and exercising of faith on Jesus Christ: And, 1. Folk had need to be clear in the common fundamental truths of the gospel; they would know what their natural estate is, what their sin and misery is, and they would know the way how to win out of that state: Ignorance often obstructs us in the way of believing, *How shall they believe on him, of whom they have not heard?* Rom. x. 14. when folks believe not, it is as if they had never heard. 2. When ye have attained to the knowledge of the common truths of the gospel, as of your sin and misery, the nature of the covenant, the Mediator and his fulness, &c. labour to fix well the historical faith of them: We are sure that many never come this length, to believe the history of the gospel; and, till that be, they can advance no further; for, as the word is, Heb. xi. 6. *He that cometh to God, must believe that he is, and that he is a rewarder of them that diligently seek him.* I say; these common simple truths of the gospel would well

well be fixed by an historical faith; and yet this would not be rested on, because, tho' they be excellent truths, yet they may be known and historically believed, where saving faith and salvation follow not. 3. Be much in thinking, meditating and pondering of and on these things; let them sink down into your hearts, that the meditation of them may fix the faith of them, and that they may deeply affect us; we would seek to have a morally serious feeling of them, as we have of the common works of the Spirit. But there are many, like the *way-side-hearers*, who, as soon as they hear the word, some devil, like a crow, comes and picks it up; therefore, to prevent this, ye would seek to have the word of God dwelling richly in you; ye would meditate on it, till ye be convinced of your hazard, and get the affections some way stirred, according to the nature of the word ye meditate upon, whether threatnings or promises. The most part are affected with nothing; they know not what it is to tremble at a threatning, or smile, as it were, on a promise, thro' their not dwelling on the thoughts of the word, that it may produce such an effect. 4. When this is done, folks would endeavour a full up-giving with the law of righteousness as to their justification, that if they cannot so positively and stayedly win to rest on Jesus Christ and his righteousness, yet they may lay the weight of their peace with God on no other thing; they would lay it down for a certain conclusion, that by the works of the law they can never be justified, and would come with a stopped mouth before God: Thus tender Christians will find it sometimes easier to give up with the law, than to close with the gospel, as to their distinct apprehension of the thing. 5. When this is done, go (as it were) to the the top of mount Nebo, and take a look of the pleasant land of promises, and of Christ held out in them; and let your soul say, O to have the bargain well closed, to have my heart stirred up to love him, and to rest upon him! O to have faith, and to discern it in its actings! for when the life of faith is so weak that it cannot speak, yet it may breathe; and tho' ye cannot exercise faith as ye would, so as to grip to and catch fast hold of the Object, yet essay seriously to do that far, as to esteem, love, and vehemently desire it; in this respect, the will is said to go before the deed; tho', as to God's begetting of faith, there be a contemporariness of the will and the deed, yet, as to our sense, the will overturns the deed; even as in another sense (tho' it makes well for this purpose) the apostle says, *To will is present with me, but how to perform that which is good I know not;* for we ought to have our will running after Christ, and believing on him, when we cannot attain to the distinct actings of it.

But it may be here objected and said, Is not this presumption? *Answ.* If this were presumption, then all we have said of the warrant of the gospel to believe, is to no purpose; Christ never counted it presumption to desire and endeavour in his own way to believe on him, for attaining of life through him. To desire heaven and peace with God, and to misken Christ and pass by him, were indeed presumption; but it is not so, to desire these through him. 6. When ye have attained to this heart's desire, if ye cannot distinctly to your satisfaction act believing on Christ, ye would firmly resolve to believe, and essay it, and say, This is the way I will and must take, and no other, as David saith, Psal. xvi. 2. *O my soul, thou hast said unto the Lord, Thou art my Lord.* Hence the exercise of faith is called a choosing of God, Deut. xxx. 19. and Josh. xxiv. And seriously, sincerely and firmly to resolve, this is our duty, when we can win to do no more; and it is no little advancement in believing, when such resolution to believe, is deliberately and soberly come under. 7. When this is done, folks would not hold at a resolution; for to resolve, and not to set forward, will be found to be an empty resolution: therefore, having resolved (tho' still looking on the resolution as his gift) we would set about to perform, and believe as we may: and when we cannot go, we would creep; when we cannot speak words of faith, we would let faith breathe; when it can neither speak nor breathe distinctly, we would let it pant: In a word, to be essaying the exercise of faith, and often renewing our essays at it; which if we did, we should come better speed in believing than we do; Thus, tho' ye were walking under a conviction, that ye could do no more at this, than a man whose arm is withered can do to stretch it forth, yet as the man with the withered hand, at Christ's word of command, essayed to stretch it forth, and it went with him; or, as the disciples, when they had toiled long, even all the night, and caught nothing, yet at Christ's word let down the net, and inclosed a multitude of fishes; so, tho' ye have essayed to act faith often, and yet come no speed, yet essaying it again on Christ, calling to it, it may, and will, thro' grace, go with you. 8. When yet ye come not speed as ye would, your short-coming should be bemoaned and complained of to God, laying open to, and before him the heart, who can change it; and ye would have it for a piece of your weight and burden, that your heart comes not so up to, and abides not so by believing: I would think it a good frame of spirit, when the not having of the heart standing so fixed at believing, is an exercise and a burden. 9. When all this is done in some measure, ye would wait on in doing thus, and would continue in this way, looking to him, who is the Author and Finisher of faith, for his influence to make it go with you. To look to him to be helped, is the way to be helped to believe; or to pray to him to better and amend faith, is the way to have it bettered and amended: it's said, Psal. xxxiv. 5. *They looked to him and were lightned, and their faces were not ashamed.* And if it be said, How can one look that sees not? It's true blind folk cannot look, yet they may essay to look; and tho' there be but a glimmering, as the looking makes the faculty of seeing the better and more strong, so the exercise of faith makes faith to increase; this is it that the Psalmist hath, Psal. xxxi. 24. *Be of good courage, and he shall strengthen your heart, all ye that hope in the Lord;* that is, if ye be weak, wait on, and he shall strengthen you; believe, and give not over, tho' to your sense ye come not speed. Beginners that are looking conscientiously to their way, tho' they have but a glimmering weak sight of Christ, and be as the man that at first saw men walking as trees; yet, if they wait on, they may attain to a more distinct seeing, and to a more close and firm gripping of Christ.

We close with this word of advertisement, That as we speak not of these things as being in man's power to be performed, so neither can they be gone about to purpose, but where there is some faith and love; yet, when they are at first looked on, they are some way more within our reach than the distinct exercise of faith, which is a great mystery. The Lord bless his word, and make it useful to you.

SERMON IX.

Isaiah liii. 1. *Who hath believed our report? and to whom is the arm of the Lord revealed?*

IF folks soberly and gravely considered of what concernment it is to make use of the gospel, and what depends upon the profitable or unprofitable hearing of it, how serious would both speakers and hearers be? This same poor, mean and contemptible like way of speaking or preaching, is the ordinary way that God hath chosen to save souls, even by the *foolishness of preaching,* as the apostle hath it, 1 Cor. i. 22. and where ministers have been tender, how near hath it lyen to their hearts, whether people profited or not? They that will read Isaiah, how he resented and complained of it, and how he was weighted with it, will easily be induced to think that he was in earnest, and that it was no little matter that made him thus cry out, *Who hath believed our report?*

We shew that four things were comprehended in the words. 1*st*, That the great errand of ministers is, to bring the glad tidings of Jesus Christ the Saviour to sinners. 2*dly*, That it is the great duty of people to believe and receive the offer of Jesus Christ in the gospel. 3*dly*, That it is the great sin of a people that hear the gospel, not to believe and receive Jesus Christ, when he is offered unto them. The 4*th*, and last thing, which now we are to speak of (having gone thorow the first three) is, That the great and heavy complaint, that a faithful minister of the gospel hath, is, when these good news are not received and welcomed, when they have it to say, *Who hath believed our report?* when it is but here one and there one that closes with Christ.

Considering these words, as they hold out the prophet's resentment and complaint, we shall from them draw four *observations,* which we shall speak shortly to, and reserve the use and application to the close of all.

Observ. 1. The first is, That it is meet for, and the duty of a minister of the gospel, to observe what fruit and success his ministry hath among a people, and whether they believe or not. Isaiah speaks not here at random, but from consideration of the case of the people, and as observing what fruit his ministry had among them: We would not have ministers too curious in this, as to the state of particular persons, neither would we have them selfy or anxious in seeking any ground of boasting to themselves; yet they would seek to be so far distinct and clear anent their spiritual case and condition, as they may know how to speak suitably to it, and how to speak of it to God; that they may say as they have ground for it, that in such a place, among such a people, *a great door and effectual was opened to us,* as the apostle saith, 1 Cor. xvi. 8. and in such another place, and among such a people, *Who hath believed our report?* as here the prophet doth. It's said, Luke x. 17. and Mark vi. 30. The disciples returned, and with joy told Christ all that they had done, and how the devils were subject to them; they made account what success they had in their ministry: So it's necessary that a minister know what success

success he hath among a people, that he may know, 1. How to carry before God in reference to them, what to praise for, what to lament for, and what to pray for. 2. It is necessary, as to the people, that he may carry right to them, for the gaining of strangers to God, and helping forward these who are entered into the way, and that he may know what report to make of them. 3. It is necessary for a minister himself, tho' not simply as to his peace, for that depends on his faithful discharge of his office, yet as to his joy and rejoicing, to know when he labours in vain, and when not, among a people.

We would not then (as a passing word of use) have you to think it curiosity, tho' something be said now and then, and asked at you, that some of you may possibly think impertinent; for it becomes a physician to seek to know the state and condition of these whom he hath under his hand and cure; and ye would not take it ill, tho' after observation, we now and then speak and tell you, what we conceive to be your condition.

Observ. 2. The second observation is, That it is most sad to a tender minister, and will much affect him, to see and observe unbelief and unfruitfulness among the people that he hath preached the gospel to. This must be a certain and clear truth, if we consider what it was that put Isaiah to this, even to cry, *Who hath believed our report?* Tho' a minister should have never so great exercise of gifts, never so much countenance and respect among a people, if he be tender, he will be more grieved and weighted with their unbelief and unfruitfulness, than with stripes and imprisonment; there will be no suffering to this in his esteem, nothing so sad a ground of complaint; this makes the prophet, Mica vii. 1. to cry, Alas and *woe is me, I am as these who have gathered the summer-fruits, as the grape-gleanings after the vintage, there is no cluster to eat, the good man is perished, and there is none upright among men*; and he insists in this complaint. How often was our Lord Jesus, the most excellent and tender preacher that ever preached, put to this complaint? All the affronts and reproaches he met with, grieved him not so much as the unbelief and hardness of heart that were in the people; it's said, Mark ii. 5. that *He looked round about on them with anger, and was grieved for the hardness of their hearts;* and it's said, Mark vi. 6. that *He marvelled, because of their unbelief;* it so affected him, that (Luke xix. 42.) it's said, that *when he came near to the city, he wept over it, saying, O that thou hadst known, in this thy day, the things that belong to thy peace!* There is a fourfold reason of this, that hath a fourfold influence on the sadning of a serious and tender minister of the gospel. 1. Respect to Christ Jesus his master, in whose stead he comes to bespeak and woo souls to Christ. What would an ambassador think of personal respect and honour, if his master were reproached, and his message rejected and despised? And can an honest and faithful ambassador of Christ look on, and his heart not be wounded, to see the gospel fruitless, the Lord's pleasure as it were marred, and the work of gathering in of souls, obstructed in his hand, and his Lord and Master affronted and slighted? 2. The respect that a faithful minister hath to peoples souls, hath influence on this. A tender shepherd will watchfully care for, and wish the sheep well, and be much affected when they are in an evil condition; and where the relation is of a more spiritual nature, and the flock of far, very far greater worth and concernment, what wonder the shepherd be more affected? as Paul bespeaks the Galatians iii. 16. *My little children, of whom I travel again in birth, till Christ be formed in you.* To be travelling and bringing forth but wind, cannot but prick and wound an honest minister of the gospel at the very heart; 2 Cor. xi. 29. Paul saith, *Who is offended, and I burn not?* The very hazard of a soul will be like a fire burning the heart that is tender and zealous of the spiritual good of souls. 3. The respect that a faithful minister hath to the duty in his hand, hath influence on this: for such a one loves to neat his duty, and to go neatly and lively about it; and the unbelief and the unfruitfulness of the people cloggs him in his duty, and makes him drive heavily: hence it is said, Mat. xiii. 58. and Mark vi. 5. that our Lord *could not do many mighty works there*, or among that people, *because of their unbelief.* Unbelief straitens and shuts the door, and makes preaching become a very burden to a faithful minister; therefore the apostle exhorts, Heb. xiii. 17. *Obey them that have the rule over you, and watch for your souls, that they may do it with joy, and not with grief, for that is unprofitable for you,* a necessity lies upon ministers to go about their work; but when the word does no more but buff on them, so to speak, it makes them to cry as this same prophet doth, chap. vi. 11. *How long, O Lord?* And 4thly, This also hath influence on their being so much weighted, even the concern of honest ministers own joy and comfort. It's true, as we hinted before, that neither a faithful minister's peace, nor his reward of grace, doth depend on it simply; *I have spent my strength in vain,* says Isaiah, chap. xlix. 4. *yet my labour is with the Lord, and my reward from my God:* As to that, there

K   is

is no neceffary connection, and it's of grace it is fo; yet, as to a minifter's fatisfaction and joy, there is a connection, as we may fee, Philip. ii. 16. where Paul faith, *That I may joy in the day of Chrift, that I have not run in vain, and laboured in vain;* and from his expoftulation with the Galatians, chap. iv. 9, 10, 11. *I am afraid of you left I have beftowed upon you labour in vain.*

I fhall not profecute the *ufe* of this neither; only fee here, that it is no marvel tho' fometimes we be neceffitate to complain of you, and to expoftulate with you; and confidering the cafe of people generally, if our hearts were fuitably tender, it would even make us burft for grief, to fee fo many fleeping fecurely and fenfelefsly in their fins, and in that pitiful pofture pofting to the pit, if God prevent not.

Obferv. 3. The third obfervation is, *That a minifter may, and fometimes will, be put to it, to make report to God of what fruit his miniftry hath, and fometimes to complain to him of the unbelief and unfruitfulnefs of the people among whom he hath long preached the gofpel.* Ifaiah (fure) is not carried to this complaint out of hatred to the people, neither from any pleafure he hath in it, nor any delight to tell ill tales (to fpeak fo) of them: The Lord needs no information, yet he complains, and that to the Lord, as we fhew from Rom. x. 16. where it is faid, *Lord, who hath believed our report?* So then, prophets and apoftles complain of this; it is Ezekiel's complaint no doubt to God, as it was the Lord's to him, *This people are a rebellious houfe, and they will not hear;* and Ifaiah fpeaks here in his own name, and in name of other minifters of the gofpel, that they may join with him in this complaint; and there is reafon for it, if we confider, 1. The relation that a minifter ftands in to God; he ought to give an account to him, who gives obedience, and who not, and what is done by his embaffage, there being no talent given, but a reckoning how it was employed will be called for. 2. The fubordination that a minifter ftands in to Chrift, wherein it is requifite he be kept, as knowing the work is the Lord's and not his, pleads for this. 3. That a minifter may be kept from carnalnefs and vanity on the one hand, and from difcouragement on the other; he ought to be acquaint with, and to hold up both the fruitfulnefs and unfruitfulnefs of the people to God. 4. It is meet for the good of the people it be fo, not to irritate, but kindly to affect the people, that when he complains to God, they may be convinced that it is to get the evil complained of amended, if fo it may be.

This complaining will, we fear, be the refult of much preaching among you; for either there muft be more faith and fruits, elfe we will have the more complainers, and the more complaints againft you.

Obferv. 4. The fourth obfervation is, *That it is and ought to be a very fad and weighty thing to a minifter, and alfo to a people, when he is put to complain to God of their unbelief amongft whom he is labouring.* It is the laft thing he hath to do, and he can do no more; and it the greateft and higheft of witnefs and ditty againft them, when a minifter hath been preaching long, and obferving the fruit of his miniftry, and is out-wearied with their unfruitfulnefs, and forced to cry, Lord, there are none, or but very few, that *believe the report* that I have brought to them: It is the heavieft and hardeft word that Chrift hath to fay to Jerufalem, Mat. xxiii. 37. and Luke xix. 42. when he complains of their unfruitfulnefs, harder and heavier than all the woes he pronounced againft the Scribes and Pharifees, on other accounts, and at leaft equivalent to them pronounced on the fame account; for the fame wo and wrath follows both, *O*, faith he, *that thou hadft known, in this thy day, the things that belong to thy peace, but now they are hid from thine eyes!* this comes as the laft and faddeft word, holding out the defperatenefs of their condition, when the powerful preaching of the gofpel hath no gracious force, nor faving effect following it, when directions prevail not, when no fort of minifterial gifts do a people good, when it comes to that, Matt. xi. 16. *Whereunto fhall I liken this generation? it is like children fitting in the market-place, crying to their fellows, We have piped to you, and ye have not danced; we have mourned to you, and ye have not lamented:* when both the fweet offers of grace, and the terrible threatnings of the law, come forth to a people, and both are followed for a long time without fruit, then comes out that word, *Whereunto fhall I liken this generation? John came neither eating nor drinking, and ye fay, He hath a devil;* his aufftere way of living and preaching did you no good, ye could not away with it: *The Son of man came eating and drinking,* in a familiar way, *and ye fay, Behold a man, gluttonous, a wine-bibber, a friend of publicans and finners:* they ftumble on both unjuftly; and fo it is ftill even to this day, many ftumble at the meffenger, caft at the meffage, and then followeth the fad complaint.

It is meet that now we fpeak to a word of *ufe;* but we profefs we know not well how to follow it, there is fo much ground to complain, and we are not (alas!) fuitably fenfible of our own unfitnefs to

follow

follow the complaint, which makes us think that it would become another better; but, what shall we say? it is the word of the Lord; and it were needful that both ye and we should forget and take our eyes off men, and remember that it is the Lord God, and some commissioned from him, that we have to do with, that so we may accept of the message. 1. Then we may say, that it is no pleasure to us to be hewing you, and speaking sadly to you (the Lord knows) would to God there were more that needed healing medicines, and that fewer had need of hewing and wounding! But the truth is, carnal security, spiritual pride, hypocrisy, and formality, are so rife, and become so much the plague of this generation, that people believe not their hazard. Neither, 2. Is it our desire or design to speak to all of you indifferently, and without discrimination; for, as the Lord saith, Matt. xi. 19. *Wisdom is justified of her children;* Tho' the generality despise this word, yet we are confident the Lord hath some that he allows not to be grieved; and we shall desire, that such may not wrong themselves, nor mar our freedom in speaking the word of the Lord to others. 3. We shall not desire to speak peremptorily as to the case of particular persons, tho' we will not deny nor conceal our fears and sad apprehensions as to many of you; only what we have to say, ye would know and be assured, that it is not spoken at random by us, but as having some acquaintance with many of your conditions, and we may gather from these what is very probably the condition of others.

And now, as to what we would say to you; some have been preaching this gospel to you, who are flitted and removed to another part of the vineyard, other some are gone to another world, and some are yet continued preaching to you; but, what fruit is brought forth by the ministry of all? If we were put to make a report of you, as we will be put to it, what could we say? We are afraid to speak our apprehensions: O how little is this gospel, as to its fruit and success, upon the growing hand among you! we shall therefore forbear to speak of that which we think hath deep impressions on ourselves concerning you, but we would have you to look thorow matters, how they stand betwixt God and you; and, if we may humbly lay claim to any measure of the judgment of discerning, may we not ask, Where is there a man or woman, amongst most of us, that hath a conversation suitable to this gospel? If we begin at the great folk, that have the things of the world in abundance, it is their work, for most part, not to be religious, but to gather and heap up riches, and to have somewhat of a name, or a piece of credit in the world; this is the farthest that many of such design: And if we come and take a look of the way of the poorer sort, they live as if they were not called to be exercised to godliness: and this is the condition of the generality, to live as if God were not to call them to a reckoning: Ye will say, We are poor ignorant folks, and are not book-learned; but, have ye not souls to be saved? and is there any other way to be saved, than the royal way, wherein believers have walked? But if we should yet look a little further through you, how many are there that have not the very form of godliness, who never studied to be Christians, either in your fellowship with others, nor when alone, or in your families? There are some, (O! that I might not say, many!) who are hearing me, that will not once in the year bow their knee to God in their families! many of you spend your time in tipling, jesting, loose-speaking, which are not convenient; yea I dare say there are many that spend more time in tipling, jesting, idle-speaking, than in the duties of religion either in public or in private. What report shall we make of you? shall we say that such a man spent three or four hours every day in going up and down the streets, or in tipling and sporting, and would not spend half an hour of the day on God and his worship? And further, how many are yet ignorant of the first principles of religion? a fault that is often complained of; and yet we would be ashamed to have it heard of, that such ignorance should be under half a year's preaching of the gospel, that is in this place under many years preaching it, and even amongst these who hold their heads very high, and are above others, who can guide and govern their own affairs, and give others a good counsel in things concerning the world; yet if we come to speak with them of repentance, or of faith in its exercise, of convictions and challenges for sin, of communion with God, of the working of God's Spirit in the regenerate, or of the fruits of the Spirit, they have not a mouth to speak a word of these things; and if they speak any thing, O! but it looks worsh, tasteless, and theiveless like. Put them to discourse of religion, it hath no gust, (to say so) it relishes not, they have no understanding of it, at least, that is experimental: doth this look like folks that have heard and received the gospel? Let me say it, The wisdom of this world, and the knowledge of Christ, are far different things; and if some of you go that length, as to get the questions of the Catechism, which is well done in itself; if we put you but to express them in other words, ye cannot; which says plainly, that ye are not masters of your knowledge. And what shall we say of others? of whom we cannot say but we get respect enough from them, yet how do selfishness and worldly-mindedness abound in them? and how graceless and Christless are they found to be, when put to the trial? We would also say to you, that there is great difference betwixt civility and Christianity; fair fashions will never pass in Christ's account for the suitable fruits of the gospel, and will never hinder us from having a just ground of complaint against you: How many have a form of religion, and want the power of it? who think themselves something, when they are indeed nothing; and their profession is so thin and hollow, to speak so, that their rottenness and hypocrisy may be seen through it. Tho' these things be but general, yet they will comprehend a great many of you that are here in this assembly; and if so, is there not just ground of complaint and expostulation with you, as a people among whom this word hath no suitable fruit? And as for you that live prophanely and hypocritically, what shall we say to you? or how shall we deal with you? We bring the word to you, but ye make no more use of it, than if ye had never heard of it; no more religion sheweth itself in you, than if ye lived among Heathens: shall we say to God, The fruit of the gospel is there? Dare we be answerable to God, or can we be faithful to you, to flatter you over, as if all were well with you? And must not our complaint then rather be this, *Lord, they have not believed our report?* Tho' we be feckless, and tho' there be ground of complaint of us, yet the word is his word, and will take hold of you. I know that folks do not readily digest such doctrine well, and it may be some think that few ministers are better dealt with than we are; but we say, that is not our complaint: we confess, if we look from the beginning of the world to this time, there will be few ministers of the gospel found to have been better dealt with, as to outward and civil things; but alas! should that stop our mouths? Yea rather, ought it not to be the more sad to us, to be dealt with, and live in civil love with men and women, who yet do not receive the gospel, nor deal kindly with our Master? Do not think that we will take external respect to us for the fruit of the gospel: As we have no cause to complain of other things, so let us not be put to complain of this, but receive Christ in your heart; let him and his precious wares have change and go off amongst you; make use of him for wisdom, righteousness, sanctification and redemption; and go not for the fashion about the means that should bring you near him, but be in good earnest: and this would satisfy us much, and prevent complaints. *Lastly*, I would ask you, What will come of it; if we shall go on in preaching, and ye in hearing, and yet continuing still in unbelief? Will there not be an account craved of us? And must we not make a report? And, if ye think we must report, can we report any other way than it is with you? shall we, or dare we say, that such a man was a civil man, and that therefore he will not be reckoned with, tho' he believe not in Christ? No, no, but this must be the report, That such a man, and such a kind of men, tho' Christ was long wooing them, would not embrace him; tho' he invited them to the wedding, yet they would not come; nay, they mocked and spurned at it; they trod the blood of the covenant under foot, and counted God a liar in all his offers; and said by their practice, that they should be happy, tho' they took not this way: Many of you, who would not take it well if we should speak this to you in particular, will find it to be a truth one day. And if ye shall say, What would we be at? The answer is at hand, *Believe in the Lord Jesus Christ, and ye shall be saved:* This is the end of the gospel, and the mean of your happiness; it is the great and the main thing that we call for, which if it be not obtained, the ground of the complaint will continue. And, do you think this any strange, hard, or uncouth thing, that when we bring to you the offer of Christ in the gospel, we bid you receive it, and flee in to him, to hide you from the wrath to come? and yet this is all we seek of you: It is neither your shame nor your skaith that we seek, but that ye may take with your sin, that ye may judge and condemn yourselves, that your mouth may be stopped before God, and that ye may flee to Jesus Christ in earnest, and close with him on his own terms. As therefore ye would prevent the greatly aggravated sin, to wit, sinning against the gospel, and the complaint of the ministers thereof against you, and the terrible vengeance of the Mediator, *Kiss the Son*, cast open the everlasting doors of your hearts, and let the gospel, and Christ, the King of glory, have access: We pray you, stand not in the way of your own happiness, refuse not to do him that much pleasure and satisfaction for all the travel of his soul, as to give him your souls to be saved. Now, God himself keep you from this folly and soul-destroying madness.

SERMON

SERMON X.

Isaiah liii. 1. Who hath believed our report ? and to whom is the arm of the Lord revealed ?

WE have spoken somewhat, these days past, to sundry doctrines, from this part of the verse, and particularly of the sad complaint which Isaiah had in his own name, and in the name of all the ministers of the gospel, that the savoury report concerning Jesus Christ is not received; and that, tho' life and salvation through him be offered to many, yet there are but few, scarce here one, and there one, that do embrace it: This is the sad result, *Lord, who hath believed our report?* Words that, being spoken by such a prophet, and so often mentioned in the New Testament, may and should, as often as we speak, hear, or read them, put both ministers and people to a holy demur, and to look what becomes of all our preaching and hearing, when this was all the fruit, even of Isaiah's preaching, as to the greatest part of his hearers.

Ere we leave this part of the verse, it will not be unmeet that we speak a little to these three, 1. To what may be the causes why, when the gospel is powerfully preached, there are so few believers. 2. How it comes to pass, seeing so few believe, that generally so many think they believe, and so few suspect their own faith. And, 3. To the necessity that lies on the hearers of the gospel, to enquire at, and try themselves concerning their faith, and to have some solid satisfaction in it.

Altho' we mention no particular doctrines now, yet, considering the doctrines we spoke to before, these things will not be unsuitable to them, nor impertinent to you.

For the *First*, The causes why so few believe the gospel: We cleared to you already, that generally the powerful preaching of the gospel hath been with little fruit; so that Isaiah hath this sad complaint, *Lord, who hath believed our report?* and our Lord Jesus hath it also on the matter, Matt. xi. 17. *We have piped to you, and ye have not danced; we have mourned to you, and ye have not lamented;* and in the same express words, John xii. 38. And when it is so with sweet Isaiah in the Old Testament, and with our blessed Lord in the New, that spoke with such power and authority, ye may see there is reason for us to enquire into the causes why it is that so few believe. In speaking to which, 1. We intend not to touch on all the reasons, that may be gathered together, of peoples not profiting under the gospel; but of these that ye have most reason to look to, and that are most obstructive of faith in you. 2. Tho' we might speak of reasons on the side of them that speak to you (for, *who is sufficient for these things?* and we shall not deny but we have culpable accession to your unfruitfulness) yet it were not much to your edifying to insist on these. 3. Neither will we speak to these sovereign causes on God's part, who in his holy justice gives up people to unfruitfulness, when they receive not the truth in love. Neither, 4. Shall we insist on these causes that may arise from the devil, who waits on, wherever the word is preached, to mar the fruit of it, as we may see, Matt. xiii. 19. the evil spirits, like as many crows, when the seed of the word is sown, waiting on to pick it up: and ye would know, that ye never come to hear the word, but there are, as it were, flocks of devils attending you; hence it is, that some are rocked and lulled asleep, some have their minds filled with worldly thoughts, some forget all that they hear ere they go out of doors; thus it is with many hearers of this gospel, their hearts are trod upon, as the way-side, by devils and foul spirits, that never a word takes impression on them. And tho' ye may think such expressions uncouth-like and strange, yet they are sadly true; Satan waited on when Christ preached, and sure he will fear no more to do so at our preaching than he did at his; if he stood at Joshua's right hand to resist him, he will no doubt be at ours: but we say, we will not insist on these. But, 5. We shall speak a little to these causes that are common in you, which ye yourselves might know, if ye would observe them; and we would exhort you to take notice of them, when we tell you of them.

1st, Then we offer, or rather assert this for a cause, the want of serious minding the great concernment of the work of your salvation, and that this preached gospel is the word of the Lord, by which ye must be saved. Alas! tho' ye have immortal souls, and tho' this word be the mean of your salvation, yet there are hundreds of you, that never lay it to heart, that your souls are in hazard, and that this word must be it that ye must live by, and live upon: I appeal to your consciences, if ye think upon this seriously; want of this *consideration* fosters security, breeds laziness, and makes and keeps you careless and carnal. I shall instance the want of it in three respects: 1. Look how ye are affected towards this word, and your own edification by it, before ye come to hear it; how few are hungering and thirsting, or preparing for benefit by it, or preparing to meet with God in it? In effect, ye come not with a design to profit; so that if it were known, it would be wondered at, wherefore ye come to hear the word: As Christ says of some, *They came, not because they saw the miracles, but because they did eat of the loaves and were filled;* so may we say of you, that ye come not to profit by the word, but on some crooked carnal design. 2. Look how ye carry when ye are come: how many sleep a great part of the sermon? So that it is a shame to look on the face of our meetings, when in every corner some are sleeping, whose consciences God will waken ere long, and the timber and stones of the house will bear witness against them. Were you in any other meeting about ordinary business, there would not be such sleeping; but when ye are waking what is your carriage? for ye may be waking, and your heart far away, or fast asleep. How seldom can ye give account of what is said? tho' your bodies be present, your hearts are wandering; ye are like these spoken of, Ezek. xxxiii. 31. *who sat before the prophet as God's people, but their hearts went after after their covetousness:* how often, while ye are sitting here, is your heart away? some in their thoughts running after their trade, some after their merchandize, some after one thing some after another. This is one sad instance of it, that there are many of you who have had preaching forty or fifty years, that can scarce tell one note of it all; and no wonder, for ye were not attentive in the hearing of it. 3. Look how ye carry after the word is heard: What unedifying discourse will ye be engaged in, ere ye be well at the door? how carnally and carelessly do many ruth unto, and go away from hearing of the word! and when ye get a word that meets with your soul's case, do ye go to your knees with it before God, desiring him to breathe on it, and to keep it warm? or do ye meditate upon it? Now, put these three together, your carriage before, in the time, and after your hearing the word, ye will find that there is just cause to say, that the most part that hear this gospel are not serious: what wonder then that it do them no good? In the end of that parable of the sower, Matt. xiii. Mark iv. and Luke viii. it is said by the Lord, *Take heed how ye hear; for whosoever hath, to him shall be given,* &c. if ye improve well your hearing, ye will get more; but so long as ye take no heed how ye hear, ye cannot profit.

A 2d ground or cause is this, That the most part of hearers never come to look on this word as the word of God, they come never almost to have a historical faith of it; it is said, Heb. xi. 6. *He that cometh to God must believe that he is, and that he is a rewarder of them that seek him diligently:* But when folk do not really believe that God is, what wonder they seek him not, that they fear neither judgment nor hell, and that they study not holiness? They say in their hearts, they shall have peace, tho' they walk in the imagination of their own hearts, and that the way to heaven is not so narrow as ministers say it is, that God will not condemn poor christened bodies; this is the language of many hearts, and of some mouths: Need there any evidences of it be given? if ye believed that the way to heaven is so strait, and that holiness is so extensive, could ye possibly with any seriousness reflect on your heart and way, and not be affrighted? But the truth is, this word gets not leave to sink in you as the word of God; therefore, saith our Lord to his disciples, Luke ix. 44. *Let these sayings sink into your ears.* There are these things I fear ye do not believe, and let me not be thought to take on me to judge your consciences, when there are so many *that profess they know God, but in works they deny him,* as it is, Tit. i. 16. when we see such things in your carriage, we know that there is a principle of unbelief whence they spring, 1. There are many of you, that really believe not there is a God, or that he is such as his word reveals him to be, to wit, holy, just, powerful, &c. else ye durst not live at feud with him. *The fool hath said in his heart, There is not a God, they are corrupt,* &c. your practical atheism and prophanity say ye believe not there is a God. 2. Ye never believed the ill of your nature: *Do ye think* (as James bespeaks these he writest o, chap. iv. 5.) *that the scripture saith in vain, The spirit that is in you lusts to envy?* Ye do not think that your heart is deceitful and desperately wicked? Tho' we should preach never so much on this subject, yet ye lay it not to heart, ye take it not to you in particular. 3. We are afraid that many of you believe not a judgment, and your particular and personal coming to it; nay, there are among you, who are like to these *mockers,* spoken of by Peter in his second epistle, chap. iii. 4. who says, *Where is the promise of his coming?* And as there were in Paul's days some that denied the resurrection, 1 Cor. xv. so there are still, who do it on the matter at least; ye have the same corrupt nature: We would think that we had prevailed to some purpose, if ye were brought really to believe, that there is a God, a life to come, and a day of judgment; and if ye did so, ye would be more serious in duty, and would come more hungry and thirsty to the word. 4. The mean and mids of salvation is not believed, to wit, that the way to peace with God, is faith in Jesus Christ, and that there is no way to

heaven,

heaven, but the way of holiness; if all your thoughts were spoken out, it would be found that ye have another mids than faith, and another way than that of holiness: And, to make out this, we need go no further than to your practice; we are sure many of you live in prophanity, and yet we have all a hope of heaven: and what says this, but that ye think not faith and holiness necessary, but that ye may come to heaven another way? and this is an old fault and deceit; it was in Moses his days, for some are brought in (Deut. xxix. 19.) saying, *I shall have peace, tho' I walk in the imagination of my own heart, and add drunkenness to thirst;* tho' I tipple daily at my four-hours, tho' I follow my lusts and pleasures, and take my fouth and fill of the world, we cannot be all saints, &c. *The Lord will not spare that man, but his anger and jealousy shall smoke against him, and all the curses that are written in this book shall ly upon him, and the Lord will blot out his name from under heaven;* and tho' this be not now believed, it shall be found verified. There are many, when they come to judgment, that will know, to their cost, the truth of many things they never believed before, as we find in that rich man, who says to Abraham, *Send some to tell my brethren, that they come not to this place of torment;* it says as much, as that he in his life-time did not believe how terribly tormenting a place hell is, and it is even so still; tho' men and women have immortal souls, yet they go on following their sinful way, and believe not that any evil shall befal them, till God's curse and vengeance overtake them.

A 3d ground or cause is, That folk never think themselves in hazard, nor suffer their hazard to affect them, and therefore they seek not after the remedy; hence the Jews, Scribes and Pharisees, rejected Christ; why? they were righteous persons, whole, and needed not the physician: and thus it is with many of you, ye will take with it that ye are sinners, but not with the gracelesness of your nature; and this makes it, that when life, and reconciliation with God, are offered, we have almost none to accept of it; why so? ye are generally, in your own opinion, good friends with God already; none of you almost think that ye have hatred at God, and so ye carelesly and unconcernedly let the opportunity of making your peace with him slip over, even like these Jews, spoken of John viii. 44, 45. who, when Christ said to them, *Ye have the devil to your father,* answered, *He had a devil, and that they were come of Abraham, and were not born of fornication:* So it is with many of you, ye could never endure to even your selves to hell,

nor take with it, that ye were heirs of wrath, as if ye had been born with other natures than the ordinary race of mankind is: and this keeps so many of you that ye get no good of this gospel, for it seeks sinners to pardon them, and enemies to reconcile them; and, till the feud be once taken with, the friendship will never be sought after, nor will it find merchants; tho', when once the enmity is taken with, the gospel hath many sweet, peaceful, and comfortable words to speak to the man afterwards.

A 4th ground is, The love of money and of the world, which *is the root of all ill.* This is given as a main cause, Matt. xiii. why the word profits not, *The seed is sown among thorns, and the thorns spring up and choke it, the cares of this life and deceitfulness of riches choked the word:* This is not oppression nor stealing, but entanglement with, and addictedness to the things of this present world; folks allowing themselves too much satisfaction in their riches and pelf, counting themselves as if all were well if they have it, and grieved if they want it, as if there were nothing but that to make happy; being wholly taken up about it, and leaving no room for the concerns of their souls, for prayer, and seeking of God, nor for challenges to work on them, they are so wholly taken up with their callings and business: for they lay it for a ground, that they must be rich, and then they give themselves wholly to all things that may contribute to that end; and that chokes and suffocates the word, that it never comes up, that nothing comes to perfection; therefore Christ says, Luke xxi. 34. *Take heed ye be not overcharged with surfeiting and drunkenness, and the cares of this life:* I am afraid that many more among you, who are civil and esteemed virtuous and frugal, shall perish in this pit of worldly-mindedness, than shall perish by drunkenness, gluttony, fornication or the like, and yet there is nothing more frequent in scripture, than words spoken to fear folk from earthly mindedness; *How hard is it* (says Christ) *for a rich man to enter into the kingdom of heaven?* and such a man is he, that is taken up with riches, and places his happiness and contentment in them whether he have more or less of them. We speak not this to foster idleness in any, but to press moderation in the use of lawful things: ye think it enough if we cannot charge you with oppression, stealing, whoring and the like; but this gospel will charge you with the love of money; and if it find the love of the world in you, the love of the Father will not be found in you. Doth not your experience tell you, that it is not an easy matter to be much taken up with the world,

world, and to win at a suitable disposition for the duties of religion, and to be painful in them?

A *fifth* ground is, folks little prizing of the gospel and the benefits that come by it; they look not upon it as their happiness to have communion with God: they who are invited to the marriage of the King's Son, Matt. xxii. will not come and the reason is given, *they made light of it*; the offer of the gospel hath no weight, it relishes not: if a market of fine things at a cheap rate were proclaimed, ye would all run to it; but ye delight not in the word of God, ye prize not the gospel and the precious wares that it exposeth to sale amongst you; and to evidence and make out this, I would ask you these few questions; and, 1. I would ask you, How often, or rather how seldom have you sitten down purposly and thanked God for sending the gospel to you? ye have given thanks for your dinner, but how often have ye given him thanks that ye have the gospel, sabbath days, and week days? 2. How little do many of you wait on the preaching of it? were there a message sent to you but from some ordinary man, let be from a great man, ye would straiten your selves and your business too somewhat, that ye might hear it; and yet it's a wonder to think how some in this place, except on the sabbath, will hardly be seen in the Church from one end of the year to the other. 3. Had ye any evident to draw of house or land, ye would seek to have it drawn very well and sure; but many of you never sought to have the evidents of heaven made sure: Ye know, how interruptions of, and threatnings to remove the preached gospel from you, never troubled you; that business of the Tender gave a proof, that if ye might bruik your ease and the things of the world, ye cared not what became of the gospel and of the liberties of Christ's kingdom among you: nay we may say, the gospel was never less set by, never more reproached, despised, and trod upon, than in the time wherein we live: and who lays it to heart? if it were well tried, there is more pains taken upon feckless particulars in a week, than ye take upon your souls in a year; and (which may be spoken to the shame of some) more time taken up in tipling, drinking and debauching, than in prayer, or any other religious duty ; And is not that an undeniable evidence, that ye make light of the gospel *they made light of it, and went their ways*, &c. saying on the matter, Care for yonder invitation who will, as for us, we have somewhat else to do,

A *sixth* ground or cause, tho' possibly it be not so rife, is a shifting of convictions and challenges, a quenching of any begun exercise in the conscience;

some of you have been made sometimes to tremble as *Felix* did, but ye shifted it, and put it off to another time, and went away to some company or recreation, that so ye might stifle it, and drive it out of your thoughts. is there any of you, but in sickness, or under some other sad cross, or at a communion, ye have had your own convictions, challenges, and frights about your soul's estate and yet ye have smothered, extinguished, and put them out again.

A *seventh* ground or cause (which is as large and comprehensive as any) is folks resting and sitting down, before they have any solid ground to rest upon, taking a counterfeit work for a real one, like these spoken of, Hosea vii. 16. of whom it's said, *they return, but not to the most High*. Some attain to a sort of out-side reformation, and they trow that on that account they are all well enough, and in good terms with God; and when such are called to return, they say as these do, Mal. iii. 7. *wherein shall we return?* they think they are returned, and that their peace is made already; they cannot endure to be bidden believe, or to lay a new foundation, for they think it's laid already: in a word, as *Laodicea* did, *they think themselves rich and increased in goods*, when yet *they are poor, blind, miserable, wretched and naked*, but they knew not, and so are well satisfied with themselves as gracious persons, resting on these and the like grounds; as, 1. It may be they pray, and think something of that. 2. They think they have faith enough, if they have a historical faith. 3. It may be they have had some resolutions, and fits of a sort of tenderness, and these they rest upon. We shall not insist to shew the rottenness of these props, but shall only say, It were in some respect good for many of you, that ye had never had the little pieces of profession ye have; There is a sort of civil, legal, formal, fair fashioned men and women among us, whose conversation and communication relishes to none but themselves; and, speak the word who will, they think that they are without the reach of it: I must say this sad word, that I think many of you have as much believing as keeps you from faith in Christ; that is, ye have as much presumption and security as makes you that ye are never serious with the Lord to amend it, and to bring you indeed to believe; so that it's a greater difficulty, to beat you off from your rotten grounds, than it is to get you right, tho' both require the omnipotent power of God: ye think ye believe always, and ye have no doubts about it, and therefore ye think ye have faith enough to do your turn: Ah! when will ye know that security is no faith, and that there is a great diffe-rence

rence betwixt presumption and solid resting by faith on Christ?

Eighthly, We think that this wrongs many of you, because ye are not among the worst sort, and others esteem well of you; ye think ye are well enough; and this makes us, that as to many of you, we know not whether to be more familiar with, or to stand at a distance from you, because ye are ready to rest on so very slender grounds. It is not the commendation of men, but the commendation of God, that ye should seek mainly after, and yet, if ye think good men esteem well of you, ye apprehend ye are good enough. This was it that made the *foolish virgins* so secure, because the wise took and retained them in their company; and this is the neck-break of many, especially when they look about them, and observe some sin in others which they abstain from; as if it had been enough in Herod, and a sufficient proof of the reality of his religion, *That he heard John gladly, and did many things on the hearing of him.*

A *ninth* ground is (and it is a very poor one) folks sitting down on the means when they have them, as if when they have gotten the gospel they were in no hazard, and could believe when they list. I make no qestion, but where the gospel is powerfully in any measure preached, there are many more secure and fearless than if they had it not; and it is very probable somewhat of this is hinted at, Luke xiii. 26. where some are brought in saying to Christ, *We have eaten and drunken in thy presence, and thou hast taught in our streets;* who when he boasts them away from him at the great day, they will in a manner hardly believe that he is in earnest, and they give this for the reason of it, that they have heard him preach, and they have run out to the fields after him; it were good to fear while ye have the word lest ye miss the fruit of it; compare to this purpose Heb. iii. at the close, with Heb. iv. 1. and we will find this commended to us: *So we see,* saith the apostle, *that they could not enter in because of unbelief; let us therefore fear lest a promise being left us of entering into his rest, any of us should seem to come short of it;* it is much, yea the first step to faith, to get folks made suitably afraid to miss the fruit and blessing of the ordinances while they have them: it is good to be afraid, to come to the church, and not to get good of the preaching, or to go and read a chapter of the Bible, and not to profit by it; always to put a difference, betwixt the ordinance and the blessing of it, and to be afraid in the use of the ordinances to miss the blessing of them.

There may be many other causes, and we would not stint and limit you to these, but sure these are causes why this gospel profits not; we may add these few, 1. There are some that stumble at the messenger, some at the message; some thought Christ a friend of *publicans* and *sinners*, and said he had a devil, and so they said to John Baptist: There are some that can abide neither free nor fair speaking, and they think it is not the word, but the speaker that they offend at; but prejudices against the carriers of the word have never done good, but much ill; and ye would guard against them. 2. Sometimes there is a stumbling at the spiritual truths of the gospel, and a sort of new-fangledness in the hearers of it, that lasts not; John's hearers *rejoiced in his light for a season;* something of it also was in Christ's hearers, but they soon turned the back on him, when he tells them of eating his flesh, and drinking his blood, and of the necessity of it, else they could have no life in them; *This* (say they) *is a hard saying, who can bear it?* If we would consider these things, we might see convincing causes of our little thriving, and they might also (thro' God's blessing) be made use of for directions to thriving; and if we could once bring you to be single and serious in hearing, and spiritually thirsty in making use of every Sermon and Sabbath for edification, we had gained a great point of you.

SERMON XI.

Isaiah liii. 1. *Who hath believed our report? and to whom is the arm of the Lord revealed?*

IF we would soberly consider the frame of the most part of men and women that live under the gospel, it would be hard to know, whether it were more strange that so few should receive the report, and be brought to believe, for all that can be said of Jesus Christ; or whether that among the generality of hearers that do not receive the report, there are so few that will let it light but that they believe: It is wonderful and strange to see unbelief so rife, and it is as strange and wonderful, that among these many unbelievers there are so few that think they want faith.

Ye remember, the last day, we proposed to answer this doubt or question, What can be the reason that, when so few believe, all almost think they believe? and then to speak a word to the last *use* tha that rises from the matter that formerly we have handled on these words. We shew you, and we think the scripture is very clear for it, that among the generality that hear the gospel, they are very rare and thin sown that do believe; and yet, go thorow them all, there will not one among many be found, but will assert, they believe, and they will (to speak so) be crabbed and picqued, to tell them that they want faith, and so the most part of hearers live and die in this delusion; a thing that experience clears, as well as the word of God, and a thing that doleful experience will clear at the great day: therefore some are brought in, saying, Luke xiii. 26. *We have eaten and drunken in thy presence, and thou hast taught in our streets;* to whom Christ will say, *I know you not, depart from me;* which doth import this much, that some will come (as it were) to the very gate of heaven, having no doubt of their faith and interest in God, or of their entry into it, and will therefore in a manner plead with Christ to be in, and who would never once doubt of it, nor put it in question, but they were believers and in friendship with him: Altho' there will be no such debate or dispute after death, or at the day of judgment, yet it says this, that many hearers of the gospel have drunken in this opinion, which goes to death with them, and no preaching will beat them from it, that they are believers, and in good terms with God, till the intimation of the sentence of condemnation do it, and the wrath and curse of God meet them in the face: and O how terrible a disappointment will such meet with in that day! May it not then very reasonably and justly be enquired, what can be the reason and cause, when this is granted so generally to be a truth that there are few believers, that yet it should be as true. that few question or make any doubt of their faith, and how this comes to pass? I shall give you some reasons of it, which if ye would think upon, and suffer to sink down in your hearts, ye would not marvel that so many are in this mistake and delusion; and it would put many of you to have quite other thoughts of your own condition than ye have. We shall only speak to such reasons as are sinful, and culpable upon your part.

The reasons then are these. *First*, The most part never seriously think on the matter, whether they believe or not, or they never put their faith to a trial. If the foolish virgin light her lamp, and never look whether there be oil in it, and take on a fair outward profession of religion, and never look what is within it, or how it is lined, to speak so, what wonder she go up and down with the lamp in her hand, and never know whether there be oil in her vessel or not, since she never considers, not puts the matter to proof and trial? The people are expostulated with (Isa. xliv. from *ver.* 9.) for making of images, that a man should cut down a tree, and with one piece of it should warm himself, with another piece of it should bake his bread, and of a third piece should make a god, and fall down and worship it; and this is given for the ground of it, *v.* 18. 19. *They have not known and understood, and none considereth in his heart:* or as the word is, *seeth to his heart;* they consider not that that cannot be a god; folks would think, that natural reason might easily discover this folly. We are persuaded that some of you will think your faith as great a folly, when there shall be as clear evidences to prove the rottenness of your faith and hope, as there were even to common sense, to prove the image made of a piece tree, not to be God; when it shall be found and declared, that tho' ye were never convinced of sin, nor of your misery and lost condition, were never humbled and touched under the kindly sense of it, never fled to Jesus Christ in earnest, nor never had the exercise of grace, yet out over the want of all these, ye would needs keep up a good opinion of your faith and hope: We say, the reason why ye entertain this conceit and opinion is, because ye never sit down seriously and soberly before God to consider the matter, nor do ye put yourselves to proof and trial. Let me therefore pose your consciences, if ye, who have this opinion, of your faith, durst assert to him, that this faith of yours is the result of your serious examination and trial; is it not rather a guessing or fanciful opinion that ye believe? And do ye think that such a faith as that will abide the trial before God, that never did abide your own trial? It will doutless be a sore beguile, to go off the world with such an opinion of faith, and to have the door shut in your very teeth: Alas! there will be no amending or bettering of your condition after death: the day comes when many of you, if God graciously prevent not, shall curse yourselves that ever ye should have been such fools, as to have trusted to your own hearts, or to have taken up this opinion of your faith without ground: We would therefore seriously recommend to you the putting of your faith more frequently to the trial, and that ye would often read and think on that place, 2 Cor. xiii. 5. *Examine yourselves whether ye be in the faith prove your own selves,* &c. O! do not think that a matter of such concernment should be left lying at conjecture and utter uncertainty; Who loseth, when ye are so palpably accessory to your

own

own ruin, by not endeavouring to put yourselves to so much as a trial? Do not say here for excuse, *We have no more grace than God gives us*; when ye never endeavoured to be so much as at the form of the duty, or to go the length ye might have gone in putting yourselves to trial: The deceit then being desperate and irredeemable, if continued in, do not, for the Lord's sake, after all that is said to you, continue beguiling yourselves.

A *second* reason is, folks settling themselves on unsound evidences and principles of peace, that will not bear them thorow before God; I do not say that they have nothing to say in word for themselves, but that all they have to say will be no ground to prove their faith, or bear it thorow before God that they do believe indeed; it will be found at the best to be but a lie, as it is said of that man, Isa. xliv. 20. *A deceived heart hath turned him aside; he feeds on ashes, he cannot deliver his soul, nor say, Is there not a lie in my right hand?* He may have a seeming reason for his faith, but it is no reason indeed. If many of you were going now to die, what reason have ye to prove your believing by? Some will say, God hath always been good, kind, and gracious to me; I was in many straits and difficulties, and I prayed and got many deliveries: Thus all the ground of thy faith is but temporal favours or deliveries, which is as if Israel should have made their receiving of temporal deliveries, and their acknowledging of them, and having some sort of faith of them, to be ground enough to prove their receiving of Jesus Christ savingly; there is a doleful proof of the unsoundness of this ground, Psal. lxxviii. 34, 35, 36, 37. *When he slew them, then they sought him, and returned and enquired early after God: they remembered that God was their Rock, and the high God their Redeemer*: They looked to God's bygone favours for them, when they were in the wilderness, and at the Red sea, and they believed he could do so still; but *they did flatter him with their mouth, and lied to him with their tongue, for their hearts were not right with him, neither were they stedfast in his covenant*; whereupon he destroyed them, and thro' their unbelief they did not enter into God's rest. It is also said a little before, in that Psalm, v. 32. *For all this they sinned still;* there may be many temporal favours and deliveries, and these acknowledged too, and yet no receiving of Christ, for making our peace with God, for removing the quarrel betwixt him and us, and for making us cease from sin. Consider, if it will be a good ground to plead with God upon, to say to him, Lord, thou must bring me to heaven, because I was in sickness and thou raised me up: I was in this and that strait, and under this and that cross, and thou carried me thorow, and brought me out of it. The Lord will say to such that have no more to say, Ye had so many evidences of my power, and yet ye sinned still; and yet this will be all the pleading and reasoning that will be found with many of you, and the sad reply you will meet with from God.

A *third* reason is, folks giving an external countenance to ordinances, and their formal going about of them: They imagine they have faith, because they keep the church, and are not open contemners and misregarders of ordinances, as some others are, because they pray, read hear, &c. It seems it was something like this, that the persuasion of these, spoken of Luke xiii. 26. is built upon; Lord, (say they) *we have heard thee preach, and have eaten and drunken in thy presence*; it is not simply, that they heard Christ preach, for many heard him preach who stoned him; but that, when others stoned him, they followed him, and were not openly prophane nor professed contemners of him and of his preaching, as these others were; such like words fall sometimes from your mouths. Ye will possibly say, What would we have of you? ye are not prophane, ye wait on preaching, and live like your neighbours, and ye content yourselves with that: Alas! this is a poor, yea, a doleful fruit of ordinances, and of your attendance on them; if there be more security, presumption, and desperate hazarding on the wrath of God, and less taking with the quarrel betwixt him and you on that ground.

A *fourth* reason is, folks hope, even such a hope, that, contrair to the nature of hope, will make the most part of you ashamed. Ye imagine ye believe, because ye hope ye believe; and that ye will get mercy, because ye think ye hope in God's mercy; and ye will not let any thing light to the contrair; nor so much as think that ye may be deceived. The opinion that folk have of obtaining mercy, that is maintained without any ground but their vain hope, is the rifest, most unreasonable, and prejudicial evil that is among the professors of this gospel: hence, if any ground and evidence of their peace be asked for, they will answer, That they believe; if it be again asked, How know ye that ye believe? they answer, We hope and believe it is so, and can give no ground for it. Many are like these spoken of, Isaiah lvii. 10. *Thou hast found the life of thine hand, therefore thou was not grieved;* they have a faith and a hope of their own making, and this keeps them off, that the word of God takes no hold on them. We preach that ye are naturally at feud with God, and offer peace and reconciliation thro' Jesus Christ; but ye are deaf, for ye think your peace is made already; and but very few come, sensible of a quarrel with God, to this word, as to the ministry of reconciliation. This is wondered at (in a manner) by the Lord himself, Micah iii. 11. where we have a people whose way is very unlike the gospel; *The heads judge for a reward, and the priests teach for hire, and the prophets divine for money; yet will they lean upon the Lord, and say, Is not the Lord among us?* none evil can come upon us. It is not for real believing that they are charged, but for their confident asserting their believing, when there was no ground for it: so it is with many; they will say, They hope to escape hell, and to get their sin pardoned, and to win to heaven, and they believe it will be so; when in the mean time there is no ground for it, but clear ground to the contrary.

A *fifth* ground is, folks spiritual and practical ignorance of the righteousness of God, whereof the apostle speaking, Rom. x. 3. saith, *Being ignorant of the righteousness of God, they go about to establish their own,* &c. that which I mean, is folks being ignorant of their natural condition, of the spiritualness of God's law, what it requires, and of the way of faith, and of the command of believing, and the nature of it: It is from the ignorance of these three, to wit, of the mischief that is in them by nature, of the spiritualness of the law, and of the spiritualness of faith, and of the exercise of it, that they sleep on in security, and think they have faith when they have it not: And tho' sometimes they will say their faith is weak, yet they cannot be beaten from it but that they believe; and their faith is up and down, as their security stands or falls. This the apostle makes clear from his own experience, Rom. vii. 9. where before his conversion he says, he was a living man, but after his conversion he begins to think that he is a dead and gone man; the reason is, because, before conversion, he knew not himself, he knew not the law, nor the nature of the covenant of grace, *before the law came* (saith he) *I was alive*; he knew not the spiritual meaning of it, and therefore he thought he observed it, and so thought himself sure of heaven, and had no doubts nor disputings concerning his interest in God; *But* (saith he) *when the commandment came, sin revived, and I died;* I saw myself then to be lost and gone, and in every thing guilty; that which I thought had been humility, I saw it to be pride; that which I took for faith, I found to be presumption and unbelief; and my holiness, I found to be hypocrisy: not that his sin grew more upon his hand, but the sin, that before was vailed, was now discovered, and stared him in the face. This is a sad truth, yet a most real truth: The good believing (as many of you call it) and the faith that ye have, is a surer ground of your strangeness to God, and of your unbelief, than any other thing ye have can be a ground whereupon to conclude, ye have faith, and are good friends with God: ye are yet alive, strangers to God, strangers to yourselves, strangers to the spiritual meaning of the law, and to the exercise of faith. If ye would set yourselves to ponder seriously this one consideration, I think ye might be somewhat convinced of it: do ye not see many that understand more of God than ye do, and that are more tender in their walk than ye are, who yet are lother, more difficulted and afraid to assert their faith and confidence in God than ye are? and they are often brangled and put to question their faith: Will ye then consider what can be the reason that ye have so strong a faith, that ye never doubted, and they are troubled with doubting sometimes, yea often, tho' they pray more, and are more diligent in the use of all the means, and holier in their conversation than ye are, and ye will (it may be) say, Well's them that are like such a person? this is the reason of it, they see their sin, and the spiritualness of the law, and the nature of faith, and are dead to the law; but ye are yet alive in your own conceit. Do ye, or can ye think, that much prayer, reading, meditation, and tenderness in folks walk, will weaken faith, and occasion doubting? or is it not rather like, that faith will be more confirmed by these, than by the neglect of them? How is it then that ye are so strong in your faith, when they find themselves so weak and doubting? or, have ye an infused faith, without the means? or, doth God deal with you in a more indulgent way than he uses to deal with his people? How is it then, that these, of whom ye cannot say but they are more tender than ye are, cannot almost name faith, or assert their confidence in God, without trembling and fear that they presume; and yet ye dare very confidently take a mouthful of it, without any hink or hesitation, and yet live carnally and without fear? Do not many of you wonder what ails some folks, what need they be so much troubled, and why do they stand in need of some to pray for them and with them, and to answer their doubts, and ye (mean while) need no such thing? and all your remedy is, that ye assure yourselves ye believe, and think the questioning of your

security

security is the very undoing of your faith. God help, ye are in a woful taking.

A *sixth* reason is, That folk drink in some carnal principles that have no warrant in the word of God, and accordingly square every thing that comes in their way. 1. They lay it for a ground, that folk should never doubt of God's mercy. We do not say that folk should doubt of God's being most real in his offer of mercy to sinners in the gospel; but from that it will not follow, that never one should doubt of God's love to them, or of their coming to heaven, whether they close with the offer or not, Are there not many whom God curseth? and should not these doubt? A 2d carnal principal is, That there is no such reality in the threatnings of God, as there is in his promises; as if he were utterly averse from executing a threatning, and as if it were a rare thing to him to condemn any: And, is there any thing more opposite to scripture than this principle is? Hath he not said in the same place, to wit, Exod. xxxiv. where he proclaims himself *to be gracious, merciful, long-suffering,* &c. that *he is a God that will not clear the guilty?* And hath not the scripture said, *it is but a remnant that are saved,* but (as it were) here one and there one, and that there are many damned for one that is saved? But know it of a certain, that he will make you one day vomit up these principles, with exquisite torment, when out of your own mouth he will convince you of your mistake and delusion. When folks want many things, they supply all with an honest mind; this supplies your want of knowledge, your want of faith and repentance, and of every thing whereof ye are said to be short: Tho' ye live and should die carnal and unrenewed, yet ye think still ye have an honest mind or heart for all that; and what, I pray, is your honest mind, but a rotten and prophane heart, that vails your hypocrisy with a pretext of honesty? Would ye think that man honest, spoke of Isaiah xliv. 19. who with one part of the tree warmed himself, and with another part made a god, and fell down and prayed to it? and yet, in your sense, he hath an honest mind, for he followed his light, which is but darkness, and the deceit of his heart carrying him away from God, tho' he cannot see it; he discerns not, *because he considers not that there is a lie in his hand, and that a deceived heart hath led him aside.* So it is with you, and if many of you saw, what is latent under that honest mind and heart, there would be nothing that would make you lothe yourselves more. A little time will convince you, that that which ye looked for most good from, was your greatest and most traiterous enemy; *He that trusteth in his own heart is a fool,* faith Solomon, Proverbs xxviii. 26. it supposes that folk are ready to lippen to their heart, and to hearken to the language of it concerning their spiritual estate; but it says also, that they are fools that so do, for it betrays them; and there is no folly comparable to that, whereby a man betrays his own immortal soul; and that he doth, who trusts in his own heart.

A *seventh* reason is, from the deceitfulness of our heart, and the natural corruption that sticks to us: There is naturally in us, pride and self-conceit: we are disposed to think any thing that is our own, tho' it be but a shew, is as good as others reality; to think our own light and knowledge, our own other parts and gifts to be as good as those of any others, whosoever they be. And with pride there is joined self-love; we cannot abide to think evil of ourselves, or to suspect ourselves: Tho' this self-love be indeed self-hatred, and is but love to our corruptions, and makes us, that when we live in hatred of God, to think that we love him; so that we cannot be induced to think that we love him not, for we know that love to God is good, and we love ourselves so well, that we cannot endure to think we want it: hence it is said of some in the last times, 2 Tim. iii. 2, 3. *That they shall be covetous, proud, boasters, blasphemers, disobedient to parents, unthankful, unholy, without natural affection, truce breakers,* &c. *having a form of godliness, and denying the power of it;* and the fountain of all is *self-love, for* (saith he) *men shall be lovers of their own selves.* And as self-love is the fountain of much evil, so it is the fountain of self-deceit, and keeps out any thing that may make men question their own condition; so that if a word come in and say, Thou hast no ground for thy faith; the heart will be ready to answer and say, It cannot be that I am a self-deceiver: and self-love, as a partial judge, will offer to vindicate the man, and so makes him shift the challenge. Now, when all these are put together, you may see how many grounds folk have to go wrong upon; and men having hearts disposing and inclining them to go wrong, and little pains being taken to discover the deceit of them, is it any wonder that they think they believe, when indeed they believe not, and be empty and toom-headed, having little or nothing to rest upon, while they think they are rich and want nothing? These are not fancied and far-fetched things, but obvious, and at hand, and may easily be gathered from your daily practice; in all which, it is our design and scope, to bring you to try your long unquestioned peace: Do not therefore think that it is impossible to be thus persuaded, as many of you are, and yet to be mistaken, (which is another ground of folks deceit; for Laodicea was very confident in *thinking herself to be rich and increased in goods, and to stand in need of nothing ; when she was in the mean time poor, blind, miserable, wretched and naked :* and the Galatians, as we may see, chap. v. 8. had *a persuasion which was not of God.*) As there may be a persuasion of a point of doctrine as being right, which yet is an error; so there may be a persuasion of a man's spiritual state, as being right, and which he will stoutly maintain to be so, while in the mean time that persuasion is not of God that calleth him, but a strong delusion: If all that be faith which ye call faith, then certainly the way to heaven is much broader than the scripture hath chalked it out, and ministers needed not say, *Who believes our report?* for all should thus believe it: It will then, and must then, turn to this, that your persuasion is not of him that calleth you; and if a deceit may ly and lurk under this persuasion of yours, ye have certainly so much the more need to put the business to a trial.

And this is the last *use*, which we cannot now insist on. That seeing so many think they believe, who believe not, and there are but few that believe the report, and indeed rest on Christ for their salvation, as he is offered to them in the gospel; it is of your concernment to endeavour to put yourselves without the reach of this complaint, and to make it sure that ye have believed, and received the report. Is there any thing of concernment, if this be not, even to make your calling and election sure? and that cannot be made sure as to you, till your faith be made sure. If we could prevail thus far with you, we would count it a blessed fruit of this and of many other preachings, even that some of you, who have never questioned your faith, might be engaged first seriously to close with Christ,

and then to put yourselves to the trial, that on distinct grounds ye may be able to say, *I know in whom I have believed, and that he is able to keep that which I have committed to him against that day.* There are many of you that talk of faith, and yet can not only not assert your interest in Christ distinctly, but cannot so much as give any solid grounds of your believing; and should not this, think ye, put you to try it? Is there not a day coming, wherein ye will all be tried, whether your alledged faith was true faith, or but presumptuous; and wherein the conscience, which is now quiet, and which it may be never kept you from an hour's sleep, shall awake and put forth its sting, and shall bite and gnaw; and ye, who shall continue under the power of this delusion, will be put to gnaw your tongues for pain and horror under the gnawings of your conscience? Ye, that never knew all along your life what these things meant, had need to stand the more in awe, and to be afraid when ye come near death. Tho' it be a sad matter, that when we should be preaching, and would fain preach the doctrine of faith, it should by reason of your delusion, be the great part of our work, to be thus digging you out of your presumption, and overturning your carnal and ill-grounded hope; yet we have the greater confidence, and the more peace to speak to, and insist on these truths, because they ly so near to the great design of the gospel, and to your immortal souls salvation: and tho' we were able to preach more plausible and sweet things to you, yet if these doctrines profit you not, these would not. Seeing therefore they are so profitable, we should not weary to speak, and ye should not weary to hear them spoken of: Would to God ye were seriously aiming to be clear and through the matter of believing, and that ye stood in need, and were more capable of more pleasant truths! if so, we might have more comfortable, tho' we will not say more profitable, doctrines to insist upon to you.

SERMON XII.

Isaiah. liii 1. *Who hath believed our report? and to whom is the arm of the Lord revealed?*

WE have spoken at several occasions to this first part of the verse; and, before we leave it, there is one *use*, several times hinted at already, to which there is good ground to speak, it being the design and purpose of these words, to hold forth of what great concernment believing is, and of what great difficulty it is; and so many being, to the ruin of their souls, mistaken about it, there is ground to draw this *use* of exhortation from it, to wit, That then all the hearers of this gospel would be exhorted to advert well to this, that they make faith sure in itself, and that they make it sure to themselves, seeing, as I said, so many are mistaken about it, and beguile themselves. The more pressingly that the gospel calls for faith in Christ, and the more weightily the Lord expostulates

lates with the hearers of the gospel, because of their unbelief, they are doubtless so much the more concerned to receive it in its offer, and also to look well that they content not themselves with guessing at faith, and that they never think that things are well with them, except they can give good proof and warrant that they are so, and that it is saving faith that they have. Seeing there are so many that satisfy themselves as being believers, when yet so few are believers indeed; the sad mistake and disappointment of many, should have so much influence upon us, as to put us to more watchfulness; and to a more narrow trial of our own state and condition, that we may know how it is with us. All that we have spoken to the doctrines of this first part of the verse, may be as so many motives to stir you up to both these; and would to God we could be persuaded to this, as the *use* of so many preachings, once to admit and take it for granted, that it is the truth of God; that there is a necessity, an absolute necessity for us to be really rolled and casten over upon Jesus Christ by faith, for attaining of life through him. Tho' this be a very common *doctrine*, and ye would think a very common *use* of it, yet it is the great thing that God requires in the gospel; and the neglect of it, or not receiving his Son, the very contest and quarrel that God hath with the hearers of it, and the cause of the ruin of so many souls that perish under the gospel; we shall therefore propose to you some considerations, that may stir you up to this; and briefly answer a question, in each of these two branches of the use.

And, *First*, For stirring you up to this receiving of Christ by faith, 1. Consider if there be not a standing quarrel and controversy betwixt God and you for sin; and if there be, as no doubt there is, consider how that controversy is to be removed; is there any other possible way but by faith in Christ? if we were preaching to such as had never sinned, and were never under the hazard of the wrath of God, there might possibly be a difficulty to persuade to a receiving of Christ; but when ye have all this in your conscience, that there is sin, and a curse following sin, and that there is no other way for removing that curse but by Jesus Christ, is there not reason to expect that ye should receive this truth? Will any of you think to stand and abide it out against God? and if not, then there is sure a necessity of believing in Jesus Christ, or of lying under the wrath of God for ever.

2. Consider, that this gospel and word of salvation is preached to you in particular: When we speak of salvation, we do not say, that Christ was once preached to the *Jews*, or that in such a far off nation there is a door opened for salvation in the gospel; but we would turn over the words of the Apostle, Acts xiii. 33. to you, and say to you in his words, *Be it known to you therefore, men and brethren, through this Man* (to wit, Jesus Christ) *is preached to you remission of sins*, &c. and this brings the gospel near you, even to your door; it lays before you the way of access to God by Christ, and puts it so close and home to you, that Christ must either have a refusal, or a welcome from you. The first consideration of your own sinfulness and misery might put you to seek after a Saviour, tho' he were at a great distance; but this other brings him to your heart and mouth: and is it fit (think ye) to neglect such a fair occasion? and will it be wisdom, when salvation follows you, and cries after you, and wisdom lifts up its voice in the streets, saying, *O ye simple ones, how long will ye love foolishness?* &c. to stop your ear, or to turn away from Christ, and to run upon your destruction? Do ye think that this gospel will be silent always, or that your conscience will be deaf and dumb always? There are many nations that have not the gospel so near them: and it's hard to know, but the day may come, when ye would be content to buy an offer of the gospel at a dear rate, and when there shall not be a tryster, nor a days-man to be had between God and you; and these days will then be remembered with horror, which now ye securely slip over.

3. Consider what will come of this, if ye do not believe the gospel. Know ye not that many perish that hear the gospel, and that upon this same very ground, that they did not receive Christ and salvation through him offered to them therein, and whereof they are now deprived? Are there not many this day cursing in hell, under the wrath of God, that they let slip and passed over so many golden opportunites of the gospel without improvement? and know ye not that it will come to the same sad pass with you, if ye do not receive it? Do men live always? Is there not an appointed time for all men upon earth? If, before we have savingly exercised faith on him for making peace with God, we be drawn to a reckoning before his tribunal, what will come of it? and are not our precious opportunities apace and always slipping by? and is not the work of faith by delays still the more difficult? are not our bonds still the more strengthned? and doth not our indisposition still grow the greater? and is it not very ordinary to see those, who have slighted the work of faith in their youth, to live stupid in their old age, and die senseless.

4. Consider

4. Consider what sort of folk they are, of whom the scripture speaks as unbelievers, and whom the word of God holds forth to be eternally secluded from the presence of God for the want of faith. Many think that it is but the grosly prophane, or such as never had so much as the form of religion, and such as others would scunner and lothe to hear them but mentioned; and it is (I say) only such that are accounted unbelievers: but the scripture speaks of some, *that seek to enter in, and shall not be able*; that desire to be in heaven, and take some pains to win in, and yet are never admitted to enter into it; and what is the reason? because they took not the way of believing, for the obtaining of life, and coming to heaven; they took the way of works, they took the way of prayer, of purposes, promises and resolutions to amend and grow better, quite overlooking Christ and the way of believing in him; and so took the way of presumption, and promised themselves peace, when there was no true peace, nor any solid ground for it.

5. Consider (which is of affinity with the former consideration) them that are secluded from the presence of God for the want of faith: They are even men and women, as we are, that lived in the same kingdom and city with us, and prayed in the same company with us that thought themselves as sure of heaven as many of us do, that were guilty of the same or like sins that we are guilty of, that have heard many of the same preachings that we have heard, and yet they perish for want of faith, for not believing in the Son of God. Why then should we think that impossible to us, that is so common and frequent in others? Is not the same nature in us that is in others? and are not our hearts naturally as deceitful and corrupt, as those of others? and so, may not we be beguiled, as well as others? and is it not the same rule that he will walk by in judging of us, that he walked by in judging of others? What can be the reason that folk will read and hear the word, and will promise to themselves heaven, when the same word clears it plainly, that destruction is that which they have to look for from the Lord? It is nothing else, but this confident and proud presumption that many take for faith. Let not your precious opportunities slip away, and beguile not your selves in such a concerning matter as faith is; ye will never get this loss made up afterwards, if ye miss faith here.

Lastly, Consider the great necessity that the Lord hath laid upon all men and women by a peremptory command and charge, to believe in the Son of God: he hath not with greater peremptoriness required prayer, nor dependence upon him, nor any other duty, than he hath required this, 1 *John* iii. 23. *And this is his commandment, that we should believe on the name of his Son Jesus Christ*: yea, it is singled out as his main commandment. If that great inquiry be made, *What shall I do to be saved?* This is the answer, *Believe on Jesus Christ*. Do ye think that our Lord (who hath so marked and signalized this command in so special a manner) will never take account for the slighting of it; or do ye think to satisfy him by your other duties, without minding this? It cannot be; suppose ye should mourn all your life-time, and your life were a pattern to others, yet if ye want this one thing, faith in Christ, ye would be found transgressors, as having neglected the main work.

Now, for the *Question*, ye will say, what is this we are bidding you do, when we bid you believe? *Answer*, when we call you to believe, we call you, 1. To be suitably affected with the sense of your own naughtiness, sinfulness, and hazard; till there be something of this, faith in our Lord Jesus hath no access, nor will ever get welcome; deep apprehensions of the wrath that is coming, and standing in awe at the thoughts of our appearing before him, contribute much to it. I am not preaching desperation to you, as some mutter; but we would press upon you the faith of the word of God, that tells you what we are; and liveliness under that impression; that ye may not be stopped or letted, till ye come to a thorow closure with Christ: the most part of hearers come never this length, and this is the reason why many stumble in the very threshold, and make never progress. 2. We call for, and commend this to you, that ye would study to be through and clear as to the usefulness and excellency of Jesus Christ, as to the efficacy of his death, as to the terms of the covenant of grace, whereby a sinner comes to obtain right to him: to be sensible of sin and hazard, without this, is only the way to make a man desperate and mad; but when this is clear, it makes an open door to the sinner, that he may see whither to run from the wrath to come. I do not only mean that ye would get the Catechism, and be able to answer to all the questions concerning the fundamentals of religion, contained therein, but that ye would also and mainly seek to have the faith of these things in your hearts, and to have faith in God, that ye may be persuaded, that he that was and is God, died for sinners; and that, by the application of his satisfaction, sinners may obtain life; and that there is a sufficient warrant given to a sinner to hazard himself upon him. The first of these

speaks

speaks the necessity of some sense, the second holds out the necessity of a general faith, according to that word, Heb. xi. *He that cometh to God, must believe that he is, and that he is a rewarder of them that diligently seek him.* We must know that there is a warrant to come, and ground to expect acceptance from God upon our coming; or else we will never come to, nor believe in Christ. The 3d thing that we call you to, when we call you to believe, is, that the sinner would actually stretch out that faith, as the soul's hand, for the receiving of Christ, and for the application of him to himself; and would actually cast himself upon the satisfaction of Jesus Christ, for covering that sinfulness that is in him; and would catch hold of, and grip to him, that is an able Saviour, for keeping the sinner from sinking under the weight of sin that he lieth under: This is the exercise and practice of faith, when it flows from the general doctrine of the necessity of believing such things to be truths in themselves; and then it is extended and put forth in practice, that we, who are so certainly and sensibly lost, must needs share of that salvation which we believe to be in Jesus Christ, and so for that, roll ourselves on him: the first piece of sense may be in a reprobate, the second piece of faith, that there is a sufficient salvation in Christ to be gotten by them that believe in him, may be in a devil; but this third, of actual use-making of the satisfaction of Christ, for paying our debt, and rolling ourselves upon him, that is the faith and exercise of it that is particular to a sound believer, and the very thing that constitutes a believer; and it is that which we commend to you, that ye may not stand and please yourselves with looking only upon Christ, but that ye may cast and roll yourselves over upon him, that Christ may get your weight, and that all your burdens and wants may be upon him; which to do, ye must be enabled by the mighty power of grace, whereof in the next part of the verse.

The second branch of the *use*, which follows upon this, is, That we would desire you, not only to follow this way of making your peace with God, but to follow the trying and proving of it to your own satisfaction, that ye may be warrantably confident that it is so. There is a great difference betwixt these, to believe in Christ, and to be clear and certain that we do believe in him; as there is a necessity of the first, without which there cannot be peace with God, so there is a necessity of the second, tho' not simply, as without which there can be no peace with God, yet upon this account, as without which we cannot be so comforted in God;

and seeing there are so many who do not believe, who yet think themselves to be believers; and seeing there is nothing more common among the hearers of the gospel, than to reject Christ offered in it, and to misbelieve, and yet nothing more common than to be confident that they do believe; there is good ground here to exhort you to put your faith to the touch-stone, that ye may know whether ye can abide the trial, and whether ye may confidently assert your own faith upon good ground, and abide by it. We would think, if it were remembered, and seriously considered, how great a scarcity there is of believers, and how rare a thing it is to get any to receive Christ, that folk needed not be much pressed to put their faith to the trial; and when there will not be one among many found, who will pass under the account of a real believer with Jesus Christ, should not the most part suspect themselves. Seeing the most part that hear the gospel are the object of this complaint, *Who hath believed our report?* or very few have believed it: Ye would study to have some well-grounded confidence in this, that ye are not guessing and presuming, and going upon grounds that will fail you at last, but that ye be in a case to say on solid grounds with the apostle, *I know whom I have believed,* &c. There is a faith and hope that will make many ashamed; and certainly in the day of judgment, when Christ shall have to do with these persons, that never once thought to be thrust away from him, they of all men shall be thrust away from him with greatest shame: O! the confusion that will fill and overwhelm them, who had a profession of Christ and yet had never the root of the matter in them, above and beyond many others. Dare many of you, upon the confidence ye have, look death in the face? It is no great matter to be confident in the time of health: but will ye then be able to comfort yourselves in the promises of God? Do not promise to yourselves the things in the covenant, except ye be endeavouring in God's way to be sure ye are believers indeed. Our life depends upon our faith, but our consolation depends much upon our clearness that we have faith, and that we are in Christ; and therefore there is much need to press this upon you: There is no way to rid you of the terrors of God, and to make you comfortably sure of your particular interest in the promises of God, but by making it sure and clear that ye are believers in Christ indeed.

There are three or four sorts of people, to whom we would speak a little here. 1. There are some who think, that if they could do other duties, tho' they should never do this, to wit, to make their calling and election sure, they would be and do well enough: are there not many of you, that never so much as set yourselves to try whether your faith would abide God's trial or not? Ah! Ah! an atheistical indifferency, a slighting of the consolations of God, aboundeth amongst many, so that they think the promises, and the consolations that are to be gotten in the promises, are not so much worth, as to be thereby put to take pains to try and see, whether they belong to them or not; but the day will come, that many of you will curse yourselves for your neglecting and slighting of this. A second sort are these, who, because they were never sure of peace with God themselves, and because they were never sure of their own faith, neither ever concernedly endeavoured to be, they think it is all but fancy that is spoken of assurance of faith, and of peace with God; they think it is but guessing at the best; there is such a sort of persons, who think they may be doing as they dow, and need not trouble themselves with such fancies, or nice things; but if ye ask them, what will come of them at last? they will tell you, They will lippen that to God. Think ye it for nought, that God hath laid so many commands on you to make your calling and election sure? and think ye it for nought, that he hath given so many marks to try it by, and that some of the people of God do holily and humbly glory and boast so much of their communion with God, of their assurance of his love to them, and of their special interest in him? do not all these say, that there is such a thing as this to be had? There is a third sort, that please themselves with meer conjectures about this matter, and the greater their security be, they persuade themselves the more that they have faith: This is as sad as any of the former, when they grant all, that folks should make their calling and election sure, and should endeavour to be sure of their faith, but in the mean time take peace with the devil, and peace with their lusts, for peace with God; and a covenant with hell and death for a real bargain with God: This is as true as this word of God is, that there are many that put by all challenges by this, and never suspect their faith; they hope that all shall be well, and they must always believe; as if that were the whole duty of faith, to keep down all challenges. A fourth sort is, even of the generation of them that have something of God in them, who fear in a manner to make all sure, and think it a piece of humility, and of holy and tender walking, to maintain doubting; even as others think it faith, to maintain presumption: they are always complaining, as if all things were wrong, and nothing right in their case, and so foster and cherish misbelief. There is such a thing as this, that marreth even serious souls in their endeavours to make their calling and election sure; and, as long as this is, they cannot win to the suitable discovery of this excellent grace that God calls them to exercise, even *faith* in the Lord Jesus. Need we make use of motives to press you to this trial of your faith, and to this giving of all diligence to make it sure, who have especially hitherto neglected it? If ye knew any thing of the vexation that unbelief hath with it, and what horror in conscience from the sense of distance from God were, ye would think it a great matter to be clear in this thing; and if it were known and believed, how this delusion and unsickerness of faith destroys the most part of men in the world, even of the visible church, durst men ly in their security as most do, without all endeavours to make it sure on good ground, that they do indeed believe? Durst they ly still under God's curse, if they thought themselves to be really under it, and did not foolishly fancy that it is otherwise with them? Durst men treasure up wrath to themselves if they thought not that the hope they had were good enough? O! but presumption beguiles and destroys many souls; and particularly this same presumption, of folks thinking themselves right when they are wrong, hath destroyed, and doth destroy, and will destroy more members of the visible church, than prophanity, drunkenness, whoredom, theft, desperation, or any other of these gross and much abhorred evils do: This is the thing that locks folk up in their sin, even their presumption, when they say on the matter, *We shall have peace, tho' we walk in the imagination of our own heart.* It is this that makes men, without fear, steal, lie, and commit adultery, &c. that they say, *Is not the Lord among us?* Is not this the thing that keeps many of you, that ye never tremble at the word of God? We have faith in God, (say ye) we lippen and trust in him. Therefore, seeing presumption is so rife, have ye not need to try your faith? If there were so much counterfeit money in the country, that it were a rare thing to get one good and upright piece of money, ye would think yourselves greatly concerned and obliged to try it well, lest ye were cheated with base and counterfeit coin; is there not need then, yea infinitely much more need, for them that would be so wise as not be beguiled about the salvation of their souls, to search and try whether their faith will abide God's trial or not?

Ye

Ye will readily move this *Question*, What then are the characters or evidences of a solid and sicker faith that will abide the trial, by which the pretended faith that is among the men of this generation may be examined and put to just trial?

I shall first name some direct scriptures, holding out some things essentially accompanying faith; and then shall add others, having more condescending characters, for the more particular differencing of this, helping to the decision of this great question.

The first mark, whereby ye may try your faith, is, the ground and rise of it, or that whereby it is begotten and cherished; *Faith comes* (saith the apostle, Rom. x. 10.) *by hearing*; doctrinal faith comes by the preaching of the gospel, and saving faith is wrought instrumentally by the same word of God, it being *the power of God to salvation;* it being this word that is the very ground of our faith. I would ask you, Wherefrom your faith comes, and what hand the word of God hath in it? There are many that have a sort of faith, not only without, but contrary to the word of God, whereby they believe that they will get heaven, while in the mean time the word of God does directly exclude them. Get ye your faith maintained, without ever knowing the necessity of a promise for that effect? Can ye maintain your peace, and not have so much as any foundation in the truth and faithfulness of God to build it upon? Love never that faith which hungers not after the word, that is supposed to be lively without being ever fed by the word, that cannot claim either its rise and original, or its growth from the word? I will not say from this or that word in particular, or at this or at that time read or heard, but from the word of God; the word is the very foundation that faith builds upon: If we look to what either accompanieth or followeth faith, there are some plain scriptures that will make that clear, as Acts xv. 9. *And put no difference between us and them, purifying their hearts by faith;* (there was indeed once a great difference between Jews and Gentiles, but now, when he hath brought both to believe in Christ, the difference is removed) there is an efficacy in it, to circumcise the heart, to purify it, and to banish lusts out of it; for it closes and unites with Christ, and so brings him home to dwell in the heart; and where Christ dwells he commands, and so whatever opposes him is banished. Faith gives Christ welcome, and will give nothing welcome to dwell with him, that is opposite and displeasing to him: Faith improves Christ for the subduing of its lusts, and mortifying its corruptions; whereas before there might be a fair out-side of a profession, and something clean outwardly, and much filthiness and rottenness within; but when faith is exercised on Christ, it purifies from all filthiness of the spirit, as well as of the flesh; it applies the promises for that end, even to get the inside made clean, as well as the outside; yea, its main work is, to have the inside, the heart, purified, that being the fountain of all the pollution that defiles the man, and brings the other necessarily along with it. Never love that faith, that leaves the heart as a swine's sty to lusts, that leaves it swarming with unclean and vain thoughts, or that leaves the heart just as it was before; or that faith, that only cleanseth the outside, and does no more; such a faith, however esteemed by man, will never be accounted for true saving faith before God. I do not, I dare not say, that believers will always discern this heart-purity or cleanness, but this I say, that true faith will set the man a-work to purify the heart, and will be making use of Christ for that end, not only to have the arm of the dominion of sin broken, but to have the soul more and more delivered from the indwelling power of it; and this will be the design that he will sincerely drive, to get the heart purified within, as well as the outward man; inward heart-abominations will be grievous and burdensom to him, as well as scandalous out-breakings.

A second place is, Gal. ii. 20, 21. *I am crucified with Christ, nevertheless I live; yet not I, but Christ liveth in me; and the life,* &c. If ye would know a companion of true faith, here is one, it hath a life of faith with it: There is one life killed, and another life is quickned; the life that is killed, is that whereby the man sometime lived to the law, *I am dead to the law* (says the apostle) a man's good conceit of himself, that once he had, is killed and taken away; he wonders how it came that he thought himself holy, or a believer, or how he could promise to himself heaven, in the condition he was in. There is another life comes in the place of that, and it is a life that is quickned and maintained by, and from nothing in the man himself, but it is wholly from and by Christ: The believer hath his holiness and strength for doing all called-for duties, and his comfort also, from Christ; and he holds withal his very natural life, his present being in the world from Christ; his all is in Christ; his stock of life, strength, and furniture, is not in himself, but he lives by a continual traffick, as it were, on bills of exchange betwixt Christ and him; when he wants, he sends a bill to Christ, and it is answered in every thing that he stands in need of, and that is good for him: He is a dead man, and he is a living man;

and wherever true faith is, there the man is dead, and there the man is living. Do not, I pray, mistake it, by thinking that true faith is but vented, puts forth itself only in reference to this or that particular, or at this or that particular time only; for faith must be exercised, not only at starts, as when we are under challenges for sin, or at prayer, but we must design and endeavour to exercise faith thro' all our life; that is, we must by faith look for every thing, that is useful and needful for us, from Christ, and be always endeavouring to drive on a common trade of living this way; we must be habituating ourselves to seek after peace, strength and consolation, and what else we need, out of the fulness that is in him. This life of faith is, to see the want of all things in ourselves, and yet to have all things, by making use of Christ in all things; contenting and comforting ourselves that there is strength in him, tho' we be weak in ourselves, and that he hath gotten the victory over all his and our enemies, and that we shall at last, through him, be victorious in our own persons; contenting and satisfying ourselves that he hath compleat righteousness, tho' we be bankrupt and have none of our own, and betaking ourselves allenarly to that righteousness for our justification before God; thus, making a life to ourselves in him, he living in us by his Spirit, and we living in him by faith: O sweet and desirable, but mysterious life!

The third place is, Gal. v. 6. *In Christ Jesus, neither circumcision availeth any thing, nor uncircumcision, but faith that worketh by love:* He doth not simply say faith, but *faith that works by love*; for faith is an operative grace, and this is the main vent of it, the thing by which it works, it works by love: faith is the hand of the new creature, whereby every thing is wrought, it having life from Christ; and we may say, that love is in a manner the hand of faith, or rather like the fingers upon the hand of faith, whereby it handleth every thing tenderly, even out of love to God in Christ, and to others for his sake; faith works, and it works by love: that's a sound and good faith, that warms the heart with love to Christ; and the nearer that faith brings the believer to him, it warms the heart with more love to others. And therefore, love to the people of God, is given as an evidence of one that is born of God, 1 John v. 1. because, wherever true faith is, there cannot but be love to the children of God, flowing from love to him that begets them. That faith, that is not affected with God's dishonour out of love to him, and that can endure to look upon the difficulties, sufferings and afflictions of the children of God, without sympathizing and being kindly affected therewith, is not to be taken for a sound faith, but to be suspected for a counterfeit.

The fourth place is, James ii. 14. *Shew me thy faith by thy works,* &c. True faith hath always found holiness with it, in all manner of conversation, in the design and endeavour of the believer; which is, withal, through grace in some measure attained. What avails it for a man to say, that he loves another, when, being naked or destitute, he bids him, Depart in peace, Be warmed, Be filled, and yet in the mean time gives him nothing that he stands in need of? would not such a poor man think himself but mocked? Even so, will not God reckon you to be but mock-believers, or mockers of faith, when ye profess yourselves to be believers in Christ, while in the mean time ye have neither indeed heart-purity, nor holiness in your out-side conversation? that is but such a faith as devils may have, that will never do you good. Ye would believe this for a truth, that there will never a faith pass for faith in God's account, and so there should never a faith pass for faith in your account, but that faith which sets the man a-work to the study of holiness, that faith which works by love, that faith which purifies the heart, and that faith which puts the person, in whom it is, to study to have Christ living in him, and himself living in Christ.

I promised to name a few scriptures, that speak out some more condescending characters of faith. And, 1. I would think it a good token of faith, to have folk feared for missing and falling short of the promises: which may be gathered from Heb. iv. 1. That stout confidence, that thinks it is impossible to miss the promises, is a suspect and dangerous faith not to be loved; it is a much better faith that fears, than that faith that is more stout, except there be a sweet mixture of holy stoutness and fear together. It is said, Heb. xi. 7. that *by faith, Noah, being moved with fear, prepared an ark,* &c. Noah had the faith of God's promise, that he should be kept free from being drowned by the deluge with the rest of the world, and yet he was mourning and trembling in preparing the ark; if there were much faith among you, it would make many of you more holily feared than ye are: Love not that faith the worse, that ye never hear a threatning, but ye tremble at it, and are touched by it in the quick. 2. It is a good token of saving faith, when it hath a discovery and holy suspicion of unbelief waiting on it, so that the person dare not so lippen and trust his own faith, as not to dread unbelief, and

to

to tell Chrift of it; there is a poor man that comes to Chrift, Mark ix. 23, 24. to whom the Lord faith, *If thou canft believe,* or canft thou believe? Yes Lord (says he) *I believe, help thou mine unbelief:* there was fome faith in him, but there was alfo unbelief mixed with it; his unbelief was fo great, that it was almoft like to drown his faith, but he puts it in Chrift's hand, and will neither deny his faith nor his unbelief, but puts the matter fincerely over upon Chrift, to ftrengthen his faith, and to amend and help his unbelief. It is a fufpect faith, that is at the top of perfection at the very firft, and ere ever ye wot: There are fome ferious fouls, that think, becaufe they have fome unbelief, that therefore they have no faith at all; but true faith is fuch a faith, that is by and befide fufpected and feared or feen unbelief; that faith is fureft, where folk fear and fufpect unbelief, and fee it, and when they are weighted with their unbelief, and cry out under it, and make their unbelief an errand to Chrift, it is a token that faith is there. 9. The third character is, that it will have with it a fticking to Chrift, and a fear to prefume in fticking to him: There will be two things ftriving together, an eagernefs to be at him, and a fear they be found prefumptuous in meddling with him, and an holy trembling to think on it; yet notwithftanding it muft and will be adventured upon. The woman fpoken of, Mark v. 28. lays this reckoning with herfelf, *If I can but touch his clothes, I fhall be whole*; and fhe not only believeth this to be truth, but crouds and thrimbles in to be at him; yet *ver.* 33. when fhe comes before Chrift, fhe trembles as if fhe had been taken in a fault, not having dared to come openly to him, *but behind him;* fhe behoved to have a touch of him, but fhe durft not in a manner own and avouch her doing of it, till fhe be unavoidably put to it. It is a fufpect and unfound faith that never trembled at minting to believe; there is reafon to jealous that faith not to be of the right ftamp, that never walked under the impreffion of the great diftance between Chrift and the perfon, the fenfe whereof is the thing that makes the trembling, I fay not defperation, nor any utter diftruft of Chrift's kindnefs, but trembling arifing from the confideration of the great diftance and difproportion that's between him and the perfon; faith holds the finner a going to Chrift, and the fenfe of its own finfulnefs and worthlefnefs keeps him under holy fear, and in the exercife of humility. Paul once thought himfelf a jolly man, (as we may fee, Rom. vii. 9.) but when he was brought to believe in Chrift, he fees that he was a dead and undone man before. I give you thefe three marks of a true faith from that chapter. *1ft,* It difcovers to a man his former finfulnefs, and particularly his former felf-conceit, pride, and prefumption, *I was,* faith Paul, *alive without the law once,* &c. a man living upon the thoughts of his own holinefs, *but when the law came, I died;* he fell quite from thefe high thoughts. A *2d* mark is, a greater reftlefnefs of the body of death, it becoming in fome refpect worfe company, more fretful, and ftruggling more, than ever it did before; *fin revived* faith Paul, tho' he had no more corruption in him than he had before, but it wakened and beftirred itfelf more; I dare fay, that tho' there be not fo much corruption in a believer as there is in a natural man, yet it ftruggleth much more, and is more painful and difquieting to the believer, and breeds him a great deal of more trouble: for fays the apoftle on the matter, When God gracioufly poured light and life into me, fin took that occafion to grow angry, and to be enraged that fuch a neighbour was brought in befide it, it could not endure that; as an unruly and currifh dog barks moft bitterly when an honeft gueft comes to the houfe, fo doth corruption bark and make more noife than it did before, when grace takes place in the foul. There are fome that trow they have the more faith, becaufe they feel no corruption ftir in them; and there are others that think they have no faith at all, becaufe they feel corruption ftruggling more, and growing more troublefome to them; but the ftirring and ftruggling of corruption, if folk be indeed burdened, and affected, and afflicted with it, will rather prove their having of faith than their wanting of it. Love that faith well, that puts and keeps folk bickering (to fay fo) in the fight with the body of death; for though this be not good in itfelf that corruption ftirreth, yet fin is of that finful nature, that it flees always more in their face that look God and heavenwards, than of others that are fleeping fecurely under its dominion. A *third* mark is, when the foul hath never peace in any of its conflicts or combats with corruption, but when it refolves in faith exercifed on Jefus Chrift, as it was with Paul, in that chapter after his converfion: That is a found faith, that not only makes peace at firft by Chrift, but that cannot (to fay fo) fight one fair ftroke in the fpiritual warfare, nor look corruption in the face, nor promife to itfelf an outgate from any affault of the enemy, but by faith in Jefus Chrift; as it was with the apoftle; who, toward the end of that chapter, lamentably cries, *O wretched man that I am, who fhall deliver me from the body of this death?*

yet immediately subjoins faith's triumphing in Christ, *I thank God through Jesus Christ our Lord;* he belike, before his conversion thought he could do well enough all alone, but it is not so now, when he can do nothing without Christ, especially in this sore war with his corruption. That is a sound faith, that makes the sinner to make use of Christ in every thing he is called to, that yokes him (I mean Christ) to work on every occasion, and particularly when it comes as it were to grappling and hand-blows with this formidable enemy the body of death, this monster, whereof when one head is cut off, another starts up in its place.

For a close of this purpose, I beseech and obtest such of you as are strangers to saving faith (who are I fear by far the greatest part) to consider seriously all I have spoken of the nature and native evidences of it, that you may be undeceived of your soul-ruining mistakes about it; and let sincere and sound believers, from all, be more cleared, confirmed, and comforted in their faith.

SERMON XIII.

Isaiah liii. 1. ------ *And to whom is the arm of the Lord revealed?*

THere are many mistakes in the way of religion, wherewith the most part are possessed; and amongst the rest there is one, that generally the hearers of the gospel think it so easy to believe, that there is no difficulty in that by any thing: they think it hard to pray, to keep the sabbath, to be holy; but the most part think there is no difficulty in believing; and yet unbelief is so rife, and faith so rare and difficult, that the prophet Isaiah here, in his own name, and in name of all the ministers of the gospel, cries out, *Who hath believed our report?* he complains that he could get but very few to take the word off his hand: and, because it weighted him to find it so, and because he would fain have it to take impression on his hearers, he doubles expressions to the same purpose, *And to whom is the arm of the Lord revealed?* which in sum is, There is much preaching and many hearers of the gospel, but little believing of it, few in whose heart the work of faith is wrought; it is but here one, and there one, that this gospel hath efficacy upon, for uniting of them to Jesus Christ, and for working a work of saving grace in them; the effectual working of God's grace reaches the hearts of but a few.

For the opening the words, we shall speak a little to these three. 1. To what is meant by the *arm of the Lord.* 2. To what is meant by the *revealing* of the arm of the Lord. 3. To the scope and dependence of these words on the former.

For the *first*, In general know, the *arm* of the Lord is not to be understood *properly*; the Lord being a Spirit, hath no arms, hands, nor feet, as men have: but it is to be understood figuratively, as holding out some property or attribute of God; by the *arm* of the Lord, then, we understand in general the power of God, the arm of man being that whereby he executeth his power, performeth exploits, or doth any work: so the *arm* of the Lord is his power, whereby he produceth his mighty acts; as it is said in the Psalms, cxviii. 15. *The right hand of the Lord hath done valiantly:* xcviii. 1. *His hand and his arm hath gotten him the victory.* And, because the power of God is taken either more generally for that which is exercised in the works of common providence, or more particularly for that which is put forth in the work of saving grace; we take it here in short to be the grace of God exercising its power, in and by the gospel, for the converting of souls, and causing them savingly to believe: so, Rom. i. 16. *I am not ashamed of the gospel of Christ, for it is the power of God to salvation to every one that believes;* not simply as it consists in speaking of good, sweet and seasonable words, but as it cometh backed by the irresistable power of the grace of God, as the word is, 1 Cor. i. 23, 24. *We preach Christ, to the Jews a stumbling block, and to the Greeks foolishness; but unto them who are called, both Jews and Greeks, the power of God and the wisdom of God;* and that it is so to be taken here, the connexion of these words with the former will make it clear; for sure he is not speaking of the power of God in the works of common providence, but of his power in the conversion of souls to Christ, even of that power which works saving faith in the elect.

For the *second*, the *revealing* of the arm of the Lord: By this we do not understand the revealing of it *objectively*, as it is brought to light by the preaching of the gospel; for thus it is revealed to all the hearers of the gospel, it is in this respect not kept hid, but brought forth clearly to them in the word: And therefore, 2*dly*, The revealing of this arm of power of the Lord is to be understood of the *subjective* inward manifesting of it, with efficacy and life, to the heart, by the effectual operation of the Spirit of the Lord; as it is said of the great

Serm. XIII. *Isaiah* liii. Verse 1.

great things prepared for them that love God, 1 Cor. ii. 10. *But God hath revealed them unto us by his Spirit:* it is that which is called, 1 Cor. ii. *the demonstration of the Spirit and of power,* which makes plain and powerful to the spirit of the hearer inwardly that which the word preacheth outwardly to the ear, and yet remain still an hidden mystery; this is the *revealing* of the Lord's arm that is here spoken of, because it is that on which believing dependeth, and of the want whereof the prophet sadly complaineth, even where there was much preaching.

For the *third,* to wit, the scope, dependence and connexion of these words with the former: We conceive they come in, both for confirmation and for explication of the former words 1. For confirmation there are (as hath been said) but few that believe, for there are but few that have this saving and effectual work of God's grace reaching their heart; tho' they have the word preached to them, yet they have not the arm of the power of God's grace manifested to them: and so he confirms his former doctrine concerning the paucity of believers under the preaching of the gospel. *First,* By asserting the fewness of them that are brought to believe, to be converted, and effectually called by the gospel; which comes to pass thro' their own unbelief: And *Secondly,* By asserting their fewness in respect of God's sovereign applying of his grace in the gospel, which is but to few; it is but few that believe, for it is but few that he makes effectual application of his grace to. 2. We say it comes in to clear and explicate the former words whether we take it by way of a reason, or of an answer to an objection: For if it be said, How can it be that *Isaiah, Paul,* yea, and our Lord *Jesus Christ* himself, should preach so powerfully, and yet that so few should believe? He answers, It is not to be marvelled at, in respect of God, as if he were frustrate of his design; no such matter: It is because the power of Jesus Christ is revealed but to few. And we take this the rather to be the meaning of these words, because when Christ is preaching and many take offence and stumble, John vi. 43, 44. he says, *Murmur not among your selves; no man can come unto me, except the Father, which hath sent me, draw him;* there must be an effectual work of the grace of God put forth on the heart, else none will believe on me: so it is said, John xii. 37, 38. *That they believed not on him; that the saying of Isaias might be fulfilled which he spoke, Lord, who hath believed our report, and to whom is the arm of the Lord revealed? therefore they could not believe, because that Isaias said again, He hath blinded their eyes,* &c. He speaketh not so, to apologize for, or to excuse their unbelief, but to shew the connexion that is betwixt these two, the not revealing of the arm of the Lord, and their not believing; even so here the Lord shews the connexion that is betwixt the efficacy of the work of grace, and believing or turning to God, that where the powerful and effectual work of his grace goeth not forth with the preached gospel, there will be then no believing nor conversion, no saving change of the person from nature to grace.

That which we would say from these words, may be drawn to three doctrines, which I shall first propose, and then clear and apply them for use. The first is, *That in the work of conversion, and begetting of saving faith, there is requisite and necessary, beside the preaching of the word, a distinct, inward, peculiar, real, immediate, efficacious, and powerful work of the Spirit of the Lord on the hearts of as many hearers as are converted by this gospel.* 2. *That it is but few of many hearers in whom the Lord thus efficaciously and effectually works by his Spirit, and the power of his grace:* It's but *here* one and there one, a very few who are thus wrought upon and converted. 3. *That there is a necessary and inseparable connexion betwixt this inward and efficacious work of the Spirit, and faith or conversion.* Where this work of grace is not, there cannot be faith; and where it is, faith necessarily must be, otherwise these two could not be commensurable, of equal extent and reciprocal, *Who hath believed our report? and to whom is the arm of the Lord revealed?* He is not, neither can be a believer, to whom it is not revealed; and he is and cannot but be a believer, to whom it is revealed. For the *first,* We say, There is in the work of conversion and begetting of faith, beside the preaching of the gospel, a distinct, inward, peculiar, real, immediate, efficacious and powerful work of the Spirit of the Lord requisite and necessary for conversion and begetting of faith, to convince of sin, and to humble for it, to enlighten the mind in the knowledge of Christ, to renew the will and affections, and to persuade and enable the soul of the sinner to embrace and receive Jesus Christ as he is offered in the gospel. We shall *first* take notice of, and clear, some words in the doctrine; and *then* confirm it. *First,* For clearing of some words in the doctrine, we say, 1. It is a *distinct* work of the Spirit, distinguished and separable from the word, tho' it goes along as he pleaseth with the word, yet it is not as if there were some power infused in to the word, and went always and necessarily along with the

the word, which is the foolish and groundless conceit of some; for albeit it accompany the word, yet it is from a distinct agent working, and a distinct work, and is separable (as I said) from the word, tho' it be wrought on the heart of the same sinner, to whose ear the word is preached. 2. It is an *inward* work of the Spirit; for, beside the outward and external preaching and calling by the word, there is an inward, powerful, effectual work and calling of the Spirit in the conversion of a sinner, which speaks to the heart, as well as the word speaks to the ear: so that this work of the Spirit, that goes along in conversion, is much more than any external perswasion of the preached word can produce. 3. We say it is a peculiar work, to difference it from what is common to the hearers of the gospel, for it's a work that is peculiar to them whom the Lord converts, and is applied to none other, but to those in whom he works faith, and whom he effectually calleth by his grace: It is a peculiar work then, and not common; for if it were common to all the hearers of the gospel, and not peculiar to some; these two could not go together and be commensurable (as we said) *Who hath believed our report? and to whom is the arm of the Lord revealed?* 4. We say, it is a *real* work, as well as powerful; a real work of the Spirit, that is not only able and powerful to produce the effect, and to convert the sinner, but real and powerful in producing and bringing of it about, and to pass, by a real influence of the Spirit, actually renewing the will, infusing and creating the habits of grace, and particularly the very habit of faith amongst others in the soul; which is quite another thing than the supposing and saying that a man hath power to believe and be converted; that there is no more requisite to his conversion, but to perswade him to put forth that power or strength, which he hath, into exercise or practice: it is a real work of the Spirit, and a powerful bringing about of the conversion of the sinner in a physical way, as they say in the schools. 5. We say, it is an *immediate* work of the Spirit on the heart, to difference it from a mediate perswasion or moral suasion (as it is called) as if there were no more requisite in conversion, but God's enlightning of the mind, and by that perswading the will to close with Jesus Christ, without any immediate work of the Spirit on the will itself. In this doctrine, we take in all these, according to the scripture, in opposition to the several errors vented by men of corrupt minds, anent the work of conversion and of saving faith: God's arm and hand must be revealed; the work and power of his efficacious grace must be put forth, for moving and inclining the heart and affections, and for determining the will itself.

We might further clear and confirm all these from that famous instance of Lydia, Acts xvi. 14. where Paul preaching to some women, it is said of her *whose heart the Lord opened, that she attended to the things that were spoken of Paul;* where we find these things differenced, 1. The Lord's powerful work on her heart, from Paul's preaching to her ear; the Lord opened her heart. 2. It is an inward work, for it is on the heart. 3. It is a peculiar work; it is not all who hear Paul preach whose hearts are opened, but it is the heart of one Lydia. 4. It is in the nature of a real work, that makes a real inward change on her. 5. It is an immediate work: for the Lord not only enlightens her judgment, but goes down to the heart, and opens it, and works a change in it immediately. Paul indeed, by his preaching, opens the way of salvation to all that heard him; from which, tho' many go away with their hearts unopened, yet the Lord hath a secret, mysterious, real, inward work on her heart, which is evidenced by the effect; for he not only enlightens her mind, but makes her willingly yield to the call of the gospel, by opening of her heart.

In the *second* place, to speak a little for confirmation of the doctrine, we would consider these four or five grounds or reasons, to shew that there is such a work of the Spirit wherever faith is begotten, and that most intelligibly in them that are at age. It is clear from these places of scripture, where there is an express distinction and difference put betwixt the outward ministry of the word, and this inward, powerful efficacious work of grace on the heart, and wherein the great weight of conversion is laid on this inward work, and not on the outward ministry of the word; as Deut. xxix. 4. where the Lord by Moses tells the people, how many things they had seen and heard, and yet says he, *The Lord hath not given you a heart to perceive, and eyes to see, and ears to hear unto this day:* they had the outward means in plenty, when they wanted in the mean time the inward power; the gift of a spiritual life, and the making them spiritually active to exercise it, was with-holden, and therefore they did not savingly perceive, see nor hear, John vi. 44. *Murmur not among yourselves; no man can come unto me, except the Father which hath sent me draw him: It is written in the prophets, And they shall be all taught of God; every man, therefore, that hath heard and learned of the Father, cometh unto me;* where there is very clearly a distinction put betwixt the outward teaching and the Father's drawing, betwixt

twixt the minister's teaching and God's teaching: it was one thing to be taught outwardly by Christ, as the Prophet of his church, and another thing to be drawn and taught inwardly of the Father; this inward teaching is called *drawing*, to shew that it is not external oratory or eloquence consisting in words, to persuade, that can effect the business, but a powerful draught of the arm of the Lord reaching the heart. There are several other scriptures full and clear to this purpose, as Psal. ciii. 3. and Acts xi. 21. A *second* ground, of kin to the former, is from the many and various expressions that are used in the scriptures for holding forth this work of the Spirit of God in conversion, that point out, not only an hand working, and a work wrought, but an inward powerful way of working and bringing about the work, as Jer. xxxi. 34. *I will put my law in their inward parts, and write it in their hearts.* Ezek. xi. 19. *I will give them one heart, I will put a new spirit within them, and will take away the stony heart out of their flesh.* Ezek. xxxvi. 26, 27. *A new heart will I give unto you, and a new spirit will I put within you,* &c. Jer. xxxii. 40. *I will put my fear in their heart, that they shall not depart from me.* It is called the Father's *drawing*, John vi. 44. as I shew. In the saints prayers, as Psal. li. it is called even as to further degrees of this work, or restoring of lost degrees, *creating of a clean heart, and renewing a right spirit within.* And many more the like expressions there are, which shew not only man's impotency and inability to convert, or savingly to change himself; but also, that to his conversion there is necessary, an inward, real, peculiar, efficacious, powerful work of the spirit of grace. 3. It is clear, and may be confirmed from the power of God, which he puts forth and applies in the begetting of faith, and in working conversion: It is not a mediate work, whereby he only persuades congruously, as some love to speak; but an immediate and efficacious work, whereby with mighty power he works conversion; *It is God* (saith the apostle, Phil. ii. 13.) *that worketh in you both to will and to do of his good pleasure:* and as he not only persuadeth, but effectually worketh; so he not only works on the judgment, to the enlightning of it, but on the will to incline and determine it, by curing it of its crookedness and perverseness, backwardness, obstinacy, and rebellion; and the power whereby he worketh this great work is said, Eph. i. 19. to be *that same mighty power, which he wrought in Christ, when he raised him from the dead: That ye may know,* saith the apostle, *what is the exceeding greatness of his power to us-ward who believe, according to the working of his mighty power, which he wrought in Christ, when he raised him from the dead, and set him at his own right hand,* &c. It is such a power that works faith, and so exercised in the working of faith, as it was in raising of Christ from the dead: Now, could there be use for such a power, if there were no more requisite to conversion but an objective suasion, or a bare proposal of the object, with external persuasion to embrace it, wherein the soul is left to itself to choose or refuse as it pleaseth? certainly, if there were no more, considering our natural enmity at God and his grace, the devil and corruption would have much more influence, and a far greater stroke upon the heart to closing up of the same in unbelief, than any outward persuasion would have as to the opening of the heart, and the begetting of faith; therefore his power is necessarily called for, and the Lord addeth it in converting sinners, else the work would for ever ly behind; and if men be spiritually dead in sins and trespasses, (as all men by nature are) as real a power must be exercised in raising and quickning of them, as there is exercised in raising and quickning of the dead. 4. It may also be cleared from some in whom this power is exercised; as some children, some deaf persons, and others, whom we cannot deny to be reached by the grace of God, and yet there can be no other way how they are reached, but by this effectual, efficacious, and immediate powerful work of the Spirit, they not being capable of reasoning or persuasion by force of argument.

We shall only add two reasons further, to confirm, and some way to clear, why it is that the Lord works, and must work thus distinctly, inwardly, really, powerfully, and immediately, in working faith, and converting of sinners. The first is drawn from the exceeding great deadness, indisposition, averseness, perverseness, impotency, inability, and impossibility that is in us naturally for the exercising of faith in Christ: if men naturally be dead in sins and trespasses, if the mind be blind, if the affections be quite disordered, and if the will be utterly corrupted and perverted: then that which converts, and changes and renews them, must be a real, inward, peculiar, immediate, powerful work of the Spirit of God: there being no inward seed of the grace of God in them to be quickned, that seed must be communicate to them and sown in them, ere they can believe, which can be done by no less nor lower than the power of God's grace: It is not oratory, as I said, nor excellency of speech that

that will do it; it is such a work as begets the man again, and actually renews him. The second is drawn from God's end in the way of giving grace, communicating it to some, and not to others: If God's end, in being gracious to some, and not to others, be to commend his grace solely, and to make them alone in grace's common or debt; then the work of grace in conversion must be peculiar and immediate, and wrought by the power of the Spirit of God, leaving nothing to man's free will to difference himself from another, or on which such an effect should depend; but if we look to Scripture, we will find, that it is God's end in the whole way and conduct of his grace, in election, redemption, calling, justification, &c. to commend his grace solely, and to stop all mouths, and cut off all ground of boasting in the creature, as it is, 1 Cor. iv. 7. *Who makes thee to differ from another? and what hast thou that thou hast not received? now, if thou didst receive it, why dost thou glory, as if thou didst not receive?* This being certain, that if the work of grace in conversion were not a distinct, inward, peculiar, real, immediate work, and did not produce the effect of itself by its own strength, and not by vertue of any thing in man, the man would still be supposed to have had some power for the work in himself, and some way to have differenced himself from another; but the Lord hath designed the contrary, and therefore the work of grace in conversion must be suitable to his design.

Use 1. The first use is for the refutation of several errors, and for the confirmation of a great truth of the gospel which we profess.

It serves, I say, *first,* for the refutation of errors, which in such an auditory we love not to insist on; yet we cannot here, the ground being so clear, and the call so cogent, forbear to say somewhat briefly this way, and the rather that the devil hath taken many ways, and driven many designs to weaken the estimation of God's grace among men, and to exalt proud nature, and that there is here a collection and concatenation of those designs and ways against the truth, which this doctrine holds forth, vented by corrupt men. As, 1. They will have nothing to be necessarily applied for the working of conversion, but the preaching of the word; taking it for granted that all men have universal or common grace, which God by his sovereignty (say they) was obliged to give, else he could not reasonably require faith of them: and upon this comes in the pleaded-for power of free-will, and man's ability to turn himself to God: Others by pleading for this notion of a light within men, become to be patrons of proud and petulant corrupt nature, as if there were need of nothing to beget saving faith but that common grace within, oratory or suasion of mouth from without; and hence they came to maintain the foulest errors, which have not only been condemned by the church of God in all ages, but have even by some Papists been abominated; and many of these same errors are creeping in, even in these times wherein we live, the design whereof is to tempt folk to turn loose, vain, and proud, and to turn the grace of God into wantonness, as if they needed not at all to depend on God and his grace, having a sufficient stock within themselves, on which they can live well enough: And it is not only the errors of Papists, Pelagians, Socinians, Arminians, or errors in the judgment, that we have to do with; but of such as overturn the very foundation of the work of man's salvation, and who, tho' pretending to higher notions do yet go beyond all these: but if it be true, that in the work of conversion, beside the preaching of the word, there is a distinct, real, inward, peculiar, immediate efficacious work of the Spirit, necessary for bringing about such an effect; then there is no common or universal grace, that all the hearers of the gospel have, nor is there any power or ability in man to believe of himself; otherwise there were no necessity of such a work as this, for the converting of a sinner, the prophet need not to cry, *Who hath believed our report? and to whom is the arm of the Lord revealed?* and Christ needed not say, *No man can come unto me except the Father draw him:* for men might come without the drawing, and believe without the revelation of God's arm: But, in opposition to that, we say, and have made it clear, that the work of conversion is brought about by a distinct, peculiar, powerful, real, and immediate work of the Spirit on the heart, whereby he not only enlightens the mind, but renews the will, and rectifies the affections. 2. There is another error that this refutes, which seems to be more subtile; for some will grant a necessary connexion betwixt the effect and the grace of God, who yet say that it is suasion or persuasion (for here we take these for the same) so and so trysted to prevail with some, that brings about the effect or work of conversion in them, and not in others where that persuasion is not so trysted; but this opinion lays not the weight of conversion on the arm of the Lord, but on some circumstances accompanying the word, and leaves still some ground of boasting in the creature. 3. A third error, which this doctrine refutes,

from the judgment without the Spirit's immediate work on it: but seeing the will is the prime seat of man's perverseness while in nature, and the principal part to be renewed; it is a strange thing to say, that in the work of conversion, other faculties and powers of the soul must be renewed, and yet that this which comes nearest to the life of the soul should be neglected, or not stand in need of renovation: but from this text it is clear, that in conversion the arm of the Lord must be revealed, and that there is a powerful work of grace, that not only presents reasons from the word to move the will, but really regenerates and renews the will: Now, what is for the refutation of these errors, serves also to confirm us in the truth of the doctrine opposite to these errors.

2*dly*, It serves to refute something in folks practice, and that is, their little sense of the need of grace. Most part come and hear preachings, as if they had the habit of faith, and as if it were natural to them; and pretend to the exercise of faith, never once suspecting their want of faith, nor thinking that they stand in need of such a work of grace to work it in them, as if it were impossible for them not to believe: hence many think that they have grace enough; and if they pray, it is that they may do well, never minding the corruption of nature that is in them: and indeed it is no wonder that such persons fall readily into error, when their practice says plainly they think they have grace enough already.

The second *doctrine* is, *That this distinct, real, inward, efficacious, powerful work of the grace of God in conversion, is not common to all the hearers of the gospel, but is a rare thing applied but to few*: It is even as rare as faith is. And what we touched on, to evidence the rarity of faith, will serve also to evidence the rarity of this work of grace in conversion; it is on as many as are believers, and are saved, that the work of grace is revealed, and no more, Jer. iii. 14. *I will take one of a city, and two of a family; and bring you to Zion, saith the Lord;* it is two or three in the corner of a parish, or in the end of a town, to speak so, who no more; all being found guilty, he is just in what he doth, in calling or not calling effectually, as he pleaseth. And yet, 2*dly*, The Lord hath thought good to call few of many, for holy and wise ends; as, 1. To hold forth his sovereignty; and that he is free, and will walk freely in the dispensing of his own grace: hence, he not only takes few, but ordinarily these that are the most mean, contemptible, silly, and in a manner foolish, of the multitude of hearers: *It is not many noble, not many wise according to the flesh, not many rich, not many learned*, that he chooseth and converteth; very ordinarily he hides his grace from these: it is but seldom that he calls and takes the stout and valiant man, and the learned scholar; but it is this and that poor mean man, the weaver, the shoemaker, the simple plough-man, &c. whom most ordinarily he calls, when he suffers others to continue in their sin. 2. That he may make all the hearers of the gospel walk in holy fear, and awe of him, he reveals his grace in few; it is not the multitude that believes, but here one and there one, that all that have the offer of grace may fear lest they miss it and receive it in vain, and may be careful to entertain and make right use of the means of grace, and may withal cherish the Spirit in his motions, and not grieve him. O! if ye knew and believed what a rare thing the work of the Spirit of grace is, ye would be feared to quench, extinguish, or put out any of his motions. 3. As to the godly, he does thus, to make them admire, adore, and praise his grace, and the power of it, so much the more.

The *uses* are three. 1. It serves to move all to reverence, adore, and admire the grace of God, and his sovereign way in it. Presume not to debate or dispute with him, because they are few that believe, and few that he hath determined his grace for; it is an evidence of his dread, a proof of his sovereignty, in which he should be silently stooped unto, and reverently adored, and not disputed with: we ought to bound all our reasoning within his good pleasure, who might have taken many, and left few, or taken none, as pleased him; and we should not think strange, nor fret that the gospel is power-all but on few; here is the reason of it, that may quiet us, the Lord hath determined effectually to call but few, and yet he will not want one of his own, *All that the Father hath given to Christ, shall come to him*, tho' none come but as they are *drawn*; a thing that we should be sensible of, but yet calm and quiet our spirits, rather wondering that he hath chosen and calleth some, than fret because he hath past by many.

Use 2. The second use is, to exhort you that are hearers of the gospel, and have not had this distinct and powerful work of grace begetting faith in you, to be persuaded of this truth, that faith and the work of grace is no common thing. The most part, alas! think that they have grace, and that it is not one of many that want it. They will readily say, It is true I cannot believe of myself, but God hath given me the grace. But I would ask you this question, Do ye think that grace is so common a thing, that it comes to you and ye never knew how, or so common that never a body wants it? if not, how cometh it then to pass, that ye think and speak of grace as ye do? We would think it a great length, if many of you could be persuaded of your gracelessness; it is not our part to point particularly at the man and woman, tho' the deeds of many of you say, within your heart, that there is no fear of God before your eyes, and that many of you think ye have grace who never had it: And therefore we would say three or four words to you; 1. Begin and suspect yourselves that matters are not right betwixt God and you: we bid none of you despair, but we bid the most part of you be suspicious of your condition, suspect, nay, be assured, that hypocrisy is not grace, and that your presumption is not faith: for, if but few get grace, then many should suspect themselves; and seeing grace is so rare a thing, do not ye think it common. 2. Neglect no means that may bring you through grace to believe, but be diligent in the use of them all, of the word, prayer, sacraments, meditation, &c. It is by these that the Lord begets grace, and by neglecting of them ye may make yourselves guilty of destroying your own souls. 3. Beware of quenching the Spirit in any of his operations or motions, of smothering or putting out any challenges or convictions; if the conscience be at any time touched, or the affections tickled, go not away, as the temporary believer doth, sitting down there without going any further; fear to strangle the beginnings of the life of grace, for grace may begin at little; and if you quench any motion, conviction or challenge, ye know not if ever ye shall meet with the like again, because when he knocked hard at your heart, ye held him out and kept him at the door; and ye may be in hazard of that terrible charge, Acts vii. 31. *Ye uncircumcised in heart and ears, ye have always resisted the Holy Ghost; as your fathers did, so do ye*. Seeing this work is no't common to all the hearers of the gospel, but peculiar to some, labour to have it made sure to yourselves, by putting it to proof and trial in good earnest.

Use 3. The third use is for you that are believers, (and would to God there were many such) to whom I would speak three or four words. 1. Learn from this to be humble. *What hast thou, man, but what thou hast received? and if thou hast received it, why dost thou boast, as if thou hadst not received?* O! but it is unsuitable to believers, who are free grace's debtors and beggars (whereof none need to think shame) to be proud and forget themselves: Thou hast nothing, believer, to boast of, but that he hath shamed thee with his grace; and shouldst thou be proud of that, as if thou had made thy self thus? Therefore guard watchfully against all puffing-up, self-conceit, and high-mindedness, and study to be humble, and to carry a low sail, else thou mayst break out into some scandalous offence, and may become a shame and reproach to the gospel. We commend humility to you above many things; for we think that in these days, folks pride is like to break their necks; for, when once conceit creeps in, they begin to think they are so far advanced in holiness, that they must not keep company with others, nor join in worship with them; and from that they go to another thing, and from that to a third, that it is hard to tell where they will halt or end; they grow so giddy, that they are scarcely like to leave so much ground as themselves may stand upon. O! think shame of pride; it is a most intolerable thing to be proud of that which God hath given, wherein ye have no more hand, and whereof you can no more boast, than they who never had it. 2. Be thankful, and give God the praise of that ye have gotten: *It becomes the upright to be thankful*: It is no little matter, to have God's power manifested in the working of faith, and conferring grace; the temporal throne and kingdom, and great things in the world, are nothing to this, it is peculiar to the Lord's own, and not common: Many get their fill of the world, who never got, nor will get this; the world is of so little value with the Lord, that (to speak so) he doth not much regard who get it, tho' it be exactly distributed by his providence; but converting and upholding grace is peculiarized to his favourites. Being therefore clear

clear that he hath bestowed grace on you, O how should ye exult in blessing God (as David did) for giving counsel to make choice of such a portion, and for his powerful determining of your heart by his grace to embrace it, for which you have not yourselves to thank, but God! 3. Be compassionate and tender towards others, considering that it is only grace that hath made the difference betwixt you and them, and not any good nature in you, which was not in them, as some foolishly fancy. Be not puft up at the faults and falls of any, but rather mourn for them, as well as for your own; and be the more humble, when ye think of the difference that grace hath made, lest ye fall; and since your standing is by grace, be not high-minded, but fear. Of all persons, it worst becomes you to look lightly on, let be to mock at the falls of others, considering who, and what, hath made the difference. 4. If it be so peculiar a privilege, to be partakers of this powerful and special grace of God that is put forth in the great work of conversion; then sure there is something peculiar called for in your conversation, even that it may in all things be as it becometh the gospel, and answerable to this grace bestowed on you; O what manner of persons ought you to be, in all holy conversation and godliness!

SERMON XIV.

Isaiah. liii 1.------ *And to whom is the arm of the Lord revealed?*

THE way of the grace of God is a very difficult subject to be thought on, or spoken of, suitably, and as it becomes; grace having a sovereign and unsearchable channel of its own, wherein it runs: yet no doubt it is very useful, now and then, to consider it, if we knew how to make use of it aright; yea, even these steps of grace, that are most cross and contrary to carnal reason, may not a little profit, when duly pondered. Thus, when the prophet hath been looking on the scarcity of faith, and on the paucity of true believers, he looks a little farther than on the external preaching of the gospel, even upon the way of God's grace; not out of any curiosity, nor from a fretting humour, because of the unsuccesfulness of his ministry, but that he may thereby get himself stayed and composed, and that he may bring both himself and others, to reverence and adore the holy and sovereign way of God therein: *To whom* (saith he) *is the arm of the Lord revealed?* it is a word like that which Christ had on the like occasion, John vi. 44. *Murmur not among yourselves; no man can come to me, except the Father, who hath sent me, draw him.*

We opened up the meaning of the words the last day; in short they come to this, as if he had said, How few are they that believe the gospel, and who take the word off the hand of his sent ministers? and how few are they, on whom the grace of God, that only can make them believe, does effectually work? the prophet pointing at a higher hand than that of the ministers in the success and fruitfulness of the gospel, and coupling these two together, the preaching of the word, and the power of God's grace, in the working of faith and conversion of sinners.

We proposed these three doctrines to be spoken to from the words. 1. That in the work of conversion and begetting of faith, beside the preaching of the word, there is a powerful, internal, immediate work of the grace of God, exercised within mens hearts, as well as the word that is preached outwardly to the ear. Wherever faith is begotten, these two go together, the word without, and the power of grace within, the one of which is distinct from the other.

2. That this powerful, internal, and immediate work of grace within, is not common to all the hearers of the gospel, but a rare and peculiar thing to some; *To whom is the arm of the Lord revealed?* it is but one, or few of many, to whom it is revealed. To these we have spoken already.

3. The third is (which indeed holds out the scope of all) That there is an inseparable connexion betwixt these two, the begetting of faith in the hearers of the gospel, and the application of this powerful work of the grace of God for working of it; so, that where this powerful work of grace is, there is faith and conversion. The prophet makes them reciprocal and commensurable; Who is the believer? He to whom the arm of the Lord is revealed; and, Who is the unbeliever? He to whom the arm of the Lord is not revealed; These two are so conjoined and knit together, as they are never separated, and so they must stand or fall together.

That we may be the more clear, we shall take up the doctrine in two distinct branches, the first whereof is, That except the powerful work of God's grace concur, the most powerful preaching of the gospel will never beget faith in the hearts of the hearers of it. The second is, That wherever this powerful work of grace goes along with the preaching of the gospel, or wherever the Lord applies his grace with the word preached, there faith is begotten in the heart, and that soul is effectually united to Christ, and savingly changed. The one of these branches serves to shew the necessity of God's grace, from the consideration of our sinfulness and impotency or inability, and of the emptiness and ineffectualness of all outward means in themselves; and so to stop all mens mouths, as being utterly unable to contribute any thing to their own spiritual good or conversion, that being the product of the grace of God. The other branch serves mightily to commend the grace of God, as being the powerful arm of the Lord that brings to believe, that calls and converts such and such persons, according to a prior engagement and transaction betwixt the Father and the Son.

As for the first of these, It will easily be believed among men and women, that have any true sense and feeling of the corruption of their nature, and find daily somewhat of the law of the members warring against the law of the mind; and we are perswaded, if all that ever received faith were brought to depone in this matter, they would bear witness, that there is no mean, that, without the effectual power of the grace of God, can bring a stranger sinner to close with Christ and believe on him; and if all that are now before the throne of God in heaven, were called to speak to this great truth, they would put their seal to it, and say, "Not unto us, but to thy name be the glory of our believing; we had never believed, if it had been left to the power of our own free-will, and if the power of thy grace had not wrought in us the very will, as well as the deed or act of believing." Yet, because this doctrine (as we said) serves to discover the sinfulness and impotency of nature, and how little we are obliged to ourselves in this great work, and to hold forth the absolute necessity of the grace of God, and how much we are obliged to it in the work of faith and conversion, and to hold forth withal the emptiness and ineffectualness of all the outward means without this grace; and because it wants not its own considerable opposition from the enemies of the truth, we shall give you some grounds for confirmation of it. The first whereof is drawn from these express instances of scripture, wherein it is clear, that there hath been much powerful preaching, and by the most eminent preachers, and yet the generality of people have been fruitless under it, and their fruitlesness hath been brought to this very ground, to wit, that the work of God's grace and his out-stretched arm went not along with it. The first instance is, Deut. xxvi. 4. That Moses was a skill'd preacher, who will deny? he being faithful in all the house of God; yet says he, after much and long preaching, and after many signs and wonders wrought, *The Lord hath not given you an heart to perceive, nor eyes to see, nor ears to hear, unto this day;* where he not only puts a difference betwixt the preaching of the word without, and the work of grace within, but shows the necessity of the concurrence of the work of grace, and lays the great weight of the peoples profiting, or not profiting, on the wanting or having of that. A second instance is in the prophet Isaiah: Were there any among all the preachers, before or since, that preached in a more evangelic strain than he did? and yet, when he hath complained of the paucity of believers, saying, *Who hath believed our report?* he fixes and stays on this as the cause, *To whom is the arm of the Lord revealed?* And chap. vi. 9, 10. he gives an account of the said commission he had from the Lord, who said to him, *Go and tell the people, Here ye indeed but understand not; and see ye indeed, but perceive not, make the heart of this people fat,* &c. where there is also a clear distinction made betwixt the inward working of grace, and the outward ministry. A third instance, and one that is beyond all exception, is in our blessed Lord Jesus, *who spake as never man spoke,* and preached with such power and life, that even carnal hearers *wondred at the gracious words which proceeded out of his mouth, for he preached with authority, and not as the Scribes;* and yet, John vi. 44. when they began to murmur at him, what says he? *Murmur not at these things, none can come to me, except the Father draw him,* none can believe, except the powerful grace of God work faith in him; there must be a higher hand than ought ye see or hear, a more powerful work than any external preaching of mine, as a Prophet of my Church, ere a soul can believe on me; and tho' his hearers were not free of the guilt of this their unbelief, but had their own sinful accession unto their continuing in it, yet our Lord looks in on the sovereign way and work of grace, and holds there, telling them that his external ministry will not do the turn, but there must be an inward, powerful, immediate work of grace for the working of faith. We add a fourth instance, and it is of that chosen vessel Paul, who laboured more abundantly than all the rest of the apostles, and yet, when he is preaching, Acts xxviii. 25. *And some believed, and others believed not,* before he dismisses the multitude; he adds this one word, *Well spake the Holy Ghost by Isaiah the prophet unto our fathers, saying, Go unto this people, and say, Hearing ye shall hear, and shall not understand; and seeing ye shall see, and not perceive,* &c. where he expressly

SERM. XIV.   Isaiah liii. Verse 1.   99

presly differenceth his external preaching from God's inward working, and tells, that so long as there was a judicial stroke on the hearts of the people untaken away, no external preaching could do the turn, as to their conversion and bringing of them to believe; which he also does, to guard against any offence that might be taken at the unsuccessfulness of his ministry by any who would be ready to say, What aileth these folk, that they will not receive the gospel? to whom he answers, Isaiah long before told the reason of it, to wit, that there is a plague on their hearts and minds, which God must remove ere they can receive it.

2. To these plain and clear instances, we may add two or three grounds or reasons; As, 1. The exceeding greatness of the work of conversion. O how great and difficult is it! Therefore it is set out by the similitudes and expressions of *raising the dead, creating a new heart*, of *removing the stony heart*, and the like, all tending to set out the necessity of an omnipotent power, or a powerful work of grace, in the begetting of souls to Christ; and if it be so great a work, what can the outward ministry do, if the power of God be not added? or what can the man himself do here? can a man quicken, raise, create, or beget himself? It is true, these comparisons are not to be extended and applied in every respect; yet they hold out, that man, being naturally dead, can no more contribute to his own quickning and raising, and to the begetting of spiritual life in himself, than a dead man can contribute to his own quickning and arising to his natural life; for which cause, the holy Ghost hath made choice of these expressions, even to hold out the exceeding greatness of the work. 2. Consider the condition that men are in when this work is wrought, and we will see they can contribute nothing to it; that they have no apetite for it, except that they are subjects capable to be wrought upon, being as it is Eph. ii. 1. *dead in sins and trespasses*: being as to their souls estate, and to their spiritual condition, like Adam's body, before the Lord breathed in it the breath of life, and made him a living soul; as his body could not move, stir, nor act till then, no more can the natural man stir or act in the ways of God, till a new principle of spiritual life be put in him. To clear it further, we would consider, that the scripture speaks of these three in the natural man; 1. Of an utter inability and deadness as to that which is good, *Dead in sins*, Eph. ii. 1. *We are not sufficient* (saith the apostle, 2 Cor. iii. 5.) *of ourselves as of ourselves, to think any good thing, not so much as a good thought.* 2. The scripture holds him out, not only as unable for good, but perverse and bent to every thing that is evil, Col. i. 21. *Alienated and enemies in our minds by wicked works, the carnal mind being enmity against God,* Rom. viii. 7. It is plainly opposite to any thing that is good, and so to the way of faith. 3. Man's mind is not only naturally perverse and stuffed with enmity, but in an incapacity to be healed while it remaineth such, Rom. viii. 7. *It is not subject to the law of God, neither indeed can be;* and therefore, in the work of conversion, there is not only an amending, but also a renewing of our nature called for; there is more requisite than the rectifying of something in the man, even the creating of new habits, and the infusing of the principles of spiritual life and motion into the soul. It is true, in some sense, the whole image of God is not absolutely removed, the faculties of the rational soul still remain; for man hath an understanding and a will, and some sort of reason, but without any tendency to spiritual life, or to any action for God; he hath an understanding, but it is wholly darkned; he hath a will, but wholly perverse, and not in the least inclined to good; he hath affections, but wholly disordered and corrupted, and set wholly upon wrong objects: so that it is with man's soul as to good, as it is with spoiled wine; wine, when wholsom, serves to cheer, and refresh: but when it is spoiled, it is quite another thing, not only not conducing to health, but it is noisome and hurtful: It is just so, we say, with man's soul; it is by the fall quite spoiled and corrupted: it is not indeed annihilated, or made to be nothing, for it retains the same faculties still, it hath (to speak so) the same *quantity* still; but as to its *qualities*, it is utterly corrupted and carried quite contrary to God; *It is not subject to the law of God, neither indeed can be:* and renovation by grace, is the taking away of the corrupt qualities, in part in this life, and wholly in the other life; and the bringing in of new qualities, for recovering the beauty of that image of God which man hath lost. 4. Consider the end that God hath in the administration of his grace, and the glory that he will needs have it getting in every gracious work, and more especially in the work of conversion; and the silence, as to any boasting, that he will have all put unto, that shall partake of it: his end, in the administration of his grace, is to bring down pride, to stop all mouths, and to remove all grounds of boasting from the creature, that he only may have the glory of conversion; that whenever that question is proposed, *What hast thou, O man, but what thou hast received? and if thou hast received it,*

why

why dost thou boast? who hath made thee to differ from another? The soul may answer, It was not external preaching, nor my own free-will, nor any thing in me, but the power of God's grace: I have nothing but what I have received: It is on this ground that the apostle, Phil. ii. 12, 13. presseth and encourageth Christians to their great work; *Work out* (faith he) *your own salvation in fear and trembling, for it is God that worketh in you both to will and to do of his good pleasure*: the Lord leaveth not to man the working of the will in himself; *And of him,* saith the same apostle, 1 Cor. i. 30, 31. *are ye in Christ Jesus, who is made of God unto us, wisdom, righteousness, sanctification and redemption, that he that glorieth should glory in the Lord,* as he said before, verse 29. *that no flesh should glory in his presence*: There is one ground of boasting, that the Lord will have removed in a sinner's justification, and obtaining the pardon of sin, by the imputation of the righteousness of Christ; but there is another ground or matter of boasting, that man might have, if he could reach out the hand to believe, and receive that righteousness, and so put difference betwixt himself and another, which in effectual calling the Lord puts to silence, and quite removes; that man may have it to say, I have not only pardon of sin, but grace to believe, freely bestowed upon me; God made me to differ, and he only; he opened my heart, as he did the heart of Lydia. Thus the Lord will have all the weight of the whole work of our salvation lying on his grace, that the mouths of all may be stopped, and that his grace may shine gloriously; that we may have it to say with the Psalmist, Psal. lvii. 2. *It is the Lord that performs all things for me*; and with Paul, 1 Tim. i. 13, 14. *I obtained mercy, and the grace of God was exceeding abundant towards me.*

The *Uses* are these. 1. It writes to us, in great and legible letters, the great emptiness and sinfulness of all flesh, who not only do not good, but have sinned themselves out of a capacity to do good; all men and women have brought themselves thus lamentably low by sin, that now, if heaven were to be had by a wish sincerely and singly brought forth, yet it is not in their power to perform that condition; and tho' it now stands upon the stretching forth of the hand of faith to receive Jesus Christ, yet of themselves they cannot even do this. How ought then sinners to be deeply humbled, who have brought themselves to this woful pass? I am afraid that many of you do not believe that ye are such as cannot believe, nor do any good, till his grace work effectually in you.

2. It teacheth you not to idolize any instrument or mean of grace, how precious and promising soever: No preaching, if it were of a prophet, or an apostle, yea of an angel, will do the turn, without grace come with it; there is a necessity of the revelation of God's arm, and of the assistance of his grace, not only to your conversion, but every duty ye go about: Ye should therefore fear and tremble, when ye go about any ordinance, lest the arm of the Lord be not put forth in it.

3. It should make you more serious in dealing with God for his effectual blessing to every mean and ordinance, seeing without that no ordinance can profit you.

4. It serves to reprove and repress pride, and to promote humility in all such who have gotten good by the gospel. Have ye faith, or any measure of holiness? what have ye, but what ye have received? from whence came your faith and your holiness? ye have them not of yourselves; these are not fruits that grow upon the tree of nature, or in its garden; but on the tree, and in the garden of free grace, and ye have not yourselves to thank for them.

5. The main *Use* of it is for confirming and establishing you in the faith of the truth proposed in the doctrine, and for confuting and overturning the contrary error, that, as it were, in contempt of the grace of God, exalts proud nature, and gives man's free-will so great a hand in the work of conversion, that the main thing that makes the difference shall not be attributed to the grace of God, but to the free-will of the creature, which of it self choosed the grace of God offered, when another rejected it. It may indeed seem strange, that the devil should so far have prevailed with Christians, that profess the faith of original sin, and of the necessity of a Saviour, as to make them look at grace as useless in this prime step of conversion and renewing of a sinner, that when the grace of God and man's free-will come to be compared, man's will should have the preference and preheminence, the highest place and commendation in the work, and that the great weight of it should ly there, and that proud nature should be thus bolstered up, that it shall stand in need of nothing for the man's conversion, but the right use making of what it hath in it self: and yet it's no wonder that the devil drive this design vigorously; for what shorter cut can there be taken by him to ruin souls, than to make them drink in this error that nature and free-will will do their turn, and so take them off from all dependence on free-grace and on Jesus Christ, and give them ground

ground of boasting in themselves? for when it is thus, of necessity they must ruin and perish: this should, sure, make you lothe this error the more; and we are persuaded, that the day is coming, wherein the truth opposite to this error, shall be confirmed on the souls and consciences of all the opposers of it, and wherein the maintaining of this error shall be found a confirmation of man's enmity at God's grace which is not subject to his law, nor indeed can be.

But there are three questions that may be moved here, to which we would speak a word. 1. If the preaching of the gospel cannot beget faith, without the powerful work of God's grace, what is the use of the gospel, or wherefore serves it? 2. If men cannot believe without the work of grace, which the Lord sovereignly dispenseth, why doth he yet find fault and expostulate with men for their not believing? 3. If grace perform all, and men can make no mean effectual, nor do any good without it, what then should men do to come by believing, and this work of his grace?

For the *First*, We shall not say much unto it; only, seeing the Lord hath made choice of the gospel to be the ordinary external mean of grace, and of the begetting of faith, there is no reason to say that it is useless; for tho' it be not the main and only thing that turns the sinner, but the Lord hath reserved it to himself as his own prerogative, to convert and change the heart of a rebel sinner, yet he hath appointed it to be made use of, as he hath appointed baptism and the Lord's supper, for many good and notable ends, uses, and advantages, that are reached and come at by the preaching of it: As, 1. By it the righteousness of God is manifested, that before lay hid; ye may by the preaching of the gospel come to the knowledge of the covenant of redemption, and of the great design that the Lord hath laid down for bringing about the salvation of lost sinners, Rom. i. 17, *Therein is the righteousness of God revealed from faith to faith.* 2. By it the Lord revealeth the duty he calleth for from men, as well as his will concerning their justification and salvation; he lets them know what is wrong, what is right, what displeaseth him, and what pleaseth him. Yea, 3. By the preaching of the gospel, he holdeth out what mens ability is, or rather what is their inability, and by his external calling gives them in it occasion to know their inability in not giving obedience to his call: and this is no small advantage, when by it they have occasion to know the necessity of a Mediator, and to seek after another way of justification than by their own works: for so it

proves a notable mean to humble men, to stop their mouths, and to make them plead guilty before God. 4. It is profitable, as the Lord is pleased to make use of it, to call and gather in so many as he hath ordained to eternal life; for tho' in itself it be not able to convert, having the power of God going along with it, it is the instrument of conversion, and the Lord ordinarily makes use of it to the begetting of faith in them that believe, as it is Rom. x. 17. *Faith comes by hearing, and hearing by the word of God,* preached; and 1 Cor. i. 24. it is called *the power of God to salvation;* and *it hath pleased God, by the foolishness of preaching, to save them that believe;* for tho' God can work without it, yet he hath thought good to make use of it, to inform the judgment, and to stir up the affections of hearers, and so it proves instrumental to the begetting of faith in them. 5. If it do not promote the salvation of all the hearers of it, yet it promotes it in all the elect, and serves to make others the more inexcusable; and in this respect it *triumphs always,* 2 Cor. ii. 15, 16. In some it is *the savour of life unto life,* in others *the savour of death unto death,* leaving them the more inexcusable, and the more obnoxious to wrath by their rejecting of the counsel of God against themselves.

I know this will be excepted against; we come therefore to consider the second question, which is this, How can the call of the gospel make men inexcusable, seeing they cannot without the effectual power of the grace of God believe? as Christ saith, John vi. 44. *No man can come to me,* that is, no man can believe in me, *except the Father who hath sent me draw him;* yea, why doth God find fault with men for their unbelief? For answer, It hath been no new thing for men to start questions and objections against the grace of God, and to be always striving to rub affronts and disgrace upon it: see Rom. ix. 13, 14, &c. where this same objection is started, and answered again and again; for when the apostle hath said, v. 13. *Jacob have I loved, and Esau have I hated;* the objection is moved, *Is there unrighteousness with God then?* Folks readily think that there is a sort of unrighteousness in God, when he takes one, and leaves another; especially considering, that the leaving of the other infers (tho' it be not any culpable cause of) the ruin of the man's soul: He answers *first* with a *God forbid,* as if it were an absurd thing so to assert; and *then* endeavours to answer it from God's sovereignty, as being debtor to none, *I will have mercy on whom I will have mercy;* and *it is not in him that willeth, nor in him that runneth, but in God that shews mercy:*

mercy: In God's administration of grace, he is debtor to no man, nor hath he any rule by which he proceedeth, but his own sovereign will. And if it shall yet be said, if God doth walk by his own sovereign will in giving grace, *Why doth he yet find fault, or condemn? for, who hath resisted his will?* Why is God angry that men will not believe, since none can come to Christ against the will of God? His indignation riseth at this proud and petulant objection, and he answers, *But who art thou, O man, that repliest against God? shall the thing formed say to him that formed it, Why hast thou made me thus? hath not the potter power over the clay, to make, of the same lump, one vessel to honour, and another to dishonour?* By the apostle's doubling of this answer, and his not setting of himself to satisfy carnal reason and curiosity, there is ground given to silence us here: It is the Lord, he is our Potter, and we the clay; it is he in whose hand we are, who can do us no wrong; and this may sufficiently serve to put a stop to all reasoning and disputing against him. Yet we may add a word further, seeing the apostle proceeds to another reason; therefore, 2. Consider whence it is that this inability to believe, or turn to God, doth come: Not from God sure; for, if he had not made man perfect, there might be some ground for the objection; but, seeing *he did make man upright, and he hath sought out many inventions*, who is to be blamed? hath the Lord lost his right to exact his debt, because man hath played the bankrupt, and debauched, and turned dyvour, and unable to pay? doth not this very objecting prove us guilty, and evidence that we have lost that which God gave to us and made us with at the beginning? When God made Adam, he had power to believe, and give God credit as to every word revealed or to be revealed; and that, now after the fall, he and his posterity want that power, they have not this privation from God's creating of them, but from their fall, they by their fall utterly incapacitating themselves for these duties that they owe to God, and for this among the rest. 3. If there were no more but simple inability among them that hear this gospel, they might have some pretext or ground of excuse, tho' it were not any real nor just excuse, as hath been shewed: but it never comes to this, as the only or main cause of their not believing; there is always some maliciousness, perverseness, and pravity in the will: It is not, *I cannot*, but, *I will not*; it is a wilful, and someway deliberate, rejecting of the gospel, that is the ground of folks not believing: And what excuse, I pray, can ye have, who do not believe the gospel, when it shall be found that ye maliciously and deliberately chused to reject it? To make this out, consider but these few things. 1. Mens neglecting of the very outward means, that thro' God's blessing prove instrumental in the begetting of faith, as of hearing, reading, prayer, meditation, self-searching, stirring up themselves to repentance, &c. whereby the Lord ordinarily brings about and furthers the work of faith. 2. Consider the carnal, careless, and lazy manner of mens going about these means and duties, which, to their own conviction, are within the reach of that power which they have: ye might hear oftner and more attentively, ye might pray more frequently and more seriously than ye often do; ye want even much of that moral seriousness in hearing, prayer, reading, &c. that ye have in other things of less concernment; ye will hear a proclamation at the cross with more attention than a preaching of the gospel, ye will hear a threatning from man with more fear than ye will hear a threatning from God's word, ye will be more serious in seeking somewhat from man, than in asking grace from God; the reason is, because your heart is more to the one than the other; Can ye then rationally think that ye are excusable, when believing is not a thing that is in your heart, and that takes you up, but ye go about the means that lead to it unconcernedly, carelesly, and negligently? 3. Consider how often ye do willingly chuse some other thing than Christ, to spend your time, and set your affections upon, laying obstructions and bars in the way of God's grace, setting up idols in the heart, and filling Christ's room before-hand with such things as are inconsistent with his company; and all this is done willingly and deliberately: ye have said in your hearts, as these did, Jer. ii. 25. *We have loved strangers, and after them we will go:* And will ye, or dare ye make that an excuse why ye could not come to Christ, because your hearts were taken up with your lusts and idols? So then, the matter will not hold here, that ye were unable, and had not power to believe; but it will come to this, that your conscience will have it to say, that ye willingly and deliberately chused to ly still in your unbelief, and that ye preferred your idols to Christ Jesus. 4. Consider, that sometimes ye have met with some more than an ordinary touch, motion, and work of the Spirit, that hath been born in upon you, which ye have slighted and neglected, if not quenched and put out, which is your great guilt before the Lord: Is there any of you, but now and then, at preaching, or when in some great hazard, or under sickness, or some other sad cross,

ye

ye have been under convictions of sin, and have had some little glances of the hazard ye were in of the wrath of God, more than ordinarily ye had at other times? and I would ask you, Have these been entertained and cherished, or rather have they not been slighted and worn out by you? and may ye not in this respect be charged with the guilt of resisting the Spirit of God, and marring the work of your own conversion and salvation? These things, and many more, which will cry loud in the consciences of men and women one day, will quite remove and take away this objection, *that ye could not do better:* ye might have done better than ye did; ye might have abstained from many evils that ye committed, and done many duties that ye omitted, and done them with more moral seriousness than ye did; but ye were perverse, and did willingly and deliberately chuse to continue in your natural condition, rejecting Christ, and the offer of salvation through him. This also serves to refute and remove that prophane principle or tenet, that many have in their minds and mouths, *That they have no more grace than God hath given them:* Will ye dare to come before God in the great day with any such objection? No certainly; or, if ye dare, God will heighten your guilt by it, and beat it back again into your throat: Then, O then, all such subterfuges will be no shelter to you before him, nor in the least able to insconce your souls against the strong batteries of the wrath of God, that will be as a storm against the wall.

SERMON XV.

Isaiah liii. 1. ------ *And to whom is the arm of the Lord revealed?*

Ministers have not done with their work when they have preached, and people have not done with their work when they have heard: That which is of greatest concernment follows, which either hath, in the want of it, influence on the sadning of both ministers and people; or, in the obtaining of it, on their consolation. . This is the things that we find Isaiah upon here, who, having preached the gospel, looks what fruit it hath, and it had in his own time, and should have in our time: it weights him exceedingly; and indeed it is very sad that Isaiah should be so much weighted in foreseeing the unfruitfulness of the gospel in our days, and that we ourselves should be so little weighted with it, and stand so senseless under it.

He calls in this word, *To whom is the arm of the Lord revealed?* partly to confirm the former word, *Who hath believed our report?* and partly to help to make the right use of it, by drawing men to the discovery of the sovereign hand of God in the matter, and of the necessity of his grace for making the gospel effectual in the hearers of it, wheresoever it comes; *Who* (saith he) *hath believed our report?* To whom is this preached gospel made effectual for faith and salvation? It is but to very few, even to as many as have the arm of the Lord; the effectual power of his special grace revealed to them, and no more.

The last *Doctrine* we proposed, and began to speak of as the scope, was, *That believing and receiving of the gospel, and the Lord's exercising a powerful work of his grace with it, are ever still knit together;* they are of equal extent. As many believe, as he stretched out his hand of power with the word to work faith in them; and as many ly still in unbelief, as his hand of power is not revealed unto: This is his scope.

We took up this *doctrine* in two branches, *First, That the most powerful means cannot work nor beget faith in the hearers of the gospel, except there be an inward powerful work of grace on their hearts accompanying them:* And this we cleared, and spoke a little to two *Questions* in the *Use*, and left off at a third, to wit, What the hearers of the gospel should do, that have the call and offer of the gospel, seeing without the effectual work of the grace of God they cannot believe? which we shall forbear to speak to, till we open the second branch of the *doctrine*, because this question relates to both.

The second branch then of the *doctrine* is, *That wherever the Lord applieth the powerful work of his grace, there necessarily faith and conversion follow;* or, *The stretching forth of God's arm in the work of his grace, hath always the work of faith and conversion, and the engaging of the soul unto Jesus Christ, following on it.* And indeed, if it be true that we cleared before, to wit, that there are as many unbelievers as there are persons on whom grace doth not thus powerfully work, or that they are all such that this work of grace is not manifested on, then the work of conversion and believing is as broad as this work of grace is; for the prophet maketh them of equal extent; Who is he that believeth? Even he to whom the arm of the Lord is revealed: and on the contrary, Who is he that believeth not? Even he to whom the arm of the Lord is not revealed, and on whom this work of grace is not manifested. By which we may see it to be very clear, that the prophet hangs the believing of the gospel on the Lord's manifesting his arm; so that, where it is not manifested, this work of faith is not brought forth; and where it is manifested, necessarily it is brought forth.

This being a *doctrine* concerning the efficacy of God's grace, which ought not to ly hid from the Lord's people, we shall a little, *First*, clear it; and then, *Secondly*, confirm it to you.

First, For clearing of it's meaning, 1. Ye would not take up our meaning in it so, as if we made every common work, that lively means may have on the hearers of the gospel, to be conversion: the preaching of the word will sometimes make folks tremble as we see in Felix, and will waken convictions and terrors in them, and put them into an amazement, and yet leave them there; for all these convictions may be, and are often resisted, as to any saving fruit at least; which we conceive to be that which Stephen points at, Acts vii. 51. while he saith, *Ye stiff-necked and uncircumcised in heart and ears, ye do always resist the holy Ghost*; *as your fathers did, so do ye*: and what he means by this, is explained in the words following, *Which of the prophets have not your fathers persecuted?* &c. even their contending with the word of the Lord in the mouths of his servants: yea, in that same place where 'tis said, *They gnashed upon him with their teeth*, 'tis insinuated that they came over the belly of the cutting conviction, which his preaching had upon them. Nor do we, 2, mean, That every common operation of the Spirit, whether illumination of the mind, or a touch on the affections (such as may be in temporaries and apostates, is clear, Mat. xiii. 20, 21. Heb. vi. 4. and downward) is conversion; there is a great difference betwixt a common work or gift of the Spirit (which in a large sense may be called Grace, because freely given) and the saving work of grace, which before we called a peculiar work: and oftimes that common operation of the Spirit is quenched and put out, therefore the apostle, 1 Thess. v. 19. exhorteth thus, *Quench not the Spirit*. 3. When we speak of an effectual bringing forth of faith by this grace of God, we would not have you thinking, that we suppose no reluctancy to be in the man in so far as he is unrenewed: for tho', where grace effectually worketh, faith follows necessarily; yet corruption being in the man, it is disposed and apt to thwart with, and to oppose grace; and the will hath its averseness to yield: but the meaning of the doctrine is this, that tho' there be such a strong power of corruption in the man to whom grace comes, and on whom it is put forth, yet the power of grace is such, that it powerfully masters and overcomes corruption, and wins the heart to believe in, and to engage with Christ; tho' (to speak so) there be something within that strives to keep the door shut on Christ, yet when it comes to that, Cant. v. 3. *He puts in his fingers by the hole of the lock, and makes the myrrh to drop*, the heart is prevailed with so, as it is effectually opened, as the heart of Lydia was to receive the word which Paul preached. Thus, notwithstanding of corruption's opposition, grace gains its point; and the Lord never applies his grace, of purpose to gain a soul, but he prevails. 4. When we speak of the power and effectualness of grace in conquering and gaining the heart and will of the sinner to believe in Jesus Christ, we do not mean that there is any force or violence done to the will, or any exerting of a coactive power, violating the will, contrary to its essential property of freedom, to close with Christ: but this we mean, that tho' corruption be in the heart, yet grace being infused and acted by the Spirit, the pravity in the will is sweetly cured, and the will is moved and made to will willingly, and upon choice, by the power of the Spirit of grace taking in the strong hold; this great work is wrought by an omnipotent suavity, and by a sweet omnipotency: and it needs not at all seem strange; for if man, in nature, be, by the power of habitual corruption, made necessarily to will evil; so that notwithstanding he doth freely and willingly choose evil; why should it be thought strange or absurd to say, that when a principle of the grace of God is infused into the soul, and acted by the Spirit of God, it hath that much influence, power and efficacy, as to prevail with the will, it keeping still its own freedom, to make it willing to embrace Jesus Christ, and yet not at all thereby wrong that essential property of the will? Sure grace is as powerful as corruption, and the Lord is as dextrous a worker, and can work as agreeably to the nature of the creature in this gracious work, as the creature can in its own sinful actings. So then, we say, when the Lord is pleased to apply the work of his grace to convert a sinner, that work is never frustrated, but it always hath necessarily the work of faith, renovation, and conversion following on the back of it.

Secondly, We shall a little confirm the doctrine; and the grounds of confirmation are these, the 1*st*, whereof is the express scriptures wherein this truth is asserted, as John vi. 44. 45. It is said in the 44. verse

SERM. XV.   *Isaiah* liii. Verse 1.   105

verse; *No man can come to me, except the Father draw him;* and on the contrary, it is as expresly set down, verse 45. *It is written in the prophets, They shall be all taught of God; every man therefore that hath heard and learned of the Father cometh unto me:* And this being contradistinguished to external preaching, and being that which is called *drawing,* verse 44. he knits believing to it, and makes believing, called *coming,* a necessary effect of it, that to whomsoever God gives that inward lesson, they shall come: which confirms the doctrine, that whomsoever the Lord teaches and schools by his grace, and calls effectually, they do necessarily believe. Another passage we have Phil. ii. 12, 13. *Work out the work of your salvation in fear and trembling; for it is God that worketh in you both to will and to do of his good pleasure:* Where the apostle makes the work of grace not only to work ability to will and to do, but to work also to will and to do actually; and grace never worketh *to will,* and leaves the man unwilling, but necessarily supposeth the man's closing willingly with Christ, with whom he worketh thus. A 2d ground of confirmation is drawn from these expressions whereby this work is set forth, and the promises comprehending it in God's covenant, wherein it is called the *giving of a new heart, a heart of flesh, the writing of the law in the heart, the putting of his Spirit within his people, and causing them to walk in his statutes,* &c. Jer. xxxi. 33. Ezek. xxxvi. 26, 27. and it is impossible to conceive aright of the fulfilling of these promises, without the including of the effect. The giving of a new heart, is not only a persuading to believe, but the actual giving of the new heart, whereof faith is a special part; which promise is peculiar to the elect, tho' the offer of it be more large, and be further extended: And what can that promise of God's writing the law in the heart be, but an effectual inclining of the heart to the will of God, or inward renovation, contradistinguished to the external ministry, that can only hold out his will in a book, and speak it to the ear? 3. This may be cleared and confirmed from the nature of the work of grace, which is such a mighty work, and so powerful, as it is impossible it can be frustrated, or disappointed; unless we could say, that grace in God, or the grace of God, is not so powerful as corruption in us, which were blasphemy: to this purpose the Apostle prayeth in behalf of the Christian Ephesians, chap. i. 19. 20. that they *may know what is the exceeding greatness of his power to us-ward who believe, according to the working of his mighty power, which he wrought in Christ when he raised him from the dead;* he speaketh so in this high strain, to set out both the exceeding stubbornness of our nature that needs such a work, and the exceeding great power of the grace of God that worketh irresistably, not only in the conversion of the elect at first, but in all the after-acts of believing; so Eph. iii. 7. the same apostle hath it,----*according to the gift of the grace of God given unto me, by the effectual working of his power;* and Col. i. 29. *according to his working which worketh in me mightily:* The power, that worketh in believers, is God's omnipotent power, which worketh effectually and mightily; and if this power be exercised in the continuing and promoting of faith, as is said before, it must be much more exercised in the begetting of faith: yea, and what need is there that he should exercise it, if not for this end, that where he exerciseth it, it may also prevail? A 4*th* ground of confirmation may be drawn from the Lord's great end which he hath before him in this work, and that is the gaining of glory to his grace, and to have the whole work of conversion attributed to it; and if this be his end, he must and will prevail by his grace in throughing the work, in order to this end: If it were left indifferent to man, to yield, or not to yield to God, as he pleaseth, the whole weight of the work of conversion should not ly upon grace, man's mouth should not be stopped; but when that question should be asked, *Who hath made thee to differ? and what hast thou, O man, but what thou hast received?* he should still have something to boast of, and the work of his conversion should at best be halfed betwixt grace and his own free-will; this would necessarily follow, if grace did not through the work, and so God should miss of his end. A 5*th* ground of confirmation is taken from the consideration of God's decree, of the covenant of redemption betwixt Jehovah and the Mediator, and of the power and wisdom of God in carrying on this work, which we put together for brevity's cause: From all which it will be clear, that there is, and must be a necessary connexion betwixt the work of grace on believers, and the effect; and that it is not in the power of man's free-will to resist it, which indeed is not freedom, but bondage. 1. Then, we say, that if we consider the decree of election, we will find, that where grace is applied, faith and conversion must follow; otherwise, if the work of grace were not effectual to convert, God's decree should be suspended on the creature's free will, and be effectual, or not effectual, according as it pleased; and is that any little matter, to make his decree depend upon, and be effectual, or not, according to

man's

man's pleasure? That which sickereth his decree, and makes it infrustrably to take effect, is, that he hath effectual means to bring about his decree. 2. If we consider the covenant of redemption betwixt Jehovah and the Mediator, we will find, that upon the one side the mediator particularly undertaketh for them that are given to him, that he shall lose none of them; and upon the other side, we have (to speak with reverence of the Majesty of God after the manner of men) the Father's obligation to make such persons in due time believers, that Christ the Mediator may see of the travel of his soul, and be satisfied, according to that promise made to him, Psal. cx. 3. *In the day of thy power thy people shall be willing;* and that other, Isa. liii. 11. *He shall see of the travel of his soul, and be satisfied; By his knowledge shall my righteous servant justify many,* &c. and accordingly himself saith, John vi. 37. *All that the Father hath given to me, shall come unto me;* where it is clear, that these who are given must necessarily come: and he also saith, John x. 16. *Other sheep have I, which are not of this fold, them also I must bring:* and it cannot be supposed, without horror and blasphemy, that this determinate, solid, and sure transaction, having all its midses included in it, and being, as to its end, so peremptory, shall, as to these midses, and that end, and as to their throughing, not be in God's hand, but in the hand of mans free-will? If it were there, O how unsicker and loose would the bargain, and God's design in begetting faith, and in bringing souls through grace to glory be! 3. If we consider the Lord's power in beginning and promoting, and his wisdom in carrying on of this work, his power whereby he raiseth the dead, and his wisdom whereby he leads from death to life; is it possible to conceive or imagine these to be applied by the Lord in the conversion of a sinner, but this doctrine must needs hold, that the work of his grace powerfully applied, hath always faith and conversion following on it; and that the Lord leaveth not it to the option of elect souls, to believe, or not to believe, as they please? He must not, he cannot be frustrate of his end and design, but he must bring them to a cordial closure with Christ by faith, in order to their salvation.

Use 1. The first use serves to fix you in the faith of this great truth: And tho' we use not, neither is it needful to trouble you with long questions and debates; yet when the like of this doctrine comes in our way, especially in such a time wherein the pure truths of God, and this amongst the rest, are troubled and called in question, it is requisite that a word be spoken for your confirmation and establishment: and we would hence have you fixed in the faith of these two; 1. Of the impotency of nature in the beginning or promoting ought of the work of grace; which belongs to the first branch of the doctrine. 2. Of the effectualness and irresistableness of grace; that wherever God begets and brings in a soul, he does it by his own powerful grace; and wherever he applies that work, faith and conversion necessarily follow; which belongs to the second branch of the doctrine: And we would the rather speak a little to this, because it is questioned by the enemies of the grace of God, than which there is nothing they set themselves more to dethrone and debase, and to exalt and cry up nature and free-will, as if it did sit on the throne, and grace behoved to come and supplicate it, and as if it might accept or reject its bill at pleasure, as to the conversion of a sinner: in opposition to which, this doctrine holds good, that wherever the Lord applies his grace, he effectually throughs the work of faith and conversion, and there is no soul that can utterly resist it; and wherever the Lord applies this grace, the grace that converts one cannot be frustrated by another: These things we hold, in opposition to the direct assertion of the enemies of grace, whereby they make the work of conversion, not ultimately to terminate on grace, but on man's free-will; and how dangerous and damnable this error is, may easily appear: For, 1. It overturns and runs cross to the whole strain of the gospel, for if we loose but this one pin, in making faith and conversion not to depend on grace but on free-will, then the whole fabric of grace falls down flat; then God should elect us because we were to elect him, contrary to the scripture, which tells us, that he elects us, not we him; and that our closing with him by faith, depends on his electing of us. It overturns our free justification by grace; for, supposing faith comes in in justification, as it doth, none being justified but by faith, and that believing is of ourselves, and that it is in the power of man's free-will to close the bargain, all is not here of grace, our justification is not free, but someway depends on free-will. It overturns the perseverance of the saints; for, if believing depend on free-will, then our perseverance depends on it also; for, if the man's free-will change, he may fall back, and break his neck in a manner at the very threshold of heaven: whereas if it be the work of grace (as indeed it is) that brings forth faith, and carries it on, and if this work of grace cannot be frustrated or restrained by the malice and hardness of any heart to

which

which it is applied, because it cures the hardness, and removes that malice; then certainly this error cannot stand. And we are persuaded, when we plead thus for grace, we have the best end of the debate, and the surest ground to go upon, most for God's honour, and most for the comfort of believers. 2. This error thwarts with the glory of the grace of God; for it is an error that strikes at the richest and most radiant diamond of the crown of the glory of Christ, it hangs election and the effectualness of God's decree, as to effectual calling, faith, justification, and perseverance, on the person himself, and makes God and Christ to be in man's common debt, and reverence, to make his decree effectual: whereas it is the glory of grace, to have all flesh allenarly in its debt and common, as having loved freely, elected, called, justified, sanctified, and carried on the work of grace, till it end and be perfected in glory, freely; which is the song of the redeemed, Rev, i. 5, 6. *Unto him who hath loved us, and washed us from our sins in his own blood, and hath made us kings and priests unto God and his Father, to him be glory and dominion.* If eternal love be free, then the expression or manifestation of it, in making us kings and priests unto God, is also free. 3. This error is exceeding destructive to the consolation of God's people: It is not a comfortless doctrine, that sounds their believing and perseverance on their own free-will! If ye were to make the bargain of grace, whether would ye think it more comfortable and sure, that the effectualness of believing and perseverance should hang on the grace of God, or on your own free-will, especially considering the pravity of your will? Doleful would your condition be, if free-will were the base or foundation, and God used no more but external persuasion: How specious soever this opinion seem to be, because it puts it in man's option to believe, and convert himself, or not, as he pleaseth; yet it overturns the whole strain of the gospel, and quite eclipseth the glory of grace, and cuts the very throat of your consolation, and is the great ground of *Popery, Pelagianism,* and *Arminianism*: to which ye would therefore so much the more advert; and we do the rather speak to it, that ye may be guarded against it, and that ye may be settled in the truth, especially since the same errors are a reviving in another shape in these days, as is manifest in that foolery of *Quakers*, who talk of a light within them, and talk so of that light, as if it were of power sufficient to convert and guide them, if it be not resisted. As also that other conceit of being above ordinances, implies something of the same error; which ye would set yourselves to abhor, as that which the devil is again labouring to sow the seed of amongst us, and labour to be confirmed in the truth: For if there be any truth at all in Christianity, these are two main truths, the utter inability that is in mens hearts by nature to exercise faith in Christ, and the efficacious and irresistable power of the grace of God, in the begetting of faith, where it is begotten; which, when we shall all appear before the tribunal of God, will be found to be so, and none will have a mouth opened to oppose them. And what absurdity, I pray, is there here, notwithstanding all the clamour of corrupt men, that God hath reserved this work of converting sinners by his grace to himself, and hath not put it in the hand of their own free-will, which supposeth men to have a stock within themselves, and hath many fearful effects following it, tending to the depreciating of the grace of God, and to the drawing men off from dependence on Christ, and to the giving of them ground of boasting in themselves, and of vanity and security, all which this doctrine of God's grace overthrows, and stops the mouth of the creature from all vain boasting, to the high exaltation of God's free, sovereign, and efficacious grace, and to the great comfort of his people?

Use 2. The second use serves to commend the grace of God to the hearers of the gospel, and especially to believers; There cannot be a greater commendation given to it, than this, that it works effectually; and indeed it could not be called grace, I mean, saving grace, if it should want this effect, even to save such as it is applied to; but this highly commends grace, that if there be mighty corruption in us, there is a strong arm of grace put forth by him, for perfecting that which concerns us, notwithstanding of this great strength of corruption. And if ye think yourselves not to be believers, and think this doctrine to be hard, that ye cannot believe without this grace, and yet would fain believe, consider that as none can believe, neither can believers stand without grace; so grace can help you to do that which ye cannot do, which is to the commendation of grace, and should make it more lovely to you: This gives encouragement to any poor soul, that is as it were *in the place of the breaking forth of children,* and layeth greater ground of confidence that they shall come speed, than if they had it in their own hand; and serves to obviate that grand objection of souls that would fain be at closing with Christ, and cannot come to him; here is a powerful arm reached forth to draw them.

Use 3. The third use serves to humble believers

who have any thing of the work of grace, and so to work them up to thankfulness to him that hath communicate ought of it to them. Is there any of you that have grace? who hath made you to differ from others? It was not yourselves, but free grace; and therefore ye have reason to acknowledge it with thankfulness, and to say, If this same doctrine had not been true, I would have been a stranger to God all my days, and remained under the dominion of Satan and sin with these that are in nature; and with *David*, Psal. xvi. 7. to say, *I bless the Lord, who hath given me counsel; my reins also instruct me in the night-seasons:* This counsel was not the common advice that all got from the word preached, but the inward counsel of the Spirit, that made his reins instruct him, and made him inwardly to follow the advice that the word gave him outwardly: and it is this inward work of the Spirit that keeps in the life of grace, as well as begets it, as it is, Psal. lxxiii. 23---26. *Nevertheless I am continually with thee: Thou hast holden me by my right hand. Thou shalt guide me with thy counsel, and afterward receive me to glory. Whom have I in heaven but thee?* &c. *My flesh and my heart faileth: but God is the strength of my heart, and my portion for ever.* The Psalmist glorieth in this, that the work of his through-bearing did not depend on his own flesh and heart, but on God, who was the strength of his heart, and his portion for ever. If believers would consider what they were in their natural condition, and how much they are obliged to the grace of God, that with power was applied in their conversion, it would stop their mouth as to boasting; make them admire grace, and sound forth its praise: and they would think grace's sweet way of prevailing, to be no coactive forcing of their will, but the greatest part of their freedom; and so far would it be from being look'd on as a violating or wronging of their will, that it would be esteemed their truest and greatest liberty. We are persuaded that the saints in heaven count it no bondage, that God hath so fully freed them from all corruption, that they served him with delight, and do so necessarily; and shall any sojourning saints here below, count it a wronging of their will, that God takes such pains on them, to subdue corruption, and to bring them to some measure of conformity to them who are above? God forbid.

Use 4. The fourth use is, To let us see, what great ground of encouragement there is here for the hearers of the gospel to set about the work of believing, and what ground there is to make them all utterly inexcusable, who shall continue in their unbelief; which may be thought some-what strange, when we say that no means can be effectual for working of faith, without the effectual grace of God be applied: But let these two be put together, 1. That tho' we be insufficient of ourselves, and tho' all outward means be of themselves ineffectual, that yet there is a sufficiency in the grace of God: And, 2. That this grace shall be powerful to work faith in the hearers of the gospel, if they make not themselves guilty of frustrating this grace in the offer of it (as they may do.) These then, who will not believe, will be found most inexcusable. But to return to the main intent of this *use*, we say, that the encouragement lies here, that tho' we be unable, we have an able Mediator, and grace is powerful; and therefore we should with the greater encouragement set about the work of believing, as the Apostle reasons, Phil. ii. 12, 13. *Work out your own salvation with fear and trembling, for it is God that worketh in you both to will and to do of his good pleasure.* Ye might possibly think it had been more encouraging to have said, Ye are able of yourselves to will and to do; but certainly, grace is a more encouraging motive than any thing in the creature: Say not then, ye cannot will nor do, for that excuse is taken away by God's offering to work both in you by his grace; but let me exhort all, both these that are begun to be believers, and those that are to begin to be believers, to be so far from disputing themselves from it, as that they rather encourage themselves to work out the work of their own salvation with fear and trembling, because God's grace, which ye have in your offer, is so powerful to work the work, and will admit of no utter opposition from corruption in you, if ye receive not the grace of God in vain that is offered to you in the gospel. If grace were so weak as we might cast it back at our pleasure, and if it were but a helper in in the work of faith and conversion, as *Arminians* make it, what encouragement could we have from it? And as to practice, is not this doctrine as encouraging? What advantage or comfort is it to undertake any thing in our own strength which is none at all? Is not this much more encouraging, to undertake in the strength of God's grace, knowing that the same work of grace, that begets faith, is as effectual to carry it on, and to make us to persevere in it, and to enable us to every good word and work: Let grace work then, and take a proof of it, and ye shall find it powerful. The Lord himself give you wisdom so to do, for your salvation and consolation.

SERMON

Isaiah. liii 1.------ *And to whom is the arm of the Lord revealed?*

IT is much to walk evenly and stedfastly under the pure doctrine of grace, and neither therefrom to take occasion to give way to loosenesss and carnal liberty, nor to become faint and discouraged, and fearful at the way of God. Corrupt nature is ready to abuse the best things: That word which we have, 1 Pet. iii. 16. that there are many *that wrest and pervert the scriptures to their own destruction*, holds true, not only of doctrinal hereties, but it holds also true in respect of mens practice, or practical errors; for some, hearing of the impotency of nature, and of the power and perfection of grace in bringing about its designed effect, are ready to think that they need to do nothing, alledging, that if grace undertake the work, it will be wrought; and if not, it will not be wrought: and thus atheism and profanity steal in secretly upon the heart, and the sweet doctrine of grace is abused and perverted by such, to their own destruction. There are others again, who it may be will not dare so to top with God, who yet have their own fainting and discouragement when they hear of this doctrine, and think it hard that they themselves can do nothing, and fear that they will never win to believe, because they cannot do it of themselves; these also fail, and make not the right use of grace.

Ye remember the *question* which we proposed to speak a little to on the last doctrine, to wit, That seeing both these branches of it are true, That except grace concur, the most powerful preaching of the gospel will not beget faith; and, That whereever the work of grace goes along with the gospel, there faith is begotten: What is called for from the hearers of the gospel, as the use of this doctrine?

Before we come to answer this question more particularly, we would, 1. Premise this word in general, That none would account the preaching or hearing of the word of God to be useless or fruitless, albeit, that without the work of grace men cannot yield the fruit which it calleth for from them: for our blessed Lord Jesus, Isaiah, and Paul preached this doctrine of grace, and the necessity of the Lord's arm to be revealed in the conversion of souls; and yet they taught the word in season, and out of season, and were gathering in some, and to some this doctrine was made the savour of life unto life, tho' to others (thro' their enmity and corruption) it became the savour of death unto death: To conclude therefore, the inconsistency, or to deny the consistency of these two, to wit, of the necessity of preaching the doctrine of grace, and of the pressing in preaching the practice of holy duties, and the use of ordinary appointed means, would reach this dreadful length, even to condemn the prophets of old, yea, and our blessed Lord Jesus himself, who says, John vi. 44. after he had preached long, *No man can come unto me, except the Father who hath sent me draw him:* And ver. 65.----*Therefore I said unto you, that no man can come to me unless it be given him of the Father.* And will any think that his hearers, who accounted this, with some others, *hard sayings, and from that time went back, and walked no more with him*, were excusable in their doing so? or that his preaching was useless, needless, or impertinent, as having a tendency to tempt men to abandon all use of means, because he preached this doctrine of the impossibility of believing in him, without this pull and draught of his Father's arm?

But, *secondly*, We shall a little more particularly, in answer to the question, speak, 1. To what uses folk would not make of this doctrine, or what things they would abstain from, as tending to a wrong use of it. 2. To some considerations for pressing this doctrine, and removing from it the construction of hardness that we are ready to put upon it. 3. To what is the native use it calls for. And, *Lastly*, To some considerations to press this.

For the *first*, When we say to all that hear this gospel, that there is a necessity of a powerful work of grace, ere this word can be profitable; ye would, 1. Abstain from, and lay aside curiosity, in seeking satisfying answers to all these objections that are moved against it, and absurdities that it is loaded with by the devil, and man's proud nature, and learn to stoop to, and reverence the sovereign dominion of God, and his deep and unsearchable wisdom and knowledge, in this sovereign way of his grace, as the apostle doth, Rom. xi. 33. *O the depth of the riches both of the wisdom and knowledge of God! how unsearchable are his judgments, and his ways past finding out!* Ye would also consider that other word, Rom. ix. 20. *Who art thou that replies against God?* or expostulateth with him; *Shall the thing formed, say to him that formed it Why hast thou made me thus?* It is good to enquire and to seek to know the use the Lord calls for of this doctrine with sobriety: but there is an enquiring to satisfy curiosity, which the Lord abhorreth; as we may gather from Exod. xix. 21.

P *where*

where the Lord, being to deliver his will faith to Moses, *Go down, charge the people*, (a word of peremptory command) *lest they break thorow unto the Lord to gaze, and many of them perish*: The Lord is not displeased that his people should endeavour to behold, and take him up aright; but when their end is not good, but to satisfy an itch of curiosity, it displeaseth him. This may be useful in many cases, and particularly in this we have in hand, to teach us sobriety in seeking to know the way of God's grace, as the Lord would have his people, Exod. xix. waiting for as much of his mind as he thought fit to acquaint them with, and to write on the two tables of stone; but he would not have them breaking in over the boundary or march which he did set to them, lest he should break thro' on them, and they should be made to perish: So would he have men, in their studying the knowledge of his ways, and particularly of the way of his grace, to keep his measures, and to contain themselves within the limits that he pleaseth to set them. 2. Abstain from carnal fretting at, and expostulating with the way of God, whether in the highest degree of upbraiding grace and snarling at it, that ye should not have the stock in your own hand; or in an inferior degree, having a heart inwardly discontent, that ye are not more able of yourselves than ye are to believe, which is the thing that the apostle opposeth, Rom. ix. 20, 21. *Should the thing formed, say to him that formed it, Why hast thou made me thus? Hath not the Potter power over the clay*, &c. especially since none can answer that question with any just reflection upon God. Who is to be blamed for that defect or inability? or whence did that inability or defect in man's nature proceed? God was gracious, free and liberal, in making man perfect; and whose fault is it that it is otherwise? 3. Abstain from, and beware of drawing desperate conclusions as to the giving over the use of the means, or of becoming more lazy and secure in the duties of holiness, and in the practice of piety, because of the necessity of his grace; but on the contrary, be the more diligent and serious, that ye have so much need of grace, and that of yourselves ye can do so little, or rather nothing that is truly good without it.

I know that profane hearts are very fertile and broody of arguments to plead this point of neglect of means, and will readily say, What is the fruit of diligence, and the prejudice of laziness? the one will do us no good, and the other can do us no ill, seeing it is grace that doth all the work. But, 1. By your laziness ye mar your own fruitfulness, and that through your own fault, and make this addition to your guilt, that ye not only continue graceless, but do so thro' your sin wilfully. 2. Ye may draw on to your natural impotency, habitual and judicial hardness of heart, and blindness of mind: It is on this very ground that many ears are made heavy, many eyes made blind, and many hearts made fat; and is that a little or light matter? 3. Tho' ye may think this little, yet that which will bear the weight of your sentence at the day of judgment, will not be your natural impotency, or that grace was not made efficacious to your conversion; but this will be it, that when God sent out his word to win you, and offered his grace for enabling you to yield, ye did maliciously and deliberately reject it. So that it will never be suffered to come to this, I was unable; because the word was wilfully rejected before it came to this.

But, *Secondly*, Because there are some others possibly that have more seriousness in the use of means, who, tho' they dare not quarrel with grace, yet it weights and discourages them because they can do so little, and they are made heartless to essay, and hopeless to come speed; and it may be that this is in some whom the Lord allows not to draw any such conclusion, but would rather have encouraged: We would say to such, that they would that they would beware of fainting or being discouraged, as if that were impossible to God and his grace, which is impossible to them; they would by all means beware of fitting up, and slacking their hand in duty, because they can do so little. We know there are some that need not much to be spoken to, for satisfying them in this point; but there are others, who are weighted with this doctrine, to whom the Lord allows more tender usage and would not have them to faint, nor be discouraged: You that are such (if any be) may know that there is ground for us to press this, and that we may remove the construction of hardness from the sovereign way of God's grace, wherein he hath thought fit to draw men unto an absolute dependence on himself. In the dispensing of it, we shall propose these few considerations: 1. That (which was hinted at before) never a man that hath heard this gospel, when he comes to count with God, shall have it to say, that the reason why he did not receive and embrace it, was his impotency and inability; but the real reason shall be found to be his wilful rejecting of it: And upon the contrary it shall be found, that there was never one that would in earnest have had strength to run the way of God's commandments, and faith to grip to and embrace

Jesus

Jesus Christ offered in this gospel, that for want of ability came short; and if so, what reason is there to complain? If none want faith, but such as would not have him, and if none would have him complain of their want of him, upon these two we have great ground of encouragement to them that have a sincere affection to be at him, and there is no ground for folk to sit up, or fall lazy in pursuing after union and communion with him in the use of means. None shall have cause to complain of their want of him, but such as with their own consent gave him over: and any that would fain have had him, shall not miss him; for this real willingness to close with Christ, being a work of the grace of God, and it being no less power that works this will than the power which doth effectuate the work of conversion, and bring it to perfection, he that begins the work will perfect it: and therefore, in this case, folk had more need to reflect upon their unwillingness to have Christ, and to close with him on his own terms, than to dispute their impotency and inability. 2. Consider what they have been, whom the Lord hath brought thorow: Were they not such as had as much need of grace as ye have? had they not the same corrupt nature that ye have? were they not as impotent and unable to do for themselves? could any of themselves do more than ye can? Consider them all that are before the throne: Was it not this same grace of God, and not their good nature, nor their free will, that did the work? and they were not expressly, or by name, included in the promises more than ye are; and ye are not expresly excluded more than they were: The Lord brought forward the work of grace in them that same way that he dealeth with you; by the preaching of his word, he brought them first to know their sinfulness, impotency, and weakness; to know that there was need of a Saviour, that their salvation was not of themselves, neither was it in them to make right use of the Saviour, and salvation offered, but in the power of his grace; and what if he be doing so to thee! and if thy condition be hard and hopeless now, it had been a hopeless and hard condition to these many that are now before the throne. 3. Consider, That there is no question but grace is effectual to carry on the work, and to make it go thorow: All the difficulty and dissatisfaction is, because God keeps the application in his own hand, which the man's heart would have in its hand; and which of them, do ye think, is most sure and encouraging? all your fainting and discouragement resolveth in this, because ye can do so little; if ye be in good earnest desirous to have grace thro' the work of faith and conversion, would ye possibly make choice of another, or better hand than God's to put it in? Is it not as suitable and sure, that his wisdom should contrive and lay down the way, as it is to his power to set it forward, and to the freedom of his grace to make application of it, and all more suitable and sure than if it were in your own hand? May ye not think shame to be discouraged on this ground, because any thing ye do ye must needs get it from God, and that that should be an obstruction in the way of godliness, which is a main encouragement to it? Is the Lord an upbraider? is there any that can quarrel him as niggardly in dispensing of his grace? *Doth not he give to all men liberally, and upbraideth no man?* and doth it not become him well to have the conduct and guiding of his own grace? 4. Consider how many the Lord hath given grace to already; and how he hath given it freely, surprisingly, and unexpectedly: If ye could bring forth any proof that never one got good of God, ye might have a pretext for your discouragement and fearing; but when as many as are before the throne are proofs of his being gracious to sinners, when so many have gotten good of God before you; and when there are several, who, to your own certain knowledge, are daily getting good of him sensibly, freely, and unexpectedly, who were as undisposed to believe as ye are, and as much fainted and discouraged as ye are; and when he says, that *he is found of them that sought him not*; is it not as likely that a poor body, that is longing for his grace, shall be satisfied as well now as ever? according to that word, Matt. v. 6. *Blessed are they that hunger and thirst for righteousness, for they shall be filled;* the soul, that fain would have holiness, shall get it. I know there will be a business made here, and a new objection started, Whether this longing or hunger be real or not? But if your longing and hunger be not real, it will not trouble you much to want; it is not to encourage or comfort such, that have no real longing, that all this is spoken; we know there is more need to make some vomit up the conceit of their ability, than to encourage them against any seen and felt inability. There are many, alas! that think little of the grace of God; with whom the error anent universal grace would agree well, they having a presumptuous conceit of faith, and that it is not so difficult a thing to believe as is alledged: We must profess, that we have not much to say to such for their encouragement; only we would let them know, that there is a time coming, when God will refute and silence them: But as for such as see their inability, and are put to any measure of suitable seriousness and longing in earnest after believing, the Lord allows that they be strengthened and encouraged; and to such we would say this, If their missing of Jesus Christ weight them, if it be their burden, that they cannot believe, and if their longing, hunger, and thirst be some pain and piece of exercise to them, so as other things relish not with them, they are so taken up with that; and if they had their souls choice, it would be this, even a satisfying sight of union and communion with him; their longing and hunger is real, and we may turn over that just now cited word to them, *Blessed are they that hunger and thirst after righteousness, for they shall be filled:* this hunger and thirst was never begotten without some spiritual physick from Christ, the great Physician, who hath provision for satisfying it: and as we use to say of the natural life, he sent never the mouth but he sent the meat with it; so we may say of this hunger, he that gives this spiritual mouth, gives always the meat with it. Would to God there were many enlarged appetites to receive; our Lord would no doubt be ready to satisfy them all: If the mouth were wide opened, the affections enlarged, and the soul sick under hunger and thirst for Christ and holiness, that sickness should not be found to be unto death, but to the glory of the grace of him who is the great Healer.

For the *third* thing that we proposed, to wit, That seeing there are many ways how folk may go wrong, and yet none should give over hope, what is the native use and exercise that this doctrine calls for? I shall speak to this *first* in general, and *secondly*, in some few steps or particular directions. 1*st*, Then in general, Ye would consider that place, Phil. ii. 12, 13. *Work out the work of your own salvation with fear and trembling, for it is God that worketh in you both to will and to do of his good pleasure:* where it is clear, that the exhortation given to them, to work out their salvation, is drawn from this same doctrine of the efficacious work of God's grace working in them to will and to do, as the great motive; God, saith he, worketh in you to will and to do, therefore work ye out the work of your own salvation: There are in this general exhortation four things implied: The *first* is the very entry or beginning of the work of salvation, that is, the exercising of faith in Jesus Christ; it is of God, therefore work at that work; as if he had said, Believe to the saving of your souls, as the word is, Heb. x. ult. *For it is God that works the will in you.* The *second* is the work of repentance, this is also taken in here; for his bidding them *work in fear and trembling,* respects their sinfulness, and necessarily implieth repentance, The *third* is their aiming at perfection in holiness, the putting forth themselves in improving of all means, and in the exercising of all duties for that end; Work *out,* says he. And, *fourthly,* It looks to the manner, that it be not carnally, or in carnal confidence, *but with fear and trembling;* and if it should be asked, How doth that conclusion flow from this doctrine, It is God's work, or he works in you to will and to do, therefore work ye out your salvation? Folk would rather think that the conclusion should be, Since God doth all this, do ye nothing: No, but the just contrary conclusion is drawn; and it hangs on these two, 1. On the efficacy of grace, it is God that works to will and to do, it is his grace that strengthneth you; and where he works the will, he works the deed; where he begins a work, he will also through and effectuate it, therefore take ye encouragement to work; as if he had said, Fight well, for ye have a brave second, tho' it be not proper to call grace a second; set yourselves to the exercise of holiness in earnest, and God will make it go with you. 2. On the consideration of sinfulness and weakness in them, which should make them work in fear and trembling; as if he had said, Seeing it is God, and the efficacy of his grace, that doth the work, be not ye vain and presumptuous: The first part says, It is God that works, and not ye, therefore be ye the more holily confident; the second part says, It is not ye, but God, and therefore do the work with fear and trembling; and both tend to this, that folk would be serious in minding and prosecuting the work of their salvation, from the first step to the last, in fear and trembling, on this ground, that tho' they have nothing in themselves, yet there is enough in God and in his grace to do their turn. How is it then, or what can be the reason, that we in our hearts do draw the just contrary conclusion to that which the Spirit of God draws here from this ground? When we have the offer of grace, and hear of the power and efficacy of it, it should as to our part provoke us to be more busy, reasoning thus with ourselves, that tho' our corruption will soon overcome us, yet it will not, it cannot overcome grace; and tho' the exercise of faith be above our reach, yet it is not above the reach of grace; tho' we be weak, yet grace is strong, and therefore we will work it out. And upon the other side, we ought to continue humble, and in fear and trembling work it out, because it is not we, but grace, that doth the work: If grace were well considered,

there

there is nothing that would more strengthen folks hands to work; and upon the other hand, there is nothing that would make folks more watchful, and to walk in holy fear, considering that we are poor beggars, and through our unwatchfulness, or conceit and presumption, may mar the outlettings of his grace, especially if we grow secure, and ungratefully forget what we receive from him.

2*dly*, I come now to some steps or particular directions implied in this *use*, because it will be asked, What then should folk do? And, before I touch on particulars, take these two caveats in the entry to them, 1. That we can propose nothing to be done by you, neither can ye do any thing of yourselves, that is a gracious act or deed. 2. That we understand not that any thing can be done by men in their natural state, that doth infer or procure, and far less deserve the giving of grace to any; but seeing God hath given directions to us how to walk in order to the working out of our salvation, we say, (1.) That it is safe to us to walk in the way he hath directed us to walk in, and in the use of the means he hath prescribed, and much more safe than to lay them aside. (2.) That there is greater suitableness betwixt the use of the means, and the finding of grace, than there is betwixt the neglect of means and the finding of it. (3.) That it agrees well with God's way in bringing about the conversion of sinners, to bring them piece and piece forward; sometimes bringing them to the use of external means, and to the performance of outward duties; sometimes convincing them of sin, and letting them see their need of Christ; sometimes discovering the worth that is in Christ, and bringing them to fall in love with him, ere they actually close with him; and making them in their practice to follow any peep or glimmering of light that is let out to them, and go the length that light discovereth the way, and makes it plain as to their duty.

Now, for particular directions, we would, 1. Bid you study to be fixed and established in the faith of these general truths that relate to man's sinfulness and misery, and insufficiency in himself, that *in us, that is, in our flesh, dwelleth no good thing*; that naturally we are dead in sins and trespasses, and cannot quicken ourselves: and in the faith of the necessity and powerfulness of grace, and that it is Christ that must give and work faith, and that grace can do the turn, and prevail where it is put on work. Ye would also consider, and believe the great hazard of missing grace, and the advantage that cometh by it: ye would meditate on these things, and on the scriptures that hold them out, and on the experiences of the saints that confirm them, that ye may not only have a glance and transient view of them, but may be confirmed in the faith of the truth of them. 2. Content not yourselves with a general faith of the truth of this doctrine, but labour to be suitably affected with these things that ye believe; and tho' every affectedness be not special grace, yet I speak to them that are ready to lay the blame and fault on the grace of God, and yet were never affected with their own gracelessness. Ye would study to be affected with the gracelessness of your nature, and let it put you to some sanctified disquiet and trouble, till, with Ephraim, ye be made *to smite upon your thigh*, and till ye be put to a holy deliberation and consultation about your own condition. A man that is under the hazard of a civil penalty, will think on it again and again, it will affect him, and he will not be at rest till he be without the reach of it; much more should ye be with the hazard that your souls are in through sin; ye are not excusable, so long as ye come not this length. 3. Add to this, diligence in the use of all outward means and duties, whereby, and wherein, the Lord useth to communicate his grace, *abounding always in the work of the Lord*, as the apostle exhorteth, 1 Cor. xv. 58. Be diligent in secret prayer, reading, meditation, conference, self-examination, hearing, keeping good company, and the like; which indeed hypocrites may do, yet they cease not for that to be duties. 4. Be sincere and serious in the use and performance of these means and duties; that which I mean is a moral sincerity and seriousness, such as a man will readily have in a civil cause that he hath depending before a civil judge, or in hearing of news, or the like, which is a thing that may be, and is often found in men that are void of a principle of grace; and yet folk are very often defective in this, and make themselves exceeding guilty before God, because they come not this length. 5. Take heed and beware of entertaining any thing that holds and bars out grace, or of doing any thing that may mar or quench the working or moving of grace: If ye cannot get Christ entertained in your heart as ye should, be sure to give it to no other; if ye cannot get corruption thrust out, nor mortified, watch against the rising or harbouring of that which ye know to be corruption, and against the incoming or rising of such evils, as ye know will keep or put away the Beloved; guard also against the neglecting of such means, as by the neglect whereof ye may grieve his Spirit. 6. Study and seek after a composed frame of
spirit.

spirit in your ordinary walk, and especially in duties of worship. Carnal mirth and jollity, loose company, and suffering the heart to go a-whoring after the things of the world, do not only provoke Christ as they are sins, but indispose us for duty, and mar the exercise of grace where it is, and keep it back where it is not; therefore the wise man saith, Eccl. vii. 3. *That sorrow is better than laughter, for by the sadness of the countenance the heart is made better.* Carnal sorrow is not to be commended, but sober sadness, or a grave and composed frame of spirit, is better than a light and unsettled frame; it being very hard, if not impossible, to keep the heart right, even where there is grace, but where there is some counterpoise or wither-weight; and it must be far more impossible to keep it right, where the work of grace is not, or but in the very first beginnings of it; and tho' I do not call this composedness of frame, *Grace,* yet it keeps folk in some capacity, as it were, to receive grace. It is said, Lam. iii. 27, 28. *That it is good for a man that he bear the yoke in his youth; he sitteth alone and keepeth silence, because he hath born it upon him; he puts his mouth in the dust, if so be their may be hope.* For tho' crosses are not always blessed to conversion, yet we may see now and then that sad times are the beginnings of better times, and even in hypocrites their sad times ordinarily are their best times. I neither desire nor allow any to bring crosses upon themselves, yet I would desire all to make the best use of any cross they are under, and to be acquainting themselves with their sin and infirmities, and with their hazard, and with such other things as may weight and compose them, without fostering discouragement and anxiety; and to love as well to speak and hear such things spoken of as may provoke to sighing and sadness, as these that may provoke to laughter; *I said of laughter,* (saith Solomon, Eccl. ii. 2.) *It is mad; and of mirth, What doth it?* and Prov. xiv. 13. *Even in laughter the heart is sorrowful, and the end of that mirth is heaviness:* tho' oft-times our laughter may not be so sinful, yet it readily more indisposeth us for any spiritual duty than sorrow doth; the heart is like a clock, whereof, when the inner wheels are set a reeling, it is not soon righted and settled. 7. I would propose Ephraim's example to you, Jer. xxxi. 18, 19. and desire that ye would, in the sight and sense of your sinfulness, weakness, and fecklesness, be bemoaning yourselves and your sad condition to God, putting up that prayer to him, *Turn thou me, and I shall be turned;* these words, flowing from suitable sense, are good; and then follows,

After that I was turned, I repented. It is observable, that in the very entry he is graciously taken notice of by the Lord; *Surely I have heard Ephraim bemoaning himself thus;* so it is with God's people, when they consider how great strangers they have been to God, how sinful and stubborn, and how impossible it is for them to mend themselves of themselves, they retire themselves into some corner, and there bemoan their case, and cry out, O what a sinful nature is this! and when will it be got amended! *I am as a bullock unaccustomed to the yoke,* says Ephraim; and the Lord tells, he heard and observed it; when possibly he thought he was scarcely (if at all) praying, but rather sighing out as it were a short ejaculation to God, O that I were amended! the last words of his prayer are, *Turn thou me, and I shall be turned;* or, Convert thou me, and I shall be converted: he sees that when all is done, he must cleanse his hands, and leave the matter to God; I cannot, but thou canst work the work: And it ends sweetly in words of faith, *for thou art the Lord my God;* and where words of faith are after serious exercise, that exercise hath oft-times faith going alongst with it: hence are these words, Lam. iii. 20. *If so be there may be hope.* Psal. cxix. *Incline mine heart, open mine eyes,* &c. and Luke ix. 13. *How much more will your heavenly Father give his holy Spirit to them that ask him?* It is good to pray for the efficacy of grace, and to offer ourselves subjects to be wrought upon, and objects to receive what grace offers to us.

As we began these directions with a word of caution, so we would close them. Do not think that things in a natural man, following his sinful course, will bring forth grace; neither conclude, that where these things only are discerned and no more in some persons, that there grace is wanting, it being to help such forward that we mainly speak to them: Only, in sum, 1. Keep clean and clear the light ye have. 2. Improve the strength bestowed. And, 3. What ye have not, put it over on God, and seek from him, who hath grace to give for working that in you; and it would seem, that in reason ye should refuse none of these three. (1.) We say, Keep clean and clear your light; for if ye detain the truth of God in unrighteousness, and make as it were a prisoner of it, by setting a guard of corrupt affections about it, ye may bring on blindness. (2.) Improve what strength ye have; for if ye improve not your strength, were it but in natural parts and endowments, that makes you inexcusable, when spiritual and gracious qualifications are denied to
you:

you: for ye have procured this to yourselves. Are there not many things that ye thought yourselves able for, that ye never seriously once essayed? much more might have been done as to repentance, love to God, charity to others, and the like; and when ye have not stretched yourselves to the yondmost in these, there are sure many things left undone that ye might have done. (3.) What ye dow not do, or find yourselves unable to do, put it on God to do for you, seriously, humbly, singly, and self-deniedly; for if ye come not to God with that which ye are unequal and unable for, ye are still on this side your duty, and without excuse. Take these then together, Improve any strength ye have, according to any measure of light God hath given you, and come to God through Jesus Christ, seek that ye want from him, and leave the acceptation of your persons and of your performances on him: this is the result of all that we have spoken of this doctrine of grace, that ye may not take occasion from the way of God's dispensing grace, to continue graceless; which if ye do, it will be ground of a most grievous challenge against you: But that ye may see an excellent consistency betwixt the sovereignty of grace, and your going about the means appointed of God, in order to faith and conversion, and the study of holiness; and that ye may go on in the use of these means, with an eye to grace, in the sense of your own insufficiency to think, as of yourselves, so much as a good thought, leaving all your duties at Christ's feet, walking before him with a stopped mouth; when any thing is wanting, standing at his door, and begging it from him; and when any thing is received, cleansing, to say so, your own hands of it, and giving him all the thanks, praise and glory of it. To him be praise for ever.

SERMON XVII.

Isaiah liii. 2. *For he shall grow up before him as a tender plant, and as a root out of a dry ground: he hath no form nor comeliness; and when we shall see him, there is no beauty that we should desire him.*
Verse 3. *He is despised and rejected of men, a man of sorrows, and acquainted with grief: and we hid as it were our faces from him; he was despised, and we esteemed him not.*

IN the former *Verse*, the prophet hath asserted the rarity and scarcity of believing the gospel, and receiving of Jesus Christ offered therein; *Who hath believed our report?* saith he, Who hath made Christ welcome? *And to whom is the arm of the Lord revealed?* To whom hath this gospel been made effectual by the power of God for the engaging of their hearts to him?

In these two *verses*, he gives a reason as it were of this, which runs upon these two, 1. The low appearance of our Lord Jesus Christ, in respect of his outward condition; it hath no outward beauty, splendor nor greatness to commend it; but is attended with much meanness, and with many afflictions. 2. The itching humour of men, who are taken up with wordly grandeur, or greatness and glory, and make little account of any thing that wants that; as if he said, It is no wonder that Christ get few to believe on him, and that few receive this gospel; for he will not come with much worldy pomp and grandeur, which the men of the world greatly affect, and are much taken up with.

To open the words a little, we shall first consider the matter of this reson, and then the consequence of it; or what influence it hath on mens offending at Christ, and continuing in their unbelief: only we shall premise two or three words to both.

That which we premise, *First*, is this, That the He, that is here spoken of, is our Lord Jesus Christ, who in the New Testament hath this text applied to him; for albeit there be no *He* so expresly mentioned in this chapter before, yet in the 13th *Verse* of the former chapter, to which this relates, the *He*, that is spoken of here, is called *the Lord's Servant;* and it is said of him, that *He shall be exalted and extolled, and made very high:* And it is not unusual to speak of Christ singularly by a relative without an antecedent, as Cant. i. 2. *Let him kiss me with the kisses of his mouth;* because Christ to believers is so singular an One, that whenever he is spoken of by way of eminency and excellency, as here, they cannot mistake him, or take another for him. 2*dly*, This want of *form and comeliness* is not to be understood of any personal defect in our Lord's human nature, but in respect of, and with reference to the tract of his life, and what accompanied his humiliation, to wit, that it was low and mean, without that external grandeur, pomp and splendor of outward things. which the world esteem to be comeliness and beauty. 3*dly*, Where it is said, *He shall grow up before him*, &c. it relates to the hearers of the report of the gospel concerning him, or to the man that believes not the report spoken of before; and so relates to the words of the first *Verse*. *Who hath believed our report?* which is certainly meant of the man that hears of him, and to whom he seems

nothing

nothing worth, because of his mean and low outward conditon; for if we should apply it to God, we cannot see how it will so infer the scope, and be the reason of the unbelief asserted formerly, for which end it is brought in here.

We come now to open the words a little; and here we would know, that Christ's low condition is two ways set down in these two verses. 1. In the second *verse*, in respect of his want of the abundance of the things of this world. 2. In the third *verse*, in respect of the accession of outward crosses and afflictions;. for not only doth he want credit, respect and esteem, but he hath contempt, despite and reproach; not only wants he great riches, but he hath poverty, and is in a poor and low condition. The first verse expresseth him negatively, to be no worldly great Man; the second *verse* expresseth him positively to be a mean and despised Man. 1. Then these words, *He shall grow up as a plant out of a dry ground*, are expounded by the words following, *He hath no form nor comeliness;* for as shrubs or scrogs growing up out of dry ground cryn and wither, when trees planted in a fat soil are fresh, fair and beautiful; so shall it be with Christ, when he cometh forth (saith the prophet) to the eyes of the world, he shall, as it were, be like a scrab in a moor-edge. Our Lord had personal and much divine comeliness in him, as we may see, John i. 14. where he saith, that *the word was made flesh and dwelt among us, and we beheld his glory, the glory as of the only Begotten of the Father, full of grace and truth;* but the comeliness, here spoken of, is that outward state, pomp and splendor which great men in the world use to have, which Christ wanted: this is confirmed by the following words, *And when we shall see him, there is no beauty that we should desire him.* There is in men naturally a delight and complacency in that which is beautiful to the natural eye; but (saith he) there shall be no such thing seen in Jesus Christ when he cometh; and therefore no great wonder that few believe on him. And that he saith *We*, it is either according to the phrase used in scripture, to make some hard thing digest and go down the better with the hearers, whereof the speaker is not guilty; or it is his expressing what is the humour generally in all men naturally; as if he had said, Had even we who are elect and godly no more but carnal eyes, we would think no more of Christ than other folk do; for we should get no satisfaction to carnal reason.

The second thing, whereby his low condition is set out, is in these words, *He is despised and rejected of men*, &c. Not only shall he want that which carnal hearts and eyes seek and look after, but he shall be so very low, that men shall set him at nought, mock and reject him: and what wonder then that he be not believed on? *A Man of sorrows;* as for the tract of his life, it shall be spent in sorrows: *and acquainted with grief;* he shall not be a Man that shall be a stranger to crosses, griefs and heaviness, but he shall be familiarly acquainted with them, and they with him. *And we hid as it were our faces from him;* a consequent of the former: as men will not give their countenance to them whom they despise; so, saith he, we shall think shame to see or look at him: he shall be the Object of mens contempt and scorn, and we shall not so much as countenance him; he shall be despised and set at nought by Herod and the *Roman* soldiers, *and we esteemed him not;* this we is the people of the Jews, who owe him more respect, esteemed him not: and hence he concludes, that it is no wonder that but few believe on him. And so in the words following he goes on to describe his humiliation, and to remove the offence that might be taken at it, *Surely he hath born our griefs,* &c. as if he had said, There is no such cause to fear and stumble at Christ for his lowness and base outward condition; for it was not for himself, but for us, that he became so low; and therefore it did not become us to think so little of him. His griefs and sorrows are human infirmities, that he subjected himself to for our sake; for the wrath of God, which he suffered for us, is spoken of afterwards. And because there is great difference betwixt Christ's bearing of infirmities, and our bearing of infirmities, he being like to us in all things, except sin; I shall, for clearing of this, name three distinctions given by *Divines*, when they discourse of this purpose.

(1.) They distinguish and put difference betwixt the *taking on* of infirmities, and the *contracting* of infirmities; the taking on of infirmities, is the assuming of the effect without the cause, of the infirmity without the sinful defect; contracting of infirmities, is the drawing on of the defect, with, and by the cause: now, we draw on the cause with the effect; Christ took on the effect, but he had no sinful defect in him to draw on such infirmities: he might have taken on the nature of man without the infirmities, if he had so pleased; but he took on the nature and infirmities, without the cause. (2.) They distinguish betwixt these infirmities which are simply natural, such as a man might have had, though he had never sinned; and these infirmities which flow from man's nature, as fallen and corrupted. The first sort may be called *Passive*, and look to suffering, as to be hungry,

hungry, thirsty, weary, sensible of that which hurts the body: The second sort may be called *Active*, and are sinful, as flowing from sin, and tending to sin; as inclination to ill, and indisposition to good, dulness as to the uptaking of God's mind, &c. Our Lord took on the first sort of infirmities, that are simply natural, and may be without sin; but he was free of the other, that imply corruption in the nature; *He was in all points tempted like as we are, yet without sin*, saith the Apostle, Heb. iv. 15. (3.) They distinguish infirmities, into these that are called *natural* and *common* to all men as men, and these that are *personal* and acquired, as flowing from some defect in generation, or are drawn on by some intemperance, grossness in the life and conversation; as some families are subject to diseases that come by generation; others draw on diseases by whoredom, drunkenness, and the like: now our Lord was free of these last, because, being conceived by the holy Ghost in the womb of the virgin, there was no defect in his generation; and being blameless in his life and conversation, he could acquire none of those infirmities: and therefore the infirmities which he bare are of the first sort, that is, such as are common to all men, and to men as men. And hence we think it probable, which some say, that as our Lord was not sick, so he was not capable of sickness, being so perfect in his constitution or complexion; which makes for the glory of grace, and saith, That our Lord behoved to die a violent death, there being no principle in him tending to a natural death, tho' notwithstanding he died most willingly to satisfy justice for sinners. And this may serve to explain these words, *That he was a man of sorrows, and acquainted with grief.*

We come now to *observe* some things from the words. And, 1*st*, From the condition our Lord is described to come to the world in, *observe*, That *the Messiah, the Lord's Servant that was to redeem his people, was to become Man*; this is here supposed and prophesied of, as the first step of his humiliation, he is called *a Man*; and it is an aggravation of it, that he was to be *a Man of sorrows*: or, taking our Lord *Messiah* to be already come, we may take the *Observation* thus; *That the Lord Jesus Christ, the eternal Son of the eternal Father, is also a true and real Man*: A common truth, yet a truth fundamental to the gospel, whereof we are not to think the less or the worse, because it is a common truth; *When the fulness of time came* (saith the Apostle, Gal. iv. 4.) *God sent forth his Son, made of a woman made under the law*: Who, as it is, Phil. ii. 6. *thought it no robbery to be equal with God,* yet took upon him *the shape of a servant, and was made in likeness of men; and being found in fashion as a man, he humbled himself, and became obedient,* &c. So, Heb. ii. 14. 'tis said of him, *That forasmuch as the children are partakers of flesh and blood, he also himself likewise took part of the same,* &c. And v. 11. *Both he that sanctifieth and they that are sanctified are all of one, for which cause he is not ashamed to call them brethren. And,* v. 16. *He took not on him the nature of angels, but he took on him the seed of Abraham; wherefore in all things it behoved him to be made like unto his brethren,* He was made even like unto us in all things, except sin. And if we look to the way of grace, there was good reason for this, that the Redeemer of sinners behoved to be Man, 1. If we consider the interposed or adjoined threatning to the covenant of works, *The day thou eatest thou shalt surely die;* there must be a satisfaction to justice, and the curse threatned must be born. 2. The curse must be [born by man; the nature that sinned must die, the party offending must satisfy in his own person, or in a cautioner. And, 3. By our Lord's becoming Man, (1.) He came to have a right, as being near of kin to sinners, to redeem them. And, (2.) By this the law hath right to pursue and exact the debt of him. And, (3.) By this, grace hath access to commend the Redeemer of sinners to sinners, Heb. ii. 17, 18. and iv. 15, 16. *Wherefore in all things it behoved him to be made like unto his brethren, that he might be a merciful and faithful High Priest,* &c. And that we have such a Redeemer, it makes God, to say so, tryftable, and grace to have access, 1 Tim. ii. 5. *There is one God, and one Mediator between God and man, the Man Christ Jesus*; and this gives man access to step in to God. (4.) This makes the mystery of godliness to shine the more radiantly, and the wisdom and love of God to shine the more conspicuously thorow it, 1 Tim. iii. 16. *Without controversy, great is the mystery of godliness, God manifested in the flesh*. And John i. 14. *The Word was made flesh, and dwelt among us, and we beheld his glory,* &c.---*Use* 1*st*. It serves to be a prop and foundation to our faith. We may say of this truth, as the Apostle, speaking of the resurrection, 1 Cor. xv. 14. says, *If Christ be not risen, then our preaching is vain, and your faith is vain*: If Christ were not Man, our preaching and your hearing were in vain. 1. By this we have an evidence that our Lord is the true *Messiah*, who was to become Man. 2. By this we see a clear way how he was liable to our debt, and how his satisfaction is communicable to us. And, 3. In this also we see a main and most attractive argument to draw sinners into Christ for the actual application of his purchase: our Lord Jesus is Man, our Brother, and made of a woman, made under the law: O! this puts a sweetness and loveliness on the Mediator, to commend him to sinners, for the engaging of their hearts to him.

And therefore, as a second use of it, Seeing there is a Man Mediator, 1. We pray you, men and women, neglect not such a salvation as is to be had by his becoming Man; but let this argument prevail with you to make use of him, that he is a true Man: and we may say, when this Son of man comes in the clouds to judge the world, it will be one of the greatest aggravations of the sin of unbelievers, that he came thus low as to be a Man for the good of men, and yet was not made use of by them. 2. Sinners, that would be at him, may on this ground be confident and cheerful: The Steward of grace is a Friend, he is a Man, their Brother, and claims kindred to them, that honestly aim to do the will of his Father; *Whosoever shall do the will of my Father*, saith he, Matt. xii. *the same is my brother, sister and mother*. Sinners wrong Christ and themselves oft-times, when they scar at this cordial consolation that by Christ's becoming Man is allowed to them; indeed if we were immediately to go to God, *who is a consuming fire*, it were no wonder that we stood at a distance; but when God is in the Mediator Christ, God-man to reconcile the world to himself, as the word is, 2 Cor. vi. *Let us*, as the apostle saith, Heb. iv. ult. *come boldly unto the throne of grace, that we may obtain mercy, and find grace to help in time of need*. O! make this use of it, because he is a Friend that sits on the throne.

2dly, Observe, *That our Lord Jesus did not only become Man, but a Man in an exceeding low and afflicted condition*. It had been much to the Son of God to have come in the shape of a Man, tho' he had been Emperor of the whole world, but he thought not that meet; for since it was his errand in his first coming, not to judge, but to save the world, he came not to be ministred unto, but to minister; and therefore, John xiii. 12. he washed the feet of his disciples. We may take both the branches of the doctrine together; our Lord Jesus not only became Man, but he was a Man without all worldly grandeur and pomp, in a low and mean condition; and not only did he want that grandeur, but he had much affliction, shame and sorrow in the place of it. Need we to prove this? Any who are acquainted with the history of the gospel know it:

he was for the whole tract of his life, not only in a low condition, but a man of sorrows, griefs, and afflictions; under much persecution, contempt and reproach. We might instance this, 1. In his birth, 2. In his life, and 3. In his death. The meanness and lowness of his condition, and the afflictions he met with, appear clearly in all these, wherein ye may behold the glory of grace and of truth; for the more low he became, the more doth the glory of grace shine, and the more also doth the glory of truth, in that he fulfilled all righteousness.

(1.) Then, for his low condition; and that, 1. In his birth, He was not born of any of the greatest queens; however the birth of Mary was noble, yet she was in a mean condition, for the time espoused to a carpenter: he was not born in a great palace, but in a common inn, which too being taken up with guests, his mother was thrust out, or constrained to betake herself to a stable, where our blessed Lord was brought forth and laid in a manger, crib or stall, out of which the beasts eat their meat, for his cradle; there the Lord and Heir of all things is laid, and hath no other cradle, neither was the room hung with rich hangings and tapestry, as the rooms of great ones use to be. 2. In his life he was low: for no sooner is he born, but his mother is forced to flee away with him to Egypt; he dare not be seen: And when he returns, he cohabits with, and serves his supposed father and his mother, was obedient to them, ran their errands, and wrought their work; therefore he is called, Mark vi. the *Carpenter*; there is no outward nor worldly pomp and grandeur here; and thus he was for the space of thirty years: and then, when he came to his public ministry, he hath no great folks for his followers and disciples, but a few poor fishermen; over and above whom he exalts not himself loftily, but humbles himself to wash their feet, and to serve them. And to hold this forth a little further, ye may take notice of some scripture expressions to that purpose; as namely that of Luke, chap. ix. 58. *Foxes have holes, and the birds of the air have nests, but the Son of man hath not where to lay his head*; That of John, chap. i. 10, 11. *He was in the world, and the world was made by him, and the world knew him not: he came unto his own, and his own received him not*. Tho' he could have made a thousand worlds at a word; yet so low was he, that he had not a foot of ground to lay claim to, or to lean his blessed head on: and if we look to Luke viii. we will find that he was provided for in his necessity by some few women, such as Mary Magdalene, Joanna, Susanna, and

others,

SERM. XVII.   Isaiah liii. Verse 2, 3.

others, *who ministered to him of their substance*: He lived upon the charity of others; and yet, 2 Cor. viii. 8. *By his poverty he made many rich*: And when he went from place to place, his diet was often a seeking, neither do we read of any great cheer he had, but of some barley-loaves and fishes; and often the disciples were sent to seek for meat to him. And, 3. When it comes to his death, O how very low is he brought there! When he is crucified, they hang him up betwixt two thieves, as the most notorious malefactor of the three; and he could hardly come under greater reproach than was cast upon him at his death: And as a dead Man, being really dead, he is laid in the grave and buried, as if death had gotten the victory over him; and so he dies a most shameful death, after he had lived a most mean and abject life.

(2.) For his afflicted condition, it is clear, if we consider, what troubles did accompany him in his life, and at his death. No sooner was he born, but (as I said) he is persecuted by Herod, so that himself and his parents must needs flee down to Egypt; and they, being but poor folks, behoved in so long a journey to meet with many difficulties: that they were but poor, may be seen by Mary's offering after her purification. And when he came forth in his public ministry, at his very entry to it, he was most terribly tempted of the devil, taking occasion of his hunger after long fasting; and all along the exercise of it, what contradiction did he meet with from the Scribes and Pharisees? How did he travel on his feet from place to place? often subject to weariness and fainting; sometimes men will not so much as give him lodging, which he suffers patiently, and rebukes his disciples for their impatience and preposterous zeal, Luke ix. Many calumnies and reproaches were cast upon him: He was called *Belzebub, a deceiver, a friend of publicans and sinners*: How did some of his friends according to the flesh snarl at him, and offer to bind him as a mad-man? What plots and conspiracies were laid and made to take away his life? and when it came to the upshot of all, Peter shamefully denied him, and all the other disciples forsook him and fled; Many other things befel him, as may be seen in the history of his sufferings, written by the evangelists. We read that he wept thrice, to let us know that it was his frequent and familiar exercise; and a little before his death we read that he was in a great agony, and did therein sweat blood, and offered prayers with strong cries and tears: but we read not that he did laugh, or that ever any worldly mirth was found in him; which clearly makes out this truth, *That he was a man of sorrows and acquainted with grief*.

For *Use*, It would take the tongues of men and angels to speak of it, it being the most remarkable and soul-refreshing subject that ever the world heard of, even that of which the angels sing, Luke ii: 10. 11. *Good tidings of great joy which shall be to all people, that unto you is born in the city of David a Saviour, which is Christ the Lord. And this shall be a sign to you, ye shall find the babe wrapped in swadling-cloathes, lying in a manger*. Sure we should not sing less, but more than angels, men being more concerned than angels in these things; and therefore, 1*st*, Behold, believe and wonder, that he *that was rich became poor, that we through his poverty might be made rich*! That he, that was Lord of all, became servant to all! That he, *that was the infinite God, the express image of his Father's person, and thought it no robbery to be equal with God, yet humbled himself, and became of no reputation, and took on him the form of a Servant*, &c. Behold, (we say) believe, and wonder at this, 1. In respect of the cause it came from, to wit, everlasting love: he did and suffered all this most willingly, there was no constraint on him; but, as it is Psal. xl. *He delighteth to do his Father's will*; *he had power to lay down his life, and to take it up again*. 2. In respect of the end: It was not to add to his own glory; for, as God, his glory being infinite, it was not, neither is capable of diminution or addition: but he became poor, that we might be made rich; he was a Man of sorrows that we might be made to rejoice; he wept, that we might laugh; he wanted, that we might have: Is not this love, stooping thus low, to be wondered at? Was there ever the like heard of, that God, the great Party offended, should come so low to recover the despicable parties offending, and that even while they were rank enemies to him? *God commendeth his love to us*, saith the apostle, Rom. v. 8. *that while we were yet sinners Christ died for us*: and saith himself, John xv. *Greater love hath no man than this, that a man lay down his life for his friends*; *but when we were enemies, Christ died for us*. Were it then an unsuitable use of this doctrine, to be beholding, believing, and wondering at his love, and to be often thinking and saying, *What is man, that God should be so mindful of him*, as to send the Heir of all things, his own Son, into the world, as his great Ambassador and Commissioner, to negotiate a peace betwixt himself and rebel sinners, which he was to purchase by becoming so very low, and by suffering so very much.

2dly, See in this the great evil and hurt of sin, and the difficulty of making peace betwixt God and a sinner who hath provoked God: Is it a little matter, that made our Lord condescend and stoop so low? O! if folk knew the evil of sin, and that, ere justice could be satisfied, the Son of God behoved to become Man, and a deeply humbled Man; the sword of his avenging justice behoved to awake against him, and smite the Man that was his Fellow, rather than that sin should go unpunished, and justice should want satisfaction. Beware lightly to boast and brag of mercy, or to think it easy to make your peace with God: And remember that *it is a fearful thing to fall into the hands of the living God.*

3dly, See in this, much condescending in our blessed Lord Jesus; and a motive as well as a copy of patience in him, who is content to be made of a woman, made under the law, who submits himself unto the law, and takes on a mean and afflicted state of life in the world: it is a wonder that Christ's members should take so ill with a mean, suffering, and hard lot, seeing their lot is far, very far from the contempt, reproaches, sorrows, weights and griefs that accompanied their Head and Lord; and it is a shame that believers minds and hearts should be set so much on these things, that he, who was and is their Lord and Master, and the Heir of all things, possessed so little of; or that they should place their happiness in whole or in part in the enjoyment of these things, or their misery in the want of them: more patience under the cross, under watchings, weariness, reproaches, *&c.* would become us much better; our blessed Lord Jesus had a great many more.

4thly, See this to be not only a motive to patience in respect of outward things, but a stepping-stone and ground of encouragement to go forward to Christ with every want spiritual and temporal. It is much that our Lord became Man, but it is more that he became a Man under griefs, afflictions, sorrows, and temptations, and was subject to death itself: and that he hath bowels of sympathy from experience of these temptations, vexations and sorrows, as they are sinless, as is clear from Heb. ii. 4. at the close; he knows what hunger, thirst, poverty, contempt, reproach, and persecution are; he knows what it is to be set upon with the violence of a temptation, tho' there was no sin in him to comply with it.

5thly, See here a most real Saviour, since he is a suffering Saviour. Why did our Lord become thus low, but that he might come under the curse in the several degrees of it, for the satisfying of justice for our sins? And see, in every piece of Christ's sufferings a reality of the grace and love of God, a reality in the covenant and bargain of redemption, a reality in Christ's satisfying of justice, and performing his engagements according to the tenor of that transaction: And seeing there is a reality in this Saviour, and in his suffering and satisfying of divine justice, and in the price that he paid to the full; *Put* not this Saviour *again to open shame*, as the word is, Heb. vi. 6. *Tread not the Son of God under foot, neither account the Blood of the covenant an unholy thing; do not despite to the Spirit of grace*, as it is, Heb. x. 29. He hath suffered enough already, let him not be a sufferer again: O! grieve him not by your unbelief, but give him credit, by adventuring your souls on him upon his own terms; yourselves will have the advantage, and he the glory. This is the pure simple truth of the gospel; do not only receive it as a truth, but receive him that it holds forth, and let your hearts close with him, and your faith feed upon him, *who became poor, that ye through his poverty might be made rich*. Happy they for evermore, who are made rich through his poverty; and miserable are they, and much more miserable eternally will they be, whose practice faith, that they think they have another way to be happy than by his suffering and satisfaction, and in disdain reject both him and it.

SERMON XVIII.

Isaiah liii. 2. *For he shall grow up before him as a tender plant, and as a root out of a dry ground: he hath no form nor comeliness; and when we shall see him, there is no beauty that we should desire him.*
Verse 3. *He is despised and rejected of men, a man of sorrows, and acquainted with grief: and we hid as it were our faces from him; he was despised, and we esteemed him not.*

IF our hearts were suitably tender, the reading of these words, knowing of whom they are spoken, would some way prick and wound them: it is hard to determine, (tho' it may be we should not make the comparison) whether there is more grace in our Lord's condescendence, or more wickedness and perverseness in the unkind and evil meeting that he gets from sinners; but surely there is much grace on the one side in his coming so low, and much wickedness and perverseness on the other side, for what meets he with, even blessed Jesus, *who is the glory and praise of all his saints*, yea *the brightness of his Father's glory? he is despised and rejected, and we esteemed him not*; even when he thus humbled himself, and took on our nature, and was and is prosecuting the work of our salvation, and evidencing his grace in an inconceivable manner.

These are the two things that are spoken of here, his condescending to be a Man, and a mean Man; and, which is yet more, *a Man of sorrows and acquainted with grief*; which if we believed, and knew really what he were, that it was even he, *by whom all things were created, who is the beginning of the creation of God, the first-born of every creature*, yea, he *for whom all things were created*, for whose glory the world and all things in it were made and continue, he for whom all things are as their last end, and thro' whom they are preserved in their being, and governed in their operations, and shall be seen to tend to his glory in the close; we would certainly wonder more at this his condescendence: And yet, alas! it is he that is *despised and rejected*, and that *we hid as it were our faces from*, and would not give our countenance: It is he by whom the world was made that is despised, and we esteemed him not: And this is the *second* thing in the words, which we are now to speak to, even the abominably unsuitable meeting that men give to our Lord Jesus, who hath so far condescended, as to leave some way his Father's glory, not to receive a kingdom of this world, but to be trod upon in it as a worm: he is despised and rejected, and we will not entertain him, nor make him welcome when he cometh: *We esteem him not*.

Only take this advertisement, for clearing of the words, and for grounding of the doctrine, That this, which is spoken of Christ's humiliation, and man's stumbling at it, is not precisely to be restricted to his humiliation in his own person only, and mens stumbling at that; for it is given as the reason of men their stumbling and offending at Christ in all times: But is to be extended to Christ in his gospel and ordinances throughout all ages, and so it comes in as the reason why so few believe on him. If ye ask the reason why men do not now believe and receive Christ in the offer of the gospel? here it is, For *we esteemed him not*, for *he shall grow up before him as a tender plant*: he shall be mean and contemptible-like to the men of the world, and in an afflicted condition; therefore he is not esteemed, therefore he is not believed on.

These two are the main doctrines to be spoken to here, 1. That *Jesus Christ, who thus condescends and humbles himself for the salvation of lost sinners, is not esteemed of but despised and undervalued*; which is implied in the words, *When we shall see him, there is no beauty that we should desire him*; and is more clearly holden out in the following words, *He was despised, and we esteemed him not*. 2. That this undervaluing and little esteeming of Jesus Christ, is the great ground of folks unbelief, or the reason why men do not believe on him, even because they think him not worthy the receiving: Two very clear truths in the words and in experience, tho' as sad in their consequents.

As to the *1st*, which is this, That our Lord Jesus Christ is usually and ordinarily exceedingly undervalued, and little esteemed of by the men of the world, to whom he is offered in the gospel: There are two things implied and supposed here, in and about the doctrine, that will clear it, and be as two reasons of it. 1. That he hath no form nor comeliness, and no beauty wherefore he should be desired; which holdeth out this, that men are ordinarily taken up with, and seek after worldly grandeur or greatness, splendor, and beauty; that it is it that filleth mens eyes, and is that which Christ wanted: This we say, is one reason why Christ is so little thought of, even because he cometh not with external pomp, observation and grandeur, nor with great temporal gifts to his followers. That which mainly is desirable to natural men, is that which hath earthly beauty in it; a very deceitful consideration and ground, tho' such an one as men are often carried away with, and therefore they despise and reject the Saviour. 2. Which is another reason of the doctrine, and also clearly implied, That our Lord Jesus Christ's humiliation and coming so low for man's sake, his very condescending and stooping for their good, is the great ground of their stumbling at him, and because of that he is the less thought of; even the very height of his grace, and that great stretch thereof, that the Son of God became thus low as to become Man, a mean Man, and a Man of sorrows, is a greater ground of stumbling to men, than if he had never become thus low. Now these two being supposed, and thus explained, the doctrine is clear, to wit, That Jesus Christ, that became Man, and performed the satisfaction due to the justice of God for our sins, is usually and ordinarily disesteemed and undervalued by them to whom he is offered in the gospel. (1.) It was so under the Old Testament, and is so likewise under the New: What is almost all the gospel spent on, but to hold out Christ upon the one side to be a Man of sorrows, and upon the other side to shew that men esteemed him not? How was he undervalued at his birth, when his mother was thrust out to a stable, and he laid in a manger? and no sooner doth he appear in the exercise of his public ministry, but his friends offend at him, and look on him as a distracted man, Mark iii. his countrymen contemn him, and were offended at him, Mark vi. *Is not this* (say they) *the Carpenter, the son of Mary, the brother of James and Joses?* And how was he esteemed, or rather disesteemed and undervalued, at his death; so that it is said, Acts xiii. 14. *They denied the holy and just One; and desired that a murderer should be granted unto them.* They rejected the Prince of Life, and chused Barabbas; and judging him not worthy to live, they cry, *Away with him:* Hence our Lord saith, Matt. xi. *Blessed is he that is not offended in me*, which insinuates, that there were but very few to whom his humiliation proved not a stumbling-block. (2.) If we consult experience, we will find this to be true. How little is he thought of among Turks, amongst whom his precious name is blasphemed, tho' they pretend more respect to him than meer heathens do? How little is he thought of among the Jews, who call him a deceiver! And if we come nearer, even to the Christian Church, and to such as profess their faith of his being the eternal Son of God, equal with the Father, that he is Judge of quick and dead, and they that look for salvation through him; yet, if it be put to a trial, how few are they that will be found to esteem of him aright; since there are but few that believe the the report that is made of him, but few that receive him as he is offered in the gospel, few that have but such respect to him as to prefer him to their idols, and that give him the first and chief seat in their hearts? And if we consider how little eager pursuing there is after him, that he may be enjoyed; and how indifferent folks are whether they have or want him; how many things men dote upon and prefer to Jesus Christ, as the Lord complains, Jer. ii. 13. *My people have committed two evils, they have forsaken me the fountain of living waters, and have digged to themselves cisterns, even broken cisterns that can hold no water*, the thing will be clear beyond all debate. We may take in another branch of the doctrine here, when he saith, *we esteemed him not*; and it is this, That even believers are, in so far as unrenewed, inclined, and not without culpable accession to this same sin of undervaluing Jesus Christ. It is indeed true, that the apostle Peter saith in his first Epistle, chap. ii. verse 7. *To you that believe he is precious*; Which place, tho' it confirm the first part of this doctrine, that to them that believe not he is not precious, but a stone of stumbling, and a rock of offence; albeit, that believers, being compared with unbelievers, have some precious esteem of Jesus Christ, yet if we consider the corrupt nature that in part cleaves to them, the degree of their estimation of him, and that it is but very little and low, in respect of what it should be; and the many peevish fits, to's and fro's, up's and down's that they are subject to, with the many suspicions and jealousies they have of him; so that, tho' they were just now fresh and lively in the exercise of their faith, and of their estimation of Christ, yet within a little, even by and by, they give way again to their jealousies; the doctrine will also hold true of them, *we esteemed him not*.

We shall give the *second doctrine* (and then speak to the use of both jointly) which is this, That there is more culpably accessory to the abounding of unbelief, than the poor thoughts and little estimation that men have of Jesus Christ: The undervaluing of him is the great ground and reason why they believe not on him: And on the contrary, if the hearers of the gospel had higher thoughts, and a more precious esteem of Christ, and valued him according to his unvaluable worth, there would be more believing in him than there is. When the gospel comes to invite men to the wedding, Matt. xxii. when Christ is roosed and commended, as to what he is, what he hath purchased, and what he freely offereth to sinners; it is said, *that those who were bidden made light of it, and went away, one to his farm, another to his merchandize,* &c. When Christ was spoken of, and the offer of life thro' him, they undervalued and despised it, and made light of the offer, and therefore turned their backs; for they thought more of the house, of the oxen, of the farm, and of the married wife, than they thought of him: Acts xvii. when Paul is preaching Christ at Athens, the philosophers and orators, these learned heads, despise and disdain him, as a setter-forth of some strange and uncouth god: If we compare this with its contrary, it will be further clear, to wit, wherever there is estimation of Christ, it proves a help to faith, and a ground of it: so, wherever Christ is lightlied, disesteemed and undervalued; it breeds in folk, and is a ground to them of these three, 1. It cools, or rather keeps cool, their love and affection to him; where he is disesteemed and undervalued, he cannot be loved; and people in that case become like these that are brought in, in, Jer. xliv. 17. saying, *It was better with us when we did bake cakes to the queen of heaven:* The Lord is counted by them to be as *a wilderness and land of darkness;* and they say, as it is Jer. ii. 31. *We are Lords, and will come no more unto thee.* And when men esteem not Christ, they seek not after him, they care not for an interest in him, they trust not to him: when a man valueth a pearl, he will readily sell all that he hath, that he may buy it; but that which is not esteemed, there will be no care to come by it. 2. It hath influence to obstruct folks giving him credit, which is of the very essence of faith; so then, where he is not esteemed of he is not, he cannot be believed on: The former says, that we will not marry him; this says, we will not trow him, nor trust the reality of his offer: Where he is not esteemed of, he is not taken up to be real, in good earnest, and faithful in what he says; his offers are looked upon as having neither solidity nor reality in them: Therefore, Rev. xix. these two are put together, first it is said, *Blessed are they that are called to the marriage-supper of the Lamb;* and then it is subjoined, *These are the true and faithful sayings of God:* So that, when Christ is not esteemed of, he is not thought worth the crediting and lipning to; and it is on this ground that the Lord founds his controversy with his professing people, Jer. ii. 5. *What iniquity have your fathers found in me, that they have gone far from me, and have walked after vanity, and are become vain?* They undervalued his word, they thought him not worth credit, and therefore they turned the back on him; the same is insinuated by the Lord, Mic. vi. 3. *O my people, what have I done unto thee? and wherein have I wearied thee? testify against me?* 3. This little esteem of Christ weakens hope or expectation of any good that men may have from him: When we esteem him not there is no expectation of getting our need supplied, and our wants made up by him, nor of attaining in him the happiness that we would be at; and therefore there are no serious addresses made to him for the same: these three, love to him, trust in him, hope from and through him, being the prime graces in a Christian, when they are weakened, unbelief most certainly in so far prevaileth: and it being Christ's worthiness, and the estimation thereof, that gives ground to all these; then sure, when he is not esteemed, but undervalued, these must also fail in their exercise, and be in utter nonentry, where he is altogether undervalued. Now, laying all these together, there can hardly be any thing more culpably accessory to the abounding of unbelief than the undervaluing of precious Jesus Christ; it is impossible that he can be cordially welcomed, where he is not at all esteemed of.

As for *Uses* of these doctrines, they are of large extent, serving to make manifest a root of bitterness, and a great neck-break of a multitude of souls, and which men and women will not easily be persuaded to believe. Let this therefore be the *first use* of it, To discover a great sin that is incident to the hearers of this gospel: Among many other things that may be charged on them, this is one, and not the least, even little estimation of Jesus Christ; so little, that when he is speaking, they count him scarce worthy the hearing: hence is the slumbering and sleeping of so many, when he is preached of; which holds out something of the nature of all men and women. This despising, undervaluing, and thinking little of Christ, is a sin that may for a long time cleave fast and close to the hearers of the gospel, and doth so to many to their dying day. It may be ye will think this a strange and uncouth charge, and that whoever disesteem him, ye do certainly esteem him much; but it were better ye were seriously and humbly saying with the prophet here, *He was despised, and we esteemed him not.* There are many who never once suspect themselves as guilty of, or chargeable with this evil; for whose conviction, let me speak but a few words: Is there not such a bitter root in you? If it be natural to all men and women, how comes it to pass that ye are free of it? Is there nothing of the seed of the serpent in you? and if there be, will there not be hatred at the Seed of the woman in you? Are ye any other sort of hearers than they were to whom this is spoken? were they not hearers of the gospel as well as ye? nay, he speaks here of hearers of the gospel in all ages, and yet ye will disdain to take with this sin, and will account it to be an uncouth, if not an unjust charge and imputation, to say of you that ye are undervaluers and despisers of Christ: but the reason of it is twofold, the first whereof is, Because ye know not what Christ's worth is, and therefore ye do neither esteem him, nor know that ye disesteem and undervalue him; whereas they, who have won to some knowledge of his worth, are always, or very often, complaining that they cannot get him suitably thought of and esteemed. The second reason is, Because ye know not yourselves, and therefore ye take self-love and estimation of yourselves to be love to him and estimation of him; ye think yourselves so well, that ye cannot endure to think that ye want any grace or good thing; and estimation of Christ being a good thing, and ye thinking that ye could not hold up your face and own the reproaching and despising of him, ye will not let it light that ye want this grace and good thing, a precious esteem of him: But there is no greater evidence that ye are lying under the power of the deceit and delusion of your own hearts, that your natural distemper and fever is not cooled and calmed, but that ye are still roving in nature and therefore, tho' ye be living in enmity at God and Christ, yet ye cannot be made sensible of it. We really think it somewhat strange, that men and women should live twenty, thirty, forty or fifty years under the gospel, and yet never be brought to groan under this enmity, nor to lay to heart this sin of undervaluing of Christ: But if it be a truth that none naturally do love and esteem him, then certainly many of you are grosly mistaken, that think ye esteem highly of him; Ah? your fancied esteem of him will be counted an undervaluing of him.

And if ye ask, What is that to undervalue Christ? or, When is he undervalued? I answer, He is undervalued, 1. When he is not matched with, or married; when the match with himself, whereof he maketh offer, is not closed with upon his own terms: For what I pray can hinder the ending of a bargain, or finishing a marriage-contract, especially when it is so full, free, and rich on the Proposer and Suitor's part, but either that folk think it is not fit for them, or that they think nothing of it at all? and this is it that hinders closing with Christ, Matth. xxii. *they made light of it, and went away,* &c. and Psal. lxxxi. *My people would not hearken to my voice, and* Israel *would none of me,* 2. When any thing is made equal to Christ, much more when any thing is preferred to him, he is undervalued and not esteemed of; when he gets little or none of folks care and labour, little of their time, little of their love and delight, few or none of their thoughts, &c. but they are quite carried away after other things; *for where the treasure is, there the heart will be also:* and were Christ our Treasure, and precious in our esteem, our hearts would be more set on him; but it is strange, sad, and even astonishing, to think, how little our spirits are exercised with the thoughts of Christ; how little they are taken up with longing for him, and delighting in him and yet we will think that we esteem him. 3. Our Lord is undervalued, when he is not made use of, and imployed, and lippened to, as an able and sufficient Saviour. If there be a learned and skilful physician in a city in all or most diseases, or an able lawyer to plead all causes; if folk have diseases to be cured, and causes to be pleaded, and yet do not imploy such a physician or such a lawyer, but go to some other, tho' far less skilful and able, they undervalue him: it is even so here, when folks have many sins, and they seek not to him for pardon; many, not only temporal wants, but also, (and mainly) many spiritual wants, and do not acknowledge him in them, neither seek to him for supply of them; many predominant evils, and they seek not to him to mortify them; and many snares and temptations, and they do not make use of him to prevent and lead them by them; and many spiritual causes to be pleaded before God, or at his bar, and they do not employ him as Advocate to plead for them. 4. He is undervalued, when folk think not themselves happy enough in him, nor sicker enough in bargaining with him, and when he doth not satisfy and fully content them, as if he were *yea and nay,* and as if *all the promises were not yea and amen in him:* when he is not credited intirely, and rested upon, he is not esteemed of: hence he complains, John v. *Ye will not come to me that ye might have life:* and Matt. xxiii. *How would I have gathered you, and ye would not!* he would, to say so with reverence, fain do them a good turn, but they will not lippen to him. O how much of undervaluing of Christ is there among believers, when they hold and draw with him, entertain jealousies and suspicions of him, scarcely credit him, and when they do at any time credit him, are in a manner ready to take back their word again! How often are creature-comforts overvalued by them? And how often are the consolations of God small with them? These and many other ways are they, even they, in some considerable measure and degree, guilty of undervaluing of Christ.

Use 2. Take with this sin, acknowledge and seek pardon for it; it were a good token of some tenderness, to be mourning for enmity against Christ, and for undervaluing of him, as well as for drunkenness, fornication, theft, or any other gross sin: And where that gracious and right mourning, that is spoken of Zech. xii. 10. comes, it will be in special for this undervaluing of Christ to the height of piercing of him: We would ask any of you that think ye repent, if this sin of slighting him hath pierced you, as it did these? Acts ii. It may be, some think themselves so cleanly and perfect, that ye have not many sins to mourn for: O dreadful mistake! but tho' ye had no more, is not this enough that ever there should have been enmity in your bosom at Christ? And should not this prick you at the very heart, that ever ye should so undervalued him? But readily they that see fewest

sins

sins in themselves, will see and take with least of this sin.

Use 3. It serves to be a warning to all men in nature to consider what their condition is. Do ye that have this enmity, and are undervaluers of Christ, know what is in your hearts? and do ye consider what posture ye will be found in, if grace make not a change, in the day of Christ? ye will be found amongst these despisers and haters, that would not have him to reign over them: How will ye dare to appear, or in what posture will ye appear before him, when he, whom ye despised, shall come in the glory of his Father, with all the holy angels with him, and shall sit upon the throne of his glory? and yet appear ye must: How will the conscience then gnaw, and the heart be affrighted? how will challenges waken, yea, sting and prick you, on this ground, that the Son of God, the Heir of all things, the Lord of lords, and King of kings, who proposed marriage to you, was undervalued, and marriage with him made light of, and that a thing of nought was put in his room and place? will not this be a horrible challenge in that day? and if ye would consider what will be their posture that mocked and buffeted him, and plucked off his hair, that nodded with the head, and cried, Aha, and bad him come down from the cross, that did scourge him, and hang him upon the cross betwixt two thieves; such a posture will all of you be in, who have despised and disesteemed him; ye will meet with that same sad sentence, *Bring out these mine enemies, that would not that I should reign over them, and slay them before me.* O what a strange punishment suppose ye, will that be, when the Saviour of sinners shall stand by and look on, till he see vengeance execute on sinners that despised him. Think on it, for there is such a day coming, when ye will all appear before him, and when your reckonings will be cast up: suffer not yourselves to be cheated into an opinion, that it will be accounted a little sin to be found under this guilt of despising Christ; and let not one of you put it off himself, and over upon another: they will be found despisers of him, that would never let it light; nay, even many that have preached him, and that would have been angry at prophanity in others, as may be gathered from Mat. vii. 22.

The *4th Use* serves to commend this to you as a piece of your duty to study to know Christ, and to have the suitable impression of Christ and of his worth, as the great mean contributive to the bringing you to credit him, and believe on him, and to the removing a main obstruction that hinders your faith, and that is the undervaluing of him: For if undervaluing of him be the great cause of unbelief, and that which mainly obstructs faith, then the esteeming of him, from a due impression of his worth, must be a great mean of, and help to faith; and the more he be esteemed of, the more will he be believed on: It hath an attractive vertue, to draw sinners to love him; a screwing vertue, to screw up the affections towards him; and withal a fixing and establishing vertue, to settle and stay the soul upon him by believing: the soul that, from the right impression of his worth, esteems of him, knows that it may lippen to him, for he is holy and true; and hence it is, that the great thing that believers take to ground their prayers upon, is some excellency in God, some one or other of his titles and attributes upon which they fix, to bear them up, under, and against any difficulty that presseth hard upon them; this fixes also their hope and expectation of attaining of any good thing that they want through him: and therefore upon the one side, we would commend to you the study of Christ's worth, and upon the other an high estimation of him, as that which will fix your faith, and love, and hope on him; this we see to be in a high degree in Paul, Philip. iii. *I account all things* (saith he) *to be but loss and dung for the excellency of the knowledge of him*, and his transcendent worth. Ye would not think it lost labour, to read and study these places of scripture, that shew what our Lord Jesus is, in his person, natures, and offices, that ye may have the faith of his Godhead fixed, and may be clear as to the excelling fulness that is in him; as namely that of Isa. ix. 6. *To us a Child is born, to us a Son is given, the government shall be upon his shoulders, and his name shall be called Wonderful, Counseller, the Mighty God, the Everlasting Father, the Prince of Peace, of whose kingdom and government there shall be no end:* And to study his excellent proprieties, his Eternity, Omnipotency, Faithfulness, Mercy, &c. common to him with the Father and Holy Ghost; and the excellent qualifications that as Mediator he is replenished with; being full of grace and truth, and in all things having the preheminency; see Col. i. John i. 14. and Heb. i. 2, 3. &c. The reason why we press you to this, is, not only that ye may have more theory and contemplation; but also, and mainly, that your affections may be delighted in him, and that your faith may, without hesitation, come to give him credit. Ignorance of Christ breeds disestimation, and disestimation makes you not to give him credit, and thus ye

a distance from him; there is no study more pleasant, more precious, and more profitable: There is here then a task for you, that ask what ye shall do? Even to read and study the excellency of Jesus Christ, and to labour to have it well fixed in the imagination of the thoughts of your hearts; it will give you notable direction what to do, even that which is well-pleasing to God, and may be very profitable to you through his blessing.

Use. 5. See here the great necessity aud conveniency of studying the disestimation of Christ that is in us, as well as of studying the worth that is in him, and what he hath out of love suffered for us; these two are put together in the text, it being needful for us to be as well acquainted with the one as with the other. We shall give you this use in two short doctrines; the first whereof is, That it is a necessary duty for the hearers of the gospel to study throughly, and to be convinced of, and clear in their disestimation of Christ, as well as of his worth and excellency, because it wakeneth up repentance, and maketh it flow, and thorowly humbleth the sinner, when he findeth this desperate wickedness and perverseness to be in himself, and maketh him kindly to lothe and abhor himself; and unless this desperate wickedness be seen and felt, that great and bitter mourning, spoken of, Zech. xii. 10. will never flow forth.

The 2*d* is, That where folk have any just estimation of Christ, and of his worth, and are sensible of the evil of unbelief, there will also be some sense of the sin of undervaluing him; and the more sense they have of the evil of unbelief, they will be the more sensible of their undervaluing of him, and will with the prophet here cry out, *He was despised, and we esteemed him not.* And from both these ye may see the necessity of studying to find out this corruption; the search and discovery whereof will insight you in the evil and perverseness of your nature, and so deeply humble you, and also serve highly to commend Christ and his grace to you; and without the discovery of this corruption, it is impossible ever to be humbled thorowly, or to have right thoughts of Christ and of his grace.

Use 6. It serves to let us see the necessity of believing in Christ, and of the employing of him; because there is no other way to be free of the challenges of misprising and not esteeming of him, but by receiving of him, and believing on him.

A 7*th Use* may be added, and it is this, That the more there be that despise Christ, and the greater difficulty there be in believing on him, the more reason have they to be thankful that he graciously works any suitable estimation of himself in, and brings them to believe on him: These who have gotten any glimpse of his glory, which hath lifted him high in their estimation, to the drawing forth of their faith and love after him, would praise him for it: It is he, and only he, that opened your eyes to see him, and gave you that estimation of him, and circumcised your hearts to love him; let him therefore have all the praise and glory of it. This is the word of God, and himself bless it to you through Jesus Christ.

SERMON XIX.

Isaiah liii. 4. *Surely he hath born our griefs, and carried our sorrows: yet we did esteem him stricken, smitten of God, and afflicted.*
Verse 5. *But he was wounded for our transgressions, he was bruised for our iniquities: the chastisement of our peace was upon him, and with his stripes we are healed.*

THIS is a most wonderful subject that the prophet is here discoursing of, even that which concerneth the sufferings of our blessed Lord Jesus, by way of prediction several hundreds of years before his incarnation: It was much that he was to be *a Man of sorrows, and acquainted with grief;* but this was more, that *he was despised, and we esteemed him not.* There is wonderful grace upon the one side, that our Lord became so very low; and wonderful contempt and enmity on the other side, that we despised him, and esteemed him not, even because of his lowness.

In the words now read, and forward, the prophet sets himself to remove the offence that men took at our Lord's humiliation, by shewing them, that although he became so low, yet he was not to be the less esteemed of for that: And the ground which he lays down to remove the offence, is in the first words of the text, which in sum is this, That there was nothing in himself wherefore he should have been brought so low; there was no sin in him, neither was there any guile found in his mouth; but he was graciously pleased to take on him that which we should have born: and therefore men ought not to stumble, and offend at his stooping to bear that which would with its weight have crushed them eternally, and thereby to make their peace with God. In the 6th verse he shews how it came

to

to pass that he stooped so low, *All we* (saith he) *like sheep have gone astray, and turned every one of us to our own way, and the Lord laid on him the iniquity of us all:* we had lost ourselves, but God, in the depth of his eternal wisdom, love, and goodwill, found the way to save us; wherein (to speak so) a covenant was transacted betwixt God and the Mediator, who becomes Cautioner for our sins, which are transferred upon him. From the 7th to the 10th verse, he goes on in shewing the execution of this transaction, and how the Cautioner performed all according to his engagement; and from the 10th verse to the close, we have the promises made to him for his satisfaction: The scope is, as to remove the scandal of the cross, so to hold out our Lord's pursuing the work of satisfaction to the justice of God for elect sinners, and the good success he had in it.

In the 4. and 5. *verses* we have three things; 1. This ground asserted, *Surely he hath born our griefs, and carried our sorrows.* 2. Mens enmity heightened from this, *yet we did esteem him stricken, smitten of God, and afflicted:* In the very mean time that he condescended to stoop so low for us, and to bear that which we should have born, we esteemed but little of him, we looked on him as a plagued man. 3. This is more fully explained, *ver.* 5. *But he was wounded for our transgressions, he was bruised for our iniquities;* he was so handled for our sins, and *the chastisement of our peace was on him,* that which made our peace with God was on him; *By his stripes we are healed,* the stripes that wounded and killed him cured us.

We have here then rather as it were a sad narration, than a prophecy of the gospel, holding out a part of our Lord's sufferings; yet a clear foundation of the consolation of the people of God, it being the ground of all our faith of the pardon of sin, of our peace with God, and of our confident appearing before him, that our Lord was content to be thus dealt with, and to *give his back to the smiters, and his cheeks to them that pluckt off the hair.*

We shall clear the words in the assertion, which will serve to clear the words of the whole chapter, and also of the doctrines to be drawn from it. 1. The thing that Christ bare, is called *griefs, and sorrows*; by which we understand the effects that sin brings on men in the world, for it is the same that in the 5. *verse* is called his being *wounded for our transgressions, and bruised for our iniquity;* it is a wounding that iniquity causeth, and meritoriously procureth: It is not sin it-self, but the effect of sin, to wit, the punishment, the sorrow and grief that sin bringeth with it, called *griefs and sorrows*; partly because grief and sorrow is necessarily joined with sin, partly to shew the extremity and exceeding greatness of this grief and sorrow, and the bitter fruits that sin hath with it. 2. How is it said that Christ hath *born* and *carried* their griefs and sorrows? By this we understand, not only Christ's removing of them, as he removed sicknesses and diseases, as it is said, Matt. viii. 16, 17. but also, and mainly, his actual and real enduring of them, as the phrase is frequently used in the scripture; *That man shall bear his iniquity;* or he shall bear his sin, Lev. v. and many other places; it sets out a real inflicting of the punishment that sin deserves, on him. 3. That it is said *our* griefs, and *our* sorrows, it is not needlesly or superfluously set down, but to meet with the offence that men take at Christ's humbling himself so low; as if he had said, What aileth you to stumble at Christ's coming so low, and being so afflicted? It was not for his own sins, but for ours, that he was so handled: And they are called *our* griefs and sorrows, 1. Because we by our sins procured them, they were our deserving, and due to us; the debt was ours, though he as our Cautioner took it on himself. 2. Because tho' the elect have distinct reckonings, and peculiar sins, some more, some fewer, some greater, some lesser; yet they are all put on Christ's account; there is a combination of them, a gathering of them all on him, as the word is, *ver.* 6. *He hath laid on him,* or made to meet on him, *the iniquities of us all.*

The meaning then of the assertion is this, Surely this is the cause of Christ's humiliation, and this makes him not only to become Man, but to be a mean poor Man, and have a comfortless and afflicted life in the world, that he hath taken on him that punishment, curse and wrath, that was due to us for our sins; and therefore he ought not to be offended and stumbled at.

Now, because Socinians, the great enemies of Christ's satisfaction, and of the comfort of his people, labour to elude this place, and to make Christ only an exemplary Saviour, and deny that he really and actually did undergo these griefs and sorrows for the sins of the elect; We shall a little clear and confirm the exposition we have given; the question is not about the taking away of sin, but about the manner of removing it: They say, That it is by God's pardoning it without a satisfaction; we say, it is by Christ's satisfaction; so the difficulty in expounding the words is, whether to expound them

them of Christ's removing our sorrows and griefs from us, or of his bearing of them for our sins, and so really taking it away. And that this scripture means not of a simple removing of them, as he did sickness, Matt. viii. 17. but by a real taking them upon himself, and bearing of them, in order to the satisfaction of the justice of God for our sins; We shall give these reasons to confirm it: 1. Because these words are to be understood of such a bearing of sorrows and griefs, as made Christ to be contemptible and despised before others: This is clear from the scope; for they are given as a reason why Christ was rejected and despised, as a Man of sorrows, and acquainted with grief, and why men should not stumble at him for all that, because it was for them. Now, if he had only removed sorrows from them, as he did sickness, it had not been a cause of his sorrow and grief, nor of any man's stumbling at him, but had rather been a cause of his exaltation in mens esteem: But it is given here as a cause of that which went before in the first part of the 3. *verse*, and also a reason why men should not stumble at him, and withal as an aggravation of their guilt who did stumble at him. Now it is clear, that the ground of the Jews despising and mocking of him, was not his removing of sicknesses and diseases, but his seeming to be given over unto death's power. 2. Because that which is called here, *bearing of sorrows and griefs*, is in the following words called a *being wounded for our transgressions*; which imports not only that he was wounded, but that our iniquities were the cause of his being wounded, and that the desert of them was laid on him. 3. This wounding is holden forth to be the *stripes* whereby *we are healed*; and *all we like sheep have gone astray, and the Lord hath laid on him the iniquities of us all*; we did the wrong, but he made the amends: And it was such a wounding, as proves a cure to us, and makes way for our peace and reconciliation with God; and such as without it there is no healing for us, for *by his stripes we are healed*: It is by his swallowing up of the river and torrent of wrath that was in our way, and would have drowned us eternally, had not he interposed for us, that we may escape. 4. Consider the parallel places to this in the new testament, and we will find that this place holds out Christ's real and actual bearing of our sorrows and griefs: I shall only name three; The first, is that of 2 Cor. v. 21. *He hath made him to be sin for us, who knew no sin, that we might be made the righteousness of God in him;* which can be no other way exponed, but of Christ's being made an offering and a sacrifice for our sins: He not being a sinner himself, but becoming our Cautioner, and engaging to pay our debt, and to tell down the price for the satisfaction of divine justice; he is reckoned to be the sinner, and our sins are imputed to him, and he is dealt with as a sinner. A 2d place is that of Gal. iii. 13. *Christ hath redeemed us from the curse of the law, by being made a curse for us; as it is written, Cursed is every one that hangeth on a tree.* The sorrows and griefs that Isaiah says here, he should bear, are there exponed by the apostle, to be his being made a curse, or his bearing of the curse that we should have born; it is not meant simply of his removing the curse from us, but it also sets out the manner how he removed it, to wit, by his own bearing of it himself, being nailed to the cross, according to the threatning given out before. The 3d place is that of 1 Pet. ii. 24. *Who his own self bare our sins in his own body on the tree;* where there is a direct reference to this place of Isaiah, which is cited for confirmation of what the apostle saith: and every word is full, and hath a special signification and emphasis in it; *He his own self bare*, the same word that is here, and *our sins*, and *in his own body* and *on the tree;* intimating the lowest step of his humiliation, *by whose stripes ye were healed*; for *ye were as sheep going astray*, &c. by his bearing of our sins, the burden of sin was taken off us, and we are set free.

I know that place of Matt. viii. 17. hath its own difficulty, and therefore I shall speak a word for clearing of it; he hath spoken *ver.* 16. of Christ's *healing all that were sick*, and then subjoins in the 17. *That it might be fulfilled which was spoken by Isaias the prophet, saying, Himself took our infirmities, and bare our sicknesses;* whereupon these enemies of Christ would infer, that this place of scripture hath no other, nor further meaning, but of Christ's curing of some sick folks, and of the deputed or committed power which he hath to pardon sins: But we suppose, that the reasons which we have already given, make it clear, that this cannot be the meaning of the place; to which we shall add *first* a reason or two, and *secondly* give you the true meaning of it.

The reasons why this cannot be the meaning of the place, are, 1*st*, Because, Acts viii. 32. this scripture is spoken of as being daily a fulfilling by Christ, and therefore it could not be fulfilled in these few days wherein he was in the flesh upon earth. 2. Because this bearing of our griefs and sorrows is such a piece of Christ's humiliation, as thereby

thereby he took on all the griefs and sorrows of all the elect at once, both of these who lived in Isaiah his time, and of these who lived before, and since his time; and therefore cannot be restricted to the curing of temporal diseases in the days wherein he was on earth, nay, not to the pardoning of the sins of the elect then living, there being many elect before and since comprehended in this his satisfaction, which was most certainly a satisfaction for the sins of the elect that were dead, and to be born, as well as for the sins of them that were then living.

2*dly*, For the meaning of the place, 1. We are not to look on Christ's curing of sicknesses and diseases, Matt. viii. 16. as a proper fulfilling of this place, Isa. liii. 4. but as many scriptures are spoken by way of allusion to other scriptures, so is this; there is indeed some fulfilling of the one in the other, and some resemblance betwixt the one and the other, and the resemblance is this, even to shew Christ's tenderness to the outward condition of folks bodies, whereby he evidenceth his tenderness and respect to the inward sad condition of their immortal souls, whereinto they were brought through their sin; the great thing aimed at by the prophet. 2. If we consider the griefs and sorrows that Christ bare and suffered, complexly, in their cause and effects: He, in healing of these diseases and sicknesses, bare our griefs, and carried our sorrows, because, when he took on our debt, he took it on with all the consequences of it; and so, tho' Christ took on no disease in his own person, for we read not that he was ever sick, yet in taking on the debt in common of the elect, he virtually took on all sicknesses and diseases, or what they suffered in the diseases, or should have suffered, he took it on together; and hereby he had a right, to speak so, to the carrying of all diseases, and in carrying of them he had respect to the cause of them, to wit, sin: Therefore to such as he cured, he says very often, *Thy sins be forgiven thee*; he studied to remove that in most of them he did deal with: And so, looking on our Lord as taking on our sins complexly with the cause, and as having a right to remove all the effects of sin, evidencing itself in the removing of these diseases, whereof sin was the cause, these words may be thus fulfilled; and so they are clear, and the doctrine also. We have here no mere exemplary Saviour, that hath done no more but confirmed his doctrine, and given us a copy how to do and behave; but he hath really and actually born our sorrows and griefs, and removed our debt, by undergoing the punishment due to us for sin.

Observe here, 1. *That sin in no flesh, is not in the elect themselves, is without sorrow and grief*: tribulation and anguish are knit to it, or it hath these following on it: Or take the doctrine thus. *Wherever there is sin, there is the cause of much sorrow and grief*; no more can the native cause be without the effect, than sin can be without sorrow and grief: It is the plain assertion of scripture, Rom. ii. 8, 9. *Indignation and wrath, tribulation and anguish upon every soul of man that doth evil*; which one place, putting the four words together, says, 1. That there is sorrow most certainly, and inseparably on every soul that hath sinned. And, 2. That this sorrow is exceeding great (which may also be the reason why this sorrow is set out in two words in the text) therefore four words are used by the apostle to express it. It is not our purpose here to dispute, whether God in his justice doth by necessity of nature punish the sinner? These three things considered, will make out the doctrine, which is, That there is a necessary connexion betwixt sin and sorrow; and that this sorrow must needs be very great, 1. If we consider the exceeding unsuitableness of sin to the holy law of God, and how it is a direct contrariety to that most pure and perfect law. 2. If we consider the perfectly holy nature of God himself, *The righteous Lord*, saith the Psalmist, Psal. xi. 7. *loveth righteousness*; and the prophet Hab. i. 13. says, *He is of purer eyes than he can behold evil, and he cannot look upon iniquity*. And though we need not to dispute God's sovereignty, yet it is clear that he is *angry with the wicked every day*, Psal. vii. 11. and he *will by no means clear the guilty*, Exod. xxxiv. 7. and that there is a greater suitableness in his inflicting sorrow and grief on a sinner that walks contrary to him, than there is in shewing him mercy; and there is a greater suitableness in his shewing mercy to a humbled sinner, that is aiming to walk holily before him. 3. If we consider the revealed will of God in the threatning, who hath said, *The day thou eatest thou shalt surely die*; We may say, there is, as they speak in the school, a hypothetick necessity of grief and sorrow to follow on sin, and that there is a necessary connection betwixt them: And this may very well stand with the Mediator his coming in, and interposing to take that grief and sorrow from off us, and to lay it on himself; but it was once ours, because of our sin.

If it be asked, What grief and sorrow this is? We said, it is very great, and there is reason for it: For though our act of sin, 1. As to the subject that sins, man, and, 2. As to the act of sin itself, a sinful thought, word or deed, that is soon gone, be finite; yet, if we consider sin, (1.) In respect of the object against whom, the infinite God; (2.) In respect of the absolute purity of God's law, a rule that bears out God's image set down by infinite wisdom, and that may be some way called infinitely pure; and sin, as being against this pure rule that infinite wisdom hath set down; and, (3.) If we consider it in respect of its nature, every sin being of this nature, that though it cannot properly wrong the majesty of God, yet as to the intention of the thing, and even of the sinner, it wrongs him; sin in these respects may be called *infinite*, and the wrong done to the majesty of God thereby, may be called infinite, as these who built Babel, their intention in that work breathed forth infinite wrong to God, as having a direct tendency to bring them off from dependence on him: And so every sin, if it had its will and intent, would put God in subordination to it, and set itself in his room: And therefore sin in some respect, as to the wrong against God, is infinite.

2. Observe, *That the real and very great sorrow that the sins of the elect deserved, our Lord Jesus did really and actually bear and suffer.* As we have expo[u]nded the words, and confirmed the exposition given of them, ye have a clear confirmation of the doctrine from them. 1. *Griefs* and *sorrows*, in the plural number, shew intenseness of sorrow and grief. 2. That they are called *ours*, it shews our propriety in them. And, 3. That it is said Christ *bare* them; these concur to prove the doctrine, that the same sorrow which the sins of the elect deserved, Christ bare: It not only says, that our Lord bare sorrows, but the same sorrows, that by the sins of the elect were due to them; and so there was a proportionableness betwixt the sorrows that he bare, and the sorrows they should have endured; he took up the cup of wrath that was filled for us, and that we would have been put to drink, and drank it out himself. Suppose that our Lord had never died (as blessed be his name, there is no ground to make the supposition) the cup of sorrow that the elect would have drunken eternally, was the same cup that he drank out for them. It is true, we would distinguish betwixt these things that are *essentially* due to sin as the punishment of it, and these things that are only *accidentally* due to it; the former Christ bare, but not the latter. To clear both in a word or two, (1.) These things essentially due to sin, as necessarily included in the threatning, *The day thou eatest thou shalt surely die:* and in the curse of the law, according to that, *Cursed is every one that abides not in all things that are written in the book of the law to do them;* are death and the curse; these are essentially the desert of sin; in which respect it was not only necessary that Christ should become Man and suffer, but that he should suffer to death, or should die; and not only so, but that he should die the cursed death of the cross, as the threatning and curse put together hold out: And as to all these things that he underwent, and met with before, and at his death, they were the accomplishment of the threatning due to us, and fulfilled in and by him in our room; so that, as he himself saith, Luke xxiv. 26. *O fools, and slow of heart to believe all that the prophets have spoken, ought not Christ to have suffered these things, and to have entred into his glory?* Therefore he behoved to be in an agony, and to sweat great drops of blood, to be crucified, and die, and to be laid in the grave. (2.) These things which we call accidentally due to sin, are mainly two. *1st*, That horrible desperation of the damned in hell, where they gnaw their tongues for pain, and blaspheme God; this, we say, is not properly and essentially the desert of sin, but only accidental; 1. In respect of the creature's inability to bear the wrath that sin deserveth; and hence ariseth not only a sinless horror which is natural, but a sinful desperation. 2. Add to this inability of the creature, the enmity thereof, whereby it cometh to thwart with and contradict the will of God; hence the desperation not only ariseth, but is increased: Now, our Lord Jesus not being simply a Creature or a Man, but God and Man in one Person, he was able to bear the sorrow and wrath due to the elect for their sin; and there being no quarrel, nor ground of any quarrel, betwixt God, and him on his own account, though he had a natural and sinless horror at the cup of his Father's displeasure, when put to his head; yet he had no sinful desperation. The *2d* thing accidentally due to sin, is the eternal duration of the wrath, or of the curse; because the sinner, being a mere creature, cannot at one shock meet with the infinite wrath of God, and satisfy justice at once; therefore the Lord hath, in his wisdom and justice, found out a way of supporting the creature in its being, and continuing it for ever under wrath, because it cannot, being finite, satisfy infinite justice: But our Lord, being God and Man, being of infinite worth and value, and of infinite strength, was able to satisfy justice, and bear at once, that which the elect could never have born; yet he had the essentials of that which sin deserved,

to wit, death and the curse, to meet with, and did actually meet with them; as the hiding of his Father's face, and the suspending and keeping back of that consolation, that by vertue of the personal union flowed from the God-head to the Man-head: And he also had the actual sense and feeling of the wrath of God, the awaked sword of the justice of God actually smiting him; so that men wondered how he could be dead so soon. We shall only add a word or two of reasons for clearing and confirming the doctrine; and for proof of it, these three things concur, 1. That sin's deserving, by God's appointment, is to have sorrow following on it. 2. That by God's appointment, according to the covenant of redemption, the Son of God undertook that same very debt that was due by the elect. And, 3. That it was God's design not to pass one of their sins, without satisfaction made to justice, but to put at the Cautioner for them all, for the declaration of the riches and glory of the free grace of God, when the sinner is liberate, and not put to pay, and for the declaration of the holy severity and justice of God, when not one farthing is owing, but the Cautioner must needs pay it; and that both these meeting together, there may be, to all generations, a standing and shining evidence of the unsearchable riches, both of God's grace, and of his justice.

This is a sweet doctrine, and hath many massy, substantial, and soul-refreshing uses: Out of this eater comes meat, and out of the strong comes sweet, this being the very marrow of the gospel, holding out not only Christ's sufferings, but that he suffered not at random, or by guess, but that he suffered the sorrows and griefs that we should have suffered: and tho' the equivalent might have been received, yet he would needs undergo the same sufferings in their essentials; which may exceedingly confirm the faith and hope of believers in him, of their exemption and freedom from the wrath and curse of God, seeing he suffered the same that they should have suffered, had not he interposed betwixt them and it, as their Cautioner and Surety.

Use 1. Hereby we may know what an evil and bitter thing sin is, that hath such effects; would to God we could once prevail thus far with you, as to make you take up and believe, that sin hath sorrow and grief inseparably knit to it, and that the sinner is miserable, and liable to death, and to the curse of God; and there is no difference but this, that sinners are insensible how miserable they are, and so in greater capacity to be made obnoxious to that misery: Do ye mind this, O sinners, *That God is* *angry with you every day?* That *indignation and wrath, tribulation and anguish, is to every soul of man that does evil?* That *God will by no means clear the guilty?* Tremble to think upon it; many of you pass as gay honest folks, who will be found in this roll: and would ye know your condition, and the hazard that ye run? 'Tis of wrath and the curse of God eternally, with desperation and blasphemy; and if that be misery, sin is misery, or brings it: and the day comes, when there shall be a storm from heaven of fire and thunder, that will melt the elements above you, and not leave a stone upon a stone of these stately buildings on earth about you; in which day, sinners will be confirmed in the belief of this truth, *That it is an evil and bitter thing to depart from the living God.*

To press this *Use* a little, there are two sorts of sinners, who, if they would soberly let the truth of this doctrine sink in their minds, they would see their folly: The first sort are these who ly quietly under bygone guilt unrepented of, as if the sorrow were past, because the act is so; but think not so: Will the just God avenge sin on his Son, and will he let it pass in you? Ye that will grant ye are sinners, and are under convictions of sin, ye had need to take heed what is following it; as ye treasure up sin, ye are *treasuring up wrath against the day of wrath:* O wrath is a heaping up in store for you. A second sort are these that go on in sin, whatever be said to the effects of it, and will confidently put their hand to it, as if there were no sting in it at all, and drink it over as so much sweet liquor: But these stolen drinks, that seem sweet in secret, will be vomited up again with pain, torment and sorrow; and either it shall be grief and sorrow to you in the way of repentance, or eternal grief and sorrow, when the cup of God's wrath shall be put in your hand, and held to your head for evermore.

Use 2. By this ye may see a necessity of making use of the Mediator Christ Jesus; it is God's great mercy that he hath given a Mediator, and that the Mediator is come; and that he hath taken on our debt. What had been our eternal perishing and wallowing in hell's torments with devils, to his sufferings? Always this doctrine saith, that there is a necessity of making use of him, and receiving of him; and therefore, either resolve to meet with this sorrow in your own persons, or betake you to him, that by his interposing it may be kept off you. Weigh these two, that sorrow, death, and the curse necessarily follow sin, and that Jesus Christ hath died, and undergone that curse for the elect sinners: and then ye will see a necessity of being

found

found in him, that ye may be free of the curse; which made Paul make that choice, Phil. iii. 8, 9. *I count all things dung that I may win Christ, and be found in him.* Oftimes the allurements of the gospel prevail not to bring sinners to Christ; but if its allurements do not prevail, will not the consideration of the vengeance of God persuade you? However, in these two doctrines ye have in sum this, the curse of God following sin, and a free and full Saviour holden out to you, by whom ye may evite the curse: ye are invited to make him welcome; choose you, death and life are set before you, whereby you are put to it, whether ye will adventure to meet with the curse, or to make him welcome. Now, God himself make you wise to make the right choice.

SERMON XX.

Isaiah liii. 4. *Surely he hath born our griefs, and carried our sorrows: yet we did esteem him stricken, smitten of God, and afflicted.*
Verse 5. *But he was wounded for our transgressions, he was bruised for our iniquities: the chastisement of our peace was upon him, and with his stripes we are healed.*

IF we had the faith of that which the prophet speaks here, and the thorow conviction, who it is of whom he speaks, we would be in a holy transport of admiration and astonishment at the hearing of it; that it is he, who is the Prince of life, that was bruised and wounded; and that these bruises, wounds and stripes are ours, were for us, and the price and satisfaction for our iniquities to divine justice; and yet, that even he, in the performing of all this, is vilipended and despised by those, whose good he is thus pursuing and seeking after: Oh, how should it be wondered at!

These words (as we shew) hold forth these three, 1. The cause or end of Christ's suffering, *Surely he hath born our griefs, and carried our sorrows;* which is to remove and take away the scandal that might arise from Christ's humiliation, described in the foregoing words: he was low indeed, but there was no guile found in his mouth; it was for no quarrel that God had at himself, but he undertook our debt, and therefore carried our sorrows. 2. The aggravation of mens enmity and desperate wickedness; that yet, notwithstanding of all this, *We esteemed him smitten of God, and afflicted.* 3. We have the exposition of the first part more clearly set down, *But he was wounded for our transgressions, he was bruised for our iniquities,* &c. where more fully he expounds what in the beginning of the 4th verse he asserted.

We expounded the first part of the words, and shew, that these griefs and sorrows held forth the due desert of sin; called ours, because they are the due and particular desert of our sins, and that which they procured: and that Christ's bearing of them was not only meant of his taking away, or removing from us our sorrows and griefs, as he did diseases, but of his real undergoing of that which we should have undergone, even such a bearing, as made others think him smitten and plagued of God, and such as wounded and bruised, even such as made him become a curse for us, and such as procured healing to us: All which proves, that it was a real undergoing of sorrow and grief.

We spoke to two doctrines from this part. 1. That sin hath sorrow necessarily knit to it, and never wanteth sorrow following it. 2. That Christ Jesus undertook the same sorrows, and really bare these same griefs that sin procured to the elect, or that by sin were due to them.

That we may proceed to observe somewhat more, and for clearer access to the doctrine, we shall speak a word to a question that may be moved here,

What is meant by these words, *our, we,* and *us?* He hath born *our* griefs, the Lord hath laid on him the iniquity of *us* all, by his stripes *we* are healed? And the rather I would speak to this, because throughout the chapter we will find these Pronouns very frequent. We know, in scripture, *our* and *us* are sometimes extended to all mankind; so *we* are all lost in Adam, and sin hath a dominion over *us* all: and that part of the words, verse 6th, *All we like sheep have gone astray,* may well be extended to all mankind. Sometimes it is to be restricted to God's elect, and so *all* comprehends only such, and all such: And in this respect, *our, us,* and *we,* and *all,* are contradistinguished from many others in the world, and take not in all men, as Gal. iv. 26. *Jerusalem which is above is free, which is the mother of us all;* which is spoken, in opposition to the bond-woman and her children spoken of before; so that this *our, us,* and *we,* are not to be extended to all individual men in the world, as if Christ had satisfied the justice of God for all; but it is to be applied to God's elect, separate in his purpose from others, and in God's design appointed to be redeemed.

redeemed and satisfied for by Christ. And the words being thus expounded, they lead us to this doctrine, That Jesus Christ, in bearing the punishment of sin, had a particular and distinct respect to some definite sinners. For confirmation of it, we shall not go out of the chapter, the scope whereof we would clear a little; and if we look thorow the chapter, we will find five grounds, to clear that these words are to be thus restricted.

For, 1. We are to expound this universal, with respect to God's purpose and covenant, the contrivance of the elects redemption, and to the death of Christ, the execution of it; and so these words, *our, us, we, all*, are and must be restricted to these; and in them we are to find out, who they are: Now, who these are, we find clear, John vi. 37, 39. in the 37th verse, where he saith, *all that the Father hath given me shall come unto me*; and verse 39th, *This is the Father's will which hath sent me, that of all which he hath given me I should lose nothing*: it is in a word these whom the Father hath given to Christ, and as many as are given will believe; and certainly these that are given to Christ, to be redeemed by him, are the same whose iniquities the Father makes to meet on him: and these are distinguished from these not given, John xvii. 6, 11. and are called *his sheep*, John x. 15, and 17. *Therefore doth my Father love me, because I lay down my life*, to wit, *for my sheep*. And all the strain of this chapter being to shew God's way of contriving and prosecuting the work of redemption, and Christ's executing thereof, according to the covenant of redemption; all this spoken of Christ's suffering must be expounded according to that engagement. 2. Whereas it is said, verse 8. *For the transgressions of my people was he stricken*; it is certain, this *our*, and *us*, and *we*, for whom Christ was stricken, must be restricted to God's people, that is his peculiar people, who are his by electing love, as Christ saith, John xvii. 6. *Thine they were, and thou gavest them to me*: they are not his, as all the world are his, but are contradistinguished from the world, as his own peculiar, purposed, designed people; sure all the world are not God's people in this sense, therefore they are called *his sheep*, and contradistinguished from these who are not his sheep, John x. 17. And therefore we are to look on these words, *our, us*, and *we*, as of equivalent extent with the peculiar people of God; he carried the punishment of the sins of all God's people, that are his peculiar election. 3. So, verse 10th, *When thou shalt make his soul an offering for sin, he shall see his seed*: hence we gather this, That these, whose iniquities Christ bare, are Christ's seed; and for these he purposely laid down his life, as these whom he expected should be saved, for satisfying of him for the travel of his soul, and for no more; and these cannot certainly be all the world, there being such contradistinction betwixt Christ mystical, or his seed comprehending the elect, and the seed of the serpent comprehending the reprobate and wicked, who are said to be of their father the devil: these are Christ's seed, who are spiritually begotten of him, and these doubtless are not all the world, and for these only he suffered; so that *our* sins here are the sins of all the seed. 4. Look to verse 11th, where it is said, *By his knowledge shall my righteous Servant justify many: for he shall bear their iniquities*: where it is clear, whose sins they are that Christ bears; it is theirs who are justified by his knowledge, or by faith in his blood; and justification by faith in his blood, and redemption by his blood, are commensurable, and of equal extent. Now, it being certain as to the event, that not all the world, nor all in the visible Church, are justified by the faith of Christ, it must also be certain, that the sins of others, who are not, nor shall be justified, were never purposely born by Christ. And this ground, as all the rest, will be the more clear, if we consider, that it is given as an argument why they must be justified, because he hath born their iniquities. A fifth ground may be gathered from the last words of the chapter, *He made intercession for the transgressors*; whence we may reason, that Christ's intercession and his satisfaction, are of equal extent, he satisfies for no more than he interceeds for. Now, it was not for all the world, nor indefinitely, and by guess, for all in the visible Church that Christ did interceed, *but for them that the Father had given him* out of the world, John xvii. verse 6. and 9. *Thine they were, and thou gavest them me*: and verse 10. *All mine are thine, and thine are mine*; Christ's death being the ground of his intercession, and it being by vertue of his death that he interceeded, his death and intercession must be of the same extent; he interceeds for such and such sinners, because he hath paid a price for them, that there may be a good account made of them at the last day.

The 1st *Use* of it serves to clear a great and precious truth concerning God's covenant, and discriminating love, whereby he hath put difference betwixt some and others. 2. It serves to stir them up, who are thus differenced, to admire at, and to commend his love, who hath been graciously mindful of them when

when others are past by. 3. It serves also to clear the other Scriptures, and this same Chapter, and to teach us, not to make common to all, the privileges bestowed on some peculiar ones, and to guard us against the vilifying and prophaning of our Lord's sufferings, as if he had no special and peculiar design in them, or as if they might be frustrated in the design of them, contrary to the promise made to him of the Father.

And therefore here, to obviate an objection, which is made from the 6 v. *All we like sheep have gone astray*; whence some would infer, that it is all who like sheep have strayed, whose iniquities Christ hath born: we say, That the *All* is not meant to comprehend them whose iniquities Christ hath born only, but to hold out the extent of straying; or the meaning is not to shew, that his suffering and satisfying of justice extended to all that strayed, but to shew, that the elect for whom he suffered had all of them strayed, as well as others: and this is like the reasoning which the apostle hath 2 Cor. v. 14. *If one died for all, then were all dead;* the meaning whereof is not, that Christ died for all that were dead, but this is the meaning, That all for whom Christ died were once dead: so here, while it is said, *All we like sheep have gone astray*, it is to shew, that the elect strayed, and esteemed him not, as well as others, and had God's curse lying on them as their due, till Christ interposed, and took it off them. The point might have also use for confirmation, but we do not follow these.

2. *Surely he hath born our griefs, and carried our sorrows*, that is *our* griefs and sorrows who are his elect, his people, his seed, who flee to him for refuge, and are justified by his knowledge, or by faith in him, and for whom he maketh intercession: hence observe, That believers would endeavour the strengthening of themselves in the faith of this, that Jesus Christ hath born *their* griefs and sorrows, and hath satisfied justice for them in particular; they would study to be in case on good ground, with the prophet, to say, *Surely he hath born our griefs, and carried our sorrows*, to make it sure, that they are in the roll of elect believers, and justified persons; to say with the Apostle Paul, Gal. iii. 13. *He was made a curse for us;* and with the same Apostle 2 Cor. v. ult. to say, *He was made sin for us, that we might be made the righteous of God in him*; and to say with the Apostle, Peter, 1 Pet. i. 24. *Who his own self bare our sins in his own body on the tree.* They speak always by way of application. So these places, whereby we confirmed the doctrine, That Christ really bare that punishment of the sins of the elect, are express in an applicatory way: And that notable place, Gal ii. 20. where, as if it were not enough to say, he loved us, and gave himself for us, he draws it nearer and more home, and saith, *Who loved me, and gave himself for me:* but that ye may not mistake the point, my meaning is not, that every body off-hand should make application of Christ's death: O the presumption and desperate security that destroys thousands of souls here, as if there were no such distinction as we held forth in the first doctrine, nor any bar to be put in the way of that fancied universal application of Christ's dying for all sinners! whereas we shew that it was for his sheep, and these given to him of the Father only, that he died, and for no more: but this is my meaning, that (as it is, 2 Pet. i. 10.) ye would *give diligence to make your calling and election sure*, and that in an orderly way, ye would secure and sicker your interest in Christ's death: not to make this the first thing that ye apprehended for the foundation of your faith, that he died for you in particular, for that were to come to the top of the stairs, before ye begin to set foot on the first step; but the orderly way is, to make sure your fleeing to Christ in the sense of sin, and your closing with him on his own terms, and your having the characters of his people ingraven on you; and then, from such premisses, ye may draw this conclusion, as the result thereof, *Surely he hath born our griefs, and carried our sorrows*; then ye may be satisfiedly confirmed in this, that when Christ transacted and bargained with the Father about the elect, when he prayed, and took the cup of his Father's wrath, and drank it out for them, he minded your names, and was made a curse in your room: the reason is drawn from the advantage of such a doctrine, as hath hanging on it the consolation of all the promises of God; for we can never comfortably apply, nor be delighted in the promises, till we come to make particular application of Christ's purpose and purchase in the work of redemption. This is it that rids marches, and draws a line betwixt us and reprobate ungodly men, and that keeps from the fear of eternal death that pursues them; and it gives some ground of hope to lay hold on, and grip to, as to our enjoying of Christ's purchase. I know there is nothing that folk had more need to be sober and wary in the search of, and in the securing themselves in, than this: yet by the same command that enjoineth us to make our covenant-state, our calling and election sure; we are bound to make our redemption sure; and having at some length spoken of the way of making sure

sure our believing, on the 1 v. we may infist the less on this, of making sure our redemption by Christ

The *1st Use* serves for information; to let you know, that there are many professing Christians, that account this a curious, nice, and conceity thing, to study to be sure, and to make it sure, that Christ in his death and sufferings minded them in particular; others may be think it impossible; and all may think it a right hard and difficult thing, and indeed so it is: But yet we would have you to consider, 1. That simply it is not impossible, else we should say, that the comfort of the people of God were impossible. 2. That it is no curious thing; for the Lord doth not lay the obligation to curiosity on any, tho' we would wish that many had a holy curiosity to know God's mind towards them, that they might not live in the dark about such a concerning business. 3. That *the secret of the Lord is with them that fear him*, Psal. xxv. 14. and even this same secret concerning redemption is with them, *and he will shew them his covenant:* And indeed it were no small matter to have this manifested.

And therefore, as a *2d Use* of the point, we would commend to you the study of making this sure; for it hath many notable advantages attending it: It would provoke to humility, and to thankfulness to him *that loved us, and washed us from our sins in his own blood*; it would make a comfortable and chearful Christian life; it would warm the heart with love to God, and to Jesus Christ, who hath thus loved us, as to give himself for us. When we commend this to you, it is no uncouth, nice, needlessly curious, or unattainable thing; nor would we have you, when ye cannot attain it, to sit down discouraged; neither would we have you take any extraordinary way to come by it; nor waiting for any new light, but that which is in the Bible; nor would we have you resolving to do no other thing till ye attain to this: But this we would have you to do, even to make faith in Christ sure, by fleeing to him, and casting your burden on him, by cordial receiving of him, and acquiescing in him; and then ye make all sure. The committing of yourselves to him, to be saved by his price paid to divine justice, and resting on him as he is holden out in the gospel, is the way to read your interest in his redemption; and this is it that we have Gal. iii, and ii. 19. where it is disputed at length, that we are heirs of Abraham by believing; and, *By the law* (saith the Apostle) *I am dead to the law, that I might live unto God: I am crucified with Christ nevertheless I live, yet not I, but Christ lives in me, and the life which I live in the flesh is by the faith of the Son of God:* Hence he concludes, *Who loved me, and gave himself for me;* And this he proves in the last words, *I do not frustrate the grace of God,* I do not disappoint it, mar it not in its end and design: It is (as if he had said) seeking a lost sinner to save, and I give it a lost sinner to be saved: For tho' God's decree be the first step to salvation, and the work of redemption follows on it, and then believing on both; yet to come to the knowledge of God's decree of election, and of our concern in the covenant of redemption, we look downward, and seek first to know, if we have a right to make application of that which was thought upon long since concerning us; and this we do, by reflecting on the way we have come to believing: If we have been convinced and made sensible of sin, and of our lost condition by nature; if we have not smothered that conviction, but cherished it; if we have not run to this or that duty for satisfying of divine justice, and for making of our peace thereby, but were necessitate to betake ourselves to Jesus Christ made offer of in the gospel for the salvation of sinners; and we have closed with him as he was offered; and if we have done so, we may thence conclude that he hath loved *us*, and given himself to save *us*: Because he hath humbled me for sin (may the serious soul say) and given me this faith to believe in him; and this is his promise which I rest upon, that I shall be saved. Or thou mayst try thy interest in his redemption thus; Whether am I one of God's people or no? Whether do I walk like them? and so go thorow the marks and signs of holiness, asking thy self, What sincerity is there in me? what mortification? what humility, meekness, love to God and his children? and what fruits of faith in new-obedience? These two, faith and holiness are the pillars that bear up the house of assurance; working and not resting on it, believing and yet not growing vain and light because of it, but so much the rather studying holiness; and to go on betwixt and with these two, till we come to read God's mind about our election and redemption: For neither believing nor holiness can make any alteration in the bargain of redemption, yet it will warrant our application of the bargain, and clear our interest in it; as the apostle Peter plainly insinuates, when he thus exhorts, *Give diligence to make your calling and election sure*: How is that? Will diligence make God alter his decree of election, or make it any surer in itself? No, by no means, but it will assure us of it; for *by so doing an entrance shall be ministred unto us abundantly into his everlasting kingdom;* by giving all diligence to add one grace to another, and one degree of grace to another, there shall be a wide door opened to us to go into heaven by; and there is no hazard in commending this doctrine to you all, even the study of faith and holiness, thereby to come to the knowledge of God's secret counsel concerning you.

And therefore, as a third *Use* of this point, Know that all of you, that prejudge yourselves of this comfort of your interest in Christ's purchase, do bring the blame of it on yourselves. If any shall profanely *object*, If God hath purposed, so many shall get good of Christ's sufferings, and no more, what will my faith and holiness do, if I be not elected? And what can my unbelief and negligence prejudge me, if I be elected? We shewed, in the former *Use*, what faith and holiness will do; and we tell you here, what your unbelief and negligence will do, and it is this, it will seclude you from all the blessings of the covenant, and bring you under the sentence of condemnation: For as the conditional promise looks to the believer and unbeliever; so it is not Christ's purchase, nor the difference God hath made in his purpose of election, that is the cause why ye are damned and not justified; but ye are damned, because ye transgressed God's law, and when salvation was offered to you through Christ, ye would not close with the offer; and ye are not justified, because ye betook not yourselves to him for righteousness, but continued in your sin, and in seeking righteousness by the law: For altho' this universal be not true, *That Christ died for all men*; yet this universal is true, that *they are all justified that by faith flee unto Jesus Christ for refuge*: Hence these two are put together, John vi. 37. *All that the Father hath given me, shall come unto me; and him that cometh, I will in no wise cast out: For I came down from heaven, not to do my own will, but the Father's will that sent me.* If it should be asked, What is the Father's will? He answers, *This is the Father's will that sent me, that of all that he hath given me I should lose nothing:* there are (as if he had said) some committed to me, to be redeemed by me, and I will lose none of them. And lest it should yet be objected, But I wot not if I be given to Christ, to be redeemed by him; he adds, *And this is the will of him that sent me, that every one that seeth the Son, and believeth on him, may have everlasting life:* In which words, we have two wills to say so, both having the same promise and effect; the first relates to the secret paction of redemption, *verse 39.* and the second is his revealed will pointing at our duty, *verse 40.* And so, if any should say, I know not if I be given to Christ, I know not if I be elected: This answer is here given, What is that to thee? It is not to be searched into at the first-hand, and broken in upon *per saltum*, and at the broad-side; that is God's secret will, and that which is his revealed will belongs to thee, and that is, to see that thou believe; and if thou believest, the same promise that is annexed to believing is annexed to election, and they sweetly tryst together, and are of equal extent, to wit, believing, and to be given to Christ? And therefore let me commend it to you, to hold you content with God's revealed will; for it is not the ground of your faith, I mean as to its first closing with Christ, that of all given to Christ, he should lose none; but this is the ground of it, That every one that seeth the Son, and believeth on him, shall have everlasting life: And we may add this word, as one motive amongst others to faith and holiness, That by your studying of these, ye may turn over the words of the Prophet here to yourselves, and say, *Surely he hath born our griefs, and carried our sorrows,* and that of the Apostle, Gal. ii. *Who loved me, and gave himself for me;* also that word of Peter cited before, *His own self bare our sins in his own body on the tree.* And O what consolation is here!

The 4th *Use* of it is, To commend the practice of this to the believer, that hath indeed fled to Jesus Christ; and to shew the great privilege that they have who are such: The practice of it is, that believers should seek to be established and confirmed in the particular application of Christ's death to themselves, not only to know that he suffered for the elect and for believers, but for them in particular, that, as it is, Heb. iv. 16. *They may come with boldness to the throne of God,* and confidently assert their interest; and as it is, Heb. vi. they may *grow up to the full assurance of hope unto the end.* We suppose there are many believers, that dare not disclaim the covenant, and their interest in Christ, who yet are fearful to make this particular application, *Jesus Christ hath loved me, and given himself for me:* But if they could knit the effects, with the cause from whence they came, they might attain to it; for the man that can say, I am fled to Christ for refuge, he may also say, that he purposely laid down his life to pay my debt; and he is warranted of Christ to make this application of his particular intention towards him. Upon the other-side, the more consolation be in this to believers, it speaks the greater ground of terror to unbelievers, because of the prejudice they sustain by the want of this; and as many of you as make not faith

and

and holiness your study, ye ly out of the reach of this consolation that flows from Christ's bearing the griefs and sorrows of his own: And therefore let the profane, senseless multitude, that know no what it is to die to the law, or to live to holiness, as ye would not commit sacrilege, stand a-back, and not dare to meddle with this redemption, till ye stoop and come in at this door of faith and holiness: And let as many as are in this way admit of the consolation, for it is the Lord's allowance upon you; but for others, if ye presume to take hold of it, the Lord will wring it from you, and let you know to your cost that ye had nothing to do with it.

SERMON XXI.

Isaiah liii. 4. *Surely he hath born our griefs, and carried our sorrows: yet we did esteem him stricken, smitten of God, and afflicted.*
Verse 5. *But he was wounded for our transgressions, he was bruised for our iniquities; the chastisement of our peace was upon him, and with his stripes we are healed.*

THESE words, and all this chapter, look liker a piece of the history of the gospel, than a prophecy of the old testament; the sufferings of the Messiah being so directly pointed at in them. We shewed that this first part of the 4th verse holds forth the cause of his sufferings, and it is applied to our Lord, Matt. viii. 17. and 1 Pet. ii. 24. As for the second part of the verse, in these words, *yet we esteemed him smitten of God, stricken and afflicted*: any who are acquainted with the gospel, cannot but know that it was fulfilled in him: And it is an aggravation of their sin who did so undervalue and and despise him, that though he condescended to come so low for us, yet we slighted him; and even then, when there was greatest love let out, we abused it, and made it the rise of the greatest malice: And for the 5th *verse* it is applied by Peter, 1 Pet. ii. 24. This whole chapter then being so gospel-like, and having a direct fulfilling in Christ, we may draw this general doctrine from it, *That our Lord Jesus Christ, who was born of the Virgin Mary, suffered under Pontius Pilate, was crucified, died and was buried, and rose again the third day; is the very same* Messiah *that was prophesied of in the old testament, and was promised to Abraham, Isaac and Jacob, whom the fathers before his coming in the flesh were waiting for.* And though this may be looked on as a very common and useless doctrine, yet it is the main ground and foundation of our faith: We may take many things for granted, wherein if we were well tried and put to it, we would be found unsicker, and in this among the rest. Now, for confirmation of it, this same one argument will make it out; we shall not follow it at length, but in the prosecuting of it shall restrict ourselves to this chapter: The argument runneth thus, if in Christ Jesus, that which was prophesied of the Messiah, and promised to the fathers, have its fulfilling and accomplishment; then he must be the same Messiah that was prophesied of, and promised to them; for these things spoken of the one and alone Messiah, can agree to no other: But whatever was prophesied and spoken, or promised of the Messiah to the fathers, to the least circumstance of it, was all fully accomplished and fulfilled in Christ; therefore the conclusion laid down in the doctrine follows, to wit, That our blessed Lord Jesus is the same Messiah that was prophesied of, promised to the fathers, and whom they before his coming were looking for: So that that question needs not now be proposed, *Art thou he that should come, or do we look for another?* Go, says Christ, Mat. iv. 4, 5, 6. *And tell John, The blind receive their sight, the lame walk, and the lepers are cleansed, and the deaf hear, and the dead are raised, and the poor have the gospel preached to them, and blessed is he whosoever shall not be offended in me*: Blessed is he, who because of my humiliation is not stumbled. Now, not to make a rehearsal of the general prophesies in scripture, all of which have their exact fulfilling in Christ, we shall only speak to two things here for making out of the argument proposed, 1, That this chapter speaks of the Messiah. 2. That which is spoken in it, is literally fulfilled in Christ.

1. That this chapter speaks of the Messiah; though of old the blinded Jews granted it, yet now they say that it speaks of some other: But that it speaks of him, these things will make it evident, 1. If we look to the 13th *verse* of the former chapter, where it is said, *My Servant shall deal prudently, he shall be exalted and extolled, and be very high;* There our Lord Jesus is spoken of as the Father's Servant or great Lord-deputy; and the Jews themselves grant that this is meant of the Messiah; and there is nothing more clear than that what is spoken in this chapter relates to him, who is called the Lord's Servant in the former chapter, as we shewed at our entring to speak of it. 2. If we look to the description of his person, it can agree to no other; for it is said, *There was no guile found in*

Isaiah liii. Verse 4, 5.   Serm. XXI.

his mouth, he was brought as a lamb to the slaughter, and as a sheep before the shearer is dumb, so he opened not his mouth, &c. He had no sin of his own, which can be said of no other; therefore this chapter speaks of him. 3. If we consider the ends and effects of his sufferings, for it is for the transgressions of his people; and as it is, Dan. ix. 26. *He was to be cut off, but not for himself:* The effects, *He shall see his seed, and by his knowledge justify many.* And the new testament is full to this purpose, there being no scripture in all the old testament more made use of, nor oftner applied to Christ, than this is.

2. What is spoken in this chapter is really and literally fulfilled in Christ; and we may shortly draw what is in it to these *five* heads, all which we will find clearly fulfilled in him. 1. To his sufferings. 2. To the ground of his sufferings. 3. To mens account and estimation of him. 4. To the promises made to him. 5. To the effects that followed on his sufferings. (1.) For his sufferings, it is said, that he should be *a man of sorrows and acquainted with grief:* that he should be *despised and rejected of men, and not be esteemed;* that he should be looked on, *as stricken, smitten of God, and afflicted;* that he should *bear our sorrows and griefs,* and be *wounded for our transgressions;* that he should be *oppressed and afflicted,* and *brought as a lamb to the slaughter,* that he should *be numbered amongst the transgressors;* and that he should die, and be buried, *make his grave with the wicked and with the rich in his death;* all which are clearly fulfilled in him: And the clearing of his sufferings, whereof we spoke before, clears this, that not only he suffered, but that he was brought so low in suffering. 2. For the ground of his sufferings, it is said to be the sins of his own elect; *He bare our griefs, and carried our sorrows:* he was wounded *for our transgressions, and bruised for our iniquities; there was no guile found in his mouth:* The greatest enemies of our Lord could impute nothing to him; Pilate was forced to say, that he found no fault in him; all which shew that it was for the transgressions of his people that he suffered. (3.) As for mens little esteem of him, it is also very clear; for he was despised and rejected of men; we hid as it were our faces from him; he was despised, and we esteemed him not: The world thought little of him; and what is more clear in the gospel than this, where it is told, that he was reproached, buffetted, spitted on, despised? they cried, *Away with him, crucify him: he trusted in God, let him deliver him;* but *God hath forsaken him.*

(4.) As for the promises made to him, *He shall see his seed, he shall prolong his days, and the pleasure of the Lord shall prosper in his hands; he shall see of the travel of his soul, and be satisfied; and by his knowledge shall many be justified,* &c. What mean all these, but that he shall die, and rise again, and have many converts; that God's work shall thrive well in his hand, and that he shall have a glorious kingdom and many subjects? Which is called afterward his *having a portion with the great,* and his *dividing of the spoil with the strong*: All this was accomplished in Christ, when after his resurrection many were won and brought in by the gospel to believe on him; and though the Jews and Heathens concurred and conspired to cut off all Christians, yet his kingdom spread, and hath continued these sixteen hundred years and above. (5.) As for the effects that followed on his sufferings, or the influence they have on the elect people of God; as many converts as have been and are in the world, as many witnesses are there, that he is the Messiah; every converted, pardoned and reconciled soul seals this truth: Hence, 1 John v. 7, 8. *There are* is it said, *three that bear witness in heaven, the Father, the Word, and the holy Ghost, and these three are one; and there are three that bear witness on earth,* the *Spirit* in his efficacy, the *Water* in the sanctifying vertue of it, in changing and cleansing his people, and the *Blood* in the satisfying and justifying vertue of it; and these three agree and concur in one, even this one, to wit, that Jesus Christ is the Son of God: And then it follows, *He that believeth hath the witness in himself,* because he hath gotten pardon through him, and therefore can set to his seal to this truth, and say, Truly Christ is the Messiah.

The *Use* is, To exhort you to acquaint yourselves with these things that serve to confirm this truth; the book of the Acts of the Apostles, and the Epistle to the Hebrews, are much spent upon it, even to hold out, and to prove Christ Jesus to be the true Messiah, and Saviour of his people: if this be not made sure and sicker, we have an unstable ground for our faith; and though it be sure in itself, yet so long as it is not so to us, we want the consolation of it: And there is a twofold prejudice that cometh through folks want of thorow clearness in, and assurance of this truth. 1. To the generality of hearers there is this prejudice, that they are so careless and little solicitous to rest on him: And as it made the Jews to reject him, who to this day stumble at him on this very same ground, that they know him not to be the Messiah, the Christ of God;

God; in whom is accomplished all that was spoken of the Messiah: So Christians not being through in it, they do not rest on him, nor close with him as the true Messiah. 2. There is a prejudice also from it to believers, who having only a glimmering light of Christ's being the Messiah, come short of that consolation that they might have, if they were through in the faith of it; there is this great evil among Christians, that they study not to be solidly clear and through in this point, so that if they were put to reason and debate with a Jew, if there were not a witness within themselves of it, the truth of the faith of many would be exceedingly shaken.

From this, that he never speaks of Christ's sufferings, but he makes application of them, he carried *our* griefs, he was wounded for *our* transgressions, &c. Observe, *That believers would look on Christ's sufferings as undergone for them, and in their room and place*. We cleared before, 1. That Christ suffered for some peculiarly, and not for all: and, 2. That believers would endeavour the clearing of their own interest in his sufferings, and that they have a right to them. Now we shortly add this 3d, of kin to the former, That believers, and such as are fled to Christ for refuge, would look on his sufferings as come under for them; and these same scriptures which we cited to confirm these, will confirm this. The reason why we would have you confirmed in this, is because, (1.) It is only this that will make you suitably thankful; it is this which is a notable ground of that song of praise, Rev. i. 4. *To him that hath loved us, and washed us from our sins in his own blood*, &c. (2.) This is a ground of true, solid, and strong consolation, even to be comforted in the applicative faith of Christ's purchase. (3.) It is the Lord's allowance on his people, which they should reverently and thankfully make use of, even to look on Jesus Christ, as wounded, pierced, and lifted up on the cross for them; and by doing this, according to his allowance, there is a paved way made for application of all the benefits of his purchase.

3. From the scope (looking on the words as spoken to remove the scandal of the cross) *observe*, (which may be a reason of the former) *That folk will never take up Christ rightly in his sufferings, except they take him up as suffering for them, and in their room*. This look of Christ, leads, 1. To take up much of the glory of grace, and condescending love to sinners. 2. It leads to take up Christ's faithfulness, that came to the world on sinners errand, according to the ancient transaction in the covenant of redemption, as he is brought in,

saying, Psal. xl. *Lo, I come, in the volume of book it is written of me, I delight to do thy will O God.* 3. It leads to a stayed look of God's holiness, justice, and goodness, in exacting satisfaction of his own Son, and in accepting of that satisfaction. 4. It gives a right view of the way of grace, and leads in to see it to be a most real thing; God the offended Party, accepting of the price, and Christ paying it: thus the believer's faith gets a sight of Christ satisfying, as if he saw his own debt satisfied by himself; it sees him undergoing the curse, and justice inflicting it on him, that the believer may go free.

The *Use* is, To shew the necessity of studying the well grounded application of Christ's sufferings as for us: Much of the reason, why Christ is not more prized, lies here, that he is not looked on as paying our debt; otherwise, when challenges of the law and of justice take hold on the soul, if Christ were seen interposing, and saying, *A body hast thou prepared unto me*; and if justice were seen exacting, Christ performing, and God accepting his satisfaction; and that, in sign and token that justice is satisfied, he is raised from the dead, justified in the Spirit, and is entered in possession of glory, as believers Fore-runner, in their name; it would afford precious and lovely thoughts of Jesus Christ, and humbling thoughts of ourselves: Therefore there is a necessity, if we would consider his sufferings aright, and prize and esteem him, that we endeavour to make particular application of them to ourselves on good grounds. 2. Upon the other hand, know, ye who have no ground to make this application, that ye cannot esteem aright of him or his sufferings, nor of the grace that shined in them, because ye have no title to, nor can, while such, have any clearness of interest in them. 3. For you that would fain have a high esteem of Christ, and yet are all your days casting at this foundation, never think nor expect to win rightly to esteem of him, so long as ye fear to make application of his purchase; and therefore, that ye may love and praise him, and esteem rightly of him, labour to come up to the making of this application on solid and approved grounds.

4. More particularly, from this part of the aggravation, *Yet we esteemed him stricken, smitten of God, and afflicted*; We have a fourfold confirmation of truth, or four precious truths confirmed. (1.) That our Lord Jesus in his sufferings did really suffer, and was really brought low in his sufferings, so as onlookers thought him a most despicable Man, and one that was stricken and smitten of God, and afflicted: Of this we spoke on the beginning of the fourth

fourth verse. (2.) We have here an evidence of the exceeding great freeness of grace, and of the love of Christ in his sufferings, in so far as he bare their sorrows, and paid their debt that counted them smitten; there was no good thing in us to deserve or procure his sufferings, but most freely he underwent these sufferings, and undertook our debt, Rom. v. 8. *God commends his love towards us, in that while we were yet sinners, Christ died for us.* And v. 10. *While we were yet enemies, we were reconciled by the death of his Son.* Can there be a greater proof of infinite and free love, than appears in our Lord's sufferings? There was not only no merit on our side; but on the contrary, despising, rejecting, being ashamed of him, reproaching him, kicking against him, and rubbing of affronts on him; Paul and others having their hands hot in his blood.

Use 1. Consider here, behold, and wonder at the free love of God, and rich condescending love of Christ: He stands not at the bar and prays for them that were praying him to pray for them; but, as it is in the end of the chapter, it was for transgressors: It was even for some of them that were seeking to take away the life of the Prince of life, and for other transgressors.

2. Know, that in them to whom the benefit of Christ's death is applied, there is no more worth than there is in others who do not share of the benefit of it, It is the opinion not only of hereticks, but some way of many ignorant professors, that these for whom Christ died were better than others; but here we see a proof of the contrary; he dies for them that accounted him smitten of God: And this he doth for two reasons, 1. To shew the riches, and freedom of his grace, that could overcome man's evil and malice, and outreach the height of the desperate wickedness that is in man, and that stands not (to speak so) on stepping-stones, but comes over the greatest guilt of sin and enmity in the creature. 2. To comfort and encourage his followers, when engaged to him, against and out-over their grossest failings and greatest miscarriages: He that loved them, when they were despising and rejecting him, and spitting in a manner in his very face, will he now give up with them, when they have some love to him, for this or that corruption that stirreth or breaketh forth in them? Thus the apostle reasons, Rom. v. 10. *If when we were enemies we were reconciled to God by the death of his Son, much more being reconciled we shall be saved by his life:* We were enemies when Christ gave himself for us; but thro' grace we are somewhat better now: Enmity and despite in us was then at an height; now it is weakened, restrained, and in some measure mortified: And if while we were at the height of enmity against him, he died for us to reconcile us to God, how much more now, being reconciled, may we expect peace and safety, and all the benefits of his purchase thorow him? Thus there is a notable consolation, from this bent of malice that was sometime in us, compared with the victory that grace hath now gotten over it; and the gradation is always comfortable, to wit, that these lusts that once did reign, and were without any gracious opposition made to them, or any protestation entered against them, prevailing it may be publickly, are now opposed and protested against: And if Christ stood not on the greater, will he stand on the lesser? And our Lord allows this sort of reasoning so much the more, that he may thereby strongly engage the heart of the believer against sin, and to the admiring of grace, and withal to the serious study of holiness.

3. It serves to let you know how much ye believers are engaged and obliged to grace, and what things you owe to it. (1.) Look to what satisfies for your debt; ye pay not one farthing of it, our Lord Jesus paid all. (2.) Look to the moving cause, it is to be attributed to nothing in you, but altogether to free grace: Some poor dyvour may by his pleading prevail with an able and pitiful hearted man to pay his debt; but there was no such externally moving cause in you to procure this of him, but he freely and willingly, and with delight paid your debt, when ye were in the height of malicious opposition to him, doing all that might scar him from it: And had it been possible that man's malice, despising and despite could have scarred him, he had never died for one sinner; but he triumphed openly in his grace over that, and all that stood in his way.

4. We have here a confirmation of that truth, that holds out man's malice and desperate wickedness; and can there be any thing that evidenceth man's wickedness and malice more, than, 1. To have enmity against Christ; 2. To have it at such an height as to despise him, and count him smitten and plagued of God; And. 3. To be at the height of malice, even then when he out of love was condescending so low as to suffer and satisfy justice for him? Ye may possibly think that it was not ye that had such malice at Christ; but saith not the prophet, *We esteemed him smitten of God?* Taking in himself and all the elect. ' Which might give us this observation, " That there is nothing more des-
" perately wicked, and filled with more enmity a-
" gainst Christ in his condescending love, and against
" God

"God in the manifestation of his grace, than when
"even elect souls, for whom he hath suffered, de-
"spise him, and count him smitten of God and
"afflicted." It is indeed very sad, yet very profitable, to walk under the deep apprehension and soul-pressure of heart-enmity against God and Christ: Are there any of you that think ye have such sinful and wicked natures, that dispose you to think little of Christ, to despise and reject him and his grace? God's elect have this enmity in their natures; and if such natures be in the elect, what must be in the reprobate, who live and die in this enmity? If this were seriously considered and laid to heart, O but folk would be humble; nothing would affect the soul more, and stound to the very heart, than to think that Christ suffered for me, thro' grace an elect and a believer; and that yet notwithstanding I should have so despised and rejected him, and accounted him smitten of God and afflicted. Let me exhort all of you to look back on your former walk, and to lay this enmity to heart; for the day is coming, when it will be found to be a biting and conscience-gnawing sin, to many. 4. In that he aggravates their enmity from this, observe this truth, which is also here confirmed, "That there is no-
"thing that gives sin a deeper dye, than that it is
"against grace and condescending love, that is,
"against Christ when suffering for us, and offered
"to us." O! that makes sin to be exceeding sinful, and wonderfully abominable; and thus it is aggravated, Heb. ii. as greater than the contempt of Moses his law; and Heb. vi. it is accounted to be a *crucifying the Son of God afresh* and a *putting him to an open shame*; and Heb. x. it is called a *treading him under foot*, an *accounting the blood of the covenant to be an unholy thing*, and a *doing despite to the Spirit of grace*. These two last scriptures look mainly to the sin against the Holy Ghost, yet so as there is somewhat of that which is said in them to be found in all unbelievers their despising of Christ: it is a sin someway hateful, even to the publicans and sinners, to hate them that love us, to do ill to them that do good to us; how much more sinful and hateful is it to despise and hate him who loved us, so as to give himself for us, and when he was giving himself for us? There are many sins against the law that will draw deep, but this will draw deeper than they all, even sinning against grace, and the Mediator interposing for sinners, and manifesting love to them: And the reckoning will run thus, Christ was manifested to you in this gospel as the only remedy of sin, and set forth at crucified before your eyes, and made offer of to you in the gospel; and yet ye despised him, and esteemed him not: And let me say it to believers, that it is the greatest aggravation of their sin. It is true, in some respect, that the sins of believers are not so great as the sins of others, they not being committed with such deliberation and full benfil of will, nor from the dominion of sin; yet in this respect they are greater than the sins of others, because committed against special grace and love actually communicated; and therefore when the believer considers, that he hath requit Christ thus, it will affect him most of any thing, if there be any suitable tenderness of frame.

5. From considering that it is the prophet that expresseth this aggravation, we may observe, "That
"the believer that is most tender, and hath belt
"right to Jesus Christ and his satisfaction, and may
"upon best ground apply it, will be most sensible
"of his enmity, and of the abominable guilt that
"is in despising and wronging of Jesus Christ:" Therefore the prophet brings in himself as one of those that by Christ's stripes were healed, taking with his guilt; *we despised* and rejected him, *we* esteemed him not, *we* judged him smitten of God: the reason is, Because interest in Jesus Christ makes the heart tender, and any wrong that is done to affect him the sooner and the more deeply, the scurf that sometime was on the heart being in a measure taken away; and interest in Christ awakeneth and raiseth an esteem of him, and produceth a holy sympathy with him in all the concerns of his glory, even as the members of the body have a fellow-feeling with the head. Make a supposition, that a man in his madness should smite and wound his head, or wrong his wife, his father, or his brother; when that fit of madness is over, he is more affected with that wrong, than if it had been done to any other member of his body, or to other persons, not at all, or not so nearly related to him: There is something of this pointed at, Zech. xii. 10. *They shall look upon him whom they have pierced, and mourn for him, as a man doth for his only son*; as if he had said, the strokes they have given the head shall then be very heavy and grievous to be born, and will be made to their feeling to bleed afresh: they thought not much of these woundings and piercings of him before; but so soon as their interest in him is clear, or they come cordially to believe in him, they are kindly affected with the wrongs done to him.

The *Use* is, That it is a mark, to try if there be indeed an interest in Christ, and if it be clear. The man whose interest is clearest, 1. His wrongs done to Christ will prick him most: If the wrongs be done by others, they affect him; if by himself, they some way faint him. Wholeness of heart, under wronging of Christ, is too great an evidence that there is little or no ground for application of his satisfaction; but it is kindly like, when wrongs done to Christ affect most. 2. When not only challenges for sin against the law, but for sins against Christ and grace offered in the gospel, do become a burden, and the greatest burden. 3. When the man is made to mind secret enmity at Christ, and is disposed to muster up aggravations of his sinfulness on that account, and cannot get himself made vile enough; when he hath an holy indignation at himself, and with Paul counts himself, the *chief of sinners*; even tho' the evil was done in ignorance, much more if it hath been against knowledge. It is no evil token, when souls are made to heap up aggravations of their guilt for wrongs done to Christ, and they cannot get suitable expressions sufficiently to hold it out, as it is an evil token to be soon satisfied in this: There are many that will take with no challenge for their wronging Christ; but behold here how the prophet insists, both in the words before, in these, and in the following words; and he can no more win off the thoughts of it, than he can win off the thoughts of Christ's sufferings.

6. While the prophet faith, when Christ was suffering for his own, and for the rest of his peoples sins, *We esteemed him not*, but judged him *smitten of God*: Observe briefly, because we hasten to a close, " That Jesus Christ is often exceedingly mistaken " by men in his most glorious and gracious works." Can there be a greater mistake than this? Christ suffering for our sins, and yet judged smitten and plagued of God by us; or, more home, even Christ Jesus is often shamefully mistaken in the work of his grace, and in the venting of his love, towards them whose good he is procuring, and whose iniquities he is bearing.

The *Use* of it serves, 1. To teach us, when we are ready to pass censure on Christ's work, to stand still, to animadvert on, and to correct ourselves, lest we unsuitably construct of him: He gets much wrong as to his public work, as if he were cruel, when indeed he is merciful; as if he had forgotten us, when indeed he remembers us still: And as to his private work in particular persons, as if he did fail in his promise, when he is most faithful, and bringing it about in his own way. And, 2. (which is of affinity to the former) It is a warning to us, not to take up hard constructions of Christ; nor to mis-construct his work, which when mis-constructed, himself is mistaken and mis-constructed. How many think that he is breaking, when he is binding up; that he is wounding, when he is healing; that he is destroying, when he is humbling? Therefore we would suspend passing censure till he come to the end and close of his work, and not judge of it by halves; and then we shall see there was no such ground for mis-constructing of him, who is every day holding on in his own way, and steadily pursuing the same end that he did from the beginning; and let him be doing so. To him be praise for ever.

SERMON XXII.

Isaiah liii. 5. *But he was wounded for our transgressions, he was bruised for our iniquities: the chastisement of our peace was upon him, and with his stripes we are healed.*

IT is hard to tell whether the subject of this verse, and almost of this whole chapter, be more sad or more sweet: it is indeed a sad subject to read and hear of the great sufferings of our blessed Lord Jesus, and of the despiteful usage that he met with, and to see such a speat of malice spued and spitted out on that glorious face; so that, when he is bearing our griefs and carrying our sorrows, we do even then account him plagued, smitten of God, and afflicted, and in a manner look upon it as well bestowed: Yet it is a most sweet subject, if we either consider the love it comes from, or the comfortable effects that follow it; that hath been the rise, the cause, and the occasion of much singing to man here below, and the cause and occasion of so much singing among the redeemed that are this day before the throne of God: and as the grace of God hath overcome the malice of men, so we are persuaded this cause of rejoicing hath a sweetness in it beyond the sadness, tho' often we mar our own spiritual mirth, and know not how to dance when he pipes unto us.

These words are an explication of the 4th verse, where it is asserted, that Christ's sufferings were not for himself, but for us: From, and by which, the prophet having heightened mens malice, who notwithstanding thereof esteemed him not, yea, judged him smitten of God; he comes again, for furthering and carrying on of this scope, to shew more particularly the ground, end, and effects of Christ's

sufferings

sufferings: Where ye would remember what we hinted before in general, That folks will never think nor conceive of Christ's sufferings rightly, till they conceive and take him up as suffering for them; and when we consider this, we think it no wonder that the most part esteem but little of the sufferings of Christ, because there are so few that can take him up under this notion, as standing in their room, and paying their debt, and as being put in prison for them, when they are let go free.

In this 5th verse we have these three, 1. A further expression of Christ's sufferings. 2. The cause of them, or the end that he had before him in them. 3. The benefits and fruits or effects of them.

There are in the words four expressions which I shall clear. (1.) *He was wounded*, to shew the reality that was in his sufferings; he was actually pierced, or (as the word is rendered in the margin) *tormented*, and the cause is *our transgressions*: and while it is said, *He was wounded for our transgressions*, he means, 1. That our transgressions procured his wounding; and, 2. That his wounding was to remove them, and to procure pardon to us. (2.) *He was bruised*, that is, pressed as grapes in a wine-press, he underwent such a wounding as bruised him; to shew the great desert of sin, and the heaviness of wrath that would have come on us for it, had not he interposed: and the cause is *our iniquities*. And those two words, *transgressions*, and *iniquities*, shew the exceeding abominableness of sin; *transgressions* or errings, pointing at our common sins; *iniquities* or rebellions, pointing at greater guilt. (3.) *The chastisement* (or, as the words bear, the discipline) *of our peace was upon him*: It supposes, 1. That we by nature were at feud with, and enemies to God. 2. That, before our peace could be procured, there behoved to be a satisfaction given to justice, the Mediator behoved to come under discipline and chastisement. (4.) *And by his stripes we are healed;* he was so whipped, that (to say so) the marks of the rod remained behind. The first benefit looks to pardon of sin, and peace with God, in the first three expressions; the second, in this last expression, looks to our sanctification, and purging from the dominion and pollution of sin: By Christ's becoming sin for us, there is a way made to wash us from all the guilt of sin, and from all the foul spots and stains that were on us by sin; and he hath thus procured holiness to us; we come easily by it, but it cost Christ dear, yea very dear.

These very sad, but most sweet, and soul-solacing words, hold out a short sum of the substance and marrow of the gospel; and because they do so, we shall speak of them summarily together: and ye would the more seriously attend, especially such as are more ignorant, that by the reading and opening up of this verse ye may be brought and kept in mind of the sum of the heads of the gospel. And to make the matter the more clear, I shall endeavour to make the doctrines drawn from it, as so many answers to six or seven questions; as, 1. What is man's condition naturally, and what is the condition of all them that get not benefit by Christ's death? 2. How is man redeemed and freed from that condition? 3. By whom is he freed, or who makes the satisfaction? 4. How doth he perform that satisfaction? 5. What are the benefits that flow from, and come to us by the satisfaction performed? 6. Who are the persons for whom Christ hath performed the satisfaction, and to whom he hath procured these benefits? 7. What is the way how these benefits are transferred or derived to those persons? And putting these seven together, we may have a short catechism in one verse.

1st, Then, What is man's condition by nature? 1. He is under transgressions. 2. Under iniquities. 3. At feud with God. And, 4. Under wounds and most lothsom diseases of a sinful nature. In a word, Man by nature is a sinner, guilty, greatly guilty, under God's wrath and curse; and at feud with God; of a most sinful and abominable nature, even sick of, and lothsom because of sin. The first is implied in this word, *He was wounded for our transgressions*, that is, our common sins; the second is holden out in the next word, *He was bruised for our iniquities*, or rebellions, which holds out great guilt; the third in that word, *The chastisement of our peace was on him*, which supposes that we were once without peace with God; the last word, *By his stripes we are healed*, supposeth that we continue in that condition filthy and polluted, and polluting ourselves more and more, greedy to drink in sin, and wounding and sickning ourselves by sin: Now, lay these four words together, they clear this truth to our judgment, and serve to point out to us the necessity of a Mediator. Again, consider them in a second notion, and they tell us, that even the elect themselves are by nature in the same sinful and rebellious condition with others, at feud with, and under the curse of God, and abominably polluted, before they be washed and healed; as the apostle asserts, Eph. ii. " We are by " nature children of wrath even as others;" and here it is plainly declared, " He was wounded for " our transgressions, he was bruised for our iniqui-

" ties, &c." Some are ready to think (as was hinted before) that the elect by nature were better than others, or that God foresaw they would be better than others; and therefore he elected them. This piece of Arminianism is in all naturally; but this text, in downright contradiction to such a groundless conceit, answers and asserts, that by nature they they are even like others, as the apostle saith, Rom. xi. 32. " God hath concluded them all under unbelief, that he might have mercy on all ;" all the elect, as well as others, are concluded under sin and wrath, that the way of obtaining any spiritual good, might be by mercy and free-grace alone.

2. How are folks freed from this sinful and miserable condition? *Answer*, 1. In general, before the quarrel can be taken away, and their peace can be made, there must be a satisfaction, which is implied in these words, " The chastisement of our " peace was upon him ;" which supposes the necessity of a satisfaction made or to be made, in respect of God's decree and commination, who said, " The day thou sins, thou shalt die ; *and* Cursed, " is every one that continues not in all things written in the law to do them. 2. And more particularly, there must be a satisfaction, because there is, 1. The justice of God that hath a claim by a standing law. 2. The holiness of God, that must be vindicate. And, 3. The faithfulness of God, that must cause be performed and come to pass what it hath impledged itself for, as well in reference to the threatning as to the promise ; for these words, " Hath he said, and will he not do it ?" relate to the one, as well as to the other. There is a great mistake in many, while they leap immediately to mercy, without minding the necessity of a satisfaction to provoked justice, and on this ground, that God is merciful ; which if it were an argument good enough, it would say, that all, even the reprobate, may get mercy : but we would consider the way that God hath laid down for sinners coming to mercy, and how that, before peace can be made, he will needs have satisfaction to his justice.

3. Who maketh this satisfaction ? The text says, it is *He* and *Him*; *He* was wounded for our transgressions, the chastisement of our peace was on *Him*: And who is this *He* and *Him* ? It is in general the Messiah, who was then to come; he who was conceived by the holy Ghost, born of the virgin Mary; who suffered and was crucified, who died and was buried, and rose the third day ; even he, who having the nature of God and our nature united in one person, " He his own self bare our sins in his body " on the tree," as it is said, 1 Pet. ii. 24. and he,

" who knew no sin, was made sin for us, that we " might be made the righteousness of God in him," as it is, 2 Cor. v. alt. even he of whom the Apostle hath been speaking here, while he says, " We " as ambassadors for Christ, as though God did be- " seech you by us, we pray you in Christ's stead be " ye reconciled unto God." And when we say it is Christ that is meaned of, we are to understand it as well negatively and exclusively, excluding all others; as positively including him : When we make him to be the only Saviour, we exclude all that men can do, with their penance, prayers, good works; and all that the angels can do : Neither man nor angel could satisfy divine justice, and make our peace with God; and therefore is is said, Acts iv. 12. " Neither is there salvation in any other ; for there " is no other name under heaven given among men, " whereby we must be saved, but the name of Je- " sus," where it is clear that all others are excluded, as it is, Psal. xl. 6. " Sacrifice and offering thou " wouldst not," *&c*. Neither penances, performances, nor any other thing will do it ; but it is, " Lo, I come, in the volume of thy book it is writ- " ten of me, I delight to do thy will, O my God." Take this then as another ground of saving knowledge, that it is our blessed Lord Jesus that satisfies justice, even he who, being God, was content to become Man, and is God and Man in one person ; he, and he only, undertaking the debt, satisfies justice.

4. How does he satisfy justice ? Answ. " He " was wounded for our transgressions, he was bruis- " ed for our iniquities, the chastisement of our peace " was on him, and by his stripes we are healed :" In which words, observe these three things. 1. In Christ's satisfaction for us, there is an actual undertaking, he becomes Cautioner, and enters himself in our room ; when all other things are casten, angels, men with their sacrifices, thousands of rams, ten thousand rivers of oil, and the fruit of the body, then our Lord Jesus comes in and undertakes, Psal. xl. 7. *Lo, I come*, he satisfies for our transgressions; which supposes that justice could not have sought our debt of him, if he had not undertaken it; therefore, Heb. vii. 24. he is called the *Surety of a better testament*, for he comes in our room and place, and undertakes to pay our debt : Even as if a man under debt were a-carrying to prison, and another able rich man should undertake to pay the debt; although the debt should ly over for a while unpaid, yet the creditor will get a decreet on the cautioner for payment of the debt, when he pleases to put at him ; so Jesus Christ enters Cautioner for our debt, and becomes liable to the payment of it,

2. Christ's

2. Christ's performance and payment of the debt according to his undertaking, implies a covenant and transaction on which the application is founded; which we shewed was also implied in the foregoing words, *v.* 4. "He hath born our griefs, and carried our sorrows." God the Father, Son, and holy Spirit, are the Party wronged by sin; Jesus Christ, considered personally and as Mediator, is the Party undertaking: The terms are, That he shall suffer, and satisfy justice for us, and that we shall go free, that his paying shall be our freedom, that the debt which he pays for us, shall not be exacted off us ourselves, 2 Cor. v. ult. "He, who knew "no sin was made sin for us, that we might be "made the righteousness of God in him:' and here, " the chastisement of our peace was on him;" it was transferred from us to him, " that by his "stripes we might be healed;" by his stripes and blanes, health was procured and brought to us. (3.) Our Lord Jesus, in fulfilling the bargain, and satisfying justice, paid a dear price; it was at a very dear rate that he bought our freedom; he was wounded, bruised, suffered stripes and punishment: So that ye may take the answer to the question in sum to be this, Our Lord Jesus performed and satisfied for all that was due by us, by undertaking our debt, and paying a dear price for sinners, according to the covenant of redemption; he came under the law, and the law struck at him as Cautioner, and he answered the law's demands, and fully and condignly satisfied the justice of God for us.

As for that *Question,* Whether Christ might not by one drop of his blood have satisfied? and such like; we think them very needless, too curious, and little or not at all edifying: But if it be asked, Why Christ paid so much? We answer, 1. It behoved Christ to pay a condign price, to give a condign satisfaction to justice. 2. It was meet that he should pay all that he paid. *First,* We say, it behoved to be a condign satisfaction; For, (1.) It behoved to be a price equivalent to all that the elect should have suffered, had not he interposed. (2.) It behoved to be proportionable to the justice of God; for God having laid down such a way of shewing mercy, that his justice should be salved, there behoved to be condign satisfaction, for the vindication of justice: which was done by Christ's suffering to the full undoubtedly; if we consider, 1. The excellency of the Person that suffered, God and Man in one Person. 2. If we consider the nature of his sufferings, that they were exceeding great, heavy, and pressing. And, 3. If withal we consider the manner of his sufferings, that it was with much readiness and cheerfulness of obedience to the Father's will: That such and so excellent a Person should suffer, and suffer so much, and suffer in such a way, this sure makes condign satisfaction; and so justice is thereby fully satisfied, and made as glorious as if all the elect had suffered eternally: Therefore we say, that his sufferings were a condign and proportionable satisfaction to justice for them whose debt he paid; by this justice is completely and gloriously satisfied. *Secondly,* We said, that it was meet that he should pay all that he paid: and so it is, if we consider, (1.) The excellency of immortal souls; a little price (as all that men or angels could have paid would have been, the finest gold, silver, or precious stones) could not have done it; *The redemption of the soul is precious, and ceaseth for ever,* to wit, amongst all the creatures, Psal. xlix. 8. (2.) The severity of justice on the just account of sin, called for such a price. (3.) God's end, which was to make both his grace and justice glorious, required, and made it meet that our Lord should suffer condignly, and in his sufferings suffer much, even all that he did suffer; and in this ye have an answer to this question, Why Christ suffered so much as the loss (to speak so) of his declarative glory for a time, outward sufferings and inward sufferings, even the bruising and squeezing that his soul was under, which made him to say, that *it was heavy unto death, and exceeding sorrowful?* Let not sinners then think it a little or a light thing to get a soul saved, the redemption whereof ceaseth for ever as to us or any creature: Behold herein the glory of grace eminently shineth forth, when there is such a price paid for that which in some respect is of so little worth; and also the glory of justice, when so great a price is demanded and paid down for its satisfaction, by so worthy and excellent a Person; and let none think little of sin, the guilt whereof could not be otherwise expiated, the chastisement of our peace behoved to be on him.

5. What are the benefits that come by these sufferings? *Answ.* 1. The benefits are such, that if he had not suffered for us, we should have suffered all that he suffered ourselves. 2. More particularly, we have (1.) Peace and pardon of sin. (2.) Healing by his suffering; so that if it be asked, What procured pardon of sin, and peace with God? We answer, It is Christ's sufferings: Or if it be asked, What is the cause of God's justifying sinners? We answer, It is Christ's satisfaction or sufferings. And it is (by the way) much to be regretted, that such is the ignorance of some, that if a question be proponed in divers words or expressions, as if it should

should be asked, Wherefore are we pardoned? Wherefore are we justified? which is one and the same; they know not how to answer: But here ye are called to remember, that Christ being wounded, and his bearing the chastisement due to you, is the cause of your pardon and justification. 2. Healing looks to sanctification, as we hinted in the exposition; so that if it be asked, How comes it to pass that a sinner is made holy? we have it here answered, that tho' efficiently it comes by the Spirit, and be his work, yet meritoriously it comes by Christ's sufferings, he bought it, *by his stripes we are healed:* And under these two words, *peace* and *healing*, we take in all things needful or pertaining to life and godliness; for by *peace* the feud and enmity is taken away, and we are reconciled to God, as Eph. ii. 14. he is said to be *our peace*, and he who came *to speak peace to all that are afar off and near-hand;* and also by *peace* we understand all the effects of peace. (1.) Pardon of sin, justification, adoption, communion with God here and hereafter; peace with our own conscience, and with the creatures; eternal peace and glory, and all good things purchased by Christ's death: For the Hebrews, under *peace*, comprehended all these good things. And under *healing*, we take in sanctification (as distinguished, though not divided, from those other things mentioned) dying to sin and living to righteousness, with the several degrees of their advance and progress, and the making of us to be without spot and wrinkle, or any such thing; so that folks have much advantage by Christ's purchase, and much prejudice thorow the want of it. By his death we are kept out of hell, and admitted to peace with God, and every thing that is good; we have liberty to pray for all that is good, and are brought in his own time and way to the possession of it: It is by the blood of sprinkling that we have a new and living way made patent to us unto the most holy, and holiness, in the way whereof we enter in thither.

6. To whom hath Christ procured all these good things? The text faith, It is *our* and *we*, the chastisement of *our* peace was on him, and by his stripes *we are* healed, to wit, the elect. Whence observe, 1. *That the benefits of Christ's purchase redound only to the elect:* There is a certain select number to whom they are applied, and not to all indifferently; it is only of as many as are healed, whose chastisement he hath born; it is only they whom the Father hath given him, to them he gives eternal life, and they shall never perish, John x. 28. They are effectually called, justified and sanctified. 2.

Observe, "That what Jesus Christ hath purchased, "and the benefits of his purchase, redound and are "extended to them that are guilty of hainous sins;" to them that are under transgressions and iniquities, that are at feud with God, and under many pollutions, and most lothsom spiritual diseases; to them who contemned and despised Christ and judged him smitten and plagued of God, as is clear from the foregoing words; and to them who have gone straying like lost sheep, as is clear from the words following.

This points at these two or three things very useful, 1. That the elect are by nature, and before Christ do them good, no better than others. 2. It shews the freedom of the grace of God, that comes over that, and freely gives pardon, peace, and healing to them. And, 3. It serves to strengthen a sinner's faith, who is sensible of his enmity and sinfulness, and to be a ground of encouragement to him to step to, and lay hold on Christ's purchase, because it was for such that he died; he may humbly, yet confidently say, Christ died even for such as me, for them that wounded and pierced him by their transgressions and iniquities, for them that were at enmity with God, &c. and alas! I am such, and will therefore on the call of the gospel come to him, and on his own terms endeavour to cast myself on him.

7. How are these benefits, this justification, pardon of sin, peace and healing, and all that is comprehended under them, derived from Christ to the sinner that by faith fleeth unto him for refuge? *Answer*, These two generals will clear it, 1. They are derived to us justly and in a legal way; Christ steps in our room, that we may come in his room. 2. They are derived to us freely; he was wounded and bruised, that we might go free, he endured stripes, that we might be healed; he got the buffets and bare the burden, and we get the benefits; there is not a grain-weight of it laid on us, as it is satisfactory to divine justice. To clear this a little more, anent the deriving the benefits of Christ's purchase to us, there must be a respect had, 1. To the covenant of redemption, the ground of his suffering for us. 2. To the covenant of grace and reconciliation, wherein the offer of these sufferings, and the benefits purchased by them to us, and the terms of both, are made.

(1.) I say, that respect must be had to the covenant of redemption, wherein it was acted in the council of the God-head, that the Son of God should become Man, and suffer, and condignly satisfy divine justice by paying the price due by the elect; and that that price being laid down, it should be made forthcoming for them for whom he paid it, and be reckoned theirs, and they set actually at liberty, when having recourse thereto by faith: And here there is a legal ground for transferring Christ's purchase to and upon us; the Cautioner satisfying, we the debtors are on that account absolved in his own order and method, and have a right to seek the application of the price, and the benefits purchased by that price: Christ stands in our room at the bar, and sentence passed on him to pay our debt; he satisfied according to his undertaking for us: And upon the other hand, we are brought in, and the sentence of justification passed on us on that account: *He,* saith the Apostle, who knew no sin, is made sin for us, that in him we may be accounted righteous, and may be declared free (as we are) by vertue of his satisfaction.

But it may be objected here, What are we then absolved from the very time of Christ's death, and forward? For answer, we would distinguish betwixt a right *to* the thing, and a right *in* the thing (as we use to speak) betwixt *jus ad rem,* and *jus in re;* the elect from Christ's death forward, and before too, have a right to the thing, but not in the thing, as to the application of it to themselves: An elect person, by vertue of Christ's satisfaction, hath a legal right to his purchase before believing; but when he comes to believe, the obstruction is taken away that hindered his application, and then he hath a new right, not only *to,* but *in* Christ's purchase; even as a person that is *minor* or mad, may have a right to a great possession, but by the law he is secluded from the use of it, till he come to *majority,* or have the use of reason: and this distinction we have as one of the clauses of the covenant, John vi. 39, 40. where 1. in the 39 *v.* Christ says, *This is the Father's will that sent me, that of all that he hath given me, I should lose nothing, but should raise it up again at the last day:* It is the Father's will that eternal life be given to as many as are given to Christ on his satisfaction, and Christ hath purchased it to them by his satisfaction absolutely as to the event; and therefore they have an accessibleness to it, a right to it, and cannot but partake of it, yet not simply, but in the way that he hath laid down: And therefore, 2. In the 40 *ver.* he saith, *This is the will of him that sent me, that every one that seeth the Son, and believeth on him, may have eternal life;* by believing they come to the application of that to themselves, which they had a legal right to before by Christ's death.

(2.) Respect must be had to the covenant of grace, which is not quite another thing than the covenant of redemption, but the making offer of it, and the benefits contained in it, in the preached gospel, when Christ sends out his ambassadors to woo and invite sinners to Christ, and to bring them to the application of his purchase: and it is by closing with, and receiving of Christ's offer, that the actual cure comes, and that by Christ's stripes our sores are healed; even as when a child that was *minor* becomes *major,* he comes to have a right to possess the same lands or sums of money, by the same law that gave him a legal or simple right to them before; or he comes to have a right *in* that, which before he had a right *to* so elect souls, that have a right to Christ's purchase before believing, while they are mad in nature, are under the curse and wrath threatned in the word of God, for not believing; but when they come to believe, they come to get an extract from the same word of their right *in* Christ's purchase, because the word says, " He that " believes, is past from death to life, and shall not " come into condemnation:" and so the same word that did condemn before believing, doth now absolve upon a sinner's believing; and we come at this absolution, by receiving of Christ's offer in the covenant of grace. And if it be asked, How comes it, that the receiving of Christ's free offer in the covenant of grace gives a right to Christ's purchase? We answer, It is by vertue of the covenant of redemption, wherein it is so transacted betwixt God and the Mediator: so that there is the offer of the covenant received, and the covenant itself, that concur for making over and deriving a complete right to wretched sinners in Christ's purchase.

Let the 1*st Use* of this be for your instruction and information, which is the end wherefore we have chosen, in this way, by this short view, to give you, in a very short sum the marrow of the gospel; and if ye remember these few questions, ye may be in a capacity, not only to answer us, but through grace to exercise faith on Christ: and we think ye will all readily grant, that these who cannot at all answer them, should not go to the communion; and therefore, that ye may take them with you, we shall shortly resume them. 1. What condition is man in by nature? Answer, Under sin and misery, even under the curse of God: or thus, every man is a sinner, and hath a sinful nature; or he is under transgressions and iniquities, is naturally lothsom, wants peace with God, and hath need of healing: let this, in the first place sink in your hearts. 2. How is man freed from this sinfulness and misery? Answer, He cannot be free from it, till there be a

condign

condign satisfaction made to divine justice; wounding and bruising must be to procure pardon, and stripes must be to procure healing, and chastisement must be to bring about our peace: That word, Exod. xxxiv. *Who will by no means acquit the guilty*, would always be remembred, and faith would look to a Saviour for satisfaction. 3. Who can satisfy? Answer, Neither man nor angel can do it, no penances, no prayers, nor performances of any mere creature will do it, but *he* only that was wounded and bruised, he who by nature is the Son of God, the express Image of his Father's Person, and who, in respect of his human nature, was born of the Virgin Mary, like to us in all things except sin; it is he that satisfies justice, and it is by no other way that we get pardon, and peace with God, and holiness. 4. What way doth Christ satisfy justice, and make peace betwixt God and sinners? Answer, He entred himself in our room, and as Cautioner undertook our debt, suffered the condign punishement that was due for our sins, and paid the price that we should have paid; he in a manner left heaven, and became Man, had a mean life in the world, drank the cup of his Father's wrath, was wounded, bruised, chastised, and died a cursed death, whereof his hanging on the cross was but a sign. 5. What benefits come to us by his sufferings? Answer, Pardon of sin, peace with God, and healing; the conscience by his blood is sprinkled from dead works, the person absolved, reconciled to God, made whole, and made at last to be without spot or wrinkle, or any such thing; and this is not, as *Papists* blasphemously speak, a putative effect, but a most real one. 6. Who are made partakers of this pardon, peace and healing? Answer, The elect have right to it, and by believing they make the application; therefore it is said here, *our* and *we*; and we may look upon the prophet, speaking in the name of all the elect, or in name of the believing elect, who on believing are actually healed: the elect then are healed; and the way how, is by faith making application of Jesus Christ. 7. How in justice can he be condemned, that was free of sin? and how can we be absolved, that were guilty? Answer, He in justice was condemned, because, as our Cautioner, he came in our room, and undertook to pay our debt; and on the same ground, we wretched sinners may in this way make application of his purchase, because it was on these terms that he undertook the debt, that we might be set free; and it is on these terms that it is offered in the gospel, that seeing he hath paid for elect sinners, they may,

upon the hearing of the offer, close with it. But how may the sinner apply it? Answer, Not only because it is free and freely offered, but by gripping to it by faith, as the prophet doth here, it is not only to apply it simply, but to step in, and rest upon it, in the terms it is made offer of. So that as, on the one part, Jesus Christ became really liable to suffering, and satisfied for our sins, when he said, "Lo, I come, in the volume of thy book it " is written of me, I delight to do thy will:" So upon the other part, the believing sinner comes to apply the price paid, by embracing the price, and acquiescing in the satisfaction, and gripping to it as his own, and by his being brought to say in faith, Let his wounding be my pardon, let his chastisement be my peace, and let his stripes be my healing. By this means, as the law had a right to Christ for his paying the elect's debt, so they, by believing, get a right to the promise of pardon and healing: for if the bargain was sicker on the one side, to procure wounding to Christ, as if he had been the sinner himself; so on the other side, the bargain is as sure; the believer is set free, and may be as really comforted, as if he had a righteousness of his own, or had never sinned.

Use 2d. Therefore there is here wonderful matter of consolation to believers, that what was justice to Christ, is grace and mercy to us; that which was pain to him, is pleasure to us; his sorrow our comfort, his wounding our pardon, his stripes our healing, &c.

Use 3d. As ye would not prejudge yourselves of these benefits which Christ hath purchased, make your peace with God through Christ; if your pardon and peace be not obtained this way, ye will never get it, but ye shall be made to pay your own debt, and be liable to wrath eternally, because of inability to pay your debt to the full: therefore step to, and make the offer welcome, how sinful and undone soever ye be; the more sensible ye be, ye are the more welcome. This is the particular use of the doctrine. O let these things sink in your hearts, that ye are sinners, great sinners, under wrath, and at feud with God; that Jesus Christ is the Saviour of lost sinners, and that there is no way to pardon and peace, but by closing with him, and laying hold on his satisfaction, that ye may be drawn to cast yourselves over on this everlasting covenant, for obtaining the benefits that Christ hath purchased. And himself bless what hath been spoken for this end and use.

SERMON XXIII.

Isaiah liii. 5. *But he was wounded for our transgressions, he was bruised for our iniquities; the chastisement of our peace was upon him, and with his stripes we are healed.*

IT were no small progress in Christianity, to know and believe the truths that are implied and contained in this same verse; the Lord, by the prophet, is giving a little compend of the work of redemption, by his saving of sinners from death, through and by the wounding of the Mediator. We did a little open the meaning of the words, and gave a sum of the doctrines contained in them, at least of some of them, which do contribute to this scope.

The prophet is here speaking of Christ's sufferings, with a respect to the cause of them, and the effect that followed them; and shews how this was indeed the mistake and blasphemous imputation that we had of, and were ready to put on him, even to judge him smitten and plagued of God for his own sins, whereas God hath another design: he was altogether without sin, but he was wounded for *our* transgressions, he was bruised for *our* iniquities; we were at feud with God, and he took on him the chastisement of *our* peace; and this is the effect, to procure healing to *us*.

We shall now speak a word to three *doctrines* further, besides what we spoke to the last day, which are these, 1. That there was an eternal design, plot and transaction betwixt God and the Mediator, as to Christ's suffering for the redeeming of elect sinners, before he actually suffered. This the prophet speaks of as a thing concluded; for the cause of his sufferings was condescended on, and the end and fruit of them was determined, which implies an *antecedaneous* transaction betwixt the Father and him, for putting him in the room of sinners: and by this transaction, justice hath access to exact the payment of this price; he interposed, and the Father exacts of him the payment of their debt, and seeks satisfaction from him for all that he bargained for. 2. That this transaction or design, concerning the redemption of elect sinners, is, in respect of Christ's suffering and satisfying of justice, fully and actually performed; he undertook to be wounded and bruised, and he was accordingly actually wounded and bruised: the transaction, as to the engagement in it, and efficacy of it, took place in Isaiah's time, and before his time; but as to the actual performance of what the Mediator engaged himself to suffer, it is spoken of prophetically by him, as a thing done, because to be done; and now it is done, and indeed long ago. 3. That the satisfying of justice, by the Mediator's sufferings, according to his engagement, proves as effectual to absolve, justify and heal these, even the grossest sinners, that come under this bargain and transaction, as if they had actually suffered, and paid and satisfied their own debt themselves: their sins are pardoned through his sufferings, their deadly wounds are healed by his stripes, as if they had never had a wound; their count is dashed and scored as clean out, as if they had never had any debt; they are acquitted and set free, as if they had never been guilty.

These three *doctrines* ly very near the life of the gospel; and the prophet, in this chapter, and particularly in this verse, is often on them. Our purpose is only shortly to explicate them to you, as a short sum and compend of the tract of the covenant of redemption; the *first* of them shews the rise of the work of redemption; the *second* shews the mids by which it is executed; the *third* holds out the effect and consequence, and the end of all.

For the *first* then, there is (we say) an eternal transaction betwixt God, and Jesus Christ the Mediator, concerning the redemption of sinners; his actual redeeming, by being wounded and bruised, supposeth this; for the Son is no more liable to suffering (not to speak of his suitableness) than any other of the Persons of the blessed Godhead, had there not been an antecedent transaction; there was no obligation nor tye on him to be wounded, and to enter into the room of sinners as their Cautioner, for payment of their debt, if there had not been a prior engagement; neither could his wounding and bruising have proven useful, or have brought healing to us, if this prior engagement had not been; and this is it which we call the *covenant of redemption*, which we would not extend so as, in all things to stretch it to the properties of these covenants and bargains which are amongst men, it being in some respect an expression used to make grace more discernable to us, that can conceive so little of grace's way. This transaction, or covenant of redemption, is sometimes called *the Father's will*, and *his law*, as Psal. xl. 8. *I delight to do thy will, O my God, yea thy law is within my heart;* and John vi. 38. it is called so, *I came from heaven not to do mine own will, but the will of him that sent me;* so also, John xvii. 14. it is called the Father's *work* in one respect, and the Son's *work* in another respect, *I have finished the work thou gavest me*

U   to

to do; which is the profecution of the fame contrivance ufually called a *covenant*, becaufe, as to the effentials, it hath the nature of a covenant, to wit, two parties agreeing, and terms whereupon they agree, and is well ordered in all things for profecuting and carrying on the defign of faving loft finners, called, Acts ii. 23. the *determinate counfel and fore-knowledge of God*; there was a plot and defign in God's counfel, concerning Chrift's fufferings, whereof his fufferings were the execution.

To clear it a little, we would confider thefe *five* things in it, 1. The parties. 2. The matter about which it is. 3. The rife and occafion of it. 4. The terms wherein the form of it ftands, or the midfes whereupon it is undertaken. 5. Some properties of this covenant.

1. For the Parties ; upon the one fide is God effentially confidered, or all the three Perfons of the glorious Godhead, Father, Son, and Holy Ghoft, who are all concurring in this covenant, it being the act of the determinate counfel of God ; and in this refpect God is the Party to whom the fatisfaction for loft finners is made, and he is alfo the Party condefcending to accept of the fatisfaction : and and upon the other fide, the Party engaging to make fatisfaction, is Jefus Chrift, the fecond Perfon of the bleffed, dreadful, and adorable Trinity, perfonally confidered, now becoming the Head of the elect, that he may have them all with himfelf to be one myftical body ; in the firft refpect, all the three Perfons, that fame one bleffed God, give the command or require a fatisfaction as God, and concur, as the infinitely wife Orderer of the decree : and in the fecond refpect, Jefus Chrift, as Mediator, undertakes to make fatisfaction, Pfal. xl. 6, 7. *Sacrifice and offering thou didst not defire*; God, as it were, making the offer, What can, or fhall be given to me, for the redemption of finners ? Sacrifice and offering will not pleafe. nor are accepted by me. Then follows the Mediator's part, *Lo, I come, in the volume of thy book it is written of me, I delight to do thy will, O my God*: for tho' in the firft refpect, all the perfons in the Trinity be on the one fide, being of one will ; yet in the other refpect, Chrift Jefus, as Mediator, comes in on the other fide, to do his will.

2. As to the matter about which this covenant is : it is about the fatisfying of juftice, and making of peace between God and loft finners ; it is that we might be pardoned, juftified, have peace made with God, and be healed. It is true, there is an end above and beyond this, even the glory of God's rich grace, and condefcending love, that ftoops fo low to fave finners ; but finners pardon, and peace with God, and their healing, is the immediate end : or, if we come nearer, the matter about which it is, is the redeeming of the elect ; for thefe words in the text, *we* and *us*, are of equal extent with them that are juftified and reconciled, and whom he actually healed by his wounds and ftripes ; fo that whoever they be who are never juftified and healed, they are not comprehended in this bargain.

3. The rife and occafion of this covenant may be gathered from thefe three. 1. There is the fuppofing of man's fin and fall ; for, whatever election doth, redemption doth muft certainly fuppofe man to be loft, and under fin. 2. There is God's decree, not to pardon fin without a fatisfaction. 3. There is God's election preceeding, or his purpofe to fave fome, for the glory of his grace, which are the elect, who are faid to be *given to Chrift*. Thefe three are the rife and occafion of the covenant of redemption ; man hath finned, the threatning muft be executed, and juftice fatisfied ; and yet God hath, for the glory of his grace, elected a certain number to life, and that muft needs ftand firm ; and thefe three feeming to thwart one of them with another, gives occafion and rife to the excellent and admirable contrivance of this way, how the loft finner fhall be faved, yet fo as juftice fhall be fatisfied, and not wronged in the leaft, and juftice fo fatisfied, that yet the decree of election by grace fhall ftand.

4. As for the terms (wherein the form of the covenant ftands) and the midfes by which thefe ends may be brought about, to wit, how the redemption of loft finners may be obtained, juftice may be fatisfied, and the glory of grace made to fhine, and how any thing that makes thefe feem to juftle and thwart might be guarded againft ; and that was it, which (to fpeak fo with reverence) put God to the confultation about it, which fhews the excellency of the covenant of redemption, and the deep draughts that are about it ; for otherwife, and properly, God needs not confult or advife : They are fhortly thefe, 1. God's offer to redeem man, if his juftice may be fatisfied, and if any refponfal perfon will become cautioner, and undertake to pay the elect's debt. 2. The Son's accepting of the offer, and undertaking or engaging to pay their debt, upon condition that his payment and fatisfaction fhall be accounted the elects, and accepted for them. 3 The Father's acceptation of this engagement and undertaking according to his offer, and the Mediator's accepting of it, and acquiefcing in it ; he holds the bargain,

(to

SERM. XXIII. *Isaiah* liii. Verse 5.

(to speak so) and so it is a closed covenant: the first is comprehended in these words, *Sacrifices and offerings thou didst not desire*, Psal. xl. insinuating that God did desire something; the second in these words, *Mine ears thou hast opened, then said I, Lo I come, in the volume of thy book it is written of me, I delight to do thy will;* which implies the Father's acceptation, as well as Christ's undertaking; and it also points at the way how the satisfaction is made effectual: especially if we compare these words of the Psalm with Heb. x. 5, 6. we will find that they relate to Christ's humiliation in general; for it is in the Psalm, *Mine ear hast thou opened;* but in Heb. x. 5. it is, *A body hast thou prepared me:* and where it is said in the Psalm, *I delight to do thy will,* the Apostle says, *By the which will we are sanctified.* The Father makes the offer on the terms of a satisfaction to justice; the Son as Mediator accepts the offer, and undertakes for the elect: Here am I, to do thy will, on the same terms that the offer is made; and the Father accepts of the Son's engagement, according to that word, Matt. iii. *This is my beloved Son, in whom I am well pleased;* he offers himself Surety for sinners, and the Father is content to accept of him as their Surety: In the one respect it is called the *Father's pleasure;* verse 10th of this chapter, *Yet it pleased the Lord to bruise him,* &c. because the terms were so proposed: and in the other respect, its called the *Mediator's pleasure,* or *satisfaction,* verse 11th, because the condition proposed is satisfying to him, *The pleasure of the Lord shall prosper in his hand.* He undertakes to pay, and God accepts of his undertaking, and obliges himself to absolve the believer: and the words following, *He shall see his seed, and of the travel of his soul, and be satisfied,* and *by his knowledge shall my righteous Servant justify many,* are promises made to him, on supposition of his making satisfaction, 2 Cor. v. ult. the first part of the transaction is, *He hath made him to be sin for us, that knew no sin;* and the other part of it is, *That we might be made the righteousness of God through him:* he accepting of the bargain, obtains a right to a justifying and absolving sentence, by vertue of his suffering; for which cause these words are added, *in him,* or *through him:* This shews the clearness of God's justice in proceeding with the Mediator; the ground of sinners justification through him; and gives sinners a warrant to make use of Christ's satisfaction as theirs, because it was so agreed upon in the counsel of the Godhead.

5. We come now to speak a little to some properties of this covenant, and shall content ourselves with three or four of them that make for the scope: As, 1. The justice and equity of it. 2. The faithfulness of it. 3. The freeness of it. And, 4. The wisdom that shines in this bargain; passing by the rest.

(1.) *The justice and equity* of this transaction may appear in these respects; 1. That the Father should be satisfied; and that he that was wronged, should have his honour restored; that the threatning given out in his law should light and take effect; that the soul that sins should in his own, or the Surety's person die; and that a suitable recompence should be made to justice, before the sinner should be absolved. 2. Justice appears in this respect, That when the Son of God, the Mediator, offers to become Man, and to endure and suffer all that the elect should have suffered, his sufferings should be accepted as a satisfaction; because the justice of God, yea, the holiness, power, and greatness of God, are as gloriously manifested in Christ's satisfaction, as if man had suffered; nay, there would not have been such an amends and satisfaction made to justice, if all creatures had suffered: Justice by this means hath more satisfaction than it could have had otherwise; and hereby the holiness of God, and the severity of his justice, as well as the condescending love of God, is the more manifested, that he himself should condescend to satisfy; therefore, Rom. iii. 26. it is said, *That he might be just, the justifier of him that believeth on Jesus:* God is just, in that he will not only have satisfaction, but an equivalent satisfaction, for the restoring of his justice to its declarative glory, wherein it suffered by man's fall. 3. Justice appears in this respect, That the Mediator satisfying justice, these for whom he suffered should be acquitted, and have the sentence of absolution past in their favours; which the rather we would take notice of, that we may know the redemption purchased and bestowed by the Mediator, is by an exact satisfying of justice, and not by removing of our sins, as he did our diseases, nor by pardoning of them by an authority committed to him; but, as I said, by a real and actual satisfying of the justice of God for them: therefore, Luke xxiv. it is said, *He behoved to suffer these things, and then to enter into his glory;* there was a necessity of it, because of the justice of this covenant, for the Son, not only to become Man, and be in a low condition, but to become a curse, and to die the cursed death of the cross.

A second property is *faithfulness* on all sides; faithfulness on the Father's side, in his word and

U 2   promise

promise to the Son; *All that are given of the Father, are made to come to him; and there is nothing lost*, John vi. 37, 44, 45. Faithfulness on the Son's side, performing all according to his undertaking, *fulfilling all righteousness*: Therefore when in the one word he says, *Deliver me from this hour;* in the next word he says, *But for this cause came I unto this hour*; it was my errand into the world, and now I am to go about it by and bye: *And I lay down my life for my sheep myself, no man taketh my life from me, but I have power to lay it down, and power to take it up again*. His faithfulness also appears in keeping all that are committed to his trust, *None of them shall perish, but he shall raise them up at the last day*. Therefore he is called the good or faithful *Shepherd*.

3. It is a *free* covenant: it is *just*, as betwixt God and the Mediator; but as to the elect, it is most *free*: By his wounds we have pardon, and by his stripes we have healing; *The chastisement of our peace was on him*; there is not one grain weight or worth to be satisfied by us: *He was made sin for us*, he was made the curse, even the wrath-pacifying-sacrifice and offering; *That we might be made the righteousness of God*, not thro' ought in ourselves, but *thro' him*, 2 Cor. v. *ult*.

4. It is a most *wise* contrivance, for if the Son had become Man and Mediator, how could justice have been satisfied, or the elect pardoned and healed? They could not satisfy for themselves, and no creature could satisfy for them; therefore the only wise God finds out a wise mids for such an end, as is the saving of the elect, in a way wherein justice and mercy, or free grace, sweetly kiss each other, and wherein they both shine forth conspicuously and radiantly.

That which we would say, in short, concerning this covenant, is this, That Jesus Christ hath undertaken to pay the elect's debt, and hath stepped in unto their room; and God hath imputed unto him their sin, and accepted of a satisfaction from him for them; and all this in a legal and just way, so as there is access before the throne of God for them to plead for the application of his righteousness by virtue of this covenant; that as really and faithfully as Christ performed his undertaking to God, and his satisfaction was accepted for them, they may as really and on good ground expect the application of it to them: For tho' all be of grace to us, yet it is a bargain on just and legal terms betwixt God and the Mediator; therefore there is a title and right in justice for the elect, when they come to Christ, that his satisfaction shall stand for them, as being members of his Body, and in whose room and place he satisfied; Hence it is said, 1 John ii. 1. *If any man sin, we have an Advocate with the Father, Jesus Christ the righteous*; and whereon is this righteousness founded? The next words tell us, *He is the propitiation for our sins*; he hath paid the price that was due by us, and we may seek the application of it to us, according to the transaction past betwixt the Father and him, now performed; which is the next point.

The 2d Doctrine is, "That this transaction and " design concerning the redemption of sinners, is " now not only undertaken, but fully performed;" as is clear, Acts ii. 23. *Him, being delivered by determinate counsel of God, ye have taken, and by wicked hands have crucified and slain*; the eternal purpose concerning this is now execute: As to the efficacy of his sufferings, *He is indeed the Lamb slain from the beginning of the world*; Because neither the Son's undertaking was questioned by the Father, nor the Father's promise questioned by the Son. To speak so with reverence of such a mystery, the Father, before his coming, trusts him upon his engagement with the salvation of so many elect souls as he had given him; and the Son, considered as Mediator, trusts the Father with the justifying of them, according to the promise made to him in the 11 verse of this chapter; but the actual performance of the undertaking was not till Christ suffered. This actual performance of the covenant comprehends these things shortly; 1. That as this plot and design of redemption was laid down, so it hath the performance by all the parties covenanting: It is actually performed according to the terms of it. 2. That it hath the real effects covenanted for, actually and really brought about: It hath with it a most real and effectual following, to speak so, whereof Christ's actual suffering was a part, and a main part.

I say, it is performed by all parties according to the terms, and hath its real effect, in these respects, 1. Christ Jesus hath, according to this covenant, sisted himself before the bar of justice, and undertaken our debt. 2. Justice hath pursued Christ for our debt, and hath exacted payment of it from him: The cup that belonged to us was put in his hand, and he was made to drink it: In which respect, it is said, *He was made a curse for us*, Gal. iii. The sword of divine justice awaked against him, and did smite him. 3. Jesus Christ, according to his undertaking, doth accept of the claim, undergoes the debt, and satisfies justice; therefore, when he stands in our room, as if he had been the guilty Person, he opens not his mouth to justify him-

himself; he says not, these are not my sins, but is as dumb, as the sheep is before the shearer, because he was our Cautioner: The everlasting covenant, to say so, stood registrate over his head, and he is made to count for all that was due by, and to us. 4. It is performed in this respect, that the Father pursues not the elect on this account to be satisfied of them, who, as soon as they accept of the covenant, are actually justified and absolved. Indeed, while they are in nature, the sentence still stands, *Cursed is he that sinneth and believeth not*: yet, by vertue of his performance of the transaction, they have a legal right to justification, and the promise to him stands good, that the elect by his knowledge shall be justified; and it hath an actual performance in all them that believe, they are really made free as he was made the sinner. 5. In respect of the manner, (1.) It is performed exactly according to the covenant, even as it was agreed upon, that for so many he should suffer and procure eternal life, and so it is; eternal life is given to so many, according to the condition of this covenant and bargain. (2.) As it was a bargain wherein Jesus was to be satisfied; so it was exactly satisfied: Christ Jesus gets nothing down, not one farthing is remitted, but satisfies all, pays down the full price; he drinks out all the wrath contained in the cup, till it come to that sweet word, uttered by him amongst his last words on the cross, *It is finished*.

The 3d Doctrine is, *That tho' elect sinners, be as well sinners by nature, and as gross sinners as others: yet by vertue of this covenant, and upon condition of their accepting of it, they may obtain, and do actually obtain, peace with God, pardon and healing, as if they had never sinned, or as if they had satisfied the justice of God themselves.* This is the very end of this transaction, *He was wounded for our transgressions, and bruised for our iniquities, the chastisement of our peace was upon him, and by his stripes we are healed*: His wounds, bruises and stripes, effectually procured justification and healing to us: And this is the ground of that which we call *imputed righteousness*, and shews how it comes to pass that we are made righteous by the righteousness of another, scornfully called *putative righteousness* by Papists: But considering what is in the former doctrines, and in this, we will find it to be a clear truth, on which our justification, and the whole weight of our salvation hangs; that the believing sinner, closing with Christ's satisfaction, is as effectually absolved from sin, as if he had never sinned; Christ's satisfaction becomes as really his, as if he had paid the debt himself: And if we consider these three, 1. The great design of the covenant of redemption betwixt God and the Mediator. 2. The faithfulness of God in this covenant, in performing his part on the terms on which the Mediator laid down a price for the elect. 3. The excellency and efficacy of the price paid with respect to the covenant; we will find that there is a clear access in law, or according to the decree of God manifested (the decree called a *law*, *Thy law is within my heart*) for the grossest sinners that come under this bargain, and close with this covenant, their obtaining peace, pardon, justification, and healing, as if they had never sinned, or had satisfied themselves, and that they may confidently expect it on this ground.

1. I say, if we consider the great end and design of the covenant betwixt God and the Mediator, we will find it to be the justification of the elect: Christ suffered, not for any sin that was inherently in himself: He had no sin; there was no guile found in his mouth, no quarrel betwixt God and him on his own account; but he was wounded for *our* transgressions, the chastisement of *our* peace was on him: To make peace betwixt God and us by his wounding, was the great design of the covenant of redemption; and can that design hold, if his satisfaction come not in the room of ours, and stand not for our satisfaction and payment? In man's law, the cautioner paying the debt proves valid for the principal debitor: And when this is the design of God in the covenant of redemption, how to get the debt of dyvour sinners paid, and themselves set at liberty, and when this is found out as the mids, *a body hast thou prepared unto me*; the covenant must be as real on the one side as it is on the other; that is, as real and effectual to make the believer in Christ just, as it was real and effectual to make Christ to be accounted the sinner, and to be dealt with as such. We may clear it further in these two, 1. By looking to Christ typified in the offerings under the law: When the sinner came with his offering, he laid his hand on the head of the beast, especially of the *scape-goat*, to shew that Jesus Christ, who was to come to be both Priest and Sacrifice, who was to bear the sins of the elect, as they were to be set free; that he was to lay his neck down to the knife of justice, that the stroke might be kept off our throat. 2. We are so justified by Christ, as Christ was made sin for us: Now our sins became really Christ's, not that he was made the sinner inherently, that were blasphemous to be thought or spoken of; but he was reckoned the sinner, and was substitute in the room of sinners, as if he had been the

sinner,

sinner, and was made to satisfy for original sin, and for actual sin, as if he had been guilty of them by committing them; therefore, 2 Cor. v. ult. he is said to be *made sin for us*, and Gal. iii. to be *made a curse for us*, and 1 Pet. ii. 24. *to bear our sins in his own body on the tree*: And if he suffered for us, and if we partake of his righteousness, as he did of our sins; then our justification really follows, and we are absolved and made righteous through his satisfaction closed with by faith, as if we had never sinned. The parallel is clear, 2 Cor. v. ult. *He was made sin for us, who knew no sin, that we might be made the righteousness of God in him*: So that Christ was made sin, in the same manner we are made righteous; that as legally as he who had no debt, was made liable to our debt, so as legally we partake of his righteousness, and are declared free: Even as the debtor is legally freed from the debt which his cautioner hath paid, and cannot be liable to it; so the believer, by Christ's satisfaction, is freed from the debt of sin, and absolved and declared righteous. And tho' this may seem strange and a wonder, to be a sinner, and yet in some respect free of sin; under guilt, and yet absolved; yet Christ's satisfaction is as real and effectual to the believer, as if he had satisfied himself, because his Cautioner hath satisfied for him.

2. If we consider God's faithfulness in this covenant, in performing his part, according to the terms of it, the matter is clear: For as the Mediator hath performed his part according to his engagement; so it is impossible but God must perform his, and must accept of the satisfaction in the name of the elect, and upon their believing justifies them: For as it was the Father's will, that he should lay down his life for his sheep, so it was the will of the Father, Son, and holy Ghost, that believers in him should thro' his satisfaction have eternal life, John vi. 39, 40. when he hath said before, *I came not to do my own will, but the will of him that sent me*, he subjoins, *This is the Father's will which sent me, that of all that he hath given me, I should lose nothing, but should raise it up again at the last day*; where the satisfaction that Christ should make is implied, and it is a great one: And what satisfaction shall he have for that? even the salvation of the elect; *This is the will of him that sent me, that every one that seeth the Son, and believeth on him, may have everlasting life, and I will raise him up at the last day*. And ver. 10. of this chapter, it is clear that he shall not want satisfaction; *for he shall see of the travail of his soul, and be satisfied*: And what is the satisfaction? *By his know-*

ledge shall my righteous Servant justify many; he shall be the cause of the justifying of many, and they shall be actually absolved in due time: And what is the ground of it? *For he shall bear their iniquities*: And therefore, as God is faithful, he shall get that, which he merited and purchased for them, applied unto them.

3. If we consider the excellent and equivalent price that Jesus Christ hath paid, and that with respect to the covenant, we have a clear ground why the believer may expect and be confident to be absolved and declared free: It is no mean price, gold, silver, or precious stones, but the blood of him that was and is God; which we say would be considered not simply, but with respect to the covenant, and to the end wherefore he suffered and shed his blood: For though it be no comfort to a sinner simply that Christ suffered; yet when he considers that it was for this end, to wit, that justice might be satisfied, and that these for whom he satisfied might be justified, and made free; the believing sinner may hence reason; If there was a reality in justice pursuing of him as my Cautioner, and a reality and efficacy in his satisfaction; and if it was full and complete, so as justice was fully satisfied by it, when there was a reality of mercy, pardon, justification, and peace with God, and of healing to and for me, their being made forthcoming to me upon the condition of believing; and in this respect, though it be grace to pardon sin as to us, yet it is justice in God to give Christ the satisfaction for the travail of his soul, as well as he gave God satisfaction to his justice: And the equivalent of that which the elect should have paid, being paid to justice by Christ their Cautioner, the Lord cannot, nor will not shun nor shift the pardoning of a believing sinner according to the covenant.

The *Uses* are five, 1. Of instruction, whereby we may have a map of God's way of saving sinners; and of the way of sinners coming to get salvation through Jesus Christ.

2. To stir us up to admire the love of God, contriving such a design for the salvation of lost sinners; the love of God, that gave his Son; and the love of the Son, that engaged to come, and hath come and paid the debt.

3. It gives a notable warrant to the faith of a sinner to take hold of, and close with Christ, and to rest upon his satisfaction for justification and healing, because he hath God and the Mediator covenanting for this very end, the Mediator engaging to satisfy, and God engaging to receive the satisfaction, and to justify all these who shall accept of it, and rest upon it.

4. It

SERM. XXIV. *Isaiah* liii. Verse 5. 155

4. It is therefore a notable ground of encouragement, and of exhortation, to take hold of Jesus Christ, and of his satisfaction: Folk would not fear at him, but lippen their salvation to him, and be sure the bargain will not fail; as it is sure that the Mediator hath satisfied, it is as sure that his satisfaction shall be made forthcoming to believers in him.

5. To reprove the neglecters and slighters of Jesus Christ, and of this offered salvation thro' him; when he hath taken the threatning and curse of the law on himself, to make out the promise to them, it must be a great aggravation of folks guilt to slight him. It serves also to comfort a poor sinner, that hath many sins and challenges, and knows not how to be quit of them: The covenant says, our sins are translated on the Mediator, that we might be set free; Christ Jesus covenanted on the terms of justice, to make way for us to covenant on the terms of mercy; God covenanted with him to pursue our sin in him, and he covenanted to impute that satisfaction freely to us: Hence is that never-enough noted saying, 2 Cor. v. 19. *God was in Christ reconciling the world to himself.* It is justice on his part, he satisfied for pardon of sin, and peace to them: But on the elect's part it is grace, God is reconciled to them, not imputing their sin to them; but it is for Christ's satisfaction that he freely forgives them their sins: So that what cost him dear, comes most freely to us; and this is no small ground of comfort to a conscience pressed with sin. God fix these things in your hearts.

SERMON XXIV.

Isaiah liii. 5. *But he was wounded for our transgressions, he was bruised for our iniquities: the chastisement of our peace was upon him, and with his stripes we are healed.*

IF there were more deep convictions amongst us of our natural deadness in sin, and of that fearful condition that naturally we ly under by our liableness to the wrath and curse of God, all men and women having by nature God's curse, as the sentence of the law, registrate against them; the reading of such a text, wherein a way of remedy is holden forth, would be more welcome to us; and we are persuaded that such a thorow conviction would not only make the word more lovely and delightsom to us, but more plain and easy to be understood by us, and to be sooner taken up by us; and one preaching would thus be more profitable and effectual than many are to you while in a secure condition: When people are not under the deep and due conviction of their sin and misery, they have no serious thoughts that the word of the gospel concerns them in particular, and that their souls stand in need of that which is spoken to them therein.

Ye may remember, we spoke somewhat from these words for clearing the way of making peace betwixt God and sinners; and for holding forth the way that God in his infinite wisdom hath laid down for setting of poor sinners, that are lying under the curse, free: For this end, there was an eternal transaction and covenant entred into by the Father and the Son, the Father demanding, and the Son accepting and satisfying, as Mediator and sinners Cautioner, what was due to justice for the sins of the elect, as was determined in the counsel of God; from which blessed bargain, all our salvation flows as from the fountain, and runs down as a river to us.

That which now we are to speak a little to, is some profitable *Uses*, which are the scope of all, and tend to lead you in to know the use of such doctrine, and not only to know it, but to engage you to make suitable practical improvement of it.

There are several sorts of *Uses* that flow from this verse, whence the preceeding doctrines have been drawn.

The *first* sort is for *Information*; which ye who are more ignorant, and have not so much light in you as to discover the way to heaven, would especially take heed to, though they be useful to all. And, 1. Ye would know and be informed in this, that all men and women, without exception, are lying under transgression and iniquities, and liable to be smitten and cursed of God, till these be taken away: But this having been spoke of in the forenoon, we need not insist on it now; but the truth is, neither law nor gospel hath gained this much ground on the great part of you, as to bring you really to know, that naturally ye are dead in sins and trespasses: and, till this be drunk in and digested, other truths cannot to any purpose profit you.

2. Ye would know and consider the necessity of a satisfaction to the justice of God, before sinners can be freed from sin, and from the curse and wrath of God, that they are under and liable to, by reason of their original corruption and actual transgressions. Do ye think that Jesus Christ did needlesly enter into the covenant of redemption, and engage to satisfy, and actually and really did suffer and satisfy justice? If men might come so easily to heaven

as many suppose, it had been needless. Would God (think ye) have wounded the Cautioner, his own dear Son, if those who ly under sin and wrath might have by another way satisfied justice, and restored him to his honour? Nay, ere this peace could be made, this behoved to be; and yet I much doubt if any do think that there is any such distance betwixt God and them, which a word of prayer, or confession, or some penance cannot remove: This is, alas! the woful ignorance of many that live under the gospel; but ye would know that a satisfaction behoved to be, and such a satisfaction as was equivalent to the wrong done, and suitable and satisfying to him that was wronged by sin, and that among all the creatures it could not be found. Yea, ye may read from this the dreadful effects of sin, and what a horrible thing it is to have your transgressions to count for with God yourselves: If sin brought such heavy things on the Cautioner, what will it bring on the sinner, who hath continued all his days in tops with God, to speak so, and would not make peace with him, when he was earnestly invited to it? Yea, we may from this know, what is that most horrible, dreadful, and confounding sentence, which is abiding all of you that stand it out, and do not make your peace with God through this satisfaction of our blessed Lord Jesus, when ye shall be made eternally to bear the wrath that sin deserves, which yet is intolerable.

3. Ye would hence know, and study to be clear and distinct in your knowledge of this precious truth, how a sinner, that by nature is under sin and wrath, and hath ground every day to look for it, may be freed from that curse and wrath: To prevent which, the Lord hath made a covenant with the Son, who is appointed Mediator for making peace betwixt God and sinners, by satisfying his justice for them, and by paying the same debt that was due by them; so that this wrath is prevented, and their peace is made by vertue of this covenant of redemption; wherein these two clauses are agreed and concluded upon betwixt these two infinitely responsal parties, 1. That Christ shall become the sinner, and be handled as a sinner; tho' there was no sin in him. 2. That the elect sinner, that by nature was a child of wrath even as well as others, shall be freed from the wrath to come by vertue of his satisfaction: These are two pillars that our salvation is built upon, and that our peace and reconciliation with God flow from: by his wounding and bruising, we are pardoned, *The chastisement of our peace was on him, and by his stripes we are healed.*

To clear this a little; This covenant would be considered, 1. As it looks to the parties, and their several actions. 2. As it looks to the execution thereof, in all the steps of it.

For the first, There are three parties that concur in their own place, 1. God is the party offended, and he is here bruising and wounding the Mediator: He is the Judge, and stands ready to execute the sentence that stands in his law against sinners, if he get not an equivalent satisfaction. 2. Jesus Christ the Mediator is the party wounded and bruised; the Mediator's part is to satisfy justice, to pay the price, and perform the satisfaction resolved upon in the counsel of God, of suitable and sufficient value for the redemption of the elect, according to his engagement; and he is actually wounded and bruised: God determined what shall satisfy, Christ Jesus accepts of the determination, engages to satisfy, and does actually satisfy for elect sinners. A 3d party is, We poor sinners, *He was wounded for our transgressions*, &c. it is the elect sinner, or the sinner, who being made in due time sensible of sin, and afraid of wrath, and who being kindly touched with the apprehension of it, and cleared anent the firmness and freeness of the covenant, and anent the fulness of Christ's satisfaction, doth by faith flee unto Jesus Christ, and submit to his satisfaction, and betakes himself allenarly to that for righteousness; Christ lays down the price, and the believing sinner pleads for interest in it, and for the benefit of it, and by faith gets title to an absolvitur from his debt and guilt. If it then be asked, What is the thing whereby a sinner is pardoned and justified, reconciled to God, and delivered from wrath and healed? I answer, It is by believing in Jesus Christ. If it be again asked, What is the ground or reason, why the believing sinner obtains that favour? I answer, Because our Lord Jesus hath sufficiently satisfied for, and fully paid the debt of so many as are brought to believe on him. If it be, 3dly, asked, How comes it that Christ's satisfaction becomes a ransom, and is accepted for such and such a believer? I answer, It is by vertue of the eternal covenant of redemption, or transaction made betwixt the Father and the Son, wherein it was agreed, that his suffering and satisfying of justice, should be accepted for believing sinners, as if themselves had satisfied; according to that of John vi. 39, 40. *This is the Father's will that sent me, that of all that he hath given me I should lose nothing: and this is the will of him that sent me, that whosoever seeth the Son, and believeth on him, may have everlasting life:* So our believing is the first immediate step, whereby we come to obtain pardon of sin, and peace with God: Christ's righteousness,

righteousness, or satisfaction, is that whereon our believing founds itself; yet so as it hath a respect to the eternal covenant of redemption, whence both Christ's satisfaction and our believing do flow, and without which we could have no warrant to expect righteousness through a Mediator; for, unless we know that Christ hath satisfied justice for elect sinners that shall believe on him, we cannot rest on him for righteousness; and unless we have an eye to the covenant of redemption, we cannot expect that his satisfaction will be accepted for us: And therefore, if we will trace these steps back again, the first rise of our salvation is in the counsel of God; the prosecution of it is in Christ's satisfaction; and the application of his satisfaction, is by our fleeing to it, and accepting of it by faith: And therefore we would learn, in our looking and stepping up to heaven, to look to these three in this order; we would first begin at faith, and in believing we would consider Christ's satisfaction, and from that we would ascend to the rise of it, to wit, the covenant of redemption, and the terms of it: All which put together, give a very clear ground of expecting righteousness through Jesus Christ. I shall illustrate it by a scripture-similitude, wherein I shall shew you how all the three concur, yet so as there is a difference in their concurrence. Ye know that under the law, there were *cities of refuge* appointed, which were types of Jesus Christ, in whom we find a shelter; in these cities of refuge, consider these three that concurred for saving the person that had committed man-slaughter; 1. God's determination, appointing such a thing, and that the man-slayer, being within such a city, should be safe from the avenger of blood; and this gave the rise to the other two that follow. 2. The city it self, as a shelter or refuge to the man-slayer. 3. The persons fleeing or running to hide themselves in it: Now the safety of the person of the man-slayer did flow from all the three. (1.) The law, appointing such a city, was the ground. (2.) The city was the shelter. (3.) The person's actual running to the city, gave him a claim and title to the privilege of the city: For tho' the former two had been, if he had not fled to the city, he had not obtained the benefit of safety: even so, the believer that would be saved, is to consider these *three*, 1. God's determining such a way of salvation to elect sinners by a Mediator. 2. The Mediator privileged as the city of refuge for this end. And, 3. The sinner's fleeing to him, which is his believing on him, and his seeking and pleading for the benefit of Christ's satisfaction, according to the terms of the covenant. Now, suppose a person to flee to the city of refuge, he is preserved in it, justice cannot follow him further than the gates yet so as he hath the benefit by God's determination and appointment of the city for such an end, and yet so as he must flee into it, ere he can plead for the benefit of the city: So, suppose a sinner to be fled to Jesus Christ by faith, he may plead for exemption from wrath, by God's determining and appointing a Mediator for such an end; and the Mediator Jesus Christ hath this privilege conferr'd on him, that he that thus flees unto him shall be safe; yet it is also suppos'd, that such a sinner hath fled to him, else he could not expect safety through him, notwithstanding of God's determining the Mediator for safety: thus we would have these three put together; and yet (as we said) they differ: for God's determination is the efficient cause and fountain of all; Christ's satisfaction is the meritorious cause, and our believing is the ground on which we have right to plead for the benefit of his satisfaction: even as the man that fled to the city of refuge, his safety was not by any virtue in his running, but by God's determination, yet his running to the city was requisite as the mids, and except he run or fled to it, he could not plead for the benefit of the city; so our believing gives us ground to plead a right and title to Christ and his satisfaction, without which we could not have that right.

But, 2*dly*, Because one will take up this under one notion, and another under another: To clear it therefore a little further, we shall again consider in the covenant these three steps, 1. The determination of it, as it is enacted in the counsel of the God-head, which in sum is this, that such and such persons shall be satisfied for by the Mediator, and his satisfaction accepted for them. 2. The execution of this covenant, where we take in all our Lord's sufferings; all the strokes and wounds that justice pursued him with, as Cautioner for the elect; and God's accepting and justifying of him, and declaring his accepting of him, and being well satisfied with what he did and suffered, by his raising him from the dead. 3. The application of his purchase, by his accepted satisfaction; which consists in these, (1.) That these that were given to Christ on this condition, that his satisfaction should stand good for them, should be justified and saved, that is, that in due time application of his satisfaction should be made to the persons given him to be saved by him; which takes in Christ's making intercession, that renewing grace, faith, &c. may be given to such persons. (2.) That the work of the Spirit, who, as the Sanctifier, begets faith, and persuades to embrace Jesus Christ, all be given them. Then (3.) Follows the believer's ver's actual coming to Christ, being sweetly and powerfully drawn to rest on him and his satisfaction; whereupon follows the application of the sentence of justification and absolution that results from the former: So that whereas it was before, *Cursed is he that continues not in all things written in the law*; now it is, *He that believeth on Jesus Christ, hath eternal life, and shall never come into condemnation*: All these go and agree well together; the covenant as the ground, Christ's satisfaction as the meritorious cause, and the application of his satisfaction by faith, which entitles and gives the believer a right to it.

The reason why we have so much insisted on this, is, That we may teach you to join respect to the covenant of redemption, Christ's suffering, and your believing, together: It will not be faith that will justify, that is, without respect to the covenant; neither will the covenant and Christ's satisfaction justify, without faith; yet ye would so put them together, as the glory of salvation through grace may not ly on faith, but on God's everlasting love, and on Christ's satisfaction. And indeed it is not little practick for a soul sensible of sin, in the exercise of faith so to lay the weight of its salvation on Christ and the covenant, as it neglect not running to Christ by faith; and so to lay hold on Christ by faith, as it lay not the weight on faith, but on Christ and the covenant: As in the comparison before used, Suppose a man, that had killed another unawares, had been taken before he wan to the city of refuge; God's determination was not the cause of that, but his not running, or his not coming at the city: So it may be that some are apprehended by the justice of God, that are less sinful than others; yet the reason or cause is not in God's covenant, nor in Christ's want of worth, but in the person's not running, or not fleeing to Christ as to the city of refuge; and therefore they are not heard to plead for immunity by vertue of that satisfaction before the bar of God.

A 2d sort of *Uses* are for exhorting and encouraging sinners to come to Christ: There is here then, 1. A clear ground to our faith, and a plain ordered and sure, a Mediator and a ransom provided, and a way laid down how to come to Christ by faith, let all of you, who come under the conviction of sin and apprehension of wrath, step to, and close with him, and plead for pardon by vertue of his wounds, and for healing through his stripes, with respect to the covenant.

There are these *four* things here that will serve to give ground for this application, if we consider, 1. The great ground of faith that is here. 2. The great reason we have to make use of this ground. 3. The great encouragement we have so to do. And, 4. The great necessity we have to make this application. A little to each of these: But we shall premise one word to all, and it is this, That considering you are all in trysting terms with God, whether ye live at a distance from him, the use will by way of exhortation reach you; or whether ye be brought to greater nearness under the sense of sin, and have some seriousness in seeking after God, it will reach you for consolation. In a word, we would exhort all, and it may be convince some, and comfort others: But to the first thing we proposed, We declare and proclaim this as a true and faithful saying, that there is here an everlasting covenant, wherein the salvation of the elect is concluded through Christ's satisfaction to justice for them, and a way laid down for making peace betwixt God and all them that will thorowly renounce their own righteousness, and lay hold on this satisfaction, even such a way as procures justification and healing to them. And for your confirmation, consider in general, if it be possible that this covenant of redemption, the sufferings of the Mediator, and the promises made to believing, can be for nought; did the Father pursue the Cautioner so hotly for nothing? or did the Cautioner pay such a ransom for nothing? No certainly; if it had not been to communicate pardon and peace, with healing by his wounds and stripes to them who were liable to condemnation, and under the dominion of sin, neither of these would have been: And therefore, for grounds of your faith, more particularly see here, 1. A full satisfaction: God hath made way to sinners peace with himself, by satisfying himself

rusalem, and to Jesus the Mediator of the new covenant, and to the blood of sprinkling. Our invitation therefore to you, is not to bid you come and count for your own debt yourselves, but to come and accept of Christ's payment of it, and of his satisfaction, whereby justice is completely satisfied. 2. See here, as another ground of faith, the justice of God, not with respect to us, but to the bargain betwixt the Father and the Son, who are the principal Parties, and we (to speak so) but parties accidentally in this covenant, the covenant being primarly and mainly betwixt God and the Mediator: The justice of it appears in this, that it hath respect to a covenant which is fulfilled on all sides; and therefore the elect's believing and taking hold of the Mediator's satisfaction, cannot but be accepted, as if he had paid the debt himself. The Father (to speak so) had the carving of the bargain, and what satisfaction his justice was to receive, to his own mind; and as it was justice on the Son's side to satisfy according to his undertaking, so it is justice on the Father's side to pardon and be at peace with the sinner that by faith flees unto Jesus Christ. 3. See in this bargain, not only justice, but mercy; as it is just, so it is a graciously free bargain; which is wonderful, and may seem somewhat strange, if not paradoxal, yet it is nothing inconsistent with the way of grace: it is just that the Cautioner should pay the debt, and yet that debt is most freely and frankly pardoned as to us; it is justice in the height as to the Mediator, but free grace as to us in the height; we come to it freely and without price, tho' it cost him dear: And that it is one of the Mediator's undertakings that it should be free to his seed, John vi. 40. *This is the will of him that sent me, that he who seeth the Son, and believeth on him, should have eternal life.* 4. Consider the reality and sureness of the bargain: it is such as it cannot fail, having such pillars to lean on, the faithfulness of God engaged on just and equal terms, and the glory of God as the end; and having a most necessary and certain effect, to wit, healing to all to whom the sovereign Medicine is applied. This stability and sureness of the covenant flows from God's engaging to the Mediator, and the Mediator's engaging to God; from the Mediator's satisfying, and the Father's accepting of his satisfaction; which being confirmed by the blood of the Testator, it becomes a *Testament*, which cannot be annulled, or altered, or changed. And if all this be so, let me put the question, Is there not good ground here to exhort the hearers of the gospel to believe in Christ, and on believing to look for life through him, and a most solid ground laid down, whereupon to build the hopes of eternal life? And therefore seeing, this is the upshot of all, that life is to be gotten freely by faith in Jesus Christ, improve this way of salvation for making your peace, under no less certification than this, even as ye would eschew reckoning with divine justice in your own persons for the least farthing of your debt.

If it be *objected* here by any, 1. We are at enmity with God, and cannot satisfy. *I answer*, This text tells you, that satisfaction is not sought from you, but from the Mediator, who hath already given it, and the Father hath accepted it for all such as shall by faith plead the benefit of it. 2. If ye shall say, We know not how to win at God, we are such as cannot step one foot forward, and so very sinful and miserable, that we know no such transgressors and wretches. *I answer*, Was it not for such that the Mediator transacted, even for such as we, transgressors, rebels, despisers of him, and such as judged him to be smitten and plagued of God? If he had been Caution only for righteous folk, there had been some reason for such an objection; but it is for sinners, for most hainous sinners: Nay, this way of reasoning and pleading says on the matter, that Christ needed not have laid down his life. 3. If it be said, We are so sinful and backsliding, so filthy and polluted that we think we are not within the reach of healing. *I answer*, This reasoning would, if it held, turn in effect to this, that ye are not within the reach of God's grace, of Christ's satisfaction; which is not only injurious, but even blasphemous to the grace of God, and to the satisfaction of the Mediator: If your sin be ugly and horrible, he suffered horrible wrath; he was wounded, bruised, chastised, &c. 4. If it be said further, We can do nothing for ourselves, we cannot come to Christ, we know not what it is to believe; or if we win to do any thing, alas! all our goodness is as the morning-cloud and early dew, that soon passeth away. *I answer*, The covenant is not transacted betwixt God and you, but betwixt God and the Mediator; and the ground of your peace, as to the procuring cause, depends on the Mediator's performing his part of the covenant in your name: and further, as for your believing, it is a piece of the Father's engagement to the Mediator, and must certainly be made as effectual as the Father must keep his word to the Son, according to these promises of the covenant. *I will put my law in their hearts, and write it in their minds; they shall all know me, &c. they shall be all taught of God; and, thy people shall be willing in the day of thy* power, and the like: All these promises were in the covenant betwixt the Father and the Son, and the application of them is but their execution as to us; and therefore, seeing such a City of refuge is cast open to man-slayers and transgressors, step humbly and boldly forward, and run into it. There is yet a fifth *objection*, which will possibly be sticking with some, and it is this, We know not whether we shall believe or not, for we know not if we be in the covenant or not. I *answer*, Would ye have thought, that he who had committed man-slaughter, would have reasoned well, if he had reasoned thus, *I know not if that City of refuge was appointed or built for me*, and when the gates of it were cast open, should fear to enter in to it on this account, when it was told him that it was appointed for such? Just so it is here. And suppose one should say, *I cannot believe*, it is as if such a man should say, *I cannot, I dow not run to the City*; nay, rather, tho' he had been feeble, yet he would have creeped, clinshed and crippled to it as he might: Even so here, in a word, a man should not dispute whose name is in the covenant, but should step forward to the Shelter and Refuge; as it is, Heb. vi. 18, 19. where the Apostle borroweth the same similitude, and says, *God hath confirmed his promise by an oath, that by two immutable things, in which it was impossible for God to lie, we might have strong consolation, who have fled for refuge to lay hold on the hope set before us*. Men in their natural condition are compared to the man-slayer, lying under the stroke of the law, or under the hazard of being pursued by the avenger of blood. Christ is compared to the city of refuge; and the heir of promise being pursued, what shall he do? Will his election simply save him? No, but he must flee unto Jesus Christ as to his City of refuge: And therefore, by all means run and flee to him, as having this fear, lest the avenger of blood pursue and overtake you; and if ye cannot run so fast as you would, yet run as ye may; and ye have this advantage, that the City of refuge is not far off, it is near you, even at your door, as the Apostle speaks, Rom. x. *The word is near thee, in thy mouth, and in thine heart*. The crippelst body amongst you all has Christ at you door, that ye may enter into him, as into a City of refuge, and that he may come in and sup with you; so that tho' ye cannot lift your feet so quickly in running to him, if ye can but in good earnest roll yourselves over upon him, ye shall be safe: Seeing then that this way of salvation is so full, so free, so equal and effectual, take heed lest ye prejudge yourselves of it.

2*dly*, To press this yet a little further, consider what good reason ye have to run: Take but this one word, Ye are sinners lying under the curse and wrath of God; and have ye any other way of obtaining pardon, or of making your peace? And if ye believe that ye are sinners and under the curse, is there not need that ye should run to a shelter from it? If we were preaching to angels that had never sinned, there might be some reason for their slighting or laying little weight upon such a word of exhortation; but seeing ye are sinners and liable to God's curse, why do ye slight a Saviour, having so much need of him?

3*dly*, Consider yet further, that ye have encouragement to run, and nothing to discourage you; What prejudice is in believing? There is no prejudice at all in this way, but many advantages; doubtless salvation will not fail them that believe: Yea, we may add from the words of the text, for encouraging to this, that the man or woman that is sensible of sin, and afraid of wrath, hath the covenant to look to, for begetting and throughing the work of faith in them with power; for if it be true, that all the midses are in the covenant, as well as the end, and if we may lay weight on the covenant for the effect, to wit, the pardon of sin, and healing, then we may also lay hold on the covenant for furthering us to that effect: I speak not this, as if folk could of themselves act faith on the covenant, before faith be given them; but I speak it to encourage young beginners, that think they have no faith at all, that they may act what they have, and may look more and more to the covenant, to be inlightened, quickned, and strengthened; and that they may say with the poor man in the gospel, *Lord, I believe, help my unbelief*, and with the spouse, Cant. i. *Draw me, and we will run after thee*.

4*thly*, And finally, for pressing of this, consider the absolute necessity that ye are under of making use of this way of salvation, of getting your peace made by Christ's satisfaction, and your wounds healed by his stripes; there is no mids, but either ye must hazard on a reckoning with God on your own score, or accept of his satisfaction: There was never a covenant made by God with man, but two; a covenant of works for perfectly righteous folks, by which covenant no sinner was ever able to come to life; and a covenant of grace, wherein Christ is made sin for us, and as many as flee by faith unto him, are made the righteousness of God through him; and therefore either betake yourselves to this way, or resolve to count with God yourselves without a Mediator and Surety: Or, if ye think

think it a fearful thing, so to count thus with God, and if it be certain, that many have been condemned for taking the way of works; let me earnestly intreat you to welcome and make more use of Christ's righteousness, for obtaining pardon of sin, and peace with God: This way will do your turn, when the other will quite fail you. But as for them who take this way, I will adventure to say in his name, that as certainly as Christ was smitten, as certainly shall pardon and healing come to them; even to as many as creep into him, and by believing lay hold on him: and on the other side, I say, in the same name, to all of you who take not this way of salvation, that ye shall most certainly be brought to reckon with God yourselves, without a Mediator, and to undergo his curse according to the tenor of the covenant of works. Thus the text sets before you life and death; God's blessing and God's curse: life, and God's blessing if ye betake yourselves to Christ, as to your alone City of refuge; and death, and God's fearful curse, if ye do it not. God himself make you wise to make the right choice.

SERMON XXV.

Isaiah liii. 6. *All we like sheep have gone astray, we have turned every one to his own way, and the Lord hath laid on him the iniquity of us all.*

YE have in the former verses somewhat of our Lord's suffering, and of his suffering for sinners, that he was wounded and bruised, &c. In this verse the prophet proceeds to clear how this came to pass, that Christ Jesus was made to suffer for the elect, the seed that God had given him; which he doth by laying down the occasion and fountain-cause whence it proceeded. 1. The occasion of it, in these words, *All we like sheep have gone astray*; all the elect, as well as others, have wandered: and *every one of us have to turned our own way*; we had denuded ourselves of all right and title to eternal life, and had made ourselves liable to God's curse and wrath thro' our sinning. 2. The fountain-cause is, *The Lord hath laid on him the iniquity of us all*; when we had all strayed, Jehovah took our Lord Jesus, as the sacrifices under the law were taken, and put him in our room, and laid on him the punishment due to us for our sins, and actually pursued him for our debt.

So the words are an answer to that question, How comes it to pass that our Lord Jesus suffered thus for sinners? It is answered, The elect had made themselves liable to the wrath and curse of God through their straying; and to keep them from that wrath, God designed and provided his Son Jesus Christ to be the Redeemer, and according to the covenant of redemption laid on him the punishment due to them for their iniquities: in a word, their sin, and God's appointing him to be Cautioner, made him liable to satisfy for all their debt.

The first part of the words hold out our natural disease; the second part holds out God's gracious cure and remedy.

In the first part we have these three, 1. The natural state and condition of all men and women, even of the elect themselves (who are mainly to be look'd on here) *All we have gone astray*. 2. This is illustrate by a similitude, *We have gone astray like sheep*. 3. It is amplified, *Every one of us have turned to his own way*: Several words being put together, to set out the desperate sinful condition, whereinto the elect, as well as others, had brought themselves.

1. Our natural state and condition is set down in this word *straying*: To *stray*, is to wander out of the way, to go wrong, to be bewildered; for God hath set a rule to men to walk by in the way to life, the rule and way of holiness; and whoever walk not in that way, do go astray, and wander out of the right way.

2. This is, as I said, illustrate by a similitude of sheep; the comparing of the elect to sheep here, is not at all to extenuate the sinfulness of their straying; tho' sometimes the innocency of that creature, in some other comparisons is insinuated: But it is to hold out the witlesness, spiritual silliness and brutishness of their straying; the scripture usually pointing out that beast to be disposed and given to wandering: And both nature and experience tells us, that in a wilderness, where there is greatest hazard, they are readiest to run on the hazard; such is their silly, and (to speak so) foolish inclination: Just so are the elect by nature.

3. It is amplified by this, *That every one hath turned to his own way*; before, it was collectively set down, *All we have gone astray*: but now, lest any should exeem himself, it is distributively set down, *every one*, even Isaiah, Jeremiah, and others, such, not one excepted. This *turning to our own way*, holds out two things 1. It is called our own way, to distinguish it from God's way, as it is, Psal. lxxxi. 13. *He gave them up to their own hearts lusts, and they walked in their own counsels:* That is, in their own inventions, or according to their own

own will, humour and inclination. 2. While it is said that every one turns to his own way, it is to shew this, that beside the common way that all sinners have to turn away from God, distinguished from God's way, every sinner hath his own particular and peculiar way, whereby in his way, he is distinguished from another sinner. There is but one way to heaven, but many ways to hell, and every one hath his different way; some have one predominant lust, some another, but they all meet here, that every one turns from God's way, every one takes a wrong way of his own.

Considering the scope, we shall shortly and passingly point at two general *Observations*, whereof the 1*st* is this, *That it contributes much for folks conceiving and considering of Christ's sufferings aright, to be well acquainted with their own sinful nature and disposition.* Men will never look rightly on Christ's sufferings, nor suitably esteem of him, nor make him, and the doctrine that holds him and his sufferings forth, cordially welcome, except they have some sense of their sinful nature and disposition: Hence it was that many of the Pharisees and hypocrites of that time wherein the Lord exercised his ministry among the Jews, never welcomed him, nor prized his sufferings; whereas among the Publicans and sinners many were brought to get good of him.

Not to insist in the *use* of this, only in a word, see here a main reason why Jesus Christ is so meanly thought of, and the report of his suffering is so little welcomed and esteemed; even because so few walk under the due sense of this, that like lost sheep they have gone astray.

The 2d general *Observation* from the scope, putting both parts of the verse together, is this, *That we should never look on Christ's sufferings, but with respect to the covenant of redemption, and God's transacting with him as our Cautioner*; therefore the last part comes in, *The Lord hath laid on him the iniquity of us all:* For albeit we know that Christ hath suffered much, yet if there be not an eye to, and some acquaintance with the covenant, the rise of his sufferings, and God's hand and end in his sufferings, it will be to no purpose; therefore, when Peter is to speak of his sufferings, Acts ii. 23. he premises these words, *Him, being delivered by the determinate counsel and foreknowledge of God*, and then subjoins his being crucified. Looking on Christ's sufferings with respect to the covenant, 1. It lets us know that Christ's suffering comes not by guess, but by the eternal counsel of God, and by vertue of that transaction betwixt the Father and the Son; and this takes away the scandal off them, which the prophet sets himself here to remove. 2. It gives faith access to make use of his sufferings, when we look to him as purposely designed for this end. 3. It holds out the love of God, Father, Son, and Spirit, towards elect sinners, that howsoever God looked angry like on the Mediator, as personating them, and sustaining their room; yet that Jehovah had the devising and designing of these sufferings, and that he sent his Son to suffer thus, it holds out wonderful love.

3. And more particularly, from the first part of the words, which is the main thing to be marked, *observe, That all men, even the elect themselves not excepted, are naturally in a most sinful and desperate state and condition:* So that if ye would know what they are by nature, this is a description of their state, *All we like sheep have gone astray, and every one hath turned to his own way*; And when it is called *our own way*, there needs no other epithet to set out the desperateness of it: That which I mean is this, that all men are naturally under these two, 1. They are under guilt before God, Eph. ii. 1, 2. *Dead in sins and trespasses, children of wrath and heirs of condemnation*, liable to the curse of God by vertue of the covenant which Adam broke. 2. (which is mostly aimed at here) There is in every one a sinful nature, a sinfulness, or sinning sin, an inclination to sin, every one hath a straying humour; so that although the similitude of sheep agree not to them in that sense, as sheep are innocent creatures, yet it agrees to them in this sense, that they are silly foolish creatures: and in this respect it is said, Gen. vi. 8. *That all the imaginations of the thoughts of the heart in man are only evil continually*; and, Eph. ii. 1. they are said to be *dead in sin*, not only in respect of their being obnoxious to God's curse, but in respect of their natural deadness, of their sinful nature, and want of spiritual life; So, Rom. iii. 9, 10. and forwards; the Apostle describes the sinfulness of man's nature at large, not only in respect of its guilt, but of its inclination to sin, and says, that *their throat is an open sepulchre;* insinuating thereby, that men naturally are like a tomb, and that the corps within the tomb is death and sin, and that all that comes from them savours of that; *Their feet are swift to shed blood, with their tongues they use deceit* &c. every member and part of the body and every faculty of the soul is bent to that which is evil. These three may further confirm it, 1. If we look in general to what the scripture speaks of men by nature, Eph. ii. 1, 2, 3. Rom. iii. and v. chapters; they being

as it is, Isa. lvii. penult. *as the raging sea, that casts out dirt and mire continually*: It is always moving and working one way or another, and more especially in a storm; so that though at one tide ye would sweep the shore never so clean, it will be as foul and dirty the next tide that cometh: So are these hearts of ours (as Peter speaks, 2d Epist. ii. and Jude ver. 23.) *foaming out their own shame*; and James saith, chap. iv. 5. *The spirit that dwells in us lusteth to envy*; It hath as great eagerness after, and as great delight in sin, as a drunkard hath after and in drink. 2. Experience also confirms it: Go through all men and women that ever were in the world (our Lord Jesus being excepted, as not descending of Adam by the ordinary way of generation) and that will be found true which the Apostle hath, Rom. iii. *There is none that doth good, no not one;* and that which is spoken, Gen. vi. *All flesh hath corrupted their way*. And what is the spring of all the abominations that are in the world, and the rise of these particular evils that are in believers and saints mentioned in scripture, as in David, Peter, and others; but this same corrupt nature, this body of death, as it is called, Rom. vii. 14. All which strongly prove a fire to be within, when there is such a smoke without. 3. We may confirm it from well-grounded reason, for it cannot be otherwise; if the root be of such a nature, can the branches be otherwise? *Who can bring a clean thing out of an unclean thing? No, not one.* Job xiv. 4. When Adam fell, the root was corrupted, and the branches cannot be fresh; the fountain was defiled, and the stream cannot be clean and clear: Hence, when Adam begot Seth, an elect in whom the Church was continued, it is said, that *he begat a son after his own likeness*, Gen. v. he himself was created after God's image, but begat children after his own image.

Though this be a commonly received doctrine, yet it is not without good reason, nor for no use insisted on so much here and in other scriptures; we shall therefore speak a little to these four *uses* of it.

The *1st Use* serves for information; and we may make it a looking glass, wherein we may see clearly our own most sinful state and condition: Would ye know what ye are by nature? This text tells you, that not only all men have strayed, but that each of us, or *every one of us hath turned to his own way*. But knowing how ready we are to shift the challenge, we would be persuaded that we are by nature liable to God's curse for Adam's sin, dead in sin, and inclined to all evil; sheep are no readier to go the wrong way, and will no more readily stray if they wanted a shepherd, than we are inclined to do. There is a common word in many of your mouths, that we are all sinners by nature; but when it is searched into, we find that there is much ignorance among you of what it means; many count themselves to be sinners, only because of their being guilty of the first sin, and so put no difference betwixt the first sin and original sin, which is an effect that flows from, and follows upon the first sin; the first sin was Adam's deed, and is legally ours, being imputed to us; as it is, Rom. v. *death reigned over all, even over them that had not sinned after the similitude of Adam's transgression*, because Adam in his standing and falling stood in our room, representing all mankind that was to come of him; but original sin is inherent in us, and cleaveth close to us, and is that which we are born and bred up with: And therefore ye would distinguish these sins, that ye may know, that ye are not only guilty of Adam's first sinful deed, but that ye have a present sinful and corrupt nature, though it be not always alike exercising and acting itself. Others again look only upon their nature as inclined to evil, and look not on it as that which makes them liable to wrath by reason of the first sin; but ye would put both together, and know, that though your sinfulness doth not consist only in an inclination to evil, that yet your sinfulness lies mainly in that, and that it will not be long a-going wrong: And it is not only your actual straying and going wrong that ye would take notice of, but also, and mainly, of your sinful nature, that inclines, disposes, and sets you on work to go wrong; it is your filthy corrupt nature, the body of death, the smell and savour whereof, to say so, is the kything of some actual sin. We may clear it in a similitude or two: We are, by this original sin, as young serpents before they can sting actually, or like ravenous birds before they come out of the nest; yet we call these serpents and ravenous birds, because they are come of such a kind: In our swaddling-clouts, we have the venomous and ravenous nature, to wit, original sin, in us; and in our actual sinning, we are like serpents when they come to sting actually, or like ravenous birds when they come to catch the prey; and our actual sin is a fruit of original sin: Or take it in this same similitude in the text, there are many sheep that never actually strayed; yet they are called straying witless creatures, because they are inclined to stray, and ready to stray: Or take it in this similitude, there are some diseases that follow such a house and family, some

are

are inclined to a confumption, fome to the ftone, fome to one difeafe, fome to another, which is from fome defect of the body; even fo it is here, that from a defect of our nature, infected by original fin, all actual fins flow.

The 2d *Ufe* is for conviction and reproof; and indeed we cannot well tell where we fhall begin here. However, the firft thing that it reproves, is our natural pride; though this be the finfulnefs of our very infancy, yet we are ready to look upon ourfelves as fomething: It is a true faying, though much mifapplied, that Job hath, Chap. xi. 12. *Vain man would be wife, though man be born as a wild affes colt;* a colt hath a wild humour, and is the moft witlefs of creatures: and this fame is it that is implied in that faying of James iv. 5. *Do ye think the fcripture faith in vain, The fpirit that is in us lufteth to envy?* which faith this much, that the moft part never trow that they have fuch a fpirit in them, that is inclined to all evil, bent to hate God and every thing that is good. 2. It reproves the great fecurity that is amongft the moft part. If this be a truth, that men and women are thus born under the curfe of God, and inclined to every thing that is evil, born enemies to God, and inclined to aggrege and heighten the quarrel, how comes it then to pafs that the great part fleep as foundly and fecurely as if they were in no hazard? if ye were all pofed, and put to it, how many of you can give a folid proof that ye are reconciled, that your peace is made, that ye are changed, and your nature renewed, and the quarrel betwixt God and you taken away? And yet if we look up and down, ye are generally as fecure and quiet as if ye were born friends with God; there are but few taken with a conviction, and faying within themfelves, Is yonder doctrine true of me? As if the fcripture had fpoken in vain, whatever it fpeaks of original fin. Ah! fhall never this be amended? Will ye never lay your finfulnefs to heart? Shall ye ftill think nothing of that which gives the occafional rife to the covenant of redemption, and to Chrift's fatisfaction? All the preaching that ye hear daily, if it be not now laid to heart, it fhall be moft terrible and dreadful to you one day; and the peace that ye now have, fhall end in red war and great bitternefs. 3. It reproves folks exceeding great unwatchfulnefs, and their trufting to their own nature, and following their own counfel: The wife man faith, Prov. xxviii. 26. *He that trufteth in his own heart is a fool.* Is it not proof-worthy for a man to be as brutifh as the very beaft that perifheth, as it is, Pfal. xlix. and yet to be as little watchful, and as much

truftful, or to truft as much to a man's own guiding, as if nothing of a mifguiding humour and difpofition were in him? We may more than allude to thefe words of our Saviour here, *If the blind lead the blind, fhall not both fall into the ditch?* Many of you think that ye are inftructed as fcribes in the way to heaven, and will be ready to fay, God forbid we fhould be ignorant of that, and what have we been doing all our days, if we be yet to learn that leffon? But we will tell you what you have been doing, ye have been like filly fheep ftraying all your days: And we would the rather fpeak to this, becaufe it is fo neceffary to be known and believed, and yet fo little known and credited; For, 1. Ye will never be rightly humbled, nor make ufe of Jefus Chrift, nor walk watchfully and foberly; in a word, ye will never believe and repent, till ye know, be convinced of, and believe this to be your natural inclination, and the finfulnefs of your nature: And yet, 2. Though this be fo neceffary, that the want of it mars the fruit of the word in you, and preaching doth but buff on you, to fay fo; how many are there, that are as little fenfible of it as the very ftones of the wall that are before us, or the boards that they lean upon, as to their own particular ftate and condition? I would but afk you, Is it poffible that ye could live fo fecurely, and fatisfied with your own cafe, if ye believed indeed that ye had fuch a finful nature, and that ye were liable to God's wrath and curfe? Or would ye give fuch way to your natural finful humours and inclinations, and fo contentedly flight Jefus Chrift, and the offers of the gofpel, as many of you do? And yet we fee amongft thofe with whom we converfe, men and women not only as fecure, as if they had no fuch natures, but even belching and foaming out their own fhame: We would have you therefore to be convinced and know, that not only ye are finners in the general, but that every one of you is fuch in particular.

To make it the more clear, I fhall give you two or three qualifications that are requifite to a fuitable conviction of your finfulnefs, 1. It would be particular. 2. It would be fenfible; ye would not in bare words take with it that ye are finners, but ye would fee and be convinced, that in this and this ye have finned, and ye would be kindly affected with it. 3. It would be diftinct, not a gueffing, but a thing that from the feeing and feeling of it ye would be clear in. 4. It would have fuch an influence on the moving of your affections, and fuch an inward working on your hearts, as that ye may lothe your nature, and yourfelf becaufe of it: We may

may see all these in Paul, Rom. vii. 10. and forward, who though he was greatly renewed, yet saith he, *I see a law in my members, rebelling against the law of my mind:* He feels and is very sensible of that which leads him in captivity; and he cries out, *Who shall deliver me?* &c. His affections are mightily stirred with it, *What I do, I allow not,* &c. *O wretched man that I am,* &c. If ye believe this to be a truth, and that Paul lived in the faith and feeling of it; then judge if there be not just ground to expostulate with most part of you, as being yet without the faith and feeling of this most concerning thing.

The *2d Use* of it serves wonderfully to set forth the glory of the free and rich grace of God, that all this business is made, and this transaction entred into, that Christ comes to satisfy, and doth actually satisfy justice for a number of such wretches that had gone astray like lost sheep. This comes in as the scope; we have strayed and done the wrong, but he hath paid the debt, and satisfied for the wrong done: And from comparing this verse with the foregoing, we may take these *five* considerations, that serve to heighten the glory of God's grace and free-love, and to shame believers, that are so little in wondering at. 1. Who is smitten? His own Son; we sinned, and he was smitten, even he who was and is the Father's Fellow; the sword awakes against him, and we go free. 2. What did our Lord suffer? *He was wounded and bruised, the chastisement of our peace was on him, he laid on him the iniquity of us all:* It was not a complimental or fashionable suffering, but he was arraigned before the tribunal of justice, and did really pay our debt, and satisfy justice for our sins. 3. Who exacted this satisfaction? Who did smite him? It is the Lord Jehovah, it is the Father; which makes the glory of grace shine the more: It is God the Father, whose heart was tender to the Son of his love, that exacts the full price of him; so that, as he said of Abraham, *By this I know that thou lovest me, because thou hast not withheld thy son, thine only son* Isaac *from me;* we may say, By this we know God's love to the elect, when he hath not withheld, nor spared his own Son from them, but hath laid on him the iniquities of them all. 4. For whom did he smite him? For sinners, for straying sheep, for covenant-breakers, for such as have gone a whoring from God and were bent to sin against him, I mean the elect. 5. When was it that he suffered for them? Even when they were straying, rejecting, despising, nodding the head at him, spitting in his face, and saying, *Away with him;* even then he is praying and dying for them. Now, put all these together, that such a price shall be exacted of such a Cautioner, and for such sinners, and at such a time, behold and see therein how God commends his love to us, as the Apostle speaks, Rom. v. 8. *in that, while we were yet sinners, Christ died for us;* when we were in our sin, not praying to him, nor in a capacity to pray or give him thanks for any thing that he did or suffered, he then died for us. Is there any thing here but freedom of grace? And does not this exceeding highly commend the love of God, that he exacts the debt due by us, of his Son; and the powerful love of the Mediator and Cautioner, that at such a time, and for such transgressors, he should pay such a price?

Use 4. Seeing this was our state, that we were *sinners,* and that yet herein was the love of God commended, that he laid on his Son the iniquity of us all; then, is there not good ground to take with the sin, and make use of the remedy; to take with sin, and close with Christ? We might take occasion here to exhort. (1.) To watchfulness, and to walk soberly and humbly, from this ground, that we have such a nature. (2.) To exhort every one to repentance, because by nature ye are all in such a sinful state and condition: It may be ground of exercising repentance, even long after your justification, and peace made with God who are justified, with whom it should be, as we see it was with David. But, (3.) Seeing by nature ye are under God's wrath and curse, and in a state of enmity with him, it mainly serves to exhort you to flee unto Jesus Christ, and not to rest till ye get the quarrel taken away. It might be in reason thought, that folks would be soon and easily induced to this, even to run unto Jesus Christ, and to welcome the gospel with good-will, for preventing the curse and wrath due to them for sin, and for subduing this sinful nature, and inclination to stray from God and his way: Therefore, seeing there is a fountain opened to the house of David for sin and for uncleanness, since there is a satisfaction given to justice for removing the guilt of sin, and since the Spirit is purchased for mortifying of sin, and making holy; let as many as think that they have gone astray, and have turned to their own way, as they would not be found still at this distance with God, make use of Christ for making their friendship with God. It is the word that Peter useth, 1 Pet. ii. ult. *All we like sheep have gone astray, but we are now turned unto the Shepherd and Bishop of our souls:* Hold, O hold you near this Shepherd, and make use of his righteousness for making your peace. If we could rightly under-

understand the words, we would see in them, 1. A motive to put us on believing in Christ; and can there be a greater motive than *necessity*? We have sinned and gone astray, he is the only Saviour, there is no other name given under heaven, whereby sinners can be saved. 2. There is also in them an encouragement to believing; it was for sinners, such as we are, that Jesus Christ suffered all that he suffered; which may be ground of hope and encouragement to step forward; and if neither our need, nor Christ's being a Saviour willing to make sinners welcome, will prevail, we know not what will do it. It will turn to this, and ye will be put to it, Whether are ye sinners? And if sinners, whether is it not a desperate thing to ly under sin and wrath? If ye be not sinners, we have no warrant to propose this doctrine to you, to invite or make you welcome to a Saviour; but it ye grant that ye are sinners, will ye contentedly ly under sin? Will ye be able to bear it out against God? Or think ye that ye will be well enough for all that? And if ye dare not resolve to ly under sin, I would ask, What way will ye win from it? think ye it easy to win from under it: Must not the justice of God be satisfied? Some of you think that ye can pray yourselves out of sin: But what need was there of Christ's sufferings if a satisfaction might have been made to justice another way? And if none but Christ can satisfy, it turns to this, that by all means ye would make use of him, else ye will most certainly drown and die in your sins. And this is the thing that we would commend to you, that under the sense of sin, and in the faith of God's condescending love, ye would flee to Jesus Christ, and give him employment, for making your peace with God, and taking away your sin, and sanctifying of you: O but this be suitable to sinners! and if ye think yourselves sinners, prejudge not yourselves of the benefit of a Saviour.

SERMON XXVI.

Isaiah liii. 6. *All we like sheep have gone astray, we have turned every one to his own way, and the Lord hath laid on him the iniquities of us all.*

EVERY expression that the Prophet useth, to set forth the grace of God in Jesus Christ to sinners by, is more wonderful than another, because indeed every thing that he expresseth is more wonderful than another: And there is so much grace and infinite love in the way of the gospel, that it is hard to know where there is most of it; whether in its rise, or in its execution; whether in the decree of God, or in Christ's satisfaction; whether in the benefits that we enjoy, or in the way by which we are brought to enjoy them: Sure, all together make a wonder passing great, a most wonderful wonder, even a world of wonders. It is a wonder, that (as it is verse 5.) he should be *wounded for our transgressions, bruised for our iniquities,* that *the chastisement of our peace should be on him,* and that *by his stripes we should be healed;* and when here he comes to explain this, and to shew how it came to pass that Jesus Christ suffered so much, he holds out another new wonder, *All we like sheep have gone astray,* &c. as if he had said, Would ye know how it comes to pass that the Mediator behoved to suffer, and suffer so much? All we, the elect people of God, have gone astray like so many wandering sheep, as well as others, not one excepted; and there was not another way to recover and reclaim us but this, *The Lord Jehovah laid on him the iniquity of us all:* To recover us when we were lost, Jesus Christ was substitute in our room by the eternal decree of God, and the iniquities of all of us who are his elect people, as to their punishment, were laid upon him. This then is the scope, to shew the rise of Christ's sufferings, and how it came to pass that our Lord suffered, and suffered so much: The occasion of it, was the elect's sin; and the fountain-cause, the Father's laying of their sin on him by an eternal decree, and making him to answer for it according to that decree, with his undertaking, which was the covenant of redemption, whereof Christ's suffering was the execution. Thus we have the fountain whence our Lord's sufferings flowed; he is, in the covenant of redemption, substitute and judicially enacted the elect's Cautioner, and takes on their debt; and being substitute in their room, justice pursues the claim, and sentence passes against him, for making him answerable and liable to the debt of their sins; which sets out, as it were, a Judge on the throne, *Jehovah;* and two parties at the bar, *we* and *him;* we the principal debtors, (and *him* the Cautioner, Jesus Christ, in our room and place: the law, by which the judge proceeds, is the covenant of redemption; and we the principal debtors not being law-biding, he is made liable to the debt; and on this ground the sentence passes against him, for satisfying what we were owing; and hereupon followed his sufferings: So then, the rise of his sufferings is, that it was so transacted by the wise, just and gracious God; and thus this *verse* comes well in,

to

to explain, aand further to clear what he asserted in the former *verse*. Though the words be few, yet they are a great compend and sum of the gospel; how therefore to speak of them, so as to unfold them right, is not easy: And because the devil, who seeks by all means to mar the beauty of the gospel, doth most fiercely assault where most of its beauty shines, and hath therefore stirred up several sorts of enemies to wrest these words, and to obscure the beauty of grace that may be clearly seen in them; we shall a little open the few words that are in this last part of the verse, *And the Lord hath laid on him the iniquity of us all*; having spoken to the former part of it the last day.

In the few words then, we have, *First*, (something spoken of iniquity, which three parties have some acts about, to wit, 1. The elect, *Us all*. 2. *Him*, to wit, The Mediator. 3. The *Lord*, to wit, Jehovah. Then, we have the express act of the Lord, to wit, his laying on him, the Mediator, the iniquity of us all. (1.) As for this word *iniquity*, by it is meant sometimes, 1. Sin formally taken; as it hath a disconformity to the law of God, and supposeth a spot and defect; and so it is commonly taken, when we pray for pardon of sin; and when David says, Psal. li. *My sin is ever before me*; and Psal. xxxviii. *My iniquity is gone over my head*: And so it is the transgression of the law of God. 2. It is sometimes taken for the effect that sin procureth, and so it is in effect the punishment of sin, as Lev. vii. the 18 and 20 verses being compared together; v. 18. it is said, *He shall bear his iniquity*, which, v. 20. is, *He shall be cut off*: and so it is clearly meant of the punishment of iniquity; For *to bear his iniquity*, and *to be cut off*, are the same thing there: And that word of Cain, Gen. iv. 14. *My iniquity*, or punishment, *is greater than I can bear*, hath a manifest respect to God's curse inflicted on him for his sin, and is, as if he had said, I will not get lived under the punishment that is inflicted upon me, for every one that finds me will cut my throat; and sometimes it is translated *punishment*, as in that of Gen. iv. 13. The Question then is, Which of these two is understood here in this text, whether iniquity or sin formally taken, or iniquity taken for the punishment thereof? These who are called Antinomians plead, that it is to be understood of sin formally taken: But though it be hard so much as to mention this, it being so blasphemous-like to assert, that our blessed Lord Jesus should be formally a sinner, and have the spots and defilement of sin on him, which we wonder that any Christian should dare to assert or presume to maintain; yet, because this scripture is alledged for it, we shall clear, that iniquity is not here to be taken for sin formally, but for sin in the punishment of it. And the *first* reason that we give, shall be drawn from the plain scope of the words; the Prophet having in the 5th verse said, that *he was wounded for their transgressions, and bruised for our iniquities*; the scope of this verse is to shew how it came to pass that Christ suffered, and suffered so much; which he doth, by declaring that it could not be otherwise, because the punishment of all the sins of the elect was laid upon him; and that which was called *wounding* and *bruising* in the former verse, is here called on the matter a *bearing of our iniquities* (for if they were laid on him, he did certainly bear them) the sins of all the elect trysted on him as to their punishment; and this shews how that Christ behoved not only to suffer all that he suffered: So in the 8th verse it is said, *He was cut off out of the land of the living, and for the transgressions of my people was he stricken*: That which is here called the *bearing of iniquity*, is there called, *being cut off, and stricken for the transgressions of his people*. And this may be the *second* reason of the exposition, as we have given it; because, when iniquities are spoken of, they are not called Christ's, as inherent in him, but they are called his people's iniquities, they being formally theirs, but his judicially and legally only: Even as the debt is formally the bankrupt's, but legally the cautioner's. A *third* reason is drawn from comparing this text with other parallel places of scripture: that which is called bearing of iniquity here, is called, Gal. iii. 13. his *being made a curse for us*; so that his bearing of our iniquity, is his being made a curse for our iniquity, and his bearing the wrath of God due to us for our sin. I shall illustrate it by a comparison, whence the *fourth* reason will clearly result: Our iniquities become Christ's, as his righteousness becomes ours; for these two are parallel, 2 Cor. v. ult. *He was made sin for us, who knew no sin, that we might be made the righteousness of God, in*, or *through him*; where 1. It is clear, that Jesus Christ is so the sinner in our room, as we are righteous in his room; and contrarily, we are righteous in his room, as he was the sinner in our room. 2. That righteousness is not so derived to us, that it is formally made ours, and to be inherently in us, but is ours only by imputation itself or the vertue of it being imputed to us; and it is upon this ground that, Rom. iv. *imputed righteousness* is often mentioned, that is, when God accounteth a man to be righteous, though he be yet a sinner in himself: Even so our sin is imputed to Christ,

Chriſt, and reckoned his, becauſe he became our Surety. And though Antinomians have a vain notion to elude this, yet the ſcripture is very clear, as holding forth a legal procedure; the debt is accounted his, becauſe of his obligation to be anſwerable for it, and in juſtice and law he is liable to it: and there is no other way that we can rationally imagine, how our bleſſed Lord can bear our iniquities; For, 1. It cannot ſtand with his abſolute purity, to have any ſpot of ſin, or to be formally the ſinner. Neither, 2. Is it neceſſary that he ſhould be the ſinner, but only that he ſhould pay the penalty due by us, it being the nature of contracts among men, that where the principal debitor ſuccumbs, the cautioner comes in his room; ſo is it here. Yea, 3. If Jeſus Chriſt were the ſinner formally, it would incapacitate him to be our Cautioner, to pay the penalty, or to ſatisfy juſtice for the debt of our ſins: We would not have ſpoken ſo much to this, were it not that this ſame place is preſſed in a moſt faſtidious manner by the abuſers of the grace of God to maintain their error; ſo then, we take this in ſhort to be the meaning of this part of the verſe, that Jeſus Chriſt did bear the puniſhment due to us for our ſins.

2*dly*, The three Parties, that have ſome acts about iniquity, are, 1. *Us all*. 2. *Him*. 3. *The Lord Jehovah*. (1.) *Us all*, and here we meet with the Arminians, another party that abuſeth and perverteth this place, as if it were to be extended to all men and women that ever ſinned, or went aſtray; for, ſay they, It is the iniquity of all them that are wrong, that is laid on Chriſt, and that is the iniquity of all men and women in the world: But (as we ſhew before) the ſcope of the words is not ſo much to ſhew the univerſality of all men, and womens ſinning, as to ſhew that all the elect as well as others went aſtray, and turned every one of them to their own way; and therefore it is reſtricted, *All we*; and the word *All* is no broader than the word *We*: now the *We* that is here meant, is the *we* who in the former words are *healed by his ſtripes*; and that ſure is not all men and women that ſin, but the elect only. And verſe 11th it is they *that by his knowledge*, that is, by faith in him, are *juſtified*; it is theſe *All*, whoſe iniquities he bare, and no more: So that, in ſhort, *us all* is not all men ſimply conſidered, but *us all*, that are elect; and thus it is neceſſarily to be reſtricted to the prophet's ſcope.

The meaning of both parts of the verſe together then is, *We all*, even the elect as well as others, *went aſtray, and turned every one of us to his own ſinful way*; and the Lord Jehovah made him to bear the puniſhment of all our ſins; and it could not be but a mighty great puniſhment, and a moſt huge and horrible ſuffering, when the Lord made the iniquities of *us all*, his elect, to meet upon Chriſt.

There is not much debate about the other two Parties, the *firſt* whereof is *Him*, that is, the Mediator Jeſus Chriſt, the eternal Son of the eternal Father, *the brightneſs of the Father's glory, and the expreſs Image of his Perſon*, who remaining God, became Man, to perform and bring about the work of our redemption according to his undertaking.

The other Party is the *Lord Jehovah*, the Judge and the Party offended; as we are uſe party offending, and Jeſus Chriſt the Satisfier: And the *Lord* is here conſidered eſſentially, as Father, Son, and holy Ghoſt, having one common eſſence and juſtice, and who being all Three one God, are to be ſatisfied; He is *Jehovah*.

But how is this puniſhment of our iniquities laid on Jeſus Chriſt? And here Socinians make as great a buſtle and buſineſs; the devil intending (if he could effect it) to blow up the very foundation of the goſpel, bends all his forces againſt ſuch places as do moſt lively hold it forth: But the words are clear and moſt ſignificant, as they are rendered according to the Hebrew on the margin, thus, *The Lord hath made the iniquity of us all to meet on him*. The iniquities of the elect are as ſo many brooks and rivulets, any one of which is hard and difficult for them to paſs over: But O! when Chriſt comes to ſatisfy for them, they are brought and gathered into a great lake, or rather into a vaſt ſea or ocean together; they all, collected and combined, met on him, and he did meet with them in a mighty ſhock; and ſure, they could not but be great ſufferings that he endured, when he had ſuch a ſea to paſs thorow: Or, the ſins of the elect were like ſo many companies or regiments of men, any one whereof they could never have overcome; but when Chriſt came to ſatisfy divine juſtice for them, as the companies and regiments of ſins (ſo to ſpeak) rendezvouſed, and brought in one formidable army together, met on Chriſt. The word is well rendred here, *were laid on him*, being the ſame word in the root that Saul uſed when he commanded Doeg to fall upon the Lord's prieſts, 1 Sam. xxii. 18. The word is, *Lay upon them*, or *lay at them*; as when one is angry with another, he will cry, *Lay upon him*; and this ſhews the exceeding greatneſs of Chriſt's ſufferings, when all the ſins of all the elect met together, as a huge and heavy hoſt did fall

fall and do terrible execution upon our blessed Lord Jesus. This then being the meaning of the words, the question is, Whether the Lord Jehovah did lay this punishment really upon Christ; or whether, as Socinians fondly imagine, he only interceeded for them? But for *answer*, 1. What sort of meaning of the words would that be, I pray? the Lord made the iniquities of us all to interceed on him, when the text says plainly, that *they were laid on him*, and on the matter that he bare them, and expresly so, verse 11th, *For he shall bear their iniquities*. Yea, 2. Consider the scope, and it comes in as a reason why Christ suffered so much: and would that (can any think) be a good reason for so great and grievous sufferings undergone by Christ, that God made him to interceed for all the sins of the elect? but, if you look upon the words in their true meaning, they are a clear reason why he was wounded, and exceedingly bruised and chastned, and why he endured so many stripes, even because all the sins of all his elect met on him, because he was made to bear the punishment of them all; also the words following clear it, *He was cut off out of the land of the living, for the transgressions of my people was he stricken;* and Gal. iii. *he was made a curse for us*. He suffered, *the just for the unjust;* he actually and really suffered that which we should have suffered: If it be asked, What is this, *to lay iniquity on Christ?* Or how is it said that the iniquity of the elect *was laid on him?* or in what respect? I answer, 1. In respect of God's eternal covenant; the punishment due for our sins is laid upon him by an eternal deliberate counsel or consultation of the Persons of the Godhead; wherein (as we shew before) Christ enters Surety for us, accepts of, and engages to pay our debt. 2. In respect of God's actual pursuing Christ, having thus engaged himself, putting in his hand the cup, and making him drink; and the bill of our account, and making him accountable. 3. In respect of God's acceptation of that satisfaction which Christ performed and paid down for them.

This being the meaning of the words, we come to point at some things from them; and the very opening of them may give us some insight in the way of the Gospel, and of a notable ground of footing to our faith: If we could rightly apprehend God making this transaction with the Mediator, we might not only have a ground to our faith, but a great encouragement to come to Christ, and to rest on him, who hath thus fitted himself in our room before the tribunal of divine justice; and it would waken and warm faith and love towards him.

But observe here more particularly, 1. *That all the elect people of God are lying under iniquity, even as others*. This we spoke to the last day, and shall not repeat what was then said. It is with respect to iniquity in the elect that all the business of redemption is transacted; and from hence, as the occasion, it hath its rise, even from God's being offended, and from the necessity of a Mediator: for this doth presuppose our debt, and a standing sentence against us, till Christ interposed for the removing of it.

2. From its being said before, that *every one turned his own way;* and here, that *the Lord hath laid on him the iniquity of us all*; observe, *That every one of the elect, beside the common state of sin wherein all are, hath his own particular guilt, that is, in his own way:* This is clearly holden out here, while it is said, that not only *like sheep we have gone astray*, but that *every one hath turned to his own way*; which, as it holds forth a way in them all different from God's way, so also a way in every one of them somewhat different from another's way; and this is called a *walking in the counsel of our own heart*, Psal. lxxxi. and a man's *own sore*, 2Chron. vi. 29. and a man's *own iniquity*, Psal. xviii. 23. because it is in a special manner his. To clear it a little, consider, that sin is peculiar to a believer, or may be called his *own way*, in these respects, (1.) In respect of his being more addicted to one sin than another, which is usually called a man's predominant. Two men may both be covetous and passionate; but the one of them may be called a covetous man, because he is especially given to that sin of covetousness; and the other may be called a passionate man, because he is especially given to passion. (2.) In respect of some peculiar aggravating circumstances. Though we will not dare particularly to determine as to persons, yet if we look thro' all men and women, it will be readily found, that there is some sin, which in respect of some or several aggravations, is in some a greater sin than it is in others; and hereby God hath given ground of humiliation to all: There is not a man (as we just now hinted) but readily he hath an evil which is at a greater height in him than in another; as for instance, one may be given more to the sin of drunkenness, another more to hypocrisy, another more to uncleanness, &c. I do not speak so much here of the divers kinds of sin, as of the several aggravations of this or that sin that they are given to; such and such a man may have aggravations, that will heighten such a predominant evil in him, far beyond what it is in others; And it is
from

from this ground that a believer, not in a complimenting way, but most really and sincerely, doth call and account himself the *chief of sinners;* because there are some aggravations that elevate his sin above the sin of others, or above that same sin in others: As a weak believer may have some one good thing in him more commendable than it is in a stronger believer; so the stronger believer may have some one sin, that, in respect of its aggravations, may give him ground to look on himself as beyond others in sin.

Use 1. It serves much for our humiliation, in as far as this adds to our sinfulness: There are none of us, but, beside the common way of sinning incident to all, we have something that is peculiar to ourselves, we have *our own way,* wherewith we are chargeable above and beyond others. We will readily all grant that we are sinners, but who of us will take with our particular and peculiar guilt that doth more easily beset us? who amongst many are as doves of the valleys on the mountains, every one mourning for *his own iniquity,* for his own plague and sore, that by several circumstances may be heightened as to its sinfulness beyond the sin of others?

Use 2. The second use, which is the scope, serves to shew the exceeding greatness of Christ's sufferings; O! what a shock he was in, when he had not only all the common sins of the elect to satisfy for, but when all their particular sins, with their respective aggravations, rendezvoused and trysted on him? It serves likewise to exalt the free grace of God, and the condescendency of our blessed Lord Jesus, who took in altogether in his making satisfaction for them, when there were several sorts of them, as if every one of the elect had been set to invent a new sin. What great and sore suffering was here, when he condescended to drink the cup, that had the wonderful effects of the sins of all the elect wrung into it? when not only in gross he takes on the sins of the elect, but this and that man's particular sins, which were all reckoned and summed on Christ's account, and for which he was made to satisfy; and wherein justice proceeded equally and equivalently. This notably confirmed the reality of Christ's satisfaction, by suffering what all the elect should have suffered eternally, or the equivalent of it; for if there had not been a proportionable satisfaction in his sufferings, wherefore serves such an enumeration of his sufferings?

Use 3. The third use serves to lead us in to know how much we are in Christ's debt, and what a great encouragement we have to believe, and withal, what notable ground of consolation believers have. I say, 1. It shows how much we are in Christ's debt: When we take a view of all our sins, and consider that there was a particular view taken of them in the covenant of redemption, not only all our common sins, but even all the particular and peculiar sins of believers were reckoned unto Christ the Cautioner, and put on his account, and he engaged to satisfy for all, and pay the whole reckoning; doth it not lay a great obligation on us to him, who counted for the least farthing of our debt? We, like a pack of bankrupt dyvours, did take on the debt, and the account was put in his hand, not only (as I just now said) of all our common sins, but of this and that particular sin, with all their several aggravations, and the sinful circumstances that did heighten them; and he satisfied for them all: And of this we would take special notice; for it may readily wrong us to look upon the covenant of redemption as a bargain in gross, there is a particularness in it, to shew not only the sovereignty, but the exactness of justice, and also the riches of God's grace, and of the great condescendency of Christ's love to elect sinners. 2. It is a great encouragement to believe; for even these sins that would fright and scar serious and exercised souls from coming forward to Christ, were all counted on Christ's score, and were all satisfied for by him. 3. It is a notable ground of consolation to believers, when they are disposed and ready to think that their particular sins are insufferable and unpardonable: they think that course might be taken with all their common evils; but as for this most sinful and shameful unthankfulness, this despising of his grace, this woful unbelief, &c. it stares them in the face, and they know not well how that will be got done away: but, believers in Christ, who are sorrowful and sadly perplexed on this account, is that *your own way?* It is transacted on Christ's score with the rest; *every one of us turned to his own way, and the Lord hath laid on him the iniquity of us all:* Oh impregnable ground of strong consolation, which is as *good news from a far country,* a none-such cordial to a fainting soul!

3. *Observe* here, " That a believing elect, or
" an elect believer, will not only be sensible of sin
" in the general, but of his own particular and
" peculiar sinful way;" or thus, "It is a good token,
" when folk look not only to sin in common, but on
" their own peculiar sinful way;" or thus, " That
" folk should consider their sinfulness, not only in
" common, but in particular, with its several ag-
" gravations." The scriptures which we cited before

fore do confirm this, as Pſal. xviii. 22. *I keeped myſelf from mine iniquity;* and 2 Chron. vi. 29. where ſaith *Solomon, when every one ſhall know his own ſore and his own grief;* or as it is, 1 Kings viii. 38. *The plague of his own heart.* This implies theſe two things, 1. A diſtinct aggravating of ſin, when a man not only looks on himſelf as a ſinner; but looks on his ſin, by reaſon of ſeveral aggravating circumſtances, as being above and beyond the ſin of others, and abhorreth and lotheth himſelf as the chief of ſinners, as David doth, when he ſaith, Pſal. li. *Againſt thee, thee only, have I ſinned:* he is not there extenuating his ſin, as if it were done only againſt God; but aggravating his ſin, as the words following ſhew, and *I have done this evil in thy ſight;* as if he had ſaid, Thy concern in the matter doth moſt affect and afflict me: *thou loveſt truth* or ſincerity *in the inward parts:* but I have been (alas!) all this time jugling and greatly playing the hypocrite, which makes it to be a wonderful great evil. And Pſal. lxv. 3. *Iniquities prevail againſt me;* and as Paul doth, who calls himſelf the *chief of ſinners,* 1 Tim. i. 15. 2dly That believers before conversion yea, and in reſpect of their natural inclination even after their conversion, are wofully inclined each of them to a ſinful way of their own, called, Eccl. xi. *the way of a man's own heart:* And of this believers would be ſenſible, not only of their ſinfulneſs in general and of their particular acts of ſin, but of their peculiar ſinful acts; and that for theſe ends or uſes.

1. It ſerves deeply to humble, and to preſs forth (to ſpeak ſo) repentance; when we conſider our own way to be ſinful beyond others, and that ſuch and ſuch a man hath ſinned, but his ſin hath not ſuch aggravations as mine, this makes the ſoul to bluſh, and to ſay, as it is Pſal. xl. 12. " Innumer-" able evils have compaſſed me about, mine iniqui-" ties have taken hold upon me, ſo that I am not " able to look up; they are more than the hairs of " mine head, therefore my heart faileth me;" he wonders at himſelf, how a man can be ſo given to ſin, and every day to add one new ſinful ſtep to another, and never to weary or give over; this makes him to bluſh and be aſhamed, as it is, Ezek. xvi. 63. The remembering of common ſins, and of this and that particular act of ſin, will not ſo effect this; but when a ſinner remembers, that ſuch a ſin hath been *his own way,* that humbles and ſtops his mouth exceedingly.

2. This adds a peculiarneſs to the grace of God, in the believer's eſteem, and maketh it ſo much the more amiable and admirable to him, as it is with Paul, when he ſaith, 1 Tim. i. 13, &c. *I was a blaſphemer, and a perſecutor, and injurious; nevertheleſs I obtained mercy, and the grace of God was exceeding abundant towards me. This is a faithful ſaying, and worthy of all acceptation, that Jeſus Chriſt came into the world to ſave ſinners, of whom I am the chief; howbeit for this cauſe I obtained mercy, that in me he might ſhew forth all long ſuffering, for a pattern to them that ſhould hereafter believe on him:* I was, as if he had ſaid, ſingular in ſinning, but grace was eminent and ſingular in ſhewing mercy, and hath caſt a copy thereof in me that is ſingularly eminent; the peculiarneſs of believers ſin, as it makes them know the aggravations of it beyond others, ſo it makes them exalt grace the more.

3. It ſerves ſome way to diſcriminate a ſound believer from a hypocrite; and a right ſight of ſin from that which is not ſo: It is not ſo much to know that we are ſinners, for the light of a natural conſcience will tell men that, eſpecially when their lives are ſo bad; but it is more to know, and rightly to take up the peculiarneſs that is in our way of ſinning, to take up the many windings and turnings of the deceitful heart in following of ſuch a ſin that it is addicted to; this makes a believer think, that there is no body's heart like his. We ſee ordinarily, that but very few, if any natural men, will take kindly with the peculiarneſs of their way of ſinning: and even when they will take with this, that they are ſinners in general; yet they ſhun to take with it, that they are given to ſuch a ſinful way of their own, and with the particular turnings, windings, and traverſings of their own hearts to that way; but few will grant that they are given to deſpiſing or ſlighting of Chriſt, to hypocriſy, ſelf-ſeeking, lying, &c. I will not be peremptory here, to ſay that every body muſt know what is their own one peculiar ſinful way; for ſome ſee ſo many predominant ſins in themſelves, that hardly can they pitch upon one by another: Nor upon the other ſide, will I poſitively ſay, that they are all gracious that ſee one ſin by another to carry ſway in them. But this I ſay, that this contributes much for the humbling of the ſinner, and for the exalting of free grace; and that the believer will ſee many windings and turnings in and to their own way, that others who are not believers will not ſee, and will ſee one predominant after another; whereas a natural man, tho' he complimentingly call himſelf *the chief of ſinners,* yet he doth not really think himſelf to be ſuch; but rather, if he be given to drunkenneſs, to filthineſs, or the like, he will readily caſt up David

David and Lot, or some others of the saints to excuse or extenuate it: But the believer can get none to compare himself with in the point of sinfulness; *Iniquities prevail over me*, saith David in the singular number; but when he speaks of the pardoning and purging away sin, he speaks in the plural, associating others with himself, *As for our transgressions, thou shalt purge them away*, Psal. lxv. verse 3.

4. Considering our sinful way, as the occasion of this transaction, and of the laying of our iniquities upon Christ, as the result of it, we have this sweet Observation, "That the elect are considered in the "covenant of redemption as foully and vilely sinful, "and with all the aggravations of their sins and sin- "ful ways; so that they cannot be fuller and more "vile in time, than they were considered to be, "when they were given to Christ to be satisfied for by him." How were they then considered? The text tells us, even as *straying sheep*: But that is not all, they are considered as such, who have had their own peculiar way of straying from God, and have *turned* aside to, and run on in their *own* sinful *way*: thus the Lord considered the elect in the covenant of redemption, thus Jesus Christ considered them in the undertaking for them, even with all the several aggravations of their sinfulness; so that they are not, nor cannot be worse in time, than they were considered to be before time: This is so ordered by the Lord, for these ends, 1. That justice might be distinctly, exactly, and fully satisfied; and that it might be known that it is so, he would needs be restored to his honour, to his declarative, or manifested honour and glory, which suffered by man's fall, and by the many great and variously aggravated sins of the elect; and would have his justice, as I said, fully satisfied: And therefore, as there is a volume of a book, wherein all the elect are written, for whom Christ should satisfy; so there is a volume of what, and for what he should satisfy, that there may be a proportional satisfaction and price told down to justice. 2. That believers may have a more full view of the way of grace, and of Christ's undertaking for them; when Jesus Christ undertook our debt, he had a full view of a sum he was to pay, he knew what he had to pay to the least farthing, and what his people's sins would cost him; and yet he scarred not to engage to satisfy, but did satisfy according to his engagement to the full. 4. It is also ordered so, for this end, even to confirm the believer's faith, when he cometh to take hold of Christ, and of the covenant: And when this objection mutters within him, Dare such a sinful wretch as I take hold of Christ, who hath been thus and thus polluted with sin? Yes, saith the text, for these sins, so and so aggravated, were not unknown to the Father, nor to the Mediator, when thou wast bargained about: Nay, these sins, with their aggravations, were expresly considered in the covenant of redemption; and there is no sin already committed, or to be committed by thee in time, that was not considered before time: What was your posture, believers, when God *passed by, and cast the lap or skirt of his love over you?* Were you not *cast out in the open field, wallowing in your own blood, with your navels uncut, having no eye to pity you?* &c. as it is, Ezek. xvi. And wherefore I pray, is this set down? but to let you know that ye are no worse in time than ye were considered to be before ye had a being; so, to heighten the love and grace of God in Christ, and to draw you in to him, that since God and Christ the Mediator, in the transaction about your redemption, stood not on your sinfulness, ye may not stand on it, when seriously taken with, but may submit to his righteousness, and say, Be it so, Lord I am content to take what thou freely offerest. And the more sinful and lost ye be in yourselves, when suitably affected therewith, the more wonderful is the grace of God in the plot of your redemption, the more strong is your consolation, and the greater ground of believing have ye; your sins do not surprize God, nor the Mediator; the bargain was made before your sins were committed, and therefore the price must reach them, even when they are all summed up together: He was content to accept of them, so as to satisfy for them; and blessed be he for evermore, that accepted of the bargain, and paid the price according to his undertaking.

SERMON XXVII.

Isaiah liii. 6. *All we like sheep have gone astray, we have turned every one to his own way, and the Lord hath laid on him the iniquity of us all.*

IN the former verse, the prophet hath asserted the most wonderful truths, and very concerning to the people of God, and yet such truths as will not be easily got digested by natural reason. 1. That our Lord Jesus was put to sore and sad sufferings, *He was wounded and bruised*, &c. 2. That these sad sufferings

sufferings were for us the elect: It was for our our sins, and what was due to the elect; he was made to bear them, *He was wounded for our transgressions, he was bruised for our iniquities*. 3. The end of these sufferings, or the effect that followed on them to us, pardon of sin, peace with God, and healing; *The chastisement of our peace was on him, and by his stripes we are healed*.

And each of these being more wonderful than another, therefore the Prophet goes on to clear their rise, which is no less wonderful; how it came to pass that he suffered, and suffered so much, and that we have such benefit by his sufferings. It could not (would he say) be otherwise, but it behoved our Lord Jesus to suffer, and to suffer so much, and for us; neither was it unreasonable that it should be for our benefit, For *we had all like lost sheep gone astray, and every one of us had turned to his own way*: And there was no way of relief for us, but by Christ's stepping into our room, and interposing for us, and engaging to pay our debt; and by vertue of that interposition and bargain, *The Lord hath laid on him the iniquity of us all*: And therefore, 1. Would ye have the reason of Christ's so great sufferings? Here it is, the elect had many sins, and he interposing for them, their count was scored out, and they were reckoned on his score. 2. If the cause and reason be asked, How it came to pass that Christ suffered so much for us? Here it is, he undertook to satisfy for our iniquities, and God imputed them to him: Even as if a dyvour were pursued, and one should step in and be cautioner for him, and being enacted surety, should take on him and become liable for the debt; the exacting it of him, is the laying it on him. But, 3. If it be asked, How it comes to pass that his sufferings become our healing, and bring peace to us? It is answered, It was so transacted and agreed upon; he was content to pay all our debt, and the Father accepted of his payment for ours: Our blessed Lord Jesus engaging and satisfying, the elect are set free, and justice, betaketh itself to him as the more responsal Party. This is the scope of the words, which though but few, yet exceeding full and significant, as holding out the fountain and fundamental grounds of the gospel; we shall look upon them in these three respects, (1.) As they imply a covenant and transaction, whereby the elect's sins are transacted on Christ, and his righteousness is made application of to them; Christ undertaking to pay their debt, and Jehovah accepting thereof, and promising that his satisfaction, made for the behoof of the elect, shall be applied to them. (2.) In respect of the effects, which are two; which though they seem contrary, the one to the other, yet they are well consistent together, and subordinate the one of them to the other: The 1*st* is justice on Christ's side; He satisfies for the debt due by the elect. The 2d is of mercy and grace to the elect, which is also implied; but, comparing these words with the former, it is very clear: He is wounded and bruised, and they are healed; the chastisement of their peace was on him; the imputing of their debt to him, makes that it is not imputed to them. (3.) In respect of the influence that the eternal covenant hath on these effects. It lays down the way how these may be justly brought about, which is the scope of all, even to shew how Jesus Christ, being the innocent Son of God, and without sin, was made liable to the debt of the elect's sin; he became Cautioner for them, and is made liable on that account to satisfy for them. It clears also how his sufferings stood for theirs; which may seem to be unreasonable and unjust amongst men, that the sufferings of an innocent party should stand for the guilty: It was so articled in the covenant of redemption, that the Son as Mediator interposing, and undertaking to pay the elect's debt, the Lord Jehovah the Creditor should not reckon it on their score, but on the Mediator's, and that he should count for it. The Prophet in this verse, almost, is striking on the sweet and pleasant string of this noble plot and contrivance of God concerning the redemption of elect sinners, called the *covenant of redemption*; which these words, considered with respect to their scope, do in all the parts of it clearly hold out: And therefore, the clearing of it, being the clearing of a main ground of our faith in reference to Christ's sufferings, and to the way how they are made forthcoming to us, and withal to the benefits that come by them to us, we cannot speak too much nor too often of it, if we would speak of it suitably to the passing excellency of the matter.

The *first Doctrine* supposed here is, *That there is an eternal covenant, and transaction betwixt the Lord Jehovah and the Mediator, wherein the whole business concerning the redemption and salvation of the elect it contrived*. There is an eternal covenant past betwixt God and the Mediator, wherein all that is executed, or will be, concerning the elect, till the day of judgment, was contrived; there is nothing relating to the elect's salvation, but it was in this transaction exactly contrived and laid down, even as it is in time executed; and it is called a *covenant* in scripture, and we call it so, not strictly and properly, as if all things in covenants among men were in it, but because materially and substantially it is so, and the resemblance will hold for the most part; the Lord having laid down in it the plot of man's salvation in a legal way, so as his grace and mercy may be glorified, and his justice satisfied, hath put it in this form, so as it may bear the name of a covenant: Wherein we have, 1. Mutual Parties, *the Lord Jehovah*, the Party offended, on the one side; and *the Lord Mediator, Him*, the Party engaging to satisfy, on the other side: Which shews the freeness of the redemption of the elect as to them, and the certainty of their salvation; and withal, the immutability of God's purpose, for the Parties are not mutable creatures, but on the one side *Jehovah*, and on the other side the *Mediator*, though considered as to be incarnate, and the Head of the elect. This whole business bred there, to wit, in the counsel of the Godhead, for promoting of that great end, the glorifying of the grace and justice of God in the elect's salvation. 2. Whereabout is it? It is about this matter, how to get the elect saved from the curse, to which on their foreseen fall and sinning they were made liable; redemption necessarily presupposing man's fall, and the covenant of works, to which the certification and threatning was added, *The soul that sins shall die*; and the elect presupposed as fallen, as well as others, are liable to the curse, except a satisfaction for them do interveen; so that the elect are considered as having sin, and as being in themselves lost. And what is the Lord Jehovah and the Mediator doing? What are they about in this covenant? It is how to get the punishment due to the elect for their sins removed from them. And these persons, *us all*, in the text, are all the elect, wherein there is implied a particular consideration of them that are designed to life and salvation, and a particular consideration of all their sins, and of their several aggravations, that there may be a proportion betwixt the price and the wrong that God hath gotten by their sinning against him. 3. The occasion of this covenant, and the reason why it behoved to be, is holden forth in the first words, *All we like sheep have gone astray, and turned every one of us unto his own way*: The elect, as well as others, had made themselves through their sinning liable to God's wrath and curse, and they were uncapable of life and salvation till the curse was removed; and so there is a lett and obstruction in the way of the execution of the decree of election (which must stand for the glorification of God's grace and mercy, primarily intended in all this work) and till this lett be removed, the glorification of God's grace is letted and obstructed: For the removal of which obstruction, there is a necessity of a Redeemer, for the elect are not able to pay their own debt themselves; now, that there may be a Redeemer, and that a price of redemption may be laid down, there is also a necessity of a covenant, otherwise the Redeemer cannot be, if a transaction do not precede, on which the Redeemer's interposing is founded. 4. What is the price, what is the stipulation, or that which the Mediator is engaged to, and that which provoked justice required? It is even satisfaction for all the wrongs that the sins of the elect did, or were to do, to the Majesty of God. Their sins deserved wounding and smiting; and the capitulation runs on this, that justice shall get that of the Mediator, that the elect may be spared. And comparing this verse with the former, upon the one side our Lord Jesus gives his back to bear their burden, and engages to satisfy for their debt, and to undergo the punishment due to them; and upon the other side, Jehovah accepts of this offer and engagement, and lays over the burden of their debt on him: As the Mediator instates and enacts himself in their room for payment of their debt, so he lays it on him, and accepts of it. 5. The end of this great transaction, to wit, of the undertaking on the Mediator's side, and of the acceptation on the Father's side, is, that the elect may have pardon and peace, and that by his stripes they may be healed; that justice may spare them, and pursue him; and that the discharge of the debt, purchased by him, may be made forthcoming to them, as if they had paid the debt themselves, or had never been owing any thing to justice.

Hence *Deductions* may be made, holding forth several points of truth; As, 1. Concerning the determinateness of the number of the elect. 2. Concerning the vertue and efficacy of the price which the Mediator hath paid, and the fulness of his satisfaction. 3. Concerning his imputed righteousness, which is, or may be called the laying of his righteousness on us, as our iniquity was laid on him: He is counted the sinner, by undertaking the elect's debt; and the elect, by receiving the offered righteousness in the gospel, are accounted righteous, by vertue of his satisfying for their debt. 4. Concerning the ground and matter of wonderful soul-satisfaction and ravishment that is here; that God should be thus minding the salvation of the elect, and thus contriving and ordering the work of their redemption; that their debt shall be paid, and yet nothing (to speak so) come out of their purse; and that by so excellent a mean as is the intervention of the Mediator; and that this

this shall, notwithstanding of the dear price paid by him, be made freely forthcoming to the elect.

Use 1. O! look not on the salvation of sinners, and the bringing of a sinner to heaven, as a little or a light business and work: It is the greatest work and most wonderful that ever was heard tell of; yea, it is in effect the end of all things which God hath made, and of his preserving and guiding the world in the order wherein it is governed, even that he may have a Church therein for the praise of the glory of his grace. We are exceeding far and sinfully wrong in this, that we value not the work of redemption as becomes, and that we endeavour not to pry into, and take up the admirable and deep wisdom of God, that goes along and shines brightly in this whole contexture. Who could ever have found out this way, when the elect were lying under God's curse and wrath, that then the Son of God should undertake to satisfy for them, and that the Majesty of God should be so far from partiality and respect of persons, that he will pursue his own dear Son for the elect's debt, when he undertakes it? This is the rise of our salvation, and the channel wherein it runs! O rare and ravishing! O admirable and amiable! O beautiful and beneficial contrivance! Blessed, eternally blessed be the Contriver.

Use 2. The second use serves to stir us up to study to know somewhat, and to know more of the way of salvation, under this notion of God's covenanting with the Mediator; not thereby to restrict God to man's law and forms, but for helping us to the better and more easy up-taking of these great things; and that we may see that the salvation of the elect is sure, forasmuch as it is laid down by way of bargain, transaction or covenant betwixt Jehovah and the Mediator, whom the Lord will no more fail in performing the promise made to him, than he hath failed in giving the satisfaction required. This would help both to clear and confirm the faith of believers, and strengthen the hope of all who are fled for refuge to take hold of him, in the certain expectation of these things engaged for in the covenant; seeing there is no less reason to think, that Jehovah will be forthcoming to the Mediator, than there is to think that he hath performed all that he engaged himself for.

The 2*d* thing here is, the native effect or fruit of the covenant, and that which the Prophet aims at; even to shew how it came to pass that Christ suffered so much, because it was so covenanted, statute and ordained, because he was by a prior contrivance and contract substitute with his own hearty consent in the room of the elect, who had many and great sins to count for; from whence observe, *That, iy vertue of this eternal covenant that past betwixt God and the Mediator, the complete punishment that was due to all the elect for their sins in their greatest aggravations, was laid upon Jesus Christ.* Jehovah laid upon him the iniquity of us all: this is frequently touched on in this Chapter, as particularly in the words going before, *He carried our sorrows, he was wounded for our transgressions, and bruised for our iniquities,* &c. and it is sufficiently confirmed in the New Testament, as 2 Cor. v. *He who knew no sin, was made sin for us;* he had no sin in himself, but by vertue of this covenant, he was made the sacrifice for our sin, and made to bear the punishment thereof; and Gal. iii. 13. *He hath redeemed us from the curse of the law, he himself being made a curse for us.*

There are two words which we shall a little clear in this doctrine; and, *secondly*, Give some reasons of it; and then, *thirdly*, We shall speak to some uses from it.

1*st*, For the two words or things in the doctrine to be cleared, they are these, *First*, What we mean by this, when we say, Iniquity is laid upon Christ? The *second* is, How is it laid upon Christ? As to the first, when we say, Iniquity is laid upon Christ, we mean these things shortly, 1. That our Lord Jesus is really made countable and liable to justice for these iniquities, as if they had been his own, by vertue of this covenant; in God's justice, he having engaged to pay the elect's debt, his engagement makes him liable to it. 2. We mean, that not only our Lord Jesus is made liable to our debt, but really he is made to satisfy for it: In short, we have done the wrong, but he makes the amends, as if he had done the wrong himself, *The Just satisfies for the unjust: He, in whose mouth there was no guile,* was made to satisfy for guilty sinners, as if he had been the guilty person himself: By the sins of the elect, God's declarative holiness suffered; creatures malapertly brake his command, and his justice was wronged; creatures topped with it, to say so, and that even after the curse was pronounced, and after they had believed the devil more than God: But our Lord Jesus comes in and makes the amends, and the holiness of God is vindicate by his obedience, and his justice vindicate by his suffering. The elect have deserved wounding, but, says the Mediator, Let the wounds which they have deserved come on me, let them be mine; and thus he makes reparation of the wrong, and the amends, because, tho' the elect be spared, yet hereby the Lord is known to be as really and as much a hater of sin, and as just

just in fulfilling his threatnings, as if the elect had been smitten in their own persons, because he punished sin in his own Son; yea, by this means he is seen so much the more to be holy, severe, pure and spotless: And, that the Son of God sweetly submits to his becoming Man, and to these terrible sufferings, for satisfying divine justice; Here, O here the spotlesness and severity of the justice of God, as also the greatness of the glory of free grace and love, shine forth conspicuously! 3. It implies this, That really there was a converting and turning of that wrath, and of these sufferings proportionably on Jesus Christ, which justice was to have inflicted on the elect eternally, if he had not interposed for them; and that altogether in a full cup, offered to him, and put in his hand: That, which would have been in so many drops an eternal hell to elect sinners, is made to meet on him in one great sea; he gets it to drink up, dregs and all: In which respect, Gal. iii. 13. he is said to be *made a curse for us*. The Lord will not pass from one farthing of what was due to him, and will be satisfied with no less than proportionable satisfaction to that which was due to justice by the elect themselves, though the Surety was his own only Son; Therefore it behoved Christ to come under the curse, in which sense he is said to be *made a curse for us*; which supposeth that he endured the same curse and punishment due to the elect's sins, in all the essentials of it: He behoved to die; and to have his soul separate from his body for a time, and for a season to want in a great measure the comfortable manifestations of God's favour and presence, and to have wrath pursuing him; and to have horror seizing upon him; though our blessed Lord, being spotless and without sin, and having a good conscience, was not capable of these someway accidental circumstances, of unbelief, sinful anxiety and desperation, that sinful finite creatures are liable to, when they come under wrath.

The second word or thing to be cleared in the doctrine, is, How are iniquities laid upon Christ Jesus? In three respects, 1. In respect of the eternal transaction betwixt Jehovah and him as Mediator, sustaining the persons of the elect: Even as one man hath another's debt laid on him, when by a law-sentence he is made liable to it; so is Christ liable to the elect's iniquity, when their account is blotted out, and the debt as it were written down in his account, to be satisfied for. 2. In respect of justice pursuing him for it: When he becometh Cautioner and full Debitor for the elect, he is put to pay their debt to the least farthing; the Lord musters up against him his terrors, and commands *his sword to awake, and to smite the Man that is his Fellow*. But, 3d, and mainly, In respect of his actual undergoing the curse, and suffering that which the elect should have suffered; for it is not the work of a court to pass a sentence only, but also to see the execution of the sentence; not only are orders given to the sword to awake and smite, but the sword falls on and smites him actually: and tho', from the apprehension of the anger of God, as Man, and without the sensible and comforting manifestation of his Father's love; and his seemingly forsaking him for a time, He prayed, *Father, if it be possible, let this cup pass from me;* yet it will not be, and he submits most sweetly to it: and not only is the cup put in his hand, but the dregs of wrath are, as it were, wrung out into it, and he must needs drink it up all; which manifestly kythes in his *agony* in the garden, when he is made to *sweat blood*; and in his complaint (if we may so call it) *My soul is exceeding sorrowful, and what shall I say?* and in these strange words uttered by him on the cross, *My God, my God, why hast thou forsaken me?* All which tells us plainly, that not only was he enacted Surety, and had the sentence past on him, but that really he satisfied, and had the sentence executed on him; that in his soul he was really pierced and wounded, and that with far deeper wounds than these were which the soldiers by the spear and nails made in his body, before the elect's discharge of their debt could be procured and obtained. What it was more particularly that he suffered, the following words hold out: But it is clear, that he suffered really, and suffered much; that not only he undertook to pay, but that he was actually pursued, and made to lay down the least farthing of whatever was due to justice by the elect: And this is the cause why these words are brought in as the reason why he suffered so much, even because so many and so great sins, with all their aggravations, were laid upon him; and if his sufferings were not great, and undergone for this end, to satisfy for the elect's debt, that they might be set free, the prophet's scope would not be reached, neither would there be a suitable connexion betwixt the latter and the foregoing words.

As for the second, to wit, some *Reasons* of the doctrine; we shall shortly give you these *three*, why the elects sins were laid on Christ, and put on his account, and why he was made to underly the compleat punishment of them, by vertue of the covenant of redemption. 1. Because it did much contribute to the glory of God; for he had designed in his eternal council, that his grace should be glorified in the salvation of the elect, and that his justice should also be glorified in punishing of sin, either in themselves or in their Cautioner: And as free grace and mercy must be glorious in saving the elect, and justice in being satisfied for their sins; so it is to that end, that since the elect cannot pay their own debt, that their cautioner pay it, and pay it fully; that the Lord, in exacting satisfaction from him in their name, may be known to be just. 2. This way makes much for the confirmation of their faith; for what can justice demand, that it hath not gotten? it is fully satisfied. And then for their consolation: Seeing the Father put his own Son to suffer, and to so great suffering for them, what is it that they may confidently expect from such a fountain? 3. This serves to hold out the wonderfully great obligation of the elect to God, and to the Mediator; for the greater their sin was, the more he suffered; the greater their debt was, the more he paid; and they are the more in his common, and the greater debtors to him, and ought the more to love him, and their duty for his sake: As it is said of the woman, Luke vii. *She loved much, for much was forgiven her;* so this way of paying the elects debt, calls and strongly pleads, and also makes way for much warm and tender love in them to Jesus Christ.

In the third place, We come to the *Uses* of the *Doctrine*: To which I shall premise this word of desire to you, That ye would not look on these things as tasteless and unsavoury; for, had we not had these precious truths to open up to you, we should have had no meetings to this purpose, no ground to speak of life to you, nor any the least hope or expectation of life. And indeed it may be sadly regreted, that amongst a multitude of professing people, these substantial truths of the gospel are so werish and little relishing to the most part; which too evidently appears in the unconcerned, wearying, and gazing posture of some, and in the slumbering and sleeping of others in our public assemblies: If our hearts were in a right frame, half a word, to say so, to this purpose, would be awakening and alarming to us; however this is a great privilege in itself: Heathens may and do know something of moral duties, but it is a privilege which we have, and they want, that the fundamental truths of the gospel are amongst us, and not amongst them.

The first *Use* serves to let us see the brightness of the glory of grace and truth, of mercy and justice, shining clearly here; Can there be any greater mercy, and more pure mercy than this, that the Lord should be gracious to sinners, and to great sinners, *that had turned every one of them to their own way;* in providing a Mediator, and such a Mediator; in providing such a help for them, and *laying that help upon One that is mighty*; and that he should have done this of his own head (so to speak with reverence) when the elect were in their sins, and when there was nothing to be the impulsive or meritorious cause of it; and that the Father should have laid this weight of punishment on Christ, the Son of his love, and pursued him at this rate of holy severity for sinners debt? O what grace and mercy shines here! And, 2. The spotless justice of God doth also here wonderfully manifest itself; O how exact is justice, when it will not quit a farthing even to the second Person of the Godhead, when he became Man, and Man's Surety! But since he hath put himself in the room of sinners, *the Lord maketh all their iniquities to meet on him;* this is matter of admiration to men and angels, to consider how justice and mercy run in one channel, and shine in one covenant, the one of them not incroaching upon the other.

Use 2. We may gather from this, some insight and clearness in the very great sufferings of our Lord Jesus Christ: for these things are here put together, 1. That he suffered for all the elect, *Us all*. 2. For all the sins of the elect, and for all the sins of the elect in their highest and most aggravating circumstances; the particular reckoning of them all, as it were, being cast up, they are all put in one score. 3. All these meet together in a great sea and shock upon him at one time, as they came from several airths, like so many rivers; or they were like so many rivers; or they were like so many regiments, or rather armies of men, all meeting together, and marshalled to fall pell-mell (to say so) on him; one sin were enough to condemn, the many sins of one is more, but all the sins of all the elect is much more; they deserved to have lyen in hell eternally, but he coming in their room, all their sins met as the violent press of waters on him: What then behoved his sufferings to be, when he was so put to it for all the sins of all the elect, and that at once?

Use 3. We may gather hence a just account of the truth of Christ's satisfaction, and a ground of refutation of the Socinian error, a blasphemy which is most abominable to be once mentioned, as if our Lord had suffered all this, only to give us an example, and as if there had not been a proportionable satisfaction in his sufferings to our debt, nor an intention to satisfy justice thereby: Every verse almost

almoſt, not to ſay every word, in this chapter refutes this; if he had not ſatisfied for our ſins, why is he ſaid to be here on the matter put in our room? And if his ſufferings had not been very great, what needed the prophet to ſhew the reaſon of his great ſufferings, in all the ſins of the elect their meeting on him? There was ſure a particular reſpect had to this, even to ſhew, that the meeting of all theſe ſins of all the elect together upon Chriſt, did cauſe and procure great and extreme ſufferings to him; he ſuffered the more that they had ſo many ſins, ſeeing their many ſins are given for the cauſe of his ſo much ſuffering.

Uſe 4. Here is great ground of conſolation to believing ſinners, *Out of this eater comes meat, and out of this ſtrong comes ſweet*; the more ſharp and bitter theſe ſufferings were to Chriſt, the report of them is in ſome reſpect the more ſavoury and ſweet to the believer, whoſe effectual calling diſcovers his election. And indeed I cannot tell how many grounds of conſolation believers have from this doctrine; but, 1. If they have ſinned, there is here a Saviour provided for them. 2. This Saviour hath undertaken their debt. 3. He hath undertaken it with the Father's allowance. 4. As he hath undertaken it, ſo the Father hath laid on him all their iniquity. 5. All the elect come in here together in one roll, and there is but one covenant, and one Mediator for them all: the ſin of the poor body, of the weakeſt and meaneſt, is tranſacted on him, as well as the ſin of Abraham that great friend of God, and Father of the faithful; and the ſalvation of the one is as ſure as the ſalvation of the other: All believers, from the ſtrongeſt to the weakeſt, have but one right or charter to heaven, but one holding of the inheritance. 6. The Lord hath laid on him all the iniquities of all the elect, with a particular reſpect to all their aggravations, and to all the ſeveral ways that they have turned to ſin; their original ſin, and their actual tranſgreſſions, with their particular predominants, as to their puniſhment: And there is reaſon for it, becauſe the elect could not ſatisfy for the leaſt ſin; and it is neceſſary for the glorifying of grace, that the glory of the work of their ſalvation be not halfed, but ſolely and ſingly aſcribed and given to God; and therefore the ſatisfaction comes all on the Mediator's account,

and none of it on theirs. 7. All this is really done and performed by the Mediator, without any ſuit or requeſt of the elect, or of the believer, or at leaſt as the procuring cauſe thereof: He buys and purchaſes what is needful for them, and pays for their diſcharge; and they have no more to do, but to call for an extract, and to take a ſealed remiſſion by his blood; the application whereof, the *Uſes* that follow will give occaſion to ſpeak to.

Uſe 5. Since it is ſo, then none would think little of ſin; which checks the great preſumption that is amongſt men and women, who think little and light of ſin, and that it is an eaſy matter to come by the pardon of it: They think there is no more to do, but barely and bauchly to confeſs they have ſinned, and to ſay, God is merciful; and hence they conclude, that God will not reckon with them: But, did he reckon with the Mediator, and that ſo holily, rigidly, and ſeverely, too; and will he, think ye, ſpare you? If he *dealt ſo with the green tree, what ſhall become of the dry?* Be not deceived, God will not be mocked.

And therefore, 6th, As the cloſe of all, See here the abſolute neceſſity of ſharing in Chriſt's ſatisfaction, and of having an intereſt therein by this covenant derived unto you, elſe know that ye muſt count for your own ſins; and if ſo, wo eternally to you: Therefore either betake yourſelves to the Mediator, that by his eye-ſalve ye may ſee, that by his gold ye may be enriched, and by his garments ye may be clothed, that the ſhame of your nakedneſs do not appear; and that ye may, by being juſtified by his knowledge, be free from the wrath to come; or otherwiſe ye muſt and ſhall ly under it for ever.

Thus ye have the fulneſs of God's covenant on the one ſide, and the weightineſs and terribleneſs of God's wrath on the other ſide, laid before you: If ye knew what a fearful thing his wrath were, ye would be glad at your hearts to hear of a Saviour, and every one would run and make haſte to be found in him, and to ſhare of his ſatisfaction, and to be ſure of a diſcharge by vertue of his payment of the debt; and they would give all diligence to make ſure their calling and election, for that end. The Lord himſelf powerfully perſuade you to do ſo.

SERMON XXVIII.

Isaiah liii. 7. *He was oppressed, and he was afflicted, yet he opened not his mouth; he is brought as a lamb to the slaughter, and as a sheep before her shearers is dumb, so he opened not his mouth.*

THO' the news of a suffering Mediator seem to be a sad subject, yet it hath been, is, and will be, the great subject of the gospel, and of the gladest tidings that ever sinners heard. This being the great thing that they ought in a special manner to know, even *Jesus Christ and him crucified;* the prophet here takes a special delight to insist on it, and in one verse after another hath some new thing of his sufferings.

Having in the former verse spoken to the occasion, ground and rise of his sufferings, to wit, the elects straying like sheep, their wandering and turning every one to his own way, and the Lord's laying on him the iniquity of them all: The elect that were given to Christ, being naturally at an enmity with God, and having run on in the course of their sinful nature to the provoking of God; and there being no way for them to escape the wrath which by their sins they had deserved, till the Lord found out this mids, to wit, the second Person his interposing as their Mediator and Surety, and engaging to pay their debt; on which followed the imputation of all their iniquities to him, according to the transaction made about them; which transaction being laid down as we have heard, the prophet proceeds to shew Christ's executing and performing of the transaction. And, because it might be thought that it was so great a matter as could have much, sad and sore suffering following upon it, to take on all our iniquities; he answers, that notwithstanding of all that, yet he took them on, and that very willingly and cheerfully: Or, because it might be thought that the former words look as if God had laid the punishment of our iniquity on him, and that he had not taken it on himself, the prophet tells us that it is nothing so, but that there was a mutual covenant betwixt God and the Mediator, and that the Mediator was as well content to bear the iniquity of the elect, as the Father was content to lay it on him; and that tho' he was exacted upon, oppressed, afflicted, and suffered sad strokes, yet he rewed not the bargain, but went on resolutely in paying the ransom of the elect, as singly as ever a sheep went to the slaughter, or as it is *dumb before the shearer, so he opened not his mouth* to speak against it.

There are three things asserted here, that serve to make up the scope, supposing the transaction to have gone before, 1. The Father's exacting the elect's debt of the Mediator. 2. The Mediator's yielding and satisfying. 3. The manner how he did it, willingly, readily and cheerfully. We shall first open the words a little, and then speak to some doctrines from them, reserving the uses to the close of all.

1st, Where it is said, *he was oppressed*, the words signify to *exact*; and we find it three ways applied in scripture, 1. To the exacting of tribute, 2 Kings xxiii. 33. where it is said, *That Pharoah-Nechoh put the land to a tribute of an hundred talents of silver, and a talent of gold*; it is the word that is here. 2. Sometimes it is applied to the *exacting of debts*; as when a man is put to the horn, and caption and imprisonment follows upon it: So Deut. xv. 2. When the Lord tells his people, *The creditor shall not exact of his neighbour, nor of his brother, in the year of release*. 3. It is applied to *the exacting of labour*, as Isa. lviii. 3. *Ye exact all your labour*; and Exod. i. 11. the word *Task masters* comes from the same root; this being the ordinary signification of the word, it is turned here *oppressing* figuratively, because such exacters and taskmasters, in their rigorous usage of these whom they exact upon, are often oppressive: And there being no noun prefixed to these words in the original, they may stand as well thus, *It was exacted of him*; That which he was engaged to pay, he was fully exacted upon for it, to the least farthing: Or take the words as they stand here, he was oppressed, that is, (as we use to speak) *stressed* or *distressed*, for our debt; he was not only engaged but according to his engagement he was put hard to it to satisfy. *2dly*, It it said, *He was afflicted*, which is sometimes rendered to *answer*: And these two agree very well together, he was exacted upon, and he answered the debt; as when a bill of exchange for such a sum is drawn upon a man and he answers it: And this exposition runs well and smoothly with the words following, *Yet he opened not his mouth*, he used no defence to elude or shift the debt; he said not that it was not his, but he answered it indeed, and in a word said nothing to the contrary. Or, taking the words as they here stand translated, *He was afflicted*, they signify the effect that follows on his being exacted upon; Though it brake him not, yet it brought him very low, even to an afflicted condition. The 3*d* thing is, That though he was brought thus low, and though it was not for his own, but for other folks debts (which usually troubles men most) *Yet he opened not his mouth;* to shew his wonderful condescendency, and the great love from which it flows, he paid the elects debt with as good will, and as pleasantly, as if it had been his own proper and personal debt; tho' he was the Son of God, and God equal with the Father, and might have brought legions of angels to destroy his enemies, yet, *as the lamb brought to the slaughter, and as the sheep before the shearer is dumb, so he opened not his mouth.* And it may be, that there is not only here relation or respect had to the sheep, as it is an innocent, harmless, simple, tractable creature, and not untoward and refractory, as a bull or ox useth to be; but also respect had to it, as it was made use of in the sacrifices: And so the meaning is, He yielded his life willingly, when none could take it from him, for performing the indenture, to say so, and for satisfying the transaction past betwixt Jehovah and him.

So, having shown you how it comes to pass, that Christ suffered, and suffered so much, and was brought so low under suffering; and having told that he was engaged to pay the elects debt, and that the Father had laid their iniquities on him; lest any might think that the Father would have spared his own Son, No, saith the prophet, *He was oppressed,* and not only so, but *afflicted* and humbled: And lest it should have been thought that the Lord Jehovah had better will to the bargain than the Mediator had; it is added, that he did satisfy the debt as willingly as the Father laid it on him, as these similitudes made use of plainly hold forth.

Take these *Observations* from the words, 1. " That our Lord Jesus, having entered himself Surety " for sinners, was really put at, and justice exacted " the debt of him, which he had undertaken and " engaged to pay." Read the whole story of the gospel, and it will make out this: It is said by himself, Luke xxiv. *It behoved the Son of man to suffer these things, and then to enter into his glory:* he must needs go to Jerusalem and suffer: And when the cup is in his hand, and his holy human nature, having a sinless fearing at it, makes him pray, *Father, if it be possible, let this cup pass from me,* yet seeing here was a necessity, that either he should drink it, or that the elect should perish: in the very next words, he sweetly subjoins, *Not my will, but thy will be done:* and so hotly and hardly he was pursued by justice, that he must needs come to the cursed death of the cross, and actually die; and, as if death had gotten a piece of dominion over the Lord of life, he is laid in the grave: So, Zech. xiii. the Lord saith, *Awake, O sword, against my Shepherd, and against the Man that is my Fellow, smite the Shepherd;* where we see, that when the good Shepherd and great Bishop of souls, hath undertaken for the elects debt, justice gives a commission as it were to its own holy revenge, to pursue the Man that is God's Fellow for that debt. That which we design to confirm in the doctrine, is not only, that our Lord Jesus suffered, but that his suffering was by justice its exacting of him the debt of the elects sin, according to the engagement that he came under to the Father: For the scope is to shew, not only that he suffered so great things, as oppressed and brought him very low; but also that he was put at by justice, in these sad sufferings, to pay the debt that he had taken on. For confirming and clearing of this a little, ye may consider, 1. The titles which he gets in scripture, he is called the *Cautioner, or Surety of the better testament,* or covenant, Heb. vii. 22. and by that title he is shewed to be instated in our room, and answerable for our debt: And he is called the *lamb,* that takes away the debt of sin, *by the sacrifice of himself;* he stepped in into our place, and kept off the stroke of the sword of justice that would have lighted on us, had he not interposed. 2. Consider the titles which his sufferings and death gets, Heb. ix. 12. He is said to *purchase* (to wit, by it) *eternal redemption for us.* And Rom. iii. 24. we are said to be *justified through the redemption that is in Jesus:* We were slaves to the devil, subject to the curse, decerned and adjudged to suffer for the wrongs that we had done to justice: And his sufferings is called *redemption,* because as the man that redeems the captive, gives a ransom for him; so he interposed and paid a ransom for us: It is also called a *propitiation,* 1 John ii. 2. *He is the propitiation for our sins,* to wit, pleasing to God, and accepted of him in the room of all the elect; and this word *propitiation,* as it supposeth God's being displeased with the elect before Christ's satisfaction, so it plainly holds forth his being well pleased with them on the account of his satisfaction. 3. Consider these scriptures that speak not only of Christ's sufferings, but of their end and scope, even the drawing of him down (to speak so) into the elects room, as verse 5th, of this chapter, *He was wounded for our transgressions,* &c. He got the stroke, and we got the cure, 2 Cor. v. 21. *He was made sin for us who knew no sin, that we might be made the righteousness of God through him;* We are sinners, and Christ is to purchase righteousness to us; and the way how he doth it, is by stepping in into our room, and becoming

coming our Cautioner, and he engages as Surety; the law wins at him on that ground; so, Gal. iii. 13. *He hath redeemed us from the curse of the law, by being made a curse for us:* we were under the curse, and liable to be pursued by it; and our Lord Jesus becomes a curse, to deliver us from it. Considering then the end of God's covenant, which is to glorify his justice and grace, that sinners may know it is an evil thing to sin and depart from God, and that grace is a very costly thing, whereunto he hath made access through the vail, which is his flesh; and considering Christ's undertaking, without which they could not be set free, it could not be otherwise. This is a truth that hath in it much of the marrow of the gospel, and tends much to humble us, and is also very much for our comfort: What was justice seeking of Christ when he suffered and was in an agony? If thou art a believer or an elect sinner, it was even exacting thy debt of him; and would it not affect an ingenuous debtor to see his cautioner dragged, haled, and hurried to prison for his debt? Even so, if we could look on Christ's sufferings as so many summons and pursevants arresting him for our debt, it could not but affect us with much sorrow for our sins, that brought him to this, and with much love to him, who was content to be so dealt with for them; and no doubt this is one of the reasons why *he will have his death remembred till he come again,* even that we may see our obligation to him, and be suitably affected with it.

2*dly*, Observe, "That the debt of the elects sins "was severely and with holy rigour exacted of "Christ to the very full worth or value." This proceeding was, as to Christ, by way of justice; whether we look to the purchase that he made, to wit, the elect souls, he laid down as good in their room; or whether we look to a transaction or bargain going before, whatever was in the stipulation, he paid and satisfied to the full, nothing was remitted or given him down; or whether we look to the curse due to the elect, that was inflicted on him, and he himself was made a curse for us, looking on the curse simply as penal, and what was bitter in it, which shews his condescendency in his sufferings so much the more.

3*dly*, Observe, "That our Lord Jesus was "brought exceeding low, while the debt of the "elect was exacted of him:" He was put to exceeding sore affliction, much straitned and stressed by the justice of God exacting of him the debt due by elect sinners. We spoke to some words before, which bare out this, as, *he was wounded, bruised,* *chastised,* &c. and now we see the effect here, when justice puts him to it; after he hath taken on the debt, he is tried, stripped as it were to the skin, pinched and distressed, ere he got it paid: If we consider our Lord Jesus as God, he is neither less nor more pinched, being, so considered, utterly incapable of any such thing; but if we look on him as Mediator, God-Man, God much withdrawing from him the influence of his comforting presence, while he hath the cup of wrath in his hand, so he is brought exceeding low, and sadly afflicted. And these *four* considerations (under which we may see him paying our debt) may clear it, 1. That he laid aside the glory which before the world was, he he had with the Father, for a time; which therefore, that it may be restored to him again, he prayeth, John xvii. 5. it having been, as to the manifestation thereof in his person, eclipsed, interrupted, and darkned for a season: hence the apostle says, Philip. ii. that *he emptied himself, and became of no reputation,* as if his glory had not been discernable for a time; he that is Judge of quick and dead, is himself judged; he that created heaven and earth, hath not whereon to lay his head; tho' all the kings of the earth hold their treasures of him, yet he was so poor, that he lived upon the alms of others; for *women ministred unto him.* 2. Not only hath he a being that is mean and low, but he is exceedingly afflicted; he suffered hunger; he is pursued, as if he had been a thief or a robber; a band of men comes and apprehends him in the night, as if he had been a malefactor or evil doer, and drag him away to the civil judge; his back is smitten, his face is spitted on, his head ratted and pricked with thorns; sentence is passed upon him, he is condemned and scourged; and when he doth not bear his own cross, (his body, being a true human body, is so faint and enfeebled) it is accounted a favour that he gets one Simon to help him to bear it, or to bear it after him; which is not marked, to shew that they did him a kindness or courtesy beyond others, but to hold out the low and weak condition he was brought into, that he was not able to bear it himself. And not only so, but he must come to death, and to the shameful and cursed death of the cross; he dies very quickly, further to point out his lowness, which was such, that death overcame him sooner than the others, because he had other things to wrestle with. 3. In his name he suffered, he was reproached, nodded at with the head, reviled, mocked, sent about as a spectacle from Pilate to Herod, back again from Herod to Pilate; he had a scarlet robe put on him in derisision; the high priests also derided him; the Jews wag the head at him, and count him not at all worthy to live, and therefore prefer a robber and murderer to him. 4. Consider his inward sufferings: O these were far more piercing! Justice laid claim to his soul, *The sorrows of hell compassed him; his soul is heavy unto the death; he sweats blood*, and cries, *If it be possible that that wrathful cup might pass from him;* and on the cross with a pitiful voice, *My God, my God, why hast thou forsaken me?* which, by the way is not an expression of any quarrelling complaint or discouragement, but of sinless nature, when he is arraigned and made to stand before the tribunal of God, affected with the horror of divine wrath, and cannot easily endure, that there should be a cloud betwixt God and him: But these soul-sufferings of his, will fall in to be spoken to afterwards; only we see here, that he was afflicted, and in sufferings was greatly humbled and brought very low: And, indeed, considering that all the elect's sins were laid upon him, and that justice was exacting all their debt of him, he could not be otherwise, but behoved to be exceedingly afflicted and sore distressed.

4thly, Observe, "That for as much as our Lord suffered, yet he did most willingly and cheerfully undergo it all; he thwarted not with it; he repented not, he grudged not, he flinched not, nor drew back:" Or, which is to the same purpose, " Our Lord Jesus, in his lowest humiliation and affliction, and all alongst his deepest suffering, shewed exceeding great willingness, desirousness and heartsomness:" That word was always true of him, *I delight to do thy will, O my God;* and the prophet holds out this as a great wonder, that tho' he was oppressed and afflicted, yet *he opened not his mouth*. We shall, for clearing of this, propose these considerations. 1. In his undertaking of the bargain, his willingness appears; when burnt-offerings and sacrifices would not do it, and when there was no obligation on him to do what he did, then comes in his free offer and consent, and that with delight, Psal. xl. " Then said I, Lo, I come; in the volume of thy book it is written of me, I delight to do will, O my God;" where we see that there was no exerting or forcing of a consent from the Mediator against his will, but a delightsom offering of it: and that word of his, Prov. viii. is very remarkable to this purpose, " Rejoicing in the habitable parts of the earth, and my delight was with the sons of men;" the contemplation and fo-sight of his incarnation and suffering for the elect was (to speak so) refreshing to him, and made him leap as it were for joy, ere the world was made, and before they had a being. 2. Consider the great things that he undertook, not only to be Man, but a poor mean Man. It had been much for him to have humbled himself to be Monarch of the whole world, as his *vain* and *profane* pretended Vicar the Pope of Rome claims to be; yet he not only will not be so, but *emptied himself*, and became *a worm*, in a manner, *and no man, an out-cast of the people*; O such a proof of his love! And when he took the cup, that bitter cup, and said, *Father, if it be possible, let this cup pass from me*, lest it should seem a thwarting with the work of redemption, and with his Father's will therein; he says, Let it come, Father, *Not my will, but thine be done*. 3. Consider the manner of his suffering, and we will see a further proof of his willingness; how little pains takes he to escape them? yea, when Peter labours to dissuade him, Matt. xvi. from suffering, he disdains and rejects the suggestion with a severe check, " Get thee behind me, Satan thou art an offence unto me, thou favourest not the things that be of God, but of men;" and when his disciples said unto him (resolving to go up again to Judea) John xi. 8. *Master, the Jews of late sought to stone thee, and wilt thou go thither again?* he will needs go up notwithstanding; and when they were going up to Jerusalem, Mark x. 32. *He went before all the rest*, to wit at a swift pace; and Luke xii. 50. he says, ".I have a baptism to be baptized with, and how am I straitned till it be accomplished?" Never did men long so much for their marriage-day, and for the day of their triumph, as our Lord Jesus did to get the elect's debt paid, and their discharge extracted and drawn out. 4. Consider his easiness and willingness to be taken; he goes forth, John xviii. to meet the band of soldiers that came with the traitor to apprehend him, and asks them again and again, *Whom seek ye?* and says as often, *I am he*: He will not suffer his disciples to draw a sword in his defence, Matt. xxvi. but when Peter drew his sword, he bade him *put it up again*, for he could have *commanded more than twelve legions of angels*: but it behoved him now to suffer, he came for another end than to oppose his sufferings; and hence he says, John x. " No man takes my life from me, but I lay it down of myself, and have power to take it up again;" it was neither Judas nor Pilate that took his life against his will, but he willingly laid it down; for either the elect behoved to die, or he himself; and since it is so, as if he said, then behold here is my life, take it, and I will lay it down, that they, poor things, may

go

go free: *And therefore does my Father love me* (says he) *because I lay down my life for my sheep: not because it is taken from me against my will, but because I willingly and of myself lay it down:* And when he is brought before Pilate and Herod, and they lay many thing to his charge, Matt. xxvi. 6. and Mark xv. *He held his peace;* so that it is said, that Pilate *marvelled*, Mark xv. He knew that he could but not have much to say for himself, as all men in such a case use to have, but he answered nothing; or as it is in the text, *yet he opened not his mouth:* The reason was, because he would not divert the course of justice, nor mar the Lord's design in the work of the elect's redemption through his death and sufferings: He came not into the world, to accuse Pilate or the Jews, and to justify himself, tho' now and then, for the conviction of enemies, and for his own necessary clearing, he did let a word fall; but, being engaged for the elect, he will needs perform all that justice called for. And in this willingness he hath a respect to two things, 1. To the Father's satisfaction; for his willing suffering is that which makes it a sacrifice acceptable and well pleasing to him. 2. To the elect's consolation, that they may know they had a willing Saviour, that had no necessity laid on him to satisfy, but satisfied willingly. And from these two arises a third, Even the glory of the Mediator's satisfaction; for herein his love to the elect shines brightly, *I lay down my life for my sheep:* This is the heart warming commendation of his sufferings, that with delight and pleasure he underwent them, as if he had been purchasing a kingdom to himself.

Now, to come to the *use* of all these *doctrines*; when they with the things contained in them are laid together, we profess we cannot tell you what excellent uses they yield. Would to God we were all in such a frame as the Eunuch was in, when he read this scripture (as the divine historian gives us an account, Acts viii. verse 32. and forward) who, when Philip had begun to preach to him on this excellent subject, was so taken, that before the sermon or discourse was at an end, being holily impatient at any longer delay, he says to Philip, *Here is water, what hinders me to be baptized?* I say again, Would to God we were all in such a frame, and that this were the fruit of such a doctrine as this to many of you, nay to all of you!

Use 1. Wonder, believers, at the exactness and infiniteness of the grace of God, and at the heart-affecting and soul-ravishing love of the Mediator! at grace in God, that spared the debtor, and exacted payment from the Cautioner, the Son of his love! Act love in the Mediator, that paid so much, and so willingly and cheerfully. If any subject of thoughts be pertinent for us, while we are about to celebrate the sacrament of the Lord's supper, certainly this were pertinent concerning a crucified Christ, instating himself in our room, to pay our debt, and doing this of his own accord, without the solicitation or interposing of any creature, and doing it, withal, so frankly and cheerfully. Was ever the like of this love heard tell of, for One, and more especially for such a One, to suffer so much, and so cheerfully, unrequired? We would have you confirmed in the faith of this great and sweet truth, that he had never better will, nay, never so good will to eat his dinner, than he had to suffer, and satisfy justice for you, tho' at a dear rate; he says, John iv. *It was his meat to do the Father's will that sent him, and to finish his work.* Have ye suitable thoughts of his love, when ye read the gospel? Have ye in the word seen him standing before Pilate in your room, not answering when he is accused, and Pilate marvelling at his silence? and did Pilate marvel, knowing, and being convinced of his innocency? and have ye never marvelled, or marvelled but very little? Sure, your little marvelling at his silence, is the more sadly marvellous, that the cause of his silence, when he was charged with your iniquities, with such and such a piece of your iniquities, with such a piece of your miscarriage, with such a vain and roving heart, with such a wanton look, with such a profane or idle word of yours, with the horrid sin of your having so abused, slighted and neglected him, &c. That the cause, I say, of his silence at such a terrible accusation and charge, and not vindicating of himself, or saying, These faults, miscarriages, and transgressions, are not mine, as he might have done, was pure love to you; O is not this strange, and yet most true! wonder then more at it.

Use 2. Here is strong consolation to believers, and wonderful wisdom in the rise and convoy of it, in uniting justice and love; out of which the consolation springs: Justice exacting upon, and distressing the Son of God, and he satisfying justice so fully, that, tho' all the elect had satisfied eternally in hell, it had not been made to shine so splendidly and gloriously: justice also on the Mediator's side, in yielding and giving satisfaction, tho' it should oppress and break soul and body: And yet love, both on the Father's and Mediator's side; on the Father's side, love, in finding out this way of satisfaction to his own justice, when there was no cure, but by the wounding of his own Son; and yet he was content rather to wound him, than that the elect should suffer, and be wounded eternally: Love on the Mediator's side, who willingly yields, and undergoes their debt, and will not hide his face from shame and spitting. What may not the believer expect from God, when he spared not his own Son for him? and what may he expect from Christ, who spared not himself for his sake? and who is that good Shepherd, that laid down his life for the sheep, and held his tongue, and quarrelled not with those that smote him; will he quarrel with a poor sinner coming to him, and pleading for the benefit of satisfaction? no certainly; but as the word is, Zeph. iii. 17. *He will rest in his love,* or as the word signifies, *He will be silent or dumb in his love;* he will not upbraid thee, nor cast up thy former miscarriages; he will not say reproachfully to thee, Where was thou so long playing the prodigal? He is better content with thy recovery, than ever he was discontent or ill pleased with all the wrong thou didst unto him.

Use 3. This word of doctrine lays down the ground whereupon a sinner, sensible of sin, may build his expectation of peace with God: The transaction, concluded and agreed upon, is the ground of his coming; and the exacting of the price, according to the transaction, is the ground of his expectation of the benefits of Christ's purchase: And there is justice for it, as the Apostle intimates, Rom. viii. 34, 35. *Who shall lay any thing to the charge of God's elect? It is God that justifieth, who is he that condemneth? It is Christ that died, yea rather that is risen again,* &c. And upon this follows the believing soul's triumph. O but there is much need to be throughly acquainted with the mutual relations that are betwixt Christ and the believing sinner, with the ground of their approaching to him, and with the good they are to expect through him!

Use 4. This word is made use of 1 Pet. ii. 21. to give us a notable and none-such pattern of patience; *Christ also suffered for us, leaving us an example, that we should follow his steps*. He did bear all wrongs patiently, and packed them up quietly (to say so) and *opened not his mouth*: He could have told Pilate and Caiaphas what they were, but spoke not a word but one to the high priest, notwithstanding all his provoking carriage, and a very meek one too. *If I have spoken evil, bear witness of the evil; and if well, why smitest thou me?* Amongst other copies then that Christ hath casten, take this for one, make him a copy and pattern of patience: It is to be regreted, that folks are so unlike to Christ in this respect; they think it a disdainful thing to pack up a wrong, and they will scorn and tush at it: But, what if Jesus Christ had been of that temper and disposition? (if it be fit to make such a supposition) ye had been without a Redeemer, and had perished for ever. When he calls you to be followers of him, and to suffer patiently, as he did, tho' most unjustly, as to men; for you to think or say that ye scorn it, and that ye are not so mean-spirited, what is it else, but to think, and to say on the matter, that the blessed Jesus, in his patient and silent carriage under all the injuries that he suffered very unjustly from men, shewed himself to be of a low and base spirit, and that ye disdain to follow his way? O intolerable, saucy, and proudly blasphemous reflection! The many contests, the many high resentments of wrongs, the great grudging, fretting and foaming at them that there are in Christians, say plainly, that there is little of the meek and patient Spirit of Christ in, and amongst us; and that many of us *know not what spirit we are of.*

SERMON XXIX.

Isaiah liii. 8, *He was taken from prison, and from judgment; and who shall declare his generation? For he was cut off out of the land of the living, for the transgression of my people was he stricken.*

WE need not tell you of whom the Prophet is speaking here; every verse, and every word almost, do make it manifest, that he speaks of Christ the Saviour; and indeed it can be applied to none other. It is the same verse, Acts viii. 24. from which Philip proceeds to preach Christ to the Eunuch. The Prophet hath been largely holding forth Christ's sufferings in the former verse, and we conceive he takes a turn to speak of Christ's exaltation and out-gate from these sufferings: It is true (as if he had said) *He was brought to prison and judgment;* he was indeed straitned and pinched, and laid very low: But prison and judgment did not keep him; *He was taken*, or, as the word is, *He was lifted up,* from both. And, for as despicable as he was in man's eyes, yet he was not so in himself; for *who shall declare his generation?* There is a wonderfulness in him who suffered, that cannot be be reached, but muſt be left with admiration; and a wonderful glory whereunto he was after his humiliation exalted: And there is a reaſon of this given, for preventing of offence: If any ſhould ſay, How then could he ſuffer, and be brought ſo low in ſuffering, if he was ſo glorious a Perſon? He anſwers, It is true, that *he was cut off out of the land of the living*, but for no offence in himſelf, but for the tranſgreſſion of God's elect, *was he ſtricken*, or the word is, *the ſtroke was upon him*. Yea, this (we conceive) is given as a reaſon of his exaltation; becauſe in the loweſt ſteps of his humiliation, he condeſcended to fulfil his engagement with the Father, in ſatisfying juſtice for the ſins of the elect, according to that of John x. 17. *Therefore doth my Father love me, becauſe I lay down my life, that I might take it again*: Becauſe, according to his engagement, he ſuffered for the ſins of his elect people, therefore he could not but have a comfortable and glorious out-gate.

There are theſe three things in the words, 1. Somewhat aſſerted concerning Chriſt Jeſus, *He was taken from priſon and from judgment*. 2. Something hinted at, which cannot be expreſſed, *Who ſhall declare his generation?* 3. There is a reaſon given in reference to both, *For he was cut off*, &c. which we ſhall expound when we come to it.

For the firſt, *He was taken from priſon and from judgment*: We conceive theſe words look both to his humiliation, and to his out-gate from it; the one being clearly ſuppoſed, that he was in priſon or ſtraits, and brought to judgment; and the other being expreſſed, that he was brought from priſon and from judgment. 1. *Priſon*, here, may be taken generally for any ſtrait, pinch or preſſure that one may be brought into; which we conceive both the words, and the Prophet's ſcope will clear; Chriſt never having been properly in priſon, at leaſt for any conſiderable time, but ſtraitned and pinched: And he was taken from that, being in his humiliation, and in his ſufferings, in the room of the elect, purſued by the law and juſtice of God. 2. *Judgment* is taken paſſively, for judgments paſt on him: and it looks not only to the procedure of Pilate, of the chief prieſt, and of the Scribes and Phariſees, but to a judicial proceſs, which the juſtice of God led againſt him; in which reſpect, he anſwered (as the words after will clear) for the ſins of God's people. The word, *He was taken*, ſometimes ſignifies to deliver, as a captive is delivered, when he is taken from him that took him captive; as it is, Iſa. xlix. 24. *Shall the prey be taken from the mighty, or the lawful captive delivered?* To which the Lord anſwers, *It, or he ſhall be taken*.

So then, the ſcope and meaning of the words is, that the Prophet ſubjoins a narration of Chriſt's exaltation upon the back of his humiliation, as it is uſual in the ſcripture to put theſe together, and in this order, as namely, Phil. ii. 8, 9. *He humbled himſelf, and became obedient unto death, even the the death of the croſs: Wherefore God hath highly exalted him, and given him a name*, &c. He was exceedingly ſtraitned and pinched for the elect's ſins; but death had no dominion over him, he had a glorious out-gate; he was taken out, and ſet free from the priſon, or ſtraits wherein he was held, and from theſe judgments that paſt upon him. The reaſon of the expoſition is drawn from the plain meaning of the words, which muſt run thus, *He was taken from judgment*, the very ſame which is in the following expreſſion, *He was cut off out of the land of the living*: That being the ordinary ſignification of the prepoſition *from*, the meaning muſt be this, that he was taken out of the condition wherein he was; it agrees alſo beſt with the ſcope of the very next words, *Who ſhall declare his generation?* wherein he propoſeth an admirable aggravation of this delivery.

The 2d thing hath a connexion with the former, and therefore take a word or two for clearing of it. What to underſtand by *generation*, here, is ſomewhat difficult to determine, the word in the original having ſeveral meanings; yet generally it looks to one or two, as it is applied to Chriſt, (1.) Either to the time paſt, and ſo is uſed by many, to expreſs and hold forth Chriſt's Godhead: and ſo the meaning is, Though he was brought very low, yet he was, and is the eternal Son of God. Or, (2.) (as commonly it is taken) It looks to the time to come; and ſo the meaning is, Who ſhall declare his duration, or continuance? *Generation* is often taken thus in ſcripture for the continuance of an age, and of one age following another ſucceſſively; as Joſhua xxii. *This altar ſhall be a witneſs to the generations to come*: ſo then, the meaning is, he was once low, but God exalted him, and brought him thorow; and who ſhall declare this duration, or continuance of his exaltation? As it is, Phil. ii. 8, 9. *He humbled himſelf*, &c. *therefore God hath highly exalted him*; as his humiliation was ſo low, ſo his exaltation was ineffable, it cannot be declared, nor adequately conceived, the continuance of it being for ever. There is no inconſiſtency betwixt theſe two expoſitions; his duration or continuance after his ſufferings, neceſſarily preſuppoſing his Godhead, brought in here, partly to ſhew the wonderfulneſs

derfulness of his suffering, it being God that suffered, for the Man that suffered was God; partly to shew Christ's glory, who, notwithstanding of his suffering, was brought thorow, and gloriously exalted: and these reasons make it evident, 1. Whatever these words, *Who shall declare his generation?* do signify, certainly it is something that can be spoken of no other, but of Christ, and that agrees to him so, as it agrees to no other. Now, if we look simply to the *eternity* of his duration or continuance, that agrees to all the elect, and well agrees to all men at the resurrection: Therefore the prophet must look here to his continuance and duration as he is God. 2. Because, *Who shall declare his generation?* is brought in here, to shew the ineffableness of it, and so to make his sufferings the more wonderful; it was he who suffered, whose continuance cannot be declared. 3. It is such a continuance, as is brought in to shew a reason why death could not have dominion over him, nor keep him; according to that, Rom. i. 4. *He was declared to be the Son of God with power, according to the Spirit of holiness, by his resurrection from the dead:* And the reason subjoined to this will some way clear it; for *he was cut off out of the land of the living, for the transgression of my people was he stricken:* Thereby insinuating, that because of the great work which he had to do, there behoved to be some singularness in the Person that had the work in hand, who, notwithstanding of the greatness and difficultness of it, came thorow, and was hereby exalted. However it be, the Prophet's scope being to set out Christ's humiliation and exaltation, his humiliation before, and his exaltation after, which is, as we said, ordinary in scripture; we conceive the meaning we have given is safe, and agreeable to the Prophet's scope.

We may observe three things from the first part of the words, *First*, " That our Lord Jesus Christ " in his performing the work of redemption, was " exceedingly straitned or pinched, or *held in*, as " the word is elsewhere rendered, bound up and " and hemmed in, as men are who are in prison:" And, by these straitnings, we mean not only such as he was brought into by men, (whereof we spoke before) but especially those that were more inward; and these being amongst the last steps of his humiliation, more immediately preceding his exaltation, and spoken of as most wonderful, we conceive they look to these pressures that were upon his spirit: And we shall instance several places of scripture, that serve to hold it out; the first is that of John xii. 27, 28. *Now is my soul troubled, and what shall I say? Father, save me from this hour.* Here our blessed Lord is troubled in spirit, and so pinched and hedged in as in a prison, that he is holily nonplussed what to say. The 2d scripture is Matt. xxvi. 38. *My soul is exceeding sorrowful even unto death,* which is like the expressions used by the Apostle, 2 Cor. i. 8. *We were pressed above measure, above strength, in so much as we despaired of life, and we had the sentence of death in ourselves;* there was no out-gate obvious to human sense and uptaking: So is it here; wherein we are not only to consider his soul-vexation, but that his soul-vexation was very great, extremely pinching, vexing, and in a manner imprisoning to him. The 3d scripture is Luke xxii. 24. *He being in an agony, prayed more earnestly, and his sweat was as if it were great drops of blood falling down to the ground;* there was such a striving, wrestling and conflicting, not with man without him, but with inward pressures on his spirit, that he is like one in a barrace, or cock-pit, or engaged in a duel with a mighty combatant, sore put to it, very far beyond ought that we can conceive of; so that *he swate great drops of blood,* and says, *Father, if thou be willing, remove this cup from me; nevertheless not my will, but thine be done:* it is in Mathew, *if it be possible,* and thereafter, *if it be not possible;* which says, there was no winning out of the grips of the law and justice, till that they were fully satisfied; and those dreadful words uttered by him on the cross, *My God, my God, why hast thou forsaken me?* hold out, that from the sinless human nature of Christ, the comfortable and joyful influence of the Godhead for a time was in a great measure suspended, (tho' the sustaining power thereof was exercised mightily on him) so that he looks on himself some way as forsaken, and left in the hand of the curse.

To clear this a little, we would consider these pressures that were upon our Lord's spirit, 1. In respect of their *cause.* 2. In respect of their *effects.*

1*st,* In respect of their cause. There is upon the one side his undertaking for the elect as their Surety, and God's justice pursuing and holding him in on the other side: So that he cannot decline being sisted at the bar of justice, because, as it is verse 6th, the sins of all the elect met upon him; and he having, as it is verse 7th, the bitter cup in his hand, which by his engagement he was obliged to drink, he stands there by the decree of God and by the covenant of redemption, tying him to satisfy; and being pursued by wrath and justice, the words come out, *Father, if it be possible, let this cup depart from me; yet not my will, but thine be done;* his

engage-

engagement hemming him in, and wrath pursuing him, he stands betwixt these two as a prisoner: and upon these two, *the Lord laid on him the iniquity of us all*, and *he was exacted upon, and answered for them;* follows well the third, *that he was put in prison;* for in these verses, the steps of our Lord's humiliation are followed out in a legal way, as before the bar of God's tribunal.

2*dly*, This being our Lord's posture, we shall consider the *effects* of this pressure of spirit, which we may draw to these *four* heads. 1. He was under the sense of great soul-pain, sorrow and trouble; for the cup of the wrath of God being bitter, which he was to drink, it could not but deeply sting his holy human nature, which was the procuring cause of his *agony*, and that which made his soul sorrowful, and brought out the *bloody sweat*. 2. Beside his grief and pain, there was a holy horror: And, considering the Party that he had to do with, it was impossible it could be otherwise; impossible for a finite, tho' a sinless Creature, to look on an angry God, and on wrath poured forth into the cup, which it must needs drink, and not have a horror at it; it were not becoming the sinless human nature of our blessed Lord, not to be affected with a holy and sinless horror at that most bitter cup, which brought out that sad cry, *Father, let this cup depart from me*; which did not proceed from any dislike he had to fulfil his engagement, or from any rewing or unsuitable resentment that he had so engaged himself, but from an apprehended sinless disproportionableness (to speak so) in his finite sinless human Nature, to encounter with the wrath of his Father; to which tho' he most willingly yielded, yet in itself it was dreadful. 3. There was a pinching and straitning of holy fear, as if there had been in him a sinless dispute or debate, What will become of this? Can a Man win through this? (though he was God as well as Man) how will this be gotten born? This looks as if death would get the victory; thus it is said, Heb. v. 7. *In the days of his flesh he offered up strong cries and supplications, with tears, and was heard in that which he feared:* He put up strong cries to be delivered, not from dying, but from the power of death; and was heard in that which he feared, to shew a holy care to prevent death, could that have been, and a sinless fear of it, lest it should swallow him up. 4. There was a pinching and straitning, from love to the Father, and to the doing of his will: and from love to the elect, and to their salvation, which pushed him forward to perform and fulfil his engagement; accordingly, Luke xii. 50. he says, *I have a baptism to be baptized with, and how am I straitned till it be ac-complished?* and hence it was that these words were uttered by him, *Father, not my will, but thine be done;* and therefore though he had power to command twelve legions of angels for his relief, yet, to speak so, love so binds his hands, that he will not use his power for his own liberation. But to guard this doctrine from mistakes, take a *fourfold* advertisement concerning this inward soul-pinching, which will help to clear somewhat of his soul-suffering that followeth. And, (1. Think not that there was any sinful or unsuitable confusion or perturbation of mind in our Lord, such as useth to be in us, there being no dreg of corruption in his mind to jumble or discompose his holy human Nature. (2.) Beware of thinking that there was any fretting or anxiety in him, or any discontentedness with the bargain: His expressions shew forth the contrary; for (saith he) *I could command twelve legions of angels*, yet he would not do it. (3.) Think not that there was any jealousy in him of the Father's love: though there was a suspension of the comfortable and joyful sense of it, yet there was not the least loosing of the faith of it, as is clear by his doubling of these words, *My God, my God*, when in his saddest pinch he cried out as being forsaken. (4.) Ye would not look on this, as holding out any distrust as to the event : *I have* (saith he) *power to lay down my life, and I have power to take it up again; and I will rise again the third day*. He knew that the covenant of redemption betwixt the Father and him stood firm and sure; but it is the consideration of God's now coming as his Party to exact the elect's debt of him, and his standing at the bar to answer for it, which puts him in this agony; and tho' considering Christ as a Man personally united to the Godhead (whereby he was keeped from sinking) he had no distrust to be carried thorow; yet considering him as a Man suffering, and that (to speak with reverence in such a divine subject) there was an eclipse of that sensible joy that proceeded from the two natures together, it is not possible to conceive of Christ in this posture, but wrath and anger behoved to be some way dreadful or terrible to him.

The *Uses* are 1*st*, To evidence the truth of what our Lord suffered, and how severely he was pinched and straitned; it was not the Scribes and Pharisees pursuing him, nor the soldiers buffetting and mocking him, and carrying him to the high priest's hall, and from Pilate to Herod, and back again, that so much troubled him; but there was a higher hand that he had to look to, and a Judge and court, to which he was now answering, that was very far above theirs.

And therefore, as a 2d. *Use* of the doctrine, Think it not such a light thing (as many do) to satisfy justice, or to give God a ransom for souls; ye see how it pinched the Cautioner, and put him as in a prison. Unspeakably deceived are they, who think that two or three formal words will make their peace with God, and that they will slip into heaven so: Be not carried away with this delusion; but consider seriously what will become of you, if ye be put to answer for your own debt, when he handled the Cautioner, his own Son, so roughly; ye that will sleep on, and scorn to let any word pick at you, or prick you, the justice of God shall prick you, and put you to straits, out of which ye will not be able to extricate yourselves; and he shall appear like everlasting burning, when the great day of his wrath comes, and when it shall be said by you, *Who can stand before it,* or abide it? It were good that ye, who are most atheistical, and who with a sort of triumph and gallantry will needs destroy yourselves, would lay this to heart, and remember that the day comes, when ye will be brought to this bar; and gravely consider, what an hell this will be, to have the desperateness of the out-gate sealed up in your consciences, and these evidences of God's hatred and these aggravations that our Lord's holy nature could not admit of, in your bosom: When wrath meets with corruption, and corruption with wrath, and when these mingle, how dreadful will your case be!

3*dly*, Let believers see here what ye are obliged to Christ; consider what he hath paid, and what the satisfaction of justice for you cost him. Folks are ready to think, that it was an easy thing to satisfy justice, and *to drink of the brook by the way;* but if sinners were sensible of challenges for sin, and if they had the arrows of the Almighty, drinking up their spirits, they would think otherwise, of Christ's drinking out the cup of wrath for them, not leaving so much as one drop of it: It is but the shorings or threatnings, with some drops of it, that any of you meet with in your soul exercises: O! believing sinners, are ye not then eternally obliged to Christ, who drunk out this wrathful cup for you?

4*thly*, There is notable consolation here to poor souls, that would fain make use of Christ. As, 1. That Christ hath stepped thorow this deep ford, or rather sea before them; and if the cup come in their hand, it is empty: Freedom from the wrath of God is a great consolation, and yet it is the consolation of them that are fled unto him for refuge. 2. It is comfortable to them, in their comparatively petty straits and difficulties, when they wot not what to do, when the law seizeth, and justice pursueth, and when the conscience challengeth; to consider that Christ was a Prisoner before them: Though he had no challenge for his own debt, yet he was challenged for ours, that he might be a compassionate high Priest, being made like to us, but without sin. Justice pursued him, the law arrested him, wrath seized on him; so that, when we are set upon by these, he will be tender of us, for *he knows our frame,* and that we cannot bear much: And therefore, on this ground, a believing sinner may go with boldness to the throne of grace, because Christ the Cautioner, who hath paid his debt, is there. It is a shame for believing sinners, to walk so heartlesly, even under these things that are terrible, as if Christ had not gone thorow them before them, and for them. 3. There is consolation here, when they are under any pinching cross and difficulty; as there is also ground for patient and pleasant bearing of it, because it was another sort of prison that Christ was put in for them. Ye may, I grant, lament over the long want of sensible presence, it being kindly to the believer to miss it, and to long for it; but ye should not be heartless under the want of it, nor complain, as the Lord's people do *lament; Is there any sorrow like unto my sorrow?* but submissively and contentedly bear it without fretting, seeing our Lord bare so much for you.

5*thly*, There is here a notable encouragement to believe, and a notable ground for the believer to expect freedom from sin, and from the pinching straits that it deserveth, because Christ paid dear for it: Wherefore was all this pinching, but to pay believers debt? But when we come to speak of his out-gate, it will clear this more.

Secondly, While it is said, That *he was brought from judgment,* which supposes and implies, that he was once at, or under judgement, even the judgment of God, who is his great party all along; *He laid on him the iniquity of us all;* and verse 10. *It pleased the Lord to bruise him;* He was the Creditor that caused take and arrest him: *Observe,* ' That ' in all the soul-vexation, in all the pinching pres- ' sure of spirit that our Lord sustained, he was ' standing judicially before the bar of God, and ' was judicially proceeded against as the elect's ' cautioner and surety.' There was no access to bring Christ to judgment, had he not engaged to be surety, and had not God laid on him our iniquities; for it was for no debt that he was owing himself, but for what by his engagement as the elect's surety he came under, and was made liable to.

That

That which I mean by his being brought to judgement, is not only that he suffered, and was occasionally condemned by a court of men, or by a human judicatory, which was rather like a tumultuary meeting, or a company of men in an uproar, than indeed a court; but whatever was before men, there was a legal and judicial procedure before God: For clearing whereof ye would consider, 1. The account whereon he suffered, and was brought before God's court of judgment, to speak so: It was not for any thing that the Scribes or Pharisees or Pilate had to lay to his charge; it was envy in them, the former at least, that stirred them in what they did: But the next words tell us what it was, *for the transgression of my people was he stricken;* the the priests and people had no mind of this, but this was indeed the ground of his judicial challenge and arraignment before God: The elect were in their sins, and he by the covenant of redemption stood liable for their debt, because he had undertaken for them as their cautioner and surety. 2. Consider who was his great party in his sufferings: It was not Pilate nor the Jews, he cared not so much for them; but it is God, and therefore he cries, *My God, my God, why hast thou forsaken me?* and therefore he makes his address to God, *Father, if it be possible, let this cup pass from me:* He cared not for answering them, but looks to a higher hand, and upon himself as standing before another tribunal; therefore it is said, verse 10. *yet it pleased the Lord to bruise him;* he looked not to Pilate, but to the Lord pursuing him. 3. Consider our Lord's submission to his being brought to judgment, not only nor chiefly before men, but before God; therefore says he, John xii. 48. *Father, save me from this hour, but for this cause came I to this hour;* Come then, Father, and let us count: He looks not only to the present dispensation but also to the ground whence it came, and to the end that God had in it: *for this cause came I to this hour,* even to have my soul troubled, and to be put to answer for the debt of my elect people according to my engagement: *Lo, I come* (saith he in that often cited xl. Psalm) *in the volume of thy book it is written of me, I delight to do thy will.* Consider, 4. The effects of his bringing to judgment: A sentence passes, 1 Tim. iii. ult. *Great is the mystery of godliness, God manifested in the flesh, justified in the spirit.* not before Pilate, but in God's court, having satisfied for the elects debt according to his undertaking, he gets an absolvitor, which reaches not only to himself, but to all them whose persons he sustained, as is clear, 2 Cor. v. ult. *He was made sin for*

us who knew no sin, that we might be made the righteousness of God in him: And the elects obtaining eternal redemption and absolution by his death, with the accruing of his satisfaction to their justification, clears that he stood there judicially at the bar of God, in their name, to answer for them. And there are *three* steps of this his judicial answer, (1.) He gets the libel of the elects debt put in his hand; Though *there was no guile in his mouth, yet it pleased the Lord to bruise him; he laid on him the iniquity of us all; and for the iniquity of my people was he stricken.* These are the persons that he undertook for, and for their debt he answers: The verity of the fact is clear, for they are under guilt; the law's claim is clear, for it is broken, and upon this the libel is put in his hand; hence it is said, *He died for us, he was made sin for us, and he died for our sins.* (2.) As the libel is put in his hand, so a sentence passes accordingly; he is found liable to the elects debt, and must answer for it, as the former word is, *It was exacted on him,* and 2 Cor. v. ult. *He was made sin for us,* and Gal. iii. 13. *He was made a curse for us,* that is, by the sentence of justice he is decerned to to bear the curse. (3.) The sentence is executed as it was past; the cup is put in his hand, and not only is he decerned and doomed to the curse, but actually he is made a curse, and all this as judicially sustaining the persons of the elect, and as their Cautioner and Surety.

Here we have some sweet and profitable *Uses.*
1. See here and take up the way of redemption contrived, so as it runs on mercy and justice, mercy to the elect, and justice to the Cautioner, their debt being fully exacted of him.

2. It learns us how to establish our faith, and also gives us a ground of believing. To make it distinct; justice behoved to be satisfied, without which no mercy could be shewed to the sinner; and God hath laid down the way by the Cautioner's interposing: Even as it is among men, the cautioner's being imprisoned, and satisfying, is the debitor's liberation; and as God hath condescended to deal with us by way of covenant, so he condescended in the covenant of redemption to proceed legally and judicially with Christ, that we might have the clearer way to make application of it.

3. Are there any here that look for redemption thorow Christ, and hope that their sins were in the libel given to him? O how warming would this be to your hearts! and how should it make them to melt in love and godly sorrow, to behold Christ standing at justice bar, and that for you! O what

an aspect would his sufferings have on us, if we were clear about our interest in him, and could hear him, in our name saying, *Father, here am I; if thou take me, let these go; thy will be done, for this cause came I here,* to answer for my peoples debt, to take with the challenges given in against them, and to undergo thy sentence for them? Then says justice, Thou must pay their debt; Content, says he, *here am I;* and so *he gives his back to the smiter, and his cheeks to them that plucked off the hair, and hid not his face from shame and spitting.* If we were clear that our share was there, and that our iniquities came in among the rest to make up the libel, and if we could aright discern him so pinched and straitned in satisfying for us, would we not think ourselves eternally obliged to him, to hate sin, and to *glorify him in our bodies and spirits which are his?* as it is, 1 Cor. vi. ult. If indeed ye be Christ's (as ye are all ready to profess yourselves to be) he pays dear for you; and if so, will not this ly upon you as a just debt to him, to glorify him in your bodies, and in your spirits? for both in body and spirit he paid for you.

It is a notable ground of consolation to believers against despondency and fear to appear before the throne of God; because our Lord Jesus Christ hath been before us, and in our name, and hath answered for us to the full, and hath satisfied all that justice could crave of us. What wakens terror at death, and makes the thoughts of Christ's appearing to be dreadful, but our looking on our appearing at the bar of God? but it is a comfort against it, that Christ our Cautioner was brought to prison and to judgment, and was also brought from both; yea, which is more, and without which the consolation is but halfed, he was brought to both for us, and he was also brought from both as our surety for all them that betake themselves by faith to him: he was carried to prison and to judgment as cautioner for the elect, and he was pursued as their cautioner, and therefore his payment of the debt as cautioner must be accepted in name of them for whom he paid the debt. Our Lord Jesus not only died and was laid in the grave, but he went further in (to speak so) he was even at the bar of justice, libelled, exacted upon, and sentenced, and the sentence executed upon him; else wo had been unto us: on this ground is that triumph, Rom. viii. " Who " shall lay any thing to the charge of God's elect ? " it is God that justifies : who shall condemn ? it " is Christ that died, yea rather who is risen again, " &c." and it is said, Rom. vii. " That we are de- " livered from the law, being dead to that where- " in we were held." The law had us in prison, and a lock on the door, and had us under irons; but our Lord came, and (as Sampson did in another case) carried the port and bars to the hill-top, " He " spoiled principalities and powers, and triumphed " openly over them on the cross ;" so that now " the prince of this world is judged; These are the " true and faithful sayings of God : We have thro' " Christ access, and may with boldness come to the " throne of grace, having him an high priest, who " is touched with the feeling of our infirmities, and " was in all things tempted like as we are." He knew not only what it was to be hungry and thirsty and weary, to be pained, and to die; but what it was to come before the terrible tribunal of God, and to be libelled for sin, tho' not for his own sin, and what it was to be sentenced and to meet with wrath; which gives to sinners a safe and refreshful shelter under him, as under the shadow of a great rock in a weary land. This is the great design of the gospel, to make proffer of the benefit of these sufferings to you, and to pray you in Christ's stead to be reconciled to God : Now God himself persuade you to it.

S E R M O N XXX.

Isaiah liii. 8. *He was taken from prison, and from judgment; and who shall declare his generation? For he was cut off out of the land of the living, for the transgression of my people was he stricken.*

EVery step of Christ's way to sinners, and every word whereby it is exprest, is wonderful; and therefore it is no marvel that the prophet doth by way of admiration cast in this word, *And who shall declare his generation?* We shew you, that we conceive these words to be these that express the prophet's turning of himself from Christ's humiliation to his exaltation : he hath insisted long in setting out his wonderful abasement, exinanition, and humiliation, which these words import, *he was brought from prison and from judgment* ; which look not only to his external imprisonment, to his coming to judgment before men, but also, and mainly and principally, to the pinches and straits he was brought into, and his arraignment before God's tribunal, and so the cause of his suffering, to wit, *for the transgression of his people,* as the words following hold out ; which was not the cause of his censure

before

before men, but the procuring cause of what he met with from, and before God.

But tho' he was brought to prison and to judgment, to death and to the grave, yet they did not, they could not detain him: *He was taken*, or, as the word signifies, he was lifted up *from prison and from judgment*, being the same word that followeth, *He was cut off out of the land of the living*; which supposes a turn and change from his humiliation to his exaltation: And these words, *Who shall declare his generation?* set out the unconceivable and unexpressible glory that Christ is exalted unto; so Acts viii. 33, 35. where these words are cited, it is said *In his humiliation his judgment was taken away*; that is, in his lowest step of his humiliation, his judgment, or that to which he was adjudged, was taken from him, and he was declared free. However, since in these words our Lord's humiliation is implied, and his exaltation expressed as following on it, we think it safest to understand it so. The words put together hold out the high degree of Christ's glorious exaltation, so as his generation cannot be declared; *He was taken from prison and from judgment*, and gloriously exalted in another manner, and to another degree of glory, than either angels or believers are, or are capable to be: For he that is exalted is God, whose generation cannot be declared; *Death having no more dominion over him*, and he *having the keys of hell and of death*. In a word, we take this, *Who shall declare his generation?* most immediately to relate to Christ's exaltation as Mediator, and to the glory wherewith he was invested, and to the dominion that he hath over all creatures: yet, considering that the prophet's scope is to set out this as wonderful, and considering that the first step of his exaltation is his resurrection, *whereby* (as the apostle speaks, Rom. i. 4.) *he was declared to be the Son of God with power*: his resurrection being singular in this respect, that he arose by his own power, and considering that, Acts vii. 35. Philip began to preach to the Eunuch Jesus Christ as the object of faith; we think it reasonable to conceive, that he preached Christ to be God, from this text, so that the Eunuch might have a solid foundation for his faith. And the subserving the scope, which is to set out the wonderfulness of Christ's love to elect sinners, who being God, yet condescended to come this low for saving of them; We may take in his Godhead mediately, from which as the former steps of his humiliation received worth and efficacy, so he was thereby sustained and born up under all these sufferings, whereby his people are saved.

From the *first* and *second* expressions put together, we shall draw *three doctrines* relating to three main articles of faith.

The *1st* whereof is this, "That our Lord had "an outgate from, and victory over, the lowest "and most pinching pieces of his humiliation and "suffering.' So that, tho' he was at prison and judgment, yet he was lift up from both, and had a glorious outgate: This takes in three things, which the same grounds will confirm, 1. That in his lowest estate and steps of humiliation, he was sustained, and carried thorow, so that all the assaults which he was put to endure and encounter with from all his enemies, wicked men and devils, did not overcome him. 2. That as he in himself was born thorow and sustained; so, in respect of God's bar at which he was arraigned, he was absolved and set free; he so came thorow by paying of the debt, that he had an absolvitor, as it is, 1 Tim. iii. *ult*. *Great is the mystery of godliness. God was manifest in the flesh, justified in the Spirit.* Our blessed Lord Jesus, being sustained by the power of his Godhead, was carried thorow in his sufferings, paid the elect's debt, and receives the sentence of absolution; even as a person (to speak with reverence in such a subject) having paid the debt for which he was imprisoned, is absolved and set free. 3. It takes in our Lord's actual delivery, he not only received the sentence of absolution, but was actually set free: so that as he was pleased to put himself in prison and in straits for us; so he was brought from every step of his humiliation, *from prison and from judgment*, from death and from the grave; *he nailed the hand writing which was against us to his cross*, as the Apostle saith, Col. ii. 14, 15. *And having spoiled principalities and powers, he made a shew of them openly, triumphing over them in it*; and as it is, 1 Cor. xv. at the close, he took the sting from death, disarmed it, and trod upon it: And there was necessity for this, even such necessity, that it was impossible it could be otherwise, as we have it, Acts ii. 24. *It was not possible that he could be holden of death*. This will be clear, if we consider these things. (1.) The Person that suffered: He was not an ordinary, nay, nor a meer Man, but God-Man, as is clear, Acts ii. 27. cited out of Psal. xvi. where it is said, *Thou wilt not leave my soul in hell, neither wilt thou suffer thy holy One to see corruption*. (2.) The end of Christ sufferings, which was to satisfy for the debt of his people: There having been no reckoning on his own score or account, he being still in God's favour, and his holy One in whom

whom his soul delighted all along his sufferings; his sufferings being for the sins of his elect, and he being to make application of his satisfaction, and of the purchase made thereby, to the elect, for whom he suffered and purchased these things, by his intercession; there was a necessity that he should come thorow; otherwise he should not have been a perfect and a compleat Saviour, *able to save to the uttermost those that come unto God by him,* as the Apostle speaks, Heb. vii. 25. *Such an high Priest became us, who is holy, harmless, undefiled, separate from sinners, and made higher than the heavens.* 3. It is clear also, if we consider the nature of the covenant, and of the promises made to him therein, upon his engaging and undertaking for the elect; as particularly verse 10th of this chapter, *He shall see his seed, and prolong his days,* his duration shall be for ever; *The Pleasure of the Lord shall prosper in his hand; and I will divide him a portion with the great, and he shall divide the spoil with the strong;* Our Lord's exaltation and victory over death being on the Lord's side conditioned to him the Mediator, as well as he engaged to suffer; hence it is said, Psal. cx. *He shall drink of the brook in the way, therefore shall he lift up the head.*

The *Uses* are *two,* The 1*st* whereof serves for clearing and confirming our faith in a fundamental article of Christianity, without which it were needless for us to preach, and needless for you to hear or believe; and that is, That our Lord Jesus suffered, and also got the victory over suffering; that *he was raised from the dead, and declared to be the Son of God with power;* intimating, that justice had gotten full satisfaction: in evidence and testimony whereof, he was declared free, which is a main thing that believers have to believe; even that we have an exalted Christ, a raised-up Saviour, who could not be detained by all the elect's guilt in prison. 2. It serves to be matter of strong consolation; it puts life in all Christ's offices and qualifications, and in all the promises made to believers; to wit, that our Lord Jesus is a living Christ, *over whom death had no dominion,* and he overcame it, *now to die no more;* So that, as it is, Heb vii. 25. *He is able to save to the uttermost those that come unto God by him, seeing he ever liveth to make intercession for them:* There is nothing that a soul needs or can desire, but it is to be had in him. And if we would look to particular instances, much consolation will arise from this ground; For, (1.) Hath a believing sinner to do with challenges at the bar of justice, is it not unspeakable consolation that their debt is paid? hence it is said Rom. viii. 33. *Who shall lay any thing to the charge of God's elect? It is God that justifies; who shall condemn? It is Christ that died, yea rather that is risen again.* It is that which gives proof of compleat payment of the elect's debt, and defiance to any challenges and accusations to come against the believer to his prejudice; because Christ hath not only died, but is also risen; justice being well pleased with his satisfaction, he is let out of the prison. (2.) If the believer hath to do with corruption, with the devil and with many enemies, is it not strong consolation that our Lord is risen and up, *that the Prince of this world is judged,* that Satan is troden under foot, and that *he shall and must reign till all his enemies be made his footstool:* (3.) Our Lord's resurrection hath a twofold further consolation with it to believers, 1. It serves to be a ground for the exercising of faith on him, that as he is risen, so (Rom. vi.) may we expect that being *spiritually* dead with him to sin, we shall be *with him raised up to newness of life.* 2. It is a pledge of believers exaltation and compleat victory over death and the grave, and over all enemies; for Christ being raised as the common Head of all believers who are his members, they by vertue of his resurrection, and by that same efficacy, shall be raised; and it is impossible they can ly under corruption. This is our great consolation who are believers, and live under the gospel, that we have not these things as a prophecy of things to come, but as a plain history of things in part done, and by and bye to be compleatly done. (4.) It hath also in it consolation in respect of temporal difficulties: What are they all? They are not sure such as Christ's were; and the day is coming, when believers shall have an out-gate from them all: And therefore, since our Lord is up, let not believers be afraid of any challenges whatsoever.

2*dly,* Observe, "That our Lord Jesus, being "raised up from his state of humiliation, is invested, "and put in a most excellent and glorious condition; even such as the prophet cannot express." *Who can declare his generation?* saith he; Who can declare how glorious he is now? Take two or three scriptures to confirm this. 1*st,* That Eph. i. 20, 21. "He hath set him at his own right hand "in the heavenly places, far above all principali"ties and powers, and might, and dominion, and "every name that is named, not only in this world, "but also in that which is to come, and hath put "all things under his feet, and gave him to be "Head over all things to the Church." Our Lord's throne

in all things the pre-eminency. The 3d place is, Heb. viii. 1. "Of the things which we have spo-"ken, this is the sum, We have such an high "Priest, who is set on the right-hand of Majesty "in the heavens;" Where Christ's exaltation is set out to be such as hath exalted him to the right hand of the Majesty on high.

Because this is one of the great articles of our faith, to wit, "That Christ rose from death "the third day, and ascended into heaven, and is "set down on the right of God." We shall add a little more to clear it; and, (1.) We would know, that this exaltation of our Lord is not to be understood of his exaltation properly as he is God, in which respect there is no up nor down in him; tho' his declarative glory was vailed for a time during his humiliation, yet in himself, as he was God, he was still glorious and blessed over all. (2.) When we speak of Christ's exaltation as Mediator, and as Man, we do not mean that his human nature hath lost the essential properties of a creature, as if now when exalted he were wholly or only God, or as if the properties of the human nature were swallowed up in the Godhead; that were inconsistent with his being true Man, and would mar and obstruct our consolation exceedingly: But his exaltation consisteth, 1. In the manifestation and declaration of the Person that was humbled and brought low, to be God omnipotent, omnipresent, all-sufficient, infinitely wise, powerful, just, &c. For tho' these properties agree not to the human nature yet they agree to his Person, and they are manifested to be in him without question. 2. In the exaltation of the human nature of Christ-Man, to an unconceivable height of glory, such as the human nature united to the divine nature is capable of, by very many degrees beyond any thing that the elect, whether angels or men, are capable of; the personal union making him capable of far more glory, and his excellent offices calling for it. 3. This exaltation consists in his absolute dominion and kingly power, which is more observably, directly and plainly manifested in the days of the gospel administration than it was under the law; so stood, when it is said, that *he is set on the right hand of God;* so that now Jesus Christ, God and man in one Person, is in highest glory, and in absolutest dominion, nearest unto God, far above that which angels or saints are capable of: As kings use to set their greatest courtiers and minions, whom they would honour most, on their right hand, and as Solomon set his mother on his right hand; so is our Lord set on the right hand of God in highest glory. It is true, that, as God, he hath an absolutely sovereign and independent kingdom; yet, as Mediator, God-Man, he hath a dispensatory kingdom next unto the Father in glory. 4. This exaltation consists in Christ's being furnished with qualifications suitable to that glorious condition wherein he is invested: And tho' these qualifications of the Man-Christ be not simply infinite, yet they are far above what we can conceive; and the qualifications of the Person God-man are infinite, in which respect he is omnipotent, all-seeing, and infinitely wise, to provide every thing that may be for the good of his Church and people, and to prevent what may tend to their hurt; omnipresent, &c.

The *Uses* are three, 1*st*, This would waken and rouze our spirits to high, holy, and reverend esteem of Christ; he is God above all gods, King above all kings; he hath gotten *a name above every name, that at the name of Jesus every knee should bow,* not superstitiously when he is named, but holily and reverently to think of him, and to worship and serve him. We conceive, among many faults and evils in believers, this is a root-evil, even low thoughts of glorious Christ; so that, because he hath become low to lift us up, we are ready to think the less of him: But O that we could behold the glorious condition he is exalted unto, and could look upon him as, ere long, *coming in the clouds with power and great glory, in the glory his Father, and all the holy angels with him!* It will furnish reverend thoughts of him, tho' not to hurt faith and confidence, yet to breed holy awe and reverence in us to him-wards.

The 2*d Use* serves to shew what a formidable Party they engage to cop with them, who slight our
Lord

be; therefore beware what ye are doing: Ye have a mighty great and strong Party to deal with; and when the great day of his wrath comes, and when he shall appear in his glory, how will you be able to abide the least touch of it? it will heighten your sin, and heighten your misery, that he whom the Father exalted was undervalued by you, that ye scorned to take a direction from him, or to submit to a censure drawn forth in his name, and said, at least by your practice, "Let us break his bands asunder, and cast away his cords from us, *but he hath set his King on his holy hill of Zion, for all that; and* he that sits in heaven will laugh, "the Lord will have you in derision." Think on it seriously, and know, that he is no mean person whom ye slight and despise; and tho' this may now seem less than other sins, yet it will one day ly heavy on your score and conscience, above many, yea, above all other sins.

The *3d Use* serves to be a motive and encouragement to them that hear this gospel to receive Christ, and for the consolation of believers who have received him. 1. It serves to encourage you all to receive him; he is no mean person that wooes, you, but *King of kings, and Lord of lords*; and if ye think it a happiness to be for ever with him, then let it move you to close with him; if ye do so, ye shall be made glorious as he is glorious; a due proportion betwixt the Head and the members being kept, ye shall *sit on the same throne with him*, and *behold his glory;* as he prayeth, John xvii. *I will that these whom thou hast given me may be with me to behold my glory.* This is certainly a great bargain; if Christ be glorious, he calleth you to share with him in the same glory. 2. It serves for the consolation of believers, who have received him: Ye have an excellent Mediator, a most glorious Head and Husband, and a most excellent Dowry, and ye shall know it to your superabundant satisfaction and joy in that day, when (as it is Psal. xlv.) ye shall be brought unto the king in raiment of needle work, and shall enter into the king's palace, and share of his glory, and see him face to face, and sit with him on his throne, even as he hath o-

"ed, and was in suffering brought very low, is "God." We find ordinarily in scripture, especially thro' the new Testament, these three going together, 1. Christ's humiliation; 2. His exaltation on the back of that; And, 3, His Godhead. His humiliation is not readily spoken of without his exaltation, nor his exaltation without his Godhead; because it is impossible to separate Christ's exaltation from his Godhead, his exaltation being the evidence of his Godhead; and the prophet's scope here being to set out Christ's exaltation, and Philip preaching of it to the Eunuch from this text, it is doubtless the contemplation of Christ's Godhead that occasioneth this admiring exclamation, *Who shall declare his generation?* which we apply, not so much to the ineffableness of his generation as to its being an evidence that he is God. There are three or four ways whereby the scripture confirms this: Let me desire you, by the way, not to look on this as of little moment, or but a common doctrine; and since there are many so ignorant, that we would be ashamed to tell what we hear from some of you concerning the Godhead of Jesus Christ, ye would take better heed to it, being a main pillar of Christian religion, without which our preaching and your faith are in vain; for he is not believed on at all, if ye rest not on him as God. But to prosecute what we proposed, to wit, these several ways whereby the scripture confirms this truth; and to this purpose, consider, 1. The express titles and names that are given to him in scripture, and some scripture sayings of him, which hold it out; three whereof we shall instance: The first is that of Isaiah ix. 6, 7. where, when Christ is prophesied of, it is said, "Unto us a Child is born, "unto us a Child is given, and the government "shall be upon his shoulders," And what is he? "He shall be called Wonderful, Counsellor, the "mighty God, the everlasting Father, the Prince "of Peace; of the increase of his government "and peace there shall be no end." Here we have these three, his humiliation, exaltation, and Godhead; his humiliation, "Unto us a Child is "born, unto us a Son is given;" his exaltation,

"Of

"of the increase of his government and peace
"there shall be no end, upon the throne of David,
"and his kingdom, to order it, and to establish it
"with judgment and with justice:" And his Godhead is interjected and put in betwixt these two, in the names and titles given to him, " Wonderful,
" Counsellor, the Mighty God, the Everlasting Fa-
" ther ;" not as personally taken, but (as the word signifies) *The Father of Eternity*, from whom all things have their being; and for the same reason, Chap. vii. 14. he is called *Immanuel, God with us*. A *2d* place is that of Phil. ii. 6. " Who being in
" the form of God, thought it no robbery (he did
" God no wrong) to be equal with God. he made
" himself of no reputation, and took on him the
" form of a servant, &c. wherefore God also hath
" highly exalted him, and given him a name above
" every name, &c." A 3d place is that of Heb. i. 1, 2, 3. " God, who at sundry times, and in di-
" vers manners, spoke in time past unto the fathers
" by the prophets, hath in these last days spoken
" unto us by his Son, whom he hath appointed
" Heir of all things, by whom also he made the
" world ;" and what is *He* by whom he spake to us ? " who being the brightness of his glory, and
" the express image of his Person, and upholding
" all things by the word of his power, when he
" had by himself purged our sins, he sat down on
" the right hand of the Majesty on high." There is here much of Christ's excellency holden forth ; he is the brightness of the Father's glory, and the express image of his Person: The beam of the sun is not liker to the sun's light, the impression of the the seal on the wax is not liker to the seal, than the Son is to the Father, (nay, the liveliest resemblances fall infinitely short of a full and exact resemblance) the Father and he being the same God, and he being compared with the Father, not simply as God essentially taken, but as the second Person of the Trinity compared with him who is the first Person; O deep and adorable mystery !

A 2d way to clear and confirm it, is to consider his works, oft-times joined with his name; the works of creation, providence, redemption, and guiding of his Church; so we have it, John i. 1. *In the beginning was the Word*, the substantial Word of the Father, the Son of his love, called the *Word*, either as expressing the Father's image, as a man's word expresseth his mind : or because, as a prophet of the Church, he hath revealed the Father's will. It is said, that this Word was not only *with God*, but *was God:* and then follows in several verses together his works, the works of crea-

tion, *all things were made by him*, &c. the works of providence are attributed to him, John v. 17. *My Father worketh hitherto, and I work ;* and the work of redemption, and his glorious going thro' with it, declare him to be the Son of God; for none but God could redeem his Church.

3*dly*, For clearing and confirming of this truth, we may take the express confession of the saints in scripture, whereon there is much weight laid; and I shall name but five or six of their confessions, which to this purpose are expresly and fully recorded : The 1st is that of Matt. xvi. 16. " Whom
" do men say that I am ? Peter answered, Thou
" art the Son of the living God :" and Christ says,
" Blessed art thou, Simon Barjona, flesh and blood
" hath not revealed that unto thee, but my Fa-
" ther which is in heaven;" to let us know that it is not a little thing to believe Christ's Godhead, as many take it to be ; and then he calls himself *the Rock on which his Church is built*, Christ's Godhead is the foundation of Christianity. A 2d is John i. 49. in Nathanael's words ; Christ tells him, *Before Philip called thee, when thou wast under the fig-tree, I saw thee;* and he having gotten this proof of Christ's omniscience, presently breaks out, *Rabbi, thou art the Son of God, thou art the King of Israel;* and that is the first thing his faith evidenceth itself in. A 3d place is, John vi. 67, 68, 69. where, when Christ is saying to the twelve,
" Will ye also leave me ? Simon answered, Lord,
" to whom shall we go ? thou hast the words of e-
" ternal life, and we believe and are sure, that
" thou art the Christ, the Son of the living God;" there is much in these words, *we believe and are sure*, that it is so. A 4th place is, John xi. 27. and it is Martha her confession, " Yea, Lord, I be-
" lieve that thou art Christ, the Son of God,
" which should come into the world." The 5th place is that of John xx. 28. where, when Christ bids Thomas reach hither his hand and put it in his side, his glory shines so full in his face, that he cries out, " My Lord, and my God ;" and his faith is summed up and compended in that. The last place that we shall name, is that of Acts viii. 37. and it is the Eunuch's confession, " I believe
" that Jesus Christ is the Son of God," which is the sum of his faith.

The 4th and last way of confirmation of this great truth, is drawn from the worship which is due unto him : He is the Object of Faith, John xiv. 1. " Ye believe in God, believe also in me;" He is the Object of prayer, Acts vii. 59. " They stoned
" Stephen, calling upon God, saying, Lord Jesus
" receive

" receive my fpirit;" and frequently elfewhere in fcripture he is prayed unto, though thefe two are not too curioufly to be feparated.

Ufe 1. The firft ufe ferves to ftrengthen your faith in this, that our Lord Jefus Chrift, who fuffered for finners, and is made offer of to them in the gofpel, is God equal with the Father; and fo he is to be clofed with, and refted on, as the brightnefs of the Father's glory: The reafon why we would have you confirmed in the faith of this, is not fmall; for it is a moft neceffary thing, and without the faith of it, all the work of our falvation will hang loofe, neither can we have any claim to eternal life; and therefore we defire you particularly who are ignorant hearers, and who have the name of Chrift often in your mouths, and yet know not what he is, to know, remember and believe, that he that is the Son of Mary, is alfo the eternal Son of God, being God before he was incarnate, and before the world was made, and the Maker of all that was made.

Ufe 2. The fecond ufe ferves to let you know, that tho' it be a moft neceffary thing to be confirmed in the faith of this truth, that Chrift is God; yet it is a greater difficulty to believe and be perfuaded of it, than the moft part take it to be: Many fad proofs whereof we have in folks words, and more in their practice, " Flefh and blood (faith " Chrift, Matt. xvi.) hath not revealed this unto " thee." It is a wonder whence fo many folks faith comes, who never found any the leaft difficulty in this; and it is a wonder that fo few are thorow in the faith of it, fo that if they were called and put to it, they durft not fwear that he is God: yea, if we would look on a little further, we would find, that the faith of this is but fcarce amongft us, not to fpeak of the grofs ignorance of many, who will fay, when afked, that he is not equal with the Father, or that he was made God, and other fuch like expreffions will they have, that are abominable to be once named amongft Chriftians; folks thro' their ignorance falling into damnable herefies on the matter, and yet not knowing that they do fo; as if our bleffed Lord were a made god, and not the fame God with the Father: For the proving of him to be God, proves him to be the fame God, there being but one God.

Ye would confider, for convincing you that it is thus with many of you, 1. The little fear that is in men and women of the Majefty of Chrift as God; they durft not walk with fo little fear of him, if they believed indeed that he were God: What made the Jews, with the Scribes and Pharifees, to fpit upon him and defpife him? but becaufe they wanted the faith of his Godhead: And have not ye the fame nature in you? Ye live in a place where the faith of Chrift's Godhead is profeffed, and is not queftioned; but your practice fays to beholders, that ye believe it not, becaufe ye fear him not. 2. That your fouls do fo little welcome the offer of the gofpel; that tells, that ye believe him not to be God. 3. That ye do not place your happinefs in believing on him, and in the way of holinefs; ye fay in effect, Wherefore ferves Chrift? ye care not for him: Hence it is, that fo many live contentedly without him, and are not folicitous about the enjoying of him. 4. Even in believers there is much unbelief of this truth; which is fadly evidenced by this, that they do not fo blefs themfelves in him, and that they do not fo reckon themfelves to have come well to, and to be made up in him, as David doth, Pfal. xvi. where he faith, and holily glorieth, *The lines are fallen unto me in pleafant places*, &c. And by the frequent difcouragement that is incident to believers, as if Chrift had not the guiding of them, and of what concerns them, or could not guide all well for their good. If he were believed to be God, it would quafh temptations, banifh difcouragements, comfort under croffes, fweeten every condition, induce to holinefs, reftrain from fin: And in a word, it cannot be told what is in the bofom of this one truth, when folidly believed; for what can poffibly be wanting to the believer in him that is God? He hath the fulnefs of the Godhead to fupply whatever they want, and fuftains the relation of a Husband to the believer, to make it forthcoming; and he is furnifhed with fuitable qualifications to make the application thereof: what then could be wanting, if this were thorowly believed, that he is God? Let me fay it to you, the faith of this would provoke to more holinefs, and to ftudy more the power than the profeffion of religion, and would help you to live a more comfortable life in every condition.

SERMON XXXI.

Ifaiah liii. 8, *He was taken from prifon, and from judgment; and who fhall declare his generation? For he was cut off out of the land of the living, for the transgreffion of my people was he ftricken.*

THESE words are a proof of that which we difcourfed in the lecture concerning Chrift's wonderful love to his people, than which, *no man hath greater, that a man fhould lay down his life for his friend;* But *he hath commended his love to us, in that while we were yet enemies he died for us:* This is the great commendation of Christ's love; and what will he refuse to his people, who in his love hath come this length to them?

In the former part of this verse, we shew, that there was a hint given of Christ's exaltation, of the exaltation and glory of the Mediator following on the back of his lowest suffering; an ineffable and inexpressible glory, which the prophet rather passeth with a sort of nonplussing silence, than insisteth in the declaration of it, *Who shall declare his generation?*

We come now to the last part of the words, *For he was cut off out of the land of the living, for the transgression of my people was he stricken.* They are added as a reason of the former, and the one part of them is a reason of the other: He said before, *Who shall declare his generation?* who can sufficiently declare and unfold, how gloriously the Mediator is exalted? And he gives this for the reason of it, *For he was cut off out of the land of the living;* the force of which is, that he humbles himself, therefore God hath exalted him, as the Apostle reasons, Philip. ii. 9. So that this is not added, as being posterior to his exaltation, but as a reason shewing the connection of his exaltation with his humiliation; and lest it should be a stumbling to any, that this glorious Person suffered death, he gives the reason of that also, which strengthens the reason of his exaltation, *For the transgression of my people was he stricken,* or (as the word is) *the stroke was on him;* he suffered, not for any wrong that was in himself, but for the sins of his own elect people. The first particularly looks to Christ's death, which was a prophecy in Isaiah's time, but is now an historical narration to us, we having the gospel as a commentary on it. To be *cut off out of the land of the living,* is to have an end put to the natural life, which is ordinarily done by death; but *cutting off,* here, signifies to be taken away, not in an ordinary, but in an extraordinary way, to be removed by a violent death, by the stroke of justice.

We may shortly take these two observes here, for the confirmation of two articles of our faith; looking on it, 1. As a prophecy, we may observe, " That our Lord Jesus behoved to suffer and die." it was prophesied of him, *That he should be cut off out of the land of the living;* and Dan. ix. 26. it is plainly and clearly asserted, that *the Messiah shall be cut off;* which being compared with the history of the gospel, we have it as a truth fulfilled; for our Lord Jesus was cut off, and as he himself says, Luke xxiv. *It behoved him, to suffer these things, and to enter into his glory.* And supposing the elect to be sinners, and the curse to be added to the covenant of works, *The day thou eats thou shalt surely die;* supposing also the Mediator to have engaged, and undertaken to satisfy justice, and undergo that curse for the elect; there was a necessity that he should die, as it is, Gal. iii. 13. *Christ hath redeemed us from the curse of the law, being made a curse for us;* which curse was evident in his death, for it is written, *Cursed is every one that hangeth on a tree.*

2d Observe, " That our Lord Jesus behoved to " die a violent death, and not an ordinary natural " one," which this expression, and that other, Daniel ix. clearly holds forth. And, considering his sinless nature that was not liable to death, and that he had not these principles of his dying in him, disposing him to die, that we sinful miserable mortals have in us; and considering withal, that the Lord Jehovah was (to speak so) pursuing him as sinners Cautioner at the bar of justice; it was meet, yea necessary, that our blessed Lord should not die an ordinary death, as men die ordinarily, through weakness or sickness on their beds, but a violent death.

Use. It serves to be a confirmation of this truth, that the Messiah behoved thus to die; therefore we say in the Belief, *He suffered under Pontius Pilate, was crucified, dead and buried:* Which shews, 1. The reality of his satisfaction, and the compleat payment that he made to justice, when he lays down that price which the sinner ought to have laid down. 2. It shews the reality of our Lord's sufferings, and that they were not imaginary, but that as he was a real and true Man, so his sufferings were most real; his soul was separate from his body, tho' the union betwixt both his body and soul and the Godhead continued still. 3. It holds forth a proof and confirmation of our faith in this, that our Lord Jesus is the Messiah that was prophesied of, and promised, in whom all the sufferings in his soul and body that were spoken of, to go before his death, were accomplished, and in whom this was also accomplished, that *he was cut off out of the land of the living;* so that, if we look rightly on the scripture, our Lord's sufferings will be so far from being matter of stumbling, that they will rather be a clear, convincing, and evident proof that Jesus of Nazareth is the true Messiah, and that in him, all that was spoken concerning the Messiah is fulfilled and came to pass.

4. It is matter of great consolation to believers, that our Lord Jesus, who is now exalted, died, and so death is spoiled, and there needs not be any great fear for them to yoke with it. This *land of the living* is not their rest, within a little they must be gone hence: Our Lord was cut off from it, and that by a shameful death, for the behoof and sake of others, and not for himself; and therefore his death cannot but be made forthcoming for them for whom he underwent it, and their petty sufferings need not much to vex them: These plainest truths, that are most ordinary, have in them most of spiritual sap, juice, and life to strengthen faith, and to furnish consolation to believers; and if they were rightly understood, and fed upon by faith, O how lively might they be! And were there no more but these two words in the text, O how much consolation do they yield in life and in death! Our Lord is gone before believers, and they may be greatly heartned to follow him.

The last part of, or the last thing in the words, seems to have some more obscurity in it; and therefore we shall insist the more in opening up of the same.

For the transgressions of my people was he stricken: These words do not look to the reason why Pilate and the priests condemned him, for they had no thoughts of the sins of God's people; tho' Caiaphas stumbled, as to himself, by guess on a prophecy of his dying for them: But they give a reason why he was *cut off out of the land of the living,* and look to the court and tribunal of God's justice, before which he was standing, by which he was to be sentenced to death for the transgressions of God's people, and also absolved: He was thus stricken in respect of God's purpose and design.

For clearing of the words, it may be required, 1. What is meant here by *my people*? 2. What it is to be *stricken* or smitten *for them?*

For the 1*st, My people,* it is a discriminating or differencing of some from others: And therefore, by *my people* here, is not meant, 1. All the world, or all that ever lived and had a being; we find not any where in scripture that these are called *my people,* or *God's people:* but whenever *my people* is spoken of, it is used to rid marches betwixt his people and other people that are not his, as John x. 26, 27. *Ye believe not, because ye are not of my sheep: my sheep hear my voice, and I know them,* which supposeth that some are his, and others not so his; and so *my people* cannot be all the world. Neither, 2. Can it be meant of the whole visible Church, who, in respect of the external administration of the covenant, are sometimes called his people, as all Israel are: There is a narrower march, or boundary drawn, John x. 26. where the Lord, speaking of them that were only externally in covenant with him, says, *Ye are not my sheep,* to shew that his reckoning there must not go upon external profession: And, verse 16. some that were not for the time professing themselves to be his people, are reckoned; *Other sheep I have, which are not of this fold, them also I must bring in.* Nor, 3. Can it be limited to them that were actually converted and believers; for he says (as I just now hinted) that *he hath other sheep that are not brought in;* and he is said *to gather together into one the children of God that were scattered abroad,* John xi. 52. So then, by *my people,* must be understood these who in God's eternal purpose are separate by the decree of election to be his own, even these whom he hath chosen to glorify himself in and by them through his grace, and to glorify them with himself; even these spoken of, John xvii. 6. *Thine they were, and thou gavest them me;* they are the people who were transacted for in the covenant of redemption, and that were given by the Father to the Son, to be redeemed by him; it was for their sins, even for the sins of the elect, that our Lord Jesus was stricken.

As for the 2*d,* What is it to be *stricken for their transgressions?* The meaning is, The meritorious cause of their stroke was on Christ, which intimates to us, that his sufferings and death were procured by the sins of the elect of God; his stroke, or the stroke that was upon him (as the word is) was the amends that justice got for their sins: in a word, the stroke that the elect's sins procured and merited, *took him out of* (or away from) *the land of the living, brought him to prison and to judgment, and made his soul an offering for sin.* Neither can this be otherways understood; for it is not said that for their good, or for their behoof only, or to be an example and pattern of patience only to them, he was stricken, as some grosly erroneous and profane men expound the words; but *for their transgressions was he stricken,* that is, it was their guilt, which he having undertaken and engaged to satisfy for, made him liable to this stroke.

In this part of the words, thus opened up, we have two notable points concerning the covenant of redemption, 1. The party for whom it is contrived and intended, and that is the elect or *God's people*; it is not all the world, nor all the visible Church members that God transacted for in the bargain with the Mediator, but *my people,* the elect of God; they

they were so considered in the transaction and in the execution. 2. The great price that was sought or required, that was offered, and that was agreed upon for the redemption of the elect, to wit, the death of the Mediator, even his dying the cursed death of the cross: This is the sum, for the transgressions of God's people, the stroke was upon him; God's design being to glorify his grace in the salvation of so many, sin having intervened to bring them under the curse. There is upon the one side the Lord's giving of them to the Mediator to be redeemed by him, and upon the other side the Mediator's accepting of them on the terms proposed; he is content to satisfy for them, to take the stroke on himself deserved by them, that they may go free. Each of these may be considered several ways, for furnishing of sweet doctrines.

1. From the first of those, Observe, 'That there "are some differenced from others in respect of God's "purpose, some chosen of God for his people, be- "side all the rest of the world." For some are here God's people ere they be born, and ere Christ die for them, John xvii. 16. *Thine they were, and thou gavest them to me*: They are supposed to be God's people in some peculiar respect, ere they be given to Christ to be redeemed by him. In a word, the Lord hath an elect people, or a people chosen to salvation in his eternal purpose and decree, an elect people, or a people chosen out of the world, which in this respect are not his people, or are not elected. There are four qualifications or properties in this doctrine, which will serve to clear it; (1.) When we say, there is such a decree of election, we say that it is a *discriminating* or *differencing decree*, wherein or whereby there is a taking of some, and not all; a taking of one, and leaving another; a taking of Isaac, and a leaving of Ishmael, a taking of Jacob, and and a leaving of Esau, as it is Rom. ix. And this discriminating or differencing, hath these four steps, 1. There is a differencing in God's purpose, in respect of the end, while all men are alike before him, some are designed to eternal life, others not; therefore, Matt. xxv. 34. it is said, "Come ye blessed of my Father, inherit the "kingdom prepared for you from the foundation of "the world;" and in this respect the book of life is said to be opened, Rev. xx. 12. 2. This differencing is in respect of God's offering and giving of them to the Mediator in the covenant of redemption, wherein some, not all, are given to Christ, John xvii. 2. "That he should give eternal life to "as many as thou hast given him out of the world;" where it is clear, that so many are given to him, in reference to whom he is to exercise his offices. 3. There is a differencing in respect of Christ's undertaking and executing his offices for them, he accepts of them, John xvii. 9. *For their sakes I sanctify my self*, I have separated my self to the office of Mediator, and offer my self for them, "That they also "may be sanctified; *and* I pray for them, I pray "not for the world;" it is of them that he maketh that sweet account, John vi. 39. "This is the Fa- "ther's will that sent me, that of all that he hath "given me, I should lose nothing, but should raise "it up again at the last day;" and of whom he saith, John x. 28, 29. " I give unto them eternal "life, and they shall never perish, neither shall "any man pluck them out of my hand." He answers and is accountable for them, and for them only; he will count for no other, as beeing redeemed by him, and to be made partakers of his glory. 4. This differencing is in respect of the promises made upon God's part to the Mediator in favours of the elect, and of the benefits that flow to them from the covenant: He hath not promised to justify all, nor to make all believe, but some only: He, as it were, saith to the Mediator, These I give thee to be redeemed by thee, and on the laying down of thy life, and satisfying for them, I promise to make them believe, and that through faith in thee they shall be justified; therefore saith Christ, John vi. 44. "Murmur not among yourselves; no man can "come unto me, except the Father who hath sent "me draw him." And who are they that shall believe on him? See ver. 37. "All that the Father "hath given me, shall come unto me, and him that "cometh I will in no wise cast him out," but will make him dearly welcome; and ver. 45. "Every "one that hath heard and learned of the Father, "cometh unto me; and John xvii. 2. That he "should give eternal life to as many as thou hast "given him." Thus you see what was meant, when we call this a differencing decree. (2.) We say, that it is a *definite decree*, both in respect of the number numbered, that is, about so many, and no more, and not all; and in respect of the number, that numbers such a man and such a woman in particular, in such a place, and not such another person; they are all particularly designed, and are therefore said to be *written in the Lamb's book of life*: It is not all who are foreseen to believe who are elected, as if election did follow believing, as the cause of the decree; but it is such a number whom the Lord engageth to the Mediator to draw, to teach and make them believers. (3.) We say it is a *decree that is free*, as to all merit in them whom

whom it reacheth; and it is free in these three respects. 1. In respect of any thing in the person or persons elected, who are supposed to be lying as the rest of the world; therefore it is said of Jacob and Esau, Rom. ix. 11. *The children being not yet born, neither having done good or evil, that the purpose of God according to election might stand*, &c. That is, God respected not the doing good or evil, in his electing of the one, and passing by the other. 2. In respect of Christ's satisfaction and redemption, which presupposeth this decree to be, and is the means by which it is accomplished; so that we are redeemed, because we are elected. The elect were God's people, when Christ did undertake and engage for them; and in this respect election is a fountain-grace, and Christ's death is not the cause of election, tho' it be the cause of all the benefits that follow upon it. 3. It is free, in respect of God's absolute sovereignty, who acts herein according to the purpose of his own will, having no reason without himself, as it is clear, Matth. xi. *Even so Father, because it seemed good in thy sight*; And Eph. i. 11. *Being predestinate according to the purpose of him, who worketh all things according to the counsel of his own will*: As the potter hath power over the clay, and makes of the same lump one vessel to honour, and another to dishonour as he pleaseth; so the Lord acts most sovereignly in the decree of election. (4.) We say, that this decree is *absolute and peremptory*; which is not so to be understood, as if it admitted of no misses in the execution of it. But this is the meaning, that the performing and bringing about thereof depends on nothing without God, neither can it be possibly frustrated; these sheep can never be plucked out of his hand, neither can they ever perish, but must needs all and every one of them actually enjoy that which is decreed for them by his decree; else they could not be called God's people, if they might not be his. Thus ye see what is the meaning of these words, *my people*, that is, his elect people, in or by the decree of election.

I shall shortly give you some few grounds from scripture, to clear and confirm this truth; the 1st whereof is taken from the names that the people of God get, from the expressions that are used in making mention of them in scripture, which will infer all that hath been said; as namely, They are called *my sheep*, John x. his sheep that he knows, as it were, by head-mark, by name and sirname, which cannot but be his. They are called *the election of grace*, Rom. xi. 5. *At this present time there is a remnant, according to the election of grace*; and v. 7. *The election hath obtained, and the rest were blinded.* It is impossible but the elect must obtain, there being an inseparable connexion betwixt the decree and the end thereof: They are said to be *written in the Lamb's book of life before the foundation of the world*, before there was any mention of themselves, or consideration of ought in themselves: they are said to be loved and beloved, and ordained to eternal life, Acts xiii. 48. *As many as were ordained to eternal life, believed*; where believing is made a fruit and effect of this decree of election, it is so far from being a cause thereof: They are called *blessed of the Father*, Matt. xxv. and these whom he blesseth, cannot but be blessed: They are called such as *are given to Christ*, holding forth a peculiar differencing of them from others: They are called the people whom he foreknew and predestinated, Rom. viii. 29. *Whom he did foreknow, them he did predestinate*, &c. and Rom. xi. 2. *God hath not cast away his people whom he foreknew*: Every one was not so foreknown; for Christ will say to many at the great day, *Depart from me, I never knew you*. Titles and names of this kind are frequent in the scripture, whereby God differenceth some from others; which hath its rise from God's purpose and decree of election. A 2d ground is taken from the opposition which the scripture maketh betwixt the elect and others who are not elected, which shews clearly that election cannot be understood of all, as if there were a general and conditional election: Hence it is said, *Jacob have I loved, and Esau have I hated*; the electing of the one is laid foregainst the rejecting of the other; so John x. the Lord says of some, that they are his sheep, and of others, *They are not my sheep*; and Rom. ix. the apostle speaks of some *vessels of mercy which are before prepared for glory*, and of some *vessels of wrath fitted for destruction*; and 2 Tim. ii. 21. some are said to be *vessels of honour*, some of *dishonour*; some are *ordained to eternal life*, Acts xiii. and *some are ordained of old to that destruction*, as Jude speaketh; some are *written in the Lamb's book of life*, and some not, Rev. xx. And wherefore is all this spoken? but to let us know that God hath freely and sovereignly in his decree put a difference betwixt some and others, which as it began (to speak so) in God's eternal purpose, so it will continue in the event. Which is a third ground of confirmation; and it will be clear, if we compare God's purpose and decree with the event and effect; for as a thing is in the event and effect, so God intended and purposed in his decree it should be: thus the Lord's final sentence at the day of judgment, is

but

but the result of his eternal purpose; the book of life, containing the names of all the elect, was written (to speak so) before the elect existed. And as it is said, Acts xv. *Known unto God are all his works from the beginning*, so in a special manner and peculiar way this great work of redemption was, and they that were to be redeemed, particularly known and written down in the book of God's decree of election; hence it is said, Rom. xi. 7. *Israel hath not obtained that which he seeketh for, but the election hath obtained*: and John vi. 37. *All that the Father hath given me, shall come unto me;* and John x. 28. *I give my sheep eternal life, and they shall never perish.* There is, Rom. viii. 30. a concatenation and linking together of things from God's purpose and decree of election, even to eternal glory, which is the result of election: And it being very clear that some are admitted and owned by Christ in the great day, and others not; this is also clear, that there was a differencing decree betwixt these, so admitted and owned, before the world was, and others not so owned and admitted; especially considering that this differencing at the great day of judgment is drawn from the decree of election, Mat. xxv. *Come, ye blessed of my Father, inherit the kingdom prepared for you before the foundation of the world was laid*; as if the Lord had said, There was a purpose and design of bringing you to heaven before the world was. A 4th ground is taken from the nature of God's covenant of redemption, which holds clearly forth the truth of this doctrine concerning election in all the steps of it: As, 1. In God's making the offer and gift of some to the Mediator; it is only some that he gives, and not all. 2. In Christ's acceptation of the offer and gift: He prays for some, he sanctifies himself for some, and for some he counts, and not for all. 3. There is not a promise in all the covenant of redemption, whether it be of grace or of glory, but it is intended for the elect only, and not for all; "I give unto them eternal life, and they shall never "perish, John x. Thy people shall be willing in the "day of thy power, Psal. cx. 3." Christ's undertaking is for them only, John x. "Other sheep I "have which are not of this fold, them also I must "bring in;" there is a necessity in the bringing in of them and of no others, because he undertook for them and for no others. We the rather take notice of, and insist so much on this, because it will much serve to clear the following doctrine concerning the redemption of the elect; for if there be a differencing of them from others by the decree of election, then there must be a differencing of them from o-thers, in Christ's laying down of his life for them, and not for any others: election is the key of all; there is such a people, and they are the object of the covenant of redemption, whose good is sought after and agreed upon therein, and not for any other.

Use 1. It serves for the confirmation of a weighty truth, and we would have you not to think little of any piece of truth. We shall not here follow the subtile cavillings of adversaries against this truth, only we would have you confirmed in the faith of it; for, 1. If ye be not clear and established in the faith of this truth, ye will be in great hazard, not only to make muddy, but to obstruct and stop the whole current and tract of grace, so that grace shall be a common thing, heaven and happiness shall go by guess, redemption shall be universal, &c. but let this truth be once well established, that God hath a peculiar people for whom the Mediator transacted, and these errors fall to the ground and evanish; for it is the love of election from which all the rest of the benefits that come to the elect flow, and this love is peculiar, therefore there cannot be a common application of it; it is the peculiarness of grace that commends it to the souls of believers, and makes it wonderful to them: That God should have taken notice of them, that were by nature separate from God as well as others; that their case being common, his love should be peculiar, is indeed just and great matter of wonder: hence comes in that song, Rev. v. 9. *Thou hast redeemed us to God, by thy blood, out of every kindred, and tongue, and people, and nation*: not all of every nation, people, tongue and kindred are redeemed, but some out of every one of these. Let this then be taken for a solid truth, that the Lord in his eternal purpose hath made a difference and separation of some from others, which is the great ground of the title that God hath to these some.

2. Clearness in this truth, serves to keep the hearts of God's people in awe of him, to lift him up very high in their esteem, as Sovereign over the creature: and if any should quarrel with God and say, Why did God so? that of the apostle comes well in for an answer, *Who art thou, O man, that repliest against God?* it is his sovereign pleasure, who is supreme Potter, and hath *power over the clay, to make one vessel to honour, and another to dishonour*. When the soul doth thus take up God as having all mankind before him as a lump of clay, and choosing out of it, and writing upon one man and not another, it must needs, in a transport of admiration, say, O what a great and sovereign God

must he be, who did determine and write down the eternal condition of men before ever the world was!

3. This to the people of God, (1.) Preacheth wonderful grace, when they, having gotten their calling and election made sure, come in and read their names in God's decree of election before they had a being; and, (2.) It is to them matter of exceeding great consolation. 1. I say it preacheth wonderful grace that freely chose them; and that, when thousands of great men and noblemen were passed by, such a poor body, that was half a fool, in comparison with them, should be chosen; according to that, 1 Cor. i. *Not many wise after the flesh, not many mighty, not many noble hath God called, but he hath chosen the foolish things of the world, weak and base, and things that are not,* to make them kings and priests unto God and his Father. 2. It is matter of exceeding great consolation to them, that it is free and sure: free, even so free, that it stops the mouth of boasting; for what, I pray, hath an elect more to speak of as a ground of boasting than a Pagan in America, or one in hell? *Who made thee to differ? or what hast thou, O man, that thou hast not received?* It is election that makes the difference: and it is sure, for their salvation is founded on God's purpose and decree, which is the solid rest of a believer; kindness began not on our side, but on God's, as Christ says, *Ye have not chosen me, but I have chosen you,* John xv. 16.

4. It says this, That all of you had need to make your calling and election sure; that is the very hinge of believers consolation, even to have the proof of it in your conscience, that ye are inrolled here, to get out the extract of this decree, that ye may see and read your names in it: Hence many streams of consolation flow out. If it be so with you, then ye were given to Christ; Christ undertook to satisfy justice for you; ye shall get faith, and more faith; ye shall get repentance and sanctification, and ye shall get heaven and glory at the end of your course. If it be said, this is much, how shall it be brought about? we answer, It is not impossible; and to make it out take but two words, that are both directions and marks, the practice whereof will give a solid proof of your inrolment in God's book, whence all these great and glorious things have their rise. 1. Where there is a yielding to Christ's call in the gospel, and a closing with him, that evidenceth election; for it is certain, that none shall, nor can come to Christ, and believe in him, but the elect; and whoever are elected, must and shall come, sooner or later, John vi. 37. *All that the Father giveth me, shall come unto me;* and John x. 4. *His sheep follow him, and know his voice;* they accept of and make welcome Christ's call in the gospel, and they that accept of it are elect: so that there is no need of any new revelation about the matter, neither needs their any torturing anxiety to know, how to come by thy name in the roll of the elect; try it by this, If thou hast given obedience to the call of the gospel; if thou hast, in the sense of thy need of a Saviour, fled unto Jesus Christ, and on his own terms closed with him, by this thy tenure or holding is sure, and by this thou hast an evidence that thou art an elect; for his sheep come unto him, and hear his voice: and as many of you as soundly believe on him, and have betaken yourselves to him for life and salvation, have the seal and witness in yourselves, that your names were in God's roll and book before the world was: but if this be not, debate, dispute and question as ye will about it, whatever may be afterwards, ye have no evidence for the time of your election. 2. Where there is real holiness, or a real study and endeavour to be holy and more holy, it is an evidence of election, and of a person's being inrolled in the volume of the book of God's decree; because holiness is a fruit of election, as is clear, Eph. i. 4. *According as he hath chosen us before the foundation of the world, that we should be holy;* never a person is really holy, but such as God designed should be holy: To this purpose, the apostle having, 2 Tim. ii. 21. spoken of election, *The foundation of the Lord stands sure, having this seal, the Lord knows who are his, and let every one that names the name of Christ depart from iniquity; but in a great house are not only vessels of gold,* &c. he subjoins, *If a man therefore purge himself from these, he shall be a vessel unto honour, sanctified,* &c. Not that election dependeth on man's holiness, but by his holiness he shall be manifested to be, and accounted an elect vessel, and may warrantably conclude himself to be such; so that true holiness brings folk to be acquainted with the great secret of election, and gives them boldness to make the application of it. There is nothing that men readily desire more to know than this, whether they be elected or not; here is a sure way to come by the knowledge of it, even to study to believe, and to be holy, and then we may be confident that our names were written in the Lamb's book of life; but if we slight faith in Christ and holiness, whatever may be in God's purpose about us, we have for present no ground to conclude our election upon, God himself fix us in these things, that have such mighty consequents depending on them.

SERMON

SERMON XXXII.

Isaiah liii. 8. *He was taken from prison, and from judgment; and who shall declare his generation? For he was cut off out of the land of the living, for the transgression of my people was he stricken.*

THE prophet hath been long in describing Christ's sufferings, and hath shown what height they came to, even *to prison and to judgment,* and to death itself, *He was cut off out of the land of the living:* Now he casts in a word to shew wherefore all this was, or what was the procuring cause that brought all this suffering and sorrow on Christ, which also was the end that he had before him in it, in these words, *For the transgression of my people was he stricken.* We shew that by *my people* here, was not meant all men and women in the world, nay, not all men who are externally called in the visible Church, but his elect only, these whom he hath chosen to be his people, and separated from others by an eternal decree of election; we shew also that these words *for the transgression of my people was he stricken,* do not contain only a reason of Christ's extreme sufferings, even of his being *brought to prison and to judgment* before men, but also, and mainly, of his being brought so before God, and of his being *cut off*: For the sins of God's people are not laid to his charge before men, but before God they are; and so it does imply an influence that the sins of the elect had upon Christ's sufferings, and a respect that his sufferings had to their sins; the elects sins procured these sufferings to him and his sufferings were undergone by him, for the satisfying of justice for their sins and for the removing of them.

I shall not insist further in the exposition of the words having opened them up the last day, but shall hint at a few *doctrines* from them; and because they are general and more doctrinal I shall be the shorter in speaking to them: Tho' it may be ye think not so much of them, yet they are not a little for your edification; and if ye are suitably sensible of sin, and of your hazard, there is no doctrine concerning the covenant of redemption, but it would be useful and refreshing to you.

There are several things implied here, concerning the efficacy of the price of Christ's death, and concerning the extent of it, as it is laid down as a price for the sins of the elect, which I shall first passingly touch upon, and then come to these doctrines that are more directly held forth in the words.

1st, Then, it is implied, that there is a people of God separated from others, and chosen by him, on whom he intended and proposed, before the world was, to glorify his grace: The very designation that they get here clears this; it is *my people,* not only of the Jews, nor my people only of the Gentiles, but my people both of Jews and Gentiles; as Christ says. John x. *Other sheep have I, which are not of this fold, them I must bring in.*

2dly, It is implied, that this decree of election is antecedaneous to, and goes before the covenant of redemption in order of nature: It flows not from Christ's death as the effect of it, but is prior to it; for if Christ's death be the mean, or price (as indeed it is) whereby the sins of God's elect people are satisfied for, then the decree of election must preceed it. Only we would beware to ascribe to God any priority or posteriority in his decrees in order of time for he is infinite in wisdom and foresight, and able to look on all things with one blink of beholding, and to decree things infinite in number at once, which we cannot conceive of, nor comprehend: But this we say, That, considering the order of things, the decree of election is not a fruit or effect of Christ's death, but prior to it, and Christ's death follows as a mean to make it effectual; he is appointed to save the elect from their sins, and from that which their sins deserved, *For the transgression of my people was stricken*: They were God's people by election before Christ's engagement to suffer and satisfy for them, much more before his actual suffering; and so their election cannot be a fruit and effect of his suffering.

Use. It serves to vindicate this truth from an error and mistake of the Arminians, who, as they overthrow the design of grace in the salvation of sinners, in other steps thereof; so do they in this, in making Christ's death to preceed election, and election to follow it; but, as we hinted before, the decree of election is sovereign, being an act of grace absolutely free: The Lord in it having designed some for manifesting the glory of his grace upon them as the end, he hath taken in Christ's death and other midses for the promoting of it.

3dly, It is implied here, that even the elect or God's people are considered as sinful in the covenant of redemption, *For the transgression of my people was he stricken;* they were considered as sinful as well as others, when they were bargained for. We need not dispute, whether they were considered as sinful in the decree of election, it not being necessary in this place, nor profitable for you; but sure in Christ's undertaking for them they are considered

considered as sinful: For God sent not Christ, neither came he into the world, to purchase life and salvation to righteous folks; but he was sent and came to lay down his life *a ransom for many* to wit sinners; and therefore it is given as the reason of his name, Matt. i. 21. *Thou shalt call his name Jesus, for he shall save his people from their sins*.

Use 1. It serves to humble the elect greatly, who, whenever they come to get grace, they get it most freely; for they were not better by nature than others whom God past by, as is clear, Eph. ii. 1. *We were dead in trespasses and sins, and were by nature children of wrath, even as others*; Peter and Paul were by nature children of wrath as well as Judas; and David was a child of wrath by nature as well as Saul, when this transaction concerning the work of redemption was agreed upon, and concluded betwixt these most responsal Parties.

2. It serves also much for the encouragement of a believer, who is sensible of sin, and afraid of wrath, and in that posture betakes himself to Christ for refuge: tho' his misbelief should make him say, with Peter, *Depart from me, for I am a sinful man, O Lord;* yet this consideration may hearten him to draw near, that Christ was *stricken* for sinners, for the transgressions of his elect people: Yea, if there had not been sin, and if the covenant of works had holden foot, there needed not have been a Saviour; and therefore sinners have here a solid ground to lay hold upon, for life and salvation.

And therefore, as a 3d *Use* of it, It is an unsafe assertion, beside the curiosity of this, that *Antinomians* maintain, which is, That tho' man had never fallen, yet Christ would have become man; for we see here that Christ's becoming man, and his being stricken, flowed from his being Surety for elect sinners; and his being Surety flowed from the covenant of redemption concerning elect sinners: To be wise without, or beside and above what is written in the scripture, is vanity, pride and folly.

4*thly*, It is implied here, that sin, wherever it is, deserves strokes, even the sins of the elect; yea we may add this to it, that not only do the sins of the elect deserve strokes in themselves, being breaches of God's law, but that there is an actual curse standing against them, till it be removed; and God's threatning, *The day thou eats thou shalt surely die*, infers a necessity of strokes. This we say is clearly implied here, because the Mediator, entering himself Surety for the elect's debt, behoved to be smitten; and when he was so smitten, sure sin must deserve much. We speak not of an absolute necessity, but God having revealed to man his duty, and added a threatning, that in the day he should eat he should die, there is a necessity in respect of God's truth, faithfulness, and unchangeableness, who had spoken the word, that strokes should follow sin; for sin cannot be removed, till the threatning be satisfied.

Use. This may point out to us, that sin is no little nor light thing, neither is the obtaining of pardon an easy business, whatever men generally think of them: There are many sad strokes that follow sin, which will hotly pursue sinners who are not in Christ; O do not then think lightly of sin, which is the fountain of such misery and wo to the sinner: If ye knew how exceedingly bitter wrath and the curse is that follows sin, ye would as soon put your head in the fire, as ye would meddle with it; if ye believed that word to be true, which is in Exod. xxxiv. *He will by no means clear the guilty*, and if ye believed God's faithfulness that is engaged to make good his threatnings, challenges for sin would be more strong and stinging.

5*thly*, It is implied here, that tho' the elect's sins deserve wrath, and that there must be a satisfaction ere they can be removed, they yet the elect cannot satisfy for themselves: *For the transgressions of my people 'was he stricken;* Christ behoved to be smitten, ere their sin could be removed. If the elect could have done their own business, they needed not to have been so much in Christ's common and debt, nor to have given him thanks for this undertaking: But this is brought in to hold forth the condescendency of his love, that when no other thing could do it, he interposed as Surety; the abominableness of sin was so great, that the Majesty of God, his infinite holiness and his spotless justice being wronged, and the finite creature not being able to make amends for the wrong done, did require this: For all mankind, yea, all the holy Angels, could not satisfy for the wrong done by one man to the infinite God; therefore he says, *I am the Saviour, and there is none else*: He gives defiance to all saviours beside himself, *None can redeem his brother's soul from death, nor give a price sufficient for it, the redemption of it ceaseth for ever* among the creatures.

Use. Study then to be suitably sensible of this: Ye may possibly think it to be but a common doctrine, but alas! ye walk not under the due and deep conviction and sense of it; hence it comes to pass, that so few think themselves in Christ's common, and that so few make their address to him. Ask the most part, how they think they will win to heaven? They will readily name many things and ways,

ere

ere they light on Christ and faith in him; if they have done a fault, they say they will make amends, or they will pray for pardon, and they think that will do the turn: Such have this language in effect, that either there is no need of satisfaction for sin, or that they can satisfy for themselves.

6thly, It is implied here, that tho' the elect have sinned, and cannot satisfy for themselves, yet it is necessary that a satisfaction be provided for them: I do not say simply, that whoever hath sinned must have a satisfaction made for them; for the Lord hath left legions of angels, and many thousands of reprobate men and women, without hope of a Saviour, or of a satisfaction: But, considering God's purpose to bring many sons to glory, and his decree of election which must needs stand, and that the elects names are written in the book of life; it is impossible that they can ly still under the curse, but must be satisfied for, and redeemed from it: *For the transgression of my people was he stricken*: My people have sinned, and must be redeemed. On supposition of the decree of election, our Lord undertook that great work; the elect cannot perish, sin cannot draw them utterly away from God: Not only shall no externals, such as devils or men, persecution, tribulation, &c. be able to come betwixt them and life, but not sin itself that is within them; his decree, being peremptory, must stand, as he says, John x. *I have other sheep, which are not of this fold, them also I must bring in*: God's purpose cannot be frustrated nor altered, therefore of necessity their sins must be satisfied for.

7thly, It is implied here, that for this end, to wit, that the elect might be saved from sin, and that God's decree of election might stand sure, Christ Jesus became Surety, and did undertake to satisfy for their sins; otherways he could not have been liable to be stricken for them, if he had not become Surety for them. That he was for the transgression of God's people stricken, says plainly that he was engaged for them, as it is, Heb. vii. 22. *He was made Surety of a better testament*; and Psal xl. 7. *Then said I, Lo, I come; in the volume of thy book it is written of me, I delight to do thy will, O my God*: These things being spoken after the manner of and borrowed from the bargainings or transactions that use to be amongst men, we may conceive the business thus, (hinted before) There is the Father's refusing of somewhat, *Sacrifice and offering thou didst not desire;* and his proposing of another thing, and that is, that the Mediator would engage for the elect: And upon the other side, there is the Mediator's offer to undertake, and his actual undertaking and accepting of the Father's proposal; when sacrifices and offerings, when thousands of rams, and ten thousand rivers of oil will not do it, *Lo, I come*, saith he: And then, for a conclusion of the bargain and transaction, there is the Father's accepting of his undertaking, he is content to take his sufferings as the price for the elect's debt; hence, John xvii. he saith, *Thine they were, and thou gavest them me*, that is, thine they were by election, and thou gavest them me to be redeemed by me, and Heb. x. 10. it is said, that *it is by this will that we are sanctified*, that is, by the will of the Father, that the Son should be Surety.

Use. Look upon the work of redemption as a great, gracious, and glorious work; about the designing and contriving whereof, the Father, Son, and Holy Ghost were occupied (to speak so with reverence) before the world was: He might have made worlds of angels, and of sinless men and women at a word, and yet he hath graciously condescended to this way for redeeming of the poor elect. We are, alas! sinfully disposed to think little of the salvation and redemption of a soul; but it is a great matter in God's account, the deepest of whose consultation (to say so) is taken up about it, and in the contrivance whereof the manifold wisdom of God conspicuously shineth forth; and as in other things therein, so in this, that there was an ancient undertaking and engaging by Jesus Christ in the room of the elect as their Surety.

8thly, While it is said, *For the transgressions of my people was he cut off and stricken*, it implies, that Christ, in his undertaking for the elect, did oblige himself to undergo all these sufferings that were due to them, and even the sufferings of a cursed death, which was the curse threatned against man for sin, *The day thou eats thou shalt surely die:* And tho' Christ becoming Surety and Cautioner, the Party is altered, yet the price is still continued to be the same, as is clear, Gal. iii. 11. *He was made a curse for us, that the blessing of Abraham might come on us Gentiles;* whereby the justice of God is vindicate, and he hath access to shew mercy to the elect, without any the least imputation to it. Nay, this way is more for the vindicating of God's justice, and for the making of his faithfulness to shine, that Christ became Man, and died for the elect, than if the curse had lighted and lain on all the elect themselves, and it is a greater aw-band on sinners against sin; I say again, that thereby the pure and spotless justice of God is more vindicated, and his faithfulness more demonstrated, when he will needs so severely, and with so much holy rigour, exact of the Cautioner the elect's debt to the last farthing, than if they had suffered themselves eternally, It shews forth also both the manifold wisdom and riches of the free grace of God: There being a decree of election, for saving of many, and for bringing them to glory; and they being under sin, there is another decree and threatning that goes forth for cursing the sinner: And these two seeming to be altogether irreconcilable, the question comes in on the one hand, How is it possible that a sinner under the curse can be saved? And upon the other hand, How is it possible that an elect of God can be damned? The wisdom of God looseth the knot: spotless justice is satisfied, by taking hold of, and falling on the Cautioner: Wonderful grace and love vent themselves in pardoning the sinner, and accepting of a ransom for him; and manifold wisdom manifests itself in knitting these two together, so as none of them can want its effect; but all turns to the manifestation of the glory of grace in the up-shot: It cannot be that the elect shall be damned, yet here stands the threatning of a just God, and his curse ready to be execute: but here is the reconciliation; the curse is execute on the Mediator, whereby God shews himself to be a hater of sin, and an avenger of the wrong done to his justice; and the elect sinner is pardoned, whereby God manifesteth the freedom of his grace, and his wonderful condescending love.

But now we come to a *6th doctrine*, which is more directly held forth in these words, and it hath two branches, " That our Lord Jesus his death " and sufferings is a proportionable price and satis- " faction laid down for the sins of the elect, and " for them only." This is in the express words of the prophet. If the question be asked, Wherefore suffered Christ all this? He answers, He suffered it as a price for transgression: If it be asked again, For whom, or for whose transgressions did he suffer? He answers, Not for all men and women in the world, but *for the transgression of my people was he stricken*, or the stroke was on him for their transgressions. The first branch of the doctrine is to this purpose, That Christ's suffering is intended to satisfy for the transgressions of God's elected people, and with respect to satisfying for their sins did he suffer: And if we take these to be truths that we marked before, as implied in the words, this will natively and necessarily follow; if he engaged to be Cautioner and Surety for the elect's debt, then his laying down his life must be on the same account, and for the same end: Now, when we speak of Christ's laying down a price to satisfy for the transgressions of the elect, we mean not only this, that his sufferings and death have a value in themselves to satisfy for their sins, but that they are so intended by him in undergoing of them, and that they are so accepted of God, according to his purpose, and according to the transaction that past betwixt Jehovah and the Mediator: They are not only (as Socinians say) to be a confirmation of the doctrine which he preached, and to be a rule and example to us of patient suffering, and of giving obedience to the death, as he did; but it is also, and mainly, to satisfy the justice of God for our debt: So then this wicked tenet of the Socinians is exceeding derogatory to the sufferings of Christ, and to the matchless love that shined in them, yea, and even to the whole design of redemption: for if Christ's sufferings be not a satisfaction to justice, we are left without all just plea and apology for ourselves at God's bar; and if we have none, then that curse looks the wakened sinner full in the face, *The day thou eats thou shalt surely die*. And however men in their security may please themselves with such dreams, and think that a satisfaction to justice is not needful, yet if the conscience be once awakened, it will not be quieted without one; and if men's faith give not credit to God's threatnings, they can have but little, or rather no comfort at all in his promises: There is therefore a necessity of a satisfaction; and if Christ's sufferings be not the satisfaction, there is not another, and so the whole work of redemption is overturned. So then, tho' Christ in his sufferings hath left us a copy how we should suffer, yet that is not the only nor the principal end of them; but it is contrived in the covenant of redemption, and intended by the Mediator, and withal accepted by Jehovah, that they should be the meritorious cause of pardon to the elect, and the price of their redemption.

This may be further cleared and confirmed, 1. From the phrase that is ordinarily made use of in scripture, *He suffered for the sins* of his people; and in the text, *For the transgression of my people was he stricken*: Their sins had a peculiar influence in bringing the stroke on him: And what influence, I pray, could they have, but as they procured the stroke to him? And if his strokes were procured by our sins, then the desert of them was laid on him, and his sufferings behoved to be the curse that we elect sinners should have suffered. So, when he is called their Cautioner, it tells that he undertook their debt; and his laying down of his life is the performance and fulfilling of his undertaking, he was lifted before God's tribunal, and being our Cautioner he was called to reckon for them, and they were put upon his account or score. 2. It is clear also from the names that his sufferings get in the scripture, where they are called the *price of our redemption, a buying* of us, a *propitiation* for our sins that pacified God, Rom. iii. 25. and 1 John ii. 2. A *Sacrifice* often, and *Ransom*, Matt. xx. 28. *The Son of man came to give his life a ransom for many*, that is, for all his elect people, to relieve them from the bondage they were under; which plainly shews the respect that his sufferings had to our sins, that they were a propitiation for them to God. 3. It is clear, if we consider that Christ's death, as to its object, is for the transgressions of all God's people; of all the elect that lived before he suffered, whether they died in their infancy or at age; and for all that lived or shall live and die after his suffering, to the end of the world. Now, what benefit could redound to them that died ere Christ came in the flesh by his sufferings, if it were as Socinians say? for his death could not be a sure pattern of patience and obedience to them: But the efficacy of his death was from the beginning of the world: He was still in that sense the Lamb slain, before his incarnation, as well as since: And if it be not meritorious in procuring salvation to elect infants, what influence or advantage can it have as to them; either they are not taken to heaven at all, or they are taken to heaven, and yet not in the least obliged to Christ for their being brought thither; or if they be obliged to him, it is certainly by vertue of the merit of his sufferings, for expiating the sins of his people. 4. It is clear from this, that in this same chapter, and throughout the gospel, all the benefits that come to God's people, as namely, justification and pardon of sin, they are attributed to this as the cause of them, as verse 11. *By his knowledge shall my righteous Servant justify many:* And if all the spiritual benefits that come to us were procured by his death, there must necessarily be vertue in it that procured them, and it must be a price and satisfaction in reference to the procuring and purchasing thereof, that he laid down sufferings had not a satisfaction in them to divine justice, tho' there might be some shew of shewing mercy, yet none at all of a satisfaction to justice: But saith the Apostle. Rom. iii. 25, 26. *God hath set him forth to be a propitiation thro' faith in his blood, to declare his righteousness, and that he might be just, and the justifier of them which believe in Jesus;* By this, God hath made it maniest, that he is a just God, that none may preposterously presume upon mercy, nor dare to bourd with sin when it is pursued in the Surety with such severity.

For *Use* and application. 1. Do not think these truths to be of little concernment to you, as alas! they, and such like truths of the gospel, are often thought of by many; and therefore they are tasteless to them, and it is a weariness to people to hear them spoken of: And yet, notwithstanding, this same truth that we are now upon, is a great ground of our faith; for if we believe not this that Christ was a propitiation for sin, we can have no ground of lippening to him, or believing on him: But, knowing and being confirmed in the faith of this truth, we have (cordially closing with him) ground from it to expect God's favour, and to be freed from the curse; because Christ as our Surety, undertook, and accordingly satisfied for us; which is the thing that makes his death to be sweet: That Christ in his death should demit himself to leave us an example, is much; yet, if we had no more by it, it would be but cold comfort, except we had it as a satisfaction to divine justice to rest upon. Tho' this may be looked upon as doctrinal only, yet it comes nearer to our practice than we are aware of; and tho' we have no Socinians in opinion and profession to deal with, yet we have two sorts that are Socinians in heart amongst us. 1*st*, These that securely sin on still, and yet hope to get mercy, and who will confess that they are sinners, but that, for making an amends, they will pray and mend their life; and they will speak of a number of things, but it may be, not one word of Christ, or of his purchase, or of their natural inclination to presume, and to slight Christ, as if they had nothing yet to look to but a covenant of works without a Saviour, or as if God had removed or would remove the curse threatned without a satisfaction, so that Christ's satisfaction is not known nor rested on by the multitude of hypocrites that live in the visible Church; and this is easily proven from this, that there are but very few who make use of him, or stand in aw to sin: If it were believed that justice required, and will have satisfaction, either of the sinner himself, or of a Surety in his room, and that Christ is the only Surety, folks would either quit their hopes of heaven, or be more in Christ's common; and that so many maintain the hope of heaven without a due consideration of a satisfaction to justice by Christ, and without employing of him, it declares plainly, that they are drunken with this error. A 2d sort are these, who being wakened in conscience; and sensible of sin, yet are as heartless, hesitating, and hopeless to get peace thro' him, as if he had not satisfied: What else does the doubting and despondency of such say, but that there is not a compleat satisfaction in Christ's death, and that therefore they dare not trust to it? otherwise they would wonder that God hath provided such a remedy, and yet adventure to rest upon it, seeing God is as well pleased with it, as if they had not provoked him at all, or had satisfied his justice themselves.

2dly, It serves to let us see what we are in God's common and debt, and how much we are obliged to the Mediator, when there was a necessity, that either he should suffer, or that we should perish; and that tho' his sufferings drew so deep, as to bring him *to prison and to judgment*, and to put him to a holy sinless anxiety and perplexity, that yet he yielded to it, and underwent all for our sakes: This is our great ground of confidence, and the strong stay of the mind of a wakened believer; and should make us wonder at the Father's love that gave the Son, and at the Son's love that was so condescending; and should make our souls warm towards him, who, when we deserved nothing but to be hurried away to the pit, was content to enter himself as our Surety, and to pay our debt: It should also be a motive to chase souls into him, knowing that where sin is, there a satisfaction must be; and that there is therefore a necessity to flee to him, and to be in him, because there is no other way to get justice satisfied; the thorough conviction whereof is that which thro' grace not only chaseth the soul to, but engageth it to close with Christ, and to rest upon him, and to give him the credit of its through-bearing, when it is ready otherwise to sink. Now the Lord himself teach you to make this use of this doctrine.

SERMON XXXIII.

Isaiah liii. 8. *He was taken from prison, and from judgment; and who shall declare his generation? For he was cut off out of the land of the living, for the transgression of my people was he stricken.*

THERE is nothing that concerns us more, than to be well acquainted with the doctrine of Christ Jesus, and his sufferings; the prophet hath therefore been much in shewing what Christ suffered in the former words, and hath largely described his humiliation to judgment and death, *For* (saith he) *he was cut off out of the land of the living*. In the words read he answers two important questions concerning his sufferings, 1*st*, To what end were all these sufferings? He answers, That they were for transgressions, even to be a satisfaction to justice for them. The 2*d* question is, For whose sins were the sufferings of Christ to be a satisfaction? It is answered expresly in the words, *For the transgression of my people was he stricken*, or the stroke was upon him; it was for the sins of the elect, and of the elect only: For this is the prophet's scope, who, having spoken of Christ's sufferings and death, holds forth the meritorious and procuring cause and end thereof; and this is the result, design and sum of all, even to be a satisfaction for God's elect people: For (as we shew) by God's people are not meaned all men in the world, nor the Jews only, for Christ hath many sheep beside them; but it is God's peculiar people, in opposition to the multitude who are not his people.

The doctrine, or rather the branch of the doctrine we left at, was this, (and it is exclusive) " That " Christ's death is only intended to be a price for " the sins of God's elect people, and was laid " down with respect to them: His death and suffer- " ings are to be looked upon, and considered only " as a price and satisfaction for their sins, and for " the sins of none other." Or thus, " Jesus Christ " in his sufferings, and in the laying down of his " life, had a respect to the elect, and intended the " removing of the sins and transgressions of God's " elect people only, and of none other." We know nothing that we can make of these words, nor of the prophet's scope in them, but this; who, as he hath been describing Christ's sufferings in all other respects, so doth he in this, to wit, in respect of the

persons

persons for whom he suffered, and of the meritorious cause and end of his sufferings; for says the text, *For the transgression of my people*, that is, of God's elect people, *was he stricken*.

This branch of the doctrine is of great weight and concernment in the whole strain of grace; for if this march-stone be lifted, and removed, grace becomes common, and as some call it, *universal*, and so to be in effect no grace at all; for grace hath a peculiar channel of its own, wherein it runs toward a certain select number, and not towards all: I do not mean of grace taken in a large sense, for so all men, as they are partakers of any mercy, or of common favours, may be said to have grace extended to them; But I mean God's special grace, favour and good-will, which is extended only to the elect, for whose sins Christ suffered: The right bounding of which doctrine shews forth both God's sovereignty, in the dispensing of grace, and the freeness thereof in communicating and manifesting of it to whom he will; and which, thus considered, is especially engaging to the hearts of them on whom he pleaseth to manifest it.

Ere I come to confirm this branch of the doctrine, take a word or two of advertisement in the entry. *1st*, That Christ's death may be considered *two* ways. (1.) In respect of itself, and as abstracting from the covenant of redemption, wherein it is contrived as to all the circumstances of it; in which sense, as his death and sufferings are of infinite value and worth, so they are (as divines use to speak) of value to redeem the whole world, if God in his design and decree had so ordered, and thought meet to extend it. (2.) We are to consider his sufferings and death, as a price agreed upon in the covenant and bargain of redemption; wherein these two or three things concur. 1. God's proposal. 2. Christ's acceptation, and design in laying down his life. 3. The Father's acquiescing therein, and declaring himself well pleased therewith. We speak not here of Christ's death in the first respect, that is as abstracting from the covenant; for, in that respect, he might have laid down his life for few or more, for some, or for all, if it had been so intended: But we speak of it in the second respect, as it is a price agreed upon in God's purpose, and Christ's design, and in God's acceptation; and thus we say, that his death is only intended as a satisfaction and recompence for the sins of the elect, and was laid down for them only.

2dly, We may consider Christ's sufferings and death in the fruits of it, either as they respect common favours, and mercies, common gifts, and means of grace, which are not peculiar and saving, but common to believers with others, being bestowed upon professors in the visible church; or as they are peculiar and saving, such as faith, justification, adoption, &c. Now when we say, that Christ's sufferings and death are a price for the sins of his people, we exclude not the reprobate simply from temporal and common favours and mercies that come by his death; they may have, and actually have, common gifts and works of the Spirit, the means of grace, which are someway effects and fruits of the same covenant; But we say, that the reprobate partake not of saving mercy, and that Christ's death is a satisfaction only for the elect, and that none others get pardon of sin, faith, repentance, &c. by it, but they only; it was intended for none others. And this we clear and confirm from, and by, these following grounds and arguments, which we will shortly hint at.

The *1st* argument is drawn from this same assertion of the prophet thus, If Christ's death be only a satisfaction for the sins of God's people, then it is not a satisfaction for the sins of all; but it is a satisfaction only for the sins of God's people, therefore not for all; for his people are not all men, or all men are not his people, but his people are a peculiar people, separate from others, in God's purpose and decree, as we cleared before from John xvii. *Thine they were, and thou gavest them me*; and the text says expresly, *For the transgression of my people was he stricken*: He respected the sins of God's people, in accepting of the bargain, and in laying down his life, and for their sins only God accepted him; yea, the very mentioning of them thus here, secludes all others; and we must expone them exclusively as taking in none others, and must look upon the things spoken of them, as agreeing to no other; even as it is said, Heb. iv. *There remains therefore a rest to the people of God*, which is certainly exclusive of all others: And hence, when our Lord speaks of them, John xvii. he opposeth them to, and contradistinguisheth them from all others; *I pray for them, I pray not for the world, but for them which thou hast given me out of the world*; to let us know, that the things prayed for to the one, are denied to the other, according to the strain of the covenant.

A *2d* ground is drawn from the strain and frame of the covenant of redemption, where we find two things clear, (1.) That as to the end and convey of it, the elect are the only persons for whose good and behoof it is intended; and if it be the elect for whom he entered in that covenant, then the advantage

"believeth on him, may have everlasting life. Which will be the more clear, if we consider the time when this is spoken; it is at such a time, when many will not come to him, and believe on him, as ver. 36, 37. " Ye also have seen me, and believe " not: All that the Father hath given me, shall " come unto me, and him that cometh, I will in " no wise cast out; for I came down from heaven, " not to do mine own will, but the will of him " that sent me;" and then follows " This is the " will of him that sent me, &c. and ver. 43, 44. " Murmur not (saith he) among yourselves; no " man can come to me, except the Father that sent " me, draw him." This ye heard of from John xvii. 2. at greater length. 2. Look on the Son's side of the covenant, and it will also be clear; for his undertaking must be according to the Father's proposing: If the Father did not propose all, but some only to be redeemed, then his undertaking must be for these some, and not for all, conform to the Father's proposal, Psal. xl. *Then said I, Lo, I come to do thy will, O my God:* Now, the Father's will is, that he should undertake for these given him; and it is not his will, that he should undertake for others, therefore he did not undertake for them. 3. Christ's sufferings and death are the executions of the Father's will, and therefore must be the execution of his undertaking, according to his engagement for the elect, and given ones; therefore these two are put together, John xvii. 9. and 19. " I pray for them, I pray not for " the world, but for them which thou hast given " me, and for their sakes I sanctify myself," that is, for their sakes whom thou had given me, and not for the world; he sanctifies himself for them, for whom he prays, for them that are given him, and no more.

(2.) This is clear in the covenant, that Christ's death is intended therein, as all other mercies covenanted are; that is to say, to whom faith, effectual calling, justification, &c. are covenanted, for these is Christ's death covenanted, and for none others; for the covenant being mutual, the repromission on the Father's part must be of equal extent elect, and to none others: and when the smallest of blessings are covenanted, and articled for none other, but for the elect, shall Jesus Christ himself, *that gift of God,* or his death, which is the chief thing articled in the covenant, be covenanted for, or applied to any others but to them?

A 3d ground is drawn from Christ's executing of his offices; for this piece or part of Christ's executing of his offices, must correspond, and be of equal extent with all the other parts, and pieces of his offices, such as his effectual teaching, interceeding, subduing to himself, &c. which are no broader than the elect, for he executes no part of any of his offices for the behoof and benefit of any but of the elect; he savingly enlightens no others; he subdues none others to the faith of the gospel; he interceeds for none other; his intercession is not for the world; therefore his death must be for none others, all these being commensurable and of equal extent; his intercession being grounded on his sufferings: Therefore, John xvii. he lays by the world expresly, as these for whom he will not pray, and looks back to the covenant, as the ground of his undertaking for the elect, given him out of the world, and not for others; and if he will not pray nor interceed for others, what reason can be given for his dying for others? when he will not do the less, which is to pray for them, it were absurd to think or say, that he will do the greater, which is to lay down his life for them.

A *4th* ground is this, Christ's death is one of the peculiar evidences of his dearest love, beyond which there is none greater, and a main proof and fruit thereof, and therefore is not common to all, but is intended for them only, whom he peculiarly loves, and designs to bring through to glory; which is clear, Eph. v. 26. *Husbands love your wives, as Christ loved his Church, and gave himself for it,* &c. Rom. v. 5. *God commends his love to us, in that, while we were yet sinners, Christ died for us:* John xv. 13. *Greater love hath no man than this, that a man should lay down his life for his friends;* there is a world of reprobates whom Christ never loved with peculiar love, and sure for these he did

not

not die: *Jacob have I loved, but Esau have I hated*, saith the Lord, Rom. ix. 13. which the apostle holdeth forth, as a sort of copy of God's dealing in reprobation and election in reference to all mankind; and where the Lord himself hath set bounds betwixt them whom he loves and hates, it is too great liberality, or rather too great presumption for any, under whatever specious pretences, to extend this his peculiar love to those whom he disclaims.

A 5th ground is taken from the effect, thus; All for whom Christ died are justified, and freed from the guilt of their sins in due time: but Christ Jesus hath not purchased and actually procured freedom to all men from their sins, all men are not justified; therefore he laid not down his life for all: For, 1. It cannot be said, that he laid down his life for purchasing and buying of such wares, and yet that he got not that which he bought; and seeing the event tells plainly, that all are not justified and brought to heaven, it cannot be that he laid down his life a ransom for all, but it must be for the elect only, that he died. 2. To say, that God exacts double payment of one and the self same debt, that he exacts from men over again that which Christ paid already for them, reflects on the justice and wisdom of God: And to say, that person that goes to hell shall be no less in his common than others that go to heaven, is no less absurd; for the apostle says, Rom. v. 10. *If while we were enemies, we were reconciled to God by the death of his Son, much more being reconciled, we shall be saved by his life* ⁖ where he plainly insinuates, that if a person be bought by Christ's death, it cannot be that he can perish; for if the price be paid by his death, and so the greater thing be done, much more will the lesser, *we shall be saved by his life* ⁖ Now this reasoning could have no force, if Christ died for any that shall perish; yea, ver. 11. of this chapter, it is said, *By his knowledge shall my righteous servant justify many, for he shall bear their iniquities ;* where it is clear, that as many (and no more) whose iniquities Christ hath taken on and born, shall be justified; for the one is given as a reason of the other: and there should be no consequents to his justifying of them, from his bearing of their iniquities, if he could by his death bear their iniquities, whom he never justified.

A 6th ground is taken from the end of the covenant, which is to put a difference betwixt special grace peculiar to some, and severe justice to others, and particularly and specially in Christ's death, which makes out what we affirm: For if, when Christ died, many were actually damned, it cannot be said that he died for these, nor that it was with them, as with believers before his death ; for it cannot be said, that the intention of his death in the covenant, could be beyond what it was at his death, the one being the execution of the other: and sure it could not be intended at his death for the damned; for it would seem a very absurd thing to say, that when Christ was to go and lay down his life, that he was going to suffer for many, that were suffering for their own sins in hell, as many reprobate sinners were before he came in the flesh; can any imagine a possibility of such a thing? Our Lord was not to be so indifferent in the administration of grace, as to cast it thus away; and can any reasonably think, that at one and the same time, the same punishment shall be exacted from Christ, and from the persons themselves, for whom he suffered? Is it possible that this could be intended in the covenant of redemption? Or is there free access to justice to pursue Christ as cautioner, when the principal debtor is actually seized upon? indeed, when the principal is set free, as the elect were, before his death, there is access to pursue the cautioner for their debt: but no such thing can be alledged for others that were already damned; but their being taken hold of by justice, is a proof that he answered not for them, nor paid their debt.

7thly, We may argue thus, If Christ died for all, then either for all indifferently, and so all were alike obliged to Christ; or for some more absolutely that must be satisfied for, and for others conditionally, on supposition that they should believe: but this last is absurd; for, (1.) The scripture makes not two considerations of Christ's death. (2.) It were absurd to say, that now it cannot be told, whether Christ died for such an one or not. (3.) Either that condition is bought to them or not: If it be bought, then it must be fulfilled; if it be not bought, then, 1. That person cannot be said to be bought, because all needful for his redemption is not bought and paid for. 2. Either that condition can be fulfilled by themselves or not: If it may be by themselves, then is free will established, and none are absolutely redeemed: If it cannot be fulfilled by themselves, and yet bought by him for them, they are determined for another end, to wit, not to get it; and what wisdom can there be in such a redemption as this?

The 1st *Use* serves for clearing and confirming of a gospel-truth of the covenant of redemption, and for the refutation of a contrary error. As we have somewhat of many errors practically in our hearts, so have we this amongst the rest, that Christ died

died for all finners; which fosters peoples security, and their groundless hope of admission to heaven: But here we see, that our Lord Jesus, so laying down his life, intended the satisfaction of divine justice for none but for his elect people; and if so, there are many for whom he never intended the benefit of his death. There are *three* particular branches of the error, which this doctrine confutes; 1*st*, Their opinion, which is more lax, and takes in the sins of all men and women in the world, and giveth them an equal share of Christ's sufferings; as if in his intention in laying down his life, and in God's purpose, he had suffered and died for all, for him that goes to hell, as well as for him that goes to heaven: But if Christ stand as Cautioner for the elect only, then sure this opinion cannot hold; for all are not God's elect, and therefore all are not indifferently redeemed: And tho' it may be that some of you think that this looks liker grace, yet it is not only absurd, as being contrary to truth, but it is absurd also, even with respect to grace; For, 1. It makes grace a common thing, a man that is in hell to be as much obliged to Christ, as one that is in heaven: And tho' it plausibly pretends to give grace a broad and large extent, yet it takes away the power of it; for if grace be thus largely extended, it is not grace that makes the application of grace, but the free-will of the creature; for grace, according to this opinion, leaves men to be saved or not as they please, and leaves itself to be overcome by man's will: And therefore these errors divide not, but go together hand in hand; for, where grace is made so large, free-will is made to have a dominion over it, and thus the weight of grace and of election are laid upon it. 2. It lesseneth the estimation of God's grace in the minds of people; for thus, they think little of heaven, and suppose that it is an easy matter to win at it; and it breeds in them a fearlesness of hell and of God's wrath: And if many of you had not drunken in this error practically, ye would not be so confident of it, nor so obstinately maintain your hope of heaven without ground; hence, alas! it is, that many will say, God is merciful, and Christ died for all finners, and for me; and so sleep it out in security. I am persuaded, that much of the security and presumption that abounds among carnal professors is from this ground, that grace is fancied to be thus broad and large: We grant, that as to the convey and nature of it, it is broad; but, in respect of the objects on whom it is bestowed, it is narrow, tho' it cometh from large bowels. 3. It exceedingly mars, and diminisheth man's thankfulness; for when a mercy is judged to be common, who will praise for it, as he would do, if it were special and peculiar? That which is a great ground of thankfulness for election, effectual calling, justification, *&c.* is because these mercies are peculiar; even so, that which makes the redeemed thankful for redemption, is because they are redeemed and bought when others are left: Hence is that song of the redeemed company, Rev. v. 9. *Thou art worthy to open the book; for thou wast slain, and hast redeemed us to God by thy blood, out of every kindred, and tongue, and people and nation.* It heightens not their praise, that all of every kindred, and tongue, and nation were redeemed; but this doth it, that when the Lord had the whole world before him, he was graciously pleased to purchase, and redeem them out of it, that, as it is, John xi. 52. *He should gather together in one the children of God, that were scattered abroad:* They therefore, I say, bless him, and wonder when they consider, that they are pitched on, who are by nature the same with these that are past by. It were a strange thing to affirm, that they who are in hell have as great ground of praise, and of saying, *We thank thee, for thou hast redeemed us by thy blood,* as these that are in heaven have. 4. This making of grace so wide and large in its extent, as to take in all, doth leave the people of God altogether comfortless. But it may be here said, How is it that it is more comfort to believers, that grace is peculiar in saving, and that but few are redeemed, in comparison of others that are not redeemed, than if we should extend it unto, and account it to be for all? Or how is this more comfortless to them, that grace is made universal? Answer, (1.) Because, if it were universal, many, whom Christ died for, are now in hell; and what consolation can there be from that? A man may be redeemed, and yet perish, and go to hell, for all that? but it is strong consolation, when this comes in, *If, when we were enemies, we were reconciled by the death of his Son, much more being reconciled, we shall be saved by his life.* If he died for us when we were enemies, will he not much more save us, being friends? (2.) Suppose a person to be in black nature, what comfort could he have by looking on redemption as universal? he could not expect heaven by it; for many expect heaven on that ground, who will never get it: But it is a sort of consolation, even to them that are without, to consider that redemption is peculiar to some; for tho all get not heaven, yet they that believe get it, and so upon their closing with Christ, the consolation presently flows out unto them; where-

as,

as, if they should lay it for a ground that Christ's death were universal, they could never have solid ground of consolation by fleeing to him. 5. This error doth quite overturn and enervate the whole covenant of redemption and peculiar love. (1.) It enervates and obscures the wisdom that shines in it, if Christ may buy and purchase many by his death, who shall yet notwithstanding perish. (2.) It enervates and obscures the love and grace that shine in it; for it makes Christ to cast away the love and grace of it to reprobates, and so cast pearls to swine. (3.) It obscures the freedom of it, which appears in his taking of one, and refusing another, as it is, Rom. ix. 11, 12. *The children not being yet born, and having done neither good nor evil, that the purpose of God according to election might stand, not of works, but of him that calleth, it was said, The elder shall serve the younger: as it is written, Jacob have I loved, and Esau have I hated.* (4.) It obscures the justice of it, if he should buy all, and yet get but some: For it being the design of God to inflict on Christ the curse that was due to sinners, and to spare them; if this should be the result of it, that many, for whom he died, and took on him the curse, should perish, he should get but some of these whom he bought, and justice should twice exact satisfaction for one and the same debt; once of the Surety, and again of the principal debtor that perisheth. Whereas, when Christ becomes surety, they are set free for whom he was surety; and it is justice that it should be so. We do the rather insist in the confutation of this error, because this is a time wherein it is one of the devil's great designs, which he drives, to trouble the clear springs of the gospel, and to revive this error amongst the rest; and there is something of it in these poor fool bodies, who speak so much of a light within, as if all were alike, and had something, which, if they use well, they may get life by: This error always leaves men to be masters and carvers of God's decree, and of Christ's purpose and design in the work of redemption, and suspends the benefit of his death, mainly, if not only, on the consent of mans free-will.

A 2d branch of this error, which this doctrine refutes, is that which is vented by some, who are not professed enemies, but in other things deserve well of the church of Christ, which therefore should be our grief to mention; and it is this, That tho' Christ hath not simply purchased redemption from sin to all men, that yet he hath taken away from all the sins of that first covenant of works, as if there were (as they say) no sin for which men are now condemned, but the sin of infidelity, or unbelief. But this is dangerous; for, 1. If this be true, that Christ's death is only a price for the sins of the elect, then there are no sins of others reckoned on this score. 2. It halveth Christ's purchase, and hardly will we find Christ's death divided, which were to say, that he hath bought a man in part or half from wrath, and not wholly: Such a dividing of Christ, and halving of his death, seems not consistent with the strain of the gospel; for as there is one sacrifice, so there is one account on which it is offered. 3. It seems to infer a good and safe condition to all them that die without sinning against the gospel, and so to infants born out of the church, that never sinned against the covenant of grace: and it pleads much for them, that never heard the gospel, yea possibly for all, if they be not obliged to believe the gospel, as it is hard to say they are, who never heard of it. 4. There are many in hell this day, who know and feel this to be an untruth, being condemned for sins against the covenant of works; therefore he undertook not their debt, nor paid for them: And, when the books shall be cast open, there will be many other sins found to reckoned for, than sins against the gospel. Are not whoremongers, adulterers, murderers, thieves, &c. to reckon for these sins? It is very sad that such things should take place with men otherwise useful, but as in other things, so in this hurtful; which we should not speak of, were it not that they are spread abroad in books wherewith many may be leavened.

A 3d branch of the error, which this doctrine refutes, is, That Christ died conditionally for all hearers of the gospel, to whom he is conditionally offered; and this is also vented by the same authors, who say, That tho' he hath not bought all men absolutely, nor died to procure life absolutely to them, yet that he did so conditionally, and upon supposition that they should afterwards believe on him: But there can be no conditional satisfaction intended here; for, 1. If respect be had only to the sins of the elect in Christ's undertaking, then none is had to the sins of all. 2. If the Father's acceptation of the price be absolute, then there is no conditional buying. 3. If it be conditional, then he suspended the effect of his death, the satisfaction for his soul-travel, on man's will: And if this condition could not be fulfilled by man, then it is an unwise bargain, and nothing of it may fall to be fulfilled; and then believing is no fruit of grace. Again, he hath either bought faith to them, as he hath done to the elect, or not: if he hath, then they reject it, and so grace is not efficacious; if not, he hath bought the end without the midses leading to it. Or thus, if it be conditional, it is either on a condition that they can fulfil, or on a condition that they cannot fulfil; If it be on a condition that they can fulfil, then it hangs grace on mens free-will, and suspends the decree of election on their receiving of Christ; If it be a condition that is in their power to fulfil, then either Christ hath bought that condition to them, or not: To say that he hath not bought the condition of faith, it will infer a strange assertion, that he hath bought life, and not the condition, the end, and not the mids; and if it be said that he hath bought it, it cannot be said that he hath done it so absolutely, because they never get it; or, if absolutely, then to the elect only, in whom it must be, and is in due time fulfilled: And so in effect it resolves in this, that Christ's purchase is to be bounded and confined (to say so) to the elect only.

There are some difficulties and objections that will readily here be removed, which we will not enter upon, only for preventing of mistakes: It stands in the way of some to hinder their believing, as they suppose, that Christ hath died for some, and not for all; and they know not if they be of that small number. If we were to speak to such, we would say, 1. God hath not elected all, and so who knows if he hath elected them? And he will not save all, and who knows if he will save them? And so the doubt will stick still, if folks will thus break in upon God's secret will and purpose, which belongs not to them. 2. Christ's death for you is not the formal ground nor warrant of your faith, nor yet of the offer of the gospel, but the Lord's will warranting you to believe, and calling for it from you, and his commanding you to rest upon Christ for the attaining of righteousness, as he is offered to us in the gospel: We are invited by his command and promise, and we are not first called to believe that Christ died for us, but we are called first to believe in him that is offered to us in the gospel, that is our duty; and folks are not condemned, because Christ died not for them, but because, when he offered the benefit of his death and sufferings to them, they slighted and rejected it: We are to look first to what Christ calleth to, and not to meddle with the other, to wit, whom Christ minded in his death, till we have done the first. The word bids all believe, that they may be saved; and such as neglect this command, will be found disobedient. 3. Tho' Christ hath not died for all, yet all that flee unto him by faith, shall be partakers of his death; and from this ye should reason, and not from his intention in dying: If ye come not to him, ye cannot have ground to think that he died for you; but if you go to him by faith, ye may expect that he will pray for you, and own you for believers. Christ casts in that word, John xvii. *They have believed thy word;* as well as that other, *Thine they were, and thou gavest them me:* And if we put these two together, the one will be found as sure a ground of consolation as the other; but it were but a poor comfort to say, that Christ died for all, and yet that they may all, or most, or many of them, perish for all that.

The 2d *Use* serves to stir them up to thankfulness for whom Christ hath satisfied, and who are fled for refuge to him: If there be any here to whom Christ hath manifested such love, that they can say he hath loved me, and given himself for me; O how are ye obliged to wonder and bless him! greater love than this cannot be; and it should warm your hearts with love to him the more, when ye reflect on God's design upon you in particular in the covenant of redemption.

Use 3d, If Christ intended his death and sufferings only for behoof of the elect; Then, as because few come to heaven, all should be the more diligent; so, because Christ died not for all, every one should aim, in God's own way, to have it made sure to himself that Christ died for him, and should be the more watchful and diligent to make his calling and election sure; because, as it is not all that are elected, so it is not all that are purchased by Christ's death. Redemption is sure in itself, and free grace appears conspicuously in it; yea wisdom and sovereignty do also appear in this, that it is not of all: therefore study ye to make it sure, by fleeing to Christ by faith, and by the study of holiness and mortification, in his strength, and through the power of his death, which will be a proof of your interest in it: This were much more suitable, than to be quarrelling with God's decrees, as some are brought in, Rom. ix. 19. *Why doth he find fault? Who hath resisted his will?* To whom the apostle answers, *Who art thou that repliest against God?* It becomes you not to dispute with God, but to seek with more solicitude, and with holy and humble carefulness to make the matter sure to yourselves: We may well raise storms by our disputes, but shall come to no peace by them: this can only be come at, by fleeing to the hope set before us.

SERMON

SERMON XXXIV.

Isaiah liii. 9. *And he made his grave with the wicked, and with the rich in his death; because he had done no violence, neither was any deceit in his mouth.*

EVery paſſage of our Lord's way in proſecuting the work of redemption hath ſomewhat wonderful in it: We heard of ſeveral of them, eſpecially in his humiliation, how very low the bleſſed Cautioner condeſcended to come for relief of the captivity; how he was put to wreſtle and fight, and what great ſtrengths or ſtrong holds he was put as it were to take in: There is one ſtrong hold (to ſpeak ſo) not ſpoken of as yet, which muſt alſo be ſtormed, and the fortifications of it pulled down by the Mediator, and that is the *grave*. The prophet tells us, that as he declined not death, ſo neither did he decline the grave; but as he was *cut off out of the land of the living*, as a wicked man in the account of men, ſo in the account of men he was taken down from the croſs with the thieves, and buried in the grave as one of them.

I ſhall not trouble you with diverſity of interpretations, but ſhall only hint at two things, for your better underſtanding of the words, in which the difficulty lieth: the firſt is this, Whether doth this relate to his humiliation only, or to his exaltation, or to both? for it cannot be reaſonably thought, but his being buried with the wicked, is a piece of his humiliation; to make it only an evidence of his humiliation, ſeems not to ſtand with the next part of the words, *becauſe he had done no violence,* &c. which is a cauſal reaſon of that which goeth before: But we anſwer, That there may be here a reſpect unto both; the firſt words reſpect his humiliation, comparing them with the truth of the hiſtory, as it is ſet down, Matt. chap. xxvii. where it is clear that he was deſtinate in the account of men, and by their appointment, to be buried with wicked men; for they thought no more of him than if he had been a wicked man. The next words, *And with the rich in his death,* look to his exaltation, and the meaning of them is, That however he was in the account of men buried with thieves, and laid in the grave as a malefactor or wicked man; yet in God's account, and by his appointment and overruling providence, it was otherwiſe; for he put a difference betwixt him and others, and gave him a honourable burial with the rich: tho' he was deſigned by men to be buried with thieves, yet, as we have it, Mat. xxvii. 57. *Joſeph of Arimathea went to Pilate, and begged his body, and wrapped it in clean linen and laid it in a new tomb;.* which in God's providence was ſo ordered, both to ſhew a difference betwixt him and thoſe thieves, and alſo to declare that he was innocent, as the reaſon ſubjoined tells, *Becauſe he had done no violence, neither was any deceit in his mouth*; and to make way for the clearing of his reſurrection, he being buried in ſuch a remarkable place, where never man had been buried before.

So then the ſum of the words is this, He was humbled in coming to the grave, and in mens account and deſtination was buried as a wicked man; yet by God's decree and providence it was ſo ordered, that tho' he was poor all his days, he had a honourable burial, ſuch as rich men uſe to have, *becauſe he had done no violence, neither was there any deceit in his mouth*: God will not have it going as men deſigned, but will have him honourably buried and laid in the grave, that thereby there might be the greater evidence of his innocency, and a more full clearing and confirmation of the truth of his reſurrection.

What is rendred *death* here in our tranſlation, is *deaths* in the plural number in the Hebrew; to ſhew the greatneſs and terribleneſs of the death which he underwent, and the ſore ſpiritual as well as bodily exerciſe that he was put unto, at, and in his death; ſo that it was a complication of many deaths in one, and at once, which he ſuffered. 2. Where it is ſaid in our tranſlation, that *He made his grave*; in the original it is, *He gave his grave with the wicked:* So that by the pronoun *He,* may be meaned, either of the Father his giving, or it may be underſtood of the Mediator himſelf his giving; and ſo the meaning is, That it came not to paſs by gueſs on God's ſide, but was by him well ordered; and upon the Mediator's ſide it ſets out his willingneſs to go to the grave, and his having an over-ruling hand, as God, in his own death and burial; as he ſaith, John x. 18. *No man taketh my life from me, but I lay it down of myſelf*: His death and burial were determined and well ordered, as to all the circumſtances of both, by a divine decree, and by an overruling hand of providence; and this agrees well with the reaſon ſubjoined, becauſe he willingly condeſcended to die; God put a difference betwixt him and others, as is clear in that of John x. 17. *Therefore doth my Father love me, becauſe I lay down my life for my ſheep.* The verſe hath two parts, (1.) Something foretold concerning the Meſſiah, and that is, *That he ſhall make or give his grave with the wicked, and with the rich in his death.* (2.) There is a reason subjoined, especially to the last part, taken from his innocency, and from the difference that was in his life betwixt him and all men in the world, that therefore God put a difference betwixt him and them in his death and burial.

First then, This point of *doctrine* is implied here, "That coming to the grave is a thing common and certain to all men." I mean, that death, or a state of death, and to be in the grave, in an ordinary way, is common to all men; and whoever wants the privilege of burial, their condition in that respect is rather worse than better. It is supposed here, that wicked men come to the grave, therefore our Lord is said to *make his grave with them*; and it is also supposed, that rich men come to the grave, therefore it is said, *and with the rich in his death*: That which Solomon hath, Eccl. viii. 8. of death, may well be applied to the grave; *There is no man that hath power over the spirit to retain it, neither hath he power in the day of death; and there is no discharge in that war, neither shall wickedness deliver those that are given to it*: The most powerful wicked man cannot prevail over it, nor is he able to resist and withstand it; these who conquer most of the world, are constrained at length to be content with some few feet of ground, and their bodies turned into dust. Job, in the 3d chapter of his book, speaks of it as common to all, to rich and poor, to high and low, to the king and to the beggar, all are there in one category: If any were freed from it, it would readily be rich men; but, as it is, Psal. xlix. 6, 7. their riches will not be a ransom for them: *They that trust in their wealth, and boast themselves in the multitude of their riches, none of them can by any means redeem his brother*, nor give to God a ransom for him; so precious is the soul, *that the redemption* of it *ceases for ever*: Amongst all mortals, there is none that can buy himself from coming to the church-yard, or from coming to the grave; but were he never so rich and honourable, he must be laid in a hole, as well as the poor man; the bravest and best-gilded tomb is but a grave: That sentence past by God must stand and will stand, *Dust thou art, and to dust thou shalt return;* the translation of Enoch and Elias, who did not see death, doth not alter the common rule, tho' it shews the sovereignty and power of God, what he can do.

Use 1. O think more on death and on the grave! these sure would be much more profitable subjects of thoughts than many things which our thoughts run ordinarily on: *It is appointed for men once to die, and thereafter cometh the judgment*. As we walk over and tread on the graves of others now, so some will be walking over and treading on ours ere long; and within a few years our bodies will be turned into dust, and our dust will not be known from the dust of others that lived before us: It were good to have the faith of this more rooted, and that we did meditate more frequently and seriously on it.

Use 2. It reproves the pride of men and women, and their lusting after earthly vanities: When death and the grave come, where will all their brave houses, and clothes, and well drest beds be? and what will become of your silver and gold? These things will not go to the grave with you: As ye brought nothing into the world, so it is certain that ye shall carry nothing out of it; the consideration whereof would be a restraint and aw-band to mens exorbitant desires. The time is coming, when six or seven foot in length, and two or three foot in breadth, of ground, will serve the richest and most honourable; and within a few years the lord provost's dust will not be known from the dust of the poor body that got share of the common contribution; the dust of both will be alike: Dress and pamper the body as ye will, that beauty will not abide with you; wherefore then serves all this pride, vanity and bravity, seeing a very little while's time will lay it all in the dust, and when all your projects will take an end? as Job faith, Chap. xvii. *My purposes are broken;* and what did break them off? *The grave* (faith he) *is waiting for me; I have said to corruption*, to the rottenness of the earth, *Thou art my mother; and to the worms, Ye are my brothers and sisters:* They and I must ly together. These that now cannot get their beds made fine and soft enough, the worms and they will ly together ere long in the grave; the chest or coffin will not be so close but they will win in, nay, they will breed in their own bodies: Do we not see this daily? Were it not then good, that, when ye are going to the burials and graves of others, ye were thinking on your own lying down in the grave? and what will be your thoughts, in that day, of all things in this world? if dead corpses could speak out of the graves, they would preach sharp warnings to them that are alive, and would say to such as are carrying them thither, Beware of putting off thoughts of death, and of the grave. Tho' this be a common point of truth, yet few walk suitably to it; but we are generally in our practice, as if it were not a truth, no more minding death and the grave, than

Use 3. As this should make folks sober in prosperity, so it should make them patient in adversity: A little time will make us all equal; and what is the matter what our condition be, if our peace be made sure with God? Heathens may shame many of us that are professing Christians, who, by the consideration of death, have been brought to be much more sober in their carriage, than alas many of us are.

2*dly*, Observe, "That the Messiah behoved to "come to the grave and be buried." It was so designed, foretold, and fore-prophesied of; *He made his grave with the wicked, and with the rich in his death.* Hence the Apostle, Acts ii. 30. citing Psal. xvi. 8. gathers, that as there was a necessity of his being in the grave, so there was a necessity of his resurrection out of it, because he should not see corruption in it; *His soul was not left in hell*, or in the grave, neither did his flesh see *corruption*: And in all the evangelists it is clear, that after death he was remarkably laid in the grave, and very particular and special notice is taken of it. Take here shortly some few reasons of this necessity according to the Lord's appointment, and no further: The 1*st* whereof is this, That the unstainedness and purity of divine justice may appear; and that therefore the compleatness and perfection of his satisfaction, as Mediator, to the justice of God, may be confirmed: If he had not been buried, it might have been questioned, whether that which folk suffer after death be a reality or not; but his three days lying in the grave, is a greater evidence of the unstainedness and purity of justice, and of its impartiality, than the imprisoning of many creatures for many thousands of years would have been: This shews him to be a just God, when sinners Cautioner is not only pursued to death, but to the grave; and therefore this is always accounted the lowest part or step of his sufferings. And in the Creed, his *descending into hell*, is spoken of, which in our excellent Catechism is expounded to be his *continuing under the power of death for a time*. 2. It is much for the manifestation of the great love of God, and of the rich condescending grace of the Mediator, who is not only content to die, but to be laid in the grave, and to suffer death to have a kind of dominion over him for a time; so that, as death had power to separate his soul from his body, so it prorogates that power during his being in the grave: His enemies, as it were, cry, Take him up now; and they *seal the stone, and set a watch* to keep him in the grave. 3. It is for the consolation of the believer, and serves mightily to strengthen him against the fear of death and the grave; so that the believer needs not be afraid of death, but may ly down quietly in the grave, because it was Christ's bed, warmed (to say so) by him, he was there before him: And the grave is now to the believer no part of the curse, more than death is; the grave will not swallow him up with a sort of dominion and right, as it doth the reprobate. 4. It serves to confirm the truth of the resurrection of Christ, more than if he had never been in the grave, as the Apostle proves, 1 Cor. xv. from the beginning to the close, even till he come to that, *O death! where is thy sting? O grave! where is thy victory?* Our Lord, by dying and being buried, hath delivered his people from both: As neither a great stone, nor a seal put on it, could keep him in the grave, but that he rose again the third day; so nothing will be able for ever to keep believers at under: And as he died to disarm death, so his entering in the grave, was to disarm the grave, and to open a door for believers to come thorow it, by his power who was dead and laid in the grave, but now is risen and alive for evermore.

The *Uses* are, 1. To shew the full conformity and agreeableness that is betwixt what was foretold of the Messiah, and what is fulfilled; and so serves to confirm our faith in this, that he is the true Messiah, who was crucified, dead and buried: This is one of the articles of our faith, foretold by Isaiah, now fulfilled and recorded to be so in the gospel. 2. It shews the severity of justice, that when any person is made liable to the lash of it, were it but as cautioner, it will exact of him satisfaction to the uttermost: Therefore, when Christ enters himself our Cautioner, it not only exacts death, and pursues him till he give up the ghost, but after death pursues him to the grave; it will needs have the satisfaction of the Mediator; and he yields to it, so as to lay himself by as a dead man. O what a revengeful thing is justice, when a sinner must answer to it! When the Mediator was so pursued by it, what will it do to others, who are out of him? Here we may apply that word, *Daughters of Jerusalem, weep not for me, but weep for yourselves and your children; if it be done so to the green tree, what shall be done to the dry?* When the fire of the vengeance of God shall kindle that lake that burns with fire and brimstone, and when sinners shall be cast into it, as so many pieces of wood, or as so many pieces of dry sticks, what will be their condition? It were good in time to fear *falling into the hands of the living God*, which is indeed a most *fearful thing*, Heb. x. 31. 3. It shews the believer's obligation to God, that so fully provided a satisfaction for him, and hath furnished him with such a ground of consolation; beside what is done for the satisfying of justice, (which is the great consolation) there is here ground of consolation against all crosses, pain, sickness, death and the grave; there is not a step in the way to heaven, but our Lord hath gone it before us: We have not only a Mediator that died, but that was buried; and O but this is much, when believers come to think on their going to the grave! Will it devour them, or feed upon them for ever? No, he hath muzled it, to say so; they rest in their graves, as in a bed, their bodies being united to him, and their dust must be counted for: It is true, the bodies of the reprobate must be raised up, yet upon another account, and not by vertue of their union with Christ, and of Christ's victory over death in their stead, as believers are. In a word they have many advantages that have Christ, and they have a miserable life a comfortless death, and a hard lying in the grave, that want him: Therefore, as the short cut to have a happy life, and a comfortable death and burial, and the grave sanctified to you, seek to have your interest in Christ made sure; then all things are yours, and particularly death and the grave, which will be as a box to keep the particles of your dust, till it restore them faithfully to Christ, to whom it must give an account. But as for you that flight and mistken Christ, ye have a dreadful lot of it, no interest in Christ living, no union with him in the grave, nor at the resurrection; and if ye did but seriously consider that ye will die, ye would also consider that it is good dying and being in the grave with Christ, and that it is a woful thing to be, and to be in it, without him.

3dly, Observe, " That all the sufferings of our " Lord Jesus Christ, to the least particular circum-" stance of them, were ordered of God, and be-" fore hand determined and concluded upon ;" none of them came by guess upon him: That he should suffer and die, and what sort of death he should die, and that he should be laid in the grave, all was before concluded and determined. When we read thro' the gospel, it were good to take a look of the Old Testament prophecies of the covenant of redemption, and of the antient determinations concerning him, as Peter doth, Acts ii. 27. *Him, being delivered by the determinate counsel of God, ye have with wicked hands crucified:* God's foreknowledge and determination fixed the bounds, and laid down the rule (to speak so) to these wicked hands in the crucifying of him, without all tincture or touch of culpable accession to their sin: And, in looking over his sufferings, we would call to mind, that this and this was the Lord's purpose, and that in these sufferings, and in every part and piece of them, the Mediator is telling down the price that he undertook to pay ; all which demonstrates the verity of our Lord's being the true Messiah.

4thly, From comparing the two parts of the first part of the verse together, *He made his grave with the wicked*, as to the estimation of men, *and with the rich in his death,* in respect of God's ordering it, Observe, " That often God hath one design, " and men another; and that God will have his " design to stand, and infrustrably to take effect :" When some would design shame to his people, he will have them honoured.

The *1st Use* serves to comfort God's people, when they are in their lowest condition, and when their enemies are in highest power; our Lord is driving on his design, and making his and their enemies to fulfil it : Pilate and the chief Priests, with the Scribes and Pharisees, are putting Christ to death; the multitude are crying, *Crucify him,* and preferring a *robber* to him : But, in all this, they were fulfilling what God had before determined to be done ; which we say is matter of great consolation, both as to our own particular case, and as to God's general guiding of the world, and especially of his Church therein : There is nothing, wherein the malice of men seems to be most prevalent, but our Lord is still gaining his point upon, and by them]; they are all the while executing God's determination, tho' to their own ruin.

2. See here an exact correspondency betwixt all the circumstances of our Lord's sufferings, and God's determination, and a concurrence of all of them for the promoting of it, in the history of the gospel ; *A bone of him is not broken.* When the bones of the two thieves crucified with him are broken, *a spear* is run at him, and *his side is pierced,* when they are not pierced; and all this, because it was prophesied of him, that *A bone of him shall not be broken,* and *they shall look upon him whom they have pierced;* and when it comes to his burial, Pilate wots not what he is doing, when yet he is fulfilling the Lord's design, in giving his body to a rich man Joseph of Arimathea, when he asked it from him to be buried by him, whereby the prophecy in the text is fulfilled ; the wickedness of some, the contingent actions of others, and the ignorance of many, concur all together, to make

out the same holy and unalterable design and purpose of God.

And therefore, 3. Let us stay our faith here, that our Lord is still working in all these confusions: And when matters are turn'd up-side-down to human appearance, our blessed Lord is not nonplussed and at a stand when we are; he knows well what he is doing, and will make all things most certainly, infallibly, and infrustrably to work for his own glory, and for the good of his people.

From its being said, that, *he gave his grave with the wicked*, as holding forth Christ's willingness to be buried, (as he saith of his death, John x. 17. *No man taketh away my life from me, but I lay it down, and take it up again*) Observe, "That "in the whole performance of the work of re- "demption, even in the lowest and most shameful "steps of it, our Lord was a most willing Conde- "scender." *He gave his grave with the wicked*: He was a most free and willing Undertaker: When, as it were, the question was put, Who will satisfy for elect sinners? He comes in and says, (as we have it, Psal. xl.) *Lo, I come, in the volume of thy book it is written of me, I delight to do thy will, O my God*; I am here, Father, as if he had said, I offer myself, and accept of the terms heartsomly, and delightsomly; *I rejoiced*, saith he Prov. viii. 28. *in the habitable parts of the earth, before the foundation of the world was laid, my delight was with the sons of men*: So it may be made evident, that in all the parts of his sufferings, and in every step thereof he did most exactly, and also most willingly, perform whatever was carved out to him; he preached and wrought miracles, and dd all with delight, as himself says, John iv. 32. *It is my meat and my drink to do my Father's will, and to finish his work*; it refreshed him, when his body was hungry and faint, to be carrying on the work of redemption, in speaking to a poor straying sinner. If we yet look a little forward, we will find, that he so longed for the saddest part of this exercise, that he is pained till it be accomplished, Luke xii. 50. *I have a baptism to be baptized with, and how am I straitned till it be accomplished?* His heart longed so much to be at it, that he would approve nor admit of nothing that might stand in the way of it; therefore he rejected Peter's advice with holy detestation, with a *Get thee behind me Satan*; he knew well what was in Judas's mind, and yet would not divert him, but bid him do what he was about *quickly*; he went to the garden, where he was known to resort, and gave his enemies opportunity to take him, and would not suffer his disciples to draw a sword to oppose them; when he was before Pilate, he would not *open his mouth*; when he was buffetted, *he gave his back to the smiter, and his cheeks to him that plucked off the hair, and hid not his face from shame and spitting*, because he knew what was aimed at in all this, and accordingly saith, Matt. xx. 20. *The Son of man came not to be served, but to serve and to give his life a ransom for many*. When his holy human nature scarred at the cup, and when he was thereby put to pray, *Father, if it be possible, let this cup pass from me*, he sweetly subjoins, *But for this cause came I unto this hour*: And the nearer it came to his death, he vented his desire after it the more; *With desire have I desired*, saith he, or with special desire have I desired, *to eat this passover with you before I suffer*; even when he was to eat the last passover, and to take his last good-night, and to be in readiness for what was coming. What could have been the mean or motive to bring it about, if he had not been willing? It was this willingness that Jehovah was pleased with, and that made his sacrifice to smell sweetly to his Father, *who loveth a cheerful giver*: And it had never been satisfactory, if it had not been willing, but extorted; and therefore saith he, John xi. *No man taketh my life from me, but I lay it down; and I delight to do thy will*, Psal. xl.

Use 1st, See here a great evidence of the love of God, and of the Mediator; behold what manner of love this is, that when it was not required, he should offer, and freely give himself to death, and to the grave! This is the love of a Friend, and beyond it, that he should have so loved his Church, as to give himself for her to death, and to the grave; well may he say, as he doth, John xv. 15. *Greater love hath no man than this, &c*.

2dly, It sheweth what great ground of consolation and encouragement a sinner hath, that would fain be at Christ, to believe on him, and to expect life and salvation through him. Our Lord was most willing to lay down his life, and to come to the grave for that end; and is it possible that he will refuse a sinner, that comes unto him, and that would fain share in the benefit of his sufferings, which was his great end in suffering? This one thing, to wit, the willingness that he had to suffer, and the delight that he had in suffering, to purchase redemption to sinners, may be a strong cordial to strengthen the heart of a swooning sinner, and a great motive and encouragement to come forward to him. Thou wilt, it may be, say, I wot not if Christ loves me: O consider these sweet words, Rom. v. 10. *If he died for us while we were*

were yet enemies, how much more shall we be saved by his life? I shall close this discourse with these two words, the first whereof is, for encouragement: If there be any body here that would fain have Christ's love, and partake of his death; take courage, seeing our Lord, out of the great desire he had to promote the salvation of sinners, *gave himself to death, and to the grave,* will he not willingly make application of his purchase to them when they seek it? That he was willing to undergo all this, is a far greater matter than to welcome a sinner coming home to him; and if he did all that he did for this very end, will he stand on it when it comes to the application? the second word is, That this is, and will be the ground of conviction to all who think little of our Lord Jesus, and of his love, and who will not part with a base lust for him, and who will not make choice of him, but will refuse, reject, undervalue and despise him, with all that he hath done and suffered; it will exceedingly aggravate your condemnation, that when he was so willing to die for the good of sinners, ye were not willing to live for his satisfaction. Think on it, O! think seriously on it: These things are the truths of God, and the main truths of the gospel, that ly very near the engaging of hearts to Christ; and if such truths do you no good, none others readily will. God give us the faith of them.

SERMON XXXV.

Isaiah liii. 9. *And he made his grave with the wicked, and with the rich in his death; because he had done no violence, neither was any deceit in his mouth.*

THIS is a most wonderful subject that we have to think and speak of, which concerns the sufferings that our blessed Lord was pleased to undergo for sinners: And this makes it to be the more wonderful, when we consider what he was made, and what his carriage was; *he was numbred with the transgressors, and gave his grave with the wicked;* and yet he hath this testimony, that there was no violence in his hands, nor any deceit in his mouth. He was a sinless mediator, not only before men, but before God.

These words, considered in themselves, hold out a little sum and short compend of a holy walk, must perfectly and exactly fulfilled in the conversation of Jesus Christ; *He had done no violence,* or there was no violence in his hands, that is, there was no sinful deed contrary to the law of God in all his practice and walk; *And there was no deceit,* or guile, *i. his mouth,* that is, no sinful or deceitful expression: in sum, neither in deed nor in word was there sin in him; he did wrong to none by his deeds, and he deceived no body by his words. This guile or deceit, as it looks to the first table of the law, imports that there was no falshood nor corrupt doctrine in his ministry; he did not beguile nor seduce the souls of any, in leading them wrong: And as it looks to the second table of the law more immediately, it imports, that he was sincere and upright, that there was no deceit, no violence or dissembling in his carriage: so that, whether we look to him as God's public servant in the ministry, or to him in his private walk, he was completely innocent, and without all sin, as the word is, 1 Pet. ii. 22. *Who did no sin, neither was guile found in his mouth:* However men accounted of him, he was an innocent and sinless Saviour.

If we look on them as they depend on the former words, they are a reason of. that difference which in his death and burial God did put betwixt him and others. Tho' he was by wicked men put to death as a wicked person, yet God in his providence so ordered the matter, that he was honourably buried with the rich; Why so? This is the reason of it, because, tho' they esteemed him a false Prophet, and a deceiver, a wine-bibber, &c. yet he had done no wrong to any, neither by word nor by deed; and therefore God would have that respect put on him after his death in his burial, and so a remarkable difference to be made betwixt him and others.

Observe hence, 1. "That our Lord Jesus, the "High Priest of our profession, that laid down his "life for sinners, is completely and perfectly holy." He hath that testimony from the prophet here, that *He did no violence, neither was there any deceit in his mouth;* He hath this testimony from the apostles, from Peter, 1 Pet. ii. 22. *He did no sin, neither was any guile found in his mouth;* from John, 1 John iii. 5. *He was manifested to take away sin, and in him is no sin;* and from Paul, Heb. vii. 27. *He was holy, harmless, and undefiled, separate from sinners.* In this respect, there is a difference betwixt him and all men in the world; and it was necessary for believers consolation, that it should be so, *It became us,* saith the apostle, *to have such an High Priest.* If we consider the excellency of his person, he could not be otherwise, being God and man in one person, and having the fulness of the Godhead dwelling in him bodily. 2. It was necessary, if we consider the

end

end of his offices: He, being to offer up an acceptable sacrifice to God, behoved to be holy and harmless; otherwise neither the priest nor the sacrifice could have been acceptable. 3. It was necessary, if we consider the dignity of his office: It behoved him to differ from the former priests under the law; and if he had not been without sin, he should not have so suffered from them. 4. It was necessary for the persons for whom he undertook these offices: Such a high priest became them, and another could not have done their turn. All these we will find to be put together, Heb. vii. 26, 27. where the apostle having said, v. 25. *That he is able to save to the uttermost these that come unto God through him,* subjoins, *For such an high priest became us, who is holy, harmless, undefiled, separate from sinners, made higher than the heavens, who needeth not daily, as these high priests, to offer up sacrifices, first for his own sins, and then for the sins of the people.* The most holy of all the priests had sins for which they behoved to offer sacrifices, so had the holiest of the people: But Christ was holy and blameless, and had no sin; and it behoved him to be so: As I said just now, his sacrifice could never have been accepted for others, if he had needed to offer up sacrifices for himself.

The *Uses* are these; not to speak how it vindicates our Lord Jesus Christ from all these aspersions cast upon him by wicked men, who called him a *glutton, a wine-bibber, a friend of publicans and sinners, a deceiver,* &c. He was holy and harmless; and ere long he will gloriously appear to be holy, when these who pierced him shall see him, and be confounded: I say, the uses are these, in reference to the church and people of God: It serves, 1. To shew the condescendency of love, and the contrivance of infinite wisdom for the behoof of sinners; such a high priest became us. Love condescended, and wisdom contrived, that he should become man, and suffer, *the just for the unjust;* wisdom set on work by grace, provided for sinners such an high priest as they stood in need of; and indeed sinners have no want here, for they have an high priest becoming them; and this is an evidence of it, that *he is holy, harmless, undefiled, separate from sinners,* &c. 2. It serves to be a great ground of encouragement to sinners, to step to, and make use of Christ's sacrifice. Our Lord had no sin, and needed not to offer a sacrifice for himself; and if he offered sacrifice for atonement, wherefore did he so? It was either for himself, and that could not be, for he was holy: or for nothing, or for no end, and to say so were blasphemy; or it must be for a real satisfaction for elect sinners, or such as should make use of him: And thus faith hath a sure ground to lay hold on, namely, that his satisfaction was real; and that it was for this end, to be made forthcoming for the behoof of such as should believe on him. And therefore, look upon Christ's suffering, and upon his innocency who suffered, and ye will find that ye have a suitable high priest, and atonement made for you: O but that is a sweet word, 2 Cor. v. ult. *He hath made him to be sin for us, who knew no sin, that we might be made the righteousness of God in him.*

3. It is ground of great consolation to them that betake themselves to Christ: Why? our Lord's sacrifice cannot but be accepted, for there was in him no guile, nothing that might make his sacrifice unsavoury. And as it commends the way of grace to a sinner, so it is ground of encouragement to a sinner to look to be accepted through him: For if the temptation should say, Thou art a sinner, and such and such a great sinner; that is nothing to the purpose; for God hath accepted of Christ and of his sacrifice; and if thou make use of his sacrifice, it cannot but be accepted for thee: Here then is the consolation, that we have such an high Priest as became us, who needed not to offer for himself, but only for the sins of the people, and of his own people.

4. It serves notably for our imitation: He was holy, and in his holy walking hath left us a copy to write after, and to walk by: And therefore, in your speaking of Christ's holiness, or in your reading of it, consider that he is thereby casting a copy to you, and bidding you *purify yourselves, as he is pure; to be holy, as he who hath called you is holy; learn of him to be meek and lowly in heart,* to be humble and heavenly minded: and in whatever respect his life and walk is proposed to us as a pattern, set yourselves in his own strength to imitate it, and *be ye followers of him as dear children;* whenever ye read of *his obedience to death,* of his holiness in all manner of conversation, and of *his fulfilling of all righteousness,* let it provoke you singly and seriously to design and endeavour conformity to him therein in your practice.

2*dly,* From the connexion of these two, That he was accounted a sinner before and at his death, and that after his death God did put that note of respect upon him, that *he was buried with the rich, because he had done no violence,* &c. but was holy and harmless in his life; Observe, "That however "holiness may suffer as long as holy persons live, "yet at death, and after death, there is ever a te- "stimony of the Lord's respect put on it:" Or thus, "Holy walkers are always separated and differenced

"from

"from others at their death; it is ever otherwise "with them than it is with others when death "comes, however it hath been with them in their "life." *He made his grave with the wicked, and with the rich in his death, because he had done no violence,* &c. This hath been confirmed in the experience of all that ever lived: The rich glutton, Luke xvi. hath the better life as to externals, and Lazarus had a poor afflicted life; but when death comes, the rich glutton goes to hell, and Lazarus goes to the bosom of Abraham. This is laid down as a certain truth, Eccl. viii. 12, 13. *Tho' a sinner do evil an hundred times, and his days be prolonged, yet surely I know that it shall be well with him that fears God, but it shall not be well with the wicked.* There shall be a change at death; and it cannot be otherwise, whether we look, 1. To the holy nature of God, who hath a complacency in holiness, as it is said, Psal. xi. ult. *The righteous Lord loveth righteousness, his countenance doth behold the upright.* Or whether, 2. We look to the word of God, which, Isa. iii. 10, 11. bids say to the righteous, *It shall be well with them, for they shall eat of the fruit of their doings:* for, *Blessed are the dead which die in the Lord, they rest from their labours, and their works do follow them:* but, *Wo unto the wicked, it shall be ill with him, for the reward of his hands shall be given him.* The same connexion that was betwixt Christ's life, tho' a suffering life, and his death, shall be betwixt the life of all his members, and their death; *If we suffer with him, we shall also reign with him.*

The uses are, 1. To let us see what is the true way to eternal well-being, when this short life shall be at an end; and it is the way of holiness: And so it serves to answer a great question, Who shall be happy at their death? Even they that are holy in their life; whose hands have done no violence, and whose mouth hath had no guile, to wit, with the full benefit of their will, and without all gracious reluctation; for absolute freedom from these in this life was proper only to our Lord Jesus since Adam's fall: Such may expect the Lord's countenance, when death separates their soul and body. Therefore take this as a mark for trial, observe and see what is your carriage, and judge accordingly; and seeing the Lord hath joined holiness and happiness together inseparably, presume not to separate them.

2. Is it so, that holiness hath a good and comfortable close of a man's life, (which is the substance of the doctrine) it would commend to us the study of holiness, as the most precious, advantagious, honourable, sicker and safe course that a man can follow; *Say to the righteous, It shall be well with him*; it is not, Say to the honourable man, nor say to the rich man, nor to the wise man, &c. God hath not chosen many of these, as is clear, 1 Cor. i. 26. but, Say to the righteous or holy man, It shall be well with him: And is there any thing that should have so much influence on men, and take them so much up, as how to be well in the close? Folk may have a fighting life of it here, and may suffer much, and be under reproach for a time, as Christ was; but if thou be holy, ere thy body be laid in the grave, it shall be well with thy soul. And as for all who have chosen the way of holiness, we are allowed to say this to you, that it shall be well with you at death, and after death, at judgment, and even for evermore: *To them* (saith the apostle, Rom. ii. 9.) *who by a patient continuance in well-doing, seek for glory, and honour, and immortality, eternal life.* O how many great and good things are abiding all the honest hearted students of holiness! Eye hath not seen, nor ear heard, nor heart conceived, what they are.

3. It is ground of expostulation with them that neglect and slight holiness; As it will be well with the righteous or holy, so they shall have a miserable and desperate lot of it, who either despise or neglect holiness, " Wo to the wicked (saith Isaiah iii. 11. " it shall be ill with him." Some of you may think that ye are rich and honourable, are well clothed, sit in fine houses, and have rich covered tables, when poor bodies are kept at the door, and are destitute of these things; and are ready to bless yourselves as being well, tho' ye care not for, nor seek after holiness: But wo unto you, for ye must die, and go unto the bottomless pit, and there ye will not get so much as a drop of water to cool your tongues in these tormenting flames; neither your riches, nor honours, nor pleasures, will hold off the heat and fury of the vengeance of God, nor in the least case you in your extreme pain; but, as it is, Rom. ii. 9. " Indignation and wrath, tribulation " and anguish (*four sore words*) will be upon every " soul of man that doth evil." O do ye not believe this? It is the truth of God, and a very plain truth, and we are persuaded none of you will dare downright to deny it. Holiness will have a sweet and comfortable close, and the neglect of it will have fearful effects following on it. What is the reason then that holiness is so little thought of, and followed, do ye believe that ye will die? and think ye ever to come to judgment, or to hear that word, " Come, ye blessed of my Father, inherit the king- " dom prepared for you; for I was hungry, and ye
" fed

"fed me; naked, and ye clothed me, &c." O what will become of many of you, when the Lord Jesus will be revealed from heaven, with his mighty angels, in flaming fire, to render vengeance to all them who know not God, and obey not the gospel; and will say to you, *Depart, ye cursed, into everlasting fire, prepared for the devil and his angels; for when I was hungry ye fed me not*, &c. This is, I grant, a general truth; yet if it be not received, we know not what truth will be received; and if it were received, the practice of holiness would be more studied; there would be less sin, and more prayer, reading, meditation, more seeking after knowledge, and more watchfulness and tenderness of folks conversation: Always in this the Lord shews the connexion that is betwixt holiness and happiness, and here ye have the copy and pattern of an exemplary walk.

3. From this, that the holiness and blamelessness of Christ, here spoken of, is marked in him as peculiar to him, for it fits him to be a high-priest, and proves that only he could be the priest that suited and became us, and that no other could do our turn, as the apostle reasons, Heb. vii. 26, 27, 28. *For the law maketh men priests that have infirmity; but the word of the oath, which was since the law, maketh the Son, who is consecrated for evermore:* From this, I say, Observe, " That all men, even the most " holy, except Christ (who was both God and Man) " are sinful, and not one of them sinless, while liv- " ing here on earth." And the reason is, because if any were sinless, then this that is said here would not be peculiar to our Lord-Jesus Christ, that *He did no violence, neither was there deceit in his mouth:* This being a singular character of our high priest, that none of his types could claim to, it exclusively agreeth to him, so as it agreeth to none other. The scripture is full to this purpose, in asserting, that not only all men are sinners, as considered in their natural condition, but that even believers are sinful in part; for the same apostle John, that saith, 1 Epist. i. 3. " Truly our fellowship is " with the Father, and with his Son Jesus Christ," saith also verse 8. " If we say we have no sin, we " deceive ourselves, and the truth is not in us," and verse 10. " If we say that we have not sinned, we " make him a liar, and his word is not in us;" and 1 Kings viii. 46. and Eccl. vii. 20. " There is no " man that doth good, and sinneth not;" plainly insinuating, that all have need of an intercessor; we shall not insist in this: only from these words compared with the scope, making it peculiar to Christ to be without sin, and implying, that none other

are so; we would consider the necessity of its being so. 1. For differencing and separating of Jesus Christ from all others, by putting this dignity on him, of being *holy, harmless, undefiled, separate from sinners*; this is his prerogative, and badge of honour, above others. 2. It is necessary for this end, to demonstrate the need that is there of offering himself a sacrifice for sinners; and that it was not for himself; but for sinners that he offered up himself: and that there is a continual necessity of making use of that sacrifice; for if there were not a continuance of sin in part, while believers are out of heaven, there would be no need of Christ's office; if we were holy and harmless ourselves, we needed not such an high priest.

Use 1. To establish us in the faith of this truth, That amongst all men there is none that were true men except Christ, that is, without sin; sin is still abiding in them, while in this world: Of none of them all it can be said, that *they have done no violence, neither is there any deceit in their mouth;* none of them could ever say since Adam fell, *The Prince of this world cometh, and hath nothing of me;* yet this is a special qualification of Christ Jesus, for his Priest-hood, that he was without sin, and behoved to be so. I am not pleading, that sinners should take a liberty to sin, because there is no perfection to win at in this life, God forbid; wo unto them that make such an use of this truth: nor do I speak of it, to allow any to dispense with, or to give way to themselves to sin; for we shew before, that Christ is here proposed, as our pattern, and we are bidden *purify ourselves, as he is pure:* But this we say, that none living here on the earth are without sin; the most perfect men that are on this side eternity, carry about with them a *body of death*, called five or six times *sin*, Rom. vii. that hath actual lustings, and a power, as a law of sin, to lead captive; and that makes the man guilty before God.

Use 2. For reproof of two sorts of enemies to this truth. (1.) These inveterate enemies of the Sacrifice of our Lord Jesus Christ, to wit, the Papist, that black train that follows Antichrist, who pleads for a perfection according to the law, as attainable in this life, laying down two grounds to prove this perfection. 1. That the inward lustings, or first risings and motions at least of the body of death are no sin. And, 2. Their exponing of the law, so as it may suit to their own apprehension, and opinion, yet so, as they say, that every believer or godly person wins not to this perfection to keep the law wholly, but only some of their grandees. This the Lord hath mercifully banished out of the

reformed

reformed Churches, as inconsistent with the experience of the saints, who *find a law in their members warring against the law of their mind, and leading them captive to the law of sin that is in their members*; inconsistent with the scriptures, which clear, that none have attained, nor do attain perfection in this life, but the contrary, that *in many things we offend all;* and inconsistent with grace, that leave sinners still in Christ's common and debt, as standing in need of his imputed righteousness: This perfection they place in inherent holiness, and habitual garce; but we insist not on it. (2.) Another sort of enemies, reproved here, are the old Familists, who are owned by these who are called Antinomians, several of which miserable persons are now going up and down amongst us, who say that the people of God have no sin in them: Wherein they are worse than Papists; for Papists make it peculiar to some only, but they make it common to all believers; and Papists make their perfection to consist in inherent holiness, but they make the nature of sin to be changed, and say, that sin is no more so in a believer, even tho' it be contrary to the law of God. We grant indeed, that the people of God are free of sin in these respects, 1. In this respect, that no sin can condemn them, they are not under the law, but under grace; in that respect, Rom. viii. 1. it is said, that *There is no condemnation to them who are in Christ.* 2. In this respect, that they cannot fall into that sin, *which is unto death*, as is clear, 1 John v. 17, 18. And, 3. In this respect, that they cannot so sin, as to ly, or be under the reign and dominion of sin, as is evident, Rom. vi. 14. the believer *delights in the law of God according to the inner man*, Rom. vii. 22. and is not in sin, neither doth commit sin, as the unbeliever doth, for the seed of God abideth in him, and is kept from being involved in that which his corrupt nature inclines the believer to. So then, what the scripture speaks, of believers being free of sin, is to be understood in one of these respects: But to say, (1.) That a believer cannot sin at all, sad experience and practice of the saints is a proof of the contrary: Or, 2. To say, that sin in a believer, is no sin, because of his faith in Christ, is as contrary to scripture; for the law of God is the same to the believer and unbeliever, and sin is the same to both; adultery is adultery, and murder is murder in David, as well as in any other man. Sure, when Christ bade his disciples pray for forgiveness of sin daily, he taught them no such doctrine, as to account their sins to be no sins; for if so, they should neither repent of sin, nor seek the pardon of it, as some are not ashamed to say they should not. That which we aim at, is, to clear it to be Christ's prerogative only to be free of sin, none other in this life can claim it; and to teach believers to carry about with them daily, all along their mortal life, that which is for their good, even the sense of sin. I know it is now an up-cast from some pretended perfectionists, to the people of God, that they think and say, that they have sin, and are not perfect; and we are by these men called Antichristian Priests and Jesuits, because we preach that doctrine: But let it be soberly considered, whether it doth better agree with Papists and Jesuits to say, that believers are without sin, or to say that they have sin? They who say that believers, or the saints, have no sin, do agree in this with the Papists, who maintain a perfection of holiness, or a conformity to the law in some in this life, and who deny the lustings of the body of death to be sin; without which opinion, tho' most gross, they would not, nor could with the least shadow of reason, maintain their doctrine of justification by works: And yet some now among us will needs call us Popish, because we say that we have sin, and that none of God's people are without sin in this life; this seems to be very strange: But that which have been the thought of some sharp-sighted and sagacious men, since the beginning of our confusions, to wit, that Popery is a working, as an under-hand design; is by this, and other things, made to be more and more apparent: Is there any thing more like Popery working in a mystery, yea more Popish than to say, that the motions of corruption in believers are no sins, that a man or woman may attain to perfection in holiness here, and yet to catry on this with that subtilty, as confidently to aver, that it is Popery to say the contrary? Nay, if the scriptures they make use of in their papers or pamphlets be well considered, we will find, that not only a perfection in holiness and good works is pleaded for, but a possibility of fulfilling the law and covenant of works, as namely, 1 Pet. i. 15. 1 John iii. 3. and v. 5. and Matt. v. ult. Will ye (say they) call yourselves saints, that are not purified even as he is pure? And will ye call yourselves believers, that have not overcome the world, &c? as if all that is commanded duty might be, or were perfectly reached in this life, and as if no distinction betwixt begun, yea, considerably advanced holiness, and intire perfection were to be admitted. That for which I mark this, is, to shew that the design of Popery seems to be on foot; the devil in some considerable persons venting these things, when the great patrons and authors of them

them ly darned and hid. And it is observable, which we have heard of late, that some ring-leaders in this time have declared themselves expresly for Popery: Tho' we have reason to bless God, that the people in this place are kept free of these things; yet this truth is worthy the vindicating, and the hazard and danger is to be guarded against by all of us, when this foul spirit is driving so hard, and prevailing with some to publish abroad this error in papers; and so seeking to draw people into the snare. Lay down but these two principles, both now mentioned, that they that have faith have no sin, and that they that want grace should not pray, what would they turn to, and resolve in? Satan's design in this, is doubtless to make all untender; and it is both sad and strange, that it is not *seen and observed*. What a terror and torture would it be to an exercised and tender Christian, and how would it put his conscience on the rack, to say to him, What a faith is this of yours, that cannot keep you altogether from sin, and that cannot quite overcome the world? God be blessed, that hath given poor believers other and better grounds in the gospel, by which to judge of their faith, so that they may own their faith as sound, though they have a mixture of unbelief with it; and yet unbelief is always a sin; and may say with that poor man, Lord, I believe, help thou my unbelief.

3*dly, Observe*, "That, to the making up of a "perfectly holy walk, there is a necessity both of "holiness in practice, and of soundness in judgment; "that no deceit or guile *be in thy mouth*, and that "*no violence be in thy hands.*" And this is needful to be taken notice of, because many have an aptitude to think, that folks may be truly holy, be of what opinion in judgment and persuasion they will; as if God had left the mind of man to be a bare empty table or board, that he might write on it, whatever he liked or pleased: But our Lord is vindicated here, from the scandal or corrupt doctrine, as well as from scandals in this practice; and therefore, as we would say on the one hand to you, who are sound in your judgment and hate error, that if ye be gross and untender in your practice, the soundness of your judgment will not prove you to be holy; so upon the other side, we would say, that though it were possible ye could be sinless in your practice, if you take a latitude and liberty, as to your judgment to be corrupt, and to vent what ye please, ye will never get God's approbation, as being holy persons: Therefore let both be joined together, soundness in judgment, and tenderness in practice. God give the right use of these things.

SERMON XXXVI.

Isaiah liii. 9. *And he made his grave with the wicked, and with the rich in his death; because he had done no violence, neither was any deceit in his mouth.*

Verse 10. *Yet it pleased the Lord to bruise him, he hath put him to grief: When thou shalt make his soul an offering for sin, he shall see his seed, he shall prolong his days, and the pleasure of the Lord shall prosper in his hand.*

WE were speaking somewhat, the last day, of our Lord Jesus his innocency; which is here compended, and summed up in these two, 1. That *there was no violence in his hands*, 2. That *there was no deceit in his mouth:* However he was accounted of among men, and by them numbered among transgressors, yet he was not so in very deed, and before God.

The prophet proceeds, and answers an objection, How came he then to suffer, if he was so innocent; especially his sufferings being ordered by God, who is said to *give his grave with the wicked?* He answers the objection, and removes the offence, by giving three grounds for this, verse 10. *Yet it pleased the Lord to bruise him, he hath put him to grief:* This is the first reason, and it is taken from the fountain whence his sufferings proceeded, God's good pleasure graciously ordered it so; it was the good pleasure of Jehovah, that so it should be. The second reason is taken from the nature, or end of his sufferings, in these words, *When thou shalt make his soul an offering for sin;* Tho' he suffered for men as a sinner, yet before God it was an offering for sin, to satisfy for, and to remove the sins of his elect people. The word may be either, *When thou,* or *when he shall make his soul an offering for sin:* But both come to one thing, which is this, That his sufferings were not such as befel other men, nay, nor such as befel innocent men; but they were ordered on a higher design, and for an higher end, even to be a satisfaction for sinners, and to make way for their freedom. A 3d reason is this, As his sufferings flowed from God's good pleasure, and were a satisfaction for the sins of his elect people; so it hath notable and noble effects. And there are *three* mentioned here, 1. *He shall see his seed,* he shall have a numerous offspring, many that shall hold eternal life of him. Men by their suffering of death are incapacitate to increase their offspring, but this is a quickening suffering and death that hath a numerous offspring. 2. *He shall prolong his days,* which seems to be another paradox; for mens days are shortned by their sufferings, and death; but tho' he be dead and buried, yet he shall rise again, and ascend, and sit down at the right hand of the Father, and live for ever, to make intercession for his people. A 3d effect, which is the up-shot of all, *The pleasure of the Lord shall prosper in his hand:* God hath designed him for a work, which is the great work of redemption, even the bringing of many sons to glory; this is the will of him that sent him, that he should give eternal life to as many as should believe on him: And this is called God's *good pleasure,* which shall thrive and prosper in his hand: He shall pull many captives from the devil, and set many prisoners free; he shall by his sufferings overcome the devil, death and the grave, and all enemies, and shall gather the sons of God together, from the four corners of the earth; and that work shall not misgive, nor be frustrated, but thrive in his hand. So then, in this text, we have much of the gospel compended in few words.

We shall speak a little to one observation more from the close of the 9th verse, where Christ Jesus his sinlesness and innocency is holden out, in these two, *There was no violence in his hands,* no sinful practice in him, *And there was no deceit in his mouth:* Which looks not only to his sinless carriage before men, and so says, that he was no liar nor dissembler in his dealing and converse with them; but also to his doctrine, and so says, that there was no doctrinal deceit in him; which is, when men lie of God to men, which is a gross sort of lying, and a deceiving of souls, in making them to take that for truth which is not truth; and in derogating from the truth, and making them to take that for error which is truth, as the Apostle speaks of such, *that they speak lies in hypocrisy.* These words, *There was no deceit in his mouth,* look to both; especially to the last, that is, the doctrinal deceit of corrupt teaching (whereof he was free altogether) I say, it looks especially to that, because he was calumniated, traduced, and called *a deceiver of the people:* That is (as if the prophet had said) most untrue of him, there is no deceitful word in all his doctrine; tho' it was imputed to him, yet he was most free of it. Thence observe, " That exact " holiness and blamelesness, takes in holiness in a " man's conversation, in respect of practice; and " soundness in judgment, in respect of doctrine." For if our Lord be a pattern of holiness, that which was in him as our pattern, is called for from us, even to be pure as he is pure; *No violence was in his hands,* he was no stealer, nor robber, nor oppressor, (to speak so with reverence) *and there was no deceit in his mouth,* the word and worship of God was not wronged by him: And he is holden forth as an example to us in both.

That which we would say further on this, shall be in a word of *Use:* where we may clear both the branches of the doctrine, to meet with two exceeding prejudicial tenets among men.

1. There are some, who, if they be not erroneous in their opinions, and sectaries, they think they are well enough, and insult over the infirmities of poor folk, that fall into these errors; and they will (like these spoken of) whore, drink, steal, and lie, &c. *and yet lean upon the Lord, and say, Is not the Lord among us? no evil shall come unto us.* Such half and divide godliness; they will not be Papists, Puritans, nor Sectaries; but there is much unholiness in their practice, much self-seeking, pride, hypocrisy, formality, deceiving, cousening, falshood; and they cover all with this, that they are found as to their profession; though only hearing, and not doing, professing, and not practising: But they would consider, that Christ faith not, Blessed are they that hear only, but, *Blessed are they that do the will of God.* O beware of this great deceit; it is a piece of Christ's innocency and holiness, that *no violence was in his hands,* there was no sinful thing in his practice, no sinful word came from his mouth; ye shall never be accounted followers of Christ, tho' ye give your bodies to be burnt for the truth (as it is to be feared few of you would do) if your conversation be not suitable; God shall never accept of your testimony: Therefore divide not these things, which God hath put together; let holiness be in your practice, otherways Papists and Quakers, yea, the grossest and most abominable heretics and ye will be utterly disclaimed.

The other branch of the *Use* is, That suppose there were never so much apprehended tenderness in folks walk, tho' they were much in duty, and tho' they would quit all they had to the poor; yet if deceit be in their mouth, if they corrupt the truth, and teach others so to do, there is a want of the half of holiness, yea, in some respect of the best and chief half of it; and the reason is, 1. Because the image of God consists as much in the truth, as in the practice; nay, if practice be not conform to truth

truth, it is no true holiness: and where error is drunken in, there is in so far an utter unsuitableness to the holiness of Christ, as well as where profanity appears in the conversation; *For there was no deceit in his mouth.* 2. Because this word of God prescribes the doctrine of faith to be believed, as well as duties to be performed; and the right grounding of faith is a main, if not the main thing wherein the image of God consists, to wit, in *knowledge*: and error is as inconsistent with knowledge, as ignorance is, yea, more, in so far as it leaves a contrary impression of untruth on the soul, which is worse than simple ignorance. 3. Because when a person miscarrieth, by turning aside from the truth to error, he also miscarrieth in his practice, at least, in so far; the right conceiving of truth, being both the ground of our faith, and the rule of our practice: As for instance, let once the conceit and fancy come in, of folks being above ordinances, no conscience is thenceforth made of sanctifying the Sabbath or Lord's day, nor of any other duty of worship; but men become almost, if not altogether Atheists. Yea, 4. The incoming of error begets a sort of presumptuous confidence; therefore Christ says, *He that breaks one of these commandments, and teacheth men so to do, he shall be called least in the kingdom of God*; he not only breaks the command himself, but he seeks to engage others to do so likwise: so that an error from the truth, is a sin against the first table, and so among the greatest evils; and the teaching and propagating of error, is a sin against the second table, because it hazards the soul of our neighbour; whereas violence in the hands hurts only his person or estate. And, 5. If we look to the rise of error, or whence it comes, we will find it to be a fruit of the flesh, Gal. v. 19. and that which flows from our corruption; and is therefore ranked in with *witchcraft, adultery, fornication, idolatry, hatred, variance,* &c. 6. If we look to the scripture-account of it, and of the propagators of it, we will find that 2 Cor. xi. 13. they are called *false apostles, deceitful workers, ministers of Satan,* not common sinners, *transforming themselves into the ministers of Christ;* and no marvel, for Satan himself is transformed into an angel of light; for their work is to gather in souls to the devil, to hale them as in a net to him, to be disciples to him. Or, 7. if we look to the effects that follow upon error, and upon the propagation of it, we will find them to be dreadful: For, as it is, 2 Pet. ii. 1. *They draw upon themselves swift destruction;* chap. iii. 16. *They wrest,* or pervert *the scriptures, to their own destruction.* In all these respects, error in judgment is as evil (if not worse) then profanness in practice. And if we look thorow the Churches of Christ, we will find that there hath been more palpable havock and destruction of souls since *Antichrist* arose, by his gross errors, and damnable delusions, than hath readily been by sin in practice; which men do not own and avouch, as they do these delusions: Think therefore seriously on this; whoever would be pure as Christ is pure, would study soundness in judgment, as well as tenderness in practice; and yet how many are readily mistaken in this, who, if they meet with some that can speak a few good words, and make pretences to a holy walk, tho' the second command be baffled and disgraced by them, and the name of God torn, and tho' the fourth command be made of none effect or price by them, it is thought but little of, all is covered with this, that they are good folks, and of a tender walk? But O! can they be good, who abuse that wherein the name and image of God are most tenderly concerned? and will God account that to be holiness agreeable to his law, that flights, depreciates, and vilifies the best part of his law? Let me therefore beseech you to take in, and to class error with other sins, and to look upon unsoundness in the truths of God, as a fruit of the flesh; and withal to look upon sound knowledge in the mind, and the form of sound words in the mouth, as being a duty, that is called for from you, as well as other duties. We the rather take occasion to speak to this, because the devil is seeking to turn men meer Atheists, Gallio's as to the truths of God, to *care for none of these things*; and as to wear out the esteem of truth, so to make people to look upon error as if there were no hurt by it (it is sad that there is not more scarring at, and keeping distance from the company of such) if they can but give a parcel of good words, and make shews of respect to piety in this lukewarm time. There is need to guard against this temper, or rather distemper, and to look well that we half not, nor divide the pattern and copy which God in his word hath cast to us, and set before us: We would study purity and tenderness in our walk, and growth in sound knowledge; and would walk humbly, under the impression of our hazard: It is sad when folks are ill girded, and yet scarcely discern it. It seems to be a winnowing time, and some are already taken off their feet, who thought not, some months or years since, to have carried in reference to the truth, as they have done; it hath been God's mercy to this place, that he hath hedged us about hitherto, at

which

which the devil hath raged not a little. Be humbled, and have an eye to him that can keep his people, and can establish them in the truth, and make them unblameable in holiness till the coming of the Lord.

We come now to the 10th *verse*; and from the first part of it, *Yet it pleased the Lord to bruise him, he hath put him to grief*, these 3 things arise clearly, 1*st*, " That tho' our Lord Jesus was most in-" nocent in his own Person, yet he was put to ex-" ceeding sore trials and sharp sufferings." For (1.) *He was bruised*, to wit, like corn betwixt the upper and neither millstones, or like grapes in the wine-press; which respects not so much his outward sufferings, tho' great *(for a bone of him was not broken)* as his inward soul-sufferings, and the inward pressures of wrath that were on his human soul. (2.) *He was put to grief*, was sore straitned and pinched; and these expressions import so much, *My soul is exceeding sorrowful, even unto death; my soul is sore troubled, and what shall I say?* and, *My God, my God, why hast thou forsaken me?* The particulars of this grief was spoken to before; and we shew in what respect he was so humbled, and that he was most sinless, and without any the least carnal mud or passion, under these expressions, in which the sense of grief vented itself most in him: Only, if it be here asked, What is the reason, why the prophet doth so much insist, in pointing out Christ's sufferings, and the extremity of them, that scarce almost is there one verse, but he hath in it some one or other new aggravation of them? We conceive the reason of it is, 1. Because there is nothing wherein the greatness of the love of God, and the kindness of the Mediator's condescending, doth appear more than in this; for, the more he suffered, the more the love of God shined, and his condescendency kythed the more; this being the great instance, and demonstrative proof of the love of God, *God so loved the world, that he gave his only begotten Son*, as it is, John iii. 16. O manifold and vastly comprehensive *So!* What is unfolded in it, eternity will but suffice fully to unfold. And this being the great instance of the Mediator's condescendency, and of his commending his love to sinners, *That while we were yet enemies he died for us*, as it is, Rom. v. the Lord loves to have this the subject of our thoughts, that we may be led thereby into the soul-ravishing, and satisfying contemplation of the love whence it came. Because there is not any one thing that lies nearer, or that is readily of greater concern to believers, than to be well acquainted with Christ's sufferings, wherein the Lord would have his people spiritually perquier: and it is of their concernment in a twofold respect, 1. As it is the ground of their peace, therefore he is called *our peace*, and a *propitiation*, for by being acquainted with Christ's sufferings, believers have a solid ground for their faith, whereby they discover access to peace with God, to pardon of sin, and justification, the Mediator having undergone these sufferings for this end. 2. As it is the ground of their consolation, considering that they have a suffering Mediator, that hath paid the price that was due by them; even such an one that knows what it was to be bruised with wrath, and is therefore very tender of, and compassionate towards souls, that are under challenges, and apprehensions of wrath: These are sweet words, which we have to this purpose. 1 John ii. 1. *If any man sin, we have an Advocate with the Father, Jesus Christ the righteous, who is the propitiation for our sins*, who was content to suffer and satisfy for them. O consider then what ye are doing, when ye read of his sufferings! for the very marrow of the gospel, and the life of the consolation of the people of God lies here. 2*dly*, From these words, *Yet it pleased the Lord to bruise him, he hath put him to grief;* Observe, " That the Lord Jehovah had the main " and principal hand in all the sufferings of this in-" nocent Mediator." It was not the Jews nor the Scribes and Pharisees, nor Pilate; but it pleased the Lord, to bruise him, and to put him to grief; as is clear, Acts iv. 27, 28. *Herod and Pontius Pilate, and the Gentiles and people of Israel, were gathered together, to do whatsoever thy hand and thy counsel determined before to be done.* In all that they did, they were but doing that which was carved out before, in the eternal counsel of God; and therefore Peter says, Acts ii. 23. *Him, being delivered by the determinate counsel and fore-knowledge of God, ye have taken, and by wicked hands have crucified and slain.* The Lord's hand was supreme in the business; and we may gather the supreme and sovereign influence of the Lord's hand, in these three respects in Christ's sufferings, 1. In respect of his appointing them; it was concluded in the counsel of God, what he should suffer, what should be the price that Jehovah should have, and the sacrifice that he would accept of from his hand. 2. In respect of the ordering and over-ruling of his sufferings, when it came to the execution of his antient decree; he, who governs all the counsels, thoughts, and actions of men, did in a special manner govern and over-rule the sufferings of the Mediator: tho' wicked men were following their own design, and were stirred and acted by the devil, who is said to have put it into the heart of Judas to betray Christ; yet God had the ordering of all, who should betray him, what death he should die, how he should be pierced, and yet not a bone of him broken. 3. In respect of his having had a hand actively in them: and as he was one chief Party that pursued Christ, it was he that was exacting the elect's debt of him; therefore the Lord looks over Pilate and Herod to him, and says to Pilate, " Thou couldst have no power over me, " except it were given thee from above;" and to his Father, " Father take this cup from me; *and* " My God, my God, why hast thou forsaken me?" He was pursued as standing Cautioner in our room; in which respect it is said, *He that spared not his own Son;* he spared him not when he cried, but would have him drink out the cup; and, Zech. xiii. 7. *Awake, O sword against my Shepherd, and against the Man that is my Fellow, smite the Shepherd.* The message comes from him, and he gives the sword a charge, and orders it to smite him: In all which respects, it is said, *The Lord bruised him, and he hath put him to grief.* It was this, more than sword, or nails, or spear, or whip, that made him cry out; another and a higher hand brought his sinless soul to more bitterness, than all the sufferings he endured from men.

Use. This leads us in to the vindicating of the sovereign and holy providence of God, in that wherein men have a most sinful hand, and are most inexcusable: Tho' Judas that betrayed, and Pilate that condemned the innocent Son of God, acted most sinfully; yet the Lord himself hath an active over-ruling hand, in carrying on his own design; and what Judas and Pilate, with other wicked men, did, was so far from being by guess, that they were the executioners of his antient decrees: And he is most pure and spotless in venting and manifesting grace, holiness and justice, when men were venting their corruptions, impiety and injustice most; therefore the holy providence of God mixeth no more, as to any sinful participation with men's sin, in their sinful and wicked actings, than the covenant of redemption mixed itself with the sinfulness of them that crucified Christ: Nay, this is a principal diamond in his crown, that he can not only govern all the natural second causes that are in the world, in their several courses and actings, and order them to his own glory, but even devils, and wicked men, and hypocrites, their most corrupt and abominable actions; and make them infrustrably subservient to the promoting of his own holy ends and purposes,

and yet be free of their sin for which they shall count to him: And as it was no excuse to Judas nor to Pilate, that they did what before was decreed of God; so it shall be no excuse to any man in a sinful course, that God hath a hand in every thing that comes to pass, who yet is just and holy in all. It may also stay our hearts, when the devil and his instruments, as it were, are running mad; that they can do no more than what God permits, nay, some way commissionateth them to do. The devil could not so much as touch a tail of one of Job's sheep, without leave asked and given: " O the " depth both of the knowledge, and of the wisdom " of God! how unsearchable are his ways, and " his judgments past finding out!" *3dly*, As we may see here, the concurrence of the Persons of the blessed Trinity, Father, Son, and Holy Ghost; the concurrence of Jehovah with the Mediator for carrying on the same design, the work of man's redemption (for it pleased them all) so, taking the Lord Jehovah essentially, as comprehending all the three Persons, we may observe, " That the Lord " is well-willed to, and hath delight in prosecuting " the work of redemption, tho' even to the brui- " sing of the second Person of the Godhead, con- " sidered as he became Man and Mediator." Not that he delighted in the sufferings, as such, of his innocent Son, for he *afflicts not willingly the children of men:* but considering the end, and the effects that were to follow, to wit, the seed that he should beget to eternal life, and the captives which he was to redeem, in that respect, it was not only not against his will, but it pleased him well, or, as the word is in the New Testament, *it was his good pleasure;* alluding, as it is like, to this of the prophet: Hence, when Christ speaks of the work of redemption, he calleth it the *Father's will,* and *work;* the Father's *will,* when he says, *I came not to do my own will, but the will of him that sent me;* the Father's *work,* while he says, *I have finished the work thou gavest me to do:* And here it is called his *pleasure,* for there was nothing without himself to move him to it; when he might have suffered all fallen mankind to ly still in their forlorn condition, it pleased him to give his son, of his own good will, to redeem several of them.

Use. If we put these doctrines together, they afford us wonderful matter of consolation, 1. That we have an able Saviour, that hath given a sufficient ransom for us, a price that cannot be over-valued. 2. A willing Mediator, that gave himself; no man took his life from him, but he laid it down of himself, and took it up again. 3. A willing Jehovah.

Isaiah liii. Verse 10.

..ah, contriving and taking pleasure in contriving the redemption of elect sinners, thro' the death of his own Son: Which reproves, and gives check to the wonderful strange mistakes that are often found with some poor souls concerning the way of peace; as some will be ready to say, O if Christ were as willing to take me, as I am to take him! as willing to welcome me, as I am to come to him! But is not this a proof of his willingness, that he was content to be bruised, and put to grief, about the work of our redemption? Others have a secret apprehension, that if God were as willing to receive and save them, as Christ is, they would have more confidence; but says the prophet here, that *it pleased the Father to bruise him*, in whose breast (to speak so) bred the plot of sinners redemption; Jehovah thought it good: He loved the salvation of sinners so well, that he was content to seem in a manner regardless of his own Son's cries and tears for a time, to make way for performing that satisfaction that was due to justice; and he did this with good-will, and pleasantly. We shall not insist more on particular *Uses*; but is there, or can there be greater ground of consolation, than this? or is there any thing wanting here to compleat the consolation? Is there not a well-furnished Saviour commissionate to give life to whom he will, who hath purchased it, that he may give it? and a well-willing, loving and condescending God, willing to give his Son, and willing to accept of his death for a ransom? and what would ye have more? The Party offended is willing to be in friendship with the offending party, and to give and accept of the satisfaction: What can tentation say? or what ground is for jealousy to vent itself here? *He that did not spare his own Son*, but willingly and freely *gave him to death for us all, how shall he not with him also freely give us all things?* as it is, Rom. viii. And if *we were reconciled to God by the death of his Son, when we were enemies, shall not we much more be saved by his life?* as it is, Rom. v. 10. There is a great disproportion betwixt Christ and other gifts, yea, and the gift of heaven itself; and shall a poor sinner have a suffering Saviour given, and may he not also expect pardon of sin, justification, faith, repentance; and admission to the kingdom? There is here good and strong ground of consolation, to them that will build on it: Let the Father, and Christ's love to you be welcome in its offers, that his end, in bringing many sons to glory, be not frustrated by any of you, so far as you can; tho' it cannot indeed be frustrated; *For the pleasure of the Lord shall prosper in his hand, and he shall see the travel of his soul, and be satisfied.*

SERMON XXXVII.

Isaiah liii. 10.------*When thou shalt make his soul an offering for sin, he shall see his seed, he shall prolong his days, and the pleasure of the Lord shall prosper in his hand.*

CHRIST and his sufferings have been a most delightsom subject to be spoken and heard of, before ever he suffered; and they should be to us now no less, but much more so, even very glad tidings to hear, that ever the Son of God was made an offering for sin.

This verse, as we hinted the last day, doth set forth Christ's sufferings, and in these three, that the design of God in bruising the innocent Lamb of God might be the better taken up. (1.) They are holden forth in the rise where they bred, or in the fountain whence they flowed, the good pleasure of God; *It pleased the Lord to bruise him, to put him to grief.* Which the prophet marks, 1. To shew that all the good, that comes by Christ to sinners, is bred in the Lord's own bosom: It was concluded and contrived there, and that with delight, there being no constraint or necessity on the Lord to give his Son, or to provide him to be a Cautioner for dyvour sinners, but it was his own good pleasure to do so. 2. To shew the concurrence of all the Persons of the Trinity in promoting the work of redemption of sinners; which was executed by the Son the Mediator, to shew, that the love of the Son in giving his life, is no greater than the love of the Father in contriving and accepting of it for a ransom; there being naturally in the hearts of the hearers of the gospel this prejudice, that the Father is more rigid, and less loving than the Son: But considering, that it was the Father, Son and Spirit, that contrived Christ's sufferings; that the Son's sufferings were the product and consequent of his contrivance? it removeth this corrupt imagination and prejudice, and sheweth that there is no place for it. It doth also contribute notably to our engagement to God, to be throughly persuaded of the Lord's good pleasure in the sufferings of the Mediator, as well as in the willingness of the Mediator to suffer; he having performed the will of the Father, in the lowest steps of his humiliation. (2.) They are exprest, and holden forth in their nature and end, they were to be *an offering for sin*;

sin; and this follows well on the former verse, because it might be said, How could he, that *had no violence in his hands, nor guile in his mouth*, be brought so low? He hath answered in part, by saying, *It pleased the Father to bruise him, and to put him to grief*. But because that does not so fully obviate, and answer the objection; he answers further, that there was a notably good end for it: Tho' he had no sin in himself, nor are we to look on his sufferings, as for any sin in him, yet we are to look upon them as a satisfaction to justice for the sins of others; even as the bullocks, lambs and rams, and the scape-goat, were not slain for their own sins, for they were not capable of sin, yet they were someway typical offerings and satisfactions for sin, in the room of others for whom they were offered; so our Lord Jesus is the proper Offering and Sacrifice for the Sins of his elect people; and his sufferings are so to be looked on by us: And this is the scope. But to clear the words a little more fully, there are different readings of them, as they are set down here in the text, and on the margin. Here it is, *When thou shalt make his soul an offering for sin*, on the margin it is, *When his soul shall make an offering for sin*: The reason of the diversity is, because the same word in the original, which signifies the second Person masculine, *thou*, meaning the Father, signifies the third Person fœminine, *his soul shall make itself*: But on the matter, whether we apply it to the Father, or to Christ, both comes to one thing; it seems to do as well to apply it to Christ: The former words having set out God's concurrence, and good pleasure to the work; these set out the Mediator's willingness, as in the last verse, it is said that *he poured out his soul to death:* and properly Christ is the Priest that offered up himself: yet, we say, there is no difference on the matter, nor as to the scope, the will of the Father, and of the Mediator, in the work of redemption, being both one: tho' (as we said) we incline to look on them, as relating to Christ. 2. *Offering for sin*, in the original, signifies *sin*; so that the words are, *when thou shalt make his soul sin*, the word being ordinarily used in the Old Testament, and thence borrowed in the New Testament to signify a sin-offering; as Exod. xxix. 14. and Levit. iv. v. and xvi. chapters, where the sin-offering is appointed; it is the same word that's here, intimating that the sin-offering was designed to bear their sin, *They shall lay their hands on the sin*, or sin-offering, because the sacrificed beast was typically to have the peoples sins imputed to it; tho' properly no man's sin is imputed to any, but to Christ. This is also clear, if we compare Psal. xl. 6. with Heb. x. 5, 6. That which in the psalm is rendered *sin-offering*, in the original is *sin*; but the Apostle, Heb. x. hath it *sacrifice for sin*; and it is the same word which he hath, 2 Cor. v. ult. *He was made sin for us*, that is, an offering for sin. By which we may see the unwarrantableness of some mens accounting Christ to be formally a sinner, because he is called *sin*, and because our sin is said to be laid on him, which, in scripture-phrase, is as much as his being a sacrifice for sin in the room of sinners.

(3.) *His soul* may be taken either simply, for *he shall be an offering for sin*, the soul being often taken for the whole person; or it may be taken more to relate to his sufferings, called *the travel of his soul*, verse 11. however it is the Person, the Man-Christ, soul and body, that is the Sacrifice, and more especially his soul, as the wrath of God was on it; and when he suffered, his soul did undergo that wrath, as well as his back was given to the smiter, and his cheeks to them that plucked off the hair.

(4.) There are two words further, which we would hint at in the exposition, for clearing of Christ's being called *an offering for sin*. 1st, We would put a difference between the offerings and sacrifices which were for sin under the law, and this offering, which is applied to Christ: The apostle says, Heb. x. *That it was impossible, that the blood of bullocks and of goats could take away sin;* They were not properly sin-offerings, but as they were types of that offering which was to come. And so, when Christ is called an offering, he is differenced from all the offerings that were offered before him by the Priests on earth, in this, that his offering or sacrifice takes away sin, by vertue of itself, according to the covenant; but these offerings of those Priests that were under the law (as is clear, Heb. ix. 13.) took not away sin by themselves, but only in so far as Christ who was typified by them was made use of. And from this we may see it clear. 1. That it was by the blood of Christ, that the fathers under the law had their sins pardoned; and that the pardon of sin was to them an effect of this offering, as well as unto us. 2. That all these sacrifices and offerings under the law were types of this one offering, and not the anniversary sacrifice only, which was offered once a year by the High Priest; which we the rather hint at, because both these are by Socinus, that enemy of Christ's satisfaction, controverted; he aiming thereby to draw souls from leaning to this offering. 2dly, What we speak of Christ's sacrifice, relates to that which be performed on earth. Tho' he be yet a Priest, and lives for ever to make intercession for us; yet this offering respects that which he offered while he was here in the world, and especially that which he offered on the cross, as it is said, Eph. v. 2. *He hath loved us, and given himself for us, an offering and sacrifice to God, for a sweet smelling savour;* and Heb. x. 12. *This Man, after he had offered one sacrifice for sins, for ever sat down on the right hand of God;* and by his sacrifice once offered up before, he went into the most holy, *he hath perfected for ever them that are sanctified*: Which is also a truth controverted by that same enemy Socinus; the clearing of it serves, not only to open up the meaning of this place, but to let us see the efficacy of Christ's sufferings, and the nature of them, that in them especially, his offering, as it brings pardon of sin, and peace with God, does consist. So then the meaning of the place is in short, That tho' our Lord Jesus had no sin, yet it pleased God, in his counsel, to appoint him to suffer, and that his sufferings should be an offering for the sins of others.

More particularly, if it be asked, What is meaned by this, *an offering for sin?* we shall clear it from the type; and, 1. It is here supposed, that there is sin on the person, and that wrath due for sin is to be removed. 2. It is supposed, that there is an inability in the person to remove the sin, and yet a necessity to have it removed, or else he must suffer. 3. There is supposed the interveening, or coming of something in the place of that person that is guilty of sin, and liable to wrath. 4. There is supposed the acceptation of that which interveeneth, by God, the Party offended; and so it presupposeth a covenant, whereby the Lord hath condescended to accept of that offering. Take it in the sin-offering goat, the scape-goat, Levit. xvi. a lively type of Christ; when he is brought into the congregation. (1.) The Priest must put his hand upon him, and confess the sins and transgressions of the people over him; which signified their acknowledgment of their sins, and a liableness to suffering because of them. (2.) It supposed their proposing of that goat, as a sacrifice to bear their sins, and to take them on him; therefore it was said, *The Priests shall put* the iniquities of the people upon him. (3.) The one of these goats was to be sent away into the wilderness, and the other was to be killed; and generally all the sin-offerings were to be killed: So that no remission of sins was without blood, and they came in the room of the sinners, bearing as it were their sin, and their punishment.

And, (4.) It is to be *an atonement*, to wit, a typical atonement: By this means, the people were to have access to ecclesiastical privileges; but they could not purify the conscience, except Christ were made use of, who was the true atonement then, as he is now, still for sin; and by vertue of his sacrifice, according to the covenant, they were to deal, for the pardon of the sins born by him.

We come now to *observe* some things from the words; and, 1. It is supposed here, that even the elect, and consequently all others, are by their sin liable to God's judgment, and obnoxious to his wrath; there were no need of a sin-offering, if this were not. The name that Christ gets here, supposes that there was sin, and that there was wrath for sin lying at the door of all men, since man fell, and brake God's command: All men are before God like Isaac, lying before his Father, ready to be killed, his Father having his hand stretched out with the knife, ready to take away his life; and our Lord Jesus is as the *ram* that was caught in the thicket of thorns, whereby elect sinners are freed, and himself made the sacrifice that was provided in their room and place. Thus, in the name that our Lord Jesus gets, we have holden out to us, the posture that all of us are in by nature, if Christ interveen not to take the stroke off us on himself, laying himself open to the stroke of justice for sin: To clear it, consider these three things, which will hold out, what this state and posture of ours is; 1. The natural sinfulness, and guilt that men are lying under, which makes them naked, and to be as that wretched infant, (spoken of Ezek. xvi.) lying in their blood, cast forth into the open field, to the lothing of their persons: This makes God and them to be at feud, and lays them open to the stroke of justice. 2. Consider the interveening of the law of God, that threatens the curse on sin wherever it is, and pronounces this sentence, that *the wages of sin is death*, and says to the sinner, as it is said to Cain, *If thou sin, death lies at thy door;* and in this sense, sinners are not only like to malefactors taken and apprehended, but like to such when sentenced to death; therefore, John iii. 18. *He that believes not, is condemned already*. 3. Consider, that men in their natural state, who have broken the covenant of works, have justice someway pursuing them to the executing of the sentence, which God in his law hath pronounced against them; and they are these shedders of blood before they betook themselves to the city of refuge, having the avenger of blood following hard at their heels: In which sense, John iii. 36.

it

bespeaks him thus, therefore thou art cursed, therefore thou art a dead man.

Soberly think upon this, and make these uses of it, 1. See here the condition of all men by nature, and your own in particular; a very terrible and dreadful condition, wherein they are like men lying bound to be a sacrifice to the wrath of God, the Lord's hand being stretched out to lay on the stroke, and the wrath of God abiding on them. Do ye indeed believe this to be your state and posture, till application be made of Christ's sacrifice, and till there be a laying of your sin over on him by faith, that ever till then ye are liable to the law's sentence, and that the curse and wrath of God abideth on you? and yet this is the state and posture of all the children of Adam, that have not got Jesus Christ put in their room: It was typical, if the people did not bring an offering as was prescribed, their sin remained in them; but it is real here, sin and wrath remain, where Christ is not made use of by faith.

The second use is for expostulation with many of you, that are still in nature (and I wish there were fewer of you in this case to be spoken to) How comes it to pass, when this is your condition by nature, that ye are so secure, and that ye have few or no apprehensions at all of the wrath of God, and of the hazard of your immortal souls? Ah? are there none such here, that apprehend their hazard? were ye ever under it? and if so, how have ye been delivered out of it? or who is come in your room? do ye think it nothing to be under sin, and the curse of God, to have wrath abiding in you, yea abiding on you? There are many of you who are sleeping sound now, and that disdain to notice challenges: But, as Solomon speaks of the man that was sleeping on the top of a mast, and complaining of that, and of them that deceived him; so shall it be with you, that can ly still securely sleeping in sin, and that put by one day after another, and do not make use of this sacrifice. All that the gospel aims at is this, that ye would seek to change rooms with Christ, that the feud may be removed, and that the quarrel that is betwixt God and you may not be continued and keeped up; especially, seeing there what a terror it will waken in your conscience one day, ye would certainly think it good news to have the sufferings of Christ spoken of and the benefit of them offered to you now.

The third use is, to stir up sinners to thankfulness, especially such of you as are blest with effectual counsel, to make the right use of this sacrifice: O consider how much ye are obliged to God, and to Christ the Mediator! The preaching of the gospel is now thought little of, and is tasteless to many; but did ye know what is your state and posture by nature, how near ye are to hell, and how near the curse and wrath are upon you, even ready to grasp at you, to tear and devour you, the Mediator's interposing to satisfy for you, would make him more lovely to you; and ye that have gotten interest in him secured, would think yourselves much, unspeakably much, in his common, to say so, and in the debt of his grace. This was the posture that grace found you in, even liable to the stroke of God's drawn sword of justice: and our Lord Jesus on the one side stepped in, and said, Hold, Lord; let that be on me, and let them go free: and upon the other side, there was God's good pleasure, condescending to accept of his offer, and saying, *Awake, O sword! and smite the shepherd, and spare the sheep*, What obligation should this lay upon you, to love and be thankful to God, and to the Mediator, who interposed to keep the stroke off you; I say, upon you who are sinners, and apprehensive of wrath? This is Christ's offer; and if ye be fled to him for refuge, he hath changed rooms with you. Ye are much (as I said) in his debt; he hath freed you of your debt, and purchased an absolution for you; and *there is no condemnation to you*, as it is, Rom. viii. 1. whereas before ye were in a manner condemned already. But the truth is, our Lord Jesus is undervalued, not only by them that apprehend not their hazard, and so make not use of him; but also in a great measure by them that do apprehend it, in so far as they give way to unbelief, and dare scarcely trust to his sacrifice.

The 2d and next thing implied here, is, "That "tho' men be naturally under sin, and obnoxious.
"to

"to the wrath and curse of God, by reason of sin; "yet there is nothing that can take away that sin, "and free them from wrath, but Christ Jesus his "offering up himself a sacrifice for sin." Therefore he is so made the offering for sin here, as it is exclusive of all other things; no other thing could do it; as it is, Heb. x. 14. *He by one offering hath perfected for ever those who are sanctified.* The blood of bulls and of goats could not take away sin; *Neither is* (as it is, Acts iv. 12.) *there any other name under heaven given to sinners, whereby they can be saved, but by the name of Jesus.* I shall not speak here of the nature of Christ's offering and sacrifice; but sure, tho' all men be under sin and wrath by nature, there is no other way to remove it, except by this sacrifice. Thousands of rams, (as it is, Micah vi. 7.) and ten thousand rivers of oil, the first born of the body, will not take away the sin of the soul; Christ's offering up of himself, in God's account, is only the sin-offering, for the removing of sin, and wrath from sinners. Is it needful to prove this? We wish it were not; but the truth is, it is hardly believed by men and women. Consider therefore shortly these three things, and ye will find it true, 1. The certification and peremptoriness of the curse that follows sin, as we may see, Gal. iii. 10. *Cursed is every one that continueth not in all things written in the book of the law to do them.* Whatever may be said of God's absolute sovereignty, whereof we will not now speak, God hath so ordered his covenant, and revealed his will in his word, that *the soul that sins shall die,* if a sacrifice be not put in its room. 2. Consider the ineffectualness of all other things to satisfy justice. Tho' we would multiply offerings, what cares God for these? *All the beasts on the mountains are his, he delights not in the blood of bulls and goats,* as it is, Psal. l. Thousands of rams, and ten thousand rivers of oil, are rejected; whether we look to penances, (whereof some foolishly talk) what can these do to God? or whether we look to mens external performance of holy duties, or to their inward convictions, challenges and mournings for sin, there is no suitable value in these things, to interpose betwixt them and God's wrath; suppose that man after the fall could perform duties without sin: Therefore the apostle, Heb. x. says, that *it was impossible that the blood of bullocks and of goats could take away sin;* there is no suitableness nor proportionableness betwixt the blood of a beast, and the soul of a sinner; far less betwixt it and the majesty of God that is wronged by sin: Wherefore, when the sufferings of a sinner are lengthned to twenty thousand millions of years in hell, the justice of God is never satisfied, nor never will be to the full; what then can other things do? 3. There is no other thing that hath a promise made or annexed to it, nor is there any other mean laid down, for the removal of sin and wrath, but Christ offering himself up a sin-offering. I know some are ready to think, that tho' there be no worth in the thing, or duty, yet God of his free grace will accept of it; but is there a promise of God's accepting any other thing for a satisfaction for sin, or for the removal of wrath, but Christ's sacrifice alone? and will or can folks expect that for which they have no promise? The scripture is plain and premptory in this, as namely, Acts iv. 12. *There is no other name under heaven, whereby a sinner can be saved, but by the name of Jesus:* He is *the Door, the Way, the Truth, and the Life,* John xiv. *The promises are yea and amen in him,* 2 Cor. i. there is greater necessity to be through in this, though a common truth, than folks think of: And for use, it aims at these two. (1.) Upon the one side, to carry down all beside, that pretends to satisfy God, or to make a sinner acceptable to him. Prayer is no sin-offering; repentance, convictions, a blameless life &c. are no sin-offerings; these things are empty, and insignificant, as to the justification of a sinner, or the obtaining of his pardon. (2.) Upon the other side, it points out the absolute necessity of making use of Christ's sacrifice, and of the betaking of ourselves to it, for the satisfying of God's justice: If there be a necessity of the pardon of sin, and of the removing of wrath, there is then sure a necessity of closing with Christ, and his sacrifice.

The first of these uses speaks to two sorts of persons, with whom the word of God hath no weight, and who, in effect think to satisfy God with nothing. 1. A prophane, graceless, secure company, who, because God keeps silence, are disposed to think that he is like themselves, and that he will never pursue a quarrel against them; much like to that man spoken of, Deut. xxix. 18, 19. *Who says in his heart, He shall have peace, though he walk in the imagination of his own heart, adding drunkenness to thirst.* We have a generation of this sort among us, who tush at all threatnings, (alas for them! O that God would be graciously pleased to make a change on them; or, if that may not be, that he would rid us of them!) who will needs live sensually, and as they list; who will needs speak and do as they please, and will not be controuled; and yet, at the first hand, will boldly and confidently assert their hope of heaven, as if they never had been sinners: Whence comes this, even from their supposing, that there is another way to heaven than God hath chalked out; they think they may be saved, tho' they never betake themselves to Christ for union with him: But whether shall their sentence or God's stand? there is a day coming, when ye shall know. Ye say, Ye shall have peace; but God says, No,; Why so? Because ye never knew what it was to make use of Christ; ye had never so much as a form, nor any the least gust of religion, but were and are still as senseless as the stones in the wall: What do ye think will become of this? God urges as it were, the offers of Christ upon you,, and ye still slight him: He tells you, that there is a necessity of union with him, else ye shall never see heaven; and ye ly still at a distance from him, and yet will needs hope for heaven: But alas! it will not be so with you. Either think on the right way, which is, by putting Christ in your room, and laying of religion to the heart in sad earnest; or dream not of coming to heaven. A second sort are they, who are not altogether so profane as the others, but will condemn them (as indeed the practice of many is lothsom) they will, it may be, pray in their families, and will not be drunk, neither will they swear, nor lie, and they will walk blamelesly; and, upon these grounds, they promise heaven to themselves very confidently; and yet they come not through the sense of their sinful and cursed state by nature, to close with Christ by faith, and to make use of his sacrifice: Such err on the other hand. Oh, when shall we be at this, not to neglect the study of holiness, and yet not to rest on it, to the prejudice of this one offering! This were a practice suitable to, and worthy of professors of the gospel; to be seriously aiming at all duties of holiness that are called for; and yet to be building all their expectation of any good from God, on the sacrifice of Christ alone; never coming to God without bringing it along with them, and looking through it to be accepted before him: There needs no more, and no other thing that we can bring will do our turn, nor be taken off our hand, if this be neglected. The Lord himself teach us this way.

SERMON XXXVIII.

Isaiah liii. 10.------*When thou shalt make his soul an offering for sin, he shall see his seed, he shall prolong his days, and the pleasure of the Lord shall prosper in his hand.*

WHatever the men of the world think of it, it is not an easy matter to get the justice of God satisfied for sin, and to get the wrath and curse, that men by sin have drawn on themselves, removed: Offerings of bullocks, and goats, thousands of rams, and ten thousand rivers of oil, will not do it; the redemption of the soul is so precious, that it ceaseth for ever that way, and by all such means: Therefore the Lord in his wisdom hath found out the means, and in his grace and love hath condescended, that his own dear Son, his Fellow, shall, as a Lamb without spot, be a Sin-offering, to take away the sins of his elect world; and this is the great consideration under which we should take up the death of Christ, as making himself therein an Offering for sin, and interposing himself to satisfy divine justice, that forgiveness might be made forthcoming to us.

The *Doctrine*, which we proposed to be spoken to the last day, was this, " That Jesus Christ is " the only Sin offering, by which sin can be taken " away, and God so satisfied, as to forbear the " punishment of the sinner, and to admit him to " peace and friendship with him." If we would enumerate all things imaginable, and invent ways and means without number to remove sin, or to make a sinner's peace with God, there is no other means but this that will do it; as we have it Heb. x. " Christ Jesus, by his once offering up of himself, " perfects for ever these who are sanctified;" and Acts iv. " There is no other name given under hea" ven, whereby sinners can be saved, but the name " of Jesus."

The *Use* is, to commend, and to demonstrate to us all, the necessity of the use-making of this one offering of Christ. If he be the one offering to take away sin, and if no other will be accepted, then there is a necessity, that he in his offering of himself be made use of: If all be under sin, and if, by the law, sin and death be knit inseparably together (as it is said, *The wages of sin is death*) and if freedom from sin and wrath, and peace with God, be necessary; then there is a necessity, that sinners be serious in this matter, to get a title to, and interest in this one Offering and Sacrifice of Christ.

In the prosecuting of the *Use*, we shall speak a little to these four things, 1. To some grounds, or reasons, to shew the necessity of sinners use-making of Christ's Sacrifice or Offering. 2. To this, what it is to make use of this Offering. 3. We shall give a word of advertisement, as to some mistakes that are about it. 4. We shall give some difference-

it

ing characters, or evidences, of a person that is making right use of this Offering, for obtaining of pardon, and for making of this peace with God.

For the *First*, that is, the reasons to evince the necessity of it; the first of them is that which we hinted at just now, If men were not lying under sin, and obnoxious to wrath, and if there were any other sin-offering, or any other way or mean to escape the curse and wrath of God due for sin, there were no such necessity: But seeing that all men are under sin, and under the curse of God and his wrath, because of it, and seeing there is no other thing that can take away sin; then there is an absolute necessity, seriously to make use of, and to have an interest in this sin-offering. 2. Consider, that the great part of men in the world, and even of them that hear this gospel, do not indeed make use of this offering, tho' they be some way under the conviction that they are sinners, and that this is the only sin-offering to take away sin: And we suppose, if ye were all put to it, ye could not deny, but ye are sinners, and that nothing can take away sin, but Christ's offering up of himself as a Sacrifice to satisfy justice. Tho' some be that grosly ignorant, that they will speak of some other thing, yet generally these that own and maintain the truth of the gospel, are under a conviction that no other thing can take away sin; and yet, even amongst these, there are many that never make use of Christ, and of his Sacrifice, to take away their sins, to remove wrath, and make their peace with God: There were many Jews, who by the daily sacrifices, which typed forth this one offering of Christ, were taught, that there was no other way to come by pardon, and peace with God, but their use-making of it; and yet the most part of them, in going about these sacrifices, were slighters of this one Sacrifice; therefore the apostle says of them, Rom. x. 13. "That, " being ignorant of God's righteousness, they went " about to establish their own righteousness, and " did not submit themselves unto the righteousness " of God." It is as certain, that many that hear this gospel, and profess Christ to be the only sin-offering, will be disowned of him on this account; therefore many are brought in, saying, Luke xiii. " Did we not hear thee preach in our streets? have " we not eaten and drunken in thy presence?" to whom he shall say, " Depart from me, I never " knew you, ye workers of iniquity;" because (as if he had said) whatever ye professed, ye never made peace with God, through and by me. And what is the reason, I pray, that so many perish under the gospel, who in word acknowledge this one offering, and that it is it only which takes away sin, but because that, notwithstanding of that conviction and acknowledgment, they are never brought actually to make use of Christ, and of this his Sacrifice and Offering; and if ye think and acknowledge, that there are many that go to hell, that have the knowledge and conviction of this truth, ye also must grant, that it is because they make not conscience to make use of it. 3. Consider, that tho' there be many of the hearers of the gospel, who do not rest on Christ, yet it is very hard to convince any of them, that they are ready to slight Christ's Sacrifice: I am sure that both the former will be granted, (1.) That nothing but Christ's Sacrifice can satisfy justice; (2.) That many do not rest on it, that so perish: But if we come to the (3.) scarcely shall we find one that will grant (except it be a tender body) that they make not use of him: They will easily be convinced, that adultery is a sin, and that they are guilty of it, if they be so indeed; that drunkenness and sabbath-breaking are sins; yea, possibly (which is more) that vaguing of the mind in duties of worship is a sin, and that they are guilty of it: But it is not so easy to convince them, that they are guilty of the sin of not making use of Christ, and of his Sacrifice; nay, they are so puft up with a good opinion of themselves, that they will laugh at such a challenge; and hence it is, that so few make use of Christ's Sacrifice, and of his righteousness, because so few are convinced, that they believe not on him; therefore, when the Spirit comes, John xvi. it is said, that *he shall convince the world of sin*; not because they did whore, drink, swear, &c. tho' convictions for these sins will not be wanting; but *because they believed not in Christ*: And hence it is, Luke xiii. 25. that these will not take Christ's first answer, *I know you not*: What (as if they said) knows thou not us? *we have eaten and drunken in thy presence*, we have professed faith in thee, and we hope to get heaven by thy righteousness; and yet he shall answer them again peremptorily, *Depart from me, I know you not*: Not that there will be much to do, or any great difficulty to convince folk in that day or any room left to debate the business; but he would tell us by this, that many die in this delusion: And if it be a thing that folks are so hardly convinced of, had they not need to be seriously solicitous, that they be not deceived and disappointed? 4. Consider how sad the disappointment will be to sinners one day, when they shall be brought to acknowledge, that they knew that there was no other name given whereby sinners could be saved, but

the

the name of Jesus; and yet that they slighted and rejected him. Ye that never seriously minded counting and reckoning with God, do ye think on this, and that the passing of the sentence, will be upon this ground, to wit, Whether ye have fled to Jesus Christ and make use of his Sacrifice or not? Will it not be a sad disappointment, to meet with a doleful *Depart from me*, on this ground, because tho' there was some conviction that this was the only Sacrifice and Sin-offering that takes away sin, that yet it was not made use of, nor made the ground of your peace with God?

But to the 2d, What is it then to make use of this Offering? I know no better way than to explain it from the typical sacrifices, that were under the law; and we may take it up in these three, (1.) It implies a thorow conviction of folks liableness to the justice of God for sin, and an utter inability in ourselves, and utter emptiness and impotency in all other means, to satisfy for sin: Thus they that brought the sacrifice to the Priest, laid their hand on the head of the beast, by which they acknowledged, that death was due unto them. So then, to have the lively sense of the due desert of sin, that is, to have the sentence of death carried about in our bosom, to have the thorow conviction of the emptiness of all other means of relief, is requisite to the right use-making of Christ's Offering. (2.) It implieth this, that there be a look had to the institution and ordinance of God, appointing this Sacrifice to be the mean of the redemption of sinners: Therefore, in those sacrifices that were offered for sin, there was a respect had to God's covenant; wherein were not only promises relating to external cleansing, and to admission to Church-privileges, but promises also relating to inward cleansing, and the pardon of sin, which was the great end of these sacrifices; and the looking to the institution of this Sacrifice, is the ground that leads us in to take up the end of Christ's sufferings, and is a warrant for our faith, in the use-making thereof; being the only sacrifice that expiates sin, and holds off wrath: And if these two things be not carried along in the use-making of this sacrifice, to wit, the conviction of sin, and the liableness to wrath; and God's institution and appointment of this sacrifice, to take away sin, and to avert wrath; our use-making of it is but will-worship. (3.) It implies this, that when the sinner is walking under the sense of his sin, and the emptiness and ineffectualness of all other things, to remove sin and wrath (as David hath it, Psal. li. 16. *Thou desirest not sacrifice, thou delightest not in burnt offerings*) there must be a looking to the worth of Christ, and of his Sacrifice, that is appointed to take away sin, and hold off wrath; and the soul's actual applying of his Offering to itself; as we may see in the iv. v. vi. and xvi. chapters of Leviticus, where there are several sacrifices appointed to be offered for several sins, and particularly that of the *scape-goat*, on the head whereof, the Priest for the people was to lay his hands: In which was implied not only their acknowledgment of sin, and of their deserving death; and of God's appointment of that to be a typical offering for the typical taking away of sin; but these two things further were implied, 1. That they did take the burden of their sins, which neither they themselves, nor any other could bear, and laid it on Christ; when justice did put at them for their debt (to speak so) they drew a bill on Christ, as their Cautioner, to answer it; and as they did put the debt in his hand, to be paid by him; so they lippened and trusted the weight of their souls to him, and to no other: So that, when God was pursuing them for their debt, saying, as it were, I will have payment of you, or else you must die; they brought the sacrifice to the Priest, to please God typically, with an eye to Christ typified thereby: Even so, for sinners to make use of Christ's sufferings, is, in the thorow conviction of sin, and of deserved wrath, to flee unto Jesus Christ, and to put him in their room; being content and desirous, that he be their Cautioner, and undertake for them, and satisfy for their debt: Yea, putting him actually to it, to pay their debt; so that they have no other answer to any challenge fot sin but this, The Cautioner that I have betaken myself to, and put in my room, will pay this debt, and answer for it: The 2d act of faith is this, When they have betaken themselves to him, and to his sacrifice, they acquiesce in, and rest upon it alone, for obtaining of the sentence of absolution: which was also implied in the people their laying their hands, by the Priest, on the head of the sacrifice: For as it implied their acknowledging that they could not please nor satisfy God of themselves, nor by any other way or mean; so it implied, that according to God's covenant, they expected his absolving of them, because of that sacrifice; and that, tho' they were desperate by themselves to satisfy, yet they had faith in God's covenant, that the sacrifice they offered, would typically satify him: Even so, the believer draws the conclusion from Christ's sacrifice, according to the terms of the covenant, that he hath absolution; and rests on and acquiesces in it: And this is called *Trusting* or *Confiding* in Christ;

when not only he casteth himself on him, but hath confidence, that the bill which he hath drawn on him will be answered by him; which is founded on the covenant, in which it is said, *Of all that come unto me, I will put none away*; as it is, John vi. 37. *Him that cometh to me, I will in nowise cast out*; and Zech. xiii. *There is a fountain opened in the house of David, for sin, and for uncleanness*: on which ground believers expect the benefit of washing, on their performing of the condition of the covenant: And when David, Psal. li. 7. prays, *Purge me*, it holds out the act of faith, drawing the bill on Christ: And when he says, *I shall be clean and white as snow*; it holds out his confident resting on, and acquiescing in Christ, for cleansing. And this is the reason, why some express faith, by *cleaving to Christ*; others, by *confident resting on him*, or by assurance: And there may be a truth in both; because the one looks on faith according to the first act of cleaving to him; and the other takes up faith according to the other act of *assured resting on him, or confiding in him*, and so, or in his sacrifice offered up once for all. In a word, to make use of this once offering for sin, is so to make use of him, as to put him in our room, and ourselves some way in his room: Not to dare to count and reckon with justice; nay, not to dare, as it were, to count with Christ; but leaving Christ in the stour (to speak so) and running away from reckoning with justice, to hide ourselves under him, who can count to the utmost farthing: Even as when God commanded Abraham to offer up his son Isaac, and when he was lifting up his hand to slay him, there came a voice from heaven, *Abraham hold thy hand*, and a ram is provided, and Isaac is loosed, and taken down from off the altar, and the ram is put in his stead and place; so there is here a changing of rooms with Christ, according to that sweetest word, 2 Cor. v. ult. *He was made sin for us, who knew no sin, that we who had no righteousness, might be made the righteousness of God in him.*

3. If it be so very difficult, and yet so absolutely necessary, to make use of Christ, and especially in his offering up of himself for the sins of his people; there is ground here for warning, and advertisement, to walk tenderly in this matter, that this sacrifice be not slighted, that this one offering be not neglected, as we would not have sin lying at our door. And here we shall point at three sorts of persons, who may be counted slighters and neglecters of this offering. The 1*st* sort are these, who think to make their peace with God, without

minding the necessity of the interveening of any thing betwixt him and them; and these go on several grounds, or are of several sorts. 1. Some are utterly careless how their peace be made, or whether it be made or not: They hope for it, and think to come at it, but cannot give an account, whether they will come at it or not; and they are careless to know the way. 2. Others go upon their presumption: They think God loves them, because they love themselves; and tho' they know they have sin, yet they think God will not be so ill, as to reckon with them; they think they are sure that God loves them, but they cannot give a ground for it. 3. Others think, God is merciful, and therefore they conclude that they will be pardoned: They cannot conceive God to be like man in his mercy, but to be far beyond him, (as indeed he is infinitely in some respect) and therefore, because, when man is merciful, he sometimes seeks no satisfaction; so neither will God, think they; not considering, that tho' God be merciful, that yet he will not shew mercy to the prejudice of his justice, but will needs have it satisfied: Such think, on the matter at least, that they would have gotten mercy, tho' Christ had never died. It is true, If God had not been merciful, never a sinner had gotten mercy; yet that is not the ground of his shewing mercy, otherwise all the world might expect mercy: For he is, and ever was, gracious and merciful in himself; and therefore there must be some other ground and way for obtaining of pardon; else it cannot be expected, because of the alone simple and abstract consideration of his mercy: And yet many will needs expect it on this ground, without respect to the Mediator's purchase. A 2*d* sort, are they that take the legal way, for making their peace with God: Not as if they thought to appear before God without sin, and holy, as the covenant of works requireth; but if they sin, they will make amends: And it is either something negative that they have not done, or something positive that they have done, or some internal qualifications, that they rest upon. 1. Something negative, they have not been so ill as other folks; and if they go to hell, they think, few will go to heaven: They have done wrong to none; and if they were about to die, they think, and, it may be, say, that they will leave a good name behind them, on the account of their harmless walk; like that Pharisee, they can say, *Lord, I thank thee, I am not like other men, nor like this Publican*: They are no drunkards, no oppressors, they neither curse nor swear; and when they see any profane persons, they are puft up with

a good

a good opinion of themselves, because they are not as profane as they. Or, 2. They will come a further length, and positively do many duties, upon which they rest; and whereof they are ready to boast, with the same Pharisee, who vaunted, *I fast twice a week, I give tithes of all I possess:* If any duty be performed, or any good be done by them, their fingers are ready (to say so) to stick to it: But, 3. and especially, If there be any inward work, as if there be any liberty, or motion of the affections in prayer; if there be, at hearing the word, some convictions sharper at one time than at another; if there be any sort of repentance, rewing, and sadness for sin, &c. these, they think, will do their turn: It is most certain, and might be cleared, both from the word of God, and from experience, that many hundreds of professors dash, and perish on this stumbling-block, Isaiah xlviii. 1, 2. where the Lord is speaking of a people, *that made mention of his name, and sware by him, but not in truth, nor in righteousness:* of whom he says, that *they call* and count *themselves of the holy city, and stay themselves upon the God of Israel*; and the ground of it is, their resting on external duties, of fasting and prayer, and the like: Expectation of happiness grounded on some feckless performances, cuts the throats of many and civil and discreet men, that are not grossly profane. A 2d sort do not altogether slight and neglect Christ himself, but they slight and neglect his offering; as if they would in a manner make use of himself, but not of his sacrifice; as Matt. xix. and Mark x. there is a man spoken of, that comes to Christ, would fain be at heaven, and asks, *Good Master, what shall I do that I may inherit eternal life?* and yet he was going on the grounds of his own righteousness: This is exceeding subtile and deceitful; and therefore ye would take the better notice of it, and how it is fallen into. A man may come to Christ, as God, for pardon of sin (and some think tho' most ignorantly and erroneously, that Christ the Son is more compassionate and ready to pardon than the Father) and may seek pardon from him; but not for his sake, or on his account: For there is a difference betwixt making Christ the Object of our worship, and making use of him as Mediator. There are many that have prayed to Christ as God, and sought pardon of sin from him; who never prayed to obtain pardon, by vertue of his offering. Folk may also desire help from Christ, to enable them to do duties, that they may thereby work out the work of their own salvation, and be helped this way to make their peace with God, who do not ground the making of their peace with God on his offering alone: These things are exceeding frequent in peoples practice, who will pray to Christ for such and such things, and yet not found their expectation of them upon this offering, or his righteousness: If we would make use of Christ's offering singly and rightly, we would eschew these, and all other wrong ways.

4. It may be asked then, What are the evidences that may give a person some clearness, that he is making use of Christ's righteousness aright, and that it is not his own righteousness, nor the making use of Christ's only as he is God, that sustains him? I answer, that this is indeed a mystery; and will require searching, and watching to observe our own condition. And more things concur than one or two, to make a full discovery of it: In speaking to this, as we desire to strengthen the presumption of none, so we shall labour to shun the weakening of the faith of any sound believer. There are then these six or seven differencing evidences, or characters of a person, that is rightly making use of Christ's offering, which difference him from others: And, 1. One that truly makes use of Christ's offering, hath not only been brought to see his need of it, but his natural propension and readiness to mistaken it, and rest upon other things beside it, for the making of his peace; whereas another man, who does not rightly make use of it, tho' he may see his sin, and so his need of it; yet he sees not, neither will take with the tendency, propenseness, and inclination of his heart, to rest upon some other thing beside it: See this difference in Paul, before and after conversion, Phil. iii. Before he was converted, he studied, as he thought, all the righteousness of the law; and no doubt offered sacrifices, which implied the acknowledgment of sin; and he thought that all was well with him: Therefore he says, *Touching the righteousness of the law, he was blameless*; and verse 6. *These things that were gain to me*, or these things that I placed my righteousness in, I thought the more sacrifices that I offered, I had the more to buy my peace by; he sees, that in his studying of holiness, he was seeking to make a stock in himself: But after his conversion, he casts all these, as to leaning to them, or making them any ground of his peace with God, or of his justification before him; he betakes himself only to Christ's righteousness, and *counts them to be but loss*. I would think it a good evidence for folks, not only to see the looseness of their hearts in duty, and that to be a sin; but to see, when ought went well with them, the inclination of their hearts ready

to account that to be gain, and to rest upon it: There is such an humour and natural inclination in all; and it is a good token when it is discovered, and becomes a burden, and the ground of a challenge; not only that they have sinned, in this, and that, and the other duty, but that they have gone a whoring after their feckless performances, to the prejudice of their esteem of Christ, and of his righteousness: *Before the law came* (saith Paul) Rom. vii. *I was alive,* I thought I had a stock to do my own turn; *but when the commandment came, sin revived, and I died.* There are many that will be convinced of sin in their performances, that will not be convinced of this sinful inclination to put these in Christ's room. A second difference or evidence is this: One that aims to make use of Christ's offering and righteousness, not only their sins will be an exercise to them, how to win over them to Christ, but it will be their exercise also, how to win over their graces and duties to him; it will be an exercise to them, not only to have such a sin in their duty taken away, but how to win over the duty itself, that they stumble not on it, to the prejudice of their trusting to Christ: whereas another man, when his duties go well with him, it is easy to him to win over them, as he thinks, because he rests satisfied with them. Paul, Phil. iii. sees not only while he was in nature, that he counted something gain beside Christ, but after conversion, he finds an inclination to it; and therefore, in opposition to this inclination, he doth with a *doubtless,* cry down all things, and count them but dung and loss for the excellency of the knowledge of Christ; taking in his gracious actions, as well as others: For the words in the text and context tell us, that he is speaking of duties performed by him, even after conversion; and that he found a necessity to cast away the good as well as the bad, in the point of justification: As a man, that is in a storm at sea, hath a greater reluctancy to cast over-board, silks, sattins, velvets, and other such fine things, than that which is more base, and of less worth; so he found it more difficult, and was put to some harder exercise, to be quit of his duties, that they should not stick to him, than to be rid of his sins. Is there any such exercise as this amongst folks, to be put to wrestling with their duties, not as being angry at them as such, but how to get them as it were cast over-board; to be jealous of any good in them, or done by them, that it pre-judge not their esteem of Christ; to be busy in well-doing all the day, and in the evening to count all their doing but loss; and to renounce it utterly, as to any putting-up by it,

or as to the making of their peace with God thereby? A third evidence is this, One that is single in making use of Christ's sacrifice, will be exercised and disquieted, when his duty is done, till there be, for acceptance, a staying and resting on Christ's righteousness. There are two sorts that utterly fail, and fall short here, 1. Some that are content with sin, and make lies their refuge. 2. Others that are satisfied with duty, if it go well with them, and promise themselves acceptance on that alone account, neglecting Christ. But the believer hath (as I just now said) one exercise of faith, how to be quit of sin; and another new exercise of it, how to be freed from resting on duty, and how to be singly engaged unto, and to rest upon Christ: his mind is not quiet in all his duties, till he come hither, even to be found in Christ, not having his own righteousness, but his. It is a good token, when folks are not only exercised to have sin mortified, and duties going with them, but also to have their peace with God grounded on Christ, and not on duty; hence it is, that a Christian will sometimes be taken up a whole day in duty, and yet have but little, or no peace, because he would be over, and through all duties, to resting on Christ, which he wins not at to his satisfaction. 4thly, One that is single in use-making of Christ, and of his offering, hath a fear of mistaking this offering of Christ, and that some other thing be put in his room, and he mistent or neglected. There will be not only a fear, lest he sin, and come short in the suitable performance of such a duty, and lest he fall under wrath; but also fear and jealousy, lest, in his unbelief and selfishness, he be going wrong in the use-making of Christ, and of his sacrifice; as is implied in the word, Heb. iv. 1. where the apostle, having spoken of many of the Israelites their unbelief in the former chapter, says, in the beginning of this, *Let us therefore fear, lest a promise being left us of entering into his rest, any of us should seem to come short of it,* to wit, through unbelief: Be holily jealous (as if he had said) *lest,* as it is chap. iii. 12, 13. *there be in any of you an evil heart of unbelief, in departing from the living God.* In a word, he will be suspecting the exercise of his faith, as much as any thing; a natural man will sometimes, it may be, suspect his duties, but hardly will he be brought to suspect his faith, otherwise he could not have the peace that he hath, such as it is: This may also be confirmed from that poor man's prayer to Christ, Mark ix. *Lord, I believe, help my unbelief.* He dare not well trust his own faith. 5thly, They that are single in their use-making of Christ's offering, not only see themselves

sinners

sinners, but they carry along with them the discovery of the naughtiness of every thing that is best in them; when they see that, to which others trust to so much, so very unsuitable, and that they are far short of what they should be at, they dare not own, nor look on it to boast of it, but it is a burden to them, to see so much sin in it: It is nothing to see sin in some outward actions, and in that which is directly contrary to God's law; but it is much to see sin in our best things, as in our faith in God, in our love to him, and in our ends in holy duties. A legal man will confess it may be readily, that he sins in every thing; but he covers all with this, that he hath a good heart to God, or a good end: The believer on the contrary sees all his good so naughty, that it is tasteless to him; he never gets any thing to rest on, or that can bear his weight to confide in, till he comes to Christ's sacrifice. 6thly, Such as are aiming rightly to make use of Christ's offering and sacrifice, esteem and think exceeding much of it; therefore they adventure heaven and their eternal salvation on it: it is that which cheers and delights them most, that Christ hath stepped in, and engaged to do that for them, which neither themselves, nor any other person, or thing could do; *The life* (saith the apostle, Gal. ii.) *that I now live in the flesh, is by the faith of the Son of God, who loved me, and gave himself for me;* And 1 Tim. i. 15. *This is a faithful saying, and worthy of all acceptation, that Jesus Christ came to the world to save sinners, of whom I am the chief.* And John heartsomly, Rev. i. 7. *To him who loved us, and washed us in his own blood,* &c. But they that endeavour not, neither aim rightly to make use of Christ's sacrifice, think little or nothing of it; they are not made glad, nor are their hearts lifted up with spiritual joy because of it: The good and glad news of a slain Saviour, are not the chief ground of their consolation, as they are to the believer. This evidence is somewhat general, yet sure as well as the former. O but it is matter of much wonder to the believer, when he thinks how that, when the stroke of justice was ready to come on him, Christ should have interposed betwixt him and the fatal deadly blow! But others esteem not of it, and therefore cannot make use of it. 7thly, They that are rightly making use of Christ's sacrifice, find it to be a difficult thing, and that which will cost them wrestling, to get it made use of aright; they breathe after it, and yet win not to that which they would be at in it: O! as David cries, Psal. li. *Purge me with hyssop, and I shall be clean; wash me, and I shall be white as snow:* they know not well what way to make use of it to their satisfaction, they would make so much use of it, or how to vent and exercise their faith on it; and when it comes to actual believing, and to the acting of their faith, they find it to be like a smooth and slippery stone, that they cannot easily hold their feet on. So Paul says, Phil. iii. *I count all things but dung, that I may win Christ, and that I may be found in him;* he cared not what he cast overboard, that he might win to that land, even to Christ and his righteousness; like sea-men in great hazard, who cast all over board, to win to the shore; it is even so with the believer, he sees that there is such hazard to go wrong, and that it is so difficult to be right, even to make the heart to submit to the way of faith, and to abide by it singly, that he is content to suffer the loss of all things, if he may be right there: But on the contrary, a man that rests on his own righteousness, be a difficulty what will to him, faith is no difficulty to him; he may have fear to come short of heaven sometimes, but he thinks that he is always exercising his faith. In a word, the believer ordinarily believes best, when he hath the deepest, and most kindly impression of his sin: As for the legal man, he can believe well, as he thinks, when he hath no challenge for sin; but when he is challenged for sin, his faith fails him. Now, from all that hath been said, ye may see the necessity of making use of this sacrifice; and how warily, and cautiously it should be done, that ye may steer a right course between gross profanity and presumption, either of which will ruin and destroy the soul: The Lord Jesus himself be your Steersman, and Pilot, that ye by his skilful conduct may stemme the port, and hold off these rocks, on which thousands of souls have split, and make shipwreck.

SERMON XXXIX.

Isaiah liii. 10.——*When thou shalt make his soul an offering for sin, he shall see his seed, he shall prolong his days, and the pleasure of the Lord shall prosper in his hand.*

SIN was easily brought into the world; a little business brought in sin, and the curse and wrath of God with it; and, without any great difficulty, men can continue in sin, and ly under God's wrath and curse: But the taking away of sin, and the satisfying of the justice of God for it is no easy matter, that (if we may so speak) did put heaven and earth both to it; there was such a contrivance of this way, and such a mean chosen, and made use of, that sin might be removed, and the curse taken away, as the like was never heard of.

The intimation and manifestation of this way, is in the first part of this verse, *Yet it pleased the Lord to bruise him:* in God's council, and by his pleasure, it was contrived, and the way found out; and the mean is set down in these words, *When thou shalt make his soul an offering for sin;* the Mediator, even he who was the spotless Lamb of God, in whose mouth was found no guile, was bruised, and put to sad suffering, to get this effectuate; that the curse might be removed from sinners, he was made the sin-offering.

We shew, that Jesus Christ is the only sin-offering, by which sin is taken away, and that it is implied here; so that it is denied to all other things, or means, to have any efficacy, virtue or merit in them, as to the removing of sin, and the curse brought on by it. This is, I say, so peculiarly applied to Christ's offering, that it is denied to every thing else; which shews, 1. How much sinners are obliged to Christ, who, when no other thing could do it, interposed himself. 2. The necessity of making use of this one offering, without which never soul can be perfected or saved. He is the alone foundation of sinners peace, and of all the consolation that they can have in the promises of God.

Now, to proceed, and to hint at some few things more from the words, wherein the end, and nature of Christ's sufferings are set forth, He in his sufferings, and offering up of himself, did step into the room of the sinful elect, that by justice exacting of him the debt that was due by them, they might escape, and be set free; hence observe, *1st,* " That
" when there was no other thing, nor mean, that
" could sufficiently satisfy divine justice, or be a
" sacrifice for sin; our Lord stepped to, and un-
" dertook, and became the sacrifice to take away
" sin;" according to that often cited Psalm, Psal. xl. 7, 8. *Sacrifice and offering thou didst not desire, in burnt-offering thou hadst no pleasure:* He is not speaking of what God required in the law, as typical; for he required sacrifices and offerings in that respect, but not to be a propitiation for the sins of the elect world, because they could not do it: And then follows, *Lo, I come,* or I am here; *mine ear hast thou bored;* it is, Heb. x. *A body hast thou given unto me;* which sets out his being put in a capacity to be a sacrifice; *I delight to do thy will, O my God.* Here there are these four things implied. 1. A liableness in the elect to the justice of God for sin; and as to all other means and ways of relief, but by this one sacrifice, a desperateness and impossibility: And considering the sentence, which God had pronounced, *The day that thou eats thou shalt surely die;* and, *Cursed is every one that continues not in all things written in the law, to do them;* no sacrifice can be accepted but this only; thousands of rams, and ten thousands of rivers of oil have no access; he did not in that respect require these, neither would he capitulate on these terms. 2. That, when no other sacrifice could do the turn, Christ Jesus came in, and was content to interpose, and to be the sacrifice for sin; *Lo,* saith he, *I come,* I am here ready to satisfy for my elect people: For this is an old design, and he had undertaken from eternity to carry it on. 3. There is implied here a great willingness, a delightsom and heartsom condescending in the Mediator, to be the sacrifice; he steps in affectionately in the room of the elect, as the sacrifice for them, to receive the stroke of justice, that they may escape and go free; *I delight to do thy will, O my God:* This is God's will, as to the work of redemption, as it is, John vi. 38. *I came down from heaven, not to do mine own will, but the will of him that sent me;* and John xvii. 4. *I have finished the work thou gavest me to do.* That *will* and *this work* is

all

all one. And, Heb. x. it is said, *By which* (or by this) *will we are sanctified.* 4. The Father's admitting and accepting of him to interpose in the room of them, for whom he offered himself, is implied here; for otherwise his offering up of himself, could not have been a sacrifice satisfactory to justice, if the Lord Jehovah had not been content so far to relax his threatning and curse in reference to the party offending, as to admit of a cautioner in the room of the dyvour sinners, to satisfy for them, of which satisfaction he accepted: All these things put together, make Christ's interposing himself as a sacrifice and surety compleat. *I delight to do thy will,* supposes not only God's pleasure, that he should interpose, but his accepting of his interposing; and this is (to speak so) the flooring, and foundation of the work of redemption: The sentence stands over the elect's head, Cursed are the guilty; Christ comes in and interposes cheerfully to take on the debt, and says, Here I am, let the curse fall on me, and let satisfaction be taken from me; and this being offered according to God's will, it is accepted, and Christ's satisfaction becomes an offering in their room.

Use. See here a desperate condition, wherein by nature we are all lying; it sets us well, in speaking of grace, to take a view of what we were: And it shews how much sinners are in Christ's debt and common, that interposed for us in this condition. Could we suitably make inquiry what case we were in, under the hand of justice, and its stroke ready to light on us; and could we behold our Lord Jesus Christ interposing for us, and the sword of justice awaking against him, and smiting him for us; and the Lord Jehovah accepting of his interposing, and making his soul an offering for sin; and him willingly, and delightsomely offering up himself in our room; we would see our obligation to God, who was pleased to contrive, admit, and accept of this way, and mean of our redemption: And could we consider, what advantages we have by this redemption, and what it cost Christ to obtain it, we would see ourselves much, unspeakably much, in his debt. The day is coming, when it will be thought a favour, and when the sweet effects of it shall be made fully forthcoming to them that now cordially close with it, and when the fruit of despising it shall be found to be bitter like gall and wormwood.

2*dly*, From its being said, *When thou shalt make,* or when his soul shall make itself, or he himself shall make himself *an offering for sin;* Observe, " That as Christ undertook, and by undertaking " interposed to come in sinners room, to satisfy for " their sins; so his death and sufferings are really " the performing of that undertaking; and his death " and sufferings are so to be looked on, and considered by us an offering for sin." Or thus, " Christ's death is the sin offering that satisfied the " justice of God, in the room of elect sinners." This is the sum or compend of all that is spoken of his sufferings. If then it be asked, what meaned they all? Here it is, he was made a sin-offering. We shall clear it a little in these three or four parts, or branches. 1. Christ is properly a sin-offering, or a sacrifice for sin; he is properly the propitiatory sacrifice for sin, that satisfies the justice of God for the sins of the elect. 2. This sacrifice was especially offered by him, in his death and sufferings; it is his suffering and humiliation that is most properly this sacrifice, for it is that which is related here. 3. That by Christ's offering up of himself, he was not only outwardly pinched, but his soul was deeply affected, and troubled: In satisfying the sin-revenging justice of God, both his soul and body were straitned, and stressed. 4. By his suffering, there is a sufficient satisfaction given to justice for the sins of his people, a propitiation, or propitiatory sacrifice, that makes God propitious to elect sinners: As in satisfying the justice of God for sin, all other things are denied to have a hand; so there is a sufficient efficacy, and worth in his sacrifice to do the turn, and by God it is accepted as such; and so there is a fair way made to them, for whom he offers this sacrifice, to escape sin, and the wrath and curse of God, and to be set free.

As for the *first* of these, to wit, That our Lord Jesus, in his dying and suffering, was properly the propitiatory sacrifice, or is properly a propitiatory Sacrifice for the taking away of sin: To clear it a little we would consider, *First,* That sacrifices are sundry ways taken in scripture. (1.) Sometimes they are taken improperly for duties; as alms, prayers, praises, &c. Psal. 11. *The sacrifice of a broken heart thou wilt not despise:* So also, Heb. xiii. 15, 16. (2.) They are taken more properly for such sacrifices as were offered under the law; as of bullocks, lambs, rams and goats; yet none of these was the true propitiatory sacrifice, as is clear, Heb. x. 4. *It was impossible that the blood of bulls and goats could take away sin:* But Christ's sacrifice is properly the propitiatory sacrifice, it being by this sacrifice that believers under the old testament became partakers of redemption, and obtained remission of sins, as well as believers do now under the new. If it be then asked, What is necessary to a

sacrifice:

sacrifice properly so taken? I answer, These four things, (all which we find to be in Christ's sacrifice,) 1. That there be some thing, or matter, set apart to be offered to God in the room of some other thing, as it was in the typical sacrifices. 2. That there be some appointed to offer the sacrifice, that there be some set apart for that very thing. 3. That there be a killing or destroying of the thing that is offered in a sacrifice; which especially in the sin-offering was necessary, to wit, that it should be killed, or destroyed; as we see in Exod. xxix. and Leviticus frequently; This had a signification, and the Lord would thereby point out man's great guilt, and the necessity of a Mediator, in order to the obtaining of pardon; for there could be no remission or pardon of sin without blood, as it is Heb. ix. 22. therefore the sinner behoved either to die himself, or to have another to die for him, and in his room. 4. The sacrifice behoved to be offered according to the manner prescribed by God, as to all rites and ceremonies injoined. Now we may see all these in Christ's sacrifice; for, 1*st*, He himself is the Sacrifice, Heb. vii. 26. Heb. ix. 26. Heb. x. 10. and frequently else where in that epistle; and 1 Pet. ii. 24. *Who his ownself bare our sins in his own body on the tree:* And when he had offered up himself as a sacrifice, *be sat down on the right hand of the Majesty on high;* he is the alone sacrifice, that comes properly in the room of elect sinners. 2. As there behoved to be one to offer the sacrifice, so Christ Jesus is the Priest, that offered up the sacrifice of himself: He is not only the Sacrifice, but the Priest: And in this he differed from other Priests, Heb. vii. 26. *Such an high Priest became us, Who is holy, harmless, separate from sinners, and made higher than the heavens;* and then follows, *Who needs not daily, as these High-Priests, to offer up sacrifices, first for their own sins, and then for the sins of the people; for this he did once, when he offered up himself.* There are three things ordinarily attributed to Christ, as to his sacrifice, to wit, That he was the Sacrifice, the Altar, and the Priest; 1. He was the Sacrifice, in respect of his human nature: Which we are not to look upon, abstracting and dividing it from his divine nature; for tho' he suffered in the flesh; yet it was the same Person, that was God, that suffered. He was the Altar, by which his sacrifice received a special efficacy, vertue, value, and commendation; as it is said, *The Altar sanctifies the offering:* So Christ Jesus according to his Godhead was the altar, which did put special excellency on his sufferings, and made them to be of such worth and value; therefore, Heb. ix. 14. it is said, *That he through the eternal Spirit offered up himself without spot unto God;* it was the suffering of the Person that was God, that made the sacrifice to be accepted. 3. He was the Priest, and that according to both his natures, each nature concurring, and that jointly, as in one Person, to the making of the sacrifice offered up to God acceptable. 3*dly,* We have in him a real destruction; but do not mistake the word: It is not so to be understood, as if he were annihilated, or had been utterly destroyed, and undone; but the meaning is this, that he was killed or put to death, and his Soul separate from his Body: in which respect, he ceased to be, what he was before, for a time; having been really slain, dead and buried. And, 4*thly,* All this was according to God's prescription and appointment in the covenant of redemption; *This commandment* (saith he, John x. 18.) *have I received of my Father,* to wit, *that I should lay down my Life for my sheep;* and most emphatically, he says, John xiv. 13. *As my Father gave me commandment, even so* (mark, *even so,* most exactly in conformity to the commandment) *do I:* It was all, to every circumstance, ordered according to the good pleasure of God, who was pleased thus to bruise him, and to put him to grief.

The 1*st Use* of it serves to teach us how to conceive and consider of Christ's death and sufferings rightly, to wit, even as a sacrifice designed by God, to come in the room of elect sinners: And how to look upon his death; not as the ordinary death of ordinary or meer men, who by necessity of nature die; but to look on it, as being appointed of God to be a sacrifice, properly so taken, for the sins of his people.

2. This serves to clear some truths, concerning our Lord Jesus his sacrifice: For we must consider it, as satisfying to justice, and meritoriously procuring the escaping from wrath, and salvation of them for whom he interposed. It is from the gross ignorance, or from the wicked denial of this ground, that the damnable deniers of Christ's satisfaction, do also deny the propriety of his sacrifice on earth, and bound it to heaven; whereas it is bounded to his death; tho' by vertue of this one offering, he continues to intercede for us in heaven.

3. It teaches sinners what is the native *Use* which they should make of this sacrifice: They should look upon it, as the only sacrifice to prevent eternal death and the curse of God; and so it demonstrates to us, that either Jesus Christ must be received by faith, and his sacrifice rested on, or we must resolve

to

to meet with wrath, and the curse of God ourselves in our own persons.

4. It serves to clear us anent the way and tract of grace; to wit, how it came to pass, that our Lord, who was innocent, and without sin, was so bruised, and put to grief: He came to be a propitiation for the sins of his people, and sisted himself in our room, as our Cautioner, as a sin-offering for us. It would doubtless quash many questions, and doubts, that arise in the hearts of believers, if it were well understood: They may say, We should have been in such and such a sad condition, this and that terrible thing would have come on us, if he had not interposed; never enough can these words be spoken, and thought of, that we have, 2 Cor. v. ult. *He was made sin for us, who knew no sin, that we might be made the righteousness of God in him.*

5. It serves for notable consolation to believers, who have betaken themselves to Christ, and have many challenges for sin to buckle with, that his death was to be properly a sacrifice for sin, and was so accepted of God in their room: So that ye see the right up-taking of Christ's death, is a matter of no little moment; *Christ crucified* being the very substance of the gospel, it helps much to keep alive the impression of our sinfulness, and of the goodness of God and gives us directions how to escape wrath, by putting him in our room. There is nothing wherein folks more readily miscarry, in making of their peace with God, than in not making the right use of Christ, and of his sacrifice and death: Some praying for pardon of sin from him, and not for him or for his sake, when they know not what they are saying, as we hinted at before: Some praying for strength from him for duty, that they may do for themselves; not considering that we are justified by his interposing in our room, and by faith's closing with him, under that consideration, as sisting himself at the bar of justice; and the Lord accepting of him in the room of elect sinners: This being well considered, gives to faith much clearness how to take him up, when the soul honestly aims to partake of the benefit of his sufferings.

Secondly, For clearing this a little further, we would know, that there are (as divines observe) *four* or *five* ways, how the death of Christ is to be considered; or how Christ, in procuring by his death redemption, peace, and pardon to sinners is holden forth in scripture. 1. He purchases redemption, and pardon of sin *meritoriously*, or he *merits* it by his death; this respects the value of Christ's sufferings and satisfaction: So that, if we consider Christ in himself, and the elect in themselves; his death and these sufferings are more, than if all the elect had suffered eternally in hell. 2. His death is considered as *satisfaction*; and this looks to the wrong that men by sin have done to God: That the finite and feckless creature durst be so malapert as to break God's command, it required a satisfaction equivalent to the wrong done; tho' the word *satisfaction* be not in scripture, yet the *thing* is; Christ Jesus, for the restoring of God to his honour that was, as to the manifestation of it, wronged by man's sin, comes in to perform the will of God, and to satisfy for the wrong done him by man, that it may be made known that God is holy and just, who will needs avenge sin on his own Son, the holy and innocent Cautioner, when he interposes in the room of the sinner: Which vindicates the spotless justice and sovereignty of God as much as, if not more than if he had exacted the satisfaction off the sinners themselves; as it is, Rom. iii. 16. *To declare his righteousness, that he might be just, and the justifier of him that believeth in Jesus.* 3. Christ's death is considered as a *redemption* of man from sin, the law, and the curse, because liable to a debt which he cannot of himself pay; and his death was in this respect a paying of the debt that man was owing, and loosing of the captive and imprisoned sinner: Even as when a piece of land is mortgaged, and a person comes in, and pays that for which it was mortgaged: So Jesus Christ comes in, and (as it were) asks, What are these men owing? and what is due to them? It is answered, They are sinners; death and the curse are due to them: Well, saith he, I will take their debt on myself, I will pay their ransom, by undergoing all that was due to them; *He hath redeemed us from the curse of the law,* (saith the Apostle, Gal. iii. 13.) *being made a curse for us, that the blessing of Abraham might come on us Gentiles.* And so Christ's death, in this respect, is to be looked on as a laying down of the same price that justice would have exacted of men: His death is the paying of our ransom, and satisfying of the account that was over our head. 4. His death is considered, as it furthered the work of the redemption of elect sinners, by a *powerful annulling* of the obligation that was against us, and by a *powerful overcoming* of all enemies that kept us captive: He grappled and yoked with the devil, and that wherein he seemed to be strongest, and overcame him; he tore the obligation that stood over sinners heads, as it is, Col. iii. 14, 15. Blotting out the hand-writing of ordinances that was against us,—and that was contrary to us, he took it out of the way, nailing it to the cross; and having spoiled principalities and powers, he made a shew of them openly, triumphing over them in it: In this respect, tho' his death be one of the lowest steps of his humiliation; yet considering him as, in it, prevailing over the devil, and other enemies, he is to be looked on as powerfully working, and efficaciously perfecting our salvation: In the former respect, he pays God the debt that was due by sinners; in the latter respect, considering the devil, and spiritual enemies, as so many jailors, keeping sinners prisoners; he by his death, wrings, as it were the keys out of his hands, and sets the prisoners free. 5. Christ's death is considered (as it is in the text) as an *offering* and *sacrifice* for sin: In this respect, it looks to God as displeased with man; and our Lord Jesus interposes to pacify him, and to make him well pleased, and that by the means of his death, God's peace, favour and friendship may be recovered to poor sinful men. All these considerations of the death of Christ, are but one and the same upon the matter; yet, thus diversified, they serve to shew, how unexpressibly much sinners are obliged Christ; what great advantages they have by him; and what a desperate condition they are in, who are without him, having nothing to satisfy justice, nor to pay their debt with.

2*dly*, We said, that this sacrifice was especially offered by him in his death; therefore he is said to offer this sacrifice on the cross: *He himself*, as Peter hath it, 1 Pet. ii. 24. *bare our sins in his body on the tree.* Heb. ix. at the close, and Heb. x. 14. it is said, *That he once offered up himself to bear the sins of many, and by his once offering he hath perfected for ever these who are sanctified.* So that his offering is to be applied to that which he suffered on earth, before he ascended, and it is in this respect, that he is a propitiatory sacrifice; tho', as I said, the vertue thereof is still communicated by him, now when he is in heaven.

Use. This serves to remove two errors, about Christ's sacrifice. The 1*st* is that which bounds and limits Christ's offering and priesthood to his going to heaven, thereby to enervate the efficacy of his sufferings and death; quite contrary to this scripture, wherein the prophet, explicating his sufferings on earth, calleth them *an offering for sin*. The 2*d* is that blasphemous conceit and fancy of the Papists, who account their abominable *Mass* a propitiatory sacrifice for taking away the sins of the quick and of the dead; which, as it is most horrid blasphemy, so it is most expressly against this text; for, if Christ's sacrifice, for the taking away of sin be peculiarly applied to his humiliation and death, which brought with it such a change, as made him not to be for a time, what he was before; then certainly there can be nothing of that now, which can bear that name; there being no other thing, to which the properties of a real sacrifice can agree, but this only. 3. I said, that Christ's offering up of himself a sacrifice, was in his soul as well as in his body; and that he was therein obnoxious to the wrath of God. That is, as he stood Cautioner for the elect, and had the cup of wrath put in his hand, he suffered not only in his body, but also and mainly in his soul, which the Jews could not reach; and he is here holden out as a sin-offering in his soul: Yea, considering that it was the wrath of God, and his curse due to the elect, that he had to deal with, his soul was more capable to be affected with it than his body; hence he says, when no hand of man touched him, John xii. 27. *Now is my soul troubled, and what shall I say?* and Matt. xxvi. 38. and Luke xxii. 44. *Now is my soul exceeding sorrowful, even unto death; and being in an agony, he prayed,* &c. That which looked like strong armies mustered, and drawn up against him, was not the soldiers that came to take him, nor the bodily death which was quickly to follow, but it was the Father's coming with his awakened sword, to exact of him the debt due by the elect, and to be avenged on him for their wrongs, and his being to step in into their room, and to be smitten with that awaked and furbished sword, and to offer himself the sacrifice, as he had long before engaged: Here, O here, was the heat and strength of the battle!

Use This shews, 1. What a dear price Christ paid for sinners. 2. The severity of the justice of God, in exacting the elect's debt off the Cautioner. 3. How much we are obliged to the Cautioner, who so willingly undertook the debt, and was so ready to pay it, though it cost him not only external and bodily sufferings, but soul-suffering, and put him to encounter with God's curse and wrath. We are persuaded, could we conceive, and speak aright of these sufferings, that there is a great mystery here: And really it is a wonder that we are not more affected with it, even to consider, that such miserable creatures should be pursued by justice, that can do nothing to avert the stroke of it; and that such a great and glorious Person, as the Son of God, should interpose himself; and that the Father should spare the poor sinful enemies, and make

way

way for them to escape, by the diverting of his justice from pursuing them, and by making it take hold of the Son of his bosom, exacting the debt severely from him. O what a wonder is this! that the Lord should pass by the enemy, and satisfy himself of his own Son! yea, that God should take on himself the place of a Mid-man, and satisfy himself! That God should be in Christ reconciling the world to himself! This, this is the wonder: Herein infinite wisdom, pure and spotless justice, holiness and faithfulness, grace and mercy, to the admiration of men and angels, appear and shine forth most radiantly. It can hardly be known, in which of these the glory of God shines most, in this great and glorious work of redemption: But of them all, we may say to you elect, and believing sinners, What could our Lord Jesus do more for your salvation? I say what could he do more, than to offer up himself a propitiatory sacrifice for your sins? In the gospel he calleth upon you to make use of it, that, by virtue of his sacrifice, your peace may be made with God; as it is, 1 John ii.

1, 2. *If any man sin, we have an Advocate with the Father, Jesus Christ the righteous;* and then follows, *he is the propitiation for our sins:* This may give abundant ground to sinners to go upon, in their application to God for pardon and peace; even this, that he hath made himself a sacrifice, for setting of them free, for whom he offered himself, a sacrifice. O sinners, admire him, employ, and make use of his moyen and court in heaven; improve, and welcome these glad tidings; and let it never be said, nor heard of, that he was offered up a sacrifice, and that ye would not admit of the benefit of it; that ye would not accept of him to be a Daysman and Tryster betwixt God and you, to remove all grounds of quarrel. O! for Christ's sake, and as ye love your souls, flep to, and seek grace to make the right use of his sacrifice, in order to the obtaining of the pardon of your sin, and the making of your peace with God: Let himself powerfully persuade you to, and prevail with you, in this incomparably greatest of all concerns.

SERMON XL.

Isaiah liii. 10.——*When thou shalt make his soul an offering for sin, he shall see his seed, he shall prolong his days, and the pleasure of the Lord shall prosper in his hand.*

WHERE there is any light and knowledge of a Godhead, amongst men, there is this impression on them, that it is a dreadful thing to have a controversy lying over betwixt God and them unremoved: And upon this ground it is, that as naturally the conscience doth challenge for the provoking of God, so men, according to the light they have, are set on to seek after this and that, and the other mean and way, to get God appeased, and the conscience quieted; and it is like that this hath descended to men from Noah, that the most part of them have thought on the mean of sacrifices, by them to make their peace with God: So the Lord taught the family of Adam, after the fall, and Noah renewed it, after his coming out of the ark: and it is probable (as I said) somewhat of this hath abiden with, and stuck to men, even when they degenerated and apostatized from God, and offered sacrifice to devils, tho' not intentionally, but unto God in their account. And indeed it is no marvel that flesh and blood be here at a stand, and made to say, *Wherewithal shall we come before God?* But we have this advantage by the gospel, that, in it, the Lord hath shewed to us, what it is that satisfieth justice, and takes away sin, and the curse; and that it is even this in the text, *Thou shalt make his soul an offering for sin:* There is no other thing that a sinner can bring with him, that can be accepted, or that can make him to be accepted of God.

We have hinted at some things from the words already, and shew, that Christ's sacrifice is called *an offering for sin,* as excluding all others, and as expressing the nature and ends of it: We shall now speak to one thing more, which is the 4*th*, implied in this expression; and it is this, "That " tho' atonement and satisfaction to God can be " made by no other sacrifice, or offering; yet " there is an atonement and satisfaction, that may " be made by Christ's offering." Hence he is called *an offering for sin:* not only because it excludes all others, but also, because he is accepted for that very end, as a propitiation for the sins of them, for whom he suffered, and offered himself in a sacrifice.

As this is denied to all other things, (as we just now said) so it is applied and appropriated to him, and his offering; as Heb. x. 10. By the which will we are sanctified, through the offering of the body of Jesus Christ, once for all. Verse 12. *This Man, after he had offered one sacrifice for sins, for ever sat down on the right hand of God.* And verse 14. *For by one offering he hath perfected for ever them that are sanctified.* This is the great thing that the Apostle aims at in that dispute, not only to cast the Levitical offerings, as to the removing of sin and the curse, and making of sinners peace with God; but to commend this *one offering, as able to save to the uttermost all that come unto God through it:* And, according to this, we have that great question answered to poor sinners, *Wherewithal shall we come before the Lord, and bow ourselves before the most high God? He hath shewed thee, O man, what is meet, and what the Lord requireth of thee.* That there is nothing but this one sacrifice of Christ, that will do the turn; and this will do it most infallibly, and most fully, as to the procuring of pardon of sin, and the making of their peace with God: So that, by the right making use of this sacrifice, a sinner may most really expect remission of sins, and peace with God, and his friendship, as if sin had never been; for otherwise Christ could not be called the *sin-offering, or an offering for sin,* if he were not accepted in the room of the sinner that comes to him.

To clear it a little, there are *four* things, in and about this sacrifice, to make out this; and to prove that a sinner, that makes use of this sacrifice, may expect the pardon of sin, and peace with God. The 1*st* is the excellency of his offering; *he offered himself,* as it is, Heb. vii. 27. and Heb. x. 10, 12, 14. The offering up of himself, and of his blessed body on the tree, was another sort of sacrifice than all these bulls, rams, and goats, offered under the law, that were but types of him. The 2*d* is the excellency of the Person that offered up this offering, which is in effect the excellency of the Priest. As the sacrifice was excellent beyond all other sacrifices, so also is the Priest above all other priests, Heb. vii. 26. *Such an High-Priest became us, who is holy, harmless, undefiled, separate from sinners;* a Priest, who is the Son, and is set over the house, as the Heir: And tho' the human nature was the sacrifice, yet (as was said before) not as abstracted from the divine nature, the Person being but one, and so the Priest offering commends the sacrifice offered, and makes that it cannot but be accepted. The 3*d* is, his willing condescending to be the sin-offering, to interpose himself, and to become this sacrifice, out of respect to the honour of God, that his justice might be vindicated and satisfied, and that thereby access might be made, for shewing mercy to the heirs of salvation: Which exceedingly commends this sacrifice; according to that of John x. 17. *Therefore doth my Father love me, because I lay down my life, that I might take it again; No man taketh my life from me, but I lay it down of myself, and take it again.* It commends his sacrifice, that he was not constrained to it, but did it most willingly, and with delight: It is true, if we look to him, as the eternal Son of God, and the second Person of the blessed Trinity, he could not but be loved of the Father, as well before his incarnation, as after; but that he says, *Therefore doth my Father love me,* it is to be understood, on account of his voluntary condescending as Mediator to do his Father's will; and out of respect to his honour engaging, and, according to his engagement, satisfying his justice for the elect: And this cannot but commend his offering, that such a glorious Person, who was holy, harmless, and undefiled, should, out of tenderness to the honour of God, and that the wrong done to it by sinners might be repaired, and out of love to the elect, should condescend to stoop so low, as to make himself a sin-offering: This regard for the honour of God, and willing condescendency to suffer for the repairing of it, is abundantly valuable, and (tho' it be a great word) above the disrespect that sinners evidenced to the honour of God, by their sinning. The 4*th* is the covenant, which is the ground of this offering, and that whereby it is regulated, and the terms of it: It was not an undertaking, as a piece of will-worship, but according to the deliberate counsel, and foreknowledge of God: wherein it was determined, that the Son of God should become Cautioner, and be made liable for the debt of the elect, and be an offering for their sins, by which freedom from sin and wrath should accresce to elect sinners: And all this being concluded in the covenant of redemption his offering could not but be accepted for us, the Lord having condescended on the articles of that covenant for this very end.

This *Doctrine* is of mighty great and notable concernment to sinners; and, were there any such wakening and rousing amongst us, that souls were put to say, and cry, *What shall we do to be saved?* The opening up of this truth, to wit, that Christ is a sin-offering for sinners, and that by his offering the atonement is made, would be much more acceptable

ceptable and refreshful: And therefore let this be the 1st *Use*, That tho' there be nothing imaginable, that can be brought before God, which will be acceptable to him, as a satisfaction to his justice; yet here there is a ransom found, by the offering whereof to God, a soul that is lying under challenges for sin, and apprehensions of wrath, may expect absolution; this is, in effect, that which Elihu says, Job xxxiii. *If there be an interpreter, one of a thousand, to shew unto man his righteousness, then he is gracious unto him, and saith, Deliver him from going down to the pit, I have found a Ransom:* Here is the Ransom, our Lord Jesus Christ stepping in in sinners room, and offering himself up a sacrifice to satisfy the justice of God; so that a sinner, in making use of that, may come to be in good terms with God. And are not these glad tidings of great joy, that an offering is provided, a ransom paid, and a way found out, how sinners, liable to the curse, may expect freedom? It is no small matter, that God hath given this subject to us to speak of, and to you to hear of; that the torturing anxiety of a soul driven almost to despair, may have this for an answer, even the blood of Jesus, *that blood of sprinkling, which purges the conscience from dead works;* which as it satisfies justice, so it quiets the conscience of the sinner, that flees unto it, and makes right use of it. It would become sinners well, to think more of these glad tidings, and to study to have them always fresh. There are many parts of the world, wherein men are sacrificing beasts, some lambs, some rams, some other beasts, and some (it may be) the first-born of their bodies for the sin of their souls; (and, which is lamentable, sacrificing these these things to the devil, on the matter at least, and not to God) and yet all that does not their turn; and not having heard of this offering, they cannot make use of it, neither can their conscience ever be quiet: But our Lord Jesus hath sent these blessed news to us, and hath shewed us what is the sin-offering, the atonement, and propitiatory sacrifice; we need not send our children through the fire, nor bring any other offering to God, to appease his wrath; he hath given to us his son, and hath accepted him for a sin-offering, and hath told us, that this shall be as sufficient and satisfying, as if we had made the satisfaction ourselves: Here, O here, is the wonder, even a wonder of wonders!

Use 2. See here the way how we come to life by Christ; it is imported in this doctrine to be by Christ's being made an offering for us: It is not our praying to him as God, nor by our holy living, nor by his working holiness in us; (tho' these ought, and will be in some measure, where he is made use of aright) but by his offering up himself a sacrifice for us, and by God's imputing it to us: And, considering that Christ Jesus is the offering in our room, and that thereby God is pacified, and sin and wrath removed, there can no other way be conceived, how we are made partakers of it, but by *imputation*. This will be the more clear, if we consider that the same way that our sins became Christ's, the same way his righteousness became ours; or the same way that justice laid claim to him for our debt, the same way lay we claim to his righteousness. Now, it is blasphemous to think, that our sin became his any other way, but that legally he entering himself as our cautioner, our sin was reckoned on his score; even so his righteousness becomes ours, by being imputed to us: So the apostle says, 2 Cor. v. ult. *He was made sin for us who knew no sin, that we might be made the righteousness of God in him,* and have his righteousness derived to us. It were good that we would learn how to win to this righteousness, even by presenting him to justice, as cautioner for our debt; and by taking hold of his righteousness, to ground our plea upon, when we come to reckon with God for our sins. And we think that there is here a clear ground, for refuting of that way of justification by any thing inherent in ourselves: For, if it be by his offering that we are justified, then it is by nothing in ourselves. Now, this name, that Christ's sufferings gets, bears out, that it is that which satisfies God, and absolves us, as the alone meritorious and procuring cause; and therefore there is no other thing, that we can derive our justification from, but his righteousness only.

Use 3. Seeing by Christ's offering there is a ransom and atonement to be had, and seeing it is offered in the gospel, we pray you, in the name of the Lord, to take hold of, and improve this offering; let every body, that hears tell that Christ is the *Sin offering,* endeavour to get him to be their sin offering: There are none that know, and find, that they have sinned, but they would think of an amends; and here it is, and there is ground to exhort you to make use of it, and to encourage you to it, because this is the very end of his suffering, and he is fully furnished completely to accomplish it. If there were no access to life by this offering, he would not be called a *Sin offering,* in opposition to all other offerings; there is ground therefore to declare this to you, that by Christ Jesus, life and reconciliation is attainable, and that it is actually

attained

attained by accepting of this offering: Such as accept of it, and rest upon it, shall find acceptation with God, and freedom from sin and wrath, by virtue thereof. It is a common question, What shall we do? we do all we can, or may: But if we were studying a long time to tell you, this is it, even to make use of Christ's offering; this, and this only will do your turn completely, and no other thing will do it.

The *4th Use* is of strong consolation to all who betake themselves to Christ: He is the sin-offering, that procures the taking away of sin and wrath, and that procures friendship with God; and there is no imputation of sin, nor *condemnation to them that are in him*, Rom. viii. 1. and hence is that triumph, ver. 34. *Who shall lay any thing to the charge of God's elect? It is God that justifieth, who is he that will condemn? It is Christ that died, yea rather that is risen again*, &c. If justice were coming to execute the sentence, what can it say to the believer? Jesus Christ hath stepped in betwixt wrath and him; and, as to God's acceptation, he alone is counted the *Sin-offering*; and as these, who under the law offered the typical sacrifices, had access to the ordinances, and were sanctified, as to the purifying of the flesh; so much more is this offering able to purify the conscience, and to purge it from dead works, and to give a fair access to the promises of life, and to the favour of God, to all them who make use of it, as if they had never sinned. I know, much of the weight of this consolation will ly on this, Whether Christ's offering be made use of? And some will say, How shall we make use of Christ's offering? And others will ask, How shall we know, if we have made right use of it? And would to God, that souls were beaten off their pride and security, and brought under the conviction of a necessity of use-making of Christ; he would discover both to them. But before we answer the question, there are two things we would presuppose. 1. We presuppose, that the soul is made sensible of its need of Christ's sacrifice, from the apprehension it hath of a quarrel betwixt God and it, and from the fear of his wrath because of sin; else the asking of such a question is to no purpose: For as we hinted before, the offering of a sacrifice implies the confession of guilt; so the making use of Christ's sacrifice, presupposes the sense of sin. Ere a soul can make use of his offering, it must know, its due was utter consumption. 2. We presuppose, that the soul is desirous to be at God, and to have peace with him, to which end Christ is the mids; and there will be no respect had to the mids, except there be a respect had to the end, as it is, Heb. xi. 6. *He that comes to God, must believe that he is, and that he is a rewarder of them that seek him diligently*; where there is implied in the corner, a desire to be at God, and an expectation of some benefit to be had from him; or, as the word is, Heb. vii. 27. *He is able to save to the uttermost all that come unto God by him*; Which implies the sinner's being sensible of his lost condition, his desire to be at God; and then Christ's offering comes in, as the mids, to bring about, and to come by that end. But these being presupposed, the great thing, wherein the answer of the question lies, How to make use of Christ's offering for the attaining of that end, of pardon of sin, and peace with God, seems to be holden out in that word, Heb. vii. 25. *He is able to save to the uttermost, them that come unto God by him*; and therein we may consider sinners desire to be at God, and the use-making of Christ, in reference to that end, in these three, (1.) To have the breach made up with God, in respect of their state. (2.) For quieting the conscience, in respect of particular challenges. (3.) For the making up of their defects in grace, as well as for the removing of sin. And as use-making of Christ in these three, points out the way of a sinner's coming to Christ, so a sinner's going on in this way, evidenceth his right use-making of him: Which will serve to answer both the questions, to wit, how to make use of Christ's offering? and how to know that we are making use of it aright?

For the first, to wit, Going to God by Christ; 1. It is opposed to stepping in to God, at the first hand. 2. It is opposed to the use-making of any other thing, in our coming to God, for making up the breach. 3. It implies the sinner's betaking of himself to Christ, as the Mid-man, by whom he expects to come to friendship with God. There are some scriptural similitudes, whereof if we could rightly conceive, and apply them to this purpose, they might serve much to clear it. There is a distance, which, like a gulf, is fixed betwixt God and man; a soul then comes to God by Christ, as one goes over a gulf by a bridge; hinted at by the apostle, Heb. x. 19, 20. *Having therefore boldness to enter into the holiest by the blood of Jesus, by a new and living way, which he hath consecrated to us through the vail, which is his flesh*. We take the force of the similitude to ly in this, That as one that hath a vail betwixt him and another, whom he desires to approach to, must go through that vail ere he win to that other; so here, Christ's flesh being the vail, he by his death hath rent it, that sinners

ners might slip through that rent, or breach, to God: that is, when all was before shut up, and close betwixt God and sinners, Christ was content that a rent should be made in his body, through which they might come to God; coming to God by Christ, in this sense, is to walk, as it were on Christ's sufferings as a bridge, and to have no other place, or ground, to stand, 'or walk on to God, but this. Again, John x. Christ calls himself the *Door, I am the door;* and John xiv. to the same purpose, he is called the *Way:* To tell us, that as none can come in to a house, but by the door, nor can come to the end of their journey, but by the way that leads to it; so heaven being shut up, and closed upon sinners, any that would have entry into it, must betake themselves to Christ by faith; for, by faith in him, the door is opened, and the way paved to heaven. It is a good token, when the way to heaven looks on the sinner, as a hard wall, or like a sinking moss or bog; and faith in Christ gives him some little hold, whereby he wins over the wall, and leads him to some little hillocks, or hard bits, or spots of ground, whereby he steps thorow the moss, or bog, to Christ: Or, when the sinner lays his reckoning to make use of Christ's satisfaction, for payment of his debt; so that, if he were to appear at the bar of justice, his answer would not be, that if he had done a fault, he had made, or would make amends; nor that he prayed, and repented, and sought mercy; but this, that he took with his guilt, and made use of Christ's sacrifice: So Paul speaking, when renewed, in opposition to what he was, while a Pharisee, says, Philip. iii. That *he counts all things to be but loss and dung, for the excellency of the knowledge of Christ, that he may be found in him, not having his own righteousness, which is according to the law, but that which is through the faith of Christ.* When he, even he, thinks on the day of judgment, and where he will hide himself in that day, when it shall be asked (and every one shall be asked the question) Where art thou? his desire and resolution is, to give this answer, I am in Christ; Lord, I have no righteousness of my own to lippen, or to trust to; I will never make mention of my painfulness in my ministry, of the tenderness of my walk, nor of any thing else of that kind; but I will betake myself to Christ's righteousness, and will say, Lord, here is much debt on my score, but there is a righteousness to which I am fled by faith, and on this I will ground all my answers: this righteousness is in Christ, as the purchaser thereof; and it is ours by faith, when we betake ourselves to it, to make it the ground of our claim: Even as if a number of men were pursued for debt before a judge, and one should come in, and say, I have paid so much; and another should say, Give me down a part, and I will pay the rest; and a third should say, Give me a day and time, and I will satisfy; and a fourth poor body should come in, and say, I have indeed nothing myself to pay my debt with, but I betake myself to the responsal Cautioner, who hath paid all for such as betake themselves to him. This is faith's answering and arguing; it will never shift the debt, nor yet admit of the final sentence of condemnation, tho' readily acknowledged to be deserved; but it interposes Christ's satisfaction, as that which will be acceptable, tho' the sinner can do nothing of himself. In a word, this way of pleading is, upon the one side, an utter denying of the man's self, and of all that is, or can be in him, for attaining of righteousness; and, upon the other side, a crediting of himself to Christ, for the attaining of that which he hath not in himself: It is not only faith (if it were possible to separate these two) to deny our own righteousness; but, by the exercise of it, there must be a stepping over on Christ, and on his righteousness, unto God.

The 2d thing, wherein the exercise of faith in the use-making of Christ's sacrifice consists, is, in reference to particular challenges: For, even when a soul hath fled to Christ, and made use of his sacrifice for pardon of sin, and for peace with God, it will not be free from challenges, and from new accounts; and therefore the exercise of faith is to be continued in the use-making of this offering, in reference to these particulars, as well as in reference to the making of our peace with God at first; in which respect, faith is called a *shield,* Eph. vi. 16. When new guilt is contracted, and drawn on, and then tentation says to the believer, Is this the goodness of your purposes, and resolutions, which have been like flax before the fire? No sooner wast thou essayed, and assaulted, but thou didst greatly succumb, and wast much foiled, and prevailed over: The soul runs to the same targe, buckler, or shield; and tho' every one of these challenges be like a fiery dart that would set the conscience on a flame, yet by faith the dart is kept off, or the venom of it suckt so out, that it burns not; and it makes the soul to say, Tho' I cannot satisfy for the debt, yet there is in Christ's righteousness, whereto I betake myself, which can do it: And if we look to that, which entertains tormenting exercises, that speak evil of the grace of God (for humbling exercises are called for, and are profitable) we will find it to be this, to wit, When souls come to dispute, and debate with challenges, and do not interpose the targe or shield of faith, taking hold of Christ's righteousness, betwixt them and these challenges ; for sometimes a soul will betake itself to Christ's righteousness for peace at first, and will look upon itself, as bound to keep, and maintain its own peace ; and will, on the matter, think that it is but a sort of baffling, or prophaning of Christ's righteousness, (to say so) to be making daily use of it, for answering of new challenges ; and such will be ready to say, Should not a believer be holy ? and we say, that he should, and that it were to abuse the spiritual armour, to take one piece of it, and not another, yea, nor all the rest : But this we say likewise, that when one makes use of the *sword of the Spirit*, he may warrantably make use of *the shield of faith also*; failing in this, that is, when Christ's righteousness is not made use of, in reference to particular challenges, mightily indisposeth many serious poor souls for use-making of the rest of the weapons of their spiritual warfare: And therefore, as ye would exercise faith in general, for reconciling you to God, as to your state ; so ye would exercise faith on Christ's offering, for doing away of particular quarrels, and for silencing of particular challenges, which is to be daily washing at the fountain. In short, as to the other question, this may be a mark of a person, that is making right use of Christ's offering for his peace, if he be daily making use of Christ's offering for his peace, if he be daily making use of his offering for quenching and silencing of particular challenges.

The 3d thing, wherein this exercise of faith in the use-making of Christ's sacrifice consists, is, in reference to the defects of our grace : We have indeed much need of Christ, and he hath much forthcoming in him, for the helping of grace, for the amending of weak faith, and love, and other graces, as well as for obtaining pardon of sin, and of peace with God, and for answering of challenges ; and yet, ofttimes, these, who are making use of Christ in the former two respects, are in hazard, and ready to think, that they should believe more, love more, and exercise other graces more, of themselves : But we are to make use of him, for helping defects of grace, as well as for these other things. By this, I mean, not only the use-making of Christ meritoriously ; and so that we should look on faith, love, repentance, and every other grace, as purchased by him, as well as peace with God ; and that we should make use of Christ's offering,

for attaining of these ; but I also mean, that we should make use of Christ, as a Priest, to make his own offering effectual, for attaining all the benefits of his purchase, considering, that he is able to save to the uttermost all these that come unto God by him. The apostle goeth on this ground, Heb. x. 19, 20. *Seeing we have such an High Priest*, and such an offering, *let us draw near with full assurance of faith*, &c. And if ye ask, What this is ? It is of largely extended use ; it is even to make use of Christ, as a Priest, not only as the Object of faith, and as the Procurer and Worker of faith, but also for the confirming of weak faith ; it is a looking to him, to get the weak faith, that we dare scarcely lippen to, made strong ; and a lippening, or trusting of our weak faith to him, to carry us through, when we dare not well lean to it. In the first respect, we do by faith lippen, and trust to Christ's righteousness ; in this last respect, we lippen, or trust our faith to him ; and look to him, not only for pardon ; but we lippen to him for making faith to keep its grips of him : And as it was with that poor man spoken of, Mark ix. who, upon the one side, betakes himself to Christ, *If thou canst do any thing, have compassion on us, and help us* ; and on the other side, being holily impatient, finding his faith like to fail and misgive, when Christ says to him, *If thou canst believe, all things are possible to him that believes* ; he cries out, in that his holy impatience, *Lord, I believe, help thou my unbelief*: He acknowledges his unbelief, as well as his faith ; and trusts Christ with the mending of his faith, and holding together the sheards of it (so to speak) when it was like to crack, and fall asunder. Our doing thus, evidenceth a more full denying of ourselves, when we dare not trust our own believing but as it is committed to Christ, and when there is a crediting of him, and leaning to him, both for the benefit we expect, and for the application of it : That word of the apostle, Phil. iii. 12. is apposite, and excellent to this purpose, *That I may apprehend that for which I am apprehended of Christ Jesus* ; as is also that of Pet. 1 epistle. 1 chapter. verse. 10. *Who are keeped through faith by the power of God.* So then, in answer to both the questions, 1. How to make use of Christ's sacrifice ? And, 2. How to know, if we have made, or do make use of it aright ? We say in short, as to the *First*, 'That there must *first* be a leaning to his merit, for the buying, or procuring of our peace, and betaking of ourselves to it for that end, 2dly, When tentations recur, and when new challenges arise, there must be a constant

stant daily betaking of ourselves to faith in his sacrifice, as to a shield, or as to a store-house; which he himself calleth *an abiding in him*, John xv. 3. There must be an use-making of Christ, as a Priest, not only to remove daily contracted guiltiness, but also to heal the infirmity and weakness of our graces, especially of faith and love, giving him credit to bring our faith and love to perfection. It is a sweet word which we have, Psal. ciii. *He healeth all thy diseases*. As to the 2d question, we say, That person may look on himself, as making right use of Christ's righteousness, that is daily making use of him, in these fore-named respects, who, if he were to appear before God, it is Christ's righteousness only that he would build on; he is also daily making use of him, to answer challenges as they recur, and dare not lippen to his own faith, but as it is committed to him; considering, that, as faith is in himself, it is daily in hazard to be extinguished; And we may add, that he so makes use of Christ, as that he dare not go to God without him; as the word is, Heb. vii. 25. *Them that come to God by him*; he comes unto God by Christ, in prayer, in praises, and in every other duty of worship: The apostle, to this purpose, says, Heb. xiii. 15. *By him therefore, let us offer the sacrifice of praise to God*. The believing soul is never right till its *all* be put in his hand. Tho' all these be not distinct, and explicit in the person's use-making of Christ's sacrifice; yet he expects that the application of the benefits which Christ hath purchased to him, shall be made forth-coming to him, by vertue of that same purchase; and that he, who is the *Author*, will also be *the Finisher of his faith*. The sum and up shot of all, is, to shew that as we have much good by and in Christ, if we could make use of it; so he calleth us to be cheerful and comforted in the use-making of it, and not to diminish our own consolation, when he hath condescended graciously thus to extend, and enlarge it, with so richly liberal and bountiful a hand.

SERMON XLI.

Isaiah liii. 10.----------*He shall see his seed, he shall prolong his days, and the pleasure of the Lord shall prosper in his hand.*

IT may be thought, and that very justly, that there must be some great and glorious design driven in the contrivance of the work of redemption, that was executed by such a mean, as the suffering of the Son of God; and that there must be some noble and notable thing following on it, that moved the Father to send his Son, and the Son to come for this work. This part of the text answers, and tells us what is the design, *He shall see his seed, he shall prolong his days*, &c. He shall communicate life to many that were dead, and shall beget a generation, that shall have life derived from him, as a seed have from their parents: And so this is a third answer, for removing of that stumbling objection, proposed in the begining of the verse, to wit, How it came to pass, that the innocent Son of God, *who had done no violence, and who had no guile in his mouth*, was put to such sufferings? We shew that there were three grounds laid down, in answer to this, *1st, It pleased the Lord to bruise him*, it was the Father's good peasure. The 2d is from the nature of his sufferings, which were to be a *sin-offering*, or *an offering for sin*, not for his own, but for the sins of the elect. The 3d is, That his sufferings should have notable fruits and effects following them, set down in three expressions, which are partly prophecies, telling what should be the effects of the sufferings of the Mediator; partly promises made to the Mediator, telling what should be his reward and hire (to speak so) for his sufferings. (1.) *He shall see his seed*, that is, many shall get good of his sufferings; (2.) *He shall prolong his days*, that is, he shall out-live these his troubles and sufferings, and shall have a glorious out-gate and reign; (3.) *The pleasure of the Lord shall prosper in his hand*, that is, the work that was given him to do, and to finish, shall thrive well, and no part of it shall fail, or miscarry. In the first promise made to him, or in the first effect that should follow on his sufferings, in these words, *He shall see his seed*; we have these three, 1. A relation implied betwixt Christ and believers; they are his *seed*, such as in the next verse are said to be *justified* by him: It is in short, many shall get

K k pardon

of sin, and justification, by his death. In this respect, it is said, Psal. xlv. *penult* verse, *Instead of thy fathers, shall be thy children, whom thou mayst make princes in all the earth*. 2. A prophecy, and foretelling of the event, that should follow Christ's sufferings; and so it holds out this, That our Lord Jesus should not only have a seed, but a numerous seed, that should be made sure to him: And it seems to be in allusion to that which is spoken of Abraham, and of others in the old Testament, of whom it is said, they should have seed, that is, that many should descend of them: But there is more here; for, whereas others, while they are living, or in their lifetime, beget a seed, which begetting is interrupted by death; the death of our Lord Jesus begets his seed, or his seed are begotten by his death. 3. Considering the words as a promise, they hold out this, That tho' our Lord Jesus suffer, and die; yet he shall not only have a seed, but he shall see his seed, he shall out-live his sufferings and death, and shall be delighted in seeing of them, who shall get the good of his sufferings: As it is said of Job, that *he saw his children*, or seed, *of the third and fourth generation*, that is, he lived long, and saw many that came of him; even so, tho' our Lord came to death, and to the grave, yet he should not only have a numerous seed, and many children, but he should live and see them; and that not only for three, or four, or ten generations, but for very many generations: And his dying should neither mar his begetting, nor the seeing of them. And this *seeing of his seed*, is opposed to such parents as are dead; and who, tho' their children and posterity be in want, yet they know it not. From the *First* of these, Observe, " That believers are our Lord Jesus his seed, they " are come of him:" Whatever their meanness and lowness be in the world, and tho' they could not claim kindred to any of externally honest rank, or quality, yet they are his seed. To this purpose the apostle bespeaks the believing Corinthians, 1 Cor. i. 27, 28. *Ye see your calling, brethren, how that not many mighty, not many wise men after the flesh, nor many noble are called; but God hath chosen the foolish things of this world, to confound the wise*, &c. *that no flesh should glory in his presence*; Tho' ye be not of any high rank or quality in the world, yet *of him are ye in Christ Jesus, who of God is made to us, wisdom, righteousness, sanctification, and redemption*: In this respect, Christ is called the *everlasting Father*, Isa. ix. 6. For he is the Father of all believers, that ever had, or shall have life; who are, Psal. xlv. pnult verse, called his *children*.

To clear this a little, ye shall take it in these four or five respects, or considerations, in which believers are said to be *Christ's seed*, or to be descended of him. *1st*, In this respect, that, as believers, they have their being of him: As children descend from off their parents as to their natural being; So believers, as they have spiritual being, descend from him, and hold their being of him; without whom they had never been believers: And in this respect they are his seed, 1. Because he *meritoriously* purchased life to them; which is the thing here mainly understood, as following immediately upon the back of his sufferings. 2. Because they have life from him, *efficiently*, as he works it in them, and by the gospel begets them; therefore he is said, 1 Tim. i. 10. to have *brought life and immortality to light by the gospel*, which was not known in many parts of the world till Christ brought it forth; in this respect, believers are Christ's seed: We are not believers born of our parents, nor have the faith which we have, of the ordinances, nor of ministers, as efficient causes thereof; but it is from our Lord Jesus, who is believers Father. Thus believers have an affinity and near relation to Christ, even to be his children: And any that would lay claim to faith or spiritual life, would see well, that it be this way kindly, and (as we use to say) leil come, from Jesus Christ, and that they be in his debt and common for it. *2dly*, They are his *seed*, in respect of the likeness that is betwixt him and them, or in respect of the qualifications that are in them; as they are said, 2 Pet. i. 4. *By the exceeding great and precious promises, to be made partakers of the divine nature*: They have of the same Spirit, for the kind, that he, as Mediator, hath in him; and it is in this respect, that, Can. vii. 1. the believer is called the *Prince's daughter*, which especially looks to the spiritual, generous, and noble qualifications, that are derived from Christ, to the believer: Hence believers are said to have the *Spirit of sons*, when all others, tho' they be the greatest in the world, have but the spirit of servants; and their generosity is nothing to that of believers, who are *made partakers of the divine nature*: We have not, says the apostle, *received the spirit of fear, but of faith and love, and of a sound mind*. Ah! there are many that claim kindred and relation to Christ, that are very unlike him. *3dly*, They are called Christ's *seed*, in respect of the care that he hath of them: Never mother was more tender of the sucking child, than he is of his believing children; therefore, saith the Lord, Isaiah xlix. 15. *A mother may forget*

SERM. XLI.   *Isaiah* liii. Verse 10.

her sucking child, but I will not forget thee: Hence is that phrase, even as to visible professors of the Church, who refuse to listen to the call of the gospel, which is much more eminently verified in believers, Matth. xxiii. *How often would I have gathered thee, as a hen doth her chickens under her wings!* So tender and respective is he to his children, as the mother is tender of the sucking child, or the hen is of her newly-hatched, and young chickens; for they are, in some respect, come out of his own bowels; his blood was shed to purchase them; so it is said, Isa. xl. 11. *He gathers the lambs with his arm, he carries them in his bosom, and gently leads those that are with young.* And, O what mafty confolation have such words as thefe in them! And what confidence may believing sinners have to come to this Mediator, that is a Mother, a Father, a Brother, and a Parent; that hath begotten us out of his own bowels, and in some respect (as we are believers) hath as a mother conceived us in his own womb! 4thly, They are called his *feed*, in respect of the portion which they get from him. The apostle says, that parents provide for their children; it is indeed eminently so here, believers come under his care, oversight, and tutory; and as a man provides for his household, his children and servants meat in due season (and the apostle says, *He is worse than an infidel, that provides not for them of his own house*) even so our Lord Jesus, as he gives believers their spiritual life, so he entertains that life, provides for them, and trains them up, and on, till he enter them into the possession of eternal life; they are made by him *Princes*, Psal. xlv. 16. entitled to a kingdom; yea, all his children are *kings*, and sit with him on his throne, Rev. ii. last verse, and are made partakers of his glory; and (to speak so) they fare as he fares, they dwell as he dwells, and behold his glory: O, is not this much, that the poor dyvour, that hath not a penny left him, nor to leave to another, should be thus dignified, as to have a claim to Christ's kingdom, to be an heir, and a joint heir with him, who is the Heir of all things! For so we come to be retoured (to speak so) and to be served heirs to all things; as it is, Rev. xxi. 7. *He that overcometh shall inherit all things:* And it goes on this ground, Heb. i. 2. that the Mediator *is appointed Heir of all things*; with whom being *joint heirs*, we are heirs too, and made to inherit all things. 5thly, They are called his *feed*, because of the manner of their coming to the possession of that, which through him they have a claim to; for they have a claim to nothing, but by being heirs to, and with him; and by believing in him, they are *heirs of the promise*, in some respect, as Isaac was: So then, briefly to recapitulate all these, would ye know the way that believers are Christ's *feed*? 1. He begets them, and they have their spiritual life of him. 2. He is tender of them, as of his own children. 3. They are furnished with qualifications, and dispositions suitable to him. 4. They have a rich portion from him, and are well provided for. 5. What good they get, is for his sake, who is their Father: Here we may allude to that word, Rom. xi. *They are beloved for the Father's sake;* by a right and title to him, they come to have a good and goodly portion,; they claim not to their portion, because of this or that thing in themselves, but by their being served heirs to Christ; being come of him, they come to get a right to what is his.

Use. As all relations betwixt Christ and believers speak out much confolation, so doth this, if we were in case to apply it; this one word hath in it, and holds forth a good condition, and is a very broad charter.

See here then, 1*ft*, What we are in Christ's common and debt, who are believers: It is much to be made a friend, to be freed from the curse of God, and to have all our debts paid; but this is more to be *his feed*, to be his own children, to have our life of him, to have our provision and portion from him. It is really a wonder, that we wonder not more at this, and other relations that are betwixt him and believers: as namely, he is the believers *Father*, and takes them to be *his sons and daughters;* he is the believers *Brother*, and *is not ashamed to call them brethren;* he is the believers *Husband*, and they are *his spouse;* he is their *Bridegroom*, and they are *his bride:* Such relations as these being pitched upon, and made choice of, to fill (if I may speak so) the faith of the believer, and that the believer may feed sweetly and delicately on them, till time come that the vail of similitudes be taken away, and they be brought to see him as he is, even face to face; and that thereby they may be helped to win to read their advantages and privileges, which they have in him. What can be the reason, then, that so few think and esteem suitably of the excellent and desirable condition of believers, and that words of this kind relish not? Here is the reason, he of whom they hold all these privileges, and by whom they are put into this notable and non-such condition, is not suitably esteemed of, and accounted precious; therefore believers in him are thought the less of. Our hearts

hearts fhould melt in love to him, and in forrow for offending him, at the the reading and hearing of fuch expreffions, whereof the fcriptures of God are ftuffed full.

2dly, Are there any that would have a good and happy condition fummed up and compended? Here it is, even to have our Lord Jefus to be a Father, and to be his *feed*, to come in as fons and daughters to him. I appeal to you all, if any condition can be put in the ballance with this; is there any honour and dignity like it, or comparable with it? Who can claim to be come of fuch a parent as is he, *who is King of kings, and Lord of lords, the Prince of the kings of the earth*, the Father of glory, his eldeft and only begotten Son, by an eternal and unfpeakable generation, who in all things hath the pre-eminency. What is your pedigree, who will fay, and boaft, that ye are of fuch a laird's or lord's houfe, and of fuch an ancient family and ftock; yea, tho' ye were of blood royal, what is it to this? What will become of mens gentility or nobility of birth, yea, of royalty of birth, in that day, when Chrift fhall fet his throne in the clouds? To have this relation to Chrift, will be more valuable and honourable, in that day, than to have been great commanders, lairds, lords, marquiffes, dukes, princes, and kings, who will all in that day ftand upon the fame level with the pooreft peafants, and when all honours and dignities, which are now fo much thought of, and thirfted after, will be laid in the duft. Therefore learn to think of this as the nobleft birth and defcent, which is through faith in Chrift Jefus; and covet, and be holily ambitious, to have the qualifications of his children. Look to the qualifications, parts, endowments, and accomplifhments, that ufe to accompay, or follow any houfes of the braveft of natural men; are there any of them comparable to the qualifications of believers? Is there a flock or race of people in all the world, fo truly generous and noble as believers are, who are come of Chrift, and are made valiant, through the exercife of faith in him, againft all occurring difficulties; regardlefs of worldly things, and taken up with, and bufied about high and noble projects and defigns; even to have heaven, and glory, and God himfelf; who undervalue, and holily difdain the things of the world, which earth-worms fo much feek after? Their qualifications kyth efpecially in this, that their defigns are heavenly, their minds elevated to, and fet on the beft things, and that they have a truly magnanimous and a valorous way of profecuting them, by ftudying the mortification of fin, and conformity to God, when others cannot endure to caft out with, and abandon a luft; they holily fcorn, and account it below them, to have their peace ftanding or falling with the ebbing and flowing of creature-comforts, which the men of the world place their happinefs in; their ftudy is to be pure, as Chrift is pure: O is there any portion like theirs? Many of you think but little of it now, but ye will think more of it in that day, when the earth, and all things in it, fhall be burnt up with fire; what will the earth-portion fignify then? Ye that now have your variety of fine and delicate meats, with your ale and wine at every meal, who fhall be found out of Chrift, fhall not get a drop of cold water to cool your tongue, under your exquifite and hellifh torments, when the poor body, that believed, and had a hard life of it here, fhall be in Abraham's bofom, and with Chrift at his table, yea, and on his throne with him; and it is upon the account of their having a title to Chrift, that they come to all that glory and happinefs. O is there any right and title like the believer's, which is founded on Chrift's right and title, which is, or may be called, the *original right* of the believer, who *is keeped by the power of God, through faith unto falvation*. If thefe be the true and faithful fayings of God, what is the reafon that men think fo little of them? Why is an intereft in Chrift fo undervalued? Believe ye, that fuch and fo much good is to be gotten by being Chrift's feed and children? If ye fay that ye believe it, how comes it to pafs that fo few have it for their defign, and that your defigns are fo much for this and that in a prefent world, and that this is fo much flighted, and that there is fo much boafting and glorying in other things, and fo little holy boafting and glorying in this?

There are two or three *marks*, which we may gather from the words, that may help to fhew when this claim is warrantably made, and which may evidence the groundlefnefs of the claim of many. And, 1. Chrift's feed hath another original than that which they bring with them into the world; there is in them a change of the ground of their hope, and that on a new account: Folks come into the world finful, children of finful parents; but when they come to be believers, they get a new life, which men cannot give, and this new life hath new actings and fruits: Ah! how many dream of a right to Chrift, who know no other birth or being but that which is natural. 2. They who are Chrift's *feed*, carry along with them the impreffion of an obligation to, and an acknowledgment of him in whatever good they have gotten;

they

they think themselves much obliged to Christ, and they acknowledge him for their life, as it is, Mal. i. *If I be a Father, where is my honour? and if a Master, where is my fear? a son honours his father*, &c. A natively and genuinely disposed child acknowledgeth his father as his father, and revereneeth and loveth his father as his father; but there are many that pretend to a being from Christ, who think not themselves in his debt and common for it, and who know not what it is to walk under the conviction of their obligation to Christ for their supposed spiritual life and being. 3. They, who are Christ's *seed*, have in them a likeness to him, as they did once *bear the image of the earthly*, so *now they bear the image of the heavenly Adam*; not that they come up in all things to be exactly like to the pattern, but it is their aim; and other things, that disconform them to him, are deformed, lothsom, and ugly in their sight: Their old inclination is burdensom to them, and is the continual ground of an inward contest and wrestling; and, in a manner, they are troubled at the very heart how to keep down what is opposite to Christ; and when their corruption over-masters them, they are the more discomposed and disquieted: They discern something in them, that is not like to Christ, and they abhor that, tho' it be never so near and dear to them, their very *self*; they see something also like to Christ in them, and they cherish and make much of it; they would fain be at more of it, and to have his image more deeply impressed on their spirits, which they reckon their greatest, yea, their only beauty.

The 3*d Use* is for direction to believers: If ye be *Christ's seed*, ye must be other sort of folks in your designs, and in your deportment and carriage: King's children ought not to carry as others; it would be highly unsuitable, yea, even abominable to see them walk so trivially and lightly, as every base, ill-bred beggar's child doth: It is no less incongruous and unbecoming, that believers should be taken with this and that vanity, that meer worldlings are take with, and hunt after.

The 4*th Use* speaks a word of consolation to believers, and holds forth the greatness of the privilege of being *Christ's seed*. It will be much to perswade a poor sinner, duly sensible of sin, to believe this, and that the Lord is in earnest, when he speaks thus; that such an one, who hath betaken himself to Christ for life, and humbly claims right to nothing, but by vertue of Christ's right, (the main thing, that our union with him is bottomed upon) who is content to be in Christ's common for life, and goes not about to establish his own righteousness, but leans to his righteousness, for life and salvation, should be *his seed*, and have all the privileges of sons derived to him; and yet it is the Lord's faithful word: Neither hath eye seen, nor ear heard, nor hath it entered into the heart of man to conceive, what good things are laid up for such a person, and that are stuffed up in these expressions of our relation to Christ Jesus.

Use 5. It may also be a quieting and comforting word to some believers, who are in affliction, poverty and straits in the world; that our Lord Jesus is a kindly affectionate Parent, more kindly and tender-hearted, than the tenderest father or mother: And indeed it may sufficiently quiet them, that they have such a kindly Overseer and Provisor, who is also a cordial Sympathizer with them, whatever their condition be; he will not deny his offspring and seed, whom he laid down his life to purchase.

The 6*th Use* may be for incitement and provocation to all that would be happy, to place it here; interest in Christ Jesus, by believing on him, brings us to have interest in the enjoying of him, and all that is his; and can there be any more sought after, or wished for? Are there any, but would think it a good life, to be here? And who are they, of whom he speaks so? It is not of some sort of strange and uncouth folk, that were once in the world, but are now all out of it, and of whom there are none now in it; it is not such as want sin, and derive their life from their own works; but it is such as are, 1. As considered in themselves dead in sins and trespasses, and without spritual life and being; and who know, that all the pains that they can take, will not acquire it; and who, it may be, are quite dead to their own apprehension and sense oftentimes; and who have judged themselves, and have the sentence of death in themselves. It is such as look to him for the obtaining of life; and who acknowledge him for any life or liveliness they have; and who expect it, and bruik it, by vertue of his purchase; which is that on which all their plea for life is founded.

Now I know, that all this will not readily clear some; there are so many things that look counterfeit like: But I am now speaking to them, who have some sticklings of spiritual life, which yet are not so lively, as they can discern them to be the stirrings and sticklings of life; and they have a body of death in them, which is ready to extinguish that life; and often they think that it is extinguished already: They have convictions of their own deadness, and that things are wrong in their condition,

tion, and are quite out of all hopes of righteousness from and by themselves, or from any thing that they have done, or can do; and they have some confused looks to Christ, but they cannot rid their feet in the matter of their faith, and duties go not so with them as they expected, and would have them. To such I shall speak a word or two, and close. 1. I would ask, Whence comes that stickling of life, or feeling of that body of death? What is the original of it? will nature discover the corruption of nature, and bring folks to be out of love with corrupt nature? Certainly, where this is, it is not like nature, but is the life of Christ; especially, when it puts folk to discern, and take up their own deadness, to quit their own righteousness, and to betake themselves to the righteousness of Christ, if they could win to be distinct in it: This looks to be from Christ, *whose Spirit convinces the world of sin*, and of the sin of *unbelief* in particular; and of *righteousness*, as being only to be had in Christ; and of *judgment*, that is, of the reasonableness that he should have a dominion over them, and that they should walk in holiness: Yet, notwithstanding of all this, they are hanging in a kind of suspence and hover, and know not whether to look on themselves as believers or not; they wot well that it is not right with them, that they are lost in themselves, and that no other way will do their turn, but faith in the righteousness of a Mediator: The thing whereat they stick and halt, is, that they know not how to through, and maintain the consent that they have given; and they cannot think, that their faith is true faith, because they know not how to follow forth the exercise of it; though they have renounced their own righteousness, and laid their reckoning, to be in Christ's debt and common, for righteousness and life, if ever they come by them: All their difficulty is, how to through their believing. Now it is not to the founding of life, that we are here speaking, but to the exercise of life, and to the finding out of life: And we say, that such an exercise supposes life to be, though it be not discernable in its exercise to the soul itself. There are many poor creatures born and brought forth into the world, that can neither talk nor walk, but must be carried and keeped tenderly, and that are someway, as if they were brought out of the womb: So is it with many believers; and it were good to be in Christ's common as for life, so for bringing life to exercise, and by diligence and waiting on him, in the use of his own appointed means, to seek to come to some distinctness in nearing, and exercising of any life, that he hath given: And it is no small encouragement to this, that Christ *shall see his seed*, that he must have saints and believers in him; which should make poor souls, that have no life in themselves, with the more confidence to commit themselves to him, upon this very ground, that the Father hath engaged to Christ, that he shall have many such for his *seed*; the which promise is performed to him, in the gathering in of poor, confused, and mind-perplexed sinners, to be in his debt for life, and to hold their life of him for ever. It will sure be no small part of the ground of saints praise in heaven, that he not only bought life for them, but that he made application of life to them, and trained them on, till he had got them fitted to speak to his praise; wherein the body of death makes many a sad stop, and makes poor believers to stammer, as it were, while they are here. But it is good news, that Jesus Christ hath bought life, and brought it to light; and that, by this gospel, he is making application of it, and declaring that he is content to bestow it freely, on all them that will be in his common for it.

SERMON

SERMON XLII.

Isaiah liii. 10.——*He shall see his seed, he shall prolong his days, and the pleasure of the Lord shall prosper in his hand.*

IT was once a riddle, how out of the strong could come forth meat, and how out of the eater could come forth sweet; it is here most clearly unriddled, and that in a most wonderful and comfortable manner: Our Lord Jesus, the *strong Lion of the tribe of Judah, is put to grief and bruised, and his soul is made an offering for sin;* and here is the sweet meat that comes out of it, *He shall see his seed, he shall prolong his days,* &c. The substance of the words is, That by his death many shall be brought to life: It is the same death that hath given us the hope we have of life, and all the ground that we have to speak of it to you; which had never been, had he not been *bruised and put to grief.*

We shew, that here is holden forth the Lord's great design in the contrivance of the work of redemption; and that these words are a further answer to the stumbling objection proposed before, to wit, how the innocent Son of God could suffer? *It pleased the Father to bruise him, when he shall make his soul an offering for sin,* &c. which justifies God in that proceeding, and serves to wipe away that reproach that might seem to stick to him. In sum, it is this, If we consider the notable and noble fruits, and comfortable effects, that follow on his sufferings and death; there is no ground to stumble at God's giving his Son, or at the Son's condescending as Mediator, to suffer, to be despised and put to death: And this is the first fruit, and effect thereof, that *He shall see his seed:* whereby is meaned, that by his death, the elect, who are given to him, do by faith in him receive a new life from him, and are taken in, under a most sweet and kindly relation to him, by their being begotten again to a lively hope, through his resurrection from the dead.

We spoke to this point, that believers are *Christ's seed;* which shews the great privilege that they are admitted to, and their great obligation to Christ on that account: They are obliged to him for their spiritual life and being; as children are obliged to their natural parents for their natural life and being; and infinitely more obliged, inasmuch as the one life is infinitely preferable to the other.

There are three things more to be observed from the words, 1. Considering them as they stand in dependence on the former; " That God's design " in sending his Son in to the world, and the Me- " diator's design in coming so low, is to have a seed " begotten to the hope of eternal life; and to have " poor souls, dead in themselves, sharing of life in " and through him; even to have many partaking " of life through his death." 2. Considering the words, as foretelling the event of Christ's death and sufferings, we have this observation from them, " That our Lord's death shall certainly procure " life to many; or thus, It cannot be, but his death " must have fruit to the saving of souls from death, " and to the making of them partakers of life." 3. Looking on the words, as a promise made to the Mediator, we observe from them, " That the see- " ing of a seed, is exceeding much thought of by " Jesus Christ, it pleased him wondrous well; " therefore this promise of a seed is made to him, " to encourage him to lay down his life."

We shall speak a word to each of these, and shall leave the consideration of the words, as they hold out, not only our Lord's outliving his sufferings, but his seeing a seed on the back of them, to the second effect that follows, *He shall prolong his days.*

For the first *doctrine*, we suppose it will be clear, if we consider how the *seeing of his seed* is subjoined to, and dependeth upon the former words anent his making *his soul an offering for sin;* which holds out this, that the great design of God, and of Christ the Mediator, in his sufferings, is to beget a people to eternal life, and to make way, that sinners, naturally dead in sin, may partake of spiritual and heavenly life, and may be begotten to the hope of eternal life through him. And what other design, I pray, could there be than this? For the Lord had nothing to procure for himself; to speak simply, there could be no addition made to the glory of God thereby: Therefore it is said, John vi. 39, 40. *This is the Father's will that hath sent me, that of all he hath given me, I should lose nothing, but should raise it up at the last day: And this*

this is the will of him that sent me, that every one who seeth the Son, and believeth on him, may have everlasting life, and I will raise him up at the last day. 1 Tim. i. 15. *This is a faithful saying, and worthy of all acceptation;* and what is it? *That Jesus Christ came into the world to save sinners:* And that, John x. 10. *I came, that they might have life, and that they might have it more abundantly.*

There are two things that we would speak a word to, for clearing of the doctrine, and then make use of it. The *1st* is, How this can be God's design, in Christ's humiliation, to beget many sons to life? *2dly*, How Christ's death contributes to this design? For the first, When we speak of God's design here, we mean not his last and ultimate design, but his immediate design in the gospel, which is subservient to that his last and ultimate design; to wit, the glorifying of his grace and justice, in giving the Mediator to satisfy justice for dyvour sinners, who are not able to satisfy for themselves; and he having chosen this as the mids to that highest end, we may well say, that this is his immediate design in the gospel, that thereby the glory of his grace and justice might be manifested. For the 2d, which is, How Christ's sufferings contribute to this end? It may be soon cleared, if we consider that there is a twofold lett in the way of sinners partaking of life, which Christ's sufferings do remove. The *1st* lett is a standing quarrel betwixt God and the elect, they having sinned, and having nothing to pay their debt; this our Lord Jesus by his death removes, he pays the debt, and tears the obligation, called *the hand-writing that was against them, nailing it to his cross,* Col. ii. And, in this respect, his death is called *a ransom for many;* and in the words before, he is *said to make his soul an offering for sin,* on the same account, to wit, that the principal debitor might be set free. The 2d lett is man's utter unfitness to walk with God: For tho' the debt were taken away, yet they have no life; but Jesus Christ by his death, hath laid down a ground how a sinner may be reconciled to God, and may partake of grace here, and to be in case to walk with God, even while sojourning in the world, in some good measure, and of the life of glory hereafter; his sufferings are not only a ransom for their debt, but also a bridge (to speak so) to step over the gulph of the distance that is betwixt God and them, unto glory, whether he as the Fore-runner is gone before them: In this sense, we have our graces, as the fruits of Christ's sufferings; the life of grace, faith, love, perseverance, &c. we have also protecti-on, preservation, and guiding in the way, till we be brought through to eternal life; as that word is, John vi. 39, 40. cited before, *That of all whom the Father hath given me, I should lose nothing:* In the first respect, Christ is surety for our debt; in the second respect, he is surety for our duty: In the first respect, we are admitted in the covenant with God; in the second, we are entertained in it by him, who lives for ever to make intercession for us.

Use 1. See here, believers, what ye are in the Father's debt for sending his Son, and what ye are in the Son's debt for coming to die for you: ye behoved to have born the curse yourselves, it he had not born it; but he took it on himself, that ye might be freed from it: Thus it stood with you, ye deserved to be shut out for ever from God, to have the sword of his justice awakened against you; and *he gave his back to the smiters, and, his cheeks to them that pluckt off the hair,* and was content that the sword of justice should awake against him, and smite him, that he might by his stripes heal you, and by his death procure life to you: Yea, it stood thus with you, and it could not be otherwise; the justice of God being provoked, and the elect being under the curse, as it is, Gal. iii. 10. *Cursed is every one that continueth not in all things written in the law to do them:* Ezek. viii. 4. *The soul that sins shall die.* Either they behoved to die, or the Cautioner; and our Lord was content to be a sin-offering, thereby to set sinners free; *To be lifted up on the cross, that he might draw all men after him:* to pay their debt, which all the creatures could never have paid: And therefore we would ask you, if you think heaven and glory to be of worth, and if ye think it to be of great mercy, to be free of wrath to come, and from the damned state and condition of the reprobate angels, and of reprobate men and women in hell, and to be admitted to enter with Abraham, Isaac and Jacob into the kingdom of God, and into these heavenly mansions; are ye not much in Christ's debt, that procured this for you, and at such a rate, that thereby life might be communicate to you, who were naturally dead in trespasses and sins? Whatever the rest of the world think of it, if any of you be born again, as ye ought in a special manner to think much of it, so ye will do in some measure; for ye are as much in Christ's common as all that is worth, who was content, that poor sinners should partake of him and of the life that is in him, to taste of death himself; and who hath said, *Because I live, ye shall live also:* In a most wonderful way, his death is the price, by which

which life is communicated to us; and it would become believers well, to be often reckoning, what they are in his debt. It is one of God's great ends in the work of redemption, even to have sinners esteeming highly of, and much ravished with his grace, and with his love brightly shining in the way thereof; yet less conscience is made of this, than of many other duties, by believers: We will lend an ear to a practical point of doctrine, and will some way aim to mind it; if we be bidden pray, we will pray; if we be commanded to mortify sin, we will endeavour it, and so in other duties: But who minds this as a duty, when we are called of God, to admire, and praise his grace and love, and humbly to glory in him, so as seriously to set ourselves to fall about it? and yet this were a most native, proper, and kindly exercise for believers, even like the work of those, who say, *Salvation to our God, that sits upon the throne, and unto the Lamb*, Rev. vii. 10. *To him who loved us, and washed us from our sins in his own blood*, &c. Rev. i. 5. To be taken up with such soliloquies in ourselves about this subject, and with such songs of praise to him, who hath given us so noble a being and life, which is conveyed to us by his blood, is sure a suitable use of this point; for, if our life be of much worth, he must be of infinitely much more worth in himself, and should be so to us, who purchased it at such a dear price.

The 2d *Use* is to exhort you, whom we suppose to be renewed, (as some of you now hearing me are, and O that all of you were) that whenever ye think of enjoying of heaven, and glory, ye would think also, whence it came to be thus with you; O think on that rock, out of which ye are hewn, as ye are believers, and are intitled to life; and this will lay the natural pride, which, alas! too often believers have going along with their hope of life, as if they were something better by nature than others, because they have hope to come to heaven: But think this also with yourselves, that there are no thanks to you, but *to him who loved you, and washed you from your sins i t his own blood*; which should make you walk softly, and with a stopped mouth; and in this case, every thought of your title unto, and of your hope of heaven, would be both singularly pleasant, and profitable to you.

Use 3. See here, that which maketh the glad tidings of Christ's death wonderfully comfortable. It is much that Christ came, and suffered; but if we add this, that his design in suffering was to beget sinners to a new and spiritual life, to raise and quicken them that were dead in sins and trespasses, to pay their debt, and to cancel their obligation, it makes it to be much more wonderful. Alas! we have great want of spiritual affections, that are not more affected with this, even with this, that the Father should send his Son, and that the Son should come into the world; And wherefore? That he might have a seed; that poor bodies, that were dead and without life, might be quickened; and that such, as had no hope of heaven, might have it. That in such a way an entry into heaven should be made to sinners, this is the wonder. Do ye, believers, indeed believe this, that the Lord's design, in all the work of redemption, was to bring dead sinners to life? This is it that makes Christ get the name of a Saviour, that the *Shepherd being smitten, God might turn his hand on the little ones*.

And therefore, as a 4*th Use*, See here a good ground, whereupon to preach to you by the death of Christ, the offer of life, and the remission of sin, as the apostle hath it, Acts xiii. 39, 40. *Be it known therefore to you, men and brethren, that through this Man is preached unto you the forgiveness of sins: and by him all that believe, are justified from all things, from which ye could not be justified by the law of Moses*: And there is never a text, that speaks of the end of Christ's sufferings, but readily it some way lays a ground, how a sinner may get life; and it is as if it were a proclamation to sinners to make the right use of what is offered to them. If our Lord Jesus had not suffered, there had not been a warrant for us to speak of life to you; there had been no treaty with sinners, no door opened for access to heaven, no ground for any to call God, *Father*: But on the contrary, Christ having suffered, and satisfied justice, it gives us ground to make this proclamation to you, *Be it known unto you, that through this Man is preached unto you the forgiveness of sins*. And these two put together, 1. That there is a sufficient price laid down for the satisfying of the justice of God, for the debt of elect sinners. 2. That this is the Lord's design in laying of the price down, even to procure and communicate life to them, according to that of John iii. 16. *God so loved the world, that he gave his only begotten Son, that whosoever believeth on him should not perish, but have everlasting life*; and that of John xii. 32. *And if I be lifted up, I will draw all men after me*: This demonstrates, that there is a sufficient warrant to make use of Christ, for pardon of sin, and for obtaining of life, through him: For readily the exception is one of two; either, (1.) That the price will

will not do the turn; and that cannot be said, for the death of Christ is a price sufficient: Or, (2.) That sinners know not what is the Lord's purpose in it; this text holds out that, and tells us, it is, *that he may have a seed.* This is the sum of the covenant of redemption; saith the Father, Son if thou wilt lay down thy life, *thou shalt see a seed,* that shall have life through thy sufferings; and the Lord would have never given his Son to die, if he had not minded the salvation of sinners, and to beget, and promote life in them, through his sufferings; and to what end is the gospel preached, by which *life and immortality are brought to light,* but that what he hath bought may be applied to sinners?

And therefore, as a 5th *Use,* We beseech you to concur with Christ in the design of his laying down his life: Is it not (think ye) great ingratitude to him, and great cruelty, to yourselves, that when the Lord hath designed such a thing by the laying down of his life, that ye should, as far as ye can, stand in the way of it? Now his design is, to have many in his common for life, that he may *have a seed;* and to have poor sinners, that are dead and lifeless in themselves, taking with their sin, and coming to him, to get justice satisfied, and a right to life, by his offering: And is this a prejudicial design, or unprofitable to sinners? why then should ye stand in the way of that? When our Lord hath designed sinners good, and hath been content to lay down his life to make life possible to you; when all his design in dying, is, to have sinners saved by their betaking themselves to him, and that by their betaking themselves to him the *second Adam,* they may get a right to life transferred to them; is it not folly and madness for sinners, to obstruct what they can this his design? The apostle makes use of this argument, 2 Cor. v. 18, 19. *He hath given us the word of reconciliation, that God was in Christ reconciling the world to himself, not imputing their trespasses unto them: We therefore, as ambassadors for Christ, as though God did beseech you by us, we pray you, in Christ's stead, be ye reconciled to God.* And what is the reason? *For he was made sin for us, who knew no sin;* and for this end, *that we might be made the righteousness of God in him.* And is not this the same argument that is in the text? Our Lord was made a *sin-offering,* that he might *see a seed;* and if so, then we would intreat you, if the bleeding bowels of Christ can have any weight with you, and if you would do him a pleasure, not to mar his design, as far as ye can, (for he will infrustrably accomplish his design) and that is to have souls brought in to make sinners peace with God, and that they may make use of his sufferings for that end. Need we use arguments, to perswade you to this, which is so much for your own good and welfare, even to save your souls; to come and be reconciled to God; to make use of Christ for life, to prevent the wrath that is to come, and to make heaven sure to yourselves; which is impossible for you, honestly to aim at, but God shall have the glory of his grace and wisdom from you? and if this be not your aim and endeavour, God will not have the glory of his grace in you, though passively he shall have the glory of his justice in punishing you eternally in hell. But that is not his great, and proper design, in sending of his Son; for he could have had his glory that way, though he had never sent him into the world: And therefore, in his name, and in his stead, we do again and again seriously beseech and solemnly obtest you, to give our Lord Jesus satisfaction in this particular. Ye that are going to hell, or are in hazard of it, come to Christ Jesus, the Prince of life, the Purchaser and Giver of life, and get life from him; come, as dead sinners in yourselves, and by the law, to get a new gift of life by his right: And we propose this suit and request in his name, who tells us that he laid down his life, to get a *seed.* This gospel comes to every one of your doors, and says to you, Will ye be obliged to Christ for life? will ye be his children? If the heart be honest, and ye can sincerely say, Content, Lord, and will creep in under his wings, that ye may be found in him, and may be covered with his righteousness, there is good ground to expect a closed bargain; for our Lord purposely died, that he might *have a seed;* and is calling upon you for this very end, and will not go back of his word, if ye be content to bargain with him: And therefore I would again say unto you, Shift not his call; It is his design to have a seed; and it should be yours to seek to be of that seed: O let him have his errand among you! The offer comes (as I just now said) to every one of your doors, and your answer will be, and must be, either *yea* or *nay;* either that ye are content to be his children, that his grace may be glorified in you; or that ye are not content, and that *ye will not come to him, that ye may have life,* as it is. John v. that ye scorn to be his seed, and children: But ah! the day comes, when ye would be glad of such an offer, and will not get it.

But, to come a little nearer in the application of this *Use,* (1.) Are there not many of you without life, yea, hundreds of you? not one among many is renewed: If ye think yourselves to be dead, this word of life and salvation is sent unto you; and sure you have need of it. (2.) There is life in Christ to be had; a fair purchase made, and a way laid down, to bring sinners to have a right to life; and are not these two, think ye, well met and trysted? On what ground then is it bottomed? Upon one of these two, or rather on both of them, implied in this phrase, of being *Christ's seed*. 1. It implies, that there be a coming to Christ, as void of life; and an actual trusting to him, for the attaining of life; that sinners, pricked with fear, or feeling of the wrath of God, acknowledge Christ as the Father of their life, and credit him with the application of life to them. 2. It implies, not only the crediting him with the application of life, but that we commit ourselves to be alone in his debt and common for it; which is implied in that word, John v. *Ye will not come to me, that ye may have life:* The use-making of Christ, for the attaining of life, is implied in the word *coming:* and that is, for slain and dead souls to go to Christ for absolution and life, called, Heb. vii. 25. *A coming to God by Christ.* And again, it is not, you will not come unto me, that ye may *buy or procure* life, or *work* it to yourselves; but ye will not come to me, that ye may *have it*, ye will not be in my common for it: The first word expresses where we get our life, and that is in Christ's sufferings; the second word, how we get it, even as the child gets life from its parent, we get it fully and freely conferred on us by him. So that the similitude says this much, Come to Christ, who hath procured your life; and trust your getting of life to him, on the terms of grace: And since this is all that Christ seeks of you, not to make your performances the ground of your pleading for life, but his purchase; and that having need on your side, and fulness on his side, ye should come and have; what hinders your closing of a bargain? This is the very thing your salvation will stand or fall on; even on your yielding to come to him, and to be in his common for life, and on your leaning to his righteousness, or not; and according as ye act faith or not on him, in this respect, so will the sentence of your absolution or condemnation pass in the great day. And therefore, let me beseech you yet again, above any thing to make this sure. And when I speak of making it sure, it is not only to have a glance of the thing in your minds, as many may have, to whose door Christ comes, when yet they will not go out of doors to him; nor is it only to have a conviction in your judgment and conscience of the reasonableness of it, as many of you have so many convictions of sin, and of the necessity of faith in your judgment, as will make you inexcusable; ye are convinced, that such a thing should be, and there it holds; the Lord draws you by his word to give assent to the reasonableness of the offer, but ye smother the conviction, ye come Agrippa's length in assenting to the truth, but come no further; ye laid your account, it may be, that ye could not save yourselves, and that your salvation was only in Christ, and ye took that for faith: But, believe me, there must be something more than that, even a laying of yourselves over on him, and a making application to him, to fill the empty room in the heart. I remember of a dying person, that had a good word to this purpose, who, when it was asked at him, How his faith did now differ from that which he had in his health? answered, When I was in health, I was convinced that I should believe; but now my soul actually casts itself on Christ. The many convictions that men have, that they should believe, will stick to them, and go with them, to hell, and make them the more inexcusable, that they held there, and went no further.

6thly, And lastly, It serves to be a ground of expostulation with many hearers of the gospel, who have heard of this noble design, and yet make no use of it. O hypocrites, formalists, and profane persons, what a reckoning will ye have to make, when this shall be found on your score, ye were dead in sin, and the Lord contrived a design to save lost sinners, in sending his Son to be *an offering for sin*; and the Son came and laid down his life; and ye were called and invited to come to him, and to have life in him; the glad tidings of redemption were preached, and made offer of to you; and ye would not be content to close with Christ, but would, so far as ye could, thwart with him, in his design, tho' it cost him his heart-blood to bring it about: What will come of this? or, what will ye answer him for it? Ye will say, it may be, That ye were content to concur with Christ, and stood not in the way of it; but it will be replied, Why then did you live and die in your sin, and bring your soul to this dreadful hazard and loss? Your conscience and God will bear it in upon you, and ye will not get it shifted, that your destruction was of yourselves, because ye would not be saved; and will that, think ye, be a suitable and satisfying answer, that tho' Christ would have saved my soul, I would not be saved by him, and then to go to hell for that? what a tormenting thing will it be in the conscience, that life was offered to me, on condition of believing in Christ, but I refused, or scorned to take it on that condition? Think on it, what ye will think to be sent to hell, because ye would not be saved freely by Christ; and to perish, because ye would not be *Christ's seed*, because ye would not take with your guilt, that ye might have life from him. What, do ye all think that ye have life? are there none sensible of their need of life from Christ? Alas that we should be put so often to repeat these words! We may almost speak to stones with as great hope of success, as to many consciences among you, that are habitually obdured, and blinded with presumption, by the god of this world, who hath put out your eyes; but the day comes, when ye will find yourselves greatly mistaken. I shall insist no further; only, seeing that ye are naturally dead in sins and trespasses, and seeing that Christ's design in dying is to *have a seed*, as ye would not prejudge yourselves of life, as ye would not be found to be despisers of his sufferings, and such as have trode the blood of the covenant under foot, study to make sure eternal life to yourselves, by betaking yourselves to him for it: or lay your reckoning to be reputed guilty of this horrid crime, with all the aggravations of it.

SERMON XLIII.

Isaiah liii. 10.------*He shall see his seed, he shall prolong his days, and the pleasure of the Lord shall prosper in his hand.*

THERE is not one reading of these words but it might put us to this wondering question, For what is it that this great design of all Christ's sufferings hath been driven? and what hath been the great end of this covenant of redemption, that hath such sharp, sore, and sad sufferings following thereon to the Mediator, who engaged in it? This world was made with little noise, (to say so) there was no engagement on God for bringing about of that work, tho' very great, as there is in bringing about this; this then certainly must be a quite other thing that hath an offering, and such an offering, as had in it the bruising and dying of the Person, that was the Son of God, interposed, for the obtaining of it. But this answers the question, *He shall see his seed,* &c. Which, in sum, is this, his life shall procure life to many dead sinners, and they shall get it certainly applied to them: And the work of the ministry (to speak so) and of the mediatory office of Christ shall thrive well in his hand; so that there is not one soul, that is designed to life and glory, but it shall be brought to the possession of it in due time.

There are two things, which we hinted at the last day, that we shall now speak a word to; and the first of them is this, " That it is an agreed u-" pon, and a concluded article in the covenant of " redemption, that our Lord Jesus shall, and must " have a *seed*." This is a most certain and infallible truth; it is an effect laid down here, as a necessary consequent of his *offering up of his soul for sin*: It is a determined thing, if we look, 1. To the certainty of the event: Our Lord Jesus Christ must have a *seed*, to wit, believers in him; that is concluded on, and promised to him. 2. If we look to the *seed* that he shall have; they are particularly determined upon, to wit, how many children he shall have, and who they shall be: That was both a promise in the covenant, and a prophecy, as we have it, Psal. xxii. where the psalmist, speaking before of Christ, says, verse 30. *A seed shall serve him, it shall be accounted to the Lord for a generation:* and this is laid down as a solid conclusion, John vi. 37. *All that the Father hath given me shall come unto me;* which supposes both a determinate number given, and the certainty of their coming: Become of the rest of the world what may, they shall undoubtedly come. And indeed, if we look to the nature of this transaction, we will find it to be a promise, and a promise of God to the Mediator, that can neither be altered, nor unaccomplished; yea, it is a covenanted promise, made on a condition, to wit, the laying down of his life, as the stipulation on his side; and that which he hath for so doing from the Father, on his side, is this, That *he shall see his seed* And when this

this is not only a promise, but such a promise as is grounded on a transaction, bearing a condition, which the Son hath performed, as he himself saith, John xvii. 4. *I have finished the work which thou gavest me to do;* there is a justice and faithfulness in the performance of the promise on the Father's side to him, that *he shall have a seed.* 3. It is clear also, if we consider the end of this transaction, which is, to glorify the grace of God by Christ's purchase, in the salvation of elect sinners; in respect of this end, it cannot fail, but Christ must have a *seed*, that the end may be attained: So then, our Lord Jesus must have, and certainly shall have, many that shall partake of eternal life by him.

The 1*st Use* of it serves to let us see the unwarrantableness of that doctrine, that leaves the fruit of Christ's death, as to the *seeing of a seed,* to an uncertainty, laying the weight of it on man's free-will; a thing that is very taking with natural men, and with conceity carnal reason: But if it were left to men's option, to receive Christ or not, then the execution of the work of redemption and the performance of such a promise, as this is, behoved to have the certainty of it subjected to man's will, and should be made effectual, or not, as he pleased: But it is God's great mercy to us, that we know it is not so: and that there is an equity here (to speak with reverence of the Majesty of God) that seeing our Lord Jesus hath done his part, the promise should be made effectual to him, and that he should *have a seed.*

Use 2. It layeth a ground, serving greatly to quiet us in the reeling of times, when the world is going through other, and turned up-side-down, and when we are disposed to wonder what will become of the Church, that is now sorely assaulted, and made to stagger; what, by the old enemy Antichrist, who is bestirring himself mightily; what through abounding security, and formality, whereby Satan is seeking to draw away many, some to error, and some to profanity: But tho' Antichrist, and the devil, with all their emissaries and agents, had said the contrary, our Lord Jesus shall *have a seed;* It may be, they are not the plurality of a kingdom, or nation, of a city, or of a congregation, but they shall be so many, as shall serve to the making out of the promise. Our Lord makes use of this, John vi. 37, and 44. where, when a number are turning away from him, he says, *Murmur not at this, no man can come to me, except the Father that sent me, draw him:* and *all that the Father hath given me, shall come to me:* I will get as many (as if he had said) as are appointed to receive my word from myself, or from my servants speaking in my name; as for others, I look not for them. It is true, we would beware of having any sinful accession to the marring of the progress of the gospel, and be suitably affected with any such thing in others; but withal, we would reverence the Lord's sovereignty, who knows how to have a care of his Church in the worst of times: And let us quiet our hearts, amidst all the reelings and confusions of these times, that our Lord shall have a *seed*, and that he shall not want any of all those that are given him of his Father, but shall raise them up at the last day.

Use 3. Seeing this is the Lord's design, it would commend to the hearers of the gospel a study to concur in this design (if we may speak so) in their public and private stations, in reference to themselves, and in reference to others: As it is the Lord's design, that Christ shall *have a seed*, so we would make it ours. We may most safely side, and strike in here with the Father, Son, and Holy Ghost, whose design runs on this; and (to speak so) they have, must have, and shall have a poor and cold game of it, who thwart with the Lord in his design, whoever they be, and in whatever station or capacity, public or private. As it is no wisdom, so it will be no advantage, to struggle or strive with God: But here is matter of great encouragement to any that would have the gospel prospering, religion countenanced, error suppressed, the power of godliness promoted, and prophanity born down; that our Lord Jesus Christ does concur with them in the same design. I know not any other design that a man can strike in with, without fear to come short in it, but this; and whosoever strike in with this, it shall not misgive them, for Christ shall *have a seed.* And tho' we cannot, nor ought not absolutely and peremptorily, to design particular persons; yet in the general, we ought to concur, to have the promise made to Christ, *of a seed,* performed to him. And indeed it is no small privilege and prerogative, that we are admitted, by prayer or any other way, to concur with him in this design; according to that memorable word of promise, concerning this matter, Psal. lxxii. 15. *Prayer also shall be made for him continually, and daily shall he be praised.*

Use 4. There is here great encouragement to sinners, that are in their own apprehension void of life, and have some sense of their deadness, and would fain be at Christ for life, and have him for their Father: Such, I say, are, by this doctrine, encouraged to step to; for it is a thing determined and

and promised: And since it is so, we may and ought to essay and endeavour that he may *have a seed*, and may be sure it will not displease him that we endeavour to offer ourselves to be of his seed. It is a foolish, and yet often a puzzling and perplexing doubt, that comes in the way of serious souls, when they offer to come to Christ, that they know not but that they may be presuming: If there be any acquaintance with God's and Christ's design, manifested in the gospel, there is no ground for such a doubt; and such a soul may as well question, Whether will God and the Mediator be pleased, that the promise made to him of *a seed* be performed? Certainly it will be displeasing to neither of them, but well-pleasing to both; and therefore the sinner would be strengthened on this ground, and take it for granted in his addresses to God, that such a thing is designed, to wit, that Christ shall *have a seed*.

Use 5. It shews what must be the condition that others stand in, who do not come and make offer of themselves to be *Christ's seed*: they do, in so far as they can, thwart with God's design: And this will come on their account, that if Christ should never *have a seed*, they would not for their parts betake themselves to him, nor be of *his seed*; but, as far as they could, would stand in the way of the performance of this promise, to him: And this will be ground of a sad challenge from God; I designed that Christ my Son should have a *seed*, and I engaged by promise to give it to him; and ye scorned and disdained (to speak so with reverence, in such a subject) to satisfy God that far, as to yield to Christ, to be of *his seed*, that that promise might have its accomplishment in you.

1. From the words complexly considered, Observe, "That Christ's having and obtaining of a "seed, his getting of souls to believe in him, is a "thing most welcome, and acceptable, both to Je- "hovah that makes the promise, and to the Media- "tor to whom it is promised.' There is nothing that pleases God and the Mediator better, than for lost sinners to betake themselves to Christ, and his righteousness, for life; it is the satisfaction that he hath for the travel of his soul; it is the recompence here promised to him; it is (to speak after the manner of men) as if the Son were saying, What shall I get, if I lay down my life for sinners? Here the Father promiseth, Thou shalt *see thy seed*, that is, many shall believe, and be justified through thy death: and this is so acceptable to the Mediator, that he says, *Lo, I come, in the volume of thy book it is written of me, I delight to do thy will,*

O my God; and Heb. x. the Apostle says, *By this will we are sanctified;* he sought no more but this, for all his sufferings and soul-travel. And that it is no less acceptable to Jehovah, that makes the promise, is as clear; therefore, in the last part of the verse, it is said, *The pleasure* (the will or the delight) *of the Lord shall prosper in his hand;* that is, the engaging of souls to believe (which is God's delight, as well as the Mediator's) shall thrive, succeed and prosper well. It is this that, John xvii. Christ calls *the finishing of the work which the Father gave him to do;* What is that? *This is they were, and thou gavest them me*: It is even his stepping in betwixt justice and them, to make way for their reconciliation through his blood; and this is very delightsom and well-pleasing to Jehovah. It is true, this delightsomness is not to be so understood, as if there were such affections and passions in the Lord, as there are in us: But it is attributed to him in these respects. 1. It is called pleasing and delightsom to him, as it agrees with his revealed will and command; and so it cannot be conceived but to be pleasing to God, as that which he commandeth, calleth for, and approveth: In which respect, the holiness of them that will never be holy, and the faith of them that will never believe, is, or may be called pleasing to God. 2. It is called pleasing to the Lord, in respect of the end, and as it is a mids to the glorifying of his grace, and the performance of his promise to the Mediator; for by this his grace comes to be glorified, and he hath access to perform what he hath promised to the Mediator. 3. It is pleasant to him, because in this the Lord hath a special complacency, and hath evidenced in his word comparatively a greater delight in sinners closing with Christ, and in their accepting of life thro' him, than in many other things: Therefore it is, that he calleth for this so pressingly; and when Christ is not thus made use of he declares himself to be grieved, and that there is a sort of despite done to him; whereas, upon the other side, he takes it (dare I speak it with reverence) as a courtesy and honour put upon him, when a soul gives up itself to him, and dare hazard the weight of its immortal soul on his word: In this respect, Abraham is said, Rom. iv. to *give glory to God,* when he trusted himself, his soul, and all his concerns to him; and we will find, that believing is accounted to be a honouring of the Father, and of the Son, if we compare the 24, and 25 verses of John v. together.

The *1st Use* serves to let you see, That not only do the Father and our Lord Jesus Christ call

sinners

sinners to believe, do warrand them to believe, and lay down grounds, whereupon they may found their faith: but they also declare, that it is well-pleasing to them, and that they shall be very welcome that come. The carriage of the father of the prodigal, Luke xv. is but a little shadow of that welcome that a sinner, in returning to God by faith in Jesus Christ, may expect; tho' indeed that parable shews plainly, how hearty a welcome returning sinners may expect; *It was meet* (saith he) *that we should make merry, and be glad; for this thy brother was dead, and is alive; and was lost, but is found again.*

Use. 2. It serves to banish away that unworthy apprehension, that is in the minds of too many, that there is greater rigidity and austerity in God the Father, than there is in the Mediator towards poor sinners. If we look to God as God, his grace abounds in the Person of the Father, as it doth in the Person of the Son; and if we look to the Son as God, he is the same just God, that will not acquit the guilty, more than the Father will do; so that there is no ground for this apprehension, which fosters a sort of blasphemous conception of the blessed Trinity, as if they were of different natures and dispositions, most unbecoming Christians: Hence is it, that many, who are ignorant of God, will speak of Christ as being easier to be dealt withal than the Father is; a conceit most derogatory to the divine Majesty, and unworthy of Christians. Indeed, if we abstract God from the Mediator, there is no dealing with him; but if we look on God, and come to him in the Mediator, there we find him easy to be dealt with: Therefore, that which is called the *satisfaction* of the Mediator, verse 11. is called here, *the pleasure of the Lord*, because he delights in the performing of his promise to the Mediator, in reference to his having of *a seed*. It is from this also, that some folks will pray to Christ, as if he were a different Thing or Being from God; and they would first make their peace with Christ, and then, by his moyen, bring themselves in good terms with God. The Mediator indeed, considered as Mediator, is different from God, who, without him, or out of him, is a consuming fire: But, considered as God, he hath the same properties, and gives pardon on the same terms; and, in this respect, we are to make use of his own righteousness for obtaining of pardon from himself, there being but one God. There is occasion too frequently to meet with this error, and I know not how many inconveniences it hath following upon it: Some think that they are always sure of Christ's friendship, but they doubt of God's, as if the Father had not the same delight to save sinners, that Christ the Son hath. And another abuse follows on the former, that there is no more use made of Christ, but by a word of prayer to him, without exercising faith on his Godhead: if there were no more to rectify this gross mistake, this alone text might do it; if ye make use of Christ's righteousness, ye may expect friendship from the Father, and from the Son; and if ye do it not, ye have no ground to expect friendship from either of them.

Use 3. There is here ground of glad tidings to sinners, and that which makes the covenant of redemption to be deservedly called the *Gospel*, and that made the angels to sing, *Glory be to God in the highest, peace on earth, and good will to men;* that there is such a covenant laid down, for bringing life to dead sinners; and that the Father and the Mediator are delighted, comforted, (to say so) satisfied, and well pleased with sinners making use of the Mediator for life. Is there then any sinner here, whose conscience lays open to him his hazard, applies the curse to him, and passes sentence on himself, and hath some desire to be at Christ, and yet wots not if he will hold out the golden sceptre? Behold, this text doth hold it out to such, and bids them come in boldly, for Christ makes them welcome; yea, the Lord Jehovah makes them welcome: It is the Father's, and Christ's delight that thou come forward. If there be a doctrine in all the scripture sweet, it is this; and, without this, no preaching, nor point of truth, would be sweet: I say, without this, to wit, that God hath not only provided a price, and makes offer of it, but is well content that it be made use of; yea, and is delighted that a sinner, dead in himself, trust and concredit himself to the Mediator, for obtaining of life through him. And can there be any question of this? For, 1. If it had not been the Lord Jehovah his delight, why then did he make such a covenant? why did he (as it were) part and sunder with the Son of his love? why did he accept of a Cautioner? and why transferred he on his own Son, and exacted of him, the debt that was due by elect sinners, and made the sword of his justice to awake against him? If he had not had a great delight in the salvation of sinners, would he have taken that way, to smite the only Son of his love, to spare them? And if it had not been the Son's pleasure, would he with such delight have undertaken, and done the Father's will, in reference to their salvation, *Lo, I come* (saith he) *I delight to* do thy will, O my God: It was the Father's will, and he had a delight in it; and it was the Son's will and delight, and he came, and, according to his undertaking, laid down his life. 2. Wherefore else are all the promises and encouragements that are given to sinners to believe? as that of Matth. xi. 28. *Come unto me, all ye that labour, and are heavy-laden*, &c. and that, 2 Cor. v. 20. where both are put together, *We are ambassadors for Christ, as though God did beseech you by us, we pray you, in Christ's stead, be ye reconciled to God*. Ministers press you in the name of God, and by vertue of a warrant from him, to be reconciled; and they have Christ's warrant, in a more peculiar manner, as the great Prophet of his Church, to tell you; it is a thing that the Lord Jehovah and the Mediator have pleasure in, even in this, that ye should be reconciled. 3. Wherefore are the many expostulations with sinners, that *they will not come to Christ for life, that they will not be gathered, that when he stretches out his hand all the day long, they will not behold him?* &c. Do not all these confirm this truth, that there is nothing he is better pleased with, than with a sinner's coming to Christ for life? Let me therefore beseech you, by the love that ye pretend to Jesus Christ, and in his name, and in the name of Jehovah, obtest you, be ye reconciled to God in Christ; let him have satisfaction; let this pleasure be done to the Lord, even to receive life from him: This is no hard nor hurtful, no unreasonable nor rigid request, I am sure; all that he requires of you, is, that ye would come to him, and get life: O! if ye could but suitably apprehend this to be that which the Lord aims at, in this preached gospel, that we might (to speak so with reverence) put an obligation on the Majesty of God, in making sure, in this his own way, the salvation of our own souls; and that we could not do him a better turn: (But I pray take the expressions right, for we cannot set forth his love, but in our own language, which comes infinitely far short of the thing) we could not find in our hearts to refuse to grant such a loving, and highly rational a request. As it is sure then upon the one side, that we cannot do that which will please him better; so it is as sure on the other side, that we cannot do that which will displease him more, than to slight his counsel in this. Though we would give our bodies to be burnt, and all our goods to the poor, he will not count it a pleasure done him, if this be not done: We would look upon this, as low condescendency, and great grace in the Lord, that he seeks no more of us, but the making sure eternal life to ourselves, as that which will be most pleasing to him; it is even as if a son should say to his father, Father, what will please thee? And as the father should say to his son, Son, have a care of thyself, and that will please me; because, by our so doing, he reacheth his great end, to wit, the glorifying of his grace and love, which sinners, by their unbelief, do what in them lieth to mar and obstruct. If we could speak seriously to you in this matter, it might be next to speak on every day: Always, seeing he hath purchased redemption to sinners at a dear rate, and all that he requires of you, is to close with him, and to seek after the application of his purchase we again earnestly pray you, be ye reconciled to God, and take heed that ye receive not this grace in vain. What can ye do that will be pleasing to God, or profitable to yourselves, without this? Or what fruit of the gospel can be brought forth, when this fruit is not brought forth, if Jesus Christ in his offices get not employment, and if his offering be not fled to for making of your peace? We may, in consideration of this great and grave subject, go from the congregation partly refreshed, that there is such a doctrine to be spoken of, tho' we cannot, alas! speak of it suitably; and partly afraid, lest we be found, as far as we can, thwarting with, and running cross unto God's good-will and design in it, notwithstanding all the favour and grace he hath made offer of to us. It were good that we carried serious meditation on this subject along with us.

SERMON XLV.

Isaiah liii. 11. *He shall see the travel of his soul, and shall be satisfied: By his knowledge shall my righteous Servant justify many; for he shall bear their iniquities.*

THIS is a great work that the Mediator hath to do; a great price that he hath to lay down for the satisfying of divine justice, and for redeeming of the lost elect: Now, what shall he have for all the travel of his soul? Here it is answered, and the terms of the covenant of redemption again compended. As for the effects and fruits of his death, spoken of in the close of the former verse, *He shall prolong his days*, that being spoken to, on the matter, from verse 8. and *the pleasure of the Lord shall prosper in his hand*, being spoken to by another lately in your hearing, from John xvii. 4. and in part by us, from verse 10. now read over again; we shall forbear further speaking to them, and come to that which follows in the 11th verse.

In this verse then there are these three. 1. An offer and promise made to the Mediator, That if he will accept of the proposal, and lay down his life for redeeming of the lost elect, it shall not be fruitless, *He shall see the travel of his soul and shall be satisfied*. 2. The way how this satisfaction shall be brought about, *By his knowledge shall my righteous Servant justify many*; that is, by faith in him, his purchase shall be applied to all these for whom he should suffer, who thereby should be justified. 3. The ground of this, which also shews the way how he shall justify many, *For he shall bear their iniquities*; that is, by his undertaking, and paying of their debt, he should meritoriously procure their absolution, and the setting of them free. In the first part, we have these three things implied. 1. A supposed condition, or restipulation on the Mediator's side, that his soul shall be put *to travel*; which expresses both the nature of his sufferings, that they shall not only be bodily, but also, and mainly, soul-sufferings, and conflicts with the wrath of God, which the elects sins deserved, as the main and principal thing articled, and that wherein the price of their redemption lay; And the greatness and extremity of his sufferings, here called *travel*, from the similitude of a woman in travel, and *the travel of his soul*: This being the way foretold, how Christ should be used; he should travel in his sufferings, to procure life to his people. 2. A promise made to him, That *he shall see the travel of his soul*, that is, he shall not bring forth wind, but shall have a large offspring, which, in the 2d part of the verse, is called a *Justifying of many by his knowledge*: This is the fruit he shall have of his soul travel. 3. The extent of this, which is, his being *satisfied*, and quiet; which looks to two things, (1.) To the certain and infallible success of his sufferings: Not one of the elect shall be amissing, none that he hath bought life to shall want it; he shall get as many justified and saved, as he conditioned for. (2.) To the great delight and complacency that our Lord hath, in performing the work of redemption, and in sinners getting the benefit of it: He shall think all well bestowed, when they come to get the application thereof, and by faith in him to be justified. From the first of these, Observe, "That the Mediator, in performing the "work of redemption, and in satisfying the justice "of God for the debt of elect sinners, was not only "put to external and bodily, but also, and mainly, "to inward, spiritual and soul-sufferings: Or, "The redeeming of lost sinners cost our Lord Jesus "much soul-travel and suffering." We have hinted at his sufferings often before, but this place especially speaks his soul-sufferings, and the inward anguish and agony that he was brought under: We shall therefore speak a little to this, it being most useful, and extensive in the fruits and benefits of it, to the people of God; and shall, *1st*. Confirm it by some places in the gospel, where we have the fulfilling of this prophecy clearly holden out to us; And *2dly*, By a fourfold reason: Only take this for an advertisement, That when we speak of the soul-sufferings of our Lord, we do not mean of any sufferings after death (as Papists falsly calumniate us) but of these sufferings especially, that were about the time of his passion, when he got the full cup of the Father's wrath put in his hand, towards his approaching to the cross, and when he was upon it, when he was arraigned, and when he was exacted upon for the elects debt, The *first* passage, to confirm it, is that of John xii. 27. *Now is my soul*

soul troubled, and what shall I say? Father, save me from this hour: Here his soul-sufferings begin clearly to shew themselves, when there was no cross, nor suffering in his body; yet he is put to such a pinch, considered as Man, that he is, in a manner, *overplussed,* and put to say, *What shall I say?* the horror of that which was begun, and was further coming on him, being beyond all expression; whereupon follows that prayer, *Father, save me from this hour*: His sinless human nature fearring some way to enter on it. The 2d passage is that of John xiii. 21. where it is said, that *He began to be troubled in spirit, and testified,* &c. But let us come forward, and put Matthew, Mark and Luke together, and we shall see what an inexpressible and unconceivable height and heap of sorrows, his soul-trouble and travel will amount to: Matthew says, Ch. xxvi. 37, 38. that *He began to be sorrowful, and very heavy;* and in the next words, *My soul is exceeding sorrowful even unto death:* And what made him so sorrowful? The next words, *Father, if it be possible, let this cup pass from me,* shew that it was the cup of his Father's wrathful justice put in his hand. Mark says, Chap. xiv. 33. that when he came to the garden, *he began to be sore amazed, and very heavy*: A wonderful expression to be used of the Son of God, that the Person that was God should be *amazed*; yet being considered as Man, he was so. Luke says, Chap. xxii. 44. that *being in an agony, he prayed more earnestly*: There is a sore exercise, and sad soul-travel indeed, when the sword of God's justice awaked against the Man that was *God's Fellow,* and when he hath the curse that was due to all the elect to encounter and meet with; this was such a combat, the like whereof was never in the world, and the effect of it is, *His sweat as great drops of blood falling down to the ground.* When there was no hand of man stirring him, nor any man to trouble him by him; but God, as a severe, and holily rigid Exactor, putting him to pay the debt, which he had undertaken to pay, according to his obligation; the inward pressure of his soul pressed great drops of blood from his body. And if we will yet look a little forward to Matth. xxvii. 46. we will find him brought to that extremity on the cross, that he cries, *My God, my God, why hast thou forsaken me?* Which tho' it say, that there was still faith in the Mediator, in adhering to the Father as his God; yet it sets out that great horror which he had inwardly to wrestle with, when there was some restraint on the sensibly comforting influence of the Godhead: Now, when all the evangelists concur so massily, emphatically, and significantly to express this, wealing out, and pitching upon such weighty words to set it forth by; we may see it to be designedly holden forth, as a special truth, that the faith of the people of God may be strongly confirmed therein.

To confirm it yet further, put these four together. 1. The estate that the elect are naturally lying in, for whom Christ undertakes; they are naturally under sin, liable to the curse of God for the transgressing of his law, which had said, *The soul that sins shall die;* and, *Cursed is every one that continueth not in all things written in the book of the law to do them.* 2. Add to this, the supposition of Christ's undertaking to be the elect's Cautioner, and to satisfy for their debt; whereby he steps into their room, takes on their debt, and (as the word is, 2 Cor. v. ult. *Becomes sin for them*) is content to be liable to, and to be pursued by justice for their debt: And tho' here there be a relaxation in respect of the persons of the elect, for whom the Cautioner stands good, yet, in respect of the curse and death due to them, there is no relaxation, but the same thing due to them is laid on him; as it is, Gal. iii. 14. *He hath redeemed us from the curse of the law, being made a curse for us*: In every thing he was put to pay the equivalent, for making up the satisfaction due to justice. And these two being put together, that elect sinners were obnoxious to wrath, and that our Lord came in their room, he behoved to be put to sad and sore soul-sufferings. 3. Consider God's end in the work of redemption, which is to point out the inconceivableness of his wonderfully condescending grace and mercy, in exacting of satisfaction from the Cautioner, and in setting the sinner free, that his grace may be so glorified, as there shall be a proof given of his justice and sovereignty going along with it: And infinite wisdom being set on work to glorify infinite grace and justice, there is a necessity, for the promoting of this end, that the Mediator shall thus satisfy; and the more full the satisfaction be, the more conspicuously do the grace and justice of God shine forth, and are glorified, according to that word, Rom. iii. 26. *To declare his righteousness, that he might be just, and the justifier of him that shall believe in Jesus.* This is the end of Christ's being made a propitiation, that God may be manifested to be spotless and pure in his justice, as well as free and rich in his mercy and grace, who, having given a law to man, will not acquit the transgression thereof, without a condign satisfaction. 4. Consider, that it is indeed a great thing to satisfy

justice

justice for one sin, that it is more to satisfy justice for all the sins of one person, which all the angels in heaven, and men on earth, cannot do; and therefore the punishment of the damn'd in hell is drawn out to eternity's length, and yet there is never a compleat equivalent satisfaction made to justice: But it is most of all, to satisfy justice for all the sins of all the elect; who, tho' they be few in comparison of the reprobate world, yet simply considered they are many, yea, even innumerable. And our Lord having taken all their sins on him, he is peremptorily required to satisfy for them all: And if this withal be added, that he is to satisfy for all the sins of all the elect at once, in a very short time, and hath the curse and wrath of God due to them, mustered, and marshalled in battallie against him, and as it were in a great body, in a most formidable manner marching up towards him, and furiously charging him; and all the wrath which they should have drunken through all eternity (which yet would never have been drunk out, nor made the less) put in one cup, and propined to him, as the word is, Psal. cx. 7. *He shall drink of the brook in the way*; the wrath of God running like an impetuous river, must be drunk up at once, and made dry by him: These, being put together, do clearly, and convincingly shew, that it could not be but an inexpressible and inconceivable soul-travel and suffering, that our Lord Jesus was put to.

The *Use* of this doctrine is large, and the 1*st* *Use* is this, That ye would take it for a most certain truth, which the scripture doth so frequently and significantly hold forth, That our Lord Jesus, in performing the work of redemption, had much sad soul-travel and sorrow: The faith of this is very useful to demonstrate the great love of God, and of the Mediator; for doubtless, the more suffering be undergone by the Mediator, the more love kythes therein to the elect. 2. It serves to hold out the sovereignty and justice of God, and the horribleness of sin. 3. In respect of God's people, it is useful, that they may be through and clear in the reality and worth of Christ's satisfaction; he having no other end in it, but to satisfy justice for their sin. 4. It is useful to shew the vanity and emptiness of mens supposed and fancied merits, and of any thing that can be alledged to be in man's suffering, or doing, for the satisfying of divine justice, seeing it drew so deep on Christ the Cautioner. And here two gross *errors* come to be refuted and reprobated; one of the Socinians, who seek quite to overturn Christ's satisfaction; and another of the Papists, that diminish his satisfaction, and extenuate and derogate from the great privilege of the pardon of sin, as if any thing could procure it, but this satisfaction of Christ by his soul-travel; both which are abundantly refuted by this text.

But to speak a word more particularly to the *First*, For clearing of which, ye will ask, What could there be to affect the holy human soul of our Lord? Or what was that, wherein his soul-sufferings did consist? But, before we speak to this, we would premise this word of advertisement in the entry, That there are two sorts of punishments, or penal effects of sin: The 1*st* sort, are such as are simply penal and satisfying, as proceeding from some extrinsick cause. The 2*d* sort are sinful; one sin, in the righteous judgment of God, drawing one another: And this proceeds not simply from the nature of justice, but from the nature of a mere sinful creature, and so from an intrinsick cause of a sinful principle in the creature. Now, when we speak of the soul-sufferings of Christ, which he was put to, in satisfying for the sins of the elect; we mean of the former, that is, sufferings that are simply penal; for there was no intrinsick principle of corrupt nature, nor ground of challenge in him, as there is in sinful creatures: And therefore we are to conceive of his soul-sufferings, as of something inflicted from without; and are not to conceive of them, as we do of sinful creatures, or that have sin in them, whereof he was altogether free.

Having premised this, we shall speak a little to these two, 1*st*, To that wherein this soul-suffering did not consist. 2*dly*, To that wherein it did consist. For the former, wherein it was not, 1. We are not to suppose, or imagine any actual separation betwixt his Godhead, and his Manhead, as if there had been an interruption of the personal union; not so, for the union of the two natures in one Person remains still; he was God and Man still, tho' (as was hinted before) there was a suspension of such a measure, at least, of the sensible comforting influence of the divine nature from the human, as had wont to be let out thereto; and yet there was even then a sustaining power, flowing from the Godhead, that supported him, so that he was not swallowed up of that, which would have quite and for ever swallowed up all creatures, as is evident in his crying, *My God, my God, why hast thou forsaken me?* Which shews, that tho' the union and relation stood firm, yet a comfortable influence was much restrained. 2. There was no sinful fretting, no impatiency, nor carnal anxiety in our Lord, all along his sufferings; for he did most willingly undergo them, and had a kindly submission in them all; as is evident by these words, *But for this cause, came I into this hour;* and, *Not my will, but thy will be done.* 3. There was not in him any distrust of God's love, nor any unbelief of his approbation before God, neither any the least diffidence as to the outgate; for, in the saddest and sharpest of all his conflicts, he was clear about his Father's love to him, that the relation stood firm, and that there would be a comfortable out-gate; as his prayer before shews, wherein he stiles God, *Father;* and these hardest like words uttered by him on the cross, *My God, my God why hast thou forsaken me?* do also shew, wherein twice over, he confidently asserts his interest, *My God, my God*; though he was most terribly assaulted, yet the tentation did not prevail over him. 4. Neither are we to conceive, that there was any inward confusion, challenge, or gnawing of conscience in him, such as is in desperate sinners, cast under the wrath of God, because there was no inward cause of it, nor any thing that could breed it; yea, even in that wherein he was Cautioner, he was clear, that he was doing the Father's will, and finishing the work that was committed to him, and that even under the greatest apprehensions of wrath: Therefore all such things are to be guarded against, in our thoughts, lest otherwise we reflect upon our innocent and spotless Mediator. But, 2*dly*, To speak a word to that wherein it doth consist? 1. It did consist (as we hinted before) in the Godhead's suspending its comfortable influence for a time from the human nature: Though our Lord had no culpable anxiety, yet he had a sinless fear, considering him as Man; and that the infinite God was angry, and executing angrily the sentence of the law against him, (though he was not angry at him, considered as in himself, but as he stood in the room of the elect, as their Cautioner, of whom he was to exact the payment of their debt) he could not but be in a wonderful amazement, as the word is, Mark xiv. 35. *He was sore amazed;* and, Heb. v. 7. it is said, *When he had offered up prayers, and supplications, with strong cries and tears, unto him that was able to save him from death, he was heard in that which he feared*; which looks to his wrestling in the garden. 2. He had an inexpressible sense of grief; not only from the petty outward afflictions that he was under; (which may be called petty comparatively, tho' they were very great in themselves) but also from the torrent of the wrath flowing in on his soul: That cup behoved to have a most bitter relish, and an inconceivable anguish with it, when he was a drinking of it, as appeared in his agony. O as he was pained and pinched in his soul! The soul being specially sensible of the wrath of God. 3. It consisted in a sort of wonderful horror, which no question, the marching up (to say so) of so many mighty squadrons of the highly provoked wrath of God, and making so furious and formidable an assault on the innocent human nature of Christ (that, considered simply in itself, as a finite creature) behoved necessarily to be attended with: Hence he prays, *Father, if it be possible, let this cup depart from me*; intimating, that there was a sinless lothness, and a holy abhorrence to meddle with it, and to adventure upon it. Tho' we have not hearts rightly to conceive, nor tongues suitably to express these most exquisite sufferings, yet these things shew that our Lord Jesus was exceedingly put to it, in his holy human soul.

The 2*d Use* serves to stir us up to wonder at the love of God the Father, that gave his own Son, and exacted the elects debt off him; and made the sword of his justice to awake against him; and to wonder at the love of the Son, that engaged to be Surety for them, and humbled himself so low, to lift them up: It was wonderful, that he should stoop to become Man, and to be a poor Man, and to die; but more, that he should come this length, as to be in an agony of soul, and to be so tossed with a tempest of terrible wrath, tho' he was not capable of tossing as meer creatures are: This, being well considered, would heighten exceedingly the praise of grace in the Church, and very much warm the hearts of sinners to him. And for pressing this *Use* a little, and for provoking to holy wondering at this love; consider these four, 1. Who it was that suffered thus? Even he that was *without guile*; he that was *God's Delight*, his *Father's Fellow*, the *express Image of his Person*, *he that made all things*, and who will one day *be Judge of all*; it is even he that thus suffered. 2. What he suffered? Even the wrath of God, and the wrath of God in such a degree and measure, as was equivalent to all that the elect should have suffered eternally in hell; which presseth forth from him these expressions which we hinted at before. 3. For whom all this was? which makes it appear to be yet more wonderful: It was for a number of lost straying sheep, that were *turned every one to his own way*, as it is verse. 6. for dyvours and debauched bankrupts, that were enemies to, and in tops with him:

Some

Some of them spitting in his face, some of them upon the consultation of taking away his life, as may be gathered from Acts ii. Yea, take the best of them, for whom he suffered, even those whom he took to the garden with him, to be witnesses of his agony; and we will find them sleeping, when he is in the height of it, and is thereby cast into a top-sweat of blood; and out of case to watch and to bear burden with him, but for one hour. It had been much for him to have suffered for righteous persons; but, as it is Rom v. *God commends his love to us in this, that while we were yet sinners, Christ died for us.* 4. The manner how he suffered, to wit, most willingly and patiently; tho' he easily could have commanded more than *twelve legions of angels* to rescue him, yet he would not, but would needs be apprehended by a number of poor worms, that will, with many mo, one day crawl at his footstool; that being the over-word of every article of the covenant of redemption on the Mediator's part, both as to the undertaking and the performance, *I delight to do thy will, O my God:* And now, for what end are all these things spoken? Is it (think ye) only, that we should speak, and that ye should hear of them, and no more? Surely no; it is a wonder, that this, which concerns us so nearly, is not more affecting to us. Are there any here that have any hope of benefit from Christ's sufferings, or that have win comfortably to apply them? Do not ye behold a depth of love here, that cannot be sounded? Is it suitable, think ye, that sinners, who have the hope of heaven thro' Christ's sufferings, should be so little moved at the hearing and reading of them? he suffers much by sinners, when his love shining forth in his sufferings is not taken notice of. I would pose you, when was your heart suitably affected with thinking on them? Or, when did ye make it an errand to God, purposely to bless him for this, that he sent his Son to suffer, and that the Mediator came and suffered such things for you sinners? This is a part, and a considerable part of your duty; and gratitude should constrain you to it: And you should not mince, nor derogate from the just esteem of his love; tho' through your own fault, ye be not sure of your interest in it, yet his condescending grace is not the less.

Use 3. Behold here, as upon the one side the exceeding severity of justice, and terribleness of wrath; so, upon the other side, the exceeding abominableness, and desperateness of sin. Would ye know what sin is, what wrath is, how just and severe the law is? read all these here, even in what is exacted by justice off the Cautioner, for the elect's sins. The most part of men and women, alas! do not believe how evil and bitter a thing sin is, and therefore they dally and play with it; they know not what wrath is, and therefore they dare hazard on it; they know not how strict the law is, and therefore they promise themselves *peace, though they walk in the imagination of their own hearts, and add drunkenness to thirst:* But, O secure sinners! what mean ye? have ye, or can ye have any hopes, that God will deal more gently with you, than he dealt with his own Son, when he was but Cautioner, and the sinner only by imputation: Ye are finite creatures, and drink in sin as the ox drinks water, and have an inward sinful principle, and an evil conscience, filled with just grounds of many challenges. Consider with yourselves, what a desperate condition, under inevitable and intolerable wrath, ye have to look for, who have no ground to look otherwise on God than as an enemy: When wrath was so horrible to innocent Jesus Christ, who had no sin, no challenge, no doubt of an interest in God, what will it be to you? Certainly the day is coming, when many of you will think ye have greatly beguiled and cheated yourselves, in thinking, that justice would be so easily satisfied as ye did: O then ye will be made to know to your cost, the nature of wrath and justice, and the nature of sin, who would never suffer these things to light before. The case of the rich glutton in hell may persuade many that the law is strict, and that sin is an ill and bitter thing, and that wrath is sore to bide: Therefore let me intreat you, as ye would eschew the wrath of God, and the lash of his revenging justice; beware of sin, dally not with it, as ye would not have it aggravated by this circumstance, above many, that ye hazarded to commit it, upon the consideration of God's goodness, that in reason should have led you to repentance.

Use 4. See here the absolute necessity that lies on sinners, who hear this gospel, to receive Christ by faith, and to improve his satisfaction for obtaining of life through him: For one of these two must be resolved on, either to come to this reckoning with justice yourselves, or to endeavour the removal of wrath by the satisfaction of Christ; there being no other way to come to freedom from guilt, and from the wrath that guilt draws on: That Christ Jesus suffered thus, as sinners Cautioner, it says, that wherever sin is, God will exact satisfaction: and where he exacts, he does it severely, tho' most justly; and if he exact it severely off the Cautioner, what will he do with the dyvour debtor, especially when he hath slighted the Cautioner, and de-

Isaiah liii. Verse 11. Serm. XLV.

spised the grace offered through him? And therefore, not only in respect of the command, but of the consequent that will follow the disobedience of it, be exhorted, if ye mind not to take your hazard of wrath, to endeavour, in God's way, to get your interest in this satisfaction which the Cautioner hath made well secured. There is here a solid ground for faith, to expect that this satisfaction will do the turn of all them who will make use of it; and a most pressing motive, to engage them that are lying under sin, to embrace, to close with, and to rest upon this offered satisfaction, that this grace be not received in vain: Is there not a testimony in your consciences of the former, and why do ye not make use of the latter? Will ye but once be prevailed with to put yourselves to it thus, What if I be made to reckon for my own sins? what horrid wrath will I meet with, when the Mediator had such sore soul-travel; even when there was a covenant-relation standing still, not doubted of, betwixt the Father and him; when formidable wrath shall be seen palpably pursuing me the sinner, having no covenant re‑ lation to support me? We would not put it to your choice, whether ye will count or not; for that must be, and shall be, whether ye choose or refuse: *It is appointed for all men once to die, and after to come to judgment; and we must all appear before the judgment seat of Christ*; But that, which we would put to your choice, is the way of coming to this judgment and reckoning; and there are but two ways, either ye must step to at your own hand, or ye must betake you to Christ's righteousness, as being thoroughly convinced of the necessity of it, and that it will do your turn. The day of the Lord will discover that many have spoken of their faith and repentance, that never really exercised the same. I shall now say no more; only remember, that *it is a fearful thing to fall into the hands of the living God*; who, when his wrath is kindled but a little, can cause the stoutest and proudest of his enemies to perish in the midst of all their designs and projects; they will all then be found to be happy *who have put their trust in him.*

SERMON XLV.

Isaiah liii. 11. *He shall see of the travel of his soul, and shall be satisfied: By his knowledge shall my righteous Servant justify many; for he shall bear their iniquities.*

ALL scripture is given by inspiration of God, and is profitable for doctrine, for reproof, for correction, for instruction in righteousness; that the man of God may be made perfect, throughly furnished unto all good works; and that his people may be *made wise unto salvation*: Yet these scriptures, wherein our Lord Jesus is holden forth more clearly, are eminently useful; he being the foundation and ground of all, to whom the law and the prophets bear witness, and they are only profitable to us, in the estate wherein we are, in so far as they relate to him, and point him out to us. And we may further say, that these scriptures, wherein his sufferings and death are holden forth, in the richness and fruitfulness of them, are singularly so; that being the very life of the covenant, and the very door, by, and through which we step from death to life; and whatever they be to others, sure they have a special sweetness in them to sensible sinners: And therefore the sum of the gospel, and of saving knowledge, is by the apostle, 2 Cor. ii. 2. compended in *the knowledge of Christ, and of him crucified;* which unfolds his very heart and bowels to us.

The prophet hath been pointing out this in several verses, and hath hinted at the effects of his sufferings in the former verse: And now, in these words, he put a new title on them, calling them the *travel of Christ's soul*; not only to set out the exceeding greatness of them, but with respect to the foregoing words, wherein it is said, *he shall see his seed*; which is repeated here, when it is said, *he shall be satisfied*: so that, as a mother is in travel, for bringing forth of a child; so, says he, Christ shall be put to soul-travel, for bringing life and immortality to the seed given him, to be saved by him: And seeing he is put to travel, he must needs bring forth, and *see his seed*. Here we may allude to that of Isaiah lxvi. 9. *Shall I bring to the birth, and not cause to bring forth? saith the Lord; shall I cause to bring forth, and shut the womb? saith my God.*

We

We have spoken of the nature and greatness of these sufferings: Now, ere we proceed to any more observations, we would speak a word further to the *Use* of this; it being indeed an eater out of which comes meat; and a strong, out of which comes sweet; these pangs having calmed and quieted the pangs and showers (to speak so) of many travelling souls, and brought forth a birth at last.

And therefore, beside what I spake to in the *Use* the last day, I would add this, that we would endeavour to have the solid faith, not only of his sufferings, but of the greatness of his sufferings, imprinted deeply on our hearts; that (I say) the sufferings of a dying blood-sweat-Christ, wrestling and struggling, even to his being in an agony, with the wrath of God, and putting up strong cries with tears, may be born in on our hearts; and that we may throughly be persuaded of the greatness of the work of redemption, and that it was a most dear and costly bargain to Christ: For it was not gold nor silver, it was not kingdoms, nor visible worlds, nor angels, that were given as a price for elect sinners; but it was the precious blood of the Son of God; nay, it was the bitter and sharp soul-travel, sadness, sorrow, and agony of our Lord Jesus, which (to speak comparatively) was beyond the shedding of his blood: And what a price do ye think this to be? That he, that made all, and preserved all in their being, and was before all things, should come thus low, as to be a Man, and a mean, sorrowful, suffering and dying Man, yea to be a cursed Man, and to go out of this life, as being under a curse, yet being always the beloved Son of the Father, and being even then, when at his lowest *the Prince of the kings of the earth*, and shining forth gloriously in the power, and riches, and freeness of his love and grace? Sure this wonderful low stooping, and humbling of himself preacheth out the love that straitned and constrained him to run upon that which was his own death; there being no hands that could have taken away his life, had he not willingly laid it down, which he did with delight: Could we make use of this, there is much here to be said for our use.

We shall draw what we would say on it, to these four heads. 1. To something for instruction. 2. To something for consolation. 3. To something for exhortation. 4. To something for reproof, and expostulation.

I say, 1*st*, It serves for *Instruction*: and ye would from it be instructed in several things, 1. How to think aright of the great severity of the justice of God, and of the horror of wrath, and of the dreadful consequents of sin, which it will most certainly have following on it. May it not make your souls to tremble to think upon, and consider, that our Lord Jesus was brought to such a pass, as to be in such an *agony*, to be so *exceeding sorrowful*, and even *amazed*; to be so troubled in soul, that he was thereby made to *sweat great drops of blood*, and to be wrestling with somewhat, that his holy human nature had a fearing at? O the desert and wages of sin, is dreadful! when the law pursues its controversy, and when justice exacts what a broken covenant deserves. Alas! the most of men believe not this; but it is here that may convince us, what an evil thing sin is, and what a dreadful thing it is to fall into the hands of an angry God. O that ye would think upon it, that ye may beware of sin by all means, and may always be minding that word which our Saviour hath, *If these be done in the green tree, what shall be done in the dry?* If it was so done with him, who in the action (if I may so call it) was performing his Father's will, and giving an admirable proof of his respect to the honour of God; what will he do to the dry sticks, the damned reprobate, who have slighted the offer of his grace, despised the sufferings of a Mediator, and disdained to be reclaimed? Hear it, and tremble, and be persuaded that the horror that sin shall bring upon the sinner, when God comes to reckon with him, is inexpressible. 2. Be instructed, and see here, how great the difficulty is of making peace with God, when once his law is broken; a thing that is little believed by most, who are disposed to think that they will get God sooner pleased and pacified, than they will get their neighbour or master pacified and pleased; which says, that either they think nothing or but very little of his wrath, or that they will soon get it put by, that a word will do that: Hence it is, that they think, that an equivalent price is not necessary for satisfying the justice of God, and for preventing of his wrath; but if it be so easy a thing to pacify God, and to satisfy his justice, why did our Lord undertake the debt? why did he become so low, and pay so dear a price, to procure a discharge of it? why was his soul put to such travel, when no shame nor reproach, nor pain of his blessed body could do it, but his soul, in the sore travel thereof, behoved to be made a sacrifice for sin? Sinners grosly ignorant mistake of the justice of God, appear palpably in this: There was never a person that was called to it, and did undertake to remove God's wrath from others, but our Lord Jesus; and ye see here what it cost him: And what do ye imagine will be the lot of others, who shall ly under it eternally? 3. See here the worth and weight of a soul, and the great moment of the salvation of a soul. Immortal souls are of much worth; and tho' men often sell them at a cheap and easy rate, yet our Lord bought souls dear: It is very true, souls, considered in themselves, are not worthy of the price laid down for them; but being considered with respect to the end for which they are designed, to wit, the glorifying of the riches of the grace and mercy of God, and their enjoying of him, they are of much worth. Ah that men should sell their souls so very cheap; when our Lord bought souls so very dear! 4. See here, the solidity, fulness and satisfactoriness of the price that Jesus Christ gave to justice, for the souls of his people: It cannot sure but be a fully satisfying price, that such a Person should suffer, and suffer so much, even to be put to soul-travel, for which there could be no reason, neither could it have any other end, but the satisfying of divine justice for the sins of the elect: And considering these his sufferings in the degree of them, which was so very high; and in the rise of them, which was God's purpose and decree; and in the end of them, which was to satisfy the justice of God, and to make his grace glorious, it cannot but be a most solid, full, and satisfying price; so that a soul may have here a sufficient ground to build its salvation upon: And the more low that the Mediator was brought by his sufferings, the more solid and sicker is the ground of our faith; yea this is the end why he came so low. See here, how greatly we are in Christ's debt, that when justice was provoked, and sinners had losed themselves, and when nothing else could be admitted, but all other sacrifices were rejected, he was graciously pleased to yield himself to be the sacrifice, by his extreme and most exquisite sufferings, most pleasantly and heartsomly, saying, *Lo, I come, in the volume of thy book it is written of me, I delight to do thy will, O my God; by the which will,* faith the apostle, Heb. x. *we are sanctified,* and by it we have access to eternal life. It had been much, if he had made a new world for believers to dwell in, nay it had been much, if he had provided angels to mollify and mitigate their sufferings, and to give them drops of water to cool their tongues in hell; but that he, his own blessed Self, should decline no soul-travel, beside bodily sufferings, to redeem them from the curse; how much, how unspeakably much are they obliged to Jesus Christ? If we were suitably sensible of our hazard, and clear as to our interest in these sufferings, it could not be, but our souls would leap someway within us, as the babe did in Elizabeth's womb, on this consideration, that a Cautioner and Saviour hath come, and paid the price that was due by us, to the justice of God; this is a greater obligation than his making of the world for an habitation to sinners; nay, a greater obligation than his giving of heaven to us, if abstracted from Christ: O! so well as it would become us in reading of these words, to stand and pause and to say, Is it so indeed, that Christ gave himself thus for sinners, and for me? This is it which opens the door of access to God, and makes a bridge over the gulf, that is betwixt God and sinners; he was smitten, that by his strokes and stripes health might be brought to us; he was content to undergo sore soul-travel, that thereby life might be brought to us:

That which we mainly aim at, in this branch of the *Use,* is, that ye would look to the mercy purchased by his soul-travel, as your great obligation, and at what a rate you have the offer of grace, and access to heaven: when he made the world, heaven and earth, sun, moon, stars, &c. he spake the word, and it was done; there needed no more, but *Let such a thing be, and it was;* but the work of redemption was of another sort, and brought about at a high and dearer rate: Therefore, among all the things which the gospel holds out, put a special price on these things that are fruits of Christ's soul-travel; and consider what a slight it will be, and what guilt it will involve you in, that he should purchase redemption so dear, and make offer of it so freely, and ye should care little or nothing for it. 6. Be instructed anent the absolute necessity of being in Christ's debt for the use-making and application of his purchase: Is there any man that can merit it, or render him a recompence for it? If not, and if there be a necessity of heaven and salvation, then sure there is a necessity of being in Christ's debt, and of making use of his purchase, for the attaining of which he hath purchased; and men are not hardly dealt with, or ill come to, when this blessed necessity is imposed upon them, not to satisfy for themselves (for, what can they bring that will be an equivalent price;) but to acquiesce in his satisfaction made to justice for them, and the rather, that they cannot bind him to make application of it. Folks are very readily given to one of these two, either to misken and pass by the Mediator, and so to presume to make a new bargain for their peace, by offering to drink themselves, for themselves, of that cup which Christ drank of, for that only was the price of souls: Or, if they esteem of Christ's satisfaction, they think to oblige him.

him, and to procure from him the application of his purchase, by their prayers and good living; but what is there in this, more than is in the former? what price is there that can be given to him, that is equivalent to his sufferings? It must therefore of necessity come to this, that as it was freely purchased, so it is freely applied: And it were very suitable for sinners to carry the faith of this along with them in their bosom; If he procured heaven to us, by his soul-suffering and travel, we cannot procure it to ourselves, and therefore a necessity lies on all that would be at heaven, to be in Christ's common for it: And this is the upshot of all that dyvour sinners may know, that they are in his common, as for his purchase, so for the application of it.

Use 2. This doctrine yields much consolation, and it is the fountain and rise of it; his soul-travel bought it all, and makes way to the bringing of us to the possession of it: And, in many respects, our consolation depends on it; we shall look upon it; as the rise thereof, more generally, in these respects, 1. That, to a poor sinner lying under the curse, there is a possibility of getting it put by, and kept off; that heaven is not desperate, and that the fear of coming before the tribunal of justice is not absolute: For our Lord hath satisfied justice; the price that he laid down was not for nought, but levelled at this very scope, as the apostle hath it, 2 Cor. v. ult *He was made sin for us, that knew no sin that we sinners might be made the righteousness of God in,* or through, *him?* And what strong consolation is this, for a sinner, under the curse of God, to have this word spoken to him, Tho' thou cannot satisfy justice for thyself, yet there is a way laid down to satisfy it for thee? The Mediator having the price that was required, proposed to him, did not stick at the terms, but held the bargain, and hath accordingly actually performed it. 2 It is a consolation in this respect, That not only is there a compleat satisfaction given to justice, but a willing Saviour, ready to make that satisfaction forthcoming, and to make it forthcoming freely. Can there be a greater proof of our Lord Jesus his love to sinners than this, that when they were considered with all their debt lying on their heads, he undertook this soul-travel for them, to procure them salvation from wrath and justice? This is more than his giving them his word for it, tho' that had been enough; it is more than the giving them his oath, thus to commend his love, as it is, John xv. 13, *Greater love hath no man than this, that a man should lay down his life for his friend:* But,

says the apostle, Rom, v. 8, 10. *God commends his love to us, that while we were yet sinners, yea enemies, Christ died for us;* this good Shepherd laid down his life for his sheep. 3. It is a consolation in this respect, that there is also a willingness in the Lord Jehovah, the provoked Party, to accept of this satisfaction, and to absolve the elect, on account of this satisfaction: For what I pray was all this soul-travel that the Lord underwent, but Jehovah his transferring of the debt of the elect on him, according to the transaction that had past in the covenant of redemption? He would never have made the sword of his justice to awake against the Man that was his Fellow, if he had not been content to accept of his satisfaction for them that should make use of it: For we have not only the Mediator, and his *satisfaction,* to look upon in this soul-travel; but also the contrivance of the covenant, called in the former words, *The pleasure of the Lord,* who, while we were enemies, gave his Son, and was content to want him for a time (to speak so) and to be a distinct Party to pursue him. Is not this then a good bargain, when we have a willing Mediator, and Merchant, content to give the price and satisfaction; and a gracious and willing God, content to accept of this satisfaction; and both of them content to make the application of it to us freely? as it is, Rev. iii. 18. Here is matter of strong consolation, the ground whereof will not fail, to wit, the Mediator's soul-travel; And the Lord Jehovah will not cast the bargain, when the poor sinners say, I have nothing to pay; but there is a price in Christ's satisfaction offered in the gospel, and the Judge says, or admits it for the sinner that lays claim to it, as if the sinner had never sinned, or had actually paid the price himself.

But, 4. Look a little further, and we will find more consolation, though this be much. Consider a sinner in a tempted condition, and under sad soul-exercise, that wots not what to do with unbelief, with the devil, and with the wrath of God, all which are like to overwhelm and swallow him up, and the heart is like to sink; here is the native and kindly fountain for such a soul to drink at, that our Lord Jesus suffered more, and that it was another sort of cup that he drank of, and drank out, and for these ends, (1.) To take away the sting and bitterness of thy cup. (2.) To procure and meritoriously to purchase a freedom and outgate from these temptations to thee. (3.) Also, that he might be made a sympathizing high Priest, and the more compassionate towards the person that should be so tempted, according that, Heb. ii. ult. For that he himself hath suffered, being tempted, he is able also to succour these that are tempted: He was tempted, that he might have kindly sympathy with tempted souls; and therefore, when such are ready to fall aswoon, he daunts and dandles them, as it were on his knee; and when they are in hazard to turn their back on the conflict, he comes up with fresh strength and recruits them: So, Heb. iv. 15. *We have not an High Priest which cannot be touched with the feeling of our infirmities, but was in all points tempted like as we are, yet without sin;* we have such an High Priest, as was not only mocked and scorned of men, and some way deserted of God, but who was tempted, tho' not from sin within (for he was without sin) yet to sin, for he was assaulted by the devil, and tempted to unbelief, and other gross sins, as is clear, Matth. iv. tho' (as he saith himself) *The prince of this world had nothing in him.* And he was not only tempted to sin, but, as if he had actually sinned, he met with wrath from all: There is a sweet and strong sympathy flowing from such bowels, as one brother hath towards another; yea inconceivably beyond the tenderest bowels, that the most warmly loving brethren in all the world have one towards another: And therefore he knows well what apprehensions, temptations riding thick (to speak so) will attempt to beat in upon poor souls, and can from experience sympathize with them. It is not so to be understood, as if there were any additional degree made to his kindness, skill, and grace, as he is God; these being infinite in him, as so considered: Yet being Man as well as God, or having a human nature, he hath from his personal experience a sympathy, and that in a human way, though infinitely above what we can conceive, with his own, under their temptations, and sad soul-exercise. And seeing the scripture holds out such a thing as this, that our High Priest is a Man that hath bowels of sympathy, it may sufficiently warrand a believer to expect much good, this and other ways from Christ; he having grace infinite in him as God, and a tender heart as Man, to befriend them, and to communicate and let out of that grace unto them: And this is great ground of consolation to believers, under any cross and piece of hard exercise, to know that we have a Mediator, who knows in experience, tho' not the sinfulness that accompanies these hard exercises in us, yet what these fears are of being shut out from God, and how dreadful a thing it is, to be at controversy with him; and is like to these, who, having come thorow a sad trial, and piece of exercise themselves, are thereby the more ready to sympathize with others under it. (5.) and *lastly,* The consideration of this may comfort believers even in their outward afflictions: It had been another sort of crosses that they would have been made to meet with, if he had not taken this cup of wrath and drunken it for them; and therefore they would be comforted, and bless God, who hath taken this soul-travel from off them, and made way for a retreat and shelter for them in him: And it should even shame believers, who are ready to think so much of any little bit of inward exercise, or of outward affliction; seeing our blessed Lord Jesus endured so much, not only outward and bodily affliction, but also so much inward trouble and soul-travel, that thereby their burden might be made light, and their yoke easy.

Use 3. For exhortation, Seeing our Lord Jesus was put to such sore soul-travel, sure it lays a great obligation on them, for whom he suffered, to endeavour to make some suitable and grateful return; seeing therefore we are so much in his common and debt, we should give him a friendly meeting in these *four,* which this calls for; 1. It calleth for love to him that vented such love to us. 2. It calleth for faith, That seeing he gave such a price for us, we should trust our souls to him. 3. It calleth for holiness and obedience, even living to him, and to the glorifying of him that hath bought us: This argument will sure weigh with you, who on solid grounds lay claim to his purchase. 4. It calleth for thankfulness and praise, in magnifying his grace and love, that hath so loved us: And are not all these very suitable and becoming, that sinners should love him; and that these who love him not, should be *Anathema Maranatha,* accursed to the coming of the Lord; that sinners should believe on him, and to be obedient to him, and thankful?

If ye believe this truth, this comfortable and soul-ravishing truth, let me exhort you, and be exhorted and prevailed with, to love our Lord Jesus Christ, and to give him that answerable respect, meeting, and welcome, that becomes; if we may plead for any thing from you, sure we may plead for this. If it be true that he engaged in such a bargain, in which, if he had not engaged himself, we had inevitably gone to the pit; and if he hath actually paid the price which he undertook to pay; let your consciences speak, if it should not melt the hearts of such, to whom the benefit of this is offered, with love to him? And if ye have the faith of the doctrine, can ye deny, but this obligation

lieth

lieth upon you? Look into your consciences and hearts and see if ye be able to shift it: And if ye had suitable palaces for entertaining him in, if ye be not bound to open to him, and give him patent entry to them; and if your eyes were fountains of tears, if it would not become you to wash his feet with them, and to wipe them with the hair of your heads? Would to God that you were under the suitable impression of this, and that ye were by the gospel, and the privileges ye have by it, constrained to love the Lord Jesus Christ! It may be some of you think, If this be all that is called for, he shall not want it. We assure you it is called for; *My son* (saith he) *give me thine heart*. But we are afraid, that tho' ye will confess, that this is your duty, and that ye should have love to him; yet the most part of you want it: For, when we speak of love to Christ, it is not a pretext or apprehension of love, that will be taken for love; but such love, as hath these qualifications; *1st*, If Christ be loved, he will be esteemed of, as the most excellent Thing, or Person, the most excellent Bargain, the most kind Friend, the most loving Husband, and as the most full, compleat and absolute Sufficiency, or sufficient One; as he is spoken of, and esteemed of by the spouse, *Cant*. v. *His countenance is like* Lebanon, *excellent as the cedars, his mouth is most sweet, he is altogether lovely:* The heart is brought to esteem of him, and to prefer him beyond all that it can set the eye upon. It were indeed somewhat, if ye were brought under a conviction, and thorow persuasion of this, that Jesus Christ is the incomparable best Thing that a sinner can have a title to: But alas! *He is despised, and rejected of men*, tho' he be *the Chiefest of ten thousands*; and men play the fool egregiously, in preferring other things to him, who is infinitely worthy of the preference unto, and of the pre-eminency above them all. A *2d* evidence of love is, the heart's longing and panting after the enjoyment of him, and after the enjoyment of him, as the most excellent Object, quite surpassing all other objects; and when the thirst and longing of the soul is so carried out after him, as it cannot be satisfied without him, which is to be *sick of love for him*, as it is, Can. ii. 5. and v. verse 8. to be in a manner swooning and fainting because of his absence, and even greening (to speak so) for his presence; to have the bent of the soul's designs and desires towards making of that glorious conquest, whereof the apostle speaks, Philip. iii. *Even to count all things to be but loss and dung; and to cast all things as it were over board, to win to him, and to be found in him*; to count of him as *the pearl of price*, and *as the treasure hid in the field*, for the sake of which, ye would strip yourselves to the skin, and sell all that ye have to buy it. *3dly*, This love to Christ Jesus hath in it a satisfying delight in him, and the soul's blessing of itself in him, its contenting itself with him, and its rejoicing in that sweetness which it findeth to be in him, as being the only attractive Object, that hath such a loveliness in it, as breeds satisfaction; which satisfaction begets a kindly warmness in the heart to him again, even till the soul be put in a holy lowe or flame of love to him. More of this love would make Christ and the gospel much more sweet, and would make every one of these words, that expresseth his love in his sufferings, to be like marrow and fatness, and would also make the promises to be like breasts full of consolation; it would withal cause, that there would not be such mistakes of Christ, nor such gaddings and whorings from him, and such preferring of idols to him, as, alas! there are. Where this love is not, there can be no other thing that will be acceptable. We shall say no more for the time, but only this, that we do appeal to your consciences, if there be not here an excellent and non-such Object of love, and if there be not here much reason to be in love with that Object? A very *Heathen* will return love for love; and should not we much more do so in this case? God himself kindle this love in us, and make us know more the great advantages of it.

SERMON XLVI.

Isaiah liii. 11. *He shall see of the travel of his soul, and shall be satisfied: By his knowledge shall my righteous Servant justify many; for he shall bear their iniquities.*

THE work of redemption is a business that was very gravely and very seriously contrived and prosecuted, in respect of God, and of the Mediator; there was much earnestness in it as to them, and yet notwithstanding (which is a wonder) men, whom it concerns so much, whose salvation depends on it, and to whom the benefit of it redounds, are but very little serious in their thoughts of it: Our Lord Jesus was in travel, soul-travel, sore soul-travel to bring about this work, and that the gospel might be preached to sinners, that they might have thereby a ground to their faith, to expect life and remission of sins through him; is it not then sad that we should speak and hear of it, and be, in a manner, like the stone in the wall, no more, or little more affected with it, than if it were a matter that did not at all concern us? The reading and hearing of these words will doubtless be a great conviction to secure sinners, that our Lord Jesus was at such pains, and put to such sore soul-travel and suffering, and that yet such sinners were never stirred, nor made serious, to have the application of this purchased redemption made to them.

The scope of these words is to shew the great inward soul-travels, conflicts, and straits that our blessed Lord Jesus had and was put to, in through-ing of the work of redemption, and in paying the price due to the justice of God for the sins of the elect. It is a wonder that ever we should have it to speak of, and that ye should hear of this subject, which is the very text, (to say so) and sum of the gospel; and therefore before we leave it, we shall speak a little more to the *Use* of it: And truly, if we make not use of this doctrine, we will make use of none; tho' I confess it is a great practique, how to draw it to use, and to conform ourselves in our practice to the use of it.

We proposed some things the last day, which we could not then prosecute; As, 1. Something for exhortation, 2. Something for reproof and expostulation; which rising clearly from the doctrine drawn from the words, we may now insist a little on them.

1*st*. For exhortation, considering Christ's sufferings, and the extremity of them, and that they were undergone for sinners, we would exhort you to love him as ye ought. There is a ground and warrant here to require it of you, seeing that love in his bosom came to such an height, that he was content to lay down his life, yea, seeing he was in such a hot flame of love, that the cup of wrath did not quench it, but his love drank and dried it up, *Greater love than this hath no man*: It is a most wonderful love, considered with all the circumstances, whereby it is heightned; and there is ground here to excite and stir you up to give him a kindly meeting, and to welcome his love with love: It will sure be a great shame, if our Lord's love stood at nothing, so that he might do the Father's will, and finish the work committed to him, which was the perfecting of the work of sinners redemption, the redemption of his lost sheep; if every trifle, or any trifle, shall quench love in our hearts to him. O what a shame will it be in the day of Judgment to many, when this man shall be brought forth loving this idol, and another man loving that idol more than Christ; this man loving his lust, that man his ease, and another man his wealth or honour, and preferring them to Christ; and when it shall be found, that they would not quit nor part with their right eye nor their right hand (which are not worth the name of *members*, being called so, because they are members of the body of death) out of love to him! Think folks what they will, that native impression of the obligation that lies upon them to love Christ, is wanting, and that divine and soul-ravishing influence, that his love should have on hearts. It is true, ye all think that ye love him, unless it be some of them who indeed love him; but, if ye could reflect upon yourselves, ye will find that ye have little or no love at all to him indeed: And therefore, for undeceiving of you, beside what we said the last day, take two or three characters of kindly love to Christ, 1. This love is never satisfied with any degree or measure that it hath attained, so as to sit down on it: It hath these two things in it, a desire be further on in love, and a weightedness

weightedness that it cannot win at growth in him: The loving soul is disposed to think, that its love to Christ is not worthy to be called love; and it breathes after it, even to have itself warmed therewith to him, and to be brought to a further nearness to him; as we may see through the Song of Solomon, and particularly Chap. vii. at the close, *There will I give thee my loves*; and Chap. viii. *O that thou wert as my brother, that sucked the breasts of my mother!* Kindly love to him, puts the soul to long for an opportunity to vent its love towards him. 2. Where this love is, the soul will be serious in praying for it, that it may attain it, as if it wanted it; and it will be much affected for the want of the lively exercise of it, and will be as much challenged for coming short in it, as it will be for any other sin: There is no benefit that it seeks more after, than to have the heart circumcised to love him; and O but it will be accounted a great benefit, to get love to Christ! And as it is one of the things that it seeks in prayer, so it is one of the things that it eyeth in repentance; it is much affected with the want of it, confesses it to him, aggreges the sin thereof against itself, from this ground, that it loves not Christ as it should. I know not if there be much of this among us: Many will be sorry if they fall in drunkenness, or in any other gross sin; but O how few repent of their want of love to Christ, and that he gets not his own room in the heart! 3. Where this love is, it is ever suspicious and jealous, lest the heart cliver and cleave to some other thing, and give it room, to the prejudice of Christ: It is a sad thing, when folks let their affections go out at random, and are not afraid, lest they out shoot themselves in loving the world, their pleasures, their credit, &c. but rather they are like the whore in the Proverbs, who says, *Come, and let us take our fill of loves*. Love to Christ hath a weanedness from these things, and a jealousy lest they usurp a room in the heart, that is not due to them; because, as John says, there is not a consistency betwixt the love of God, and the love of the world in the heart: And therefore it is the watchful care of a poor believer, to keep out inordinate love of the world, and of these things that the heart is given to go a-whoring after; hence David prays, Psal. cxix. *Incline my heart to thy law, and not to covetousness;* and, *Turn away mine eyes from beholding vanity.* There is in too many a sort of rooted confidence that they love Christ, and they never suspect themselves of the contrary, when yet some other thing hath his room.

2*dly*, There is ground here to exhort you to believe on him, as the prince of life, and the Saviour, that is well fitted and qualified to give repentance and remission of sins: and this is the very native use that flows from this doctrine, even to lay a solid ground of faith to a soul lying under the sense of sin, to step forward to God's bar, with confidence, considering Jesus Christ crucified, and put to soul-travel for elect sinners, who should betake themselves to him; which if it had not been, there had not been any ground for faith: and the lower he came in his sufferings, we have the more native and broad ground of faith, and the stronger motive to draw us to take hold of him, and to found and fix our faith on his satisfaction. To clear this branch of the use a little, 1. Consider here a ground for faith, in a fourfold respect; And, 2. The force of the motives that arise from these grounds, pressing a sensible sinner to exercise faith on them; or on him by them; And 3. The necessity that we are under, so to do.

For the first, 1. In general, there is ground here to bring the heart to be through in the historical faith of what is spoken concerning the truths of the covenant: For, doth not this soul-travel of our Lord say, that men are lying naturally in a sinful condition, and obnoxious to wrath; that there is a covenant past betwixt the Father and the Son, for delivering of elect sinners out of that condition, and that by the sufferings of the Mediator; and that, by our betaking of ourselves to him, we may be freed from sin and wrath? Otherwise, why did the Mediator come thus low, except it had been true that man was under a debt that he could not pay? And why did the Father send his Son, except he had been really minded that he should offer himself up a propitiatory sacrifice to God for man's sin? And his accepting of the satisfaction tells plainly, that he was content, that the cautioner's payment should stand for the principal debtors. All this supposeth a covenant, which is as real, as if we had seen, and had been ear-witnesses of the reading over of the covenant in all the articles of it. We wish that many were come this length, as to be confirmed in the historical faith of the general truths of the gospel, summed up in Christ's sufferings: And there cannot be any serious reading or hearing of Christ's sufferings, but there must also be some considering of their rise and end; if it be otherwise, we do but superficially run over them. 2. As this shews the Lord's seriousness in pressing the offer of redemption on sinners, so it calleth you to be serious in accepting of it; according to that in John xii. *When I am lifted up, I will draw all men after me;*

where Christ's lifting up is made an attractive to draw lost sinners after him. And can there be a greater ground of faith, or a stronger motive to persuade a sinner to be reconciled to God, and to rest upon Christ's satisfaction, in order to that, than this, that Jesus Christ hath purposely laid down his life, and undergone suffering, even to such an extremity, to bring it about? 3. When we say that Christ's soul-travel calls for faith; it requires this, and gives ground for it, that they that betake themselves to Christ for justification before God, may confidently commit themselves to his guiding in all other things: For, will he not be tender of them in these, when out of respect to them, when there was not a covenant betwixt him and them (tho' they were mentioned in the covenant of redemption) he laid down his life, and suffered such things for them? May we not, from this, reason, as the apostle doth, Rom. viii. *He that spared not his own Son, but gave him to the death for us, how shall he not with him also freely give us all things?* Can there be a greater ground for sinners, that fear to give him credit, to trust him with all things that concern them, than this, that he suffered so much for them? 4. Having betaken ourselves to him, it serves to confirm our faith, and to bring us to the quieting of ourselves in resting on him, and acquiescing in him: For, what more could we require for our settlement and quieting than this, that he who hath come so low, and condescended so far for the behoof of poor sinners? Therefore, in all these respects, let me exhort you, and in his name, *who was made sin for us, that we might be made the righteousness of God in him*, obtest you, not to keep at distance from him, but take with your sin, by faith to flee unto him, and to the efficacy of his blood; O yield yourselves by faith to him, for use-making of him for your justification. And a little more particularly, let me here speak a word to two sorts of persons, 1. To them that are yet strangers to God. 2. To them that are looking towards Christ. And (1.) For you that are strangers to God, whose hearts were never yet affected with the conviction of the necessity of believing, who can ly down, and rise up, without serious thoughts of your soul's estate, or of the necessity of making sure your peace with God; I beseech you, lay to heart your condition, and beware of trampling the blood of the covenant under your feet; let not the grace that is offered to you in this gospel be heard and received in vain; but, by the acknowledgment of sin, and of God's justice to which ye are liable for the same, timeously betake yourselves to Christ's sufferings, for a shelter from the wrath of God, that will be as a storm against the wall. This we press as the great use of this doctrine upon you, that ye improve the cup of wrath that the Mediator hath drunken, for your exempting from the curse that is due to you, and that cup that ye deserved to have drunken eternally. (2.) For you, who, under the conviction of sin, are looking towards Christ; let me intreat you not to stay on this side of the *City of refuge*, but step forward, and improve the soul-travel of the Lord for your spiritual ease, settlement, quiet and comfort, as well as for keeping you from wrath, otherwise it will bring bitterness in the end: If ye make not use of Christ's sufferings, if ye betake not yourself to him, and do not trust him for justification and life, ye will make yourselves guilty of his blood, and will be found treaders of it under foot.

And therefore, let me here speak a word to the second thing proposed, that is, the grounds, or reasons, or motives, that should press you to make use of these sufferings; and of the grounds of faith, that they hold out unto you. And, 1st, In general, let me ask, is there not need that ye should do so? is there not guilt, and hazard of wrath because of guilt? And if so, why stand ye at a distance from the Saviour? If it were sinless saints and angels that were exhorted to make use of him, it would be the less wonder, that there were so little thinking of a Mediator; but when it is sinners that are called upon, and sinners in such imminent hazard, it is indeed a wonder that there is not greater flocking unto him, and pressing on him: If there had not been need, would the Father have so pursued the Son? Or, do ye think that it was for a complement that he laid down his life? which sure he would not have done, if salvation could have been had any other way. 2dly, And more particularly, as ye would consider the marvellous grounds that he hath laid down for faith to rest upon, so ye would consider the many motives that ye have to press you to rest on these grounds, which we shall draw to these four. 1. The fulness and sufficiency of the ground that is given to faith in Christ's sufferings; which, the deeper they draw on his soul, faith hath the fuller and better ground to make use of them. 2. The power and ability that are conspicuously in him, to make application of his purchase: He hath encountered wrath, and hath overcome; he is absolved and justified before God, and *is exalted to be a Prince and a Saviour, to give repentance to Israel, and remission of sins;* and, having satisfied justice, and defeated the devil, and being thus

thus exalted, he can bring through, and land fair, such sinners as betake themselves to him: And these two, to wit, a sufficient price paid for the debt of the elect; and a sufficient Prince and Saviour, able to save to the uttermost all that come unto God through him, and who is exalted, and sitteth at God's right hand to make intercession for us, as they are a solid ground for faith to rest on, so a strong motive to press believing. 3. The great faithfulness of God, that brightly shines, and wonderfully appears here, who, according to the covenant, sends his Son, and pursues the quarrel against him, and in so doing keeps the promise made to Abraham; and the great faithfulness of the Mediator, in coming and performing all that he undertook for the elect: Both of them are so faithful in performing all that was covenanted, to the least *iota* thereof; as is evident by what our Lord says, *I have finished the work which thou gavest me to do.* Seeing therefore there is such exact faithfulness in keeping, and fulfilling of all that passed in the covenant of redemption, and of all that was promised to the fathers; and seeing the Mediator hath said, *That of all that come unto him, he will cast out none,* nor put them away; is there not here a strong motive to believing? Will not the Lord Jesus be as faithful in keeping the promises made to comers unto him, as the Father and he have been in performing of what was covenanted concerning their redemption? The 4th is the great love of God and of the Mediator, that eminently shine here, in their willingness to make the application: As he is faithful, so is he willing to be employed; and what greater evidence of love would we have than this, that our Lord Jesus hath delighted so much in the salvation of sinners, that he laid down his life, and endured much sore soul-travel, for this very end? *We beheld,* (says John, chap. i. 14.) *his glory, the glory as of the only begotten Son of the Father, full of grace and truth:* In his humiliation, he was glorious in both these; glorious in his truth, making his faithfulness to shine, in exact keeping of what was agreed upon and promised; glorious in his grace to poor sinners, in making application of his purchase, freely and fully: Yea, the more that he was obscured by his humiliation, the more did his grace shine forth; how much more glorious will he be in these, when he is now exalted? 3dly, If these two perswade you not to believe on him, to wit, the grounds that he hath given for believing, and the powerfully pressing motives to make use of these grounds; consider the absolute necessity that ye ly under of making use of these grounds, without which ye will never be able to shift the wrath of God. Is there any that can give God a recompence? *The redemption of the soul is precious, and ceaseth for ever,* as to you: Or, If any could have been able, why did the mediator come thus low? And where should have been the glory of grace and truth, that hath shined so radiantly in his sufferings? And therefore, from all these be exhorted to give him the credit of your salvation, by making use of his righteousness, and by founding your plea before God on his sufferings, as ever ye would have your souls saved: Otherways ye can expect nothing, but to fall under the rigour of justice, and to be made to satisfy for your own debt to the uttermost farthing; and when will that be? Dare the most innocent amongst you step in to satisfy justice for themselves? If not, is there not a necessity to make use of his sufferings for that end, which he hath made attainable by his tearing the vail of his own flesh, that sinners may step in with humble boldness to the holy of holies? This is the end of our preaching, and of your hearing, which, when it is not singly aimed at, and endeavoured to be reached, we are useless in both.

And therefore, 2dly, May we not expostulate with you, that are hearers of this gospel, and yet continue strangers to Christ; that can hear of his sufferings, and of his having been in agony, for this very end, that sinners might have a warrant to their faith, and yet have never to this very hour actually fled unto him to find shelter? I know that many will not take with this; and therefore, in more close application of this use (seeing here lieth the great treasure of the gospel, which, if it be not, what can be improven to any purpose?) We shall speak a word to the generality of hearers, who are strangers to the right use-making of Christ's righteousness: And tho' ye may think this to be a hard charge, and cannot well endure to be expostulated with as unbelievers; yet let me ask you, 1. Do you think that all of you will go to heaven? If not, but that it is a truth, that the most part of the hearers of the gospel will perish; then sure all are not believers; for all believers will go to heaven, and not one of them shall perish: And tho' ye will not now believe this, the day is coming, when ye shall, if grace prevent not, see and find it; when believers will be taken in with Christ, and others shut out. Many of you may think that this doctrine is needless; the more needless that many of you think it to be, it is so much the more needful, and useful to be insisted on with you. 2. If ye say, ye have faith; I ask you, Whence came it, and how got you

you it? I know, many of you will say, We believed always since we had understanding to know good by ill: Yet, when ye are put to tell what it is, ye know not how to answer, nor can ye give the least satisfying account of it; and yet ye question not but it will be well with you, and never once feared to go to hell: And is that faith, think ye? Alas no, it is a plain counterfeit, and a very cheat. Others are ready to say, We believed not always, yet we believe sometimes, to wit, when we do some duties, and abstain from gross evils; but when challenges come from the neglects of duties, and for the commission of sins, we want it, and have nothing of it; and when death comes, such are forced to say, We fear we have been beguiling ourselves: whence comes this? but even from this ground, that they would never suffer it to light, but they had faith; which yet will never be accounted to be faith, because it hath not Christ's righteousness for the ground of it; and therefore, when any challenge is awakened, it is a seeking and quite gone: Whereas true faith will in some measure stand it out against a challenge, and will abide the trial of a challenge, on the account of Christ's righteousness fled to. 3. We ask you this question, Are ye sure of your faith? Ye will say, We hope so, and believe so; and this is all ye can say: Which in effect comes to this, We groundlesly presumed so. And it is observable, that if ye be put to a second question, What ground have ye for your faith? Ye have none at all: If ye be asked, Whether ye be certain that ye are believers? Ye will answer, No body is certain, God knows that. Is not this strange? and hath it not in it an utter inconsistency, that men and women should confidently assert and maintain their faith, and yet, when they are put to prove it, they will tell you that they are uncertain, and that none can be certain of it? Therefore, think it not strange that we expostulate with you; that ye have been so long hearing of Christ, and that yet ye have little, or rather no faith at all in the use-making of his righteousness. But to make this the more convincingly clear, we shall give you four characters, whereby true faith may be tried and known; which will serve also to discover the unsoundness of the faith of many. (1.) It may be tried by the ground that it leaneth upon; solid faith hath for the ground of it Christ's righteousness and satisfaction, his sufferings, the price that he paid to justice for sinners debt; that *He, who knew no sin, might become sin for us,* as it is, 2 Cor. v. ult. Ye that say, Ye hope to come to heaven, and will assert strongly that ye believe: Try it I beseech you, by this, What is it that warrands you to believe? or, whereon is your faith founded? Is it Christ's righteousness that gives your faith a ground? Ye will say, Yes, and who do otherwise? are there any, but they expect life through Christ? But deceive not yourselves, there are many that have some sort of respect to Christ, who do not at all rightly respect his sufferings: Many will look upon Christ as a Sovereign, and as one that can pardon them their sins, and will pray to him for pardon of them; who yet never seriously lay the weight of their obtaining pardon on his death, but expect pardon immediately, without an interveening satisfaction; yea, they never look upon that as needful. Others again look only to Christ's ability to save, and will pray to him as to an able Saviour; and here also, by such, his righteousness and merit is shut out, as if it were superfluous and unnecessary. A third sort look to his mercy, and think that he is very kind and gracious, and that as one man forgives another, so will he forgive them; and do not respect his righteousness, nor found their faith and expectation of pardon upon him, as upon one that hath satisfied justice by the travel of his soul, that pardon might come to them who come to him. But, where true faith is, the soul begins to look on itself, as arraigned before the tribunal of justice, and libelled, as unable to pay its own debt, judges itself, and hath not only some piece of exercise to be freed from a challenge (which is all the faith that many have) but hath serious exercise, how to have the challenge answered, by betaking itself to Christ's satisfaction: From these grounds, that a satisfaction is given, that this satisfaction is made offer of in the gospel, and that the soul is content to make use of it, it draws the conclusion anent pardon: It hath interveening, betwixt the consideration of its guilt, and its application of pardon, both the covenant of redemption on God's side, and the covenant of reconciliation on the sinner's side, which the soul doth eye, as that which gives it warrant to lay hold on Christ's sufferings; which the other, who presumes, doth not: The believing soul says, If this satisfaction had not been, I could never have expected mercy. (2.) In the solid faith of a believer, there is an use-making of Christ crucified, allenarly, as the meritorious cause of justification and life; so he is exercised in this, to be allenarly settled on him as such: As for presumptuous souls, as they find it easy to believe, so they find it easy to believe, and to rest on him only. But as the true believer hath it for one piece of exercise to him, how to win to Christ; so it is a second piece of exercise to him, to get him rested on only, and to get him, as crucified, made the ground of his faith; as the apostle insinuates, when he says, 1 Cor. ii. 2. *I determined to know nothing among you, but Christ Jesus, and him crucified:* Where we have three grounds of saving faith, or knowledge, 1. Jesus Christ; 2. Him as crucified; and, 3. A determining to know no other thing, but him, to rest upon for life and salvation: It is in this respect that the apostle, Philip. iii. 8. doth count all things to be but loss and dung, and cast, as it were, all over board, that he may win Christ, and be found in him. Many find it no difficult business to rest on Christ only, and to keep out other things from being joined with him, and never once suspect themselves in this by any thing; but the believer (as I just now said) hath here an exercise and difficulty to get Christ alone rested on, so that nothing else be in the least rested on, because he knows nothing else to be a sure foundation, and because he knows that it is natural to him to rest on other things beside Christ. (3.) The true believer is taken up, not only to have a sure ground to build on, but also to have his own gripping at, and building, on that ground, made sure: It is his exercise to have it out of question, that his faith is true faith, and not presumption or guessing; to have the grace of faith actually and really taking hold of, or apprehending Christ: Whereas another that presumeth, and hath only an opinion, or conjecture, in place of faith; as he is in his own opinion easily brought to Christ, so he finds it easy to exercise believing on him; he will, it may be, grant that he cannot sanctify the sabbath-day, and yet he can believe, as if believing were less difficult than to sanctify the sabbath: So many will grant, that they cannot pray, and therefore do decline the worshipping of God in their families; who, yet will confidently say, they can believe, and that they do believe always, as if believing were less difficult than to pray for a quarter, or half a quarter of an hour: But, where solid faith is, the exercise of it is a difficult thing; and the person that hath it, hath a holy jealousy of it; and the experience of many others, and of himself, sometime telling him, that he may be mistaken, he is often trying it, and doth not, nay, he dare not trust much to it, and is put often with that man spoken of, Mark ix. to cry, and sometimes *with tears, Lord, I believe, help my unbelief:* He dare not trust much to his own grip, and therefore hath recourse to Christ to get it sickered, and to have him taking and keeping the grip of his grip, as it was with the apostle, Phil. iii. 12. (4.) When believers have betaken themselves to Christ, they have a new exercise, to know that it is so indeed. It is not only an exercise to them how to ground their faith right, how to quit all other things, and to betake themselves to Christ only, and to cast their burden on him; but it is an exercise to them, to be clear that it is Christ indeed that they rest on, or to be clear that they have rested on him. It is no good token when folks are soon satisfied with their believing, and never put it to the trial; and this is it that makes many go on guessing, till they come to death, which makes a divorce betwixt them and their fancied faith, and discovers it to be but a delusion: Whereas it is believers work, to try whether they have, and to know that they have believed, which they win not soon to know; and the reason is, because the sense of sin, the apprehension of wrath, and their love to God, and to Christ the Mediator, with their desire to enjoy him, suffer them not to be quiet till they be sicker. We may see all the four together, Phil. iii. 7, 8, 9, 10. where the apostle, speaking of his case when he was *a converted Christian,* in opposition to what it was when he was a Pharisee, and thought himself to be very well, and a strong believer, saith, *What things were gain to me, I counted loss for Christ: Yea, doubtless I count all things to be but loss for the excellency of the knowledge of Christ Jesus my Lord, for whom I have suffered the loss of all things; and do count them but dung, that I may win Christ, and be found in him, not having mine own righteousness,* &c. The Object he would be at, is *Christ:* the manner how, is, *Not having mine own righteousness;* the mean through which, is *faith* in him; this is it that brings him to union with him: And then he would know experimentally, that he doth know him savingly, as a believer in him, by finding *the power of his resurrection,* by having *fellowship in his sufferings* and by being *made conformable to his death;* whereby he would prove, and make out, to his own quieting and consolation, that he is indeed a believer. The believer is never right till he be in Christ, and it is his exercise to be quite rid of all other things, and to rest upon him alone; neither doth he rest here, but he must be clear that he is in him, and that he hath fellowship in his sufferings, and conformity to his death: This we would recommend to you as your main study as ever ye would comfortably evidence to yourselves, your believing in him.

O o   SERMON

SERMON XLVII.

Isaiah liii. 11. *He shall see of the travel of his soul, and shall be satisfied. By his knowledge shall my righteous Servant justify many; for he shall bear their iniquities.*

THE bargain of redemption is a great bargain, and we may say that it is a good bargain, wherein the greatest things that ever were imagined are transacted: The sum whereof is in these two, 1. What shall be the satisfaction that must be given to the infinite justice of God? Or, what shall be the amends that must be made to God for the satisfying of his justice for the sins of all the elect? And that is compended in these words, *The travel of Christ's soul.* That is the condition, or these are the terms, on which only the Lord Jehovah will tryst, (to speak so) and he will tryst on no other terms. 2. What shall be the satisfaction that the Mediator shall have for all his sufferings, and soul-travel? And this is summed up in these words, *He shall see of the travel of his soul, and shall be satisfied;* upon which two stands the covenant of redemption: And hence it is, that all things relating to the salvation of the elect, are so sicker and firm, that there is no possibility of the misgiving or failing of whatever is here transacted upon.

We having spoken somewhat of the price, which the Son, the Mediator, was to give; and of the soul-travel which he underwent in the paying of it: We shall now speak of the words, as they hold out the promises made to the Mediator; and it is twofold, 1*st,* *He shall see of the travel of his soul:* Which words being an explication of the former, and looking also to these which follow, there is a word to be supplied, which will take in both, and it is *fruit,* *He shall see the fruit of the travel of his soul*; that is, He cannot but have a seed, and a numerous offspring, because of his soul-travel, in bringing them forth: And so the promise, in this respect, shews the certainty of the effect, that is, that he shall most certainly bring forth in his travelling. The 2d promise is, That he *shall see* the fruit of his soul-travel, or his seed: It is much to have a seed, but it is more to see it; it is not only this, that Christ shall have a numerous issue, but that he shall out-live death, to see and oversee, and be a Tutor to them, tho' by his death he purchase life to them.

We shall from the first promise take two observations: the 1*st* is this, " That our Lord Jesus, " by his suffering and soul-travel, shall certainly " attain the fruit he aims at in it; his death and " sufferings shall not be fruitless, but shall certainly " have the intended fruit." Whatever we take the fruit to be, whether we take it out of the former words, it is a *seed that he shall see,* or have; or whether we take it out of the following words, it is the *justifying of many*; both these come to the same thing, and it shall certainly come to pass, and be made effectual in the up-shot of it; as the Lord himself saith, John xii. 24. *Except a corn of wheat fall into the ground and die, it abideth alone; but if it die, it bringeth forth much fruit*: Where he compares his own death to the sowing of seed, which, when sown, doth rot, and then springs up, and hath fruit; So (as if he had said) my death shall be a seed, or seed-time, whereon abundant fruit shall follow, for the good and salvation of many. This doctrine supposes, 1*st*, That our Lord Jesus had a respect, in the laying down of his life, to the salvation of his own elect people; or thus, That our Lord Jesus, in the laying down of his life, had a design and purpose to save the elect, as often he saith, *I lay down my life for my sheep;* and here they are called a *Seed,* and *Fruit* and such as are *justified* in due time. 2. That this purpose should by his sufferings be certainly made effectual; this being the Father's promise to him, *He shall see his seed, or the travel of his soul, and he shall be satisfied,* it cannot be frustrated. And we may further confirm it from these grounds, 1. Because it is a covenanted and transacted business betwixt the Father and the Son, and is here promised: If therefore there cannot be a failing of the transaction and bargain, it must certainly have the full effect. 2. Because the Mediator hath faithfully fulfilled his part of the covenant; and if he hath been so faithful on his side, then Jehovah on the other side of the covenant, who hath in it promised satisfaction to him for the travel of his soul, cannot but perform his part also: The Mediator performed his part, even till it came to these sweet words, uttered by him on the cross, *It is finished;* and therefore, as I said, the other part, that *He shall see the*

the fruit of his soul-travel, must also be performed. 3. It is also clear from the end and design of the covenant of redemption betwixt the Father and the Son, and of Christ's laying down his life, which was to bring about life unto, and to make it forthcoming for all them that the Father had given him; and to, and for no more; nor to, and for no fewer: Therefore he saith, *All that the Father hath given me, shall come unto me;* and, *I give them eternal life, and will raise them up at the last day.* Now, this being the end of the covenant, and of Christ's death, and the mean whereby the glory of grace is manifested, that life might not only be purchased to the elect, but also actually conferred on them according to the Father's and the Mediator's design in the covenant; Christ Jesus cannot but have the promise made good unto him, there being an engagement of, and on the Godhead (to speak after the manner of men) as to the reality, certainty and success of the performance, and for making out this promise to the Mediator.

The 1st *Use* serves for instructing and clearing of us in several things controverted by unsound men: For if this be a truth, that our Lord's sufferings and soul-travel cannot but have fruit, and the fruit that he aimed at therein; then, 1. There is a definite, particular and certain number elected, to partake of the benefit of Christ's sufferings; because there is only such a particular number that is given to Christ to be redeemed by him, and that do actually partake of the benefit of his sufferings, which cannot fail. 2. That Christ's sufferings are not intended as a price and satisfaction for the sins of all and every one; for so he should not see the fruit of the travel of his soul, but should in a great part miss and lose it, if he had intended that the travel of his soul should have been undergone for Judas, as well as for Peter. 3. There is here a ground for the certainty and efficacy of the grace of God in converting elect sinners: For Christ Jesus cannot lose these who are committed to him to be redeemed, more than he can lose the fruit of his sufferings; then sure faith is not left pendulous on man's free-will, but it is put out of question, as to all his own, through his undertaking: As he saith, *No man can come to me, except the Father draw him;* so he saith, *these that are given me, shall* and must *come to me;* there is a putt, or a powerful draught of the spirit of God, which is nothing else but the efficacy of his grace, by which this is made infrustrably sure, and not left contingent. 4. See here the truth of the perseverance of the elect and regenerate saints, who are appointed to be the fruit of his soul-travel, and a satisfaction to him for the same; for if they should fail, and not persevere to the end, the promise made to the Mediator should be cast loose, and not be necessarily performed and fulfilled. 5. See here how the salvation of elect sinners depends on the engagement betwixt God and the Mediator: Their redemption depends on his paying of the price, and their attaining the benefit of it depends on God's engagement to the Mediator; therefore we are said, 1 Pet. i. to be *keeped by the power of God through faith unto salvation.* It serves withal to clear the sovereignty of God, and the freeness of his grace, when sinners cannot pretend to have any hand in the work, to mar the beauty and efficacy of grace that shine therein.

Use 2d. There is here, 1. Something for the encouragement of such as would fain believe in Christ. And, 2. Somewhat for comfort to, and for confirmation of them, who have betaken themselves by faith to Christ. 3. It serves withal to encourage them who would be at believing, and find difficulty in the way, while they are breathing after him: It is certainly promised, that *He shall have a seed, and shall see of the fruit of the travel of his soul:* such therefore may expect that they shall come speed, who would fain be at that which is the fulfilling of God's engagement to the Mediator; for it was transacted in the covenant of redemption, that his suffering should be for the good of elect sinners, and that the Father should make application of his purchase made thereby to them. I say, it serves to comfort, encourage and confirm such as are fled to Christ, and find their own difficulty how to win through; for they have a good Cautioner to make out their faith, and what concerns their salvation: God's promise to the Mediator shall not be for nought, nor in vain, but shall have its accomplishment. If poor sinners were left to their own guiding, the bargain should never take effect, nor be made out; but it may encourage, and comfort the poor believer, tho' it should also humble him, that the business is put in another and better hand than his own: This hath strengthened the wavering hearts of many believers before, that both sides of the covenant, as to their forthcoming and performance, depend on the Father, and on the Mediator; the Mediator undertaking the payment of their debt, and the Lord Jehovah undertaking to draw them in to the Mediator, and by his power to bear them through, till they get all that the Mediator hath purchased for them, conferred on them.

2*dly,* Observe, " That all the benefits and advantages

" vantages, that any have ever gotten, or shall get
" that lead to life eternal, and which concur to
" promote the work of their salvation, are the fruits
" of Christ's purchase, by his soul-travel." Is a
sinner brought to believe? It is a fruit of his suffering: Is a sinner glorified? It is a fruit of the same:
And therefore, when in the one word it is said, *He
shall see his seed;* It is said in the next word, *He
shall see of the fruit of the travel of his soul;*
to shew that a soul's engaging to Christ by faith,
whereby the person becomes one of his seed, flows
from his sufferings, and is a fruit of the travel of
his soul, as it is, 2 Cor. v. *ult. He was made sin
for us, who knew no sin, that we might be made
the righteousness of God through him,* or in him;
where our *righteousness*, and what conduces to our
justification, is derived from his being made sin, or
a *Sin-offering* for us: And Gal. iii. 13. it is said,
that *Christ hath redeemed us from the curse of the
law, being made a curse for us, that the blessing
of Abraham might come on us Gentiles;* whatever
is comprehended under that blessing, as taking in
both the end and means by which we come by it,
flows from his being *a curse for us,* and from his
being brought under sad suffering, and sore soul-travel for us. In this *doctrine* ye would consider
something for clearing of it, or rather take the
doctrine itself several ways, and it will help to clear
itself. (1.) Then, when we speak of the fruit of
Christ's sufferings, we mean, not only that our justification, the pardon of our sins, and our entry into heaven, are fruits of it; but that our believing,
repentance, holiness, and every thing that leads
thereunto, are fruits of it also: Therefore it is
promised to Christ, Psal. cx. 3. *Thy people shall
be willing in the day of thy power.* And that these
that are given to Christ shall come, is a promise;
as well as it is a promise, that these that come shall
be justified: And the one follows upon Christ's engagement, as well as the other. (2.) If we take
the doctrine thus, That there is nothing that a
sinner gets, that leads to life and salvation, but it
is a fruit of Christ's purchase; we get neither repentance, nor faith, nor holiness, nor any other
such thing, but on account of Christ's satisfaction.
Or, (3.) Take it thus, Whatever is needful for
compleating of them that are Christ's seed, whom
he hath purchased, whatever they want or stand in
need of, whether righteousness, holiness, repentance, faith, hope, &c. all are purchased by him,
and are the fruits of his death and soul-travel;
this riseth clearly from the words, *He shall see of
the fruit of the travel of his soul,* That is, He
shall see sinners believing on him, and repenting
for sin, as well as he shall see them glorified: Which
will be clear, if we consider these two reasons,
1. The nature of the covenant, wherein all the
promises concerning sinners salvation are comprehended: There being but one covenant of redemption, and that being a promise of this covenant, to
circumcise the heart to love God, and to *write his
law in it,* as well as to pardon sin; and all the
promises of the covenant depending on Christ's stipulation, and these things in the promises flowing
from the covenant betwixt God and the Mediator;
sinners can have no right to any thing that is promised, but by a covenant; neither can they have
any access to them, but through Christ's suffering.
2. It is clear, from the end of the covenant, that
whatever sinners stand in need of, they must be in
Christ's common for it: Now, if we had faith, or
repentance, or any other grace, from ourselves, or
on our own account, we should not be in his debt
or common for all that we need, as indeed we are,
according to that, 1 Cor. i. 30, 31. *He is made
of God unto us, Wisdom,* to be our Guide and
Teacher; *Righteousness,* to be our Justifier, and
the meritorious cause of it; *Sanctification,* to be
the Worker and Procurer of it; and, in a word,
compleat *Redemption*: And this is subjoined as the
reason of all, *That he that glories,* or rejoices,
may glory, or rejoice in *the Lord*; that is, whether
there be a looking to faith or repentance, or any
other grace, there may be no cause to be vain or
proud of it, but that knowing these to be from
Christ, and fruits of his purchase, all the praise of
them may be to him alone.

The *Use* of this is large; it speaks something
more generally to them that are strangers to Christ,
and who think that they would be at him; and
something to them that are in him; and something
to both. And the *1st* thing that it speaks is this
(which we have often heard of, but cannot hear of
it too often) even the great and glad tidings, and
very good news, which we have to speak of through
Jesus Christ, That redemption is purchased by him
to poor sinners; and that through him there is access to life, and peace, and reconciliation with God,
from which through sin we had fallen, and run ourselves under a forfeiture of, and from which we had
been barred up eternally, except he had suffered:
There was a wall of separation and partition standing betwixt God and us, which by his sufferings
was demolished and broken down, and thereby a
door of access to God struck up, even *through the
vail of his flesh.* These should be refreshing and

fresh news to us every day, as indeed they would be, if we rightly knew, and, believed the benefit of God's friendship, and what were our hazard in lying still in nature, and what was the price that Christ laid down, to purchase for sinners friendship with God, and delivery from his curse; that it behoved to cost him sore soul-travel, ere any special grace could be bestowed on sinners; and that this same gospel that is preached to you, is a fruit of the travel of his soul; and that, in making the covenant of redemption, this same was a part of the indenture (to speak so) that these good news might be published in this same place, and these glad tidings spoken of among you. And therefore, 2*dly*, Put a great price on the means that may further your salvation; oh' repentance, faith, holiness, peace with God, &c. for they are the fruits of a very dear purchase, and the results of a great and sore conflict, which the Mediator had with the justice of God, ere there could be access for a sinner to any of them: There was not so much paid to get the world created, as was paid to buy faith, repentance, access to God, and an entry to heaven, to run-away sinners; nothing was paid for the one, but a mighty great price for the other. And therefore, 3*dly*, We would expostulate with many of you, how it comes to pass, that ye think so little of these things that Christ hath purchased; and that ye think so little of faith in him; and that so many of you take a counterfeit for it, try not if you have it, trouble not yourselves tho' ye want it; and that other things of little value are much esteemed of, and overvalued by you. Is there any thing comparable to that, which Christ hath put such a price on, that he gave his own life for it; and that God hath put such a price on, that he promised it to Christ, as a part of the satisfaction for the travel of his soul? and yet it is lightly valued by many, yea, by most men and women: The day will come, when ye will think faith to be of more value, and will think the pardon of sin, and an interest in Christ's blood, to be valuable above the whole world, though ye had it, when ye shall be brought to reckon with God for the slighting thereof. And therefore, 4*thly*, Seeing this is a truth, that every thing that leads to life eternal, is a fruit of Christ's purchase; take the right way to attain it. The exhortation implies these two; 1. That ye make a right choice of, and put a just value on these things, that ye should choose and value. 2. That ye take the right way for attaining of these things. (1.) Then, would ye know what is to be valued and chosen? It is, certainly these things, that God and the Mediator esteem of, and that the congregation of the first-born esteem of: The things that Christ hath purchased, and which are the fruits of the travel of his soul, are most excellent; and therefore mind, study, and seek after these things, that may lead your souls in to life eternal; seek after faith and repentance, to have your peace made with God, to have the heart purified, to be of a meek and quiet spirit, *which in the sight of God are of great price*, as the apostle Peter speaks; to have pardon of sin, and holiness, for adorning the gospel of God; and to have glory, that ye may see God and enjoy him: These things are the best things, this is undoubtedly *the better part, which will never be taken from them*, whose choice thro' grace it is. God will give great estates, countries and kingdoms in the world, to men, to whom he will not give so much faith as is like a grain of mustard-seed, nor a drahm of true holiness, because he thinks much less of the one than the other, and because the one is not so like God, nor will it have such abiding fruit as the other.

(2.) What way may folk win to make this choice, and to attain these best and most valuable things? No other way, but that which this doctrine holds out: If all things that lead to life and salvation be fruits of Christ's purchase, then sure it is by vertue of Christ's purchase alone, that ye must come by them; pardon of sin comes by the blood of sprinkling; peace with God, grace, and more grace, the the exercise of grace, and growth in holiness, faith in all its exercises and advances, and every other grace, comes by his sufferings; as also doth glory, because he hath purchased these graces of the Spirit, as well as pardon of sin, and heaven. Often Christ is mistken; and passed by here; many think they shall obtain pardon of sin, and go to heaven without him; others, tho' they will not own that, yet fall in the second, and would make use of him for pardon of sin, and for paying of their debt, if they could repent and believe in him; but till they find these in themselves, they fear to come unto him: Whereas, the sinner that is convinced of sin, and of his hazard, would lay down this as the first step of his way in coming to Christ. Any repentance, and believing, and the making of the heart willing to close with, and to cleave to him, is the fruit of Christ's purchase, and I must be in his common for it, for there is no other possible way to get it. The first airth (to speak so) that a wakened and sensible sinner should look unto for pardon and peace, for repentance, faith and all things, would be to Christ, and his sufferings, whence all these come. Sinners at first are disposed to take too far a look, and so mistake in the order of things; therefore, when the sense of sin pinches them, and they set about to believe, and find that their hearts are very averse from believing, and can hardly be brought to it, then they are fainted, when they consider and find, that, if it stood but on this, even to consent to take Christ, they cannot do it: But then, and in that case, the Lord minds that they should be much in his common, for faith, and repentance, and for a soft and tender heart, and that they should seek these from him, as well as pardon of sin, considering that all this is Christ's purchase, and that there is a possibility to win to it this way, when they can win to it no other way; if ye would take this way, even to eye and look to Christ as the Author and Finisher of faith, and be in his common for it, through his grace it should go better with you: This is it which the apostle hath, Heb. xii. where he calls, to *lay aside every weight, and the sin that easily besets us, and to run the race with patience that is set before us*; and if it should be said, How shall that be done? even by *looking unto Jesus the Author and Finisher of our faith*; and then follows, *Who for the joy that was set before him, endured the cross and despised the shame*; thus leading folk into his sufferings, as the solid foundation of their faith.

Use 2. See here ground for quashing the natural pride that is amongst men and women, as to spiritual things: How so? where is the ground for this? Here it is, because all is Christ's purchase; which may also give a check to these, who, because they have nothing in themselves, think not that they shall come-speed upon this ground; as it doth to these others, who have gotten something, and are proud of it. To clear it a little, we would consider, that there is a pride in folk, ere they come to Christ, they cannot well endure to be in Christ's debt for every thing; they will take pardon of sin from him, but they would have faith and repentance of themselves, as some money in their purse to bring with them to him, that they may buy it: But where will you, I pray, get faith, or repentance, if not from him? are they not his gifts, and fruits of his purchase? Which, if it were well considered, there would be no access to the proud reasonings of unbelief: Dare ye say but these things are the fruits of Christ's sufferings, and his gifts? and if so, must ye not be in his common for them? And as it silenceth the reasonings of unbelief, so it stops the mouth of the sinner, and humbles him much more than if he had these things in, or from himself, and were only to be in his common for righteousness and justification. 2. We would consider, that there is often some pride and conceit in them that have faith, disposing them to think themselves to be better than other folks: But, if ye have faith, whence is it? or who hath made you to differ? Is it not a fruit of Christ's purchase? and will ye be vain or conceity of that which is the purchase of another? This is a spiritual poor pride, that stinks in the nostrils of the holy Lord, so to abuse his goodness, as to be proud because he hath bought and bestowed that which ye could never have procured nor attained yourselves: If then folks have nothing, it is good to mind this, that Christ hath purchased what sinners stand in need of, and that it may be had in and from him; and if folks have any thing, they should not be proud or conceity of it, but mind that what they have is a fruit of Christ's purchase, and that therefore there is no ground to be proud of it.

The 3d *Use* serves to shew what great obligation lies on sinners, that get any special good from God: It is Christ that hath purchased all, and therefore they ought to improve all that they have gotten for him who hath bought all; as it is, 1 Cor. vi. 20. *Ye are not your own, ye are bought with a price, and therefore glorify God in your bodies and in your spirits, which are God's:* Whatever ye have of faith, of repentance, of holiness, or of ability to serve and honour God in your station, it is bought with a price, and a dear price; and therefore glorify God in the right use making, and managing of it. We would think it no little progress and advancement in religion, if ye were brought to walk under the suitable impression of your engagement to Christ, as holding all that ye have, and all that serves for your through-bearing of him; for what do we, or can we do? It is Christ that buys all, and that confers all; we can do nothing of ourselves but abuse his purchase: And, were it not that the sickerness and stability of our covenanting depends on the first covenant, even the covenant of redemption, transacted betwixt these two responsal Parties, Jehovah and the Mediator, we would quite mar and break all the bargain betwixt God and us, and cast all loose every day, if not every moment.

The other promise is, that *he shall see his seed:* And, as we hinted before, it is one thing, to *have a seed,* and another thing *to see a seed;* the former promise looks to his *having* of a seed, and this to his *seeing* of that seed: Whence observe, "That

" not only is there *a seed* promised to Christ, but
" also the *seeing of a seed*; not only fruits, but
" the improving and managing of these fruits: Or
" thus, That not only is there a seed promised to
" Christ, but the overseeing of that seed is also
" promised." He shall have no other tutor (to
speak so) to leave his children to, but to himself;
he shall die, and shall by his death beget a seed,
and yet by his death he shall become the Overseer
of that same seed, that by his death is begotten:
There is much of the dignity of Christ's office,
and of the comfort of believers here, that Jesus
Christ is not only the Procurer of our life, but the
Overseer of it; hence is that conclusion of the A-
postle, Heb. vii. 25. *Wherefore he is able to save
to the uttermost all that come unto God by him, forasmuch as he lives for ever to make intercession for
them:* He hath not only purchased life, and many
good things for believers, but he is living to make
the application of his purchase to them; and therefore is able to save to the uttermost all that come
unto God by him: Indeed, if he had been prevailed over by death, there might have been great hazard and doubt, if not utter despair of ever attaining his purchase, and a great crack (to say so) or
breach in our consolation; but when he is Execu-
tor of his own testament, and by his Spirit makes
the application, what is, or can be wanting? We
shall say no more, but that here it is clear, that we
have a living Mediator, as himself says, Rev. i.
18. *I was dead, and am alive, and live for evermore*; and therefore, sinners, step forward to his
sufferings, and seek the application of his purchase,
since he lives to make it; it will no doubt be great
ground of challenge against you, who slight his
sufferings, and keep at a distance from him, since he
is alive, and since what is much accounted of by
him, even the fruits of his sufferings, is by you
set at nought, who neglect, refuse, or despise him,
and the benefit of his sufferings. O what an aggravation of your guilt will this be, when he is
looking on, to see what comes of the fruit of his
sufferings, and soul-travel, to be found thus to
slight, and in a manner to affront him! He knows,
and takes notice of the breathings of faith, where
they are, and is well pleased with them, and with
the least mintings at it; he knows also, who despise him, and refuse to believe in him, and hath all
put on record. God give us wisdom to make the
right choice.

SERMON XLVIII.

Isaiah liii. 11. *He shall see of the travel of his soul, and shall be satisfied: By his knowledge shall my
righteous Servant justify many; for he shall bear their iniquities.*

AS it is a most wonderful work that our Lord
Jesus hath in hand, and a mighty great har-
gain, that cost him the travel of his soul; so it
may be thought, that it must be a very great price
that our Lord Jesus hath to expect, as his satisfaction for all that sore labour and travel: This is
it that the text holds forth, *He shall see of the
fruit of the travel of his soul*, which in sum is this,
he shall see poor sinners getting good of him, justified by his grace, and admitted to friendship
with God, and that to his satisfaction, as the words
following clear, *he shall be satisfied*, to wit, as
to that fruit, and shall acquiesce in it, as his satisfaction for all the travel of his soul.

We told you, that there were three things in
these words, 1. The price that is called for from
the Mediator, in performing the work of redemption, and making reconciliation betwixt God and
sinners, to wit, *the travel of his soul*, the sad and
sorely pinching straits and pressures that he was put
to, and brought under, not only in his body, but
also in his soul. 2. The promise made to him, u-
pon his undertaking and paying of the price, *he
shall see of the travel of his soul*, that is, the
fruits and effects of his soul-travel; it shall not be
for nought, but shall certainly have fruit, he shall
have a numerous issue. 3. There is here holden
forth the Mediator's acquiescence in the bargain so
proposed, that he undertaking the condition of laying
down his life, on these same terms that he shall
see a seed, he requires no other satisfaction, and
therefore he accepts of it, and acquiesces in it, as
the result of this design, *and shall be satisfied*.

Having spoken of the former *two*, we come now
to speak of the *third*; and we may consider it in
these three respects, 1. As it looks to Christ's design, who is like to one that is running a race, and
hath the prize before him, and in his eye; and this

is implied here, that he hath something before him, in laying down his life, which he shall not miss, but shall reach and be satisfied in it: So many are given him, for whom he enters Cautioner, or on condition that his righteousness shall be made forthcoming to them, and that none of them shall be without, or want it. 2. As it looks both to the number, and certainty of the effects and fruits, in respect of them that are given to him; *He shall be satisfied*, he shall have, tho' not all men and women, yet a sufficient number, even as many as shall satisfy and content him; and whatever was intended by him, in the laying down of his life, he shall want nothing of it, but shall be satisfied in it; and thus the words are to be actively understood, to wit, of God's actual performing of that which shall be satisfying to the Mediator. 3. It may be looked on as the effect and consequent following upon the former promise; and so it is to be understood passively, for the delight that he takes in the fruit of his sufferings, and in the seeing of sinners getting the good of them; and so the meaning is, that he shall be fully contented, and throughly well satisfied with, yea, even delighted, and (to speak so) comforted in this, for all the travel of his soul, when many shall be brought to believe in him, and to get good of him.

To clear it further, we may take the words as alluding to several similitudes, as, 1. To that of hungry and thirsty persons, who are said to be satisfied, when their hunger and thirst are removed, by meat and drink; which implies, that Jesus Christ, in his pursuing and performing the work of redemption, had a holy hunger and thirst, and this his hunger and thirst is satisfied in their salvation, and what leadeth to it; as himself saith, John iv. 32. (where he makes use of this same similitude) *I have meat to eat that ye know not of.* 2. It may allude to a man's taking pains in planting of a vineyard, or orchard, to whom it is a satisfaction when all the trees grow, thrive well, and bear fruit; and so the meaning is, that our Lord Jesus shall be at vast expence, and great labour and pains, in making sinners to become trees of righteousness; but that all these for whom he suffered, and was at all this expence and pain, shall hold so well, and be so fruitful at length, that he shall be fully satisfied in them, and think all well-bestowed: Or, 3. We may take it in allusion to a woman in travel, who is said, John xvi. 21. *to have sorrow while her pains are upon her; but so soon as she is delivered, she no more remembers her sorrow, for joy that a man-child is born.* And this similitude is here especially alluded unto; therefore our Lord's sufferings are called *travel*, because of the pains that he was put unto in them, and because the end of them was to bring forth children, before called *his seed*: As if the prophet had said, Our Lord Jesus shall be put to great sorrow in suffering, but he shall bring forth; and, as a woman hath joy in the man-child brought forth, so shall he have more comfort and delight in the bringing forth of believers, than he had sorrow in the procuring of life to them, tho' that was very great.

From the words, thus considered and explained, take these *two observations*, 1. "That our Lord "Jesus is exceedingly delighted, satisfied, and "well-pleased with poor sinners making use, and "getting good of his suffering: It is a thing most "satisfying, and well-pleasing to him. 2. That "seeing our Lord Jesus is so well pleased with sin- "ners making use of him, there is all equity and "reason for it, that he should have this satisfaction." And this follows not only on the former, but clearly riseth from the words; for this satisfaction is allowed him for his soul-travel: And as it is just, that they that labour should partake of their labour, and that the hireling should have his hire; so it is not only satisfying to Christ, that sinners get good of him, but it is just, he having purchased it at so dear a rate.

For the first of these, That our Lord Jesus is exceedingly delighted and satisfied with sinners making use, and getting good of him; if there were no other scripture to confirm it, this same is sufficient: Would ye then know what Christ aims at in his sufferings, what will content and satisfy him, as a recompence for all his soul-travel? it is even this, to *see of the fruit of the travel of his soul*, to have sinners getting good of him, and saved by him; and there is nothing but this that will satisfy him: It were a great matter to have the faith of this settled and rooted in our hearts; if we could rightly take up what he hath suffered, how low he hath condescended to come, even to be a Man, and a *Man of sorrows and acquainted with grief*, to be reproached and mocked, to take on him the curse, and to be in pain and soul-travel; and then, if we could rightly take up what he aimed at, and designed in all this, and what he accounted to be a recompence to him for it all; even this, that when his gospel is preached, such and such poor sinners, under hazard of wrath, and challenges for sin, should, through closing with him, be brought to answer all their challenges by this; our Lord Jesus hath satisfied justice for sinners: And when poor sinners

sinners are under the sense of a hard heart, that they should cast their eye on the same ground for a remedy of that spiritual malady and plague, even his sufferings, which have purchased the mollifying of the heart, as well as justification, and pardon of sin; and when a sinner is disconsolate and dejected, because of sin and divine displeasure, that he should be cheered, and comforted in his sufferings: this, even this, is refreshing, and is delightsome to him: We say, it were much to get this throughly believed, that sinners are not half so fain to come in under his sufferings for shelter and refreshing, as our Lord Jesus is (to speak with reverence) to see them sheltered, refreshed, and thriving; the very mentioning of this ought to be *as marrow to the bones*.

But, for further clearing of it, we would speak a word. 1. To what this delight and satisfaction is. 2. To some grounds, to confirm the truth of it, that our Lord Jesus is indeed delighted to see poor sinners coming to him, and getting good of him.

For the *First* of these, we did, when we was speaking of these words, verse 10. *The pleasure of the Lord shall prosper in his hand,* shew how it was a delightsom thing to Jehovah: And now, speaking of it from the 11th verse, in reference to the Mediator, we shall take it up in these particulars, 1*st*, There is in our Lord Jesus, not only a delight in sinners getting good of him, as it is a thing he calls for, and is agreeable to his revealed will, and as being required of them as their duty, in which respect it is acceptable to God, and cannot but be acceptable and well pleasing unto him: Neither, 2*dly*, Is this delight only in respect of the end of his sufferings, which were undergone to make a way for, and to strike open a door to the throne of grace, through the vail which is his flesh, that poor sinners might come to the fountain and wash, and have access to God through him; which being the end he had before him in his death, cannot but be acceptable to God, because it was his end in giving of his Son to die; and so it is delightsom to the Mediator But also, 3*dly*, It is so in these two respects further; sinners coming to him, resting on him, and getting good of him, is his delight. 1. In respect of the honour that is done unto him; when a sinner believes on him, he counts it the putting of the crown on his head, as it is. Can. iii. 11. See also, to this purpose, John v. 23, 24. And tho' there could have been a possibility of honouring God before, yet there is no honouring of the Mediator, till folk make use of his sufferings by faith; and it is on this ground that Christ complains, when he is not made use of: And therefore when sinners give him credit, by committing the saving of their souls to him, and by making use of his offices for that end, and for his performing in them that wherefore they were appointed, it cannot but be acceptable and well pleasing to him. 2. In respect of that sympathy, that our Lord Jesus hath with his own members; for tho' the Mediator be now glorified in heaven, yet he hath a human heart and affection still, tho' inconceivably glorious, and so a kindly sympathy with them and is some way affected with both their good and their ill: And, considering him thus, he hath a delight in the good and welfare of his people; and their being delighted in, and satisfied with him, proves a delight and satisfaction to him.

For the *next* thing, to wit, the clearing and confirming of it; it might be cleared and confirmed from many grounds, but we shall only touch on some, that may make it out most convincingly, that it is most delightsom to Jesus Christ to see sinners making use of him, and getting good of his sufferings: And this his delight may be drawn from eternity, and carried on to eternity. 1. In the making of the covenant of redemption, it was delightsom to him to enter in it, as is clear, Psal. xl. *I delight to do thy will, O my God*: The bargain was no sooner proposed (if we may speak so to that which is eternal) but heartily it was closed with by him; and this is confirmed, Prov. viii. 30, 31. where the substantial wisdom of the Father is brought in, saying, *Then I was by him, as one brought up with him; and I was daily his delight, rejoicing in the habitable parts of his earth, and my delights were with the sons of men*: Our Lord Jesus, before the world began, was delighted in the fore-thought that such a thing was a coming, that in such and such parts of the world, such and such poor sinners should be called by his grace, and get good of his sufferings; as a man in a long journey or voyage, may be delighted in the foresight of the end of it, before he come at it. 2. Look forward to his executing of his office of Mediator, and to his going about the work of redemption, and we will find that he does it with delight Therefore, John iv. when he is sitting on the well side, and is weary with his journey, and hath neither to eat nor to drink, he falleth a preaching to a poor sinful woman; and when 'the disciples would fain have refreshed him with that which they had bought, he says to them, *I have meat to eat that ye know not of*: and when they did begin to wonder what that could be, he says further to them

them, *It is my meat to do my Father's will, and to finish his work:* And what was that? A poor whorish woman is spoken to by him, and brought, by his speaking, to acknowledge him to be the Messiah, and to accept of him as such; and by that blessed work, his hunger and thirst were satisfied: So, Luke xxii. 15. he saith to his disciples, *With desire have I desired to eat this passover with you, before I suffer:* And, Luke xii. 50. *I have a baptism to be baptized with, and how am I straitned till it be accomplished?* Tho' the drinking of that cup was terrible to him, and tho' mockings and reproaches were not pleasant in themselves; yet the love that he had to sinners good, mastered all the bitterness that was in these, and made them sweet. 3. There is nothing that he more complains of, nothing angers and grieves him more, than when he is not made use of. *Ye will not* (faith he, John v.) *come unto me, that ye may have life;* to shew that the best entertainment that they could give him, was to come and get life from him: And it is told us, that *he was angry and grieved for the peoples unbelief and hardness of heart;* yea, *he weeps* over them because of this, Luke xix. all which prove the great delight that he had and hath still, in sinners getting good of him. And frequently in the Song, as chap. ii. and 6. he is said to *feed among the lilies;* there is all his entertainment that he gets in the world, he feasts on the fruits of his own Spirit in them that welcome him. I shall name but one place more, and that is, Psal. cxlvii. 10, 11. *He delights not in the strength of a horse, nor in the legs of a man, but in them that fear him;* the following words clear it more, what it is that delights him, *In them that hope in his mercy,* that is, in them that draw in to him by believing, he delights in those beyond all the world.

Use 1. It were a desirable thing to be believing this. Are there any so prophane, but are ready to think, that if they knew what would please God, or Christ, they would do it? The question is here answered, that this is pleasing, and only pleasing to him; if this be wanting, there is nothing that will please him, even what ye make use of Christ's sufferings, and employ him in his offices, for getting the good that may be had by them: This is it that ye are called to, and which delighted him; and if this be not, tho' ye would give *him thousands of rams, and ten thousands of rivers of oil, yea the first born of your body for the sin of your souls,* it will not satisfy him, nor be accepted; because this alone is the satisfaction that he will have for his soul-travel.

I shall a little explain this, and then prosecute the use of it. Ye will ask then, What is the fruit of Christ's soul-travel that satisfies him? I answer, That we take in under it, not only, 1. That ye should aim to be at heaven; neither, 2. this, That ye be serious in the duties of holiness, as if these were well pleasing to God, without respect to Christ's sufferings; but it is the use-making and improving of Christ's sufferings for attaining of these: When folk by this mids, by this new and living way, step forward to heaven, and seek to be serious in the study of holiness; when they that could not walk in the way of holiness, do now walk in it, *leaning on their Beloved,* and study to live by faith in him; this is it mainly wherein his delight and satisfaction doth ly, even when a poor sinner is brought to make use of him for peace and reconciliation with God, for through-bearing in all called-for duties, for his consolation, and for his admission to heaven in the close: And therefore they do not only fail here, who are prophane, living securely, never minding heaven, their peace with God, nor the study of holiness, neither only these, who cast the law and its reproofs behind their backs (these are lothsom to God and Jesus Christ)· but by this, these are also reproved, that do not improve the sufferings of Christ for peace and reconciliation with God, for righteousness and for strength, for comfort and encouragement, and who hope not in his mercy; the reason is, Because, tho' it were possible they could make progress in holiness, and attain to comfort and peace that way, yet it would not be thus the fruit of the travel of Christ's soul, he being past by, and so could not be satisfaction to him: But where a poor sinner sees that he cannot come to God of himself, cannot make his peace, nor can he walk in the way of holiness, so as to please God, and so flees to Christ for refuge, and makes use of his purchase; there lieth Christ's delight, to see such a sinner come and hide himself under the shadow of his sufferings: And in this respect, the more hardly a sinner is put at, it is the more satisfaction to him, that he in his death and sufferings be made use of, because, this way, the sinner's life is more intirely the benefit of his sufferings; and that such a person hath any strength, comfort or peace, and is admitted to heaven, it is allenarly through the travel of his soul, which is his great satisfaction.

And therefore we would, 2*dly,* Commend to you, that as ye would do Christ a favour (to speak so with reverence; and O what a motive is this for vile sinners, the dust of his feet, to be put in a

capacity

capacity to do him a pleasure) endeavour this especially, that, as to you, Christ may see the fruit of the travel of his soul, and be satisfied, and that all his kindness offered to you may not be fruitless: This is the great hinge of the gospel, as to that which is pressed upon you; and this is the wonderful motive that is given to press it, that it is delightsom to Christ, and therefore ye should believe on him: It were encouragement enough that it is profitable to yourselves; but if ye had hearts of stone, this should move you to it, that our Lord Jesus seeks no more satisfaction from you, for all his soul-travel, but that ye make use of his sufferings, that ye do not receive this offer of his grace in vain, nor be fruitless under it. In a word, we have here laid before us (and think upon it) the most wonderful, inconceivable, and inexpressible suit and request of him who is the Creator, to us poor sinful creatures; and what is it? I have been (says he on the matter) in sore travel and pain for you; now, I pray you, let it not be for nought, let me see the fruit of it: And (to speak it with reverence of the Majesty of God) it would say this to you, Let not our Lord Jesus rue of his sufferings; for as many as hear of this offer, and do not credit him with their souls, they do what they can, to make him repent that ever he became Man, and suffered so much, when he is thus shifted, and unkindly requited by them, to whom he makes the offer: And this is a very home and urgent pressing of the necessity of making use of him, when such an argument is made use of; for thus it stands with you, and his offer speaks this, either make use of Christ, and of his soul-travel, for saving of your souls, that so he may be satisfied; or if ye slight him, ye not only destroy and cause to perish your own souls, but ye refuse to satisfy Christ for his soul-travel, and do what in you lies to mar and defeat the end and design of his sufferings; and is not this a great and strongly pushing *dilemma?* The result of your receiving or rejecting of Christ will be this, if ye receive him, ye satisfy him; if ye reject him, ye say, ye are not content that he should be satisfied: And what can be expected to come of it, when Christ suffered so much, and when all that was craved of you, was to make use of him, and when it was told that that would satisfy him, and yet that was refused? What a horrible challenge will this be in the great day? And therefore, to press this *Use* a little, we shall shew you here, 1. What it is that we exhort you to; and, 2. What is the force of this motive. *1st,* We would commend to you in general, that ye would endeavour the salvation of your own souls; this is it he cries to you, Prov. i. 22. *How long, ye simple ones, will ye love simplicity, and ye scorners delight in scorning? turn ye at my reproof,* &c. He aims at this, that ye should get your souls saved from wrath; and this should not be prejudicial, nor at the long-run unsatisfying to yourselves, and it will be very satisfying to him. 2. It is not only to aim at salvation simply, but to aim at it by him, to aim at pardon of sin and justification through his righteousness and satisfaction; and that ye would bring no other argument before God to plead upon, for your peace with him, but this; and that ye would aim at holiness, as a fruit of his death, *He having purchased a peculiar people to himself, to be zealous of good works,* as it is, Tit ii. 14. and that ye would aim to do holy duties, by his strengthning of you; and that ye would live by faith in him, which is *your victory over the world,* and the very soul of the practice of all holy duties. And, 3. That ye aim to have a comfortable, refreshful and cheerful life in him, and by what is in him, as if it were your own, it being legally yours by faith in him; to be stopping your own mouth, as having nothing in yourselves to boast of, and (as I just now said) to be clearing and delighting yourselves from that which is in him; and as it is, Psal. cxlvii. even to be *hoping in his mercy.* In a word, it is to be studying peace with God through him, to be studying holiness in his strength, and to be studying a comfortable and cheerful walk, through the grounds of joy that are given you in him, which is very reasonable. Would ye then do him a favour, and have him delighted and satisfied, do but this, give him your souls to be saved by him, in his own way; come to him, sensible of sin, and founding your peace on him, tho' weak in yourselves, yet strong in him, *on whom, as the mighty One, God hath laid help:* and studying holiness in his strength, drawing vertue from him only, to mortify your lusts; that it may be known that Christ hath died, and is risen again, because grace shines in such a person: And be comforted in him; *He that glorieth let him glory in the Lord,* having given up with creature comforts and confidences, with your own gifts, parts, duties, &c. and having betaken yourselves to the peace, strength and consolation that are in a Mediator, and which run through the covenant of grace, and flow forth from him, as the fountain from whom all the graces and comforts that come to us are derived. 2dly, For the force of the motive, consider seriously, if this be not a pinching strait that ye are put to: If this be it wherein our Lord's satisfaction lies, and wherein

shameful and abominable guilt, that when the business of your own salvation stood on this, even on your satisfying of Christ by yielding, ye refused, disdained and scorned it, and would not make use of him for your peace, and would not in his strength study holiness, though your own souls should never be saved, nor he satisfied for his soul- and may look like presumption to look a promise in the face, and to offer to make application of it to the poor sinner's self; yet seeing it is a thing so pleasing to Christ, that it satisfies him for all his sufferings, essay it upon this very account, remembring always, that *He delights in them that hope in his mercy*: And to him be praise for ever.

SERMON XLIX.

Isaiah liii. 11. *He shall see of the travel of his soul, and shall be satisfied: By his knowledge shall my righteous Servant justify many; for he shall bear their iniquities.*

IT is a great work that our Lord Jesus hath undertaken, in satisfying the justice of God for the sins of the elect, and he hath at a dear rate, and with great expence and travel, performed it: Now it is but reason that he should again be satisfied, that so Jehovah's satisfaction and the Mediator's satisfaction may go together; and that is the thing that is promised here in these words. What this satisfaction is which is promised to him, as the great thing in which he delights, and by which he is satisfied, in the undertaking and performing of the work of redemption, it is also set down here, *He shall see of the fruit of the travel of his soul, and shall be satisfied:* which, in a word, is this, he shall see many, who had perished if he had not suffered, getting good of his sufferings, and to be benefited by them; who, by his taking on him the curse, and by his undergoing his soul-travel, shall be freed from the curse, and made to partake of the benefits, privileges and comforts that he hath bought by so great and precious a price.

We proposed this as the main *doctrine* from the words the last day, "That it is great satisfaction "to our Lord Jesus, to see sinners making use of, "and getting good of his sufferings." Or thus, "That sinners making use of Christ's sufferings "for their good, is his satisfaction, for all the soul- "travel, and sufferings that he endured." *He shall see of the fruit of the travel of his soul, and shall be satisfied.* I shall insist no further in clearing and confirming this, but come close to the *Use* of it; and if any point of doctrine have use, this may have, and hath it, to the gladning and making joyful and fain the hearts of lost sinners, that our Lord Jesus should suffer so much, and seek no more satisfaction for it all, but to see sinners improving his sufferings for their good, to have a seed brought forth by his soul-travel, and to have them getting life by his death, and the blessing by his bearing of the curse; and yet this is it that this doctrine bears forth.

We may draw the *1st Use* to these *four*, from and by which we may learn and know in some measure, how to answer this question. Seeing we have heard so much of Christ's suffering and soul-travel, what shall we give to Christ for all that? how shall we satisfy him? If there were any affected suitably with thankfulness from the hearing of Christ's being brought so low by his sad sufferings, this would be, and could not but be their question. Here is an answer to it, That our Lord Jesus seeks no more as a satisfaction for all his sufferings, but that ye improve them for your good: This will delight and satisfy him, ye cannot do him a greater pleasure, nothing will be more acceptable; nay, nothing will be acceptable to him, nor taken off your hand, but this, even to see you coming in to him, and making use of his sufferings for your own good, that as to you in particular, his sufferings may not be in vain, and for nought, but that ye improve them, and so improve them, as that ye may not live and die in the case that ye would have been in for ever, had he not suffered, that is, under the dominion of sin and Satan, under the wrath and curse of God, in an anxious heartless life, without God, and without hope in the world? It is even this in a word, That hearing of his sad sufferings, and of the design of them, ye may betake yourselves to him for pardon of sin, for sanctification in both the parts of it, and for consolation, and that in the end ye may get your souls saved, on the account of his sufferings, and by vertue thereof. 1*st* then, Ye would seek to be reconciled to God, as the apostle, 2 Cor. v. 20, 21. exhorts, *We as ambassadors for Christ, and in his stead, beseech you to be reconciled to God*; and the argument whereby it is pressed, is the same that the doctrine holds forth, *For he was made sin for us, who knew no sin, that we might be made the righteousness of God in him*: hence it follows also, chap. vi. 1. *We beseech you, receive not this grace of God in vain*. Are there any of you, who are convinced that Christ should be satisfied, and that he should not be at all this travel and pains for nought, and that think ye would fain satisfy him, if it were in your power? Behold, our Lord hath told you what will satisfy him; it is not thousands of rams, nor ten thousand rivers of oil, but that his sufferings be so improven by you, as the native fruits of them may follow and be found in you; that, considering the woful case ye are in by nature, ye may make use of his satisfaction to divine justice, as the alone atonement, and may by faith take hold of it as the ground of your peace: If this be not, Christ will be to you as if he had never suffered. 2*dly*, It calls for holiness and mortification of sin: This is much pressed, Rom. vi. from verse 2. to 14. and by this same argument, to wit, That seeing Christ died for believers, we should die with him; that being it wherein the power of his death kythes, even in the mortification of our lusts, which he came to destroy: But when folks live as they had wont to do, in their prophanity and looseness, there is nothing of the fruit of the travel of his soul to be seen in them. 3*dly*, Christ travelled for the consolation of his people: And this is another fruit of his death and sufferings, that these who have betaken themselves to Christ, may comfort themselves on this ground, That once, and that ere long, they will get the mastery over a body of death, and will get both Satan and it bruised under their feet, through him, *who was delivered for our offences, and rose again for our justification, and who hath blotted out the hand-writing of ordinances that was against us, nailing it to his cross*, and that *through the vail, which is his flesh, there might a way be made patent to us unto the most holy;* and that with confidence we might approach to God, and in his sufferings drown all our challenges. And indeed believers are behind, and greatly at a loss, who have betaken themselves to Christ, and yet live as anxiously and uncomfortably, as if they had not a slain Mediator to comfort themselves in, who, by his sufferings, soul-travel, and death, hath made a purchase of so great things for them. And, in a word, the up-shot of his sufferings is, to get the souls of believers in him, carried unto heaven, and keeped there perfect, till the body be raised, and in a perfect state re-united to the soul, at the great day; according to that of the apostle, Eph. v. 26, 27. He gave himself for his Church, that he might sanctify and cleanse it, and present her to himself a glorious Church, without spot and wrinkle, or any such thing: And when souls are not taking the right way to heaven, he hath nothing of the travel of his soul from such, more than if he had not undergone it, nor suffered at all.

Use 2. If this be Christ's satisfaction for all the travel of his soul, that he see sinners getting good of his sufferings; then, if any motive be weighty to move people to give him their souls to save, this must sure have weight with them; even that thereby he may have satisfaction for his soul-travel: And therefore we would exhort you, on this ground, to give him your souls to be saved by him, in order to his satisfaction. And what is spoken in common, take it as spoken to every one of you in particular, men and women, old and young, rich and poor; if ye would do Christ a favour and pleasure, give him employment for pardon of sin, for peace with God, for sanctification, for consolation, and for access to heaven: Or, if ye would know what motive we would use to persuade you to make use of this gospel for all these, take this for one, and a main one, That it will satisfy, and even (to speak so with reverence) comfort Christ for all the travel of his soul, and for all the hard labour that he endured; even as it satisfies a wooer for all his pains and patience, in waiting on after many refusals and slights, when he gains the woman's consent, and when the match is made up: So it will satisfy him, when he sees souls, by vertue of his sufferings, brought to believe on him, and to lay the weight of their salvation upon him; for then he sees it was not for nought that he laid down his life: And truly, if this motive prevail not, I know not what motive will prevail.

But, to make it the more clear and convincing, consider these things, 1. What it is that Christ seeks, when he seeks satisfaction for the travel of his soul; he even seeks your benefit and good: If he had sought that which would have been painful to you, ye would, I suppose, have judged yourselves obliged readily to have gone about it, had it been (as we use to speak) to have gone through the fire for him; but now, when this is all that he seeks, that by making use of his sufferings ye may be justified, made holy, comforted in your life, and brought to heaven at your death, should it not much more engage you to give him this satisfaction? 2. Who seeks this satisfaction, and to whom is it to be given? Is it not to our Lord Jesus Christ? There is very great weight in this part of the argument, that by believing on him, and making use of his sufferings, we not only satisfy and save ourselves, but make glad the heart of our Lord Jesus Christ, who, being considered as God, needs no satisfaction, neither is capable of any additional satisfaction from creatures, he being infinitely happy, and fully satisfied in the enjoyment of his own all-sufficient Self; nothing from without can be added unto him; Yet he having condescended to become Man, and Mediator betwixt God and man, to reconcile lost sinners to God, he is graciously pleased to account it satisfaction to him for all his soul-travel, to have sinners making use of him for their good; and if there be any weight in the satisfaction of One that is great and good, and good to us, this hath weight in it, that our doing so will satisfy him, that is matchlesly great and good, and superlatively so to sinners. 3. Consider the ground on which this satisfaction is pleaded for, and it will add yet more weight to this argument; it is satisfaction to him for his *soul travel*: And can any find in their hearts to think but he should be satisfied on this account? Is there not reason for it? *Who* (as the apostle says, 1 Cor. ix. 7.) *goeth a warfare on his own charges? who plants a vineyard, and eats not of the fruit thereof? or who feedeth a flock, and eateth not of the milk of the flock?* Ah! should our Lord Jesus bestow all this labour and pains for nothing? And further, 4. Whose satisfaction is it that is sought? (This consideration is somewhat diversified from the 2d, and would not therefore be look'd on as any tautology) Is it not his, who is Lord of all, and who will one day be Judge; when, if we had all the world, we would give it to please him; and who will pronounce the sweetest or the saddest setence upon us, according as we have satisfied him, in this, or not. Considering that it is he who desires this satisfaction from us, should there not be an holy diligence, eagerness, and zeal to get that performed, that will please and satisfy him; especially when the improving of his sufferings may do it? But, 5. From whom requires he this satisfaction? Is it not from them, who like sheep have gone astray? From these who have many iniquities lying on them, and are lying under the curse of God by nature? From these, who must either be healed by his stripes, or else they will never be healed, but will die of their wounds? May not this make the argument yet the more strong, that he is not seeking this satisfaction of strangers, but of his own people, nor of righteous folk, but of sinners, who are lying under the curse, and whose happiness lies in giving him this satisfaction? And when it is thus with you, that either your sins must be taken away by him, or else ye must ly under them for ever; that either he must bear the curse for you, or ye must bear it yourselves; if these things be obvious, as indeed they are, O! give him the satisfaction that he calls for, and let him not be put to say, as it is, Isaiah. xlix. 4. *I have laboured in vain, and spent my strength for nought, and in vain.*

2dly, To press this yet a little more (altho' it should be sad to us, that there should be need to press that so much on us, which is so profitable to us, and satisfying to him) even that we would make use of him for our spiritual good and advantage; these considerations will add weight to the argument, 1. What esteem Christ hath of it; he thinks it as it were to be payment, and a sort of compensation for all his labour and sufferings: The price was not gold nor silver, nor any such thing, which he gave for sinners; but it was his precious blood, his own life, who was the Prince of life, and the Prince of the kings of the earth: And O what a vast and infinite disproportion is there betwixt his life, and all our lives! and yet he accounts it a sufficient reward, if we will but give him ourselves to be saved by him in his own way, and will make use of his death and sufferings of him for that end? If he had commanded us to run here and there, and to undergo some long and very toilsome voyage, or some hard piece of labour, or to bestow of our means and substance, yea, all of it, to please him; it had been very reasonable on his part to have demanded it, and most unreasonable on ours to have refused it: But our Lord lays weight on none of these things, as separated from the laying the weight of our souls on his righteousness; the reason is, Because the making use of his righteousness, and the improving of his sufferings for our justification and salvation, shews that he in his sufferings is esteemed of, and he seeks no more but that. 2. Consider how good reason ye have to satisfy Christ, and yield to him, and to improve his sufferings for your own salvation: Is there any that dare say the contrary? Will not historical faith say, that there is good reason for it? If there be any love to him, or to your own souls, will it not plead for this? If ever ye think to be pardoned, is there any other name given, whereby ye can expect it? Is there any holiness, or comfort, but from him? any hope of heaven, but through him? and will not this bind the conscience of any, that is not desperate, to judge, that he from whom all this comes should be satisfied? 3. Consider at what a rate he hath purchased these benefits of the pardon of sin, of peace with God, of sanctification, and of the hope of heaven, &c. and how he hath brought them about: Did he not engage in the covenant of redemption, and hath he not performed all that he engaged for, in taking on our nature, in being in an agony, in sweating drops of blood, in being buffeted, mocked, reproached, and in dying, to procure life and peace to sinners? If we could rightly discern his sufferings, and the benefits that we have by them, it would say, that there is good reason, that he should have a kindly meeting, who hath done and suffered so much to obtain these to us. 4. Consider the cheerful way of his suffering, and of his laying down of the price, how well pleased he was to undergo it for his people; so that he saith, John x. *beth my life from me, but I lay it down, and take it up again*; Psal.

sons, having the least measure of natural or moral ingenuity, to give him a meeting? Very Heathens will love those that love them, much more ought ye to satisfy him in what he requires, who hath done so much for sinners. 5. Consider what he seeks as a satisfaction (hinted at before) If it were a great matter, or which were to your prejudice, there might be some shadow of a ground to refuse; but when it is no more but to make use of his sufferings for your own good, how can it be refused? It is in this case, as if the patient's health would satisfy the physician, as if a poor man's receiving of a sum of money would satisfy the rich friend, who is pleased to bestow it; or, as one that is naked would satisfy another, by putting on the clothes laid to his hand by him: What reason is there to refuse such offer? And yet this that Christ calls for, is, even as if the physician should say to his dying patient, I will be satisfied greatly, if thou wilt take this potion that is for thy recovery, health and cure; and will not be content, if thou take it not, tho' the ingredients stand myself very dear; besides that, it is for thy good, and will recover thee: Or, as if the Father should say to the child, I will not be content, if thou put not on such a fine suit, that stood me so much money; in a word, that which makes the dyvour sinner happy, is that which satisfies him. 6. Consider, if Jesus Christ get not this satisfaction, what will become of it; if ye please him not in this, he will be highly displeased, no other thing will satisfy him, tho' ye should pray and weep an hundred years, and do many good works; if he get not this fruit of his soul-sufferings, to wit, that ye improve them for your soul's good and salvation, he will be continually displeased: Therefore it is said, Psal. ii. *Kiss the Son lest he be angry*; And that is nothing else, but to make use of him in his offices; and it says, that there is no way to please him and to eschew his anger, but this: And indeed, if ye anger him, ye anger him that can be your best Friend and your greatest Foe. 7. Consider further, how our Lord Jesus seeks, and presses for this satisfaction from you; he sends forth his friends and ambassadors, to woo in his name;

the

and to beseech you to be reconciled, and to tell you, that it will not be thousands of rams, nor your first-born, that will do the business; but that ye must humble yourselves, and walk with God, which necessarily supposeth the use-making of Christ: If there had been no pleading with you in his name, there had not been such sin, in not improving his satisfaction; but when he pleads so much and so often for this, and intreats every one in particular to satisfy him, saying, as it were, Let me see of the travel of my soul, let me have this much satisfaction for all my sufferings, that ye will make use of my righteousness; and when he is so very serious in beseeching and intreating, it should, no doubt, make us more willing to grant him what he seeks. 8. Ye would look upon this, not only as a discourse in the general to sinners, but ye would also look on it, as addressed to every one of you in particular; and therefore remember, that ye will all be called to give an account of this matter, and it will be asked you, What became of such and such an offer of grace, and whether ye gave him the satisfaction that he called for, or not; according to that word, Acts xvii. 31. *He hath appointed a day, wherein he will judge the world in righteousness, by that Man whom he hath ordained, whereof he hath given assurance to all men, in that he hath raised him from the dead*, He would have judged the world, tho' Christ had not come; but he will have a day wherein he will call all the hearers of the gospel to an account, especially as to this, to wit, What welcome they have given to Christ? And seeing such a day is coming, when folk will be called to an account, what use they made of him; with what face will many come before him, when it shall be told them, that he craved no more satisfaction from them for all that he suffered, but that they would have improved his sufferings for their own good, and that yet they would not give him that much? Doth not this say, that there is need that we should look well what fruit there is of his sufferings that there may be more than if he had not suffered at all? 9. Consider the great weight that will be laid on this sin, of refusing to believe, and to satisfy him in this, to wit, in improving of his sufferings, above all other sins: This is a sin that will be found to be against equity, thankfulness and ingenuity, that when he had done and suffered so much, he was so ill requited; yea, it will be found to be a wilful and malicious sin, that, when your good and his satisfaction were joined together, ye would rather choose to destroy yourselves, than to satisfy him, in saving yourselves, through use making of his sufferings. There are two remarkable words to this purpose,

Heb. vi. 8. in the 6th Chap. it is said of such, that *they crucify to themselves the Son of God afresh, and put him to an open shame*; that is, they do displease and anger him, and do what in them lies to to cast reproach upon him, as if he were no Saviour at all; or an insufficient Saviour, to put him to suffer over again, in his wanting of satisfaction for his sufferings; as it is a great pain for a mother to be in travel, but it is another, and, in some respect, a greater pain, if the child die in the bringing forth: In the 10th Chap. verse. 28. it is called, a *treading under foot the Son of God, and an accounting the blood of the covenant to be an unholy thing*: and in the 16 verse. before it is said, *There remains no more sacrifice for sin, but a certain fearful looking for of judgment*; and it is upon this very account, (as we did, at another occasion, make use of these two scriptures to a like purpose, and did thus caution our application of them against mistakes) for what greater indignity can be put on him, than, when his satisfaction depends on the improving of his sufferings, yet people will not do it? As nothing pleases him better than to improve his sufferings, so on the contrary, there is no sin that doth displease him more, than when they are not improven: And if ye will not now believe this to be a truth, yet, when the Lord shall call you to account for it, ye will find it to be a most certain and sad truth, that he called you to believe, and that ye would ly still in your unbelief, ignorance and prophanity; that ye destroyed your own souls, and made his sufferings as useless, as to you, as if there had never a door been opened to sinners to heaven, by them. Is there any of you that will be able to answer to this challenge? If not, then let him have this satisfaction, by improving of his sufferings, that he may find (to say so) that his death hath not been for nought, as to you: Study to have him great in your esteem, and to have yourselves saved by the vertue and efficacy of his sufferings, otherwise the challenge will be unanswerable; considering, that he declared that this would satisfy him, and ye knew that it would have pleased him, and removed the quarrel, and saved yourselves; and that withal, by this means, a comfortable sentence at judgment might have been procured to you, and that yet ye disdained to do it. And therefore, since it stands so with you, be intreated to make earnest, and greater earnest of believing and of the great work of getting your own souls saved, which he hath thought so much of, else it had been better for you that ye had never had a delightsom hour in the world; and sad will the encounter be, that ye will have

with

SERM. L. with him, and with your own conscience in that day, when it shall have this to tell you, that ye cannot now expect any good or favour from the Judge, because when he would have saved you, ye would not have it so, but would needs run on your own damnation. And therefore we say again, Either give him satisfaction, by improving of his sufferings, and by making earnest of the business of your salvation; or, resolve to meet with a most terrible Pursuer of the quarrel against you: The wrath of God is dreadful, but much more the vengeance of the Mediator, who, because ye would not give him his will in your salvation, he shall have it your ruin and destruction.

4. There is here a sweet word of consolation to poor souls, that fain would have sin taken away, and are afraid to presume: Our Lord will never be angry, that ye make use of his sufferings for your own good; nay, he accounts it a satisfaction to him, that ye improve them; that, when ye find yourselves arrested for sin, ye put it on his score, and draw a bill on him to pay your debt; that, when you find yourselves under that, which, to you, looks like the dominion of sin, ye look to his cross for vertue to crucify, kill and subdue it: If therefore (as I have often said) ye would do him a favour or pleasure, make use of him; be assured, that the more weight ye lay on him, ye do him the greater pleasure; and this is all the amends that he seeks for all the wrongs ye have done to him, and all the satisfaction that he seeks for all the good turns he hath done to you, that ye come to him, thus to make use of him; and it is good reason, even all the reason in the world, that he get this amends made to him, and this satisfaction granted to him.

SERMON L.

Isaiah liii. 11. *He shall see of the travel of his soul, and shall be satisfied: By his knowledge shall my righteous Servant justify many; for he shall bear their iniquities.*

THERE are two things of great concernment for men to know, for sinful men to know; (if any thing be of concernment) the one is, How the justice of God that is provoked may be satisfied? or what it is, by which provoked justice is satisfied? And the other is, What the way is, how we come to get that satisfaction applied to us? or, what is the way to get the benefit of it made ours? And both of them are answered in this verse clearly and shortly: The first is holden out in the first part of the verse to be the *travel of Christ's soul*, which hath a special look to the covenant of redemption, and to the condition on which it is accomplished and performed, that is, his *soul-travel*, under which all his sufferings are comprehended: The other is in the latter part of the verse, *By his knowledge shall my righteous Servant justify many, for he shall bear their iniquities*; this holds forth in short the gospel-way, how a sinner may be brought to get the benefit of Christ's satisfaction; these two being the sum of the gospel, to wit, Christ's purchase, and the application of it to sinners.

In this last part of the *verse*, we have these *five* things to be considered, which express this, 1. The great benefit that flows from Christ's sufferings, and it is *justification;* which in a word is this much, to be absolved, acquitted and set free from the guilt of sin, and from the curse of God; *justifying* here being opposed to *condemning:* So that, when it is said, *They shall be justified;* the meaning is, that these that were before obnoxious to the curse, and that were by the law to be condemned, (according to that word, *Gal.* iii. 10. *Cursed is every one that abides not in all things written in the law to do them*) shall now, thro' the benefit of Christ's sufferings, be declared free, and set at liberty, even as a debtor is set free by the interveening of a responsal caution r. 2. The parties made partakers of the benefit, and they are called, *many;* tho' they are few, being compared with the world, yet in themselves they are many: *They shall come,* or many shall come, *from the east, and from the west, and from the south, and from the north, and shall sit down with Abraham, Isaac and Jacob in the kingdom of heaven.* And, comparing this word with the last words of the verse, it says, that they are as many as these are whose iniquities he bare, and the payment of whose debt he undertook. It is not to be taken universally for all, but for some singular selected persons, whose iniquities he bare. 3. The fountain from which, or from whom this benefit flows to many: It is the Lord's *righteous Servant, he shall justify many*; where the effect is attributed alone to him. 4. The way how Christ justifies: It is not simply, by forgiving, (as he indeed hath power to forgive sins) but *meritoriously*, to wit, by his satisfying for them; therefore it is added, *For he shall bear their iniquities;* he shall take on their sins, and pay their debt:

debt: And therefore, when they come before the tribunal of God, the guilt of their fins is taken off them through his merit. 5. The great mids, or mean, by which this benefit is derived to these many: It is *by his knowledge*; which is not to be taken *subjectively*, for the knowledge that he hath, but *objectively*, that is, he, by making himself known by believing: Or, it is *by his knowledge*, not *actively*, but *passively* taken; not his knowledge, whereby he doth know, but that whereby he is known; it is in a word, by faith, according to that, Phil. iii. 8, 9, 10. *I count all things* (faith the apostle there) *loss for the excellency of the knowledge of Christ Jesus my Lord*, &c. and he expones what that is in the next words, *That I may be found in him, not having my own righteousness, which is according to the law, but the righteousness of God, which is by the faith of him.* These may afterward be more fully cleared, as we come to speak of them more particularly.

There is here then a brief compend of the gospel, and of the way of sinners reconciliation with God; so that if ye would know, (1.) How a sinner is justified, or wherein it consists? Here it is, it consists not in the infusing of grace, nor in the sanctifying, or making of a profane person holy, tho' that doth accompany always and follow justification; but in the absolving of a sinner from the guilt of sin, or in acquitting the guilty. 2. Would ye know the ground on which this goeth, or how it comes to pass, that the just God can justify an ungodly sinner? It is because of Christ's righteousness, and of his satisfying justice, or paying of the sinner's debt. 3. Would ye know how it comes that this man, and not another, comes to get Christ's satisfaction made his, and hath his debt thereby taken off? It is by his knowledge, and by faith in him; (called *knowledge* here, because it necessarily presupposes the knowledge of him) it is by acknowledging of him in his offices, and by submitting and betaking of ourselves to him by faith; because it is articled in the covenant of redemption, that his righteousness shall be made forthcoming to all them that by faith betake themselves to him for shelter: So that hereby the ungodly are declared righteous, because, through the Cautioner's payment and satisfaction, their sin is not imputed to them; and they are declared free, because of his paying of their debt for them. 4. Would ye know the reason of this, how it comes that faith justifies in its resting on Christ? It is not because of any worth in itself, nor because of any account that is made of its worth, but because it rests on

Christ's righteousness, and takes hold of the benefit of Christ's purchase: Therefore it is added, *Because he shall bear their iniquities*, because by faith they take hold of his sufferings and satisfaction; whereby their sin is taken away, and God becomes well pleased with them for his sake. This then is a most material place of scripture, and we had need, in entring upon it, to have an eye to this *righteous Servant*, that he would be pleased to make the meaning of it known to us, and to give us the right understanding of this great mystery.

First, In general, observe here, in what estate men are naturally, and as abstracted from Christ: They are unjustified, and lying under God's curse, obnoxious to his wrath; this is supposed: Consider men then in their natural estate, this is it, they are even obnoxious to the wrath and curse of God, which is ready to seize upon them for their breach of God's covenant, and for provoking of him by sin; if men thought seriously on this, how could they sleep, or have peace, not knowing when they may be arrested, and put in prison, till they pay the uttermost farthing, which will never be? O that ye knew and believed this, who are ready to defy any that will offer to charge you with one penny of debt, and who walk up and down without all fear of your hazard? Lay your natural estate to heart, and ye will have quite other thoughts of yourselves.

2*dly*, Observe the way how freedom from this debt of sin, and from liableness to the curse, is derived; and to this, many things concur, each of which hath its own place. 1. The Mediator and his satisfaction; this is the ground of the freedom. 2. The covenant of redemption, and the promise made to the Mediator in it, *He shall see his seed*, &c. *He shall see of the travel of his soul, and shall be satisfied; By his knowledge shall many be justified*, &c. wherein it is articled, that those for whom he suffered shall be pardoned and set free: And it is this that gives sinners access to expect the benefit of Christ's sufferings: otherwise, tho' Christ had suffered, they had not been the better of his sufferings, if this covenant had not been, which gives them warrant to lay hold on the same: ere faith can act on Christ's sufferings, it must have this ground laid down, That it hath a warrant by vertue of this covenant to lay hold on them. 3. The knowledge and offer of this mysterious contrivance of grace, is also necessary, and doth concur to bring about the freedom: This must be manifested, that there is such a Saviour, such a satisfaction, and such a covenant, wherein

the

the ground is laid down, and a warrant given, by vertue of this covenant to make use of Christ's satisfaction, and to come by the benefit of it; this is implied in that word, *His knowledge*: So, *Rom.* x. it is said, *How shall they believe in him, of whom they have not heard?* which says plainly, that there cannot be faith, except knowledge preceed. I observe this the rather, because many think to come to heaven without knowledge, and so continue still in their ignorance: But ere there can be found faith, there must necessarily be some measure of knowledge of these things that are necessary to be known; as that we are sinners, and that we are lost in ourselves, that Jesus Christ is the alone propitiation for sin, and that, according to the covenant of grace, they that believe on him shall be absolved and set free. 4. There is a concurring of faith, for taking hold of this benefit of offered salvation through Christ: How faith concurs with Christ's satisfaction, in order to the making of our peace with God, we shall not now stand to speak particularly; only in general, it is by his knowledge that it justifies: For, tho' he have sufficient righteousness, and tho' the covenant give warrant to take hold of it, yet, if there be not an actual taking hold of it, it will not profit us; therefore, Rom. iii. 22. and ix, 30. it is called, *The righteousness which is by faith in him*; and Rom. iv. 5. the apostle saith, *To him that worketh not, but believeth on him that justifieth the ungodly, his faith is counted to him for righteousness*. It is not faith without its Object Christ, nor the Object Christ without faith; but it is faith taking hold of him as its Object, by which we have access to plead for absolution: Without Christ, our faith will do us no good; and without faith, Christ will not profit us; for, without faith, we have no title to Christ: And each of these would be put in their own room and place; Christ in his room, and faith in its room, as the condition on which his purchase is made offer of to us.

More particularly let me, *First*, Consider the title that Christ gets in these words; he is called the Lord's *Servant*, and his *righteous Servant*.

1st, As for *Servant*, It looks to him as Mediator, as this whole *Chapter*, with Chapter xlii. 1. and liii. 13. do abundantly clear: Christ Jesus then, as Mediator, is the Lord's Servant: or he, in performing the office of Mediator, is his Father's Servant; so the Lord calls him, *Psal.* lxxxix. 19. when he says, *I have laid help upon One that is mighty, I have found David my Servant*, &c. For he is there speaking of Jesus Christ, with whom the covenant of grace, as with the Head of the confederated party, is principally made. It imports these *Four*, which may be as so many reasons of this designation. 1. An humiliation, and inferiority in respect of God, as it is said, *Phil.* ii. *He humbled himself, and became of no reputation*:: In which respect, he himself says, that *the Father is greater than he*; and that *he is sent*, that he came not to do his own will, but the will of him that sent him. This holds forth a great wonder in the dispensation of grace, that the Father's Fellow and Equal, he that was Lord and Master of all, should become a Servant in the work of redemption, for the saving of souls: This must sure be a great work, wherein the Son becomes a Servant, as it must be a greater wonder, that grace so far condescended, as to make him, who is the Prince of life, to become a Servant: And we would look at it as a much greater, and far more momentuous business, than we use to do, to get a soul saved. 2. It imports his prerogative, as being singularly and eminently God's Servant; he is called, *Heb.* xiii. 20. *The great Shepherd*; so may he be called the great Steward and Deputy over all the Lord's house; So then, he is a singular, choice, and non-such Servant; *Behold*, says Jehovah, *Isaiah* xlii. 1. *my Servant whom I uphold, mine Elect in whom my soul delighteth*: Tho' all be God's servants, yet in this respect, he is singularly, and solely a Servant, as he is great Lord-deputy, made Head over all things to the Church, who was before all things, and is preferred to all things. This is very comfortable to believers, to consider, that tho' our Lord Jesus be a Servant, yet he is a choice and singular Servant, Administrator, and Steward for their good, it being for them that he becomes a Servant. 3. It imports the particular task or work that is laid on him, and the commission that he hath gotten to follow forth and prosecute that work; which is the main reason of this designation of a *Servant*, because he is intrusted with carrying on the great work of the redemption of elect sinners: Therefore he says, *I came not to do my own will, but the will of him that sent me, and to finish his work*; and, *I have finished the work which thou gavest me to do*; because he is particularly intrusted with the bringing about of that work. He hath gotten so many given him to redeem and save, to whom he is appointed a Shepherd, a Head, and Overseer or Bishop? Therefore he calls himself the *good Shepherd*, and is called by the apostle, the *Shepherd and Bishop* (or **Overseer**) of souls: And of all that

that are given him he loseth none, but maketh account of them all. And this is yet more comfortable, when we consider that Christ is not a Servant simply, but a Servant commissionate to gather in souls, to bring home the lost sheep of the house of *Israel*; this is his office and service, even to satisfy for the sins of such, to destroy the power that the devil hath over them, and so subdue sin in them. 4. It imports this, that the work which he performs, in the redeeming of souls, is so acceptable to God, and doth so mightily concur and co-operate, to the promoting of his design, that the Lord owns every thing that he performs, as performed by his great Ambassador, and by him, who hath the trust of all the affairs of his house committed to him; so that our Lord Jesus, in performing the work of redemption, cannot but be acceptable to Jehovah, because it is a performing of that with which he hath intrusted him: Therefore, *John* iv. he says, that *it is his meat to do his Father's will, and to finish his work*; and to this purpose, he says to his supposed father, and to his mother, *Luke* ii. 49. *Wist ye not that I must be about my Father's business?* It is his business, because it is so on the matter, it is so accounted of, and comes to be so in the end; and therefore in the 10*th verse* of this *Chap*. it is said, *The pleasure of the Lord shall prosper in his hand.*

2*dly*, As for his being the Lord's *righteous Servant*; he is not only a Servant, but an excellent Servant; not righteous simply, as he is God only; nor righteous simply, as he is Man; but righteous, in the administration of his offices, and in the discharge of the great trust committed to him. Whence observe, ' That our Lord Jesus, in per' forming of the office and work of Mediation and ' redemption, is most trusty and faithful.' There is not any the least fault or failing in his performing of it: He is the Lord's Servant, that never wronged his Master, who never miscarried in his commission, nor mismanaged it in the least; saith he, *I have finished the work which thou gavest me to do.* If we look a little to the qualifications, that shine eminently in the administration of his office, they will make out this; for he administrates them. 1. Wonderfully wisely. 2. Very tenderly. 3. Most diligently and effectually. 4. With all faithfulness: Thus doth he intirely and holily, without the least touch of unrighteousness, perform all the trust committed to him, and that both towards God, and towards the sheep; so as he is eminently, by the Lord's own testimony, *his righteous Servant*, with whom he is well pleased, and cannot but be well pleased. It will not be needful to separate these qualifications of his service in the administration of his offices: In speaking to them, we shall only desire you to take notice of some few places of scripture that hold them out, the first whereof is that, Isa. xl. 11. *He shall feed his flock like a shepherd, he shall gather the lambs with his arm, and carry them in his bosom, and gently lead those that are with young:* Never shepherd was so careful of his flock, for he feeds them, and in feeding them waits diligently on them, and takes them to these places where it is best for them to feed: He thinks fit now and then, it is true, that dogs be hounded at them, yet he is so warm to, and tender of them, that he gathers them with his arm, and he is so dexterous and skilful in conducting them, that he gently leads them that are with young; that is, such of them as are in pangs of the new-birth, he will by no means over-drive: To speak it with reverence, he is as a skilful midwife, to make those that are with child safely to bring forth; well then may he get this name, of the Lord's *righteous Servant*. The next place is, Isa. xlii. 1, 2, 3, 4. *Behold my Servant whom I uphold, my Elect in whom my soul delighteth; I have put my Spirit upon him, he shall bring forth judgment to the Gentiles: He shall not cry, nor lift up, nor cause his voice to be heard in the street: A bruised reed shall he not break, and the smoking flax shall he not quench: he shall bring forth judgment unto truth,* &c. Is there not here a wonderful commendation that the Father gives to the Son, and that the gracious Master gives to the righteous Servant in his offices? He is his elect choice Servant, in whom his soul delights; he does not cry, nor lift up his voice; he is busier about his work, than in making any din about it; there is no frowardness in his way, but he is tender of souls, that are like to a bruised reed, and smoking flax; he will not break the one, nor put out the other; where a soul is weak, or wounded, he will not break or bruise it, by a rough touch, or word; and where there are the least breathings of sincere desires after him, he will not quench, nor stifle them: And tho' the task be great that he hath in hand, he fails not in going through with it; he sits not up, nor is he discouraged under it, notwithstanding of all the wrath he hath to meet with in his way: Therefore when the cup is put in his hand, at which his holy human nature some way shrunk and scarred, yet he takes it pleasantly, saying, *But for this cause came I unto this hour;* and
pro-

prosecuted his work couragiously and constantly, till he bring forth judgment to victory, and till he gain his point: This shews him to be a most choice and faithful servant. A 3*d* place is Isa. lii. 13. *Behold my Servant shall deal prudently*, &c. It cannot be imagined, what a spiritual canny and dexterous way he hath in the saving of souls, and how wisely and prudently he pursues that work. There is a 4*th* place, Psal. lxxxix. 19, 20. *I have laid help upon One that is mighty, I have exalted One chosen out of the people, I have found David my Servant: The enemy shall not exact upon him*, &c. He is so dexterous and powerful, that the devil shall gain no ground of him, but he shall gain ground of him, and defeat him; so that we come after only to gather the spoil. *He is able to save to the uttermost* (as it is, Heb. vii. 26.) *all that come unto God through him*; and near the close of that Chap. it is said, *Such an high Priest became us, who is holy, harmless, separate from sinners, made higher than the heavens.* These are his qualifications, he is an holy and harmless high Priest, a sweet and (to say so) illess Mediator, by whom there was never any hurt; his ill was never heard of, in the place where he was: He was undefiled, pure and spotless, in the management of all the trust committed to him; there was never any thing done by him, of which it could be said, that it might have been done better: He is separate from sinners, and so another kind of high Priest than those who were before him; and all this, both as to God, so as he could say, and go to death with it, *It is finished;* and as to them that were intrusted to him, so as he could say, *Of all that thou hast given me, I have lost none*; he makes a full and faithful account of all committed to him.

This is a plain, and yet a most useful truth: For *use* of it, behold here, and wonder at the way of grace, that not only gives a Mediator, but such a Mediator, who (as it is, Heb. iii.) *is faithful over the house of God:* This is the very life of our consolation, that we have an able Mediator, a good Shepherd, a wise, prudent tender One, and faithful; and indeed it would well become us to wonder more that the Lord in the way of his grace hath thus condescended; and it should exceedingly provoke us to be thankful on this account, that not only there is a way of grace, but such a way of grace found out and established, whereby we have such an high Priest, that manages all so well, and so dexterously. O have ye ever suitably prized this, that God hath given such a righteous and faithful Mediator and Servant! I fear many suffer this most observable dispensation to pass without due observation. Though the Lord Jehovah speaks not of him, without commending him; yet wretched and ungrateful we, can, alas! speak of him, and hear him spoken of, with hearts very little affected: Believers may be ashamed of this; we think lamentably little of him, we esteem not suitably of him; when we see him, there is scarce any form or beauty seen in him, wherefore we should desire him; we do in a great measure undervalue this way of grace's administration, that should be in a special manner ravishing to us, that we are thereby brought under such a tutory.

The 2*d Use* is for believers comfort and encouragement; O but they are happy, that have committed themselves to him, as to a faithful Shepherd and Overseer! They may be sure that he is a notable and non-such Overseer, as might be more fully cleared, if we would descend to the particulars of believers need: Have they little grace? is it scarce smoking? he is not a rigid task-master, like to the *Egyptians*, nay, nor like to the law, he quenches not the smoking flax. Are they staggering because of apprehended or real weakness, and their hearts shaking like the trees in the wood, or rather like so many straws? they may with comfort give him the oversight of them; he will not break the bruised reed, he will bear the heaviest end of his own yoke. Have they a straying disposition? Are they like young wanton lambs leaping out from the rest? He will gather them with his arm; and when he takes a rougher way, yet grace shines still in it. Are they fainting and swooning? he will take them into his bosom; he will lead the blind, he bears the weak, he hath a way of supporting his own that is most tender; *My grace* (says he to Paul) *is sufficient for thee; my strength is made perfect in weakness*. Are there any of them with child, (to speak so) or is their bringing forth quick and lively? He gently leads those that are with young, and will not suffer them to miscarry, in the bringing forth; he will *not put new wine into old bottles, he will not cause to travel, and not make to bring forth:* The Lord hath given believers such a Servant as they stood in need of, even a righteous Servant, suited every way to their condition, who will not be behind, nor wanting, in looking to the least wrigling (to speak so) under his care and over-sight.

It serves therefore, in the 3*d* place, to reprove the suspicions and jealousies that believers have often of Christ, who are disposed to say with the
Psalmist,

falmift, Pfal. lxxvii. *I said, My hope and my strength is perished from the Lord; will the Lord cast off for ever? will he be favourable no more? is his mercy clean gone for ever? doth his promise fail for evermore? hath he forgotten to be gracious?* &c. Nay, the jealoufy and mifbelief of fome ferious fouls will fometimes talk at this rate, I may give it over, this work will never go with me. Beware, I befeech you, of this; for the language of it is, that our Lord is not a righteous Servant: Let therefore your fpirits be calmed, and pray the Lord to command a calm in them which are committed to him. Befpeak your fouls, as David did his, Pfal. xlii. *Why art thou cast down, O my soul? and why art thou disquieted in me? Trust in God;* for he is faithful (as if he had faid) that he hath the overfight of me: And effay, with Paul, to be in cafe to fay, *I know whom I have believed*, and fo fhall not be afhamed; *I am perfuaded that he is able to keep that which I have committed to him, against that day*; I know that he is fuch a Chrift, that I commit myfelf to, who is fo fkilful, dexterous, tender, and faithful in keeping that which is given to him. And is not this moft comfortable, and a notable ground of quietnefs, that our Mediator is fuch as cannot mifcarry? and may it not fhame believers, when either they adventure upon any thing alone without him, or when they commit themfelves to him, and yet do not fo intirely truft him, but entertain fufpicions and jealoufies of him, and think, becaufe their fpark is not a fire or a flame, but fmokes only, that therefore it will die out, and be utterly quenched, as if he could not keep it in, and increafe it, and becaufe they cannot guide themfelves, think that they will utterly mifcarry, as if he had not arms to carry them? Indeed prefumption is to be abhorred, but fuch as are fled into him would truft in him fo far as to keep up their hearts in him, and would ftudy to be cheerful in him,

and to walk up and down in his ftrength; this is certainly called for from you: Therefore be content to be born by him, where you cannot go your felf.

Use 4. Is he fuch a righteous Servant? Then let me fay, Are there any of you that need to fear, or to have the leaft hink, or hefitation, to commit yourfelves to him? And fhould it not be a motive to prefs you to give him credit? For he fays, John vi. 39, 40. that it is his commiffion and fervice to keep them which are committed to him, and to raife them up at the laft day, and to give them eternal life; and he is righteous and faithful in performing of it: If fo, then credit the falvation of your fouls to this righteous Servant; *commit your souls to this righteous Servant in well-doing to him, as unto a faithful Creator;* never be at peace, nor at cafe, till ye be under his charge and keeping; and though ye be as little lambs, as weak wriglings or heavy with young, it is the lefs matter, if ye be of his flock, ye fhall be preferved: Is it poffible that ye can be right, if ye be from under his care and cuftody? Nay, it is utterly impoffible, that ye can be fecure, but under his care; and it is as impoffible, but that ye muft be fafe, if ye be under his care and overfight; and therefore endeavour to be within the reach of it, and to count yourfelves happy, when ye do fincerely give him credit; and to believe that ye are in greateft hazard, when ye take moft on yourfelves. What a fhame will it be to many, who have heard that Chrift was fuch a Servant, and yet they would not take his fervice to bring them through to heaven? Thus it ftands with you, to whom he is fpoken of in the gofpel, ye fhall be found either to have accepted or rejected him, according as by faith ye yield yourfelves to him, or by unbelief ye refufe to clofe with him: Let not this word flip, as many have done. And the Lord himfelf make you wife, to make choice in time of the fervice of this righteous Servant, for your juftification and falvation.

SERMON LI.

Ifaiah liii. 11.------*By his knowledge shall my righteous Servant justify many.*

IF we had fuch thoughts of the falvation of our own fouls, as the Lord had, and ftill hath, of the falvation of fouls, we could not but be more ferioufly concerned about them, and more taken up, how to get them faved: This work of the falvation of finners did before the world was (to fpeak fo with reverence) take up the Perfons of the glorious Godhead; and was fingled out, and made choice of, as an employment worthy of the Son of God, who was chofen for this very work, that by him many might be juftified and faved; for the accomplifhment of which, he became a Servant: Muft it not then be an excellent work, that none but he could be trufted with, who is Heir of all things, and by whom the world was made?

We fhew you the meaning of thefe words the laft day, and obferved two things from this defignation, that our Lord gets here. " 1. That our
" Lord

"Lord Jesus, in the work of mediation, and of
" the redemption of sinners, was God's Servant."
Not so much to denote his being inferior, as Mediator, to the Father; as to hold forth his being commissionated for this service, and the Lord accepting of him in it. " 2. That our Lord Jesus
" did excellently discharge this trust committed
" to him." Therefore he is not only called a *Servant*, but *my righteous Servant*, as having most faithfully acquitted himself, and as being fully approven and accepted in the trust committed to him. When the Lord speaks so of Christ, it ought mightily to engage us to be much in love with God, who hath given such a faithful Mediator and Servant; and with Jesus Christ, that condescended to take the trust of poor sinners salvation, and that doth so kindly discharge it. There are some things here, that may be passingly hinted at, and then we shall come more closely and particularly to the words.

1. Then, observe, "That it is a privilege and
" prerogative to be God's Servant." Therefore it is mentioned here, as a piece of the Mediator's privilege: It is true he was singularly and eminently a Servant, even the Lord's choice Servant, in whom his soul delighted, and does delight, above what any other can be capable of; yet to be a servant to God, to take direction from him, to do his will, to seek his honour, to give obedience to him, in what he calleth for, is certainly a privilege, and a great one; yea, it is spoken of as a privilege of glorified saints in heaven, Rev. xxii. 3. "His servants shall serve him:" And if it be a privilege in heaven, we would think it so here on earth; and yet, if the language of our hearts were known, there would be found a secret disdaining of, and repining at service to God, and a saying on the matter, *Let us break his bands asunder, and cast away his cords from us.* But, know ye what ye are doing? even disclaiming and despising that which is your great privilege: All these that are in heaven, and all those who are in a right frame on earth, count it their privilege to be his servants; and we are commanded to pray, "Thy will be done
" on earth, as it is done in heaven;" or, Be thou served on earth, as thou art in heaven: Therefore it ought to be accounted of, as a privilege, as a great and glorious privilege, to be his servants.

2. Observe, " That the Lord can tell exactly
" and infallibly, how every servant carries himself;
" who are ill and slothful, and who are good and
" faithful servants; who are righteous servants according to their measure, and who not." Will he take notice how Christ carries himself in his service and trust, and will he not take notice of others? Most certainly he will; and therefore, Mat. xxv. and Luke xix. he calls the servants to a reckoning, to whom the talents are given; and as they have made use of them, and improved them, or not, so doth he commend and reward them, or not: There are none of us, but have gotten some one talent and trust or another, and no doubt, there will be much to reckon for; I am afraid, that when he calls us all to an account, though there will be some to whom it will be said, *Well done, good and faithful servant*; there will be many to whom it will be said, *Thou evil and slothful servant*: And the *slothful servant* will be found to be the *ill servant*; and, amongst other aggravations of his guilt, this will be one, that he was unlike to Christ the righteous Servant.

3. Observe, "That the right improvement and
" discharge of the trust committed to us, and of
" our service to God, is a commendable and honourable thing." It is recorded here, to Christ's commendation, that he was a *righteous Servant*, even faithful over the house of God, in all things: and proportionally is the commendation of the ordinary under-servants, when they, in their places and stations, perform their service honestly and faithfully, so as they may be accepted of God on his account: The day is coming when every man's work will be rewarded; and as we sow, so we shall reap; in that day, if we had all the world, we would give it, to hear that word from Christ's mouth, "Well done, thou good and faithful servant;" but few will get that testimony. Ye think it much now, to get a name of fidelity amongst men, and to be esteemed such as keep your word, and will not break your promise, nor parole, (and it's good in so far, that it be so) but many such will be found to have broken many a word to God, and falsified many a promise: Think upon it, and lay it to heart, that it will be better to have a word of testimony from God in that day, and to have it said to you by him, Faithful servant, thou improved well the little that I gave thee; it was laid out, and expended, not so much to buy and to put on brave clothes, nor to buy or build fine houses, as it was for me, and for my honour; whatever place, station, capacity or employment thou wast in, thou endeavoured to do good in it; and when thou couldst not do for my work, for my people, and for my honour, thou wast praying for them; and when thou had an opportunity to hear my word, thou didst not slight, nor let that slip:

This

This, I say, will be better than a great name and testimony from and amongst men; but alas, we fear that it shall be said of many, Ye had many opportunities of getting and doing good, but what use made ye of them? It had been better that ye had never had them, it had been better that ye had never had a groat or two pence, than to have had all these riches; and to have had none, rather than to have had such and such a lucrative or gainful place and employment, which ye improved not for God. It is a sore matter, that we should preach, and ye should hear these general truths of the gospel, from day to day, and that yet they do not sink into your hearts. Ye will not readily deny, that there is a day of reckoning coming, and that it will be a great favour to be commended of him in that day; and yet, how few do by their practice evidence, that they lay weight on it? It is very sad that religion should be so trifled in. Many of you will come to the church, and seem there, and in your other carriage, as if ye were going to heaven; when, in the mean time, ye have few serious thoughts, either of heaven or of hell: But in that day wherein ye shall stand trembling before his tribunal, and shall there receive the sentence of an evil and slothful servant, ye will find to your cost, that there was weight in these truths, that now ye take but little notice of.

4. In general, Observe, "That it is singular, " proper and peculiar to our Lord Jesus, to be " God's approven Servant, so as to be without all " ground of challenge, in the discharge of his du- " ty and trust." And indeed there is no righteous servant, in this sense, but he only, who according to the very rigour of the law, was such; the law could not charge him with any the least violation of it, or want of conformity unto it, for " he ful- " filled all righteousness." We spake to this on verse 9. and shall not now insist on it: Only it is a sore matter, that this truth should be called in question, and called an untruth in those days; and that men should say, that this designation and title is not proper to Christ, but that it is common to all true Christians, as if they were all free of sin; and that not by the imputation of Christ's righteousness to them, but by their own doing of righteousness: Lord save us! what a high injury is this to the Son of God? and what gross ignorance is here of the corruption of man's nature, which in the best and holiest of mere men is never in this life finally expelled, as the scriptures of the Old and New Testament most convincingly clear! and what a wronging is this of the truth of God, which holds forth our Lord Jesus, as singled out to be, and who

is designed by this name, *The Lord's righteous Servant!* Now, if there were any more properly so called, we could not say that it were meant of him. But it is not very profitable to insist in speaking of these dotages and foolries.

But to come more particularly to the benefits that flow from, and come by this *righteous Servant*, and from the service intrusted to him, and so faithfully managed and discharged by him: " By " his knowledge (saith Jehovah) shall he justify ma- " ny;" that is, his service is to absolve sinners, and set them free from the guilt of sin, and from the curse that naturally they are under, and liable to.

Looking on these words in the connexion with the former, we shall observe three or four things, ere we come to the more close and particular consideration of the words in themselves.

The *1st* of which is this, " That the justifying " of many sinners, even of all the elect, is the spe- " cial trust committed by Jehovah, to the Media- " tor; It is in this especially wherein his service " consists." Would ye then know, what is the employment of this righteous Servant? It is even this, " he shall justify many;" he shall procure their absolution from the guilt of sin, and from the curse of God, and shall set them free from the judgment which the law hath against them, whereby they are laid under the curse, for disobedience thereunto: This we may consider, 1. As it relates to God; and so it imports, that the justification of sinners is very acceptable to him: For it is that for which he hath given a commission to the Mediator; and what he hath commissioned him in, the performance of it must needs be acceptable to him: Therefore, that which is here called *the Lord's service*, is called *the Lord's pleasure*, verse 10. to wit, to see a poor sinner brought in by the Mediator, and on the account of his satisfaction justified; he is pleased with, and takes it well. 2. It may be considered as it looks to the Mediator; and so it speaks out the Mediator's design and work: It is that wherein he is employed, and with which he is taken up, even to get elect sinners brought from under the curse of God, and freely justified through himself; So that, if ye would know what is the sum and effect of Christ's errand and work in the world, here it is, *he came to save sinners*, as it is, Tim. i. 15. *He came to seek and to save that which was lost*, to bring home the lost sheep on his shoulder, to seek and find the lost groat, and to reclaim prodigals, as it is, Luke xv. This is his meat and his drink, his work and business, as himself says, John iv. 34. " My meat is to do the " will of him that sent me, and to finish his work;"

and

18. he bids sinners *come and buy of him eye-salve, gold, and white raiment*; he hath eye-salve for the blind, gold to inrich the poor, garments for the naked; and in a word, every thing that is needful for sinners. It is comfortable to hear that Christ is a Servant; but to hear that this is his service, to justify sinners, and that he is so well fitted for it, makes it so much the more comfortable: and were we suitably sensible of sin, and did we thoroughly believe this truth, our hearts would *laugh* within us, as Abraham's once did, to know that this was given to Christ in commission to justify sinners, and that he is so well fitted for this business that he is commissioned about and employed in; especially now, when he is so busy about this work and employment, for tho' he be ascended on high, yet *he hath received gifts for*, and given them to *men, even for the rebellious, that God the Lord might dwell among them*; as it is, Psal. lxviii. compared with Eph. iv. This is the end of the ministry and ordinances, even to further this work of the justification of sinners, that by acknowledging and making use of Christ, this work may be brought about, and this effect made to follow: This is the end of fasts and communions, even to arrest perishing sinners a while, to tryst and treat with him about the concerns of their souls; these are special seasons for putting him to exerce his office in justifying of them: And this day this scripture is fulfilled in your ears, and ye should let it sink in your hearts, that our Lord Jesus is pursuing his commission, and performing his service, keeping up the treaty, and inviting and persuading sinners to come to him, that the pleasure of the Lord may prosper in his hand. And therefore know assuredly, that this is it, that Christ is employed in, and taken up with, even to get sinners freed from the guilt of sin and from wrath by his righteousness; it is not only, nor mainly, to get them brought to the church, and to his supper, or to get them made formal, and to abstain from cursing, swearing and profanity, (tho' these will follow of will) but it is to get them brought in to himself, and justified. And we have these two words to say to you further in this matter, 1. There is here good ground of encourage-

" should raise him up at the last day;" which is in sum, " that by his knowledge many should be " justified." And it is added, " For he shall " bear their iniquities," to anticipate and answer an objection: For a sensible sinner might say, How can I be justified, that have so many sins? here is a solution of that doubt, he " shall satisfy for them." All these words are (as it were) big with child of consolation, being the very heart and life of the gospel, as any thing that comes so near to Christ's commission, and unfolds so much of it, is. A 2d word is this, That ye mistake Christ's errand, work and service very far, who think to content him, and put him off with this; who would give him the name of a Saviour, and yet would be at the saving of yourselves without him; who would compliment him (as it were) with fair generals, but will have none of his physick, or of his cures, nor will renounce your own righteousness, and make use of his, for your justification: this says one of these four, Either that he is not commissionated, and trusted for this end; or, that he is not meet for that trust; or that he is not faithful in it; or else, that ye can do your own turn without him, and that there is no need of his office: And which of all these can abide the trial before God? And yet it shall be upon one of these that ye shall be found to have cast at Christ, and to have refused to permit him, (so far as ye could hinder and obstruct) to do his Father's business; and if ye adjust not accompts with him, there will be a most dreadful reckoning betwixt God and you.

2dly, Observe, That this particular trust anent the justifying of sinners, our Lord Jesus doth most righteously, diligently, dexterously, tenderly and faithfully discharge. It was his Father's will, that he should be baptized, and fulfil all righteousness; and more especially that he should justify many: In this he is very skilful and faithful, and it is on this account he is called *the good Shepherd*, and that he is said to *lay down his life for his sheep*: that he is called, *a faithful high Priest*, and is said to be One that is *able to save to the uttermost those that come unto God through him*; and that he is

arm, he carries them in his bosom, and gently leads those that are with young; and chap. xlii. 3. that *a bruised reed he will not break, and the smoking flax he will not quench:* And it is said, 1 John ii. *If any man sin, we have an Advocate with the Father;* and who is he? *Jesus Christ the righteous;* righteous in the faithful managing of his trust, by making sinners peace with God. Would ye know then, in what respects, or on what account it is, that Christ is called a *righteous Servant?* We answer, In these respects, 1. Tho' we have failed and broken the law, yet he hath not; and God will not look down on him. 2. In this respect, that he pleads for no sinners pardon, but he can fully pay their debt, and hath done it: If he seek one thing from God, he yields in another, and according to the covenant of redemption exactly proceeds; for he is a propitiation: He seeks nothing but he pays for it, and wrongs not him in the least who hath trusted him; the Lord Jehovah is not a loser, but hath his honour restored by him. 3. In respect of his keeping faith to the persons that have need of him, for whom he hath undertaken: He is not only faithful to the Master, but to the children and servants; he owns and acknowledges them, when they come to him under their necessities, and is forthcoming to them, every way suitable and answerable to his place and trust, in doing good to sinners.

Use. Had we sensible sinners to speak to, sinners groaning under a body of death, with pricked hearts crying out, What shall we do for the wrongs that we have done to God? Sinners under holy fear to spoil and mar the bargain, and to hazard their own souls; had we (I say) such sinners to speak to, there are good news here to them: The trust of saving souls is committed to a faithful Shepherd; it is not committed to yourselves, for so it had been a doleful trust; but it is committed to him, that hath gotten the sheep by name given to him, to be kept by him, and he will not suffer them to miscarry, nor to go quite wrong: And what more would ye have? A salvation and a price is much, but it is more to have a Saviour to make the application of his purchase, Bishop of souls to justify and carry sinners, and if any such do trust him with the salvation of their souls, he is faithful, and will not suffer them to perish.

3dly, From comparing these words, "By his "knowledge he shall justify many," with the former, "He shall see of the travel of his soul, and "shall be satisfied;" We observe, "That our "Lord Jesus is never satisfied with sinners, nor "content till he be employed by them in this piece "of service, even to justify them by his know- "ledge, or by faith in him." He gets not satisfaction for the travel of his soul till this be, and this is it which satisfies him: He cares not for compliments, great professions of respect to religion, and Hosanna's, without this; he wept over Jerusalem, notwithstanding of these, because of the want of this: He cares not for Martha's cumbersom service, but is content of Mary's sitting down to hear and receive his word; if he get not this employment, no other thing will content him, as we may see in these three parables, Luke xv. when the lost sheep is amissing, he is not satisfied till it be brought home; the making the house clean will not please him, if the lost piece of money be not found; the finding whereof brings out that, Come and rejoice with me: And when the prodigal returns then, and not till then, are uttered these joyful words, "This my son was dead, and is alive; he was lost, and is found: Then comes the mirth, and all the minstrels are yoked. Would ye lay the hair of your head under Christ's feet, would ye give him thousands of rams, and rivers of oil, and the first-born of your bodies for the sin of your souls; all these will not please him, if ye get not yourselves to be justified by his knowledge; nothing will content and satisfy him but that: The reasons are, 1. Because he gets not his work, intrusted to him, carried on otherwise (if I may speak so) for as the Father delights to see the work which he hath trusted him with prospering, so doth he. 2. Because he gets not the native credit and honour of his office, till he get this, but counts himself to be like to an Ambassador, who comes to woo a wife for the King his

his Master, who is well treat and entertained, but gets a refusal of what he came for: It was the disciples commendation, John xvii. that they received his word; though all other things could be, if this be not, he never gets kindly respect. 3. Because, without this, folk can never love Christ; for it is this benefit of justification and pardon of sin, that much engages to love and praise him: *Because* (say and sing the redeemed, Rev. v. 9.) *thou hast redeemed us to God by thy blood, thou art wo thy to receive all praise, dominion, power, and glory.* It is impossible that they can suitably esteem of him, and love him, who are not justified by him; and therefore they that believe not on him to justification, are called *despisers of him, and treaders of the blood of the covenant under foot*; and they fall under that sad complaint which is made, John i. 11. *He came to his own, and his own received him not; he was in the world, and the world was made by him, and the world knew him not.* There is then a necessity laid upon you, either to give him employment in this, or to ly under his displeasure, and to be made countable for standing in the way, so far as ye could, of his satisfaction. The Lord hath so moulded the way of his grace, that not only he doth invite and allure sinners but also he lays strong bonds on them for their good, and leaves it not indifferent to them, to make use of Christ, or not, for their justification; but they must either take this way, or have God and the Mediator to be their enemies, in the greatest measure, and in the highest degree: Choose you then, whether ye will satisfy Christ Jesus or not. How shall he be satisfied? will ye say: Even by your betaking of yourselves to him, and by improving his righteousness, for your peace with God, and for your justification before him; humbly pleading guilty at the bar of justice, and begging pardon and acceptance on the account of his satisfaction, and by faith extracting your discharge and absolution, that so the application of his purchase being obtained, the conscience may be quieted on that ground. And do ye think this a matter to cast out with Christ about, that he would have you justified, and that ye will not; that he would have you washen in his blood from your sins, and that ye had rather ly still in them? Think ye this reasonable? And yet thus it stands with you; and we declare it to you in his name, that Christ and ye shall never be friends, except on these terms, that ye take with your sins, and natural enmity against God, and welcome heartily the news of a Mediator, and embrace his righteousness, trampling your own under your feet, as to all expectation of justification by it: that in a word ye do by faith take hold of the offer of salvation through him in the gospel, resigning yourselves absolutely to him, and founding your humble plea before God thereupon. This is the shield of faith that quenches the fiery darts of the devil, and that which gives wings to the soul, to flee to heaven upon; and we wot well this is no unfriendly message nor evil bargain, and ye may have it of him: He is indeed a dexterous and skilful Handler of souls, that commit themselves unto him; why do you not then, in his own way, hazard your souls on him? Were sinners hazard known, and what solid confidence they may have, in putting their souls in Christ's hand, they would be thronging in upon him, to get hold laid on his offer, which is like a banner displayed, and spread out in this word of the gospel, to which every one may put his hand: This is the very sum of the gospel, to pray you to be reconciled to God, to admit of the Mediator, and to give him a commission (to speak so with reverence) or rather to intreat him to make your peace, that is, to give him the credit of saving you; that if justice were pursuing you, ye might be found in him, not having your own righteousness, but his, and in him have one answer to all challenges; not thinking yourselves the less sicker and sure, that ye have given up with your own righteousness, and betaken yourselves to his. Who knows but souls might be getting good at such a time, if this were made use of, and believed? O so faithful as he is! he dare give his word and seal, that he will keep to you; and this is his end in word and sacrament, that sinners might be brought to trust in him, in giving him the employment to justify them; that they, being in themselves blind, may come to him for light; being poor, may come to him for gold to enrich them; being naked, may come to him for garments to clothe them; being ungodly, may come to him that he may justify them: But alas, people are for the most part senseless and regardless of their sin and misery, and therefore he gets no employment from them: Many sit very brave and fine here, and have no legal bar on them to keep them from the communion, who yet have sleepy and senseless souls, and are ruining and destroying themselves; this we assure you is the condition of many of you, who never knew to make use of Christ, and of his righteousness, and yet will boast of your faith, and of your good heart to God. Away with your old presumptuous faith, take with your unbelief and presumption; say not ignorantly, that ye shall do as you can, tho' ye cannot do as ye would: Ye are unsound at the heart, mistaken about your spiritual state; and know that the devil by a deceitful heart is speaking out of you such language; for it is enemies we are commissionated to reconcile, and it is b st sinners that Christ came to seek and save; and ye see not yourselves to be such, and therefore ye care not for such offers of grace: But ah! many of you, if grace prevent not, will get a cold welcome from Christ at that day, and will be made sadly to smart, for the slighting of many precious opportunities, which God did put in your hand, and whereof to make use ye had no heart.

SERMON LII.

Isaiah liii. 11.------*By his knowledge shall my righteous Servant justify many, for he shall bear their iniquities.*

THERE hath been much spoken from this sweet scripture of our Lord Jesus his sufferings, and somewhat also of the promises made to him, that his sufferings should not be for nought: In these words, we have a compendious explication of the effects that flow from them, by which he shall be satisfied for them all; which ye may take up in these four, 1. The great benefit itself, that is holden out here, and that is *justification*. 2. These to whom it shall come, it is *many;* so that his having a seed, spoken of, verse 10. is exponed here by this, that *many shall be justified.* 3. The way how this is derived to them, *by his knowledge;* which we shew, is to be understood of faith in him. 4. The ground from which this flows, and on which it is built, and that confirms it; *For he shall bear their iniquities;* and as it is in the following verse *he bare the sins of many*, and therefore they must be justified; it being but reason, that these many, whose iniquities he bears, and whose debt of sin he pays, should be justified.

We may speak more particularly to the explication of each of these, as we come to them. We shall then first expone and give the meaning of this word *justification*, or to *justify*, ere we come to the doctrine, because it will serve to clear it, and will make way for it, and so much the rather as it is the very hinge of the gospel, and that on which our salvation depends, tho' yet but very little and very ill understood; there being many that cannot tell what it is, tho' there be not many words more frequently mentioned in the scripture, and tho' it be that whereby a person is translated from the estate of enmity, into the state of friendship with God.

As for this word to *justify*, or *justification*, then, there are three senses given of it, two whereof are erroneous, and the last only is according to the mind of the Spirit of God speaking in the scripture, which we shall clear and confirm.

1st, Some take this word *physically*, as if it were to make just, by the infusing of habitual grace, or by a physical and real change; and, so taken, it is the same with that which we call sanctification: But in all the scripture, we know not one place, where necessarly the word is so to be understood; although this acceptation of the word, is the great rise of the Popish error, in that controversy concerning justification. *2dly*, Others take it for God's revealing, manifesting or declaring the way how a guilty person comes to be just: And so to justify, is for ministers to teach the way to people, how they may live holily; as it is said, Dan. xii. 3. *They that turn many to righteousness*, &c. By which sense, some wickedly and blasphemously detract from Christ's satisfaction, as if his justifying were no more, but a teaching of sinners the way how to be justified, to wit, by living holily and justly. But the word that follows in the text, *For he shall bear their iniquities*, cuts the throat of that exposition; for it is by Christ's bearing of the punishment of the elects iniquities, and for paying of their debt, that they come to be justified; therefore the one is given for a reason of the other. *3dly*, Considering the word according to the meaning of it in scripture, we take it for a *legal*, *forensick*, or *court word*, borrowed from mens courts, wherein a person arraigned for such a crime is either condemned or absolved; and when he is absolved, and declared to be acquitted or made free from that which is laid to his charge, he is said to be justified: So is it before God, and in his court; justification is the freeing of a sinner from the charge that the law giveth in against him, and the absolving and declaring of him to be free from the guilt of sin; and from the punishment thereof, which by the sentence of the law is due to him. The former two senses run to the making of a man to be inherently holy, or without a fault; which is, as if a guilty man, or a criminal, being sisted be-

fore

fore a civil court of judicature, were declared to be innocent: But this true meaning of the words sets out a man arraigned before God's tribunal, and charged with guilt, and found faulty, but absolved, and acquitted, not because he wants sin, but because his debt is paid, and his sins satisfied for by a Cautioner. Even as a man, that is called before a civil court for such a sum of money, and is found liable to the debt; but his cautioner coming in, and paying the debt for him, there is both in reason and law just ground why that man should be absolved, and declared free of the debt: So is it here, Christ Jesus taking on and satisfying for the debt of the elect, and procuring absolution for them for whom he hath paid the price; there is reason and ground in law that they should be justified and absolved. All these opinions agree in these two. 1. That men naturally have sin, and that they must count for it. 2. That this justification, whatever it be, where it is, doth fully absolve and acquit the sinner, and makes him free of sin, as to the guilt, the punishment, and consequents of it, death and the curse, as if he had never had sin. But the difference lieth here, that this last acceptation of the word, absolves a man, tho' he have sin in himself, by the interposing of a Surety and Cautioner, who pays his debt, and procures the sentence of absolution to him: And in this sense, justification is, as if a man were standing at the bar of God's tribunal guilty, and having a witness of his guilt in himself; and God, out of respect to the Mediator his satisfaction, and payment of his debt, which he hath laid hold upon by faith, does pronounce that sinful person to be free, absolved, and acquitted from the guilt and punishment of sin; and doth accordingly absolve him upon that account. So then, justification is not to be considered, as God's creating and infusing of gracious habits in us, but the declaring of us to be free, and acquitted from the guilt of sin, upon the account of Christ's satisfying for our debt.

This we will find to be very clear, if we consider how the word is taken, both in the Old and New testament, as namely, Isaiah v. 23. *Wo unto them that justify the wicked for a reward, and take away the righteousness of the righteous from him;* and Prov. xvii. 15. *He that justifieth the wicked, and he that condemneth the just, even they both are abomination to the Lord;* where the plain meaning of the word can be no other than this, that when a judge pronounces a man to be just, altho' he be unjust, it is a wicked thing, which the Lord abhors: And so, Psal. li. 4. *That thou mightest be justified when thou speakest, that is, that thou mightest be declared to be so;* and Matth. xi. 19. *Wisdom is justified of her children.* 2dly, We will find this meaning of the word to be clear, if we consider justification, as distinguished from sanctification; for in that Popish sense, they are both made one and the same: but they are distinguished in scripture; as, 1 Cor. vi. 11. *Such were some of you, but ye are washed, but ye are sanctified, but ye are justified;* where he looks on these two benefits of justification and sanctification as distinct, and distinguisheth the one of them from the other: Now, sanctification being the grace that renews our nature, and makes an inward spiritual change, justification must needs be that act of God's grace, that takes away the guilt of sin, and makes sinners to be friends with God, through Christ's righteousness; and so it is a relative change of their state. 3dly, It will be clear, if we consider to what it is opposed in scripture: It is not opposed to sinning, as sanctification is; but to these two, 1. To the charging of a sinner with somewhat unto condemnation: And, 2. To the act of condemning. Now the opposite to condemnation is absolution, as is clear, Rom. viii. 33. *Who shall lay any thing to the charge of God's elect? It is God that justifies, who shall condemn?* &c. God's justifying is put in as opposite to the charging and libelling of the elect, and to the condemning of them, therefore none of these can be: And so justification there, looks both to the part of an Advocate pleading and declaring a man to be free, and to the part of a Judge pronouncing him to be absolved and justified; which well agrees to our Lord Jesus, who justifies his people both ways. 4thly, It may also be cleared from parallel scriptures, where justifying is called reconciling; as 2 Cor. v. 18, 19, 20. *God was in Christ reconciling the world to himself, not imputing their trespasses unto them, and hath committed to us,* &c. And how that comes to pass, is told in the last verse *For he made him to be sin for us, who knew no sin, that we might be made the righteousness of God in him;* So that to be made the righteousness of God; is to be justified; and to be justified, is to be made friends with, or to be reconciled to God; and that not by working a moral change, but upon the account of Christ's satisfaction, bringing us into friendship with God. So, Eph. i. 6. where to be *justified*, is exponed to be made *accepted in the Beloved:* And what else is that, but to be in good terms with God, to have him passing by all quarrels, as having nothing to say against us, but accepting us through Christ as

righteous

righteous? So, Acts xiii. 38, 39. *Be it known unto you, that through this Man is preached unto you forgiveness of sins; and by him, all that believe are justified from all things, from which ye could not be justified by the law of* Moses. A place that clearly holds forth that as all the elect are naturally chargeable by the law, as been guilty of the breach thereof, and that they cannot be absolved from it by ought in themselves; so they are through faith in Jesus Christ freed from it; As if the Lord had said, Ye are freed from the sentence of the law, because through Christ is preached unto you remission of sins; and there is a way laid down for your absolution, who believe, from the guilt of sin, and from all the consequents of it. 5*thly*, It is clear from the text, because it is such a justifying, as hath in it Christ's being sentenced in our room, as the cause of it: Now, he was sentenced in our room, not by having sin infused in him, which were blasphemous to think, but by having our sin imputed to him; and therefore our justification must be our absolution, by having his righteousness imputed to us, as is clear throughout this chapter: Therefore it is said, *He hath carried our sorrows, and born our griefs; he was wounded for our transgressions, he was bruised for our iniquities, by his stripes we are healed, he laid on him the iniquity of us all;* and in these words, *By his knowledge shall my righteous Servant justify many, for he shall bear their iniquities.* It is a justification that comes to us by Christ's taking on our debt; and this we cannot imagine to be otherwise, but by a legal change, or by a change of law-rooms; he coming as Surety in our room, and we having absolution by vertue of his satisfaction: So that the meaning of the words in short is, as if the prophet had said, Would ye know what ye have by Christ's sufferings? even this, to wit, that *many, as many as whose iniquities he bore and satisfied for,* shall be acquitted and absolved from the guilt and punishment of their sin, through his satisfaction; they shall be freed from the sentence and curse of the law, which they deserved; and shall be declared righteous, through the righteousness of their Cautioner, which they have laid hold upon by faith.

Hence observe, " 1. That all men and women, " even all the elect themselves, are by nature liable " to an arraignment before the justice-seat of God." That they are justified, supposes a bringing of them, as it were, before his tribunal, ere they can be justified, and have the sentence of absolution past in their favours: The apostle takes this for granted, Rom. xiv. 10. *We shall all stand before the judgment-seat of Christ;* and Heb. ix. 27. *It is appointed for all men, once to die, and after that comes the judgment;* there is a solemn decree past, that as all men shall die, so every man shall be brought to a reckoning and judgment: And Acts xvii. 31. *He hath appointed a day in which he shall judge the world in righteousness,* &c. and that cannot be reversed: See 2 Cor. v. 10. *For we must all appear before the judgment-seat of Christ;* we *must*, there is an unavoidable necessity of it. For further clearing and confirming of this, ye would know, that there are *three* courts, that especially the hearers of the gospel are liable unto, which we would make ourselves for; they are all put together, Rom. ii. 12, 15, 16. There is, 1*st*, The court of the word, wherein God keeps a justice-seat, or tribunal, condemning the wicked, and absolving the righteous; as Christ says, John. xii. *The word which I speak shall judge you in the last day:* And this is it that the apostle hath in that forecited place, Rom. ii. 12. *As many as have sinned in the law, shall be judged by the law.* A 2d court is the court of the conscience; and this is more broad and extensive, reaching all men without, as well as within the church; wherein God hath his own way of libelling, and accusing of, and passing sentence upon sinners; as verse 14, 15. *When the Gentiles, who have not the law, do by nature the things contained in the law, these having not a law, are a law unto themselves; which shew the work of the law written in their hearts, their conscience also bearing witness, and their thoughts the mean while accusing, or else excusing one another.* A 3d court or judgment-seat, is that which is more discernable, distinct and terrible, and that is the judgment-seat of God, when he shall conveen all and every one before himself immediately, and shall judge and pass sentence upon them; whether this be done to a particular person, or to the whole world, as verse 16. *In that day, when God shall judge the secrets of men, by Jesus Christ, according to my gospel.*

Use. We would have you confirmed in the faith of this truth, that there are none of us, but we are liable to all these courts; and therefore ye would live so, as ye may be in a posture fit for this appearing: Many of us, alas! live as if we were never to be called to an account, and as if there were no tribunal that we were to appear before.

2*dly*, Observe, " That all men and women, even " the elect themselves, are naturally, and as in them " selves, obnoxious to condemnation, and liable to " the sentence of it before God's tribunal." For Jesus Christ his justifying of them, and procuring their

their absolution, implies this much, that they, as considered in themselves, are liable to, and cannot receive another sentence than that of condemnation: It says, that not only they have sinned, but that, because of their sin, they are liable and obnoxious to condemnation; that for their sin God's curse is due to them, John iii. 18, 36. *He that believeth not, is condemned already;* and, *He that believeth not, shall not see life, but the wrath of God abideth on him:* The sentence is standing against him unrepealed, even that sentence which we have, Gal. iii. 10. *Cursed is every one that continueth not in all things written in the book of the law to do them.* The sinner comes no sooner to look to the court of the word, nor to the court of his own conscience, but that sentence is laid before him; and when he comes before God, he can expect no other thing, the Lord proceeding according to the rule of the word: So, Rom. iii. 19. *We know that whatever thing the law saith, it saith to them who are under the law, that every mouth may be stopped, and all the world may become guilty before God;* which supposes a liableness to his curse, and a subjection to the judgment of God, as the word is rendered on the margin; there are none, as considered in their natural condition, who have a word to say against it. To clear it a little, ye would consider two things in the law, as it is a covenant of works, under which all men are by nature, 1. The directive, or commanding part of it, that carves out man's duty, and so is the rule of righteousness to men and women; and what is not conform to the commands and directions of it, is sin, and hath a guilt with it: This is most certain, that the law, even as to believers, is a rule of righteousness, according to which they are to walk. 2. There is in it the sentence of a curse, whereby the person that sins, is not only declared to be guilty, but liable to God's wrath and curse; this may be separated from the former: The law was, no doubt, a law of righteousness to man in his innocency, and is so to the believer still, who is absolved from the curse of it; but yet the believer, as considered in his natural condition, is not only guilty, but stated under the curse: And this is the meaning of the doctrine, that naturally not only are all men sinful, but they are stated under the curse of God; the law says on the matter, Man and woman, thou hast not abiden in what is written, and therefore thou must die, thou art liable to the curse, which will light, if it be not prevented. If there were any need of reasons to prove this, they are not wanting: It is so, 1. That the Lord may humble all flesh, as the apostle says, Rom. iii. 19.

That every mouth may be stopped, and that all the world may become guilty before God. It is so ordered, that his grace may shine the more conspicuously; when the person is found guilty, and obnoxious to the curse by the law, grace shews itself to be wonderful, in pulling the sinner from under the lash of the law: As Isaac was set free, and a sacrifice was accepted in his room; so the sinner is set free, and the Mediator in his satisfaction is accepted in his room: To this purpose it is said. Rom. xi. 32. *God hath concluded them all in unbelief, that he might have mercy on all:* not that he shews mercy on all that are in unbelief, but this is the meaning, that it might be mercy to all that should get good of the Mediator, and alone mercy to the elect, both of Jews and Gentiles. It is on this ground, that, Eph. ii. 3. the apostle not only saith, *Ye were dead in sins and trespasses;* but also, turning it over on himself, he adds, *And we are all the children of wrath, even as others,* liable by sin to the curse of God, if it had not been graciously prevented.

Use 1. Let all of us take a view here of our natural condition, and indeed it were the better for us that we were more frequently viewing it: What is it, will ye say? It is even this, ye are all liable to appearing before God's justice-seat; ye are all guilty, and, by the sentence of the law, under God's curse, and condemned already; because God hath said, *He that sins shall die:* We are, I say, all thus by nature.

Use 2. It gives a great commendation to the grace of God in Christ Jesus; it makes grace wonderfully glorious, that takes the sinner, at this nick, and in this pinch. We shall not dispute here, nor is it needful, nor edifying, whether God might have forgiven sin freely, without any intervenient satisfaction to his justice, seeing he hath declared his mind concerning that in his word, Exod. xxiii. 7. *I will not justify the wicked;* and chap. xxxiv. 7. *That will by no means clear the guilty;* and Gen. iii. *The day thou eats,* or sins, *thou shalt surely die:* This is it that puts a man, as considered in his natural condition, to be as it were in hell, while he is on earth; and puts him in such a near capacity to the wrath of God, if we may so speak, and to the actual undergoing of it, that there needs no more but the blowing out of the breath to put him in the pit; yea, while he is living, he is a prisoner in chains, till the day of execution come, if grace reprieve him not. Ye would think much of grace, O how very much! if ye were seriously comparing these two together, to be so near hell, and yet, as it were, to have a ladder set up for you to ascend to heaven by, and that in such a way, as by Christ's becoming a curse! They will certainly never think much of the grace of God, and of the love of Christ, they will never think much of their own hazard, nor will they ever in earnest make use of Christ's righteousness, who have not some quick and lively impression and sense of this their condition by nature; and therefore, whenever ye go to read, to hear, to pray, to meditate, &c. take up yourselves, as naturally arrested before the court of God, and obnoxious to his wrath; this would lay your pride, and make Christ's offers in the gospel lovely to you.

Use 3. This shews, that these, who get any good of Christ, are much in Christ's debt and common, and have in themselves no cause to boast of it. If this be true, even of the elect, that they are all once under the sentence of condemnation, else they could not be justified and absolved by Christ; ye that think yourselves to be something, what have ye to boast of? *Who hath made you to differ? and what have ye, but what ye have received?* It sets you well therefore to be humble, and to put a price upon Christ, as the apostle doth, on the same consideration, Gal. ii. 20. when he says, *Who loved me, and gave himself for me;* that makes him relish sweetly to the believer; and this is the ground of his triumph, Rom. viii. 33, 34. *Who shall lay any thing to the charge of God's elect? It is God that justifieth, who is he that condemneth? It is Christ that died, yea, rather that is risen again,* &c. This way of justification makes Christ's death wondrous lovely, and it is on this that the song of the redeemed is founded, Rev. i. 5. *Unto him that loved us, and washed us from our sins in his own blood, and hath made us kings and priests unto God and his Father, to him be glory and dominion for ever and ever, amen;* and of that new song, Rev. v. 9, 10. *Thou art worthy to take the book, and to open the seals thereof; for thou wast slain, and hast redeemed us to God by thy blood,* &c. It is an evil token, when folks can talk at a high rate of their hope of being justified, when in the mean time they have so little estimation of Christ, and their hearts are so little warmed with love to him, who is so lovely to believers; and when they can so confidently make application of his purchase to themselves, and yet cannot tell when their heart was ever in the least measure ravished with the consideration of Christ's love, neither did it ever relish to them, nor were their hearts ever in the least engaged to him, on that consideration.

Use 4. All of you, who are lying in this natural condition, and know not what is your hazard, who are living in your profanity, or at best in your hypocrisy, civility, formality, not regenerate or born again, but have still the same faith and love that ye were born with, and no other, what is your posture? Ye are not in Christ, but lying naked, obnoxious to the wrath and curse of God, condemned already; and what if your breath go out in this doleful condition? what if a palsy or apoplexy overtake you suddenly? what if a stone fall upon you, ere ye go home out of this place? There is even but that much betwixt you and hell; ye are liable to be arrested before the court of God's justice, and how will it be with you when ye come there, and when it shall be said, that such a person hath broken the law, and therefore God's curse is due to him, and therefore, Away with him? For *he judgeth according to mens works*. Are there none of you afraid of this? do ye believe it to be a truth? O that ye did, who are lying contentedly and secure in your natural condition, and it does not trouble you? Will you yet ly still contentedly in this dreadful state? Is it possible that ye can be well in this condition, though ye would heap up riches as the sand? Ye cannot look into the Bible, nor into your own heart, but it curses you; ye cannot look to the bar of God's justice, but the sentence meets you, *Depart from me, ye cursed*. This is the truth of God, and if ye think there be any here lying still in black nature, (and we are not, sure, all renewed) think then upon your case; O that ye saw your posture! The hand-writing coming forth on the wall did not so affright Belteshazzar, as the curse would affright you, if it were believed. And, 2*dly*, If this be your natural condition, and if ye believe it to be truly so, we would expostulate with you, and even wonder, 1. How comes it to pass, that so many of you ly still in your natural condition, and endeavour not a change of your state? It will be wondered at by angels, and by all the elect, yea, and even by the reprobate that never heard of Christ, that so many heard the gospel, and had the offer of Christ, and yet did not stir up themselves to make use of him. Is it not a wonder that folk can sleep secure under the curse of God, *and bless themselves, till their iniquities be found to be hateful?* To be in this condition, and to sleep quietly under it, will have a doleful wakning. 2. How is it that so few take pains to try how it is with them? If any of you were lying under a decreet of an hundred pound Scots, ye would not be so secure, till ye knew that ye were freed of it; And if it be true, that this is your condition by nature, to be under the standing sentence of the law, and the curse of God, how is it, ye never try if ye be come out of that condition? I ask the most profane men amongst you, Were ye never under this sentence? If ye say, Not, the word of God will stand up against you, and say to you, that ye lie falsly; and if ye be under it, is it not hazardous to be so? But I fear, that many of you dream, that the curse of God wears away as ye grow up. 3. Think ye never of coming to judgment, and of God's proceeding in judgment against you? think ye never that ye will die, and after death come to judgment, according to the general appointment past upon all men? How cometh it, that ye are not thinking on it, and what may be the Judge's procedure towards you? He will judge you according to this word; and all that are out of Christ, and not justified by him, will be cast into the pit of hell: There is no new sentence to be past, or to be executed upon you, but that which was standing over your head before. 4. Know ye how long he may treat with you, or how long ye may be in a capacity to get your state changed? Are there not many taken suddenly away, of whose state we shall not judge? but may it not be so with you? why are ye then so secure, and why decline ye the word, and refuse to let it search you, while ye know not whether the curse be removed, and whether the sentence be changed, or recalled? Some of you perhaps will say, The Lord knows that, it is not for us to know; and that says, that ye do never so much as essay to know, and to win to clearness about your state: Others of you will, it may be, say, That ye hope all will be well; and yet that at the best is but a guessing: And ye would be loth to speak so of a decreet that were past against you, about a sum of money, in any poor court of judicature on earth; and will ye suffer this terrible sentence to stand over your head, in the court of God's justice, and not study to be distinct, and at a point, upon solid and good grounds, that it is repealed? If ye did really believe that it was once so with you, and that yet ye are in hazard of this sentence, ye would not, ye could not, I am sure, ye should not be at rest, till ye knew that it were removed; it would put you to make use of Christ in good earnest for your peace, and to seek after an extract of the repealed sentence, and of your absolution, sealed up in your bosom: And this is the thing that we aim at in all this, even that as ye would not have a terrible meeting with God before the bar of his justice, that ye would seek to have the curse, that ye are naturally lying under, removed, and to have your peace made with God, and to have some well-grounded clearness about it, that ye might live comfortably, and die with solid confidence and Christian courage, without which ye can do neither.

SERMON LIII.

Isaiah liii. 11. *He shall see of the travel of his soul, and shall be satisfied: By his knowledge shall my righteous Servant justify many; for he shall bear their iniquities.*

THE way of absolving a guilty sinner, in the justice of God, is the great sum and scope of all the gospel; even to shew how a lost sinner, obnoxious to the sentence of a transgrest law, may, without prejudice to the justice of God, come to be justified: We are persuaded, that there is nothing of greater concernment to sinners; and if we knew our debt, and our hazard, we would think, that there is nothing of greater concernment to us in particular. The sum of the covenant of redemption runs on this, and it is the great thing aimed at in all this chapter, wherein the prophet lets us see, 1. What is the great thing that satisfies justice; and, for this end, much hath been spoken of Christ's sufferings and *soul-travel*. 2. He lets us see, what is the benefit that comes to us by Christ's sufferings, and that is *justification*, or absolution from the guilt of sin, and from the curse which it deserves. 3. He lets us see the way how this benefit is derived, and it is *by his knowledge:* This, saith he, shall be the great result of Christ's sufferings, *Many shall be justified;* and this shall be the way how it shall be derived to these many, and that is, *by his knowledge*, or by faith in him, resting on his righteousness and satisfaction.

We opened up the meaning of the words the last day, and pointed at two *Doctrines* from them, 1. "That all men and women have a judgment "to abide before God, an arraignment and indict- "ment there, to which they must answer." They must all come to get a sentence from God. 2. "That all men naturally are liable to the sentence "of condemnation. This is supposed here; for, in as far as sinners are only by faith in Christ justified, in as far the sentence of the law, and of the covenant of works, is standing against them, and over their heads, who are not by faith united to Christ Jesus, and justified by his righteousness.

The 3*d Doctrine* (which is almoſt the very words of the text) that now we intend to ſpeak to, is this, "That tho' all men naturally be obnoxious to the "ſentence of the law, and to the curſe of God; "yet there is a way laid down, how a ſinner, ſo "obnoxious, may be juſtified, and freed from that "ſentence, and this is by faith in Jeſus Chriſt "only." If any doctrine be of concernment for us to know, and to be well, and experimentally acquainted with, this is of concernment to us; *By his knowledge ſhall my righteous Servant juſtify many.* There are *three* things in this doctrine implied, which by one and the ſame labour will be proven; and therefore we ſhall put them together. 1. That altho' all men be naturally obnoxious to the wrath and curſe of God, yet he hath appointed a way how guilty ſinners may be juſtified and abſolved. 2. That the way of attaining to this benefit of juſtification, and freedom from the curſe, is by faith in Chriſt's righteouſneſs; it is *by his knowledge,* ſaith the text. 3. That there is no other way by which a ſinner, obnoxious to the curſe, can be juſtified, but by faith in Chriſt's righteouſneſs allenarly: This laſt branch of the doctrine ſays not only, that there is no other mean to ſatisfy juſtice, but Chriſt's merit and ſatisfaction; but that there is no other way, but the way of faith, to win to the application of his ſatisfaction: Whereby many queſtions may be anſwered, and many errors in doctrine and practice confuted; but our preſent purpoſe is to ſhew, how a guilty ſinner may be juſtified.

And therefore we ſhall, 1. Give you a general view of the truth of the doctrine, by confirming it from ſcripture, in all the parts of it. 2. We ſhall ſpeak more particularly to the ſeveral branches of it. And, 3. To the way of attaining juſtification, in the ſeveral cauſes of it, as it is here holden forth.

For confirmation of the general doctrine, ye ſhall, 1. Look upon ſome ſcriptures, and, 2. To ſome grounds of reaſon.

As for the confirmation of it by ſcripture, if we look through the goſpel, it is our Lord Jeſus Chriſt his own doctrine which he preached, and the way which he laid down therein, for juſtifying and ſaving a ſinner; ſo, John iii. where it is three or four times repeated, as, ver. 16. *God ſo loved the world, that he gave his only begotten Son, that whoſoever believeth on him, ſhould not periſh, but have eternal life:* ver. 18. *He that believeth on him, is not condemned, but he that believeth not, is condemned already, becauſe he believeth not in the name of the only begotten Son of God:* ver. 36. *He that believeth on the Son, hath everlaſting life; and he that believeth not the Son, ſhall not ſee life, but the wrath of God abideth on him;* and, ver. 14. 15. *As Moſes lifted up the ſerpent in the wilderneſs, ſo muſt the Son of man be lifted up, that whoſoever believeth on him, ſhould not periſh, but have eternal life:* And that is all one as to ſay, He that believes ſhall be juſtified; Mark xvi. 16. *He that believeth, and is baptized, ſhall be ſaved; but he that believeth not, ſhall be damned.* Theſe are the terms on which the apoſtles are by Chriſt warranted to preach the goſpel, and to make the offer of life to every creature; and therefore, if we look forward to their preaching, we will find it to run in the ſame ſtrain, as Acts xiii. 38, 39. *Be it known unto you therefore, men and brethren, that through this Man is preached unto you the forgiveneſs of ſins; and that by him, all that believe, are juſtified from all things, from which ye could not be juſtified by the law of Moſes:* Where, while Paul is ſumming up the whole meſſage that he had to deliver, he goes upon the ſame ground; and wherein we have theſe three clearly holden forth, 1. That all men are liable, as in their natural eſtate, to God's curſe, and by the law cannot be juſtified. 2. That there is a way laid down, thro' Jeſus Chriſt, to come by juſtification and remiſſion of ſins. 3. That the way, how ſinners come by this, is faith in Chriſt; *All that believe are juſtified:* Look to the Epiſtles, eſpecially theſe written to the Romans and Galatians, where this queſtion about juſtification is expreſly and of purpoſe handled, and we will find, that it is the ſum of both; as Rom. iii. where, having ſaid, ver. 23. That *all have ſinned, and come ſhort of the glory of God,* and ſo, that all are liable to God's judgment, he ſubjoins, ver. 24. *Being juſtified freely by his grace, through the redemption that is in Jeſus Chriſt;* where is the great mean of our juſtification: And then he adds, ver. 25. *Whom God hath ſet forth to be a propitiation through faith in his blood;* where we have the mean of application, to wit, *faith:* And chap. iv. 5. *To him that worketh not, but believeth on him that juſtifieth the ungodly, his faith is counted for righteouſneſs;* which place demonſtrates this, That an ungodly perſon, taking hold by faith of Chriſt's righteouſneſs, may be, and is juſtified and abſolved, and freed from the guilt of ſin, as if he had never ſinned: So, Gal. ii. 15 16. *We who are Jews by nature, and not ſinners of the Gentiles,* or not without the covenant, as they are, *knowing that a man is not juſtified by the works of the law, but by the faith of Jeſus Chriſt, even we have be-*

lieved in *Jesus Christ, that we might be justified by the faith of Christ, and not by the works of the law, for by the works of the law shall no flesh be justified;* which place shews not only this, that through faith in Christ is justification and life to be had, but it also excludes all other ways of justification, *Knowing that a man is not justified by the works of the law, but by faith:* But that which we are now speakin to, is only the positive part of the doctrine, to shew that a guilty sinner, obnoxious to the curse, may by faith come to be justified, and made free from the guilt of sin, and from the curse, as if he had never sinned, nor been under the curse.

For further confirmation of the doctrine, ye would consider these *four* grounds, and ye will see from them good reason for it: Only remember this, that justification looks always to a judicial procedure, (as we hinted before) wherein the Lord is (as it were) on the throne, and the guilty sinner at the bar, pleading through Christ's righteousness and satisfaction to be absolved; which is even as if a debtor, arrested for debt, should plead for a liberation, not because he is not owing the debt, neither because he hath paid the debt, but because his Cautioner hath paid it for him: This being supposed and remembred, ye would (we say) consider these grounds or reasons for confirming the doctrine; 1. The sufferings that Christ hath endured, and the satisfaction that he hath made, in the room of sinners, as the next words hold out, *For he shall bear their iniquities;* and ver. ult. *He bare the sins of many:* Nay, this is the great scope of the chapter; therefore we said, *That he hath born our griefs, and carried our sorrows,* and that *the Lord hath laid on him the iniquity of us all;* this makes a ground of confirmation. 2. Consider, how that there is not only a sufficient price paid, but there is a covenant of redemption warranting him to pay it, and accepting it off his hand, as complete payment and satisfaction for the elect's debt: And except there be a look had to this covenant, faith hath not a sufficient ground to rest on for justification through Jesus his satisfaction, because otherwise, we see not a reason why his sufferings can be accepted for us; for suppose (if such a supposition may warrantably be made) Christ to have suffered, yet it was free for God to have accepted that as a satisfaction for our debt, or not: But the consideration of the covenant of redemption removes that doubt, and gives faith a ground to lay hold on Christ's sufferings, as satisfactory to the justice of God; because in the covenant of redemption, it is so transacted and agreed upon betwixt God and the Mediator; therefore the apostle, speaking, Heb. x. 8, 9. and forward, from Psal. xl. of this covenant, shews, that when sacrifices and offerings will not do the turn, Christ comes in, saying, *Lo, I come, in the volume of thy book it is written of me; I delight to do thy will, O my God: By which will* (saith the apostle) *we are sanctified:* And had there not been such a will, his sufferings had not been useful to us. 3. Consider the offer that is made in the gospel to sinners, which is the object of our faith: For the covenant of redemption is not the ground and object of our faith; tho' it clears the ground and reason of our faith; but it is God's offer in the gospel, according to that place, Mark xvi. 15, 16. *Go ye and preach the gospel to every creature; he that believeth, and is baptized, shall be saved:* He warrants them to go and make it known to all to whom they shall preach, that there is remission of sins to be had through faith in Christ; and this is a ground to faith, when God makes offer of Christ's satisfaction in the gospel, on condition that we believe, and accept of him; when we by faith close with the offer, it gives us, as it were, an assignation to Christ's purchase: The gospel says, as Paul doth, Acts xiii. 38. "Be it known to you, "that through this Man is preached to you remis-"sion of sins, and by him all that believe are ju-"stified;" and faith consents to that, as giving God credit, and accordingly closes with, and rests upon it, as the ground of its plea before God: So that when the question comes to be asked, What have ye to answer the law, and to pay your debt with? Faith, or the believing sinner, answers, I have nothing of my own, but there is a satisfaction in Christ, according to the covenant of redemption, which is holden out and made offer of to me in the gospel, and is given and allowed to me, for defence against what the law or justice can say; and I betake me to that: And this is the native and kindly act of faith in justification, when it makes use of this defence, and trusts to it alone. This is even it that Paul hath, Phil. iii. 9. compared with ver. 8. *I count all things loss, that I may win Christ, and be found in him;* that when it shall be asked, Paul, where art thou? I may have it to say, I am here, Lord, even in Christ, and in his righteousness: This is the ground of his plea, having given up with his own righteousness as to his justification before God, and he will have no other defence but that. 4. Consider the end of all these, to wit, of Christ's sufferings, of the covenant of redemption, and of the offer of the gospel; it is the praise of the glory

ful in keeping his promises, and therefore he is *the justifier* of them that believe in Jesus: The other place is, Eph. i. 6. where, when the apostle hath spoken of election, predestination, and adoption, he sets down the end of all, to wit, *To the praise of the glory of his grace, wherein he hath made us accepted in the Beloved:* And this is a ground that makes all sure; for God cannot fail to justify the sinner that believeth in Christ as he is offered in the gospel, because that is the very end of his justifying sinners, the praise of the glory of grace, which he will not miss, but must certainly and infrustrably come by.

The *Uses* are four in general. The *1st* whereof is for information, and it is such a lesson of information, as, without it, all the preaching of the gospel is to no purpose; and the hope of eternal life were utterly desperate, if such a doctrine were not in the gospel, that through faith in Christ a sinner may be justified. Would any know then how they may be absolved? This answers the question, and tells us that it is through faith in Christ's righteousness, and no other way: And if we digestedly believed the former two doctrines, 1. That we must all come before the tribunal of God; And, 2. That we are all obnoxious to the curse of God; we would think this were a very concerning question to be put, How such a guilty sinner may be absolved and justified? And indeed, if we be not clear in this point, it is, as to any fruit, in vain for us to preach, and for you to hear, or to think of coming to heaven; which is in a word, That a sinner, through resting on Christ's righteousness, according to the covenant of grace, may come to be absolved, and freed from the guilt of sin, and from the curse, as if he had never sinned, nor been liable to that curse.

For further clearing of this *Use*, Consider, 1. What *justification* is. 2. What we mean by faith. And, 3. What are the *causes* of this justification spoken of in the text. *1st*, By justification, in this place, is not to be understood the making of a person perfectly holy, nor to have grace infused into him, for that is sanctification; but it is to be absolved, and declared free, in respect of the guilt of sin, and of the word, tho' indeed justifying faith doth presuppose that; neither by faith do we mean such a faith whereby a man doth at the very first believe that he is pardoned, and which puts away all doubting, and lifts him in his own conceit to the height of assurance about the obtaining of the thing; it is the Antinomian presumption, to believe at first hand, that I am justified and pardoned: But it is such a faith, that takes hold of Christ's righteousness, made offer of in the gospel, that I may obtain justification and pardon of sin through him; according as it is said, Gal. ii. 16. *We believed in Jesus Christ, that we might be justified by the faith of Christ:* It is an actual closing with the offer of Christ's righteousness, and a submitting to the terms of it, for justification: the soul's founding of all its defence before God, on Christ's righteousness and purchase offered to it in the gospel, and resting on it for life and salvation: As, suppose there were a multitude of rebels, to whom pardon were by proclamation offered, on condition that at such a time they should lay down their arms, and come in; and if one of them were challenged, and called to a reckoning, after his coming in, for his rebellion; the ground of his plea would not be, that he never was out in rebellion, but that such an offer was made, and that he did hazard his life on it: So it is here, a sinner is a rebel against God by nature, and being in rebellion, hath the offer of pardon and life made to him, on condition that he close by faith with Christ's righteousness, and the sinner doth by faith give God credit, and hazards his soul on that; whereas unbelief (to follow the similitude) is, as if a rebel, hearing of such a pardon offered, would not think that a sure way to come off, but would either plead innocent, or take him to some other shift: This then is the faith that I mean of, which actually closes with, and makes use of God's offer of Christ's righteousness for absolution. *3dly*, Consider the *causes* of justification: and there are three in the words. 1. The *meritorious* cause, that he hath procured and bought this benefit, is Christ's satisfaction, his *bearing of our iniquities; he shall justify many, for he shall bear their*

their iniquities. 2. The *instrumental* cause, condition, or mean, or way, how that benefit is derived to us, is *faith*, called here *his knowledge*; it is the true faith we spoke of just now; faith taking hold of such a promise, and resting on God's faithfulness for the making out of it; it is this which gives the soul a title to Christ's righteousness, which formerly it had not, and makes Christ's purchase of due to belong to it, by vertue of God's offer; and consequently the benefit of justification is derived to it, by its taking hold of the offer, which otherwise it could not partake of. 3. The formal cause, wherein justification properly consists, is this, even God's absolving or judicial pronouncing of the sinner to be free, and his accounting of him as righteous, on account of Christ's righteousness imputed to him, and taken hold of by his faith. Where the sentence is past, we need not curiously enquire: It is like, as the sentence of condemnation stands in the word, while the sinner is in unbelief; so by believing in Christ, he hath absolution in the word, as John iii. 18. *He that believeth in him, is not condemned;* and this sentence of the word is as effectual for absolving of the sinner, as if the sentence were pronounced in an immediate way, or with an audible voice from heaven, by God, with the sinner's name, and sirname in it: And therefore let me commend this, with the other places I named before to you, that from them ye may learn to take up the way, how a sinner is absolved and justified; it is Christ's satisfaction that makes the amends, and is the meritorious cause; it is God's word that makes the offer of that satisfaction; and it is our faith, begotten and quickened by God's Spirit, that taketh hold of it; and justification itself is God's absolving, and accepting of the person, as righteous in his sight, who is fled to Christ's righteousness. And thus, though God's grace and mercy be the *efficient* cause that admits of the ransom, yet neither is grace in us the *formal* cause, nor is grace in God the *meritorious* cause, but it is that which lays down the way how a satisfaction shall be provided, and accepts of it when provided, and of the sinner on account of it, when by faith he betakes himself to it.

Use 2d. Seeing there is such a way of justification provided, and by the gospel brought to light, revealed and made manifest, as the word is, Rom. i. 17. and iii. 21. Since, I say, that mystery, which before was hid, is disclosed, and life and immortality brought to light by the gospel; let me earnestly intreat you, that ye would make use of this mean and way of justification, for the obtaining of absolution before God: The end of preaching (as we said) is to reveal this righteousness; and the end of the revealing of it is, to engage sinners to make use of it; of which tho' we should preach to you from the one end of the year to the other, if ye do not betake yourselves to it, so as to close with it, and heartily to submit unto it, it will all be to no purpose.

For pressing of this *Use* a little further, consider the great concern and moment of this application, and what may induce you, seriously to mind it: And, to this purpose, 1. I would pose and put you to it, if ye believe that by nature ye are liable to God's curse, and that ye must compear before his judgment-seat; and if ye be found in nature when you compear, that will be a woful and dreadful sentence, that ye will meet with from God: And if withal ye believe this, that by justification, ye may have sin pardoned, be reconciled to God, and have the curse removed from you, and be put in such a state as if ye had never sinned: If, I say, ye believe these things to be the truths of God, is not this of your concernment, whether ye be made friends with God, and have your sins pardoned, or not; whether ye shall be eternally happy, or eternally miserable; whether ye shall get God's blessing, or ly for ever under his curse: If this, I say, be of your concernment, then surely obedience to this exhortation, is of your concernment, because there is no other way to win to absolution but this. 2. Consider, That it is the very design of the gospel, and of this benefit that is made offer of to you therein, which all the nations that have not the gospel want, the privilege being denied to them: God makes offer of a way to you, how ye may be justified; and ye profess your desire to learn it; and to get it practically made use of, and improven, and (as Paul hath it, Philip. iii. 8, 9, 10.) that ye may know Christ; that ye may win him, and be found in him; and it is the sum of the gospel, as we have it, Acts. xiii. 38. *Be it known unto you, men and brethren*, *that thro' this Man is preached unto you remission of sins, and by him all that believe are justified*: This is even the time that the Lord is making this proclamation, that was before prophesied of, and published by Isaiah, *By his knowledge shall my righteous Servant justify many;* this is it that is even now revealed, declared, and made manifest to you, that by Christ Jesus alone righteousness is to be attained: And if it be of such concernment, that, for this very end,

end, God hath sent his Son to die, and hath sent this gospel to declare and make offer of this benefit of his death unto you; it is no doubt greatly of your concernment, to make use of it, when it comes to you. 3. Consider, that if the Lord's proclamation of it have not that effect, to engage you to Christ Jesus, for the obtaining of righteousness thro' him, it will leave you in a worse condition than it found you in: It is not now, whether ye will perish or not? tho' that be a great matter (the most barbarous *Heathens* will readily think, that God's justice is terrible to meet with) but it layeth these two in the balance; It is either a most inconceivable condemnation, beyond what others, who have not heard the gospel, will come under, if the offer be slighted; or eternal salvation, if it be embraced: *Wo to thee* Chorazin, *wo to thee* Bethsaida (saith the Lord, Mat. xi. 21, 22.) *For if the mighty works which are done in thee, had been done in* Tyre *and* Sidon, *they would have repented long ago; and it shall be more tolerable for* Sodom *in the day of judgment, than for* Capernaum, who, because *they were lifted up to heaven*, in respect of a glorious dispensation of gospel-ordinances, and improved them not *shall be cast down to hell:* And whereon is this dreadful denunciation founded; Even on this ground, just now hinted at, the gospel was more plainly and powerfully preached to them, than it was to Tyre and Sidon, to Sodom and Gomorrah, who had Lot's testimony;, but Christ's and his apostles testimony, in a manner swallowed up that, which testimony they slighted. Now, pose yourselves, whether this gospel hath not sounded loud in your ears? have ye not heard it? yes verily: We may here allude to that word, Rom. x. 16. doubtless ye have heard, the sound thereof is come to you, and ye shall never have that to object, that ye heard it not. This text, and this same sermon on it, and others will bear witness, that, thro' Jesus Christ, ye had a way laid down to you for remission of sins and for justification: And what will follow? either you must betake yourselves to Christ's righteousness for justification, and study to be holy; or else ye will bring upon yourselves a more terrible condemnation than came upon the inhabitants of Sodom and Gomorrah, who were consumed and burnt quick, by fire and brimstone from heaven: And therefore there is ground here for all to look well about us, what use we make of this benefit offered to us, that we miscarry not, and make not ourselves most inexcusable, for slighting of it.

I shall here speak a little to some sorts of people, that ought mainly to lay this to heart. 1*st*, To some that are so utterly careless and indifferent in making their peace with God; that to this day all warnings, threatnings, and dispensations that they have met with, could never prevail with them, once to make them that far serious, as to ask that question, What they should do to be saved? to whom much preaching is but a beating in the air, to whom such preaching is fruitless, and Christ useless, it is of these that he speaks, Mat. xxii. who being invited to the wedding, *They made light of it, and went away, one to his farm another to his merchandize:* There is a generation of such persons amongst us to this day, who never thought seriously of the gospel, nor of this doctrine, which is the substance and life of the gospel, and without which we can enjoy no mercy nor benefit holden forth and made offer in the word; but slight pardon of sin, and think little of justification who will, the day is coming, when it will be much thought of, and when many of you, if God prevent not, would give all the world for an offer of it, and would be glad to be burnt with the world, or covered with, and smothered under a hill or mountain, rather than to come and receive your fearful doom and sentence from the Judge, because ye had this favour in your offer, and made not use of it. A 2*d* sort are a prophane company, who if their carriage be looked on, it says plainly, nay it openly proclaims, that such men believe not that there is a judgment coming; otherwise they durst not for a world live as they do: Is this, think ye, the way to be justified, to be laughing, sporting, gaming, tipling, and trifling away your time, in spending it in decking and dressing of your bodies, in bestowing of more time in one day on the body, than ye do in eight, or many more days on the soul; to be glutting in the world, to be following the desires of your hearts, and the sight of your eyes? Prophane as ye are, think upon it, for we declare even unto you, that there is a way how the ungodly may be justified, held forth, and offered in this gospel; and if ye contemn it, God shall vindicate his grace, and your trampling on it shall return on your own head. A 3*d* sort are such as have never taken with their sin, nor with the feud betwixt God and them: We invite the filthy to come and wash, sinners to come and get pardon; the ungodly to come and be justified; but alas! we cannot get sinners that walk under the due sense of their sin to preach to; I dare say, that to many of you,
the

the doctrine of justification is in some respect needless, I am sure for the time useless; for ye were never convinced of your sin, nor of your hazard, but thought that ye were always sure of your justification; you never evened yourselves (to speak so) to hell; God always, ye think, loved you; and perish who will, ye will not perish: These, and such as these, have been your thoughts of yourselves, and of your state; and we have more difficulty to get you prevailed with, to think seriously of making your peace with God, than we would readily have in this to prevail with *Pagans*, or with adulterers and murderers, whose natural conscience would sooner be awakned than yours. Justification is not a serious matter to many of you, ye think to slip thro' God's judgment: If ye be asked, Whether or no ye be absolved? Yes, that we are, will ye say, long since: But ah! how came ye to be absolved? was ye ever chased, and did ye ever flee for refuge to the hope set before you? was ye ever pursued by the law to Christ? and were ye ever made cordially to close with him, and to found your plea on his righteousness? It will be strange, if so many shall slip into heaven, and never know how: We grant, there may be some brought in, who have not distinctly discerned the manner how; but that almost whole congregations, and country-sides should be made friends with God, and never know, or at least never kindly take with the feud, we profess, we see not through it, it is to us an unintelligible riddle and a paradox: therefore be intreated to reckon over again; tho' there be a justification, thro' the blood of Christ to be gotten, yet assure yourselves that ye are not in the way to it, while ye continue senseless of your sin and of your hazard. A 4*th*, sort are these, who think that they have nothing to do with this doctrine; they are rich, they are wise, they are of honest rank, and have a name and commendation in the place where they live, and they have, may be, some schoolcraft, and learning, and therefore they are persuaded that they cannot miss justification; and where is there one person amongst many, if it be not some poor body, even it may be poor in the world, that ever thinks that the severity of the law, or the threatnings thereof, concern them? But, are there any more ways to heaven, but one? or is there one for the rich, and another for the poor? do not all come in at this door? is not this the way, even to take with your sin, and to flee to Christ for life? And yet, are there not some amongst you, that cannot endure to think of hell, to dread it, or (as we use to speak) to even yourselves to it? because ye are thought something of, able to do your turn, and have some parts, and abilities: But there are many more rich, more wise and learned folk than you are in hell, that were never absolved before God, nor never shall; yet there is a propensness in great men, in rich men, and in men of parts, to slight this doctrine: But such have in some respect more need to give all diligence to make your calling and election sure, than many others, and yet ye go not so far as they do, who yet go not the just length. A 5*th* sort, are such as never knew any inward work, or exercise of the Spirit of God upon their consciences, but have lived with a sort of wholeness of heart all their days: If any be called to take notice of this doctrine, they are called to take notice of it; *There is a generation,* saith Solomon, Prov. xxx. 12. *which are pure in their own eyes, and yet are not washed from their filthiness;* they conclude they are absolved, but never look inward, to see if there be ground to bear that conclusion. 6*thly,* and lastly, There are a sort that are formal, and hypocritical; they were never grosly prophane but they were as little truly and seriously religious: Ye had need, therefore, to take heed whereon ye found your peace, and beware that ye take not the form of godliness for the power of it, especially when the form is come to so great a height. And seeing this way of justification is holden out to you through Christ, we exhort and beseech you all, and especially those of such sorts as we have named, to look well that this grace be not received in vain. In a word, these two sorts should take special heed to this doctrine, 1. Some that mind not religion at all. 2. Others, who, if they mind it, mind it not in the way of grace, but as it were by the works of the law: We declare to you, that justification is by faith in Jesus Christ, and by resting on his righteousness; as many as take that way, they may be assured to come speed; and they that misken, and slight that way, shall never win to heaven; *for there is no other name given, whereby a sinner can be saved, but the name of Jesus only; he is the way, the truth, and the life, and no man cometh to the Father but by him.*

SERMON LIV.

Isaiah liii. 11.------By his knowledge shall my righteous Servant justify many.

THERE is (as I said lately) nothing of greater concernment to a sinner to know, than these two, 1. What it is that satisfies justice, and makes a sinner acceptable before God? 2. To know how that may be attained, or what way it is to be applied? And this verse, shortly, but very clearly, answers both. 1st, That which satisfies justice, *is the travel of Christ's soul*, or his sufferings. 2. The way how this is applied, derived, or communicate, is set down in the latter part of the verse, *By his knowledge shall my righteous Servant justify many, for he shall bear their iniquities:* This is the effect of Christ's sufferings, that many by them shall be absolved from the guilt of sin, and from the curse; and this is the way how these many come to be thus absolved, it is by believing on him; for thus his satisfaction is accounted theirs, as if they themselves had satisfied. We proposed, the last day, this *doctrine* to be spoken to from the words, "That there is a way through faith in Christ, "and resting on his sufferings, by which a sinner, "obnoxious to God's curse, may attain to be justified and declared free before the throne of "God." This doctrine implies these *two* things in general, 1. That there is such a thing possibly attainable by a guilty sinner, as justification. 2. That justification is to be attained allenarly by faith in Jesus Christ, resting on his righteousness; *By his knowledge shall he justify many;* As there is a necessity to be absolved, so there is a necessity to take this way for absolution; because this, and this only, is holden out to be the way how justification is attained: It is by Christ's *knowledge*, which in short is by faith in him.

We discoursed somewhat of the positive part of this truth the other day, which is of great concernment; the understanding thereof being the very hinge of the gospel, and that wherein, in a special manner, the gospel and covenant of grace differs from the law and covenant of works; and pointing out a way for coming by righteousness and life through Christ, in opposition to the law as a covenant of works, that holds out a way to righteousness and life through our own performances.

We touched also at some *uses* of the doctrine, for directing of you to the believing use-making of Christ, for coming at peace with God; it would follow now, that we should speak a little to that use of refutation, that flows natively from this doctrine: For if this be the way, and the only way of the justification of a sinner before God, to wit, by or thro' faith in Christ's righteousness; then all these ways that lead not sinners to resting on Christ's righteousness alone for justification and peace, must be inconsistent with the gospel, and so to be rejected and abhorred, whether they be in doctrine or in practice: And we choose the rather to speak a word to this, because it will clear the doctrine of justification by faith the more, when we come to see and consider these corruptions and errors that are foisted in by heterodox men, in this great truth of God, to the preventing and corrupting thereof; and it will the more provoke us to thankfulness to God, who hath graciously delivered us from these snares, errors and corruptions; an error and mistake here, about the substance of this truth, being such, as, though we held all other truths incorrupted, will ruin us.

There are, we suppose, *four* sorts of errors especially, that contradict this grand truth, anent justification by faith in Christ's righteousness, to which we shall speak a little. The 1st is that old rooted error of *Papists*, who, in this point, enervate and overturn the whole way of the gospel: And because this is it that a great part of the Christian world hath been deluded with, though it be in those days little thought of by many, and because it is not one single error, but as it were a chain of very momentuous and fundamental errors; we shall insist a little, in laying it out before you: and ye would not so much look on it, as a controversial, or meerly speculative, as a grosly practical error, and such as is naturally rooted in all men; ye would also look upon it, with holy fear and jealousy over yourselves, lest inadvertently ye slide into it; and withal, ye would look on it, and make use of it, as a motive, to provoke you to love the truth more, and to be, as I said, the more thankful to God, who hath freed you from that dark, heavy and comfortless way of justification by works, which is now impossible.

It may be that this error of *Papists* will not be thought much of by some, when they hear that they speak of justification by Christ, and by

his

his merits, and by faith, as well as we *Protestants* do; but it is the more dangerous that they do so: and therefore, ere I shew their way of justification, and the inconsistency of it with the gospel, I would have you to advert to these *Three* things, 1. That in this matter of justification, though *Papists* acknowledge the name, yet they do not acknowledge the thing itself; and so, upon the matter, the controversy is not so much, what justification is, as whether there be such a thing as justification at all, taking it to be a thing distinct from sanctification, and regeneration, which they in effect deny: For if the form constitute justification, and if to them, the form of justification, be the infusing of habitual grace in the soul, then it is nothing different from regeneration and sanctification; and therefore, when they speak of justification, they speak of it in this sense: For a justified person, to them, is a man renewed, and made holy, even as to calify, or to heat water, is to make that hot which before was cold; so justification to them, is to make a sinful person just, because of inherent righteousness in himself. 2. When they speak of justification, they make a two-fold justification: The *1st*, whereof is that which they call the justification of a wicked person, or of an unrenewed man, when grace is at first infused into him, which they grant a man cannot of himself condignly merit: The *2d* is of a man's growing, or increasing in grace, when he attains to more grace, and to more glory; grace and glory being of the same nature, (wherein they and we do not differ.) And to this *Second* justification, they make necessary a man's proper merit of works; for they say, That the first justification will not do a man's turn, who is come to age, though to a child it be sufficient; because their attaining of glory, who are at age, is the proper hire of their works, which supposes holiness: And therefore, when they say, that Christ's merit procures justification, their meaning is, that it procures the *First* justification, but not the *Second;* that is in effect to say, that it buys habitual grace, as a stock to a man, wherewith he may trade: But when they come to speak of heaven and glory, which is obtained (as they say) by the *Second* justification, that is come at by the man's own trading with that stock of habitual grace; and so the man's trading, or trafficquing with this stock, comes in, as that which procures, wins, and merits the prize. 3. Though they use the same names that we use, as of *faith*, and *pardon*, or *remission of sins*, yet there is very great difference betwixt them and us, as to the thing; for they count nothing to be faith, but historical faith, which the devils have: and for remission of sin, they divide and distinguish betwixt the removing, or remission of the blot of sin; and the removing, and remission of the punishment of sin; and they say, that in the *First* justification, the blot of sin is expelled, by the infusing of habitual grace, even as darkness is expelled by the coming in of light: But as to the punishment of sin, they leave a man to satisfy in part for himself, after his justification.

Now, (as we said) because there is not one error or two here, but a concatenation, or chain of many errors, therefore, for further clearing of the truth, and discovering of these errors, ye would consider, that when the question is proposed, this is the great state of it, What that is, on which a sinner may ground his peace before the tribunal of God's justice, as a solid defence, to answer all the challenges of the law, and whereupon he may expect to be absolved, and admitted to heaven? They say, that it is inherent holiness, wherewith a man's soul is sanctified, renewed and made conform to the image of God, which (say they) is of that nature, that it cannot but make the person acceptable to God; so that, in coming before God's tribunal of justice, he hath in himself wherewith to answer all his challenges, or all the challenges that the law can bring against his inward and habitual grace and sanctification: It is true, they grant, That God works this grace in them, and that men are not naturally born with it, and that Christ's merit procures the bestowing of this grace; but yet they say, Though a man do not merit this first grace, yet he must dispose himself for it, by the exercise of his free-will, faith, alms-deeds, and the like; and so he makes himself congruously meet for, and capable of sanctification, and habitual grace, without which God does not bestow it: and, if we look to the *instrumental* cause, they take in the sacraments of baptism, penance and extreme unction, as means whereby God worketh that grace, (and that, as they say, by the very work wrought) if he be a man come to age, and if there be not opportunity of getting the sacrament, he hath it in his vow, which comes in place of the sacrament; by which means, they have these *Two* effects: The *First* is a positive bringing in of grace into the soul; the *Second* is privative, whereby the blot or spot of sin is expelled, as heat expels cold, or light expels darkness: and this they call remission of sin, which grace shuts, and drives it out, so that the soul is not polluted with it: And because all this takes in but the guilt of sin, which they say is removed in the *First* justification; they have a *Second* justification, whereby they say that the punishment of sin is removed, and whereby they merit Glory; and here come in their *donations, fastings, pilgrimages, peregrinations,* &c. whereby they make amends to God; and because they cannot win to make a full amends here, they have their *purgatory* and *soul-masses;* and so they have not only God to satisfy, for the wrongs which they have done to him, but heaven to procure by their own merits: For they lay down this as a ground, that glory in its full being is the proper reward of merit, which, say they, is not founded on God's promise, for that were to merit *congruously* only, and not *condignally;* nor is it founded on Christ's merit, for that were to reward his merit, which to them is absurd, though they grant an intrinsick worth to be in both; But it is merit in strict justice, on and by which they expect heaven and glory: and having heaven (as we say) to procure by their own merit, because they cannot thus merit it, especially if man's nature be look'd on as corrupted; they invent two things, or forge two devices for that; 1. To deny concupiscence to be sin; And, 2. To distinguish betwixt mortal and venial sins; and venial sins they make to be consistent with merit, in which they take in a world of things as not deadly: And if a man have not merit enough of his own, they have a treasure of merits of many saints, who have satisfied for more than their own guilt amounted to, and have merited more than heaven to themselves; and the *pope* being by them supposed to have a right and power to dispense these merits, he gives to them that want, a right to such and such a saint's merits: And when all is done, they confess that this way of justification is not certain, that it cannot give peace, that it may be lost, and that, being lost, it cannot be recovered, but by a new grace gotten by the sacrament of penance; the very rehearsing of which things may let you see, how unlike their justification is to the gospel, and to the way of justification that it lays down; and what ground of thankfulness we have to God, who hath not only contrived, but revealed unto you, a more solid and comfortable way of justification. 1. Though their way hath much pains, and labour and toil in it, yet ye see what it amounts to, and how much uncertainty, anxiety, and horror do accompany it; neither do they ever attain to justification before God by it. And this is the 2d thing we would speak a word to, even to shew that this way of justification is inconsistent with the gospel, and that wherein a soul can neither have solid peace nor comfort: And we shall speak a little to this, 1. In general, and then, 2. more particularly. 1*st*, In general, their way of justification is the re-establishing of the covenant of works; for it supposeth, that God hath conditioned life to none, but on condition of their works, which in their value are meritorious. It is true, they *First* allow to Christ's merit this much, that he hath thereby procured this merit to their works. And 2*dly,* That he hath procured to them habitual Grace, to work these works; though (as we said before) they must dispose themselves for that Grace. But that doth not alter the nature of a covenant of works, seeing the terms are still the same: For, consider; Adam before the fall, he was to expect life according to the terms of the covenant, *Do this and live;* and here the terms of the covenant are the same, tho' their use be different; and if the scriptures do oppose these two, that *if it be of grace, it is no more of works;* and contrarily, then sure this way of justification, that puts a man to the same terms of the covenant that Adam had to expect life by, must necessarily be inconsistent with the gospel. This will be the more clear, if we consider, how they themselves illustrate their meriting by the works of the saints, by Adam his meriting of life while he stood; the which meriting flows from an intrinsick worth in the works themselves, without respect to Christ's merits; and if the covenant of works hath these same terms, then their justification, no doubt, must be a re-establishing of that covenant. 2. The scripture speaks of our obtaining justification and righteousness always in this sense, to wit, by God's imputing the righteousness of Christ to us, not only for coming at the first grace, but for attaining heaven and glory; it is that which Paul leans to, when he comes before God, Phil. iii. *That I may be found in him, not having mine own righteousness, which is by the law, but the righteousness which is through faith of Christ;* he lays by the one, and betakes himself to the other, as his only defence, and that whereon he doth ground his plea before God. Now, this being the scripture way of justification, and their way being quite contrary to it, (for if they were asked, How think ye to answer before God? they behoved to say, By the merits of our good works) it must needs be inconsistent with the grace of the gospel, and that which *Paul* would by no means hazard his peace upon. We will find nothing more frequently mentioned in scripture, for the making of our peace with God, than covenanting with God, the imputation of Christ's righteousness, and justification by faith: But all these *three* are here, in their way of justification, shut out and excluded; for they have no such thing as covenanting, they scorn the imputation of Christ's righteousness, as but a putative and imaginary thing, and they cannot endure justification by faith.

But, 2*dly*, and more particularly, Behold and consider how universally it corrupts, and even destroys the doctrine of the gospel. 1. It corrupts and destroys the nature of grace; for it hangeth it on man's free-will, he must dispose himself for it, and gives him liberty to choose, or reject it as he pleaseth; and it makes that flow from man himself that satisfies God's justice, as if remission of sins were not free: And in the *second*, justification and admission to heaven and glory, it utterly excludes grace, and takes in merit, and makes heaven the proper reward of man's own merit. 2. It enervates the merit of Christ, and his purchase, though it seem in words to acknowledge it; because it neither admits of the merit of Christ, as the satisfaction to justice, by which the punishment is taken away; nor to be that by which life is procured: but it takes in works, satisfaction by penance, whippings, pilgrimages, &c. and all that it leaveth to Christ's death, is the procuring of a new covenant of works, and the buying of a stock of habitual grace to man to send for himself: but lays not the removing of the punishment on Christ as our cautioner in our name satisfying the justice of God for our sins; but it leaves it on ourselves, and on our keeping the covenant of works, as that whereto the promise is made. 3. It overturns the nature of God's covenant; for either it makes no covenant at all, or it transforms the covenant of grace into a covenant of works, putting us to expect life through the merits of works; for they will have no promise of life to be made on condition of Christ's merit, laid hold upon by faith, but on condition of our own works alone: for though they pretend that it may be called Christ's merit, because, say they, he hath procured grace to work these works; yet in effect their way of justification is to restore us to that covenant which Adam had, and to ability to keep the same terms, though, as we said, the rise be different. 4. It is inconsistent with our natural state; for it supposes man before conversion to have a free-will to good, and ability to dispose himself to receive grace, and gives him a hand in turning himself to God, as if he were not dead in sins and trespasses; and so the sovereignty of God is bounded and limited to wait on a man so disposed, and so disposing himself. 5. It destroys the nature of God's law, as if it were consistent with his holy law, to have such and such lusts abounding within, and did not exact a reckoning for such breaches of it, as they call venial sins. 6. It overturns the scripture-doctrine concerning sin, for it makes many sins to be in effect no sins. 7. It corrupts and destroys the nature of all the sacraments, and makes new sacraments that God never appointed; and gives them power to work that which God never gave them, as if the very works wrought did confer grace. 8. It is inconsistent with the justice of God; as if, forsooth, such poor trifles and toys as these which they invent, were satisfaction enough to his justice: yea, as if some men could more than satisfy justice, and could not only merit heaven to themselves, but also help to merit heaven to others; and as if God were bound in proper justice to the creature, and that not only on the account of this promise, but also, if not mainly, on the account of merit of condignity: all these things are involved in this Popish way of justification, and inconsistent with the truth of the gospel; and we have touched on them, to let you see, that it is not one error that is here, but a complication of errors: and truly, if there be not an abhorrency of Popery, because of this gross error of justification, there is but little ground to expect, that men will keep at suitable distance from it in other things.

And therefore, from what hath been said, take a few *directions*, as your *use* of it; and if we were tender, it might do us good, now and then to get a little view of such errors. 1*st*, Then see here the necessity of being more distinct and clear in God's way of justification, in the way how peace is made betwixt him and a sinner, when we see how many errors follow and creep in after one error; and when we consider, how Popish priests and Jesuits are moving, and how this same error, which hath so many errors with it, is stealing in, ye had much need to be well acquainted with the truth, and to be guarding yourselves against error, especially when some lay so little weight on it, that they call it a striving about words, which faith that there is but little abhorrence of the thing. I am apt to think, that the most part of them that are called Christians, could not well tell how to oppose Popery, Arminianism, or Antinomianism, if they were tempted to embrace them, or any other error or nerefy; and when withal we confider how naturally we are inclined to fhuffle by the covenant of grace, and to cleave to the way of works, or to turn the covenant of grace into a covenant of works, we would try well, what we incline to in this point, whether in our judgment, or in our practice, left we fall from that which is right in practice at leaft, if not in opinion alfo. I intreat you to ftudy this, as a main point of Chriftian religion, even that ye may know and be clear in your knowledge of the way, how God accepts of, and juftifies a finner. 2*dly*, Know, that this error of Popery in particular, is not of fo little concernment as many think it to be: It is a wonder that men fhould think, differences about matters of religion to be fo light, and fo little a matter, as if it were but the change of outward ceremonies, or of words; hence it comes to pafs, that there is fo little care and zeal to prevent the rife, and fpreading of errors: we fhall only commend to you *three* things, for guarding you in reference to this error. 1. Sift yourfelves often before the tribunal of God's juftice, till your hearts be brought under fuitable impreffions of God's holinefs and juftice, of the feverity and ftrictnefs of his law, and of the neceffity of your anfwering to it in your own perfons, or in the perfon of a cautioner; and then confider, what will be your defence in fuch a pofture. 2. Carry always alongft with you the impreffion of your original fin, and natural corruption, and of the finfulnefs of your practices: this will make you lothfom and abominable in your own eyes, and Chrift precious; and fuch a foul will not be in fuch hazard of putting his own merits in the room of Chrift's. 3. Think upon that which in God's offer is prefented to you, as the way of making your peace; though ye would ftudy holinefs, in order to that end, when ye are fo finful, and when divine juftice is fo fevere, it looks not like the way to peace. But when we confider God's offer in this gofpel, as it is held forth, Acts xiii. 38, 39. *Be it known unto you, men and brethren, that through this Man is preached unto you forgivenefs of fins; and by him, all that believe are juftified from all things from which they could not be juftified by the law of Mofes;* and the invitation that is given, Ifa. lv. to them *that have no money to come and buy* freely, *without money, and without price;* and fee God calling his call on another ground than your holinefs, and putting in your offer Jefus Chrift and his righteoufnefs; it is a raifing and rouzing up of the foul, to expect abfolution before the throne of God, on a more folid foundation, that will bear its weight. We would beware of taking that way of juftification, and of making our peace with God, that feems to be moft rational like to our corrupt nature; for, as many fay, to be forry for fin, to ftudy to make amends, and to do what they dow, feems to be the moft reafonable way, and agrees beft with our corrupt nature: but that is not it which will do your turn, but the way which God hath holden out, and that is, by his knowledge, by faith in the righteous Servant. 3*dly*, See here, how much we are obliged to God, for holding out to us the right way to life. If ye look to many nations abroad, the way to life is holden out to them on this ground, even their own inherent holinefs, their own good works, their giving of confiderable parts of their eftates, their penances, &c. which yet can never quiet the confcience, nor fatisfy God's juftice: Yea, our own predeceffors in this nation were drowned in the fame errors, and were as foolifhly and fenflefly fuperftitious as the inhabitants of any other nations, before the light of the gofpel brake up among us; accounting fuch and fuch fins to be no fins, leaning to their merits, to the merits of faints, to indulgences, to foulmaffes, whippings, and a number of things of that kind: And now, that God hath mercifully freed us of thefe foolries, how much are we obliged to him? Hath ever Scotland been thankful as it becometh, for this mercy? We do, by our unthankfulnefs, darken and obfcure the freedom of grace, that by this gofpel is preached unto us; and there needs no other evidence of it but this, that many are to this day as ignorant of the way of juftification of finners, and as abftract from, and as great ftrangers to the right way of making ufe of Chrift's righteoufnefs, as if it had never been revealed unto them; or if they know, and can fpeak any thing of it, all the ufe they make of it, is to turn the grace of God into wantonnefs; and, becaufe holinefs is not the ground of making their peace with God, to take the more liberty to loofenefs: thefe are not fruits of the gofpel, other fruits muft be brought forth, or elfe ye will repent it, when ye cannot mend it. Let it therefore affect you, that God is fo ill requit for his goodnefs; and ftudy to be more thankful to him, that we may fpeak of thefe truths, and difcover thefe errors, and that we are not judicially blinded as many other people and nations are. 4*thly*, Pity them that are lying under darknefs of their delufions and errors, and pray for them: It is a fore matter, that the moft part of the Chriftian world fhould have the name of Chriftians, and yet fhould maintain fuch

doc-

doctrine, and lay down and hold such a way, as keepeth from benefit by Christ Jesus; yea, as denies on the matter, that he is come: For this is indeed the spirit of Antichrist, and of the man of sin, that takes souls off from Christ; and yet how few make conscience to pray for these poor people, and that God would pursue the whore, and break up and skale that market spoken of, Rev. xviii. and would discover his truth, and make his gospel to be purely preached to them that are sitting in the region of darkness, and in the shadow of death; ye would pity bound up and imprisoned souls in this error, and pray for their reclaiming, and that God would keep this land from it: It is an old seated and rooted error, and the rest are but foolries in comparison of it; this is the devil's great engine and army, others are but vapours, to say so; which may tell us, that speaking and hearing of such a business is not altogether useless. What if the day should come, that all our Bibles, and every English book that serves to hold out truth, and to discover error, should be taken from you, and ordered to be burnt, and that books stuffed with their errors should come in their room? Many of you think little or nothing now of the light and liberty of the gospel which ye enjoy; but if heaven be so much worth, this gospel is of much worth to you, and this truth of it in particular. 5thly, Let not this gospel be preached for nought; O! receive not this grace in vain, that is, this grace offered to you in the gospel, and the clearing of such truths to you. O what a challenge, and aggravation of our guilt will it be, when we come before the throne! when many other nations will be condemned, because they leaned to their own merits, and made no use of Christ; and many of us shall be condemned, because tho' we professed an indignation at these errors, yet we made no more use of Christ than these, who by their doctrine excluded him. If our predecessors could speak, what would they say? would it not be this, It is just that ye perish, for ye had Christ and his righteousness clearly preached to you, which we had not, and yet ye slighted him? Therefore take hold of, and improve the opportunity. God hath clearly revealed this truth to the land, and to this place; walk in the light while ye have it, else your condemnation will be the greater, as it is, John iii. 19. 6thly, Seeing God hath given us this singular mercy, even the clear revelation of the way of justification by Christ's righteousness and merits, let us not, through our evil conversation, make the truth of God to be evil spoken of; turn not the grace of God into wantonness. It was an evil that soon arose in the primitive church, and which the apostle disputes against, Rom. ii. 3, 6. Because he preached justification by grace, and not by the works of the law, some were ready to abuse that sweet doctrine, and to say, *Let us sin, that grace may abound; and let us do evil, that good may come of it, whose damnation,* says he, *is just:* And he follows out these objections, and insists in answering of them; and O but this is damnable, from the abounding of God's grace, to take the more liberty to sin! And yet, what other language have the lives of many, but this, Because justification and happiness are not built on our works, therefore we may live as we list? despitefully and presumptuously reflecting on the way of justification by faith, and on God who hath contrived it: But if any of you will abuse God's grace, and sin the more, God shall charge it on your own heads, this gospel shall never do you good, God will require it of you; your sins are multiplied, and your plagues shall be multiplied above any that have lived under black Popery. I dare say, many of you would probably have had a greater restraint on you from sin, and would have been more charitable, and forward in many external good works, if ye had been profest Papists, than now ye are, being profest Protestants; a judicial stroke on you, for the abusing of grace: And is this the fruit of the gospel? No certainly; grace was never preached, that men should grow cold and indifferent in the practice of good works, but that, through the laying hold on Christ's righteousness, they might have peace with God; and that, through the study of holiness, God might be glorified: Therefore study the exercise of faith so, as ye seclude not holiness; and study holiness so, as ye mar not the freedom of grace; and put these two together, which are the compend of the gospel, when suitably practised.

SERMON LV.

Isaiah liii. 11.------*By his knowledge shall my righteous Servant justify many*, &c.

THIS blessed death and soul-travel, of our Lord Jesus, hath been good news to many; and it is the ground of all the hope of life that ariseth from the word to a sinner: It should never be tasteless nor disrelishing to us, in mentioning, reading, or thinking of it; but it should in reason make sinners glad, that ever there was such a subject to be spoken of, and to be considered; it behoved certainly to be a great business, that brought the Son of God to die; the salvation of sinners is a great work, though many of us think but very little of it.

The sum and scope of Christ's sufferings and death, are briefly holden forth in these words, *By his knowledge shall my righteous Servant justify many*; Where we have, 1. The great benefit that comes by his death, which is *justification*, or the absolving of sinners from the guilt of sin, and from the curse of God due to them for sin: by Christ's interposing himself to become a Sin-offering, there is a way laid down, how sinners may be relieved. 2. The parties made partakers of this benefit, and they are called *many*. 3. The way how it is derived to these many, it is *by his knowledge;* that is, by, or through faith in him.

We have spoken somewhat of the benefit itself, *justification;* which is the thing aimed at, for the most part, in preaching, and in all other ordinances, that God may, by the righteousness of his Son in the gospel, carry on the justification of sinners, through their knowledge of him, or by causing them to rest upon his righteousness by faith, in order to their salvation. It is sad, that in this point, which is of so great concernment, so many should go so far wrong, and mistake so grosly, that it is no great matter, in some respect, whether they be called *Christians*, or not; this being the advantage of a *Christian*, that he hath a way to justification, and absolution from sin and wrath before God, revealed to him, which others have not; who, if he come short of this, or fall in gross errors about it, he had little or no advantage beyond *Heathens*, who may have more of the fat of the earth, and of the things of the world, than these who are within the visible church have: But in this, in a special manner, the *Christian* excels and goes beyond the *Pagan* or *Heathen*, that he hath a way laid down to him, how he may come to be reconciled to God, and freed from wrath, and from his curse due for sin; which we have shewed to be by fleeing to Christ, and by faith resting on his righteousness and satisfaction: For Christ the Cautioner having paid the debt, by laying down a price fully satisfactory to divine justice; and this satisfaction being offered in the Gospel, upon the condition of receiving him; a sinner giving his consent to God's offer, and closing therewith, may confidently expect, according to that offer to be justified, and no other ways.

We shew you one particular, great and gross error, wherewith these, who are under the darkness of *Popery*, are wofully carried away; which we did the rather touch upon, because tho' it be a doctrinal error in respect of them, and disputed for by them; yet, in respect of the practice of many *Protestant Christians*, it is very rife and ordinary, that is, to mistake, err, or go wrong in the way of making of their peace with God: And there are *three* sorts especially, who do exceedingly mistake, err, and go wrong here; these of whom I mean, and am now speaking, are not such as are maintaining, disputing, or writing for such errors, but such as count themselves to be sound Protestant Christians, and haters of the gross Popish error, that we spake somewhat to the last day. The *first* sort are these who to this hour never laid down any solid reckoning how to make their peace with God, or what way to come at absolution before him; these persons do in practice deny, whatever may be their professions, that there is any such thing as a reckoning to be made betwixt God and them; or that there is a necessity of justification, for preventing of their eternal ruin and destruction: they live from their birth, with a hope of coming to heaven, without looking how they may pass this great step of justification before God, they never saw nor laid to heart their need of it; are there not many hearing me to day, that are of this number? who will needs keeps up confidently their fancied hope of heaven, and yet never knew what it was to answer a challenge for Sin, or a threatning of the curse, for the breach of God's law, from Christ's righteousness; nor did they ever sist, and arraign themselves before God's tribunal, as guilty; nor did they ever think seriously of their charge, nor

of

of their summons, nor of the way of making their peace with God, by taking hold of Christ's righteousness. A *second* sort are the generality of legal Professors; I do not say, that they are legal in their practice; that is, that they make it their business to keep the law, for they are as little concerned, or careful in that as any; but they are legal in this respect, that when it comes to the making of their peace with God, they know nothing but the law to deal with, as that man spoken of, Matth. xxv. that got the one talent, and was utterly careless to improve it; yet, when it comes to a reckoning, he stands and sticks to the rigor of the law; *Master,* saith he, *lo, here thou hast that which is thine;* just so, such will be ready to say, We have no more grace than God hath given us, we have a good heart to God, we are doing what we dow or can. Here come in prophane men, meer civil men, and hypocrites; and more especially the meer civil men, who do much in the duties of the second table of the law, and they will profess that they do mind judgment and a reckoning; but, as if they had been bred and brought up in a *Popish* school, they foist in a legal righteousness, instead of Christ's, as the ground of their justification before the tribunal of God. Ye may take these instances of this sort of persons, which are very common, and who in their practice almost in every thing agree with the *Popish* doctrine. The 1*st* instance is of such persons that know nothing of the imputation of Christ's righteousness, yet if we speak of it, they will fall out in such expressions as these, We can do nothing of ourselves, there is no goodness in us, its God's grace that must do our turn; yet in the mean time it is not Christ's righteousness, they lay down to themselves as the ground of their justification, but the good which they have done as they suppose in Christ's strength, and the grace which is given them to work, and do that good by; which is the same thing with the *Popish* way of justification, as if Christ had procured an ability to us to keep the law ourselves, in order to our being justified thereby: Hence they will believe, pray, hear the word, praise, and go about other duties, and will profess that they acknowledge Christ in these, and that they have the grace from him to perform them; He furnishes the flock, and they trade with it, and so for the attaining of life, they are obliged to their own trading; which is in words to pretend grace, but really to put our own works and righteousness in the room of Christ's righteousness, as the ground, or meritorious cause of justification; for the grace given to us, enabling us to work, is not Christ's righteousness, but our own, because given to us, and working in us; and so it is always ourselves and our own righteousness, not Christ's and his righteousness, that we rest upon. A *second* instance of some folk, that speak of Christ, and of attaining life through him, yet it is not in respect of his merit, but in respect of his strength; for such will say, We hope through Christ's strength to come to heaven; their meaning wherein is, that he will help them so to repent and believe, so to be holy and resist temptations, as they shall come to heaven thereby, as the deserving cause of their coming thither. It is true, there is something right here, when in its own place; if whole Christ were rested upon, justification being put in the first place, and his merit rested up for that, it were good that his strength were leaned to, and made use of, for performing the duties of sanctification: but when his strength is rested upon as the alone thing, and when we look not to Christ's purchase and merit as the ground of our acceptation, but to Christ as enabling us to do duties, to the end that we may give God a recompence thereby; at the best it is but he and we together: This certainly is wrong; for nothing is proposed as a satisfaction to God's justice here, but what is immediately our own. A *third* sort are somewhat wiser, who, it may be, think, that any thing that is in themselves, is not worth the naming; but, partly through Christ's matter, and partly through what they have, and can do themselves, or by these joined together, they hope to be saved. This was the doctrinal error of the *Galatians*, who attributed justification to Christ, and to the works of the law jointly. This way ascribes to Christ's righteousness this much, that it makes our own righteousness to be accepted, as the ground of our justification before God, which in some respect is worse than the covenant of works; for the covenant of works sought a perfect righteousness; but this way offers an imperfect righteousness, and to amend, and to eke out our imperfect righteousness, it takes in the righteousness of Christ; but there is no such covenant, or way of justification in scripture; for God made but two covenants for men to attain life by, one of *works,* which is now impossible; the other of *grace,* by which only it is possible to attain justification and life: This makes a third covenant, or contrivance, by a mixture, partly of some works in us, and partly of some grace in Christ, to make up what is lacking in our works; and yet this way is very pleasing to our nature, and that to which we are much inclined for justification; for men are naturally disposed to think that they give Christ enough, when they allow his righteousness to make up what is defective in their own. It is true indeed, that Christ's merits do wash our duties, but our duties come never up to be the ground of our justification in whole, or in part; which is evident from this, that, ere Christ make our duties or performances acceptable, he makes our persons first to be accepted; and that once being, then any thing performed by us, in Christ's strength, according to the will of God, is acceptable also.

But now we proceed further in the words of the text; and, before we come to the causes of our justification, we shall briefly *observe* two or three things that ly obviously in our way; the 1*st*, whereof is this, that the absolving of a sinner, through the imputation of Christ's righteousness, is the proper and native result of Christ's purchase, and the great intendment of it; his sufferings and soul-travel were undergone, to procure justification to *many*: So that if we would know what is the fruit of Christ's soul-travel, here it is, *by his knowledge shall many be justified*; therefore, Rom. v. 9. it is attributed to his blood, *being justified by his blood, we shall be saved from wrath*; and, 2 Cor. v. ult. *he was made sin for us, who knew no sin, that we might be made the righteousness of God through him*; that which I mean is this, that Christ's intendment in his dying was to redeem, and really and actually to procure absolution and justification before the throne of God, to so many as should believe on him; or we may take the doctrine these two ways, which yet come both to the same account. 1. Thus, That the thing which Christ intended in his death, was not a mere possibility, that sinners might be justified, nor to lay down a conditional way of their justification, whereby they might come, or not come to it, and so to make it possible; but that which he intended was, that their justification might follow absolutely; I do not mean instantly, and without the interveening of a condition; for here his *knowledge* comes in, as the condition: but that which I mean is, that he died, that their justification might actually and certainly follow as a fruit of his purchase. In a word, his death and sufferings were not to make justification possible to all, but that so many as he bargained for might be absolutely justified; or that *many*, that is, all the elect, might be actually justified, because *he shall bear their iniquities*, therefore by his knowledge they shall be justified.

We *observe* it for these *ends* or *uses*, 1*st*, To give an answer to that question, What is the native result of Christ's death to his people? We say, It is their absolute and actual justification. These that would extend the grace of God, and the death of Christ, so broad and wide, as to leave out none, say in effect, that the design thereof was to lay down such a way as makes it possible to all to be justified, and yet such a way as makes it possible that none at all shall be justified; for it hangs justification on the free-will of the creature; and so, in striving to make grace broader than God allows, they come to make it none at all, by leaving it on man's free-will, whether it shall be effectual or not, but, blessed be God, the covenant of God was not on these terms; for it is said here, *That by his knowledge he shall justify many*. 2*dly*, It gives us these two practical *uses*. 1. It shews what should be our intendment, in our use-making of Christ's death, and that is, that we may be justified, and absolved by it, even to make use of it for attaining to pardon of sin, and peace with God: If this be overlooked and neglected, all other fruits of it are useless; it will avail but little to be a member of the visible church, to be baptized, and to be admitted to the Lord's supper, to have literal knowledge of the principles of religion, to have a gift of preaching, or of prayer, &c. these will not justify: The peculiar thing aimed at in Christ's death, and that which his people aim at, and have to rejoice in, is *justification through his knowledge*, which is always to be understood without prejudice to the study of holiness.

2. It gives us this *Use*; Whoever would have absolution before God, would know that this was the very thing engaged for by Christ, and his intendment in his death, that sinners, believing in him, might be absolutely and actually justified by him; it was not simply to propose justification to them, but that absolutely they might be absolved from the curse of God due to them for sin: and now, may I not ask, whether this is more encouraging to sinners, to have Christ procuring justification only conditionally to them, or to have the thing absolutely conferred upon them? this is a ground whereupon believing sinners lift up their heads confidently, and expect justification through his righteousness: it is this that was promised to

Christ

Christ, and it is this that is the native fruit of his death, without which it will be fruitless: and this may remove the great obstruction that readily a sinner, when he is serious, seeth lying in his way, to wit, the want of righteousness, and the fear of not being absolved; the want of inherent righteousness in himself, which makes him liable to the curse of the law; when he seeth upon what terms Christ died. *First*, To procure a righteousness to them that wanted righteousness. And, *Secondly*, Upon these terms, that sinners through faith in him, might be justified, and freed from the guilt of sin, as if they never had sinned themselves. Considering this to be his intendment, according to the terms of the covenant of grace, what have they, or what can they have, to fear or fright them from expecting the fulfilling of this promise? because the contrivance of the covenant of redemption, is to buy justification absolutely, and not the possibility of it only; not to buy grace to us, whereby to justify ourselves, but justification itself, so as we may be beholden to him alone for it.

Again, 2*dly*, When we say, that the justification of a sinner is the proper result of Christ's death, it may be thus understood, that the righteousness whereby a sinner is justified, is immediately Christ's death and purchase, as to the meritorious cause thereof: so that if we look to what justifies a sinner, as to the meritorious cause of it, the knitting of these two together, *He shall see of the travel of his soul, and shall be satisfied;* and, *By his knowledge shall my righteous Servant justify many*, doth hold it forth to be Christ's death and purchase; the travel of his soul is, and must be the ground on which a lost sinner is justified before the throne of God. This both confirms what we formerly proposed concerning this doctrine, and also shews that the justification of a sinner is not by inherent holiness. Whence comes it, I pray, that makes a sinner acceptable before God? It is not from habitual, nor actual inherent grace, but from Christ's righteousness, laid hold on by faith, that gripeth and adhereth to it: but from the latter part of the words, we will have more particular occasion to speak to this, where these two are knit together; *By his knowledge shall my righteous Servant justify many, for he shall bear their iniquity*; therefore we do now pass it.

The *Object* of this benefit is *many*; many ordinarily in scripture implies these two things, 1*st*, A great number, and so it shews the extent of the object; that is, that Christ shall purchase and redeem many, or by his death procure justification to many. 2*dly*, A restriction, and thus *many* is opposed to *all*; and so the meaning is, there shall many be justified by Christ's death, but not all; and therefore, as none can from these words plead for an universality in justification, so neither can they in redemption, for he only bare their iniquities, whom by his knowledge he justifies.

Looking on these *many*, in this twofold consideration, we may take these *Observations* from it. 1*st*, Taking it extensively, *Observe*, 1. That the righteousness of Christ is of itself able to justify many; it is a righteousness that can satisfy for the sins of many; or thus, That in the covenant of redemption, there is an intended application of Christ's righteousness and purchase to many. 2*dly*, That there are many, who shall indeed partake of Christ's righteousness, and be justified by it; it is not one, or two, or a thousand, but as it was intended to justify *many*, so it shall be actually applied *to many* for their justification. 3*dly*, Comparing the former words, *He shall see of the travel of his soul, and shall be satisfied*, with these words, *By his knowledge shall my righteous Servant justify many*; *Observe*, That Christ is not satisfied for the travel of his soul, except many be justified by it; or thus, It is Christ's satisfaction, how many there be that make use of him, and that, by making use of him, come to be justified by him, as afterward we will see: These many are all these that believe, all these that have this true and saving knowledge of him, and do rightly acknowledge him.

The making out of one of these doctrines will make them all out, that Christ's righteousness is able to justify many; that many shall be justified by it; and that it is his satisfaction and delight, that many may be justified, and get this good of it: it is said, Matth. xx. 28. That *he came to lay down his life a ransom for many*, and Rom. v. 15. That *the gift of grace, which is by one man Jesus Christ, hath abounded unto many*; and verse 19. *As by one man's disobedience many were made sinners, so by the obedience of one shall many be made righteous*. Let but these *four* things be put together and considered, and if it be found, that there is no just ground to quarrel these doctrines, 1*st*. The native worth, and intrinsick value that is in the satisfaction of Christ; it is *the blood of God*, of the Person that is God: it is an offering that flows from a willing and cheerful Giver, which makes it the more acceptable; he was content with delight to pay the price; there cannot be a limiting or bounding of this worth or value, because there cannot be any bounding or limiting of the Person that gives the value to it, if it be considered in itself. 2*dly*, Consider the freeness of the offer, which takes in *many*: our Lord communicates very freely what he hath bought very dear; and it is done with respect to his taking in of many, to take away all exceptions from the poor and needy, and from them that want money. 3*dly*, As the terms are free, so the offer is very broad, and comprehensive, as we see, Isaiah lv. 1. *Ho, every one that thirsts, come to the waters;* and Rev. xxii. *Whosoever will, let him come, and take of the water of life freely.* And we find these expressions, *all that believe;* and, *whosoever believes,* to be frequently used in the scriptures; which takes in all that will yield themselves to him on the terms of the covenant, to close the bargain with him. 4*thly*, Consider God's end in the justification of sinners, which is to make his grace to shine, and to triumph, and to make its victory over man's sins conspicuous and glorious, by being beyond it; not in respect of the number of persons, but in this respect, that as Adam's one sin brought death on many, so the death of Christ hath brought justification to many; as it is Rom. v. *The judgment was by one to condemnation, but the free gift is of many offences unto justification.* Whereas Adam's one offence brought death to many, here the relieving of one sinner is the procuring of freedom to many, because in that respect Christ is a satisfaction for many offences. But it may be *objected* here, Is it not said, that the way to Heaven *is strait, and few there be that enter in thereat?* They are thin sown, to say so, that are heirs of this inheritance. *I answer*, by a distinction; Though they be comparatively few, yet, considered in themselves absolutely, they are many, or they are simply many, though comparatively but few: consider and compare them with the multitude of reprobates that are even in the visible church, they are few; yet if ye will consider them in themselves, they are many: and it is most true that is spoken, Rev. vii. 9. *I saw a number which no man could number:* if we look since the beginning of the world, how some are taken in this age, and some in that, some of this nation, and some of another, they will be found to be but few, when all nations are put together; yet in themselves they are many. There are these *three uses* of it, which may be reasons why it is put in here. The *First* is, to let us see the largeness of the extent of the worth of Christ, and of the allowance of grace, in reference to the justification of sinners through him; which should make us stand, pause, and wonder. It had been much, if grace had saved but one, more if it had saved a thousand, or twenty thousand: But O! what ground of admiration is it, when many are saved by it! This is the native end, why it is put in here, even to shew, that it is not for nought that Christ died, it shall be a blessing to many. I mark it, because, though the presumptuous thoughts of many lead them to extend the merits of Christ to all in the visible church; yet it may be, that in others there are too narrow limiting thoughts of the extent of his merits, and of the allowance of grace, as to the number of the elect that shall be saved: it being certain, that as we are in hazard, and ready to abuse any thing; so this, if it be said that they are *many* that are justified, we are ready to exclude none; and if it be said that they are *few*, we are ready to make grace as it were a nigard and churl, and to contract and narrow too much the application of it.

The second *use* of it, (which is a second reason, why this word *many* is put in here) may serve for encouragement to sinners, and to hearten them to essay to get this benefit of justification made their own: many trow (and in some respect it is a truth) that it is a singular and odd thing to come by justification; and hence they conclude, that they will never get it; and indeed, if the thought of its singularity and rareness made them careful to win at the thing, it were a profitable use of it; but, when it makes them heartless to attain the thing, it is a wrong and prejudicial use of it: but sinners, there is here ground of encouragement, provocation and up-stirring to you, to seek after justification through Jesus Christ, because there are *many* that are the objects of it. The righteousness of Christ is a righteousness that will save *many;* it is an article of the covenant of redemption, that Christ shall get *many;* the promise will give title and right to many, he will not be content, if he get not *many*. Now, putting these together, it cannot but be very great encouragement to seek, and a strong ground to expect justification on this account, because, 1. That which a believing sinner gets, is justification, pardon of sin, both original and actual, and its complete actual justification, not only the procuring the offer of it, but the application of it, *justification from all things, from which we could not be justified by the law of Moses,* and justification never to be reversed.

versed. 2. This justification is designed for, and allowed to *many;* the stepping in of some before others doth not wrong them: and there needs not be disputes about election; for the text says, that the allowance of grace is to *many*. 3. It is Christ's satisfaction that he gets many to be justified; and the more that step to, to lay hold on this benefit, he hath as it were the more satisfaction. And if the sinner should say, I know not if I be included in that number; the terms of the covenant run to all that believe: if there be a flying to Christ by faith for refuge, there needs not be anxious disputing, whether the sinner will come speed; but there should be a stepping forward. *Many* have gotten good, and *many* will get good, and there is room sufficient for as many as will yield themselves up to Christ, and rest upon his righteousness; it is a large mantle that covers thousands, and the Lord will have thousands to be hidden under it, and justified by it.

3*dly*, It serves to be a most terrible ground of inexcusableness to these, to whom Christ's righteousness is spoken of, and offered in the gospel, who yet neglect to make use of it, that he was content to lay down his life, and that as a ransom for many. None needs to say, I knew not if I would be welcome; he said, It was for *many:* and though he said not, it was for *all*, yet it is for *all* that will believe in him; and therefore it is not, nor shall not, because he hath confined the benefit to few, that ye are, or shall be excluded; but because, tho' he extended the benefit to *many*, yet ye excluded yourselves: and none of you, who hear this gospel, shall have it to say, I betook myself to Christ by faith, but he refused to admit of me, and he would have no more than he had. There are many who please themselves with such a word as this, when they hear that many will be saved; but it will be the dearest bought doctrine that ever ye heard: It had been in some respect better, that ye had heard that it was but two or three that will come to heaven; because the hearing of *many's* coming thither, will greatly aggravate your guilt, who neglect so great a salvation.

Therefore take two or three *caveats* of this *Doctrine*. And, 1. Beware of being secure because there are *many* that shall be justified, there are many more that shall perish; compare these that perish with these that will be saved, and it will be found, that they are but a handful that will be saved, and that swarms and multitudes will go to hell: Therefore, when ye hear that the door is opened to many, let it encourage you to enter in; but remember this, that more will be excluded, and perish, than will enter in and be saved. The scripture says, *Many are called, but few are chosen,* even in respect of the called within the visible church. 2. Consider that grace is enlarging of this benefit: to take in many, will be your greatest challenge and aggravation, that shall miss, and come short of it; *Therefore let us* (as it is, Heb. iv.) *fear, lest having a promise left us of entring into his rest, any of us should seem to come short of it.* When this door is opened to us, we would by all means fear coming short, or not entring, through unbelief; for it will be worse with us, than if the door had never been opened. Folks ordinarily think not so much to miss or come short of a privilege, which but one or two have access to; but when it is such a privilege as is made attainable by *many*, the missing of it galleth and tormenteth the more; and when *many* shall come from the east, west, south and north, and shall sit down with Abraham, Isaac, and Jacob in the kingdom of heaven, what weeping and gnashing of teeth will it cause to them, who shall be secluded? And therefore, 3. Beware of thinking that there is the less diligence or fear required, because we say, that *many* will be justified; for, tho' there be many that are redeemed, and *many* that shall be justified, yet all these come to be justified through Christ's *knowledge:* And therefore such as are ignorant and profane can but take little or no comfort hence, while they continue to be such. Tho' there be many that are justified, yet none but believers are justified; and none can warrantably look on themselves to be believers, but such as are sincere students of holiness: I would not therefore have you laying weight, either on *many* or *few's* being justified, except by way of motive, but on the way that ye take to come by the end, tho' a great many more were saved than will be; if ye take not the way of faith and holiness to come to salvation, ye will not get yourselves shrouded in the croud, but tho' there were never so few damned, ye shall make up the number. In a word, it is ground of encouragement to a poor sinner, that would fain be justified in God's own way; it is also ground of shame and confusion of face to the unbeliever, that restrains the benefit of Christ's purchase, and shuts himself out, when grace doth make use of such expressions to bring him in; and it will be ground of conviction to all that have so wide a door opened to them, and do not strive to enter in. It may be many of you think little of this now; but in the day when *many* shall be taken into the kingdom of heaven, and others shut out, it will be known to be a matter of the greatest concernment. If once we could be induced to be in earnest in this one thing, there were a great point gained on the hearers of the Gospel; and till it be seriously minded, there is nothing that we can do in religion, that will be to any purpose.

SERMON LVI.

Isaiah liii. 11. — —*By his knowledge shall my righteous Servant justify many*, &c.

IT is a great matter to have the solid impression of Christ's fulness on your spirits, and to be throughly persuaded that there is a righteousness to be had in him; yet the consolation is not full, unless there be a clearness in the way how this righteousness is applied and come by, and a kindly yielding to follow that way: For, tho' we know that Christ died, and that there is a righteousness purchased, yet there are many that are never justified, and that shall never be saved by it; and therefore it would not be so much to know that there is such a thing, if he had not laid down a way how we may be partakers of it; which way can no more fail and misgive, than Christ's righteousness can: and these words hold out the way, *By his knowledge shall my righteous Servant justify many;* that is, Through faith in Christ many shall be made righteous; his satisfaction shall be accounted the believers, whereby it shall come to pass, that they shall be as really justified, as if they had born their own iniquities, because his bearing of them shall be accounted theirs.

We spake, 1. Of this general, That there is such a thing as justification, or God's absolving of a sinner, who by his own iniquity is liable to the curse. 2. That this justification is the proper effect of Christ's death. 3. From the objects of it; That they are *many*, yet not all, who are justified, *many* being put as a mids betwixt two extremes, neither including all, nor only taking in a very few. Having put by these more general doctrines, we would now speak a little to this great benefit of *justification*, in reference to the particular *causes* that concur to the attaining of it, which will lead us to a more distinct uptaking of it: there is ground for them all in the *text;* and therefore we shall put them together, that we may have a short view of this great benefit complexly.

There are commonly *six causes* assigned to, or made necessary to concur in justification, tho' we know not well how to express them, so as ye may take them up, because of the ignorance of many of you. 1. There is the *efficient* cause, and that is God, the Party that doth justify. 2. The *end*, or *final* cause, and that is his own glory. 3. The *meritorious* cause, or that which procures it, or the ground on which God justifies, and that is Christ's merit. 4. The *inward instrumental* cause, by which we get a title to, and an interest in Christ's merit, and that is faith. 5. The *formal* cause, or that wherein justification consists, and that is imputation of Christ's righteousness to the sinner upon his acceptation of it, and the absolving of the sinner by vertue of his righteousness. 6. The *external instrumental* cause, and that is the word of God, by which this justification is revealed, and wherein God declares and passes the sentence.

For the *first*, ye would, for clearing of it, remember what we spake in our entring on this doctrine, that this word *justification* is a legal, forensick, or judicial word: and we are to conceive of God, who is the Party offended, as the Judge; and of the sinner arraigned, and brought before his tribunal to be judged, as a delinquent: the law gives in the libel or indictment, founds the challenge or accusation; the sinner's conscience and actions are so many witnesses, proving the breaking of the law, and him to be obnoxious to the curse on that account. In this we say that God is the *efficient* cause, and so we may take the words, *By his knowledge shall my righteous Servant justify many*, actively and efficiently to look to Christ, as having this power, as he is God; which is proper to God alone, as is clear, Rom. viii. 34. *It is God that justifies.* 1 Cor. iv. 4. *Tho' I know nothing by myself, yet I am not hereby justified, but he that judgeth me is the Lord:* And this is a reason of the former, to wit, that no other can absolve but God, the Party offended, who is Judge.

We mark it for this practical *use*, which the Apostle makes of it, which is to bid us lay less weight upon others thinking well of us, or absolving us, and on our own absolving ourselves; the Lord chargeth some thus, Luke xvi. 15. *Ye are they which justify yourselves before men, but*

God knows your hearts: Paul will not justify himself, for that is God's place and prerogative. How many are there, who take another person's testimony for God's, and think, that since others love, respect and commend them, they are in a good condition, and well enough? But, alas, is that person God? Except mens testimony be founded on the grounds that are held forth in the word (and if so, then it is God's testimony) it will not do the business, nor avail you any thing; except there be a sentence of absolution pronounced and past by him, their sentence, or yours, will be recalled; though many of you do not down-right profess this, yet many of you practically fall into it: always remember that it is God that justifies, and that his absolution is different from mens, and from your own; many have good thoughts of you, and so may ye of yourselves, when God may have none.

For the 2*d*. to wit, the *Final* cause, it is clear here also, by comparing the former verse with the word going before, in this same verse; and ye may take it in this *Observation*, That the glory of God, and of the Mediator, is the end that God hath before him, in the justifying of sinners; therefore it is called the Lord's *pleasure*, or delight, and the Mediator's *satisfaction;* because he hath proposed to himself therein the glory of his grace especially, and also of others of his attributes, as his end, and so hath a kind of longing desire and thirst after; for the Lord, being absolutely glorious, cannot but love his own glory; and being the infinitely pure, all-sufficient Good, he cannot but love himself and his own glory; and therefore for attaining of this end, he justifies and absolves poor sinners. Now God is glorified here two ways, 1. He gets the glory of his grace, that is exceedingly magnified thereby, as is clear, Eph. i. 5. *Having predestinated us to the adoption of children by Jesus Christ to himself, according to the good pleasure of his will, to the praise of the glory of his grace:* It is the Lord's pleasure, to glorify his grace; and this proves to be the glory of his grace, when a sinner liable to wrath is fully justified, and intitled to heaven. 2. He gets thereby the glory of his justice and righteousness, which takes in the glorifying of God's holiness and wisdom: He is seen here to be a holy God, who will needs testify his dislike at sin, wherever it is; a just God, that will needs punish it; a gracious God, that will pardon; and such a wise God, as finds out the way, how both to punish and pardon, without any the least imputation, either to his justice, or to his mercy and grace; and so he shews himself to be infinitely just, gracious, wise and holy, in the justification of sinners: these we may see, Rom. iii. 24, 25, 26. *Being justified freely by his grace, through the redemption that is in Jesus Christ,* there justice and grace shine clearly: justification is free, yet there is a price laid down, and a satisfaction made to justice; and the 26. verse shews the end, to wit, *To declare his righteousness, that he might be just, and the justifier of them who believe in Jesus.* He hath indeed taken a way, how to pardon sin, but so as it is through a redemption, or by the exacting of a price, that he may be seen to be just, who will not pardon sin without a satisfaction; justice kythes in this, that Christ is put to pay a great price: and that he may be seen to be gracious, he hath laid down a way, how the price, that was to be paid by Christ, might be imputed to, or reckoned on the account of the guilty sinner, and that he might be thereby absolved: And thus justice and grace may kiss each other, in this admirable contrivance. And although none almost except Socinians deny the justice of God, in the justification of sinners; yet as they do doctrinally in substance deny it, so many of us, who profess to abhor their doctrine, do practically deny it also.

And therefore, as the 1*st Use* of it, let me speak a little to unbelievers, and ask you, What think ye will become of you? ye must either betake yourselves to Christ's satisfaction, or ye must resolve to satisfy for yourselves: Secure hypocrites think of nothing but of grace, and that God will always be gracious, and never suffer themselves to think of the necessity of a satisfaction to be made to his justice; and thus they slight, and on the matter deny his justice, as if he were not to be glorified in that attribute, as well as in his grace and mercy; whereas there is no other way to declare God to be just in the justification of them that believe, but this, which brings them to Christ's satisfaction.

Use 2. It is ground of notable consolation, and encouragement to a poor exercised soul, sensible of sin, whereupon to expect justification: It is God's end, in justifying sinners, to set out the glory of his grace: and is it not much, that God should contrive such a way for glorifying of himself, as should carry along with it good to us, yea, such a way as should resolve in our good, which comes in as a subordinate end, to the glorifying of his grace, as the ultimate end? may not this be an encouragement to them, to seek after justification on these terms, and for this end?

Use

Use 3. It shews, That as many as submit not to the way of this righteousness, and of justification by grace, are thwarting with God's end; they set themselves to hinder and obstruct it, even that he should not be glorified in his justice and mercy: they do what they can, that God should neither be just nor gracious; but he shall be just in condemning them, whether they will or not: though he be not glorified in his grace, as to them, they setting themselves, what they can, to let it; yet in his justice he shall most certainly be glorified. O that men and women believed how deep their guilt draws, who are standing in the way of the glorifying of God's grace! it will be found, in some respect, to draw deeper than the guilt of these abominable sins of adultery and murder, in the day of the Lord: and yet many of you will be found to have done this, and to have come short of righteousness.

For the 3d, that is the *meritorious* cause: take it in this Doctrine, *That the meritorious cause, that procures our justification, and with respect to which God justifies a sinner, is the alone merit and satisfaction of Christ Jesus.* And this arises from the text, on these two considerations, *1st*, Because this justification is laid down, as an effect of Christ's soul-travel, and suffering: if justification be the proper and immediate effect of Christ's sufferings, then his soul-sufferings must be the meritorious cause of it, we cannot imagine another: He purposeth, by his sufferings for the elect, that they shall by his knowledge be justified; therefore they must be absolved, and justified, by his interposing to take on our debt, and so his sufferings must be the procuring cause of it. The 2d consideration is taken from the words following, *He shall justify many, for he shall bear their iniquities*: if Christ's bearing of our iniquities be the ground of our justification, or that by which it is procured, then his sufferings must be the meritorious cause of our justification, or that on account whereof we are justified; because his bearing of our iniquities can no other ways be the cause of our justification, but by his interposing to merit the same to us by his sufferings. Would ye know, as if the prophet had said, how Christ's sufferings shall be the cause of our justification? here it is, he shall bear our iniquities, and therefore our justification flows therefrom: the Lord, by the prophet, hath so knit these two together, that his sufferings both go before, and are subjoined to *his justifying of many*, that it may be put out of question, that the Mediator's sufferings is the alone meritorious cause of his pronouncing the sentence of justification, and of accepting and accounting us as righteous before him.

This is not in so many words professedly controverted, or denied by the Papists, with whom we here deal: for they grant, that Christ by his sufferings procures grace, and God's acceptation of our good works, in so far as they are rewarded, beyond their condignity: but, to make the difference betwixt them and us the more clear, we shall put in *four* words in the doctrine, and speak a little to them; we say then, that Christ's satisfaction is not only the meritorious cause of justification, but also, 1. It is the nearest and most immediate cause. 2. The alone meritorious cause. 3. The meritorious cause, as contradistinguished from, and opposed to our works, and inherent righteousness. 4. It is the meritorious cause, as inherent in him, and as imputed to us. These *four* are clear in the *text*, and may very well be put in the doctrine.

1st, Then we say, it is not only the meritorious cause, but the next immediate cause, *causa propinqua* (as we use to speak in schools) of our justification; so that if it be asked, What is the cause or ground on which God absolves a sinner, or the next immediate thing, that he hath a respect to in his justifying of him ? It is Christ's merit, his soul-travel and suffering: Papists deny this, and make the next immediate cause to be the grace infused in us, that which is called, *gratia gratum faciens*: but if ye ask the prophet, what is the ground, I mean the next immediate cause, on which justification is derived to many ? he tells us, that it is not the inherent righteousness of these who are justified, but that it is Christ's *soul-travel*, and *his bearing of our iniquities*: hence, 1 Cor. i. 30. Christ is called our righteousness, *He is* (saith the apostle) *made of God unto us, wisdom, righteousness*, &c. Not only by Christ have we a righteousness, that makes us acceptable to God, but his righteousness is ours, and God's respecting of us, in, or throught it, making us acceptable.

2dly, Not only is his righteousness the meritorious cause, but it is the only meritorious, or the alone meritorious cause; and herein Papists and we differ: They grant, that Christ's satisfaction is the meritorious cause; but remotely only, as it procures inward or inherent grace, by which we merit; but they will not have it to be the only meritorious cause, but will needs have our own works to merit also, and that properly; whereas the prophet speaks of justification, as the effect of Christ's soul-travel only; and if so, then

these

there can be no other thing admitted, for there cannot be two social or joint meritorious causes; therefore throughout the scripture, when the merit of justification is attributed to Christ, it excludes all other things, and is opposed to our own works; which is the *Third* thing.

3*dly*, Then we say, That Christ's righteousness is the meritorious cause of our justification, as contradistinguished from, and opposed to our own inherent righteousness, or works; and herein also Papists and we differ: they grant indeed a meritorious influence to Christ's righteousness; but that is (say they) as it makes our own righteousness meritorious, not as contradistinguished from, and opposed to our own righteousness, but as having influence on it. Now these are directly opposed in scripture; I shall only name that one clear place, Phil. iii. 9. *That I may be found in him, not having mine own righteousness, which is of the law, but that which is by the faith of Christ*; where Paul is consulting, and resolving what he will take himself to, as his defence at the bar of God; we see, 1. That it is his scope and design, that, in the day of judgment, he may be found in such a case and posture, that he may be able to abide the trial. And, 2. That he speaks of *Two* righteousnesses, the *One* is his own, that is the inherent grace which he hath gotten, and the works which he hath done: the *Other* is the righteousness of Christ without him, which is by faith: Now, when he lays his reckoning, he is so far from joining these two together, as con-causes, or social causes of his justification, that he opposes them; *That I may be found in him, not having mine own righteousness;* without my own, or, *not having my own*, &c. *in him*, as having given up with, denied and renounced my own righteousness: He will not admit of that, on any terms, in less or in more; so clearly doth he, as to his justification before God, seclude his own righteousness, and betake himself to Christ's righteousness alone, as contradistinguished to his own.

4*thly*, We say, That Christ's righteousness, as it is in him, and imputed to us, or made ours by imputation, is the alone meritorious cause of our justification and salvation; so as that which he hath purchased is reckoned and accounted the sinner's, as if it were his own inherently and personally: This I also gather from the words, *By his knowledge shall my righteous Servant justify many, for he shall bear their iniquities:* Would ye know, as if the prophet had said, how Christ is the meritorious cause of justification?' Thus it is, because he shall bear their iniquities; if he hath taken on the burden of their sins, and had their sins imputed to him, then it will follow by proportion, that they are justified by the imputation of his righteousness to them. And there is nothing that the scripture doth more inculcate than this, that we are justified by the righteousness of Christ, without us, and imputed to us, or reckoned ours; we by faith laying holding upon it, and God's accepting of it for us, makes it become ours; and yet there is nothing that we do more practically err in, and which Papists do more scorn and flout at, wholly enervating the way and contrivance of grace, by excluding and shouldering out the righteousness of Christ, calling it, in derision, a *putative*, or merely farcied, and imaginary righteousness, (as if there were no reality in it) and by bringing in, and establishing their own righteousness; though it be very clear from this, and many other scriptures, that Christ's righteousness must be ours by imputation, because he bare our iniquities: He became our righteousness, by paying of our debt, as our Cautioner, and no other ways; the scripture never speaks of his being our righteousness, by procuring ability to us to pay our own debt.

I shall clear this 4*th* Branch a little further, because it will serve to clear the rest, that is, That Christ's righteousness, as it is in him, and imputed to us, is the only meritorious cause of our justification; and if we consider, *First*, The way of justification that is used among men, this will be the more plain; There being two covenants, by the one of which life was once attainable, and by the other of which it is now attainable; 1. The covenant of works, which absolves a man that never brake it, which is, as when one among men, or before mens court, is declared to be free, because he was never owing the debt. 2. The covenant of grace, that provides a Cautioner to pay the sinner's debt, upon whose payment thereof, had recourse to by faith, there is access in law to the sinner to call for absolution: Even as it is in mens courts, though the principal debitor hath nothing to pay, yet if the cautioner pay the debt, it is the principal debitor's clearing; and if he should be again charged to pay the debt, his immediate defence would be, that the cautioner had paid it already; So is it here, the Lord hath borrowed, and made use of this way, that is used among men, to make the mystery of justification, which passeth in the court of God, the more clear to us: it is as if one should alledge, that such a person is owing so much, and he should say, I cannot be charged with it, and upon what ground? no, becaufe I am not owing the debt, but becaufe fuch a one has paid it for me; fo fays the apoftle, Rom. viii. 34. *Who fhall lay any thing to the charge of God's elect? It is God that juftifieth, who fhall condemn? It is Chrift that died,* &c. The defence propofed before the tribunal of God, is Chrift dying, and that is as much as he hath paid the price, or debt; who then can charge it on the principal debitor? And the frame and contexture of the words fhews, that it is a judicial procedure; for they fuppofe a charge or libel, and a fentence; and the meritorious caufe of the fentence of abfolution is, *that Chrift hath died.*

2*dly*, If we confider the nature of the two covenants, and compare them together, it will be clear, the Papifts confound the two covenants; for *works* to them is the condition of both covenants, making ufe of that place, Matth. xix. 17, 21. *Keep the commands; if thou wilt be perfect, fell all thou haft, and give to the poor;* quite contrary to the fcope of it: For therein Chrift is putting the man to a thing impoffible to himfelf, to bring him to fee the neceffity of a Mediator, and difcover his unfoundnefs, when he will not forego his great poffeffions for him: But the fcripture doth clearly difference the covenant of grace, and the covenant of works, that they are oppofed; for the covenant of works faith, *Do this and live;* and the covenant of grace faith, *If thou fhalt believe with thy heart in the Lord Jefus, and confefs with thy mouth, thou fhalt be faved:* and therefore the account of one's being juftified in the covenant of grace, muft be different from the account whereon one is juftified in the covenant of works, otherways they could not be oppofite; the covenant of works refpects the inherent righteoufnefs, as the condition; the covenant of grace refpects faith, taking hold of the righteoufnefs of Chrift; and therefore his righteoufnefs muft juftify, as being in him without us, and as imputed to us: it cannot be our righteoufnefs within, that juftifies; for fo, it fhould be the fame with the covenant of works; for though Chrift did procure inherent righteoufnefs to us, it makes no difference in the condition itfelf, which is works.

3*dly*, It will be clear, if we confider how the fcripture fpeaks of Chrift's righteoufnefs becoming ours, even as our fins became Chrift's, and was the caufe (if we may fo fpeak) of his condemnation; that is, as he became liable to the curfe, that as he ftood a legal Perfon in our room, he became guilty, and liable to the payment of our debt; for otherways it is abomination once to fpeak of his condemnation; and if his righteoufnefs become ours, as our fin became his, then certainly his righteoufnefs is the caufe of our juftification, as it is in him inherently, and in us by imputation only. The blafphemy of Antinomians is moft detestable, and not at all pleaded for, even by Papifts; and therefore we ftand not on it here. Now our fin became Chrift's by imputation, therefore his righteoufnefs muft be ours the fame way: If it then were afked, How we are juftified? The text anfwers, *He fhall juftify many, becaufe he fhall bear their iniquities:* the prophet makes his fufferings to be the antecedent, whereof our juftification is the confequent; for his bearing of our iniquities is given as a reafon of our juftification; this is alfo clear, 2 Cor. v. ult. *He was made fin for us, who knew no fin, that we might be made the righteoufnefs of God in him:* in which words the Spirit of the Lord doth fo explain, bound and inculcate this, that there can be no rational exception againft it, nor evafion from it; *He was made fin,* that is, a fin-offering, or an offering for our fin, though there was no guile found in his mouth; though he had no fin, neither was capable of fin, yet he was made a facrifice for our fin: as *he was made fin,* fo are we *made the righteoufnefs of God in him.* If any fhould afk, What is it to be made righteous? the apoftle anfwers, Even as Chrift was made fin, the fame way are we made righteous; and that is, by imputation of Chrift's righteoufnefs to us, and not by our own merit; we have no more merit than he had fin: But as he was accounted to be the finner, though free of fin in his own perfon; fo a believing finner is accounted righteous, though without any merit in himfelf, becaufe God hath engaged in his covenant, to make Chrift's righteoufnefs forthcoming to the believer: Though that were enough, yet the Spirit of the Lord addeth a further word, *in him,* to anfwer that queftion, Whether Chrift hath procured inherent holinefs to us, that thereby we may be juftified? No, faith he, that is not the way; our righteoufnefs is *in him,* and not inherent in us: even as the fin imputed to Chrift is inherently in us: fo the righteoufnefs, whereby we are juftified, is inherently in him.

4*thly*, It may be clear from this, that frequently it is called a righteoufnefs that is attained by faith, and that it is oppofed to our own righteoufnefs and working; now it cannot be conceived, how we can get a righteoufnefs by faith, but by pleading that his righteoufnefs may be imputed

unto

SERM. LVI.   *Isaiah* liii. Verse 11.   341

unto us, Rom. iii. 22. It is called *the righteousness which is by faith;* and ver. 25. *Whom God hath set forth for a propitiation, through faith in his blood;* and chap. iv. ver. 5. *To him that worketh not, but believeth on him that justifieth the ungodly, his faith is counted for righteousness:* Faith taking hold of his righteousness offered to sinners in the gospel, his righteousness so taken hold of, becomes a propitiation to pacify God towards the sinner, as if he had satisfied in his own person: Even as if a company of men had been out in rebellion, and a proclamation of pardon comes forth from the king, because he is satisfied by a great friend, who hath paid their ransom: Which proclamation of pardon runs on these terms, Whoever will lay down arms, and come in, and accept of the king's pardon, that is procured, and made offer of, shall be acquitted of the guilt of rebellion, and received into favour; who, whenever they are challenged, will plead their absolution on that friend's procurement, and offered on such terms in the proclamation: Now suppose (as I hinted before, not long ago) that when these rebels have yielded themselves, and accepted of the terms, if any of them should be called to answer at the bar, or the king's bench, as being challenged for his rebellion; his answer and defence would be, That such a proclamation was made to us, and I laid down my arms, and accepted of the pardon; this in justice would be admitted, and sustained as relevant, because that procurement or procured pardon becomes the person's, according to the terms of the proclamation: It is even so here, we are rebels to God, Christ Jesus steps in, as the great Friend of sinners, and satisfied justice; and thereupon the proclamation comes out, as it is, Acts xiii. 38, 39. *Be it known unto you, men and brethren, that through this Man is preached unto you the forgiveness of sins; and by him all that believe are justified from all things, from which ye could not be justified by the law of Moses:* When the sinner is arraigned before the tribunal of God, he hath two acts of his faith; one that submits to God, and to his way of absolving sinners, and another that pleads for absolution, not on the terms of his own innocency, but on the terms on which Christ's satisfaction is made offer to him; and so faith justifies, as it takes hold of the meritorious cause, and builds its defence at God's bar, on Christ's righteousness alone; it is the procurement of the Mediator that it pleads upon, and in this sense the imputed righteousness of Christ, and the righteousness of faith, are one and the same, because faith takes hold of the righteousness without us, which can be no other but the righteousness of Christ.

5*thly*, It is clear from the plain and direct expressions of scripture to this purpose; take but these few, as Rom. iv. 3. and 22. compared with Gen. xv. 6. *Abraham believed God, and it was counted to him for righteousness;* he had the promise of Christ to come, and received and rested on it; it was not his faith, but the promise of the Messiah rested on by faith, that was imputed to him for righteousness; and ver. 6. *Even as David describeth the blessedness of the man to whom God imputeth righteousness without works;* It is not, Blessed is the man who is holy, (though such a man is seriously studying to be holy, albeit not in order to his justification thereby) but *blessed is he to whom righteousness is imputed without works;* and he confirms it from, Psal. xxxii. *Blessed is he whose transgression is forgiven, and whose sin is covered; blessed is the man to whom the Lord imputeth not iniquity.* Blessed is the man to whom the Lord imputes righteousness, tho' he have it not in himself, and to whom he imputes not sin, though he have it in himself; so, 2 Cor. v. 19. *God was in Christ, reconciling the world unto himself, not imputing their trespasses unto them.* Jesus Christ is the Reconciler of the world to God by his own merit; being God and Man in one Person, the efficacy of his sufferings reconcileth the world of the elect: and how is this purchased reconciliation applied? By *not imputing their trespasses unto them.* That which here is called *justification,* is there called *not imputing of transgression,* through that righteousness which Christ hath purchased, or through offering up of himself a sacrifice to God, to satisfy his justice.

6*thly*, We might say, That this way of justification, through the imputation of Christ's righteousness, ought to be admitted according to Papists own grounds; For, 1. they grant that young children, who cannot merit, are justified and admitted to glory by Christ's merit, as the immediate and proxime cause of their justification; and why not also of those that are at age? Is he not the common cause? what absurdity is in the one more than in the other! Is not the justification of both alike free? Though there be difference in the manner of application, yet in the meritorious Cause there is no difference; and seeing to children, Christ is the meritorious cause of their justification, why not also to these come to age? 2. They will grant an imputation of the righteousness and merits of

X x   other

other saints to them that want of their own, as to the removal of temporal plagues, and the taking them out of purgatory; and if they grant that there may be an imputation of the merits of saints, why deny they the imputation of the merits of Christ, as to the removal of eternal wrath? Is there any probability, that there can be any imputation of the one, and not an imputation of the other? 3. They allow an imputation of Christ's merits, as to the procuring of the first grace, without all faith apprehending him; and if, by their own doctrine, it be not absurd to speak of Christ's merit, as to the infusing of grace at first, why shall it be thought absurd to speak of Christ's merit, as to the procuring of glory? 4. They grant, that there is an imputation of Christ's righteousness, as to the procuring of glory, in a higher degree, (though they say, that it is a far better life, which comes by our own works) and why not, as to the procuring of glory in a lower degree, yea, both of grace and glory, and of every good thing? We have insisted on this the more, 1. Because it is the main foundation of our faith, and the end of it, and the great scope of the gospel. 2. Because there are so many mistakes about this, and a gross mistake in this is remediless, when we come before God. Even before the tribunal of men, if we make a wrong defence, it hazards our cause; so is it here, for to have a hiding-place in Christ, and under the covert of his righteousness, is our only defence before the dreadful tribunal of God. 3. Because it serves much to clear this truth; for we would have you knowing, that it is not enough to speak of Christ's merit, as the cause of our friendship with God; a Papist will do that, who yet leaneth not to Christ's merits alone, but to his own, ar least in part, and in conjunction with Christ's; and therefore we would now and then speak of this, because there is such horrible ignorance of it, though a fundamental truth. How many gay honest folks (as they are called and accounted) are there among us, that cannot tell how they came to be justified, or what is the ground which they have to rest on, if they were going to die? Is it not absurd, that men should be called Protestants, and live so long under the clear light of the gospel, and yet be ignorant of this main point of the Protestant religion?

Therefore, 1. Make this *Use* of it, to inform yourselves in the causes of your justification, and to turn them over into questions and answers to yourselves; so that if ye ask, what is the efficient cause of justification? It is God the Party offended. What is the final cause of it? It is his glory. What is the meritorious cause? It it Christ's merits, or his righteousness imputed to us. What is the inward instrumental cause? It is faith, *&c.* according to the solid answer given in our Catechism, to that question, What is justification? *It is an act of God's free grace, wherein he pardoneth all our sins, and accepteth us as righteous in his sight, only for the righteousness of Christ imputed to us, and received by faith alone;* where the efficient cause is God's free grace, Christ's righteousness the only meritorious cause, and the only inward instrumental cause, faith alone; the formal cause, God's pardoning our sin, and accepting of us as righteous: Remember well, that it is not Christ's righteousness, as having a merit in it, to procure inherent righteousness, but as it is imputed unto us, and accounted ours, that justifies us; thus ye will remember the difference betwixt Christ's righteousness and our own. And as for the external instrumental cause, it is holden out in these words of our Catechism, in the description of faith, *as he is offered to us in the gospel:* all these causes must in ordinary dispensation concur to our justification, and the pardoning of our sins.

The 2*d Use* serves to teach us to be on our guard against the Popish error of justification by works: though we are here mercifully keeped free, yet the land is tempted in several corners of it, to shuffle by Christ's righteousness, and to bring in mens own righteousness or holiness, as the ground of their acceptation before God: There are some spottings of it within a few miles to this place; and since this error draws souls away from that which is their right and only defence before God, that is Christ's righteousness, it cannot but ruin them; which should make you all to look well about you, and upon this account to abhor it: It is one of the great delusions of the man of sin, which being once admitted, will, with your own consent, bring you again in bondage to a covenant of works.

Use 3. Follow this way in your practice in your seeking after justification, renounce your own righteousness, and lean to Christ's righteousness alone. What better are many of us in our practice than Papists? If ye ask many, What is it that satisfies the justice of God? Some will answer, 1. Their good prayers, or their good works; and if they have done a fault, they shall make amends. 2. Others will say, That they have a good heart to God, and they mind well, though it is but little they do we. 3. Others will thank God, that they have been keeped from gross evils, and that he hath helped them to pray, and to wait on ordinances; and tho' they

they have no righteousness of their own, yet God hath helped them to do many good things; and thus all that they lean to, is still within them. 4. Others will say, We warrant you, we can merit nothing, but we hope, through Christ's righteousness, our holiness and prayers will be accepted; not as duties, or fruits of faith, but they think to make these two concur, as the ground of their justification; *to wit,* Christ's righteousness, and their own performances together. And, What is all this but black and abominable Popery? And yet, if we go through the generality of professors, great folk, and mean folk, we will find few, but, by one or other of these ways, they delude themselves; and that but very few have Christ's righteousness, as the immediate ground of their justification and defence before God: Be ashamed therefore, that ye are so ignorant of this point, and be exhorted to study it as the main thing, if ever ye think to stand before God's tribunal; and to carry your cause; be exhorted, I say, to be clear in this defence, which only will be found relevant before God, and nothing but this, *to wit,* the satisfaction of Christ, taken hold of, and rested on by faith.

The 4th *Use* serves for notable consolation to a poor sinner, that hath no righteousness of his own, and who without this would never have peace. What would any of you think or say, if ye had your prayers and good works to hold up to God, for the ground of your justification? But here is a way for the most profane and graceless to be justified; which we do not mention to foster profanity, or an indifferency as to the having or wanting of inherent grace and holiness, God forbid we should: But to hold out the excellency of this way of justification by grace, whereto, if ye kindly submit, ye may come to be justified. It is not your own righteousness, whether ye have less or more of it, that justifies you; for to that ye must be denied, and endeavour to make this sure and sicker: therefore let not this grace be offered to you in vain; if ye slight it, it will be a fearful challenge, and will make you one day stand with a silent mouth, and an empty hand, when ye shall be charged, because ye have not laid hold on this righteousness, which only can answer all challenges; and ye shall stand naked before God, because ye had this robe of Christ's imputed righteousness, for covering of your nakedness, in your offer, and would not put it on. This is it that bare through David, Abraham and Paul, and all other believers; yea, that which (to say so) bare through our Lord Jesus, who *was justified in the Spirit,* as he stood in the room of elect sinners; and believers in him may be fully assured of their justification, through his imputed righteousness, not that which is his essential, but cautionary righteousness; therefore throng in to make use of it. And let God himself bless thro' Christ what hath been said to you to this purpose.

SERMON LVII.

Isaiah liii. 11.────*By his knowledge shall my righteous Servant justify many, for he shall bear their iniquities.*

THESE words shew the great scope and design of the covenant of redemption, and of Christ's sufferings agreed upon therein, which have been so much insisted on in the former verses; and that is in a word, that there may be a ground laid down, how a sinner may be justified; therefore there is the greater need, that this point be well studied, in all the causes of it.

It follows now, that we consider this part of the words, which holds out the mean, by which this benefit is made ours, and that is, *by his knowledge,* which holds out the *instrumental Cause* of our justification; it is ordinarily so called, and we see no cogent reason inducing us to a change of the designation. *Faith* here is called *Knowledge,* not as if it were a bare speculative notion, such as devils may have; but because knowledge is a notable antecedent to faith, and faith is consequent to, and supposes preceeding knowledge, as we may see, Rom. x. *How shall they believe in him, of whom they have not heard?* Thus, faith is exprest by knowledge, John xviii. 3. *This is life eternal, to know thee, the only true God, and Jesus Christ,* &c. Now, it cannot be eternal life, to know, by a mere notional or speculative knowledge, for several reprobate men exceed many believers in this; but it is to know so, as to believe in God, and to rest on the Mediator for life through him, as it is, 2 Pet. i. 3. *He hath given unto us all things that pertain to life and godliness, through the knowledge of him,* &c. Mere speculative knowledge cannot be the condition of the promises, for they are made to the man that believes; which believing, takes in, not only the act of the mind, knowing and assenting, but of the will, consenting and closing with the Object known: And this will be the more clear from these two,

two, 1. That by knowledge here, is meaned that by which justification is made ours, or applied to us, and that which intitles us to it: Now, mere speculative knowledge doth not that, but it is faith embracing him, who is made known. 2. If we compare that which is attributed to knowledge here, with that which is attributed to faith elsewhere, Rom. v. 1. *Being justified by faith, we have peace with God;* and Rom. iii. 25. *He is the justifier of him which believeth in Jesus;* we will find, that what is called *Knowledge* here, is called *Faith* there: so that we may, without hesitation, take the meaning of the words thus, *My righteous Servant shall, by faith in him, justify many,* who, by his bearing of their iniquities, shall be absolved and set free. Therefore, what is spoken of knowledge in the doctrine, we may look on it as agreeing to, and meant of faith.

We shall here insist a little on this *Doctrine,* which is implied in the words, That justification through faith, or the obtaining of the pardon of sin, through Christ's righteousness, taken hold of by faith, doth necessarily presuppose knowledge in the person that may expect it; or thus, Faith, where it is saving, and such as justifies, hath always knowledge going along with it, otherwise faith could not be called *Knowledge;* there may be knowledge without faith, but there can be no faith without knowledge; and so consequently a sinner cannot expect justification without knowledge. For making out of this, ye may consider these things. 1. Faith is of itself nothing, but as it lays hold on some object. How can faith lay hold on an object, except it know it? as the word is, Rom. x. *How can they believe, except they hear?* Can any person rest on an unknown Mediator? That sure were not faith, but a blind guessing; it is just, as if ye should say that ye believe such a thing, when yet ye cannot at all tell what it is; which is not faith, but, as I said, blind guessing and presumption. 2. Faith, as justifying, is always holden forth, as making use of, and giving credit to that which is revealed in the word: hence, we that hear the gospel, have that revealed to us therein, binding us to the belief of it, that Heathens have not; as it is, Rom. i. 17. *I am not ashamed of the gospel of Christ, for therein is the righteousness of God revealed from faith to faith,* where it is necessarily presupposed, that the revealing of the righteousness of the gospel (which here comprehends the knowing of it) must go before faith; and as a person grows in faith, he grows in the knowledge of it. Hence also, they are said to be strong in faith,

who are strong in knowledge; and they are said to be weak in knowledge, who are weak in faith, Rom. xiv. 1. and xv. 1. Because they knew not that the ceremonial law was taken away, and particularly the difference of meats, and so durst not hazard on some things, which their Christian liberty gave them access to. 3. Consider, that, in justification, God would have a sinner to proceed as a man doth, who tables his defence before an earthly tribunal of justice; who, if he plead well, and on relevant grounds, he comes the better to: and as it is dangerous, in a weighty cause depending, to have an ignorant advocate, who puts in a wrong defence, so is it here, and in this case, to be ignorant; hence, Rom. x. it is given, as the reason of the Jews miscarriage in the point of justification; *But being ignorant of the righteousness of God, they went about to establish their own righteousness;* that is, being ignorant of that which God would accept for righteousness, they thought to patch up one of their own: and so is it still, for some hope to come speed by their prayers, others think to come speed by their good heart to God; a third sort puts in their good works, if not in express words, yet practically; all which may let us see the necessity of knowledge to justification. 4. Consider, that there must be repentance, ere a sinner can be justified, which supposeth knowledge; for he must needs know his sin, and that his own righteousness will not do his turn: and so long as he is ignorant, he cannot repent, nor renounce his own righteousness; for, while he is so, he cannot know what is sin, and what is not sin; what is faith, and what is presumption, unless it be by guess; and folk will never be suitably affected with sin by guess. The apostle Paul says, (as it is, Rom. vii. 9.) *Before the law came, I was alive;* that is, before it came to him, in the knowledge of its spiritual meaning, and broad extent of it: while he was a Pharisee, he was alive, in his own esteem; *But when the commandment came, sin revived, and he died;* he then saw need of another righteousness than his own. We preach to you sometimes the necessity of repentance, and of your being humbled; and that ye should deny your own righteousness, and betake you to Christ's; but, except there be knowledge of your unrighteousness, it is as if we should bid you wash where there is no spot seen. 5. Look forward to the duties of holiness, which are necessary, though not to justify you, yet that ye may live as it becomes justified persons; though not to make your peace, yet to glorify God, and to keep up friendship with him. Now, can any know, or do duties, who are ignorant? Hence it

comes

comes to pass, that some hazard on sin, taking it to be duty, and fear sometimes at duty, as if it were sin. 6. Consider your own peace, and in order to it, there is a necessity of knowledge, else there will be still a doubting whether ye are right or wrong; hence it is sa'd, Rom. xiv. *He that doubteth, or doth doubtingly, is damned;* for he hath a sentence in his own conscience against himself, though he may be doing that which on the matter is right. 7. In a word, ignorance puts us out of case to make use of many notable opportunities and privileges; we know not what use to make of the word, of the sacraments, or of Christ: how many have lived a considerable number of years strangers to the advantages that are to be gotten by him, through their want of knowledge? therefore, John iv. Christ says to the Samaritan woman, *If thou hadst known who it is that asked it of thee, thou wouldest have given him drink, and he should have given thee living water;* where he insinuates, that her ignorance was a great cause why she keeped at such a distance from him. It is hardly possible, that so many poor souls would abide at such a distance from Christ, if they knew him: There is no desire after that which is unknown; and therefore many do live at such a distance from Christ, because they have not so much as the literal knowledge, or historical faith of his worth.

The *uses* are *three*. 1. Take it for granted, if ever ye would see the face of God, that there is a necessity of knowledge; for knowledge is a piece of God's image, as well as holiness; and knowledge is commanded, as well as holiness. Knowledge was placed in the first man Adam, as well as holiness; and when we are renewed after the image of God, in conformity to the second Adam, we are renewed *in knowledge:* and not only so, but knowledge is a mean of the exercise of faith, of repentance, and of holiness; and if such a thing be needful, by the necessity of a mids, in order to an end; if obedience to a command; or, if the thing itself that is to be known, be needful; then knowledge must be needful. It is true, we would beware of extremities here; as either to say, on the one hand, that there must be such a high degree of knowledge; for in the speculative part of knowledge, (to speak so) reprobates may go beyond believers; or upon the other hand, to think that knowledge is enough, and that there needs no more but knowledge, as alas many do rest upon their knowledge: and therefore we would beware of separating of these two, knowledge and faith.

If it be asked here, What knowledge is requisite to justification? I would speak a word to this question, not so much for satisfying of curiosity, but for your instruction, who are more ignorant; and to shew the necessity of the thing and to give you a short view of these things that are necessary to be known about this matter: and therefore, 1. Ye must know God that justifies you, ere ye can be justified; as it is, John xvii. 3. *This is life eternal, to know thee the only true God, and him whom thou hast sent, Jesus Christ;* If ever ye be absolved before such a judicatory, ye must know your Judge; that there is one God, that he is one in his essence, and that there are three Persons, yet so, as the Trinity of Persons doth not hinder or obstruct the unity or oneness of the God-head, 1 John v. 7. *There are three that bear record in heaven, the Father, the Word, and the holy Ghost; and these three are one.* Study then to know God, who is your Judge, not so much out of curiosity, seeking to know how the Persons differ, as to their manner of subsisting, as how to be fixed in the faith of the thing. 2. Ye would know yourselves, and what may be charged on you before God; can men carry rightly before a judge, or before a judicatory, if they know not how it stands with them: and this will lead to know the state and case wherein ye were made at first, and the covenant of works, which God made with man at the beginning, when he gave to him the promise of life upon condition of obedience; and that ye are liable to the curse, due for the breach of that law and covenant, else ye will never know your hazard; and knowing the breach of the law, and covenant of works, it will make you, through God's blessing, to seek after justification, which otherwise ye will never do. And so ye are to know, that the first covenant was broken by Adam, and that this made him and all his posterity liable to the curse, as being guilty of his transgression; and this takes in the knowledge of original sin, even of the sinful estate wherein ye were born, and of your actual sins. 3. Ye must know, how a sinner, lying in such a state and case under sin and wrath, may come to be absolved; and this leads you in to know, that there is a new covenant made through a Mediator, in which there is a promise of life and salvation, through believing in him, which, Rom. x. is called *the law of faith,* which gives a sinner ground of hope to be justified by the righteousness of a Cautioner, and leads him in to know the defence, that he may and ought to plead upon before

two natures, he might be God and Man in one Person; in reference to which, he must needs be known; for if we know him not to be Man, we cannot understand how divine justice is satisfied; and if we know him not to be God, we cannot understand how the human nature can be sustained, and supported and carried through, in satisfying the justice of God. And withal, a necessity of knowing how the Mediator procures this justification: and this leads us in to know his offices; how he was a Priest, and interposed betwixt God and sinners, and made himself an offering for our sin, and maketh intercession for us; how he was a Prophet, and how, when the thing was unknown, to wit, how a sinner might have peace with God, he revealed it of old by his prophets, in the old testament, and his apostles and ministers in the new testament, and doth by his Spirit enlighten the soul, to take up the difference betwixt justification by faith, and justification by works; how he is a King, to subdue sin in us, to mortify our corrupt nature, that will still boast till it be subdued, to guide us in his way, to fight our spiritual battles in us, and for us; and to take course with all his and our enemies: otherwise, if we know not this, though we are justified just now, we would be led captive by sin and Satan to our ruin within an hour; but knowing him to to be King, it gives faith footing to expect through-bearing and victory. 4. As we must know what Christ is, so we must know what is in Christ, and what is communicated and applied to sinners by him, and so the condition of the covenant of grace, which is faith, whereby we come to be united to Christ; and that this faith is not a bare assenting to the truth, but a closing with, and a resting on him: for we can never believe, except we know what faith is. 5. It is needful, that we know what duty is called for from a justified person, to wit, repentance and holiness; because, though he justifies none for repentance, yet he justifies none but penitents, and he requires repentance from all whom he justifies; *Except ye repent*, saith Christ, *ye shall all likeways*

fy and confirm the believer's right to him, and these good things promised through him. Let me intreat you, believers, and as many as look for justification, to study throughly to know, that these things are necessary to be known; even to know God, and yourselves, and what ye may be justly charged with before him, that your mouths may be stopped; to know Jesus Christ, and his offices, (for ye can never upon any ground expect justification, except ye know who hath procured it); to know what God requires of these who are justified: In a word, study so much as may bring you to know your lost estate, and the remedy thereof, and how to found your defence, when ye come before God, &c. And if ye would study thus to know God, and know yourselves, and your natural condition, and Jesus Christ, and the way how ye come to be justified through him, and your duty to him, and so make a catechism to yourselves out of these few heads, it were a short and sure way to come to knowledge.

The *2d Use* serves for reproof and conviction to them that ly still in ignorance, which is a most sinful and dangerous condition: for if knowledge be a duty, and if ignorance be a sin, and such a sin as hazards the soul, then what a woful case are many of you in, who now hear me? lay aside all other sins, I would be ashamed to speak of the great ignorance that is among you! how many of you are there, that cannot give any tolerable account of your Catechism? who know not your natural state and condition, nor the way how to come at peace with God, nor any ground for your faith to rest upon, nor Christ, nor his offices? and alas, if it be so, what better are ye than heathens? sure ye are much worse, because ye have despised knowledge; can the gospel give you faith, to whom it never gave knowledge. There are several sorts of persons, to whom I would here speak a word, 1. There are some that never lay the necessity of knowledge to heart, betwixt whom and Turks and Pagans there is in this respect but little difference; and yet such will

will be ready to say, We live, and do as well as we may; that there may not be a quarrel or controversy betwixt God and us: But is it possible but there must be a quarrel, if it were but on this alone account, that ye think there is none? O that ye would consider, what a sin ignorance is! when the devil appeared in the world, he made it a great part of his first work, to extinguish and put out the light of knowledge, and by this means he labours still to keep folk in ignorance; hence the apostle says, 2 Cor. iii. *If our gospel be hid, it is hid to them who are lost, whose eyes the god of this world hath blinded.* Profanity and error are great baits and snares, but ignorance carries more to hell than both these do; for ignorance fostereth and cherisheth, if it do not also beget, profanity and error; as the apostle Peter insinuates, when he says, that the ignorant or *unlearned, wrest,* or pervert *the scriptures unto their own destruction.* Much ignorance, and conceit of knowledge, will soon and easily shake people loose, and make them a prey to error, and also to profanity: Must not ignorance then be an evil thing, when it leads the way to so many other sins, and at last to hell and destruction? Hence it is, at least in part, that the kingdom of Satan is called the *kingdom of darkness;* and sure they are very proper subjects of his kingdom, who are ignorant: And is it possible, think ye, that people can think of God, or of their duty aright, or have any solid peace, who are in that condition? They are just like to one sleeping on the top of a mast, in great hazard, and yet utterly senseless of it. Look but to *two* or *three* words, that hold out the dreadful danger and hazard of your condition, who are ignorant; The *first* is that, 2 Thess. i. *Christ will come in flaming fire, to render vengeance to all them that know not God, and obey not the gospel.* The 2d is, Hos. iv. *My people perish for want of knowledge.* The 3d is, Isa. xxvii. *This is a people of no understanding; therefore he that made them, will have no mercy upon them.* Think not then little of ignorance, neither think yourselves to be well, so long as ye live in it. A *2d* sort will readily grant, that ignorance is an evil thing, and that knowledge is good and desirable; but yet they take no pains to have their ignorance cured and removed, or to attain knowledge: they are secure and confident, tho' poor, blind and wretched, and make their ignorance a cloke of excuse for their other sins; hence some will say, We have been poor ignorant bodies, and we hope that God will not lay sin to our charge. O what delusion and desperate danger is here! If it be asked, (and it would become us well to enquire into it) What can be the reason of this horribly gross ignorance that is among us, which is such, that we are almost hopeless of many of you, if some extraordinary work of God's Spirit fall not in on your minds and hearts? Very readily these go together, the most ignorant are the most senseless, and the most ignorant are the most confident. The causes of this may be several; as, 1. Folks undervaluing the practice of religion; let the most ignorant persons be in earnest in the practice of religion, and they will readily through God's blessing, as seek after, so come at some measure of knowledge: This is a fountain of your ignorance, that ye are not in earnest in religion; *Then shall ye know* (saith the prophet Hosea, chap. vi.) *if ye follow on to know the Lord.* Excuse not your ignorance, and want of knowledge, by your not being book-learned, by your want of time and leisure, and by other such shifts: If ye were in good earnest, and serious in seeking after the knowledge of the things of religion, ye would soon in some measure understand, and take them up; but ye come and hear, and sit for an hour, and take no heed what is spoken: ye will not read the Catechism, nor ask a question about what ye are ignorant of, nor will take heed to what is said, when others are examined. There are none of you, but if ye were in earnest, ye might come to some good measure of knowledge; because they were sometime as ignorant as ye are, and as incapable, who yet have come to knowledge, and these will be witnesses against you, who had the same gospel, the same seasons and means of knowledge, and yet continued still in your ignorance. 2. Many of you do not ponder the sinfulness and hazard of ignorance; for ye continue as secure, as if God would never lay it to your charge. Ye would not readily ly in the sin of drunkenness, or of swearing, or of any other such things, without a challenge; but ye can ly still in your ignorance, and in the sin of not profiting by the means which ye are under, and yet dispense with yourselves therein; and ye secretly say within yourselves, If we be well otherwise, we hope knowledge will not be required of us: But will not, think ye, God's image be required to be in you? Are not faith, repentance and holiness required? and can any of these, I pray, be without knowledge? Do ye see any touched with the impression of their sin and guilt, but as soon they fall to the study of knowledge? and

and who continue to be ignorant, but stupid bodies, that never saw their hazard? which is an ordinary companion and attendant of ignorance. A 3*d* cause is negligence and slothfulness. The wise man says, *The hand of the diligent maketh rich*, and slothfulness brings on poverty: in every thing, if ye compare folks together, ye will find, that wherever any are soberly and seriously diligent, God blesses it; so that we may gather and conclude their diligence from their knowledge. There are many here, who I suppose are very ignorant; but let me ask you, What time and pains have ye ever bestowed on the study of knowledge? Ye hear the preaching, and ye read a chapter of the Bible now and then; but that is not enough, for ye may be present here, and yet not hear to any purpose. How many come to hear the preaching of the word, from whom, through their own fault, devils come, as so many crows on new-sown land, and snatch away the word that is sown? and it is never known that such seed was sown. For most part, ye either hear negligently, or ye quickly forget all that ye hear; ye never speak of it in your families, neither take ye any time for reading and pondering the Catechism. How many of you did ever set any days or hours apart to study knowledge? Ye will cry out against pretended enthusiasms and inspirations, as delusions, and there is good reason for it; but, how shall ye get knowledge, if ye will be at no pains for it? Your practice says, ye expect it should come by immediate inspiration, without all use of ordinary and appointed means. 4. Others will say, that they would fain know, but they are very dull and incapable; and it is often true, that they are so: But, are such in earnest, out of love to knowledge, studying to come by it? It is said of some, 2 Thess. ii. *Because they received not the truth in love, God gave them up to strong delusions, to believe a lie.* There are many, who study knowledge, but not from a right principle, nor from a right motive; it may be, that they may get their token to come to the Lord's Supper, to eschew shame when they are examined, or that they may be able to talk: It is just with God to let such want knowledge. 5. Folks go not about the use of ordinary means, as having therein need of God's blessing, and of his Spirit to help them rightly to take up his mysteries; they pray not for knowledge as God's gift. How many of you, when ye take up the Catechism to read, fall down on your knees to seek God's blessing on your reading thereof! When John is speaking of the benefits that come by Christ, this is by him put in among the rest, *And hath given us an understanding, that we may know him that is true,* 1 John v. 20. If therefore ye would know God aright, seek his blessing in the use of his own appointed means. Ye study the knowledge of God, even as if ye were to read a common human history; if ye seek a blessing to your meat, why seek ye not a blessing on the means of knowledge, which is as necessary to the soul, as meat is to the belly? how often hath David such a suit to God, when he says, Psal. cxix. *Open mine eyes, that I may see the wondrous things of thy law; teach me thy statutes,* &c. he thought no shame to pray for knowledge; sure if we prayed more for it, we would thrive better in it. Other reasons fall in, in the *directions,* anent the study of knowledge, which we shall give you.

The 3*d Use* serves to exhort you to, and to commend the study of knowledge to you, as a necessary, commendable, and profitable duty. Can we hope to prevail with you in any thing, if we prevail not with you in this, even to lay the necessity of knowledge to heart? will not the excellency of the Object, the authority of God commanding it, the advantages that come by it, with the prejudices that attend and follow the want of it, commend it to you? will ye ever be persuaded to seek after faith and holiness, that will not be persuaded to study knowledge? It is a wonder how many of you can have the confidence to say, that ye keep your hearts to God, when ye are so void of the very form of religion, which much consists in knowledge; for it is that wherein it is keeped, and whereby through grace it is suitably exercised. Sure ye can never have the power of religion, who want the form of it; therefore let me exhort you all, especially such of you as have some eminency above others, to study knowledge: let the more aged study it; and let these that are younger study it; if the time of youth go over without it, it is one to many if ever the loss be recovered and made up again; and ye that can read, have time and parts, study the knowledge of God; many of you will be very sad and dreadful spectacles in the great day, when ye shall be charged with this, that ye never judged precious Jesus Christ to be of that much worth, as once to put you seriously to the study to know him; this is no fable nor fiction, but a sad truth. When men value and esteem any thing, be it science or art, they will be at pains and give diligence to know it, because they prize it: therefore, for helping you to the study of knowledge, take these few *directions,* and a *caveat* or two in the

about this in private weekly; it may be, it were fit that some of you did so daily, ye spend much time more idly; if ye knew the hazard of ignorance, ye would even take some set time to study knowledge, and this would not need to be counted any wronging of, or incroaching upon your Christian liberty; as ye stint some time for prayer, may ye not stint some time to read the Catechism, or to go to some family where ye that cannot read yourselves, may have one to read it to you? And to several, I may add for a help to this, that ye would take a part of that time, which ye spend on tippling; is it not obvious, that the person that is oftest in the hostler-house, or in the tavern, is ordinarily the most stupidly ignorant? Tell me whether it is better spent time to take an hour, in two or three days, and bestow it in reading of the scriptures, or of some good and edifying book, whereby you may come to knowledge, and to grow in it, than to take several hours, every day almost, in an ale-house, or tavern. Many of you, as it is well known, will sit down in such places at four or five o'clock in the afternoon, and continue till eight or nine at night; how much ye drink, I speak not of that, but sure ye mispend much precious time, and much debauch your own spirits? What if, by such doings, ye be laying a ground for this challenge? Sir, you lived in such a place, under such means, and you spent your time so and so; you might have been freed from the guilt of mispending of your time, and of your ignorance, had you taken a part, or the whole time, and spent it in the study of knowledge; would not this be better for your families, better for your souls, and better for your bodies? Would it not prevent much sin, and much reproach? And therefore, if ye lay weight on the good of soul and body, bestow more time in the study of knowledge: that sin of tippling brings alongst with it many other sins; and were it not well done, to put some duty, and even this duty in particular, in the place of it? Others of you that drink and tipple not away so much of your time, ye know what time ye spend walking on the plain-stones, and in pratling and talking of idle and unedifying subjects, in drolling up and down the streets, when ye are not at all called to do so. 3. Make conscience to improve the means of knowledge which ye have; read especially the Bible, and also the grounds of religion, compendiously summed in the Catechisms lesser and larger. Ye have frequent preaching and catechising; at every diet study to get something, and put every day's lesson to another, and this would, through God's blessing, increase your knowledge; for instance, take this lesson to day, that nothing can justify but the righteousness of Christ, laid hold on by faith; take another with you the next day, and let not one day's lesson shoulder out another: let the husband and the wife, the children and servants, compare their notes, or what they remember of sermons together; be often speaking of what ye hear in your families. Ye have, it may be, some neighbours, who would be content that ye come in to them; or, it may be, they have children who can help you: make use of such means and persons, and that would both help your knowledge, and evidence your love (when sincerely gone about) to the communion of saints. 4. Be about the use of the means, with an eye to God for his blessing on them; pray to him for opened eyes, and, that he would give you an understanding to know him. There is a stupidity in many of you, that makes all that ye hear to go by you, and as it were to slide off you; so that if it were known, some would wonder how there could be such ignorance amongst them that frequently hear the gospel. 5. Any light of knowledge that ye have, be tender of it in your practice; God ordinarily refuseth to give more, where that which he hath given is not used well; where men *do not like to retain God in their knowledge*, or where *the truth is detained in unrighteousness*, it provoketh God so give you up to a reprobate mind, as the apostle tells us, Rom. i. *If ye continue in my word*, (says Christ, John viii. 31, 32.) *then are ye my disciples indeed, and ye shall know the truth, and the truth shall set you free*: And, John vii. 17. *If any man will do his will, he shall know of the doctrine, whether it be of God, or whether I speak of myself.*

He that goeth confcientioufly and conftantly about the duties of holinefs that he knows, (for he muft make confcience of all, elfe he will thrive in none) he fhall increafe in knowledge.

There are alfo fome things that more generally conduce to knowledge, as that, magiftrates, minifters, elders, parents, mafters of fchools, and mafters of families do their refpective duties. 1. Then let me defire you to fee to the education of the youth; I mean of the children of the meaneft and worft, to bring them up at fchools: it is fad to confider, how many young ones of gracelefs, carelefs, and ignorant parents, are brought up to the devil; it were no great bufinefs to help them that cannot entertain them at fchool. O that we were all willing to contribute for fuch a work! it might help them to know fomething of God, or to be civil at leaft; it would alfo remove the excufe, that we frequently meet with from many, to wit, that they cannot read; and if parents will not be ferioufly concerned in this themfelves, God requires us to take fome courfe to bring up their young ones in the knowledge of God; and truly, if this external eafy mean be neglected, we can expect little of other means; if this were minded, it might be an ornament to the city, and the burden would not be fo very great, if it were once put to the trial. Will ye that are parents, and able, be induced to put your children to the fchool? If ye be not able, make it known. I know there are fome who will drink more in one day fometimes, than would keep their children at the fchool for many days; and I fuppofe, that there are but few who can fay, that it is mere neceffity that lets them. Are there any of you that can fay, ye would fain bring up your children at fchool, and ye fpake to magiftrates, or to church-feffions for help, and that it was refufed you? It is your part to feek for help, that are really unable, and it lieth on you, to fee to it yourfelves who are able; and while ye neither do yourfelves, nor feek help from others, ye are utterly inexcufable. 2. I would commend to you the neceffity of ufing private means, and that ye would not lay all the weight of your profiting on your being in the church, and on your coming to be catechifed, or to hear others catechifed; but give diligence in private to come to knowledge, elfe it will be long ere ye thrive and profit. Ye that are in one family, when ye come home from fermon, confer together now and then, and be fpeaking of what ye hear on the Sabbath, betwixt Sabbath-days; and when ye can get any to anfwer a doubt or queftion to you, make ufe of the opportunity: though we could go through you all twice a year in examination and catechifing, it will not do your turn if this be neglected: But as ye would be careful to keep your children at fchool, fo ye would be bufy in your families, at all family-duties; this was wont to be the old way of God's people, and it would make hearing of fermons profitable. 3. I would commend you to careful attendance on, and confcientious ufe-making of the miniftry of the word, the great ordinary mean of knowledge; and that ye who are moft concerned would be thinking of the great conveniency, if not neceffity, of more labourers. If it were known how numerous a people we are; how many hundreds every one, who labours among you, hath under his charge: how little time we have to go through you all particularly, and what abounding ignorance there is in the greateft part of the people; I fuppofe it would be thought, that the charge of any one of us might require two to difcharge it fuitably; which we do not prefs to fpare our own labour and pains, but to ftir you up to a neceffary duty: the effecting of the thing is not impoffible, and it is a work and duty well becoming you, and worthy of you; the Lord himfelf perfuade you to mind it. I fhall clofe up all with a caveat or two. 1. Beware of placing over much religion in knowledge, or of being puft up with your knowledge, when ye attain to any meafure of it. 2. Beware of counting mere knowledge to be faith; but when ye come to know and difcern the object, be fure that ye take hold of, and reft upon that which the eye of faith difcerns: the land is, to fay fo, afar off, and within the vail; caft therefore the anchor of hope there. 3. Beware of thinking, that ye merely of yourfelves can acquire any found and faving knowledge, or pump it out of yourfelves: we bid you not ftudy the knowledge of God, as ye ftudy other common things; there are here requifite humility, fear, reverence, love to the truth, dependence on God, prayer to him, and acknowledgment of him: let me again ferioufly commend this ftudy to you, and through it let me commend Chrift unto you, *whom to know is life eternal;* to him be praife for ever.

SERMON LVIII.

Isaiah liii. 11.——*By his knowledge shall my righteous Servant justify many, for he shall bear their iniquities.*

IF any thing should be studied with diligence, sure this should be, even to be clear how we may come to be at peace with God, how we may be absolved and justified, when we come to reckon before him: it is no curiosity, singly and diligently to make enquiry here, altho' the unfaithfulness and pride of some unhappy men have made the study of it unpleasant, by corrupting and making crooked God's plain and straight way of making of our peace with him, and of our being justified before him.

We entred to speak of the great mids, or mean by which this righteousness, that justifies a sinner before God, is derived; or, by which we come to have a title to, and an interest in it: and as we have great need to be clear in that righteousness, which will be a relevant defence before the tribunal of God's justice, that we propose not one that will be casten and rejected; so we have as great need to be clear in the way, how that righteousness may be made ours, seeing many are, and will be condemned, notwithstanding of Christ's righteousness, because there is no application of it made by them to themselves.

We shew you, that by *Knowledge* here is meaned *Faith*, as the scriptures in the New Testament (which hold out justification to be by faith) make clear, it being evident, that no merely speculative knowledge can intitle to this justification; yet it is called knowledge, 1. Because faith necessarily presupposes knowledge: if it be not a part of it, yet certainly it is a necessary antecedent of it. 2. Because, though there be not an evidence to reason in all the things which we believe, yet there is a certainty; and faith gets this name, because it makes men certain of these things which it takes up, as if it were a science or knowledge. 3. To distinguish it from all other sorts of knowledge, and to bound and include it, mostly at least, within this Object, Christ, to speak so; therefore it is said, *By his knowledge*, or as the word is better rendred, *By the knowledge of him shall my righteous Servant justify many*; which shews, that it is not knowledge taken largely that he means of, but knowledge with respect to Christ, the great Object of it, as it is, 1 Cor. ii. 2. *I determined to know nothing among you, but Jesus Christ, and him crucified:* And saith Paul, Phil. iii. 8. *I count all things to be but loss, for the excellency of the knowledge of Jesus Christ my Lord.* Ye will ask then, how doth knowledge and faith differ, seeing wherever there is faith there is knowledge, though not contrariwise, wherever there is knowledge there is faith? We shall not stand upon this, but shortly we conceive, that knowledge discovers the Object, and faith takes hold of the Object, and rests upon it; knowledge is the eye of the new creature, discovering such a thing; and faith is the hand that catcheth hold of, and grips that thing that is discovered: or thus, knowledge is like to the head, that takes up such a thing in a notion; and faith is as the heart, that closes with it; therefore, Rom. x. it is said, *With the heart man believes unto righteousness, and with the mouth confession is made unto salvation.* I know many take knowledge for faith, which at the best is but historical faith; and it is as if a man who is a drowning should see another casting in a rope to him, and he sees and knows such a thing, but takes no hold of it, and therefore perishes; or, as a sea-man's discovering good ground to cast anchor on, but not casting forth his anchor thereon, is exposed to the violence of the storm, and so ship-wrecked; knowledge discovers the ground, but faith casts the anchor on it: it is much to get you brought up to know, but much more to get you brought to know the difference that is betwixt faith and knowledge; hence it is, that many say, that they believed ever since they knew good by ill, because they never looked on faith, but as the knowing, professing and declaring such a thing to be true; but it is one thing to know a physician, and another thing to employ him, and to make use of his physick.

We spake of this general doctrine, that knowledge is a necessary thing, as being presupposed to faith, and particularly the knowledge of Jesus Christ; Therefore it is called, *The knowledge of him*, because it is Christ's Jesus which is the Object of faith; therefore our study of knowledge would especially be with reference to him. There are *two* sorts of persons, who are not utterly ignorant, and yet are defective here; 1. There are some that love and study to be scholars, but Christ is not the object of their knowledge; it is not the knowledge spoken of here, to be well skilled in philosophy, in tongues, in mathematicks, &c. which we discommend not; nor is it to be able, specula-

tively

Jesus, and him crucified. A second sort, are such as want not affection to truth, nor love to piety, yet to them the studying of this doctrine, that concerns Christ, and his offices, is somewhat tasteless and wearisom; they would be at hearing of duties, cases and questions spoken of, though we may in some respect say, that none of these are objects of faith properly, at least as it is justifying, but means and midses to guide you to make use of, and to carry suitably to the privileges that are in the covenant. Hence many have good affection, that are very shallow in their knowledge of Christ, and think but little of preaching, and books that hold out the doctrine concerning Christ, because they come not in so close to practical things and cases; whereas, if they were better settled in the knowledge of Christ, it would answer all their cases, and loose all their questions and doubts: let therefore these be well looked to, and this, by no means, be nauseated or slighted; though knowledge of the truths of God be necessary, yet it is especially the knowledge of Christ that is necessary.

There is another thing supposed here, that serves to clear the doctrine of justification, which we shall observe, ere we speak of faith itself particularly, because it is antecedent to it; and it is this, That the gospel is a necessary external mean for promoting of our justification: For faith, as we have shewed, presupposes knowledge, and knowledge presupposes the revelation of God's mind in the gospel; and if knowledge be necessary to faith, then the gospel must be necessary, for it is said, Rom. i. 17. That *by it the righteousness of God is revealed from faith to faith;* there is great need to observe all the steps of this doctrine well, and this among the rest; the gospel is not a thing that bred in nature's breast, or a thing that men by nature have the knowledge of; nay, it is foolishness to the wise men of the world, as we may see, 1 Cor. 1. *We* (says the apostle) *preach Christ crucified, to the Jews a stumbling-block, to the Greeks foolishness;* Faith comes by hearing, as it is, Rom. x. 17. *and hearing by the word of God;* and in the same chap. ver. 14, 15. *How shall they be-* our knowledge; then there must necessarily be something to reveal it: I speak here of the ordinary way of God's revealing himself; what he may do extraordinarily towards dumb and deaf persons, to idiots and young children, I meddle not with that, but leave it to himself as a secret, which he thinketh not fit to impart to us. I call the gospel the *external mean* of promoting our justification, in four respects, 1. Because it lays before us the object of our faith; for *in it* (as it is, Rom. i. 17.) *is the righteousness of God revealed,* &c. and Rom. iii. 21, 22. *Now the righteousness of God without the law is manifested,* &c. We would never know the way how a sinner comes to be at peace with God, and to be justified without the gospel. 2. Because it not only reveals the object of faith, but it makes offer of it; and hereby a sinner, that hears the gospel, hath warrant to embrace and make use of Jesus Christ's righteousness, and to rest upon it: and therefore, if temptation should say to the sinner, Though Christ died, what is that for thee? Faith hath this to reply, The gospel calls me, and that warrants me to come to him, and to make use of his death; the *promise,* as it is, Acts. ii. *is to as many as the Lord our God shall call:* and in this respect, the promise is our right and evident, whereby we come to have a claim to Christ. 3. Because God makes use of the word preached, for engaging of sinners to Christ, and for making them to take hold of him; it is true, that it is not powerful of itself, and without the Spirit, yet it is the ordinary mean that God makes use of; therefore faith the apostle, 2 Cor. x. 4. *The weapons of our warfare are not carnal,* though they be weak in themselves, yet *they are mighty through God, to the pulling down of strong holds.* And in this respect, the gospel not only offers life, but, through God's blessing, as a mean, begets life; and, by the Spirit accompanying it, sinners are engaged to take hold of Christ, and to rest on him for salvation. 4. Because this word being taken hold of, and closed with, contains the pronouncing of the sinners *absolvitur,* or of his absolving sentence, when he says, *If thou believest, thou shalt be justified and saved;* upon supposition of believing, the

SERM. LVIII. *Isaiah* liii. Verse 11.

the sentence stands good to the believer, *Thou art past from death to life; there being no condemnation to them who are in Christ Jesus.*

The *1st Use* serves to clear that which we hinted at before, in naming this for a cause of justification; though it be the *external instrumental cause*, yet it is a cause.

The *2d Use* serves to teach you to put a price on the gospel; it is the bane both of profane secure sinners, and of a sort of vain and giddy people among us, that they prize not the preaching of the gospel, as the external instrumental cause, that concurs in the justification of sinners; but if ever ye be absolved, ye will be beholden to this preached gospel; I will not say always to the preaching, but sure to the gospel that is preached. This on the one hand reproves these who will be ready to say, that they have faith, who yet never knew the gospel to do them good, and such also who seldom come to hear, and who never care for preaching; and upon the other hand, it reproves these, who, when they fall a tottering, reeling and wavering, and begin to incline to error, cast at the preaching of the gospel, having, it may be, slighted it before in their hearts; whither when Satan once gets them, he tosses them in a great measure, as he pleases, and makes them so giddy, by frequent turning about, that they scarcely leave to themselves a foot-broad of scripture-ground to stand upon: But as ye respect the glory of Christ, the good of your souls, and your absolution before God, esteem much of the gospel; for *it is the power of God to salvation:* and if ever ye come to heaven, it will be by this gospel, as the external mean; these nations that never heard it will think you to be most desperately wicked and miserable, who have had it, and yet so unworthily slighted it.

For pressing of this *Use* a little, take *Two* or *Three doctrines* in reference to it. 1. Walk under the conviction of the necessity of the gospel, for there is no absolution without it; it is true, God might have taken another way, but on the supposition, that he hath appointed faith to be a mids to justification, and that faith supposes knowledge, then certainly knowledge doth suppose a necessity of hearing the gospel: ye will never value preaching, nor any other ordinance of Christ, if ye see not a necessity of them, and know them not to be for your good. 2. Study to know what is the main end and design of, and what is the advantage that is to be had by the ordinances. Many come to the preaching of the gospel, to hear and learn some lesson for informing their judgment; some come to get directions, in reference to some particular duty; some to get a doubt loosed; none of which are to be disallowed in themselves, but rather in so far to be commended: but how few come to it, as to a mean to carry on, and bring about their justification; and to bring them out of black nature, into a state of grace? It is the sum of Paul's preaching, and the end of it, as the divine historian shews, Acts xxvi. 18. *To open blind eyes,* to turn them from *darkness to light, and from the power of Satan unto God, that they may receive forgiveness of sins, and an inheritance among them that are sanctified by faith that is in him.* 3. Aim in your practice to carry on this design, even to put a close to the treaty anent justification betwixt God and you. When ye come to the preaching, and hear us declare in the name of the Lord, that a believing sinner hath access to have his sin taken away, and to be justified through the imputation of Christ's righteousness; ye would step to, hearing this proclamation made of the pardon of sin, by one of Christ's ambassadors in his name, and accept of, embrace and cordially close with it, if it were just now, at this very occasion. 4. This would be the great design both of preachers and hearers; of preachers, to follow that way of preaching most, that lays open the mystery of faith in Christ; and of hearers, to love that way of preaching best, not so much that which fills the head with notions, as that which serves to help to close a bargain betwixt God and you. This was Paul's great design in preaching, as we see, 1 Cor. ii. 2. and 1 Cor. i. 23, 24. He no doubt taught other things, but he compended all in this, or levelled all at this, as the scope; and this was his main design in his preaching, and pressing of other things.

The *3d use* serves to make a sad discovery of many of you. Is this gospel the external mean of justification? Then see if ye ever knew any benefit ye got by it. Ye will be like to say, that ye are in friendship with God; but how I pray you, came ye by it? There is little change to the better in your knowledge, and as little odds in your practice: ye are as much given to covetousness, tipling, lying, swearing, pride, vanity, &c. as ever; and are these, think ye, the fruits of justification? do ye think that to be justification, which is neither from the word, nor conform to it? If God would commend this to your hearts, I think it might alarm you to more serious thoughts of your condition. I put it to your conscience, if ye can conceive any difference betwixt

twixt you, and thefe that never heard the Gofpel? Ye are baptized, and hear preaching, &c. But, alas, it is none of thefe that juftifies; they are only ufeful, as they lead you forward to the ufe-making of Jefus Chrift. Again, let me afk you, what effect hath preaching upon you? Hath it convinced you of fin? no; how then can it convince you of righteoufnefs? Therefore, if ye would make fure juftification indeed, try it by the word. 1. What was it that put you to feek after righteoufnefs, and juftification? Was ye ever convinced of the need of it? and if ye have been convinced, was it by preaching of the word? 2. If ye have been convinced of your fin and mifery, where fought ye for a remedy? was ye led in through the word, to feek a plaifter to heal that wound of conviction? 3. What was it that warranted you to take hold of that word, or that gave you a right to it? I know that ye will fay, that it was Chrift holden out in the word, that ye did betake yourfelves to; but what weight laid ye on God's call in the gofpel, warranting you to lay hold on the promife of righteoufnefs and pardon of fin through Chrift? I know there are many, who, though there had not been a call from God, would have confidently ftepped forward to the promife; but were ye ever like to Peter's hearers, *pricked in your hearts*, and made to fay, *Men and brethren what fhall we do?* Or, being fome way pricked, was it God's call, holding out the promife *to you, and to your children, and to as many as our God fhall call*, that brought you to reft on the promife? God hath defigned preaching for this end; and ye would try, if ever ye was put to it, to look to God's call, that gave you warrant to believe; for there is nothing more certain than this, that wherever faith is ficker and well built, 'tis grounded on God's call, and doth take his faithfulnefs for its backbond (to fay fo) and warrant.

More particularly, we come to fpeak of this word, as it refpects the *inward mean*, or the *inward inftrumental caufe* of juftification, which is *faith*; for there is this order and method. 1. The finner is convinced, and made fenfible of fin, and brought to reckon for it, in his own confcience before God. 2. There is Chrift's being holden forth, interpofing himfelf to take on the finner's debt, and fatisfying the juftice of God for it, which is the meritorious caufe. 3. There is God's offer in the gofpel, holding out Chrift's righteoufnefs to loft finners, and calling them to make ufe of it. 4. Upon this, there is faith's receiving of the offer, and refting upon Chrift, and his righteoufnefs for life; which (to fpeak fo) is the inward inftrumental caufe, taking hold of the external, and as I faid of Chrift in it. 5. And laftly follows God's imputing the righteoufnefs of Chrift to the finner, and abfolving him, by vertue of that righteoufnefs, from the guilt of his fin, as if he had never finned.

In fpeaking of this inward inftrumental caufe, *Five* things would be cleared; which we fuppofe are implied in the words. 1. The neceffity of faith, holden out, as the mean, by which juftification is come by. 2. The immediate Object of juftifying faith, and that is Chrift's fufferings, or Jefus Chrift, as fuffering, travelling in foul, and paying our debt. 3. The act of this faith on this Object, which is not a bare fpeculative knowledge, or a meer hiftorical faith, but fomething that really acts on Chrift, with refpect to his fufferings. 4. The effect of this faith, taking hold on Chrift and his fufferings, and that is juftification, which is not the making a finner to be juft by inherent righteoufnefs, but the actual abfolving of him from the guilt of fin, and from God's curfe; the changing of his ftate, and the bringing him from under the curfe, into good terms with God. 5. The manner how faith concurs in producing, or bringing about this effect; wherein we have this general, that faith hath a peculiar influence in the juftification of a finner, that no good work nor any other grace hath. There is none of all thefe things but it is in this miferably declined generation (wherein the devil fets himfelf mightily to obfcure truth, as the Lord by the gofpel doth clear it) controverted: I fhall only endeavour to clear the pofitive part, and let you fee what is truth in thefe things, whereby ye may be brought to difcover and abhor the errors that are contrary thereto.

The 1*ft Doctrine* then is this, That, before a man can be juftified and abfolved from the curfe of God due to him for fin, there is a neceffity of faith in our Lord Jefus Chrift. This is clear from the words, and from what hath been faid in the opening of them up; if it be *by his knowledge*, or *the knowledge of him*, that *many are juftified*; then it cannot be that they are juftified before they come to the knowledge of him, or from eternity. Only in paffing, take two or three words of advertifement, and then we fhall confirm the doctrine, 1. When we fpeak of juftification, it is in refpect of our being abfolved and freed, not from the pollution of fin, but from the guilt of it, as it makes us obnoxious to the curfe: the

the clearing of the effect will clear this more: 2. When we speak of faith, it is not to be understood as it were a declaration, or manifestation of our justification; or, it is not to be understood of faith in the height of full assurance, and as it is a plerophory, but of faith, as it is a laying hold upon Christ. 3. When we speak of the necessity of faith in order to justification, we mean not, as if there were such an absolute necessity of it in itself, that God could not do otherwise, or justify without it; but we mean a necessity, in respect of the order which God hath laid down, and held forth in the Gospel, which is by the knowledge of his Son to justify many. And from these considerations many arguments of our adversaries are made very little regardable, yea utterly void.

For confirmation of the doctrine, then, 1. Consider these scriptures, that expresly limit, confine and bound justification and pardon of sin to the person that doth believe: So, Rom. i. 17. *The righteousness of God is revealed from faith to faith; as it is written, The just shall live by faith*, Rom. iii. 24, 25. *Being justified freely by his grace, through the redemption that is in Christ Jesus, whom God hath set forth to be a propitiation through faith in his blood*, &c. Col. iii. 22. *God hath concluded all under sin, that the promise by faith of Jesus Christ might be given to them that believe.* Acts xiii. 38, 39. *Through this Man is preached unto you forgiveness of sins, and by him, all that believe are justified from all things; from which they could not be justified by the law of Moses.* Consult these scriptures, and ye will find, that Paul clears both these questions. 1. Who are justified? All that believe. 2. When are they justified? When they believe. 2dly, Consider these scriptures, that place all men before believing into a state of wrath; and they will furnish a second ground for this; as, John iii. 18. *He that believeth on him, is not condemned: but he that believeth not, is condemned already;* he lies under the covenant of works, and is condemned, as considered in himself tho' God may have a purpose to make a change of his state: So, Eph. ii. 1, 2, 3. *You hath he quickned, who were dead in trespasses and sins, wherein in time past ye walked, and were children of wrath even as others,* &c. And ver. 12, 13. *We were sometimes without Christ, being aliens from the common-wealth of Israel, and strangers from the covenant of promise, without hope, and without God in the world: But now in Christ Jesus, ye who sometimes were far off, are made near by*

the blood of Christ. And ver. 8. *By grace are ye saved, through faith, and that not of yourselves, it is the gift of God; not of works, lest any man should boast.* It is faith that gives the title, which we had not before. 3dly, Consider, that the scriptures do expresly make believing to precced justification, and make justification to be an effect, or rather a consequent of faith, to which faith necessarily concurs; as all these places, which say, that we are justified by faith in Christ, do clear: as, Rom. v. 1. *Being justified by faith, we have peace with God, through our Lord Jesus Christ;* which place looks on faith's concurring in justification with a kind of causality. Rom. iii. 22, 25. *The righteousness of God, which is by faith of Jesus Christ unto all, and upon all them that believe,* &c. Eph. ii. 8. *By grace are ye saved, through faith.* See more fully to this purpose, Gal. ii. 16. where the Apostle designedly, as it were, sets himself to confirm this truth; for, speaking of the way how sinners come to be justified, and as it were entring into the debate, he says, *Knowing that a man is not justified by the works of the law, but by the faith of Jesus Christ, even us, we have believed in Jesus Christ, that we might be justified by the faith of Christ.* In which place we have three things considerable to make out the point; 1. He compares the concurring of faith to justification, in the covenant of grace, to the concurring of works to justification, or to the obtaining of life, in the covenant of works; as works did justify in the covenant of works, so does faith in the covenant of grace: Now certainly the performing of works, in the covenant of works, behoved to go before justification that way; therefore the want of works made Adam to come short of justification by works. 2. He looks on faith, and speaks of it, as concurring to justification, with a respect to Christ; and never looks on it in this matter, as a grace considered in, and by itself, but as acting on Christ in a peculiar manner. 3. In express words, he says, *We have believed in Christ Jesus, that we might be justified;* which clearly implies, that they could not be justified before they believed: And we may well and easily gather, that the justification here meant is that which is real and actual, and not the declaring of a man to be justified to himself, else works might declare a man to be justified to himself, as well as faith; but he contradistinguishes faith and works here, and opposes the one to the other.

The *first use* serves for clearing of this truth;

That there is a necessity of faith's taking hold of, and resting on Christ, ere we can be absolved and justified; and so both these errors of Antinomians fall to the ground, 1. That by which they assert, That these who are justified, were justified from eternity, and were never under God's curse. And, 2. That faith is not necessary to the attaining of justification, but only to a person's knowledge that he is justified; and so they say, that faith enters us not in the covenant; which is false, it being the terms or condition, on which God proposeth and promiseth pardon in his covenant; as is clear, John iii. 18. *Whosoever believes shall not be condemned, but shall have everlasting life.* And Mark xvi. 16. *He that believes, and is baptized, shall be saved;* with this opposition, *He that believeth not shall be damned;* Faith being it which enters us in the covenant: for either sinners are justified before they can be in covenant with God, which is an absurdity, and inconsistent with God's covenant; or it is by faith that they entred in the covenant. There is here also a clear discovery and confutation of a 3*d* error of Antinomians, concerning the nature of faith, that it is persons believing, that they are justified: No, not so; for, as the apostle says, Gal. ii. 16. *We have believed that we might be justified;* we believe, in order to justification: And to say, as Antinomians do, would do much to infer universality of justification, as well as of redemption. It is God's mercy, that this error is discovered, and that we have this truth pointing out to us, that justification must have faith going before it, and alongst with it.

The 2*d use* serves to demonstrate the absolute necessity of believing, and taking hold of Christ. If absolution and justification be necessary, faith must be necessary: And therefore, if Christ be preached to you, and if by him all that believe are justified; take hold then, I beseech you, of the offer; receive, embrace, close with it, and let your very hearts open to it, without which ye can never expect to be justified before the tribunal of God. Now let God himself bless this same word to you through Jesus Christ.

SERMON LIX.

Isaiah liii. 11. --- --*By his knowledge shall my righteous Servant justify many, for he shall bear their iniquities.*

SOME further and more serious apprehensions of our sin and hazard would make the reading of these words to be refreshful and welcome to us; the stayed thoughts of an arrestment laid upon us, to appear before God's tribunal, and to reckon for our debt, would make us think much of a Cautioner; the want whereof make the glad tidings of the gospel to be tasteless, and without relish: This is the great scope of these words, to shew how a summoned sinner, arraigned at God's bar, may be justified, and freed from the charge he is liable to; for, says the prophet, *By his knowledge*, who is the Surety of the covenant, *shall many be justified.* That which we last left at was this, That faith in Christ, receiving and resting on him, is necessary for the attaining of justification; so that in God's way, these are so linked and knit together, that never one shall be justified but a believer; tho' there be a righteousness in Christ, yet it shall be derived and communicated to none, come to age, but to these who by faith betake themselves to Christ: What way the Lord takes with infants, elect infants I mean, is not that which the prophet aims to speak of; tho' it be Christ's righteousness that is communicated to them, as well as it is to them who are at age, yet as to the manner of communicating it, God hath his own way, which we know not.

Now that we may learn, in speaking to these truths, not only to get some light for informing of our judgment, but also some help for our practice; take two or three *uses*, ere we proceed any further.

The 1*st use* then is, To let you see the absolute necessity of believing in Christ Jesus, and that it is as necessary for the attaining of our justification, as Christ's dying is; for our justification is an effect flowing from several causes, and the want of any of them will mar it: There must necessarily be a concurrence of them all, to bring it about; and therefore, tho' there be an excellent worth in Christ's righteousness, yet there is a necessity of faith, to lay hold upon it, and to make it ours: God's order in the covenant bears this out, wherein he hath knit the promise of pardon of sin, and of justification, to faith, and resting on Christ; and there is good reason for it, as, 1. The Lord will have a sinner to know what he is obliged to Christ, which faith contributes much unto; for faith stands not in the way of the freedom of justification, but rather commends it; for the Lord would have us know, that we hold our life

life of him: And not to receive him by faith, is an evidence of highest presumption; therefore it is said, Rom. iv. 16. *It is by faith, that it might be of grace:* God hath chosen this way, that the freeness of his grace, in pardoning of sin, may be seen. 2. The Lord by this lets the unbeliever know, that the reason of his own ruin is of himself; there shall not be one unbeliever found, that shall have it to say, that the blame lay on God, or on Christ, because the offer was made to them on condition of receiving it by faith, and they not performing the condition, their guilt is aggravated by their slighting of the offer: It is true, that we are not now dealing with them, who downright deny the truth of this doctrine; but, alas, what better are they, who do in their practice deny it, and live senslesly and securely under the gospel? We conceive that there are *Three* sorts of persons, that have need of a word to be spoken to them here. 1. Such as live carelesly, and securely (as we just now said) as if God required nothing of them at all: as they were born, they know not how; so they live, they know not how; and when they are pressed to a change of their state and way, they make excuses, partly from the sinfulness of their nature, that they can do nothing, partly from the abundant grace of God, that he must do all: but it will never excuse you, that ye wanted grace, and had a sinful nature; for whom, I pray, can ye blame for it? ye that make a bachel of his mercy, if ye continue to do so, shall never get good of it; for he hath said that he will justify and save none but the believer: There is none other that hath the promise of pardon; it is not made to any thing that is to be brought forth, or done by your own strength, or by the strength of nature, or of free-will; but God hath laid down this order and method, and made it known that ye should believe and receive the offer of Christ in the gospel; renounce your own righteousness, and betake you to Christ's righteousness, otherwise ye cannot on good ground expect to be justified. 2. Others will set about many things that are good; but the works of believing they can never be brought to mind or own: they will make a sort of conscience of prayer, of keeping the church, of reading the scriptures, &c. but to give obedience to the command of believing, they mind it not, they can live and die without it; this was the woful and soul-ruining practice of the Jews of old, as we are told, Rom. ix. They took much pains to come by righteousness, but *they attained it not, because they sought it not by faith, but as it were by the works of the law, for they stumbled at that stumbling stone;* when they had gone a part of the way, as it were, and come to the stone of believing, there they fell and brake their necks. Hence there are many, who promise heaven to themselves, and think that they have done something for it, who yet never laid hold on Christ for their justification; but let me tell you, that though ye could go the greatest length in holiness that ever any did since Adam's fall, it will not avail you, if ye neglect faith in Christ: I say not this to dissuade you from the duties of holiness, God forbid; but to divert you from seeking justification by them: study the duties of holiness, but seek always by any means to be found in Christ, and in his righteousness, and not in the righteousness of your duties, as to your justification. It is true none that have any tolerable measure of knowledge, will profess down-right, that they lean to holy duties; yet many are so ignorant, that they cannot distinguish betwixt faith and works; and there are not a few, who have a hope of heaven, such as it is, who never knew any thing of the exercise of believing. A 3d sort are these, who, because of some common favours that they have received, as evidences of God's care and kindness, conclude their justification. It may be some have had now and then deep convictions, or have win to tears in prayer, or at a sermon: Others, it may be, have had some joy now and then, at hearing the word: Others will, it may be, dream of such and such heavenly things, and have, as they suppose, a vision of them in their sleep, and some joy will follow on it when they are awaked: Others may have met with many deliveries by sea and land, and God hath dealt well with them, and their children, in external things; but alas, these things may befal unbelievers: not one of them, nor all of them together, if there be no more, will justify; ye would rather try these things, whether they be sound, and evidences of special love, or not, by your believing; if they have faith in Christ carried along with them, it is well; if ye can say, that *after ye believed, ye were sealed with the holy Spirit of promise,* and that your joy followed upon your closing with, and resting upon Christ, ye have no reason to question it; but where such tastes go before, and are without believing, it is suspicious like; there are many of you that have multitudes of things, that ye lean to, beside Christ, and never seriously put yourselves to the trial, whether ye be indeed fled to him.

2. *Use.* We would commend this to you, as a ground of trial of yourselves, if ye be justified, if

ye have seriously taken with your sin, and embraced God's offer of the righteousness of Christ, and rested on it; make this once sure, that ye have been sensible of sin, that ye have been beaten from your own righteousness, that ye have fled to Jesus Christ, and closed with his righteousness offered in the gospel; then this will natively follow, that by his knowledge thou art justified; his word speaks it out plain to thee: It may be that some think this to be a broad mark, and that others will think it narrow; yet it is a solid mark, and no other thing is or can be a mark, but as it implies this. Though some may presumptuously gather from it a broad conclusion, yet it will be found to be as straitning and searching a mark, when well considered, as other marks and evidences are, that we cannot at first so easily lay hold upon; and, therefore we would say, that it is not every one that thinks he believes, but it is such as really believe, who have this evidence; and for preventing of mistakes, we shall follow this evidence of justification, to wit, faith, to the very rise of it. 1. It supposes a charge and summons, as it were, given to the persons, to appear before God. 2. There is a sentence discovered, standing against them, and over their heads, by the covenant of works: now, what can ye say to these *Two?* where I desire you not so much to speak your light, as your practice and experience; what a charge, or summons was put in your hands? Have ye read the libel of your sins? and have ye seen the breaches of the law, and your liableness to the curse of God for the same? If so, then what means the good opinion that many of you have of yourselves? This is even the thing that the apostle saith of himself before his conversion, Rom. vii. 9. *Before the law came, I was alive; but when the commandment came, sin revived, and I died:* That is, before the charge was put in my hand, and I summoned to appear before God's bar, I had a good opinion of myself, and I thought that all was well; but when I came to take up the law in the spiritual meaning, and broad extent of it, I saw myself lost, and gone, and that conceit fell. These *Three* then usually preceed faith, 1. That a person hath had a good opinion of himself. 2. That this person is summoned or charged to answer at God's bar. 3. That the person is made to pass sentence on himself, as lost and undone, by reason of the law's sentence, and curse standing over his head unrepealed. Now, how hath it been with you as to these? The most part are quite of another disposition than Paul was; they think they are well enough, because they never discovered their rotten condition: but try well how it is with you; go in and see if ever ye discovered in yourselves, 1. An inclination to establish your own righteousness. 2. Was ye ever under a work of the law humbling you? And 3. Was ye ever in your own apprehension lost? If so, then ye are such as Christ came to call. 2*dly*, In the next room consider what ye betook yourselves to, for answering that charge, and for a remedy of that lost condition; there is no remedy but the offer of Christ's righteousness in the gospel. Some being charged with guilt, betake themselves to prayer, and that is well done in so far; but if ye hold there, and go no further, it is not right: it is here, as it was with these, who lived under the law, who, when they had sinned, made use of sacrifices, and the greatest part held there, and went no further; whereas the believer looked through the sacrifices to Christ: so, if ye hold at prayer, and other duties, and go no further, these will not profit you; but know ye what it is to go to prayer, and in prayer to go to Christ, and rest on his sacrifice for your acceptance? I fear there is great ignorance here; the most part know not what they have done, when they were charged; or, if they did any thing, they prayed; or, if they went any further on, they look to the promise of God's mercy; but that is not far enough gone. How many such are there, who have made their prayer their only intercessor, and have presumed to step in on God's mercy, without a Mediator? 3*dly*, Suppose that ye have betaken yourselves to Christ, as to the remedy; come on, and try how your union hath been made up with him, where did ye seek and find him? Christ Jesus is to be found in the gospel, in the ministry of the word; therefore that is put in on good reason in the definition of faith given to us in the Catechism, *That it is a resting on him, as he is offered in the gospel:* but I fear and suppose that many have another Christ (to speak so) whom they have gotten without knowing, or making any use of the word, or offer of the gospel, *which is the power of God for salvation to them that believe.* 4*thly*, Wherewith did ye take hold on him? or how did ye act on him? Was it by faith, or not? There are many, who act on him as they think by prayer, not as the meritorious cause, but as the efficient cause of justification, praying for pity and pardon from him; but this is not to take hold of Christ's righteousness by faith: others think, that if they can love and serve him, and please him with duties, they will engage him to give them pardon; and in this they have to (speak so) an underhand covenant of works: they will do

some-

something to please the Mediator, and wherein they come short, they expect that he will make it up; and this is very ordinary in practice. If ye ask some, What hope have ye of justification? They will answer, Through Christ's righteousness, and that is good in so far; but ask them again, How they will get it? they will answer, That they will do what they dow or may, and they hope that he will pity them: ye would look in upon your own hearts, and see whether it be not secretly making something of this kind the ground of your title to Christ, and of your justification. And yet all this may be, and often is in them that will not stoop to the way of grace, nor submit themselves to the righteousness of God. They will speak of Christ's righteousness, and yet they will needs give him some compensation; and so come, never really, to renounce their own righteousness, and to flee unto his, and to hold it up as their defence before God. Take but an impartial view of these steps, and many of you, who suppose that ye are believers, will not be found to be so, nor justified before God, because ye lay not claim to it by faith, but, as it were, by the works of the law.

Use 3d. There is here ground for all that neglect Christ, and do not by faith take hold of him, to look for a most dreadful sentence; and ground for others, who seek righteousness through faith, to look for a most comfortable sentence. 1*st*, then; Is this a truth, that justification is through faith in Christ? Then many of you are not justified, and, if the Lord prevent it not, ye will never be justified: If so, then it must be a most dreadful thing, not to believe. If ye would know what is your condition, ye may read it, John iii. 18, 36. *He that believeth not is condemned already, and he shall not see life, but the wrath of God abideth on him*; and, Gal. ii. 10. *As many as are of the works of the law, are under the curse; for it is written, Cursed is every one that continues not in all things written in the book of the law to do them*. If ye really believed this, many of you would be under horror, to hear what a sad condition ye are in, even *condemned already*, and having the wrath and curse of God *abiding on you*; because the word curseth and condemneth all that are not in Christ by faith. This, I fear, belongs to very many, who are altogether secure and careless, and yet are in reputation amongst us: and is it not very sad to be professing fair, to have the offer of life, and to be treating with God about your peace, and yet to be still in the state of enmity with him, so that if death were within twenty four hours march to you, ye could have nothing to expect, but the ratifying of this sentence of God's curse upon you? We are sure there is as much in this, as might, in reason, put you, by all means, to study, 1. To be believers, for without faith ye are never over the borders of God's curse; which may lay a chase to you, and put you to the necessity of fleeing to Christ for refuge. 2. To take some pains to try, whether ye be in faith, as the apostle exhorts, 2 Cor. xiii. 5. *Examine yourselves, whether ye be in the faith, prove yourselves; know ye not your own selves, how that Christ is in you, except ye be reprobates?* His meaning is, Know ye not, that this is a truth, that ye are in a reprobate or unapproven condition, except Christ be in you; and Christ is in none, but in the believer: If so, ought ye not to try yourselves, if ye be in the faith, if ye be believers. There is no ordinary way, to win to the sure and comfortable knowledge of it, but by trial; and if ye be not believers, is there not reason, and is it not of your concernment, to endeavour, by trial, to come to the knowledge of it? As this is ground of terror to the unbeliever, so it is ground of notable consolation to the believer, who, if he were even put to the reckoning with *Paul, I was a blasphemer, a persecuter, injurious;* yet here is hope for him, that he shall be found in Christ, not having his own righteousness, but Christ's: believing in Christ will obtain justification to such a person; his righteousness taken hold of, and put on by faith, is as pleasing and acceptable to God, as the unrighteousness of the sinner is displeasing to him. This was it that made David to sing sweetly, Psal. xxxii. *Blessed is he whose transgression is forgiven, whose sin is covered; blessed is the man to whom the Lord imputeth no iniquity;* to wit, through the imputation of Christ's righteousness, as the apostle clears, Rom. iv. As the first branch of the use shews the necessity of faith for chasing sinners to Christ, so this branch is a sweet motive to draw them to him; and if there were more sensible sinners amongst us, whose own righteousness misgives them, and who are brought to that pass, that the Jaylor and Peter's hearers were in, crying out, *What shall we do to be saved?* This word, *Believe in the Lord Jesus, and ye shall be saved,* would make them come in cheerful, as he did, from the brink, not only of temporal, but of eternal death. 'Tis this faith, by which we have access to stand before God: ye would therefore be earnestly intreated to betake yourselves to it, and to Jesus Christ by it, for your pardon and peace, even for your justification before God.

2*dly*, Consider these words, as they hold out the

in him, as suffering, as satisfying for sin, as in soul-travel, bearing our iniquities. Hence *observe*, That Christ Jesus, his righteousness, holden forth in God's promise of free grace, is the native and proper Object, that saving and justifying faith takes hold of, and rests upon; or, to the same purpose, The saving grace of faith, that justifies, is that faith that does peculiarly apply and rest upon Christ, Jesus, holden forth in God's promise in the gospel, as the righteousness of a sinner that believes on him; hence the prophet calleth it here, not knowledge more generally taken, but *the knowledge of him*, and that as he is holden out in this *chapter*, to wit, as Surety for sinners, and suffering for their debt. This will be clear, if we consider all these scriptures that make offer of the pardon of sin; for it is offered, not on condition of faith in a more general notion of it, but on condition of faith *in him*; so Rom. v. 22, 24, 25. *The righteousness of God, which is by faith of Jesus Christ, unto all, and upon all them that believe.: Being justified freely by his grace, through the redemption that is in Jesus Christ, whom God hath set forth to be a propitiation through faith in his blood.* Rom. v. 1. *Being justified by faith, we have peace with God, through our Lord Jesus Christ*, John i. 12. *To as many as received him, he gave power to become the sons of God, even to as many as believe in his name*; where the faith that hath the promise of justification, and the privilege of adoption annexed to it, is called the *receiving of Christ, and believing on his name*.

It must also be cleared, and confirmed by good reason. 1. Faith does not justify as it is considered in itself as an act, but as it relates to, and unites with Christ, as the meritorious cause of justification. 2. Neither does faith justify as it looks to every object which the word holds forth, but as it respects Christ offered in the gospel, whom it receiveth, because there is no other thing that can bear the soul's weight and burden: Therefore he, as offered in the gospel, must be the Object of faith, at it is saving and justifying. 3. The terms of the covenant, and God's offer clears it also; for God's offer of justification is not on these terms, that a

be counted to us for righteousness; which may also confirms this truth.

The *Uses* of this *doctrine* are such, as serve both to clear the nature of faith, and to direct us in our practice.

The first *Use* then serves to clear the truth; as the Papists corrupt many truths, so they corrupt this truth, concerning the nature of justifying and saving faith, in these *Three*, 1. In the *Object*. 2. In the *Subject*. 3. In the *Act* of it. As for the *Object* of this faith, they make it to be every thing that God reveals, and sometimes they take in their own *Traditions*; the reason is, because they give not faith a causality in justification, nor the capacity and place of a thing, acting on Christ peculiarly; but take it in as a common grace, or at the best, as a grace that is radical, and gives life to other graces, but never as taking hold of Christ's righteousness: which quite overturns the way of justification through faith in him; for faith, that layeth not hold on his righteousness cannot justify: and their making the Object of faith to be so broad, doth enervate both the immediate merit of Christ's righteousness, and the exercise of faith on it. 1*st*, Then we grant, that there is a historical faith requisite, as to the whole word of God; yet we say, That the faith that justifies is properly that faith that singles out the righteousness of Christ, and takes hold of it: so that it is not our believing that the world was made, that there will be a day of judgment, nor our believing that a Saviour of sinners is come into the world, and hath suffered, &c. that justifies; but it is a closing with, a receiving of, and resting on that Saviour; a singling out of the promise that makes offer of him, (as for instance, where it is said, *If thou believe on the Lord Jesus, thou shalt be saved*) and pitching on that, and resting on him holden out in the promise: faith gives the soul footing here, whereas before, its case was very desperate. 2*dly*, We may clear what we are to look to, as the object of justifying and saving faith, by our putting in these *three* words, or expressions in the *doctrine*, to wit, *Christ Jesus his righteousness holden forth in the promise of God's*

God's free grace in the gospel; and which are needful to be taken in, though it be not always necessary, that we be explicit in the uptaking of them. 1. There is need of taking in *Christ's righteousness*, because it is our defence at the bar of God's justice; even as a debitor, whose debt the cautioner hath paid, hath that to answer when he is charged for it, that his cautioner hath paid it. 2. There is need to take in this, *Holden forth in God's promise in the gospel*; because, tho' Christ be the Object of justifying faith, and his righteousness be the ground of the soul's defence before God, yet God's promise must be looked on by faith, for the use-making of Christ and his righteousness, and as a warrant to rest on him, and to expect justification through him: And thus faith hath Christ's fulness, or his full and complete satisfaction, for righteousness; and God's faithfulness impledged, that the believer shall be accepted through it: And it is on this ground, that faith sometimes looks on God as *able*, sometimes as *faithful*; therefore it is said, Heb. vii. 25. *He is able to save to the uttermost*; and Heb. i. *Sarah judged him faithful who had promised*: Whereupon there is a closing with the offer in the promise, and a looking to obtain that which is promised, as if they had a righteousness of their own; and this the apostle calls *the law of faith*, Rom. iii. 27. because to justification there is, beside the payment of the debt, a law, declaring the man to be absolved, requisite; and the sinner, having God's offer and promise, that upon his accepting of Christ's Christ's righteousness he shall be justified, instructs that his debt is paid by his Cautioner, and that therefore he ought to be, and is accordingly absolved: And tho' God's promise be not so properly a law, yet the apostle calleth it so, and it is a solid defence to the soul that is fled to Christ, who may thus reason, I have no righteousness of my own, but Christ's righteousness by proclamation is offered to me in the gospel, and I have heartily received it, and God is faithful to make good his promise to me; and this looks to Christ as he is revealed in the gospel. 3. There is need to put in this word, *The promise of God's free grace*; because hereby the sinner is made to see whence the promise came, and of what nature it is, and gives ground to take hold of the promise, and of that which is made offer of in it. The promise is of free grace, therefore it is always called the covenant of grace; so, Rom. iv. 16. *It is of faith, that it might be by grace, to the end the promise might be sure to all the seed*: For, if it were not of grace, the sinner would never think himself sure, nor would he know if such a sinner might take hold of such a promise; but, considering that the promise is of grace, and his acceptance is of grace, as is often repeated, Eph. i. ii. and iii. chapters, these *Three* are the great warrant that a sinner hath to roll himself over on a complete Mediator; a faithful God promising to answer all grounds of fears, doubts and jealousies; and free grace, which answers all challenges that may come in to hinder his closing with, and resting on the promise: For if it should be said, How darest thou lay hold upon the promise? The answer is, It is free, it is not *the mount that may not be touched*, but it is *Jesus the Mediator of the new covenant*, &c. It is grace that is the rise, the end, and the condition of it: These are the *Three* on which faith yields itself to Christ, and which are the Object of it, on which it dare hazard, and on which it does hazard; and these *Three* are revealed in the gospel of the grace of him that is faithful, and cannot deny himself: May we not then say, O sinners, if ye will believe, that ye have a good resting place, *a sure Foundation, a tried Corner-stone*, as it is, Isa. xxviii. cited Rom. ix. where the apostle hath it, *He that believes on him, shall never be ashamed*: There is a sufficient Surety, a full Mediator, there is a faithful God that will keep his word, and there is a free covenant and promise, softer for a bruised soul to roll itself over upon, than any bed of the finest downs is for a weary and crazy body; this is a *chariot paved with love for the daughters of Jerusalem*. Single out Christ from all that is in the world, without slighting any part of it, and believe in him, and lippen to him; let him have another weight and lift of you than ye give to any other thing, he is able to bear it, and God will never quarrel you for so doing, but will keep his word to you that do betake yourselves to, or that have betaken yourselves to him; *He that believes shall never perish, nor come into condemnation*. O! know what a ground ye have to rest upon, it is even the substance and marrow of all the word of God, ye have Christ and his fulness, God and his faithfulness, grace and its freeness: and are there such *three* things beside? or is it imaginable, or possible that there can be any beguile, or failure here? spare not then to lay the weight of your souls upon it; let it be the foundation of your peace, and let it answer all challenges that may be, whether for many, or for great and grievously aggravated sins: only by faith take hold of this righteousness, and rest upon God's faithfulness, and free promise, to make it forthcoming to you: But upon the other side, O how greatly will it aggravate your guilt, that had

had such a remedy in your offer, such *a tried Corner-stone, elect and precious*, to rest upon, and yet made no use of it! Let me exhort, beseech, and even obtest you, *that ye receive not this grace in vain;* but as Christ is laid *for a sure Foundation*, so come to him, and build upon him, that ye may not *be ashamed* in the day of the Lord, when all that believe not, how presumptuously soever they may hold up their heads now, *shall be ashamed and confounded world without end*. O happy, thrice happy will they all be found to be then, *who have trusted in him*.

SERMON LX.

Isaiah liii. 11.--- ---*By his knowledge shall my righteous Servant justify many, for he shall bear their iniquities.*

THE knowledge of Christ was wont to be much thought of by the people of God, and to be in high estimation among them; and we may say, we wot well it was deservedly so, considering that it is by his knowledge, that justification was derived to them, and is derived to us: This is that which the Lord is clearing by the prophet here, to wit, how the benefit of Christ's sufferings and purchase may be derived and communicate unto a sinner; which these words, (though but few) as purposely made use of, do clear, even that his sufferings should not be in vain, but that he should see a seed; and tho' that seed should not be *all* men, yet they should be *many:* And the way how these many should come by the benefit of his sufferings, is also held forth; and that is, *By his knowledge*, who is the righteous Servant. We shew you, that this doth upon the matter look to faith, and is meant of it; and confirmed it by other parallel scriptures, which say, that *through faith in him, all that believe are justified*. We came also to speak of this faith which justifies, and did propose *Five* things to be spoken of concerning it, (and indeed if any thing be of concernment, this is; if a right to Christ and his purchase be of concernment, then sure it must be of concernment to know, how we come by that right) 1. The necessity of it. 2. The Object of it. 3. The act of it. 4. The effects that flow from it. 5. The manner of its concurring in the attaining of justification. We spoke of the *first*, to wit, of the necessity of faith, and shewed, that though there be a full satisfaction laid down to merit and procure justification, yet it is applied to none but to believers, and not till they believe.

2. We spoke also to this, that faith, as it justifies, looks not to all the word of God as its object, but mainly and principally to Christ, and to the word only, in so far as it holds out Christ in the promises and offers of God's grace, as it is here called the knowledge of him, or faith in him.

We now proceed to hint a word for clearing of a question, and it is a new and very late one, to wit, Whether justifying faith lays hold on Christ as a Saviour and Priest only; or whether it lays hold on him, not only as a Priest to save, but also as a King to command? Though this doth not look at first blush to be of any great moment, and that such an inconsiderable like difference is not to be stood upon; yet we will find that this last wants not its own influence on altering the common and ordinary, and (as we conceive) the solid received doctrine, concerning the way of justification, if we should admit it: And therefore we answer the *Question* from the *Text*, That Christ, considered as suffering, and bearing our sins, and so as offering himself in a sacrifice, is the Object that justifying faith, as such, takes hold of; therefore the connexion of these two is clear in this verse, *He shall see of the travel of his soul and be satisfied:* and *by his knowledge shall many be justified;* and again it is subjoined, as the reason why many shall by faith in him be justified; *Because he shall bear their iniquities*. By the knowledge of him that offered himself in a sacrifice, many are justified; and many are justified, because he bears their iniquities; which will infer this, that faith considers him as satisfying for the iniquities of his people, in its acting on him for justification, and pardon of sin. It is true, Christ's offices are not divided, and it is not true faith, if it take not hold of him, and make not use of him in all his offices; but as there are several evils in us, which his offices do meet with, and are suited unto, so should faith take hold of them, and make use of them for curing and removing of these evils: He is King, Priest, and Prophet; and faith takes hold of his, as a King, to command and subdue us to himself; as a Prophet, to illuminate us, and cure our blindness; and as a Priest, to satisfy divine justice, and to procure the pardon of sin; as we are not to separate, so we are not to confound these: We use not to say that Christ as a Prophet doth justify us, nor that as a Priest he doth illuminate us; no more should we, nor can we well say, that as a King he satisfied justice for us; the same blessed God is wise, righ-

righteous, holy, faithful, just, merciful, &c. yet he is diversely considered in respect of our conceiving and use-making, according to our need; so is it here. For clearing whereof, take these grounds. 1. The scripture speaks of, and points Christ out in his sufferings, as the Object of justifying faith, Rom. iii. 25. *Whom God hath set forth for a propitiation through faith in his blood:* where the blood of Christ, and he as suffering, is purposed as faith's Object: so 1 Cor. i. *We preach Christ crucified.* 1 John ii. *We have an Advocate with the Father, Jesus Christ the Righteous, and he is the propitiation for our sins;* where he is holden forth in his sufferings, as the propitiation that faith layeth hold on, John iii. 14. *As Moses lifted up the serpent in the wilderness, so must the Son of man be lifted up, that whosoever believeth on him,* &c. where Christ lifted up, and as dying on the cross, is made the Object of justifying faith; even as the brazen serpent lifted up was the object that they looked to, when they were stung, and cured. 2. It is also clear from the law's libelling and charging us for the debt of our sin, that makes us liable to condemnation; and faith being the mean of our justification, and absolution from the debt, it must needs look to the Cautioner's paying of our debt, and so answering the charge, which was done in his death; for he paid our debt, satisfied the penalty of the law, and came under the curse, in suffering death; as is clear, Gal. iii. the 10. ver. being compared with ver. 13. So, Rom. viii. 34. *Who shall lay any thing to the charge of God's elect? It is God that justifies, who shall condemn? It is Christ that died;* which is brought in as faith's answer to the charge. The charge cannot be denied; for we are guilty of so many sins, and therefore liable to condemnation; but, saith faith, Christ hath died: It proposes him dying as a satisfaction for answering the charge, and for obtaining of absolution. 3. Christ as suffering and satisfying justice is our righteousness, and therefore must be the Object of faith, as it is justifying, whereupon it pleads an absolution before the throne of God; so that, when we come to plead and found our defence before God's throne, it is not on this, that Christ is a King, and hath subdued us; but it is on this ground, that he is our Priest, and hath satisfied justice for us, and paid our debt, and procured a discharge to us: So the apostle, speaking of Christ's sufferings, Col. ii. says, *that he blotted out the hand-writing of ordinances that was against us, and took it out of the way, nailing it to his cross:.* It is Christ as suffering that is the ground of our peace, and therefore faith as justifying must so consider him. Tho' we desire to move nothing needlesly, yet laying it once for a ground, that justifying faith lays hold on Christ as a King, this will follow as a consequence, and, as we suppose, as a reason, that our obedience to Christ as a King hath the same influence, and the same causality in our justification, that faith's resting on Christ's satisfying for us as a Priest hath;' because as Christ's priestly office gives us a warrant to rest upon him for justification, so would his kingly office, (if it were the object of justifying faith as such) when taken hold of for our obedience. We have touched upon this, 1. That ye may see the warrantableness of this doctrine which is received in the churches of Christ, and that ye may consider Christ as *the high Priest of your profession,* and plead justification from his sacrifice, acting faith upon him accordingly. 2. That we may put a bar against the introducing of justification by works, under one pretext or another, how specious soever, seeing the scripture so directly opposes faith and works in our justification; for if we once admit that Christ as King, is the Object of justifying faith as such, it would overturn the distinct way of faith's acting upon Christ's righteousness, for answering the charge put in the sinner's hand by the law; and when the soul getteth a challenge for sin, would put it to look what obedience it hath given to Christ as a King, to answer that challenge or charge by; and would in the same manner also put the soul to gather the ground of its peace from the one, as well as from the other, that is, both from Christ's righteousness, and from its own obedience, not only as an evidence, but a social cause, or not only to its own sense, but as to the effect: But we leave this as a thing to be regretted, that when there is ground enough of stumbling, because of our ignorance and blindness, there should, and that very unnecessarily, be such new occasion of stumbling to souls cast in the way of faith.

We come now to speak of the *Act* of faith as justifying, called here *knowledge,* and the *knowledge of him,* to shew that it points at justifying faith; for if it were not so, it were the same with common knowledge, whereby we believe any history of the Bible: but this being justifying knowledge, it must be knowledge of another kind. We shall here clear, 1. Wherein the act of justifying faith consists. 2. Remove some mistakes about it, and make some use of it.

For the *first,* We suppose there are these *four* requisite, in, or to justifying faith, though not always in the same degree. 1. That there be a distinct

stinct knowledge in some measure of the object; an antecedent that faith presupposes, and for which cause faith gets the name of *knowledge* here and elsewhere in scripture, the antecedent being put for the consequent: For faith hath always knowledge with it, tho' knowledge hath not always faith. 2. That there be an assent to the thing known; as when we know that we are sinners, and that it is the blood of Christ that must cleanse us from sin, we must assent to the truth of these, as Christ says, John viii. *If ye believe not Moses his writings, how shall ye believe my words?* If ye assent not to the truth of what he hath written, how can ye believe my speaking? Both these are in the *understanding:* and if there be no more, this makes but historical faith. 3. When the soul knows it is a sinner, and under the curse, and that Christ is a Saviour, and that there is salvation to be gotten by such a mean, and that he is an able Saviour, and hath *assented* to the truth of these; there is a *consenting* of the heart to that truth conditionally proposed, and made offer of, that is, to receive Christ as he is offered in the gospel; which in scripture is called a *receiving* of him, John i. 12. *To as many as received him,* &c. And this is an act of the *will,* respecting Christ as offered, and a bargain proposed that will make the soul happy, where faith accepts. 4. There is a resting on Christ received as a good bargain, which is also an act of the heart, or will, called in scripture a *committing ourselves to him, a leaning on him,* or *rolling ourselves on him ;* which we conceive to be the same that Paul hath, Phil. iii. 9. *That I may be found in him:* When the soul places its safety here, and lippens to Christ's righteousness alone, as contradistinguished to its own; these *two* last acts are properly the essence of faith as justifying, and they are well holden out in the Catechism, where faith is described to be *a saving grace, whereby we receive and rest upon Christ, as he is offered in the gospel.* We shall illustrate it in a comparison made use of before, to this purpose: Suppose there were a number of rebels, that had incurred the prince's displeasure, and were guilty of treason by the law; suppose also the prince's son, or some courtier, hath satisfied for them, and procured their pardon and peace; upon which there comes out a proclamation, that if they will submit, and yield themselves, and lay down their arms, they shall be pardoned, and admitted to friendship, as if they had never rebelled: Those rebels must know, 1. That there is an act of favours past, and a proclamation made on such terms. 2. They must have a general faith and assent to the thing, and that there is no question but such a thing is done. 3. There is a consultation by the understanding with the will, if they will admit of, and receive it, and trust themselves to it, And then, 4. There is the heart's consenting to accept of the offer of grace, on the terms of the proclamation, and a resting on it, which is a lippening of their defence to it, that if ever they should be called to an account, they will make use of such an act of grace, and of the proclamation for their defence and safety, and lippen to it, and and to his faithfulness who made the proclamation, believing that he will fulfil his word and promise: It is just so here, in a sinner's acting faith for justification. We may instance and illustrate it also in the example of the prodigal, wherein we may find something of all this: When he had been in the height of his distraction and madness, in his natural condition, it is said, *He came to himself,* he knew and believed that there was meat enough in his father's house, and resolved to go home; upon his knowledge follows his resolution, and his will consents, *I will arise and go,* which supposes his faith of an offer of meat, on condition of his going; and then there is that whereon he grounds his defence, *I will say, Father, I have sinned ;* I will disclaim all, and betake me to thy grace, implied in the word *Father:* He resolves to table his defence on this ground, and upon this comes home.

More particularly, 1. Knowledge of the object rested upon is necessary, Rom. x. *How can they believe on him of whom they have not heard?* It is not possible we can believe what we know not. And as every other step hath some doctrinal mistake, and some practical, so hath this. The doctrinal mistake is that error of Papists, unworthy to be refuted; they say, There is no knowledge requisite to faith; yea, some of their prime men have said, That faith is rather ignorance than knowledge; but surely then faith would not be called knowledge, if it might rather be defined ignorance; but this they maintain, to keep the people in ignorance of the gospel; and it is the ground of many more errors, and much delusion: It is even as if a blind man could go well in a slippery place, where are many pits; for knowledge is no less necessary to faith, than eyes are to such a man. The practical errors in this, are such as we find in many of you, who think ye can believe well; but ask, and put you to it, ye cannot tell what: Many of you are obstinate maintainers of implicit faith, while ye say, ye have faith, and yet cannot tell what it is, nor whereon it is grounded; but we say, that knowledge

SERM. LX.   *Isaiah* liii. Verse 11.   365

-ledge is so necessary to faith, that if it be not a part of it, yet it is necessary antecedaneous to it, and presupposed; therefore, if ever ye would be accounted believers, study knowledge, and the knowledge of Christ crucified, at least so far as to ground your faith upon. It is sad that so many will maintain the reality of their faith, and yet are grosly ignorant of the fundamentals of religion; knowledge is the very rise of, and first step to believing; and yet it is hardly possible to brangle the vain confidence of many, whom it is as impossible to bring to knowledge.

2. There is an *Assent* requisite to the object known, which is that we call *Historical Faith*, and this is to be confirmed in the general truths contained in the gospel: as, that Adam was made according to God's image, that he fell, and brake the covenant of works, and made himself, and all his, liable to God's curse; that we are by that covenant under God's curse; that Christ Jesus the Son of God, according to the covenant of redemption, entred himself Cautioner for the elect; that he really died and paid their debt; that his purchase is made offer of in the gospel; and that, according to the covenant of grace, there is a real absolution from sin, and an eternal happiness to be had at the great day, through embracing of him. There must be an assent to the truth of these things; for it is impossible, that they, who think not themselves sinners, and that mind not a day of judgment, and a reckoning, will ever close with Christ, and lippen to his righteousness. I fear there are but few hearers of the gospel, that come the length of devils in believing, and yet all will needs be counted Christians. We would here, upon the one hand, disclaim the Popish error, that placeth all the essence of faith in the understanding, which is somewhat strange, seeing they scarce think knowledge of the thing to be believed necessary; the reason is, because they know, or at least own, nothing more of the concurrence of faith in justification, than is obedience to a commandment: they think it is a duty and obedience to a commandment, to assent to any truth; therefore they take this general historical faith to be the only faith, as they take holiness to be the only ground of their peace, when they are called to an account; and thus faith, as a part of their holiness, comes in, but they admit of no particular respect to faith's taking hold of Christ's righteousness, as the immediate ground of their peace. Upon the other hand, we would seclude the vain faith of many professors, who some way believe all that is in the Bible, so as they question nothing

therein, they know no other faith but this; yet if this were justifying faith, the devils should have it, *For they believe and tremble;* they believe there is a God, that Christ is the Son of God, that they that believe shall not perish, that God is faithful, *&c.* But this historical faith is not enough, 1. Because (as I just now said) it may be in reprobates and devils. 2. Because the scripture expresly differenceth this sort of faith, from saving faith; many were called believers, to whom Christ would not commit himself, as it is, John ii. 24. For, though they believe it to be truth which he spake, yet they rested not on him; so in the parable of the sower, Matth. xiii. there are three grounds that receive the seed, which imports, in two of them at least, a kind of believing; but the fourth ground is only good. 3. Because this faith acts upon every revealed truth alike, and assents to all passages recorded in the Bible alike; as on, and to that, *Paul left his cloke at Troas,* and the like; as it acts on that, *This is a faithful saying, that Christ came into the world to save sinners,* and such like; but, according to that ground formerly given, faith, as it justifies, acts on Christ only; and therefore this bare assent to the truth of the word cannot be justifying faith, because it acts no otherways on Christ, than it doth upon other things; ye would therefore know a difference in your practice betwixt these two, the crediting the truth of a thing, and your actual receiving, and resting upon that truth: as for example, A man proposeth marriage to a woman, and she believes that he is in earnest, and not in scorn, yet there is a great difference betwixt that and her actual consenting to marry him; so is it here, the man may believe that Christ doth really make offer of himself to him, and yet be far from cordial receiving of him; or take it in the example made use of before, Suppose that some of the rebels we spake of, believe the proclamation to be a truth, yet thinking it hard to be under the bands of government, they do not embrace it. If it be *objected* here, that the scripture often calls justifying faith a believing *that Christ is the Son of God,* which is no more than this assent of the judgment, or historical faith; For *answer,* It would be considered of whom the scripture there speaks. 1. It is of Jews for the most part, who had the faith of the Messiah generally among them: And no question, the believers of them, such as the proselyted eunuch, Martha, and Mary, had the faith of the Messiah's satisfying divine justice, and of their justification through his satisfaction: But the great question of the Jews was, Whether Jesus the Son of Mary was

A a a   the

the Messiah or not? and it being revealed, and believed that he was, the other followed, they rested on him of will, (to say so) as the Messiah. 2. Believing of Christ to be the Son of God, doth not exclude, but include their consenting to the receiving of Christ; but it holds forth also their assent to, and persuasion of that truth that was then debated, that he was indeed the promised Messiah, and the Son of God; for the devils confessed him to be the Son of God: and none will say, but there was more in their believing him to be the Son of God, than in the devils believing it, who never believe unto salvation, as they did. 3. Consider, that as sometimes knowledge is put for faith, so this assent may be put for faith, where yet more is implied in it; especially considering that, Rom. x. faith is called, faith of the heart, *With the heart man believeth :* Now, believing with the heart being an act of the will, these testimonies setting out faith to be a believing Christ to be the Son of God, must imply a lippening to him following upon it: we are therefore never to look on these places as comprehending a bare assent only, but as including also, and carrying alongst with it, the cordial receiving him, and of resting upon him.

For the 3*d*, to wit, the *receiving Act* of faith, which differs from the former, as we shew in the examples hinted at before; it looks to the covenant of redemption betwixt Jehovah and the Mediator; it accepts of the terms of the covenant, as they are proposed in the gospel, and consents to the bargain; and as God proposes the righteousness of Christ, it submits to the same; which Paul, 1 Tim. i. calls *a saying worthy of all acceptation,* to be welcomed and believed as such; and the believers mentioned, Heb. xi. are said, *not to have received the promises, but to have seen them afar off, and to have embraced* (or saluted) *them:* This receiving is no physical, or natural act, as if we were to receive such a thing by the mouth, or bodily hand; it is an act of faith in the heart, proportioned and suited to this spiritual bargain, or marriage, proposed in the covenant of grace; and it is like a man consenting to a civil bargain, or like a woman's consenting to marry a man: As when it is said to sinners, Ye are naturally dead in sins and trespasses, and under God's curse; but, be it known to you, that we preach remission of sins to you through the blood of Christ; faith considers this offer, accepts of, and welcomes it.

The 4*th* and last act, *is a resting on him,* which is still the same faith, but another act of it; not as if there might be a receiving, and not resting, or a resting, and not a receiving; or as if we were to difference them in respect of time; but faith is said to receive, as it respects the gospel-offer of Christ, and his satisfaction; and it is said to rest or rely, as it respects Christ, and his satisfaction; the thing offered and received, with regard to the charge to which it is liable: It is here that it rests, and to this it betakes itself, as to its defence, when challenged: it is difficult to difference these two, or peremptorily to say whether Christ's righteousness be received, or rested upon; yet it is made our defence, because it is closed with, and we make them two acts of the same faith, though it is hard to make the one of them to be the effect of the other, or the one of them to be antecedent to the other, in respect of time at least; as a proclamation of pardon being made to rebels, they say, This proclamation gives a freedom from the law's pursuit, because they have embraced it; and these rebels make that the ground, if ever they be challenged, whereon they found their defence: they have this to lippen to, and upon this they rest; though none of these acts can well be said to be before, or after the other, in respect of time. For clearing of this a little more, consider, that this resting may be looked on, either *passively,* or *actively; passively,* in respect of the believer's acquiescing in Christ, and assuring himself that all shall be well; this is not that act of faith that is called for to justification, but supposes the person to be justified, for he must be justified ere he can rest, or acquiesce in it. *Actively,* in respect of our resting on him that we may be justified, as the apostle hath it, Gal. ii. 16. And this, Isa. v. 6. is called a *taking hold of God's covenant;* it is an actual committing of ourselves to him, that we may win to peace, or a leaning on him, as suppose one were to rest upon a staff: it doth not only imply the effect, his having of ease; but also, and firstly, his leaning to or resting on it, in order to ease; therefore it is said, Matth. xi. 28. *Come unto me, all ye that are weary and heavy laden, and ye shall find rest:* The act that justifies, is this last and active act, the act of coming, or leaning, or resting; and the passive act of acquiescing, or assurance, is that which follows upon it, as a fruit and effect of it : And therefore we humbly conceive, that it is not safe, to define justifying faith by *Assurance;* or to say, that wherever faith is, there is assurance: it is rather a resting on Christ that we may have rest; and a ground of defence, and reason to be proposed, if we should be quarrelled for, or charged with the debt of sin.

The *Uses* are, 1. To remove the difficulties; as namely, it may be asked here, Is there no confidence

fidence nor assurance in this active act of faith, which is the essence of it? We answer shortly, There are *three* sorts of confidence pleaded for, that are far from the nature of faith, and yet faith wants not its own confidence and assurance, if it be taken in a right sense. The 1. is for a man to believe, that Christ died for him in particular, on the first hand, and to think that he hath no more to do, but to believe that Christ died, and suffered for him, and that thereupon he is justified; for this layeth a ground for universal redemption against the current of the scriptures, and can never be a ground of interest in Christ's righteousness: It supposes that to be done already, and admits not the soul to concur by believing for coming to the application, and yet this is very rife amongst people, I believe that Christ died for me, and shed his precious blood for me: and so long as they can maintain this presumption, and not suffer themselves to admit of any debating, and questioning, whether they have ground and reason for it, or not; they think they have faith enough: but this is no act of faith, nor of the nature of true justifying faith; which is to take hold of Christ offered, that we may come to be absolved through him: therefore, whenever the scripture puts us to believe, it commands us to take hold of Christ offered, and not at first hand to believe, that he died for us in particular; I suppose many are carried away with this presumption, that will, to their cost, at last find it to be otherwise. 2. Others think that all faith consists in this, to believe that God loved them from all eternity, and that they are already justified, which is the Antinomian way; they believe not that *they may be justified*, which was Paul's way, Gal. ii. 10. but they believe that they *are* justified, and this also presupposes universal redemption: and to press it upon you, were to bid you all believe that God hath loved you, and pardoned you from all eternity, which were to bid you believe a lie; for we wot well from the scriptures of truth, that God hath not loved all from eternity, and yet this is the faith that many of you presumptuously practises; we are all naturally some way Antinomians, Papists and Arminians in our practice; and the way of error is more consistent, and current with our nature, than the way of truth: But, O! presumptuous hypocrites, will ye daringly, and without any ground, believe God's love to you? God shall shake you out of that confidence, and blow upon it, and make it evanish: ye cry out on them that live in error, yet ye practise these same errors (to speak so) as fast as ye can; we cannot by much preaching get you brought to the knowledge of the truth, but ye can drink in error ere ye hear of it, and it will ruin your souls, if grace prevent not; and many of you shall find that thus you have destroyed yourselves. A *3d* sort of rotten confidence, is that which some have, who cannot say they are for the time justified, yet they have a persuasion to get heaven, and to be justified ere they die, or that at death they will be sure of it, and they wot well they shall not despair. This is also naughty presumption, and continued in, as hazardous as utter desperation, and killeth more souls than despair doth; for such rest quietly in their hope of being freed from wrath, and having their peace made with God, and yet never go to Christ to have it done: this is like that man's presumption, that says, Tush, *I shall have peace, tho' I walk in the imagination of my own heart*: God is gracious and merciful, and I hope he will not be so severe as he is called: The Lord called this a belying of him; for he says in his word, that *there is no peace to the wicked;* and the foolish presumer says, *I shall have peace:* shall his word or theirs stand? They say, Jer. v. 12. and vii. 9. *The temple of the Lord, the temple of the Lord are these*. They make a fair shew of attendance on ordinances, and yet *steal, murder and commit adultery, and say, We are delivered to all these things*: Is not this a gross belying of the Lord? God shall beat back many of your vain confidences in your faces, and your faces wax pale; when God shall cause your charge and summons to come unto judgment, sound in your ears, these and such like confidences will never bear you through, it is not these we speak of.

Yet, *2dly*, We say, that the right exercise of faith wants not its own confidence, comfort and assurance, when taken in a right sense, much whereof is attributed by some to the definition of faith; for some mistake faith, and others are mistaken or misunderstood in their speaking of faith; some divines that write of faith, speak of its being an assurance, defining it at its height; yet generally they take in, and presuppose the active act of faith resting on Christ. Others define it by these two acts, a receiving of, and resting upon Christ; Therefore we would not conceive of them, at least of many of them, as making this assurance to our sense to be essential, and absolutely necessary to the being of justifying faith; much less would we think, that they misken, and pass by the true acts of receiving and resting upon Christ; only some of them (which we humbly think is their mistake) having to do with Papists, who place faith in the understanding, add an assurance of faith to the former acts; in which we say there is a ground of confidence, or a conditional assurance: upon supposition that souls receive Christ, and rest upon him, they may be confident, that that is a ground that will not fail them; they may be confident that he will not deceive them; a confidence in this, that they may step to, or lean upon Christ, and not fear that he fail them, or that they may without all fear of hazard cast themselves on Christ; therefore he is called a *tried, elect, precious Corner-stone, a sure Foundation;* and indeed that is no small ground of confidence, that when a soul comes to Christ by believing, it may be sure he will not fail it. 2. Being sure that we have committed ourselves to Christ, (which supposes faith's being put to exercise and practice) there may be a confidence in this respect, we may be sure he will not fail us in particular, 2 Tim. i. 12. *I know in whom I have believed, and that he is able to keep that which I have committed to him, and that I shall not be ashamed.* He puts both these together, I know that he is able, and that he will not fail me, I shall not be ashamed: So, Rom. viii. *I am persuaded, that neither death nor life,* &c. *shall be able to separate us from the love of God that is in Christ Jesus:* If souls have received the offer, they may be sure it will not misgive them. 3. Add, That this actual, or active resting on Christ, may be separate from the sense of it, or from the passive act of faith, or quietness that follows on resting on Christ; for there is a resting on Christ, which is very faith itself, and not the effect: *Come, and ye shall find rest:* Coming is before finding of rest, to our sense at least. We are not to knit this passive *rest*, with the other active act of *resting,* as if it were impossible to rest on Christ, without present sensible ease: beside, it is this active resting that gives us right to Christ, and not the passive, Gal. ii. 16. *We believed that we may be justified:* This necessarily goes before our believing that we are justified.

To close with a word of more particular *Use,* Let me exhort you to lay less weight on your bare thinking that ye believe, on your present ill-grounded hope and peace. Aim, and endeavour to act, and exercise faith on Christ actively, receiving and resting on him for winning to peace: This practice of faith is the over-word (to say) of the doctrine of justification; that seeing there is such ground of justification laid down, the righteousness of Christ, and that it is proposed to you; and seeing this is the very act of justifying faith, to receive and rest on Christ, as he is proposed and offered; when this offer is made to you, let your faith receive, take hold of, and consent to the bargain; and ground and found your defence here, for answering all challenges that the law and justice may present against you: That there was a Saviour offered to you, and that ye received him, and rested upon him, will be a ground that shall bear you out, when you come before God; and except this be made sure, our speaking, and your hearing of faith, will be to no purpose.

SERMON LXI.

Isaiah liii. 11.------*By his knowledge shall my righteous Servant justify many, for he shall bear their iniquities.*

THIS is a great assertion, and of mighty moment, wherein to the knowledge of Christ, the justification of many is attributed: and indeed, if we knew what an advantage and benefit it were, there would be nothing more studied than how to obtain it; for it is the very inlet, and opens the door to glorification; and if to be happy in the enjoyment of God be a benefit of great concernment, then this of justification must be so.

We proposed to speak of the way how this benefit is applied, and that is by faith, set out under this expression, *his knowledge,* or the *knowledge of him;* and touched on the benefit of faith, and the necessity thereof for attaining justification, God having so ordered it in the covenant, that none others should be justified, but such as have faith. 2. We spoke also to the Object of this faith, Christ Jesus as our righteousness and peace: So that Christ becomes in a peculiar manner the Object of faith, beside any other thing; because it is only in Christ it can find a shelter, therefore it is only to Christ that it flees, when it is pursued. 3. We spake likewise of the nature of this faith, or its act, it being the heart's trusting itself to Christ's righteousness, whereon it hazards the weight of its peace, and relies here: And as all the terms of justification are borrowed from law, wherein there is supposed a charge, a tribunal, and a judge; so is this resting in like manner; it is in effect an arraigned person's making of Christ's righteousness his legal defence against all challenges: the substance of the phrase is in that of Phil. iii. 9. *That I may be found in him,*

SERM. LXI.   *Isaiah* liii. Verse 11.

him, *not having my own righteousness,* &c. Where, presupposing a libelling and charge, whereto does the apostle betake himself? and what is his refuge? It is Christ and his righteousness, even to be found in him; as if the question were proposed, Paul, what wilt thou do in the day of judgment? what wilt thou lean to for a defence in that day? To which he answers, Not to my own righteousness, but this is it, even to be found in him; which he expones to be, the having of his righteousness by faith, that is the righteousness of Christ by faith taken hold of by me; which faith shuts up as it were Paul in that righteousness, and hides him so, as he is past over, as if there were no unrighteousness at all in him.

The *effect* of this faith follows, when a person is chased, and hath fled unto, and laid hold on Christ; the effect, I say, is, he shall be justified. We may consider this several ways; and, for explication's sake, I shall shortly put by some of them.

1. Then, according to the exposition of the words, take this *observation*, That there is such a thing as justification distinct from sanctification. That benefit of justification follows on faith's taking hold of Christ, because it is such a benefit as follows Christ's taking on our sin; *By his knowledge shall he justify many, for he shall bear their iniquities.* Now sanctification is not that, but the infusing of holiness in us, and is the work of God's Spirit, inwardly working a change in the man. We did some way clear and confirm this in the exposition of the words, and shew you how sanctification differeth from justification; *Now ye are justified, now ye are sanctified,* says the Apostle, 1 Cor. vi. making them distinct benefits. To clear it a little further, *two* things are to be considered in sin, both which are to be removed by Christ, but differently; 1. Something that defiles and pollutes us, and makes us disconform to God's image; hence sin is in the scripture compared to boils and sores, and menstrous clothes, and is called *filthiness.* 2. There is a guiltiness that follows on this, whereby we are not only presupposed unclean, but are made liable to the law's certification, wherein it is said, *Cursed is every one that continueth not in every thing written in the book of the law to do it.* Now, if we speak of the removing of these two, justification takes away the guilt of sin; when the sinner is pursued before God's tribunal, he is discharged by the imputation of Christ's righteousness, to which he is fled for refuge; the law absolves him, not because he wants sin, but because

the Mediator hath satisfied for his sin, and that satisfaction is by faith laid hold of: sanctification takes away the pollution and blot of sin; the person that had these boils and sores is cleansed, or healed, or is a healing, and under cure (for there is no compleat healing while on this side of heaven) As, suppose a man, by transgressing the law, had wounded himself, in wounding or hurting another; there is here both a guilt, and a deformity; a guilt in transgressing the law by hurting his neighbour, and a deformity in wounding himself: Justification is as if the penalty of the breach of such a law were not exacted, by the interposing of a cautioner; and sanctification is like the healing of the wound in a man's self, by taking or application of some physick or plaister: So is it here, justification sets us free from the guilt, and sanctification cures us of the wound of sin. Man's fall was a guilt, and by that fall he wounded himself; and by Christ both are removed from the believer: by his satisfaction he justifies, and by his grace and Spirit he sanctifies him.

Use. We observe it only in passing, because it serves to clear all that concerns justification; and therefore, when we speak of justification by Christ's righteousness, 1. It is not as if we had a righteousness communicate to us, and were made actually holy, but it is the imputation of Christ's righteousness to us; the confounding of these two does ill, and is very prejudicial, not only to the Papists, but to others, who think they are justified, when they think they have some good frame, which being wanting, they suspect their justification. 2. The meaning is not as if Christ's righteousness were our sanctification, which is the error of the Antinomians, who make all sanctification to be justification, even as the Papists make all justification to be sanctification; therefore we would learn to distinguish these two, yet not so as to separate them.

2dly, Observe, That this effect, justification, is not only, nor mainly, the sense of being pardoned and absolved; but it is real absolution and pardon itself; because this justification that follows faith, is that which Christ hath purchased by his soul-travel, and bearing of our iniquities, and entitles the justified person to him, and makes him to be of his seed; and that is, not to have the sense that we are justified, but actually to be justified. And here there is another mistake to be adverted to, to think justification to be the evidence of what is past before we were born; yea from eternity: The justification here spoken of, is that which

which makes us stand before God, is opposite to works, and to the curse, and frees us from it; but the sense of justification is not that, whereby we stand before God, and is opposite to works and the curse: And therefore take this advertisement, that justification is not to be sensible of our justification, but it is really to be so, whether we know and be sensible of it or not, and that by vertue of Christ's righteousness apprehended by faith.

The *Third*, and main thing in this effect, is, That laying hold on Christ by faith, as he is offered in the gospel, does before God serve to the justifying of a sinner, and the absolving of him from the guilt of sin; that is, when a sinner, sensible of sin, is brought to lay hold on Christ's righteousness, then follows God absolving of him, as if he had never had sin, or had satisfied for his own sin; which is not only holden out here, but is frequently spoken of through the *Epistles*, and is the justification that stands in opposition to the way of works; to wit, when a poor sinner, sensible of sin, is perswaded by God's Spirit to flee unto, and rest upon Christ righteousness offered in the gospel, upon which follows God's absolving of him. This *Doctrine* takes in the substance of the text, *By the knowledge of my righteous Servant shall many be justified.*

There are several things that will fall to be cleared in the prosecuting of this, which we shall speak to shortly, for clearing of that question of the Catechism, *What is justification?* because this *doctrine* holds out the *form* of it, and deduceth it in this order, 1. A sinner is here supposed to be living under God's curse, according to that, Gal. iii. 10. *Cursed is every one that continues not in all things written in the law:* This is man's condition by nature. 2. It is supposed that Christ becomes Cautioner for elect sinners, and takes on their debt, and satisfies for them, on condition that if they shall believe on him, they shall be justified, and have his satisfaction imputed to them; and that the Lord Jehovah accepts of the Mediator's satisfaction, and engageth to make out the condition. 3. The Lord in the word of the gospel hath revealed this, and hath comprehended the way of a sinner's justification in the gospel-covenant, and promises and makes offer of it to all that hear of it, saying, *He that believes in the Son shall not perish, but have eternal life; and all that believe on him shall be justified from all things, where from they could not be justified by the law of Moses:* This is the external instrumental cause of justification, that holds out the way to life, which supposes the former. 4. When this is made offer of in the gospel there is the operation of God's Spirit on the soul, enlightning the mind of the sinner, convincing him of his hazard, chasing him to Christ, and powerfully perswading him to take hold of his righteousness made offer of to him; whereupon the soul comes to put forth the act of faith, and to rest upon his righteousness; as when it was said by Philip to the eunuch, Acts viii. *If thou believest, thou mayest be justified;* The soul answers, *I believe in Christ the Son of God;* whereupon it becomes a bargain: And this is the inward mean, or instrumental cause, of justification. 5. Follows God's imputing to that sinner, that receives Christ as he is offered, and rests upon him by faith, his righteousness; and Christ's payment and satisfaction to justice is counted his, and according to this his sins are pardoned, for the merit of that righteousness, and he himself is accepted and accounted righteous, as if he had never sinned; and he hath such a sentence past on him, as is held forth in these words of Psal. xxxii. 1. *Blessed is the man whose transgressions are forgiven, whose sin is covered, to whom the Lord imputes no iniquity:* and in these, Rom. viii. 1. *There is therefore now no condemnation to them who are in Christ Jesus,* &c. Even as, before he fled to Christ, there was a curse standing against him: And this is an act of God, the sovereign and efficient cause, *To declare his righteousness that he might be just, and the justifier of him that believes in Jesus,* as it is, Rom. iii. 26. which is the final cause.

We may confirm this, either as to the positive part, that by believing a sinner is justified; or as to the negative part, that there is no other way possible, whereby a sinner can be justified, but by believing: So that this great effect follows from a sensible sinner's taking hold of Christ's righteousness by faith. Ye may look upon a few scriptures to this purpose, as namely, Gal. ii. 16. where this apostle, entring in the debate, lays down this conclusion, *Knowing that a man is not justified by the works of the law but by faith in Jesus Christ, even we have believed in Jesus Christ, that we might be justified by the faith of Christ:* as if he had said, We have taken this way for the attaining of this end, *believing that we might be justified.* The apostle speaks here. 1. Of a justification by faith, which is opposite to works; and as he ascribes it to faith, so he denies it to works. 2. He makes it exclusive, and will have no other thing to concur in the manner at least, by faith; *Knowing* (saith he) *that a man is not justified by works, but by faith.* 3. He holds out his own, and other believers

believers practice; *Even we have believed, that we might be justified;* as if he had said, We took this way of faith to be absolved before God, which by the law, or the works of the law, would never have been. See also to this purpose, the *epistle* to the Romans, 1, 2, 3, 4, and 5. chapters, especially the 3, and 4. In the 3d chap. v. 25. when he is summing the doctrine of justification into a compend, he says, *Whom God hath set forth to be a propitiation through faith, to declare his righteousness for the remission of sins,* &c. Where Christ's righteousness is called a *Propitiation through faith,* and faith is holden out as the channel in which justification runs; and in the words following, the believer is holden out as the object of it; so chap. iv. it is holden out in the instance of Abraham, particularly in ver. 5. *To him that worketh not, but believeth on him that justifieth the ungodly, his faith is counted for righteousness:* where the Apostle proposes *Two* ways of a person's aiming to be justified, the 1. whereof is, When a man worketh, and on that account seeks to be justified, and that way is rejected. The 2. is, When a man hath no works, or worketh not on that account to be justified by them, but by faith betakes himself to Christ's satisfaction; and that way is established, for that man's faith is counted for righteousness, and is the ground of his peace before God: we gave some scriptures before for this, and shall not therefore now insist. There is also good reason why it cannot be otherwise, 1. If we consider what man is in himself ungodly, rebellious, having nothing to present unto God; but when a righteousness is represented to him by way of offer, and he is through grace brought to accept of the offer of the righteousness of another, nothing can be conceived to be brought to receive it, but his faith: And if Christ's satisfaction be his justification, and if it be faith that takes hold of it, we have a clear reason why justification is attributed to faith. 2. Consider, That this contributes most to God's end, which is, to glorify himself, especially in his grace, in the justification of sinners, even to hold forth the manifold riches of his grace; and nothing contributes to this so much, and so well, as that which speaks the sinner to be empty: and nothing empties the sinner more than faith; it being the great act of faith, to bring the soul off its own bottom, and to stop all boasting; to drive it out of itself to be found in him; therefore *it is said to be of faith, that it might be of grace,* Rom. iv. 16. As if he had said, If it were by any other thing, it could not be by grace. But faith claims nothing but the righteousness of Christ to rest on; he hath paid the price, and made the satisfaction, and that satisfaction is mine, saith faith, because it was offered to me, and I have been brought to lay hold on it. And the nature of this pleading stops the mouth of the creature, and proclaims justification to be alone the effect of God's grace, and of Christ's procurement. 3. Consider, that if it depended on any other thing, our justification could never be perfect; when we speak of justification, and call it perfect, it is not so to be understood, as if faith were perfect; but Christ's satisfaction, which is our righteousness, and which faith lays hold on, is perfect, though our faith's grip be weak; hence it is, that the weak believer is justified, as well as the strong; all who look unto Christ, though with a weak-sighted eye, get salvation through him, as well as Abraham, because his righteousness is perfect, which weak faith takes hold of, as well as strong faith. Now if justification were founded on ought within us, it could never be perfect, but *by him all that believe are justified from all things from which they could not be justified by the law of Moses;* and one of them made as free as another. It is not here, as if one part of the debt were scored and blotted out, and not another; but all is blotted out, because the righteousness presented before God's tribunal, and imputed to us, which is the defence that faith gives in, is perfect. We may compare strong and weak faith to two advocates, the one more able, and the other weaker, pleading the same cause before a just judge; strong faith pleads more strongly, fully and distinctly, weak faith pleads not so fully and distinctly; but both pleading on the same ground, God the Judge judgeth not according to the distinctness, or undistinctness of the pleading, but according to the defence, or reason given in, and absolves both alike, and the weak believer is as fully pardoned as the strong is.

The *Uses* are many and comfortable; 1. It serves for our direction. If any were asking, how they may come to be justified? This doctrine answers. By faith in Jesus Christ, by taking with your sin, and taking hold of Christ's righteousness offered to you in the gospel, and by making that your defence before God: And is not this a lesson worthy the learning, which the whole word of God aims at, even to instruct you how to make your peace with him? It is by the knowledge of Christ, or by faith in him, by resting on him, as he is offered in the gospel; and this cannot but be a solid and sicker way of justification, because we have God's word for it; it is founded on his faithfulness, and on the transaction made betwixt God and the Mediator. We have also the experience of all the saints for it; Abraham before the law, David under the law, and Paul since the law, all of them were led the same way. Ye would take notice of this, not only as the great question in catechizing, or examination, but as the ground whereon ye build your peace, if ye were dying; there is a perfect righteousness in Christ, made offer of to you in the gospel, on condition ye will receive him as he is offered; and if ye so receive him, it shall be yours, and ye shall at God's bar be absolved; the righteousness of Christ shall be as effectual for your absolution, as if it were inherent in yourselves, and faith shall unite you to him, and make you one with him: In a word, ye must all come before God's tribunal; and there are but two defences to be proposed, either something in yourselves, as your love and charity, or good carrriage and duties; or to take with your sin, to condemn yourselves, and to flee to Christ, and present his righteousness, as the righteousness of the Cautioner that hath paid your debt; and according as ye take the one way, or the other, ye may expect to be justified, or not; and this *Doctrine* rejects the one way, and owns and confirms the other, which is by faith.

And therefore, 2*dly*, (which is the great *Use* of all this *Doctrine*) Here there is ground laid down to any that would be justified, how they may win to it, and a warrant to propose justification, as a thing attainable through faith in him; ye have it in your offer on these terms, and therefore let me earnestly intreat you to accept of the offer; if this be the way of justification, take this way: seeing there is an absolute necessity of faith in every one that would be at justification, make it sure that ye are indeed fled to Christ, and that it is his righteousness, which ye make your defence before the bar of God's tribunal. We shall branch forth this *Use* of exhortation in these *Two* or *Three* words. 1*st*. When Christ is spoken of in the gospel, let him be by faith received; and if ye would know what this is, labour, 1. To know, and to take up the difference betwixt self-righteousness, and that righteousness which is by faith; for many are so ignorant, that they know neither the one nor the other, or at least not the one by the other. 2. When ye are come to know the difference betwixt these two, and are soberly weighing what ye should lippen to, in your coming before God; with indignation shuffle out, and cast by, disclaim and renounce your own righteousness, and grip to the righteousness of Christ: here faith will have a double work, upon the one hand to reject self-righteousness, and upon the other hand to rest upon the righteousness of Christ alone, according to that, Philip. iii. 9. 3. When ye have gotten your own righteousness casten, and Christ's righteousness closed with, there is a necessity to cover and hide yourselves in it, that ye may never so much as in the vaguing conceit of your mind, be found out of it; it alludes to the city of refuge, wherein, when once entred into, and abiden in, the person was safe; but if he was at any time found without, he was in hazard to be killed by the avenger of blood: which held out not only the act of faith fleeing to Christ; but its abiding in him, being hid in him, containing and keeping itself in him, and continuing to plead its defence on that ground: there may be, in a fit of sad exercise, a renouncing of our own righteousness; but when that is over, and we begin to conceit something of that which we have done, we are ready to forget Christ's righteousness, and to lean to our own; and that is in a manner to come out of Christ, and from our city of refuge, if ever we were in him: faith, as it betakes itself to Christ, so it states itself in Christ, where only it dare abide the trial. 2*dly*,. We would commend this to you, as the great ground of your peace and hope, even that ye would put it to the trial, and make it sure, whether ye be in the faith or not; it is true, there are many beguiled in this, and take themselves to be in the faith when they are not; and others question their faith, and their being justified, without just ground; yet it is impossible to win to clearness of interest in Christ, or to the having of any solid and comfortable hope of enjoying God, except there be some clearness that we are in the faith, and have indeed betaken ourselves to Christ; which cannot be win at, without putting it to the trial: other evidences serve to clear our justification, as they clear our faith; and as they prove faith, so they conclude and prove our justification, and the out-gate promised. Now, if believing be such an evidence of justification, and of a well-grounded hope of heaven, is there not reason we should put it, in good earnest, and frequently, to the trial, and seek to know whether we be in the faith or not? The Apostle, 2 Cor. xiii. 5. doubles his exhortation to this purpose, *Examine yourselves, if ye be in the faith, prove your own selves, know ye not your own selves, how that Jesus Christ is in you, except ye be reprobates?* We do the rather press this, because, if we were serious in the trial, there would, through God's blessing, be more faith in some, and less presumption in others; and these that have faith, would have more peace and comfort in it. But that which makes many content themselves with a counterfeit instead of faith, is, that they put it not to the trial; and that which makes them who have faith to want peace, and live in much anxiety, is, that they do not more prove themselves, as to their faith: These are then the *two* main points of believers duty, By faith to take hold of Christ, and to rest on and in him; and, By trial to make it clear and sure to themselves, that they are believers: And these *two* are the great up-shot of all this doctrine, To persuade us to believe, that we may be sure; and, To persuade us to study to be sure and clear in it, that we may be comforted thereby.

SERMON LXII.

Isaiah liii. 11.--------*By his knowledge shall my righteous Servant justify many, for he shall bear their iniquities.*

THE doctrine of justification through faith in Christ Jesus was wont to be much thought of among the people of God: It is called, Gal. iii. 8. *The preaching of the gospel to Abraham*, when God foretold him of a way of justification and salvation, through Christ's coming of him, *That in him all the nations of the earth should be blessed:* This was the telling of good news to him, and we are sure it is as good news now as ever it was, and would be so to us, if we could look on it spiritually, as they did; for there is as great hazard in sin, and the curse is as terrible and insufferable, and the love of God as fresh now, as they were then.

We have for some days been speaking of this doctrine of justification, and it will be much to speak and hear of it profitably. We desire not to insist on what may be unuseful, but we conceive there is some necessity in insisting on this: it is our own negligence and ignorance that makes many things of this kind to be very unuseful, even so that we scarcely conceive them; and we are made heartless in speaking of them, because to many they are, as if spoken in a strange language; which is, and should be for a lamentation.

The last thing we proposed, was, to hold forth the mean by which justification is attained, to wit, *Faith;* which we observed, to shew how faith concurs in the attaining of justification. Few or none ever denied faith to be necessary for the attaining of justification, neither can any that read the word of God with the least consideration, but have that impression of it; but the great thing, wherein the difference lies, and wherein men miscarry, is, in attributing to faith the right or wrong manner of its concurrence, in the attaining of this effect. Tho' these things may, at first blush, look like meerly notional speculations, and such as do not concern Christians practice; yet there is no error in doctrine about this matter, but there is something in folks practice, that looks like it, and is influenced by it; and it is mens inclination to error in practice, that makes them as it were to err in errors in judgment.

We shall *observe* two generals further, and proceed. The *1st* whereof is, "That faith hath a peculiar way of concurrence for the attaining of "justification, which can agree to no other grace, "nor work, nay nor to faith itself, considered as a "work." Therefore *justification of many*, is here derived to them *by knowledge*, or by faith in him, that is, by faith in Christ, as secluding all other things; it is by faith that justification is derived and applied to us, and by faith we come to have right to it, and an interest in it.

The *2d* is, "That however faith concur for attaining of Justification; yet it is not faith of itself, or by any virtue or efficacy in itself, but as "taking hold of Christ as the Object of it, that it "justifies." Therefore it is said to be *by the knowledge of him*, or by faith in him; it is by receiving him, uniting us to him, and resting on him, that we are justified.

We shall shortly explicate both these branches, and then come to some practical use of them together.

1. Then, we say, That there is something in justification attributed to faith, that cannot agree to any other thing; which is implied in many scriptural phrases, and in this *text*, in as far as it is said, that *by his knowledge*, or by faith in him, justification is attained: and therefore, when we are said to be justified by faith, we affirm that faith hath a peculiar way of concurring for the attaining of justification, which can agree to no other grace, as to repentance, love, meekness, patience, &c. nor to prayer, alms-deed, or any other good works, or work. For confirming of this, consider,

B b b

'der, 1. That we are said to be justified by faith, in opposition to works; and that there is something attributed to faith, which is denied to works: Generally this is clear in these epistles written to the Romans and Galatians; particularly, Rom. iv. 2, 3. "If Abraham were justified by works, he hath whereof to glory, but not before God; for what saith the scriptures? Abraham believed God, and it was counted to him for righteousness. Now to him that worketh is the reward not reckoned of grace, but of debt; but to him that worketh not, but believeth on him that justifieth the ungodly, his faith is counted to him for righteousness;" where, most clearly and convincingly, believing and working are directly opposite, the one to the other; and Gal. ii. 16. "We who are Jews by nature, knowing that a man is not justified by the works of the law, but by the faith of Jesus Christ" (or, as the word is, no not by faith, that is, a man is not justified by works, but by faith) "even we have believed in Jesus Christ, that we might be justified by the faith of Christ, and not by the works of the law:" Where the apostle cannot more purposely and pressingly make a difference betwixt any two things, than he doth betwixt these two, justification by works, and justification by faith. And in all this discourse it cannot be said, that the apostle only excludes works in respect of merit, or works as they look to the works of the ceremonial law; for he opposeth faith, and all sorts of works, or works in whatsoever respect, as inconsistent: it is not one or two sorts of works, but all sorts of works of the law; and there can be no works, but such as are commanded by the law, which are excluded. Now, if the apostle exclude all these, what are the works that we can be justified by? 2. Consider the peculiar phrase, that the scripture useth to this purpose; and, where we are said to be *justified by faith*, there is a sort of causality attributed to faith, that can be attributed to no other grace, nor works: hence the righteousness of Christ, is called the *righteousness of faith*, and we are said to be *justified by faith in his blood*. So, Phil. iii. 8, 9. *I count all things to be but dung, that I may win Christ, and be found in him, not having mine own righteousness, which is of the law, but that which is through the faith of Christ, the righteousness which is of God by faith*. And Rom. iii. 25. *Whom God hath set forth to be a propitiation through faith in his blood*. Many more such phrases there are; and truly it would look very unlike the scripture, to expone these scripture-phrases of a righteousness of works, or by works. 3. Consider how the apostle opposeth the two covenants, the covenant of works made with Adam, and the covenant of grace made with believers in Jesus Christ, Rom. x. 5, 6. Moses *describeth the righteousness of the law, that the man which doth these things shall live by them*. The righteousness of the law speaks of *doing*, by which we come to be justified; *But the righteousness of faith*, or the covenant of grace, *speaketh on this wise, The word is near thee, even in thy mouth, and in thy heart; that if thou confess with thy mouth the Lord Jesus, and shalt believe in thy heart, that God raised him from the dead, thou shalt be saved*. Where the apostle opposeth these two covenants, not in respect of merit only, as if the one were inconsistent with grace, and not the other: but he opposeth them in this, that the righteousness of the one covenant is in *doing*, and the righteousness of the other covenant is by *believing*; and therefore, according to this opposition, whatever is a man's *doing* is not the ground of his peace, and justification before God, because the righteousness of his *doing* is the condition of the covenant of works; and the righteousness of the covenant of grace is quite of another nature, to wit, *Believing in him who justifieth the ungodly*. 4. Consider, that the thing, that is the ground of our justification before God, is Christ's righteousness inherent in himself, and imputed to us, for the covering of our nakedness; because he, as our Cautioner, hath paid the debt: hence it follows, that faith hath another way of concurring in justification, than any other thing can have; because it is faith which receives and puts on that righteousness, which no other thing doth; *That I may be found in him*, saith the apostle, Philip. iii. 9. *not having mine own righteousness, but the righteousness which is by the faith of Christ*: So that to be *in him*, is to have his righteousness, and this righteousness is put on by faith. Only take two words of advertisement, ere we come to clear the other branch of the doctrine. The first is this, When we speak of the peculiarness of the way of faith's concurring in justification, so as no other grace or work doth, we design not to weaken or cry down the necessity of repentance, and of other graces, nor of good works, the very thoughts whereof we abhor, but to give every one of them their own, and the right place: And therefore it is a gross calumny to say that we affirm, that the study and practice of holiness and good works is not necessary; we only cry them down on this account, that when we come before God, our works, or holiness, are not to be presented to him as the ground of our justification, and absolution, but the righteousness of Christ, that faith takes hold of; and in this we say, that faith peculiarly concurs as no other grace doth, because it is fitted with an aptitude to receive and apply Christ's righteousness, which no other grace is: As we say it is by the eye that a man sees, though, if he had not a head and brains, he would not see; so though faith and holiness, or good works, be not separate, yet faith is as it were the eye of the soul, that discerns and takes hold of Christ's righteousness. The 2d is this, That when we speak of good works, we speak of them as the Apostle doth, Tit. iii. 5. where he saith, *Not by the works of righteousness which we have done, but according to his mercy he saved us*: and by good works, denied in the point of justification, we understand all that is our own *doing*, not excluding only some things that were so accounted in the time of darkness, as alms-deeds and the like, but (as we have said) all that is our own *doing*.

The 2d Branch is, That this peculiarness of faith's concurring in justification, is not from any efficacy in faith, or from faith considered as our deed or work, but as it acts on Christ, as the Object of it; and therefore, when it is said, Rom. iv. 3. That *Abraham believed God, and it was accounted to him for righteousness*; the meaning is not, as if God had accepted his believing, as an act or work for his righteousness; and that it was accounted as a perfect grace; but the meaning is, that Christ Jesus the promised seed, received by faith, or his betaking of himself to the righteousness of Christ holden out to him in the promise, was accounted his righteousness, as if he had had an inherent righteousness of his own; and so faith is imputed, not in respect of its act, but in respect of its Object; by his union with Christ through faith, Christ's satisfaction became his. To clear it a little, take these Considerations, 1. Consider faith as a grace in us, and so it cannot be imputed for righteousness; for in that respect it is a work, and is excluded by the apostle's opposition, made of grace and works: it must therefore be faith considered as acting on its Object. 2. Consider that in scripture, to be justified *by Christ, by his blood, and by faith*, are all one, because when it is said, we are justified by Christ, or by his blood, it takes in Christ and his blood laid hold on by faith; therefore sometimes *Christ*, sometimes *faith*, is called our righteousness; because as Christ, considered as suffering and satisfying, is the meritorious cause of our justification, so faith is the instrumental cause taking hold of his satisfaction, which is our righteousness: both are necessary in their own way, and Christ's righteousness implies faith, and faith implies Christ and his righteousness; the one implies the other necessarily. 3. Consider the phrases used in Scripture to this purpose, as where we are said *to be justified by faith*, it ever respects Christ; and where we are said *by faith to put on Christ*, it is not faith considered as righteousness of itself, but it is faith considered as acting on Christ, and his righteousness; therefore it is the righteousness which is by faith, the righteousness which is in Christ, and by faith, taken hold of by us; and becoming ours.

The *uses* are several, *1st*, For information and conviction; and we would, (1.) be informed in, and understand well the meaning of this doctrine. When we say, that faith is necessary to justification, and concurreth in attaining of it, as no other thing doth, that ye may give it its right place, and may make no confusion of these things that are distinct, 1. We deny not works, notwithstanding of all that we have said, to be necessary, more than we do faith; but the great difference is anent the giving of faith and works, or faith, as it is a work, an equal share, in respect of causality, in our justification: And therefore we would beware with Papists to attribute a sort of condignity to faith, as if it merited eternal life, which flows from their ignorance of God's covenant; for they think, that since he commands us to believe and promiseth life to believing, that there is a merit in believing, as they fancy there is in prayer, alms-deeds, and other duties, or good works; but in this respect, as it is a work in us, the apostle excludes faith, and makes our justification free; whereas, if faith in justification were considered as a work meriting our justification, it should not be free. And altho' there be no Papists in profession here amongst us, yet it may be there are some, and that not a few, that think God is obliged to them, because they believe, and that expect heaven and life eternal on that ground; even as when they pray, they think they should be heard for their praying; and when they give alms, that they should be rewarded for the same as a meritorious work. 2. Neither do we understand, when we say that faith is necessary to justification, and concurreth in the attaining of it;

that by believing we are disposed to be holy, and so more enabled to justify ourselves; which is also a Popish error, wherein, I fear, many professors of the gospel amongst us ly who think they are obliged to their faith, because it disposeth them to hear, read, pray, and the like, and so enableth them to work out a righteousness to themselves, whereby they expect to be justified; this is another fault, and error to be guarded against; for though we give faith a radical vertue, to keep life in other graces, yet so considered, it is still a piece of inherent holiness, and pertains to sanctification, and not to justification. 3. When we say, that faith concurs in the attaining of justification, we do not say that it concurs in the same manner that repentance, prayer and good works do concur: But it may be said here. Seeing we grant, that good works and duties are necessary, what then is the difference? I answer in these two, *1st*, Faith is the proper and peculiar condition of the covenant of grace, and not our works, or holiness, whereof faith, considered as a work, is a part: Works the condition of the covenant of works, for it says in this manner, *The man that doth these things shall live by them;* but the covenant of grace, in opposition to it, says, *If thou believe with thy heart in the Lord Jesus, and confess with thy mouth, that God raised him from the dead, thou shalt be saved;* as it is Rom. x. What works is in the one covenant, faith is in the other covenant, and that as it is opposed to works, and to faith itself, as it is a work in us. *2dly,* There is a peculiarness in faith's concurring for the attaining of justification, in respect of its instrumentalness, in taking hold of Christ for our justification, or in receiving and resting upon him (as we said before) for that end: for, when Christ is offered in the gospel, faith flees to him, receives him, takes hold of him, and rests on him: neither repentance, nor prayer, nor any good works, hath an aptitude, and fitness to receive Christ, and present his satisfaction to God as the ground of the sinner's defence, as faith hath: and therefore it is so often said by divines according to the Scripture, that faith is the instrumental cause of our justification; which we shall clear in two or three similitudes, which the Scripture makes use of, 1. Christ compares himself to the brazen Serpent lifted up in the wilderness, John iii. 14. Man by sin is stung deadly, as the Israelites were by the fiery serpents: Christ Jesus as suffering, and hung, or lifted up upon the cross, is proposed to our faith to look upon, as the brazen Serpent was proposed to them that were stung, and put up on a pole for that end; and as there was no healing to the stung Israelites, except they looked to it, and the cure followed to none but to these who did behold it; so Christ Jesus proposed as the Object and meritorious Cause of justification, justifies none but such as look to him by faith; and although they were to look to the brazen serpent, yet their look gave them no efficacy to the cure, but it flowed from God, ordaining that as a mean of their cure; even so it is not from any efficacy in faith considered in itself, that sinners are justified, but it is from Jesus Christ the Object, that faith, eying him lifted up as the Saviour of the elect, and his satisfaction as appointed of God for that end, doth justify: and therefore it may well be called an instrumental cause, because it is not Christ abstractly considered, that justifies, more than it was the serpent considered abstractly, without their looking to it, that did cure, but Christ considered, and laid hold on by faith; but in this respect, faith is said to justify, even as the eye looking to the brazen serpent put them in capacity of the cure, though the cure flow from God's appointment, and not from their looking; so is it in faith's concurring for the attaining of justification. A *2d* similitude is that of miraculous faith, we find it often said by the Lord in his working such cures, *Thy faith hath made thee whole;* there, was no efficacy in faith itself for producing the cure, but it was the mean by which the cure was transmitted to the person under such a disease; so it is in believing, in order to our justification; it is by believing on Christ, that our spiritual cure in justification is transmitted to us, and we are said to be justified by faith, because by faith, it is conveyed to us. A *3d* similitude, for clearing that faith may well be called the instrumental cause of justification, may be this, Even as the advocate's pleading may be called the instrumental cause of the client's absolving; as, suppose a man, whose cautioner had paid his debt, were cited to answer for the debt, his advocate pleads his absolution and freedom from the debt, because his cautioner had paid it; although the debt was paid, yet the man had not been absolved, if it had not been so pleaded on his behalf; So the concurrence of faith in the sinner's justification, is to table Christ's satisfaction for his defence before God, and to plead his absolution on that ground: The believing sinner's faith says, It is true I was owing so much debt of sin, but Jesus Christ my Cautioner, to whom I am fled, hath

satis-

satisfied for it; therefore I ought to be absolved: and the law allows of this sort of pleading, and upon this ground; in which respect faith concurreth in attaining, and may well be called the instrumental cause of our justification. I shall say no more on this *Use*, but these two words, We may partly regret our great ignorance, that we know so little of the use of faith in our justification; and partly we may lament the great confusion that is in these times, wherein men are set to overturn such a clear truth, as if faith had no instrumentality in our justification, but as if it, and other duties and works, were equal sharers, and alike in it; Which, 1. overturns the nature of God's covenant of grace, in making works the condition of it, as if there were no difference betwixt the two covenants of works and of grace. 2. It hath this miserable ill attending it, that it shoulders out Christ's righteousness, and shuffles in an inherent righteousness of our own, as our defence, when we come immediately before the throne of God; whereas the Gospel puts us to a righteousness without us, and imputed to us. This way leads us to seek righteousness in ourselves. Whether works, or faith as a work, be made the ground of our justification, it is all one; for if faith, considered as a work in us, disposing us to holiness, and as a part of sincere holiness, be the thing presented to God, as the ground of our justification, it is still something within us, and such a thing, as is still imperfect, which would miserably mar poor souls comfort: whereas the righteousness of Christ, laid hold on by faith, being made the ground of our justification, it affords solid consolation; for though faith in us be weak and imperfect, yet his righteousness is perfect: and, as it was not the Israelites looking, as we said, that was the ground of their health and cure, but God's appointing of such a mean for their cure looked to; otherwise they that were weak sighted, and had bleared eyes, might think themselves not in such a capacity of healing, as these who were strong, and more clear sighted, whereas they were all alike cured, if once they looked; even so is it here.

A 2d *Use* of this, and the other doctrine formerly spoken of, is for direction, and practical information. Would any know justification by Christ? here is the way: it is by faith in him, when Christ Jesus and his satisfaction is made offer of in the gospel, for justifying all self-condemning sinners that lay hold on him; sinners by faith fleeing to him, and resting on him, get a title to his righteousness, that cannot but save them; so that if it were, 1. asked, What is that, which a man appearing before the throne, dare hazard to present to God, as the ground of his defence? It is answered, Christ's righteousness, his satisfaction. 2. If it were asked, How comes one to have title and right to that righteousness, so as he may own and present it for his defence? It is answered, that it is attained by believing in him. 3. If it be asked, How comes faith to get a title to that righteousness? Is it by any virtue or efficacy in Faith, as a work in us? It is answered, No, but it comes to get title to it, by going out of itself, by receiving and taking hold, and making use of the worthiness that is in Christ's righteousness, which is as a garment, able to cover the sinner's nakedness, and to hide all his spots; and, as a complete ransom, to pay all his debt: and thus we see here, upon the one side, a necessity of faith, in order to justification; and, upon the other side, a warning, not to count grace, and the righteousness of Christ, the less free; that faith hath an instrumentality in the application of it, faith having *two* things that it pleads upon; 1. Emptiness, and need in itself; whence it arrogates nothing to its own pleading, but, 2. founds its defence on the good ground it hath to propose; and therefore, as, upon the one hand, we would know that there is a way to come by justification, by taking hold of Christ's righteousness by faith: So, upon the other hand, we would be afraid to let any thing stick to us from our faith, as if we had a meritorious or efficient hand in, or were to be thanked for our winning to justification; for, as a beggar, in receiving an alms, can alledge no merit to be in his receiving, or caling for it; so no more does faith's receiving mar the freedom of our justification, by any merit in it.

Use 3. Seeing faith concurs instrumentally in the attaining of justification, there is here clear ground to exhort you, by faith to receive Christ, and to commend to you the exercise of believing, because without it ye cannot be justified, and by it ye shall certainly be justified.

Use 4. Here, O! here is ground of consolation to poor sinners, sensible of sin, trembling at God's bar, as being obnoxious to the curse, that by receiving of Jesus Christ, they may be absolved from the debt of sin, and freed from the curse; therefore, if there be any such here, put forth your hands, and receive what is in your offer; open your soul's mouth wide, and let in Christ, and he will fill it: faith having, as to our spiritual life, the same place that the mouth hath to the body, for justification is derived by faith in him to the sinner.

Use 5. This serves exceedingly to humble a sinner, whether it be a sinner aiming, and seeking to be justified, or a sinner that hath attained justification, in so far as there is no ground of boasting here. If ye be aiming to be justified, it may humble you; for what can ye contribute to it? Being enabled, ye can indeed receive what is offered, and that is all; neither can ye receive, except ye be enabled, as is said. It serves also to humble such as are justified: Have ye righteousness? It is not your own, but Christ's; it is he only that did the turn. If it should be said, ye believed, and may boast of that; I ask, What did ye when ye believed? Did ye any more but this? Ye pleaded guilty, and did consent to take Christ's righteousness, and the pardon of sin through him freely; and what matter of boasting, I pray, is here? None at all. Thus this doctrine contributes, both to make these who are seeking pardon, and these who have gotten pardon, humble; *Where is boasting then?* (says the apostle) *It is excluded: By what law? By the law of works? No, but by the law of faith,* as it is, Rom. iii. 17. The believing sinner does nothing, and hath done nothing towards the procuring of his own justification, but gets all freely. We can never think, nor speak aright of justification, but it lays our vain humour, and stops the mouth from boasting, while it saith, *What hast thou, O man! but what thou hast received? and if thou hast received it, why dost thou boast, as if thou hadst not received it.*

We shall close and shut up the whole of this doctrine, by proposing some few considerations, as conclusions from it. 1. See here a necessity of being acquainted with the truths of the gospel; and with this truth in particular, concerning justification: (whereof, alas! many are very ignorant) Seeing there are so many ways to go wrong, and so many do go wrong about it, we had need to be the more clear in the right way: if there were more knowledge of this, and of other truths, we might speak and hear with more profit; and if ye did not please yourselves with mere and airy notions, but justification, that is of the very marrow of the gospel, and is deservedly accounted to be *articulus stantis, aut cadentis ecclesiæ*; but ye would come to it in fear, being jealous of your own ignorance, and shallowness of capacity rightly to take it up, especially when new questions are rising, and started concerning it: and as Paul and David studied this way, and held it forth to others, as the way whereby they went to heaven, and whereby others must come to it; so we commend to you to follow them. A 3d consideration is, If faith be so necessary to justification, as without it ye cannot be justified, is there not reason that ye should study to be distinct, and clear that ye have faith, and that ye are indeed believers? this is one of the great uses of the doctrine: if there be no way but faith, and if in studying this one way many go wrong, then, as ye would make your calling and election sure, study to make this sure, by putting yourselves to the trial, if ye be taking this way, as the apostle most pathetically exhorts, 2 Cor. xiii. 5. *Examine yourselves, if ye be in the faith, prove your own selves,* &c. It is truly matter of wonder to think, how so many men and women are so soon satisfied in the matter of their believing, which yet is so tickle and difficult a business: we would have none to be jumbled and confounded about it, who desire to be serious in the thing; yet we would have all wakened, and put to diligence. Many men have taken pains to go wrong in this matter of justification; and how few of you have taken pains to go right in it? and how is it, that many of you win so easily at it? seeing the apostle, Rom. ix. calls it *a stumbling stone* to many, and *a rock of offence:* surely if it be so, your coming at it by guess, and ignorantly, is to be suspected; and therefore, on this consideration, ye would be awakened, to put yourselves more seriously to the study of it, and to try yourselves, if ye be come well to it; for it is the special, yea, the only ground of your peace before God. There are many of you, who in a manner think it impossible to miscarry in this; for ye know that there is no way to be justified but by faith; and yet, if many of you were put to it, ye know not the manner nor way how faith justifies,

which

which shews that it is not so easy a matter as ye think it to be. A 4th consideration is this, That in speaking of justification, and faith's peculiarness, or peculiar way of concurring in it, ye would beware of crying down works, as to their usefulness, or necessity; this was an error that soon entred in the church: as soon as Paul cleared and pressed the doctrine of justification by faith, some arose, who (as James shews in the 2d chapter of his epistle) affirmed, that works were not needful, but faith would save them: *No*, says James, *that faith is dead and vain that wants works*. And therefore remember, 1. That though we tell you that works are not properly the condition of the covenant of grace, yet we say that faith and works are never separate in a justified person; sound faith cannot but work, and put on the study of holiness. 2. We say, Although works concur not in the obtaining of pardon of sin, yet we say they are needful to salvation, and to folks entry into heaven; for the apostle saith, Heb. xii. 14. *That without holiness none shall see the Lord*: Though it is faith that makes our friendship, yet it is by holiness that it is entertained, and it is holiness whereby our communion is kept up with God; therefore, Col. i. 12. we are said by it, *to be made meet to be partakers of the inheritance of the saints in light*: For it transforms us to God's image. 3. Works are necessary, though not to procure our peace, yet for the entertaining of our peace; and except we have works, we cannot have a solid proof that our justification by faith is real; and in this respect, James says, chap. ii. that Abraham was justified by works, that is, by his works he was declared to be a justified person: as to the justification of his person, he was justified by faith, before Isaac was born; but by his offering up of Isaac, and other fruits of his faith, he was declared and manifested to be a justified man, and made suitable to the covenant that he was engaged in with God. Therefore, as the sum of all, be exhorted to study the exercise of faith and holiness, so as every one of them may have its own room and place; for that will be your advantage, and without this no other thing will advantage you. Now God himself, that calleth for both, sanctify and enable us for both.

SERMON LXIII.

Isaiah liii. 11.------*For he shall bear their iniquities.*

IT is a thing that can neither be easily believed, nor yet understood, how *by Christ's knowledge*, or by faith him, *many shall be justified*; in these words, the prophet adds a reason, that both confirms and clears it: It shall be, saith he, that many shall be justified through faith in him, *For he shall bear their iniquities;* he shall take on, and pay their debt; and so, (as I said) it is a reason confirming the former truth, and shewing that it cannot be otherways, but they must be absolved through faith in him, because he bears the punishment due to them for their sin. It serves also to clear how justification is attained by faith, to wit, not by any vertue or efficacy that is in faith, abstractly considered, as if believing of itself did the turn, but by vertue of Christ bearing their iniquities, and making satisfaction for them, which faith lays hold on; so that, when he said, *By his knowledge shall many be justified;* it is not by any efficacy attributed to their believing, but by vertue of Christ's righteousness, and satisfaction, which only faith gives a title to; and is the means, and way by which a believer comes to it, and so (as I have said) it serves for explication of the former truth: So that, if the question be asked, How can sinners be justified by believing? It is here answered, Because Christ shall take on their debt, and the righteousness purchased by him shall redound to them, and be reckoned theirs. It is the same, on the matter, with that which we have, 2 Cor. v. *ult. He that knew no sin, was made sin for us;* and what follows, *that we might be made the righteousness of God in him;* which clears, that this way of justification, which the gospel holds out, is not (as I just now said) by any efficacy, or worth in faith itself, nor by any inherent qualifications in the person that believes; but this is the ground of it, Christ's *bearing of our iniquities:* the elect were sinners, and Christ hath taken on him their iniquities, therefore they cannot but upon their fleeing to him by faith, be justified; when they plead his satisfaction for their defence before God, their absolution must needs follow. This is the scope of these words, which are as it were the bond knitting all the rest together, and containing the foundation whereon our justification is founded. There are only *Three* words here that need a little of explication. 1. By *iniquity* is not meaned sin formally taken. We shew, when we spake of the 6th verse, That Christ was not the sinner formally con-

considered, that being inconsistent with his holy nature, and with the personal union of the Manhead with the God-head; but the meaning is, that he took on him the punishment due to our iniquities, or the punishment that our iniquities deserved. 2. When he is said to *bear* their iniquities; it imports a burdensome bearing, or his bearing it with a weight, and that there was a weight in it, as it is said, ver. 3. and 4. *He was a man of sorrows, and acquainted with grief; surely he hath borne our griefs, and carried our sorrows;* and therefore the apostle, 1 Pet. ii. 24. saith, *He his own self bare our sins in his own body on the tree,* when *he was made a curse for us,* as it is Gal. iii. 13. He did bear our sins, by coming under the curse that was due to us for them. In a word, his bearing of our iniquities is a real satisfying of the justice of God for them, by interposing his own blessed back, and taking on the strokes that were due to us. 3. When it is said, *their iniquities,* it relates to the *many,* that, in the former words, are said to be justified through his own knowledge: it is spoken of the iniquities of the elect, and believers, who through Christ are made friends with God; and therefore these being the *many,* they cannot but be justified, because Christ hath paid their debt, according to his engagement. These words, as almost every other verse of this chapter, contain the substance of the gospel; take shortly *five* or *six observations* from them, which we shall put together. The 1*st* is, That the person who is to be justified by faith in Christ, is naturally lying in iniquities; this is supposed, while it is said, that Christ *shall bear their iniquities;* even the iniquities of them, who are to be justified, through faith in him: so it is said before, *The Lord hath laid on him the iniquities of us all, and we all like sheep have gone astray;* these, and many other scriptures; nay, the whole current of the scriptures, confirm the point, and put it beyond debate.

I observe it for these *Ends* and *Uses,* which will shew why it is so frequently marked. 1. That the freedom of God's grace may kyth the more in their justification: they are sinners even as others are, and it is grace that makes the difference; therefore their justification must be free. If then any would have good, or have gotten good by the gospel, and by Christ offered to them therein, let them know that it is freely. 2. That a believer, who is justified, should be very humble; for he was a sinner as well as others, and is still a sinner in part: therefore it becomes him to walk softly, with a stopped mouth, and to be tender and compassionate towards other sinners. There is not a believer, but the weight of his iniquities would have borne him down to hell, had not Christ interposed, and taken them on him; and therefore he ought to be both humble, and thankful. 3. That sinners, who have the offer of Christ's righteousness in the gospel, may not despair, how great soever their sins be. Indeed, if they resolve to continue in sin, or to sin that grace may abound, they have no ground to expect pardon; the apostle doth, with abhorrency, reject the drawing of such conclusions from the grace of God, Rom. iii. But for a guilty sinner, that hath no good in himself, to commend him to Christ, to lean to, and to believe in him, who justifies the ungodly, is a doctrine which the same apostle approves, and gives an open door to them that desire to abandon sin, and to expect justification through Christ's satisfaction; thus a door is set open to you, to believe in him who justifies ungodly sinners, to betake yourselves to him who is the Saviour. 4. To confound and stop the mouths of all self-righteous men, as having nothing to do with Christ. He came to take on iniquity, and to bear it; *he came to seek and to save that which was lost,* and hath not a commission to save self-righteous folk; *For he came not to call the righteous, but sinners to repentance;* and so long as they continue in that condition, they cannot look on themselves, as persons whom he came to call, neither can they take any comfort in, or from his coming.

The 2d *Observation* is, That wherever iniquity is, it is a burden, a heavy burden. There is nothing more heavy than sin, it being that which presses the guilty person to the lowest hell. It brought the fallen angels out of heaven to the pit. Ye may take an instance or two of its weight on a sinner, when he becomes sensible of sin. Psal. xxxviii. 4. *My iniquities,* says David, *are gone over my head, as a heavy burden they are too heavy for me:* It is true, sins are not always weighty to folks sense, yet in themselves they are weighty, and some time they will be found to be so, by the sinner. So, Psal. xl. 12. *Innumerable evils,* says the Psalmist, *have compass'd me about, my iniquities have taken hold of me, so that I am not able to look up: they are more than the hairs of my head, therefore my heart faileth me.* In a word, if the wrath of God, and his curse be heavy, sin must be heavy; is not that heavy, which damned, and drowned the old world, and will burn and bury in ashes this world that now is standing? Is not that heavy, which hath brought on so many

thou-

thousands and millions to hell? And that made our blessed Lord to cry, yet without all sinful anxiety, *My God, my God, why hast thou forsaken me?* and, *My soul is heavy to the death.* And is it not that which makes the Lord say, that *he is pressed*, with his professing people's sins, *as a cart is pressed with sheaves?* All the indignation, and opposition of the men of this world, is nothing to him, in comparison to the sins of his people; he can break through briers and thorns, and consume them together; but the iniquities of his people are said to press him, to shew the abominable lothsomness and weightiness of them.

Use 1. It may make us wonder, that men and women think so little of sin. There are many that will tush at a challenge or threatning for sin; but let me say it, that mountains of lead, yea, though all this world turned into one mass, or lump of lead, it should not be so heavy, as sin should be to you; your drunkenness, filthiness, covetousness, lying, the vaguing of the mind in private duties of worship throughout the week, and in publick duties on the Lord's day; your neglect of prayer in secret, mocking at piety, &c. shall (however light now) one day be found to be weighty, when, as it is, Rev. vi. 6. *Ye shall cry to hills and mountains to fall upon you, and hide you from the wrath of the Lamb.* A mountain would be thought light in that day, but the face and wrath of the Lamb shall be terrible; therefore either give up with sin, and study holiness, or make you for this dreadful posture, that ye would wish to have a hill or a mountain tumbling on you, and yet shall not get that wish granted. What mean ye, O Atheists! and desperately secure pleasers of yourselves, with your idols, that ye dare thus to ly and live under this burden! Will ye be able to come before the throne of God with it upon your back? It is a truth, that sin is such a burden as will sink you to the pit, if ye seek not in God's way to shake it off in time.

2dly, If it be such a burden, make this *twofold* use of it. 1. Beware of keeping still upon you the burden of bygone sins, but take with them, seek to be suitably affected with them; betake yourselves with all speed to Christ, and cast yourselves and your burden on him; it is for this reason that faith is called a *leaning on Christ*, because, when the burden of sin is like to break the sinner's back, faith casts himself and his burden on Christ. 2. For the time to come, study holiness, and take on no more of this burden; always remembring, that when ye take on the debt of the least sin, or seek to hoodwink (as it were) the conscience, and to put out the eyes of it, that ye may sin the more securely, and with the greater liberty, ye are all the while but heightning your burden, and making the weight of it the more intolerable: And is that wisdom, think ye, to be taking on a burden of that, which will press, crush, sink and drown you eternally, under its grievous and unsupportable weight?

3dly, *Observe*, That, for as heavy a burden as sin is, Christ stooped down, and took it on his blessed back, John i. 29. *Behold the Lamb of God, that taketh away*, or beareth, and by bearing, taketh away *the sins of the world*, 1 Pet. ii. 24. *Who his own self bare our sins in his own body on the tree.* So *the just suffered for the unjust*, Heb. ix. ult. *He was once offered to bear the sins of many.* Whether it was the same very burden that the elect should have borne, or the equivalent of it, we will not now debate, having spoken somewhat more particularly to it before; either of them being according to the terms of the covenant of redemption, and accepted of the principal creditor: yet it would seem he did bear the curse in the essentials of it, and in that respect came under the same burden; he died, because he was threatned, *The day thou eats, thou shalt surely die*, and *the soul that sins shall die*; and he died a cursed death, because a cursed death was threatned, as it is Gal. iii. 10. compared with 13. and so came under the curse: Here is love indeed, and a true friend's kind turn, that when sin was such a heavy burden, Christ came in betwixt the elect and it, and took it on himself, and stood at the bar of God, as chargeable with our debt, which was really charged on him, as it is, Isa. l. 6. *He gave his back to the smiters, and his cheeks to them that pluckt off the hair; he hid not his face from shame and spitting:* all these buffetings of profane soldiers, were but little to that weight of wrath that was laid on him, to the making of him groan; to that cup, which in the garden he drank out, and which made him sweat blood, and cry out, *My soul is exceeding sorrowful and heavy even unto death;* and, *Father, if it be possible, let this cup pass from me; yet not my will, but thine be done:* O! what a weight was it, that made him so cry out? There needs no more to prove that he bare our sins, and that there was an exacting of him what we were owing, and that his sufferings are indeed a satisfaction to justice for them, even for the sins of all the elect.

The *Uses* are two, 1. It serves to hold out and confirm this truth, That our Lord Jesus his sufferings were a real satisfaction to justice, for the sins of the elect; and that by his sufferings he was indeed put to bear their iniquities; and that they were not only, nor mainly for example, though we may well make that use of them; but he was made liable for our debt; we sinned, and he suffered and satisfied for our sin; we debauched our stock, and played the bankrupts, he paid our debt.

2. It serves hugely to commend to us the love of God, that gave his Son; and of the Mediator, that came to buy and redeem elect sinners at so dear a rate, and to take on such a weighty burden, to ease them of it. Were there any here (as we hope there are) that know the weight of sin, O! but they would think much of this, even of Christ's taking on the burden of sin, and casting it by, having satisfied justice for it, and loosed the knot of the law, and of the curse that tied it to them; to become man was much, but to bear the burden of our sins was more: Angels wonder at this, that he who is their head should become so low, as to sist himself before God's tribunal, and to undergo the suffering of death, and to take on the weighty burden of the elect's debt, and to satisfy for it. If we were in a right frame of spirit, we could not hear this word, but it would ravish our hearts, and put us to a pause, and holy *non-plus*; but the most part, alas! walk lightly under the burden of sin, without ever considering what Christ hath done to remove it from off his people; nay, I am afraid that believers, who have ground to be lightned, through Christ's condescending to bear their burden, do not as they ought acknowledge him, who hath taken the burden off them.

4thly, From comparing these words with the former, *Many shall be justified, for he shall bear their iniquities*, *Observe*, Christ's bearing of their iniquities, and his satisfaction for our sins, is imputed to us, as the immediate ground of our absolution, and justification before God; so that if it were asked, What is the ground on which a sinner is justified before God? The Text answers, Because *Christ hath borne their iniquities*, he hath paid the debt: even as (to make a comparison for clearing of it) when a debtor is pursued, and hath nothing to pay, yet he pleads that the debt cannot be exacted of him, because his cautioner hath paid it; and the ground on which that debtor is absolved, is his instructing that the cautioner hath paid the debt, which being done, he is set free: so is it here, the believer he is God's debtor, Christ Jesus is his Cautioner, who hath paid his debt; who, when he is brought to the bar of God, and somewhat is laid to his charge, he pleads upon the ground of Christ's satisfying for his debt, and that therefore he ought not to be put to answer for it himself; according to that word, Rom. viii. 34. *Who shall lay any thing to the charge of God's elect? It is God that justifies, who shall condemn?* and the ground follows, *It is Christ that died,* he hath paid the debt.

Use. Among other things, there are two consequences that follow upon this doctrine, that serve to clear the doctrine of justification. 1. That the righteousness, whereby we are justified, is imputed to us, and accepted of God, as if it were our own: Ye are sometimes hearing of imputed righteousness, and it is a great concernment to you to know it well; yet I am afraid, that many of you are very ignorant of it; I shall therefore, in a word or two, explicate it, by comparing the two covenants: The righteousness of the covenant of works is an inherent righteousness, as it is, Tit. iii. 5. *Not by works of righteousness, which we have done;* it is a righteousness of our own doing, made up of our praying, hearing, and other duties, as they are acts of ours: The righteousness of the covenant of grace, is an imputed righteousness, that is, when Christ's doing and suffering is accounted ours: take both in this comparison, The righteousness of the covenant of works is like a debtor, or tenant, his paying of his own debt or rent, by his managing his business providently and dexterously, and none other is troubled with it; the righteousness of the covenant of grace is like one, that hath spent up and debauched all, and hath not one penny to pay his debt or rent with, but hath a worthy, able and responsal cautioner, who hath paid for him: Both being pursued, and brought before the judge; the first man is absolved, because what he was owing, he paid it at the term precisely; the other man granted, that he was owing the debt, but pleads that his cautioner hath paid it, and the law accepts of the cautioner's payment, and pursues the debtor no further, but absolves him: so it is here, when the believer comes to stand at God's bar, it is nothing in himself that he pleads upon, but it is Christ's sufferings; who said on the cross, *It is finished;* the debt of my people is fully paid: and faith pleading for absolution on that ground, according to the law of faith, he is absolved, as if he had paid the debt himself, or had been owing none. If then it should be asked, Believers, what ground have ye to expect to be justified? The prophet answers here, *Christ hath borne our iniquities*, and this is the believer's defence: and therefore see here a possibility to reconcile these *two*, that some men scorn and flout at, as irreconcileable, to wit, How one can "be a sinner, and yet righteous; he may be sinful in himself, and yet righteous, through the imputation of Christ's righteousness. So, 2 Cor. v. ult. " He " was made sin for us, who knew no sin, that we " might be made the righteousness of God in him." Rom. iv. 5. " To him that worketh not, but be- " lieveth on him who justifieth the ungodly, his " faith is counted for righteousness."- The man, ungodly in himself, is justified thro' the satisfaction of Christ, imputed to him for righteousness, and laid hold on by faith; as if he had not sinned, or had actually satisfied himself.

2*dly*, This consequence followeth, that it serves to clear how faith justifies: as when we say, " Faith is our righteousness, and is imputed to us "; for righteousness," we are not to look on faith properly, as a grace in us, and divided, or abstrac-ted from the object; no, by no means: but as it is a laying hold on the object; it is *faith in him that justifies*; and, *Through his knowledge shall many be justified*, because *he shall bear their iniquities*: Faith justifies by vertue of Christ's satisfaction, and as taking hold of it; faith does not justify, as it is an act of grace in the sinner, but as a closing with Christ the Object of it; even as in the similitude we made use of before: It is not enough that the cautioner hath paid such a man's debt, but that the man must instruct it by producing the discharge, the production whereof is the cause of his absolution in law; yet the vertue that makes the discharge so to concur, is not the discharge itself, but the cautioner's payment, or satisfaction, mentioned, and contained in the sinner's discharge: Even so is it here, it is Christ's righteousness that concurreth, as the meritorious cause of the sinner's absolution; and faith concurs as the instrumental cause, in the pleading of that defence; whereon justification follows as an effect of these causes. We know not when, or if ever hereafter, we may have occasion to speak so much to the doctrine of justification; therefore let me press the study of it upon you again and again: Seek to know what this imputed righteousness is, and how different from that which is in yourselves; what is the true meaning of it, as a main hinge of the gospel, without which the covenant of grace can never be understood aright; the ignorance whereof makes many live in security upon the one side, and keeps many in much anxiety upon the other.

5*thly, Observe*, That although Christ Jesus hath borne the iniquities of many, even of his own people, yet not the iniquities of all men and women, but only the iniquities of them that shall be justified, and brought to the actual possession of that which he hath purchased: This may be made out from these *three* in the Text. 1. The relative *their*, it is *their* iniquities, which are borne by Christ, that shall be justified; and who these are, the former words tell, *through his knowledge shall be justify many*. 2. The connexion made by the prophet betwixt these two, *many shall be justified, for he shall bear their iniquities*; all, whose iniquities Christ hath borne, shall be justified. It could not be an argument to prove their justification, if Christ should bear the iniquities of others, or of all men and women, multitudes of whom are never justified; for it might be objected, that Christ bears the iniquities of those many who are never justified, which would be quite contrary to God's covenant, and exceedingly mar the consolation of the believer; beside that, it would make the prophet's reasoning here inconsequent and impertinent. 3. Consider these words, not only as they stand in connexion with the former, but as they are a reason why in justice such should be absolved; and so they will also clear the doctrine: for, so considered, they imply that it is just, that the believer should be justified; even as when the cautioner hath paid the debt, it is just that the principal debtor should be absolved; and upon the other hand, it is not just that the debtor, for whom the cautioner hath not satisfied, should be absolved: the words will bear this twofold consequence; for he knits these two, their being absolved, and Christ bearing their iniquities, and being made liable to their debt; and he consequently disjoins these two, Christ's not bearing the iniquities of others, and their not being absolved; and so, although Christ hath borne the iniquities of *many*, that is of the elect, and hath satisfied and suffered for them, yet not for all, but only for the *many*, who in due time shall thro' his knowledge, that is, through faith in him, be justified; and these who are left to pay their own debt, Christ never died for them: it were very unlike the prophet's reasoning, to say, that such a man is in hell, and yet Christ bare his iniquities.

Use 1. It serves to confirm the former truth. Would ye know whose iniquities Christ hath borne? It is of as many as are justified; the iniquities of such he bare, and of no more.

2. It serves to provoke you, that have gotten in Christ this privilege, to be very thankful: This is it that makes the song of praise heartsom, Rev. v. 9. *Thou hast redeemed us to God, by thy blood, out of every kindred, tongue and nation;* because it is not a common, but a peculiar special mercy, if any be so.

6thly, From the connexion, *observe*, That although Christ hath not borne the iniquities of all men and women, yet he hath borne the iniquities of all that believe; and none ever believed on him, but they may conclude that he hath borne their iniquities, and on that plead their justification, thro' his satisfaction: although there be a restriction on the one side, yet there is none on the other; all are not justified, but these only whose iniquities he hath borne; yet all who, through his knowledge, or faith in him, are justified, their iniquities he hath borne. And hence it will follow, That never a person believed, but Christ hath borne his iniquities. Not that the man's believing is the cause of Christ's bearing, for his bearing of the man's iniquities is the cause of his believing; but it is to shew the connexion, betwixt his bearing, and the man's believing, and that his believing is the evidence of Christ's bearing of his iniquities. And this is more comfortable than the doctrine of universal redemption a thousand times; for it joins Christ's dying and the justification of all that believe on him: So that there are none, that by faith betake themselves to him, but they may expect freedom from the curse, and absolution before the throne of God; whereas the doctrine of universal redemption saith, that Christ died for all, yet all shall not be saved, and I wot not whether I shall be saved or not: and what ground of anxiety is this? But this doctrine hath solid consolation in it. Christ hath not died for all simply, but for all believers, he hath borne all their sins; but I have betaken myself to him by faith; therefore he died for me, he hath borne my iniquities, and I shall never bear them myself, but be justified.

I suppose we need not to stay on the confirmation of this. 1. It is impregnably proved from the reasoning of the prophet in this place; all that are believers cannot but be redeemed and justified, because he hath borne their iniquities, who by faith betake themselves to him. 2. If faith in Christ be a saving fruit of his death, and if none can believe but these, whose iniquities he hath borne; then, wherever faith is, the person may conclude, that Christ hath borne his iniquities, and that he shall be justified: But faith in Christ is a saving fruit and effect of his death, for he hath purchased it among the rest of these spiritual blessings spoken of, Eph. i. 3. where we are said to *be blessed with all spiritual blessings in him;* And it being a promise of the covenant of grace, it cannot but be purchased by the death of the Testator Christ Jesus; therefore, &c. 3. It is clear also from the apostle's reasoning, Rom. v. 10. " For if, when we were enemies, we " were reconciled to God by the death of his " Son; much more, being reconciled, we shall be " saved by his life:" Will he not, who hath paid such a dear price for us, to purchase reconciliation to us, make it out, by bestowing on us the fruit of his purchase?

The 1st *Use* serves to vindicate this our doctrine, concerning Christ's dying for, and bearing the iniquities of believers only; which is most unjustly loaded with reproaches, and debated against by mens cavillings, as if it were a comfortless doctrine; sure it is more comfortable, more sure, and more agreeable both to the wisdom and grace of God, than the doctrine of universal redemption is: For, put these together, That all believers are redeemed and justified, that Christ hath borne their iniquities; that faith is a saving grace, and a fruit of Christ's death; that such as believe, may conclude their justification; and that Christ will make out the benefits of his purchase to them: What want believers, that may be for their comfort? Whereas, if we should lay it for a ground, that Christ died for *all*, what comfort were in that? For all are not justified and saved, but only believers: yea, by the doctrine of universal redemption, tho' ye were even now believers, ye could not conclude that ye should be saved, because ye might fall from it again: But our doctrine of justification hath solid consolation; for, Rom. i. 16. " It is the " power of God unto salvation, to every one that " believes." And, Rom. iii. 2. " It is unto all, " and upon all them that believe:" And it makes the believer sure of his perseverance, for it is an express article of the covenant. We shall only say this, that ye will find, that all, that, in doctrine, or practice, make the way to heaven widest, they make it most unsicker and unsure, and they are in greatest confusion: and indeed it is impossible it can be otherways; for, if men go once out of God's way, which is the strait and narrow way, they can never be sicker and solidly sure, because there is no ground of confidence in it.

The 2d *Use* serves to answer a *Question*, that some out of curiosity puzzle themselves with, which, if well, soberly, and wisely followed, would be no curiosity, and it is this; How shall I know if Christ died for me? *Answer*, Make it sure that ye believe, and then ye shall be sure of the benefits of his death; for if he hath borne the iniquities of these that believe, and if there be no way to make it sure he hath borne our iniquities but by believing, it is a needless stir and noise that is made, about
the

to this, is their never throughing and making it clear to themselves, whether they have believed; and therefore, if ye would see your election, and interest in Christ's death, put the matter of believing to a point; for it is the door whereby ye win into other secrets of God, such as election is; and there is no other way to win to it: therefore these two are knit together, John vi. 39, 40. "This is the will of him that sent me, that of all that he hath given me I should lose nothing;" and if it should be asked, How shall I know, who are given to Christ, to be redeemed by him? The next verse answers, "This is the will of him that sent me, that every one which seeth the Son, and believeth on him, may have everlasting life, and I will raise him up at the last day." Would ye then know who are given and redeemed? They are believers, I mean, of such as are come to age; for none will make the question concerning infants? And therefore, if ye would know the way of coming to the knowledge of your justification, redemption, and election of God; begin at the lowest step of believing, and make that sicker, and all the rest will follow of will: but if ye mistken and overlook this, and will go up to the top of the ladder, *per saltum*, and at the first; it will be just with God, that ye

should not perish, but have eternal life: If thou be a believer, thy name is there, Christ hath borne thine iniquities; and what consolation is that to them, who are clear anent their faith? But, alas! it says there is much rotten, unsound and slippery faith among us, and also much faith that is but little lively, that there is so little solid comfort following it.

Use 4. It serves to demonstrate the necessity of believing, the advantages of it, and the necessity of our endeavouring to be clear that we do believe; if these two go together, justification and believing, then there is a necessity of believing; and if these two go together, clearness about our believing, and the knowledge that Christ did bear our iniquities, then there is in some respect a necessity, that we know we believe; otherways we can have little or no comfort in Christ's bearing of our iniquities, and of our being given to Christ to be redeemed by him: from these two the advantages of believing may appear; therefore, to make all sure, justification, Christ's bearing of your iniquities, and and your being given to Christ, make it sure that ye are in the faith; and this way give all diligence to make your calling and election sure: And the Lord himself prevail with you so to do.

SERMON LXIV.

Isaiah liii. 12. *Therefore will I divide him a portion with the great, and he shall divide the spoil with the strong; because he hath poured out his soul unto death: And he was numbred with transgressors, and he bare the sins of many, and made intercession for transgressors.*

THERE hath been a compendious sum of the covenant of redemption delivered by the prophet in this chapter, wherein, what is required as the price for elect sinners from the Mediator, is holden forth, on the one side, in a large description of his sufferings; and what is proposed, as the fruit that should follow, and as the satisfaction that the Mediator should have for his sufferings, is on the other side also laid down; as, that " he should " see his seed, and prolong his days, and the plea-" sure of the Lord should prosper in his hand: " That he should see of the travel of his soul, and

" be satisfied; and that by his knowledge many " shall be justified." In this verse, we have a summary recapitulation, and repitition of this mutual bargain; only it is proposed in a different method: for before, what was required, and undertaken by the Mediator, was first set down, and then the promises made to him were next set down; here the method is altered, and the promises made to the Mediator are first down, and the conditions required of him last set down; it is like, to shew the oneness of the covenant, and the mutualness of the terms of it; and that though, as to our conceiving,

and

and up-taking of it, there be something first, and something last, yet with God there is no such thing, but it is one present act: The promises made to the Mediator are two expressions, with an inference in the word *Therefore*, knitting this to what went before; *I will divide him a portion with the great, and he shall divide the spoil with the strong.* In short, the similitudes here used, are taken from conquerors, and victors, who have been in a war and fight, and having defeat and routed all their enemies, and put them off the field, have a notable outgate, victory, and triumph, and a great spoil, as the fruit of war; and so the meaning is, that the Mediator, by his undertaking to satisfy for the elect, should have a great fight and combat with many enemies, but he should lose nothing by it, he should have a notable outgate, an excellent victory, and glorious triumph, great glory and spoil: so that there was never war like his, nor enemies like these that he had to encounter with; so there should never be such victory, triumph and spoil, as our Lord Jesus should have. The word *portion* is not in the original, but well supplied. It is only, *I will divide him many*, as the word is often used, and *he shall divide the spoil with the strong;* that is, he shall, in dividing the spoil, be above the strongest.

The words infer, and take in these *Three*. 1. A great defeat, and victory over all the Mediator's enemies, the devil, death, and the curse; he gets a great victory over them, and gives them a great defeat, so that they are quite beat off the field, as *dividing of the spoil* imports, Psal. lxviii. 12. *She that remained at home divided the spoil;* and, Isa. ix. 3. *As men rejoice, when they divide the spoil.* 2. The great number of captives, that our Lord, in his victory, and triumph, takes and brings off; that is, he gets a great booty, which is that spoken of in the words before, *By his knowledge shall many be justified;* and it is that which is exprest in that Psal. lxviii. 18. *Thou hast ascended on high, thou hast led captivity captive;* that is, these that were formerly captives thou hast redeemed from their captivity, and led them captive that carried others captive; as the people of God pray, Psal. cxxvi. 4. *Turn again our captivity.* 3. It takes in the excellent victory, the great triumph and glory, that the Mediator should have by this means; " He is exalted above every name " that is named, that at the name of Jesus every " knee should bow, of things in heaven, of things " in earth, and of things under the earth. For further clearing of it, we shall recommend to you two or three places, in which, it is like, there is an allusion to this; as that, Col. ii. 14, 15, " Blotting out the hand-writing of ordinances " that was against us, and contrary to us, tak- " ing it out of the way, and nailing it to his " cross," tearing, as it were, the obligation that the law had over the elect, by his paying of their debt: " And having spoiled principalities and pow- " ers, he made a shew of them openly, triumph- " ing over them in it." There is his victory and triumph: He combats with, subdues, and treads under foot, all his, and his peoples enemies, by satisfying the justice of God for the elects debt; and spoils them of many souls that were led captive by them, and triumphed openly over them, declaring himself to have gotten the victory in a most majestick manner. A 2d place is, Phil. ii. 8, 9. " Being found in fashion as a man, he hum- " bled himself, and became obedient unto death, " even the death of the cross: wherefore God " hath highly exalted him, and given him a name " which is above every name, that at the name of " Jesus every knee should bow, of things in hea- " ven, in earth, and under the earth, and that " every tongue shall confess that Jesus Christ is " Lord, to the glory of God the Father. This is his victory, triumph, and glory, such as none in heaven or earth ever had, or shall have the like. A 3d place is that, Eph. ii. 20, 21, 22. " He raised him from the dead, and set him at " his own right-hand in the heavenly places, far " above all principality, and power, and might, " and dominion, and every name that is named, " not only in this world, but also in that which is " to come; and hath put all things under his feet, " and gave him to be Head over all things to the " church:" whether they be devils, or good angels, or men, saints militant, or triumphant, he is above them all, all are made subject to him, and he is the Head of his church.

The expressions run in different persons. The *first* is in the first person, " I will divide him a " portion:" It is a promise of God the Father to the Mediator, for his attaining the victory; as it is said, Eph. i. 20. " God raised him from the dead." The 2d expression is in the 3d person, *He shall divide the spoil;* to shew that the Mediator, God-Man, concurred in the attaining the victory: Therefore, Rom. i. 4. he is said *to raise himself:* And in that it is said, *I will divide, and he shall divide;* it is to hold out the Mediator his attaining and possessing of what was promised, and to shew that there is nothing promised to the Media-

tor,

tor, but actually he is, and shall be put in the full possession of it.

The last part of the words holds out the conditions on the Mediator's side, in *Four* expressions, 1. *Because he hath poured out his soul unto death;* that is, because he willingly condescended to die, he yetted, or poured out his soul to death. 2. *He was numbered with transgressors:* he had a reproached and shameful life, and a reproached and cursed death; he was thought the worst in the world, so that Barabbas a murderer was compared unto him. It also points out the respect that his death had to a satisfaction for the sins of the elect; he was legally numbred, and counted amongst transgressors, tho' he was no trangressor. 3. *He bare the sins of many;* which expones the former, and says this much, that not only he simply died, and died a shameful death, but that he died for this end, to bear, and by his bearing to remove, the sins of the elect; for it relates to the *many* that in former words are said to be *justified by his knowledge:* And it cannot be but these *many* shall be justified, because he did bear their sins, as to the punishment, and curse due to them; and whose sins soever are born by Christ, these are and shall be justified: and therefore he must be victorious, and have a glorious triumph and outgate, because he lays down his life for his sheep, as it is John x. 17. *Therefore doth my Father love me, because I lay down my life, and take it up again:* And by the way it is a strange thing, that the only begotten Son of God should be loved on this account, accepted, and glorified in this work, even because *he poured out his soul unto death,* out of zeal to his Father's glory, in prosecuting the work of sinners redemption. 4. *And he made intercession for the transgressors:* which points out the application of his death, and the benefit thereof to *many,* whose sins he bare. He died to take their sins away, and interceeds to have his purchase made effectual; for tho' this be applied usually to his prayer on the cross, yet that is but one particular of his intercession, which is of a larger extent; and therefore it is noted as a condition required of the Mediator, that he must not only die, but also interceed, that the benefits of his death might be made forthcoming for them, for whom he died.

Thus ye see, we have the sum of God's covenant here: As if the Lord were proposing to the Mediator; Now, Son, if thou wilt pour out thy soul unto death, and thereby bear the sins of my elect people, and make intercession for them, thou shalt lose nothing by it, thou shalt have a notable victory, and triumph, and a great spoil. In the words before, the Mediator having accepted the terms of the covenant, and performed them, though not actually at that time, but in the purpose and decree of God, which now are actually performed; therefore the promises are turned over in a concluded covenant, and in an absolute right to him.

What needs further explication, we shall endeavour to reach it, as we speak to the *observations;* and because the words for the most part yield the same doctrines that have been spoken to before, we shall not insist in them.

1st, Then, from the repetition, *observe* in general, That the nature and terms of the covenant of redemption, betwixt God and the Mediator, is a profitable doctrine, and useful to be understood, and believed by the people of God; therefore it is so clearly proposed, and again and again repeated, and laid before their eyes; and summed and repeated in this *verse,* to keep them in mind of it. These that know the covenant of redemption, as that which hath in it the sum of all the foundations of our faith, and the ground of our access to God, and of our peace with him; they will easily grant that, that it is very necessary to be studied, known and believed: for, *First,* By it we know what we may expect from God, because what we are to expect is promised to Christ in this covenant, us to our head; *this portion with the great and this dividing of the spoil with the strong:* He hath it as our head. 2. Because we know by this covenant, how we come by these things promised; and that is, *by pouring out of his soul unto death, bearing of our sins, and interceeding for us;* which supposes, and includes our betaking of ourselves unto him by faith. 3. Because, by this covenant, the rich and free grace of God hath its due glory: for there is nothing considered here, as the reason of setting captives free, but Christ's paying of the price; it comes freely to us, as a gift bestowed.

2dly, And more particularly, *observe;* That though our Lord Jesus Christ, in the work of sinners redemption, had a sore combat and fight, yet he hath a glorious outgate, triumph and victory; it was the greatest, sorest, and most furious onset and assault that ever was heard of, that our Lord Jesus encountred with: As the remembrance and consideration of what hath been spoken, of his *being in an agony, and sweating drops of blood;* of his praying, that *if it were possible, that cup might*

might depart from him; of his crying, *My God my God, why hast thou forsaken me?* &c. will most convincingly make out, the justice of God pursuing him for all the guilt of the elect, principalities and powers being in his tops; the devil, the prince of this world, having all his instruments yoked, and at work, some to nod the head, some to mock and scourge him, &c. yet he did abide it all out; *he gave his back to the smiters, and his cheeks to them that pulled off the hair, and hid not his face from shame and spitting;* and had a most glorious victory, and triumph over all. What we said in expoüning of the words, clears it somewhat, and that word, John xii. 13. *Now is the judgment of this world, now shall the prince of this world be cast out;* to point out his victory over the world, and the devil: and that word, Col. ii. 14, 15. *He spoiled principalities and powers;* he unclothed them, and left not (as we use to speak) a whole rag on them; he by a strong hand pulled all the elect from them, and left none of them in their possession; he brake open the prison doors, and set them all at liberty. This was indeed a great victory; he also hath a great spoil of many captives, and great glory, being exalted in our nature, *at the right hand of the Majesty on high, having a name above every name, that at the name of Jesus every knee might bow:* and that passage, Eph. i. 20, 21. is to the same purpose, *he hath put all things under his feet,* &c. If we look to reason, it cannot be otherways. 1. If we consider what our Lord Jesus was in his person, being the Son of God, he cannot but be glorious, John xvii. 5. he prays, *Father, glorify me with that glory which I had with thee before the world was.* Tho', by being man, he became of no reputation, and a vail was drawn over the declarative glory of the God-head in his person for a time, yet he remained still the Son of God, and glorious in himself; and it cannot be but he, that is God, must be glorious in his exaltation, when that vail that obscured his glory is taken away. 2. His office, as Mediator, and Head of the elect, proves it. He, that was appointed Head over all things to the Church, could not but be great and glorious; and therefore, when that of Psal. x. 10. is cited by the apostle, Acts ii. 24. and xiii. 35. it is said, *that it was impossible that death could keep him.* 3. It will be clear, if we consider the work itself wherewith he was intrusted; it being a work that was so well liked of, and approven by. God, he could not but have a glorious victory and outgate; therefore says he, John x. *My Father loveth me,*

because I lay down my life for my sheep, And Phil. ii. 8. it is said, *Because he humbled himself, and became obedient unto death, therefore God hath highly exalted him.* It was the contract betwixt God and the Mediator, that he should first become low, and then be exalted; and therefore he behoved to be exalted, and made very glorious.

Use 1. Learn, not to undervalue, nor to vail and obscure the glory of the Mediator, from the consideration of his sufferings; for tho' he was low, yet he is now exalted; he had a most noble, excellent and glorious victory and triumph over all his enemies. There are none of us all, but shall at the day of Judgment, when he will be seen to be Judge of quick and dead, (which is a part of his triumph) having so many redeemed slaves (to speak so) at his back, having a confirmation of this truth in our bosom. And indeed it is no little part of religion, to get this point deeply impressed on our hearts, That our Lord Jesus, who was once low, is now exalted to such glory: look to it, and we will find a great part of our deadness and unsoundness here, that his greatness bulks not suitably in our eye; alas! we do very much undervalue him: but his humiliation being for us, it should not make us think the less of him, nor make us lessen the high esteem we should have of him, but should in reason make us think the more of him, and put the greater price on him.

Use 2. It is a most comfortable doctrine, in reference to all ups and downs of the time, and to all the straits that his church and people can be put to; it cannot be ill with Christ, and it shall not be ill with them: He may have contests, but he shall get, yea, he hath gotten the victory; he once died, to die no more: all that he hath now to do, is, to make application of his purchased redemption, and to divide the spoil; to notice (which he doth most narrowly) what of his purchase is yet in the devil's possession, and to rescue and set it free. He hath gotten the possession of the kingdom, and it must, and it shall go well, let the world rage, and let the sea roar, and the floods lift up their voice, and the mountains be cast in the sea. Whatever confusions and overturnings come, or whatever troubles be, our Lord Jesus hath gotten the victory, and is dividing the spoil: He will take no other division, than what Jehovah hath made, and carved out to him; it will not be what devils or men, what great men, kings, princes, parliaments, potentates, armies, &c. are
pleased

pleased to give, or allow to him; but he must needs have the portion promised him, *with the great, and the spoil with the strong;* he shall certainly get that, and none shall be able to bereave him, or take a bit of it from him; yea, none shall possess a foot-broad of ground bestowed on him and his followers: He shall have a church and ordinances dispensed therein, where he intends it, and souls shall be gathered to him from all quarters, as they were given to him: and maugre all the malice and proud opposition of devils and men, all that the Father hath given to him shall come to him, without all peradventure, or possibility of misgiving; they shall not, by all their opposition and persecution, be able to keep any one of the gifted ones from coming to him, in the season agreed on betwixt Jehovah and him. And, *2dly,* It is comfortable to God's people, as to their own particular case; corruption is a strong and formidable enemy; the devil is a restless enemy, and goeth round about, like a roaring lion, seeking whom he may devour; the world is a deceitful, ensnaring enemy, and doth often, in a manner, even overwhelm them: But our Lord Jesus hath the victory, and parting of the stakes, (to say so) or the dividing of the spoil; these that remain at home, the fecklessest boy or girl, lad or lass, shall divide the spoil. This is it that Job comforts himself with, Chap. xix. " I know that my Redeemer liveth, and that he shall stand at the latter day " upon the earth," to wit, as sole and absolute Conqueror, the victory being intirely on his side; " with these eyes shall I see him, and no other " for me, though worms destroy this body. Believers, O Believers! there is a good day coming; he hath gotten the victory, and so shall ye; " the God of peace shall bruise Satan under your " feet shortly:" and whatever wrongs ye suffer, and whatever straits ye be under now, while the wicked are in prosperity, there will be a new decision, yea, a new division ere long; all shall be snatched from wicked men, but your cup shall run over; there shall be no more fighting, no more parties to give you battle, or to oppose you, when he shall have beaten all enemies off the field: It will be a poor and sorry portion that many will get in that day, who did not lippen and trust to Christ's spoil, when ye believers shall be sharers with him in it.

Use 3d. This says, that it is both hard and sad to cop with Christ, and to be found in opposition to him: I speak not so much of publick contests, such as Pilate, Herod, the Scribes and Pharisees had with him, and which many great ones of the earth still keep up against him, who will find the smart of their opposition ere long; but of all that contend with him in his ordinances, and who say, by their practice at least, " Let us break his bands " asunder, and cast away his cords from us," as it is, Psal. ii. " And we will not have this Man " to reign over us," as it is, Luke xix. He will say, " Bring out these mine enemies, and slay " them before me:" Beloved hearers, this day is coming, when all of us will stand before him, and shall see him divide the spoil; and wo, wo will be to that person that day, that would not submit to his government: O what a dreadful thing will it be to be slain before the Mediator, to have the Prince of life taking holy pleasure in thy death, because thou sided with the devil, and the lusts of thine own heart, because thou resisted and quenched his Spirit, and barracaded the way of his access to thee, and would not let him in, to reign in thy heart, nor yield thyself as a subject to him! But it shall be well, unspeakably well with Christ, and all that are his, in that day. He and they shall triumph most gloriously; the splendor, spiritual state, and majesty of that triumph, shall infinitely transcend all that hath been looked at with wonder, in the most glorious triumphs of the greatest emperors, kings, or captain generals in the world.

3dly, Consider what this spoil is, even to *see his seed,* and to *justify many,* and to get them brought in to him, and made partakers of his grace and glory. Observe, " That it is a Part of Christ's " victory, triumph and glory, to get the devil de- " feat in, and dung out of souls, and to get them " converted, justified and saved through his blood." When he is triumphing over enemies, as it is, Col. ii. 14, 15. what is he doing? He is even tearing the bond that was above the elects head, and blotting out their debt; in that he triumphs most gloriously: so, Psal. lxviii. " Thou hast ascended on " high, thou hast led captivity captive;" there is his triumph and spoil, even a company of poor slaves redeemed by him; *The weapons,* says the Apostle, " of our warfare are not carnal, but spiritual, and " mighty through God, to the bringing down of " strong holds, and leading every thought and i- " magination lifted up against God captive unto " the obedience of Christ;" there is Christ's victory and triumph: What are the strong holds that he batters, storms and takes in? He makes some proud hearts to stoop and yield to him, and carries some, that were rebels to him, captive to his obedience: O happy captivity! It is not meant in respect of thraldom and bondage, but in respect of

D d d

volun-

His portion and spoil, What doth our blessed Lord Jesus take to himself? What doth this David claim or take to him as his spoil, who is alone the Monarch of this great universe? It is a number of poor sinners, *Come to me,* says he, *ye blessed of my Father, inherit the kingdom prepared for you:* He hath no more, he seeks no more, but so many souls as he minded to do good to; *When the Lord divided the nations,* as it is, Psal. cxxxix. *He chose* Jacob *for his portion.* If we consider a little more particularly, we will find the justification and salvation of sinners to be our Lord Jesus his victory, triumph and spoil, because herein he is victorious, and triumphs, and gets the glory of his obedience, faithfulness, grace, power and love; the glory of the Mediator shines manifestly and conspicuously in all these here. 1. The glory of his *obedience,* when he hath it to say, as it is, John xviii. 9. *Of all that thou hast given me, I have lost none:* He gets so many souls committed to him of the Father to redeem; and when he hath done, and performed the work, and brought them in, he hath the glory of his obedience to his Father, who saith to him, *Thou art my beloved Son, in whom I am well pleased.* 2. The glory of *his faithfulness;* according as he did engage and undertake to Jehovah, he hath keeped his word: and there is a necessity lying on him, that it should be so, that of all committed to him, he should lose none, but present them without spot or wrinkle, or any such thing; therefore he is called the *faithful Shepherd,* because he loses none of the sheep that are given him. 3. The glory of *grace,* and *infinite love;* the more that are saved, the more grace and love shines forth in paying their debt and ransom, and in bringing them in to be partakers of his *love;* therefore, John xvii. he says, *That the love wherewith thou hast loved me may be in them, and I in them;* he would have the love communicated by the Father to him, to be in them, that it may be known that he hath loved them, as the Father hath loved him: there cannot be such a proof and demonstration of love as this; it is evidenced in his exaltation as their Head, and in their being brought

1 Pet. i. they are *said to be keeped by the power of God, through faith unto salvation.* In a word, as it was the manner of old, for conquerors to ride in triumph, and all their prisoners led before or after them, at their back; so our Lord, for manifesting the glory of his grace, faithfulness and power, brings so many sinners through to glory, and hath a greater train than ever any conqueror had; and he counts it his glory and triumph to get many lost souls saved, John xvii. *Thine they were, and thou gavest them me, and I am glorified in them;* How is that? *I have given them thy word, and they have received it;* he counts himself glorified in sinners submitting to him, in their believing on him, and in their taking pardon from him. Now, let me say, that if we were wailing and making choice of a *Doctrine,* to warm the heart of a sensible sinner, to shame unbelief out of the world, and to give impregnable ground to hazard on Christ, here it is, that our Lord Jesus placeth his victory, glory, triumph and spoil in this, even in doing good to sinners, and in having sinners getting good of him; it is his portion, when (to say so) the world is dealt, that he gets a number of lost sinners to save as his share; and though he be the Heir of all things, and the First-born, yet he loves that better than a thousand kingdoms; when he hath his spoil and prey at the taking, this is it, and he chooseth no other: O sinners! do ye think this little? or do ye think little of this? Had he placed his glory, in crushing under foot all the prisoners of the earth, or in bringing the world to nothing, who could have said, What doest thou? But when he placeth his glory and triumph in this, to overcome the devil, to cast him out of souls, to relieve poor sinners, and to bring them in to acknowledge him as the *Author of eternal salvation,* and as *the Author and Finisher of their faith;* if ye would have something to wonder at, is it not here? He will burn the world into ashes, and leave it, and will cast many kings and great men into hell; and yet he gathers poor elect sinners out of that burnt heap, as it were, as the thing he hath designed for his spoil: he hath no more, and he seeks no more,

(as

salvation, as is wonderful in this respect, that he counts it his glory and triumph to have many sinners saved, when he might have glorified himself in sending us all to hell: May we not wonder at this? and yet we ought to believe it, and the little faith of it makes it to be so little wondered at. Ah! sinners for the most part believe not that Christ thinks so much of the saving of sinners; and therefore they wonder not at it, are not suitably affected and taken up with it.

Use 2*d.* There is here a sweet and solid ground for quieting and settling the faith of sensible sinners, who would have footing to their faith. Christ counts it his glory and triumph to save such as ye are, and if ye perish that would fain be at Christ, and his righteousness for life, Christ shall want his glory and triumph: And may not that serve and satisfy you, that your salvation is his glory and triumph, which he will not come short of? The Father hath here promised it, and he shall not, he cannot want it; sinners he must have, and shall have to be saved, because his victory, triumph and spoil depend on it: A wonderful condescension of grace (which is not easily believed) that all these are linked and coupled together, and through other, as it were, sinners salvation, Christ's victory, triumph and spoil, and God's glory in his grace, love, faithfulness and power! Ye reflect no doubt on God's faithfulness, who suspect and are jealous of your salvation, if indeed ye do, by faith, betake yourselves to Jesus Christ.

Use 3*d.* Doth Christ think so much of the salvation of sinners, that he counts it his victory and triumph, his portion and spoil? Then, 1. All that give not Christ their souls to be saved, do what they can to lessen Christ's portion, and to

there is here a strong and effectual motive to persuade to faith in Christ, and a stronger and more effectual cannot be thought upon: It will be Christ's triumph to pull you out of the claws of the devil; and if he do it not, ye on the matter allow the devil some way to get the victory over Christ, which is yet impossible, but the devil will certainly have victory over you, to whom ye will be slaves and drudges for ever. There is also here ground of great terror and dreadful warning to such as yield not to Christ, because they do what they can to impede his victory, when he comes by his ordinances, *to turn them from darkness to light, and from the power of Satan to God,* they thwart with him; the day is coming, when this doctrine will be comfortable to some, and terrible to others, when there shall be none of us, but we shall see it confirmed with our eyes, when he (as a man sorting and sharing his spoil after the victory) shall say to these on his right hand, *Come, ye blessed of my Father, inherit the kingdom prepared for you;* and to others; *Depart from me ye cursed, into everlasting fire, prepared for the devil and his angels;* even as if a conqueror should take some prisoners, and make them sons and heirs, and set them upon thrones, and should cast others into perpetual prison, who loved not liberty: And indeed it will be a fearful prison to be in hell, with the devil and his angels. Either we will be part of Christ's portion and spoil in that day, or he will refuse, disown and reject us, leaving us to be an everlasting prey to the devil; happy they whom he chooseth, and wo to them eternally whom he casts as refuse ware: God give us wisdom to lay these things to heart.

SERMON LXV.

Isaiah liii. 12. *Therefore will I divide him a portion with the great, and he shall divide the spoil with the strong; because he hath poured out his soul unto death: And he was numbred with the transgressors, and he bare the sins of many, and made intercession for the transgressors.*

THIS covenant of redemption is a great bargain, there was never such parties as the Lord Jehovah, and the Mediator; and we may say, there was never such conditions and articles in any bargain, as are in this. The verse now read

ator, *I will divide him a portion with the great; a fair and large victory, and a good and glorious out-gate; and he shall divide the spoil with the strong:* As these that are conquerors and victors use to share most largely and deeply in the spoil, so our Lord Jesus shall have a rich spoil, a large booty, many redeemed souls, a bride whom he shall present blameless to the Father; these are the spoil, the jewels that he fights for, and the prey he chooseth: When the world is burnt, and the rest are sent to hell, he gathers out so many for himself. 2. The conditions on the Mediator's side are four, he comes to this victory and triumph, because *he hath poured out his soul unto death,* because *he was numbred with transgressors,* because *he bare the sins of many,* and because *he made intercession for transgressors,* therefore shall he be sure of all this.

Although there be no express name of a covenant here, yet ye see the thing; because as in covenants amongst men there are two parties, and their engagements are mutual, and the performance of these engagements in the one depends on the performance of them in the other; so is it here. 1. The Parties are Jehovah, and the Mediator. 2. There are two things promised to the Mediator; a glorious victory, and a rich spoil, the justifying of many. 3. The conditions on the Mediator's side, on which the performance of the promises depends; he condescends to die, and to die willingly, to be numbred with transgressors, to bear their sins, and to make intercession for them; this Jehovah condescends to accept of; and upon this, *many,* to wit, all elect sinners, are *justified through faith on him,* as it is verse 11.

1. From the promise made to Christ, (where the person is changed) *I will divide him a portion with the great, and he shall divide the spoil with the strong,* I will grant him such a thing, and he shall obtain it, take this general *observation,* as the reason of it; " That all the promises made by Jehovah to the Mediator are certain, and shall actually be performed." I will grant this to him, and he shall get it. The connexion doth also confirm it; *Because he hath poured out his soul unto*

diator God-man, in whom the Father is well pleased; and the Mediator having performed what he undertook for the elect, there is no ground to question the performance of the promises made him.

Use. And it is a very comfortable one; Look, whatever is promised to the Mediator, in reference to particular, private, or publick mercies, all shall be most certainly and infrustrably performed; Christ is the Party to whom the promises are made, and Jehovah cannot fail to perform what is promised to the Mediator, more than the Mediator hath failed in performing what he undertook: Now it is promised to the Mediator, Psal. cx. 3. " Thy " people shall be willing in the day of thy power, " in the beauties of holiness, from the womb of " the morning, thou hast the dew of thy youth:" Where there are these things promised to Christ: 1. That his people shall be made willing in the day of his power, which is exponed in that, John vi. 44. *No man can come to me, except the Father who hath sent me draw him;* God takes away the stubbornness, and frowardness that is in the elect, and makes them pliable to embrace, and receive, and give up themselves to Christ. 2. That his people shall be numerous, the youth of his womb shall be numerous, as the dew in the morning. 3. They shall be holy and shining in holiness, *In the beauty of holiness;* again it is promised to the Mediator, that all believers in him shall be justified, as it is verse 11. *By his knowledge shall my righteous servant justify many;* and this is according to that, John vi. 39, 40. *This is the will of him that sent me, that of all that he hath given me I should lose none; and this is the will of him that sent me, that every one that seeth the Son, and believeth on him, may have everlasting life:* The poor sinner that by ..ith betakes himself to God's promise, the promise cannot fail him, because the Mediator is considered as the Party, to whom the promise is made: And the absolute salvation and redemption of believers is in the same place promised; though they be in hazard through many sins, indwelling lusts, temptations and snares, to be drawn away, yet " they shall have eternal life, they shall " never

" never perish, none shall pluck his sheep out of
" his hand, he shall see his seed, of all that are
" given him, he shall lose none:" This would
commend believing to us, as a sure and ficker bargain, because the ground of our faith is articled
betwixt God and the Mediator; and it is as impossible that it can fail, as it is impossible that God
can be unfaithful, and that the Mediator can fail
in that wherein he is engaged. Again, if ye look
to promises of publick mercies, as that he shall
have a church in the world, and that she shall
be continued and preserved, &c. These promises
shall certainly be performed, as that, Psal. ii. 6.
*I have set my King upon my holy hill of Zion; ask
of me, and I will give thee the Heathen for thine
inheritance, and the uttermost ends of the earth
for thy possession;* a fruit of which promise is our
preaching, and your hearing the gospel here this
day: And the promises, Psal. lxxxix. from verse
20. and forward, " With him my hand shall be
" established, and my arm shall strengthen him;
" the enemy shall not exact upon him, nor the son
" of wickedness afflict him; I will beat down his
" foes before his face, and plague them that hate
" him; I will set his hand on the sea, and his right
" hand on the rivers; I will make him my first
" born, higher than all the kings of the earth; my
" mercy will I keep for him, his seed shall endure
" for ever; if his children forsake my law, then
" will I visit their transgression with the rod; ne-
" vertheless, my loving-kindness I will not utterly
" take from him, nor suffer my faithfulness to fail:"
There is, Hos. iii. a promise of the ingathering of
the Jews: and, Isa. ix. 6. it is said, that *the government shall be upon his shoulders, and of the
increase of his government there shall be no end;*
and, Rev. xi. 15. it is proclaimed, *The kingdoms
of this world are become the kingdoms of our Lord,
and of his Christ:* All these, and many the like
promises, shall be accomplished, though the world
should be turned down every month once,
let be every year: The ground of the church's
continuance, and preservation, is not, because such
and such persons govern; otherwise, what would
have become of the church, when Antichrist prevailed? but the promises made to the Mediator.
Here lieth the Christian's peace, when he hath to
do with challenges; it is impossible that the believer in Christ can perish: And here is insured the
church's preservation, even by God's promise to
the Mediator, that he shall have a seed, and that
many shall be justified, that he shall divide the spoil:
And tho' we see but very little appearance of the
spreading of the gospel among the Jews and Pagans,

or where Antichrist reigns,
now for many years rathe
extended; yet there is not
but it shall be accomplish
ground of our peace, and o
er, as it is, Psal. lxxii. " I
" for him continually, and
" ed:" Two sweet exerc
for that which is in the pa
kingdom come, and daily to
coming of his kingdom.

But, 2*dly,* What is spok
tor's part, we take it for g
thing spoken of, but it is,
the Father engages to pe
promises are made to him,
ed whatever he undertook
long ere the Messiah came
as a thing done in the prete
as yet it was not actually
because it was as certain a
done. *Observe* hence, "
" Christ's undertaking, a
" nant of redemption, bu
" tually performed." O b
sal and faithful Parties in
God, and Adam who br
played the traitor; but it i
and the Mediator, *Emma*
the other side: Therefore t
Mediator's performing acc
ing, as well as there is fa
forming whatever he hath
mised to him. Ye shall on
stimonies for this: The 1
xvii. 5. *This is my belove
well pleased;* He undertoo
and hath accordingly perfo
ther is well pleased. A 2d
he appeareth before the Fa
argument for his glorifyin
glory, which he had with
world was: *I have glorifi
finished the work which*
have gotten a task and piec
me, and now it is performe
he hath on the cross, is ren
It is finished; now the t
and I have no more to do,
the victory, and to the di
a 3d testimony, is our Lo
heaven, and the glory tha
the day of judgment, wh

consummate: That shall be a proof and testimony, that he left nothing undone, that was given him to do; that he bare the sins of many, that he gave his back to the smiters, and his cheeks to them that pulled off the hair, and that he satisfied justice freely, and ascended to heaven, as it is, 1 Tim. iii. 16, " Great is the mystery of godliness," saith the apostle, " God was manifested in the flesh, justi-
" fied in the spirit," fully absolved, as having performed all whatsoever he undertook, " seen of an-
" gels, and raised up unto glory."

Use. This is also, though a general, yet a very comfortable doctrine to the people of God, in as far as from it they may know, that there is no more to be paid to the justice of God for the sins of the elect; it hath gotten full satisfaction, the Cautioner hath paid all their debt, and is now exercing his offices, for applying to them his purchase, making intercession for them, overseeing them, proving a Tutor to them, guiding them, and all that concerns them, and his church; even doing all things well, managing the affairs of his Father's house, as a Son, and he cannot but guide all things well:
" Other sheep," saith he, " I have, which are not
" of this fold, them I must bring in, and they shall
" hear my voice, and I give them eternal life, and they
" shall never perish:" A most pregnant ground of comfort to the believer, that his eternal well-being, cannot but be sure and sicker, because it hath the Father and the Mediator their faithfulness engaged for it; if Jehovah perform the promises made to the Mediator, and if the Mediator perform his engagement to Jehovah, and raise up believers at the last day, then it must follow, that their salvation is sure. This is the main ground on which believers peace is founded; and here we may allude to that, Heb. vi. " He hath sworn by two immu-
" mutable things, wherein it is impossible for God
" to lie, that the heirs of promise, who are fled
" for refuge to lay hold on the hope set before
" them, may have strong consolation:" Even so here, there are two immutable things, to wit, God's promise to the Mediator, and God will and must keep his word to him; and the Mediator's engagement to God, and he will and must keep his word to him: And indeed we have good proof of both already; for it was this engagement that made the Father send the Son of his love, out of his bosom, to be incarnate, and to undergo the work of elect sinners redemption; and it was this engagement that made the Mediator die, of whom the Father exacted the price, till he declared himself satisfied, and well pleased: Now, when these things that seemed most difficult are accomplished, what can fail?

1. Then there is here ground to fix our faith upon; and indeed there is need to fix it rightly: The ground that our salvation, and perseverance in the faith is founded on, is not our continuing to pray, to believe, and to love God, but this engagement betwixt the Father and the Son; and it is the cause procuring the other, as a necessary and infallibly certain effect; it is mainly on this, that believers should rest quiet and confident. 2. It should make believers humble and chearful, seeing, though they be weak in themselves, yet here they have a grip and hold for every hand, as it were; Jehovah's word, and the Mediator's word for their through-bearing. 3. It should much commend believing, and the state of a believer, who have such ground of assurance: The greatest monarch on earth hath not such ground of assurance for his dinner or supper, as the poor believer hath for eternal life; for, the word spoken by Jehovah to the Mediator, and the undertaking of the Mediator to Jehovah, cannot fail; and the believer hath that to rest upon, as the ground of his assurance.

More particularly, the articles on the Mediator's side are (as I said) in these *four* expressions, [He hath poured out his soul unto death, he was numbred with the transgressors, he bare the sins of many, and made intercession for the transgressors.] 1*st*, He must *die*, expressed in these words, *He hath poured out his soul unto death;* which implies *three* things, 1. That it is an article of the covenant of redemption, and of the Mediator's undertaking, that he should die for sinners; and so it is a needless, curious and unwarrantable dispute, Whether fallen man might have been redeemed any other way, or whether a drop of his blood was not enough to redeem man? because we see here it is determined and articled in the covenant of redemption, that he should die; Jehovah will have the Mediator dying; and be possible what may to God's sovereignty, (which we would not make to clash with his justice, nor his justice with his sovereignty) this may bound and limit us, that it is concluded in this covenant of redemption, that the Mediator shall lay down his life; and it being concluded, it is certain, 1. That God hath given man a law, threatning him, that if he should break that law, he should die. 2. That all mankind, and so the elect, have broken that law, and so are liable to the threatning and curse. 3. That the Mediator became Cautioner, and undertook to satisfy for the elect's debt; it was necessary that he should die, because he undertook to pay their debt, and to satisfy for their sin, which was death by the law to them:

them: And so the justice of God is vindicate; He cannot be called unjust, nor partial, nor unholy, though he do not actually punish every sinner, that hath sinned in his own person, because God's holiness and justice appear conspicuously, that he would rather execute what was due to the elect, on his own Son, than that their sins should go unpunished: And, considering the nature of the Mediator's death, that it was a violent and cursed death, that which had extreme anguish and sorrow going before, and alongst with it; it shews that the Lord hath purposely taken that way, to make it known, how bitter a thing sin is, how terrible a thing his wrath is, and how holily severe his law is, and to let all know that it is a dreadful thing to come in tops with him, who did so put his own Son to it.

Use 1. This *Doctrine*, tho' it hath been spoken to before, is a sovereign doctrine, yea, the sovereign doctrine, and the corner-stone of all religion, that Christ hath died for the sins of his people: It gives us access to preach the gospel, which is therefore called, *the preaching of Christ crucified*. Know therefore, and believe, that the Mediator died, and that it behoved him to die; for it was required as a condition of the covenant of redemption, to be performed by him; to which he yielded, and consented. O what love is here, to article such a thing before sinners had any being! It was more than to be hungry and thirsty, and weary; he behoved to die, and to be made a curse: When sacrifices and burnt-offerings will not do, he says, *Lo, I come, in the volume of thy book it is written of me; I delight to do thy will, O my God!* I heartily accept of the bargain.

Use 2. It speaks a sadly alarming word to all you who are secure Atheists, and care not for the wrath of God; O what will become of you, when the wrath of God and you shall meet! If sin brought the Creator to death, O what wrath shall ye come under, when ye shall be put to reckon for your own sins! The smiting of the Shepherd was more than if all the sheep had been smitten; and though now ye think little of sin, yet the day comes, wherein ye shall know to your cost, that *it is an evil and bitter thing to depart from God*, and that *it is a fearful thing to fall into the hands of the living God*.

Use 3. See here the necessity of making use of Christ's death; either ye must do it, or die, and come under the curse of God yourselves; there is not a mids: If ye have sin, how will it be gotten put by, and satisfied for; not by your prayers, let be by a laughter or smile, nor by your living of an honest life, as ye call it; Christ had infinitely more of this than any of you, and yet he got not sin so put by: We may here allude to that, Eccl. viii. 8. *There is no discharge in that war, neither shall wickedness deliver those that are given to it.* Death, when it hath a commission, and God's terror backing it, O how will it handle the secure stubborn sinner, when the hand of God shall pursue him eternally! Alas! what are many doing that never fear the wrath of God, that suspend, put off, and delay the closing of their accompts, and all endeavours to die to sin, and to live to righteousness, and either pass over their days as Atheists, or as formal hypocrites? and such are some of you that hear me this day, who never seek to be found in Christ, nor to improve his death to the mortifying of sin: What will ye do in the day when ye shall be called to a reckoning? Ye will curse the day that ever ye heard the gospel, and that this was concluded, that Christ should die; it will be the favour of death to you thro' all eternity, and will be the most soul-searching and tormenting word that ever ye heard; and ye will wish that the work of redemption had never been heard of, nor resolved upon.

Use 4. It is a comfortable and encouraging word to sensible sinners; such, betaking themselves to Christ, may be sure to get good of him, for he hath paid the price already, and hath given his word for it, *That such as believe in him, shall never perish, but that he will raise them up at the last day.* Ye would not think, that it will be displeasing or dissatisfying to the Father, or to the Son, that ye come to him, and take hold of him; for it was for that end, that God sent him, and and that he laid down his life, and died; (but he dies no more) it will be no trouble to him, but satisfaction to his soul, for all the travel of it, to make application of his purchase to you: And seeing it will not displease, but be most acceptable to him, that ye believe on him, and be saved by him; and since not believing, rubs shame in a manner upon him, why do you not betake yourselves unto him by faith, for his satisfaction, and your own salvation?

2*dly*, He not only died, but it is said, *He poured out his soul unto death;* which implies two things.
1. The intenseness of it, it was an uncouth and strange death; not only was his body afflicted, but his soul was poured out. 2. It looks to his goodwill, readiness and chearfulness in dying; Father, (as if he had said) must I die? and wilt thou have my soul sorrowful and heavy? I am content to be so, thou shalt have my life: He comes not prig- ging

ging to die, (to speak so) but casts down his blessed life at his Father's feet, and plentifully gives it out to the uttermost; so that he will not, as it were, leave one drop of his blood, but will needs pour and yett it out in abundance, even all of it.

Hence *Observe,* " That our blessed Lord Jesus " was most hearty in laying down his life for sin- " ners, was most chearful in undertaking, and most " willing and chearful in executing what he did " undertake." He makes not two words of the bargain, (to speak so) but when sacrifice and offering will not do it, as it is, Psal. xl. then says he; *Lo, I come, in the volume of thy book it is written of me; I delight to do thy will, O my God.* There is no standing, nor disputing here on the Mediator's side, but a present willing and heartsom undertaking: Therefore, Prov. viii. he says, *Though he was continually with the Father, even from everlasting, yet his delights were with the sons of men, rejoicing in the habitable parts of the earth;* Ere ever the world was made, ere ever there was a sinner in being to be redeemed, he rejoiced before hand, thinking there would be such an opportunity to manifest his good-will, grace and mercy, and if we look through the gospel, how often will we find this made good? *No man taketh my life from me,* but (saith he) *I lay it down of myself, and I take it up again:* And when they came to take him, and Peter drew his sword, he said, *Could not I have commanded twelve legions of angels: but all that is written of me must be fulfilled:* I have bargained to lay down my life, and it must be; and, *I have a baptism to be baptised with, and how am I straitned till it be accomplished?* And when it came to be accomplished, though he gave evidences of his power, in *making them fall backward,* who came to apprehend him, yet he raises them again, and goes with them; and when they mock him, and buffet him, and nod the head at him, and bring him to the bar, and question him, and when they said, *If thou be the King of Israel, come down from the cross, and we will believe thee;* which we may think he could have done, though they were but tempting him; yet in all these he was silent, and never opens his mouth, till he comes to that, *It is finished:* He never spake a repining word: It was wonderfully much to suffer, and to die so chearfully, but to pour out his soul unto death, to take his life in his own hand, and to be so holily prodigal of it, as to pour it out, there having never been such a precious life, and so precious blood poured out, this was much more.

Use. It shews what esteem ye should have of souls, and every one of you of your own souls:

Our Lord Jesus poured out his soul unto death for souls; he values souls so much, that he gave his precious life for them: Therefore it is said, 1 Pet. i. 19. *We are not redeemed with corruptible things, as silver and gold, but with the precious blood of Christ:* If he esteemed so much of souls, what will it be thought of, when ye waste your souls, and ye know not whereon. He bought souls dear, and ye sell them cheap, for a little silver and gold, or for that which is worse, and far less worth: What an unsuitableness is here betwixt Christ's estimation of souls and yours, betwixt his buying them at so dear a rate, and your casting them away, for that which is very vanity? What do the most part of you get for your souls? Some a bit of land, some a house, some a feckless pleasure, some a sport, some the satisfaction of their lusts, or a moment's sinful mirth; O pitifully poor bargain! what will become of the mirth, or lust, or pleasure, of this house, or of that land, when kings, and great men will ly crawling, like so many worms before the Lamb? Ye will not get your houses or land with you, ye will not get leave to wear your brave clothes, ye will have no silver nor gold in your purse in that day; and suppose ye had it, the redemption of the soul is precious, and ceaseth for ever by any such price: 'Tis a wonderful thing, that when Christ esteems so much of souls, that sinners should esteem so little of them; is it not just that such souls go to hell, when they esteemed them so little worth?

Use 2. It should teach you to love, and heartily to welcome this Lord Jesus Christ; what argument of love and of trust, what motive to welcome him can there be, if this be not, that he spared not his life, but poured it out unto death for sinners? How long shall we halt betwixt Christ and Belial? We dow not endure to mortify a lust, to want our sport and laughter, or a bit of our credit or honour, though it should cost us the want of Christ: But, O ingrate fools! is that a becoming requital to him that took his innocent soul in his hand, and poured it out for sinners, and when he was some way melted like lead in the fire of God's wrath, was content to yett it forth abundantly, out of love to their salvation? Should it not rather call for love to him, for trusting and welcoming of him, and to suffering for his sake, if he call you to it? Will ye skar to hazard your life for him, that poured out his soul for sinners! It would do a soul good to think how willingly and chearfully he suffered; But, alas! how reluctantly, and unwillingly come we under suffering for him? However, let

me

me commend these *three* words to you. 1. Love him, *For even Publicans will love those that love them*; and give Christ love for love. 2. Credit and trust him, do not look for ill at his hand; what ground is there to suspect him? It is his glory to do good to sinners, and he counts them his triumph and spoil; and to make conquest of them, he poured out his soul unto death, or, as the word is, Phil. ii. *He emptied himself;* which seems to look to this word of the prophet. And is not that warrant sufficient for you, to trust and credit him, and to lay the weight of what concerns you upon him? And, 3. Welcome him, which is a fruit of faith and love; he is a sweet Wooer, he is that *good Shepherd, that laid down his life for his sheep;* He gave himself for his church, as it is, Eph. v. Therefore, I say, welcome him; this is the great thing the gospel aims at; such expressions are a great depth, and it would require time to read, to ponder them, and to wonder at them; and we would be much in praying for a right uptaking of them.

3*dly*, From the connection, *because* he hath poured out his soul unto death; *Observe,* " That " our Lord Jesus his willing condescending to die, " is most acceptable to the Father." Therefore, he says, *I will give him a portion with the great, and he shall divide the spoil with the strong,* because he hath done so and so; and all the promises made to him confirm this: That is a wonderful word, John x. 17. *Therefore does my Father love me, because I lay down my life for my sheep.* The only begotten, and well beloved Son of the Father, cannot but be loved; yet, he says, *Therefore,* or on this account, *does my Father love me:* That is, I am Mediator, the Father's Minister, Steward, or Depute, in this work of redemption of sinners; and because I so willingly and chearfully lay down my life for them, he hath given me this victory and glory. So well pleasing to God is the willing and chearful death of the Mediator, that it should be admired by us, and should have this weight laid on it by us, that seeing chearfulness in obedience is so acceptable to God, we should study it, for he loves a chearful giver, and chearfulness in any duty: It is much we have this word to speak of to you, many nations never heard of it, and ye would make some other use of it, than if ye had never heard of it; O but it will be dreadful to such as have heard it, and do slight it! their souls shall be poured out into hell, even squeezed, and wrung eternally by the wrath of God; therefore look not lightly on it, do not think all this transaction of grace to be for nought, if we were serious; we would wonder what it means. Alas! we think little or nothing to make our peace with God, and yet all this business is, ere the matter can be brought about. It is a great evidence of the stupidity, senslesness and absurd unbelief of many, that they think nothing of sin and wrath, and of the hazard that their souls are in; and that they look at peace with God, as an easy business: But one day it will be found to be a great matter to be at peace with him, that sin is bitter, and wrath heavy; and that to be in good terms with God, is better than a thousand worlds: God himself make you wise to think seriously on it in time.

SERMON LXVI.

Isaiah liii. 12. *Therefore will I divide him a portion with the great, and he shall divide the spoil with the strong; because he hath poured out his soul unto death: And he was numbred with the transgressors, and he bare the sins of many, and made intercession for the transgressors.*

THERE was never bargain so seriously entred in as this betwixt Jehovah and the Mediator, never bargain was of such concernment and weight: It is therefore no marvel it be insisted upon. The prophet hath been holding forth the terms and conditions of it on both sides, and now he sums them up in the last verse, that the business may be left clear and distinct; setting forth what the Lord Jehovah engageth for to the Mediator, and what the Mediator engageth for to Jehovah; only with this difference, that in the former part of the chapter, the Mediator's engagement is first set down, and then what are the promises that the Lord Jehovah made to him; but in this verse, where the covenant is resumed, what the Lord engageth for to the Mediator is first set down, and then what the Mediator is to perform in the last place; to shew (as I said) the mutualness of the covenant of redemption, and that it is but one bargain, one link whereof cannot be loosed on either side.

In the last part of the verse, what the Mediator is to perform, is set down in four expressions, as past and done, because of the certainty and efficacy of the Mediator's sufferings, and of his performing what he undertook, and of divine justice its acceptation thereof. The *1st* is, *because he hath poured out his soul unto death*: It was proposed to the Mediator

diator to die, which he undertook, and in the execution, goes chearfully about it; *He poured his soul unto death,* without any prigging; grace and love (to speak so with reverence) were so liberal and prodigal of the life of our Lord Jesus, for the salvation of lost sinners; that his blessed Soul was separate from his Body, and he made obnoxious to the curse, which most willingly he under-went; his life or soul was poured out unto death. The 2d is, *He was numbred with the transgressors;* which implies three things, 1. It supposes that he was indeed no transgressor, there was no guile found in his mouth; yet he behoved to stoop so low, as to be reckoned among, or numbred with transgressors. As the former expression holds out the painfulness of his death, so this holds out the ignominy of it: He not only died, and behoved to die, but he was looked upon as a despicable person, even so despicable, that Barabbas, a thief and robber, was preferred unto him: Of this we spake from verse 3. *He was despised and rejected of men.* 2. It implies mens ingratitude, that when our blessed Lord came to redeem them, they did not count him worthy to live, but looked upon him as a transgressor; this was also fulfilled in the history of the gospel, as John xviii. 30. they say unto Pilate, *If he were not a malefactor, we would not have delivered him unto thee.* 3. It implies the low condescendence, and depth of the love of our Lord Jesus Christ, which hath no bottom; he will not only die, but die a shameful and cursed death, and take on reproach and ignominy with the debt of sinners; when they are despising him; the Cautioner must not only die, but die a shameful death: some deaths are creditable and honourable, and men will with a sort of vanity affect them; but it behoved not to be so with our Lord Jesus, when he entred himself sinners Cautioner; he must not only die, but be despicable in his death, as it is, chap. l. 5. *He gave his back to the smiters, and his cheeks to them that plucked off the hair, he hid not his face from shame and spitting;* because it was so articled and agreed upon; *When he was reviled, he reviled not again:* O what condescending-love shines forth here, in the Mediator! It was much to pay the debt, and die, but more in his dying, to be counted the transgressor; much to be Cautioner, but more to be counted the dyvour: As if some wicked and perverse officer, seizing on the cautioner, should not only arrest him for the debt, and exact it off him, but account and call him the dyvour debtor; yet he bears all patiently. It would learn us to bear reproach for him; he bare much more for us, than we can bear for him: He was railed on, reviled, buffeted, and spitted on; they in derision, said, *Hail king of the Jews;* they mocked him, nodded the head at him, hanged him up betwixt two thieves, as the most eminent malefactor of the three; and Mark saith, chap. xv. 28. That *this scripture was fulfilled, which saith, And he was numbred with the transgressors:* God had appointed it; and the Mediator had condescended to it; and therefore it behoved to be: We spake to the matter of this before, and will not now insist on it any further.

The 3d is, *He bare the sins of many;* which is also casual, as the former are: It is put in here, 1. To shew the end of his dying, and the nature of his death; his death was a cursed death, but not for his own sin; but for the sins of others, even to pay the debt that was owing by his elect: The *many* here, are the same *many* spoken of in the former verse, *who by his knowledge are justified.* It is not the sins of *all* that Christ bare, but the sins of *many;* and the *many* whose sins he bare, are the *many* that are justified; and all who are justified, their sins he bare, and of no more: so that as many as have their sins born by Christ, are justified; and whoever are justified, had their sins born by him. 2. It shews also, how the sins of these *many* are taken away, it was by Christ's bearing the punishment due for their sins; this is that which we spake to, from verse 6. *The Lord hath laid on him the iniquities of us all:* In a word, it is this, the Mediator articleth, and agreeth to take on the guilt of the sins of the elect, tho' not their sins themselves, formally considered: he took the deserving, or burden of their debt: Of this we have also spoken before, and will not therefore insist any more particularly on it.

The 4th and last article, or part of the condition required of the Mediator, is, *He made intercession for the transgressors.* There was more required of him, than to die, and to die such a death for the elect's sins; he must also make application of his death, and he will do that likewise; whereupon is founded his intercession, that the benefit of his death and satisfaction may be applied, and made forthcoming to them; which is set down in these words, *He made intercession for the transgressors;* wherein also we are to carry along the thoughts of his condescending love, who not only will satisfy for the elect's debt, and procure to them righteousness and eternal life, but when they continue in opposition to him, will make intercession for the application thereof to them; he having a number given to him, not only to pay their debt, by dying for them, but also actually to apply the benefits of his death and purchase to them, according to that, John vi. 39. *This* is the will of him that sent me, that, of all that he hath given me, I should lose nothing, but raise them up at the last day: These four do plainly and summarily comprehend the Mediator's engagement in the covenant of redemption, as to his priestly office; and having spoken somewhat to the first three, we shall insist a little on this last, concerning his *Intercession*.

For clearing whereof, when he prayed on the cross, Luke xxiii. 34. *Father, forgive them, for they know not what they do;* this was in part fulfilled: But his praying, or making intercession for transgressors, is to be considered two ways, 1. As he was a Man under the law, and so he was to pray for other transgressors, than the elect only; as Stephen, following his example, did, Acts vii. 60. when he said, *Lord, lay not this sin to their charge.* 2. As he is Mediator, and so he prays only for the elect; as is clear, John xvii. 9. And his intercession, thus considered, is always effectual, and runs in the channel of the covenant of redemption, and is commensurable and of equal extent with his death. His intercession, in the first sense, is more largely extended; he might, considered as Man under the law, have interceeded for his enemies, that were not elected: Therefore we take his intercession here in the second sense, as he is Mediator. And as Matthew, chap. viii. 17. applies his bearing of our griefs, and carrying of our sorrows, spoken of, verse 4. of this chap. to his carrying of our temporal bodily infirmities; So there may be an allusion to this, in the Lord's prayer on the cross. We mark this distinction, because Arminians, that pretend to an universal redemption, plead also for an universal intercession: And on this ground, they say, that Christ prayed for many that went to hell. But we answer, that our blessed Lord Jesus did not there, if he prayed for any such, interced as Mediator properly, but as Man under the law; even as in his prayer in the garden, when his holy human nature sinlesly scarred at the bitter cup, he prayed, *Father, if it be possible, let this cup depart from me*; and it was agreeable to the human nature, to seek innocently to eschew the drinking of such a cup; but when, in the same prayer, he speaks as Mediator, he says, "Not my will, but thine be done; and, for this cause came I unto this hour:" So when he preached as Man, and a Minister of the circumcision, he says, "O Jerusalem, Jerusalem, how often would I have gathered thee, and thou wouldst not!" Whereas, if we consider him as Mediator, he doth what he will, and calleth none but they come, and willeth none to be gathered, but such as are gathered: The intercession here meaned, is that which is an article of the covenant of redemption, and a piece of Christ's priestly office, to which the promise in the first part of the verse is made; and therefore we have here clear access to speak of it, according as the New Testament holds it out to us.

1. Then we observe this *Doctrine* from it, "That according to the covenant of redemption, our Lord must not only die, but also interceed for transgressors, or sinners; or, It is a part of our Lord's office, agreed upon in the covenant of redemption, that he should be Intercessor for transgressors." It is on this ground that it is said, Psal. cx. 4. *The Lord hath sworn, and will not repent, Thou art a Priest for ever, after the order of Melchisedek;* He is a Priest after Melchisedek's order, and not after the order of Aaron; and, Rom. viii. 34. he is said to be *at the right hand of God, making intercession for us*: It is said likewise, Heb. vii. 25. that *he is able to save to the uttermost, all that come to God by him; seeing he ever liveth to make intercession for them.* So, 1 John ii. 1. it is said, *If any man sin, we have an Advocate with the Father, Jesus Christ the righteous:* And frequently elsewhere, it is in scripture attributed to him. If it be asked, Why behoved Jesus Christ the Mediator, to be an Intercessor: We answer, For these *three* reasons: 1. It was suitable to the glory of God, that the great Lord-deputy, appointed for the ingathering of elect sinners, should be furnished with this office; and his intercession is derived from it, Heb. vii. 35. *He is able to save to the uttermost, seeing he ever liveth to make intercession for us:* He cannot sit up, nor fail in proving himself to be an able Saviour, because he lives for ever to interceed. 2. It is suitable and meet for the glory of the Mediator, and of his priesthood, that he should not be a Priest for a time only, but for ever; therefore, when he is brought in as a Priest, Psal. cx. compared with Heb. vii. he is preferred to the order of Aaron, and is said *to be a Priest for ever, after the order of Melchisedek; by so much as he is Surety of a better testament: They were many, because they were not suffered to continue; but this Man, because he continueth for ever, hath an unchangeable priesthood.* It was meet, in respect of the consolation that believers in him have from this his intercession; there had been a defect in the consolation of believers, if he had not been Intercessor; but seeing, as it is, Heb. x. 19. *We have such an high Priest over the house of God, we have boldness to enter into the holiest, by a new and living way;* and *may draw near with full assurance of faith.* And

that which gives us this boldness, is that, (as it is, Heb. iv. 15, 16.) "We have not an high Priest which cannot be touched with the feeling of our infirmities, but was in all points tempted like as we are:" Then follows, "Let us therefore come boldly to the throne of grace, that we may obtain mercy, and find grace to help in time of need." 4. We may add, that it is suitable, for this reason, to wit, if we consider, and compare the type with the antitype, Exod. xxx. 10. and, Lev. xvi. compared with Heb. ix. The high priest had sacrifices prescribed to him for himself, and for the people, when he went once in the year, into the most holy, with the blood of the sacrifice; which signified, that Christ, after the laying down of his life, "was to enter in to heaven, there to appear in the presence of God for us," Heb. ix. 24.

This is a point which may yield us many and great *uses*, as, 1. For *information*, to clear us about Christ's intercession. 2. For *consolation*, to shew us the advantages that flow to believers from it. 3. For *direction* in duty, to learn us what use we should make of it. And, 4. For *reproof* and *conviction*, for, and of the sin of our much slighting and neglecting this part of Christ's priestly office.

As for the *first*, It serves, we say, for *information*; and to let us see that we have an excellent high Priest, who is not only answerable to the type, in dying, but also in interceeding; who died, that he might make application of what he purchased by his death.

For further clearing and prosecuting of this *use*, we shall speak a little to some few questions; As, 1. What this intercession is? 2. Who interceeds? 3. For whom? 4. For what? 5. How this intercession is performed? 6. What are the grounds on which it is founded?

For the *first*, What this intercession is in general? And for clearing it, ye would consider, what it is not; and, 1. There is here no humbling of the Mediator in way of supplication, as he prayed when on earth, or as we pray, or as one man intreats or interceeds with another; that way of interceeding is inconsistent with his exaltation, his humiliation being perfected, and he being now exalted at the right hand of God. 2. It is no verbal thing, no bringing forth or uttering of words; there is no such language in our Lord's intercession: and so we are not to conceive of his intercession, as if he had made a formal prayer; that manner of dealing, or proceeding, is not now betwixt God and the Mediator. 3. Neither doth this his intercession consist in any new particular act of his will; as if he did act or will something that he did not before; therefore he is said to *live for ever, to make intercession, and to abide a Priest continually*: His intercession is continual, as is clear, Heb. vii. 3, 25. his being in heaven, and appearing there in our name, is his intercession. And therefore, 2. Let us see, in the next place, what it is? And more generally, we may take it up in such expressions, as the scriptures make use of to hold it out by; and in the similitude and analogy whence it is borrowed; for it is a borrowed thing, as the covenant of redemption is, from compacts among men, because we cannot take up divine and mysterious things, except they be exprest after the manner of men for our capacity; Such as this, as if a king's son were interposing for a person not in good terms with the king, or for whom he would have some benefit from the king his father: The similitude seems indeed to be drawn from this, yet it must not be astricted thereto; therefore, 1 John ii. 1. he is called an *Advocate with the Father*; and yet he doth not advocate our cause verbally, as we said before; And, 1 Tim. ii. 5. "There is one God, and one Mediator betwixt God and men;" where the apostle is speaking of praying: And here he is said to make intercession for us, as the high priest did in the name of the people. In a word, it is our Lord Jesus Christ his making of what he hath purchased, and hath engaged to him in the covenant of redemption, effectually forthcoming for the behoof of the people, as if he were agenting their cause, as an advocate in heaven; which is so held forth, for the help of our faith; that the Mediator having made his testament, and confirmed it by his death, is looking well that his death, and the benefits purchased to elect sinners thereby, may be made effectual; and is as it were lying as agent and advocate at court, to procure and bring about this business, according to that, John xvii. 19, 20. 24. "For their sakes I sanctify myself, that they also may be sanctified, &c. Neither pray I for these alone, &c. and, Father, I will that these whom thou hast given me, may be with me where I am." It is even that all may be made good to them, for whom he sanctified himself; and the effectual making out of that which he hath purchased to them, that is called his *intercession*.

2*dly*, Who makes intercession? It is not enough that Christ, as man, makes intercession; but it is Christ Mediator, God and man in one Person; It being an error of the Papists, to make the intercession of Christ to be a thing performed by the human nature only, which lesseneth the consolation of believers, and is inconsistent with the union of the two natures, and detracts from the weight that his Godhead gives to his intercession.

3dly, For whom does he intercede? There are here extremes on both hands to be eschewed. 1. Some make his intercession over broad, as if he interceeded for all the world: this he expresly denies, John xvii. 9. *I pray not for the world;* and his intercession being grounded on his death and satisfaction, it must be of equal extent therewith, and must relate to the covenant of redemption, wherein so many were given him to be redeemed by his death. 2. Others make his intercession too narrow, in making it only for them that actually believe: He also refutes this opinion, John xvii. 20. by saying, *Neither pray I for these alone, but for all that shall believe on me through their word:* And it is always on this ground that he interceeds, to wit, because *they are given;* so that it is for the elect, converted or unconverted, that he interceeds. The reason why we mark this, is to overturn thereby two corrupt distinctions that are made use of, to bring in an universal intercession, as well as an universal redemption. (1.) Some make his intercession common to all; but we, according to the scripture, acknowledge no such intercession to belong to Christ, especially as Mediator: however, he might, as man, under the law, have prayed for some that shall not be actually saved, as he commands one man to pray for other men, yet not for all men simply. (2.) Others make a conditional intercession for all, as they make a conditional redemption of all, and make both absolute for believers only, which is also corrupt; for, considering the object of his intercession, as Mediator, to be only the elect, as indeed they are, it overturns both this, and the former opinion: if he prayed not for all, he died not for all; the one whereof is grounded on the other.

4thly, For what doth he intercede? In general, for all that is conditioned to him, in the covenant, for the behoof of his people; he prays for the fulfilling of all the articles of the covenant, as that all the elect, who are not regenerate, may be regenerate, and made believers; that many through his knowledge may be justified; that these that are regenerate, and believers, and by faith have betaken themselves to him, may be justified, pardoned, and received in favour, friendship, and fellowship with God; that believers may be keeped from temptation; that temptations may be prevented, and they made to persevere; that Satan may not make their faith to fail them, as he designs; and the Lord gives account of his design, Luke xxii. 32. *Satan hath sought to winnow you, but I have prayed that thy faith fail not;* that they and their prayers and services may be accepted; that the suits and supplications that they present, and put up in his name, may get a hearing; that they may be carried on in the gradual advances of sanctification, to the end of their faith, the salvation of their souls; that they may be glorified, and be where he is, to behold his glory: In a word, he interceeds for every thing needful, and for every thing promised to them, his intercession being as broad as his purchase.

5thly, How doth he perform this part of his priestly office for his people? It is performed by his entry into the most holy place, in our nature and name, as having satisfied justice, and vanquished death, where he appears before God for us; so that we are to look to Christ's being in heaven, not simply as glorifying himself, or as glorified in himself, for himself, but as our Head and Forerunner, to answer all that can be said against his elect, for whom he suffered and satisfied, as it is, Heb. ix. 23, 24. *It was therefore necessary, that the patterns of things in the heavens should be purified with these, but the heavenly things themselves with better sacrifices; for Christ is not entred into the holy places made with hands, which are the figures of the true, but into heaven itself, now to appear in the presence of God for us;* so that our Lord Jesus, by his entry into heaven, doth declare (I mean materially) his victory in our name, and appears there, as a publick, and not as a private person: his entry into heaven is not to be looked on as the entry of Moses, or of Elias, but as the entry of him who is Head of the elect, whose entry there is a declaration of what he would be at: As by the power of his Godhead, he conveyed himself in thither; so he hath possession in our name, and according to the covenant declares, That these whose room he sustains, may and must be admitted to glory; and we must conceive a special efficacy in his being there; for procuring to them what he hath purchased. 2. His intercession is performed through the efficacy of his blood and satisfaction, flowing from the nature of the covenant, which hath a moral real cry, for making effectual what he by his death hath procured; as the apostle, speaking of Abel's blood, and of making application of Christ's blood, Heb. xii. 24. saith, *It speaketh better things than the blood of* Abel; for Abel's blood had a demerit in it to cry guilt, and could not but have a curse following it, because God had cursed the shedder of blood; but Christ's blood, considered as the price of redemption for the elect, hath an invaluable and upconceivable merit and worth in it, and must have a cry for the blessings purchased to them by it. 3. He performs this his intercession by his constant care, and by his continual willingness, and actual willing, that what he hath purchased for his elect people may be applied to them, that such and such persons may be brought to believe, that upon their believing they may be pardoned, delivered from snares and temptations, keeped in favour with God, may be accepted in their performances, &c. for he had that prayer, John xvii. 20, 24. and he continues to have that same sympathy; his way on earth was always sinless, but now is glorious and majestick, suited to his glorified state; he continues to interceed according as he intended; and his actual willingness is a main part of his intercession, which is not in renewing of acts (to speak so) but in his continuing desire and willingness, that what good he hath purchased may be conferred, according to the covenant; for Christ in heaven is still a true Man, and hath a will, as he had on earth, continuing to seek that they may be glorified with him, for whom he satisfied: And this actual willing, desiring and affecting, that such a thing should be, is called his intercession, because it cannot but be so esteemed, as to have the effect to follow, according to the covenant, as he says, John xi. 41, 42. *I thank thee, Father, that thou hast heard me, and I know that thou hearest me always*. This, as to his actual willing, cannot but be in heaven; however, we are sure that he is there, and in our name, and that his death and blood-shed hath an efficacy to bring about what he hath purchased; and that his will and affection are the same, and have an efficacy with them, and the effect certainly following, so as nothing can go wrong there, more than a man that hath a just cause in a court of judicature, and an able advocate, with much moyen, to agent and plead it before a just judge, can be wronged, or lose his cause.

6thly, The grounds of his intercession, are, 1. The excellency of his Person, who, though he be Man, yet he is God also, *equal with the Father, the brightness of his glory, and the express image of his Person, and upholding all things by the word of his power*, as it is, Heb. i. 2. which cannot but add weight to his intercession, as well as to his satisfaction, the Person that interceeds being God. The 2d is his satisfaction, which is the ground of his intercession; for upon his satisfaction he maketh intercession, even as if a cautioner would say, I have paid such a man's debt, and therefore he ought to be absolved: Therefore, 1 John ii. 1, 2. these two are joined, "We have an Advocate with the "Father, Jesus Christ the righteous, and he is "the propitiation for our sins:" So Rom. viii. 34. they are joined, "It is Christ that died, who is "at the right-hand of God, and maketh interces-"sion for us." 3. The covenant of redemption is the great ground on which his intercession is founded; such and such persons are given to Christ, and such privileges and benefits offered to be conferred upon them, on condition the Mediator would undertake, and satisfy for them; and he having undertaken, and paid the price, there is good ground for his interceeding, for the making application of the purchase; therefore he says, John xvii. *Trine they were, and thou gavest them me*, &c. This gives him right to plead and interceed for them, seeing he hath endured soul-travel for them, he ought to see his seed, and to have many justified, and freed from the curse and condemnation that they were obnoxious to, as the fruit of that sore soul travel.

In and from the consideration of these, we may gather what is the nature of Christ's intercession, and how we may make use of it, and how particularly we should beware of a carnal mistake in many about his intercession, as if he were praying in heaven, as a distinct Party from God. It is true, he is a distinct Person of the glorious Trinity, but not a distinct Party in interceeding, as some ignorantly conceive of him; and therefore think him easier to have access to than the Father, and therefore will pray him to pray the Father for them; as if, when they prayed to him, they were not praying to the Father, or as if there were not one Object of worship. This flows from ignorance of the nature of Christ's intercession, and is unbecoming a Christian; for, supposing a man to rest by faith on Christ, the Father is content and well pleased to pardon him, as well as the Son is, because he is engaged in the covenant of redemption so to do; and, if he be not a believer, neither the Father nor the Son will respect him: Our use-making of Christ's intercession doth consist rather in the founding of our hope of speeding with God on it, as on his satisfaction, than in putting up words of prayer to him, to interceed for us, as if he were to pray in heaven, as he did on earth, or as one man interceeds for another. The point is sublimely spiritual, and someway tickle; and I indeed fear to enter on more *Uses*, at least for the time: Only remember, that he is an Intercessor; and learn to make right use of him as an Intercessor: And the Lord himself make the benefit of his intercession forthcoming to us.

SERMON

SERMON LXVII.

Isaiah liii. 12.------*And he made intercession for the transgressors.*

IF Christ were known in the greatness and vast extent of his worth, O how lovely would he be! How incomprehensibly full are his offices of grounds of consolation to his people! But the mean and low thoughts we have of him, and the poor consolation we feed on, do evidence much ignorance of him, and much unbelief of the solid worth and fulness that is in him, and in his priestly Office in particular; and yet, O how full of consolation is it! *Such a high Priest became us,* Heb. vii. 26. even such a high Priest as sinners had need of: There hath been much spoken of one part of his priesthood, to wit, his *sacrifice*, and offering up of himself, in the former *verses* of this chapter. Now, ere the prophet close, he gives a hint of the other part of his priestly Office, to wit, of his *intercession,* a main commendation of Christ's fulness; it is that which evidenceth him to be a Saviour, *able to save to the uttermost such as come unto God through him, because he lives for ever to make intercession for them;* as it is, Heb. vii. 25. And it is a piece of the consolation of God's people, that Jesus Christ hath this office by the Father's allowance, and that it is articled in the covenant of redemption betwixt the Father and him, that as he shall " pour out " his soul unto death, be numbred with trans- " gressors, bear the sins of many, so he shall make " intercession for the transgressors;" Therefore, Heb. vii. 21. he is said " to be made an high " Priest with an oath, by him that said unto him, " Psal. cx. 4. The Lord sware, and will not re- " pent, Thou art a Priest for ever, after the or- " der of Melchisedeck." He was a Priest on earth, by offering himself in a sacrifice, and by interceeding for elect sinners; and he is a Priest in heaven by his intercession, and therefore is preferred to all the priests on earth, " Who did not continue by rea- " son of death, but he continues for ever;" and none can start him wrong, to speak so with reverence of him.

We shew, in our entring on this *verse*, that this his intercession is not to be astricted to his prayer on the cross, that was but one evidence or particular instance of it; but it takes in his whole intercession, because the scope of the Prophet here is to hold out, as what God promised to him on the one hand in the covenant of redemption, so on the other what he interceeds for; and so his intercession, looked on in the covenant of redemption, takes in his whole intercession, especially as it is gone about in heaven, by vertue of his sacrifice once for all offered up when he was on earth.

We *observed* the last day, That according to the covenant of redemption, our Lord Jesus Christ behoved not only to die, but to be an Intercessor; or, that it belongs to our Lord's priestly office, agreed upon in the covenant of redemption, not only to offer up himself in a sacrifice, and to die, but to make intercession for his people; *He made intercession for the transgressors;* or as all the rest may read in the future time, so this, *He shall make intercession for the transgressors;* but for the certainty of the thing, it is set down in the preterit, or by past time, the Father did take his word, and so it past as done in the court of heaven.

We cleared this point, and proposed *four uses* of it, the *first* whereof was to inform us anent Christ's fulness, to discover his unsearchable riches, and to let us see what an excellent high Priest we have, that continues an Intercessor: Not only hath he once for all offered up his Sacrifice, as the high-priest under the law did once a year, but hath entred within the vail, to interceed, and thereby to make the benefits of his purchase effectual and forthcoming to them for whom his sacrifice was offered; even as Lev. xvi. (where the rules for the high priest's offering are given) after he had offered the sacrifice, he took the blood, and entred within the vail; and by the sacrifice, and his going in to pray, he made atonement for the people typically: answerable to this, our Lord Jesus, *by his once offering, hath perfected for ever these who are sanctified;* and by his going within the vail, he executes this part of his priestly office, in interceeding for transgressors.

In prosecuting this *use*, we answered some *questions*, which now we shall not insist to repeat; only there is a short *question* or two, that further may be asked, which will clear the former, ere we go to the next *use;* and the first is, If our Lord, before he came in the flesh, discharged this part of his priestly office? The reason of the question or doubt is, because in the New Testament, his intercession is always, at least very ordinarily, subjoined to his ascension. The second is, How his intercession now differs from his intercession before his incarnation, or in what respects the consolation of believers, that flows from his intercession, is stronger now, than the consolation of believers

flowing

flowing there from, was before he was incarnate? As for the *first*, it cannot be denied, but Christ was Intercessor, since he had a church in the world; for it is a part of his priestly Office; and he was made a Priest, by the eternal oath, in the covenant of redemption, Psal. cx. 4. *The Lord hath sworn, and will not repent, Thou art a Priest for ever:* And he is said to have *an unchangeable Priesthood*; and there being but one way of access for sinners to heaven by Christ, who is called *the Lamb slain from the beginning of the world*, it must be holden for a sure conclusion, that his intercession is as old as his sacrifice: And he was Intercessor before his incarnation, in these three respects. 1. In respect of his office, being designed to be Intercessor; for (as we said) being designed to be Priest, and being Mediator before his incarnation, he behoved to be Intercessor also; for that way he did mediate; and the benefits that came to sinners from the beginning were the effects of his intercession; therefore, 1 Tim. ii. 5. it is said, *There is one God, and one Mediator between God and man, the Man Christ Jesus;* and there was never another real Mediator, however Moses might be called a typical one. 2. He was Intercessor before his incarnation, in respect of the merit of his future sacrifice. He did not before his incarnation interceed by vertue of his sacrifice actually offered, as now he doth; yet there was vertue which flowed from his sacrifice to be offered, to the people of God, as well then as now, when it hath been long since offered: The sins of all that ever were pardoned, were pardoned on the account of his sacrifice, and so also the spiritual benefits that did redound to them, did redound to them through his intercession then, as now, by vertue of the same sacrifice, because of the nature of the covenant, wherein it was agreed, that his sacrifice should be of the same efficacy before his incarnation, as after: For the day and hour was agreed upon, when he should offer that sacrifice; therefore it is said, that in *due time*, and in *the fulness of time*, he came and died. 3. He was Intercessor before his incarnation, as after it, in respect of the effects that followed on it, to the people of God then and now. The people of God, before his incarnation, had communion with God, and access to him, though not generally, in that degree of boldness; they presented their prayers through, and were beholden to the same Christ for a hearing, as we are; and therefore his intercession before his incarnation extended to them, as to us, in these respects, but with this difference. That he procured these benefits to them by vertue of the covenant, and the efficacy of his blood to be offered; and now he procures them to his people, since his incarnation and ascension, by vertue of the same ascension, and by vertue of the efficacy of the blood offered.

As to the 2d, How his mediation and intercession now differs since his ascension, from his intercession before it, as to the strengthning of the consolation of the people of God? For answer, 1. We lay down this for a conclusion, That though our Lord Jesus was Mediator, both before his incarnation, and now; yet since his ascension, he hath a new way of mediation and intercession, that exceedingly abounds to the strengthning of the consolation of his people; therefore it is ordinarily subjoined to his ascension, because of his new manner of discharging that his Office. It is true, there is no addition to that grace which is infinite in him, as if he could be more gracious; or as if, in respect of the covenant, there could be larger promises, as to essential things contained therein; but by taking on our nature, he hath a new way of being affected, and a new way of venting his affection to us, and is capable of another manner of touch with the infirmities of his people now, that he hath human bowels, though glorified and glorious; and the faith of his people hath a ground superadded, whereupon to expect the communication of that grace, mercy and goodness that is in him, though all the effects that followed to his people, before his incarnation, had respect to his future incarnation; so these effects had respects to his future intercession, in our nature, as well as to his dying, and laying down of the price: for these that were admitted to heaven ere he came in the flesh, were admitted the same way that we are.

But 2. and more particularly, if it be asked, Wherein this addition to the consolation of God's people by his intercession, after his ascension, kythes, or manifests itself? We may take it up in these *six* steps, which will also serve to illustrate the manner of his interceeding. 1. It kythes in this, that he appeareth in heaven in our nature; now the Man Christ is in heaven interceeding, and as Advocate answering for pursued sinners, or as Ambassador and Legate, agenting the affairs of them that are given him of the Father, as it is, Heb. vi. 24. *He is not entred into the holy places made with hands, but into heaven itself, to appear now in the presence of God for us;* where the apostle having been speaking of the excellency of his priesthood before, and comparing him with the type, he tells, that he is not entred into the typical tabernacle, but into heaven itself, to appear there in the presence of God for us: And this is a solid ground of consolation to a poor believing sinner, that he hath Christ in his own nature in heaven interceeding, that what he hath performed before, by vertue of his office, and of the efficacy of his sacrifice to be offered, when he should be incarnate; he now being incarnate, and ascended, performs it, we having God in our nature, become a Man like unto us, to care for the things of his people: and if any new question arise, or debate be started, to entertain the treaty, and to effectuate and make out their business, that nothing that concerns them misgive. 2. Their consolation is stronger in this respect, that he is in heaven, by vertue of the efficacy of his sacrifice already offered; as the high-priest, when he had offered the sacrifice, took the blood with him within the vail, and interceeded for the people, so our Lord Jesus is not now interceeding by vertue of his sacrifice to be offered, but by vertue of his sacrifice already offered, having entred into heaven, and taken the efficacy of his sacrifice with him, to enter it (to speak so) in the book of God, to stand on record: nay, he standeth there himself, to keep the memory of his blood fresh; and by each appearance of him there, who is never out of the sight of the majesty of God, there is still a representation of the worth and efficacy of his sacrifice, and for whom, and for what it was offered. 3. There is, by the Man Christ his being in heaven, this ground of consolation superadded, that he hath a sympathy with sinners otherwise than before, not as to the degree, nor as to the intenseness of his grace and mercy, (as I hinted before) but as to the manner how he is affected: so that he hath the true nature and sinless affection of a Man, and so hath bowels to be wrought upon, which kythed while he was on earth: Although we cannot take up the manner how he is touched, yet he is touched otherwise than God abstractly considered can be, and otherwise than an angel in heaven can be touched, as we may see, Heb. ii. 17. and iv. 15. *We have not an high Priest, which cannot be touched with the feeling of our infirmities, but was in all things tempted as we are, yet without sin:* And it behoved him to be like unto his brethren, that he might be a merciful and faithful high Priest, and have compassion on the ignorant, and them that are out of the way: He is sinners Friend, that is Intercessor, and such an Intercessor, that interceeds, from the impression that the holy and inconceivable sympathy, which he hath with his members, hath upon him, as his expression to Paul speaks forth, Acts ix. *Saul, Saul, why persecutest thou me?* counting himself a Sufferer with his people, which cannot but have its own influence on his interceffion, and add to the consolation of his people, that what he interceeds for the procurement of to them, is some way on this ground, as being a favour to their glorified Head. 4. Beside this sympathy, he hath a longing (to speak so) to have all the wants and defects of his people supplied and made up, and to have all the promises made to him, in behalf of the elect, fulfilled: not any such longing, as may in the least incroach on, or be inconsistent with the glory, and glorified state of our blessed Lord Jesus; but considering, that there is a near relation betwixt him and his followers, he being the Head, and they the members, and that he hath a sympathy and affection according to that relation, it is answerable and suitable, that he should desire, and some way long for the perfecting of his body the church, which, Eph i. is called, *The fulness of him who filleth all in all:* And he hath, no question, though a most pure and regular, yet a most kindly and strong desire and longing to have his body perfected, to have the elect gathered and brought in, as he had on earth a longing to have the work finished, which was given him to do: And this cannot but be a weighty part of his interceffion, and very comfortable to his people, his longing to have such and such a person converted, such and such a person more mortified and more perfected, and made more conform to him. There is a word, Heb. x. 13. that gives ground for this, *From henceforth expecting till all his enemies be made his footstool:* and what is spoken of this *expecting* of what is there mentioned, may be applied to other things: He is sure expecting, till all these promises, concerning his seeing of a seed, and the justifying and glorifying of many, be fulfilled, because that was promised him in the former *verse;* and expecting till he divide the spoil with the strong, as is promised in the former part of this *verse.* Now, our Lord Jesus having laid down his life, what is he doing in heaven? Even longing till these promises be fulfilled; not that he hath any longing that implies a defect in him simply, for he is absolutely glorified and glorious: yet such longing as is consistent with his glorified state, as (if we may make the comparison, though in every thing it be not suitable) the souls in heaven are perfectly glorified, yet they have a longing for the union of their bodies, for the perfecting of Christ's Body mystical, and for the union of all the members in a soul and body with the Head: So Christ, considered as Mediator, God-man, in heaven, hath a longing and holy desire, which agrees with his office, and is a qualification thereof, and doth nowise interrupt his happiness, that what concerns his elect may be perfected; therefore it is said in the *verse* before, *He shall see of the travel of his soul, and shall be satisfied*, importing, that it is a kind of new satisfaction to him, to get a sinner brought in to believe in him, and that he was waiting and longing for it. 5. He hath an actual waiting and continuing desire, that what he hath purchased to such and such persons may be applied; and this is not simply to will, for he had that on earth, but a declaring of it in heaven, that such and such things may be made forthcoming, and made effectual for the behoof of his members, that what he intended, in laying down his life, may be brought to pass: it is the Mediator God-man willing, whose will, as Man, being perfectly conform to the will of God, cannot be (to speak so) gainsaid, in whatsoever he willeth for the persons given him; and this is answerable to that, John xvii. 24. *Father, I will, that these whom thou hast given me may be with me where I am*, &c. I will, that such and such things engaged to me for them may be made good; that such and such persons be pardoned and brought through; that they may be preserved from temptation, may have their prayers heard; that they may be made to persevere, and may be glorified: So that we cannot imagine a case wherein God's people have need, and a promise in the covenant, but there is an actual willingness in Christ to have the need supplied, and the promise applied, according to the terms of the covenant. 6. We may take in here, not only Christ's willing that such a thing be done, but his effectual doing of it: And as this is a piece of his intercession, so it holds him forth to be a notable Intercessor; compare John xiv. 13, 16, 26. and xv. 26. and xvi. 7. In the xiv. chap. verse 13. he says, *Whatever ye ask in my name, I will do;* which we suppose respects Christ as Mediator, to be trusted as great Lord-deputy in our nature, to answer the prayers of his people, when put up according to the will of God. The xvi. chap. ver. 26. speaks of the Father's sending the comforter: and chap. xv. 26. of the Mediator sending the Comforter: So doth chap. xvi. 7. in one place it is, *What ye ask, I will do;* and in another place, it is, that *the Father will do*: it is all one; but it is to shew, that what the Father doth, he will do it by the Son, the Mediator, and he will actually perform it: and these three expressions, *I will pray the Father*, and *I will send*, and *the Father will send*, hold out this, that as the Father doth by the Son, so this is a part of Christ's intercession, effectually to procure and send out to us what we have need of. 7. In all this, there is in the Man Christ, an adoration of the Father, which, though it be not such as is unsuitable to his exalted and glorified state, yet is it becoming well him that is Man, and in that respect is at his right hand, to give to God. I shall only say further here, that tho' we cannot tell how he interceeds, to satisfy ourselves fully, yet this is clearly held forth to us, that whatsoever is needful, by his being in heaven, we may confidently expect it will be performed from the Man Christ, from him who is God-Man in one Person; and so his intercession with the Father is his actual procuring and doing such a thing, and that not as God simply, but as Mediator: Therefore these two words are put in the forecited expressions, *Whatsoever ye ask in my name, I will do it, that the Father may be glorified in the Son, and whom the Father will send in my name;* that is, by vertue of my procurement, by vertue of my sacrifice and intercession: and the sending of the Comforter shews, that it is performed by him that is God-Man, out of the respect he hath to his members, and on the account of his office, which he pursues for their edification: and so there is enough to answer the question, and abounding consolation to his people, which is the next *Use*.

Use 2. To shew the notable consolation that flows from this part of Christ's office. O what savouriness and unsearchable riches are in this part of his name, that our Lord Jesus, as Intercessor, appears in the presence of God for us! We shall speak here of these *five* things; 1. Wherein this is comfortable? or to the extent of it. 2. To the advantages that follow on it. 3. To the grounds of this consolation, which are confirmations of it. 4. To this, at what times, and particular occasions the people of God may, and ought in a special manner to make use of, and comfort themselves in it. And, 5. On what terms this consolation is allowed, that they grow not vain and proud of it.

For the *first*, Our Lord's intercession gives a *fourfold* extent of consolation, that makes it wonderful. 1. In its universality, as to the persons to whom it is extended, not indeed to all men in the world, but to all that will make use of it; and tho' it were simply of universal extent to all men in the world, yet it would comfort none but such as made use of it. And that vanity of the Arminians, that extends Christ's death and intercession to all, can truly say no more for solid comfort; for they are forced to say, That Christ died, and intended his death for many that will never get good of him: but we say, All that he intended should get good of his death, do get the intended good of it; yet, we say, that whoever will make use of him, shall get good both of his death, and of his intercession: So, Heb. vii. 25. *He is able to save to the uttermost, all that come unto God through him.* Though the cause seemed to be desperate, and the sentence pronounced, *Cursed is he that continues not in all things written in the law,* yet he is able to save them; therefore, 1 John ii. 2. 'tis said, *If any man sin,* O strange words! *We have an Advocate:* What! an Advocate for *any* man? yea, for any man that will make use of him: For, as we shew before, though 'tis true that his intercession is bounded to his elect, yet 'tis as true, that he refuses no cause that is honestly given him to plead; *If any man sin, we have an Advocate:* He will not say to such poor souls, I will not be for you, I have done all that I may, but it is gone against me; neither will he prig (to say so) with you; he will not say, I will have this or that, ere I undertake your cause for you; but, *if any man sin:* If any man see his need, and will imploy him, whether he be a great man, or mean man, whether he be poor or rich, bond or free; whether he be an old sinner that has lived long in security, hypocrisy or prophanity, or be a fitten up professor, whether he be young or old; if any of you all that are here will come to him, he will not refuse to be imployed by you: *By him therefore* (as the apostle exhorts, Heb. xiii. 15.) *let us offer praise to God continually:* And as praise, so the sacrifices of other duties, and they shall be accepted. As the offer of the Gospel runs on an universality, and excludes none, but these that by their unbelief exclude themselves; So his intercession runs on an universality, If any man sin, and will imploy him, he is an Advocate at hand: And seeing it is Christ, and Christ as Intercessor for transgressors, that we are speaking of, as the ground of sinners consolation, let me in passing defire you to remember, that he is pointing at you, men and women; and if there be any of you, that have a broken cause to plead, any debt that ye would fain be freed of, any sin to be pardoned, or your peace to be made with God; here is an Advocate, and the very best, offering himself to be imployed. Such an Advocate as said, John xi. *I thank thee, Father, for that I know thou hearest me always:* This was true while he was on earth, and will be true to the end of the world. 2. The extent of this consolation appears in respect of all cases: As his intercession secludes no person, that will make use of him; so it secludes no case, though it looked like a lost cause, and though the conscience had pronounced the sentence, God is greater than the conscience, and who can loose from it; though the act were past in the law, he can cancel it; And here comes in the triumph, Rom. viii. 33, 34. *Who shall lay any thing to the charge of God's elect? it is God that justifies.* Will the devil, the law, the conscience, or any thing, lay ought to the charge of the man whom God justifies? No, why so? *It is Christ that died:* But that is not all; Alas! may the soul say, how will I get good of Christ's death? I cannot apply it, and make use of it: He answers, that *He is also risen again, and sitten down at the right hand of God, and there maketh intercession for us;* to wit, that his purchase may be applied: and there needs no more; ye will get no more, ye can seek no more, and that closes the triumph. There is no sin, before nor after conversion, no sin of ignorance, no sin against light, no enemy, no temptation, whatever it be, but that word answers all, *Who can lay any thing to the charge of God's elect?* Where Christ takes the sinner's case in hand, who will stand up against him? he is too strong a Party. If Satan stand at the high priest's hand, it is the Lord that rebukes him, Zech. iii. that as it were boasts him from the bar. 3. The extent of this consolation appears, in respect of the degree and height of the perfection of the salvation that comes by Christ's intercession, to all that make use of him, in all cases, Heb. vii. 25. *He is able to save to the uttermost:* The word is very significant, he is able to save perfectly, to perfection, and to perfection at the height of perfection; and what more would ye be at? He can save from corruption, and put without the reach of it; he can save from wrath, that it shall not come near you; he can save from all the effects of sin and wrath; he shall not leave a tear on the cheek of any of his own, ere all be done; and that is the ground of it, *For he lives for ever to make intercession for us.* If any should say, He may save from one sin, but not from another, or he may bring me a piece of the way to heaven, and then leave me there; 'tis folly, says the Apostle, to think so, *For he is able to save to the uttermost, because he lives for ever to make intercession:* Although his death seem to be transient, once for all perfected, yet that cannot mar the application of the benefits purchased by it; for he is Intercessor, and he that procured thy entring in the way, will carry thee on in it; he that procured a sanctified conviction to come in, will through it; he that procured thy justification, and pardon of sin, will also apply it to thy conscience, and bring forth an intimation of it, when he thinks fit, and sanctify thee throughly: and this is indeed great consolation to a sinner, that he who hath begun the work will perfect it; and he will not leave it, till it be at such a height of perfection, as it can be desired to be no higher. 4. The extent of this consolation is such, that it reacheth to all times. There is not a believer in any place or case, that is wrestling with any difficulty, that can come wrong to Christ; he is ever in readiness to be imployed; there is never an hour or moment that he hath his door shut: he died once, but now lives for ever, to die no more; and he lives for ever, to make intercession: he is entred into immortality, to make effectual what he hath undertaken in favours of his people; he is always at the bar, and when his own are but little imploying him, he is minding their affairs night and day, watching over them every moment. See Luke xxii. where the Lord saith, *Peter, Satan hath sought to winnow thee, but I have prayed for thee, that thy faith fail not*: Satan gave in a bill against Peter, when he had no mind of it, but the Lord repelled it: the greatest cheat, of the most subtile adversary, that steals out decreets, cannot circumveen him; he is still waiting on at the bar, that nothing come in against his people to their prejudice; and if it do come in, it is that he may crush it in the first motion. O how doth the consolation of believers stream out here? *He will not cry, nor lift up, nor cause his voice to be heard on high; a bruised reed will he not break, and the smoking flax will he not quench, until he bring forth judgment unto truth:* he will not contend, nor say, Man or woman, how is this, that thou hast put thyself in the mire, and would have me to take thee out of it; that thou brings a broken plea to me, and seeks of me to right it? He will not ask, whether ye have money, all his imployment is free; nor will he put you back till the morrow, nor bid you wait on till another time: morning and evening, and at midnight he is ready; and when the elect sinner hath little thought, he is watching over his need, preventing many temptations, keeping from many ill turns, casting many challenges over the bar, that the devil and the law put in: Therefore study his offices more, and this among the rest; we much wrong him, in not studying of them, and acquainting ourselves with them, that we may feed upon them. Himself open up his name to us, and to him be praise.

SERMON LXVIII.

Isaiah liii. 12.------*And made intercession for the transgressors.*

O THAT sinners were seriously considering how much they are obliged to Christ! he hath, in the former words, *poured out his soul unto death* for sinners, and was wounded for transgressors; and yet that was not all, though sin was our Lord's death, he hath not casten out with sinners, but having gotten the victory over all enemies, and sitten down at the right hand of God, *he makes intercession;* and to make it the more full, it is said, *he makes intercession for transgressors*: All his offices have an eye to sin and sinners, and this part of his office among others.

We began to speak of an *use* of comfort that flows from this; and truly, if any doctrine be comfortable, this is, that sinners have an Advocate with the Father: What would sinners do, when their peace is broken, and there is a door shut betwixt God and them, and his back is turned on them, and the conscience is wakened, and they cannot think on God but it is troublesome to them, if they had not a Friend in court, with whom the Father cannot but be well pleased?

This consolation being a main part of the use of this doctrine, and the ground of believers boldness with God, in the following of it forth, we proposed *five* things to be spoken to. 1. To shew the largeness and extent of the consolation that flows from this ground, and of this we spake. 2. The particular advantages that the scripture attributes to Christ's intercession, and the consolation that is in them. 3. The particular times, when especially believers are called to make use of this consolation. 4. Some grounds warranting them to make use of it. And, 5. Some caveats, or advertisements to them that would warrantably comfort themselves from it.

To proceed now, and to speak to these last *four* things. 1. The particular advantages that the scriptures attribute to Christ's intercession; and if ye look through them, we will find that there is nothing that may be useful to a believer, either as to a particular or publick mercy, but it is knit to Christ's intercession.

1st, For private mercies. 1. Look to the beginning and growth of our spiritual life, and to the pouring out of the Spirit; it is made the fruit of Christ's intercession, John xiv. 16. *I will pray the Father, and he shall send the Comforter:* and, John xvi. *If I go not away, the Comforter will not come.*
This

This is the consolation of a believer, labouring under deadness of spirit, barrenness and unfruitfulness, that the pouring out of the Spirit is a remedy of that, and the pouring out of the Spirit a fruit of Christ's intercession: it is this that procures the first conviction of the Spirit to an elect lying in nature; it is this that continues these convictions, and procures the Spirit's quickening of them, John xvi. 8. If it should then be asked, how a person, lying in black nature, gets any good? It is answered, that it is Christ's intercession, that does the turn. 2. It is from Christ's intercession, that we are keeped from many temptations, or when they affault, that they prevail not utterly over us: the devil lies always at the wait, and we are often secure; but our Lord Jesus (to say so) watcheth the stot, or rebound of the temptation, and wards it off, as to the designed prejudice, Luke xxii. 32. *Simon, Simon, Satan hath desired that he may have you, that he may winnow you; but I have prayed for thee, that thy faith fail not:* There are many temptations that he keeps off, that they beat not on us, and when they affault us, he breaks the power of them, that the believer succumbs not under them: Hence it is, that we are keeped on our feet, otherwise, what would become of us? When David fell in adultery, and Peter denied his Master, what would have become of them, had it not been for this? There would be no living for us, in the multitude of temptations, if he were not interceeding for us. What could we foresee of Satan's snares? What strength have weak and witless we, to resist temptations? What could we do with the spear of corruption, when it rises like a flood upon us, and Satan inforceth his assaults upon us, as if he were speaking with man's voice, or mouth, bidding us do this and that? But there is an Intercessor, that pleads our cause. 3. We have, by this intercession, the preventing of many judgments temporal and spiritual: When the ax is laid to the root of the tree, and it is found barren, and justice cries, and the command comes out, *Cut it down, why cumbreth it the ground?* How comes it, that the ax strikes not? Why is it not hewed down? There is an efficacy in Christ's intercession for sparing of it a while longer, as it is, Luke xiii. 6. *The dresser of the vineyard says, Spare it for this year,* and it is granted. O but we would have a most sinful and miserable life, if there were not an Intercessor at God's right hand! 4. Disposition for duty, and help in the performance of duty, flows from his intercession: it is this, that makes us pray, and that gives us boldness in prayer, and in other duties, that *there is such an high Priest over the house of God,* as it is, Heb. x. 19, 20, 21. It is this that gives us ground of approaching to God, and to expect a hearing; as it is, Luke xiii. 7, 8. it is his digging and pains, that makes the barren fig-tree fruitful. 5. It flows from this, that our prayers are heard; tho' there be much infirmity in them, and that they are not cast back in our faces as dung, but are made savoury to God; it is thro' the efficacy of his intercession. We have a type of this, Rev. viii. 4, 5. where John sees an angel come and stand at the altar, " having a golden censer, " and there was given unto him much incense, that " he should offer it up with the prayers of all saints, " and the smoke of the incense which came up with " the prayers of the saints, ascended up before " God:" It was savoury and acceptable to God, and made the prayers of all saints acceptable; for the weight of God's accepting their prayers, is laid on the smoke of his incense: it is he that takes the mangled, and half prayers of his people, and presents them to God; and when they would be cast back, as the supplication of an enemy, he, as great Master of requests, through the acceptation that he hath with God, makes them acceptable: we should have no ground to pray with confidence, nor expectation to be heard, if there were not a golden censer in his hand. 6. We have from his intercession an answer to all challenges: There is much debt on our score; the law pursues hard, and curseth us for our habitual enmity, and all the particular acts of it; and his intercession is the last defence, on which the triumph of faith rises, by the other steps, Rom. viii. 33. *Who shall lay any thing to the charge of God's elect?* Is it because they want a charge? No, for there is the devil, the law, and the conscience to charge them; but, *It is God that justifies, who shall condemn? It is Christ that died, yea, rather is risen again, who is at the right hand of God, and maketh intercession for us:* We have an high Priest there, that hath paid our debt, and pleads, that the application of his purchase may be made forthcoming; and who, I pray, will lay any thing to our charge in that court, where God is Judge, and Christ is Advocate? 7. More particularly, our Lord, by his intercession, taketh away the guilt of our holy things, for when we approach to God in worship, there is a carnalness and pollutedness in the best things we do, much irreverence, much unbelief, much want of humility, zeal, sincerity and tenderness; so that *all our righteousnesses are but as filthy rags:* but the high Priest, Exod. xxxviii. 28. hath on his forehead, *Holiness to the Lord; and his office is, to bear the iniquities of*

Father: However our prayers and praises, and other parts of service, be but little worth; yet he makes them acceptable, and procures that they be not rejected, when he is for this end employed, and made use of. 8. We will find that strength to bear thro' under a cross, and a good outgate from under the cross, comes from him, as Intercessor: O so advertent as he is, when his own are under the cross! his bowels are then moved, tho' not as they were on earth, yet certainly they want not their own holy motion, suitable to the glorious estate whereunto he is exalted: Therefore, Acts ix. he cries from heaven, *Saul, Saul, why persecutest thou me?* And Stephen, when a-stoning to death, sees him *standing at the right hand of God*, executing this part of his priestly office: One part whereof, is to keep off a cross; and another part whereof, is to help to get it honourably born, and to get victory over it. 9. Our perseverance in the faith, and perfect glorification, is a fruit of Christ's intercession; so that his own cannot but persevere, and be glorified, because he intercedes for them. This is it that is spoken to several times, John xvii. especially verses 15. and 24. In the 15th verse, *I pray for them, that they may be kept from the evil:* He prays for them, that they may be kept from the evil of sin, especially; he prays for them, that they may be kept, that they fall not from the truth; and, verse 24. *Father, I will that those whom thou hast given me, be where I am, to behold my glory.* That longing and effectual desire and will of his, presented by him in heaven, is continuing still effectual for all the saints in the church militant; there is ground of quietness and comfort from his intercession; and, by vertue of it, to have hope, that not only present, but coming snares and temptations shall not prevail: Therefore the apostle, Rom. viii. 38. to his speaking of Christ's intercession, subjoins his highest triumph, *I am persuaded, that neither death nor life, principalities nor powers, things present, nor things to come;* and because it is impossible to number all things, he says, *nor any other creature, shall be able to separate us from the love of God, which is in Christ Jesus our Lord.* Now, if all these

heavy to the church, and publick work of God; in reference to all which, we will find consolation from this ground. The *1st* is the fear of a scarcity, or weakness of the publick ministry; that being the great gift which he hath given, for the edifying of his body; and it being a prejudice to the church, when she hath not pastors *according to God's own heart.* But compare Psal. lxviii. 18. with Eph. iv. 8, 12, 13, 14. and we will find that his intercession answers all that fear: in the Psalm, it is said, *Thou hast ascended on high; thou hast led captivity captive, thou hast received gifts for men;* which supposeth his seeking of, or making suit for them; or, as the word is, Thou hast received gifts *in the man,* that is, being in our nature, he procured them: And, Eph. iv. it is said, *He gave gifts to men;* and compare these *two* places with a *third,* to wit, Acts i. 4. where he bids his apostles *tarry at Jerusalem, till he send the promised Spirit;* and immediately after his ascension, as it is, Acts ii. he poured it out, which abode on them, in the *likeness of cloven tongues of fire:* It is likewise said, John xi. 39. that *the Spirit was not given, for Jesus was not yet glorified:* All which shew an influence, that Christ's ascension hath on the pouring out of the Spirit, and on the gifts given to men, whether ministers or others. There is nothing amongst men readily less cared for, than a ministry; some would have none at all, others would have them of such a stamp, as would please and humour them; but our Lord hath received gifts to be given unto men; and he hath poured out such gifts on the apostles and others, hath what gifts he pleaseth, and sees needful for his church's edification, yet to give: And that he gives such gifts to men, that his people are not praying much for; whence is it, but from his intercession? Therefore, Rev. i. we will find that he delights in this property, as a piece of his spiritual state and grandeur, *That he holds the stars in his right hand;* such is his respect to them, and his it is to dispose of them. 2. It is a greatly exercising difficulty to the church of God, to think of the mighty opposition that is made by enemies; Mahomet, Heathens, Antichrist, false Brethren, threat-

threatning to swallow up the little flock, the church of Christ, which is like a bush burning with fire, and not consumed: But for this there is a consolation in Christ's intercession, according to that word, Heb. x. 13. *He sat down on the right hand of God, from henceforth expecting, till his enemies be made his footstool;* He hath this for his suit at the Father's bar, and is backing it: Upon this it followed, and as a fruit of it, that all the first persecutions were broken; on this it hath come to pass. that Antichrist's kingdom is tottering; and it is on this ground, that his bearing-down, and utter-breaking will be accomplished: Hence it is most emphatically said, 1 Cor. xv. 24. that *he must reign till he hath put all enemies under his feet;* according to the promise made by Jehovah to him, Psal. cx. 1. *The Lord said to my Lord, Sit thou on my right hand, till I make thine enemies thy footstool.* He cannot be an Intercessor, but his enemies must down: For who, I pray, will be able to stand, when he gives in his complaint against them? Who will plead Antichrist's and other persecutors cause, when he appears against them? And he is so certain of his enemies being made his footstool, that he is waiting till he see it done; he must reign till then, maugre all the malice and might of devils and men.

3. It is a difficulty to the church and people of God, to think on such great confusions as are in the world; there are but a few judicatories that are for Christ; but few governors, higher or lower, that do consult his honour, or regard him; it is others that have the throne and court, and the guiding of things, than friends and favourers of his interest, for most part: but here the consolation lies, that there is a court in heaven, that gives out orders, where the church hath an Agent constantly lying, where the devil and the world hath none; Jesus Christ is the church's Agent and Intercessor there: Daniel, chap. x. 13. hath a word to this purpose, *The prince of the kingdom of Persia withstood me one and twenty days, but Michael the chief Prince came to help me:* And, verse 21. *There is none in all the court of Persia that holdeth with me in these things, but Michael your Prince.* The great Intercessor was at court, looking that nothing went wrong, seeing that no decree were past to the prejudice of the people of God, and his work. In the time when they were building the temple, *He* (Zech. xvi. 13.) is said *to build the temple of the Lord, to bear the glory, and to be a Priest, sitting and ruling on his throne,* having the government committed to him. What hazard then is there here, when heaven guides all, when the church hath an Agent at the court, to see (as I said) that nothing go wrong, when Michael the Prince is there, and sees all the acts and decrees of the court, and readeth them, yea, draweth them, and look well that there be nothing in them hurtful to his church: And O! may we not, and should we not thank God for this? 4. A *fourth* thing that troubles the church of God, is the abounding of offences in herself, and the spreading of error, which, like a flood, threatneth to drown the church; and great stormy winds come, that are like to blow down the house of God; offences and stumblings abound, and error, which (I just now said) as a flood is like to drown all: When the devil is put from the throne, and gets not violence acted, he turns about, and falleth on another way, and spues out his flood of error, to devour the woman and her child; but our Lord hath a vote here also. After the persecution of the Heathens is over, Rev. vii. 1, 2. John sees an angel ascending from the east, the great Lord-keeper, or Chancellor of the Father's council, the supreme Deputy over all under-officers, that hath the keeping of the great seal of the living God, and there is nothing relevant or valid till it be sealed by him: And mark the time when he appears; it is when the winds are holden, and ready to blow, as verse 1. but he cries with a loud voice, " Hurt not the earth, " nor the sea, nor the trees, till we have sealed the " servants of God in their foreheads." Stay, saith he, a little; ere these winds blow that will take the most part off their feet, ere that delusion go forward. there are some servants of God that must be marked, and put without the reach of the hazard, and the winds shall get leave to blow: What reason then of anxiety is there, or could be here, if the solid and lively faith of this Intercessor, and Advocate, his being in heaven, and thus interceeding, were in our hearts?

2dly, As to the particular times and occasions when the people of God should more especially make use of this ground of consolation, and comfort themselves in it. (I speak not of Christ's intercession simply, but of the consolation that flows from it) 1. In their languid and lifeless conditions, when the body of death comes in on them, like the waves of the sea, and is ready as it were to drown them; they ought to comfort themselves in this, that they have an Intercessor, that can rebuke that: when temptation is violent, and a person fears he be undone, he hath a grip here to hold himself by: Jesus Christ is Intercessor; he prays, that my graces fail not, that my faith and patience be not undone, that the devil get not his will of me: the man would be be desperate, if he were not in heaven, and interceeding; but he gathers confidence from this ground, and says, " I shall not die, but live, and see the salvation of God; for he is able to save to the uttermost all that come unto God through him, seeing he ever liveth to make intercession for them:" And therefore, altho' I cannot win out of the grips of this temptation, yet he can rebuke it, and break the force of it; and hence is that comfortable word, Heb. ii. last, *For that he himself suffered, and was tempted, he is able to succour them that are tempted.* Sometimes it will not meet with believers condition, that Christ suffered; but this doth, when he comes on, and finds that he was *tempted:* It is true, there was no corruption in him, and temptations had no sinful influence on him; and the more comfort to us, he is the stronger to overcome in us: yet he was set on, and affaulted by the temptation, he was tempted; and this is a consolation. When Joshua the high priest is in his duty, Zech. iii. and the devil is at his right hand, to resist him, and mar him in it, and he can do or say little himself, he boasts him with authority from marring his servant in his work. A great consolation it is, when the temptation is strong, and we weak, when the devil is violent, and we are despairing to resist him, that there is a high Priest at hand, whose office is to do it. A 2d time is, when challenges are very fresh, when the charge of one's debt given in, is long and large, and the law is severe in exacting, and justice in pressing, and pressing hard, and the conscience cannot deny, nor resist, and the man hath nothing to pay his debt, and he is like to be dragged to the prison, and there is none to undertake for him; there comes in that word, 1 John ii. 1, 2. " I write " these things to you, that ye sin not,". I give none a dispensation to sin; but, " if any man sin, we have " an Advocate with the Father, Jesus Christ the " righteous." And this is the ground of Paul's triumph, so often mentioned, Rom. viii. 34. " Who " shall lay any thing to the charge of God's elect? " It is God that justifies," &c. Tho' the charge should be given in, what is the matter? There is a way to be freed of it, there is an Advocate at the right hand of God in heaven, who became Cautioner for, and paid the elect's debt, and is now interceeding for them; and who can lose the cause, when he pleads it? And here he quiets and comforts himself, giving a defiance to challenges, and all that can be libelled against him. A 3d time and occasion is, under a cross condition, when Christians have the world on their tops, and there is confusion in publick things, and there is darkness and indistinctness in our private condition; it ought to comfort us, that we have an Advocate in heaven, who pleads our cause, and will not despise the suit of the poor and needy. A 4th time is, when we ourselves cannot interceed for ourselves; when we pray, but our prayers are much mangled, and little worth, and we think shame to look upon them; we would then look upon what account our prayers are put up: if on the account of Christ's intercession, a sigh, a groan, a broken word, nay, a breathing will be accepted; the Interceffor hath his own incense to perfume it with, and it is accepted on the weight that it hath from him: and tho' our prayer be but as the shadow of a prayer, if there be honesty in it, it is a comfort, it will be accepted on that account; *Whatsoever ye shall ask the Father in my name, I will do:* And, Rev. viii. he accepts the prayers of all faints, the weakest as well as the best; for the best goes not up but by his censer and incense, and the weakest goes up the same way: And there is, in some respect, no distinction of believers, and of their fervent or not fervent prayers there, if honest; the fervour of Christ's intercession, and the favour of his incense, makes all go up, and be accepted, because the reason of God's hearing of our prayers is not in us, else he should hear none of them; but it is in his intercession, which is of equal worth and extent to all honest prayers of sound believers; *He is able to save to the uttermost, all that come unto God through him,* tho' there be no ability nor worth in themselves, because *he lives for ever to make intercession for them.* But the two last things will clear this yet more.

3*dly,* Tho' this may seem strange like, yet it is true, if we consider the grounds, warranting us to make use of his intercession, and to draw this consolation from it; and they are *four,* 1. That his intercession supposes a defect in us, a libel and charge given in against us, else, what needed we to have an Advocate and Intercessor? If our plea were just and good, as from ourselves, we needed not one to undertake for us, the Judge would absolve us; but the defects that are in us, give access to this part of his office, which supposes us to have infirmities, else we needed not an high Priest, if we were like Adam in his innocency, for he needed not an Intercessor; and therefore in the text, it is *for the transgressors* that he makes intercession: And, 1 John ii, 2. *If any man sin, we have an Advocate,* &c. 2. All the weight of Christ's intercession, and the grounds whereon he pleads, are in himself, and therefore none need to stand a-back, because there is nothing in themselves; *We have an Advocate with*

SERM. LXVIII. *Isaiah* liii. Verse 12.

with the Father, Jesus Christ the righteous; and he is the propitiation. Christ hath in him a fulness to pay the debt himself, and he pleads on that, and on nothing in the creature: He says not, Let them be pardoned, because they have not sin, nor because they have such and such qualifications, but because I have been a propitiation for them, I have paid their debt; therefore he is called *the Righteous*, because he hath reason for that which he seeks; he hath paid for what he seeks, and therefore it cannot but be granted. 3. There is a freedom in the application of all, the application is free grace every way, and that is clear from the parable of the barren fig-tree: What could the tree say, when justice pleaded it should be cut down? There is nothing in it to procure a delay, but the Gardener stands up, and bids spare it, and he will take pains on it, and apply what is needful: Causes are not here cast back because the party is poor, nor because he hath much debt on his score; no, *If any man sin, he hath an Advocate*, the thing is obtained without money and without price: Would ye then have a Priest that suits you well? Ye shall have him, and have him freely; if ye employ him to undertake for you, he will do it freely, and it is his honour so to do. 4. It is free and effectual, it cannot misgive: For who pleads? Is it not the Son? Before whom pleads he? It is before his own Father, who heareth him always: For whom doth he plead? It is for them who are the Father's own elect, and his also; *Thine they were, and thou gavest them me; and all mine are thine, and thine are mine:* It is for them whom the Father loves as well as he. What does he seek and plead for? For that which is covenanted; and he pleads for it, according to the terms of the covenant: Therefore it is sure, that tho' heaven and earth may be mixed and overturned, yet none can loose a link here; it is impossible, but what he interceeds for, he must obtain; and for whom he interceeds, he prevails, and that is for all that employ him.

4thly, For *Advertisement* or *Caveat*. It may be asked here, May all comfort themselves in Christ's intercession? Some will think, that were good; but in truth, it would make the consolation of all unsure: therefore, there are *four* qualifications of a person that may, and only may warrantably take the consolation whereof we have spoken, 1. It is a person that hath betaken himself to Christ's satisfaction; for there are *two* parts of the priestly office, his *sanctification* and his *intercession;* and there is no dividing of them, nor making use of them, but in the right order. First he satisfies, and then he interceeds; and he must be taken, and made use of in this order, first in his satisfaction to divine justice; and it is on this ground that we must found our righteousness, and plead for absolution: And whoever have made this use of his satisfaction, may, in the second place, comfort themselves in his intercession; because it is grounded on his satisfaction, 1 John ii. 2. For whom he interceeds, for these he is a propitiation, and he is a propitiation for all who by faith have betaken themselves to him: This is the very hinge of our consolation, even to take with our debt, and betake ourselves to him, according to the covenant, lippening for salvation on that ground. 2. It is these who are essaying and practising themselves in the duties of holiness, wrestling with a body of death, and exercising themselves to godliness, that may warrantably comfort themselves in Christ's intercession; as Paul, who, Rom. vii. being put to it, in the conflict with his corruption, comforts himself thus, *I thank God, through Jesus Christ our Lord*. Tho' they be sorely harrassed with a corrupt nature, yet they may expect an outgate, through vertue of his intercession: Therefore, Rev. viii. Christ's incense (as I have often said) and the saints prayers, go, and go up together. Laziness and security hath not this consolation; but if a person be praying, and be serious, tho' weak in it, he hath an Advocate, who, when it comes to be asked, What shall be thought of such an one's sacrifice? pleads that it may be accepted. 3. It is the person that not only is aiming, and minting to do duty, but is denied to it, laying no weight on it, despairing ever to get victory over corruption in his own strength, or to come by the hearing of his prayers through any worth that is in them, and not daring to step forward his alone, but leaving all he does at Christ's feet, to make it acceptable; which leads us to the *fourth* thing requisite, *viz.* When persons, whether their doing and duties be of worth or not, Jesus Christ is made by them the upshot of all; they lay weight on him to get them done, and to get them accepted when they are done, and without him all would be desperate in their esteem: This was typified in the peoples giving the sacrifices to the priest to be offered; and tho' it were but two turtle-doves, or two young pigeons, they were brought to the priest, as well as other sacrifices. But such as consider not the enmity and sinfulness that is in themselves, and adventure to step in to God without him, cannot lay claim to this consolation, which runs always on this ground, Heb. vii. 25. *He is able to save to the uttermost, all that come to God through*

him,

Isaiah liii. Verse 12.

him, seeing he ever liveth to make intercession for them. Is there not then ground of consolation here, and such as there is reason to bestow a preaching upon it, to teach us how to clear ourselves in it, and make use of it, and how to chear ourselves in it: Ye that seclude yourselves from this consolation, O but ye spill and mar a good life to yourselves, and hazard your own cause, that will most certainly go against you, because ye put it not in the right hand; which the Lord give you wisdom to amend, and give us all the right use of this, through Jesus Christ.

SERMON LXIX.

Isaiah liii. 12.--------*And made intercession for the transgressors.*

IT were a very great consolation, and a main furtherance in all religion, to get this solidly believed, that Christ Jesus, *who is the express image of his Father's Person, and the brightness of his glory,* is now in heaven in our nature, and hath it for his work, to be interceeding, and interceeding for transgressors: We are every day reaping the good of this intercession, in reference to many evils that are keeped off us, and in reference to many mercies bestowed on us, that we pray not at all, or but little for; and we come never to hear a preaching, but we are beholden to it, it being a peculiar fruit of his intercession, that gifts are given to men, and that the gospel is sent through the earth; and if ever any get good of a sermon, it is by vertue of this intercession, seeing he hath said, that *he will pray the Father, and that he will send the Comforter;* and whenever we come to hear a preaching, there would be (to say so) a reviving of the thoughts of Christ's intercession, and a stirring up of ourselves to get the faith of it lively in its exercise.

That which we spake to the last day, was concerning the comfort that flows from this; and indeed, if any doctrine be comfortable, this must be comfortable, that we have such a Friend in the court of heaven, invested in this office of an Advocate and Intercessor for us.

Use 3*d.* Of exhortation. Seeing there is such an office wherewith Jesus Christ is invested, and such an Officer that bears this office, to be an Advocate for sinners, then sinners would be exhorted to learn to improve and to make use of this Advocate, and of his office; since he hath this office of an Intercessor. O do not despise such a mercy! neglect not such an advantage, but learn to make use of him, and in your worship-applications to God, to approach by, and through him. The ground of this *use of exhortation* is clear in the words, and from the nature of the thing: For, if Christ Jesus bear these offices, and if he bear them for us, then sure we should improve them. If he be a King, we should make use of him, for subduing sin in us; if a Prophet, we should improve that office, for attaining of light and saving knowledge from him; and if he be a Priest, to satisfy divine justice, and to make intercession, we should improve both parts of that office. The necessity of our improving of Christ's intercession appears from this, if we consider in what terms we stand with God: Have we any boldness or access of ourselves? Is not the door shut on us? And is there not a stated controversy standing betwixt God and us? And have we any access but by his moyen? The necessity of it is further clear from the order that God hath laid down in the way of his administration of grace: Why, I pray, hath he appointed a Mediator and Intercessor? Is it not for good reason? Even for the consolation and encouragement of sinners to draw near, who, if they be in earnest, cannot but be affected with fear to approach unto God; and is it possible to come unto God, and not by this door? And were it not ingratitude to neglect it, seeing he hath contrived this new and living way of access unto him?

But to descend to more particular discoursing of this matter, which is as difficult a thing to speak of aright, and to practise suitably, as any part of religion, if especially he himself teach us not; for sometimes we will make use of his sacrifice and satisfaction, when we know not how to make use of his intercession; for either we do all our alone, and mistken the Intercessor, or we will do nothing, and give it over as desperate, as if our business were quite broken and hopeless, and as if it were needless or useless to lay any weight on Christ's intercession: And thus, whether we apprehend ourselves to be in a better, or in worse case, he is much mistken and neglected. That therefore we may the better know how to make use of Christ's intercession, we shall, 1. In the general, shew what it is to improve it. 2. Speak to some particular cases, wherein it in a special manner is to be improven. 3. Satisfy and remove some objections, or answer some questions that may be moved about it. 4. We shall give some characters of one that is serious and tender in improving of his intercession.

For

For the *first*; It is indeed a thing so difficult to improve Christ's intercession aright, that we cannot easily tell how to conceive of it, being a considerable part of the mystery of faith, to go to God by a Mediator and Intercessor. However, we shall, 1. Shew some mistakes that are to be eschewed. 2. We shall shew wherein it more properly consists, which is, in the exercise of faith in him, with respect to his intercession. 3. We shall illustrate it by some similitudes, for the further making out of it. 1*st*, Then, when we speak of improving Christ's intercession, and of going to God by him, we would have these mistakes eschewed. 1. Beware of thinking, that there is a going to the Mediator in a distinct, or different manner from what is in going to God, for he is God; or, that we may go to God at one time, and to the Mediator at another time, as if we would first speak a while to the Mediator, and then speak to God; or would first make our moan to the Mediator to pacify God, and when God were calmed, to speak to him; as if he were to make moyen with God for us, as a courtier makes moyen with the king, the offended party, for a rebel: We would beware of this, for it divides in our apprehension the Godhead, that is indivisible; for if we consider the Mediator as the Object of our worship, he is to be considered as God, tho' we may, and are also jointly to consider him as Mediator, and on that account to make use of him; and if we consider him as God, we must consider him as the same God with the Father, and the Holy Ghost: But to have this imagination of him, that we are to speak to him, as another Party, or not as God, is to make him another thing, which is unbecoming that apprehension and estimation that we ought to have of the Unity of the blessed Godhead. 2. Beware of thinking, that there is a greater facility or easiness to have access to the Mediator, than to have access to God; or that it is more easy to have access to the *second* Person of the Trinity, than to the *first*, or *third* Person. We are afraid that there be mistakes here also, as if the Mediator were more easy to be dealt with than the Majesty of God; or, as if there were more easy access unto him; whereas, he being the same God, and so considered, there are the same grounds, whereon sinners may have access to the Father as to the Son. For, if we look on a sinner repenting, and believing, he is as welcome to the Father as to the Son; but if we consider the sinner as not repenting and believing, he is so, neither welcome to the Father, nor to the Son. It is true, the Son being considered as man, there is a sympathy, that the *second* Person, united to our nature, hath, which is not in God abstractly considered; yet this is not so to be understood, as if the mercy of the Mediator, having the two natures so united in his Person, were of larger extent than the mercy of God, or as if he could be merciful, when God is not: For there cannot be a greater mercy than that which is infinite, and that is the essential attribute of the Father, Son, and Holy Ghost; only this sympathy in the Mediator is to be considered, to strengthen and confirm our faith in our application to God, that we have him to approach to in our nature; but it is not to give us any new ground of having access easier to Christ than to God, but (as we said) only to confirm our faith, in having access to God: Hence it is, that Jesus Christ is always proposed as the means, whereby, and through whom, a sinner comes to God; so that we have access with boldness, not to the Mediator as a distinct Party, but to God through and by him. Therefore there is the same common way of application to God, and to Christ, the same covenant and promises, the same exercise of repentance, of faith and of prayer, which gives us access to God, and that gives us access to the Mediator. 3. Beware of placing this improving and use-making of the Mediator's intercession, in words or petitions directed to the Mediator; which, I apprehend, is the use that the most part make of his intercession; to put up such petitions, as I am afraid to speak of; as namely, O Mediator at the Father's right hand, plead for me! as if the Mediator were a distinct Party from the Judge, to whom we must speak for interceeding with the Judge, which still leads us to look on the Mediator as another different Party, or as having other terms whereupon he dealeth with sinners, or as if there were another way of making use of him, and of application to him, and on other grounds, than of, and to God; the contrary whereof we have shewed: Whereas the use-making of his intercession consists rather (as after will appear) in faith's application to God in him, and laying weight on his intercession for access, and acceptance of our persons and services; when we make it the ground of our address to God, the ground on which we draw near; and this we may and should do, when we name Christ, or pray to him as God, with respect to his office of being Intercessor: even as we look to him by faith, to get sin pardoned; there is a looking to him as God, with respect to his offering and satisfaction to the justice of God, on which account we expect to be pardoned.

But, 2*dly*, To explicate this a little more, we shall

kenning Chrift, and do all that they do, as if they were conftantly friends with God, and in good terms with him, and had need of none to make their peace, or to keep up and maintain their peace with God; which is in effect the way laid down in the covenant of works, when Adam was a friend: Another extreme is in the defect; and that is, when perfons go to God by Chrift, yet do not lay weight on his interceffion as becomes; when not only they want confidence, which the other hath, tho' on a wrong ground, but do not lay the burden on the right ground, but go to God faintingly and difcouragedly, as fearing to truft or lippen to Chrift's interceffion. There is neceffity to guard againft both thefe; for there muft be fuch an ufe making of Chrift's interceffion, as we dare not go by him, and yet a concurring act of faith, putting us to go to God by him, and to lay the weight of what we feek and expect on him, and on his interceffion. Now, the things that are prefuppofed to the ufe-making of Chrift's interceffion, guard againft the firft extreme; and thefe things wherein the ufe-making of it properly confifts, guard againft the other extreme.

Firft, Then thefe things prefuppofed, are, 1*ft*, A conviction of our natural finfulnefs, not only of the diftance that is betwixt God and us, but of the quarrel and enmity, and that by our deferving we may juftly have the door of accefs to God fhut upon us; that is it that puts the finner to afk for an Interceffor, and to make ufe of him, as thefe who have provoked a great perfon, fear to go their a-lone to him, but feek for the mediation of fome fpecial friend or favourite. 2*dly*, There is prefuppofed a confenting to, and acceptation of Chrift's fatisfaction, as the ground of our peace with God; for there is no accefs to his interceffion till this ground be laid, becaufe all the efficacy that is in Chrift's interceffion, refults from, and is founded upon his fatisfaction, 1 John ii. 2. *If any man fin, we have an Advocate with the Father, Jefus Chrift the righteous, who is the propitiation for our fins.* He procures nothing by his interceffion, but thro' the vertue of that blood, which he offered in a fa-hopes of prevailing with God) if his fatisfaction be mifkent, will be to no purpofe; for, as we fhew in the firft ufe of this point, he interceeds only for his own people, who are believers in him, and have clofed with his fatisfaction; and, as we fhew from Rev. viii. it is only the prayers of all faints that are offered up by him: I mean, none can comfortably conclude that he interceeds for them, but believers and faints; and therefore, till his fatisfaction be refted on, as the ground of our peace, we can look for no benefit by his interceffion. 3*dly*, There is beyond this required, the conviction and impreffion of our own unfuitablenefs, to keep up friendfhip and fellowfhip with God, through our remaining corruption, and the prevailing of temptation, without a Mediator; and withal, an approbation of God's way, who hath appointed a Mediator for that end; and a loving to keep up communion with him by a Mediator: So that, fuppofe we were clear that our fins are pardoned, yet we would know, that this conviction and impreffion is neceffary to put us to make daily ufe of this part of the Mediator's office: For we may have conviction of the *firft* part, that is, that we cannot make our peace without Chrift's fatisfaction; and yet we may be defective as to our walking under due conviction of the *fecond*, that is, of a neceffity of keeping up of our communion with God, by vertue of his interceffion: Which is, as if a rebel, being reconciled, and made a friend, by the procurement of fome great perfon, yet having to do with the king, fhould not dare to go unto him, without the man that was inftrumental in making his peace; or, we may allude to Abfalom's coming home by Joab's procurement, who was three years thereafter at Jerufalem ere he faw his father's face, and had a new dealing with Joab for that end: So it is very fuitable to the way of grace, and fhews, that our being and ftanding in grace is free, not to dare to go in to God, even when our peace is made, without the Mediator. 4*thly*, Upon the back of all this, there is a neceffity of the faith of the Mediator or Interceffor his being at the right hand of God, ready to agent our caufe, through whom we may have accefs, when

there

there is reason enough in ourselves, why we should be kept at the door, and though we dare not go ourselves alone, yet to adventure to go through him to God. And though this be but the doctrinal faith of the thing in general, yet it is necessarily presupposed, as well as the rest, that when a challenge rises, and the conscience says, How dare thou go to God? Faith may answer, Because there is a Friend there in our nature. When the sinner is convinced of sin, the conscience challengeth, and the law condemns, and there is some sad expectation of the drawing forth of the sentence; there is an act of faith, that convinces of a Saviour, whose satisfaction, if it be made use of and improven, all will be well. This, we say, is necessarily presupposed to the use-making of Christ's intercession.

2dly, These four being presupposed it follows, that we shew what properly it is, to make use of Christ's intercession or wherein it consists. And, 1. When faith hath laid hold on Christ's satisfaction for peace with God; in the improving of his intercession, there is an act of faith, whereby we actually bestir ourselves to approach unto God, upon the weight we lay on his intercession, that when the soul sees itself secluded, considered in itself, yet it will go forward, lippening to that; so that if a challenge come in its way, and say, What ground hast thou to look, that thou wilt be welcome to God? the soul says, None in myself, but there is a Friend before me, with whose satisfaction I have closed for my peace, and I lay this weight on his office, and on God's call to make use of him, that on the ground of his moyen with God, I dare hazard to go forward: Even as if a rebel, after his peace were made, had some business to do with the prince; and hearing that there is a friend at court, yea, the same friend that made his peace, he thinks that a good time, and fit season to go and present his suit, expecting to come speed through his moyen: and this always keeps the weight and honour of our obtaining any thing we seek, as a prerogative to Christ, and stops the person's own mouth from looking to any thing in itself to boast of; even as the rebel hath no cause to boast of his getting a hearing from the prince, but gives the thanks to him, who, as he made his peace, so also procured him a hearing; and it is according to that word, Heb. x. 21. *Having an high Priest over the house of God, let us draw near, with full assurance of faith, expecting a hearing;* and that, Heb. iv. 15, 16. *Seeing we have an high Priest; who was tempted in all things, like as we are, yet without sin,* *let us therefore come boldly unto the throne of grace, that we may obtain mercy, and find grace to help in time of need:* This is the *first* step of improving Christ's intercession, when the justified sinner is at a stand, on some new challenge for guilt, and dare not go forward, nor adventure to approach unto God, on this account and ground, that there is a Mediator and Advocate at his right hand, to hazard (if we may speak so) or rather with confidence to go forward, and present his suit to God. 2. There is an act of faith, as in undertaking, so, in expecting and on-waiting upon God, for obtaining a hearing of our suit, on this account, that Jesus Christ is an Intercessor in heaven for such as imploy him; and this guards against both the failings before mentioned, to wit, against anxiety on the one hand, and presumption on the other; against anxiety and fainting, when, as there is not only a proposing of our desire, but an on-waiting for, and expectation of a hearing from God; against presumption, and turning carnal, when the expectation of a hearing is not founded on our own righteousness, but on the intercession of Christ: This is it which we have, Dan. ix. 17. compared with Jonah ii. 4. In the ii. of Jonah ver. 4. he says, *Then I said, I am cast out of thy sight, yet will I look again toward thy holy temple;* the which look was in effect a looking toward the intercession of Christ the Messiah, the temple with its sacrifices having been typical of him, and the mercy-seat that was there, being typical of his intercession: It is as if unbelief had suggested to Jonah, Now Jonah, what will become of thee? thou art a gone man, and needs not pray any more; *Yet,* says he, *I will look again towards thy holy temple;* and though he knew not well, now being in the belly of the whale, where the temple stood; yet his faith having a suitable exercise on the Messiah signified by the temple, and his looking being an act of faith, carried in his suit to God, which was accepted: and indeed this is a main thing, by which a poor believer, cast down, wins to his feet again. The other place is, Dan. ix. 16, 17. where, when he is serious, and doubling his petition, he hath these words, *Cause thy face to shine upon thy sanctuary, which is desolate for the Lord's sake:* and to let it be known what he mean'd, by saying, *for the Lord's sake,* which looks to him who was to be Intercessor in our nature, he expones it in the following words, *O my God, incline thine ear, and hear; open thine eyes, and behold our desolations, for we do not present our supplications before thee, for our righteousnesses, but for thy great mercies:*

our expectation of a hearing on that account; and let it bear the weight of it, as well it can. 3. The right improvement of Christ's intercession hath this act of faith, that altho' there seem to be many difficulties and long off-puttings, yet faith, upon the account of his intercession, will continue its expectation of a hearing, and its looking for, of what the person hath sought, and stands in need of; whatever cross dispensations thwart its expectation, and whatever signs of anger appear in the way of its obtaining, it waits on for all that. Tho' Jonah be in the belly of the whale, and the weeds wrapped about his head, yet will he look towards his holy temple: So, tho' a soul have no life, nor sense, no inward feeling, nor arguments in the mouth, yet acting on Christ's intercession by faith, it will not leave, nor give over its suit, considering, that tho' it hath no ground of expectation of good from itself, yet from Christ's intercession it hath, which is the improvement of that, Heb. vii. 25. *He is able to save to the uttermost all that come unto God through him*, &c. If there were never so strong objections from unbelief and carnal reason, and if it should be suggested ye have such and such difficulties, that cannot be overcome, lying in the way of your salvation, and there is nothing in you concurring to make out your salvation; yet faith says, *He is able to save to the uttermost;* or, as the word is, he can save to the full, or to the yondmost; and what is the ground? *Because he ever lives to make intercession.* And this is the main thing to be taken notice of, in improving of his intercession, when the sinner hath presented his suit or request to God, through the Mediator, to get his mind quieted, on the account of Christ's intercession, that it shall be answered: Even as a man, who having a cause to plead, and getting an able advocate, who says to him, I will warrant your cause, quiets himself, because of his undertaking; so proportionably there is a weight laid on Christ's intercession by faith's lippening to him, which makes the soul to be without anxiety: And this continued act of faith doth not at all foster sin, but strengtheneth rather to oppose sin, quiets the mind, and tain'd, whether it be a mercy in preventing such and such a stroke, or the bestowing of such and such a favour; and that is, when faith derives not that mercy from, nor attributes it to its own praying, tho' it did pray, and pray somewhat seriously, but derives it from, and attributes it to the vertue and efficacy of Christ's intercession, and counts itself obliged to that, as the rise of all the person's good, and again by him returning thanks to God for it: And this is a little proof of improving Christ's intercession. Sometimes, when we want what we would have, and are restrained, we will improve all means to obtain, yet when we have obtained, there is but little acknowledgment of him therein; which acknowledgment is our duty, insinuate, John xiv. 13, 14. *Whatsoever ye ask in my name, I will do, that the Father may be glorified in the Son.* And in this sense we ought to walk in the use of every mercy, as bearing the acknowledgment of Christ's intercession, and to be affected with love to God, and should withal have a new impression of its obligation, to be forthcoming for God, upon the account of his intercession: Whereas the most part of folk take their mercies, and think not themselves to be in his common for them; neither do they own him with thankful acknowledgment of them, when they have gotten them; even as a man, who had gotten a favour through the mediation of another, and should forget him, would be very ungrate. The making use of Christ's intercession, in this respect, is the improving of it, for the awaking of our thankfulness, and the confirming of our obligation to him. If we look through our life, is there any day, or hour, but we stand in need of something, and be enjoying something? And the improving Christ's intercession thus, would make the thoughts of Christ always fresh and lovely to us; but we seek, and get, and enjoy, as if a Mediator were not in heaven: But as we acknowledge him in praying to him, when we have need; so, when any thing is gotten, we should acknowledge, that we have received it and do enjoy it, on the account of his intercession, who obtained it for us.

3*dly,*

3dly, We said, that this might be illustrated by similitudes; and there are these *three*, whereby it may be illustrate. The *first* is (if we may call it a similitude) the comparing of the use-making of his intercession, with the use-making of his satisfaction (wherein there is a resemblance) we make use of his satisfaction, when we are convinced of our natural sinfulness and enmity, and that we cannot make our own peace ourselves; yet hearing of his satisfaction, and having an offer of it, and believing that it is able to do our turn, we hazard on that ground to close with God in the covenant; and though the sense of peace come not for a long time, yet we with confidence wait for it, because the ground we lean on for it cannot fail. Proportionable to this, we make use of Christ's intercession, when under a challenge, we are convinced of a quarrel, and dare not approach to God; yet hearing tell, that there is an Intercessor in heaven, who will undertake for them that imploy him, we hazard confidently on that ground, to propose our suits unto God, and notwithstanding of difficulties, expect and wait for an answer. It may be *objected* here, that it seems there is no difference betwixt the improving of his satisfaction, and the improving of his intercession. *Answer*, There is no difference, in respect of the things sought, nor in respect of the acts of faith, whereby we make use of the one, and of the other, nor in respect of the grounds whereupon; for Christ hath paid the debt of them for whom he interceeds, he hath purchased the same things for which he maketh intercession, they are the same acts of faith that make use of both: It is the same covenant and offer, that warrants us to come to his satisfaction for peace; that warrants us to make use of his intercession for the application of peace: There is only this difference, that by his satisfaction he procures us peace, and a right to it; and our peace is made, by his laying down before God the price, which we by faith take hold of; but when he interceeds, he hath nothing to pay, but interceeds for what he hath purchased: Therefore the scripture hangs the application of his purchase upon his intercession; He hath bought peace, and every good thing that we stand in need of, by his death; and, by his intercession, he procures and makes the application: Therefore, it is on this ground that the Spirit is poured out. As among men, it is one thing to make peace, and another thing to bring the offending person into familiarity with the offended party; so it is the same faith acting on Christ's satisfaction, for being brought into covenant with God, as the meritorious cause, that acts on Christ's intercession, for application of that which he hath purchased, but under a different consideration, looking on his satisfaction as procuring, and on his intercession for application of the same things. A *second* similitude to clear it, is, the people under the law, their making use of the high priest; there were two parts of the high priest's office, or two things wherein the people made use of him, 1. For offering sacrifice, 2. For intercession; the high priest went into the most holy once a year, and sprinkled the blood, and prayed for the people; in which time they were standing without, praying, in the hope of having their prayers made the more acceptable. This was, by God's appointment, typically to prefigure our Lord's intercession in heaven: It is true the high priest's praying for them was nothing to the soul's advantage, of him or them, if Christ was not made use of, both by him, and by them; yet he was typical, and to shew this much, that they were to improve Christ's intercession, as well as his sacrifice and satisfaction: Therefore, Luke i. 10. when Zacharias went in to pray, the whole multitude of the people was without praying. A *third* similitude (which we have hinted at in our going along) is drawn from that way which is used among men, for bringing two parties that are at odds and variance to be reconciled, and at one; which, though we are not to conceive in that carnal manner, yet it holds as to the substance of the thing, as if the offending party durst not go his alone to the party offended, but should carry along with him a friend, that hath place and power to prevail with the other: When he undertakes to go along with him, contrary to his deserving, he will expect confiden.../ to get a good hearing; and if any should say to him, How dare you go to such an one, whom you have so provoked? he would answer, Because I have a friend before me, that will make moyen for me; and when by that friend's moyen he gets a favourable hearing, and his suit granted, he comes away rejoicing, professing his great obligation to that friend: So it is here, as to the thing; though, as was said, we would guard against carnal conceptions, or taking up God and the Mediator as distinct Parties, to be made application to. We shall insist no further for the time: O that there were seriousness to improve his blood and satisfaction, for washing us from the guilt of sin, and for making our peace with God; and his intercession, for upholding our peace and communion with God, and for the attaining of every good that he hath purchased and promised, which is the sum of all! God help us to the practice of it, and to be conscientious in it.

SERMON LXX.

Isaiah liii. 12.------*And made intercession for the transgressors.*

ALTHOUGH this be a most necessary thing, and that whereof we have daily and hourly use, even to be improving Christ's intercession; and altho' it be one of the most excellent and most comfortable things that a Christian hath to look to in his walk, there being no condition, but there is a ready help for it here: Yet this is our sinful misery, that either through our blindness, or our indifferency, we are much out of capacity to improve aright so rare a privilege: For as much as we have heard of it, are there many of us that can tell how Christ's intercession is to be improved? Sure we may know, that if ever we do it, there is no thanks to us for the doing of it; and indeed it is of such a nature, that we even cannot well tell, whether it be better to speak of it, or to be silent, being so little able to make any thing plain, of such a mysterious, yet very concerning thing.

Ye may remember the *doctrine* that we proposed to speak to was, "That our Jesus Lord Christ hath "this for a part of his office, to make intercession "for trangressors." Being a real Priest, he not only offers a sacrifice, but goes in, and hath gone within the vail, with the vertue of his sacrifice, to appear before God in heaven for us: As all the offices of Christ are advantageous, and would be studied by us, and we would study them well; this hath many advantages with it, and we would improve it, lest we frustrate ourselves of the cluster of privileges that is in this one doctrine, that Jesus Christ makes intercession for transgressors, or sinners.

We shewed the last day, wherein the improving of Christ's intercession doth consist: We shall now instance some cases, wherein believers, in a special manner, are to make use of it. 2. We shall give some directions for clearing some questions, or for answering some doubts about it. And, 3. We shall assign some characters of such as are rightly improving Christ's intercession.

For the *first*, Christ's intercession ought to be made use of, in as many cases as are possibly incident to a believer; and therefore we are not to restrict it to one case more than to another, altho' indeed there be some, wherein more especially we are called to improve it. Now, to clear it, that there are some cases, wherein, in a special manner, the believer is to make use of this office, of Christ's interceeding for transgressors: It may be instanced in these, 1. A believer hath either liberty, or he is in bonds; and there is a special, watchfulness called for in both these cases, that the intercession of Christ be not slighted.

1st, When he hath liberty, and his spiritual condition thrives, he prays, and his heart melts in prayer; he hath what he would have, the exercises of religion become pleasant, and he hath no will to come from them. In this case the believer is to beware, lest he be stoln off his feet, and misken Christ's intercession; for then he is ready to think that he cannot but be heard, and his prayers cannot but be heard, because he gets liberty to put them up; and it is then often, that there is hazard to lay least weight on Christ's intercession. To improve Christ's intercession aright in such cases, these *two* are to be adverted to, 1. That his intercession be acknowledged as the fountain and procuring cause of that liberty and liveliness; and so we are to carry a stopped mouth before God, and not to boast of it: For (as we shew) the pouring out of the Spirit is a special fruit of Christ's intercession, it being by vertue thereof that gifts are given, and grace to worship God in a spiritual manner. 2. That we beware of thinking that our prayers are in a fitness, or that they put us in a fitness of access to God, because of that liberty, except by vertue of Christ's intercession, more than if we had not a word to say: There is in our unbelief and presumption, a secret inclination to lay the weight of our acceptance on our own liberty; whereas, Rev. viii. the prayers of all saints must come up before God, having the smoke of his incense to make them acceptable; in which respect, in a case of liberty, Christ's intercession is made use of and improven, when we are denied to our own liberty, and it is not made the ground of our confident application to God, but Christ's intercession only. Again, 2. When the believer is in bonds, in some eminent manner, so that he cannot pray, he scarce hath a word to speak to God; he goes, it is true, about the duty, but he comes not speed, his prayer relishes not to himself; he is like one speaking, but not praying, his heart is not warmed; neither is there, at least to his own apprehension, any connexion betwixt his words; whereupon he is ready to think, that his prayer is as good as no prayer, because of that inclination that is in all of us, to rest on our own praying, without making use of the intercession of Christ: The reasons why in this case we would press the use-making of his intercession, are these, 1*ſt*, Lest we faint and grow weary in prayer, which cannot but befal us, if his intercession be not made use of. 2*dly*, Lest we lose the estimation of the excellent worth of Christ's intercession; which is exceeding derogatory to him that is *mighty to save, and on whom help is laid*; and it is especially for such a time and case, that he is holden forth for an Intercessor. Now, there is a *twofold* improvement of Christ's intercession called for in this case, when the believer is in bonds, and cannot so much as sigh, but it is called in question, whether it be accepted, tho' yet the man is serious. 1. There is an improving of it, for obtaining of that which we have been aiming at, tho' we cannot tell our own tale (to speak so) nor open our cause, nor make known our requests to God; yet, to expect what we have been aiming at, and seeking after, by vertue of Christ's intercession, for as ill set together as our prayer hath been, because it is founded upon the intercession of the Mediator, and we expect a hearing on that account allenarly; it being his intercession that makes our prayers acceptable, it can make such a poor prayer acceptable also: Whereupon the soul rests quiet, and expects a hearing on this ground, because, as we said, the prayers of all saints go up from his censer, and with his incense; and none are cast back, that are put up through him, and by vertue of his intercession: Hence sometimes looks, sometimes thoughts, sometimes broken words and groans come up before God, are acceptable, and get a return; the reason is, because, through the intercession of the Mediator, the prayers of all saints are acceptable. This is even as if a man should credit his able advocate with the managing of his cause, altho' he cannot (to speak so) mouth-band his own tale, nor express himself satisfyingly to himself in it; hence we have these words often, John xiv. 16. *Whatever ye ask in my name believing, ye shall receive; and, whatever ye ask in my name, I will do it*; that is, when ye ground the expectation of your hearing, and speed-coming in prayer, on me, and my mediation. When folks, because of their short-comings in prayer, give over the expectation of a hearing, and a return, they give over, in so far, the laying of due weight on his intercession: only ye would remember the terms, on which a person is warranted to make use of his intercession; for, when we follow not his way, in the improving of it, we cannot expect to come speed, or get good by it. 2. A believer in his bonds would expect a loosing, through the vertue of his intercession: And this is another way, how we would improve it in this case, when we are bound up, and (to speak so) langled, that we cannot stir in prayer, then we would have an eye to the efficacy of Christ's intercession, (that is of continual vigour and efficacy, even when we are very dead, indisposed, and lifeless) for the attaining of liberty and liveliness: This is indeed to cast a look to him, and singly to improve the efficacy of his mediation, when we cannot speak one word, to work up ourselves to a disposition for that work; and these two go well together, to be improving his intercession, for obtaining what we need for the time present, and for the time to come, and when we are in bonds, to be improving it for liberty and freedom.

2*dly*, There is an use-making of Christ's intercession called for, both when we aim to obtain any thing, and when we have obtained that which we would be at. 1. In our aiming to have or obtain, we would improve it, that our addresses to God may be in his name, and our faith of obtaining may be founded on Christ's intercession, and not on our own, and that our faith may be stayed and fixed in expectation of the thing: The improving of Christ's intercession in this respect leads us, 1*ſt*, To the right way of prosecuting our suits to God. And, 2*dly*, It quiets and fixes us in expecting of an answer; and, when this is wanting, Christians are either discouraged, and know not how to pursue their cause, or else they are carnally secure and presumptuous, which is very ordinary; for either, as I have said, we are under an anxious fear, so that we know not how to go about duty with any hope of success; or else we grow secure and slack, and careless in duty.

3*dly*, There is an use-making of Christ's intercession, when we have obtained any benefit, which keeps the soul in his common and debt, and in acknowledging itself to be his debtor. This makes Christians, when they have gotten any thing, to be

it keeps, as I said, the person humble and holily afraid, when it hath gotten, as well as when it was seeking; and it makes wary in using and fearful to abuse any benefit received, lest it be found a wrong and indignity done to Christ and his intercession.

4*thly*, We may instance the improving of Christ's intercession, both in a most sad, and in a most chearful condition; in reference to both which, we should make use of Christ's intercession : and it being readily one of these conditions that we are in, either a more sad, or more chearful one, we should think ourselves defective and faulty as to our duty, when we suit and conform not our way to our condition.

1. If it be a more sad condition, whether we be spiritually sad, the soul being heavy, and refusing to be comforted, or whether we be under a temporal outward disconsolate condition, there is an use-making of Christ's intercession called for in both; for a believer cannot be in any so disconsolate a condition, but he may draw refreshing from this fountain, in reference thereto; and when we make not use of his intercession in each, as it occurs, either anxiety and discouragement grows, or we turn to some unwarrantable and crooked mean or way for an out-gate from such a disconsolate condition.

Now, to make use of, and to improve Christ's intercession aright, in such a disconsolate condition and case, 1. The soul would gather, and compose itself, to search and see what is useful in Christ's intercession for its ease, seeing that sad case cannot be imagined, but Christ's intercession is a cordial for it, upon which, as a solid ground, the soul may be quiet, that it cannot miscarry in that, for which it is now in so much bitterness, seeing Christ Jesus hath the management of its case and cause : Hence it may reason thus, Although I was unwatchful, and this condition came on me unawares, and I was surprised with it, yet it is not any surprise to him : He was not sleeping, though I was; he knew what was coming, tho' I knew not; therefore this will not hurt nor pre- means; whereas, when we use not the means, or use them without due respect to Christ's intercession, the business becomes heartless, hopeless, and desperate.

2. If our condition be, or seem to be more solacious and chearful, there would be an improving of Christ's intercession, lest our chearfulness grow carnal, which it cannot otherwise be, but when he is acknowledged to be the Author of our solace and chearfulness; when he is depended upon for the continuance of it, and when the praise of it is returned to him, it bounds the heart, that there is no access to grow carnal : in which respect, these things wherein others grows carnal, such as health, strength, meat, drink, apparel, commodious dwelling, the recovery of themselves, of their children, or of other near relations or dear friends, from sickness, &c. are thus spiritualized and made spiritually refreshing to the people of God, because there is an uptaking of them, as coming through Christ's intercession, and a returning of thanks to him for them; hence, Heb. xiii. 15. it is said, *By him therefore, let us offer the sacrifices of praise to God*, there being the same access to praise in our spiritual chearfulness, that there is to pray in our heaviness and difficulties : He that is the ground, on which we ought to found our prayer, is also the ground on which we ought to build our praises; and it is he that puts life in and value upon the one and the other.

5*thly*, We may instance it in this case, when the believer is under challenges, it is then a special season to make use of Christ's intercession, and to put the libel in his hand to answer it; which is done by faith's resting on him as a Priest, for the obtaining of an absolution from that charge, altho' we cannot answer it ourselves, yet expecting an answer through him, according to that famous place, Rom. viii. 34. *Who shall lay any thing to the charge of God's elect ?* Who will libel them ? Among other reasons of the interrogation, which hath the force of a negation, this is one; *It is Christ who died, yea rather who is risen again, who is at the right hand of God, making intercession for us.*

This furnisheth an answer to the charge put in their hand: or, when the believer is under calmness and tranquillity, his intercession would be improven; for there cannot be a sanctified calmness, without depending on him, by vertue of whose satisfaction and procurement we have it, and by vertue of whose intercession it is continued.

The *reasons* why we have hinted at these things, are, 1. To hold out to you the concernment of Christ's intercession; for we cannot be in that case, but the believer hath therein to do with it. 2. To shew our great obligation to God, who hath given us such an Intercessor for all these cases: In this one word there is stored up a treasure of consolation, for all cases that a Christian can be in. 3. That we may be helped to our duty of improving and making use of him, according to the several cases we are, or may be in: For tho' his intercession be mainly to be made use of, when we come to pray; yet not only then, but at other times, and in other cases, as when we fear any hazard, when we need any good thing, when we expect it, or would be chearful on the receipt of it; and when we are in any difficulty, and know not what to do, we will find something called for from us, in reference to his offices, and to this in particular. 4. Because this use-making of Christ's intercession, commends Christ, and makes him lovely to us: And indeed, that which makes believers think so little of him, is in part, at least, the little improving of his intercession, which should be made use of in the least things, if it were when we need any thing, in our thought to look up to God, through him, and to found the hope of our getting it on this ground, because there is an Intercessor. If this were the practice of believers daily, they would see a necessity of thinking much of him; O when will we be serious and constant in the use-making of this part of his office! 5. Because it may serve also for ground of conviction to many that are called Christians, and who go through many cases and difficulties, and yet know not what it is to acknowledge him in his intercession. O it is a sad thing for folks to bear the name of Christians, and yet if they want any good thing, and can get it another way, they neglect and misken him; and if it be well with them, and if they obtain what they would have, they sacrifice to their own net, and he is slighted.

The next thing in order is, to remove some *objections*, and to answer some *questions* concerning this improvement of Christ's intercession, in the manner that we have spoken of; and there will readily be store of them in our carnal minds. Now, for the removing of these objections or doubts, I shall lay down some grounds for direction, that may answer any doubt of that kind, which may arise, partly from the doctrinal, partly from the practical part of this doctrine; it being a puzzling piece of exercise to some, that they think they know not how to improve Christ's intercession, or that they never did it aright, or possibly both these may be their exercise.

The 1*st* ground I would lay down, is this, That ye would remember, that there is an unsearchableness in this mystery of the Godhead, in the mystery of God's becoming Man, and in the mystery of the Mediator his taking on these offices, to exercise them in our nature; and, in speaking or thinking of them, there is a necessity to silence that which our curiosity would propose, for satisfaction about them; as, namely, How there are, or can be three Persons in the God-head, and yet but one God? How one of these Persons can be Man? and how it is, that by him we have access to God the Father, Son, and Holy Ghost? There is silence required in the *how* of these things, which leads to the next direction.

2*dly*, We would study satisfaction in the matter of the truth itself, rather than to be poring into the manner or *how* of profound mysteries, especially such as concern the blessed God-head, which *is higher than the heavens, broader than the earth, and deeper than the sea;* That is, (as we hinted at before) we would study rather to know that there is such a thing, than *how* it is: As, in this particular, we know that the Son of God became Man, took on our nature, and in our nature died, rose again, and ascended to heaven, sat down on the right hand of God, and makes intercession for us; these are clear: But if we ask *how* these things can be, that God can be Man, and that two natures can be in one Person, and how God can interceed, they are things much above our reach, and not so properly the object of our faith, (I say, as to the *how* of them) and our consolation lies not so much in knowing *how* such a thing is, as in knowing *that it is:* And I make no question, but there are many who pray in faith, because there is an Intercessor, who, if the question were asked, how he performs that work? they could not tell well, if at all; these that can tell most of it, are but very ignorant of it, and can tell but little: The Lord, in his goodness, hath so ordered the matter, that he hath given grounds for the faith of his people, to walk on in their duty, but will not satisfy their curiosity. And truly, if we will seriously reflect, we will find, that these things which most readily vex us, are questions about the *manner*, and not about the *matter* of things: we do not doubt, that the Son of God is God; that the holy Ghost is God, and that he proceeds from the Father and the Son; that the second Person of the Trinity became Man, &c. But the perplexing question is, *How* these things are, or can be? The Lord hath made it necessary to be believed, that there is one God, and three Persons in the Godhead: But to be in reason satisfied, as to the *how*, or manner of their subsistence and operations, that is not required as necessary; so it is here, in this matter of Christ's intercession: And therefore this second direction is, that ye would study clearness in the grounds that ye are to go upon, in the use-making of his intercession; but ye would not be curious in seeking satisfaction about the *how*, or manner of it.

3. In our addresses to God, and in our improving of Christ's intercession, we would beware of imagining, or framing in our imagination, representations to ourselves of him, who is the Object of our worship; or of the manner of the Mediator's intercession, as if we had seen him, or heard him with our bodily eyes or ears; a thing that sometimes is fashious and troublesom, as well as it is sinful, and which we are not called to; yea, if it were possible to attain to any representation of this kind, yet it is but a representation of our own forming, and so a breach of the second command: And therefore, in going to God through the Mediator, never represent to yourselves one Party standing beside, or by another, for that is but a diverting of the soul from the exercise of faith on a purely spiritual and simple Object, and derogatory to the Majesty of God; and whenever such representations are made, or rise in the imagination, or in the mind, God would be looked to, for crushing of them. It is from this that many of our doubts and questions arise; and there is no loosing of them, but by the abandoning of them: If there were a possibility to conceive something like God, yet the Lord abhorreth that; and Deut. iv. 15. and xii. 30. all similitudes and representations of God are discharged.

4. In our addresses to God through the Mediator, we would rest our faith on what is revealed in the word, seeking rather to take up God and Christ, as they are revealed in it, than, without the word, to seek satisfaction to our curiosity: We would, from the word, study to take up the attributes of God, his omniscience, omnipotency, omnipresence, wisdom, grace and mercy, purity and holiness, sovereignty, and absolute dominion in guiding all; and as being at such an infinite distance from, and infinitely above all creatures, that thereby a right impression of God may be wrought in the heart: We would likewise study clearness in the promises, both concerning Christ and his offices; and, in applications to God, we would fix our faith on these known grounds, believing we shall be heard; and being quiet on that. Moses, Exod. xxxiii. is under a vehement longing to see God, *I beseech thee*, saith he, *shew me thy glory*; the Lord tells him, that he cannot see it, and live, *but he will make his goodness pass before him*, he will let him see as much as is meet; and, chap. xxxiv. when he gives him his answer, it is not any glorious visible brightness he lets him see, but he proclaims his name to him, *The Lord, the Lord God, merciful and gracious*, &c. And comparing the words with the scope, it says, that there can be no saving uptaking of God, but as he is revealed in the word: And that way we are to be fixed in the faith of the excellency that is in him; and in going to him by prayer, through the Mediator, we would guard against any representation, and fix our faith on clear promises and attributes, as scripture holds him forth.

5. We would endeavour rather to have a composed frame of spirit, with holy reverence, in the exercise of fear, faith and love, and of other spiritual graces, than to fill our understanding with things merely speculative, and less practical and profitable; and supposing that we are in some measure clear in what is revealed of God, and of his attributes and promises in the word, in as far as may found our faith, and warrant us to put up such and such suits to God through the Mediator, and that we come to him in holy reverence, we are rather to exercise our graces, and have an eye downward, in reflecting on ourselves, seeking to be clear in what is called for in a worshipper of God, than to be curiously poring and prying into the Object of our worship himself: And therefore let this be well studied, even to be up at that wherein we are clear, and which we do not question, nor make any doubt of, as, namely, that we should be in a composed frame of spirit, in holy reverence, and under the due impression of the Majesty of God, and then there will be the less hazard, if any at all, of going wrong; whereas, if we divert from this, and seek to satisfy ourselves in the *how*, or manner of up-taking of God, we will but mire ourselves, and

and mar the frame of our own spirits, and bring ourselves under an incapacity of going about duty rightly.

This much we have spoken on the *third* part of the use of *exhortation*, wherein we allow a sober and solid up-taking of the things of God, and in as far as may be profitable for founding of our faith, and for guiding of our practice, but not to satisfy curiosity; for if we once go to chase, and follow question upon question, in what concerns the doctrinal, and speculative part of this doctrine, we will run ourselves a-ground. And therefore, God having made these things wherein our duty necessarily lies clear, that there is no hazard to go wrong in single following of it, we should study these things that are clear, (which might be another direction) and holds us with, and at, what we are clear in, and not suffer our minds to run out on either groundless or unprofitable speculations. God himself help to the suitable practice of these things; and to him be praise.

SERMON LXXI.

Isaiah liii. 12.-------*And made intercession for the transgressors.*

IT is a great mercy, that God hath bestowed such a Mediator on sinners, that he hath given such an high Priest, that can be touched with the feeling of sinners infirmities, so as to make intercession for them; and O but it is a great mercy to be helped to make right use of him! When these two go together, to wit, a Saviour offered, furnished with all these offices of *King, Priest* and *Prophet;* and a soul sanctified and guided by the Spirit of God, in making use of him, according to these offices; it is a wonderfully and unconceivably gracious dispensation: And it is no doubt, a very valuable mercy to be helped to make use of this part of Christ's office, to wit, his intercession; this is that, whereof we have begun some few days since to speak to you: And, for the better clearing of it, we endeavoured to answer some doubts, or questions, that, it may be, have arisen, and been tossed in the minds of some, while we have been discoursing of, and opening up this matter. That which we would now speak a little to, is a subject of that nature, that, considering our shallowness in uptaking of these things, we cannot easily tell, whether it be better to speak of, or to forbear the speaking of any doubt or question, lest one occasion another; and therefore, most certainly, there would be much sobriety here, and an abandoning of all sinful curiosity, lest unseasonable and intemperate desires to know, either what is not to be known, or what we cannot know, mar, and obstruct our improvement of what we do, or may know. Several things doubted of may be moved and objected here; but we shall only speak a word to the clearing of these four, 1. Something concerning the Object of worship, and particularly of prayer in general. 2. We shall consider how the Mediator is the Object of our prayer, or how he may be prayed unto. 3. A word more particularly, in reference to the form of some particular petitions, and to what seems most warrantable from the word in these. 4. We shall answer some practical doubts that have, or may have some puzzling influence on the consciences of some Christians: But, as I said, we had need, in speaking and hearing of these things, to be awed with some deep impression of the Majesty of God on our hearts, lest we meddle carnally with matters of a most sublimely spiritual and holy nature. For clearing of the *first* then, we lay down these assertions: The 1st whereof is, That as there is one worship, so there is no formal Object of worship but God; this is clear, because the worshipping of any with divine worship, as namely, with believing in them, or praying to them, supposes them to have such attributes of Omniscience, Omnipotency, Supremacy, *&c.* as are only agreeable to the Majesty of God; for we cannot pray to One, but we must believe that he hears us, and so that he is Omniscient; that he is able to help us, and so Omnipotent; that he is above all, and so Supreme; as it is, Rom. x. 14. *How shall they call on him, in whom they have not believed?* There can be no divine Object of worship to settle the soul upon; but where the essential attributes of the Godhead are; and it is on this ground, that we reject invocation of saints and angels: Adorability being the essential property of the Majesty of God, as well as eternity and immutability are; there can be no adoring or worshipping of any, but where there is adorability in the Object that is worshipped by that worship; and there is none capable of worship but God, supremacy being due and essential to him only. 2. That tho' there be three Persons in the glorious and blessed Godhead, distinct, yet there are not three distinct Objects of worship, but one Object of worship only; The Father is not one Object of worship,

worship, the Son another, and the Holy Ghost a third; but the Father, Son, and Holy Ghost, are that same one Object of worship; and when we pray to one, we pray to all. The reason is clear, Because, tho' there be three Persons in the Godhead, yet there is but one essence of the Godhead: and the divine essential properties (which are the grounds on which we adore God) are essential, and agree to all the Persons of the Godhead; the Father hath not one Omnipotency, and the Son another, neither are there two Omnipotents, but one omnipotent God; and so in other attributes they are the same essential properties of the Godhead, and incommunicable: And therefore, tho' the Father be another Person, and (as they use to speak) *alius*, yet he is not another Thing, or *aliud*, but the same God, with the Son, and Holy Ghost: And altho' the Persons have a real distinction amongst themselves, yet none of them are really distinct from the Godhead; and so there is but one Object of worship; and therefore, tho' sometimes all the Persons be named, yet it is not to shew away distinction in the Object of our worship, but to shew who is the Object of our worship, to wit, one God, yet three Persons, one in three. 3. That tho' in prayer to God, we may name either the Father, the Son, or the Holy Ghost; yet whosoever we name, it is always the same God, Father, Son, and Holy Ghost, that is worshipped; and this followeth well on the former, and may be the use of it: For, if the Father be God, and if we worship him as God, we cannot worship him, but we must worship the Son and Holy Ghost with him, because they are the same God, having the same essential attributes: And therefore, 4. Whensoever we pray to, and name one of the Persons, we would not conceive that he is less worshipped, that is not named, or that we pray less to him that is not named; as it may be in the same prayer, when a person begins at first, he names the Father, and when he has proceeded a little, he names the Son: Men would then beware of thinking that there is a difference in the Object they are praying to; or, as if they began to pray to one of the Persons, and now they are praying to another, as a distinct Party; for it is still the same God, who is the Object of worship. We observe it, to teach you calmness, soberness, and composedness of frame, in approaching to God; wherein folks would beware of curious tossing in their mind, and imagination, what may be the Object of their worship, and of suffering it to run in an itchingly curious way on the distinction of the Persons; but would stay their mind upon one God in three Persons, and seek after no more.

The 2d is, How the Mediator is the Object of our prayers, or may be prayed unto? And for clearing of this, we would propose these considerations, 1. That it is a certain truth, that the Person that is the Mediator, is the Object of our worship, and may be prayed unto, because he is God, the second Person of the Godhead; and therefore, Acts vii. at the close, a direct prayer is put up to him by Stephen, *Lord Jesus*, saith he, *receive my spirit*. 2. We say this, That the adoration and worship that is given to the Mediator, is not of any distinct kind from that adoration and worship that is given to the Father, and to the Holy Ghost, but the same supreme divine worship, for he is the same God with the Father and Holy Ghost; and altho' he be a Mediator, it derogates nothing from his Godhead: And the scripture speaking of no divine worship but one, we are therefore not to conceive him to be worshipped with less confidence, fear, or reverence, than the other Persons of the Trinity; for there is no such worship in scripture: and to give himself, would derogate from the Majesty of Jesus Christ, who is God equal with the Father, and the Spirit; for, altho', as Mediator, he be inferior to the Father, yet the Person whom we worship, is God equal with the Father, and the Holy Ghost. 3. The worshipping of Jesus Christ Mediator, and the giving of him divine worship, is not the worshipping of any other Object, but of the same, to wit, God, who is made flesh, and is manifested in our nature, by the union of the second Person of the Godhead, with the human nature which he has assumed and taken to him; upon which it follows, that Jesus Christ must be the same Object of worship, and that our worshipping of him, is the worshipping of God, and that our praying to him, is praying to God the Father, Son and Spirit: And there is reason to take heed to this, because, when we in prayer are speaking to the Mediator, thoughts may steal in, as if we were not so immediately and directly speaking to God, as when we name the Father. 4. Consider, that Christ Jesus being worshipped with this divine worship, as the one Object of worship, (for as we shew there cannot be two Objects of divine worship) it will follow, that Christ Jesus as God is worshipped; for tho' it be the Person that is Mediator and man, that is worshipped, yet it is not the Person as Man, but as God, that is worshipped: And the reason is clear, because it is not Christ Jesus as man, but as God, that hath these properties of God, to be omniscient

ent, omnipotent, infinite, supreme, adorable, &c. And therefore, as, upon the one hand, we say, that Christ-God died, and suffered, because he being God and man in one Person, the Person that was, and is God, died and suffered, tho' the Godhead did not suffer, neither can suffer: So, upon the other hand, we say, that Christ-man is prayed unto as God; but tho' there be an union of the two natures in the Mediator's Person, and tho' the properties of the one nature be sometimes attributed to the other, because of the straitness of the union, yet we must still keep the properties of each nature distinct, and in our worship-application to him, consider him accordingly: As to be finite, agrees to his human nature, and is to be attributed to that; and to be infinite, agrees to his divine nature, and is to be attributed to him in respect of that. To clear it a little, (if it be possible for us to clear it) we must conceive, in our worshipping of God in the Person of a Mediator, a threefold Object of our worship: (for so divines use to distinguish, and we would hold us close by them) 1. The *material* Object, or the Object which we worship, that is the Person we pray to. 2. The *formal* Object of our worship, or that which is the ground or account on which we worship that Person. 3. The Object of our *consideration*, in our worshipping of that Person, on that account. As for instance, (1.) The Man Christ Jesus, is the Person whom we worship, or pray unto. But, (2.) The formal Object of our worship is Christ's Godhead, and we pray to him on that account, because he is the Eternal, Infinite, Omnipotent, Supreme, &c. in respect of his divine nature. (3.) In our worshipping of this Mediator, on this account, or ground, the mind may be swayed to it, on consideration, that the Person whom we worship as God, is also Mediator and man; and this proposes no new Object of worship, but gives a motive to induce us to worship him, and warms the heart with love to him: As, when we go to pray to him, the mind may consider him as One that died; now, so considered, he is not the Object of our worship, because it holds him out as humbled, and suffering, yet our so considering him, strengthens faith to expect what we need from him; and it induces to pray to him, and engages to love him: Even as the people of Israel, in praying to God, sometimes used that title, *Our Redeemer that brought us out of Egypt;* yet the ground, and account on which they worshipped him, was his being the eternal, infinite, and omnipotent God; and the consideration of his works were but motives to induce them to worship

him, and to strengthen their faith, in expecting what they stood in need of from him: So is it here; for if it were possible to conceive, that the Mediator that died, were not God, we would not pray to him, for God is the alone Object of divine worship; yet to consider, that he is God, and yet died, is an inducement to us to pray to him, and it strengthens our faith, to consider, that as he is God, so also man, One that died, and hath also entred himself in this near relation to us.

For the 3*d*, (which will help to clear the former) that is, the forms of such petitions as may be used in petitioning the Mediator; we need the less to stand on it, if (as hath been said) we hold us by these grounds, 1. That there is but one Object of worship. 2. That this one Object of worship, is God. 3. That in worshipping the Mediator, we do not divide that Object of our worship. Yet we shall speak a word for clearing, 1. What form seems most allowable here. 2. For clearing of somewhat, which we hinted at the other day, anent one particular form of petition.

1. Then, this is clear, that we may pray directly to the Mediator, by naming him, as Stephen does, Acts vii. at the close. 2. That the Mediator, when prayed to, may be considered as such by us; for there is a difference betwixt that which is considered by us, in the act of our worship, and that which is the Object of that act; and (as we said) the motive that induces us to that act, is the up-taking of him as Mediator. 3. That he may be designed *Mediator* and *Redeemer*, and may get these names and titles, because they serve to strengthen our faith, and to warm our affections to him; even as when the people of Israel prayed to God, they remembered, that he was their Redeemer and Deliverer, and had wrought so and so for them; and these were motives to induce them to pray, and served to strengthen their faith in praying to him; yet the ground and account on which they worshipped him, was his own infinite glorious Majesty. 4. It is clear, that when the Mediator is prayed unto, something may be sought from him, that agrees to the office of the Mediator: For instance, he may be prayed unto, to take to him his government, and to exerce it, to give gifts unto men, to gather his own elect, to make his will effectual for the ingathering of them, &c. yet even then a difference would be put betwixt the Object of our suit, and the matter we suit for, which belongs to him as Mediator; yet as God, he is the Object of our suit and prayer. This
seems

seems to be hinted at, Psal. xlv. when the Psalmist, speaking to the Son the Mediator, says, *Gird thy sword upon thy thigh, ride prosperously; let the King's arrows be sharp in the hearts of his enemies;* Which upon the matter seems clearly to relate to Christ's executing his office as Mediator: Yet look to the title he gives him, and the ground or account on which he puts up his prayer, it is the consideration of him as God; therefore, he says, *O thou most mighty!* a divine attribute, pointing him out to be God: And, *Thy throne, O God,* (faith he) *is from everlasting,* &c.

Now, as for the 2d thing, If all this be granted, it may then be asked, why we seem not to be satisfied with that manner of expression, or form of petition, which we hinted at the other day, *Lord Jesus, make intercession for me, plead for me, with, or before the Father;* seeing we allow such a petition as this, *Lord Jesus, make me partaker of thy intercession,* and the like, as warrantably, when put up with reverence and faith, the same Object of worship being invocate with them both? *Answer* 1. We say, that the use-making, and improving of Christ's intercession, is not to be restricted to this manner of expression, or form of petition; and it was for this end that we observed it: For it cannot be said, that only we make use of Christ's intercession, when we use this form, and so it is not essential, nor necessary to the use-making of Christ's intercession: This is the fault that is in it, as if there were no use-making of his intercession, but when this form of petition is used; whereas, we shew, that it is mainly the exercise of faith, resting on his intercession, whereby it is improven; and one may be using this form of words, and yet not be improving his intercession; and another may not use this form of words, and yet be improving it, when faith is exercised on it: And therefore, to improve his intercession, is rather by the exercise of faith to rest on it, than in any such form of words to pray to him; and we would not think, that Christ's intercession is made use of, when the Father is prayed unto, or when such a form of words is used, but place it in the exercise of faith alone. 2. We say, if such a petition be well understood and qualified, it is not simply sinful or evil; if so be our meaning amount to this much, Lord Jesus, let me be partaker of the benefits of thy intercession; even as we may pray, Lord Jesus, let me be partaker of the benefits of thy satisfaction: Yet we say, it would be well understood and qualified; and a person, in putting up such a petition, would advert well, that he be not praying to any other object of worship, but God, and that his meaning be the same, as if he were praying to the Father, and said, Father, let me be accepted through the intercession of the Son: And thus the one is an improving of Christ's intercession, as well as the other; for altho' the altering of the nomination of the Person may strengthen faith, yet it is never to be so understood, as if there were a different Object of worship, or, as if there were less access to Christ's intercession, or to the benefits thereof, in the one form than in the other. Yet, 3. We say, there is often a readiness to miscarry in this form of petition; for ye would consider and examine, (1.) If it doth not often flow from a mis-informed judgment within, and if it had not a tendency in it to obscure the nature of the unity of the Object of our worship, and readily disposing to, or flowing from this opinion, that praying to the Mediator is not the same that praying to God is, as if there were two distinct Objects of worship. Or, (2.) If there be not a readiness to consider the Person that is Mediator, to be of less glory and majesty than the Father, and to consider the Father to be of less loving-kindness and tenderness to sinners than the Son, and other things of that kind, which move people to put up a suit, in such a form, which makes it more difficult to keep the thoughts of one Object of worship under such a form, than otherwise. Yet, (4.) We say, it may be used by, and accepted of God, from many that have not that distinctness and clearness in the ridding of their thoughts in this mystery, that is requisite, because there may be real faith under such a form of words, (tho' infirmity in the use-making of Christ's intercession) and God respects that wherever it is: And under such a form, there may be those two, 1. A soul-sensibleness, that the person hath no access to God, but through a Mediator. 2. A resting on the Mediator for acceptance; and where these two are, tho' the form be used, it may be accepted; although if faith be, though this form be not, it mars not the person's acceptation: For no question, many of the people of God, both before Christ came, and some time after, had not that distinctness in use-making of the intercession of Christ, as now is holden forth, as Christ says to his disciples, John xvi. 24. *Hitherto ye have asked nothing in my name;* and Cornelius, mentioned, Acts x. and others, their prayers were accepted of God, tho' they rested by faith on the Mediator, in a more confused dark way, and had not that distinctness in them, of use-making of him,

which

which was afterwards more clearly revealed. And therefore, 5: and laftly, Tho' we will not be peremptory in condemning such a form altogether, yet we think it largely as safe to abftain from any fuch form of words, in the ufe-making of Chrift's interceffion, as may have in them any appearance of, or tendency to the dividing of the Object of our worfhip, or the Mediator from his Godhead, efpecially in praying with, or for others, where it may ftumble more than edify; and when it is ufed, it would be very warily, and well guarded, remembring always, that the improving of Chrift's interceffion confifts more in faith's refting on it, and in making addrefs to God through him, and according to the ufual manner of the fcripture, than in any other thing or way whatfoever.

The 4th thing we propofed to fpeak a word to, was fome *practical doubts* or *queftions*, that may puzzle fome Chriftians, who, having obferved what hath been fpoken on this fubject, may be ready to think, and fay, that the improving of Chrift's interceffion is to them a greater myftery than ever it was: Many times they have prayed, and minded it not; and when they mind it, they are not diftinct in their improving of it, and they are never like to mind it. For *Anfwer*, 1ft, Ye would look to what is effential to the improving of Chrift's interceffion, and make that fure; and if ye afk what it is, it takes in thefe *four*, which where they are, his interceffion is made ufe of; tho' there may be unclearnefs in many other things; 1. That a perfon pray to God, that he be called on and worfhipped. 2. That our addreffes be not founded on any thing in ourfelves, but that there be a renouncing of our own righteoufnefs, as it was with Daniel, chap. ix. 18. *We do not prefent our fupplications unto thee, for our own righteoufnefs*, &c. 3. That there be a believing of our acceptation through Jefus Chrift; tho' there be a diftance betwixt God and us, yet that there is a way, through the ufe-making of Chrift, to come over that diftance, and to win at nearnefs to him. And, 4. Upon that account to enter our fuit, and to put up our prayers to God, with the one word difclaiming our own righteoufnefs, and with the other pleading on the account of God's mercy through Chrift, as Daniel doth, *Not for our righteoufnefs, but for thy mercies fake, and for thy name's fake*: Now, I fuppofe, that fouls fhould not be able to anfwer the feveral queftions about the Object of worfhip, and the way of improving of Chrift's interceffion; yet, if they call upon God, if they renounce their own righteoufnefs, not knowing any ground in themfelves to lean to, or to put up their fuit on, and make ufe of Chrift for the ground of their acceptance with God; and if it were afked them, What gives you ground to expect a hearing of your prayers? they would anfwer, Even the fame that gives us ground to expect pardon of fin, and we would never expect to win to either without a Mediator; they are amongft them who are improving Chrift's interceffion, and fuch would filence and hufh other queftions, if they be clear in this. 2*dly*, We anfwer, That there may be a real ufe-making of Chrift's interceffion, and it may be accounted fo, where there is much indiftinctnefs in the up-taking of it; as thefe inftances clear, of Cornelius, Acts x. and of the difciples, John xvi. who prayed not on the account of their own righteoufnefs, or of the covenant of works; (for they made confeffion of their fins) yet the Mediator, and his interceffion, was not fo diftinctly, as fuch, confidered by them; in their fo doing, for they did not diftinctly take up him, as Chrift fays, *Hitherto ye have afked nothing in my name;* yet there was an actual refting on him by faith; and their prayers were no doubt accepted of God, he not being fo diftinctly known to be the Interceffor, as now he is: and therefore there is required a more diftinct ufe-making of him now, and not a refting on him indefinitely, but particularly and diftinctly, he being clearly revealed now to be the Mediator. 3*dly*, We anfwer, That believers may fometimes be making ufe of Chrift's interceffion, in approaching to God by him, and yet they themfelves not know diftinctly that they are doing fo, as we fee in the difciples, John xiv. 4. Chrift fays, *Whither I go ye know, and the way ye know;* and, verfe 6. fpeaking of coming to the Father by him, he fays, *I am the Way, the Truth, and the Life;* and yet, verfe 5. Thomas fays, *Lord, we know not whither thou goeft, and how can we know the way?* and the Lord turns it over to him, and fays, that *they have both known him and the way.* As alfo, believers may fometimes, through want of clearnefs and diftinctnefs in this, what it is to make ufe of Chrift's interceffion, or becaufe they want that meafure of diftinctnefs they would be at, think that they are doing nothing, as to the ufe-making of his interceffion; and yet the work of God's Spirit, though they know it not well, may be leading them: for it is in this, as it is in the ufe-making of his fatisfaction; a believer may be making ufe of Chrift's fatisfaction, and be juftified by it, when he knows not that it is fo, or poffibly cannot

not well tell what it is to make use of it; which may quiet any risings or reasonings that may be in their minds about this matter. 4*thly*, We answer, That explicit thoughts of Christ's intercession are not always necessary nor requisite for the use-making of it; even as we are to design God's glory, to be our main end in all our undertakings, so we are to pray in the name of Christ; but as it is not requisite, that there be always, and all along with the action, an actual minding of God's glory, but that being laid as our principle, which we walk by, and the strain of our walk and conversation to that end, it is and will be accepted before God, altho' there be not, in and along with every thing we do, explicit thoughts of his glory: So is it in our praying in Christ's name, and in improving of his intercession; there may be a virtual, tho' not an actual and explicite resting on it, the soul having laid down that for a ground and principle, that it is not for any thing in me that I do expect a heaven, but it is through Christ; and all the confidence that I have to be heard, it is through him. 5*thly*, We answer, That a poor soul, that wots not well what to do in this case, would eye God's promise, to be guided in the use-making of Christ's intercession, without anxiety, as it is, John xvi. 26: *In that day ye shall ask in my name;* as if he had said, It hath been your fault, that ye have not hitherto prayed in my name, at least with that distinctness that ye ought; but, I give you my word for it, *ye shall pray in my name:* And when through confusion we are ready to faint, we would eye this promise, to be guided in the use-making of his intercession. 6*thly*, We would learn rather to hold us in our worshipping of God, with that which is practical, and serves to bring us under an awe and reverence of the Majesty of God, than give ourselves to that which doth indispose and disquiet us: And I shall close all with this word, that we would even admire, how souls are carried and brought to heaven, that we should be suffered to pray, and that God breaks not out upon us; and we would study to be deeply humbled for our ignorance of God, and of Christ, and would think ourselves to be much in his debt and common, for teaching us to make right use of him, seeing we are so ready to miscarry, even when we desire and endeavour to make use of him.

SERMON LXXII.

Isaiah liii. 12.------*And made intercession for the transgressors.*

THE greatest privileges that we have by the gospel, do often hold forth the greatest aggravations of our sin, as being against so great and excellent privileges. Now, that the Lord hath given us a Mediator, and that this one part of his mediation, to wit, to make intercession for transgressors, or sinners, is one of the great privileges of the gospel, is beyond all doubt; and therefore we had need to fear, lest by our abusing, and not improving aright of this privilege, it prove an aggravation of our guilt: And this is the last thing that we would speak a word to, from these words, That seeing our Lord Jesus is invested with this office, to be an Intercessor, then it must be a ground of expostulation with, and reproof of these, who shall be found slighters of his intercession; for, if it be a duty to improve his intercession, and if it be a mercy that we have it, and if many advantages be gotten by it, then it must be a grievous sin, a matter of just challenge, and great shame, that sinners should have such an Advocate and Intercessor provided for them, to take and plead their cause so freely, and to manage it so dexterously as he doth, and not to slight him, and not to put that trust in him, as to commit their cause to him.

In prosecuting of this *use*, we shall, 1*st*, Shew that there is such a sin, as not improving of Christ's intercession, and how it is fallen into. 2*dly*, The causes of it, or whence it comes, that folks so much mistken this part of Christ's office. 3*dly*, The great inconveniencies that follow on it, and the great prejudices that are sustained by it. 4*thly*, We shall hint at some symptoms and evidences where this sin is. And, 5*thly*, Speak a word to the remedies in opposition thereunto.

For the *first*, That there is such a sin, it may be clear, from a few considerations, that may be obvious to every one of us. 1. It may be clear, from the effect; what is the cause that so many come so little speed in prayer, that they pray, and yet get not a hearing; so that, in the day of judgment, it will be found, that many prayed, and that their prayers were cast back as dung upon their faces? *They sought to enter, and were not able,* as it is, Luke xiii. And this will be found to be the reason of it, that they went to God, but
mistken'd,

misken'd, or took not notice of him, who is *the Way, the Truth, and the Life*: for, where Christ's intercession is improven, there is an effect following; for God hath laid it down for a solid ground, that *whosoever believeth in him, shall not perish*, and *whatsoever ye ask in my name, it shall be granted*: And therefore, where there are many petitions put up to God, and no answer at all, there is sure a crack and default in folks making use of Christ; for God is faithful, and will perform his promise. *Secondly*, and more particularly, All the members of the visible church may be reduced to these *three* ranks, and we will find a defect, as to the use-making of Christ's intercession in them all, tho' not of the same degree, or rather not of the same kind. 1*st*, Either they are profane, and have not so much as a form of religion; and such do slight Christ and his intercession altogether. Or, 2*dly*, They are hypocrites, that make a fashion of prayer, but come not to God by him, but, at the short cut, proudly step forward, and put up their suits upon the account of their own righteousness; as they ground their justification on it, and not on Christ's satisfaction, so they put up their prayers to God, on the account of their own righteousness, and not on the account of Christ's intercession. Or, 3*dly*, They are such as have something of God in them, and so are believers; and, even in such, there is often a great defect, as to this, as Christ says to the disciples, John xvi. 24. *Hitherto ye have asked nothing in my name*. He chargeth them not simply for not praying, he grants that, *but ye have not asked in my name*, Ye have not made use of my intercession as ye should have done: Altho' there be not such a defect in them as there is in the former two sorts; yet there is a great short-coming, and not an improving of Christ's intercession, as they should. And therefore, *Thirdly*, It will be more clear, if we consider the particular cases incident to believers, when we will find, that but very scarcely Christ's intercession is improven in any of them; as, 1*st*, If the believer hath liberty in prayer, he is ready to sit down on it, and to conclude, that he cannot but be heard, because he hath liberty: And there is not so single an eye had to Christ's intercession; and often it is more difficult to hold off this sin, when liberty is enjoyed, than when it is wanting, because, tho' liberty be good and desirable in itself, yet, through our corruption and pride, it is often abused: Even as when Christians win to some good measure of holiness, it is in some respect more difficult to rest upon Christ's righteousness, than if that measure were not attained; so is it here more difficult, some way, to rest upon Christ's intercession, when we have liberty in prayer, than when we are in bonds, and under restraint. 2*dly*, Upon the other hand, if we look to a believer, when he is straitned, and it goes not well with him in prayer, there is then ordinarily a great defect in making use of Christ's intercession, as if it could not in that case avail us; and upon this follows anxiety and fretting, and the believer is ready to conclude, he will be nothing the better of prayer, and that it is better to pray none, than to pray so; whereas an eye to Christ's intercession would give the mind some quietness. 3*dly*, If there be an ill and very necessitous case, or if there be challenges, and some commotion, discomposure, and disquiet in the spirit, there is readily little respect had to Christ; if quietness and calmness be, there is also hazard of sitting down on that, and we readily forget that we hold it of him; and indeed it will be found difficult, either to have or to want, and in either the one case or the other, to be making right use of his intercession. Now, when I speak of this sin, it not only reproves them that pray none at all, which smells of gross Atheism, but also these who shuffle by Christ, and step forward at the nearest, as if they were not to come to God by him, as it is, Heb. vii. 25. and John xiv. 6.

Secondly, The *Causes* of this sin, and whence it comes to pass, that folks so slight the use-making of Christ's intercession, 1. There is a great difficulty in the thing, it is tickle. 2. There is a natural aversion from, and enmity at that thing in us. 3. There is a readiness to pitch on some other thing, and to misken and overlook this. Now, let all these *three* be put together, and we will see the reason and way how folk slide and fall into this fault.

1*st*, I say, there is a difficulty in the thing, it being one of the most purely spiritual, sublime and denied things in all the gospel, one of the greatest exercises of faith; and we know, that all such things have to our nature a great difficulty. 1. It is a difficulty to bring a man to be but formal in religion. 2. There is a difficulty, when he is made formal, to make him serious, even in a legal manner, and to be any thing affected in the exercise of repentance, and of other duties, so that he be not grosly dissembling. 3. When he is made thus serious, it is a difficulty to bring him over that seriousness, and to draw him from resting on these duties, which he hath been drawn to: I say, it is a great and difficult work to get a man brought to the performance of holy duties, and as great a work to get him brought over them, and from resting on them, to rest on Christ's righteousness for his justification, and on Christ's intercession for the acceptance of his prayers: And therefore, when the Lord hath once gotten his disciples to pray, and honestly yoked and engaged therein, he trains them on to pray in his name, and so to get their prayers rightly qualified. 2*dly*, If we consider our nature, we will find, that there is an averseness and backwardness therein to it, as there is an averseness in us to all things that tend to the making us deny ourselves, and lay the weight of every thing on Christ; that which thwarts with our pride, stands and sticks at our stomachs, (to speak so) and goes not well down with us: Of such nature is this, for our use-making of Christ's intercession implies, that we of ourselves are at a distance with God, that we have broken covenant, and are not to be trusted without a Mediator; and there is in our nature a secret sort of disdain at this, we cannot naturally endure it: Hence, Rom. x. it is said of the Jews, that being ignorant of God's righteousness, they did not submit nor stoop to the same, but sought to establish their own righteousness. 3*dly*, There is a readiness to pitch and condescend almost on any other sin, rather than on this; and therefore folks may be longer under it than under many, and yet not be challenged for it: They will readily be challenged for lying, swearing, Sabbath-breaking, and the like; but they sleep more securely in this sin, than in most others: It is a sin easily fallen into, and a sin not easily recovered from, or win out of, because it is a gospel-sin, that the light of nature reacheth not, and that the conscience hath not such an awe in convincing of. It is against nature's light to neglect prayer, or to take God's name in vain: But this runs in the channel of the gospel, to pray in the name of Christ, and to make all our addresses to God through him; the sinful neglect whereof, cannot be discovered, but by gospel-light: and we find by experience, that many will be convinced of, and have challenges for out-breaking sins, who yet will have no challenges for the neglect of this duty; even as it is easier to convince folks of a breach of the law, than of not believing in Christ: many will grant, that ignorance of God is a sin, and that irreverence and wand'ring in prayer are sins, who yet will stand and stick at this, and cannot be gotten convinced, but that they still believe in Christ, and make use of his intercession.

For the *third*, to wit, the inconveniencies and prejudices of this evil, they are very many; we shall only hint at them, for they are directly opposite to the good that comes by the improving of Christ's intercession. 1. It makes many prayers to be fruitless and frustraneous: Tho' folks should weary themselves in prayer, yet it is all but lost labour; and the Lord will say, as it is, Isa. i. *Though ye make many prayers, yet I will not hear them*, if Christ's intercession be neglected; but one word put up in Christ's name hath a gracious hearing. 2. It makes many prayers and other duties also to be lifeless; no duty goes with folks, neither can it go with them, when Christ is slighted, seeing it is by faith in him, that we have life derived to us, whereby we are made lively in every thing. 3. It hath much anxiety following on it, to be praying, and to have no expectation, nor ground of expectation of a hearing; for if we look no further than to something in ourselves, it is but a poor foundation of quietness and peace. 4. It hath this prejudice, that it inures, habituates and accustoms us to a low esteem of Christ, and makes us want many sweet experiences that we might have of his usefulness and worth; and it fosters a disrespect of Christ: whereas the use-making of his intercession keeps always up an esteem of him, and makes the thoughts of him fresh; and it is ever well with the soul, while he is esteemed of; and it is impossible it can be well, when he is not in request.

Now, ye may easily gather what all this aims at, even that ye may not satisfy yourselves with the form of duty, but that ye may look that it be rightly discharged, so as Christ in his offices, and particularly in his priestly office, and more particularly in his part of it, be made use of: It may be, there are some here that have been called Christians, these twenty, thirty, or forty years; but I would enquire at you, What use have ye made all the while of Christ's intercession? The neglect of this is a sin against mercy, a sin against your own souls and the cause of many other sins: Therefore take it among your other reproofs, that not only ye have neglected prayer, lived in ignorance, and taken his name in vain, but that ye have also long professed faith in Christ, and yet have not made use of Christ's intercession. This will be amongst your saddest challenges, when ye come to sickness, and to your death-beds, and ye will have it heavily charged on you, that there hath been great slighting and miskenning of Christ,

even

even when ye thought that ye were praying to him.

In the 4th place, To clear it yet further, we shall, 1. Hint at some symptoms or evidences of neglecting of Christ's intercession. 2. At some characters of a person that is making use of Christ's intercession aright. 3. At some directions that may help to the suitable performance of this duty. And 4. At some motives and encouragements to it.

1st, For the symptoms or evidences of miskenning, and slighting of Christ's intercession. 1. This is one, when there is little walking under the impression of the need of his sacrifice, when folks walk whole-heartedly (to speak so) and without due conviction of the distance that is betwixt God and them; for Christ's intercession flows from his satisfaction, and the improving of his satisfaction flows from the conviction of our natural distance from God: When folks are not sensible of their enmity, and of their vileness, and see not their need of washing, when they have a heal heart, few challenges, little exercise of repentance, and of self-lothing, it is a great evidence that there is little or no use made of Christ's intercession. The 2d symptom is deep security, and much self-confidence; where these are, Christ's intercession is little or not at all made use of; When a soul makes no question of, nor hath any doubt about its own peace, or about its praying, or getting a hearing, this is indeed self-confidence, and does flow from the former, to wit, ignorance of our distance from God, which is clear both from experience, and from scripture; they that make least use of Christ's intercession, and have most carnal confidence, have readily fewest challenges: Thus the Pharisee stands, Luke xviii. and prays, saying, *Lord, I thank thee*, &c. The greatest part of such folks prayers is thanksgiving on carnal grounds; whereas the poor Publican dare not come near; but when the Pharisee comes boldly forward, he *stands afar off*, and says, *Lord, be merciful to me a sinner*, who (as if he had said) have a respect to the covenant of grace, and so to the improving of Christ's intercession; it is certainly an ill token when folks sit down with confidence to their prayers, and rise up from them, without all fear of being denied, and said nay. A 3d symptom of not making use of Christ's intercession, is, when folks have too much anxiety, which is a fault that a believer may easily fall in, when he hath no ground from himself to propose to God for a hearing, and when he cannot answer his own challenges, and is therefore discouraged; which says, that he lippens not much to Christ, and to his intercession. A 4th symptom is, when duties of worship become burdensom, when it wearieth folk to pray, to sanctify the Lord's day, &c. when these are fashious and cumbersom to them; the reason whereof is, because they take the burden wholly or mostly on themselves, and lay it not over on Christ; whereas, were he rightly made use of, it would be found to be a truth, that *his yoke is easy, and his burden is light*, as himself saith, Matth. xi. 30. A 5th symptom is, when folks are not thankful for any mercy they receive, and are not wondering how it comes, that they get such mercies as they have, when they think little of their daily bread, of ordinances, of access to pray, &c. Souls that are improving Christ's intercession, think much of any mercy, because the least mercy is quite without the reach of the merit of ought they can do, and must come to them by the mediation of Another: Thus every mercy becomes a double mercy, as it is considered in itself, and as it comes to them by vertue of Christ's intercession; therefore the believer, improving Christ's intercession, wonders at every thing he meets with from God; that he is admitted to pray, or to praise; for he knows, that it is from free grace, thus admitting sinners through and by a Mediator.

As to the 2d, to wit, the characters, or evidences of a person's making use of Christ's intercession; the 1st may be this, A constant use-making of Christ's satisfaction, when the soul is never quiet, but when it hath a respect to that; and this use-making of Christ's satisfaction hath in it always, either more implicitly, or more expresly, an use-making of his intercession, and leaves the weight of duties and mercies upon him: Hence a soul will be under thorow conviction of its enmity, and very much edged and eager in its desires after peace, and will have expectation of obtaining it through him. A 2d evidence is, When folk in their approaches to God, have faith and fear going together: anxiety and fear, without faith, are not good, and self-confidence without fear is as ill; but when faith and fear go together, it is good; fear, arising from the impression of our own unworthiness and discovered distance; and faith, from the discovery of Christ's fulness, keeping the mind quiet, looking over its own unworthiness, to his worthiness, like that spoken of No-soul itself. 3. They that make use aright of Christ's intercession, betake themselves to it, when in a manner they have given over, and been formerly hopeless, like these spoken of, Psal. cvii. *Then they cry in their distress*, &c. Many have a confidence, because they were never brangled nor shaken, and have win to quietness this way; even as it is in the matter of making peace with God, many will profess that they always had it, even from their youth up, they never doubted of it, which speaks its unsoundness: but it is a solid evidence of faith, when the soul hath once been brangled and shaken; and this gives it confidence, that Christ hath satisfied, and makes intercession, and they betake themselves to that. 4. Where Christ's intercession is improven and made use of, it will be ground of rejoicing and comfort to think on it, when souls themselves can do but little, being bound up, and under bonds, yet they chear themselves, and bless God, that they know they have an Advocate: I apprehend, there are many to whom it was never refreshful, nor matter of gladness, that he is an Advocate, or that he stands in such relation to plead for sinners; surely such have not made use of him. A 5th evidence is this, When any thing is attained, the improving of Christ's intercession makes thankful and humble: if the soul have liberty, it is not puffed up with it, because it considers, that it is a mercy come through Christ's intercession; it hath received it, and therefore should not boast; it is not of its own procurement, but it is obliged to free grace for it. 6. The soul that is improving Christ's intercession, when it obtains not, it gives not over, but continues adhering and waiting for attaining of that which it is seeking; the cause of such a person is never quite desperate: If it be a thing conditional, it is submissive; if it be simply necessary, it is dependent, and will not quit, nor give over, because, tho' it obtain not to day, it knows it is possible to attain it, and that it will in due time be attained; it lays not the weight of its obtaining on its own prayers, but on Christ's purchase and intercession: and tho' the believer may be some-intercession. It is here as in justification, it is one part of his exercise to do duty, and another part of his exercise to be denied to it, and made to betake himself to Christ's righteousness allenarly for his acceptation; but other persons that make no use of Christ's intercession, if they get words, and any a bit of tenderness, they think all is well enough; but it is a believer's exercise, to see that his mind miscarry not in the use-making of Christ. 8. Souls that are improving Christ's intercession, their confidence is not up or down, according to their liberty, words or reasons they win to make use of in prayer; but they are up or down, according as they win to get the thing they seek, committed to Christ. Hence, a word or look will sometimes quiet the soul, when at another time, many hours prayer will not do it: For this is sure, so long as the thing rests on ourselves, the soul gets never a kindly lair; and that which puts it off ourselves, over on Christ, is the exercise of faith, and not liberty, nor the multitude of words. At another time, a believer will rise from prayer, and not seriously look, whether Christ have been depended on, or not, but is quiet, because he hath prayed; whereas, when Christ's intercession is improven, he is quiet on that ground, that it is God that is prayed to, through Christ; it is that which gives him ground of confidence to expect a hearing, and on that his soul rests, when he hath done praying. And therefore we would commend this to you, in place of many questions that might be moved on what ye have heard, even to carry a distinct answer in your bosom to these *two*, whether when ye are going to pray, or when ye have done with prayer, 1. To whom are ye to pray, or have ye been praying? That it is the great God, that one God, the Maker of all things, who ought alone to be worshipped, that being properly and formally the Object of your worship, and particularly of this your prayer. 2. Upon what ground do ye hazard to put a suit to this great God, and what is it that gives you confidence to expect an answer? It is that, not for any righteousness or worth in yourselves, or in your prayers,

but

but for Jesus Christ, for his satisfaction and intercession's sake: When ye can give a distinct answer from the conscience, in reference to these two, tho' there be not such distinctness in other things, to wit, that it is God ye pray to, and that ye expect a hearing on Christ's account, it is right.

For the *third* thing, What is it, that will help us to make use of Christ's intercession? (1.) Consider that it is our duty. Souls often mind not, that God hath not simply bidden them pray, but commanded them to pray in the name of Christ; he hath not bidden you simply approach to him, but to approach to him, in and by Christ; this would be remembred, else we forget the half of our duty, to wit, the manner how we should come to God, which is a main, if not the main part of it. (2.) We would remember, and think upon our condition by nature, that upon the one side, God is a consuming fire, and we on the other, like dry stubble; and that there is no approaching to him, without a Mediator: There were the less hazard of going wrong, if folk were walking under the suitable impression of their sinfulness and misery by nature; the want whereof, makes too much forwardness, in stepping to God without Christ. Therefore we commend to you all, and especially when ye go to prayer, to endeavour to be under deep impressions of your own sinfulness and baseness; as we see it was with Abraham, Gen. xviii. *Behold, now I have taken on me to speak to the Lord, who am but dust and ashes.* (1.) Mind the promise of God's hearing you through Christ, and his promise of leading you in all necessary truth, and so to perform duty in this manner: Mind, I say, *1st*, The promise of hearing, that it is not a promise to hear us simply in what we pray for, but in what we pray for with other requisite qualifications of prayer, and with this in particular, that it be in Christ's name: Hence is *asking in his Name*, so often mentioned, John xiv. ver. 13, 14. and xvi. ver. 23, 24, 26. To mind, that there is a promise of hearing, draws a soul to pray to God; and to mind that the promise is made to praying thus qualified, to wit, that it be in Christ's name, binds the soul to this way, because otherwise it forfeits the promise, if it observe not the due qualification; I fear, there are too many, who look on the promise, as absolute: It is true, tho' there are absolute promises in the covenant, yet there are other promises that have qualifications and conditions, whereof this, anent hearing of prayer, is one; and we are to expect the performance of the promise, when we seek after the qualification and condition. *2dly*, Mind Christ's promise, whereby he hath engaged, as to lead us in all necessary truth; so in this part of it, to put up our prayers in his Name, John xvi. 24. *In that day ye shall ask in my Name.* To consider aright of this promise, gives some ground of confidence to win at the performance of it, and holds the soul in dependence on him, and makes it to be quiet in the duty of improving Christ's intercession; and indeed this is a main part of religion: Learn therefore, to put these things together, 1. Think it a mercy, that ye have a warrant and access to pray. 2. That ye have a promise to be heard. 3. That ye have a Mediator to interceed for you. 4. That a promise is given you to learn how to make use of him; and tho' that the use-making of his intercession aright be difficult, and many do mistken and mistake it, yet that by the eying of the promise, ye may win to the right use-making of it; ye would by any means eye the promise, that ye be not mistaken: It may be there is a look now and then to liberty, and it is good in itself; but there may be a defect here, that ye look not to Christ to be helped to pray with liberty, and to be guided to pray in his Name, so as to lay the weight of your being heard, on Christ's intercession.

4thly, When there hath been an eying of the promise, not only for the thing we seek, but also to be guided in the seeking of it, ye would be often taking a review of yourselves in, and after prayer, whether ye be indeed praying, and have prayed in Christ's name, that when the soul looks back, and sees that it hath much miskenned and neglected Christ, it may take itself in this evil, and disclaim it, and settle itself on a right ground. In a word, there would be looking well on the one side, that Jesus Christ be the ground we build on; and on the other side, that when we eye Christ, and build on him, we be not afraid to hazard on him: for into one of these extremes we readily run, either to lippen and lean to some other thing than Christ; or, if we see no other thing to lean and lippen to, and be necessitate to eye him, we distrust him, and are loth to hazard on him.

5thly, And lastly, If we consider well, we will see good ground, 1. To press, 2. To encourage us to this way, not to be doing duty only, as men under the law, but as Christian men under the gospel, with respect to Christ's satisfaction and intercession. And, *1st*, For pressing it, consider that there is a neceſſity of it in reference to as many prayers as are accepted of God: if it be neceſſary to get a hearing, it is neceſſary to pray in Chriſt's name. It may be, many think it to be but an indifferent thing, that we have been preſſing, all the while that we have been ſpeaking of Chriſt's interceſſion; but indeed it is of more moment than our preſſing you to any external duty, for the external duty of prayer, tho' it muſt needs be gone about, is yet but the carcaſe, this is the ſoul and life of prayer: And therefore let me exhort and obteſt you, never to ſatisfy yourſelves with a legal performance of the moſt ſpiritual duties in themſelves, except ye win to a Chriſtian way of performing them, that is, that they be done in Chriſt's ſtrength, and that ye reſt on him for the acceptance of them; it is as neceſſary to worſhip God in and by a Mediator, as it is to worſhip the only true God, and not to worſhip a falſe or ſtrange God. I make no queſtion, but the moſt part of the hearers of the goſpel do deſtroy themſelves here, by reſting on their legal performances, and not making uſe of Chriſt. 2dly, For your encouragement conſider, that it is moſt advantageous and profitable; theſe words in the promiſe are broad and full, *Whatſoever ye aſk in my Name, I will do it*; and the promiſe is frequently repeated, in theſe forecited chapters of John. O what calmneſs, tranquillity, peace, victory over anxiety, what patience in waiting, whether when in bonds or liberty, do flow from the exerciſing of faith on this ground, to wit, that we have an Advocate in heaven with the Father! Further, conſider the great ground of confidence that hath been given us, that we ſhall come ſpeed in this way, which ſhould ſtir us up, hearten and encourage us to it; which will manifeſtly appear, if we join theſe *two* together, 1. That this bleſſed Advocate is our Brother; that he was made like unto us in all things, except ſin; that he is a fellow-feeling high Prieſt, that is touched with our infirmities; that he refuſeth to grant no ſuits of his people, that are for his glory, and their good; that he ſaves all to the uttermoſt that come unto God by him: None could ever ſay, that he refuſed to take their cauſe in hand, when they indeed committed it to him. 2. That when a cauſe is committed to him, it cannot but carry, and be ſucceſsful; for as he is Man, ſo he is God, and he is heard always: This bleſſed Mediator (as I ſaid juſt now) refuſeth the ſuit of none, and no ſuit is refuſed him. And now, what can we ſay more to you, for your up-ſtirring and encouragement to make uſe of him? It is no ſtranger that we have to go to, and there is good ground of confidence, that when we go, we ſhall come ſpeed: Therefore, let him ever be gone unto more and more; and bleſs God heartily, that he hath given ſuch an high Prieſt unto ſinners, *who is able to ſave to the uttermoſt all that come unto God through him*. Now, to this God, who can effectually teach us to make uſe of the Mediator every way, and particularly in his interceſſion, ſuitably and ſucceſsfully; and who is *able to do exceeding abundantly above all we aſk, or think, according to the power that worketh in us, be glory in the church by Chriſt Jeſus, throughout all ages, world without end*, Amen.

F I N I S.

www.ingramcontent.com/pod-product-compliance
Lightning Source LLC
Chambersburg PA
CBHW051725300426
44115CB00007B/468